THE SOVIET THEATER

THE SOVIET THEATER

A Documentary History

Edited by
Laurence Senelick and Sergei Ostrovsky

Yale UNIVERSITY PRESS

NEW HAVEN AND LONDON

All pictures come from the Laurence Senelick Collection.

Yale University Press books may be purchased in quantity for educational, business, or promotional use. For information, please e-mail sales.press@yale.edu (U.S. office) or sales@yaleup.co.uk (U.K. office).

Design and typography by Concord Editorial and Design.
Printed in the United States of America.

Library of Congress Cataloging-in-Publication Data

The Soviet theater : a documentary history / edited by Laurence Senelick and Sergei Ostrovsky.
    pages ; cm
 Includes bibliographical references and index.
 ISBN 978-0-300-19476-0 (cloth : alk. paper) 1. Theater—Soviet Union—History. 2. Theater—Soviet Union—History—Sources. 3. Theater and state—Soviet Union—History. 4. Theater and state—Soviet Union—History—Sources. I. Senelick, Laurence, editor. II. Ostrovsky, Sergei, editor.
 PN2724.S65 2014
 792.0947—dc23

                    2013044557

A catalogue record for this book is available from the British Library.

This paper meets the requirements of ANSI/NISO Z39.48–1992 (Permanence of Paper).

10 9 8 7 6 5 4 3 2 1

For Inna Solov'ëva and Anatoly Smelyansky, sine qua non

Gather up the fragments that remain, that nothing be lost.

—Gospel of St. John

Theater is a living spiritual and intellectual focus, a place for social self-awareness, a vanishing point where all the lines of force of the age meet, a seismograph of the times, in space, an area of freedom, an instrument of human liberation.

—Václav Havel, *Disturbing the Peace*

Contents

Preface

The Soviet theater may be the best documented in history. With the possible exception of France, no other government devoted so much of its attention to theatrical matters and generated so much paper in that regard. The administration and its bureaucracies produced legislation, transactions, and red tape. In addition, Russian artists were "people of the word." Following the example of the Moscow Art Theater, directors and companies preserved records of rehearsals, stage plans, sketches for designs, photographs, every scrap of paper associated with a production. A lively theatrical press proliferated editorials, reviews, roundtables, profiles, character studies, and surveys. In a society in which any public utterance might be subjected to close scrutiny by the powers-that-be, individuals expressed themselves privately in letters, diaries, journals, and personal memoirs. At times it seems as if almost every Soviet citizen concealed a written testament to his individuality in the face of enforced conformity.

The oft-quoted remark in Bulgakov's novel *The Master and Margarita* that "manuscripts do not burn" looks less paradoxical in view of the Russian reluctance to destroy documents. Unlike the Nazis, the Soviet political police seldom conducted conflagrations of written or published material. A sheaf of papers might be confiscated, but most usually, it was preserved in the government archives, either as collateral evidence or in case its author might return to favor. Occasionally, material in danger of such confiscation might be privately secreted away. The most famous case of this is the Meyerhold archive. In 1939, a few days before Meyerhold's arrest, his wife, herself about to be murdered, entrusted the archive to Sergey Eisenstein, who hid it in his dacha. It was intact and available for publication when Meyerhold was rehabilitated in 1955.

The resurfacing of this documentation was important to the continued health of the theater. Many of those who had fallen into disfavor had become nonpersons, their names and careers erased first from playbills and programs, then from the histories. The document was often the only testimony that a certain person had existed and accomplished anything. Rather than obliterating, the Soviet authorities became expert at retouching, refashioning reality so that, instead of a gaping lacuna, a softened, reassuring image could be provided. This explains why, with the collapse of the Soviet Union, a favorite form of publication is the collection of documents. Sometimes a publishing house is founded solely for the purpose of making public a mass of documentation.

When the USSR imploded in 1991, it provided fresh new opportunities for scholarship. Archives and collections were opened to researchers, but, as many realized, the window might be slammed shut again at any time. We therefore decided to take advantage of the opportunity and plunge into the mass of material to compile a history of the Soviet theater based on original documents. A generous grant from the National Endowment for the Humanities enabled us to devote two years to exploring archives in Russia, Israel, and the United States, in the process collecting a vast fund of material, much of it unpublished or never republished after its first appearance in a periodical.

The topic was attractive in its seeming discreteness: it could be bounded by the dates 1917, when the October Revolution marked the beginnings of Soviet power, and 1991, when the USSR disintegrated. Conversely, the field was vast, seeming to cover all the constituent republics and divagating into such topics as émigré theater. With such an *embarras de richesses*, we would have to be highly selective. Until the materials had been collected and sorted, however, it was unclear where our emphases would lie. Eventually, certain productions and individuals retained their prominence, whereas others proved to be of equivalent interest.

Another factor that impelled this project was that no comprehensive history of the Soviet theater existed in English. Books either included chapters on it or were devoted to specific periods or individuals. Certain figures, such as Meyerhold, Vakhtangov, Stanislavsky, Bulgakov, and Lyubimov, were given pride of place, for obvious reasons, but turning the spotlight on these eminences left large tracts of activity in shadow. Separate monographs were devoted to such topics as children's theater, puppetry, the Yiddish stage, and censorship, but the close focus blurred the context. Earlier attempts by its participants to write of the Soviet theater's evolution, such as those of Nikolay Gorchakov and Yury Elagin, were often distorted by parti pris and were wielded as weapons in the Cold War.

Yet, to leach out the political element would be a different kind of distortion. In 1988, the veteran Soviet theater critic Konstantin Rudnitsky published a survey of Russian and Soviet theater from 1905 to 1933, intended for an English-language readership. Rudnitsky was steeped in the subject and had personally suffered from the Stalinist attack on "cosmopolitans" in the 1950s. Yet the only mention of Stalin in his book was in a picture caption, and Rudnitsky's choice of dates clearly showed a reluctance to deal with the repressions and purges that arrived with the Second Five-Year Plan. The brilliant theatrical achievements of the 1920s and early 1930s therefore come across, in Rudnitsky's account, as either spontaneously generated or stimulated by the artistic creations of others.

The fact is that, by definition, the Soviet theater was so tightly intertwined with politics that what happened in it has to be seen as a reaction to the constantly changing policies of the government. We are not dealing with independent artists creating in a vacuum, nor even with theater folk responding to the tastes of an audience. Art for art's sake plays no role here. In the USSR, almost from the first, the theater is, in one way or another, a reflection of the government's mood. How theater is to serve society is dictated from above: one may oppose that diktat or find idiosyncratic ways to serve it, but it cannot be avoided.

A history that would encompass the whole arc of development was needed. We decided that the story could best be told, not by a magisterial narrative voice, but by a polyphonic compilation. Consequently, our definition of *document* is a very catholic one: it includes legislative and state records, protocols, minutes of meetings, and official pronouncements. These are amplified by memoirs and diaries, personal accounts, letters, journalism, reviews and criticism, passages from plays, parody, and satire. We decided that to rely wholly on previously unpublished matter would severely narrow the picture; in many cases, important documents had appeared in Soviet collections but were barely known in English. So we cast our net even wider to take in whatever could provide detail and variety. We have been careful to provide a wide spectrum of opinion, for even when homogeneity was most prescribed by Party congresses, individuals still found ways to make their voices heard. We have also drawn on the testimony of outside observers, foreign visitors whose reactions, often naive or poorly informed, provide valuable counterpoint.

These documents cover the period just prior to the revolution of February 1917 to just following the dissolution of the Soviet Union in 1991. In many cases, they offer more information on the decision-making process—the behind-the-scenes meetings of committees and government agencies, internecine hostilities, financial considerations—than has hitherto been available to the reader with no Russian. The finished production, judged by eyewitness testimony and criticism, has to be viewed in the light of those conditions that led to its creation. Many of the documents illustrate "how the sausage is made," ugly though the process may be. So many English-language accounts of the Soviet theater assume that its practitioners followed their own bent that this documentation may serve as a useful corrective.

To be as compendious as possible and to make the most salient points, we have excerpted and filleted the documents. Excisions are indicated by an ellipsis within brackets ([. . .]), whereas an ordinary ellipsis (. . .) is repeated when it occurs in the original document. Even with radical abridgement, we have had to curtail coverage of many of the Soviet nationalities; however, the accomplishments of the Georgian, Ukrainian, and Jewish theater in the first half of the Soviet period were so outstanding that they had to be included, if only succinctly. For the same reason, an intended chapter on émigré theater was abandoned, particularly because its relation to the Soviet stage was at most polemical.

We have followed common practice in the names of theaters: the Moscow Art Theater, the Red Army Theater, the Satire Theater, and many others are given in English, whereas the Bol'shoy, the Maly, and the Kamerny remain in Russian.

However, to use Aleksandrinsky, Mariynsky, and Mikhailovsky for the former Imperial Theaters in St. Petersburg obscures the fact that these are simple adjectival forms of (Empress) Alexandra, (Empress) Maria, and (Grand Duke) Michael. So we have preferred to use those names.

Wherever possible, individuals have been identified by full names, birth and death dates, and a modicum of information. This has proven to be impossible in some cases. Once a footnote identifies an individual or an entity, the information is not repeated. Unless otherwise noted, all the translations are by Laurence Senelick.

THIS PROJECT BEGAN as long ago as 1994 and was generously funded for two years by the National Endowment for Humanities, so our first acknowledgment goes to it. Later grants from the Faculty Research Council of Tufts University and the Institute for Research and Exchange (IREX) aided the continuation of the work. A great many individuals assisted us along the way. The list of libraries and archives consulted, which is given at the top of the bibliography, should serve to indicate how many of their curators and staff members aided the project. To cite individuals, we are very grateful to the following.

In the Russian Federation, Mikhail Shvydkoy, former minister of culture; Vyacheslav Nechaev of the Central Theater Library; Raisa Ostrovskaya of the Ermolova Museum; Aleksandr Popov, Anatoly Smelyansky, and Oleg Tabakov of the Moscow Art Theater; Inna Solov'ëva of GITIS; Aleksandr Chepurov of the Alexandra Theater, St. Petersburg; Nataliya Gladkova, dramaturg of the Satyricon Theater; the archives and press offices of the Museum of the Red Army Theater, the Bakhrushin State Theater Museum, the Central State Archive of Art and Literature, and the Vysotsky Museum; Aleksey Bartoshevich, Dina Goder, Vsevolod Ivanov, Mikhail Kozakov, Boris Liubimov, Sergey Nikulin, and Arkady Ostrovsky. A fuller list of the archives consulted appears at the head of the bibliography.

In North America, Jeanne Newlin, Martha Mahard, and Annette Fern, formerly of the Harvard Theater Collection; the Russian Research Center at Harvard University; the Nicholas Butler Library of Columbia University; Dina Brode, Sharon Marie Carnicke, J. Douglas Clayton, Timur Djordjadze, Dr. Catherine Evtukhov, Donald Fanger, Spencer Golub, Marjorie L. Hoover, Felicia Londré, Irena Makaryk, John Malmstad, Anna Muza, Olga Partan, Joseph Price, Nicholas Rzhevsky, Joel Schechner, Rama Sohonee, Jurij Striedter, Manon van de Water, Andrew Wachtel, and Don B. Wilmeth.

Elsewhere, the Society for the Advancement of Friendship with the USSR, London; the Bibliothek of the Freie-Universität Berlin; the Wissenschaftskolleg zu Berlin and its former librarian Ghesine Bottomley; Claudine Amiard-Chevrel, Marie-Christine Autant-Mathieu, Philip Bullock, Christine Hamon-Siréjols, Fausto Malcovati, Cynthia Marsh, Anthony J. Pearson, Béatrice Picon-Vallin, Herta Schmid, Maria Shevtsova, E. Anthony Swift, Andrzej Wirth, Boris Yentin, and Stuart Young.

Several well-wishers and abettors of this project have passed from the scene before they could see the fruits of their efforts. Among them are Jean-Norman Benedetti, Victor Borovsky, Oleg Efremov, Daniel Gerould, Simon Karlinsky, Alma Law, Paul Schmidt, Richard Stites, Marianna Stroeva, and Benjamin Tsemakh.

In a work of this kind, book dealers are of inestimable value in providing valuable material. Thanks go to Oriental Research Partners; Panorama of Russia; Southpaw Books; Lydia Rozovsky; Barbara Cavanagh of Motley Books; Daly Books of East Otis, Massachusetts; Richard Stoddard; Jonathan and Lisa Reynolds of Dramatis Personae; and Willem Meeuws of Oxford.

Several of Professor Senelick's former graduate students at Tufts University contributed in many ways, first and foremost Professor Dassia Posner of Northwestern University, who, in the course of her intensive archival research in Moscow, discovered Tairov's (possibly) last letter in the Russian archives. The long-suffering members of the seminar on Soviet theater read earlier recensions of this work. The staff of the Department of Drama and Dance have been very efficient in reproducing material and preparing it for mailing, particularly Rita Dioguardi and Chris Mascara.

The editors and officers of Yale University Press have to be thanked for their enthusiasm in accepting this work for publication, their exemplary patience in waiting for it to be finished, and their courage in accepting it in its entirety.

Note on Transliteration

The system of transliteration from Cyrillic is meant to be reader-friendly to someone who does not know Russian. When a name is already familiar in English in a conventional spelling—Meyerhold, Eisenstein, Tchaikovsky, Chaliapin, Chagall—we have retained that spelling. "E" at the beginning of a name is rendered as "E" rather than as "Ye"—so Evreinov, not Yevreinov. The soft sign has been dropped from some names and words well known in the West, for example, from Gorky and Gogol, but not from Ol'ga, Bol'shoy, or Khar'kov.

Cyrillic	System used in this book	Pronunciation
Аа	a	*f*ather
Бб	b	*b*ank; (at the end of words) to*p*
Вв	v	*v*et; to*w*el; (at the end of words) dea*f*
Гг	g	*g*et; (at the end of words) brea*k*
Дд	d	*d*addy; (at the end of words) ve*t*
Ее	e	m*e*t; m*i*tt; *y*eah
Ёё	ë	b*o*rder; *yo*re
Жж	zh	vi*s*ion; pu*sh*
Зз	z (except when it indicates a German *s*)	*z*eal
Ии	i	ch*ee*se; *i*f
Йй	y	unstressed vowel
Кк	k	*k*ept
Лл	l	*l*og
Мм	m	*m*ama
Нн	n	*n*o
Оо	o	(stressed) *o*rder; (unstressed) *a*rtistic
Пп	p	*p*age

Рр	r	*r*ake
Сс	s	mi*ss*
Тт	t	*t*en
Уу	u	sp*oo*n
Фф	f	*f*orm
Хх	kh	*h*ah; a*ch*
Цц	ts	i*ts*
Чч	ch	*ch*ief
Шш	sh	*sh*oe
Щщ	shch	fi*sh ch*owder
Ъъ	omitted	no sound value
Ыы	y	ph*oo*ey
Ьь	omitted	no sound value
Ээ	é	vet; d*a*y
Юю	yu	*you*; s*ui*t
Яя	ya	*ya*hoo

Diphthongs

-ай	ay	*eye*
-ый	y	*i*ts
-ий	y	*e*ven
-ия	iya	tri*age*
-ье	'e	*ye*ah
-ьи	'i	*yi*p

Abbreviations and Acronyms

agit—agitatsionny (agitation; agitational)

Akdrama—Leningradsky (Petrogradsky) gosudarstvenny akademichesky teatr dramy (Leningrad [Petrograd] State Academic Dramatic Theater; then, Rossiysky Teatr Dramy im. A. S. Pushkina [Russian Drama Theater named for Pushkin])

AKhRR—Assotsiatsiya khudozhnikov revolyutsionnoy Rossii (Association of Artists of Revolutionary Russia)

Akmuzo—Tsentral'naya muzykal'naya sektsiya Glavnogo khudozhestvennogo komiteta Akademicheskogo tsentra Narkomprosa (Central Musical Division of the Chief Artistic Committee of the Academic Center of Narkompros)

AKTEO—Tsentral'naya teatral'naya sektsiya Glavnogo khudozhestvennogo komiteta Akademicheskogo tsentra Narkomprosa (Central Theatrical Division of the Chief Artistic Committee of the Academic Center of Narkompros)

AN—Akademiya Nauk (Academy of Sciences)

ASSR—Avotnomiya sovetskaya sotsialisticheskaya respublika (Autonomous Soviet Socialist Republic)

BDT—Leningradsky Bol'shoy Dramatichesky Teatr (Leningrad Great Dramatic Theater)

CPSU (B)—Communist Party of the Soviet Union

Éktemas = Géktemas

FÉKS—Fabrika éktsentricheskogo aktëra (Factory of the Eccentric Actor)

GABT—Gosudarstvenny akademichesky bol'shoy teatr (State Academic Bol'shoy Theater)

GAKHI—Gosudarstvennaya akademiya khudozhestvennykh nauk (State Academy of Artistic Studies)

GATOB—Gosudarstvenny akademichesky teatr opery i baleta (State Academic Theater of Opera and Ballet)

GÉKTEMAS—Gosudarstvennye éksperimental'nye teatral'nye masterskie (State Experimental Theater Workshops)

GITIS—Gosudarstvenny institut teatral'nogo iskusstva (State Institute of Theatrical Art)

GIZ—Gosudarstvennoe izdatel'stvo (State Publishing House)

GLAVLIT—Glavnoe upravlenie po delam literatury i izdatel'stv (Chief Directorate for Literature and Publishing)

Glavmuzey—Otdel po delam muzeev i okhrane pamyatnikov iskusstva i stariny Narkomprosa (Department for Museum Affairs and the Preservation of Artistic Monuments and Antiquities of Narkompros)

Glavpolitprosvet—Glavny politiko-prosvetitel'ny komitet Respubliki (Chief Politico-enlightenment Committee of the Republic)

Glavpolitput'—Glavny politichesky otdel Narodnogo komissariata putey soobshcheniya (Chief Political Department of the People's Commissariat for Communications)

Glavprofobr—Glavnoe upravlenie professional'nogo obrazovanniya Narkomprosa (Chief Directorate of Professional Training)

Glavrepertkom—Glavny komitet po kontrolyu za repertuarom Narkomprosa (Chief Committee for the Inspection of the Repertoire of Narkompros)

Glavtop—Glavny toplivny komitet (Chief Fuel Committee)

GOMETs—Gosudarstvennoe ob'edinenie muzykal'nykh, éstradnykh i tsirkovykh predpriyaty (State Union of Musical, Variety, and Circus Enterprises)

gos.—gosudarstvenny (state)

Gosagitteatr—Gosudarstvenny agitatsionny teatr (State Agitational Theater)

Gosbot—Gosudarstvenny Bol'shoy operny teatr (State Great Opera Theater)

GOSET—Gosudarstvenny evreysky teatr (State Jewish Theater)

Gosizdat—Gosudarstvenny izdatel'stvo RSFSR (State Publishing House of the RSFSR)

Goskontrol'—Komissiya gosudarstvennogo kontrola (Commission of State Inspection)

Gospokaz—Gosudarstvenny Pokazatel'ny teatr (State Exemplary Theater)

GOSTIM—Gosudarstvenny teatr imeni Meyerkhol'da (State Meyerhold Theater)

GPU—Gosudarstvennoe politicheskoe upravlenie (State Political Directorate) [secret police]

GtsTM—Gosudarstvenny tsentral'ny teatral'ny muzei im. Bakhrushina (State Central Theatrical Museum named for Bakhrushin)

gubkom—gubernsky komitet (provincial committee)

gubkompart—gubernsky komitet partiya (provincial party committee)

gubolitprosvet—gubernskoe politiko-prosvetitel'noe otdelenie (upravlenie) (provincial politico-enlightenment department [directorate])

guboprodkom—gubernsky prodovol'stvenny komitet (komissiya) (provincial rationing committee [commission])

GULAG—Glavnoe upravlenie ispravitel'no-trudovykh lagerey (Chief Administration for Corrective Labor Camps)

GUM—Gosudarstvenny universal'ny magazin (State department store)

GUTs—Gosudarstennoe upravelenie tsirkami (State Directorate of Circuses)

GVYRM—Gos. vysshie rezhissëtrskie masterskie (State Advanced Directors' Workshops)

GVYTM—Gos. vysshie teatral'nie masterskie (State Advanced Theatrical Workshops)

IMLI—Institut mirovoy literatury im. A. M. Gor'kogo Akademii nauk SSSR (Institute for World Literature named after Gorky of the Academy of Sciences of the USSR)

IZO—Otdel izobrazitel'nykh iskusstv Narkomprosa (Department of Visual Arts of Narkompros)

KGB—Komitet gosudarstvennoy besopasnosti (State Security Commission)

KhPSRO—Khudozhestvenno-prosvetitel'ny soyuz rabochikh organizatsiy (Artistic Educational Union of Workers' Organizations)

KINO—Kinematografichesky otdel Narkomprosa (Film Department of Narkompros)

Komgosoor—Komitet Gosudarstvennykh sooruzhenny (Committee of State Construction)

Komtruda—Narodny komissariat truda (People's Commissariat of Labor)

KP—Kommunisticheskaya partiya (Communist Party)

KPRF—Kommunisticheskaya partiya rossiskoy federatsii (Communist Party of the Russian Federation)

krasnoarm.—krasnoarmeysky (Red Army)

LEF—Levy front (Left Front of Arts)

LGAORSS—Leningradsky gosudarstvenny arkhiv Oktryabrskoy revolyutsii i sotsial-isticheskogo stroitel'stva (Leningrad State Archive of the October Revolution and Socialist Construction)

LGITMiK—Leningradsky gosudarstvenny institut teatra, myzyki i kinematografii imeni N. K. Cherkasova (Leningrad State Institute of Theater, Music, and Film named for Nikolay Cherkasov)

LGTMA—Leningradsky gosudarstvenny teatral'ny muzey (Leningrad State Theater Museum)

LITO—Literaturny otdel Narkomprosa (Literary Department of the People's Commissariat of Enlightenment)

LGSPS—Leningradsky gorodsky Sovet professional'nykh soyuzov (Moscow Municipal Council of Trade Unions)

Mastkomdrama—Masterskaya kommunisticheskoy dramaturgii (Workshop of Communist Drama)

MAT—Moscow Art Theater

MATsIS—Masterskaya tsirkovogo iskusstva (Workshop of Circus Art)

MDT—Maly Dramatichesky Teatr (Small Dramatic Theater)

MGIK—Moskovskoe gos. institut kul'tury (Moscow State Institute of Culture)

MGKT, MKT, Moskat—Moskovsky gosudarstvenny kamerny teatr (Moscow State Chamber Theater)

MGSPS—Moskovsky gorodsky Sovet professional'nykh soyuzov (Moscow Municipal Council of Trade Unions)

MGU—Moskovsky gosudarstvenny universitet (Moscow State University)

MK—Ministerstvo kultury (Ministry of Culture)

MKhAT—Moskovsky khudozhestvenny akademichesky teatr (Moscow Art Academic Theater)

MKhT—Moskovsky khudozhestvenny teatr (Moscow Art Theater)

MONO—Moskovsky otdel narodnogo obrazovaniya (Moscow Department of People's Education)

MOSPS—Teatr imeni Moskovskogo oblastnogo Soveta professional'nykh soyuzov (Moscow Regional Theater of Trade Unions)

Mossel'prom—Moskovskoe ob'edinennie predpryatiy po pererabotke produktov sel'skokhozyaystvennoy promyshlennosti (Moscow United Enterprises for the Distribution of Agricultural Industrial Products)

MSRD—Moskovsky Sovet rabochikh deputatov (Moscow Council of Workers' Deputies)

MTK—Moskovsky teatr klounady (Moscow Clown Theater)

MTsRK—Moskovsky tsentral'ny rabochii kooperativ (Moscow Central Workers' Cooperative)

MTYUZ—Moskovsky Teatr Yunogo Zritelya (Moscow Theater of the Young Spectator)

MUZO—Muzykal'ny otdel Narkomprosa (Musical Department of the People's Commissariat of Enlightenment)

MVD—Ministerstvo vnutrennykh del (Ministry of Internal Affairs)

narkom—Narodny komissar (People's Commissar/iat)

Narkomfin—Narodny komissariat finansov (People's Commissariat of Finances)

Narkomnats—Narodny komissariat po delam natsional'nostey (People's Commissariat for Matters of Nationality)

Narkompros—Narodny komissariat prosveshcheniya (People's Commissariat of Enlightenment)

Narkomtrud—Narodny komissariat truda (People's Commissariat of Labor)

Narkomvoen—Narodny komissariat po voennym delam (People's Commissariat for Military Affairs)

Narkomyust—Narodny komissariat yustitsii (People's Commissariat of Justice)

narobraz = otnarobraz

NÉP—Novaya ékonomicheskaya politika (New Economic Policy)

NVKD—Narodny komissariat vnutrennykh del (People's Commissariat for Internal Affairs)

OGIZ—Ob'edinënie gosudarstvnnykh izdatel'stv (Central State Publishing House)

OGPU—Ob'edinënnoe politicheskoe upravlenie (Unified State Political Directorate)

OGT—Opytno-geroichesky teatr (Experimental-Heroic Theater)

OLP—Otdel likvidatsii posledstviy (Department of Liquidation Consequences)

ONO = otnarpobraz

ORU—otdel rukopisey (Department of Manuscripts)

OSPS—Oblastnoy sovet professional'nykh soyuzov (Regional Council of Professional Unions)

otkomkhoz—otdel kommunal'nogo khozaystva (Department of Communal Agriculture)

otnarobraz—otdel narodnogo obrazovaniya (People's Education Department)

Poarm—politichesky otdel armii (Political Department of the Army)

Pogub—politichesky otdel gubvoenkomata (Political Department of the Provincial Military Committee)

Podiv—politichesky otdel divizii (Political Department of Military Divisions)

Proletkul't—Vserossiysky tsentral'ny komitet proletarskikh kul'turno-prosvetitel'nykh organizatsiy (All-Russian Central Committee of Proletarian Cultural-Enlightenment Organizations)

PTO—Petrogradskoe teatral'noe otdelenie (Petrograd Theatrical Department)

PTU—Petrogradskoe teatral'noe upravlenie (Petrograd Theatrical Directorate)

PUR—Politicheskoe upravlenie Revvoensoveta Respubliki (Political Directorate of the Revolutionary Military Council of the Republic)

RABIS, Sorabis—soyuz rabotnikov iskusstv (Union of Art Workers)

Rabrin—raboche-krest'yanskaya inspektsiya (Worker and Peasant Inspection)

RAMT—Rossiysky akademichesky molodëzny teatr (Russian Academic Youth Theater)

RAPP—Rossiyskaya assotsiatsiya proletarskikh pisateley (Russian Proletarian Writers' Association)

RATI—Rossiyskaya akademiya teatral'nogo iskusstva (Russian Academy of Theater Arts)

repertkom—repetuarny komitet (Repertoire Committee)

Revvoensovet—revolyutsionny voenny sovet (Revolutionary Military Council)

RKI—raboche-krest'yanskaya inspektsiya (Workers' and Peasants' Inspectorate)

RKKA—Raboche-krest'yanskaya Krasnaya Armiya (Workers' and Peasants' Red Army)

RKSM—Rossiyskii kommunistichesky soyuz molodezhi (Russian Communist Union of Youth)

RKT—raboche-krest'yansky teatr (workers' and peasants' theater)

RMO—Russkoe muzykal'noe obshchestvo (Russian Musical Society)

ROABTs—Rossiyskoe obshchestvo artistov var'eté i tsirka (Russian Society of Variety and Circus Artistes)

ROSTA—Rossiyskoe telegrafnoe agentstvo (Russian Telegraph Agency)

RSDRP—Rossiyskaya sotsial-demokraticheskaya rabochaya partiya (Russian Social Democratic Workers' Party)

RSFSR—Rossiyskaya Sovetskaya Federativnaya Sotsialisticheskaya Respublika (Russian Soviet Federal Socialist Republic)

RTO—Russkoe teatral'noe obschestvo (Russian Theater Society)

RVSR—Revolyutsionny Voenny Sovet Respubliki (Revolutionary Military Council of the Republics)

SGO—sovet gosudarstvennoy opery (Council of the State Opera)

SIT—sovet gosudarstvennykh teatrov (Council of the State Theaters)

SNK = Sovnarkom, Sovet Narodnykh Komissarov (Council of People's Commissars)

Sorabis = Rabis

Sovdep—Sovet deputatov (Council of Deputies)

Sovnarkom—Sovet narodnykh komissarov (Council of People's Commissars)

Sovtrudoborony—Sovet truda i oborony (Council of Labor and Defence)

Soyuzgostsirk—Vsesoyuznoe ob'edinenie gosudarstvennykh tsirkov (All-Union Association of State Circuses)

SPb—Sankt-Peterburg (St. Petersburg)

SNK—St. Petersburg Sovnarkom

SPD—Soyuz tsirkovskikh deyateley (Union of Circus Workers)

SR i KD—Sovet rabochikh i krasnoarmeyskikh (krest'yanskikh) deputatov (Council of Workers' and Red Army Soldiers' [Peasants'] Deputies)

SSR—Sovetskaya sotsialisticheskaya respublika (Soviet Socialist Republic)

SSSR—Soyuz Sovetskikh Sotsialisticheskikh Respublik (Union of Soviet Socialist Republics)

STD—Soyuz teatral'nykh deyateley (Union of Theater Workers)

STDM 17–21—*Sovetsky teatr. Dokumenty i materialy. Russky sovetsky teatr 1917–1921. Dokumenty i materialy* (Soviet theater documents and materials. Russian Soviet Theater 1917–21), ed. A. Z. Yufit (Leningrad: Iskusstvo, 1968)

STDM 21–26—*Sovetsky teatr. Dokumenty i materialy. Russky sovetsky teatr 1921–1926. Dokumenty i materialy* (Soviet theater documents and materials. Russian Soviet Theater 1921–1926), ed. A. Y. Trabsky (Leningrad: Iskusstvo, 1975)

Temusek—teatral'no-muzykal'naya sektsiya Moskovskogo otdela narodnogo obrazovaniya (theatrical-musical section of the Moscow Department of People's Education)

TEO—Teatral'ny otdel Narkomprosa (Glavpolitirosveta, Proletkul'ta) (Theatrical Department of Narkompros)

Teresvat—Teatr revolyutsionnoy satiry (Theater of Revolutionary Satire)

TIM—Teatr imeni Vs. Meyerkhol'da (Meyerhold Theater)

TOK—Teatral'ny osoby komitet (Theatrical Special Committee)

TRAM—Teatr rabochey molodëzhi (Theater of Young Workers)

TsDKZh—Tsentral'ny Dom kultury zheleznodorozhnikov (Central House of Culture of Railway Workers)

TsDRI—Tsentral'ny Dom rabotnikov iskusstv (Central House of Art Workers)

Tsentoteatr, TsT—Tsentral'ny teatral'ny komitet Narkomprosa (Central Theater Committee of Narkompros)

TsGALI—Tsentral'ny gosudarstvenny arkhiv literatury i iskusstva (Central State Archives of Literature and Art)

TsIK—Tsentral'ny ispolnitel'ny komitet (Central Executive Committee)

TsK—Tsentral'ny komitet (Central Committee)

TsKA—Tsentral'ny Teatr Krasnoy Armii (Central Theater of the Red Army)

TsKSM—Tsentral'ny Komitet soyuza molodëzhi (Central Committee of the Union of Youth)

TsT = Tsentroteatr

TsTSA—Tsentral'ny Teatr Sovetskoy Armii (Central Theater of the Soviet Army)

TsTsI—Tsentr tsirkovogo iskusstva (Center for Circus Art)

TsSTsI—Tsentral'naya studiya tsirkogo iskusstva (Central Studio of Circus Art)

TsUT—Tsentral'noe upravlenie teatrami (Central Theatrical Directorate)

TYUZ—Teatr yunogo zritelya (Theater of the Young Spectator)

UONO—Uezdny otdel narodnogo obrazovaniya (Regional Department of People's Education)

UZP—Upravelenie zrelishchnymi predpriyatnyami (Directorate of Entertainment Enterprises)

VChK—Vserossiyskaya chrezvychaynaya komissiya po bor'be s kontrerevolyutsionney i sabotazhem (All-Russian Special Commission for the Fight against Counter-revolution and Sabotage)

VGIK—Vsesoyuzny gosudarstvenny institut kinematografii (All-Union State Film Institute).

VKhUTEMAS—Vysshie khudozhestvenno-tekhnicheskie masterskie (Higher Artistic-Technical Workshops)

VLKSM—Vsesoyuzny Leninsky kommunistichesky soyuz molodezhi (All-Union Lenin Communist Youth League)

VO—voenny okrug (military district)

Vsebyurvoenkom—Vserossiyskoe byuro voennykh komissarov (All-Russian Bureau of Military Commissars)

Vseprofsovet—Vserossiysky sovet professional'nykh soyuzov (All-Russian Council of Professional Unions)

Vserabis—Vserossiysky professional'ny soyuz rabotnikov iskusstv (All-Russian Professional Union of Worker's Arts)

Vsevobuch—vseobshchee voennoe obuchenie (general military training)

VTO—Vserossiyskoe Teatral'noe Obshchestvo (All-Russian Theatrical Society)

VTsIK—Vserossiysky Tsentral'ny ispolnitel'ny komitet Sovetov (All-Russian Central Executive Committee)

VTsSPS—Vserossiysky Tsentral'ny sovet professional'nykh soyuzov (All-Russian Central Council of Professional Unions)

VUOAN—Vsesoyuznoe upravlenie po okhrane avtorskikh prav (All-Union Directorate for the Protection of Actors' Rights)

VUZ—Vysshee uchebnoe zavedenie (Institution of Higher Education)

THE SOVIET THEATER

Introduction

I N 1897 the first Conference of All-Russian Theater Practitioners took place; its very existence testified to the growing importance of the theater as a profession in the Russian Empire. It dealt with such matters as unemployment and benefits, the proletarian element, and bringing theater to the common people. Although the conference was riven by anti-Semitism, for the theater was one of the few professions in which Jews could make a name (usually an assumed name) for themselves, its progressive elements inspired the creation the following year of the Moscow Art Theater (MAT) and the New (Novy) Theater, an affiliate of the Moscow Maly.

On the eve of revolution, every town in the Empire, even the most primitive, could boast a space given over to the performing arts. They ranged from palatial, as in Odessa and the fashionable resort of Kislovodsk, to meeting rooms in assembly halls in remote hamlets. By 1914, there were 153 professional theaters throughout Russia.

The hierarchy of Russian theater could be easily mapped. At the top stood the Imperial Theaters, lavishly subsidized by the monarchy and constituting an elaborate and separate bureaucracy almost equal to a state ministry. Because their administrators, with a few notable exceptions, were usually government officials rather than artists, their tastes were markedly conservative. In Moscow, the Bol'shoy (Grand) Theater, founded in 1776, was given over to spectacular productions of ballet and opera. The specialty of the Maly (Small) Dramatic Theater, founded in 1820, was apparent in its nickname "The House of Ostrovsky"; its troupe, studded with stars who excelled at emotionally saturated acting, perpetuated performance traditions in the classics. St. Petersburg, as the seat of government, followed a similar pattern on a more munificent scale in its three imperial playhouses. The Empress Maria (Mariynsky) Theater was exclusively reserved for opera and, especially, ballet; its aesthetic agenda was set by a coterie of avid balletomanes, and its corps was the hunting preserve of grand dukes and other nobility. The Empress Alexandra Theater (Aleksandrinsky or, as its habitués called it, the Aleksandrinka) performed drama in Russian; its stars were all-powerful and declamatory, and they usually dictated a repertoire that spotlighted their talents. Younger directors, such as Meyerhold, had begun to introduce innovations in the choice of plays and their methods of staging, and the stage designers could be brilliant; but for the most part, the Alexandra clung to the tried-and-true. Given its official nature, the dramatic treatment of social issues and even unionization among the workers were ticklish subjects. Last and definitely least, the Grand Duke Michael (Mikhaylovsky) Theater was reserved for performances in French and German by foreign, though resident, troupes, which automatically limited its audience to an elite crowd.

After the imperial monopoly on theater in the capitals was revoked in 1880, few managers leaped to the challenge of offering rival attractions. The abiding problem was the lack of a theatergoing public large enough to ensure a profit. Even a manager so astute at audience pleasing as Mikhail Lentovsky, who offered spectacular *féeries* and sensational melodramas, regularly courted bankruptcy and had to be bailed out by the merchants who made up the bulk of his public. The commercial class, in fact, accounted for a considerable part of the audience at most private enterprises, with an admixture of the intelligentsia.

The most successful of these privately run companies were Korsh's Theater in Moscow and Suvorin's Society of Literature and Art Theater in St. Petersburg (also known, confusingly, as the Maly). Korsh, a former lawyer and ticket broker, shrewdly varied his repertoire, offering the latest boulevard hits to the ordinary playgoer and matinees of literary classics and novelties to university students and educated classes. It was Korsh who persuaded Chekhov to write for the stage. Suvorin, the millionaire tycoon of a publishing empire and a hard-bitten monarchist, offered similar fare, but titivated by more glittering stars and a more culturally ambitious choice of plays. With his government connections and large private income, Suvorin was less dependent on the box office than Korsh. He was typical of a new breed of self-made entrepreneur who chose to be a patron of the arts and cultivate high culture outside the framework of imperial bureaucracy.

The success of these two enterprises emboldened the founding of the Moscow Art Theater in 1898. Its cofounders came from disparate backgrounds. Konstantin Alekseev, scion of a wealthy textile manufacturer who acted as an amateur under the stage name Stanislavsky, had led a sheltered life, indulged in all his artistic activities. Nemirovich, a professional writer and prize-winning playwright, was the son of a Serbo-Ukrainian military officer and an illiterate Armenian mother; he taught classes in drama at the Moscow Philharmonic. Their original intentions were to create an edifying theater open to the working classes, but the lack of municipal subsidy and government restrictions forced them to turn it into a joint-stock company, with most of the shares held by an art-loving industrialist from Stanislavsky's circle. Its style and its artistic choices made it a de facto house for the professional classes and the intelligentsia. Despite ambitions to cover world drama, they found they were best at Chekhov, Hauptmann, and Gorky and were frustrated in their attempts to break out of the box of "psychological realism."

The founding principles of the Art Theater and its governing practices, for all the taunts they attracted, were highly influential. The troupe was made up not of raffish barnstormers and ladies of easy virtue but of respectable middle-class families and gymnasium graduates. Plays were staged only after long and arduous rehearsals, and their mises-en-scène attempted to re-create everyday life or an historical period, with heavy reliance on lighting and sound effects. The acting was subdued and nuanced, with much attention to pauses; individual performances were subjugated to the ensemble. Audiences were not allowed to enter late or in their overcoats and galoshes.

Gradually, the Art Theater gained a reputation as the most serious and high-minded company in the Russian Empire; throughout the provinces, directors copied their techniques. The MAT itself, however, underwent a number of crises, both financial and artistic. They found themselves outstripped in innovation and audacity by the experiments of their competitors. On the eve of revolution, they were facing artistic bankruptcy. They tried to remain up to date by staging plays by the faux symbolist Andreev, the mystagogue Merezhkovsky, and the Chekhov epigone Surguchev, but these were half-hearted efforts, received with faint enthusiasm by their public. A set of Pushkin one-acts, produced for an anniversary, only showed their ineptitude at verse drama. The Revolution caught them unprepared to welcome change.

By the time of the revolutionary upheavals of 1905, with a weakened censorship, the theater world was splintered by a number of movements and philosophic theories. Political thinkers wanted plays to rouse spectators to take action. The mystical anarchists and the symbolists, led by Vyacheslav Ivanov, called for a communal bonding (*sobornost'*) that would abolish the boundary between stage and audience to unite the two into one collective enactment of religious character. Nikolay Evreinov preached the special nature of the theater and located "the instinct for theatricality" at the root of all rites and all arts. He also introduced monodrama, proposing that the action onstage be seen through the eyes of a single protagonist. Eclectics insisted that every play required its own idiosyncratic mode of production: this was the credo of Mardzhanov and Tairov at the Free Theater and of Fëdor Kommissarzhevsky in several posts. The actors were supposed to be "synthetic," versatile in every style of performance. The MAT's chief rival, Nezlobin's Theater, did well copying whatever was in fashion. Meyerhold, whose studio at the MAT in 1905 was not allowed to open, pursued his experiments in symbolism at Vera Komissarzhevskaya's theater in St. Petersburg, then tried out historical and decorative staging at the Imperial Theaters, while simultaneously exploring Asian and commedia dell'arte techniques in small studios. Evreinov and others pursued similar tracks, with historical reconstructions at the Antique Theater and miniature monodramas at the Crooked Mirror cabaret.

The decade leading up to the outbreak of the Great War provoked such anxiety, turmoil, and uncertainty in the Russian populace that no single style could express it. The consequent proliferation of theatrical styles led many to posit a "crisis in the theater" and, in the case of the critic Yuly Aykhenval'd, to declare its irrelevance to modern society. Audiences expected the theater to reflect the greater convulsions within the Empire but also to take their minds off current events. While the plays of Leonid Andreev and Mikhail Artsybashev were popular as overwrought expressions of sexual neurosis and intense angst, audiences were also flocking to satirical revues, bedroom farce, and musical comedy.

The divergence between these two extremes was, in fact, an instance of the Russian ambivalence about theater that goes back to the first years of the Muscovite grand duchy. The very words *teatr* (theater), *aktër* (actor), and *pesa* (play) are foreign imports that do not show up before the reign of Peter the Great. Earlier, the standard terms for performances are *potekha* and *poteshny*, "fun, amusement," usually provided by jesters and other professional entertainers. The Orthodox Church set its face against such ungodly activities, but, under the influence of Jesuit academies and Lutheran pastors, plays based on biblical stories began to be performed at court. Occasionally, the two strains—professional entertainers and amateur performers—coexisted, as when minstrels (*skomorokhi*) acted the Chaldeans in the Fiery Furnace play. *Deystvo* (enactment), a term specially applied to triumphal celebrations in Red Square and Uspensky Cathedral, came to be the standard term for any kind of performance. It was later revived by Bolshevik activists to describe mass open-air re-creations of revolutionary events.

However, as the monarchs invited in more and more foreign acting troupes, first Italians, then French and Germans, and the nascent Russian drama based itself on foreign models, native literati called for a national theater. It would not only be distinguished by its exploitation of Russian life as subject matter but would use the drama to correct and reform Russian manners. A task was laid on the Russian theater that it be instrumental in enlightening the nation.

This theme is harped on continuously throughout Russian writing. It so obsessed Gogol, who felt he had to be a messiah, that it destroyed his talent. The critic Belinsky, followed by Chernyshevsky and Dobrolyubov, preached the need for the theater to instruct its audiences and lead them out of darkness. Ostrovsky deplored audiences's enthusiasm for Offenbach when they should be imbibing lessons from dramas of Russian life by himself and his contemporaries. In the latter half of the nineteenth century, frequent attempts were made to create a *narodny* (people's, national) theater, although there was no consensus on how this was to be done or for what reason. Stage European and Russian classics, said some; no, only folk dramas, said others. It is to advance literacy, said some; no, the main goal is to prevent alcoholism and similar wastes of time, said others. Theater groups were formed in peasant villages and factories and may be seen as the seeds of the later Proletkul't movement. One of the reasons Russian acting and directing have been so focused on reality is that realism is viewed as more accessible, a better medium for instruction. Yet, for all its abstruseness, the symbolists' concept of *sobornost'* was advanced with the same corrective goals in mind. Hence the notions of "theater for itself" and "theater as such," of "retheatricalization of the theater," whose influence, although in conflict with the characteristic cultural tendency of the socialist revolution, nevertheless would make itself felt on almost every form of spectacle born after the Revolution. The conflict was apparent in the activities of the Proletkul't itself.

In short, there was a deeply rooted belief among most educated Russians that theater had to be more than mere entertainment. Even if it did not deal in crude messages, its sophistication, polish, and high level of artistry were supposed to edify and improve the spectator. One was to leave the playhouse spiritually elevated and morally improved. This tradition would fit neatly within the scheme for the arts promoted by the Communist Party and the Soviet state. Inspired by socialism, the theater would uplift the intellectual and ideological status of the masses and indoctrinate them in the new political realities. It would serve to advance socialism.

The belief in high art as a means to national salvation that had taken root in the nineteenth century meant that the Soviets could condemn cubism, formalism, and other nontraditional forms of art as counterrevolutionary, without abandoning the ideal of the social significance of art. As Svetlana Boym has put it,

> if the Russian political heritage is not admirable, the Russian artistic heritage is. The writers offered a different kind of double agency, cultural mediation, and translation. If there is a single indisputably positive outcome of Russian–Western cross-fertilization, it is the birth of classical Russian literature. Writers were often regarded as "foreigners in their own land," and yet, since Pushkin, they were also unofficial legislators of the people, in Russia more than anywhere else.[1]

Substitute "artist" for "writer," and the same holds true for the theater.

Only in societies where art and literature are taken so seriously are they regarded as potent and dangerous. The Soviet conviction that culture matters was evident in the attention paid to even minor details of theatrical activity by the highest levels of the state bureaucracy. Unilateral decisions by theater staff were out of the question: every measure taken had to be scrutinized, discussed, and approved, starting with the theater's Party committee and moving up through various censorship bodies before reaching the Politburo or the Central Committee.

Marx had held that in the communist utopia, artists as a separate caste would cease to exist. Conditions would be such that everyone would be free to be an artist: it was a world in which all workers were Sunday painters, poets, or actors. Lenin, more pragmatically and, perhaps, more cynically, did not trust to the organic evolution of this condition. The proletariat needed guidance by an intellectual elite. As early as his pamphlet *What Is to Be Done* (1902), he had stated that the economic struggle can "generate only a trade-union consciousness" in reforming

---

1 Svetlana Boym, *Another Freedom: The Alternative History of an Idea* (Chicago: University of Chicago Press, 2010), 4.

existing society. To radicalize the movement and to provide a "revolutionary consciousness" that could create a new society, there needed to be a "vanguard party"
of full-time "professionals" "from without" that would lead the proletariat to this
end. True revolution required the "profound scientific knowledge . . . born in the
brains" of Marxists sprung from the "*bourgeois intelligentsia*" (Lenin's emphasis).

So, from the very outset of the Revolution, these two concepts were set on the
road to a head-on collision. Lenin and his chief deputy in the art world, Lunacharsky, maintained the importance of the high culture of the past and the value of
the bourgeois intelligentsia in preserving it until such time as the proletariat was
mature enough (and socialist enough) to take over. Those further to the Left took
the position that art had to be made by and for the proletariat and that all vestiges
of bourgeois culture should be extirpated. Expediency and maximalism were at log-
gerheads. Neither side had a clear victory. At the same time, when Stalin eliminated
that stalwart of the utopian position the Proletkul't and repudiated the policy of
"proletarianization" of the culture, he was also calling for writers to be "engineers
of the soul" by submerging their need for individual expression in service to a
greater cause. Both the bourgeois intellectual and the proletarian amateur were
transformed into cogs in the machine for perfecting socialism. Creative activities,
to be orthodox, had to contribute to building that movement; the best way to take
part in the struggle was to join the Communist Party and trumpet its policies.

Subsuming all artistic endeavor into one giant purpose had been stipulated
in another of Lenin's statements: "In the Soviet Workers' and Peasants' Republic,
every educational endeavor, both in politics and in education generally—and in art
particularly—must be permeated with the spirit of the proletariat's class struggle
for successfully accomplishing the aims of its dictatorship."[2] The theater, of all the
arts the one that speaks most immediately to the public, therefore required intense
supervision and repression. The reactions of spectators had to be foreseen and
regimented so that the correct political lesson could be learned. Paradoxically, the
twentieth-century Russian theater has long been considered, and with some justice,
a cornucopia of invention, innovation, and unbridled creativity. The names Stanislavsky, Meyerhold, Mayakovsky, Tairov, Eisenstein, Bulgakov, Okhlopkov, Éfros,
and Lyubimov are bywords for theatrical brilliance. Nevertheless, every action
in the theater between 1917 and 1992, whether traditional or experimental, Party
dictated or dissenting, amateur or professional, was taken in reaction to a political
event, decree, or atmosphere. Unlike a painter who might hide his most personal
creations in the cellar, showing them only to trustworthy visitors, the theater artist
had to work out in the open. That so many extraordinary accomplishments saw the
light of day is all the more remarkable given the obstacle course set in their path.

Lenin grew irritated by theater that seemed to shirk its civic responsibility; he
blamed both the bourgeois Art Theater for wasting its talents on such sentimental

2   Vladimir Lenin, draft of resolution "O proletarskoy kul'ture" [On proletarian culture], in *Sochineniya* [Works] (Moscow: Gos. Izd-vo, 1926–27), 14:409.

trash as *Cricket on the Hearth* and the futurists for perversion and obscurantism. Such "deviations" had to be brought into line. In 1919 a decree was enacted to "unite the theatrical field," and a Central Theatrical Committee was created as part of the People's Commissariat of Enlightenment. This was part of a general trend as the Soviet government began to centralize, indeed, to overcentralize, every aspect of society, including the realms of art and culture. Political ideology became the touchstone of worth. Artists were refashioned as "cultural workers" and, as individuals, had to be subordinated to the collective. Companies were given more importance than stars, and the greatest merit was attached to works that furthered the social struggle. Ideology trumped aesthetics in matters of art.

"Bliss was it in that dawn to be alive, but to be young was very heaven." Wordsworth's response to the outbreak of the French Revolution may be applied to the Russian Revolution only with conditions. The instability of daily life, the privations, the terror unleashed by the Bolsheviks in their own insecurity prevented even true believers from being wholly elated by the turn of events. Even so, many artists seized on the opportunity to impose previously sidelined or experimental styles on the public. In the early absence of censorship, anything went. The ferment of ideas and experimentation made the first couple of decades a golden age of theater. The most fertile of these movements was futurism, whose proponents had greeted the Bolsheviks with enthusiasm. The futurists, notably Vladimir Mayakovsky, took on the task of completing the social revolution by "an October 25 in the realm of art."

The notion of an artistic avant-garde is essentially a twentieth-century invention. It arises in the earliest stages of a society's modernization, at a point when the new technologies are still found to be exhilarating. Only gradually do their oppressive elements become apparent. History is flashing by so quickly that the present cannot be grasped, but the future seems to hold out glowing promise. This belief that humanity is rapidly approaching the greatest change it has ever experienced, a change for the better, typifies the creed of the avant-gardist. The past, even the recent past, is regarded as remote and irrelevant.

Young Soviet artists shared this belief. They embraced all the outward tokens of modernism—machinery, speed and efficiency, rejection of tradition—and, to a greater or lesser degree, folded in the communist insistence on the primacy of the proletariat. At the same time, they could not abandon their own personal visions and extreme forms of expression, often running headlong into the need for comprehension and acceptance by the masses.

The Soviet system perpetuated tsarist systems of control and censorship, but in a far more programmatic and consistent manner. The task of the prerevolutionary censor had been to ban and proscribe, to prevent the public from coming in contact with ideas deemed subversive or injurious. The Soviet regime practiced both proscription and prescription: it determined not only what was harmful but also what was wholesome for the community. It is therefore possible to talk of Soviet art and theater not simply as a continuation of long-standing Russian traditions but as a distinct network of ideas and practices. The agglomeration may at first seem too eclectic: proletarian *samodeyatel'stvo* (do-it-yourselfism), living newspapers, socialist realism, biomechanics, circusization, the synthetic actor, and conflictlessness appear to be warring extremes. What they have is common is that, at one time or another, each was seen as a means of promoting socialism and a new Soviet way of life. What they also have in common is an attempt to appeal to a new audience.

Theater fever took hold from the start. During the harshest days of the Civil War, despite the cold, privations, anguish—perhaps because of it—the theaters played to full houses. In Moscow alone, dozens of new theaters opened their doors. Itinerant companies performed under the roughest of conditions. In 1920, more than a thousand professional troupes functioned in the Red Army. During the first months of 1920, the 16th Army of the Western Front alone welcomed 259 performances, attended by 149,470 spectators. To make the theater accessible to the people, in the year following the Revolution, the workers were given free admission to all theaters. If we are to believe Stanislavsky, the acting profession formed under the old regime felt "impotent at the sight of this mass unleashed on the theater."

During the New Economic Policy of the 1920s, radical experimentation ran amok and alarmed the authorities. Although many of the prominent practitioners paid lip service to the homilies of socialism, they went their own ways in terms of staging and design. While Meyerhold proclaimed that biomechanics and constructivism were fully consonant with a working-class vision, they were also the purest expression of the modernist avant-garde. The fad for exploiting circus, music hall, and silent film techniques was a nod to popular entertainment, but it was also a direct legacy of futurist manifestos. The best playwrights were confecting satires, not tributes to the revolutionary cause.

The consolidation of power under Stalin drastically reduced the variety on offer. In the early 1930s, political opposition to the Central Committee had been overcome, the New Economic Policy had been rescinded, the first Five-Year Plan was under way, agriculture was in the process of being completely collectivized: in short, in the jargon of the times, there was "a socialist offensive on every front"—including the cultural front. In 1931 a theatrical conference organized by the Proletarian Writers' Organization rejected the prerevolutionary cultural heritage, accused the Moscow Art Theater of "bourgeois realism," and advocated the substitution of itself for existing theaters. These proletarian literary organizations were themselves swept away in 1932 to make way for a Union of Soviet Writers. The theatrical arms of Proletkul't were reorganized into "theaters of Leninist komsomols." That same year, Stalin for the first time qualified writers as "engineers of souls" and spoke of "socialist realism." The First Congress of Soviet Writers in August 1934 heard from the mouth of Andrey Zhdanov a definition of socialist realism that was incorporated into the statutes of the Writer's Union. Socialist realism, opposed on one side to futurism, on the other to critical realism, became henceforth the "fundamental method"—to quote Zhdanov—for all the arts.

The classics now made up a large part of the repertoire, and the Art Theater was extolled as a pattern for all theaters in the USSR. Maksim Gorky was largely responsible for this change. Since his return to the USSR in 1928, after a seven-year residence in Italy, Gorky accomplished an enormous amount of work as an organizer, theorist, and dramatist. His programmatic article "On Plays," published in 1933, demanded a civic drama reflecting the new man and honored the psychologically realistic drama founded on character conflict: "The indication of class is not enough to express the living man," he wrote. In 1932 the Moscow Art Academic Theater had added to its title "named after Gorky."

Stalin's performance as general secretary of the Central Committee of the Communist Party was the fullest incarnation of centralization and hierarchy. Unlike Lenin, who cared little for the theater (when in London, he had visited only music halls), the general secretary took an avid interest in every aspect of it, reading plays in manuscript, bestowing preferment on actors, ordering openings and closings, censuring reviews, and judging prizes. His opinions were usually less predictable and less dogmatic than the policies pursued by his underlings, owing to the vagaries of his taste and his acquaintance with individual artists. Nevertheless, during his regime, theatrical activity was subjected to the closest scrutiny from above and the harshest directives of any time in Russian history since Tsar Aleksey Mikhaylovich banished the *skomorokhi*. The importance attributed to the theater can be seen in the institution of such distinctions as Meritorious Artist or People's Artist of the USSR as well as in the number of arrests and convictions of actors and directors during and after the Terror.

These punitive measures were also part of the centralization process, the ruthless homogenization of multinational cultures within a gigantic Eurasian state. The accusatory labels may have changed over time—"internal émigrés" and "bourgeois nationalists" in the 1920s, "wreckers" and "revisionists" in the 1930s, "rootless cosmopolitans" in the 1950s—but the aim was always to make the entire nation toe the general line (*zagib* or *peregib*).

A British historian has questioned the singularity of Stalin's influence in the arts, asking whether attempting creative work in the arts under Stalin was a qualitatively different proposition from the way it was, and is, under

> systems governed by religious or commercial ideology and practice. For what creative person anywhere at any time, no matter what their readiness to oblige, has not been hindered as well as helped by the people whose job it is to commission or subsidize works of arts, then produce and monitor them?"[3]

This seems a remarkably ingenuous formulation. Under Stalin, the artist, particularly the theater artist, had not only to pledge allegiance to formal policies pronounced ex cathedra; he also had to fear arbitrary punishment dictated only by

3   G. S. Smith, "Stalin on top," *Times Literary Supplement* (August 7, 2009), 11, speaking of Prokof'ev.

the whims and moods of a supreme leader. When one considers that the various layers of bureaucracy were themselves subject to these whims and therefore unsure of the criteria for praise or condemnation, it becomes clear that "ideology" under Stalin was not a wholly reliable standard by which to make art.

This may help to explain why the history of the Soviet theater is most usually told through the careers of its stage directors. The Communist emphasis on self-governing companies failed to take into account the growing prominence of the director during the fin de siècle. The Moscow Art Theater had been mocked by traditionalists for the subservience of its actors to the direction of Stanislavsky and Nemirovich-Danchenko. (Indeed, Stanislavsky, who began as a dictatorial director in the style of the Saxe-Meiningers, would, by the end of his life, revert to the idea of the actor as fount of creativity.) However, the Art Theater model began to prevail, and many of those who had begun their careers at this time—Vakhtangov, Meyerhold, Tairov—became the movers and shakers of the first two and a half decades of Soviet rule. Their ideas and their personalities were stamped on their productions so indelibly that this individualism led, in some respects, to their repression and persecution. During the 1920s, when the government itself was undergoing flux, their personal styles could be exercised with some latitude. With Stalin installed as the ultimate authority, there was no room for individual initiative. A common practice under Stalin and his successors was to transfer or merge companies and blur their creative profiles, to prevent the strong individuality of their leaders overshadowing the theater's primary responsibility to the system.

The teeming creativity of directors and designers against such odds is all the more noteworthy in the face of Soviet playwriting. They had to make bricks with very little straw. The Revolution did not unleash an Elizabethan age of great writing for the stage. The best dramatists of the earlier period, satirists such as Mayakovsky, Bulgakov, Érdman, and Shvarts, or experimenters such as the Oberiu group, met with brief runs, prohibitions, or coterie audiences. The plays that held the stage were either calculated audience pleasers or more or less explicit restatements of current government policy. What drew the public was not so much the scripts as their treatment. After the Great Patriotic War, a new school of playwrights, among them Arbuzov, Rozov, Volodin, Roshchin, Vampilov, and, later, Petrushevskaya and Gorin, could inject more personal attitudes and idiosyncratic voices into drama. But even its strongest apologists cannot point to the advent of a Soviet Gogol or Chekhov.

The Great Patriotic War sent the theater in two extreme directions: the established companies were evacuated far into the interior, and contingents from them traveled to the various fronts to remind the troops of the national culture for which they were fighting. The need to defend the motherland put all other agendas in the shade. Immediately after the war, a rare sense of relief prompted a respite from messages and incentives. The interlude was brief. The last years of

Stalin's reign saw the theater under attack again: starting on the ideological front, with an insistence on lack of conflict in drama and cold war, it rapidly devolved into finger-pointing at specific persons. The critical establishment, which had been created through the Writer's Union expressly to preserve uniformity of opinion, was now accused of being a nest of vipers.

Even after Stalin's death, reform was limited. Whatever energies survived after the war were devoted to hostilities against the West. The great theatrical titans of the 1920s and 1930s were dead or demoralized. The bureaucratic armature that had built up around the theater over the previous three decades was intact, if rusty: screws might be loosened or tightened, but it held fast. Until 1991, the Soviet Union counted 640 state theaters, with forty-five in Moscow alone (for an agglomeration of eight million inhabitants). The actors and technicians were all salaried functionaries, who had to spend three or four years in specialized technical schools to be eligible for employment. Actors' salaries were based on the number and importance of their roles. Older students, from thirty to thirty-five, might study for two years to become directors; the graduate competitions awarded state positions to those who excelled. The permanent troupes, well protected by unions, played without interruption for years a rota of some twenty plays. This rigid system did not allow for the freedom for actors to move from troupe to troupe without special permission; repertoires and budgets had to be endorsed from above.

However, even though the framework remained in place, the audience had changed. Theatergoers who had grown up after the war regarded the cataclysms of the first half of the century as recent history, not personal experience. A liberalizing of the theater came not from government fiats but from below, from the concerted effort of a new generation. It wanted to improve and perfect the socialism it had been taught, not overturn or replace it. The Sovremennik and the Taganka were the only two new official theaters to be created after World War II. The young actors and critics who planned the Sovremennik were inspired by the Théâtre National Populaire of Jean Vilar, which had visited the Soviet Union now that the "window to the West" had been reopened. In other words, they were not rebels with a cause, opposing the government; they were hoping to reignite the revolutionary ideals that had become obscured by years of cowardice and compromise. Even Lyubimov's Taganka claimed a descent from Vakhtangov and Meyerhold; its Brechtian methods, in its formative phase, were in the service of dusting off such icons of Revolution as Mayakovsky.

The first signs of new life began in the repertoire, particularly in the Baltic republics and amateur studios. The classics were rediscovered: innumerable reinterpretations of Gogol, Tolstoy, Ostrovsky, and Chekhov; adaptations of Dostoevsky; even the occasional remarkable staging of Shakespeare (Tovstonogov's *Henry IV,* Lyubimov's *Hamlet,* Éfros's *Othello*). First as a trickle, then as a flood came the so-called absurdist European plays by Jarry, Pinter, Albee, Witkiewicz,

Camus, Beckett, Ionesco, Mrożek, and eventually Genet; the indigenous Russian absurd (vaudevilles, the Oberiuts), the "lost dramatists" of the 1920s (Érdman, Babel, Bulgakov, whose works were still censored on the state-supported stages despite the rehabilitation of their authors), contemporary plays of social criticism by Petrushevskaya and Sadur. By the late 1980s, a frequent two-way traffic between foreign troupes and Russian directors enriched the thinking of and the influences on the Soviet theater.

Even so, the new theaters found themselves sidelined. The Sovremennik was not taken seriously by the theatrical bureaucracy, which undermined it by wooing away its director Oleg Efremov to head the moribund MAT. The Taganka, although the hottest ticket in Moscow and a must-see for theatrical tourists, was never awarded an official prize or even allowed a souvenir album. Their most audacious productions were regularly banned or emasculated, often for the most trivial of reasons. They were at best "licensed dissent," tolerated but not encouraged by the powers-that-be. The case of Anatoly Éfros was similar: he was transferred from one theater to another, his authority as director subverted, his creative decisions questioned.

Much of the originality and audacity fled to the margins, to the innumerable studio theaters that sprang up in cities throughout the Soviet Union, ranging from clown and mime shows to full-fledged repertory companies. The existing legislation had not foreseen this development, and there was a hectic scramble to enact new regulations that could both control and nourish the phenomenon. Most of it came too late.

Under Brezhnev, audiences flocked to the theater to hear allusive references to political life: gestures, postures, metaphoric stage designs could constitute a language easy to decipher but difficult to censor. Television and the first whiff of freedom of the press drew audiences away from the theater: the rapidly shifting pageant of news provided a novel attraction. The theaters, in response, began to slough off their mantle of civic engagement. They tried out their own freedom to engage in theatricality for theatricality' sake, to amuse and provoke. A new breed of directors emerged: some, such as Anatoly Vasil'ev, proclaimed an interest in advanced philosophical experimentation; others, such as Lev Dodin, wanted to put together teams that would create collectively; still others, such as Sergey Zhenovach, Pëtr Fomenko, and Valery Belyakovich, were eager to explore neglected genres and authors. In many cases, there was a distinct turning away from politics as a subject for drama. The audience, which the Soviet pioneers had conceived as a mass responding in unison, fragmented into individual coteries.

By the time the Soviet Union disintegrated, theaters in its republics were still active and numerous, but a "Soviet Theater" could no longer be identified, either as a branch of government or as an individual enterprise. With the introduction of consumer capitalism, state subsidies were reduced or removed; theaters had to woo patrons, often corporations, to sponsor fresh productions or convert portions of their buildings into restaurants and casinos to generate income. However, the freedom from state control led to considerable diversity. The Soviet past was now available for remodeling. Instead of Evreinov's spectacular reenactment of the storming of the actual Winter Palace, the Russian stage now preferred what the Polish director Tadeusz Kantor has called "the storming of the Winter Palace of Illusion."[4]

---

4   Tadeusz Kantor, *A Journey through Other Spaces: Essays and Manifestoes, 1944–1990*, ed. and trans. Michal Kobialka (Berkeley: University of California Press, 1993), 221–22.

CHAPTER ONE

The Revolution, 1917–1919

D URING THE GREAT WAR, the Russian theater marked time, entertaining the civilian population with frivolous diversions and calls to patriotism, while sending groups of performers to the front lines to entertain the troops with song and recitation. The theater journals regularly reported the injuries and deaths of young actors who had joined up in a fit of war fever. The February Revolution and the establishment of the prophetically named Provisional Government introduced louder notes of uncertainty. The Bolshevik takeover in October, with its contingent bloodshed and civil conflict, turned a confused situation into a rout. Institutions dependent on government subsidy had no sense of how they were to exist; those dependent on the box office saw empty houses because of unsafe streets and devaluation of currency. As the bulwarks of society collapsed, the theater seemed increasingly irrelevant.

The Bolsheviks' interest in the theater was manifested, from the earliest days of its accession, by the promulgation of legislative measures. On November 9, 1917, a fortnight after they seized power, a decree of the Soviet of the People's Commissars (Sovnarkom for short) placed the theaters under the authority of the arts division of the brand-new State Commission for Enlightenment, which was to become the People's Commissariat for Enlightenment (Narkompros). (The word *Proshveshchenie* was chosen instead of that for Education or Instruction, in line with the concept of the masses as *chërny,* or "benighted.") In January 1918, by order of the People's Commissariat for Enlightenment, the theaters of Moscow were placed under the authority of the division of art and enlightenment of the Moscow Soviet; subsequently, the provincial theaters passed progressively under the authority of local Soviets. At the same time, a theater section (Teatral'ny Otdel; TEO) was organized by Narkompros. It was tasked with running the theater as a branch of the government and "giving the provinces directives of a general character concerning the operation of theatrical activity, with the intention of unifying it."

With an early recognition that artists could have a powerful influence on public consciousness, the Bolsheviks set out to attract writers, philosophers, artists, composers, and theater people to their cause. In line with this idea, the leadership of the TEO section was entrusted to individuals with theatrical experience. Although the first administrator was Trotsky's wife, Ol'ga Kameneva, she was teamed with

Vsevolod Meyerhold, who had run the Petrograd section of TEO and who would succeed her in August 1920. From March 1918 to February 1919 the brilliant poet Aleksandr Blok directed the repertoire division and was instrumental in founding the Bol'shoy Dramatic Theater (BDT) in St. Petersburg. Stanislavsky's favorite student, Evgeny Vakhtangov, took on the management of the directing division in 1919. Most of them greeted the Revolution sincerely and enthusiastically and believed in its statements of utopian aims.

Although Marxism was antireligion, the millennial atmosphere churned up a remarkable number of works on biblical or mystical themes. The Art Theater's production of Byron's *Cain,* Vakhtangov's projects for Old Testament plays, Tairov's staging of Claudel's *The Tidings Brought to Mary;* Boris Glagolin's concept of Christian communism; *Zagmuk,* the Maly Theater's play of a slave revolt in Babylon; Mayakovsky's *Mystery-Bouffe;* and even Meyerhold's *The Dawns* are variegated manifestations of this impulse to clothe apocalyptic events in traditional religious imagery.

Almost immediately, conflicts arose concerning the appropriate path for Soviet culture to take. Once all the theaters were put under Meyerhold's supervision, he called for radical reforms, a renunciation of the culture of the past, and a repudiation of those who thought differently in the fields of ideology, art, and literature. Left-wing radicals, working through an organization called Proletarian Culture (Proletkul't), urged the new state to reject the historical legacy of world culture, which, they declared, was elitist. The party leaders, however, among them Lenin, Lunacharsky, Trotsky, and Bukharin, were conservative in their tastes and held fast to the traditional touchstones of the prerevolutionary intelligentsia. They declared the country to be heir to all that was best in world culture.

Throughout this period, the central figure was the first Commissar for People's Enlightenment Anatoly Lunacharsky. An old-style *intelligent* down to his pince-nez and rolled r's, he was renowned as a public speaker, had impeccable credentials as a Marxist from his teens, and had been a card-carrying Bolshevik from 1903. Lunacharsky saw his task as reconciling the aims of the Revolution with the needs of the artistic community and, ideally, merging the two. He proved for at least a decade to be an effective mediator. Through his efforts the best theaters of the tsarist era were preserved from destruction, radical artists were given latitude for their experiments, and the attempts of governmental agencies to interfere with creative activities were closely monitored and, occasionally, chastised. Over time, as maximalist positions became more entrenched and the state tightened its grip on the entire culture, Lunacharsky's intercessions were less effective, and eventually, he was edged out of the picture entirely.

Lunacharsky's first major project was to rescue the theaters from indigence and disorganization and bring them under state control. On August 26, 1919, the Soviet government adopted the decree "On the Unification of Theatrical Activity," which rounded out the earlier measures. This decree, signed by Lenin, turned out to be the constitutive charter of the Soviet theater; it nationalized "all theatrical property (buildings, properties), in view of their cultural value," and centralized the whole economy of the theater under a Central Theatrical Committee (Tsentroteatr) answering to the Narkompros. It also instituted a censoring function by calling for an inspection of the repertoire by the authorities (either the Tsentroteatr or a local section of the Narkompros) to make sure it was serving the socialist ideal. The unification was not fully integrated, however: the decree distinguished those theaters "recognized as useful and artistic" (themselves divided into several categories, all subsidized by the state) from theaters "managed by entrepreneurs or private organizations that do not guarantee a superior level of culture."

Theater histories often give the impression that the Revolution welcomed with open arms untrammeled experimentation in the arts and gave its blessing to the discovery of new forms. A minority of artists may have seen the overthrow of the tsarist regime as an artistic opportunity, but the policies of the Bolshevik Party and the Soviet government were far from iconoclastic. Quite the contrary. Their concern was to make the Russian cultural legacy available to a proletarian audience and allow the disinherited to take possession of what had been withheld from them. The program adopted by the eighth Party Congress in 1919 indicated that "it is necessary to offer and render accessible to workers all the art treasures that emerged from the exploitation of their work and that heretofore have been at the exclusive disposal of the exploiters."

The concern with preserving the theater as a medium of traditional culture can be seen clearly in the founding of the Bol'shoy Dramatic Theater in 1919. Its founders, among them Blok and Maksim Gorky, meant it to be a temple of high culture and traditional drama. To match the sublimity of an apocalyptic era, the repertoire needed to be made up of Shakespeare, Schiller, Goldoni, Molière, and Rostand.

Chaos Out of Order

Soviet historians mark October 25, 1917, as the official opening date of the Bolshevik Revolution, when the cruiser *Aurora* fired on the Winter Palace. Theater history sets the date somewhat earlier, in Petrograd, on February 25, 1917, when a fur-swathed audience left the opulent Alexandra Theater, after attending the opening night of *Masquerade,* to hear gunshots in the bitterly cold streets. The police were firing on a mob at the Nikolaev railroad station. The event signaled the outbreak of the February Revolution, but it also bore a symbolic meaning. Vsevolod Meyerhold, the most controversial and prominent stage director in Russia, had planned and rehearsed Lermontov's romantic verse melodrama for seven years; all the resources of the Imperial Theaters had been put at his disposal. Everything that appeared onstage, from the hundreds of costumes to tea services, had been especially designed by Aleksandr Golovin and constructed specifically for this production. Its costliness and sumptuousness marked the climax of both Meyerhold's work with traditional forms of romantic theater and the open-handed patronage of the court. It has also been read as a requiem for the society of bejeweled aristocrats and profiteers who filled the stalls. This, the last production at the Alexandra as an imperial playhouse, was like a burst of royal fireworks answered by the artillery of the imminent overthrow.

When the performance had ended, the star, Yur'ev, who was celebrating his silver jubilee, was heading to take his curtain call when he was approached by two actresses.

Yury Yur'ev, *Zapiski* [Memoirs], ed. E. M. Kuznetsova (Leningrad: Iskusstvo, 1963), 2:232–35. Yury Mikhaylovich Yur'ev (1872–1948), leading man at the Alexandra Theater (1893–1917), who played Molière's *Dom Juan* and Arbenin in *Masquerade* for Meyerhold; in 1918 he founded the St. Petersburg Theater of Tragedy and in 1919 helped cofound the BDT.

"Go away, go away at once," E. N. Roshchina-Insarova[1] said on the way. "I don't know if we'll get home today."

"Why not?" I asked, bewildered.

"Why not? Didn't you hear? There's shooting in the streets..."

I lent an ear... And indeed, somewhere in the distance, the muffled sound of gunfire could be heard. [...]

[Yur'ev got his ovation and a party and was trying to find a way to get all his bouquets and wreaths home.] My intimates and friends, who had taken on that mission, seemed to have great difficulty, because the horse cabs had disappeared. They tried to phone for a taxi, but taxis refused to come. By fair means or foul, they secured two motor cars and one horse cab. It was impossible to take everything, most of the unwieldy stuff had to stay in the dressing room until the next day.

The electricity on the street was out. Only Nevsky was lit by a searchlight from the Admiralty. It was dark, empty; a sinister silence prevailed. Despite the unremitting, rather terrifying situation, we got home to Kamennostrov Prospect without any obstacles. [...]

On the next morning, February 26, the day seemed to dawn calmly. The usual traffic on the streets, although every so often mounted patrols would turn up. In the afternoon a telephone call from V. A. Telyakovsky.[2] Again, as yesterday, a notification that the show might not go on. Around five, Telyakovsky let me know that the show would go on.

I had a hard time getting to the theater... Soldiers everywhere, patrols... They were dispersing the mob, which included, evidently, many curiosity seekers. There was a large group near the theater. Excited by something... It turned out that they had just carried off the corpse of a student, killed by a stray bullet, lodged in one of the side

1 Ekaterina Nikolaevna Roshchina-Insarova (actually Pashennaya, 1883–1970), prominent actress in St. Petersburg, noted for emotional nuances, "the poet of renunciation and self-sacrifice."
2 Vladimir Arkad'evich Telyakovsky (1861–1924), director of the Imperial Theaters 1901–17, a supporter of talent, but conservative in his literary tastes.

doors (across from Tolmazov Lane), where the student had been killed. Eyewitnesses were offering details of the incident...

[...] The mood was tense to the *n*th degree, not at all to do with the show. Minds were occupied with other things; it was hard to concentrate.

The performance, despite intense coordination, went without élan: the performers, understandably, were unfocussed and inattentive.

The next day, February 27, a call from Telyakovsky.

"The show has been changed... mobs of workers are moving along the Liteyny, heading for the Tauride Palace... Reports from the police department have been inauspicious... A bloody clash is bound to happen... Don't leave the house!"

And so, the performance of *Masquerade* set for February 27, 1917, did not take place.

THAT SAME DAY, the Socialist revolutionary Aleksandr Kerensky helped form two provisional committees to deal with the conflict. Unrest was the order of the day, with strikes, queues at bakeries, the police firing on crowds, public meetings, and deliberations of the Duma, until, on March 14, a Provisional Government was appointed, with Kerensky appointed minister of justice. For many in the theater, narrowly focused on their rehearsals, this was all white noise. Typical was the atmosphere at the Moscow Art Theater's first studio.

> Sof'ya Giatsintova, *S pamyatyu naedine* [Alone with my memory] (Moscow: Iskusstvo, 1989), 164–65. Sof'ya Vladimirovna Giatsintova (1895–1983), actress at the Moscow Art Theater from 1911 and leader in the MAT First Studio, where she played Maria in *Twelfth Night*.

Rehearsals for *Twelfth Night*[3] were long and hard... and we didn't notice when the February Revolution took place—life had already been turned inside out by the war, and one more reversal did not strike us as so unusual as to pay it the attention it deserved. Even the abdication of the tsar[4] somehow made no special impression—in those days it was much more important to earn approval at rehearsals. True, we all went to hear Kerensky[5] at the Bol'shoy Theater, where we even ran into Stanislavsky.[6]

Kerensky entered to tempestuous applause, stood there for a moment—and jumped onto the table. He spoke of waging war to its ultimate victory, all the while working

---

3   The MAT First Studio's production of Shakespeare's comedy opened on December 25, 1917, with Mikhail Chekhov as Malvolio.

4   On March 15, 1917, Nicholas II abdicated the Russian throne for himself and his heir Tsarevich Aleksey and was placed under house arrest in Tsarskoe Selo.

5   Aleksandr Fëdorovich Kerensky (1881–1970) was made minister of justice in the Provisional Government on March 14–15, 1917, and became its head on July 21, as prime minister and commander in chief of the Russian armed forces.

6   Konstantin Sergeevich Stanislavsky (actually Alekseev, 1863–1938), cofounder of the Moscow Art Theater in 1897. Scion of a millionaire industrialist sprung from peasants, he began as an amateur actor and, at the MAT, promoted innovative approaches to acting, playing leading roles in Chekhov, Gorky, Ibsen, Ostrovsky, and Turgenev.

himself up into a kind of inspired hysterics. It impressed the listeners. Sitting in the dress circle, I saw how the stage was watered with a golden rain: to support the army, women took off their rings, bracelets, necklaces, wept and showered Kerensky with flowers. He was always referred to as a poseur. I never quite followed the meaning of his speeches, but, when I heard that hoarse voice with an intonation that went straight to the soul, with a temperament like his, he would surely have been enlisted by the Art Theater. What can you do—I have a one-track mind.

[...] The October Revolution also took us completely by surprise. No one, including Stanislavsky, was prepared for it or could figure it out. We considered that something extraordinary and meaningful had happened, but we had no direct relationship to it. Therefore, we had to go on working on new "given circumstances,"[7] that is, trying not to hear the gunfire in the streets and to proceed with the last rehearsals and techs for *Twelfth Night.*

PAYING LITTLE HEED to the new government, street life and free expression were revitalized. Walls blazed with advertisements and announcements. "Concert meetings" of public speakers were frequently held.

> A benefit performance at the Maria Theater for widows and orphans of the February Revolution, April 1917. Meriel Buchanan, *Dissolution of an Empire* (London: John Murray, 1932), 201–2. Meriel Buchanan (1886–1959), daughter of the British ambassador to the Russian imperial court, served as a nurse for wounded soldiers in St. Petersburg during World War I; she left Russia in January 1918.

For the first time that night the real, devastating change which had been made by the Revolution came home to me in its full force. Here was indeed the same blue and white Opera House, here were the same glass chandeliers, the same blue velvet curtains. But the Imperial Arms and the big golden eagles which had surmounted the boxes had been torn down, leaving gaping holes which had not been filled up, the men who showed people to their places had cast off their gold-braided Court uniforms and wore plain grey jackets which made them look indescribably shabby and dingy, soldiers in mud-stained khaki lolled everywhere, smoking evil-smelling cigarettes, spitting all over the place and eating the inevitable sunflower seeds out of paper bags. A few *nouveaux riches,* who had known how to profit from the Revolution, lolled in the boxes, over-dressed, over-scented, over-jewelled; the stalls were filled with long-haired men and short-haired women whose high woollen blouses and unwashed appearance showed that the doctrine of liberty was one that preached a contempt for beauty.

---

7 *Predligaemye obstoyatel'stva,* a phrase adapted by Stanislavsky from Pushkin, to indicate the conditions the playwright and the play provide an actor in determining a character's behavior.

ALTHOUGH the Provisional Government professed its intent to aid the Allies in winning the war, the army began to disintegrate, as "delegates" from the capital arrived at the front to announce that the officers no longer had any authority. Orders and counterorders reduced the efficacy of an already demoralized force. The Bolsheviks promised voters an immediate separate peace.

> Aleksandr Kugel', editorial, *Teatr i Iskusstvo* [Theater and art] (June 24, 1917), 478. Aleksandr (Avraam) Rafaylovich Kugel' (1864–1928), influential and artistically conservative editor of the Petrograd magazine *Teatr i Iskusstvo*, cofounded the Crooked Mirror cabaret in 1908.

Right now, the actor's most real and important work, and, I would say, his great historical task, is to set out for the front to counterbalance the corrosive and ruinous sermons about peace with Germany, or—what comes to the same thing—ignorance about the war against it, or—what is still worse (because it is even more senseless)—the transformation of a national army in wartime into a weapon of the International. The actors should establish concert parties of a patriotic character . . . Every actor who feels that he is a son of Russia [. . .] can and must direct all the passion of his heart and talent to inspire people to perform heroic deeds and to stir up feelings for our country [. . .] Go then, actors, if love of your country lives within you, go to the front, to the soldiers, rouse their emotions and raise their spirits! And you, oh tender and delicate actresses, go there and use your soft and womanly voices to appeal for a struggle on behalf of the honor and dignity of Russia.

> B. Nikonov, *Obozrenie teatrov* [Theater survey] (July 7, 1917; August 23, 1917). Boris Pavlovich Nikonov was a novelist and writer on legal matters.

Not a single real talent has yet spoken out in the language of freedom during this "free period" . . . The talented remain silent, disturbed and frightened by the terrible dregs, the confusion, and the disorder that our revolution has harbored . . . Can songs of beauty and light conceivably be sung when the spectacle of a shameful struggle against our country is going on? This struggle has almost become a slogan of the day. The spectacle can make one cry out from pain, or swear, or tear one's hair, but it cannot make one write songs or create inspired works of art! . . . Something incomprehensible has occurred. [. . .] The hopes have been crushed underfoot by criminals. People have grown stupid, squandered their humanity, incinerated their souls, and run away from the enemy at the front, and here they sing savage songs all night long . . . One does not feel like believing that this is life itself.

> Aleksandr Blok, "Letter on the theater," September 1917, in *Sobranie sochineny v shesti tomakh* [Collected works in six volumes] (Moscow: Pravda, 1971), 5:392–94. Aleksandr Aleksandrovich Blok (1880–1921), Symbolist poet, whose

poem *The Twelve* (1917) glorified the Revolution. After 1917 he took an active part in running theater through the TEO and with Maksim Gorky in 1919 organized the Bol'shoy Dramatic Theater. Shortly before his death, he complained that artistic freedom was being taken away in the Soviet Union.

I protest that state theaters must exist, because, unfortunately, at the moment no one but the government can provide artistic institutions autonomy and independence.

Can such theaters exist without compromise? They have to exist without compromise, and the government itself needs them to.

The theater is a mighty force for education. The theater must train the will. [...]

Anyone who believes in a better future is bound to know that this is a brief, transitional period; it has to be endured until the race of sated, apathetic, and squeamish people, long hated by all actors and artists, whatever their schools, will forever abandon the brightly lit theatrical auditoriums and sink to the depths where it is foredoomed to sink; another race, irrepressibly bursting upward—a race of people, spiritually starved, alert and sensitive—will still not fill those auditoriums.

I don't know how long such a time will drag its weary length along; maybe it will be a protracted period; maybe great art, the theatrical in particular, will no longer be needed by the new people just as it was long unneeded by the old; but this is a secondary question—not only for art but for every artist.

In any case, the government must make an experiment and try to set up a test budget; if it will go to the end, art will deign to accept external backing from it. [...]

From a government that has grasped the whole world in its tentacles, that knows no bounds, that is not in control of its forces, that has led Europe into the military debacle in which it now finds itself, one can expect anything.

It does not pay for a government of any regime whatever to close the doors of theaters any more than the doors of universities. It is but a small twitch of the tentacles, a twitch on the periphery, at first almost unnoticed in the center. The power of the government (the notorious awful "might") is such that at first no one—neither society nor individual—is able to mount opposition to the destruction of whole institutions (theaters) and individuals (artists).

But if this occurs, then woe betide the government in future. Its tentacles will shrivel up, weaken; the response to all its sinister past activities will be unheard of, and savage anarchy will overshadow all the horrors of its past wars; there will be a blind revolt by people long dwelling in darkness, the proper retribution for those who declare that man can be satisfied with bread alone.

And the stone age will return. And again, suddenly and secretly, a poor man, still hunted down by beasts, still savage, will smile; again he will begin to use a stone to scratch his poor fancies, poor designs, attracted by that same inexplicable and irresistible power of art.

V. Vodin, "Rayonnye teatry" [Neighborhood theaters], *Teatral'naya gazeta* [Theater Gazette] 38 (September 24, 1917), 4–5.

"Bread and circuses" is the age-old demand of the general public even in our times, when the weariness at political struggles is tangible, but when ever newer and newer sources of spiritual strength are still needed to carry on the unending battles and skirmishes, in particular, to hearken to the imperious voice of the people demanding "shows." And it is dangerous, fraught with ruin for culture to hand the masses over to the power of, namely, "shows," shows that, what's more, are coarsely sensual. There are queues at the entrances to the movies as long as those at the entrances to the bread shops. And this evil is no less than "the bread lines"; here the spectator either roars with laughter at the never-ending adventures of the Glupyshkins[8] (and this is far from the least of the frivolities) or, with sinking heart, watches a crime serial. And later, from this people whom we keep segregated from Shakespeare, Tolstoy, Ostrovsky, Gogol, we will demand political maturity, almost an Athenian democracy. By supporting the movies, we increase the power of a mob that has no spiritual relation to cultural achievements; and it is criminal for the leaders of democracy at the present time to drop from their hands such powerful weapons as theater in the struggle against the base appetites of the human soul. And I would like to believe that Moscow, the socialist municipality of Moscow, will not refrain from supporting theater, that eternal tribune of beauty and freedom, through all the outlying districts of the city. I am sure that "the masters of Moscow" need only send out the call, and there will forgather for this great, truly great task all those who hold art dear, who believe that theater is the mentor of the general public.

> Playwrights bent every effort to exploit current events, as was demonstrated in advertisements from the last page of *Teatr i Iskusstvo* 10 (1917).

S. A. Mirovich. Contemporary comedy in two acts. *Vova the Revolutionist*. Price 2 r. A comic farce in 1 act forbidden by the censor. *Oy, Something's About to Happen*. Price 1 r.

New play (topical). *The Last Monarchists* (*Shturmer, Lenin and Co.*). Original comedy in two acts. By Al. Pav. Burdvoskhodov. Price per copy 3 r.

The Revolutionary Wedding (*A Life for Love!*), play in three acts, trans. E. Shidlovskaya. This play monopolized the 1917–12 [*sic*] season at the Odessa Dramatic Theater. By A. I. Sibiryakov. Suitable for production even in small theaters. Ten characters. Effective roles for the heroic lover and the dram. ingenue.

Lenin and Co. (*Enemies of Freedom*). Political caricature in one act from the life of the Bolsheviks. 2 m. and 2 f. roles. Price 1 r., 50 k.

The Nocturnal Orgies of Rasputin (The Tsar's miracle-worker). Set in a private room in a restaurant, roles: The Tsarina, Vyrubov, Rasputin, Minister Protopopov.

For Thee My Fatherland! play in one act in two scenes by E. Shidlovskaya. The play

---

8   Glupyshkin, the Russian name of Cretinetti, the immensely popular comic figure created by André Deed in slapstick films from Itala Studios (from 1909).

is accompanied by music by V. Pergament (Introduction. Intermission. Oriental song and hymn). Benefit role for a young leading lady. Price 1 r., 50 k., with piano score.

The Murder of Gapon (*The Mystery of the Dacha in Ozerki*). Drama in one act by S. A. Alesin, rep. of the Petr. and Moscow Theaters.

Comrade Directors! A. Kireev-Gatchinsky presents the latest novelty of the season: *The Anarchist,* 1 m., 2 f. Owes its exceptional success to its topicality.

THE BOLSHEVIK coup d'état burst on the public in Petrograd on October 25, 1917, when the Peter and Paul fortress and the cruiser *Aurora* on the Neva shelled the Winter Palace and the Admiralty. In Moscow, efforts to resist broke out. Richard Boleslavsky, a member of the Moscow Art Theater before the war, had joined the Polish Lancers. On leave, he rejoined the company.

> Richard Boleslavsky with Helen Woodward, *Lances Down: Between the Fires in Moscow* (Indianapolis, Ind.: Bobbs-Merrill, 1932), 72–74. Richard Valentinovich Boleslavsky (Bolesław Ryszard Srzednicki, 1887–1937), Polish actor and director, member of the Moscow Art Theater (1908–19) and the First Studio (1913–19). During the First World War, he served with the Polish Lancers but left Russia when his fellow cadets were executed. He later was with the Kachalov Group in Prague (1921), founded the American Laboratory Theater in New York (1923–30), and became a successful Hollywood film director.

On a certain October night in 1917, the [Art] Theater was crowded. The play, Knut Hamsun's *In the Grip of Life.*[9] In the third act I had but few cues, though I had to remain on the stage. I sat on a large couch facing the audience.

[...] The first row, the most expensive seats, belonged to solid people, thoughtful and elderly. To-night they were shrunken, devitalized, absent. Secret minds behind the masks were on the fever which was tormenting the land.

During intermissions the telephones were besieged. Lobbies and corridors hummed with excitement. A man at a telephone would turn to the crowd and say in a hushed voice, "Fighting in Petrograd! Bloody fighting... Government troops against the Soviets." Another man would come in from the street white and breathless, but a little pompous with his news: "Navy has gone in with the Communists... Cruiser *Aurora* going to bombard Petrograd... Sailors turned the fortress at Cronstadt over to Lenin... all the officers drowned."

The bell rang and the curtain went up for the last act. The audience obediently hurried back to its seats. Like automatons, like robots of the intellect, they sat and listened. We went on with the show.

During the fourth act Colonel Mödl,[10] Chief of the Moscow police, came back-stage and called up his office on our separate line. Actors crowded around the telephone

9 *Livet i Vold* (1910) had first been staged at the Moscow Art Theater in 1911 by Konstantin Mardzhanov, with Ol'ga Knipper in the role of a diva.

10 Colonel Ozv Al'fredovich Modl' had been a decorated officer of the 2nd Siberian Rifle Regiment during the Russo-Japanese War of 1905.

booth. He spoke in monosyllables, he listened for a long time. We could not make out what he was saying, but his face was twitching and with his right hand he was pulling nervously at the white aiguillettes on his shoulders. Only once his voice came stifled through the walls of the booth. He shouted into the transmitter, his face red with fury. "Burn it... Burn everything... Burn it at once!" After which he rushed out and whispered to General Stakhovich,[11] "Can I get a civilian suit here? Petrograd is in the hands of the Communists." Stakhovich took him to a dressing-room. Ten minutes later, Mödl appeared in an old workman's cap and a shabby overcoat belonging to a minor character in some play. The disguise was poor. The clothes, worn and humble and too small for him, merely drew the eye to his healthy, fragrant face. You could see that its little beard and mustache had been groomed by the best barber in town. And shabby men have no such white and shining teeth. He was as incongruous as an English race-horse harnessed to a plow.

Our old tailor and dresser, Baldin, a plain peasant who was a friendly and honest little workman, came rushing out holding Mödl's uniform.

"Your Excellency... Your Excellency... what shall we do with this?" Mödl blew up. "Bitch it!" He released the safety catches on two automatics, stuck them in his pockets, and went out, slamming the door behind him. The little tailor stood aghast, his round face all agape.

Stakhovich addressed him with elaborate graciousness. "My friend, I advise you to preserve this uniform. Tomorrow you may be appointed to wear it." Baldin, from his four feet ten, looked up at Stakhovich's six and two, blinking his eyes. [...] Later he folded it carefully, hung it in a wardrobe and pinned a card on it on which he asked somebody to write: "Left by His Excellency Colonel Mödl. The lining of the left armpit slightly damaged. Mothballs put in, October, 1917."

The fourth act continued. The spectators of the first row were still there, more ghostly than before. Through the long last act till the final curtain they sat like a row of condemned. The curtain rose three times while they applauded mechanically. They stood with a sort of reverence as at a mourning service, until a voice shouted from the gallery: "All power to the Soviets!" Nobody turned around. Nobody looked up. No one picked up the shout and no one objected to it. As if hit over the head by a stick, the spectators shrank still more. But the applause stopped. The curtain went down for the last time in silence. We all hurried to take off our make-up.

Teatr i Iskusstvo 43 (October 22, 1917), 743.

Concerning the question of closing the theaters in Moscow. The Soviet of Professional Union of Actors has also convened an extraordinary meeting of its members. It unanimously resolved:

1. The theater world of Moscow brings together in its professional constituency an enormous mass of workers, whose number, including the families here, consists of

11 Aleksey Aleksandrovich Stakhovich (1856–1919), cavalry colonel, adjutant of the Moscow governor-general; shareholder and investor in the MAT from 1902; member of the MAT board of directors; actor from 1907. Founder of the MAT cooperative society.

some tens of thousands of persons. The right to work, relevant not only to the communal, but also the individual's living welfare, is an elemental and inalienable right of every citizen.

2. The artistic and cultural significance of the theater does not need to be defended. In these troublous days of our social degeneration the theater, irrespective of its forms, plays an exceptional role, as a factor in social unity grounded in artistic enjoyment and spiritual refreshment.

3. The theater is an indispensable agent for the beneficial stimulation of wide circles of society. In great measure the power of the theater's material support of the nation is expressed by state taxes, which provide the government tens of millions of rubles.

4. The economic costs of fuel and lighting are remarkably immaterial, for the quantity of electric energy required by the theaters does not exceed 2 percent of its general usage throughout Moscow.

In view of the foregoing, the meeting determined:

a. to affirm that the closing of theaters in Moscow, from time immemorial the focal point of artistically theatrical life in Russia, both deals a deadly blow to national culture and social life, and deprives a mass of many thousands of a livelihood while, to a remarkable degree, reducing the revenue of the nation's charitable and governmental funding.

b. to take all measures open to the Union to prevent the calamity threatening the theater, in implementation whereof to commission a specially appointed delegation [...] of representatives of the professional union of Moscow actors.

Together with that, the meeting expresses a profound conviction that its voice—the voice of many thousands of the working masses, the voice of art, the voice of generally-accepted cultural and creative and social forces—must meet with a wide and sympathetic response from both society and those of its leading organs to which the country entrusts the preservation of all the values of its material and spiritual welfare.

ELECTED to the team of delegates, mentioned in the resolution, were K. S. Stanislavsky, A. Yu. Yuzhin, A. P. Petrovsky, A. D. Koshevsky, M. F. Lenin and M. S. Narokov.[12] On October 27, the Military-Revolutionary Committee of Petrograd informed Batyushkov,[13] Chief Deputy for State Theater, that it had appointed M. P. Murav'ëv Commissar of State and private theaters. He in turn ordered the

12 Aleksandr Ivanovich Yuzhin (actually Sumbatov, 1857–1927), Georgian prince, dramatist, leading romantic actor at the Maly Theater, Moscow; he became its director in 1919. Andrey Pavlovich Petrovsky (1869–1933), MAT actor, director, teacher; also worked in Korsh's and at the Alexandra Theaters as well as in the provinces. A. D. Koshevsky, comedian and operetta performer. Mikhail Frantsevich Lenin (actually Ignatov, 1880–1951), actor; at the Maly Theater 1902–51. Mikhail Semënovich Narokov (actually Yakubov, 1879–1958), who accused his fellow actors of political "semi-literacy."

13 In November the apolitical literary critic Fëdor Dmitrievich Batyushkov (1857–1920) was elected chairman of the General Meeting of State Theater Artists, which refused to recognize Murav'ëv's authority; he was dismissed by Lunacharsky December 12.

theater staffs to stay at their posts or otherwise be punished for opposition to the Bolshevik authorities.

Sergey Bertenson, *Vokrug iskusstva* [Around art] (Hollywood: Sergey Bertenson, 1957), 236–37. Sergey L'vovich Bertenson (1885–1962), in 1917 assistant to F. D. Batyushkov [see note 13] in administering the Petrograd state theaters; in 1918 became secretary to the MAT administration. Accompanied the Kachalov Group in its travels in Europe 1918–22; then, as Nemirovich-Danchenko's secretary came to the United States with the Musical Studio 1922–24. He accompanied Nemirovich to Hollywood and settled there.

On October 27, 1917, posters appeared in the streets announcing the deposition of the Provisional Government. Immediately the Bolsheviks made their first attempt to rule the theaters: a military–revolutionary committee appointed its own commissar over all the state and private theaters—an actor of the Suvorin Theater Murav'ëv. He issued an appeal in which he directed all the actors and theatrical staff to remain at their posts. Similarly, anyone who refrained from fulfilling his obligations, it was explained, would be subject to a form of punishment, as an individual opposing the new regime. This appeal was distributed in the state theaters by our commandant Bespalov, who quickly forgot his officer's vocation and his order of Vladimir with swords of which he was very proud, and immediately played a very active role in propagandizing for the recognition of the Bolsheviks, for which he was sharply condemned by his colleagues—the union of soloists of the Maria opera. Unions in that dark time sprang up like mushrooms after rain, and at the Maria Theater, beyond the general union of all the staff, there also appeared a separate union of performers and soloists of the opera troupe, which for some reason wanted to be distinguished from the performers of the chorus and orchestra. To Bespalov's side, there immediately came Graff, a stagehand and machinist of the Maria Theater, one of the most efficient, quiet, dependable, courteous, and loyal staff members, a few individuals of the working-class personnel, and . . . Meyerhold. For a long time now he had already propagandized for the idea that art and revolution were bound by family ties, and gradually began to grow closer and closer to the revolutionary proletariat. At the Alexandra Theater, followers of the new regime also appeared in the person of Pashkovsky[14] and the equally untalented actress Tiraspol'skaya,[15] about to be dismissed, and the assistant lighting director Brovkin. The last was a typical representative of that less-than-semi-intelligentsia who were educated out of propaganda pamphlets, and invariably larded his talk with ready-made, hackneyed phrases from the "political primer." [. . .]

14 F. Kh. Pashkovsky, actor, from January 16, 1918, chairman of the Provisional Committee at the Alexandra; from February 22 to March 11, actively worked for the autonomy of the state theaters.
15 Nadezhda L'vovna Tiraspol'skaya (1867–1962), actress at the Maly 1895–1902 and the Alexandra 1903–56; in her long career, she aged from Juliet to Ranevskaya (*The Cherry Orchard*) to Mrs. Higgins (*Pygmalion*).

In local committees of workers and staff a ferment began, but on the whole Murav'ëv's appeal had no success [...]

[The troupe of the Alexandra Theater replied:] Quoted in Murray Frame, *The St. Petersburg Imperial Theaters* (Jefferson, N.C.: McFarland, 2000), 157–58.

The artists of the Russian Dramatic troupe of the State Petrograd theaters, at a General Meeting on October 28, 1917, having listened to the instruction sent by the self-appointed commissar of state and private theaters and signed by Mikh. Murav'ëv, resolved that:

1. Acknowledging the authority of the Provisional Government in the person of Commissar F. A. Golovin[16] and Chief Deputy F. D. Batyushkov, they cannot entertain the instructions of impostors unacknowledged by the whole of Russia. Therefore, they are returning the instruction to the sender;

2. Protesting against those who sent this instruction and the threats set forth therein, they are temporarily halting performances.

Resolution of the Union of Workers of the Petrograd State Theaters in regard to the proposed strike, October 31, 1917. Quoted in Frame, *St. Petersburg Imperial Theaters*, 158–59.

1. In view of our political immaturity, and not having a clear idea of the revolution that has taken place, we, the workers in the state theaters, cannot officially attach ourselves to any existing political party.

2. And as we are materially dependent on each working day, we resolve with real duty to fulfill to the letter the obligations of our service. And that is why we cannot bear responsibility for the cessation of performances in the theaters.

THE MOSCOW RESISTANCE devolved into a small band of military cadets trying to defend the Kremlin, before they were overpowered and slaughtered (November 12–14). This period is recorded in the Performance Diary of the Moscow Art Theater, kept by directors and stage managers on a daily basis. It makes for a chronicle of increasing deterioration, absences of actors and staff, dereliction of duty by caretakers and watchmen, and unrest in the audience. Rats ran wild.

Day Officer's Journal. Khudozhestvennyy Teatr. Tvorcheskie ponedel'niki i drugie dokumenty 1916–1919 [The Art Theater: Creative Mondays and other documents 1916–1919], ed. Z. P. Udal'tsova (Moscow: Moskovsky Khudozhestvenny Teatr, 2006), 353–54.

---

16 Fëdor Aleksandrovich Golovin (1867/8–1937), as a member of the Cadet party, had chaired the Second Duma in 1907; the Mensheviks appointed him to look after and liquidate the Ministry of the Court, making him responsible for the care of the imperial family.

October 28 [1917]. 11:40 a.m. [. . .] In the box office a new [ticket sale] (today Saturday), in the vestibule lots of the public. [All] the box-office attendants at their places. In the street machine gun fire, apparently shots from ordnance. In the military hospital (in Lyanozov's house)[17] a commotion. Constant delivery of the wounded. The telephones don't work. A detachment of soldiers with machine guns has set up along the lane across from the theater. The soldiers are carefully setting their sights in the direction of B. Dmitrovsky Boulevard, Tverskaya. They've taken them off somewhere. No one knows whose they are: the Bolsheviks or the Provisional Government's. A lot of our audience in the street. No panic evident.

12 noon. [. . .] Vl. I. [Nemirovich-Danchenko][18] advises that the performance be canceled. Lots of calls coming into the theater, it's impossible to phone out of the theater. The gunfire goes on. In the lane another flail of soldiers—guns at the ready.

12:20. A motorized cart drove by—lots of wounded.

At the corner of Gazetnaya and Tverskaya, where a new building is going up, they say cadets have dug in and they will take them by storm. The wounded are carried past in people's arms.

[. . .] Along the sidewalk on the theater side those wounded in the stomach are carried on stretchers (I was standing at this time at the window in the main lobby), and immediately after them some curiosity seekers walk, primarily women, and after them a few young ladies are distributing to one another tickets they've just bought at the theater box office; across the way, near Meyer's shop, an officer walked over to a cab driver and began to pay him for a trip! (12:45).

Vl. I. Nemirovich-Danchenko is definitely for calling off today's performance, we don't reckon that we'll be able to play tomorrow or the day after. Koreneva[19] phoned, asked about the performance, and not just her, the phone kept ringing with similar questions. Constant firing, sometimes handguns, sometimes more often machine guns—like iron shutters being slammed! So it's impossible to phone out. [. . .]

1:15 p.m. A request came from the Belostok hospital to allow a detachment of orderlies into the theater—for rest and reorganization. At 1:20 the vestibule of the dress circle was filled with students and sisters of mercy. The public prosecutor Staal'[20] arrived from the Palace of Justice. He had to get to a meeting of the City Council—but it is impossible.[21]

---

17 At the outbreak of World War I an infirmary was set up next to the theater building in Kammerherr Lane; it was subsidized by one-time voluntary subscriptions and 2 percent of the salaries of the theater staff.

18 Vladimir Ivanovich Nemirovich-Danchenko (1858–1943), prize-winning dramatist and pedagogue, cofounder with Stanislavsky of the Moscow Art Theater; liberal in political sympathies and an efficient organizer.

19 Lidiya Mikhailovna Koreneva (1885–1982), actress at the Art Theater from 1904 to 1958; in this period she usually played ingenues.

20 Aleksey Fëdorovich Staal' (1872–1949), public prosecutor of the Moscow Palace of Justice.

21 The building was located on the site of what became the Lenin Museum and then the Historical Museum behind the Kremlin.

A serious battle, judging by rumors, at the National Hotel. Fifty-six (Bolshevik) regiments have settled in there. Word is that they are firing exploding bullets.

Staal' says that forces are coming from the front to defend the Provisional Govt.—to Moscow and Petrograd.

The gunfire continues. [...] I decided to keep four watchmen on day duty, for more than their board.

They've been getting their board. The medical orderlies on day duty left. There's shooting now along Dmitrovsky Blvd, on the way to the Continental. At the corner of Kuznetsky and Dmitrovsky Blvd a boy of ten was killed, trying to run across the street.

On the street they say that the Maly Theater was riddled with bullets.

[...] *I. M. Moskvin*[22]

THE OCTOBER REVOLUTION found young actor and director Evgeny Vakhtangov at a crossroads. Despite his allegiance to Stanislavsky's system of psychological realism and his socially advanced views, diverse ideological tendencies and artistic trends were contending within him. He was typical of many artists in his political fence sitting during this turbulent period.

> From Vakhtangov's diaries. *Evgeny Vakhtangov. Sbornik*, ed. L. D. Vendrovs-kaya and G. P. Kaptereva (Moscow: VTO, 1984), 271–72. Evgeny Bagrationovich Vakhtangov (1883–1922), Stanislavsky's amanuensis at the MAT and brilliant actor and director at the First Studio 1911–19; he would become a leading theatrical visionary of his generation.

October 29, 1917. On the night of Friday, October 27, they began shooting in Moscow. Today is the 29th. Nearby, on Ostozhenka, by Mansurov Lane, fusillades went on nonstop all day. There was rifle, revolver, and cannon fire. For two days now we haven't gone outside. We were unable to get bread today. We feed ourselves on what there is. At night we darken the windows so the light can't filter through. Newspapers aren't available. Who is shooting whom and what for we don't know. Our telephone doesn't work for outgoing calls. No one who phones us knows anything either. Who will prevail—"Bolsheviks" or government forces—is unknown for the second day in a row. Trams have stopped running. There's water and light. When will this end?

October 30, 1917. Today at 10:30 p.m. the electricity went out. At 3:00 in the morning it went on again.

October 31, 1917. The telephone hasn't worked all day. We are completely cut off and know nothing at all. The shooting goes on nonstop. Judging by the groups that

---

22 Ivan Mikhaylovich Moskvin (1874–1946), actor, at the MAT from its founding to the end of his life. A skillful character actor with a fine comic touch, he later became a deputy to the Central Committee.

flit through the streets near Brusilov's[23] apartment—in our direction this situation supports the "Bolsheviks."

We sat like this for six days until November 1.[24]

DESPITE GROWING DISGUST with the war and the regular surrender of Russian troops, fighting continued sporadically on the western front. An effort was made to continue the amusement brigades that had been frequent under tsarist command. Hostilities concluded with an armistice on December 14, 1917.

> Report on mobilizing actors to form troupes and transporting them to the front. No earlier than November 9, 1917. *STDM 17–21*, 295–96.

There were nearly a thousand actors mobilized.

Thirty-six troupes have been organized.

Only twenty-five troupes could travel to the front in teams of two hundred and ninety-two individuals, because there were no means of transport for the remaining nine troupes.

In the following directions:

to the Southern front twelve troupes,
to Vologda a troupe,
to Samara five troupes,
to Simbirsk two troupes,
to Tsaritsyn two troupes,
to Kursk four troupes.

For organizing the troupes the Vsebyuirvoenkom assigned eight hundred thousand rubles, five hundred thousand have been spent.

Everywhere the performances have enjoyed great success.

Opinions give a thorough impression of delight from the satisfaction obtained.

Over sixty-five thousand Red Army men have seen the productions.

True, many troupes did not have time to celebrate the October Revolution holiday because of bad railway transport and numerous attendant military circumstances.

However, it can be said that the first experiment of the expedition seems to have been a success, if we set aside a certain amount of local lack of organization.

A number of applications are currently arriving from the front with the request to send more troupes.

The repertoire consists of complete plays: *People of Fire and Iron, The Weavers,*

---

23 Aleksey Alekseevich Brusilov (1853–1926), top tsarist general, supreme commander of the Russian Army in the Provisional Government; in 1917 he mounted an unsuccessful offensive against the Central powers. After the October Revolution he sided with the Communists and served as inspector of the Red Army Cavalry.

24 This last phrase was written in pencil, obviously a few days later.

Innocent though Guilty, A Child of Nature,[25] operas: *Evgeny Onegin, Rigoletto, Pagliacci,* etc.; one-act plays, operatic excerpts, recitations, dance numbers, vocal, instrumental, circus acts, etc.

The whole repertoire was approved by the All-Russian bureau of military commissars, of the agitational-enlightenment section.[26]

IN ACCORDANCE with Marxist principles, the workers and peasants were to be treated to the fruits of civilization. Theaters were to be made accessible to a proletariat unaccustomed to the etiquette and decorum that had once reigned in these palaces of culture.

> Vladimir Nelidov, *Teatral'naya Moskva. Sorok let moskovskikh teatrov* [Theatrical Moscow: Forty years of Moscow Theaters, 1931] (Moscow: Materik, 2002), 347–48. Vladimir Aleksandrovich Nelidov (1869–1926) had been an official for the budget of the Imperial theaters 1893–1900, head of the repertoire of the Moscow Maly Theater 1900–1907, and head of its dramatic troupe 1907–9; first husband of the actress Ol'ga Gzovskaya.

Illiterate people, won over by the propaganda and without restraint, were admitted into the theaters. At one time they were let into the theaters for free. The tickets were distributed through organizations. Well, of course, the first pancake fell flat, and how. In the first days after the October Revolution a riot (true, the theaters were still closed) by a gang of workers from some factory smashed up the Maly Theater and carried off whatever could be borne away, especially the actors' clothes, for most of them kept all their civilian "wardrobe" in the theater. By the time the troops showed up a week later, the theater had been turned into a pigsty.

They found the guilty parties. The head of the troupe, Osip Andreevich Pravdin,[27] gave an answer typical of the times to the question of one of the "powers-that-be" what to do with the culprits: "Open a school for them." "The pigs already have one." "Then open another one."

When the theaters reopened, I was witness to the following. [. . .] There sits a couple. He and she. He is in a waistcoat and Russian blouse, she in a kerchief. They are holding a bag of candy. They both hold on to it, and, not taking their eyes from the stage, "fumble" in the bag and carry on chewing.

---

25 A mixed bag: *Lyudi ognya i zhelezi,* a drama by M. N. Zotov; *Die Weber* by Gerhard Hauptmann, a panoramic account of a strike; Ostrovsky's melodramas *Bez viny vinovatye* and *Dikarka.*

26 This section was created in April 1918, with theatrical, musical, cinematic, and sport divisions. In April 1919 it was merged into the Politotdel of the Revolutionary Military Soviet of the Republics (RVSR).

27 Osip Andreevich Pravdin (actually Oskar Avgustovich Treyleben, 1849–1921), character actor, expert in Molière; began in Helsinki, at the Alexandra Theater 1875–77, the Maly from 1890; he headed the Maly troupe after the February Revolution.

Konstantin Stanislavsky to A. I. Yuzhin, November 8, 1917. In *Sobranie so-chineny v devyati tomakh,* ed. A. M. Smelyansky et al. (Moscow: Iskusstvo, 1988–99), 8:356.

Just last night I learned from O. V. Gzovskaya[28] the horrible details of the sacrilege committed on the Maly Theater.

I feel grief and rage. It is as if they had raped my mother, as if they had insulted the memory of Mikhail Semënovich.[29] I would like to go to you and with my own hands cleanse the dear theater of the foulness churned up by the unleashed insanity. I would like to tell you many warm words now. But, happily, unleashed insanity cannot insult art and its glorious representatives.

All civilized Russia is with you. In misfortune it loves and values you more than in good fortune.

May God grant that we shall soon forget this dreadful nightmare so that with redoubled energy we can carry on with distinction the work begun this season. [...]

Alekseev-Stanislavsky

From the editorial pages of *Teatr i Iskusstvo* 44–46 (November 12, 1917), 762–64.

November 12, 1917, Petrograd. A new tempest is blowing over Russia and in particular over Petrograd. [...] In regard to the inactivity of the theater at the present time we consider it a double sin and a double apostasy. The theaters have before them such broad cultural tasks that it would be outright incomprehension of its great role to get mixed up in the struggle of political parties, for sufficient unto the day is the evil of each of them. All kinds of audiences—both those who groan under what is going on and those who triumph and celebrate a victory—are needed by the theater: the former to be refreshed and to forget themselves, the latter to take thought and reflect. The inactivity of the theater is to add the coup de grâce to the chaos and spiritual oppression we are undergoing at the moment. [...]

Current Events and the Theater. Current events are reflected in the theaters, of course, in the sorriest ways. The drop in the box office began on the fifteenth of October, influenced by rumors of the arrival of the Bolsheviks. From Monday the 23rd the fall of the box offices took on a threatening character, and from Wednesday the 25th it was catastrophic. On that day some theaters performed, others didn't. From Thursday performances were definitely terminated at K. Nezlobin's Theater, "The Crooked

---

28 Ol'ga Vladimirovna Gzovskaya (1889–1962), star of the Maly Theater 1905–10, 1917–19, and the Moscow Art Theater 1912–16. In 1919 she emigrated to Germany but returned to Russia in 1932.

29 Mikhail Semënovich Shchepkin (1788–1863), Ukrainian actor born a serf, who became a leading actor at the Moscow Maly Theater (1823–63), considered the father of Russian realistic acting and theatrical ethics.

Mirror," Saburov's "Passage" Theater.[30] The last tried to perform on Saturday, but the box office was so pathetic that they didn't even perform on Sunday. "The Palace" played on Sunday to a box office of 280 rubles; the Liteyny Theater tried to perform a couple of times; the Troitsky closed on Monday. The Alexandra Theater[31] came out on strike on Saturday, partly in protest against the appointment of Mr. Muraev'ëv[32] as commissar of theaters. At the People's House, performances at times went on, at times were canceled. "The Musical Drama"[33] was firmly kept going and forced the performers to sing operatic trills to the sound of gunfire. The plight of the theaters that did perform was most painful; actors didn't show up, owing to the raising of bridges and the like. During the day many theaters had no lights and had to call off rehearsals. Once a week premieres played to a full house—*Round Dance* at the Crooked Mirror, *Salome* at the Troitsky Theater, *King of the Jews* at Nezlobin's, *Eternal Love* at the Liteyny, *The Doll*[34] at the Palace. The oddest thing is that during the time that all the theaters trying to perform even on Sunday had fifteen to twenty attendees, both the "Nevsky"[35] and the "Troitsky" farce theaters made around fifteen hundred rubles, and both those theaters went on performing the whole time, to the greater satisfaction of informed democracy.

In Moscow from October 28 to November 7 the theaters have been inactive, except, however, for certain theaters of miniatures. So, the Petrovsky Theater of Miniatures bravely worked the whole time. The Bol'shoy Theater underwent exceptional damage. One missile exploded on the roof and another beneath the roof. The scene shop, where two missiles fell, was damaged. The auditorium and the stage are quite all right. In all the lobbies and dressing rooms window frames are damaged and the windows shattered, and many of the costumes and properties have been plundered. The Maly

30 Konstantin Nikolaevich Nezlobin (actually Alyabyev, 1857–1930) managed a theater in Moscow 1909–17, which had great appeal for a middle-class audience; emigrated after the Revolution. The Crooked Mirror (Krivoe zerkalo, 1908–18, 1922–31), an innovative theater of miniatures specializing in parody; founded by A. R. Kugel' and directed by Nikolay Evreinov. Saburov's Passage Theater (Teatr S. F. Saburova, 1912–25), chiefly a house for farce and comedy featuring the actress E. M. Granovskaya.

31 Palace (Palas-Teatr, 1910–22), an operetta house featuring brilliant performers. Liteyny Theater (1909–18), intended as an imitation of Paris's Grand Guignol, came to specialize in comedy. Troitsky Theater (Troitsky Teatr Miniatyur, 1911–18) staged satiric sketches, one-act plays, and operas. Alexandra Theater (Aleksandrinsky Teatr, 1832 to present), a state-subsidized imperial playhouse dedicated to performances of drama in Russian, its company studded with stars.

32 Mikhail P. Muravëv, former stage manager at Suvorin's Theater in Petrograd; appointed commissar of state and private theaters by the Military-Revolutionary Committee. He resigned in early November 1917.

33 People's House (Narodny Dom Imperatora Nikolaya II, 1900s–1930s), in Alexandra Park, contained a spacious New or Opera Theater from 1912, where the great bass F. M. Chaliapin often performed.

34 *Round Dance* (*Reigen*) by Arthur Schnitzler; *Salome* (*Salomé*) by Oscar Wilde; *King of the Jews* (*Tsar' Yudeysky*) by Grand Duke Konstantin Romanov; *Eternal Love* (*Ewige Liebe*) by G. Faber; *The Doll* (*La Poupée*), comic opera by Edmond Audran.

35 Troitsky Fars A. S. Polonskogo (1916–18) and Nevsky Fars (1904–18) specialized in traditional bedroom farce and piquant operettas, usually translated from the French.

Theater[36] and Nezlobin's Theater suffered minor damage. At the Maly Theater all the best costumes have been plundered, the actors' dressing rooms broken into. The losses amount to hundreds of thousands of rubles.

On November 8 a general meeting of all the staff and workers was called to clarify the further work of the theater.

On November 8 all the private theaters reopened, except for the Art Theater.

At the general assembly of stage and theater workers of Moscow held at Yuzhny's Theater, a resolution was announced by the entrepreneurs who had shows running at the time of the break to pay the salaries of all those in service.

PROTECT THE THEATERS!
(Letter to the editor)

When it became known that the government had passed into the hand of the Bolsheviks, members of the Theater Commission of the Executive Committee of the Soviet of Workers' and Soldiers' Deputies turned to the comrade city head in charge of the Cultural-Enlightenment Department, Comrade Lunacharsky,[37] with the request to take measures to protect the theaters; Com. Lunacharsky immediately sent a letter to the Military-Revolutionary Committee, informing it that, finding it necessary to take measures to preserve the Petrograd theaters, he charges it to take those measures to be executed to the Chief Plenipotentiary Theatrical Commission, namely, me. Members of the Theater Commission present at the Smolny Institute worked out lists of theaters and the military units close to them, which would assume the protection. Muster rolls with the request to mount protection out of 150 men of various regiments were sent to the Military-Revolutionary Committee. Yesterday, having with great difficulty procured automobiles, I, accompanied by the secretary of the Theater Commission, Slobodsky, and a member of the Theater Commission, Kiseleva, visited all the state theaters, the Musical Drama, the Maly Theater, the Liteyny Theater, the theaters of Nezlobin, Saburov, Troitsky, Mardzhanov,[38] and other theaters, finding nowhere a single soldier on guard. The disorder in the city increased. The number of arbitrary searches, accompanied by thefts, increased. The Domestic Committees have organized protection for their own homes, and only the theaters remained undefended from the criminal element. [...]

I direct an impassioned appeal to all theatrical workers: do not drag the theaters into the political struggle and protect them from destruction by the benighted masses of brutalized people, but everyone individually, as a free citizen, should join a party fighting for the salvation of the fatherland. [...]

stage director of the Maly Theater, *Mikhail Murav'ëv*

---

36 The Maly Theater, known as the House of Ostrovsky and as the second Moscow University, was the oldest extant theater in Russia, unofficially dating from 1755; in its building on Theater Square from 1825.

37 Anatoly Vasil'evich Lunacharsky (1875–1933), narkom of enlightenment. See headnote.

38 Mardzhanov's was the Free Theater (Svobodny Teatr) in Moscow, the seedbed for the Kamerny Theater.

Teatral'naya gazeta [Theatrical gazette] (November 14, 1917).

A general meeting of the theater workers of Moscow passed the following resolution: "To declare Tuesday November 7 a day of mourning for the theater as a token of grief and sorrow over the bloodshed and the cruel acts of destruction, on that day no performances or shows will be given."

A COUNCIL of the Russian Theatrical Society had also made an appeal not to perform on November 13 as a token of mourning of those slaughtered by the Bolsheviks. The Art Theater resumed performances on November 21; all the rest of the theaters, except for the state-supported theaters, which had suffered especially from destruction during the October Revolution, had reopened on November 8.

Moscow Art Theater Daily Reports, 249, 355, 361.

November 21 [1917]. The first day of performance after the October Revolution. Other theaters, besides the state-run ones, began on November 8. Ours entered into an agreement with the state-run ones to open when we jointly recognized that civic conditions made things at least minimally possible for the theaters to function. We settled on November 21, i.e., that day at two o'clock when the election ended at the Constituent Assembly, and if they proceed freely, without force and coercion, that will signify the possibility for theatrical activity. So it happened.

However, it is impossible to say whether external conditions have implemented the peaceful and concentrated course of the performance. The audience is still panicky. Rumors, creating a mood of panic, never stop. The streets are completely unsafe. Besides, the trams run only until nine o'clock.

We began with productions sold before the Revolution.[39] The tickets were then all sold out. The audience had the right to get their money back. However, today at the matinee and evening (*Blue Bird* and *Three Sisters*) the box office was quite full. The composition of the matinee audience was almost normal—the standard intelligentsia, the so-called refugees; very few workers or soldiers—the occasional ones, but very few. The composition of the evening audience cannot be defined. The very lowest democracy—if one may use the expression about workers and soldiers—again, as at the matinee, was almost absent, that is, no more than used to come to the Art Theater. I mean that its (democracy's) victory has not yet brought it to the Art Theater. But also the absolute absence of our beloved bourgeoisie. Most likely there was a mixture of a

---

39 These were *The Village of Stepanchikovo* from Dostoevsky, Chekhov's *Three Sisters*, Ostrovsky's *No Fool Like a Wise Fool*, Hamsun's *In the Grip of Life*, Gorky's *Lower Depths*, Chekhov's *The Cherry Orchard*, and Saltykov-Shchedrin's *Pazukhin's Death*.

very non-Muscovite average intelligentsia with clerks from Moscow department stores and shops. As if there were a sort of transference from Korsh's.[40] [...]

V. Nemirovich-Danchenko.

November 27 [1917]. Having inspected the journal, I have seen with sorrow that there is no entry for November 22—say what you will, an exceptional date in the life of the Art Theater. That is the day when the Maly Theater almost *in corpore* came to the Art Theater first to express thanks for the sympathy shown by the Art Theater regarding the insult visited on the Maly Theater by Red Army soldiers from October 27 to 31, and then to support the idea of the amalgamation of the Maly and the Art—an amalgamation, i.e., finding points in common not only regarding the operative partial agreement, as this was concerning the resumption of performances, but in general the administration of the organizations, and even in the community of artistic work. [...]

V. Nemirovich-Danchenko.

November 26 [1917]. *Evening. Cherry Orchard.* In [the directors'] room there is an insidious spring in the sofa. When you get up it plays a whole chord. All these little noises, squeaks, trampling create that atmosphere of backstage life that prevents one from acting and observing in peace.

K. Stanislavsky, A. Sanin.[41]

It is essential to focus the attention of everyone taking part in *The Cherry Orchard* (and maybe other plays!?). Everyone has acted himself well into the play and the roles. It's all nice and cozy, and they're beginning to live for themselves, their personal lives. Much of this is valuable and good. But, living for themselves, they forget about the play, about Chekhov, his ideas and feelings, which are to be conveyed to others, they forget about the through action and don't keep to the outlined path. Here's the result: while one performer is carrying on an important scene, speaking an important thought, another carried-away performer is very nicely and realistically overdoing the details, trivia, interpolating a new mise-en-scène—one kills the other. The result is a general vividness, authentic, lifelike, but as in life a hodgepodge, and not the clearly and simply manifested life of the spirit, purified of the extraneous, as it ought to be in art. One must avoid overstatement, one must remember the main points of the play and the through action.

K. Stanislavsky.

---

40 Korsh's Theater, Moscow, opened in 1882 and served a middle-class audience with a shrewd mixture of well-acted boulevard drama and literary classics; after the Revolution it was renamed the Comedy Dramatic Theater and was liquidated in 1932.
41 Aleksandr Akimovich Sanin (actually Shenberg, 1869–1956), actor and director; at the MAT 1898–1902, 1917–19, an expert at crowd scenes, especially in historical drama. Emigrated 1922.

December 8 [1917]. I note a woeful incident during the performance (*Village of Stepan-chikovo*): a suicide in the auditorium.

The scene "His Excellency" was proceeding. A shot rang out, when Moskvin exited the stage, and Gaydarov[42] entered and had already begun the scene between uncle and nephew. An officer shot himself, sitting in the top gallery, in the sixth row in the middle on the far left side. The commotion in the audience forced the curtain to be rung down. In about two minutes, after they had carried out the suicide, calm was restored. Bebutov[43] spoke from the stage that the actors considered it possible to carry on the performance, the audience replied, "Please do," and the scene began with Gaydarov's exit . . .

Because this scene was followed by "The Chase" and "Mishino," they hurried to restore order in the corridors, but it was not entirely normal, because, with or without instructions, the ushers themselves carried the corpse into the lobby (upper) and accordingly in the next intermission the lobby had to kept closed to the public. Naturally, it would have been more proper to take him into the boardroom. In any case, a huge amount of blood all the way down from the upper gallery to the lobby had to be quickly mopped up and rinsed away. [. . .] During the next act they removed the corpse.

The suicide was a young officer. He shot himself in the right temple, the bullet passed through the left and lodged in the ceiling. When the suicide was removed, he was already dead. His head was drenched in blood, and there is still a great deal of blood in the lobby where he lay. No documents were found in his pockets.

V. Nemirovich-Danchenko.

IN DECEMBER 1917 the Soviet of Workers' Deputies organized free performances for workers. The Moscow Art Theater's shareholders protested, to no avail.

Aleksandr Yakovlevich Tairov (actually Kornblit, 1885–1950), actor and director, had worked at Mardzhanov's Free Theater (1913) and in 1914 created the Kamerny Theater. He promoted the idea of the synthetic actor, capable of playing everything from Greek tragedy to musical comedy and pantomime. Even he, who had previously displayed no interest in politics, was caught up in the revolutionary fervor and issued a manifesto proclaiming, in a very peculiar way, his sympathy with the socialist agenda.

---

42 Vladimir Georgievich Gaydarov (1893–1976), actor at the MAT 1915–20; worked abroad 1920–32; in the troupe of the Leningrad Drama Theater 1938–68; second husband of Ol'ga Gzovskaya.
43 Valery Mikhaylovich Bebutov (1885–1961), assistant director at the MAT 1912–18; in the First Studio 1913–18; as a director, collaborating with F. F. Komissarzhevsky and Meyerhold, he became an antagonist of the MAT. At the RSFSR 1 Theater he promoted "Theatrical October"; codirected some productions; later produced memoirs of Meyerhold.

Aleksandr Tairov, *Proklamatsiya khudozhnika* [An artist's proclamation] (Moscow: M. Shlugleyt and A. Bron-Stén, 1917), 11–13, 21.

Today is a great day in Moscow.[44]

Even in our great era, it is worthy of special attention.

So far the Revolution has accomplished an enormous work of liberation—it has destroyed the endless obstacles in which the ousted regime entangled life, it has blown up ground overgrown with tall, poisonous weeds to prepare the ground for a new planting.

And so today for the very first time, new seeds will be sown onto the soil, today for the very first time, a foundation will begin to be laid for that majestic building, whose name is the Rights of the People.

Today for the very first time, the new architects of ancient Moscow turn to the ballot boxes and bring to them, along with their ballots, all their desires and hopes for a renewed life. [...]

The artist is an individualist from birth.

"Art is the most vivid form of individualism known to the world," says Oscar Wilde.

Individualism and true freedom and strength can flourish only under socialism.

Only under socialism will the destitution, the humiliatingly distorted and broken life and creative work of many great artists, vanish, not to mention that of a whole rank of other talents, perhaps even geniuses who perish unknown to anyone, in the cold and obscurity of garrets and cellars.

Only under socialism will an opportunity be fully provided for them to reveal their individuality [...]

Only under socialism will an opportunity be given to anyone who has the flame of talent blazing within him, for it will not be extinguished by overwork [...]

Only under socialism, freed from the cares of "daily bread," from importunate worries about the morrow, will the artist be liberated, for, well provided for materially, he ought not to cater to the tastes of the majority, but, on the contrary, asserting his individual will in his creative work, will establish these tastes himself.

Then true individualism will prevail, then everyone will freely be able to assert his spiritual "self," then all people without exception will become life's creators, rather than its slaves. The flourishing of individualism now, under private property, is inevitably grounded in slavery.

Only by transforming a large part of society into slaves and forcing it to die of starvation and monotonous labor, which is fatal to creativity, is a minority in the position to strengthen its individualism nowadays.

For individualism to flourish, slaves are undoubtedly required.

As one vivid example of this, take ancient Greece.

And slaves will be needed under socialism as well.

But under socialism, these slaves will not be people but soulless, compliant machines. [...]

---

44 The article was published in *Vlast' Naroda* (People's power) on election day for the Moscow City Council.

"Art for the people"—this is where a danger is outlined for the true democratization of art.

As if there could be two different kinds of art: one for the non(?)-people, and the others for the people!

Is art really a railway train with Pullman cars for the "clean" public and unheated cattle cars for the people!

No, art is integral and valuable in and of itself, art is for all whose soul possesses either a conscious or an unconscious thirst for beauty. Everything that is created by a man's talent, everything that bears the true mark of creativity, everything that enters into the concept of *art as such*—all this and only this is the subject of the democratization of art.

NEVERTHELESS, the Kamerny Theater carried on its wholly aesthetic program, without concern for the class struggle. On December 21, 1917, Tairov produced two charming trifles, Lothar's *King Harlequin* and Debussy's *Toy Chest*.[45] His justification for the former was that it showed the dethroning of kings and set up the actor as revolutionary activist.

> Yury Sobolev, "Harlequin enthroned," *Teatr* (November 30–December 3, 1917),
> 4. Yury Vasil'evich Sobolev (1887–1940) was a critic, historian of literature and
> theater, and biographer.

The Kamerny Theater has with indubitable success brought out *King Harlequin*, a "presentation with masks" by R. Lothar.[46] This remarkable and witty piece provides excellent material for the performers. There is a good deal of paradox, but the story of Harlequin, who, by a trick of fate, became a king, is told attractively. No doubt, however, there is a flight of that shallow aestheticism, whose stamp is on all the "style moderne" issuing from the Munich workshops, where real wisdom is exchanged for beautiful words, cheap allegory is passed off as original symbolism. Idiosyncratically both with that "modernism" and that method of staging, which has become a cliché for the Kamerny Theater—the performance made use of those external outlines, long familiar in the past work of A. Ya. Tairov. Onstage are the same little screens, little scraps of cloth, painted squares and triangles, those same truncated little columns, the same fantastical costumes, which impede movement, and those same unbelievably graphic makeups that turn faces into lifeless masks. This fracture is also expressed in the manner of performance, at times using details of original acrobatic refinement. But the inadmissible forms in which the outward aspects of the performance are expressed did not prevent the appearance of that sincere temperament, that passionate and bright youthfulness, that plasticity rare in Russian actors and that charm permeated with details of inspiration that mark Mr. Tseretelli's impersonation of Harlequin. [. . .]

45 The ballet *La boîte aux joujoux* (1913).
46 Rudolph Lothar (actually Spitzer, 1865–1943), Austro-Hungarian writer whose erotic "play of masks" *König Harlekin* was translated into fourteen languages.

THE DEBUSSY, performed as a marionette play, later toured to Petrograd.

> Mikhail Kuzmin, "The toy chest," in *Zhizn' iskusstva* [Life and art] (April 1, 1919). Mikhail Alekseevich Kuzmin (1872–1936), poet and playwright, aesthete and musician, was a fixture on the St. Petersburg literary scene; his neomystery plays were praised by Aleksandr Blok.

First of all, the utterly enchanting music of Debussy, second the splendid performance of Miss Koonen[47] and a great many moments of witty and moving stage direction. [...] The director and performers revealed a real love, understanding, and in places even the dearest inspiration and invention for this pantomime, which so deserves it all. The scene of the Doll's dance, the transmission of flowers, the death and resurrection of the Tin Soldier, the prayer and joy of Koonen in the second scene, are, in my opinion, irreproachable. The doll-like expressive gestures and face, the half-childish, wide awake and yet depraved coquetry, the wooden empty-headedness—all this was presented by Miss Koonen with idiosyncratic grace, deliberate and unconstrained.

VSEVOLOD ÉMIL'EVICH (KARL THEODOR) MEYERHOLD (1874–1940) was to become the towering figure of the early revolutionary theater. After a period as an actor with the Moscow Art Theater, he formed his own itinerant troupe, which toured for several years; he then spent two years directing Vera Komissarzhevskaya's theater in Petrograd, introducing symbolist drama and stylized stagings. His next stint was at the Imperial Theaters, where his work on plays and operas alternated with experiments in studios on Asian theater techniques and commedia dell'arte. He was the first prominent theater artist to become a card-carrying Bolshevik.

When Meyerhold came to Moscow in August 1917, Tairov suggested that the two of them and Nikolay Evreinov create a single experimental theater, where each would preserve full creative independence. When one considers that Meyerhold and Tairov soon became bitter enemies, it is unlikely that such a fellowship would have lasted long, but it demonstrates the mood of cooperation that existed in the first days of the Revolution.

> Meyerhold to Aleksandr Tairov, October–November 1917, Petrograd. In *Perepiska* [Correspondence] (Moscow: Iskusstvo, 1976), 191.

Dear Aleksandr Yakovlevich, don't be angry. We Petersburgers have every right to indulgence. Things here are going very badly indeed. You know Annenkov's[48] capacity

---

47 Alisa Georgievna Koonen (1889–1974), a dusky beauty, acted at the MAT 1908–12, then joined the Free Theater, where she met Aleksandr Tairov; they married and opened the Kamerny Theater, whose star she became 1913–50.

48 Yury Pavlovich Annenkov (1889–1974), director, influenced by futurism and the World of Art, whose work tended to the caricatural; an early participant in mass spectacles.

for work, and yet I could not get from him a presentation of materials for the confer-ence.[49] He was with me today. I showed him your telegram. Annenkov promised to send everything necessary in the next few days.

I am sending you *The Exchange*[50] together with the directorial instructions, but I ask on receipt of this letter to send me posthaste the dimensions of the stage: (1) the width along the footlights, depth from the footlights to the farthest line upstage, and the height of the stage; (2) does it have a proscenium; (3) if there is no proscenium, what fills the space between the first row of stalls and the stage? (an orchestra pit?); (4) the arrangement of audience seating (pit, where the boxes are); (5) which seats have obstructed views; (6) what is the arrangement of the lighting; (7) are there footlights?; (8) what kind of curtain—does it draw or go up and down?

I would like to commission Yakulov[51] for *The Exchange*.

As soon as I get your specific answers to the questions about the stage arrange-ments, I will immediately embark on a preliminary plan (prior to discussions with the designer), and then I'll ask Yakulov to come here for a couple days.

Congratulations on your successful opening.[52]

Don't be angry that there was no interview, but it's Evreinov's[53] fault, for having begged off.

Greetings to Koonen and Ékster (ah, Ékster!).[54]

Your affectionate *Vs. Meyerhold*

THE EXCHANGE, codirected at the Kamerny Theater by Meyerhold and Tairov, opened on February 20, 1918; it was not popular with audiences. Tairov regarded it as the first postrevolutionary failure at the Kamerny. Henceforth, he and Mey-erhold were to be enemies.

Boris Sergeevich Glagolin (actually, Gusev, 1879–1948) in prerevolutionary times was a popular actor of heroic and romantic roles, including Sherlock Holmes and a male Joan of Arc (one of Evreinov's experiments). He served as director of the

49 A conference of deputies from the professional unions that met on August 22, 1917, in Petrograd, aiming to form a single All-Russian Professional Union that would control all the theaters.

50 *The Exchange* (*L'Échange*) by Paul Claudel (1914) was vaguely concerned with American capital-ism in the person of a "captain of industry."

51 Georgy Bogdanovich Yakulov (1884–1928), whose geometrical constructivist scenery was one of the problems with *The Exchange*. He remained as one of the Kamerny's leading designers.

52 *Salome* by Oscar Wilde on October 9, 1917; the Kamerny Theater had been closed from February 20 to October 8, 1917, owing to material difficulties.

53 Nikolay Nikolaevich Evreinov (1879–1953), playwright, director, theorist. He promoted the idea of theatricality as a constant in human life; reconstructed historical staging methods; and experimented with monodrama. The reference is to a joint interview with Meyerhold, Tairov, and Evreinov, planned but never realized.

54 Aleksandra Aleksandrovna Ékster (actually Grigorovich, 1882–1949), a colleague of Vladimir Tatlin and Kazimir Malevich, promoted cubo-futurism in art; her colorful and geometric sets and costumes were seen at the Kamerny from 1916. She also occasionally designed for the MAT studios and the Odessa People's Theater.

Khar'kov Theater from 1917 to 1923; during that time he was court-martialed by the Whites as a Bolshevik sympathizer but exonerated (1919). He was to lay his ideas for a Christian communism before Lenin in 1924, without a favorable response. He emigrated to New York in 1927.

> Boris Glagolin, "The creative paths of the theater" [Tvorcheskie puti teatr] (Khar'kov: Eparkhial'naya tipografiya, 1917), in *Avangard i teatra* [Avant-garde and theater], ed. G. F. Kovalenko (Moscow: Nauka, 2008), 79, 88, 104.

Now our first obligation is to plunge headfirst into work, to inject it with our enthusiasm as citizens, and not to dissipate it in public meetings and the street. There have been enough streets in the past and public meetings in the present. It will be a sorry matter if all theater conferences wind up doing nothing but organizing "unions"; if theaters, in commemoration of the great days, are open to all those who, having lost all shame in the eagerness to take advantage of a moment of "freedom," show an absence of any moral responsibility.

At present the most dangerous thing of all is for the theater to serve politically the autocracy of the mob that considers itself a creator fully invested with power. Servitude to an autocracy of ignorance and the majority incurably infects the theatrical organism, which is unhealthy enough without that. A dangerous time, when not only general celebration but also general truth prevails in the street. At such moments of universal creativity and inspiration, art leaves its own temple, as Mark Twain's pauper prince[55] left his court, long to go astray and be misled. [...]

The theater, like any art, is indispensable to the socialist order, to neutralize the populace from abnegation of responsibility and complacency, capable of planting the cross on the farthest perfection of communal life. The individual creation of new forms—like the expansion of the limits of knowledge, as the instigator of efforts toward the best and energy for life, as the source of the moral enrichment of the individual and the exhibition of its paragons—is among the proper tasks of socialism. [...]

The theater of Christian martyrdom is the source of faith and the theater in their idealism. [...]

Order Out of Chaos

On December 12, 1917, Lunacharsky announced that the former Imperial Theaters were henceforth to serve the Soviet cause and, in January 1918, confirmed their autonomy. He abolished the existing bureaucratic structure, transferring its functions to a yet-to-be-created Theater Council (*Teatral'ny sovet*) with representatives from each of the troupes, including the technical staff. He also continued the state subsidies.

---

55 The first Russian translation of Mark Twain's novel *The Prince and the Pauper* (1881) appeared in 1884.

Anatoly Lunacharsky, address to the actors and workers of the State Theater of Petrograd about the requirement that workers of state theaters deal with the new government, December 12, 1917. STDM 17–21, 37.

You understand perfectly well how important it is to regulate the relations of actors and workers of the state theaters with the government itself.

It goes without saying that the new government does not demand of works in any field whatever, least of all theater, a definite political credo. We demand from you no oaths of allegiance, no declarations of loyalty and obedience. The disgraceful times, when you were in a position of servitude to the tsar's court, have passed, never to return. You are free citizens, free artists, and no one will encroach on your freedom.

But there is a new master in this land—the common working man. The land is undergoing an extremely grievous moment. Therefore it is no longer so easy for the new master to dispense the people's money. The working man cannot support the state theaters, unless he is convinced that they exist not for the entertainment of aristocrats but to satisfy the deep cultural needs of the working class. Democracy, the public, must come to an agreement with the actors. This agreement is in the highest degree possible. Its preliminary condition is the mutual understanding between me, the individual empowered to act for the workers' democracy in this area, and representatives of all the companies and groups of the state theaters. [...]

The theater is a single unit. Not one question relating to it, financial or legal, can be settled without negotiations with every category of worker of a given stage.

Once again, I ask all the workers' councils of the operatic and dramatic theaters, actors, supernumeraries, choruses, orchestras, and technical staff to send a delegation to me at the Ministry of People's Enlightenment to negotiate the most important questions that concern us. [...]

BY EARLY JANUARY, the Theater Council was in place, though not functioning, with subsidiary Khudrepkoms (Artistic Repertoire committees) for each theater answerable to it. The purpose was to simplify contact between the individual theaters and the Theater Council with a minimum of red tape. It never actually went into action, rendered superfluous by the creation of the Theater Division of Narkompros on February 18, 1918.

Alexandre Benois, from his diary, Moy dnevnik 1916–1917–1918 [My diary] (Moscow: Russky Put', 2003), 406–8. Alexandre Benois (actually Aleksandr Nikolaevich Benua, 1870–1960), designer and critic, a luminary of the World of Art movement and brilliant designer of ballet and opera, emigrated to Paris in 1926.

Wednesday, January 10/23, 1918. I find myself deeply depressed by a meeting in the Winter Palace which I happened to attend [...] Lunacharsky "buttonholed" me and dragged me to the meeting, which was being held just then in Yatmanov's[56] office. It

---

56 Grigory Stepanovich Yatmanov, coworker in the Narkompros in 1918.

turned out to be something of a preliminary conference on organizing artistic soviets. There for the first time I saw both Mrs. Kameneva[57] and Comrade Avramov, as well as another rather silent gentleman and, finally, "General Volkov's heir," the notorious Flakserman.[58] Into Mrs. Kameneva's hands have been delivered all the theatrical affairs in the Russian State, except, however, the former Imperial Theaters, now state theaters "in whose affairs (Lunacharsky's words) we shall not especially meddle—they will obviously manage themselves." This means that Meyerhold has been given special treatment, having been able to captivate and "tame" this "official" (Lunacharsky) too. Mme. Kameneva is a tall lady with a swarthy face, with the expression of a "salamander," who dresses not unpretentiously all in black. She sat next to Lunacharsky and repeatedly interrupted Anatoly in the midst of his most eloquent effusions, demanding, for instance, that he explain this or that proposal by means of graphic diagrams; in general, she displayed an exceptionally "nauseating" efficiency. She is the same as Mariya Fëdorovna A[ndreeva],[59] but even more self-confident, probably, *à la longue*,[60] even more insufferable. Avramov has a very strange face—a red beard, eyes reminiscent of those of various denizens of the zoo (the gnu, the mountain goat, the wolf) or "beasts from the island of Dr. Moreau."[61] He was wearing a velvet double-breasted jacket. However, he smiled (!) at me on our introduction (whereas Kameneva barely said hello) and throughout the entire meeting kept prudent silence. Flakserman took no part in the discussions but constantly burst out of the next room and, furiously stamping his boots, proudly proceeded to the back room, where a stenographer was typing. During his boss's most impassioned speech he walked up to the table and, unceremoniously, totally blocking our view of him, grabbed the rubber stamp and began there and then to slam it on the prepared papers. Érist[62] later explained to me that this striking, well-built, handsome, long-legged ephebe clad in a military uniform was Lunacharsky's favorite. He gave off a sense of remarkable energy (or the *semblance* of energy), but my presence probably provoked him to overdo his military manner. Any business entrusted to the hands of such a punk kid must inevitably crumble to dust.—The meeting itself was filled up with an unstaunched flow of oratory from Anatoly. He is a decent and no doubt well-intentioned fellow, but what a revolting defect this garrulousness and love of hearing himself talk! What boundless frivolity, what trust in *words* and what scant attention to life! He could barely keep his seat. He will inevitably be devoured by more single-minded and forceful personalities—probably Kameneva herself. Again there

57 Ol'ga Davydovna Kameneva (born Bronshteyn, 1883–1941), Trotsky's sister; from December 1917 the head of the TEO of the Narkompros, then of the Artistic-Enlightenment politdel of MONO.

58 Benois later confessed he couldn't remember what made Flakserman notorious. While still a student, Yury Nikolaevich Flakserman (1895–1995) was appointed by Lunacharsky to the Ministry of the Court; he later moved from administration to scientific work on aerodynamics.

59 Mariya Fëdorovna Andreeva (actually Yurkovskaya, 1868–1953), actress, at the MAT 1898–1906, until she left with her common-law husband Maksim Gorky. A card-carrying Bolshevik, she took an active part in organizing the Bol'shoy Dramatic Theater in Petrograd in 1918 and served as Petrograd Commissar of Theaters and Spectacles 1919–21.

60 French, over the long haul.

61 H. G. Wells's novel of a mad scientist turning beasts into men, *The Island of Dr. Moreau* (1896), is said to have influenced Mikhail Bulgakov as well.

62 F. F. Érist, opera director at the Bol'shoy Theater 1927–28.

came appeals "not to repeat the mistakes of the past," along with demands to *preserve* the same monuments created by the past, and so on. Lunacharsky wants to establish eight soviets in all. The first for palaces and museums [...], the second pedagogical, the third, fourth, and fifth literary [...], beyond that two theatrical ones (the sixth to run the state theaters, the seventh all the other theaters in general; poor, poor artistic freedom!—and to think all this is done in the name of "liberation"), and finally, the eighth is the musical one. The focal point of all these soviets is the person of the commissar himself. [...] Later Yatmanov privately defended to me and Érist a different scheme to be headed by colleagues—this would be the State Soviet for Artistic Affairs; for all my hatred of collectives, in this case I agreed with him, because it would be too awful to give full unchecked and unilateral control to such a dreamer as Lunacharsky.

THE Proletarian Cultural and Educational Organization (Proletkul't, for short) was the brainchild of Aleksandr Aleksandrovich Bogdanov (actually Malinovsky, 1873–1928), political economist and scientist, social democrat, and belated ally of Lenin. He had, as early as 1909, attempted to form an organization to provide the proletariat with a cultural education, and his plan was adopted with alacrity by Lunacharsky. The basic concept was not simply to educate the proletariat in preexisting culture but to foster an exclusively proletarian culture that would eventually supplant the bourgeois variety. Art and thought were to be used to organize the proletariat in the social struggle. Its most perfervid adherents were too impatient to wait for the organic dissolution of bourgeois art but called for the burning of museums and the impeccably proletarian origins of anyone who took in the movement.

> The invention of the Proletkul't. From the materials of the First Moscow Municipal Conference on Proletkul't, February 23–28, 1918. Report of Comrade Bartinsky,[63] "On people's theater," *STDM 17–21*, 329–30.

General Theoretical Positions

1. Definition of "people's theater"

People's theater is theater for the people in the all-round sense and widely accessible so as later to become a theater of the people by way of stimulating amateur performances among the broad masses.

2. Goals of the people's theater.

a. educational, b. pedagogical, c. aesthetic.

3. The repertoire of a people's theater that meets these goals must be as far as possible classical, artistic, serious, and with close ties to a systematic cycle of lectures on history, chiefly the history of Russian and foreign literatures and art. [...]

---

63 K. L. Bartinsky, actor, came to the conference as a member of the Culture-Enlightenment Commission of the Presnesensk district of Moscow.

Resolutions

I. It is necessary to create in Moscow local people's theaters, located as far as possible in the venues of local clubs, so that dramatic club schools can be organized in them.

II. To organize such theaters, but specifically to seek funding, locations, troupes, and so on, to elect a permanent commission from three members of the conference and charge it first of all to address the question of support for local theaters in the Commissariat of People's Enlightenment and simultaneously explore the possibility of establishing an all-Moscow fund for local theaters by the united professional democratic unions and consumers' societies.

III. It is desirable that the Proletkul't:

1. deal with issues concerning local theaters and the repertoire of the proletarian theater;

2. create a socialist literary–artistic circle of proletarian theaters, writers, theater workers, and other areas of the artistic–educational field;

3. the convocation of periodic conferences of workers for each issue: music, theater, movies, museums, etc. [...]

Report of Comrade Ignatov[64] "On the Proletarian Theater"

4. Built on these basic principles, the repertoire of proletarian theaters must be made up of play, which awakens in the masses creative energy, a joyous acceptance of life, audacity, a thirst for tireless struggle for a socialist future; plays that awake in the masses a competition in the sublimely heroic, in knowledge, in a struggle for the triumph of socialism and demonstrating that such a struggle is the only road to the perfection of the human personality. A proletarian theater must carol constructive labor of the creative human being as one of his wondrous capabilities and thereby evoke, arouse, modulate in the masses a stalwart, unyielding, and joyous will to labor. [...]

"A repertoire for the people's theater," *Zhizn' iskusstva* [The life of art] 4 (1918), 7.

Repertoire for the People's Theater, worked out by the theatrical department of the Commissariat of Enlightenment.

Russian theater: Averkiev—*Frol Skobeev*; Aleksandr Blok—*The King in the Square*; Gogol'—*The Inspector General*; Kapnist—*Chicanery*; Knyazhnin—*The Mead-vendor*; Krylov—*Trumphus*; Lunacharsky—*The Royal Tonsorial Artist*; Mey—*The Maid of Pskov*; Ostrovsky—*The Voivode, You Can't Live As You List, Innocent though Guilty, The Ward*; Pushkin—*The Stone Guest, The Miser Knight, The Feast in Plaguetime, Scenes from the Age of Chivalry*; Pisemsky—*Lieutenant Gladkov, Laws unto Themselves*; Aleksey Remizov—*The Devil's Pageant*; Sukhov-Kobylin—*Tarelkin's Death*; Tikhonov—*The*

---

64 V. V. Ignatov (1884–1938), secretary of the Petrograd Proletkul't, then member of the presidium of the Central Committee of the All-Russian Soviet of the Proletkul't.

Lone Wolf; Turgenev—*The Freeloader*; Tolstoy—*The Power of Darkness, And a Light Gleams in the Darkness*.

Original farces: Grigor'ev—*The Piemen of Baghdad*.

Translated farces: *The Caliph's Amusements, The Love Potion*; Karatygin—*Don Quixote*; Lensky—*That's What I Call Pills, or It Melts in the Mouth*.[65]

Ancient theater: Aeschylus—*The Oresteia* (abridged); Sophocles—*Oedipus the King*; Euripides-*Alcestis* (with Gluck's music); Aristophanes-*Lysistrata* in Vil'brandt's translation; Plautus-*The Twins* (tr. S. E. Radlov).

English theater: Shakespeare—*King Lear* (tr. A. V. Druzhinin), *Julius Caesar* (tr. P. A. Kozlov), *The Winter's Tale* (tr. P. Gnedich).

German theater: Büchner—*Danton's Death*; Grillparzer—*The Girondins*; Gutzkow—*Pugachëv*; Sudermann—*Johannisfeuer*; Lessing—*Nathan the Wise* (tr. V. Krylov); Schiller—*Wilhelm Tell* (tr. F. Miller), *Don Carlos* (tr. M. M. Dostoevsky), *The Conspiracy of Fiesco in Genoa* (tr. V. Krylov), *The Maid of Orleans* (tr. Zhukovsky); Schnitzler—*The Green Cockatoo*.

French theater: Beaumarchais—*The Marriage of Figaro* (tr. A. N. Chudinov, abridged); Verhaeren—*Dawns* (tr. Chulkov); Voltaire—*The Cranks* (tr. Ryzhova and Solov'ev); Hugo—*Ruy Blas, Les Misérables*; Zola—*The Wolf's Jaws, Thérèse Raquin*; Magnin—*Prince Lugonia*; Molière—*The Bourgeois Gentleman* (tr. V. Ostrogorsky); Regnard—*The St. Germain Fair*; Rolland—*The Storming of the Bastille*; Sardou—*Fatherland* (*Count de Rizoor*), *Thermidor*; Scribe—*Bertrand and Raton, The Ladies' Battle*.

Melodrama: *The Haunted House, The Kidnapper, The Two Orphans, The Two Urchins, The Children's Doctor, Clara d'Auberville, The Spanish Courtier, A Mother's Blessing*.

Italian theater: Gozzi—*Princess Turandot, The Serpent Woman, Love for Three Oranges*.

Spanish theater: [Calderón]—*The Constant Prince* (tr. Bal'mont); Lope de Vega—*The Sheep's Well*; Cervantes—*The Siege of Numantia, Interludes*; Tirso de Molina—*The Seducer of Seville*.

Scandinavian theater: Ibsen—*The League of Youth*.

ON MARCH 11, 1918, a Charter of Autonomous State Theaters (Ustav avtonomnykh gosudarstvennykh teatrov) was agreed on by representatives of the state theaters and the government. A Council of State Theaters (Sovet gosudarstvennykh teatrov) was created to regulate relations between state and autonomous troupes, although it was quickly eclipsed by the Narkompros Division of State Theaters.

---

65 An adaptation of the French *féerie Les Pilules du diable* (1839).

Anatoly Lunacharsky and department head Ol'ga D. Kameneva, "Situation of the Narkompros TEO," June 29, 1918. *STDM 17–21*, 41.

[The Theatrical Division of the People's Commissariat of Enlightenment is established in Petrograd to carry out all matters relating to theater in the Russian Federated Republic.]

All matters relating to the Section's jurisdiction will be discussed by colleague specialists in the corresponding branches of the Section, whose appointment will be confirmed by the Commissar of Enlightenment.

The Theater Section has the right to the closest and quickest implementation of those tasks to establish branches in locations under the jurisdiction of the Section on principles confirmed by the Commissar of Enlightenment.

At the head of the Theater Section, under the jurisdiction of the Commissariat of Enlightenment, there is to be an individual, appointed by the Soviet of People's Commissars, with full authority to decide all matters relating to the internal order of the Section and having the right, in case of the commissar's absence, of direct communication with the Soviet of People's Commissars.

THE TEO was not allowed control over the state theaters, which irritated the maximalists, among them Kameneva and Meyerhold, who wanted to appropriate the former imperial playhouses.

Vsevolod Meyerhold, "On work and recreation," August 7, 1918. In *Stat'i, pis'ma, rechi, besedy* [Articles, letters, speeches, talks] (Moscow: Iskusstvo, 1968), 2:4–5.

Now, when the whole infrastructure of Russian life is being reconstructed, every citizen in the land must know that for the building of a new, socialist government, we need to have a new reserve of strength. Everyone will become a worker, in whatever trade he works—in the trade of intellectual labor or manual labor. Everywhere what is indispensable is an exceptional reserve of strength, courage, and joyous excitement.

In order not to squander his strength, the worker and consequently every citizen will strive to fight for the greatest amount of recreation, not to work less, but by means of recreation to increase ever newer and newer reserves of strength and have leisure time not only for recreation but for self-education. Hence the government will strive to organize the life of the workers of individual territories so that recreation will flow into the conditions of cultural–educational organization with modern conveniences. But the chief concern of the government is that both labor and recreation be instilled with the necessary plans for superb hygiene.

I am delighted to note the government's order to close *at night hours* all sorts of cafés, clubs, cabaret theaters, and teahouses that offer variety entertainments. All these places of recreation are needed by the worker, but they must be open during the day, not at night. [...]

Nelidov, *Teatral'naya Moskva*, 347.

For a future historian of the theater of our period it may be of interest to learn that on the anniversary of the revolution, October 28, the theaters were instructed to put on: the Maly, *Woe from Wit*; the Art Theater, *Mistress of the Inn* by Goldoni; the Bol'shoy, *Boris Godunov*; and the erstwhile Private Opera, *Lohengrin*. [...]

THE TROUPE of the Alexandra Theater had moved out of town for its summer vacation.

> Stella Arbenina, *Through Terror to Freedom* (London: Hutchinson, 1929), 107–8, 128–29. Zoe Stella Whishaw, Baroness Meyendorff (1885–1976), of an English family long resident in Russia, was an actress married to an aide-de-camp of the tsar. The couple was imprisoned and persecuted but made it to Reval in 1918, Berlin 1921–22, and England 1923. As Stella Arbenina, she acted in all these cities.

Our group, of thirty-five members, went to Vologda[66] to play repertory there during the summer. It consisted of two leading ladies (Danilova[67] and myself), two ingénues, two "character" and two "old" women; the male contingent of the company was equally large; then there were about a dozen students for small parts and crowd work; and the business manager and his staff completed the number.

We travelled in a reserved carriage. [...] One of the reasons why the Alexandra Theater company had chosen Vologda for their summer abode was that one could still get decent food there. [...] All was quite peaceful in town when we arrived there in May, and there were no signs of the approach of any fresh tragedies. [...] Our theater was extremely popular, and we played to crowded houses every night. [...]

[On July 18, 1918, the imperial family was murdered, and the news was announced on July 20.]

They were dark days that followed for us in Vologda. The performances went on at the theater (we did not dare close down for fear of being arrested as counterrevolutionaries), but we played to empty houses. The population of the town was silently mourning the tsar's death. Our audiences consisted chiefly of "Red" officers and soldiers, drunk for the most part, who slouched about the theater in the intervals, using insulting epithets when speaking of the imperial family, whose martyrdom would be on their consciences forever; bursting into yells of coarse laughter, priding themselves on the ghastly crime their comrades had committed [...]

On August 1 the Czechs took Ekaterinburg; on the third Archangel was occupied by the Allies. Martial law was proclaimed in Vologda, and the theater was closed. At first the actors, who all depended entirely on their salaries for a living, hoped that it might not be for long and that the theater would be reopened; but after a few days it

---

66 A small town on the Siberian railway, five hundred miles east of Petrograd.
67 Danilova, actress who took part in Vakhtangov's amateur productions.

became clear that there was no chance of it. Salaries were discontinued and contracts canceled owing to force majeure. [...]

The Moscow Art Theater

Serge Orlovsky, "Moscow theaters, 1917–1941," in Martha Bradshaw, ed., *Soviet Theaters 1917–1941* (New York: Research Program on the USSR, 1954), 5–6.

In the winter of 1918 a group of actors from the Art Theater was invited to give a concert for one of the Red Army divisions near Moscow, in return for a special ration. They took the actors in sledges to a former country house, then occupied by soldiers. In the huge, twin-lighted hall stood small iron stoves, red-hot. The hall was packed with soldiers and sailors who were awaiting the performance. Steam rose from their damp overcoats and galoshes; the blue smoke from cheap tobacco blinded the eyes. First, in evening dress and patent-[leather pumps], Vsevolod Alekseevich Verbitsky[68] came out. The silent auditorium heard with surprise the words of Aleksandr Blok, incomprehensible to them:

> ... I sat at the window in a crowded hall,
> Somewhere a violin sang of love—
> I sent you a black rose in a goblet
> Of gold, heavenly, ai ...[69]

Verbitsky finished in complete silence. The next selection, from *The Brothers Karamazov,* they didn't listen to and exchanged indignant comments. "What is that bourgeois mumbling about there?" shouted someone from the hall. Then from the crowd appeared the forcible figure of the commissar, loaded with machine gun ammunition belts and a huge Colt at his belt. Stopping the actors with a gesture, he loudly announced: "Here now, let's have the accordion player! And lock up this smart group—swindlers! I myself will take care of them in the morning!" An army accordion player quickly replaced *The Brothers Karamazov,* and the hungry artists of the Moscow Art Theater, frightened to death, were led under guard to a distant cold room, where they sat till dawn. Only toward morning did one of the actors think to try the door, which seemed locked. It was open, and everyone dashed out, up to their knees in snow, in evening dress, to go on foot to Moscow, forgetting the rations about which they had dreamed the day before. Thus, comparatively happily, ended the first trial of the "patronage" system for actors. [...]

THE URBAN ECONOMY had entirely broken down in Moscow. For everyday necessities, particularly food, the populace was dependent on the black market. Shortages of fuel, electricity, and raw materials complicated the routine of day-to-day performances.

68 Vsevolod Alekseevich Verbitsky (1896–1951), actor at the MAT 1924–50, one of the creators of the MAT Second Studio.
69 "V restorane" (1910), one of Blok's most famous love lyrics, was often set to music.

Art Theater daily reports, 260, 524, 300, 311–12.

January 9 [1918]. *A Month in the Country*[70] (117th perf.) [...] A far-from-full audience led to hesitation over whether there should be a performance today.

Vl. Iv. Nemirovich-Danchenko came before the curtain and turned to the audience to decide the question: Vl. Iv. pointed out that although the actors courageously arrived for the performance, they are disturbed by the mood of the street and the fact that the audience will have to go home late; the audience replied to this with the fervent wish to see the performance and broke out into applause; some members of the audience declared that they were ready to be sacrificed for the sake of art and risk danger to their persons. Then Vl. Iv. asked the audience for a three-minute pause to consult with the performers, after which he informed the audience that the actors shared the audience's mood (readiness to take risks for the sake of art), drew on fresh strength, and as soon as they had focused their concentration would start the show. [...]

Today neither the refreshment room or the property man took the trouble to procure grapes or raisins (to represent raspberries in Act II).

April 29–May 5, 1918. By decree of the All-Russian Trade Union of Art Workers performances and shows were forbidden on Thursday, Friday, and Saturday of Holy Week and on Sunday and Monday of Easter Week (April 29–30 and May 1–5); however, by decree of the authorities, May 1 was ordered performances to be given for a democratic public.

October 29 [1918]. *Woe from Wit.* [...] Instead of Sushkevich, Svarozhich played without a rehearsal. At the last or next to last time Pavlov[71] played without a rehearsal...

I understand the need for understudies, but... *Woe from Wit*!!! without a rehearsal!! In what backwater is the theater located! After this, how can one ask respect and genuine creativity of others? Why shouldn't the performers be given advance notice? We should find one little minute, amid our affairs. After all, I have a scene with him, and an important one.

The basin in our washstand looks unscrubbed since the last performance of *Fëdor*, the faucet is clogged, rusty—and dirty water stands in the basin!! Quite the picture of gradual ruin and decay.

K. Stanislavsky.

December 15 [1918]. Matinee: *Lower Depths.*[72] Began 12:45. Ended 3:55. [...]

I direct your attention for the third time that my bunks have lost their covers, now there is no way to block caps, the wooden block for caps got broken and still isn't fixed,

---

70 *A Month in the Country,* Turgenev's comedy of 1850, was first staged by the MAT in 1909 with stunning pastel sets and costumes by Mstislav Dobuzhinsky. Stanislavsky played Rakitin, but by 1918, he had been replaced by Vasily Kachalov.

71 Boris Mikhaylovich Sushkevich (1887–1946), actor, director, teacher; at the MAT First Studio–MAT 2 1908–33. Konstantin Georgievich Svarozhich (actually Trusov), actor at the MAT 1913–19. Polikarp Arsen'evich Pavlov (1885–1974), actor at the MAT 1908–22; he became a leading figure in the Russian émigré theater in Paris.

72 *The Lower Depths,* Gorky's play of lowlife, opened in 1902 at the MAT, which had a monopoly on it until after the Revolution. It was a staple of its repertoire.

and after all, don't there exist people in charge of things, and aren't there workshops?! I direct your attention, while it's not too late, before the material covering Anna's bunk rots away, to ask the designers to make a sketch of it and order a new one; if they can't give me cords, then at least thin white strings, dyed or not dyed black, but if dyed, then soon and not just before the performance, otherwise you'll stain their hands. In general, whoever it was who abandoned the prop shop left it forlorn as an orphan. There are simply no props at the performance! Good Lord, what's going on? This is just like yesterday with the money in *Ivanov*,[73] there wasn't any, and, despite my sending to Ivan Kupriyanovich for some, there was none, and when I went myself and said something, they gave me three, even French paper francs turned up! Which means, they do exist? Since there's nobody left—then maybe seek and ask help of the Governing Board, but don't be content with the fact that times are hard and there's nothing anyone wants to do, make a scandal that you'll shut down the Theater, but do not be content, otherwise the scandals themselves will shut it down! It's unbearable, disgusting, everyone is bawling or meets with indifference or laughter! [...] It's not the bourgeois speaking in me, longing for his slippers, but the actor, and not only for his own convenience but for that of others, less experienced and seasoned performers who sometimes play Bubnov. Let the foreman or one of the workmen try to talk for just a couple of minutes in a curled-up position, in which we now have to lie without the missing mattresses and blankets. [...]

What a performance! Smyshlaev was late, Afonin's costume was so torn in Act II that he couldn't walk over to us and speak his lines; S. V. Khalyutina[74] didn't show up for the crowd scene in Act III, and the ones standing around, instead of speaking the words for her, only kept repeating her name under their breath. Or is the audience the kind that will put up with this?

V. Luzhsky.[75]

A. V. Lunacharsky, "Remarks at the meeting of the Special Conference on the Theatrical Question," December 10, 1918. *STDM 17–21*, 48.

I don't believe there was any meddling in the repertoire of the Art Theater, but I will say that, of course, the government authorities cannot be indifferent to this. Besides, outside government help, a private theater cannot exist. [...] Private patronage has gone forever. One cannot raise prices above certain norms. How are we to make both ends meet? The result is either the theaters go hungry or the government will have to

---

73 *Ivanov*, a comedy-drama (1887–88) by Anton Chekhov, was revived by the MAT in 1904 as a memorial tribute to the author.

74 Valentin Sergeevich Smyshlaev (1891–1936), actor, director, teacher; at the MAT First Studio–MAT II 1913–31; the only member of the troupe to be a card-carrying Bolshevik and member of the Proletkul't. Boris Makarovich Afonin (1888–1975), actor, teacher; at MAT First Studio–MAT II 1909–13, 1916–36. Sofiya Vasil'evna Khalyutina (1875–1960), actress, teacher; at the MAT 1898–1950; Vakhtangov took her drama courses.

75 Vasily Vasil'evich Luzhsky (actually Kaluzhsky, 1869–1931), actor at the MAT from 1898 in sixty-four roles; often codirected with Stanislavsky, tasked with staging crowd scenes.

finance the theaters, but in that case, it has the right to regulate their life. [...] Some sort of order has to exist, not in the ideological sense, God forbid, but there has to be a commission that decides what theater is to be financed and to what degree. [...]

Nelidov, *Teatral'naya Moskva*, 348.

Once *Uncle Vanya* was on at the Art Theater. In the first act, there was so much going on in the auditorium that before the second act began, K. S. Stanislavsky firmly and sharply addressed the audience, demanding that they "respect the actor's work." [...]

Arthur Ransome, "*Uncle Vanya* in 1919," in *Six Weeks in Russia in 1919* (London: Allen and Unwin, 1919), 92–93. Arthur Michell Ransome (1884–1967), an English reporter during the Russian Revolution, married Trotsky's secretary before retiring to England, where he became an inspired children's writer and fisherman.

The subject of *Uncle Vanya* was a great deal more remote from the Russian audience of to-day than was the opera of *Samson and Delilah* which I heard last week. And, if I realized that the revolution had come to stay, if I realized that Chekhov's had become a play of historical interest, I realized also that Chekhov was a great master in that his work carried across the gulf between the old life and the new, and affected a revolutionary audience of to-day as strongly as it affected that very different audience of a few years ago. Indeed, the play seemed almost to have gained by the revolution, which had lent it, perhaps, more irony than was in Chekhov's mind as he wrote. Was this the old life? I thought, as I stepped out into the snow. If so, then thank God it has gone!

Nikolay Massalitinov, "My remembrances," in N. M. Vaganova, *Russkaya teatral'naya émigratsiya v tsentral'noy Evrope i na Balkanakh* [Russian Theatrical Emigration in Central Europe and the Balkans] (St. Petersburg: Aleteyya, 2007), 217–18. Nikolay Osipovich Massalitinov (1880–1961), actor and director at the MAT 1907–22; abroad during the Civil War, he carried on as a member of the MAT Kachalov group, then of the Prague Group; chief director of the National Theater of Sofia, Bulgaria, 1925–44.

A council of all the artistic, administrative, and technical personnel of the MAT was created. To this council was invited the narkom of enlightenment A. V. Lunacharsky. Vl. I. Nemirovich-Danchenko posed him a direct question: how does the narkom of enlightenment regard the Art Theater?

Lunacharsky spoke at great length with his usual eloquence as a gifted public speaker. He acknowledged the achievements of the MAT in the past. "But now you are a dead organism," he said, "you are a museum piece. To tell the truth, workers are still interested in you, as children are interested in a pretty plaything, but their horny hands will, of course, soon break this plaything. To keep this from happening, the

Soviet government is taking pains to wrap you in cotton, in a museum—lie down there—vegetate! We do not need you! But there is still time for you to come to your senses. The bourgeois individualism that divided people is over forever. Now the time has come for collectivism, which will bring happiness to all mankind, and the task of art is to illumine this new path" and so forth, all in the same spirit.

In reply, Konstantin Sergeevich pronounced an inspired courageous speech that there has never been, is not, and never will be a special proletarian art. There is only one art—the eternal one. Art in capital letters, which reflects the life of the human spirit. "Sooner or later," he said to the narkom, "you will inevitably come to this conclusion! All of the current incentives of the Soviet authorities in this regard will only bring harm." (Stanislavsky was thinking of the Proletkul'ts.) "You are destroying art, not creating it. It is impossible to think up, invent any new art. If it is to be born, it will be born on its own."

Stanislavsky's speech was met with a unanimous ovation; obviously, it made an impression even on Lunacharsky—at least he promised to do something for the MAT, and I believe he will. The agonizing season of 1918–19 somehow came to an end.

The First Soviet Play

The dynamic young futurist poet Vladimir Vladimirovich Mayakovsky (1893–1930) had, in 1911, cofounded, with the poet David Burlyuk, the cubo-futurist literary group Hylaea, which offered a "Slap in the Face of the Public Taste." He had published several influential collections of verse between 1910 and 1916, which were intended to be read aloud from the stage. However, he first came to public notice in December 1913 with his play titled, owing to a censor's error, *Vladimir Mayakovsky*, as part of a double-bill with the futurist opera *Victory over the Sun*. He enthusiastically welcomed the events of October 1917 as "my revolution." That November he attended a meeting of writers, artists, and stage directors convened by Lunacharsky at the Smolny Institute to advance future cooperation between artists and the Bolshevik regime. Mayakovsky threw himself wholeheartedly into literacy campaigns and public poetry readings, eager to replace the art of the past with a new aesthetics for the twentieth century.

> Vladimir Mayakovsky, "Open letter to the workers," *Gazeta Futuristov* [Futurist Gazette] (March 15, 1918).

Comrades! [...]

To you who have taken over Russia's legacy, to you who (I believe!) will tomorrow become masters of the whole world, I pose the question: with what fantastic structures will you cover the site of yesterday's fires? What songs and music will pour from your windows? To what bibles will you open your souls?

I observe in astonishment how famous theaters resound with Aidas and Traviatas, with their Spaniards and noblemen; how in the poems you listen to, the same aristo-crats' hothouse roses are blooming; how your eyes are goggling in front of pictures showing the pomp of the past. [...]

Only the eruption of the Spirit of Revolution will rid us of the rags of antiquated art.

AS EARLY as August 1917, Mayakovsky had conceived of a revolutionary play that would link the genres of mystical religious enactment (mystery) and farci-cal comedy (bouffe). *Mystery Bouffe* was an extravagant rewrite of Genesis, with the bourgeois Clean and the proletarian Unclean seeking salvation in their own ways. He proposed it as a celebration of the first anniversary of the Revolution. Unable to find a director in Moscow willing to take it on, on Meyerhold's initia-tive and Lunacharsky's command, Mayakovsky read it at the Alexandra Theater in Petrograd, where a performance, possibly at the former Grand Duke Michael Theater, was mooted.

> Konstantin Derzhavin, "February and October in the Theater," in *Sto let. Alek-sandrinsky teatr—Teatr Gosdramy* [A hundred years: The Alexandra Theater of State Drama] (Leningrad: Diretsii leningradskikh gosudarstvennykh teatrov, 1932), 428. Konstantin Nikolaevich Derzhavin (1903–56), literary and theater scholar, studied directing under Meyerhold; secretary of the TEO Narkompros 1921; dramaturg of the Leningrad Bol'shoy Dramatic Theater 1933–36.

The reading of this play evoked a harsh, negative response in a considerable part of the troupe, not only in reaction to its "futuristic" texture but chiefly because it came across as some sort of symbol of the presence within the walls of the Alexandra Theater of the most real Bolshevism, with its "mockery" of religious feelings, especially feared by a great many of the actors. While listening to *Mystery Bouffe,* a number of actors crossed themselves in horror at the blasphemies scattered throughout it.

> Levky Zheverzheev, "Stenographic record of memoirs," in V. Katanyan, *Mayakovsky. Literaturnaya khronik* [Mayakovsky: Literary chronicle], 4th rev. ed. (Moscow: Goslitizdat, 1961), 138, 102. Levky Ivanovich Zheverzheev (1881–1942), art critic, member of the theater-history section of the Petrograd Division of the TEO Narkompros; in 1919, with Meyerhold, created the Her-mitage Theater for popular performance—it put on shows at the Georgiev Hall in the Winter Palace from July to November 1919.

Serving at the time as chief of the "autonomous" troupe of the theater, the actor D. Kh. Pashkovsky proposed to listen to the young poet's play, recommended for production by the narkom of enlightenment Com. Lunacharsky.

The reading began in a deathly silence. The greenroom, packed to bursting with actors, responded with suspicion and animosity to both the narkom's recommendation

1.1. Poster for *Mystery Bouffe,* designed by Vladimir Mayakovsky, Conservatory Theater of Musical Drama, Petrograd, 1918. The drawing shows the old world canceled out.

and the intervention of D. Kh. Pashkovsky. At the time, despite the decree, in a corner under the roof, a little icon continued to hang, and the very title of the play, "Mystery," in association with "bouffe," immediately took aback some of the "old Alexandrites."

Meyerhold begins. The word goes out:

"Comrades, we know Goethe, we know Pushkin, now prepare to perform the greatest poet of modern times Vladimir Vladimirovich Mayakovsky."

Vladimir Vladimirovich, thoroughly uninhibited, steps up to the lectern. He sits down. Then there's a whispering, everyone is shocked... Act I. Interval. Nobody says a word... When things get as far as the scene in heaven, my attention is diverted to Apollonsky and his wife, Stravinskaya.[76] Apollonsky was a very religious man, he almost leaps up, but remains and does not leave...

Yet even here the reader's enthralling mastery made the most powerful impression on the listener. In the intervals I heard, along with obvious indignation and sneering as to the subject matter, remarks from individual actors: "he reads magnificently," "what an actor he would be," "what a noble and truly well-placed voice."

It was decided that such a new play would be out of place in an old theater. Zavteo[77] Mariya Andreeva suggested a circus.

---

76 Roman Borisovich Apollonsky (1865–1928), actor at the Alexandra Theater 1881–1920, created the role of Treplëv in *The Seagull* (1896). N. A. Stravinskaya, an actress at the Alexandra, codirected Ibsen's *Lady from the Sea* with Meyerhold 1917.

77 *Zaveduyushchaya otdelom teatra i zrelishch Soyuza kommun Severnoy oblasti:* Director of the Department of Theater and Spectacles of the Union of Communes of the Northern Region.

Mariya Andreeva recalls the event. TsGALI, quoted in A. Fevral'sky, *Pervaya sovetskaya p'esa: "Misteriya-buff" V. V. Mayakovskogo* [The first Soviet play: "Mystery Bouffe" by Mayakovsky] (Moscow: Sovetsky pisatel', 1971), 62–63.

I had a run-in with Vladimir Vladimirovich regarding his *Mystery Bouffe,* which he wanted to stage in the very first year [after the Revolution]. I considered that no one would understand it, and yet it cost a crazy amount of money. I was connected with an endless number of all sorts of people, and every one of them said, "What is this thing? What rubbish!" When Mayakovsky got offended, it didn't bother me much, because I always had good relations with him and wished to help him.

IT WAS ultimately codirected by Meyerhold and Mayakovsky at the Theater of Musical Drama in Petrograd.

Vladimir Solov'ëv, "One of my remembrances of Mayakovsky," in Katanyan, *Mayakovsky,* 149. Vladimir Nikolaevich Solov'ëv (1887–1941), director and critic, a specialist in commedia dell'arte, assisted in the directing. He later ran the Leningrad Youth Theater.

After painstakingly having explained the laws of prosody to the assembled actors, Mayakovsky taught them to recite rhythmically the complicated verses. Sitting on a chair, lightly shaking his head and rapping on the table with a pencil, Mayakovsky gradually became carried away, got up, broke away from his place, jumped onto the chair and began to conduct like a veteran choir master, infecting the actors with his temperament. Obviously, working together with the actors gave Mayakovsky something new in his understanding of the theater and drama. More and more often he began to come to rehearsals, bringing typed-up notes with new variants of specific verses, and sometimes whole sections. In the practical work the poet with the actors tried out new, stageworthy, and theatrical qualities of the text of *Mystery.*

Mayakovsky's work with the performing collective was not limited to rehearsing the choral partitions. The actors often turned to him for advice, with the request that he read this or that role. Mayakovsky's reading gave a great deal to the actors. In his conversation with the actors, in individual remarks concerning the nature of the role to be performed, Mayakovsky seemed in his treatment to hold up the formulas of the romantic theater with its sharp division of all the characters into two scenic levels: the universal and the grotesquely ludicrous. From the performers of the "seven pairs of the unclean" he demanded a firm, tough-willed principle, heroic emotion and plastic monumentality. In the treatment of the "seven pairs of the clean" he enthusiastically allowed a manner of exaggerated parody, with its crude devices of satiric buffoonery and popular farce.

THE PRODUCTION opened on November 7, 1918. Mayakovsky played several of the roles himself, and the designs were by the painter Kazimir Severinovich Malevich (1879–1936). Malevich had designed the cubo-futurist scenery for *Victory over the Sun*; in 1915 he had founded the geometric-abstract school of Suprematicism. His designs for *Mystery Bouffe* were carried out by a young artist, A. A. Lappo-Danilevsky. Although Malevich served on the Narkompros arts council in the early years of Soviet power, by the 1930s, his avant-gardism had fallen out of favor.

> Kazimir Malevich, conversation with Aleksandr Fevral'sky, September 15, 1932, in Fevral'sky, *Pervaya sovetskaya p'esa*, 69–70.

I did not appreciate images being organized around a subject in Mayakovsky's poetry, I preferred the subjectlessness of Kruchënykh.[78] My approach to the production was cubist in nature. I took the proscenium arch to be the frame of a picture, and the actors as the contrasting element (in cubism, each object is a contrasting element to the other). Planning the action in three or four levels, I tried to arrange the actors in space principally on a vertical, in accord with the efforts of the most up-to-date painting; the actors' movements had to be in rhythmic accord with the elements of the scenery. On a single canvas I painted somewhat flatly. I treated space not as illusionary but as cubist. I considered my job to create associations not with a reality existing outside the bounds of the frame but with a new reality solely from the standpoint of a painter.

> Vladimir Mayakovsky, "Tol'ko ne vospominaniya" (1927), in *Polnoe sobranie sochineny v 13 tomakh* (Moscow: Khudozhestvennaya literatura, 1960), 12:149–58.

The theater's administration did everything in its power to sabotage the production. Entrance doors were locked, even nails were kept under lock and key [...]

Posters were delivered on opening day—with painted outlines only—and a declaration was immediately made that no one be allowed to paste them up.

I painted the posters myself.

Our maid, Tonya, went to the Nevsky with the posters and nails and put them up wherever she could. They were immediately torn down by the wind.

And then, as evening came on, actors began to disappear, one by one.

I had to assume, on the spot, the roles of "A Mere Man" as well as Methuselah and one of the devils.

The next day *Mystery* was scrapped, and to the joy of the academicians, *Macbeth* again began to bore us. How else could it be? Lady Macbeth was played by Andreeva herself. [...]

---

78 Aleksey Eliseevich Kruchënykh (1886–1968), futurist poet, who, with Velimir Khlebnikov, composed the libretto for the avant-garde opera *Victory over the Sun* (1913), for which Malevich designed abstract sets and "volumetric" costumes.

> Aleksandr Blok, *Dnevniki 1901–1921* [Diaries 1901–20] (Moscow: Khudozhest-vennaya literatura, 1965), 434–35.

November 7. Celebration of the anniversary of October. At night with Lyuba to Maya-kovsky's *Mystery Bouffe* at the Musical Drama (until six o'clock with the actors' recep-tion). A historic day—for Lyuba and me—complete. During the day, both of us to town: decorations, processions, rain, by the grave [of the victims of the Revolution on the Field of Mars]. *A holiday.* At night a hoarse and doleful speech by Lunacharsky, Mayakovsky, lots of people. This day will never be forgotten.

EMBOLDENED by the enthusiastic reception awarded the play (though not the production) by the Communist press (though not by the first-night audience), Mayakovsky began to proclaim an even more maximalist position in relation to the arts in the new society.

> Vladimir Mayakovsky, intervention at the debate "The proletariat and art," December 22 and 29, 1918. In *Sobranie sochineny v vosem' tomakh* [Collected works in eight volumes] (Moscow: Pravda, 1968), 1:403.

[Doubting the effectiveness of appearing before an audience that was made up primar-ily of the intelligentsia, Mayakovsky turned away from those "habitués of the Empire (music hall)" to address the workers in the gathering:] We welcome the speaker's call for the creation of a proletarian art. But can one invite to this affair all people of art for no particular reason, as is being done now? You say: "a warm welcome." We say: show your credentials. Whose envoys are you—the heart that beats with the proletar-ian revolution or a wish for orders from a new master? [...] The new has to be dis-cussed with new words. We need a new form of art. To erect a monument to a metal worker is no great thing; you have to do it so that it is different from a monument to a printer, erected by the tsar. The Revolution, which divided all Russia into two camps, has drawn a boundary line between rightist and leftist art as well. On the left are we, who portray the new; on the right are those who regard art as a means of all kinds of acquisition. This is perfectly understood by the workers, who have joyfully accepted our manifestations. There is no classless art. Only the proletariat will create the new, and only we, the futurists, are traveling the same road as the proletariat.

The Move to Centralization

In February 1919 Narkompros altered the administrative structure of the state theaters once again by establishing directorates (*direktorii*) in each one, to plan the repertoire and maintain artistic standards. They replaced the Khudrepkom, but their members were increasingly appointed by Narkompros. Among the resolu-tions adopted by the eighth Congress of the Communist Party in March was the declaration that "there are no types of art or science that should not be linked to the great ideas of Communism and the infinitely variegated work of creating a Communist economy." All nonacademic mass education, including theater, "must affect Communist propaganda."[79]

Tasks of the Theater Section, in *Sbornik dekretov i postanovlenii po narodnomu obrazovaniyu* [Collection of decrees and resolutions concerning the people's education] (1919), 1:140–43.

[The aims are] the general guidance of theater work in the country on a broad nation-wide scale . . . to give localities directives of a general character on administering theater work, in the interests of unifying this last and aiming at a systematic and (insofar as is possible) uniform application to life (within the limits of local conditions) of the Theater Division's tasks . . . to create a new theater connected with the rebuilding of the state and society on the principles of socialism.

From Resolution of VIII Congress of the RKP(b), "On political propaganda and cultural-educational work in the village," March 18–23, 1919. *STDM 17–21, 22–23.*

The plan for educational activity in the village must include intensive co-ordination among:

1. Communist propaganda.
2. General education.
3. Agricultural education.

1. Political propaganda in the village must be carried on for both the literate and illiterate [. . .]

The movies, theater, concerts, exhibitions, etc., so far as they can penetrate the village, to which all sorts of force must be applied, indispensable to benefit Communist propaganda, both directly, i.e., through their content, and in combination with lectures and public meetings. [. . .]

2. General education—in and out of schools (including artistic institutions: theaters, concerts, movies, exhibitions, pictures, etc.), striving not only to cast light of the most various knowledge on the benighted village but, in general, to enable the operation of self-consciousness and a lucid outlook on the world—must be closely associated with Communist propaganda. [. . .]

79 *VKP (b) v rezolyutsiyakh i resheniakh s'ezdov, konferentsii i plenumov TsK. Partizdat TsK VKP (b) 1936* [VKP (b) resolutions and decisions of congresses, conferences, and plenums of the Comm. Party], part 1, 313.

> Bulletin no. 1 of the Repertoire Section, April 13–18, 1919. *Vestnik Teatra* [Theater herald] 20 (1919), 9–10. *STDM 17–21, 45–46.*

[The Repertoire section intends to issue periodic bulletins to make recommendations for a contemporary repertoire.]

First, a classical repertoire, time tested and standing for superior artistic value, will be made the basis of the bulletins.

Second, special attention will be devoted to those plays that are, in subject matter, consonant with the revolutionary period—plays in which "a re-evaluation of values" defines the emotional spirit of the drama.

Third, attention will be paid to specific questionnaires formulated by the TEO and that make particular demands—the lists will include plays with the following features: (1) plays that reflect modern life; (2) plays easy to produce; (3) plays from the life of peasants and workers; (4) plays of so-called merry theater, satisfying a lively demand for unmediated laughter. [...]

IN MAY 1919, after several meetings by professional unions, categories for theaters were established, to govern salaries in dramatic theaters. The actors were subdivided, depending on their line of business, into five categories. All theaters were differentiated into three groups.

> "Guilds and unions," *Vestnik teatra* 19 (1919), 8.

first group—large theaters with a clearly expressed artistic program;
second group—large theaters which have no definite tendency;
third group—little theaters.

Payment for actors' work is dependent on the theatrical group, the category, and the type to which the actor belongs. Besides the basic wage, it is proposed that amortized payments be made for the use of personal costumes, makeup, etc., at the rate of 25 percent for actors and 50 percent for actresses. [...]

> "Renovating the theater," *Vestnik teatra* 29 (May 27–June 1, 1919), 5.

One of the fundamental questions in this respect: which direction is the proper one for the profession of the new theater to take? Which theatrical "party" is closest of all to a workers' and peasants' theater? Is it to move to the "right"—the naturalism of the Art Theater's Chekhov productions, to the "left"—as far as the cubism of Claudel's *Exchange* at the Kamerny Theater, or to take a middle path of stylization, what Gaydeburov[80] calls "realistic impressionism"?

80 Pavel Pavlovich Gaydeburov (1877–1960), actor, director, devoted to bringing quality theater to the masses, organizing the Low-Priced Theater at the Ligovsky People's Palace, St. Petersburg, 1903–14, and, in 1905, the First Itinerant Theater.

If it would seem that the truth is acknowledged that the working class is the heir to all the values, all the achievements of artistic culture, the general line of conduct is clear-cut: *all* tendencies are legitimate, and the choice among them will be made by the working class itself.

[...] Let's go further, let's go outside the theater. How ridiculous, how absurd are these buildings in the style of the Louises or the Empire, so usual for our theaters! A new era must provide new architectural style as well, and until there is one, is it not proper to take from the old what is fittest for the new: after all, is not the Hellenistic theater, with its arrangement of seats for spectators, far more satisfactory to the demands of the new era?

ON AUGUST 26, 1919, the Soviet government adopted the decree "On the Unification of Matters Pertaining to the Theater." The whole theatrical economy was centralized by the institution under the People's Commissariat for Enlightenment of a Central Theatrical Committee (Tsentroteatr). However, to paraphrase George Orwell, some theaters were more equal than others. The decree distinguished theaters "recognized as useful and artistic" (themselves divided into several categories, all subsidized by the state) and theaters "managed by entrepreneurs or private organizations that do not guarantee a superior cultural level." Finally, it stated the principle of an inspection of the repertoire by the organs of power (Central Theater Committee or local section of Public Enlightenment) so as to make sure they served the socialist ideal.

"On the unification of matters pertaining to the theater," the SNK[81] Decree no. 98 of August 26, 1919, signed by Lenin. *Sovetsky teatr* [Soviet theater] (1967), 1–11.

[The decree establishes that] (1) The Central Theater Committee (Tsentroteatr) of the People's Commissariat of Enlightenment will be established to regulate activities in Russia; (2) TEO[82] becomes the executive branch of the Tsentroteatr; [the Bureau of State Theaters will be incorporated into the TEO. Clause 3 outlines the powers of the organization:] Supreme supervision of all theaters, both state owned and established under certain branches (military, co-operative, soviets, etc.). [Clause 4 is the cornerstone of the decree:] All theater property (facilities and chattels) is declared national property as cultural valuables [except for the private property of actors (addendum to article 8). This is reaffirmed in clause 5, which establishes that] effective as of the date of this publication, the exportation abroad, destruction, devaluing, or selling of theater

---

81 Sovnarkom, short for Sovet Narodnykh Kommissarov or Council of People's Commissars, the main executive body of the Soviet government, established by the All-Russian Congress of Soviets in 1917. In 1946 it was renamed the Council of Ministers.
82 Theater Department of the People's Commissariat of Enlightenment.

property is banned without permission of the Tsentroteatr (for national theaters) or of the Narobraz[83] (for local theaters).

[The decree establishes that theaters are divided into two groups: autonomous and nonautonomous. According to §10 of the decree, the first group consists of] theaters that the Tsentroteatr recognizes as of cultural value, and as to local theaters, it is being left to the discretion of local Soviets, so long as theaters are headed by reliable and stable collectives.

[The second group of theaters (§16) comprises] theaters that were at the disposal of private impresarios or institutions that do not guarantee a high-quality level of culture or, finally, theater groups that were newly created and still do not have a distinct profile.

[The Tsentroteatr is licensed (§19) to transfer those theaters whose acting companies have become strong enough into the autonomous groups.]

As to the autonomous theaters: they are funded by (§9), have to report annually to (§10), and are subject to audit by (§§12, 13) the Tsentroteatr, which also is to provide theaters with the repertorial guidelines without infringing on their artistic integrity (§17). As to the nonautonomous theaters, the decree establishes that (§16–17) they are allowed to use the theater property conditional on electing representatives of the Tsentroteatr of the Department of People's Education (ONO, alias Narobraz) to their governing bodies (§18)–a mandatory practice for all the ordinances of the TsT, both administrative and artistic.

The decree further provides guidelines for the Tsentroteatr's right to set the price of theater tickets, to take charge of ticket distribution, provide subsidies, etc. Finally, §§21–24 assert the TsT's rights to administer state theaters, circuses, and public festivals. Many variety and circus enterprises are deemed to perpetrate "unwholesome elements," and food and drink are to be banned from performance venues.

[Chapter 2 of the decree defines the membership of the Tsentroteatr, stating that the People's Commissar of Enlightenment and its members are in part (7) appointed by the Collegiate of the People's Commissariat of Enlightenment and in part (3) elected by the All-Russian Central Council of Trade Unions (VTsSPS).]

Lunacharsky, in *Puti razvitiya teatra: sbornik* [Paths of theatrical development: Anthology], ed. S. N. Krylov (Moscow: Teakinopechat', 1927), 30.

I personally introduced a resolution in the Council of People's Commissars that a certain sum must be allocated, not just for maintaining the traditional theaters, but for giving substantial aid to the new theaters as well. I was told that the state's central budget was so impoverished that we can take into our boat only the most valuable old theaters from the general current of culture in which the old values are submerged.

83 Department of People's Education (same as ONO).

From Protocol no. 305 of the session of the Lesser Council of People's Commissars on renaming the former Imperial Theaters,[84] August 14, 1919. *STDM 17–21, 26.*

Resolved:

(17) To propose to the People's Commissar of Enlightenment to rename the Maria, Alexandra, and Michael Theaters in Petersburg and to call them by the names of distinguished individuals. (Accepted unanimously with the assent of the speaker.)

V. Ulyanov (Lenin) [...]

Order of the People's Commissar for Enlightenment A. V. Lunacharsky, in charge of government theaters, to I. V. Ékskuzovich,[85] October 14, 1919. *STDM 17–21, 65.*

In the case of firewood shortages I order you under no circumstances to close the state theaters but to reduce the number of productions per week. Until the prices of theater seats are set, I authorize you to set them.

From Protokol no. 363, November 17, 1919. *STDM 17–21, 28.*

Resolved:

1. (a) to propose to the Fuel Commission not to allot the theaters firewood from the government supply.

(b) To propose to the Tsentroteatr in agreement with the Moscow Council of workers and Red Army deputies to reduce the number of theaters functioning in Moscow, taking into consideration the dimensions of the auditorium, the hall's need for fuel, and the general fuel demands of the building.

(c) To offer the Tsentroteatr and the theaters the right to lay in stocks of fuel on their own, under the supervision of the Fuel Commission. [...]

V. Ulyanov (Lenin) [...]

Anatoly Luncharsky, December 1, 1919. *STDM 17–21, 28.*

Given the repeated addresses to me by state and subsidized theaters to set benefits for individual performers, I declare for the present that conditions do not allow for annual or occasional benefits, with the exception of jubilee benefits (for example, the twenty-fifth or fiftieth anniversary of stage activity) for performers whose services are acknowledged by the administration of a given theater or the Profsoyuz of a given

84 In 1920 the Imperial Maria (Maryinsky) Theater became the State Academic Theater of Opera and Ballet; the Imperial Alexandra (Aleksandrinsky) Theater became the Petrograd State Academic Dramatic Theater; and the Grand Duke Michael (Mikhaylovsky) Theater became the filial of the State Academic Theater of Opera and Ballet (after 1926 the Maly Theater of Opera and Ballet).
85 Ivan Vasil'evich Ékskuzovich (1882–1942); first superintendent of state theaters, appointed 1918; director of state academic theaters in Moscow and Leningrad 1924–28.

town, which are completely allowed. In case of disagreement between the artistic collective of a given theater and the Profsoyuz, the question of deciding a benefit will be conclusively decided by the People's Commissar of Enlightenment.

> Lunacharsky to I. V. Ékskuzovich on renaming state theaters and the MAT "academic," December 7, 1919. *STDM 17–21*, 28.

"(3) This number will henceforth include the Maria, Alexandra, Michael theaters in Petrograd, and the Bol'shoy and Maly Theaters will be designated "State Academic Theaters" [Gosadurstvennye akademicheskie teatry or Akis] and the Art Theater "Art Academic." [The *direktorii* are renamed *direktsii*.]

New Theaters with a New Repertoire

Around this time, Vakhtangov acquired such widespread popularity in Moscow as a leader of young people's collectives that "demand" for Vakhtangov grew to absolutely immense proportions and far exceeded any possibilities for independent projects on his part. A group of Jewish amateur actors from Poland and Belorussia decided to go professional under the name Habima ("The Rostrum"); as ardent Zionists, they chose to perform in Hebrew rather than Yiddish. They turned to Stanislavsky, who folded them into the MAT Fourth Studio and asked Vakhtangov to take charge. Two years had passed since he had begun work at them. His diary gives evidence of how this work captivated him: he diligently studied ancient Hebrew, became engrossed in reading the Bible, read Jewish writers, dreamed of staging biblical stories. His project fitted the apocalyptic mood that obsessed many intellectuals.

> Vakhtangov becomes acquainted with the Habima troupe (after October 12, 1917). In *Evgeny Vakhtangov. Dokumenty i svidetel'stva*, ed. V. V. Ivanov (Moscow: Indrik, 2011), 1:385.

1. N. L. Tsemakh.
2. *Gnesin* Menakhim Natanovich—former Hebrew teacher, acted a lot in Palestine and Haifa.
3. *Rozenblyum*, L. A.—engineer, amateur (absent today).
4. *Vardi*—graduated high school in Palestine, made lots of appearances as a reader and raconteur, penchant as a comedian.
5. *Kogan* Sh.[86]—actor on the Yiddish stage, has also acted a few times with "Habima."
6. *Topitser* Yakov—educated as a pharmacist, acted lots of time in Russian and Yiddish amateur productions.
7. *Persits*—student, amateur.

---

86 Actually Shlomo Kon or Koén.

8. *Bregman*—student.
9. *Rovina*—former schoolteacher, acted a few times with us (in Warsaw).
10. *Starobinets, R. M.*—mediocre education, graduated the conservatory, acted in Russian with amateurs.
11. *Élias*—former Hebrew teacher.
12. *Rabinovich* (amateur actress).
13. *Shkol'nikova*—with the highest education, acted lots of times in Russian.
14. Likhtenshteyn.[87]

Vakhtangov, from Notebooks, October 25, 1918. In *Evgeny Vakhtangov,* 273.

A good idea to commission a play like this:

1. Moses (slow of speech). Wife. Aaron. Maybe he saw an Egyptian beating a Jew. Killed him. That night, in his tent, too excited to sleep, he talks about it . . . At night God speaks with him. God orders him to go to Pharaoh and gives him as a sign the ability to perform miracles. (The rod.) Moses, suffering for his people, fired up at the thought of freeing his people, prepares for the morning to go to Pharaoh.
2. Moses before Pharaoh. A speech.
3. At Pharaoh's.
4. In the desert.
5. Moses confronts the people with the tablets.
6. They wander for ages.
7. Diaspora.
8. Night. Far in the distance, beyond the scope of the senses, a fire. During the night is heard a song of hope of thousands of approaching breasts. Here come, here come the people to build their freedom. Curtain.

Vakhtangov, "To all students of the Studio," December 18, 1918. In *Evgeny Vakhtangov,* 283.

If you are no stranger to a feeling of refinement, if art for which you are training rouses within you a nobility of taste, if you want everyone who comes into your house to take

---

87 Rozenblyum, Topitser, Bregman, and Shkol'nikova soon left the troupe. Naum Lazarevich Tsemakh (1887–1939), founder and leader of Habima until 1927; worked with Vakhtangov as pedagogue and director; played Reb Azriel and the second batlan in *The Dybbuk.* Menakhém Natanovich Gnesin (1882–1952), actor with Habima 1917–23 and 1928 to his death; played Sender in *Dybbuk.* David Vardi (1893–1973), actor with Habima 1917–23 and from 1938; played first batlan and Mikhaél in *Dybbuk.* Ruvim (Reuven) L'vovich Persits, actor with Habima 1917–25. Khana Davydovna Rovina (actually Gurevich, 1890–1980), actress with Habima from 1917; played Lea in *Dybbuk* and became the grande dame of the Israeli theater. Rimma Mikhaylovna Starobinets, studied with Vakhtangov at the Habima studio 1917–18. Miriam Élias (1897–?), actress with Habima 1917–24; played Khanan in *Dybbuk.* Tamara Leonovna Rabinovich (later Robins, 1898–1965), actress with Habima from 1917; played Lea in *Dybbuk.* Isaak Likhtenshteyn, student at Moscow University, member of the Socialist Revolutionary Party.

away an impression of purity, cultivation, delicacy, and a flair for beauty—the most indispensable features of a group of artists—you must *immediately* get together and decide what is to be done about *students smoking in the Studio.* [...]

Vakhtangov, "On the new tasks of the theater after the Revolution." Vakhtangov's diary 1919. Translation in *The International Theater* 2 (1934), 17.

The theater department[88] must tactfully and delicately *give* all types (in the artistic sense) of theaters *to understand* that their future life along the paths that they have laid down will be at best only a new page of their *old* life. The revolution has put an end to the growth of the theaters that have existed up to now. It has, so to speak, cut off all new possibilities along the old, although perhaps reliable, tracks. If they do not wish to become "old theaters," museum theaters, they must change their lives, and change sharply. [...]

We must "listen to" the people. We must go into the crowd and lay an artist's ear to the beating of its heart. We must gather creative strength from the people. We must *contemplate* the people with all our artistic being. [...]

Some time must pass before artists can appear from among the people. Perhaps a great deal of time. Homes must be patiently created from which they can make their appearance, so that those who worked in the old art may be the creators of the new. They must understand how badly people have lived until now, and how wonderful is that which is now happening to humanity—that everything old is ended. They must learn to love the new people.

V. Kerzhentsev, *Tvorchesky teatr. Puti sotsialisticheskogo teatra* [Creative theater: The ways to a socialist theater], 3rd ed. (Moscow: Izd. Vserossiyskogo Tsentral'nogo Ispolnitel'nogo Komiteta Sovetov R., S. K. i K. Deputatov, 1919), 60–61. V. Kerzhentsev (actually Platon Mikhaylovich Lebedev, 1881–1940) became a Bolshevik in 1904; twice arrested, he fled abroad, where he studied the latest theatrical trends in Europe and the United States. Returning to Russia 1918, he edited *Izvestia* and campaigned for street theater and national celebrations. For his later career, see chapter 6.

In older theatrical forms it is customary to welcome the rise of the "prologue," whereby such simple means (the reading of an address to the audience) achieve an intimacy between the house and the stage.

A "prologue" can be created by the most various means. In dramatizing a novel its role will be to enact a narrator, always closer to the spectator, more comprehensible and more "his own" than the actor.

For plays of an "exaggerated" style, such as [Gogol's] *Wedlock* or *The Inspector General*, the "prologue" might be a kind of medium between the prompter and the

---

88 The theater department of the People's Commissariat for Education in which Vakhtangov was manager of the stage-directing section.

author. He is dressed in a costume of the 1830s; before the action begins he introduces to the spectators the whole cast with short character sketches (using Gogol's original words); during the action he (sitting like a reader to one side, in a special nook, or in a downstage corner) follows the script and prompts the actors when they stumble. I do not think this conspicuous prompter will weaken the effect in any way. A truly engrossed auditorium will never be deflected from the stage by the presence of "prologue" near the footlights. [...]

The spectator must be prepared for the play not by mechanically sticking dialectics onto the theater but by the ways I have shown, i.e., a preliminary reading, discussions, lectures. On the other hand, the spectators must absolutely be given a short introduction to the play and a character sketch of the author in printed form. The program will include not only the cast list and the actors' names, not only an account of the play in two or three short sentences, but also a short lecture about the play, which might be read aloud, as well as musical notation for some of the tunes, words to the songs, etc.

THE BOL'SHOY DRAMATIC THEATER was founded in 1918 in revolutionary Petrograd as "a theater of tragedy, romantic drama, and high comedy," organized by Maksim Gorky, Anatoly Lunacharsky, Mariya Andreeva, Aleksandr Blok, Nikolay Monakhov, and Yury Yur'ev. The intention was to spawn a heroic art, in tune with the times, with a repertoire grounded in Shakespeare and Schiller. Performances began on February 15, 1919.

> Nikolay Monakhov, report on the first three seasons of the BDT, May 30, 1922. *STDM 17–21*, 241–42. Nikolay Fëdorovich Monakhov (1875–1936), operetta and dramatic actor, served in the troupe of the BDT from 1919 to the end of his life.

On February 15, 1919, despite all sorts of predictions that the effort would end in failure, the Bol'shoy Dramatic Theater opened with Schiller's tragedy *Don Carlos*. The opening was marked by an outstanding success.

How this came about, even now, looking back, I cannot say. There were six or eight of us who created it who did believe in its success, but the rest either had grave doubts or simply no faith in it. But the success of the beginning encouraged all the workers, and there was general fervor for the work to come. Involuntarily, everyone stuck together, knit together, a general language, a generality of tastes appeared, and, most important, the theater suddenly became unusually near and dear to everyone. Everyone showed up at rehearsals and performances: both those involved and those uninvolved. Then there began that general life when the individual "me" disappears and changes into the powerful, robust "we"—the Theater. [...]

And in the first short season, in three months, the theater also staged Shakespeare's *Macbeth* and *Much Ado about Nothing* and *The Destruction of Jerusalem* by Järnefelt.[89]

89 *Titus,* a pacifist drama by the Swedish playwright Arvid Järnefelt (1910).

The season closed on March 15, but after a week's break we began to work on the revolutionary play *Danton*,[90] intended for echelons of the Red Army sent to Red Gorky. As you see, *from its very inception the theater was destined exclusively to serve the masses and only the masses, and the theater joyously proceeded to such enviable work.*

[...] The third season of the Bol'shoy Dramatic Theater opened with *King Lear* by Shakespeare in a production by Lavrent'ev and a magnificent design by Dobuzhinsky.[91] The second production in the roster was *The Merchant of Venice*, directed and designed by A. Benois.

Third came *The Blue Bird* by Maeterlinck, staged by N. V. Petrov.[92] [...]

THE STATE EXEMPLARY THEATER, Moscow, was founded in 1919 by I. N. Pevtsov and V. G. Sakhnovsky[93] to educate the people via the classics.

> Fëdor Stepun, "In search of a heroic theater," *Literaturny sovremennik* [Literary contemporary] (Munich) 1 (1951), 71–76, reprinted in *Byvsheevsya i nesbysheevsya* (New York: Izd. imeni Chekhova, 1956–57), 2:240–43. Fëdor Avgustovich Stepun (actually Friedrich Steppuhn, 1884–1958), philosopher and literary critic, dramaturg of the Exemplary Theater of Revolution 1919–20, was exiled to Lithuania in 1922 and eventually became a prominent figure of "Russian Berlin."

To the possible question from Party echelons as to why we have decided to take such a path, I offer the answer that, considering the proletarian of the future to be a kind of "superman," we could hail its accession to power in no worthier way than with the super-art of the past.

[It opened with *Measure for Measure*, directed by Khudoleev[94] and with scenery by Georgy Yakulov.] The workers and soldiers reacted in an especially lively fashion to the dialogue between the hangman and the clown. Perhaps they sensed that these figures were contemporary.

[The next production was Stepun's version of *Oedipus the King*.]

90 *Danton* (1900) by Romain Rolland was written for a people's theater.
91 Andrey Nikolaevich Lavrent'ev (1882–1932), actor at the MAT 1902–10, then on the Alexandra stage; one of the founders of the BDT. Mstislav Valerianovich Dobuzhinsky (1875–1957), designer, a member of the World of Art, whose elegant, pastel scenery appeared in many theaters, including the MAT, before the Revolution; he worked abroad from 1924, settling in the United States in 1939.
92 *The Blue Bird* (*L'Oiseau bleu*), a fairy-tale play by Maurice Maeterlinck, had been a perennial favorite at the MAT. Nikolay Vasil'evich Petrov (1890–1964), director, who did his earliest work for cabarets and mass spectacles; he directed at the Alexandra 1910–33.
93 Illarion Nikolaevich Pevtsov (1879–1934), actor, expert at playing neurotics, who became a member of the Moscow Dramatic Theater in 1915 and was a luminary of the Pushkin Theater from 1925. Vasily Grigor'evich Sakhnovsky (1866–1945), director, a student of Fëdor Komissarzhevsky, opposed to realism. Posthumously condemned for formalism.
94 Ivan Nikolaevich Khudoleev (1869–1932), a leading man at the Maly Theater 1893–1918, 1921–23, with directing experience.

M. F. Lenin staged Sophocles's tragedy to coincide with the convocation of the first meeting of the Third International in March 1919, which occasion granted us the right to attract to the production all the forces we needed for the staging. Lenin, of course, played Oedipus. [...]

I explained my concept for *Oedipus* to our artistic council: "Nothing is to be archaic. Our task is to show not ancient Greece but contemporary Russia. We are displaying our own tragedy in Sophocles's only because the contemporary Russian drama is not intense and monumental enough to reflect all the intensity of our own times. An impenetrable fate hangs over Russia, as over ancient Thebes. And the wisest of us, those who—like Oedipus—once guessed the riddle of the Sphinx, do not know what to do. Typhus, like the plague, cuts people down, and groans are heard throughout the land. Like the King of Thebes, we do not know wherein our guilt lies, but we feel its burden on our shoulders. Blinded, our faces wet with blood, we go out into the dark night... Oh Lord, what will become of us? That is what must be got across to the audience. [...]

Downstage [Yakulov] constructed an interesting construction of geometrically simplified staircases and platforms and filled the upstage area with an architectural structure that rose steeply upward and represented a stylized variant of the ancient theater. As the curtain rose, along the stairs and bridges upstage, symbolizing the death-dealing progress of the plague, descended to mournful music to the steps of the palace a solemnly mournful train of citizens. Glière[95] wrote the music. Like the scenery, it represented a free, modern transcription of ancient motifs. [...]

Researching [an appropriate form of speech], I came up with the possibility of performing ancient tragedy by the metrical scheme of the Orthodox liturgy. Of course, this does not mean the mere transference of this scheme from the church to stage but rather its free transposition, different for the protagonists and the chorus. We wanted above all to abandon the arbitrariness of psychological individualism, alien to the religious essence of tragedy, and to achieve a reading free of any affects, sincere, profound, and simple [...]

Stepun, *Byvsheesya i nesbysheesya*, 2:248–49.

My attempts to sneak up on proletarian culture from behind and create under the Commissariat of People's Enlightenment, not a theater of Marxist agitation, but "a theater of tragic enactment" could not, of course, be crowned with success. Aware of this, I was not very surprised when shortly after the production of *Oedipus*, in his capacity as semiofficial representative of the Commissariat, Vsevolod Émil'evich Meyerhold appeared, and, having assembled the company, took it on himself, straight from the shoulder, to excoriate our "reactionary ideology and eclectic–decadent repertoire."

The speech of this talented director, who burned all his life to be thought the last word in the era, was the most typical figure of revolutionary futurism, which at the time led the offensive along the whole "October" cultural front. Before us he paraded, if

---

95 Reyngol'd Moritsevich Glière [Gliér] (1874–1956), composer of what would become the prototypical Soviet ballet, *The Red Poppy*.

not all the concepts, then the whole vocabulary of Marxist ideology refracted through cubism. The programmatic speech for the prosecution was uttered with great, but purely histrionic, flair.

As a result of Meyerhold's appearance, the theater underwent a radical transformation. There was no room for me in the new theater. So, not yet having flowered, my theatrical career was cut short.

FËDOR FËDOROVICH KOMISSARZHEVSKY (1882–1954), director, was the brother of the great actress Vera Komissarzhevskaya. In 1914 he founded his own theater in Moscow with an eclectic repertoire in a "synthetic" style. He had hoped the revolutionary government would take an active part in reorganizing the theater but was discouraged by the remnants of the ancien régime and the expansion of an interfering bureaucracy. He emigrated in 1919 and, as Theodore Komisarjevsky, popularized Chekhov in England.

> Fëdor Komissarzhevsky to A. V. Lunacharsky, June 1919. *Mnemozina* 4 (2009), 340–42.

Anatoly Vasil'evich,

I write to you because I see that almost tragic situation in which the Russian theater in general is about to find itself, despite the fact that our government seems altogether to sympathize with its development and its embarking on new paths.

I begin with the fact that the struggle currently going on in the "sections" of the theatrical mechanism, if it has still not quite destroyed the Russian theater, threatens to destroy it soon enough. You understand what I'm talking about. The provincial theater is doomed to control by all sorts of ridiculous ignoramuses, who play the role of Shchedrin's Pompadours,[96] who manage the business worse than the old self-seeking entrepreneurs. And the Moscow theaters—some to the hum of the struggle of the theatrical powers—live happily in their hackwork [*khaltura*], reliving long hackneyed old stuff or resuscitated vulgar soldier shows; others—the few—play everything that comes their way, in the good old-fashioned way, decently, even well, thanks to a respectable or good (in the old terminology) troupe, but they have no profile in consequence of the absence of leading ideas and artistic leadership; still others try to make art, working almost 24 hours a day, because, to make art nowadays, you have to waste a good deal of time and energy, and you need much more faith in this art and love of it; but in this work they are prevented, prevented all the more since the more original this art, the less it suits various size requirements, tariffs, all sorts of unions, committees, exec-coms; hindered by all sorts of comptrollers who understand nothing about art, every possible discussion about "proletarian" and nonproletarian art by persons who themselves, I am totally convinced, do not

---

96 *He-Pompadours and She-Pompadours* (*Pompaduri i Pompadurshi*, 1863–74), "a Satire on the Art of Government" by N. Shchedrin (actually Mikhail Evgrafovich Saltykov, 1826–89). Pompadours are provincial bigwigs and functionaries; the name puns on *dur,* "fool."

fully understand what is "proletarian" or "bourgeois" art and a work of art in general.

At this time in the provinces they are paying actors a lot (eight thousand r. a month and more), while in the capital, they're cutting salaries until the unions establish new rates of pay, force actors to do hackwork [*khalturit'*] without a living wage, of course, and this is driving the stage to ugliness and forcing them to flee Moscow.

The *apparat*, which should have been regulating theatrical life on behalf of the government and concerning itself with the theater, is not only badly organized but is a total mess.

And under these conditions they still talk about the nationalization of the theaters or the centralization of the management of theaters in this disorganized *apparat*.

Having worked two seasons running, I have experienced all this myself. Working like an ox, I created right after the March Revolution two theaters with my own hands, and I know how I fought for every inch of this road I traveled. This struggle cost me a good deal of spiritual suffering and the momentary desire to give up the theater entirely, and I won't even mention the physical effects on me.

[...] But these achievements of mine did not protect me from the pleasure of being expelled by the collective troupe of the theater I created (the Soviet Opera)[97] and did not protect my other theater from remaining without a building, for the building promised us (Nezlobin's theater) remains Nezlobin's, because the collective stirred up all sorts of unions and committees, because it knows how to give a shove when and where necessary, take refuge in the work I once did with them, and which they also threw out, as the collective of the MSRD theater threw me out. [...]

The pitiful remnants of the Zimin troupe,[98] which even in its full team was made up almost entirely of the merchant's lackeys, rises under the protection of TEO of the People's Commissariat of Enlightenment (enlightenment!). The theater "named after" my sister,[99] which is infinitely dear to me—after I left it, convinced of its complete inability to work artistically with that team of actors and directors who are there at present, after this collective started to give a hideous turn to the idea dear to me, invested in that theater, after this theater went down quite a false path, which had nothing in common with my sister's name—now rises under the protection of Narkompros. Meanwhile, all my requests and even demands to have my sister's name removed from that theater, to which I *have* the right, remain of no avail. Because once (once!) Meyerhold got involved in this, wrote something in defense of the necessity of the name "Komissarzhevskaya"! The same Meyerhold, from whom Vera Fëdorovna parted on account of the decided schism in their views on art, Meyerhold, who never appreciated or understood Komissarzhevskaya herself or her ideals. Why in such a case not ask the King of Siam or the first comer about it? [...]

97 In the premises of Zimin's Opera, Komissarzhevsky opened the Workers' Soviet Opera on November 7, 1918, with a revision of Beethoven's *Fidelio*, retitled *Liberation*, the action transferred to revolutionary France.

98 Zimin's troupe, a private opera company founded in 1904 by Sergey Ivanovich Zimin (1875–1942); it employed some of the best singers and designers in Russia.

99 Komissarzhevskaya Theater, founded in Moscow in 1914 by Fëdor Komissarzhevsky and Vasily Sakhnovsky, as a chamber theater. It was closed in 1919 but reopened in 1924–25.

ONE of the first experimental theaters in Petrograd was located in the Hermitage Theater at Hall of Arms of the Winter Palace with an audience of Red Army men and workers. It opened on July 12, 1919, with Molière's *Doctor in Spite of Himself,* followed by Tolstoy's *First Distiller* (*Pervy vinkokur*), directed by Yury Annenkov. It was the first example of what was to become known as circusization.

> Viktor Shklovsky, "Dopolnenny Tolstoy" [Tolstoy embellished], *Zhizn' iskusst-va* (1919). Quoted in Yury Annenkov, *Dnevnik moikh vstrech* (Moscow: Zakha-rov, 2001), 298–99. Viktor Borisovich Shklovsky (1893–1984), literary critic, ideologue of the futurist movement, was in the 1920s collaborator with the leftist literary fronts LEF and Novy LEF. He moved to Finland in 1922 but returned to Russia in autumn 1923.

The First Distiller by Lev Tolstoy, embellished by Yu. Annenkov—I write without any irony or admiration, but simply to state a fact—has something clear and revealing in its composition.

Annenkov approached Tolstoy's text like this. He treated it as a scenario and developed it, inserting accordion players, urban jingles (*chastushki*), an eccentric clown, acrobats, and so forth. The motives for these insertions were as follows: the urban jingles were inserted as songs of the peasants, as they grew tipsy on the devil's swill. The accordion players and the round dance were also inserted in the drunk scene, the acrobats were presented as devils, i.e., the circus was brought into the play as a depiction of hell. And finally, the eccentric clown, in a red wig and "uniform" pants, was brought in for no reason at all. He merely—this red-nosed buffoon—happened to be there, and he wandered around hell as if he were a café singer.

[...] Every reproduction of a work of art is its re-creation—a rearrangement that, after closely examining the copies, is made from one and the same work of art over the space of, say, twenty years. Annenkov's rearrangement is good by the very fact that it does fancy itself a copy.

> Yury Annenkov, "The merry sanitarium," *Zhizn' Iskusstva* (1919), in *Dnevnik,* 301.

A sensation! A resplendent gala performance! A boneless man! Musical eccentrics! Flights through the air! Trained elephants! Stunts galore! The red clown Bim-Bimi! Homeric laughter! A resplendent monster performance! *Grande et brillante représentation!*

It is for you, inveterate, infirm city dwellers. Haste to the circus—it is an ersatz sanitarium for you. With an ironic smile you walk past the brightly colored circus posters, because from childhood you were taught to attend "serious" theaters. The profoundest delusion! Hurry to the circus: the circus is the best sanitarium for inveterate and chronic skeptics [...]

The circus is not art, you insist. The profoundest delusion. The art of the circus is one of the subtlest and most magnificent art forms...

The art of the dramatic actor is the most approximative of all the arts. It is the least absolute of them all. The actor can change the shape of the performance every day, sometimes raising, sometimes lowering the degree of perfection in playing his role, and, nevertheless, the show will go on to its end. Semi-colon; ellipsis... You leave the theater with the oppressive feeling of having looked into the mirror.

The circus is something else again. The circus performer's art is complete, for it is absolute. The slightest mistake in a gymnast's calculations, a second of confusion—and he loses his balance, falls off the trapeze, the act miscarries, there is no art. Nothing approximative, nothing untested. The precision and delicacy of the performance is no longer a quality but a requisite condition, a law.

The art of the dramatic actor is inspired dilettantism. The art of the circus performer is always complete mastery [...]

No semicolon; no ellipsis. A whole palisade of exclamation marks!!!!!!

[...] Two years ago V. É. Meyerhold, in an article on the circus, asserted that a circus show awakes in the spectators a heroic element. Could an aviator first decide to loop the loop, returning to the airfield after a performance of Chekhov's *Three Sisters*? No, but once he had seen the bewildering tricks of gymnasts, without a second thought he would turn the controls of his Blériot, to hang upside down three thousand meters above the earth. [...]

IN WINTER 1919–20 Yury Annenkov delivered a lecture, "Theater to the Very End," at Courses in Mastery of Scenic Design for future directors and designers. One of its main points was that the hardest thing for masters of the stage is to divine the appropriate rhythm for a performance, the correlation of various rhythms of the performance. It is this rhythmically organized movement that creates the theatrical form. "We need graphic rhythms of movement" (*Dom Iskusstv* [The House of Arts] 2 [1921]). He expanded this point in another article.

Yury Annenkov, "Rhythmic scenery," *Zhizn' iskusstva* (November 18, 1919), quoted in E. I. Strutinskaya, "'Teatr chistogo metod' Yu. P. Annenkova" [Annenkov's theater of pure method] in *Russkaya avangard 1910-x-1920x godov i teatr* [Russian avant-garde of the 1910s to 1920s and the theater], ed. G. F. Kovalenko (St. Petersburg: Dmitry Bulanin, 2000), 347.

Theatrical movement is expressed by the movement of thoughts, the movement of feelings, the movement of speeches, the movement of the actor onstage, the movement of sounds in the orchestra.

Therefore the element of stasis is in disharmony with the essence of theater.

Movement is determined by rhythm. Rhythm determines the character of movement, its psychological significance. [...]

Let us suppose that the hero despairs on learning of the death of his beloved. The set designer draws nervous zigzags of jagged lightning on disturbing patches of black, which underlines the cogency of rhythm, intensifying the sensation of spiritual gloom and mournful feelings. At that point a jolly fellow comes onstage; the rhythm of his feelings, his movement, is contrary to the rhythm of the hero succumbing to despair. The scene designer introduces the rhythm of the rollicker against backgrounds of leaping, dancing—iridescent, red, yellow, gold patches, circles, spirals. With the entrance of a girl tenderly in love there will be gently poured into the scenery rhythms of elegy, subtle streams of light blue filaments. A moving pattern of colored rhythms, fighting among themselves and resolving into a general harmony or one triumphing over another, according to the progress of the play. The more characters there are, the more variegated the nature of their feelings, the more complicated the task of the theatrical scene designer will become.

A NEOLOGISM, *khaltura*, entered the language. A malformation of *kultura*, "culture," it was the sarcastic response of artists to the call to pitch their creativity to the level of the proletarian audience. (A rough translation might be "cultcha.") With stage companies breaking up, many actors took to or were assigned freelance work. The verb *khalturit'* combined the idea of moonlighting with that of doing hackwork.

Lunacharsky, "Theater and revolution," *Vestnik teatra* 47 (December 23–28, 1919), in *Sobranie sochinenii v vos'mi tomakh* [Collected works in 8 volumes] (Moscow: Khudozhestvannaya literatura, 1964), 3:93.

Khaltura is a dual phenomenon. On one hand, it is the actor, impoverished in the wake of Revolution, trying to obtain much-desired sustenance—by the provisional retail sale of his art in a most unseemly guise, that falls outside the bounds of art—and on the other hand, it is the colossal thirst of the masses: Red army soldiers, workers, even peasants—to see a play, to rise to the level of some sort of amusement, for which they are ready to devote grain, sugar, etc., the stuff of their livelihoods from their ever more depleted stores. It is not the people's fault that instead of a fish, they are given a snake, and instead of bread, a stone. At any rate, they are hungering and thirsting for art. [...]

Nelidov, *Teatral'naya Moskva*, 334–35.

Externally theaters changed considerably. The decorum of the former imperial playhouses vanished. They became filthy, untidy, cold. The ushers retained their livery, but without eagles on the galloons, they let their beards and mustaches grow instead of side whiskers and began to look like the devil knows what. Evening dress on the musicians in the orchestra disappeared. All coats of arms disappeared. In the imperial, ministerial, and other boxes, they seated comrades. And not the best ones—either outwardly or inwardly. The productions gradually "wore out." Frequent raids and subsequent arrests scared off many people. You go to hear Chaliapin or see the ballet, and as you walk in: "Your papers!" And without the slightest provocation, if you please. You're lucky if you get off with a two-or three-week detention. I saw no happy faces at the theater. Fear reigned supreme.

[...] In 1919 I go to the dress rehearsal of *Madame Angot*[100] at the Art Theater. Onstage one of the characters says, "Excuse me, she forgot that in a time of revolution one cannot speak the truth." The audience was about to chuckle, but in a second, all mouths shut tight and people looked around fearfully. Would they be denounced?

Discipline, the original inner discipline, weakened. Need forced every single actor to have recourse to so-called hamming and such-like to "cobble together" a performance or concert for flour, sugar, etc., "to run it up" two or three times in an evening.

[...] I once even encountered a hearse (without a canopy) with actors sitting on it like birds on a perch. "Where are you off to?" "To moonlight [*khalturit'*]."—"Well, God bless."

ONE of the longest lived of these new theaters was a Yiddish-speaking studio that grew out of the amateur Jewish Folk Music Society, created in December 1916. Yiddish theater had been banned under the tsars and Jews deprived of most civil rights. The Society intended to coordinate theatrical ventures involving Jewish casts and crews. It began to move into the professional sphere in Petrograd in 1919, under the leadership of Aleksey Mikhaylovich Granovsky (Avrakham Azar or Azarkh, 1890–1937). Moscow born and raised in Riga, he had studied theater in St. Petersburg, Berlin (with Max Reinhardt), and Stockholm, and directed at the neoclassical Theater of Tragedy in Petrograd before founding the Yiddish studio theater. Many regarded him as too "Westernized" to run a Jewish company.

Aleksey Granovsky, protest at meeting of February 5, 1917, after a series of public readings of Yiddish drama was approved. Quoted and translated in Jeffrey Veidlinger, *The Moscow State Yiddish Theater: Jewish Culture on the Soviet Stage* (Bloomington: Indiana University Press, 2000), 22. © 2000 by Jeffrey Veidlinger. Reprinted with permission of Indiana University Press.

We...must have new people who will dedicate themselves fully to the new theater, for professionals will destroy it...It is first necessary to open a theater school. Jewish theater has to be created from the beginning; it has nothing—we possess neither a voice nor a body. Having set about work, we absolutely must refuse creative pursuits. In the meantime academic work is needed, and actors, who are at least literate in respect to the stage, are needed.

---

100 *La fille de Madame Angot,* an operetta by Charles Lecocq, was the first production of Nemirovich-Danchenko's Musical Studio.

> The Commissariat of Jewish Affairs, in conjunction with the Theatrical De-
> partment of the Commissariat of Nationality Affairs, began work on founding
> a Yiddish-language theater in Moscow, writing to the Theatrical Department
> of the Commissariat of Enlightenment in October 1918 (correspondence
> between Collegium of National Minorities and Theatrical Section of the
> Commissariat of Enlightenment, October 1918–May 1919), ll. 3–4; quoted and
> translated (with revisions) from Veidlinger, *Moscow State Yiddish Theater*, 23.

In the matter of building a new theater for the Jewish proletariat, we are entering a
new beginning. Jewish theater is simply fairground booth entertainment (*balagan*) in
which the pride of place is occupied by operettas, melodrama, and lame boulevard
shows with national–chauvinist content . . . In all cities in which there are Jewish
workers, social democrats are erecting dramatic circles in which there could be good
strong dramatic work.

THE ACME of revolutionary symbolism in the Proletarian Culture Movement was
P. Kozlov's Wagnerian *Legenda o kommunare* [*The Legend of the Communard*],
staged by Aleksandr Avel'evich Mgebrov (1884–1906) in 1919. The critics found it
"petty bourgeois," and Mgebrov, a professional actor of white-collar antecedents
(he had worked at the MAT from 1906 to 1908) was forced out of the movement.
The play makes a fetish of the collective but is couched in the style of prerevolutionary god seeking.

> Aleksandr Mgebrov, *Zhizn' v teatre* [A life in the theater] (Moscow: Academia,
> 1932), 2:488.

The first scene shows the completely fantastic birth of the Communard. This takes place
somewhere on a mountain overgrown with some sort of invisible forest which is not
unlike the columns of a cathedral, an aquatic plant, or an octopus. On the mountain
and in the woods. [. . .] there is (of course) a cave, and in the cave is a sage. An ancient
volume lies before him. Next to the sage, leaning on a sword, is Thought. Below is an
anvil upon which the Son of the Sun and the Son of the Earth are working on a piece
of steel from which they are forging the Communard's heart. Dark forces move and
hiss maliciously behind fantastic bushes. They keep appearing and disappearing, so
that one can imagine the fantastic world from which the author extracts his idea of
Communism. The Sage, Thought, the Son of Earth, the Son of the Sun, and, finally,
Happiness give birth to this idea. They bear it through hammer blows on the same
anvil to which the ancient volume bears witness. The dark forces tremble, but the Son
of the Sun and the Son of the Earth keep forging. Happiness throws flowers on the
anvil, and Thought awaits the sunrise.

MARIYA ANDREEVA was been a leading actress at the Moscow Art Theater from
its founding until 1906, in such roles as Portia and Hedda Gabler. She left it because

her lover Gorky became convinced it was reactionary in its political outlook. A confirmed Bolshevik, she returned to Russia in 1913 and served as commissar of theaters and spectacles in Petrograd from 1919 to 1921.

Mariya Andreeva, "Revolution and theater," November 4, 1919, in *M. F. Andreeva. Perepiska. Vospominaniya. Stat'i. Dokumenty. Vospominaniya o M. F. Andreevoy* [Correspondence. Remembrances. Articles. Documents. Remembrances of M. F. Andreeva] (Moscow: Iskusstvo, 1961), 267–69.

The most responsible and important thing in the theater is the repertoire, and it is the most difficult task facing the leaders of theatrical matters.

You cannot invent a language, you cannot artificially create it by a wave of the magic wand, off the top of your head—the people create it, it is constructed by strict, undeviating laws, and its obvious creator—the poet, the wordsmith—appears only at the topmost point of the pyramid that concentrates the whole complex of experience of the innumerable grains of sand that constitute its body, he is the only focus, concentrating all the rays of light. [...]

Our old state academic theaters attempt with might and main to change their previous aspects. The more accessible they become to the wide masses, the more eloquently the figures speak: in summer 1918–19, the state theaters gave 126 school performances, 75 performances for trade unions, and 33 for the Red Army. In the summer season, performing in the communal summer theaters and parks, the troupes of the Maria theater—opera and ballet—offered sixty-seven performances, the Alexandra theater eighty and seventeen performances for the Red Army. The Maria put on sixteen performances for the Red Army in the summer season.

The new communal theaters, re-created or reorganized from the old municipal theaters, People's Houses, the former Society for the Advancement of the People's Sobriety in summer 1918–19 offered these performances at popular prices: for schools 75, for trade unions 35, for the Red Army 100 and for the instruction of the Petrograd Soviet of Workers' and Red Army Deputies 108 performances.

For the summer season, 416 performances were given in all with 59 for the Red Army, so that the general attendance for the summer season comes to 712,672 persons in a brief two months.

At the front the communal and state theaters put on 153 performances, performed plays from the classic repertoire, wherever possible, as in Pskov, Novgorod, Cronstadt, Schlüsselburg, and less complicated things, such as *The Wreck of the "Hope,"*[101] *The Green Cockatoo, The Birth of the Marseillaise*; gave concerts and abridged operatic performances. [...]

---

101 Herman Heijerman's *Op Hoop van Zegen* (1900), a Dutch play about the scuttling of a ship for its insurance and the effect of this on a small fishing community. It was the initial production of the MAT First Studio in 1913. Arthur Schnitzler's one-act "grotesque," *Der grüne Kakadu*, takes place on the eve of the French Revolution.

The Civil War, 1919–1921

THE ARMISTICE with the Germans had humiliating results: without an army, the Bolsheviks could not prevent the Central powers from penetrating Russia. Their acceptance of the treaty of Brest-Litovsk, which stripped Russia of all the territory gained since the time of Peter the Great, was met with general indignation. The Ukraine and the Baltic countries, subjugated by Germany, pursued their own separation from the former Empire. In September 1918 a Directorate, made up of diverse factions, formed at Ufa to coordinate the struggle against the Bolsheviks. Resistance increased from the East and the South. With the end of the war, however, the White forces lost almost all their European backing and fought on in disarray.

The year 1919 was decisive, as the Whites launched four offensives. This concerted attack confirmed the Reds in their tyrannical methods, tightening controls and instituting ruthless terrorism. Atrocities became the norm on both sides. The White advance also impelled the Bolsheviks to look for enemies within. Many of the intelligentsia hastened to leave the country—for Riga, Berlin, Paris, Harbin, or New York. Those who remained were not fully trusted, and mass arrests were made of intellectuals and cultural figures, particularly those who had once belonged to the liberal political parties. Among those detained were the Moscow Art Theater's leading figures. Protests were lodged by such influential individuals as Gorky, but to little avail. The hard line of the Cheka, the security arm, often prevailed over the more tolerant policies of Lunacharsky's Commissariat of Enlightenment.

The calls from the Left to launch the arts from point zero grew more strident. Meyerhold demanded that all preexisting professional theaters be abolished and replaced by proletarian, provincial, amateur and Red Army theaters. From the creation of TEO, the great traditional theaters had been constituted as a group apart. In 1920, the academic theaters, that is, the former Imperial Theaters as well as the Art Theater and the Kamerny Theater in Moscow, came under the direct administration of the Narkompros, which kept them carefully shielded from radical innovators. Meyerhold and Tairov staked out adversarial positions, which is all the more paradoxical when one notices that they shared many attitudes: they both believed in a "theatrical theater," in the vitality of the popular arts and the commedia dell'arte as inspiration for actors, in the need for the actor to be versatile, and in the musical underpinnings of theater. They both rejected naturalism. Perhaps it was this very similarity that bred their mutual animosity.

By 1921, military operations had ended, and what remained of Russia was under the authority of the Communist government. With the pressure lightened, the centralized government, a leftover from wartime, was retained and reinforced. It was ruling over a destroyed country, racked economically by inflation and deficits. Five-sixths of industry was gone, transport for anything but military purposes had broken down, and the suppression of private trade initiatives led to an active black market. The peasants, having smoked out the rural gentry, ran their own communities, although the state made a claim to a certain percentage of the produce. The result was that farmers produced only enough for their own needs, and a devastating famine emptied the cities, partly by flight, partly by starvation. The horrors were exacerbated by a prolonged drought and a malaria epidemic.

Outside the Centers

Pëtr Kogan, "The intelligentsia in the theater in the country," *Vestnik teatra* (*Theater Herald*) (March 23, 1919), 14. Pëtr Semënovich Kogan (1872–1932), expert on Western European theater, gave public lectures for TEO Narkompros and taught at Moscow University; he also penned articles on dramatists for the Brockhaus-Ephron encyclopedia.

"In organizing the Club, thanks must be expressed to the local agronomist N. A. Subbotin, who not only in words but in deeds spared no forces to open the functions of the Club and attract to it as many vital forces and material means as possible."

This passage is from a letter from the country. We present it unaltered. It is infused with a feeling of gratitude to the intelligentsia, by whose energies the village of Panino, Pavlov district, Nizhegorod gubernia, was enriched by a cultural institution. For the first time the settlement saw onstage things by Chekhov and other authors. The local schoolteacher, postmaster, surveyor, and others acted "in the presence of an enormous confluence of people," as the correspondent reports. A people's house is opened, the opening of a reading room and a teahouse is proposed. In short, the local intelligentsia is absorbed in a new, until recently forbidden activity, the enlightenment of the common people, and the rural settlement is drawn into the circle of wholesome spiritual interests. Whining Chekhovian cultural loners, who find themselves out of work, make way for vital, active builders of a new life in various corners of Russia.

Unfortunately, this picture of friendly, comradely work of the intelligentsia in a rural settlement is far from typical of our whole young republic. [...] What are the reasons for this hostility to the local intelligentsia? [...] "When a show was first put on in our village," reports a correspondent from the hamlet of Foshny, Maloarkhangel' district, "they played a play from the life of the workers." And the author notes with joy that the spectators "were not in tailcoats and hats, but in rustic sheepskin coats and plain kerchiefs," that the play depicted "the oppression, when factory owners and mill owners got rich on the labor, sweat, and blood of the workers and held banquets." [...]

THE CONSTANT churning up of society by revolution, civil war, and famine was hardest on children. The number of orphans and abandoned youths on the streets swelled so greatly that they were classified as a distinct caste—*bezprizorniki,* the homeless or those without shelter. One of the earliest Soviet children's theaters was created to accommodate them.

Asja Lācis, "Orël 1918/19. Proletarian Children's Theater," in *Revolutionaer im Beruf* [Revolutionary by trade], ed. Hildegard Brenner (Munich, Germany: Rogner und Bernhard, 1971), 24–34. Asja Lācis (Russian name Anna Ernestovna Latsis, 1891–1979), Latvian director and actress, studied in Moscow before the Revolution, then worked in Germany in the 1920s, serving as assistant to Brecht and Piscator. She ran an agitprop theater in Riga 1925–26. She was the life partner of Bernhard Reich and an intimate of Walter Benjamin.

In 1918 I came to Orël. I was supposed to work as a stage director in the Orël Municipal Theater, in other words smooth sailing. But things worked out otherwise. [Having observed the *bezprizorniki* on the streets and the abandoned children in the orphanages, she decided to organize a children's theater in the large mansion in which she was domiciled, a plan approved by Ivan Yur'enev,[1] the local director of education.] We planned on fifteen children, hundreds showed up.

I was convinced that children could be stimulated and cultivated through acting. It would have been simple to find a suitable children's play, cast it, rehearse the children, and prepare a production. That certainly would have kept the children busy for a while but would hardly have advanced their development. [...] I wanted to bring the children to the point that their eyes would see better, their ears hear more acutely, their hands create necessities out of unformed material. To that end, I broke up the work into sections. To develop their sense of sight, the children painted and sketched. This section was led by Viktor Shestakov,[2] who later became one of Meyerhold's stage designers. A pianist took charge of musical education. Then there was technical training: the children built props, structures, animals, figures, etc. Other sections of my model school in Orël were rhythm and gymnastics, diction and improvisation. Hidden powers, liberated by the work process, abilities to be cultivated, we united through *Improvisation.* The play would arise out of it. Children would act for children. [...]

With the children who came to Turgenev House from the state institutions, there were no difficulties. But for a long time I could get nowhere with the *bezprizorniki.* When I appealed to them in the marketplace for the first time and invited them to visit us, they derided me, threatened me with sticks, and consigned me to a place for

1 Ivan Mikhaylovich Yurenev, president of the All-Russian Bureau of Military Commissars and member of the Revolutionary Military Soviet of the Republics.
2 Viktor Alekseevich Shestakov (1898–1957), designer of a number of Meyerhold's productions at GosTIM and the Theater of Revolution 1922–27, with a fondness for platforms and stairs; from 1946, chief designer of the Moscow Komsomol Theater.

which there may be no word in German. But I came back. They got used to me and our dispute, so that when I had stuck it out for a long time and kept coming back, they would gather around, greeting me with a yell as an old acquaintance. [...]

I had chosen a children's play by Meyerhold, *Alinur* (from Oscar Wilde's fairy tale "The Star Prince").[3] The children knew nothing of my plan. I gave them a scene from it as a base for improvisation: robbers are sitting in the woods around a fire and boasting of their deeds. In the middle of one such scene, a bit later, the first visit of the *bezprizorniki* to our house took place. The children jumped up and wanted to run from the intruders. They looked alarming: paper helmets on their heads, armed with tree branches and pieces of tin, in their hands pikes and sticks. I persuaded the children to go on improvising and pay no attention to the intruders. After a while, Van'ka, their leader, walked into the circle of players, tipped his group a wink—they pulled the children aside and began to play the scene themselves. They bragged about murders, arsons, robberies, seeking to outdo one another in atrocities. Then they stood up and shouted with scornful disdain at our children: "That's what robbers are like!" Consequently I had all I could do to apply full pedagogic discipline and interrupt their wild and shameless talk—for I wanted to gain influence over them. I won the game in fact—the *bezprizorniki* came back and later became an active force in our children's theater. [...]

To AVOID the disturbances and food shortages in the capitals, many actors began touring. This was a risky enterprise, since the fortunes of war might change the occupiers of a city overnight. Like Brecht's Mother Courage, the actors might have to switch flags and allegiances on the spot.

Vadim Sherubovich, "Organization of the summer departure," in *O starom Khudozhestvennom teatre* [About the Old Art Theater] (Moscow: Iskusstvo, 1990), 178–83. Vadim Vasil'evich Shverubovich (1901–81), son of Vasily Kachalov,[4] was a member of the group of MAT actors stuck in southern Russia and Czechoslovakia 1919–22; he later accompanied the MAT to the United States 1922–24. A prisoner of war of the Germans during World War II, he joined the Italian resistance and was later imprisoned in a Soviet camp. Eventually he became dean of the MAT Studio School 1958–81 and a founder of the Sovremennik Theater.

In March 1919 an idea was born: the whole [Moscow Art] theater, with their families, would move to some peaceful and well-provisioned places—Siberia, the Ukraine (Little Russia as it was then called), the Caucasus. In the diary that I kept in those years (chiefly

---

3   *Alinur-tatarchonok* (*Alinur the Tatar Lad*) by Meyerhold and Yury M. Bondi, an adaptation of Oscar Wilde's story "The Star Child," was one of the plays recommended on September 18, 1918, by the TEO Narkompros for production by children's theaters.

4   Vasily Ivanovich Kachalov (actually Shverubovich, 1875–1948), elegant, velvet-voiced leading man of the MAT 1900–1948; when he and a group of colleagues were cut off from Moscow during the Civil War, he formed the Kachalov Group, which toured Europe to 1923.

about high school activities), I wrote on March 26, "Vasya (as I called my father) came and informed me: the theater has decided to leave Moscow, with all conveniences: a private train, provisions; they'll set up a cooperative society." This project was discussed at length both in our family and with our friends. On the whole it didn't meet with sympathy. Éfros, Dzhivilegov, Kayransky[5] didn't agree. Kayransky said, "You can't run away from the Revolution." To tell the truth, shortly thereafter, he wound up in Odessa, where the Revolution had chased him, and he hid from it in a madhouse.

[. . .] Konstantin Sergeevich [Stanislavsky] was definitely and categorically against it; so was Mariya Petrovna [Lilina]. Vladimir Ivanovich [Nemirovich-Danchenko] (as I have said) would be attracted to this idea, and then he would cool toward it. But there were individuals who, once they understood that they would not succeed in organizing the whole theater for this trip, that it was difficult, cumbersome, unwieldy, decided to organize a smaller excursion. They were I. N. Bersenev, N. A. Podgorny, and N. O. Massalitinov.[6] They were energetically aided by a former official of the Court Ministry, who had served in Petrograd in the administration of the Imperial Theater and who had just recently been taken into the Art Theater, S. L. Bertenson.

[. . .]

L. D. Leonidov[7] rented the municipal theater in Khar'kov, and the group began to prepare for the journey. [. . .] The group was organized as a fellowship based on stamps, that is, each member received as his salary a percentage of the total profits indicated by the stamps allotted to him. So, Kachalov received five stamps, Knipper[8] four, Bersenev three as actors and one as members of the governing board. [. . .]

THE CONTINGENT of MAT actors, including Kachalov and Ol'ga Knipper-Chekhova, took its repertoire of Chekhov plays to the Ukrainian university town

5   Abram Markovich Éfros (1888–1954), critic and translator; before the Revolution published widely in theater periodicals; then ran the design section of the MAT and its Musical Theater 1920–26. Aleksey Karpovich Dzhivilegov (1875–1952), theater historian and art critic; evacuated during World War II, he taught at the Perm Theater Studio. Kayransky, actually Aleksandr Arnol'dovich Koyransky (1884–1968), writer and designer, who emigrated to Paris and then to New York, where he helped Stanislavsky write the first version of My Life in Art; on the faculty of the American Laboratory Theater.

6   Ivan Nikolaevich Bersenev (actually Pavlishchev, 1889–1951), a dynamic character actor at the MAT from 1911, organized tours of actors during the famine of 1918–19. Later director at the MAT 2, Moscow Trade Unions Theater 1936–38, Lenin Komsomol Theater from 1938. Nikolay Afanas'evich Podgorny (1879–1947), actor at the MAT 1903–47, a founder of the Second Studio in 1913; he later controlled the company's finances and made sure it toed the Stalinist line. Nikolay Osipovich Massalitinov (1880–1979), actor at the MAT 1907–22, settled in Sofia, Bulgaria, in 1925, where he became a leading actor and director of the People's Theater.

7   Leonid Davydovich Leonidov (actually Berman, 1885–1983), impresario, managed the MAT's Russia tours in 1917; stayed abroad when the Kachalov group was stranded abroad; later managed the MAT tours to Europe and the United States 1922–24, brought jazz to Berlin, and settled in Paris.

8   Ol'ga Leonardovna Knipper-Chekhova (1868–1959), actress, charter member of the MAT, who created many of the heroines of her husband, Anton Chekhov.

of Khar'kov, then under Bolshevik sway. One night in June 1918, some of them, including the star actress, went to a party thrown by a cooperative at the Menshevik Club. There was a ban on alcohol and a curfew in the city at the time.

N. O. Massalitinov, "My remembrances," in N. M. Vaganova, *Russkaya teatral'naya émigratsiya v tsentral'noy Evrope i na Balkanakh* [Russian theatrical emigration in Central Europe and the Balkans] (St. Petersburg: Aleteyya, 2007), 219–20.

Suddenly—about two in the morning—there was a knock at the door! I noticed that our hospitable hosts blanched and suddenly began to throw all the prohibited drinks off the balcony into the garden. The knocking continued and became ever more urgent—the door finally opened. A squad of Chekists[9] entered with an official in charge—a Lett. In broken Russian he exclaimed, "Ah, here's the booze-fest!" Later, noticing Ol'ga Leonardovna and the administrator's wife, he added, "And a couple a wh—s as well!" He explained that everyone present was under arrest and demanded that we follow him. In vain our hosts pleaded with the Chekist not to make a scandal, explaining to him that we are guests, actors of the famous Art Theater. He was adamant. One of the hosts hurried to phone the colonel—the commandant of the town—and tell him about what had happened, and he quickly dispatched a squad of soldiers headed by an officer, who decisively explained to the Chekist that he would be resisted if he attempted to put us under arrest. After a long altercation between the two officers it was decided to conduct each of us to our hotels in the escort of a single soldier and a single Chekist. So, this occurrence ended happily for us.

Our Khar'kov tours ended on June 22. The day June 23 was Monday—a day of rest, when there were never performances, and only on Tuesday, June 24, could we put on the performance of *The Cherry Orchard* [which had been canceled the previous week by the Soviet authority for the funeral of Karl Liebknecht and Rosa Luxemburg[10]]. We performed it successfully. During the intermission before the third act, gunfire began in the streets. The doors to the street were closed and, with the agreement of the audience, the show went on. When it was over and we went into the street (it was still light out, because watches in Khar'kov were set ahead three and a half hours), the White Guard faction entered the city. So, quite unexpectedly for us, a front formed between us and Moscow. Our situation was irremediable: we had traveled light, many of us hadn't even taken our overcoats, because of the June heat. One of our comrades,

9 Chekist, member of the Cheka (acronym for the All-Russian Extraordinary Commission for the Struggle against Counterrevolution and Sabotage, established in December 1917 by a decree of the Sovnarkom a month after the Communist seizure of power). On June 18, 1918, it had put down the anti-Communist rebellion of the Left-Socialist Revolutionaries.

10 Karl Liebknecht (1871–1919), German socialist, and Rosa Luxemburg (1871–1919), Russian Marxist, cofounded the antiwar Spartacus League, later the Communist Party of Germany; they were murdered in Berlin after the Spartacist uprising and were henceforth regarded as martyrs to Marxism.

P. A. Podgorny, risked returning through the front to Moscow, but we were obliged to stay in Khar'kov.

The union of Khar'kov actors announced a "White Army Day." All actors without exception had to take part (recitations, scenes, and circus acts). V. I. Kachalov and I headed for the Union to explain that we had left our nearest and dearest in Moscow, who might suffer—we couldn't take part! But all our attempts to persuade them were in vain: we were compelled to organize a free concert. So N. N. Sinel'nikov,[11] the director of the Khar'kov Theater, and I had to ride in a horse cab all around the public squares and closed buildings, where the performances were to take place, to confiscate receptacles for voluntary donations and drive them to the bank, where they were locked in our presence, and we signed a receipt. For this forced participation we all received letters threatening that, when the Soviets were back in power, we would be shot. Whether this was a serious threat or blackmail I don't know; but when our group decided to stay in one of the cities to wait out the end of the Civil War, our wives raised a hue and cry: "They'll kill you!" and we had to clear out in the rear of the White evacuation. But for a rather long time we performed in Khar'kov, filling out our repertoire with a dramatization of *The Brothers Karamazov*. We rehearsed it at the hotel. I remember, when the actor playing Mitya shouted, "I am innocent of my father's blood!" the door opened, and the police came in with the public prosecutor. We had to explain that no one had killed anyone, it was only a rehearsal.

THE MAT ACTORS eventually found themselves cut off from Moscow, and most of them were unable to return until 1922. Their venture had been a private enterprise, undertaken for the personal benefit of the actors. The Bolshevik government sponsored other companies to visit the hinterlands. The former official of the Maly Theater, Nelidov, put together a scratch troupe to tour the following year, when the political situation had stabilized but bureaucratic interference was still a problem.

Vladimir Nelidov, *Teatral'naya Moskva. Sorok let moskovskikh teatrov* [Theatrical Moscow: Forty years of Moscow theaters, 1931] (Moscow: Materik, 2002), 343–44.

Now let's talk about touring in the revolutionary period. There was a trip to Smolensk in summer 1920; our ensemble was invited for cultural–educational purposes. We were free to select our repertoires. We were never under constraints. In the dramatic portion of our performances we included such works as the second act of Andreev's *Life of Man*,[12] capable of standing on its own as an independent play, and scenes from

11 Nikolay Nikolaevich Sinel'nikov (1855–1939), director, whose reforms and innovations in Moscow and the provinces presaged many of Stanislavsky's; managed Nikolay Solovtsov's Theater in Kiev 1913–17.
12 *The Life of Man* (*Zhizn' Cheloveka*, 1907) by Leonid Andreev, an allegorical play about the struggle of Man against Fate, first produced simultaneously by the Moscow Art Theater and Meyerhold. The second act is a scene at a ball.

Dostoevsky, Pushkin, and Turgenev. The musical portion also consisted of classical works.

We were assigned a six-wheeled non-Pullman third-class carriage with a double compartment in the middle with a table and chairs. The carriage had a kitchen and a conductor. On this occasion the train left on time and arrived in Smolensk on the dot; we had made 440 kilometers in fourteen hours.

Up to Mozhaisk—100 kilometers from Moscow—everything went normally. After Mozhaisk the "local authorities" began to make their presence felt. Frequent inspections of documents, an attempt to plant "our guys" in the carriage, or else to uncouple the carriage entirely. What's more, courtesy and asking nicely had no success at all, but the phrase, "Fine, we'll wire Lunacharsky right away" produced the necessary results.

[...] Our thirteen performances went splendidly to packed houses. But I mention Smolensk chiefly to tell about the communists who were meeting there. Our performances were put on under the aegis of one of them. He held a very important post. He was a young man of very handsome appearance with remarkably beautiful hands, which led to his nickname: Thoroughbred.

The first time I appeared before him was on the fifth day to receive our general fee—250,000 rubles per performance for six persons. The price of bread at the time was 250 rubles a pound, white rolls 1,000–1,500 rubles. And about two days before this a decree had been issued in Smolensk that anyone who had more than ten thousand in cash would be answerable to the Cheka.

I go, I receive a million, I sign for it, and I ask: "And where do I find the Cheka?"—"What do you care?"—"Well, I'd better go there in person, after all, I'm holding a million."—"Please understand that an actor is bound to be exempt for the right reasons."—"What about a shoemaker?"—"Same thing."—"Well, then who's the decree meant for?"—"Speculators."

[...] After about the eighth performance, I'm summoned to a certain important military commander. You can see at a glance that he's a boor, who seems to be playing a big shot out of a bad movie. It's obvious at once that he's a blockhead. "Your performances, comrade, are good, yes, good. And I've decided to order you all to the front. The railway carriage of an international society, a kitchen. You'll get a fee. You'll play six weeks."—"We won't go."—"I'll make you."—"You can move us by force, but we won't perform."—"Why not?"—"We're tired—number one, we have engagements in Moscow—number two."—"Then I'll take revolutionary measures."—"So shall we." The traditional "we'll wire Lunacharsky" followed. End of discussion, and we returned safely to Moscow.

Mark Mestechkin, *V teatre i v tsirke* [In the theater and at the circus] (Moscow: Iskusstvo, 1976), 16–19. Mark Solomonovich Mestechkin (1900–1981), after working in Moscow theaters 1919–26, took a course in clowning and, from 1930, was artistic director of the variety and acrobatic ensembles and, from 1948, director of the All-Russian Union of State Circuses.

Meanwhile the situation at the front grew very tense once again. The Red Army had to evacuate the city. In late August 1919 a group of young actors decided to leave Kiev with the 12th Army.

We abandoned the city late at night. On the Dnieper, near Turkhanov Island, a barge was waiting for us, which was so overloaded that doubts arose as to whether it would keep afloat. My father, who was accompanying me, wept to think we would never meet again. My comrades' parents were also very moved.

The 12th Army and our group reached the small Ukrainian town of Konotop. We repaid the army with concerts, but our hearts cherished the dream of putting on a full production. This was more pertinent to us as dramatic actors, but unfortunately we hadn't enough people.

Once we mentioned our dream to the commander. And then one fine day on the streets of Konotop, the order appeared: "All present and former actors and actresses are commanded to appear at the Political Administration of the Revmilsovet [Revolutionary Military Council] of the 12th Army to be assigned duties as actors."

Martial law was in force, an order was an order, and all at once old men and women were mobilized: many of them had formerly played only in amateur shows. Nevertheless we picked up the missing actors and could put on productions . . .

Our best production was H. Heijermans's play The Wreck of the "Hope." We played this show for Red Army soldiers under all sorts of conditions, often even in public squares. But the most memorable was the performance during which the news arrived that Kiev had been liberated by our forces. Without removing our makeup, we left the stage, recited V. Mayakovsky's "Left March,"[13] and then announced that Kiev was liberated. The house responded with an ovation and singing revolutionary songs. It was impossible to go on with the show.

It was a Georgian, Konstantin Aleksandrovich Mardzhanov (actually Koté Mardzhanishvili, 1872–1933), who brought a certain amount of stability to the Ukrainian theater at a time when Kiev was bandied back and forth between contending factions. He had staged Hamsun and Ibsen at the MAT (1910–12) and founded the Free Theater with Tairov and Koonen (1913–14) before being appointed commissar of theaters in Kiev by the Narkompros (1919). His revolutionary credentials were impeccable: in 1909 he had been expelled from Odessa for having the "Marseillaise" played during Heijermans's play The Wreck of the "Hope."

Georgy Kryzhitsky, "Mardzhanov in Kiev," quoted in E. Beskin, "K. A. Mardzhanov," Teatr i dramaturgiya [Theater and drama] 2–3 (1933), 35–38. Georgy Konstantinovich Kryzhitsky (1895–1975), director and critic, worked with

13 Levy Marsh (1918–19), which praises the bravery, discipline, and hope of the proletariat in its fight against counterrevolution, marks a major shift in Mayakovsky's poetry from futurist provocation to mass appeal. It ends "The Commune will never fall / Left! / Left! / Left!"

Mardzhanov, Teresvat, and the Crooked Mirror. A founding member of Fabrika éktsentricheskogo aktëra (Factory of the Eccentric Actor; FÉKS), he was exiled from Leningrad 1938–43 and appointed director of the May Republic Theater.

In those years [Mardzhanov] conquered theatrical Ukraine, sometimes as "the leading director of the Ukraine," sometimes as "the leading director of Kiev" (at that time they did not recognize lesser qualifiers), sometimes in the role of chairman of a commission for nationalizing the theaters. In those days the theater was the only refuge of culture, and never had the contrast between the stage and the audience been so striking. There, behind the footlights, in brocade and powdered wigs, strutted the heroes of Molière and directors who excelled in sophisticated stylization, while here, before the footlights, swarmed the gray military overcoats of Red Army men heading for the front or just come from the front and the frozen faces of philistines. In that setup Mardzhanov presented one of his best productions—*The Sheep Well* [*Fuente Ovejuna*] by Lope de Vega[14]—at the former Solovtsov Theater in Kiev. The hall was packed with Red Army men. It was a tempest. The Comandarm, having cleansed the Ukraine of Petlyura's forces,[15] told Mardzhanov after the performance that he would send all the men heading for the front to see *The Sheep Well*: they will be sure of victory. The precision of the groupings and mise-en-scène. The juiciness of the grotesque buffoonery along with the innate tragedy. And the colorful scenery and costumes of Isaak Rabinovich[16] appear to be his first work for the theater.

MARDZHANOV was soon to be eclipsed by a native Ukrainian. Aleksandr (Lesja) Stepanovich Kurbas (1887–1942), inspired by Henri Bergson's idealism and folk drama, arrived in Kiev in 1916 as a young actor determined to reform the Ukrainian stage. He founded the Youth Theater in 1917 to present a European repertoire in Ukrainian and toured the provinces during revolution and civil war. The occupation of Kiev by Bolshevik detachments forced the Youth Theater to merge with the State Dramatic Theater. With the entrance of Denikin's White forces, actors fled for their lives. One group moved to Kamenets-Podolsk, others to neighboring provinces. Kurbas remained in Kiev and helped found the Theater of Taras Shevchenko. There he decided to stage Shevchenko's poem "Haydamaky," about

---

14 *Fuente Ovejuna* (1619) deals with a village uprising against local injustice and hence was popular with revolutionary theaters. Mardzhanov's production ended with the audience joining the cast in intoning the "Internationale." The Solovtsov Theater in Kiev, founded in 1891, kept up a high standard and underwent a renaissance under Nikolay Sinel'nikov 1913–17.

15 Simon Vasil'evich Petlyura (1879–1926), Ukrainian politician who protected Kiev from the Bolsheviks January to February 1918 and was de facto head of the Ukrainian state 1918–20. Emigrated 1923 and was assassinated in Paris by an anarchist.

16 Isaak Moiseevich Rabinovich (1894–1961), designer, who worked in Moscow from the early 1920s, with radical scenography for the MAT, the Jewish State Theater, the Bol'shoy, and the Vakhtangov; he helped design the Palace of Soviets.

outlaws living along the Dnieper who revolted against Poland in 1734, as a three-act play. The result was a huge success, played over all the Ukraine.

> Les' Kurbas's address to the cast, from stenographic notes taken by Yakiv Savchenko, "*Haydamaky* by Shevchenko-Kurbas," *Bol'shevik* (May 1920), in Yosip Hirniak, "Birth and death of the modern Ukrainian theater," trans. Michael Terpak, in Martha Bradshaw, ed., *Soviet Theaters 1917–1941* (New York: Research Program on the USSR, 1954), 271.

The production must be monumental, that is, internally dynamic but externally static. Monumentality is primarily simplicity, clarity, and an overall meaning of form and content. This is an art of great passions and large-scale sufferings which correspond to the many national and social trends of all humanity. It becomes evident from this why the accent is on a *pohutovyi* [homespun, folksy] presentation, not on the details of the portraiture, but on its idea of national and social context. Everything is clear, sharp, and simple. The pantomime is performed strictly to music. In the love scene, there is lyricism rather than sentimental "thrills" that hint directly of romantic experiences. Great movement, statuesque monumentality.

> Les' Kurbas, director's diary for *Macbeth*,[17] "Z rezhysers'koho shchodennyka," *Bila Tserkva* (June 26, 1920), 32. Quoted in Irena R. Makaryk, *Shakespeare in the Undiscovered Bourn: Les Kurbas, Ukrainian Modernism, and Early Soviet Cultural Politics*, trans. Irena R. Makaryk (Toronto: University of Toronto Press, 2004), 56–57, trans. rev. © University of Toronto Press Incorporated 2004. Reprinted with permission of the publisher.

What great actors once delivered unconsciously, we must deliver both consciously and consummately. Therein lies the solution to the theatrical crisis among the great past, the unknown future, and the gray present. First, the musical rhythm of everything onstage is the frame of time . . . The greater the artist of the future, the more attention he will pay, in his play or production, to [rhythm], to [making] all strokes of meaning, [all] scenes follow in such a rhythmic succession that they will evoke in the viewer an analogous rhythm and will force the heart of the viewer to beat more evenly, quickly, or more staccato.

Before the catastrophe in the play—a livelier movement in the tempo of the scenes. Thus a comprehensible art places naturalism beyond the pale of art.

Now I consciously want to try this in *Macbeth*, to stage this problem as a foundation of the production, and when confirmed to accept this as the basic method, in my view, an entirely correct one.

What are "pauses" in important, decisive moments of a play! Are they not a wide, broken up *grave*, a quivering chord of pain where the rhythm of the striking of chords, the composer and the tempo, the performer—or one and the other—are the director?

17 This first production of *Macbeth* was unfavorably reviewed as unnecessarily crude. Kurbas's second attempt, in 1924, was more successful (see chapter 3).

Hence, rhythm: in the strokes of movement, in significant words or actions, in the pauses of silence (beyond words or in insignificant words)—(beautiful words), as an accompaniment—the pause for the right hand of the player.

Needs development: the sensation of some scene as a particular example of rhythm. Art only begins here.

And further: the problem of tempo, the painterly rhythm of poses and gestures. These are the essential elements of directing and of dramaturgy. All else is naturalism, not art.

Needs development.

Les' Kurbas, June 3, 1921, in Oleksandr Zaporozhets', "Uroky: Spohady pro Lesia Kurbasa" [Lessons: Interview about Les' Kurbas], *Kyiv* 2 (February 1987), 142; quoted in Irena R. Makaryk and Virlana Tkacz, eds., *Modernism in Kyiv: Jubilant Experimentation* (Toronto: University of Toronto Press, 2010), 362. Oleksandr Zaporozhets' (in Russian, Aleksander Vladimirovich Zaporozhets, 1905–81) acted in Kurbas's First Studio before becoming an important Soviet developmental psychologist, an expert on child development.

The basis of theater [is] movement, not words. Without movement there can be no theater, just as without words there can be no literature. Movement should be of primary importance for an actor, because the material of his art is the living human body in motion. Acting involves the play of the entire body, not of just one of its parts. Words and language are only a partial expression of the total movement, this total play of the body is on an equal level to gesture, mime, or motion. Because of this, the ideal actor is the one who acts with his entire body; and the one who excels only in speech, in the art of verbal expression, without expressive movement—he is merely a declaimer.

WITH the Ukrainian theater in the hands of Ukrainians, Mardzhanov went to Petrograd, where he directed the mass spectacle *Towards a Worldwide Commune* (1920) (see later). He then returned to Tbilisi (Tiflis) to Sovietize the Georgian stage, encourage the writing of plays in Georgian, and popularize Western classics.

Akaky Vasadze, from the actor's diaries. K. Mardzhanov, *Vospominaniya* (Tbilisi: Zarya Vostka, 1958), 2:259–72. Akaky Alekseevich Vasadze (1899–1978), a Georgian actor at the Rustaveli Theater, where he played Oedipus in 1956.

February 25, 1921. Tbilisi.

A red banner flutters over the courtyard.

The Georgian SSR!

A new era has begun in the history of the Caucasian people, who, quickly healing their wounds caused by three years of government by the Mensheviks, have turned to the great creative work in all branches of economy and culture.

On the cultural front everywhere are felt enormous inner displacements, only the Georgian theater is at an impasse. The 1921–22 season could single out only one successful production, A. Tsupunava's[18] *Who Is to Blame?*

The season ended and the actors dispersed with a feeling of oppressive dissatisfaction. No plan, no clear prospects! No one is preparing for the next season... Maybe, the actors will have to be requalified for a different profession? But such is the custom: anyone who has once breathed the dust of the stage is afflicted with the theater forever... And here we are—hopeless, "sick"—in September 1922 again at the dear "theatrical hearth and home."

[...] The 1922–23 season opened with a play by Sh. Dadiani,[19] *Adversity,* followed by a revival of *Who Is to Blame?* And the possibilities of the Caucasian theater were exhausted. Then the Narkompros convened representatives of theater, literature, the community. They discussed the causes of the situation, sought a way out and couldn't find it. Suddenly the bitterness erupted that had been building up for three years. It was especially targeted at directors. It seemed as if the stagnant situation couldn't be budged and there was no way to build a bridge across the precipice between the actors and directors. Some asserted that the actors were weak and a real theater could not be created with such talents.

A proposition was made to create a studio to train actors. Possibly in a couple of years the theater would be on its feet. But who was to run the training of the cadres?

"Would you take it on?" the chair of the meeting asks one of the directors.

"Me? Not on your life!" he replies.

Everyone feels that the comrade who brought forward the proposal to create a studio does not believe in its reality.

"Then who will take this thing on?"

Then they start naming names... This one won't do, that one's too weak. More debates, more rivers of words and finally... a proposal—to close the theater.

"May I?" rang out from the floor.

The chairman turned his gaze, full of hope, in the direction of the voice.

"Suppose we ask Koté Mardzhanishvili what he advises?"

"There is no quick way to resolve the question of closing the theater," replies the man with the silvery hair. "A. I. Yuzhin[20] wants to schedule his tours to the Rustaveli Theater.[21] Grant him the venue for two months, and after that I will try to prepare a play... Let's see, perhaps we have all the talents to create a Caucasian theater."

---

18 Aleksandr Razhdenovich Tsupunava (1881–1955), Georgian director, who started at the MAT; at the Paliashvili Opera and Ballet Theater from 1918.

19 Shalva Nikolaevich Dadiani (1874–1959), Georgian author and actor, creator of the Modzravi Dasi or Mobile Troupe 1909; after the Soviet occupation of Georgia, he overcame his initial hostility and became an adulator of Stalin and a member of the Supreme Soviet.

20 Yuzhin was the Georgian prince Sumbatov and regularly toured to the Caucasus.

21 Rustaveli Dramatic Theater, Tiflis (Tbilisi) became the showplace for the best productions of Mardzhanov and Akhmeteli throughout the 1920s; but after they had been liquidated, it did not find its voice again until the 1950s.

They conferred and passed the resolution: "To postpone the decision to close the theater and discuss it again after K. A. Mardzhanishvili's production."

"The theater has found its director!" thought many who attended the meeting, as they hopefully left the Narkompros building. [...]

Agitki and Street Theater

Agitki were short skits offering propaganda on the evils of religion or the virtues of personal hygiene, performed with minimal decor in trains moving from town to town and village to village as well as from trucks and streetcars.

René Fülop-Müller, *Geist und Geschichte des Bolschewismus* [Spirit and history of Bolshevism] (Zurich, 1926), 187–88. Fülöp-Müller was the pseudonym of Philipp Müller (1891–1963), a Romanian-born, Vienna-educated writer and chemist; fascinated by Rasputin, he traveled to Russia and wrote books on the Revolution and Russian theater; he emigrated to the United States in 1939.

The erstwhile enemy is constantly ridiculed and combated in symbolic form on the open street, with the masses encouraged to join in. A favorite genre is to contrast the past and the present in the form of radical images. First come tsarist soldiers in blue uniforms with fixed bayonets, leading through the streets a group of political prisoners, followed by red gendarmes escorting white police officers in chains. The next manifestation is a colorful company of priests, generals, and speculators, who are exposed to public ridicule because, although garbed in the most elegant clothes, they wear thick ropes around their necks. During a demonstration against England a gesticulating dummy was set up in the middle of the square to represent an English diplomat in the act of delivering an ultimatum. An immense worker's fist puts an end to this political action with a punch on the nose of the foreign statesman. On a similar occasion the Englishman was represented by a gigantic effigy in tails and top hat carried on the roof of a car. Whenever the speaker referred to England, he directly addressed the effigy. Soon the crowd, too, turned against it with threatening gestures. The "Englishman," in the meantime, strolled up and down elegantly and arrogantly, a monocle casually inserted in his eye socket, until a Bolshevik worker swinging a hammer sprang onto the roof of the car. With one blow he forced the figure, which pleaded for mercy, to its knees, at which point he turned to the crowd to ask whether the "Englishman" should be spared or not. As might be expected, the mob howled in unison: "Strike him down!" whereupon the worker raised his hammer and let it fall three times with full force on the effigy's head. A man in the crowd picked up the soiled and crushed top hat, collected the fragments of the monocle, and, displaying them to the assemblage, proclaimed in triumph, "That's all that's left of our enemy!"

2.1. The Pushkin (formerly, Imperial Alexandra) Theater, Petrograd, on May Day 1919. The banner reads "Hail May 1. The military review of the revolutionary forces of the international proletariat."

INSPIRED BY French Revolutionary festivals and ideas of communal theater pro-mulgated by European reforms and pre-Revolutionary Russian symbolists, the Bolsheviks promoted mass spectacles (*massovye deystva*) as a counterblast to Orthodox religious rituals. They aided in imposing an ideological vision of history on the masses, with the continuity of class struggle and the ultimate victory of the Russian proletariat. The first of these spectacles to celebrate the Revolution took place on May 25, 1917, and in summer 1918 the capture of Azov from the Turks was reenacted on the banks of the Voronezh River.

"May First," *Zhizn' Iskusstva* 127–28 (May 3–4, 1919), 3.

The holiday of the workers of the whole world—the radiant day the first of May—appeared in the fullest sense a triumphant display of all the artistic forces of Petrograd. The celebratory performances, concerts, and spectacles in all the state, communal, regional, and private theaters and prolet'kults actually required the full mobilization of artistic forces. And this mobilization was quickly accomplished, with complete success.

All the stage workers eagerly answered the call, for this call issued from the work-ing class itself.

A special success on May 1 was had again by the organized flying squads of actors, serving the remote, suburban districts.

Unfortunately the original project, worked out on a grand scale, had to be consid-erably reduced for purely technical difficulty and the lack of means of transmission; nevertheless, even in the form in which it was realized in reality, the ideas of the organization of flying squads of actors proved all its liveliness and necessity for further development [...]

The most varied programs of the flying squads, with which they appeared in the districts ("Petrushka,"[22] limericks, improvisation, solo and choral numbers), guaranteed their success with the spectators.

Teatral, "May Day Spectacles"

On May 1, all the suburbs of the city and the workers' districts were served by itinerant theaters (in motor cars) with a varied program, set up by the Theater and Spectacle Section. [...]

The shows of the itinerant theaters ended at 6:00 p.m. At that time in Ekateringof Park, in the Putilovsk Factory district, a festival began. On an open platform a varied entertainment was set up, performed by the best talents of the miniature and variety theaters, accompanied by an orchestra.

THE MOST important spectacles put on in Petrograd were *The Overthrow of the Autocracy* (March 12, 1919) and *Play of the Third International* (May 1, 1919), staged as war games; *From the Power of Darkness to the Sunlight* (May 1, 1919), the only Proletkul't mass spectacle, held in a factory district outside the city; *The Mystery of Emancipated Labor* (May 20, 1919); *From Darkness to Light* (November 6, 1919); *The Blockade of Russia* (June 20, 1920), directed by Sergei Radlov on Pleasure Island; Mardzhanov's *Towards a Worldwide Commune* (July 1920); and the most celebrated, Evreinov's *Storming of the Winter Palace* (November 7, 1920).

TEO Section on Mass Performances and Spectacles, Appeal to Create Mass People's Theater, *Vestnik Teatra* 50 (1920), 3. STDM 17–21, 66.

Before the Revolution the art of the theater was fettered by capitalist exploitation. Now it enters the road of free development. Whenever the people break the chains of slavery, they direct their gaze to the theater. As the most powerful means of struggle for freedom of masses, theater at such moments has striven to leave stuffy buildings and go on the streets and has taken forms we now call mass spectacles. "We must refrain," says Rousseau, "from those boring shows, which bring together in dark buildings a small clutch of people, confused and unmoving, wasting time in silence and immobility. No, people, your holidays are not like that. Under an open sky, in space, must you assemble." [...][23]

Let our motto be the words of one of the first fighters for mass theater, Romain Rolland: "A free and happy people needs holidays more than theaters, it will be its own beautiful spectacle, and we must prepare future people's holidays for the people."

22 This was Lunacharsky's "Bolshevization" of the traditional puppet play, performed with live actors.
23 Jean-Jacques Rousseau's *Lettre à M. D'Alembert sur les Spectacles* (1758) argued that the theater was an immoral source of pleasure and a waste of time, substituting the artificial for a genuine community.

2.2. "Toward World Communism," a mass enactment on the steps of the Petrograd Stock Exchange, 1920, on the occasion of the Second Comintern Congress of the Third International. Banners read "Land to the People," "Power to the Soviets," and "The Blood of Hungarian Workers Calls Us to Vengeance."

All hail the collective creativity of the masses!
All hail the holiday of May 1!
All hail the liberated theater!

Konstantin Mardzhanov, rough draft for a scenario of a mass revolutionary celebration, 1920, Petrograd. Mardzhanov, *Vospominaniya*, 107–8.

Bases of the Scenario

The scenario must be in three parts:
1. Humanity of the past—its enslavement.
2. The present—struggle and victory.
3. The future—a bright life.

Part I

Tableaux of a free life.
The advent of priests.
The enslavement of the human spirit and hence the body.
The appearance of a tsar, at first as the representative of god on earth, then the subjugation of god to the tsar. Stages: the idol, the tablets, the cross at the feet of the tsar.
Forced labor in the name of the cross: Byzantium, the Holy Roman Empire (the first free thinkers are burned with books on the bonfires of the Inquisition). France.

Louis. The French Revolution. The throne is occupied by capital. The Communist manifesto. The Paris Commune and its destruction.

Part II

Capital on top, served by tsar and religion.
War on behalf of capitalism.
The Russian Revolution.
A compromise government.
The October Revolution.
Russian alone—blockade, famine, struggle, collapse.
Russia advances. The Soviet republic.
Movement in Europe. The Third International.

Part III

Members of the Third International stir up the workers in Europe.
Victory of the workers in Europe.
Annihilation of the weapons of war, inequality of peoples, all forms of capitalism.
Triumph of science and art.
Science annihilates death.
Art defeats god.
Spirit and matter merge in a single celebration.

> Anatoly Lunacharsky, "On people's festivals," *Vestnik teatra* 62 (April 27–May 2, 1920), 13; reprinted in *Sovetskoe dekorativenoe iskusstvo. Materialy i dokumenty 1917–1932* [Soviet scene design: Materials and documents 1917–1932] (Moscow: Iskusstvo, 1984), 106–7.

We must, however, be on our guard against mere entertainment. Many people believe that collective creativity means a spontaneous, independent manifestation of the will of the masses. But until social life teaches the masses some sort of instinctive compliance with a higher order and rhythm, one cannot expect the crowd to be able to create anything on its own except boisterous noise and the colorful back-and-forth movement of people in holiday costumes.

A real celebration should be organized like anything else in this world that has a tendency to produce a highly aesthetic impression. [...]

Popular celebrations should definitely be divided into two quite different acts. Into a mass demonstration, in the proper meaning of the word, which assumes a movement of the masses from the outskirts to a single center, or, if there are too many people, to a few centers, where some central action, such as an elevated symbolic ceremony, takes place. This might be a performance, grandiose, ornamental, pyrotechnical, satirical, or ceremonial, or it might be the burning of enemy insignia, etc., accompanied by loud choral singing, harmonious and polyphonic music, expressing the nature of celebration in the proper meaning of the word. [...]

The second act would be celebrations of an intimate kind either indoors, where the premises are turned into a kind of revolutionary cabaret, or outdoors: on trolley platforms, moving trucks, or simply on tables, barrels, etc.

Here all kinds of activities are possible, such as fiery revolutionary speeches, the recitation of satiric verse, clown acts with some caricature of enemy forces, or topical dramatic sketches, and much, much more.

But it is essential that any such improvised variety show be tendentious in all of its numbers. It would be good if it were simply instilled with uncontrollable, uninhibited laughter, etc.

P. Kudelli, "A new spectacle at the portal of the Stock Exchange," *Petrogradskaya Pravda* 159 (July 21, 1920). Reprinted in *Sovetskoe dekorativnoe iskusstvo*, 111–12. Praskov'ya Frantsevna Kudelli (1859–1944), Bolshevik worker for women's rights, was a reporter on *Izvestia* and *Pravda* and, from 1922, a member of the Commission on Party History.

The portal of the Stock Exchange, whither in times gone by only the trotters of stockbrokers and those seeking to get rich quick used to drive, has once more been rattled by an unwonted spectacle. On May Day we saw [*The Anthem of Emancipated Labor*] and on July 19 a grandiose new dramatized mass enactment, *In Favor of a Worldwide Commune,* in honor of the Second Congress of the Third International took place.

[...] Unfortunately, to be blunt, we cannot offer a wholly favorable reaction. *In Favor of a Worldwide Commune* encompasses far too many complicated events from the First International down to our days, including the February and October of the Great Russian Revolution. [...] The haste in staging it could be felt in everything—the scenario itself and its performance.

The scenario did not present a clear picture of the life of the era. We saw nothing but the dramatization of dry editorials, written to give a historical outline from the First to the Third International. The dryness led to tedious viscosity and utterly inartistic prose. [...]

Now, as to the crowd. On seeing a black, two-headed eagle, crudely swaying from a noose, many of them shouted out "Autocrats," on seeing beneath it a stationary idol, voices called out, "Nicholas, Nicky boy."

I repeat, there was no way to be captivated or animated by the spectacle, to be penetrated by the tragic element in the mass struggle, because, as a matter of fact, there was no tragic element, nothing but the dramatization of prosaic and often irrelevant editorials. [...]

Nikolay Evreinov, "Vzyatie Zimnego dvortsa" [The storming of the Winter Palace]. *Krasny militsioner* [Red militia man] (November 7, 1920), 1–2.

An artillery shot rings out. Light breaks through to a white platform and illuminates the worn stones of the ancient hall. On a dais, the Provisional Government, headed by

Kerensky, accepts loyalty oaths from the former dignitaries, generals, and financiers, as the band plays an out-of-tune *Marseillaise*. On a red platform, against a background of brick factories, the *Internationale* strikes up, and, to this music, individuals in the throng and then hundreds of voices yell, "Lenin, Lenin!"... While those on the white platform spend their time at all kinds of meetings, the proletariat on the red platform begins to coalesce around its leaders... Then comes a depiction of General Kornilov's[24] revolt in July. After this, the Provisional Government is protected only by military cadets and the Women's Battalion,[25] and it flees to the Winter Palace. Then, the windows of this last citadel of Kerensky light up. The Reds have now organized their own military detachments and point the Winter Palace out to each other... Machine guns stutter, rifles fire, and the artillery thunders... The din carries on nonstop for two or three minutes... But suddenly, a rocket flares up and everything instantly goes quiet, so that the air can be filled with new sounds. A chorus of forty thousand voices is singing the *Internationale*. Five-pointed red stars start to light up over the darkened windows of the Winter Palace. An enormous red banner is raised above the building itself... The show is over, and the Red forces begin to parade.

"The storming of the Winter Palace (Impression)," *Izvestiya Petrogradskogo Soveta rabochikh i krasnoarmeyskikh deputatov* [Truth of the Petrograd Soviet of Workers and Red Army Deputies] (November 9, 1920). *STDM 17–21*, 273–74.

The discharge of an artillery gun announces the start of the show. The square is darkened. A few minutes pass in tense expectation, all eyes are focused on the stage, which is silent [...] Music rings out. [...] The crowd of many thousands watches with bated breath as the action unfolds. Laughter and barbed quips greet the appearance of Kerensky, who pompously receives the homage of his admirers. "Now he's cut down to size groveling at the doors of ministers and bankers abroad," one can hear from a group of workers. "Yeah, he's got a hard time making a buck," responds a young Red Army soldier, his eyes glued to the stage.

The rapid change of events on the stage attracted the strained attention of the viewers. The July attempt to overthrow the detested Provisional Government of Kerensky, which ends in the temporary defeat of the proletariat, elicits a deep sigh of disappointment. [...] But now the chorus, heralding the power of the soviets, resounds louder and louder and with growing confidence. The supporters of the Provisional Government, panic stricken, flee in all directions. Kerensky and his ministers save themselves in automobiles; their hasty flight delights the audience. The proletariat has triumphed!

24 Lavrenty Georgievich Kornilov (1870–1918), tsarist general who led troops against the Provisional Government in St. Petersburg; after this failure, he organized the Volunteer (White) Army and led it until the retreat from Rostov-on-Don. He was killed during an ensuing battle.
25 Fifteen all-female combat troops were created by the Provisional Government to encourage the demoralized male combatants in the war to carry on fighting. The most famous unit was that stationed to guard the Winter Palace and ridiculed by Eisenstein in his film *October*. They were demobilized by the Bolsheviks in late 1917.

"Hurrah," shouts the chorus from the stage. "Hurrah, hurrah!" respond the spectators.

There begins the impetuous assault on the Winter Palace. The viewers are electrified: an instant and it seems that the crowd will crush the barrier and together with the automobiles and mobs of soldiers and workers throw itself to storm the last bastion of despised Kerenskyism.

But now the cannonade stops. The palace has been taken, and above it unfurls the red flag. The orchestra strikes up the "Internationale," which tens of thousands of voices pick up.

It is only now that one can behold the multitude of people. The square is packed. Without any exaggeration it can be said that on Uritsky Square that evening, there were no fewer than one hundred thousand people. [...]

ONE OF THE BEST of the agittroupes was the Teresvat (Theater of Revolutionary Satire), founded in the ancient Belorussian town of Vitebsk in 1919 by the poet M. Ya. Pustinin (actually Rozenblatt, 1884–1966). The town had a population of sixty-six thousand, half of them Jews. One of its native sons, the painter Marc Chagall,[26] returned there after study in Paris and was named its Commissar of Arts in 1917. He founded the Vitebsk College of Arts, where Él Lissitzky and Kazimir Malevich taught, and organized a number of impressive street festivals to celebrate the many holidays instituted by the new government.

> L. V. Mikhevich, "Vitebskie ulichnye prazdnestva 1917–1923 godov" [Street celebrations in Vitebsk 1917–23], in *Russkaya avangard 1910-x-1920x godov i teatr* [Russian avant-garde of the 1910s to 1920s and the theater], ed. G. F. Kovalenko (St. Petersburg: Dmitry Bulanin, 2000), 148.

Celebratory events virtually swamped the city. By March 1919 the city of Vitebsk officially observed:

January 1–2. New Year.

January 22. Remembrance day of January 9, 1905.

March 12. Day of the overthrow of the autocracy.

March 18. Day of the Paris Commune.

May 1. Internationale Day.

November 7. Day of the Proletarian Revolution.

By this decree [GAVO f1821, op.1, d.313, l.54] the eight religious holidays which had been observed by the old-style calendar were deemed nonworkdays, in addition to those listed above. In record time the number of holidays increased. To the March

---

26 Marc Chagall (actually Mark Zakharovich Segal, 1887–1985), a student of Bakst and Dobuzhinsky, had already had a one-man show in Berlin in 1910. He was deposed by the supremacist Malevich as commissar and moved to Moscow to work with Granovsky's Yiddish theater troupe. Fed up with Granovsky, he taught orphans in the village of Malakhovka before emigrating to Berlin 1922. He settled in Paris 1923.

8 and February 23 celebrated in Vitebsk, they added March 16, "City Day," October 27, "Day of Nestor's Chronicle." There were holidays without definite dates, such as "Cooperator Day," "Week of the Red Ploughman."

TERESVAT became a common term for agittroupes that toured to the front lines, Siberia, and the Urals, giving more than two hundred performances to more than two hundred thousand spectators. The movement reached its peak of popularity in 1920–21. Meanwhile, summoned by Lunacharsky, the Vitebsk Teresvat moved into an old railway station in Moscow, where it opened on November 7, 1920. Its troupe expanded to 350 persons, headed by David Gutman, with the participation of such writers as Mayakovsky and Il'ya Érenburg.

Moscow and Petrograd

> Statistics from "Teatral'naya i muzykal'naya Moskva," in *Revolyutsionnaya Moskva. Tret'emu Kongressu Kommunistichestogo Internatsionala* [Revolutionary Moscow: To the Third Congress of the Communist International] (Moscow: Krasnaya Moskva, 1921), 539–56.

In 1914, just before the world war broke out, Moscow numbered twenty-one theaters, among them two state and nineteen privately owned. Three years later, i.e., by late 1917, the number of theaters had grown to thirty-two; a new category of theater appeared—Soviet (one)—and a mighty rise in the number of private theaters (twenty-nine) is notable, 1917 being a period of maximal growth and the start of the crisis. As a direct consequence of the October Revolution, there was a decline in the importance of private theaters. In 1918 the general number of theaters rose to forty-five owing to the intensive growth of Soviet theaters, whose number in 1918 reached eighteen (one Central Mosc. Sov. Work. and Peas. Dep. and seventeen regional). The theaters of national minorities amounted to three (Jewish, Lett, and Ukrainian). The year 1918 saw a new decline in the number of private theaters, which continued in 1919. Their number lessened to fifteen in a general number of forty-three theaters functioning in Moscow in 1919. [...] In 1914 the Moscow theaters gave 1,876 performances, or 89–90 performances on average for each theater. The average number of performances at one theater in 1917 (given the strong and constant growth of the number of theaters) was reduced to seventy-seven and in 1919 to sixty-four. [...]

In 1919 the number of performances in theaters not only approached the norm of the prewar period but remarkably surpassed it. So, for the first half-year 1919, in forty-three Moscow theaters, 2,470 performances were put on, or an average of 57.5 performance in each theater in a six-months period. [...] The 1918–19 repertoire counted 240 plays by 136 authors. The most popular at that time was L. Andreev. Both Soviet and private theaters staged him simultaneously eighty times in all. Great success was enjoyed in that season by the plays of Gorky on the stages of the Maly, Soviet, and private theaters. By number of productions, first place belongs to Ostrovsky. His plays were on the stages of all theaters. The Maly Theater put him on seventy-five times, the Soviet forty-five, and the private thirty-two. [...]

EVEN IN 1920, when the theater epidemic was subsiding, the Red Army and Fleet had more than 1,800 clubs, to which 1,210 theaters and 911 dramatic circles were attached.

> Lunacharsky, "Report on improving the state of Moscow theaters," February 16, 1920. *STDM 17–21,* 65–66.

In addition, I report that the general number of participants of the collectives of these theaters are as follows:

Bol'shoy Theater—	1250 persons
Maly Theater—	491 "
Art Theater and its studios—	523
	2264 persons [...]
Kamerny Theater	152 persons
Model Theater	260 "
Children's "	100 "
	512 "

A grand total of 2,776 persons.

> The repertoire of the Moscow theaters in early June 1919 was as follows. "Programmy i libretto Moskovskikh teatrov," *Vestnik teatra* 31–32 (1919), 16–20.

The Art Theater: *The Lower Depths* by Maksim Gorky; *Uncle Vanya* by Anton Chekhov; *Tsar Fëdor Ioannovich* by A. K. Tolstoy; *The Cricket on the Hearth,* from Dickens.

The Art Theater First Studio: *Youth* by Leonid Andreev.

The People's House named for the worker Pëtr Alekseev: *Across the Ocean* by Yakov Gordin; *The Lower Depths* by Maksim Gorky; *Innocent though Guilty* by Ostrovsky; *Vanyushin's Children* by S. Naydënov; *Trilby* by G. G. Gé.

The Palace of the October Revolution named for Yu. M. Sverdlov: *The Carmagnole* by Georgy Chulkov; *Sten'ka Razin* by Vasily Kamensky; on the open-air stage, circus acts; in the Veranda Theater, musical evenings.

The Studio Theater of the Kh.-P. Union of Workers' Organizations (former Sohn Theater): *The Tales of Hoffmann* by Offenbach; *I Pagliacci* by Leoncavallo; *Marriage on Compulsion* by Molière; *The Tempest* and *The Merry Wives of Windsor* by William Shakespeare; *The Abduction from the Seraglio* by Mozart.

> Living conditions in Petrograd. Viktor Shklovsky, *Khod konya: sbornik statey* [A steed's gait: Collected articles] (Moscow: Gelikon, 1923), 23–25.

I burned my furniture, my sculpting stand, my bookcases, and my books—books that were priceless and innumerable. If my hands and feet felt like wood, I would warm them and wait interminably for the arrival of spring. [...] Frost congealed on the walls of houses, freezing the wallpaper. People slept in their overcoats and practically in their galoshes. Everyone gathered in the kitchen; stalactites were proliferating in the other rooms. People felt sorry for one another, and in the empty town they grew close [...]

Hunger... We ate strange things: frozen potatoes and rotten turnips, and herrings, whose heads and tails had to be cut off lest they stink. We cooked in the oil used to dry paint, in boiled linseed oil for paints, and in boiled lead salts. We ate unhusked oats with horse meat tender from decomposition... Hunger and jaundice. We were immersed in hunger, like a fish in water, birds in air [...]

And the town is great, the town kept alive... In our dark apartments—oh, the darkness, the soot from the tiny night light, and the anticipation of light!—we would gather to go to the theaters. We stared at the stage. Hungry actors performed. Hungry writers wrote. Scholars kept on working. [...] We gathered and sat in our overcoats by stoves fueled by books. Our feet were sore; our pots cracked because of the cooking-oil shortage. And we talked about rhythm and literary form. [...]

> Changes in admission. H. G. Wells, *Russia in the Shadows* (London: Hodder and Stoughton, 1920), 35–36. Herbert George Wells (1866–1946), the eminent English novelist, had first visited Russia in 1914 to interview Gorky; he returned in 1920 to see Lenin. His articles, sympathetic to Bolshevism but regarding it as "naive," first appeared in the London *Sunday Express*.

For a time, the stablest thing in Russian culture was the theater. [...] When one faced the stage, it was as if nothing had changed in Russia; but when the curtain fell and one turned to the audience one realised the revolution. There were now no brilliant uniforms, no evening dress in boxes and stalls. The audience was an undifferentiated mass of people, the same sort of people everywhere, attentive, good-humored, well behaved and shabby. [...] One's place in the house is determined by ballot. And for the most part there is no paying to enter the theater. For one performance the tickets go, let us say, to the professional unions, for another to the Red Army and their families, for another to the school children, and so on. A certain selling of tickets goes on, but it is not in the present scheme of things.

> Shklovsky, *Khod konya*, 51, 59, 61–63.

Every unit has its little theater. There is a theater attached to almost every organization. We even have a school of instructors in theater work with a section for preparing prompters attached to the Baltic Fleet... I would not be astonished if the Murmansk Railroad or the Central Nail Factory were to be training actors and not just for themselves but for others as well. [...]

No one knows what to do with the dramatic clubs. They propagate like infusoria.

Neither the fuel shortage, the food shortage, nor the Entente[27]—nothing—could hold back their development. [. . .]

Life is hard and its hardness cannot be concealed. [. . .] the road to yesterday is blocked off.

And so, man flees to the theater, to the actors, since (according to Freud[28]) we take refuge where we have a psychosis in any mania as if it were a monastery, that is, we create our own illusion of life, an illusion of reality, instead of the difficult reality of reality.

You probably remember Dostoevsky's description of a theater in his *Notes from the House of the Dead*.[29] To cover one's shorn scalp with a wig, to dress up in gay clothes, to enter someone else's life—all these were what captivated the prison workers doing dramatics. Dostoevsky says that they turned out to be good actors... These millions of [dramatic] clubs must not be closed; man must not be forbidden to emote.

> The young actors who had fled Kiev, with mandates from the 12th Red Army, arrived in Moscow in autumn 1920. Mestechkin, *V teatre i v tsirke*, 16–19.

Moscow in the early 1920s was a strange city... On the snowy streets lay fallen horses, in the evening shots rang out, fuel and foodstuffs were in very short supply... In those years as in prerevolutionary times, actors had to provide their own wardrobes. I owned a few costumes: a morning coat, a tail-coat, a frock coat. To some degree these things helped [me and my friend Volodya Nelly[30]] in the early period: we dropped in on secondhand dealers, sold some of our clothes, and somehow managed to exist.

When at last the "wardrobe stock" was gone and there was nothing more to sell, we tried out for jobs at the "Free" Theater on Triumphal Square (now Mayakovsky Square), a theater run by B. S. Nevolin and D. G. Gutman.[31]

At that time the troupe of the "Free" Theater was preparing *Fuente Ovejuna*, and it was suggested that we audition with excerpts from this play. The role of old Estevan was being rehearsed by the elderly actor M. S. Narokov,[32] and when I came on in Estevan's makeup and costume and started to recite a monologue (I was twenty), the audience

27 The so-called Little Entente of 1920 of Czechoslovakia, Romania, and Yugoslavia against Hungary. Since Russia had dropped out of the Triple Entente, France saw these three as replacement allies.

28 Freud's ideas were known and practiced in revolutionary Russia: in 1917 the first Russian psychoanalytic journal was published, and in 1924 a State Psychoanalytic Institute opened. All this was to be suppressed under Stalin.

29 Dostoevsky's *Zapiski iz mërtvogo doma* (1861) is a fictionalized account of his time in a prison camp.

30 Vladimir Nelly, Ukrainian actor at the Lesya Ukrainka Theater in Kiev.

31 Boris S. Nevolin (actually Boruch Zisea Kosio, d. 1948), director of the Intimate Theater in Petrograd 1915–17; administrator at the RFSFR 1; became an opponent of Meyerhold after the latter canceled Nevolin's production of *Fuente Ovejuna*. Emigrated to Finland and Germany, where he made films; married to the cabaret artiste Dela Lipinskaya. David Grigor'evich Gutman (actually Girshevich, 1884–1946), director and playwright, who created the itinerant puppet theater Revolutionary Petrushka in Tula, touring the front with agitprop. With a knack for improvisation, he headed the Moscow Terevsat 1920–22 and the Moscow Satire Theater 1926–29.

32 Mikhail Semënovich Narokov (actually Yakubov, 1879–1958), after an extensive provincial career as an actor before the Revolution, brought his impassioned playing to the Maly Theater 1920–49.

burst out laughing. I was totally confused and depressed. Imagine my amazement and delight when Gutman came up to me and said I was accepted into the troupe of the "Free" Theater...

Gutman was one of the most talented directors of the theater of miniatures I have ever met. [...] This artist of irrepressible imagination and subtle taste was to play no small role in the organization and establishment of the Moscow Theater of Satire. [...] Once at a rehearsal Gutman remarked to an actor, "Do it more economically, more simply, not so many gestures." "I'm looking for the kernel of the role," explained the actor. To which Gutman replied, "This isn't a grain elevator, it's a theater—here you have to act."

Nelidov, *Teatral'naya Moskva*, 349–51, 356–57.

The Moscow theater proletkul'ts [...] met in requisitioned private residences. The Central Proletkul't was located in Morozov's[33] former home on Vozdvizhenka, a tasteless copy of some Portuguese castle. The famous artist V. A. Serov[34] had called this building "a Lisbon townhouse," but others have referred to it as "the oyster works" because those mollusks embellished its walls.

There were nearly ten such proletkul'ts in Moscow; the Central one had more than one hundred students, and the others fifty to sixty. After an examination people were accepted as specialists, and the most promising were given subsidies. Altogether nearly six hundred persons out of the Moscow population of two million.

The instructors of stage art were almost exclusively actors of the Moscow Art Theater, as familiar with Stanislavsky's system of stage creativity. The essence of this system can be defined as learning art by really experiencing life.

On the recommendation of the Moscow Art Theater actor and member of its artistic council V. G. Gaydarov, I myself was first invited to the Central Studio as a lecturer on theater history. Heading the studio as its leaders were two Communist sisters. Greater "bureaucrats" in the worst sense of the word I have never seen in my life. [All the obtuse officialdom of the tsarist regime] paled in comparison with these sisters. They, thank God, didn't meddle in the teaching, but headed the "synod."

[...] A few days went by, when all the teachers were ordered to assemble. And the question of the day was our relation to proletarian art. Aha, they're fishing for counter-revolutionaries! We showed up.

At this time they were forming troupes of the best students, who were preparing performances, like students in schools in the past. And so as part of our interrogation, the question arose of the rapid casting of students in propaganda productions. Untrained students.

One of the instructors of the studio, a Moscow Art Theater actor, stood up and declared that the students' unpreparedness prevented this, and, if the performances

33 Savva Timofeevich Morozov (1862–1905), millionaire industrialist and patron of the arts, founding shareholder in the MAT, and, from 1902, one of its administrators.
34 Valentin Aleksandrovich Serov (1865–1911), painter in the World of Art movement, famous for his portraits, among others, of the actress Ermolova.

at the front are an "urgent matter," then let them detail some of the students, but then they should be regarded as forever ruined for the stage, for such a frivolous relationship to stage art is to prostitute the theater. All this was conveyed trenchantly, precisely, courageously, and with temperament. The auditors applauded. The Communist sisters hissed, "Counterrevolution." They couldn't forgive that the extremely inept play *Mariana*,[35] inspired by Communism, had been canceled after the dress rehearsal. The instructors informed them that it was impossible to put on such a play.

Then came the famous question "of one's relationship to proletarian art." Another instructor stood up and declared that a definitive answer could be given to this question as soon as we were told what "proletarian art" is. Examples offered were: "The Tale of the Fisherman and the Fish" (the proletariat in action); *Fruits of Enlightenment* (aristocrats), *Brothers Karamazov* (minor gentry), *King Lear* (crowned head), etc. Is this art proletarian or bourgeois? A deadly, gravelike stillness condensed. Never again did they inflict such interrogations on us. [...]

Other courses were given at the Proletkul't: history of literature, stage practice, movement, dance, diction and declamation; there were also courses in "politeracy" (they taught Communism). How was the teaching received? Here's how. I attended various lectures. The literature instructor was speaking, and specifically for two hours running on Homer's *Odyssey*. I look at the faces. They exhibit boredom. They yawn. Someone has rolled under the divan and is sleeping there. I attended the propaganda lectures. I saw how the listeners were making roosters out of paper. Then they would chew this paper and try undetected to throw it at the lecturer. But the next day these same people with the enthusiasm of youth would discuss [a speech of Trotsky or Lunacharsky.]

VALENTIN SMYSHLAEV, who had trained at the Moscow Art First Studio, was the only member of MAT to be a card-carrying Bolshevik; the Party put him in charge of mass spectacles in Moscow and the Proletkul't's Arena Department.

> Diary of V. S. Smyshlaev, Moscow, August 30, 1919, in *I vnov' o Khudozhest-vennom. MKhAT v vospominaniyakh i zapisyakh 1901–1920* [And more about the Art Theater: The MAT in memoirs and notations], ed. Mariya Polkanova (Moscow: Avantitul, 2004), 123–24.

Last night K. S. Stanislavsky and Moskvin were arrested by a decree of the MChK [Moscow Cheka]. All day today from early morning I ran around to various persons and offices, trying to free the old man as soon as possible, mainly. After all, he's a dreadful coward and at the moment a pauper; if they don't let him out again, he, I'm guessing, will undergo [*perezhivaet*][36] God knows what. Today's arrests were prompted, they

35 *Mariana*, a play of rural life in 1918 by A. Serafimovich, in a production by Valentin Smyshlaev, had opened the Second Central Theater Studio March 22, 1920.
36 An ironic remark, since Stanislavsky's system of acting was based on *perezhivanie* or reexperiencing emotions.

say, by the discovery of some Cadet organization, and more than sixty persons were arrested in Moscow, among others, the son of V. V. Luzhsky. [...] In V. I. Nemirovich's apartment an ambush has been laid; he's not in Moscow, he's living at his dacha. I picked up all this information at those offices at which I happened to be today on behalf of the old man. I was at the MChK for the first time—I barely got in to see the commandant despite my Proletkul't credentials and Party card. The functionaries there have an iron discipline. The commandant showed me an order from Dzerzhinsky,[37] which said, among other things, "Failure to carry out this order in every detail will subject the functionary to immediate arrest." I went to Kameneva—she put her tail between her legs. She did hardly anything at all. [*Crossed out.*] I went to Dzerzhinsky. [...] All in all I pushed all the buttons I could. It's a pity that Lunacharsky isn't in Moscow, otherwise I'm sure the old man would already be free. It's all fear and trembling at the theater [*crossed out*]. They took the old man for no reason, he's got nothing to do with anything, I'm sure, he isn't guilty... After all, in politics, he's a child.

Moscow, September 11, 1919

Stanislavsky and Moskvin were released the same day at 6:00 p.m. [...]

Then I went to the Proletkul't—stayed there about an hour and then headed back to the TEO Narkompros—to a meeting of the Tsentroteatr, the new Central Theatrical Office in which I function as a representative of the Proletkul't with a right to a consultative voice.

The meeting began at half past three. [...] The principal question of today's meeting was the merger of TEO and Tsentroteater. Some piquant things were explained to me there. (1) It seems via the merger the Cent. Comm. of Proletkul't has assigned a few million to Tairov—the Kamerny Theater! Why the Kamerny Theater? What's that got to do with the Proletkul't? Then three and a half million for the former Zimin's Opera.[38] But the worker–peasant theaters and clubs are assigned only two million in all, and then only through the proletkul't merger—nothing more is assigned from anywhere, even from the division for worker–peasant theaters of TEO—not a kopek. A piquant situation, I repeat! Tomorrow at the Cent. Comm. of the Proletkul't I'll kick up a fuss. They put through a merger of our proletkul't, and all kinds of scum, like Tairov, will get all kinds of possibilities to work at our expense; we'll be stripped bare—you can't do much with two million—when you consider the whole of Russia has to be covered. Ooh, that Tairov, he's a clever bastard! [...]

THE MOSCOW ART THEATER was in a parlous state. Stanislavsky's textile factory had been nationalized and his house confiscated, leaving him confused and desperate.

37 Feliks Édmundovich Dzerzhinsky (1877–1926), head of the Cheka from 1917; narkom for transport 1921 and chairman of the Supreme Council of National Economy 1924. Noted for his harshness in ordering mass executions and torture.

38 Zimin's Opera, a combination of the private troupe of the industrialist Sergey Zimin with the amateur Singers for Private Opera (1904), staged premieres of Russian and European works in settings by painters from the World of Art; nationalized in 1917, it was finally closed in 1924.

The only new production he attempted was of Lord Byron's poetic drama *Cain*, with the somewhat misguided idea that it was relevant to current conditions. It ran for nine performances. Meyerhold, who had personal affection for Stanislavsky but devoutly wished to see the Moscow Art Theater eradicated, published an article attempting to distinguish the creativity of one from the obsolescence of the other.

Vsevolod Meyerhold and Valery Bebutov, "Stanislavsky's isolation," *Vestnik teatra* (May 1, 1921).

In the motley bazaar of theatrical life, head and shoulders above all the rest, one may distinguish the figure of Stanislavsky, wandering alone. He is forced to be isolated as an artist, for that is what Nemirovich-Danchenko makes of him. [...] Just thinking about it—what a tragedy! We are on the brink of a tragic event. A little bit more, and (oh horrors!) we will lose our favorite from the stage... It will happen if Stanislavsky doesn't reject the art foisted on him by the literary-bourgeois management of the Art Theater and return to himself—in fact to the genius of pure theatricality. [...]

[He is a] Gaul by nature, a lover of ludic situations and jokes natural to the theater. [He must recall his particular gifts: he possesses] a healthy and agile body, a voice of enormous range, a face ready to express mimicry without makeup, an eye of a color, noted by Lensky,[39] as the most useful for the stage. [Stanislavsky ought to recognize the fact that he is] a man born for a theater of exaggerated parody and tragic distinction.

Meyerhold

Named on September 16, 1920, director of the TEO, replacing Kameneva, Meyerhold moved to become the most important person in Russian theatrical life. At that time he launched the password of "Theatrical October" and joined the Bolshevik Party. For him, as for the theorists of the Proletkul't, the Revolution had so far taken place only in the social and economic sphere; now it must be carried out in the artistic sphere, especially in the theater. He made TEO's organ *Vestnik teatra* the voice of Theatrical October, organized the Studio of Communist Drama (Mastkomdram), and, co-opting the company of the defunct "Free" Theater, founded his own troupe with the unadorned name RSFSR 1.

Aleksandr Gladkov, "Meyerhold's renown," *Vospominaniya i razmyshleniya* [Reminiscences and reflections], in *Meyerkhol'd* (Moscow: Soyuz teatral'nykh deyateley, 1990), 2:14–16. Aleksandr Konstantinovich Gladkov (1913–76) spent five years in Meyerhold's studio; he was jailed for stealing books from the Lenin Library. On his release in 1942, his play *Long, Long Ago* was performed

---

39 Aleksandr Pavlovich Lensky (actually Verviziotti, 1847–1908), actor, director, leading man at the Maly Theater 1876–1908, a proponent of Ibsen and master of makeup.

successfully; he served as a war correspondent for the TASS news agency and left memoirs of Pasternak and Meyerhold.

Only contemporaries of Meyerhold's *renown* can conceive its dimensions.

In Moscow of the 1920s his name was constantly repeated. It flashed from the posters, from newspaper kiosks, from almost every page of the theatrical press, from the caricatures and cartoons of *Krokodil, Semkhach,* and *Chudak*;[40] it resounded in the debates at the House of the Press, from the academic rostrums of GAKhN,[41] in the hostels of *rabfak* [worker's schools] and *vuz* [institutions of higher learning], the theaters of parody and miniatures, in the monologues of Smirnov-Sokolsky,[42] the lyrics of Gromov and Milich,[43] the witticisms of Mendelevich and Polevoy-Mansfel'd.[44] It was the thing to confer all sorts of honorary titles on him: he was dubbed an honorary member of the Red Army (there is a photo of him in a Red Army uniform), an honorary member of the Red Navy, an honorary miner, and so on. Young Nâzim Hikmet,[45] who was studying in those years in Moscow at the University for Workers of the East, dedicated his first poem to him; it was called "All hail to Meyerhold!" [...] The poet Vasily Kamensky,[46] author of the poem "Sten'ka Razin," popular in those years, [...] wrote, "Stride twenty years ahead, Meyerhold. You are an athlete of reinforced concrete—the Edison of trillions of volts!" And the noisy pupils of the famous FON[47] of Moscow University, when greeting Meyerhold, created a scandal with the chorus, "Stepping leftward we march ever forward, forward! Meyerhold, Meyerhold is our comrade! Comrade Meyerhold!" One theater journal once advertised a subscription for art workers to build two airplanes: "Ermolova"[48] and "Meyerhold." This was during the heyday of Meyerhold's activity and while Ermolova was still alive.

40 *Krokodil* (*The Crocodile*) and *Chudak* (*The Crackpot*) were humor magazines founded by Mikhail Kol'tsov (1922 and 1924, respectively).

41 Gosudarstvennaya Akademiya khudozhestvennykh nauk (State Academy of Artistic Sciences). Under the leadership of the philosopher Gustav Shpet in the 1920s, it tried to maintain a wholly aesthetic approach but came increasingly under party control in 1929. Shpet was removed and executed 1937.

42 Nikolay Pavlovich Smirnov-Sokolsky (actually Smirnov, 1898–1962), cabaret performer, who debunked hypocrisy and bureaucracy in a black velvet jacket, red cummerbund, and white jabot.

43 Arkady Mikhaylovich (Moiseevich) Gromov (1896–1973) and Vladimir Samoylovich Milich (?–1965), a satirical duet, began in Odessa and became famous throughout Russia in the early 1920s for their cross-talking clown act, promoting propaganda.

44 Aleksandr Abramovich Mendelevich (1896–1958), variety artist from 1920 at Moscow and Leningrad music halls, both in sketches and as a solo raconteur. Evgeny Avgustovich Polevoy-Mansfel'd (1869–1930?), short story writer who used his comic fiction for agitprop at clubs and soldiers' smokers 1918–21.

45 Nâzim Hikmet Ran (actually Mehmet Nazim, 1902–63), Turkish poet and "romantic communist" who traveled to Georgia and Moscow 1921–22 and became influenced by Mayakovsky and Meyerhold; imprisoned in Turkey 1938, he escaped to Russia 1951 and settled there briefly before taking Polish citizenship.

46 Vasily Vasil'evich Kamensky (1884–1961), futurist poet and playwright; one of the first Russian aviators.

47 Fakul'tet obshchestvennykh nauk (Faculty of Social Sciences); although the one at Moscow University was packed with Communists, it and all the others had been liquidated by late 1924.

48 Mariya Nikolaevna Ermolova (1853–1928), grande dame of the Russian theater, at the Maly

Meyerhold's name was literally known to all, even among those who never went to his theater. For philistines it was almost as scary as the word "credentials" for Glupich-kin's neighbors.[49] In the verbal landscape of Moscow of the 1920s it was as obligatorily present as the current locutions: "hands off...," "in the face of...," "our reply..." Only Mayakovsky's name could compete with it, and even if they had not been friends and collaborators in art, all the same ears and eyes put them side by side in a myriad of all possible contexts. [...]

In the stenographic record of a debate on *Dawns* (late 1920) a conscientious pencil of the stenographer notes in brackets: "Unbelievable shouting." Then "Terrific yell-ing." There is even a gap in the text marked by ellipses and again the note "The racket here is such that you can't make out a thing—everyone is howling, almost came to blows"... What raised such a storm? At bottom a mere procedural question about extending the time allowed for debate to an opponent of Meyerhold at that time, A. Ya. Tairov. Yet another characteristic stroke. Tairov said that if there was anything of beauty about Meyerhold, it was his fez (in those years V. É. wore a bright red fez). Meyerhold shouted to that, "I suppose you would prefer a white one?!"... At the de-bate partisans of the *Dawns* production walked along the streets in orderly ranks with placards congratulating Meyerhold.

[...] The very word "Meyerhold" during his lifetime meant more than the name of a single individual, although this individual actually existed, ate, drank, slept, wore a jacket, rehearsed in his uncomfortable theater, took bows from the stage, took part in debates.

This word brought some together into groups and estranged others. It was a battle flag, a password, that did not need even nominal explanation in commentaries, the cause for disputes, the target of parody and jokes and not one but several chapters in the history of the Russian theater. [...]

Vsevolod Meyerhold, speech to a meeting of coworkers of the TEO, October 11, 1920. *STDM 17–21*, 67–68.

What was the chief sin of the Theater Section, the chief flaw in its structure? You had a whole series of subsections, which were carrying on, perhaps, good and reasonably intense work, but these sections were carrying on their work in the rooms in which they were located; they were too little concerned with the coordination of their work with the work of those sections that were located near them. Everything went on "every which way," and there was no pivot in the Theater Section around which all this work revolved. That is the basic flaw in the TEO structure.

The theoretical part, i.e., that part of the theatrical work that leads from the time

---

Theater, Moscow, from 1866. Regarded as a voice for progress, she was admired by Lenin, who attended her fifty-year jubilee 1920.

49 In Nikolay Érdman's satire *Credentials* (*Mandat*, 1925), staged by Meyerhold, the feckless hero Glupichkin is feared and envied by his neighbors because he has led them to believe, erroneously, that he has a Communist party card.

of the Academy of Art so desired by Com. Lunacharsky, was in the academic plan insufficiently academic, in its practical institutions insufficiently practical. [. . .]

The TEO had no Central Governing Board of Theater. We must unify the theatrical affairs of the Republic, but where are we to find the levers for such a unification? The central governing body of theater is the section that ought to be the moving spring. [. . .]

MEYERHOLD converted the old Sohn Opera House on Triumphal Square into the "Free" Theater and then into the RSFSR 1 Theater, retaining only the young members of the former troupe. His company included such fresh talents as Mariya Babanova, Igor Il'insky, and Ol'ga Demidova. The repertoire proposed was ambitious, including *Hamlet* and a comedy of Aristophanes, to be improved by improvisation. In the event, only two of the plays listed were realized.

> Boris Alpers, *Teatr sotsial'noy maski* [The theater of the social mask] (Moscow: OGIZ-GIKhL,1931), 22–24. Boris Vladimirovich Alpers (1894–1974) served as secretary at Meyerhold's studio 1913–15; as artistic director of the Ligovsky People's, New Drama, and Proletkul't theaters in Petrograd 1921–24; from 1922, as first chairman of Repertkom in charge of state theaters; and as chief dramaturg at the Moscow Theater of Revolution 1924–27. He became a professor at GITIS and a theater historian.

It was an ordinary assembly hall, with patches of moisture on the walls and a damp and hazy atmosphere. There were no ticket collectors at the doors of the theater, [which] stood wide open, and in the winter, snowstorms would sometimes invade the lobby and the theater's corridors and make the audiences turn up their overcoat collars . . . The railings had been stripped off the boxes. The seats and benches for the audience had been greatly knocked about and were no longer arranged in rows. You could crack nuts or smoke shag tobacco in the lobby. Red Army units and groups of young workers made up the new audiences. They were assigned their tickets by allotments and filled the theater with noise and excitement.

THE RSFSR THEATER opened on November 7, 1920; Meyerhold chose a Belgian author, dramatizing Émile Verhaeren's poetic drama *Les Aubes* [*Dawns*] to be played in the style of the agitational theater, with a cubist set by Vladimir Dmitriev. It described a social revolution in a medieval Flemish city and was codirected and coadapted with Valery Bebutov. On May Day 1921 Meyerhold revived *Mystery Bouffe* in a revised and expanded version that made it more topical and more animated.

> Vsevolod Meyerhold, "On the production of *Dawns* at the RSFSR 1, 1920," *Stat'i, pis'ma, rechi, besedy* [Articles, letters, speeches, talks] (Moscow: Iskusstvo, 1968), 2:13–14.

Humanity has reached a phase when all relationships and concepts are changing. If, prior to 1917, we treated a work of literature with a certain degree of care and caution, nowadays we are no longer fetishists, we do not kneel down and exclaim in prayer, "Shakespeare! Verhaeren!..."

The auditorium has changed to such a degree that we are forced to reconstruct our relation to it.

A different audience, which will not put up with much now—when every spectator imagines that he is a model of Soviet Russia...

Now we stand on guard for the interests not of the author but of the spectator.

In the interests of the auditorium, the audience acquires decisive significance.

But, we are asked, why didn't you create a new drama yourself, instead of busying yourself with mutilating the classics?

Here is why:

From every work we first extract the scenario, sometimes preserving its individual passages, but isn't that how those who acquired such posthumous respect behaved in their lifetimes? Isn't that how Sophocles, Shakespeare, Schiller, Tirso de Molina, Pushkin behaved?...

Or were they overcome with awestruck veneration for dead canons?

Mestechkin, *V teatre i v tsirke*, 20–21.

A characteristic of this production was the rejection of the usual box set so as to bring the action and performers closer to the spectator. The actors who took part wore neither makeup nor wigs. The scenery was built from sketches by the designer V. V. Dmitriev.[50] It was "abstract" and in no way resembled ordinary stage settings.

The orchestra pit was open during the time of the action, and there, as in the ancient theater, a distinctive chorus was located. From that spot the performance was commented on, individual remarks were uttered. It was like a living crowd taking part in the performance, since the orchestra pit was connected to the stage by stairs. The slogans of the people's leader Hérénien, a role played by A. Zakushnyak[51] with great nervosity and temperament in a special manner that owed nothing to the old theater, were caught up by the performers on the steps and "in the orchestra." The prophet was played by A. Mgebrov. Standing on a cube, he recited his monologues in a frenzy with eyes ablaze.

Opening night was set for November 7, 1920. This was a period of memorable events in the life of our country. The last remnants of the White Guard had been wiped out, so the people's struggle for Oppidomagne [the city in the play] was relevant to the

---

50 Vladimir Vladimirovich Dmitriev (1900–1948) had been a student in Meyerhold's courses; his designs for *Dawns* had begun as a class project. He left Meyerhold to work for the MAT and the Vakhtangov in a more realistic mode. He introduced the birches into *Three Sisters* (1940).

51 Aleksandr Yakovlevich Zakushnyak (1879–1930) had a long history with Meyerhold, having acted in his Fellowship Society for New Drama and at the Vera Komissarzhevskaya Theater before the Revolution.

spectator. The performance was exciting for its revolutionary subject; it spontaneously resonated with what the country was going through in those years.

I happened to play the role of the messenger. Appearing onstage, the messenger gives information about how the battle for Oppidomagne is going. Whenever anything important happened in our land, the performance would be interrupted, and a periodic report would be delivered. I remember the profound impression made by the announcement that the valiant Red Army had captured Perekop.[52] Naturally, the auditorium reacted tempestuously to the joyous news. After this the action would turn back to the plot of Verhaeren's play.

We would get the news directly from ROSTA [Russian Telegraph Agency]. What's more, sometimes for want of transport, the bulletin would be brought by bicycle.

Young people attended the revolutionary performances of *Dawns* with immense enthusiasm. The shows ended with patriotic mass meetings, and the "Internationale" which concluded the performance was sung not only onstage but in the auditorium as well. Not by accident have I called *Dawns* a revolutionary performance: [...] the staging, as I've said, was extremely stylized, but to some degree, it symbolized the heroism and dynamics of our life.

After the show, which ended comparatively early, Meyerhold gave most interesting lessons in biomechanics[53] in the lobby of the theater.

Shklovsky, *Khod konya*, 66–67.

Verhaeren has written a bad play. The revolutionary theater is being created in haste, and hence the play has been hastily accepted as revolutionary. The text has been altered. There is talk on the stage ... about the regime of the Soviets. The action has been made contemporary, although I cannot say where an Imperialistic War is going on with spears and shields. In the middle of the second act, it seems, a messenger comes on and reads a dispatch about the losses of the Red Army at Perekop ... But because the action has been made contemporary, the dispatch is torn out of all context, and the artistic effect it was supposed to produce is not achieved.

[...] Of the three groups, which, according to the director's ideas, have to act in this diversion—the actors on the stage, the proletarian culture movement among the musicians, and the public in the orchestra seats—the public has downed tools. It is much livelier at any other meeting than it is at this one, in its costumes and "contre-relief" cavalry trousers.[54]

---

52 A turning point in the Civil War, when, in 1920, the Red Army seized and razed the town of Perekop in the isthmus connecting the Crimea and the Ukraine, and put to flight General Vrangel's White Army.

53 See chapter 3.

54 *Contre-relief* was Tatlin's term for a type of sculpture made of natural materials and designed to be hung. Contre-relief trousers would appear to be sewn from materials other than those usually employed by tailors.

Natal'ya Krupskaya, "The production of Verhaeren's *Dawns*," *Pravda* (November 10, 1920). Nadezhda Konstantinovna Krupskaya (1869–1930) was Lenin's wife.

Instead of "the beggars" and the "oppressed," substitute "the proletariat"; instead of "the government," "the bourgeoisie"; instead of "hostile troops," "imperialistic troops." The "Regime of the Soviets," the "Social Revolution," and other such things appeared on the stage. And a wonderful legend is turned into a trivial farce, while all the charm of *Dawns* disappears. The action takes place outside of time and space; it deals with the followers of Hérénien, who concludes a compact with the government and simply acts with insufficient prudence. In a Russian environment, the environment of the class struggle, Hérénien is a traitor, a traitor who has swallowed the bait of flattery. A hero outside of time and space may be forgiven, but to have the Russian proletariat act like Shakespeare's crowds—whom any conceited fool can lead wherever he wants—is an insult.

Telegram from Vsevolod Meyerhold to Lenin, December 27, 1920, *Stat'i, pis'ma, rechi, besedy*, 2:23.

Dear Leader!

The company of the RFSFR Theater no. 1, the theater's Artistic Council, and the whole technical and service staff express the warmest desire to see you at the new variant of the production of *Dawns* on December 28.

Knowing how busy you are, the company asks you, if you cannot be there on December 28, to attend one of the next performances of *Dawns*. [...]

———————————

MAYAKOVSKY was persuaded to endorse a Moscow production of *Mystery Bouffe*; he revised the text to make it more topical, adding a new prologue to twit the Art Theater and its admirers. The episode in Hell was expanded to provide opportunity for clowning. Journalists hostile to Meyerhold called for a cessation owing to the production's "enormous costs" and "harmful content," but Mayakovsky won over members of the Central and City committees and the Workers and Peasant Inspection by his own reading of the play. After what he referred to as "interminable rehearsals" in the "unheated" RSFSR 1 Theater, the revised play opened on October 1920.

Vladimir Mayakovsky, prologue to the second version of *Mystery Bouffe*, 1921, in *Mayakovsky: Plays*, ed. and trans. Guy Daniels (Evanston, Ill.: Northwestern University Press, 1995), 45–47. © 1968 by Washington Square Press, Inc. Northwestern University Press edition published 1995 by arrangement with Josiane Rodriguez-Daniels.

Spoken by one of THE UNCLEAN.
In just a minute
we'll present to your view

our *Mystery Bouffe.*
But first I must say a few words.
This play
Is something new.
Without help, nobody has yet succeeded
in jumping higher than his head.
Likewise, a new play must be preceded
by a prologue, or else it's dead.
First, let me ask you:
Why is this playhouse such a mess?
To right-thinking people
it's a scandal, no less!
But then what makes you go to see a show?
You do it for pleasure—
isn't that so?
But is the pleasure really so great, after all,
if you're looking just at the stage?
The stage, you know,
is only one-third of the hall.
Therefore,
as an interesting show,
if things are set up properly,
your pleasure is multiplied by three.
But if the play isn't interesting,
then you're wasting your time
looking at even one-third of what's happening.
For other theatrical companies
the spectacle doesn't matter:
for them
the stage
is a keyhole without a key.
"Just sit there quietly," they say to you,
"either straight or sideways,
and look at a slice of other folks' lives."
You look—and what do you see?
Uncle Vanya
and Auntie Manya
parked on a sofa as they chatter.
But we don't care
about uncles and aunts:
you can find them at home—or anywhere!
We, too, will show you life that's real—
very!

But life transformed by the theater into a spectacle most extraordinary!

In the future, all persons performing, presenting, reading, or publishing *Mystery Bouffe* should change the content, making it contemporary, immediate, up to the minute.

—*Mayakovsky.*

Mystery Bouffe through the eyes of spectators of the 1920s. Answers to questionnaires, preserved at the Bakhrushin Theater Museum. *Teatr* 1 (1990), 81–87.

[Some of the negative answers were extremely curt: "These are all Jewish tricks." "Shame on the author." "Pity the wretched actors." "Coarse, vulgar, insipid."]

May 3, 1921. Male. Adult. Miner. First-grade education. Goes to theater once a month. Liked it—a fighting play. I liked the acting, but not all of it. Most of all, I liked the menshevik.[55] Too realistic for the general tone, or so it seemed from the gallery. Liked the costumes. Lighting was disgusting. Staging should be in the open air, in the street. The play is revolutionary, but the theater is shabby, the theater needs to be redecorated.

May 7, 1921. Female. 18 years old. Proletarian. Second-grade education, dramatic workshop. Goes to the RSFSR every 2 weeks. Every time to *Mystery Bouffe,* to the rest seldom. Liked the play a lot. It's true to life. It has enormous meaning in the sense of agitation. Not much cohesion to the acting, i.e., one of the actor-workers should be playing one of the leading roles.

Careless attitude of some of the actors to the stage. Remarkable costumes. Very good staging and scenery. Wonderfully beautiful and appropriate lighting. No better built actor could be desired. The intermissions are boring, disgusting, like the III category. It's a great step forward. New wine, but new bottles [i.e., theaters] are needed. I liked the performance a lot, but not the theater, a barracks or [indecipherable].

Comrade comedians[56] of the RFSRF

I pay close attention to your theater and waited impatiently for these productions. I'm from the provinces myself...I came to Moscow to study, and your theater interested me very much. That's why I can't limit myself to a few phrases and want to say something more to you. I will speak about each act in detail. Act I is good. Lots of action. Although, in my opinion, it's not good enough that the workers are plastered, they have little power and fervor. After all, can people who have gone through heaven, hell, unafraid of the flood, be so inert? However, the lamplighter and the blacksmith are good...The female workers are more like boarding-school girls than female workers. Act II. Hell isn't fit for the devil either. Lazarenko[57] is an even greater rebuke to the clumsiness and fatness of your devils. Not one decent devil, except for the one who sits

55 Igor' Vladimirovich Il'insky (1901–87), actor, director, one of Meyerhold's most reliable interpreters in comic roles; transferred to the Maly Theater 1938.

56 At the RSFSR 1 Theater, the actors were called "comedians."

57 Vitaly Efimovich Lazarenko (1890–1939) was an acrobatic circus clown active in the agitbrigades for whom Mayakovsky wrote routines; he was invited by Meyerhold to play the Devil in the revised *Mystery Bouffe.*

alone on the stairs. On the other hand, heaven is a pleasure [...] one shortcoming: you dissipated all of Mayakovsky's dynamic, licked the play too smooth ... One doesn't feel the triumph of the workers when they overcome. However, the audience is far from wrong to call out V. É. Meyerhold or Mayakovsky; one way or another, I grant you the lion's share of the glory and success. Indeed, you solidly fought for *Dawns*, and to be perfectly frank, it was very unsuccessful. Comrades, I want very much to speak of your many faults and qualities, but there's no more room. I will impatiently await the debate,[58] and now, until we meet again soon. I will see you all again at the next performance. All hail the free comedians!

May 12, 1921. Male. Adult. Worker-intellectual. Finished middle school, self-educated, higher technical courses. After October, went to theater every day to 1918, now once a month. Really enjoy the play—it's life itself, although I don't understand futurism. Yes, I liked the acting, although I didn't understand it all, for the acoustics are bad. I'm on the side of realism, but I think for *Mystery* the scenery is unique. The staging is splendid. Hurrah, Mayakovsky. I consider your production a great achievement.

June 11, 1921. Male. Twenty-two years old. Peasant. Attended teacher's college. Go to theater nearly once a week. I liked it because it clearly expresses the era—that's number one. Number two—it dared in concept to be independent, novel, and idiosyncratic in form. I liked the acting because there's no clichés, you feel the soul, work and search for new forms and means to display, and recreated experience are apparent. The makeup is good, characteristic, clear, understated. Same for the costumes. The staging and scenery are splendid, gripping and heroic. I like the simplicity of the theater building. I am pleased by the theater and the performance.

Tairov and the Kamerny Theater

From the time he founded the Kamerny (Chamber) Theater in 1914, the meticulous and refined Tairov rejected, as did Meyerhold, "psychologism" and naturalism. In his book *Notes of a Director* (1921), he opposed "the truth of art" to Stanislavsky's "truth of life." With Meyerhold, Evreinov, Komissarzhevsky, and Vakhtangov, he was a proponent and exponent of "theatrical theater." At no time should the spectator forget that he is in the theater. However, Tairov's idea of theater was grounded on the virtuosity of the actor, a "synthetic performer" capable of playing every genre from high tragedy to musical comedy and harlequinade. Tairov lay far more emphasis on declamation and musical utterance than did Meyerhold. It was no coincidence that his adaptation of *Princess Brambilla* was advertised as "a capriccio on E. T. A. Hoffmann by the Kamerny Theater." Tairov's repertoire was, on principle, highly eclectic and drawn in large part from the Western theater. In no doctrinaire way was it "revolutionary," for Tairov believed that propaganda

58 This was a period when public debates and discussions of new plays were regular events.

theater in the wake of a revolution was like "mustard when a meal is over." This would prove to be a tough bone of contention.

Abram Éfros, *Kamerny Teatr i ego Khudozhniki, 1914–1934. Al'bom* [The Chamber Theater and its designers, 1914–1934: Album] (Moscow: VTO, 1934), vii–ix.

We felt he was one of us [critics, painters, and designers]. He was a comrade who had done a life's work. We could not cross the threshold of his laboratory, without at the same time sensing that the novelty of his productions was created not by him alone but by us as well. We were his spectators as much as his accomplices. We not only watched and rejoiced but also hastened to help him, correct him, and even quarrel with him. We lived by his labors. This is an historical fact. The theatrical generation 1914–24 measured its stature by the Kamerny Theater. [...]

Of all the stars of young theaters that arose on the eve of war and revolution, he alone was fanatical, consistent, and even inimitable. But his narrowness was fertile, his inimitability salvational. His foes said that Tairov was obstinate rather than inspired. His friends rejoiced at Tairov's steadfastness and gave it the appropriate name of principle. Tairov did not need individual discoveries or partial changes. [...]

Like the rest, he counted on a small circle of an elite audience. He entered, as they did, the ranks of the theatrical opposition. [...]

In 1920 the Kamerny Theater was named an academic theater, lifting it above the threat of abolition. This gave Tairov the confidence to attack Meyerhold's *Dawns* and the whole Theatrical October movement (see earlier). He published his *Notes of a Director* in 1921, laying out his aesthetic program of the synthetic unity of the arts and calling for the "Theatricalization of the Theater." Meyerhold, always spoiling for a fight, accused Tairov of shallow aestheticism.

Vsevolod Meyerhold on Tairov, *Teatral'naya Moskva* [Theatrical Moscow] 33 (1920), 14. *Stat'i, pis'ma, rechi, besedy*, 2:37–43.

Not until the publication of *Notes of a Director* had it been so clear to me that the Kamerny Theater is an *amateur* theater.

Only an amateur who wants to become an acrobat is able to achieve the techniques of the balletic art in his acting. But where in an acrobat, juggler, boxer, or fencer could you come up with such affected poses (against which Fokine[59] fought long enough in ballet), such tiresome flitting about, and those wrists tracing circles and ellipses along planes that are invisible but dreamed up by these "Kamerniks" in their "atmosphere," and these leaps out of the wings, and the skipping around the stage of these ever elegant,

---

59 Mikhail Mikhaylovich Fokin[e] (1880–1942), ballet dancer and choreographer; at the Maria Theater from 1898, soloist with Diaghilev's Ballets Russes; between 1921 and his death, he lived in Europe and the United States, never returning to Russia.

no matter what, dandies, and this prancing in the style of Louis XIV, even when it would have seemed the crudest acting techniques of American silent-film comedians would have been more appropriate.

Poor are the actors to whom Tairov "dedicates my book" ("to my comrades-in-arms and students, to their tempestuous youth, their ardent heart, their steadfast desire for theatrical mastery"). What ignorance they are mired in at every step under such a leader who tries to correct Craig[60] (and the designer, the actor, and the stage director), a matter that Tairov is powerless to comprehend. Look, in 1921, Tairov repeats on every page much of what was written by leaders of the theatrical revolution in Russia and the West from 1905 to 1917, and, not having figured it out even now, he inexcusably distorts much of it. [...]

However, we think the most ghastly thing is what Tairov posits in his chapter on the spectator. If one can escape from a technical impasse by replacing the designer Ékster with the designers Vesnin[61] or Yakulov, by making a clean break with the contemporary, by asserting the conviction that theatrical art can manage even without the spectator, that the spectator appears to be unnecessary as an incentive for the actor, that there's no reason to abolish the footlights, etc., etc., Tairov has embarked on a more dangerous path. [...]

The most up-to-date new spectator (I mean the proletariat), the most capable in my opinion of freeing itself from the hypnosis of illusionism, and specifically under those conditions that it must (and I am sure will) know that what it's watching is acting, will approach that acting consciously, for through acting it wants to express itself as coactive and *creating a new essence*, since for a living being (as for a new human being reborn in communism), every kind of theatrical essence is only an occasional pretext to proclaim in the spotlight's excitement the *joy of a new everyday life*.

> Anatoly Lunacharsky to Vsevolod Meyerhold, Moscow, 1920–21. Meyerhold, *Perepiska* [Correspondence] (Moscow: Iskusstvo, 1976), 211.

1. In my opinion, Tairov has to be brought into the fold of the TEO.

2. To outflank him, by *me* and *you* going to him at his theater and discussing with the collective the advantages of going into government work for the TEO.

> Samuil Margolin, "The contradictions of the Kamerny Theater," *Teatral'noe Obozrenie* 6 (1921), 5–6. Samuil Akimovich Margolin (1893–1953), theater critic and director, gave guest lectures at the MAT Third Studio in 1921.

---

60 Edward Gordon Craig (1872–1966), English director and designer who planned the MAT *Hamlet* 1909–12. His visionary book *On the Art of the Theatre* had been translated into Russian before the Revolution.

61 Aleksandr Aleksandrovich Vesnin (1883–1959), designer, a colleague of Vladimir Tatlin and Lyubov' Popova, who designed agitprop decorations for Moscow and Petrograd 1918–20; best known for his scenic constructions at the Kamerny Theater.

Tairov claims that even in 1917–18, he set out "finally on my path to the theater of *emotionally saturated forms*," a theater he describes as the "theater of Neo-Realism." But where on earth is this *saturated emotion* on the stage of the Kamerny Theater?

The Kamerny Theater never was and never can be an emotional theater, for *in its very essence* it is the *polar opposite of emotionality*, whenever it submits to the theatrical laws of Tairov about the actor's inner technique. And if the show *Princess Brambilla*[62] set the blood racing at the Kamerny Theater, that is because in that production Tairov himself retreated, perhaps unconsciously, but retreated from those canons that the Kamerny Theater always obeys. If isolated moments in the characterizations of Koonen and Tseretelli move us, this is also due to "retreating from the canons." [...]

Can one really conjure up emotion from *magical wonderlands* and suppose that there are other emotions besides those of our boring world, besides anger and entreaty, hope and expectation, rapture and sorrow, etc., etc.? You can invent anything you like, of course, and should invent or rather fantasize, for the gist of theatrical art lies in the fantastical. But emotions are not invented, not conjured up out of the void. Emotions come from what exists, emotions are always of the earth and the earth is their sole element. [...]

No, the internal technique of the actor, to use Meyerhold's words, is the very weakest link in *Notes of a Director* and the Kamerny Theater, where there is only the actor's external technique [...]

Radical Experiment and Its Opponents

Lenin reproached the Proletkul't's scorn for the legacy of the past and condemned it in a letter of the Central Committee, dated December 1, 1920.

> Central Committee of the Russian Communist Party (Bol'sheviks), "On the Proletkul'ts," *Pravda* (December 1, 1920). *STDM 17–21, 23–24.*

The Proletkul't arose before the October Revolution. It was proclaimed an "independent" worker's organization, independent of the Ministry of People's Enlightenment at the time of Kerensky. The October Revolution changed the perspective. Proletkul'ts continued to remain "independent," but now this was "independence" from the Soviet authorities. Thanks to this and a number of other reasons, the proletkul'ts teem with elements socially alien to us, petty bourgeois elements that sometimes seize the leadership of the proletkul'ts into their own hands. Futurists, decadents, partisans of an idealistic philosophy hostile to Marxism, and, finally, simply losers, journalists, and philosophers risen from the ranks of the bourgeoisie have somehow gotten mixed up in all the operations of the proletkul'ts. Under cover of "proletarian culture," they have offered the workers bourgeois views in philosophy (*machism*). And in the realm

---

62 Subtitled a "capriccio," Tairov's production of *Princess Brambilla*, based on E. T. A. Hoffmann's novella, opened at the Kamerny May 4, 1920, with sets by Georgy Yakulov and music by Henri Forterre.

of art they have inculcated the workers with absurd, perverse views (*futurism*) [...]

The CP not only has no desire to shackle the initiative of the workers' intelligentsia in the realm of artistic creativity; on the contrary, the CP wants to create a more wholesome, normal organization for it and give it the possibility to be fruitfully reflected in every aspect of artistic creativity. The CP is fully aware that now that the war is over, interest in issues of artistic creativity and proletarian culture in the ranks of the workers will keep growing. The CP values and respects the striving of progressive workers to put on the agenda questions of the individual's richer spiritual development, etc. The Party will do all it can so that this matter will actually fall into the hands of the workers' intelligentsia, so that the workers' government will give the workers' intelligentsia whatever it needs.

> Sergey Radlov, "For the two hundred and first and last time about the crisis in the theater" (1921), in *Desyat' let v teatre* [Ten years in the theater] (Leningrad: Priboy, 1929), 53–60. Sergey Érnestovich Radlov (1892–1958), actor and director, developed the notion of "synthetic democracy," encouraging improvisation and popular entertainment; he founded the Theater of Artistic Popular Comedy (1920–22) and, at his Theater-Studio (1935–38), was reputed to be the best Russian director of Shakespeare. The last phase of his career unfolded in Latvia.

The repertoire of the contemporary Russian theaters (the best ones, of course): *Wilhelm Tell, Uncle Vanya, King Lear, Hedda Gabler, Antigone, Jealousy* [M. Artsybashev], *The Imaginary Invalid, Not a Farthing, Then a Whole Shilling, Oedipus the King, Vanyushin's Children, The Death of Tintagiles, The Sunken Bell, The Reds and the Whites.* If the theater is especially advanced, one might perhaps add Mayakovsky's *Mystery Bouffe,* Aeschylus's *Oresteia,* Kuzmin's *Eudoxia,* or Aleksey Remizov's *Judas Prince of Iscariot.*[63] [...]

Yes, of course, it's a distinguished repertoire, a treasury of world genius, the cherished ideals of thinking and suffering humanity, colossi and titans of philosophic thought, a powerful weapon of cultural–educational influence on the masses... yes, yes, of course, you're absolutely right, and there probably ought to be such auditoriums in which literate actors will loudly recite the poetry of Sophocles, Shakespeare, Pushkin (as for the Hauptmanns, Ibsens, Maeterlincks, Chekhovs, I think the new man can do without them), but is there in this the living life of an actor's theatrical mastery?

Imagine this: would it ever strike you to ask Al'tman, Lebedev,[64] Chagall, for

63 Kuzmin's *Komediya o Evdokiy iz Geliopilya* (1908) was one of his "miracle plays" based on a saint's life; Remizov's *Tragediya o Yude printse iskarotskom* (1909) was a synthetic pastiche of a medieval mystery play.

64 Natan Isaevich Al'tman (1889–1970), designer, who provided cubo-futurist decorations for the First Revolution anniversary in 1918 and the grotesque makeups and distorted settings for Habima's *The Dybbuk* (1922); became chief designer for the Jewish State Theater 1924–28, later specializing in Shakespeare. Vladimir Vasil'evich Lebedev (1891–1967), painter, friend of Mayakovsky and Malevich, whose colorful and dynamic work was seen in costume designs and illustrations for children's books.

cultural–educational reasons, to paint pictures using the techniques of Leonardo da Vinci, Botticelli, Rembrandt, Goya, Styka,[65] Manet, Rubens, Cézanne, Repin, Tiepolo, etc., or would you be satisfied in expecting them to produce good pictures in their own styles?

—Of course, but the actor's art is an art of reproduction: he borrows inspirations from the author and transsubstantiates them into his images . . .

—Please stop: the actor is the same kind of artist, who has his own craft, his own technique, which must not and cannot change from day to day at the whim of this or that dead celebrity!

At every moment you throw the actor into the embrace of now Sophocles, now Calderón, now Chekhov, and think that he can acquire a kind of technique of his own, grope toward his own abilities, while Sophocles and Calderón and that very Chekhov each requires his own, special performance style utterly unlike that of his colleague in the repertoire. Eclecticism, that worst of malaises of our novice century, definitely obsolete in painting (the funeral of the World of Art[66]), continues to develop in the most disgraceful and barbaric form in the diseased body of our theater.

Rococo, baroque, Renaissance, pre-Raphaelite, classical, archaic, Hellenistic, Egyptian, Japanese, Assyrian–Babylonian style—to hell with the lot of them! What are we, after all, living artists or some sort of encyclopedia!

Comrade painters, improvise your pictures in the style of the twentieth century!

Composers, write music in the style of the World War and the Russian Revolution!

Poets, frame your verses in the style of 1921!

Actors, refuse to concoct mixed salads of Sophocles, Vermishev,[67] and Schiller, learn to write poems and create your own repertoire, calculated on your specific and unique actor's technique, a technique of 1921!

—What is this, a belated Futurist manifesto? A poor man's imitation of Marinetti?[68]

—Certainly not. There's no talk here of burning down museums or renouncing tradition.

To learn from the great predecessors in craftsmanship is every artist's obligation. One must not explore the dramatic technique of Shakespeare or Lope de Vega with self-reliance and naïvety. But the study of playwriting is only a means to create new and masterful plays. To turn the whole thing into a performance, to force the spectator to become engrossed in remote eras and think: so that's what it was like, is a boring, pedantic, and irrelevant activity.

---

65 Jan Styka (1859–1925), Polish painter of portraits and vast Christian allegories.

66 The World of Art (Mir Iskusstva), the St. Petersburg movement led by Sergey Diaghilev, Léon Bakst, and Aleksandr Benois 1898–1904, promoting art for art's sake and reevaluation of eighteenth-century art and Russian traditions; also the name of its magazine.

67 Aleksander Aleksandrovich Vermishev (1879–1919), revolutionary poet and journalist who fought the White Guard and was tortured to death by them.

68 Filippo Tommaso Marinetti (1876–1944), Italian theorist of futurism; in 1909 he published the Futurist Manifesto; in 1914 he visited Russia, where he was greeted cordially by the St. Petersburg avant-garde.

[...] The style of our age. Does it have a style? Forgive me but that is one of the dumbest questions frequently asked by not very observant people.

Imagine, artists, the storm and terror of our impetuous days and that glorious creativity of yours will create the style. It is already to be sensed immediately, doubly and disruptively.

Express trains, airplanes, the avalanches of people and carriages, silks and furs, concerts and vaudeville, electric lights and lamps and arc lamps, and lights and thousands of lights, and more silk, and silk slippers, and silk hats, telegrams and the radio, top hats, cigars and tennis rackets, shagreen bindings, mathematical treatises, apoplectic napes, self-satisfied smiles, brilliance, whirlwinds, flights, brocade, ballet, luxury and abundance—

over there, in the West,

and humdrum uninhabited rural towns, stern faces, Pompeian skeletons of dismantled houses, and wind, and grass between the stones, automobiles without car horns and car horns without automobiles, and sailor's bell-bottoms and leather jackets, and struggle, struggle and the will to struggle with all one's strength, and new, cruel and audacious children, and dry bread.

Old words, new voices:
Bread, love, blood... [from the book *Ships* by Anna Radlova[69]]

all this exists and all this awaits materialization in your hands, artists.

The theater demands sustenance that is living, stageworthy, and plentiful.

Modern plays—wretched bookish literature—are sapless straw.

The great elders—the Shakespeares and Sophocleses—are dry rusks.

Give us juicy, nourishing fodder—modern dramas *for the theater,* and not for the reader. Poets, cast off your comfortable poetic dressing gowns, get off your soft poetic sofas, come to us on the rough wooden platforms, learn the laws of our lives, understand that your raw material is the actor and only then the word, do not print, do not publish, do not jot down what you have created, but stage, stage tens and hundreds of your fleeting and living creations, let us have a breathing spell from all the great and not-so-great ancestors, teach the actors to perform new plays of nowadays—and no one will ever have to write another article about the past crisis in the theater.

IN DECEMBER 1921 *Comrade Khlestakov,* an update of Gogol's *Inspector General* by D. Smolin,[70] was put on in Moscow at Gostekomdram to almost universal disgust. The play had a short run, and the theater was soon closed.

---

69 Anna Dmitrievna Radlova (born Darmolatova, 1891–1949), poet and translator.
70 Dmitry Petrovich Smolin (1891–1955) had translated Aristophanes's *Lysistrata* for Nemirovich-Danchenko's Musical Studio at the MAT; he later became a screenwriter.

"Egor Kamenshchikov" [Yury Annenkov], *Comrade Khlestakov, Pravda* (December 1921), reprinted in Yury Annenkov, *Dnevnik moikh vstrech* (Moscow: Zakharov, 2001), 317–18.

Gostekomdram (State Theater of Communist Drama)...

There was an organization that dared to open a theater under this name.

There were audacious people who announced themselves to the nation not only as masters of state and communist drama but even—

Universal.

The city puts up with this audacity. But let's see what sort of audacity these Gostekomdram folks have.

On Saturday they showed their first work—*Comrade Khlestakov.*

The masters of communist and universal drama lagged behind the real masters.

A run-of-the-mill production about communism, obviously, consists for them wholly in the formula:

Steal what's there to be stolen!

And with clear consciences they have stolen from the directors Tairov, Granovsky, Komissarzhevsky, and Meyerhold.

The spectacle turned out to be indescribable:

Princess Brambilla, Mystery Bouffe, The Marriage of Figaro all at once and simultaneously in one scenic space.

"This collection of clichés, not to mention setting the teeth on edge, was done with a great lack of talent and a schoolroom awkwardness. Utterly disgusting."

SERGEY MIKHAYLOVICH ÉYZENSHTEYN (1898–1948), after training as an engineer and staging amateur theatricals in the Red Army, came to Moscow in 1920 and joined the Proletkul't. He was assigned to design *The Mexican,* an extravaganza based on Jack London, but chafed at the unimaginative approach of the director, Valentin Smyshlaev.

Sergey Eisenstein to his mother, March 14, 1921. From Andrey Nikitin, *Moskovsky debyut Sergeya Éyzenshteyna. Issledovanie i publikatsii* [Moscow debut of Sergey Eisenstein: Research and publications] (Moscow: Indergraf Servis, 1996), 128–30.

The first three ([March] 10, 11, and 13) rough previews of *The Mexican* have just taken place and ... so far it's had the greatest success with all the people I know who've seen it. There are still no reviews—for at present they're still considered rehearsals. The "ideologues" (idiotlogues) of our establishment are in seventh heaven, and no wonder—it's the first production of theirs that is not only not a failure but even a draw. On the directorial side the effects are colossal—everything I predicted a month ago when in complete disagreement with Smyshlaev about directing (in this realm he is the most perfect dilettante), he quite distanced himself from them. On the other hand, the costumes have won over everyone (the most malicious have hypercriticized only a few of them, true, for good reason, but some are already popular). For the scenery I share the laurels with Nikitin.[71] [...] before next month we'll "tone down" the scenery a bit so that it doesn't drown out the costumes. But [...] it's bright, clear, and theatrical, and the last is the most important thing. My share of the directorial composition and general staging (putting the boxing match at the finale onstage, and not offstage), the running of the interludes (adverts for the boxing match in the last act) in the last intermission, all the layouts and blocking were very successful. Smyshlaev's "internalized" work based on the Stanislavsky system is most harmful, it's incapable of understanding and appreciating all the splendor of the sharply etched rhythmic etching of the mises-en-scène and movements. The "cubist" head of one of the characters didn't work because of lack of time—half an hour before the performance, it had to be slapped together any old way. It was harshly criticized, but I'll redo it and am sure that victory will be mine. [...] In general the main thing I've managed to achieve is the theatricality of the spectacle so that even I enjoy watching it. [...]

Sergey Eisenstein, apologia for *The Mexican* (1921). Nikitin, *Moskovsky debyut*, 138–39.

1. In each act a crowd made up of individual groups (4 admirers, 4 for the first riot, 4 advertising clowns, 4 (Negro, gar [*sic*; in English in the original], cowboy and policeman), etc. etc., and a general crowd.

2. In all things the action is to be purely external. Spectacularity.

3. Don't outline the action of the characters, but bring out the character from the action [...]

4. Theatricality based on mathematical contraries and schematic oppositions: groups and movements. [...]

6. The gendarme is the only comic (with the look of a comic figure, but, in essence, "terrifying") figure against a tragic background (grotesque contrast) and the only tragic figure (Rivera in Act II) against a comic (also only in appearance) background (also in Act II). [...]

9. An emotional, lachrymose, "Nordic" (Strindberg!) "psychic" drama refashioned into a "Southern" outburst of passion—in great splotches of tragedy, and not in the finicky embroidery of a sentimental play of "broken hopes."

10. Rid Rivera of "wishy-washiness," of any neurasthenic and pathological elements, for he is unswerving in matters of action, his character should grip the spectators from the first act and not simply excite their curiosity. [...]

71 Leonid Aleksandrovich Nikitin (1896–1942), painter and designer; later worked for the Second Moscow Art Theater. He was arrested 1930 as a mystical anarchist and died in a labor camp in Krasnoyarsk.

Intrigues of Act III
(twenty-two persons in tiers)

Left

1. The romance "of the girl and the Negro."

2. The Jap makes advances to the old maid with the green sunshade (her excitement), then to the fat Negress.

3. The miner, the Negress, the American and Negroes (intoxication), then they drag in the Jap, who had flung himself at the "Salvation Army lassie" with the dark glasses.

4. The old Hindu is impassive.

Right

1. The Dandy makes advances to the "girl." Scandal—the pimp beats her. The elderly gentleman indignantly picks a fight with the pimp. His wife faints. They carry her out.

2. Fruitless efforts of love of the Negro dancer (from the café) for two girls swallowed up by Ward.

3. The romance of the coachman and the Negress past her prime.

Shouts [in English in the original] and whistles from the street urchins.

N. L'vov, review of *The Mexican*, *Vestnik Teatra* (April 5, 1921).

In essence, the play is created by the theatrical collective itself. Only the plot is taken from Jack London. All the rest, the characteristics of the figures, the text, whole scenes, is created by the studio itself. This play is constructed so that there is broad scope for interpolated scenes and improvised insertions. Therefore the studio has proceeded not from the play but from its own theatrical concept [...]

Bourgeois America is colorfully and wittily depicted, with its totalizator,[72] yellow press, raucous, pervasive, garish advertising. [...] Equally colorful was the crowd of spectators at the circus. Here the studio displayed unusual generosity: the spectator could not take in all the motley, variegated mass, living its own particular interesting life in every corner [...]

The studio rejected naturalism entirely. Act I [...] is written in verse, take places in a cubist set, with a nod to symbolism. Acts II and III in a circus are broad buffoonery, sometimes a fairground booth...

For the most part the director of *The Mexican*, V. S. Smyshlaev, has succeeded in this production in smoothing the way to realizing one of his basic ideas—the merging of the stage with the auditorium.[73]

In this regard, there is great significance to the interlude after Act II, when publicity men for the Kelby circus and reporters opposed to them address themselves directly to the auditorium and vie with one another in trying to get the spectator on their side.

---

72 A machine for registering bets and dividing the amount wagered among the winners.

73 In sending a copy of this review to his mother, Eisenstein pointed out that "2/3 if not 3/4" of the ideas in the production were his own and that the crowd scenes and the interludes were both designed and directed by him.

A fight in the very stalls, leaps into boxes, entrances from the audience conclusively eliminate the footlights. [...]

The play has no ending: an apotheosis, a symbolic procession of the Revolution was rehearsed but not staged. [...]

The Creation of GOSET

Under the tsars, the Jews had been deprived of civil rights, their advancement in the professions strictly limited. The theater offered one road to advancement, but theater in Yiddish was prohibited. The Revolution, many of whose leaders had Jewish antecedents, offered fresh opportunities. Aleksey Granovsky, who had studied with Max Reinhardt, was appointed director of the Jewish Theatrical Society in March 1918. In 1919 he founded a Yiddish studio theater in Petrograd, intended to reinterpret the image of the Jew for the world. He adopted a polyphonic, choric approach; although the material would be drawn from traditional Jewish folklore and music, the technique would be acrobatic, stylized, and exquisitely modulated. His discovery of the actor Solomon Mikhoéls[74] greatly assisted his work.

> Walter Benjamin, "Granovsky tells his tale," *Die literarische Welt* 4, no. 17 (1928), 1f; reprinted in *Gesammelte Werke* (Frankfurt-am-Main, Germany: Suhrkamp, 1972), 4:518–20. Walter Bendix Schönflies Benjamin (1892–1940), German intellectual, became the lover of Asja Lācis, who invited him to visit Moscow in 1926; under the influence of Bertolt Brecht, he exchanged his earlier attraction to mysticism for Marxism.

"I had never seen a Jewish theater. [...] I'd never been an actor. [...] My ensemble came out of an acting school. In 1919, Grimberg, a commissar under Lunacharsky, asked me to open a school for Jewish actors. Nothing programmatic, and not as an actor, but from the start as a teacher and director. The troupe that formed naturally at the time did not have the sharply defined character it possesses today. In particular, its own special province, the so-called satirical–grotesque folk play, had yet to be discovered. The first drama we put on couldn't have been more remote from this. And yet it was not an arbitrary choice, not an accident, and it involved the same formative principles that shape us today. It was *The Blind* by Maeterlinck. In it I thought I would be able to develop techniques and exercises for my directing in the most obvious way. Namely, to let movement arise out of stillness, stillness, to establish the statuesque position as the original principle, but to invest it with so much energy that each musical change of mood would allow a more expressive movement to be produced from within. And the same thing with speech; for what stillness is to the context of mime, silence is to

74 Solomon Mikhaylovich Mikhoéls (actually Shloime Vovsi, 1890–1948) studied law at Petrograd University before joining Granovsky's Yiddish studio theater in 1919. He became GOSET's artistic director 1929 and was one of the USSR's greatest actors, excelling as King Lear. After he was murdered in Stalin's campaign against cosmopolitans, his theater was closed 1949.

the context of speech. If anything attracted me to this one-act, it was its abundance of statuesque moments. But the audience, which hadn't a clue about any of this—how could it?—was disconcerted, simply in seeing a Jewish troupe do this play, and remained aloof, for quite a long time."

Often in his early years Granovsky played before two or three spectators, and even they hissed.

> Granovsky's general principles for the theater, handwritten manuscript, Bakhrushin State Theater Museum, Moscow.

- GOSEK is the first and only attempt to create a permanent performing arts theater for the Jewish people.
- Because of the political situation, it has previously been impossible to create such a theater.
- Moscow was chosen as a location, being the cultural and artistic center of the life of the whole Republic.
- Unlike any other nationality inhabiting Russia, the Jews are the only ones to have no territory of their own.[75]

> Granovsky's work with his actors. Solomon Mikhoéls, *Dos yidishe kamer teatr* [The Jewish Chamber Theater] (Petrograd: n.p., 1919), 17–24.

Feelings contended within our hearts: the great will to create onstage something from the realm of Jewishness and deep-seated doubts of our own abilities . . . after all, who were we—lonely dreamers with vague aspirations; what did we bring with us—nothing but oppressed and shackled limbs and inner tension, total ignorance and impotence in stagecraft and stage technique—nothing . . . Yet each of us had something—an ardent will and readiness to make sacrifices . . . And our leader told us that was enough. [. . .]

[He taught us that] the word is the greatest weapon of stage creativity. Its value lies not only in speech but in silence . . . Our natural condition is silence . . . The word is a whole event, a supernatural human condition . . . The intervals of silence between uttering sentences or words are the background from which the great, significant word emerges . . .

The natural condition is static . . . Movement is an event, a supernatural condition . . . Every motion must begin with stasis, which is the general background from which the significant movement emerges . . . A movement must be logically articulated into its basic elements the same way a complex algebraic formula is broken down into its simple multiplicands.

---

75 A Jewish autonomous oblast' in the Khabaraovsky Kray in the Far Eastern USSR was created 1928; a tiny station on the trans-Siberian railway was turned into its administrative center, Birobidzhan.

WHEN THE THEATER, first known as GOSEKT (State Jewish Chamber Theater), then GOSET (State Jewish Theater), moved to Moscow in 1920, Granovsky's influence was temporarily effaced by that of Marc Chagall, who had been invited to design the first production, three one-acts by Sholem Aleichem,[76] in a ninety-seat room in the flat of a Jewish businessman on Great Chernishevsky Street.

> Marc Chagall, "My work in the Yiddish theater," in *Di Yidishe Velt* [The Jewish world] 2 (1928).

They suggested that I do the murals for the auditorium and scenery for the opening production. Aha, thought I, here's an opportunity to shake up the old Yiddish theater—with its realism, naturalism, psychology, glued-on beards. I set to work. I hoped that at least a few of the actors of the Yiddish Chamber Theater and of Habima [...] would take to the new art and abandon the old ways. I made a sketch. On one wall, I intended to provide a general direction introducing the audience to the new Yiddish People's Theater. The other walls and ceiling displayed *klezmerim,* a wedding jester, female dancers, a Torah scribe, and a couple of lovers hovering over the scenes, not far from all sorts of food, bagels and fruit, laden tables, all painted in friezes. Facing them, the stage with its actors. [...]

Some time later, [Mikhoéls] gleefully declared to me, "You know, I've studied your sketches, I understand them. As a result, I've altered my role completely. Everyone stares at me and can't understand what's going on." [...] The day before the theater opened, they collected piles of really old, worn-out clothes for me. In the pockets I found cigarette butts, dry bread crumbs. I painted the costumes quickly. I couldn't even go into the hall that night for the first performance. I was smeared all over with paint. A few minutes before the curtain rose, I ran onstage to touch up the color in several costumes, for I couldn't stand "realism." And suddenly a clash: Granovsky hangs up an ordinary, real dishcloth! I moan and groan, "An ordinary dishcloth?"

"Who is the director here, me or you?" he replies.

Oh, my aching heart, oh dear oh dear!

I was invited to do the decor for *The Dybbuk* at Habima. I didn't know what to do. Those two theaters were at war with one another. But I couldn't refuse to go to Habima, where the actors didn't act but prayed, and, poor souls, still worshipped Stanislavsky's theater. [...]

A year later I was told that Vakhtangov sat for many hours in front of my sketches when he was preparing *The Dybbuk.* And, as Tsemakh[77] told me, they invited someone

---

76 The popular Jewish writer Sholem Aleichem (actually Shlomo J. Rabinovich, 1859–1916) first tried his hand at playwriting in 1905 for the New York Yiddish Theater. His character Menakhem Mendel is the paradigm of the *luftmensh,* or impoverished middleman, desperately trying to eke out a living.

77 Nahum Lazarevich Tsemakh (1887–1937), leading actor of Habima, where he played the Prophet in *The Eternal Jew* and the Tzaddik in *The Dybbuk.* He settled in the United States in 1928.

else to do the scenery à la Chagall. And at Granovsky's, I hear, they Chagalled it up all over the place.

Solomon Mikhoéls, Chagall's influence on my role Menakhem-Mendel Yak-
enhoz in *Middlemen*, 1921. Joseph Shein, *Arum moskver yidishn teater* [About
the Moscow Jewish theater] (Paris: n.p., 1964).

On the day of the opening, Chagall walked into my dressing room. After mixing his colors, he set to work. He divided my face into two parts. One he painted green, the other yellow (as the saying goes, "green and yellow is a mournful fellow"). Chagall raised my right eyebrow two centimeters higher than the left one. The wrinkles around my nose and lips spread all over my face [to] emphasize Menakhem-Mendel's tragic fate.

I looked in the mirror and was convinced that the makeup created the dynamics and expressiveness for the character. The artist [. . .] put a finger to my eye, withdrew it, and, standing back a few paces, scrutinized me, adding regretfully, "Oh, Shloime, Shloime, if only you didn't have your right eye, I could have done so much."

Abram Éfros, "Khudozhniki teatra Granovskogo," *Iskusstvo* (*Art*) 2 (1928).

[Chagall] turned the actors and production into categories of plastic art. He did not design real scenery but mere panels, texturing them variously, meticulously, and in detail, as if the spectator was supposed to stand before them at a distance of several feet as at an exhibition. [. . .] He did not want to hear about three dimensions, about stage depth. Instead, he positioned all his set pieces in parallel planes along the apron just as he was used to hanging his paintings on walls or easels. [. . .] The spectators saw multiple perspectives: painted objects contrasted with real objects. [. . .] With his own hands, he painted every costume, turning it into a complex combination of blotches, stripes, and dots and strewing them with all sorts of snouts, animals, and scribbles. [. . .] Of course, under those conditions, the integrity of the spectator's impressions was total. When the curtain went up, Chagall's wall panels and the scenery and the actors onstage simply mirrored one another. But the nature of this ensemble was so untheatrical that one might have asked, why dim the house lights? Why are these Chagallian creatures moving and talking onstage rather than standing motionless and silent like a canvas?

[. . .] The best moments were those when Granovsky carried out his system of "dots" and the actors froze in mid-movement and gesture from one minute to another. The narrative line was turned into a follow-the-dots. It required incredible technique, which Mikhoéls possessed, in the role of Reb Alter to unify Chagall's static costumes and images with the unfolding of dialogue and action. The show was built on compromise and kept teetering back and forth. The dense indomitable Chagallian Jewishness conquered the stage, but the stage was enslaved and took no part in it. [Chagall], of course, considered us tyrants and himself a martyr. He was so deeply persuaded of this thereafter that for eight years he never worked in a theater again. He never realized that he was the clear and indisputable winner [. . .]

CHAPTER THREE

The New Economic Policy, 1921–1926

FACED WITH the critical situation prevailing throughout Russia, in early 1921 Lenin put in force what he called "a tactical retreat." He pushed through a New Economic Policy (NÉP) that was at bottom an oxymoron: communist capitalism. The government was to remain steadfastly socialist in principle but not in practice. Private enterprise on a reduced scale was permitted again; food allotment was replaced by a limited market economy. This brought about a revival of urban life and an improved standard of living, with an accompanying rise in prices. A new bourgeoisie, the so-called Népmen, arose, a class of middlemen, profiteers, agents, and small shopkeepers who owed no allegiance to the Bolsheviks. To counteract this trend, all opposition to the Party was outlawed. There were rigorous purges within the Party, while the country as a whole lost its stomach for politics and turned to practical matters. After Lenin's death in 1924 the nation was run by a triumvirate: the Party secretary Iosif Stalin, Trotsky's brother-in-law Kamenev, and Zinov'ev, president of the Third International. Stalin used the dissensions between the Old Bolsheviks and the young Communists to whip up a class-war frame of mind.

In 1922, more than two hundred eminent scientists, philosophers, artists, and writers—on direct orders from Lenin—were exiled for their unwillingness to accept the new regime. Foreign travel was still allowed, with special permission, until the borders were closed in 1926.

Glavlit, the Chief Administration for Literary Affairs, was established in 1922 to prevent the publication of overtly counterrevolutionary works. It was preventative rather than prescriptive and did not interfere with basic literary freedom in matters of form and content so long as the political interests of the new regime were not adversely affected. The first Party edict on literature came in 1925, and, although it recognized the difference between "fellow travelers" and "socialist writers," it declared neutrality between contending parties:

> The Party cannot absolutely commit itself to any one trend in the sphere of literary form. While controlling literature in a general way, the Party can no more give support to any one faction (factions being classified according to differences of view about style and form) than it can decide by resolution

questions of family life. [...] There is every reason to believe that a style consonant with the new era will be created, but it will be created by different methods,
and so far there is no sign of a solution to this question. Any attempt to tie the
Party down in this respect at the present stage of cultural development must be
rejected. Therefore, the Party must declare itself for free competition between
the various groups and trends in this field. Any other solution of the question
would be a bureaucratic pseudo-solution. In exactly the same way it would be
inadmissible to ordain by Party decree the legalized monopoly of literature and
publishing by any one group or literary organization.

The result for the arts was a relative golden age, a period in which experimentation
could flourish and even be encouraged.

The extent of this freedom should not be overstated, however. On October 26,
1922, the Politburo approved a resolution to make maximum cuts in state subsidies for all theaters and to close the Maria and Bol'shoy theaters if they could not
become self-supporting within the next six months. The reasons for these closures
were not aesthetic or ideological but wholly financial. The measures were tabled
for further consideration and, when they came up again in 1925, were not acted
on. In the event, none of the academic theaters was closed down, a signal of the
ideological "Great Retreat." Lunacharsky's protection of the "cultural legacy" led to
a rehabilitation of the classics and the eventual triumph of the Stalinist grand style.

Nevertheless, the return to the box office as a factor in the repertoire intensified the competition among the various artistic schools. At a time when public
discussions of premieres were frequent and vociferous, Lunacharsky had a hard
time reconciling the demands and needs of the proletarian movement, the so-called
avant-garde and the traditionalists. Among the latter were the heads of the government, conservative in their tastes yet still demanding a new form of theater aimed
directly at the proletariat. On February 9, 1923, a decree of the RSFSR Sovnarkom
created the Glavny Komitet po kontrolyu za repertuarom (GRK or Glavrepertkom) pri Glavnom Upravlenii po delam literatury i izdatel'stva (Glavlit) (Chief
Committee for the Inspection of the Repertoire under the Chief Administration
of Literary and Publication Matters). It was not under Lunacharsky's control and
initiated a weakening of his influence on theatrical matters.

During this period, Meyerhold was the towering figure, casting his equals in
the shade. He seemed to be ubiquitous at premieres, rehearsals, public meetings,
and debates as well as in print. His embrace of constructivist stage design and
biomechanical acting was copied by theaters, studios, and schools throughout the
USSR. Young directors emulated him unthinkingly. If he exploited jazz or clowns
or Japanese screens or cinematic techniques, those elements were quickly copied
and made part of the everyday vocabulary of theatrical practice. Meyerhold's noisy
declarations of allegiance to the government, his self-advertisement as an imple-
menter of socialism and an enabler of proletarian art, put him on the moral high

ground in disputes with such rivals as Tairov. His remarkable intellect and verbal skills enabled him to find topical rationales for even his most extreme experiments.

The centrality of Meyerhold and his epigones means that the term avant-garde is not really appropriate in this case. During the NÉP period, his methods and those of his colleagues constituted the mainstream. Constructivism was pursued by government agencies in the textile and porcelain industries, in architecture, in posters, and in other branches of commerce; radical design was evident even in political banners and decorations. Biomechanics became the favored form of physical culture.

Vakhtangov's Achievements

With the Moscow Art Theater disabled, insecure, and, eventually, absent, its Studios came into prominence. The First Studio, founded in 1912, had been the nursery for Stanislavsky's acting system, providing opportunity for such young talents as Vakhtangov, Mikhail Chekhov, Serafima Birman, and Boris Sushkevich. From 1919 it was funded from the MAT budget. Its most ambitious production, staged in larger premises on Triumphal Square, was Strindberg's *Erik XIV* (1921), with Chekhov, at his most neurasthenic, in the lead.

In February 1919 Vakhtangov was invited to assume the administration of the directing section of TEO. In 1920, out of the former university group the Moscow Dramatic Studio, he founded the Art Theater Third Studio, which comprised a remarkable team of actors and directors, among them Ruben Simonov, Boris Zakhava, and Boris Shchukin, destined to play leading roles in the history of Soviet theater. There Vakhtangov mounted the one-acts Anton Chekhov's *The Wedding* and Maeterlinck's *The Miracle of St. Anthony* in 1921 and Carlo Gozzi's eighteenth-century Venetian fairy-tale *Princess Turandot* in 1922. Vakhtangov occupies an original place between Meyerhold and Stanislavsky. Trained in Stanislavsky's embryonic "system," he nevertheless felt that a more "theatrical" presentation was needed: a flamboyant style that was infused with authentic emotion. Some of his inspiration came from the commedia dell'arte, with *Princess Turandot* the consummate example.

Despite failing health, Vakhtangov was indefatigable. His reputation for pedagogy meant that he was often approached by amateur groups to whip them into shape: besides his work with the Hebrew studio Habima, he created the Kamenny Bridge people's theater, ran the Gunst Theater, and taught at the Chaliapin Studio, the Armenian studio, and the Tchaikovsky cinema studio.

Meyerhold and Vakhtangov had first met at the Third Studio of the MAT at a performance of *The Miracle of St. Anthony* in late 1921 or early 1922, although they had both seen work by the other for years. Vakhtangov addressed Meyerhold as "Dear Master."

Vsevolod Meyerhold to Evgeny Vakhtangov, January 3, 1922, 11:25 p.m., Moscow. In V. É. Meyerhold, *Perepiska 1896–1939*, ed. V. P. Korshunova and M. M. Sitkovetskaya (Moscow: Iskusstvo, 1976), 213.

Dear *Collega,*[1]
in your quiet office I talked and relaxed with soldiers of Your Army.
The minutes went by beautifully, only it was a pity you weren't there.
I very much want to have a meeting. Will you show us your *Turandot* soon?[2]
The soldiers of my Army are eagerly awaiting you. [. . .]

Evgeny Vakhtangov, "Two talks with students," April 10, 1922. In *Evgeny Vakhtangov [Sbornik]*, ed. L. D. Vendrovskaya and G. P. Kapterev (Moscow: Iskusstvo, 1984), 429–37.

Meyerhold understands theatricality to mean a kind of spectacle in which the spectators never forget for a second that they are in theater or stop accepting the actor as a craftsman playing a role. Konstantin Sergeevich [Stanislavsky] demanded the opposite, that is, that the spectators forget they are in the theater and feel themselves in the same atmosphere and environment that the characters in the play are inhabiting. He was delighted when spectators came to see *Three Sisters* at the Art Theater, not as a visit to the theater, but as paying a call on the Prozorov family. He considered this the theater's highest achievement. Konstantin Sergeevich put it this way: "As soon as the audience sits in its seats and the curtain parts, that's when we carry them away, make them forget that they are in a theater. We lead them to us, into our environment, our atmosphere, the milieu onstage at the moment."

With us, though, as we understand the theater, we lead the audience into the milieu of actors who are doing their theatrical job. Konstantin Sergeevich wanted to get rid of theatrical banality and be done with it once and for all. And anything that was the least little bit reminiscent of the old theater he labeled "theatrical," and at the Art Theater, "theatrical" became a term of abuse. True, whatever he rebuked was in fact banal, but, obsessed with expelling banality, he also lumped in with it real, essential theatricality, and real theatricality consists in presenting a theatrical work's theatricality. What do we need to make a performance theatrical?

First, the kind of execution, the kind of actor's authority that provides the spectators a constant sense of the actor's skill. When talent is crafting something, when stage authority is in the hands of a true craftsman, then there is the ring of theatricality. But when an untalented actor starts to imitate a talented craftsman, adding nothing of his own, then there is the ring of theatrical banality.

For example, this is how emotion works. When a talented craftsman, who feels his role, presents it with theatrical emotion, the audience accepts it, and the actor's emotion sets it alight. But when an untalented actor starts to imitate him (outwardly,

---

1   In Roman letters in the original.
2   *Princess Turandot* opened at the Third Studio of the MAT on February 28, 1922.

of course), without any internal combustion, the audience is unaffected and the actor fails to infect it. Especially if an untalented actor keeps admiring himself throughout his whole performance.

That the theater has to have a painted curtain, an orchestra, ushers invariably dressed in a luxurious theatrical uniform, impressive scenery, impressive actors who know how to wear costumes and show off their voices and temperaments, that the theater has to have applause—there is no doubt that this is because all these things are elements of true theatricality. But when all this is accomplished tritely, when tritely dressed ushers walk around the theater, when a third-rate orchestra is in place, when an untalented actor tries to show off a temperament he doesn't possess, when he struts around in his untalented costume, then it all has the ring of theatrical banality. Konstantin Sergeevich came down hard on all of this, started to throw it all out, seek the truth. This search for the truth led him to the truth of emotional experience,[3] that is, he demanded real, natural emotional experience onstage and forgot that an actor's emotional experience has to be conveyed to the audience by theatrical devices. And Konstantin Sergeevich was himself compelled to use theatrical devices. You know that the Chekhov productions wouldn't work without people talking offstage, the sound of crickets, an orchestra, street noises, cries of peddlers, a clock striking onstage. And these are all theatrical devices invented for Chekhov's plays.

K. I. KOTLUBAY:[4] So what is mood?[5] Are you saying it isn't a theatrical advance?
[VAKHTANGOV]: No, there shouldn't be any moods in the theater. In the theater there should only be joy and no moods. In general theatrical moods don't exist. When you look at a naturalistic picture, do you feel a "mood"? It makes an impression on you by means of its subject, but in the meantime you forget the craftsmanship. [. . .]

Of all the Russian directors, the only one who's had a feeling for theatricality is Meyerhold. In his time he was a prophet and therefore was not accepted. He was ahead of his time by a full decade. Meyerhold did the same thing as Stanislavsky. He also got rid of theatrical banality, but did it by means of theatrical devices. [. . .] But, captivated by theatrical truth, Meyerhold threw out emotional truth [. . .]

The theater should be filled not with naturalism, not with realism, but with fantastical realism. Properly discovered theatrical devices give an author authentic life onstage. [. . .]

Vakhtangov, from a diary, Vsekhsvatsky Sanitarium, March 26, 1921. In *Evgeny Vakhtangov*, 333–34.

---

3 *Perezhivanie*, literally "experience," a word Stanislavsky adopted to describe the process the actor must undergo to re-create or relive authentic emotions.
4 Kseniya Ivanovna Kotlubay (1890–1931), actress and director, Vakhtangov's assistant at the MAT Third Studio from 1913; director at the MAT and Musical Theater 1922–31.
5 *Nastroenie* (mood, atmosphere) was a key word in Stanislavsky's approach to directing; it involved harnessing all possible stage effects to bring the spectator into the world of the play.

[Theater that relays a series of facts, everyday life, representational, naturalistic, domestic] theater should die. "Character" actors are no longer needed. Anyone who has the ability and determination should feel the tragic elements (even comic actors) of any character role and should learn to present himself grotesquely.

The grotesque is [both] tragic and comic.

[...] Tairov, it goes without saying, is talented. He does not know the actor at all. The students of the Art Theater are essential to him. He will never create an eternal theater... But he has a sense of form and truth, both banal and penetrating. The spirit of a human being is inaccessible to him—the deeply tragic and deeply comic are inaccessible to him. His theater [...] is vulgar (every fad is vulgar until it's over). The Art Theater can be put under a glass bell and displayed like a museum piece. And the Kamerny, which changes its style annually, naturally ends up with vulgarity. [...]

Let kitchen-sink realism in the theater die! [...]

I want to direct *The Seagull*. Theatrically. As it is in Chekhov. [...]

Chekhov's work isn't lyric, but tragic. When a person shoots himself, it isn't lyrical.

It is either Bathos or Bravura. Neither Bathos nor Bravura was ever lyrical. And Bathos and Bravura both have their tragic masks. And so the lyrical tends to be vulgar. [...]

Sof'ya Giatsintova, *S pamyatyu naedine* (Moscow: Iskusstvo, 1989), 203.

In the Studio the main event in 1921 was Strindberg's *Erik XIV* as staged by Vakhtangov. The production provoked a varied response—from unbridled excitement to complete revulsion. But its exceptionally talented qualities were granted by everyone. [...]

I could briefly define the atmosphere of the production in two words: anxiety and doom. The stage was filled with anxiety—oblique, aslant, the seemingly broken lines of the dark gray backdrop, cut by the zigzags of lightning, at the back of which rocked a cradle of golden royal furniture, the blue of courtiers' cloaks, the deep ruby red of the headsman's getup. The designer Nivinsky,[6] who had entered the history of scene design a year earlier with the mounting of *Princess Turandot,* broke up the stage floor with some platforms, staircases—the action proceeded simultaneously or in turn in various places, tragically froze some characters, others restlessly scurried about. The actors crossed the stage on diagonals or abruptly changed direction—the sharp movements corresponded to the "angularity" of all the design details. Anxiety grew stronger every moment and became sinister, when along the backdrop the dowager queen slithered, inhuman in her ruthless hatred. Birman[7] stretched out, her face contorted by "cubistic" makeup, as called for by the whole production, spreading wide the sleeves of the black costume, as if she had spilled on the stage an invisible chalice of deadly poison.

6 Ignaty Ignatyevich Nivinsky (1880–1933), designer, invited by Vakhtangov to design *Erik XIV*; went on to do the same for *Princess Turandot* (1922) and for several plays for the MAT 2. Her chronology is inaccurate: *Princess Turandot* opened the following year. See later.

7 Serafima Germanovna Birman (1890–1976), actress and director, who began at the MAT in 1911 and became a stalwart of the First Studio and later the Vakhtangov Theater; when it was dissolved, she moved to Lenin Komsomol 1938–58. She excelled at outlandish characters and later played the monstrous Grand Duchess Efrosiniya in Eisenstein's films *Ivan the Terrible I* and *II*.

Michael Chekhov, *Put' aktëra* [An actor's path], in *Literaturnoe nasledie* [Literary legacy] (Moscow: Iskusstvo, 1986), 1:90–93. Mikhail Aleksandrovich Chekhov (1891–1955), nephew of Anton Chekhov, gained fame as an extraordinary actor in the MAT First Studio (1912–21), then ran his own studio (1919–21), before becoming artistic director of the MAT 2 (1924–27). His use of the "psychological gesture" and endorsement of the mystical theories of Vladimir Solov'ëv and Rudolph Steiner led to an arrest warrant. He emigrated to Berlin in 1928 and spent the rest of his career in Europe and the United States, as actor, director, and, especially, teacher.

The problem of the interrelationship between director and actor is complex and difficult. You can deliver dozens of lectures on the theme, but they lead nowhere if the director doesn't have a *feeling for the actor.* And Vakhtangov possessed this *feeling* to perfection. He himself talked about it as a feeling which comes when a person is taken by the hand and carefully, patiently led wherever he needs to go. It was as if he invisibly stopped by the actor and led him by the hand. The actor never felt that Vakhtangov was forcing him, but he couldn't avoid submitting to the director's concept either. Carrying out Vakhtangov's tasks and ideas, the actor felt they were his own. This unique ability of Vakhtangov's eliminated the question of who had final say in interpreting roles: the actor or the director. [. . .] He was never sentimental with actors, and the actors never impeded his concepts with their whims and obstinacy.

[. . .] Vakhtangov possessed yet another quality indispensable to directors: he knew how to *show* the actor what constitutes the main outline of his role. He didn't show the whole image or play the role with the actor himself, but he *showed, acted out* the blueprint, the design, the contour of the role. When staging *Erik XIV,* he used this means of showing me the outline of the role of Erik over the length of a whole act of the play, without spending more than two minutes on it. After his demonstration, the whole act in all its details came clear to me, even though Vakhtangov hadn't touched on them. He gave me the main, firm outline, within which I could later organize the details and circumstances of the role. He had a special talent for *demonstration.* [. . .]

Thanks to this amazing ability of Vakhtangov's, we talked very little during his rehearsals. All the work was channeled into demonstrations, displays of images, etc. He had a wonderful understanding that if an actor talks a lot about his role, it means the actor is lazy and delaying the moment of actual rehearsal. [. . .]

Konstantin Stanislavsky on the grotesque; from last conversation with Vakhtangov, early 1922. *Stat'i, rechi, besedy, pis'ma* [Articles, speeches, talks, letters], ed. G. Kristi and N. Chutkina (Moscow: Iskusstvo, 1953), 255–58.

It intrigues me when people start saying that this super-conscious supreme creation of a genuine artist, which you please to call "the grotesque," can be created by your students, who have in no way shown their merit [. . .], students who are unaware of the inner workings of their bodies, who have achieved a very high degree of physical flexibility from dancing lessons and calisthenics, these charming "puppies," their eyes still tightly shut, prattle about the grotesque . . .

No, this is a delusion! You have simply collected guinea pigs for your research and perform your experiments on them with the aid of your intuition, experiments validated neither pragmatically nor scientifically, the experiments of a talented man, which succeed for the same reasons they fail—by accident. You don't even try what is so essentially necessary for the grotesque, to study an approach to the super-conscious (where the grotesque lurks) through the conscious.

[...] Alas and alack, if, when you've created your grotesque, the spectator asks, "Tell me please, what's the significance of the two crooked eyebrows and the black triangle on the cheek of the Miser Knight or Pushkin's Salieri?"[8] Alas and alack, if you explain in reply, "Don't you see, this is how the artist intended to depict a keen sense of sight. But because symmetry is boring, he introduced this displacement...," etc. This is the pitfall of the grotesque. It dies, and in its place is born a mere rebus, exactly like the silly, simple-minded puzzles contributors to illustrated papers make up for their readers. What do I care how many eyebrows and noses the actor wears? Let him have four eyebrows, two noses, a dozen eyes, go ahead. So long as they are justified, so long as the actor's inner creativity is so great that it goes beyond two eyebrows, one nose, two eyes to manifest the creative inwardness of the infinite spiritual content. [...] To exaggerate what doesn't exist, to exaggerate emptiness—such activity reminds me of blowing soap bubbles. [...]

HABIMA'S FIRST PRODUCTION, *The Dybbuk* or *Demon Lover,* was a creation of the Yiddish folklorist Solomon Rappoport, who wrote under the name S. Ansky or An-ski.

Natan Al'tman [the production's designer], *Evgeny Vakhtangov,* 390.

Vakhtangov knew nothing of the Jewish language or shtetl life or folk customs, legends and superstitions, in other words, everything on which the play *The Dybbuk* was based. As he said, he involuntarily had to be guided by instructions from members of the studio. They pulled him in the direction of naturalism, but the play was ecstatic and heroic–tragical... The people whom I portrayed in sketches were tragically broken and hunched, like trees rooted in dry and barren soil. They were tinged with tragedy. The forms themselves had to act on the spectator, because the words the actors uttered in old "Hebrew" were for the most part incomprehensible to the listener. Their movements and gestures had to be like dancing.

When I brought the sketches to Moscow, Vakhtangov had already finished Act I. They were very distinct from what Vakhtangov had done. I don't know what he felt, when he saw the sketches for the first time, but I do know that he canceled everything he had done and started to work, having put my sketches aside. The work on the production went on in a kind of incredible excitement, almost a state of ecstasy [...]

8   *The Miser Knight* and *Mozart and Salieri* are two of Pushkin's "Little Tragedies" (1826–27), meant to illustrate dominant emotions—avarice in *Knight* and murderous jealousy in *Salieri.*

"*The Dybbuk,*" *Ékran* [Screen] 20 (1922), 6.

To be at Vakhtangov's is to feel oneself in the present every moment and to feel the present in oneself.

Many people consider this play to be hysteria in the theater. But the stage of *The Dybbuk* has an entirely different content—what it lives by, what makes it blaze, and what infects us—and that is something else: ecstasy. [...]

Éngel's[9] music resounds like old synagogue biblical psalms. It has dolefulness and passion, both expectation and a breakthrough into elements of the eternal and the infinite.

Natan Al'tman's scenery in all three acts, including the synagogue and the square by Sender's house, the chapel of the Wonder Rabbi Reb Azrael, comes from everyday life and from the fantastic: it is real in its fantasy and fantastical in its reality.

The rhythm of the action is confusion. The tempo is alarm.

Khanan the madman, for whom living is fasting, celebrating is seeing visions, dreaming is loving, is as pale as a man on death row and as inspired as a character in a Van Dyck painting with his refined face. Someone said that Khanan (Élias)[10] has the face of Erik XIV, but this is not true. Sometimes Khanan, it seems to me, is a prince of darkness, Lucifer, Satan himself, a strange combination of Satanism and saintliness.

Khanan is the *harbinger of ecstasy* in the play, and emanating from him, *ecstasy* infects everything.

Here everyone speaks, moves, feels, thinks, loves, curses, and blesses *ecstatically.*

Here they are all fanatics, obsessives, enthusiasts. There is not one calm face— really only Sender, Leah's old aunt, and the three respectable women in holiday dresses, Leah's kinfolk. But . . . not always.

Anxiety, excitement, feverishness, an uplift of spirit is the world of Habima theater. And when the Yeshiva students dance with Sender in the synagogue in their terrible and overheated dancing—oblivious to the corpse of Khanan who had died on the instant of a heart attack, hidden by the Wayfarer's shroud—their dancing becomes the dancing of dervishes.

The ecstasy of Habima's theatrical stagecraft comes from the East, from the dervish, from weird legends, from *1001 Nights,* and also from the present, from today.

The dance of the beggars with the bride, with men and women writhing around her, hunchbacks, the lame, blind, crazed and wretched, is terrible in its peculiar witchery.

When the square is suddenly emptied, the beggars rise from under the earth like fantastical creatures, yes, exactly like chimeras, and throw themselves into a frenzy at the empty table cleared of the wedding banquet.

Yes, this is what all of Vakhtangov's art is like—fantasy is in reality, reality in fantasy. [...]

9   Yuly (Joel) Dmitrievich Éngel (1868–1927), music critic for the newspaper *Russkie Vedomosti,* one of the first promoters of Jewish folk music, which he collected with S. An-ski; founded the Society for Jewish Folk Music 1908. Emigrated to Berlin 1922.
10 Khanan was played by an actress, Miriam Élias (1897–?).

Nikolay Volkov, "*The Dybbuk*: Descent into hell," in *Vakhtangov* (Moscow: Korabl', 1922), 19–20. Nikolay Dmitrievich Volkov (1894–1965) was a theater scholar and critic and author of a two-volume monograph on Meyerhold (1929). He adapted *Anna Karenina* (MAT, 1937) and *War and Peace* (1946).

The second act of *The Dybbuk*—the wedding act—is the third and last work of Vakhtangov that stands beneath the sign of duality (I'm referring to *Erik XIV* and *The Miracle of St. Anthony*)[11] . . . No longer with one, but with three devices he fashions the world of the dead. Vakhtangov has swapped the statuesque manner for a group of three heavily made-up women. Their hardened doll-like faces convey to the general order of the action a sense of inertia, one-dimensionality, prim stupidity. For the interpretation of Sender himself, the bridegroom, his teacher and the matchmaker—Vakhtangov demands identical fixed movements. For each of them he finds some strictly defined—not exactly gestures but gesticules [*zhestikov*]. They make them independent of what they are experiencing at any given moment. Ludicrously disconnecting body and soul, Vakhtangov extracts the effects of comedy from the broken parallelism of human psychophysicality. Finally, in an exaggerated manner, Vakhtangov elaborates the theme of the beggars invited to the wedding feast. These monstrous faces, deformed bodies, distorted movements are taken directly from Leonardo's caricatures . . . Vakhtangov in *The Dybbuk* shows how cruel is his talent, how close is his soul to the beauty of ugliness. With avid curiosity he stares into the teeming clouds of human wreckage he has called into life. He intensifies it all and intensifies the tempos of this whirlwind of gray debris. And then suddenly he cleaves them with the white light of Leah. The lily of Leah is the bright Ariel among the mob of Calibans. Her dancing in the chimerical round dance of human monsters is exceptional in its power. Vakhtangov does not spare the ghastliness, he lays it on with the webbed feet of toads, apelike contact. The breath of the rose-maiden mingles with the breath of the plague . . . The tragic angle of Vakhtangov's talent is united with the comic. He has a satiric vision and a keen feeling for everyday inertia . . .

Mikhail Zagorsky, "*Turandot* 1922," *Teatral'naya Moskva* 30 (1922), 11–13. Mikhail Borisovich Zagorsky (1885–1951), theater critic and historian, was Meyerhold's literary manager at RSFSR 1 Theater.

Of course this is not the *Turandot* of the fantastical Carlo Gozzi[12] any more than it is a magical performance of the commedia dell'arte. If Gozzi were to be resurrected today, he would be horrified by what one of the best of his "fairy-tale comedies" has been turned into on the stage of the Third Studio. As great would be the indignation of those Italian mummers who, sent through Wells's "time machine"[13] from the sixteenth

11 Maurice Maeterlinck's *Le Miracle de Saint Antoine* (1904) is a one-act play about the battle of skepticism and faith. Vakhtangov staged it with great success 1921.
12 Carlo Gozzi (1720–1806), Venetian count, who tried to revivify the commedia dell'arte through his dramatic *fiabe* or fables.
13 H. G. Wells's novel *The Time Machine* (1895) sends the Time Traveler into the future to discover that the human race has evolved into two distinct species, the civilized and the brutes.

century to the twentieth, would see on the stage of this studio the lack of respect with which the "barbarians" treat the whole canon of the popular theater of masks.

And at the same time, this is far from being an imitation of past experiments in this direction made by Meyerhold and Komissarzhevsky, far from the researches of Miklashevsky.[14]

So what's it all about?

It's all about Vakhtangov living . . . in 1922, after having lived in 1918, 1919, and 1920.

During those same years, in the same era, in Petersburg, there also lived the Russian scientists Pavlov and Bekhterev.[15]

Neither Vakhtangov nor I nor the rest of the thousands of Muscovites knew about the work of those Petersburg scientists.

And they didn't know of our existence.

And so, for some time now, both Vakhtangov and I and the rest of the thousands of Muscovites had been feeling that theatergoing was simply "uninteresting."

But life—oh, how interesting and gripping!—a single development of the intrigue at the Geneva convention[16] is worth something—but the theater is a void—no excitement, no stimulation, no arousal—no way!

[. . .] If in life our reflexes are stimulated by the telephone, the streetcar, the automobile and the airplane, then *no* sword of Romeo, sighs of Juliet, frigidity of Turandot, or ardor of Calaf will be able to stimulate the slightest emotion in us.

[. . .] Hence the unescapable conclusion:

Whatever we stage *nowadays* in a theater from the old repertoire must first of all depict *our* relationship to it, the relationship of a contemporary to what happened at that time . . .

Otherwise . . . the reflexes are unmoved. Otherwise . . . there is no stimulus. Otherwise . . . there is no exclusively *active* staging of a production.

So there arises the theater of Irony. [. . .]

And now comes *Turandot* . . . A subtle and malicious irony no longer merely mocks, but guffaws right in our face with all these resurrected characters from a naive fairy tale about a wicked princess and a clever prince. This is not the amiable laughter we would have encountered in brilliant Count Carlo Gozzi if, in 1922, he had seriously tried to revive his long-drawn-out and hard-bitten debate with Goldoni[17] about the destiny of popular comedy. This is the laughter of every living being along with life at

14 Konstantin Mikhaylovich Miklashevsky (1866–1944), theater scholar and film director, a student of Meyerhold; as a result of the experimental work at Interlude House before the Revolution, he wrote the first Russian monograph on the commedia dell'arte. Emigrated to Paris 1925.

15 Ivan Petrovich Pavlov (1849–1936), professor of physiology at the Russian Academy of Sciences 1896–1924, who developed his theory of conditioned reflexes by working with dogs at the Institute of Experimental Medicine. Vladimir Mikhaylovich Bekhterev (1857–1927), founder of the Institute of Psychoneurology, expert on the higher nervous system, who studied reflexes as the foundation of human behavior.

16 The Second Geneva Convention for the Amelioration of the Condition of Wounded, Sick, and Shipwrecked Members of the Armed Forces at Sea (1906).

17 An acrimonious debate in 1757 between Gozzi and the Venetian playwright Carlo Goldoni over the merits of improvisation over written comedy impelled the latter to move to Paris.

all those who, in the twentieth century, with clever mien, are developing the actors' "emotion" [...]

This is the most important thing:

In the studio, there is a director who has audacity, resourcefulness, wit, and a living heart. He sees well and keenly, his lips smile ironically at the past while his eyes peer sagaciously into the future.

And he is living among us:

In 1922.

> Émmanuil Beskin, "*Turandot* on the Arbat," *Teatral'naya Moskva* 30 (1922), 9. Émmanuil Martynovich Beskin (1877–1940), theater critic and historian and editor of *Rabis'* (1927–34) and *Teatral'naya Moskva* (1921–22), authored more than two thousand articles.

By and large, the theater apparently wanted to see *Turandot* from the angle of an ironic farce, a grotesque, and to reject psychologism. They were right to do the latter but missed the former. There was no style to the performance. This was a "cabbage party,"[18] based on the theme of *Princess Turandot*. To do this with a one-act play doesn't matter much. There was some fine joking. But when they "cabbagize" four acts, and when, even through this senseless "Satiriconery,"[19] you can glimpse Gozzi every so often and take an interest, it dispels boredom and reaches out to the aromatic pages of the original in a really modern artistically theatrical transcription of the Venetian fable.

The platform and decorative panels are dead, static and "cute" with a saccharine boudoir "prettiness." The constructivism is a kind of setting, a frame.

If *The Miracle of St. Anthony* seemed to take a step away from the naturalistic positions of the Art Theater, then in *Princess Turandot,* the studio fully "returns to its bosom." A new form is meaningful so long as it's an imitation of old material. It's a fake. Like a paper rose, it smells only of... glue.

The "glue," the work on the show was immense. But it's all a gimmick, not an artistic organism. I think it's most accurate to say there was nothing of *Princess Turandot.* There was a "cabbage party" where they roasted Count Carlo Gozzi. We had fun. And that's all.

DYING OF CANCER, Vakhtangov was too ill to attend the opening night or any of the subsequent performances. When the premiere was over, Nemirovich-Danchenko sent him a note.

18 *Kapustnik,* skits and parodies privately performed by actors on the eve of the "Great Fast" (Lent), when the theaters were closed in the pre-Revolutionary period. From 1910 the MAT cabbage parties were a hot ticket and formed the basis for the cabaret the Bat.

19 *Satirikon,* a daily satiric journal published out of St. Petersburg 1908–14; at various times its editors were the humorist A. T. Averchenko and the caricaturist N. V. Remizov (Re-Mi).

3.1. The finale of *Princess Turandot,* directed by Evgeny Vakhtangov, designed by Ignaty Nivinsky, Moscow Art Theater First Studio, 1922. Note the straight chairs in the audience.

Nemirovich-Danchenko to Vakhtangov, "Inscription on a portrait on the night after *Princess Turandot,*" in *Evgeny Vakhtangov,* 427.

Many thanks for the great artistic joy, the wonderful achievement, the noble audacity in solving the newest theatrical problems, for adding luster to the name of the Art Theater.

Evgeny Vakhtangov to Nemirovich-Danchenko, April 8, 1922. In *Evgeny Vakhtangov,* 427.

Yesterday, after each act of *Turandot,* they phoned me and let me know how you were reacting to the performance. After your discussion with the students that night, four of them came to me and told me in detail what you said. I was extremely anxious, as was the Studio [...]

I am sorry that I am very weak and ill and can't come to you right now and thank you for the joy. I'm sorry it is hard for me to write and I can't collect my thoughts to tell you everything that has captivated me...

Mikhail Kuzmin, *"Princess Turandot,"* Zhizn' iskusstva 18 (1923), 15–16.

The production, conceived as a demonstration of devices of abstract art, is worth examination only from the standpoint of its devices.

Movement as movement, gesture as gesture are more precise in Tairov, the circus element and principles of Italian comedy are more systematic in S. Radlov, the master of ceremonies is freer and busier in Baliev,[20] the eccentrism is more eccentric in the eccentrics. The most powerful aspect of the staging is the intonations, achieving in some places (the asking of the riddles) high elaboration, but they are spoiled by too much local, suburban character and an abuse of the device of a lack of correspondence between the subject and the intonational nuance. Surprising the first time, repeated ad infinitum, this device becomes annoying and leads to boredom. The same for the misplaced stresses of Pantalone (co-nun-drúms, ho-néstly, emper-ór). Inappropriate music (Chopin's mazurka) or the repetition to stupefying effect of one and the same more or less idiotic theme is also used beyond measure.

The unusual diligence and hard work, the confirmation of certain technical achievements—those are the strong aspects of the performance; superfluous systematization, heavy-handedness and the absence of any inner meaning in this bare demonstration are its defects. About the dubious taste and notorious quality of certain improvisational devices I say nothing. Perhaps it was the same with Gozzi, and the Moscow *Turandot* is trying naturalistically to impersonate the by no means naturalistic actors of that time.

HALF of the Kachalov Group of the Moscow Art Theater returned to Russia in 1922, after three years abroad, and were immediately invited to a performance of *Princess Turandot*.

> Vadim Shverubovich, *O starom Khudozhestvennom teatre* [About the Old Art Theater] (Moscow: Iskusstvo, 1990), 389–90.

Places for all of us were reserved in the eighth row. It was the first performance we had seen in Moscow after a three-year absence. What happiness that our reception by a Moscow new to us, a new Soviet theater began with this wonderful production! It contained all the freshness and infinite talent, subtlety and purity characteristic of Russian art. The purity of concept, purity of feelings... This is disinterested, sincere acting in the theater, the acting of children, in which every child is uniquely brilliant.

And at the same time it was the most "European" production of all we saw in Europe. How wonderfully refined and elegant was Zavadsky,[21] with what exquisite virile grace he wore evening dress! Where were the Viennese and Berlin theatrical "fops" and "romantic leads" now!... And the dazzling femininity of Mansurova and the gowns of Lamanova,[22] indeed they were not in fashion, they were ahead of European fashion.

---

20 Nikita Fëdorovich Baliev (actually Mkritich Balyan, 1877–1936), actor at the MAT and founder and master of ceremonies of the cabaret the Bat, founded 1910; he later took it abroad to London, Paris, and New York.

21 Yury Aleksandrovich Zavadsky (1894–1977) began as a designer at Vakhtangov's studio in 1915; both as an actor and in life, he strove to be charming, refined, and elegant. He later ran the Third Studio and acted at the MAT 1924–31. He fell into disfavor while running the Red Army Theater but later became chief director of the Mossovet Theater while teaching at GITIS.

22 Tsetsiliya L'vovna Mansurova (actually Vollershteyn, 1897–1976), Vakhtangov's favorite student, played the role of Princess Turandot; later a leading actress at the Vakhtangov Theater. Nadezhda Petrovna Lamanova (1861–1941), the leading couteriere of pre-Revolutionary Russia and dressmaker to the Empress Alexandra, began to design stage costumes at Stanislavsky's behest.

Could we have imagined that the young men here knew how to wear evening dress so elegantly and the girls "toilettes"? And the charming, half-childish splendor of the zanni... What could be better!

Turandot was the first page of that magic book we were able to leaf through that bright spring. After it came the merry, witty, splendid *Angot,* then *The Rose Pattern* at the Second Studio, where it was so exciting to see friends grown up and mature as actors and suddenly Finochka from *The Green Ring* and the young people from *Youth;*[23] bold, intelligent, deeply modern *Erik XIV,* after which all the modernism of Berlin seemed derivative, artificial, and heavy-handed compared with the internally justified audacity of M. A. Chekhov, S. G. Birman...

And what about *Phaedra* at the Kamerny? And *The Inspector General* with the grotesque and at the same time absolutely lifelike Moskvin as the Mayor and the fantastic, improbably sincere Khlestakov of Chekhov? And *Evgeny Onegin* at the Stanislavsky Opera Studio in Leont'ev Lane?... All bright, full-value, genuine, organic, principled, and, most important, pure. [...]

Meyerhold and Constructivism

Shverubovich, weaned on the principles of the Art Theater, left Meyerhold out of his roster of enlivening and "pure" productions in 1922. Yet it was Meyerhold who bestrode this narrow world like a colossus. At the beginning of the century, he had embraced the esoteric doctrines of the Symbolists to promote ideas of a "conventionalized" (*uslovny*) theater. Now he leaped on the bandwagon of constructivism and a socialist theater for the people, throwing in his lot with the leftist movements in art. His first postrevolutionary theater was meant to be utilitarian, from its barebones name, Theater of the RSFSR 1, to its unadorned interior; with a production of the grotesque comedy *The Magnanimous Cuckold* by the Belgian playwright Fernand Crommelynck, he realized his first integrally "constructivist" and "biomechanical" mise-en-scène. It was the logical culmination of the theory of "conventionalized theater": Meyerhold created a show in which the movement of bodies conclusively outweighed the word. The "construction" erected onstage was not scenery but a machine for acting; costumes were replaced by uniform blue overalls, work clothes for acting. Biomechanics rejects the "psychological" acting founded on Stanislavsky's "reexperiencing" and offers instead the virtuosity of corporeal expression, nurtured by physical culture, experiments in commedia dell'arte and the theater of the Far East. The actor is compounded with the acrobat and the juggler. The frequent use of masks or stylized makeup to typify each character by a

23 *La fille de Mme Angot* (*Doch' Ango*, 1920), an operetta by Charles Lecocq, staged by Nemirovich-Danchenko at his Musical Studio; it ran for 1,101 performances. The others were productions of the Second Studio: *The Rose Pattern* (*Uzor iz roz*), an adaptation by the symbolist poet Fëdor Sologub of his novel *The Hon. Miss Liza* (*Baryshnaya Liza*, 1920); *The Green Ring* (*Zelënoe koltso,* 1914) by Zinaida Gippius, about the political confusion of the younger generation—at the Second Studio, Finochka was played by Alla Tarasova; *Youth* (*Mladost'*), a "short story in dialogue" by Leonid Andreev that opened in 1918 and ran to 1924.

certain number of outward traits relieves the spectator of any hesitation as to who he is supposed to be. The practice of "preacting" is a technique of "distanciation," a collection of mimetic procedures by which the actor is detached from his role and can comment on his acting; it reveals the debt Meyerhold's aesthetics owed to the Chinese and Japanese theaters as well as its influence on Bertolt Brecht.

These tenets were implemented even more programatically in Meyerhold's production of Sukhovo-Kobylin's phantasmal nineteenth-century comedy *Tarelkin's Death*; they affirmed the principle by which the "construction" must be a simple machine for acting. The sinister farce was turned into a clown show full of circus stunts. Meyerhold's social and political sentiments were prominent in his modern repertoire: *Earth Rampant* (1923), an adaptation by Sergey Tret'yakov of Marcel Martinet's *La Nuit*, a hymn to world revolution; *D.E.*, an adaptation of a novel by Il'ya Érenburg that contrasted a decadent capitalist West with an increasingly powerful USSR (1924); *Roar, China* by Tret'yakov, a homage to the revolutionary struggle of the Chinese people (1926).

> Él Lissitsky, "The scene painter advances towards architecture," 1922, in Sophie Lisitsky-Küppers, *Él Lissitsky* (London: Thames and Hudson, 1968), 327–30. Él Lissitzky (actually Lazar Nikolaevich Lissitsky, 1890–1941), architect and artist, was a cofounder of constructivism.

A great stock of energy had accumulated that could not be released in architecture because no building was going on [owing to the financial crisis]. This energy found its release in the theater. Originally painters found satisfaction in theater because it afforded opportunity for painting decorative canvases on a large scale and enriching them with effects of artificial light. The stage settings of Lentulov, Fedotov,[24] and others are examples, but they were not satisfying for very long. Soon the painters themselves began, in harmony with the evolution of painting, to put forward three-dimensional spatial ideas of set design. The scene painter advanced toward architecture. [...]

The basic principles of the designer in creating scenery were as follows:

1. the scenic, acrobatic movements of the actor modify the apparatus of the play;

2. the apparatus, itself modified as a result of its mechanical construction, conditions the movements of the actors which are deduced from it;

3. these factors simultaneously lend the whole structure the illusion of reality. [...]

THE RSFSR 1 THEATER had its subsidy withdrawn on the ludicrous charge of overspending. It struggled along throughout the summer of 1921 but closed in September. The State Higher Theater Workshops (VUKhTEMAS) opened in

---

24 Aristarkh Vasil'evich Lentulov (1882–1943), painter with a powerful influence on the Russian cubo-futurists; designed for the Kamerny and Bol'shoy theaters. The graphic designer Ivan Fedotov (1881–1951) had provided abstract settings for *Lohengrin* at Zimin's Opera in 1918 and continued to design for the stage into the 1930s.

October 1921, under Meyerhold's administration, and there he taught classes to working-class youth and military veterans. To them he introduced his program of biomechanics and reflexology.

Vsevolod Meyerhold, "The actor of the future and biomechanics," June 12, 1922. In *Stat'i, pis'ma, rechi, besedy,* 2:486–89.

In the past the actor always conformed to the society for which his art was intended. In future the actor will have to coordinate his acting even more to industrial conditions, since he will be working in a situation where labor is no longer penal servitude but a vital and joyous necessity.

Under these conditions of ideal labor, art, naturally, must have a new foundation.

We are used to making a rigid division of each person's time between *labor* and *relaxation.* Every worker tried to spend as little time as possible on labor, and as much as possible on *relaxation.* Whereas such a desire may be considered normal under the conditions of capitalist society, it is wholly inappropriate to the proper development of a socialist society.

[. . .] The crucial question is to ration breaks for relaxation. In ideal conditions (of hygiene, physiology, and comfort) even a ten-minute break can completely replenish a person's energy.

Labor has to become easy, pleasant, and uninterrupted, and art has to be used by the new class as something *vitally important,* that is, fostering the labor process of the worker, and not just for entertainment. We will have to *adjust not only the forms of our creativity* but *our methods* as well.

The actor working for the new class will have to reexamine all the canons of the old theater. The whole acting profession needs to be repositioned. The actor's work in a new society must be regarded as a product necessary to the proper organization of labor of all citizens.

In addition to determining the proper ratio of relaxation to labor, it is also *important to find those active movements* that will help to optimize the entire working time. By observing the labor of an experienced worker, we can see in his movements (1) the absence of superfluous, unproductive motions; (2) rhythm; (3) the proper positioning of his body's center of gravity; (4) balance. Movements based on these principles are "danceable," the experienced worker's process of labor always recalls a dance, and here labor verges on art. The sight of a man working properly is a pleasure.

It is completely related to the work of the actor in the theater of the future.

In art we are always dealing with the organization of raw material.

Constructivism demands that the artist become an engineer. Art has to be based on a scientific foundation; the artist's creativity must always be of a conscious nature. The actor's art is based on the proper organization of raw material, that is, the ability to manage properly the expressive capabilities of his body.

The actor is a combination of organizer and what is to be organized (that is, the artist and the raw material). The actor's formula must be the following equation:

$N = A^1 + A^2$, where N is the actor, A^1 is the constructor who creates a concept and gives orders for its implementation, and A^2 is the actor's body, the agent implementing the orders of the constructor (A^1).

The actor should train his material—the body—to make it able to implement the tasks imposed from outside (by an actor or a director) instantaneously.

Since the aim of the actor's performance is to carry out a particular task, an economy of expressive abilities is required to ensure *the most efficient implementation of a task.*

The methods of *Taylorization*[25] are as natural for the actor's work as they are for any other labor targeted to achieve maximum productivity.

The consequent rules: (1) that relaxation be included in the working process in the form of pauses and (2) that art perform a specific vital function, instead of being just entertainment—that it require a vast *economy of time conservation* by the actor. Since art is part of a worker's overall time table and has only a certain number of temporal units assigned to it, that time has to be put to use in the most optimal way. This means that we cannot unproductively waste one and a half to two hours putting on costume and makeup. The actor of the future will work without makeup and in a *prozodezhda,*[26] that is, a special costume constructed to serve as an actor's casual clothes and also ideally suited for those motions and creative ideas that the actor will be implementing onstage in the process of acting.

Taylorization will allow us to play in one hour as much as we manage to supply now in four hours.

What the actor needs for that is (1) a natural *ability for reflex stimulation*—those who have this quality can be cast to type, based on their physical potential; (2) an actor must be *physically stable,* meaning that he has to have a sharp eye, a sense of balance, an awareness of where his body's center of gravity is at any time.

Since the art of the actor is the art of plastic forms in space, it is essential that an actor study the mechanics of his body. It is vitally important, since any instance of the use of force (even in the human body) is subject to the existing laws of mechanics, and the plastic art of an actor in a stage space is a manifestation of the force of the human body.

The major shortcoming of the modern actor is his total ignorance of the laws of *biomechanics.*

[...] There are many questions that have no definite psychological solutions. Building a theater on a psychological foundation is like building a house on sand; it will inevitably collapse. On the other hand, a theater built on *physical elements* can at least count on clarity. Every psychological state is determined by certain physiological processes. By finding the right solution for his physical state, an actor enters into a state

25 Taylorization, the scientific management of labor formulated by American efficiency expert Frederick Winslow Taylor (1856–1915); he used time and motion study to break work into its component parts and prescribed enforced standardization of methods.

26 *Prozodezhda,* a special uniform designed by Popova for Meyerhold; *proz* suggesting both "prosaic" (*prozaicheskaya*) and "industrial" (*proizvodstvennaya*), *odezhda* meaning "clothing." It was to serve as a basic working uniform for actors.

3.2. *Prozodezhda* for Actor No. 4 by Lyubov'
Popova, *The Magnanimous Cuckold,*
directed by Vsevolod Meyerhold, RSFSR 1
Theater, Moscow, 1922.

of *excitation* that infects the audience, involves it in his acting (what we used to call "a gripping performance"). This is the essence of acting. The *moments of excitation,* colored by one or another emotion, are the result of a long string of positions and situations.

As he practices this system of *emotional genesis,* the actor always has a solid foundation of physical motivation.

Gymnastics, acrobatics, dance, rhythm, boxing, and physical combat are certainly very useful fields of study, but they can be beneficial only so long as they are auxiliary to the main course of *biomechanics* essential for every actor.

MEYERHOLD drew his actors and designers from the workshops. The instructor Lyubov' Sergeevna Popova (1889–1924), a member of Kazimir Malevich's Suprematicists who taught for the Protletkul't during the Civil War, designed the "machine for acting" and the work-clothes costumes for his production of Crommelynck's *Le Cocu magnifique* [*The Magnanimous Cuckold*] at the former Sohn Theater, which had been reopened under the name "The Actors' Theater." The play concerns a miller so insanely jealous that he forces his wife on all the male inhabitants of his village to maintain control. Popova's construction suggested a mill with moving parts.

Sergey Tret'yakov, "*The Magnanimous Cuckold,*" *Zrelishcha* [Spectacle] 8 (1922), 12–13. Sergey Mikhaylovich Tret'yakov (1892–1939), playwright and a member of Mayakovsky's LEF movement, initiated the montage of attractions and preached a "factographic" approach to drama.

I don't like theaters and rarely go to them. What I most like to look at is how steam engines work, how streets are paved, how houses are built, how telegraph poles are climbed and wires are stretched.

[...] Love of industrial processes, interest in the utilitarian application of a thing and the techniques of its structure are characteristic for our times and are found in unquestionable connection with the heightened industrial schemes and projects of the Russian Revolution and economy. The forest and brick laying are regarded with greater interest than a house; a blueprint with greater interest than a painting [...] In the theater, rehearsals and the setting up of the scenery, its installation, provide more amusement than the polished plywood (imitation mahogany with the shavings of the process work tidily swept away) of the finished production.

The Cuckold gives satisfaction. It is a rehearsal, diffusing the aroma of work. Its *prozodezhda* does not refer us to psychology, everyday life, and history. On the contrary, the outlines and hues of the clothes offer basic associations to the industrial worker of this very day. The human body, as expressive material, set in motion, whose purpose is action, not reexperiencing, is turned to good account in diverse and far-flung ways. [...]

A word about the plot. People insist it's a farce. But to my mind, from a literary standpoint, it is not a farce but the most grievous tragedy. Jealousy that turns a man into a fool, and all that ensues from that. And inescapably. When I tried to switch the trajectory of my approach on to the rails of psychology, I was horrified—from the viewpoint of the play—by the sheer scream of a man impaled on a stake. Pornography? The question is a subtle and complicated one. To my mind, pornography is not so much a question of creativity (productivity) as a question of reception.

I watched not only the play but also the audience. I saw disapproving mamas, yawners surfeited with theatrogorging and snickering drivelers. But I also saw attentive and happily chortling workers (and by no means at the "dirty bits" in the script) and children, completely entranced by the funny and headlong action.

To sum up, I think that instead of taking children to namby-pamby neighborhood children's theaters, it would be better to take them to *The Cuckold.* [...]

Aleksey Gvozdev, "The ethics of a new theater," *Zhizn' iskusstva* 22 (1922), 9–10. Aleksey Aleksandrovich Gvozdev (1887–1937), professor of Russian literature and theater at Leningrad University, took part in GosTIM's tour to Germany 1925 and wrote one of the first monographs on Meyerhold 1926.

Meyerhold's *The Magnanimous Cuckold* is the answer of the inspired artist of the theater to the question of contemporaneity. The answer, given within the bounds of a mature theatrical mastery, freed of the traditions and routine that hovered over stage art in the course of the nineteenth century, in the era of realism, aestheticism, impressionism, and other "-isms," from whose circle other theaters are powerless to escape. Having repudiated the legacy of the not-so-distant past, Meyerhold absorbed the whole living and daring spirit of the revolutionary years, and along with it the best of the ancient traditions of the art we call the art of the theater. *The Cuckold* is a work of our time, passed through the purifying fire of revolutionary dislocations and reappraisals. But anyone familiar with the stage technique of the West and East over the course of the theater's development will find in this remarkable production many elements hallowed by the primordial traditions of stage art. [...]

Meyerhold has transformed this farce into a stupendous drama, its outcome bordering on tragedy. And this has been accomplished quite without a deficit in comic merriment. On the contrary, it is hard to imagine a more provocative, merry spectacle, more replete with amusing, mirth-raising acting. And yet this mirth is not the kind we indulge in at the Passage[27] or the operetta, or at the French theater. No, here, with Meyerhold, our mirth is purified by a sort of mountain air, a sort of broad expanse of a new humanity of the future. Here are no flabby aesthetics, no racy eroticism, no half-baked technique and discordant dilettantism, no catering to the taste of the theatrical mob. [...] Here a new artistic word rings out, renewed in its ethical content, and this achievement of Meyerhold's theater I consider the most valuable accomplishment of our theatrical present. An accomplishment for me indissolubly bound to the fact that this theater has accepted the Revolution through and through. Hence the involuntary regeneration of farce into drama, the phenomenon of a human being in a framework of laughter and joking.

It is from this viewpoint that one also has to scrutinize the directorial method of the show, its graphic means. The abolition of scenery and its replacement with a workbench casts off the everyday, temporal envelope from the play and eliminates that smack of bourgeois culture which is inherent in French farce. The same tendency also affects the replacement of everyday costume with the *prozodezhda*. A blue worker's jacket, with which the character is invested, slaughters all the usual associations connected with a costume and casts off any flight of philistinism, all the petty, humdrumness in our passions and feelings. And that mighty circus action, that whirlwind of acrobatic gestures with which the ensemble's acting bubbles, in short all the dynamic of the spectacle created on a biomechanical basis, brilliantly distributed in the construction, grips the spectators to the very end, eliminating from his reception all the elements of routine and passive contemplation. By dint of such a constructed spectacle, the heroine's genuinely human tragedy and the great blindness of her jealous spouse affect the spectator with the pure resonance of a true drama. [...]

> Rich, "Eighty of us," *Érmitazh* [Hermitage] 7 (1922), 8. *Érmitazh*, a magazine that contained current theater programs, was founded in 1922 to support Meyerhold; it became *Zrelishcha* (Spectacle) 1922–24.

These are the basic laws of biomechanics: the body is a machine, the one working it is a machinist, finding the center of gravity, balance, stability, the obligatory point of resistance, the coordination of physical movements in the stage space, orientation in space, in the placement of bodies, the law of vocal reflexes, gesture as the result of a

27 Saburov's Passage Theater 1912–25 in Petrograd specialized in bedroom farce and low comedy.

movement of the whole body, laws of running and walking, the meaning of "parade" in exercise, the Taylorization of movements, measuring by eye, arm, leg, and torso movements as efficient external work, and so on.

The biomechanical system has been practiced in Moscow for only a year. At the year's end Vs. Meyerhold and his instructor were invited to teach it in the following institutions: the Proletkul't, the Tekruzhok [Technical Club], the Trekhgorny Manufacturing Plant, the Jewish Studio (of Loyter[28]), the Bol'shoy Theater, the Actor's Theater, Meyerhold's Free Workshop.

The State Higher Theatrical Workshops are the laboratories of biomechanics, whence it will be disseminated.

Biomechanics is the most brilliant discovery on the theatrical front in the whole world. For directors it opens up the most extraordinary possibilities. Every aspect even of the present-day theater will with the aid of biomechanics receive a jolt such as the theater has never seen. Example: *The Magnanimous Cuckold*. But even in *Cuckold*, biomechanics has still not reached its apogee, for not all the actors yet master it.

Mass spectacles are becoming not a dream—a magic carpet, but a genuine reality. The magic carpet, transformed by humanity through its labor from a fairy tale into amazing reality—the airplane—is no longer a miracle out of a fairy tale. So through biomechanics we no longer have to dream, theorize, and conduct bad experiments with the mass spectacle—we know: in five, six years we shall see such celebrations of theatrical practice just as we shall joyously achieve a new everyday life.

The work processes, illumined by the laws of biomechanics, will be turned into that wholesome labor as art, labor as joy, the aspiration of all workers in all countries. [. . .]

André Van Gyseghem, "Throwing the stone," in *Theatre in Soviet Russia* (London: Faber and Faber, 1943), 29–30. André Van Gyseghem (1906–79), English actor on the London stage from 1930, made several trips to the Soviet Union between 1933 and 1939, working with Nikolay Okhlopkov at the Realistic Theater. He was able to observe biomechanical exercises in action.

1. *To concentrate the attention of the pupil*—the hands are clapped twice together in a downward movement, the arms hanging loosely.
2. *Preparing to run*—with a jump, turn and face the right, landing with the left foot in front.
3. *Preparing to run*—knees bent, right hand in front, left hand behind.
4. *Running.*
5. *To arrive where the stone lies*—stop running with a jump, landing on the left foot and with the left shoulder in front.
6. *Return to normal position.*

28 Naum Borukhovich Loyter (1890–1966), assistant director and actor at GOSET in the 1920s; chief director at the Moscow Proletkul't 1925–29. His brother Éfraim (1889–1963) ran the Jewish Kultur-Lig in Kiev and Moscow 1919–24.

7. *Prepare to get the stone*—rise on the toes and drop on to the right knee. Lean the body backward and then forward.
8. *Lifting the stone*—pick up the imaginary stone with the right hand, rise, swing the right hand, rise, swing the right arm round in a wide circle—swing it round to the left—front and back again to behind the body, where it hangs. The left shoulder is high, the right low, the right hand at about knee level. The knees are bent slightly.
9. *Preparing to run with the stone*—move backward a few steps.
10. *Running with the stone*—the stone still in the right hand held behind the body, left shoulder being raised.
11. *Arriving at the place from which to throw*—stop running, always with a slight jump, landing with the left foot in front.
12. *Preparing to throw the stone*—swing the stone over to the left front and grip the right wrist with the left hand.
13. *Swinging the stone*—swing the body weight onto the right foot—sweep the right arm back and swing it in a circular motion, still clasped by the left hand. Release the left hand and the circle widens until the whole right arm is swinging in a huge circle from the shoulder.
14. *Looking for the object to be hit*—the circular movement stops, the right arm (and stone) held out in front while the student looks.
15. *Rejudging the distance*—run a few steps forward, jump and stop.
16. *Preparing to throw*—swing the stone back, and the right leg.
17. *Throwing*—swing the right arm forward and the left back.
18. What is the result? Preparation—kneel on the right knee, clap the hands, and listen with the right hand cupping the ear.
19. *The mark is hit*—point forward with the left arm, lean back with the right arm on the right hip.
20. *Finish*—rise, facing inward, and clap twice as at the beginning.

———————————————

TARELKIN'S DEATH lacked the mass appeal of *Cuckold*; the set's moving parts often broke down, the barnlike building was unheated in the winter, and eventually the Sohn Theater's electricity was cut off.

Vsevolod Meyerhold, "Another breakup?," *Érmitazh* 7 (1922), 3.

Not until the very end of last year was I finally able to resume my work as director, interrupted by the breakup of the RSFSR 1 Theater.

Everyone knows under what conditions I was forced to bring it into being, and therefore it is no wonder that in this season I succeeded in staging only two productions, which nevertheless attracted general interest, while the second, judging by the reviews in the press and the public remarks of a series of competent persons, met with general approval. However I ought to declare that *my further work within the bounds of the Republic will be cut short*, because the only theater in which I work as a director (and not as a copyist)—the Actor's Theater—by official information communicated to me, is being removed from my authority and transferred to the Children's Theater AKTEO. [...]

In case I am deprived of the possibility of independence and activity (in my present tendency) as a director, which will inevitably result from the breakup of the Theater of the Actor, I actually and automatically *will be forced to refrain from its surrogates* [...] *and in general end activity in the Republic,* activity which evidently is considered so harmful and repulsive that its liquidation seems to be an indelible item on the agenda of the Tsentroteatr.

> O. Blyum, "The Meyerhold blockade," *Érmitazh* 8 (1922), 3–4. Oskar Venia-minovich Blyum (1886–87 to after 1927), director in charge of the Second MONO Theater (formerly Nezlobin's Theater), Moscow, edited the *Avant-Garde Almanac.*

Right now Meyerhold stands outside contemporary theatrical life. He is a déclassé individual, in our eyes leading a completely isolated existence. He is out of place on a par with happily competent mediocrity—Why? Because everyone connected with the collective guarantee of insignificance and charlatanry who has gone through the hell and high water of marketplace success—everyone, everyone, everyone who has known how to swell his sails with the fair wind of governmental favor and puff out his cheeks with the conceit of self-advertisement—stands as one man in the role of an indignant Molchalin[29] every time someone makes an attempt to break into the crypt of our theatricality.

No one encroaches on Korsh's theater: because every office-stool "Faun"[30] un-derstands that this is a "Golden Business." Nor is a finger laid on a single one of the MAT studios because the ink-stained souls who still feed on the stale columns of the *Russkie Vedomosti*[31] cannot exist without *The Deluge* or *The Green Ring.* But it's open season on Meyerhold for any poacher, because what he creates is unneeded by these creatures, confirmed in their aesthetic worldview "on behalf of polished opera-pumps and starched cuffs." [...]

On the other hand, Meyerhold, who has given us *Dawns* and *Mystery Bouffe,* who in *The Cuckold* opened up perspectives of an original theatrical rebirth, who fertilized all the achievements of the Proletkul't in the realm of theater, who vivified the stagnating idea of workers onstage—has been poisoned every hour of the day.

It may be that not everything Meyerhold has done is perfect. Maybe not every aspect of his activity is on the same level of perfection. I see no need to bring this up now. It is enough that he worked—at a time when others were picking their noses. He

---

29 Molchalin, the devious, social-climbing government secretary in Griboedov's *Woe from Wit.*
30 *Der Faun* (1906), a comedy by Hermann Baur, about a demigod who enters society.
31 *Russian Intelligencer,* a high-minded but highly conservative Moscow newspaper with a relatively limited number of subscribers.

created—at a time when the rest were off to the market. He provided ideas and sowed seeds—at a time when others were feathering their governmental nests. And now what concerns us is not a critical analysis of Meyerhold's creativity but the ultimate achievement of an essential immunity for this lucid, individual artist, deprived of the basic necessities.

MEYERHOLD'S THEATERS repudiated the bohemianism of actors and regarded themselves as laboratories. Their work was appraised by NOT (Nauchnaya organizatsiya truda; Scientific Organization of Labor), which ranked the actors of the Theater of Revolution. Mariya Babanova,[32] who had played Stella in *Cuckold*, received a score of 98 out of 100, surpassing the runners-up, who stuck at 89.

Mariya Babanova's score as an artist-worker. *STDM 21–26, 232–33.*

I. Talents with elements of influence on the spectator

a. Clarity in the line of business	—5
b. Presence of excitability and ability to use it	—5
c. Inner gifts (charm, humor, infectiousness)	—5
d. External gifts (size, face, eyes, figure)	—4
e. Range	—5
f. Plasticity	—5
g. Sense of rhythm	—5

II. Elements of external technique

1. Voice

a. purity of pronunciation (absence of dialect and impeccable diction)	—4
b. resonance (strength, fruitiness)	—5
c. versatility (range, registers)	—5
d. musicality	—5

2. Body

a. face (mimicry)	—5
b. hands	—5
c. legs	—5
d. figure (neck, shoulders, torso)	—5

III. Elements of internal technique

a. stage sense and clarity	—5
b. capacity for relationships and coordination	—5
c. ability to hold a pose	—5

32 Mariya Ivanovna Babanova (1900–1983), worked for Meyerhold at the Theater of Revolution, but left when her roles went to Zinaida Raykh; as Arbuzov's *Tanya* (1939), she created a new Soviet woman onstage.

> d. artistry (sense of proportion, artistic flair)   —5
> e. absence of routine and stale conventions and possession
>   of contemporary technique   —5

MEYERHOLD'S CONTROL extended to the Teresvat; he renamed it the Theater of Revolution and took over as artistic director. Many members of the troupe distrusted his leadership.

> Vasily Komardenkov, *Dni minuvshie* (*iz vospominany khudozhnika*) [Days gone by (from the remembrances of a designer)] (Moscow: Sovetsky khudozhnik, 1972), 94. Vasily Petrovich Komardenkov (1897–1978), designer for Teresvat 1919–22, designed Toller's *Wretched Eugene* at Radlov's Comedy Theater 1920; noted for the simple lines of his scenery.

[Meyerhold] said that, in the Theater of Revolution, he did not intend to innovate, that the chief task of the director was to find a realistic theatrical form, worthy of the theater's name, and to prove to the infidels that he, Meyerhold, could work as a realist. For innovation he had his own theater with a young, fresh troupe that was bursting to experiment.

THE SIGNATURE PRODUCTION of the Theater of Revolution was *Earth Rampant* (*Zemlya dybom*), which opened on March 4, 1923. It was Tret'yakov's adaptation of an antiwar play, *La Nuit* (1921) by Marcel Martinet, which had been published in Russian with a preface by Trotsky. Meyerhold formally dedicated the production to Trotsky, which proved to be an embarrassment later on. To create an appropriately military atmosphere, the stage was littered by Popova with realia—motorcycles, machine guns, a field kitchen, searchlights—while the acting style required emphatic speech and stark gestures. Meyerhold was named a People's Artist of the Republic on March 28 and celebrated his jubilee on April 2.

> Yury Annenkov, *Dnevnik moikh vstrech* (Moscow: Zakharov, 2001), 307.

I have forgot whether this took place at the opening (4 March 1923) or at one of the subsequent performances. The house was packed. Not far from me, in one of the boxes, accompanied by a few handsome commanders, sat People's Commissar for War and President of the Revolutionary War Soviet of the Republic L. D. Trotsky,[33] in a military uniform, following the action onstage with great attention.

---

33 Lev Davidovich Trotsky (actually Bronshteyn, 1879–1940) played a leading role in the 1905 Revolution as chairman of the St. Petersburg Soviet; commissar for foreign affairs 1917–18; commissar for war 1918–25, leading the Red Army during the Civil War; member of the Politburo 1919–27, opposing Lenin. Under Stalin, he formed a "combined opposition" with Zinov'ev and Kamenev until he was exiled from the Party 1927, expelled from Russia 1929.

3.3. Construction by Lyubov' Popova for *Earth Rampant,* directed by Vsevolod Meyerhold, RSFSR 1 Theater, Moscow, 1923.

As always, in a Meyerhold production, there were many interesting discoveries. The play's theme was the Civil War, the destruction of tsarism, the rout of the White Army. On a screen, inserted into the constructivist scenery by L. Popova, appeared political slogans. When the spectators read on it that "the performance is dedicated to the People's Commissar for War Lev Davidovich Trotsky," everyone stood up and, to applause, joined in singing "The Internationale." Trotsky also listened to it on his feet. Later, through the auditorium, real armored cars, motorcycles, and trucks rode onto the stage, also evoking applause and exclamations: "Glory to the Red Army! Forward to the Dictatorship of the Proletariat!" etc.

During one of these acts, by chance turning to Trotsky's box, I saw that he was no longer there. I thought that perhaps the production was not to his taste, and he had left the theater unnoticed. But two or three minutes later, Trotsky unexpectedly appeared *onstage* and, between the actors who parted in two in a picturesque manner, delivered a short speech, appropriate to the course of the action, devoted to the five-year anniversary of the founding of the Red Army. After a stormy ovation, the action continued to unfold onstage in the most realistic manner, and Trotsky returned again to his box.

Vsevolod Meyerhold, "From his appearance at the Jubilee Celebration," April 2, 1923. In *Stat'i, pis'ma, rechi, besedy,* 2:53.

I am proud to belong to the Russian Communist party, and all my work will be work for the proletariat. On this very day I have learned a great deal—it has demonstrated to me how I am to act in future. In the past, single individuals helped me; today it's thousands. Today the youth of the youngest class has welcomed me; in those welcomes I have derived strength for further struggles and work. All hail the younger generation!

A. Matskin, "Time to leave," *Teatr* 1 (1990), 32. Aleksandr Petrovich Matskin (1906–?) was a theater scholar and literary critic.

Nâzim Hikmet wrote a poem:

> A great theater
> is a gorgeous grain elevator,
> a wardrobe to supply GUM,[34]
> the silk of the scenery—
> on the petticoats of peasant girls!

[A telegram]: "Trotsky sends his greetings. The Red Army . . . in the name of the four services of the military (infantry, cavalry, artillery, and air force) deliver to Meyerhold the Red banner of victory."

DURING the performances, collections were taken up, which eventually went to purchasing a plane that was named "Meyerhold."

The year 1923 was the centenary of Aleksandr Ostrovsky's birth. Lunacharsky hoped to curb some of the more unbridled experiments by proclaiming "Back to Ostrovsky," requiring each of the major theaters to stage one of his plays. Meyerhold's contribution was *A Lucrative Post,* a humdrum production that proved popular with audiences. Nothing prepared the critics for Meyerhold's deconstruction of the beloved comedy *The Forest,* which opened on January 19, 1924. It initiated his practice of disarticulating classic plays into a number of episodes.

Vsevolod Meyerhold on *The Forest.* Aleksandr Gladkov, "The art of the director," in *Vstrechi s Meyerkhol'dom. Sbornik vospominany* (Moscow: Vserossiyskoe Teatral'noe Obshchestvo, 1967), 2:292–93.

In our *Forest,* at first there were thirty-three episodes, but because the performance ended very late and the spectators missed the last streetcar, I heeded the management's pleas and abridged it to twenty-six episodes. The performance, which had lasted over four hours, now ran three hours and twenty minutes. Time passed, and the management informed me that the performance was again taking four hours. I concluded that the

34 Gosdarstvenny Universalny Magazin, the massive department store off Red Square.

actors, on their own, had put back some of the scenes I'd cut. I show up, I watch—but nothing of the sort! It was simply that they were overacting the remaining twenty-six episodes. I reprimand them. It doesn't help. I call a rehearsal and with aching heart cut the production to sixteen episodes. For a while the performance runs two and a half hours, but then again expands to four hours. Ultimately, the show half fell to pieces, and we had to rehearse it anew, reestablishing all the rhythms and temporal proportions within the production. Once I had to post an order that if the scene between Pëtr and Aksyusha, which was to last two minutes, ran a minute longer, I would impose a penalty on the actors.

> Vladimir Nemirovich-Danchenko to Ol'ga Bokshanskaya,[35] February 3, 1924.
> In *Tvorcheskoe nasledie* (Moscow: Moskovsky Khudozhestvenny teatr, 2003),
> 3:63–64.

Meyerhold has staged *The Forest.* (This is worth reporting.)

In general, there is nothing on his stage, except the construction for the given performance. No curtain. The back wall of the stage and the sides are open. Upstage people walk across whenever they have to, as if there were no performance or audience.

In *Forest* stage left, there is a tall scaffolding, as if depicting a road (from Kerch to Vologda), leading from upstage left of the audience roughly to center stage (where the prompter's box normally is). At the top of the scaffolding Arkashka and Neshchastlitsev meet. At the right side they set up furniture, whatever is needed for rooms or servants' halls. Stage center stand "gigantic steps." The play begins with the meeting of Arkashka and Neshchastlivtsev. But soon their famous dialogue is interrupted, and the action shifts to the right: scenes from Ostrovsky's Act I take place there. That's how the whole first section works (the whole play is divided into thirty-three episodes. In the first section there are about a dozen of them.) The dialogue of Arkashka and Neshchastlivtsev is divided into five to six parts. And the first act is similarly divided. The act moves back and forth. On one side for a while they act at Gurmyzhskaya's, or they sit and drink tea or catch fish or sleep (Arkashka and Neshchastlivtsev), while on the other side they play cards, iron laundry, give Gurmyzhskaya a *pedicure.* The scene of Pëtr and Aksyusha in Act II (doleful, lyrical in Ostrovsky) takes place on the giant steps. At first Aksyusha runs around by herself, Pëtr watches, then he joins in, then both of them. And, as they run, they speak the lines. Here's how the characters look: Gurmyzhskaya is an actress of thirty-five, in a field jacket, a short skirt, polished high boots, with a whip, in an enormous red wig. She is all in *yellow.* Bodaev is a rural police officer with a big *green* beard. And Bulanov is in a green wig, in a lawn-tennis outfit. Milonov is a priest with golden hair and beard. Aksyusha, of course, is in a *red* dress. Vosmibratov is all in black (get it: a member of the Black Hundreds[36]). I watched only the first part. I couldn't take any more. It was very boring. But, they tell me that further on, there

---

35 Ol'ga Sergeevna Bokshanskaya (b. Nyurenberg, 1891–1948) worked at the MAT from 1919 to her death; secretary to the administration and personal secretary to Nemirovich-Danchenko.

36 Black Hundreds, extreme right political organizations, supported by the tsarist police, which, after 1905, promoted anti-Semitic pogroms and promoted the monarchist cause.

3.4. The concertina scene in Ostrovsky's *The Forest,* directed by Vsevolod Meyerhold, Meyerhold Theater, Moscow, 1924.

were passages that are successful—especially Pëtr's playing the concertina, so remarkable that it prompted applause. The actors, except for Arkashka (Il'insky), are all bad.

> Walter Benjamin, *Moscow Diary,* ed. Gary Smith, trans. Richard Sieburth (Cambridge, Mass.: Harvard University Press, 1986), 40.

December 23, 1926. The celebrated concertina scene in *Forest* is truly quite beautiful, but it had become so splendidly and romantically lodged in my imagination through Asja's description of it that I initially had difficulty finding my way into it when I encountered its reality onstage. The whole production is full of splendid moments: the scene in which the eccentric ham actor is fishing and creates the illusion of the catch wriggling on his line with mere quivers of his hand, the love scene played out as they run in a circle, the entire scene on the catwalk that leads down to the stage from a scaffold. For the first time I clearly grasped the function of the constructivist use of the stage; it had never been this evident to me with Tairov in Berlin[37] and even less so in photographs.

MEYERHOLD not only directed but codesigned, with his ex-student Il'ya Shlepyanov, *D.E.* [i.e., *Daësh Evropu; Hand over Europe*], an agitsketch or agitposter by

37 Tairov's company first played Berlin in 1923.

3.5. The moving screens designed by Meyerhold for *D.E.* by Podgaetsky, Meyerhold Theater, Moscow, 1924.

Mikhail Podgaetsky confected from the novels *The D.E. Trust* by Il'ya Érenburg and *The Tunnel* by Bernhard Kellerman, with a dash of Upton Sinclair. In seventeen episodes and ninety-five roles, it confronted the capitalist West with a triumphant international of workers and soldiers. It opened on June 15, 1924.

Mark Mestechkin, *V teatre i v tsirke* (Moscow: Iskusstvo, 1976), 48–49.

Unfortunately, the grotesque figures of the repulsive characters in the production came across more sharply than the images of the positive heroes, rendered a bit schematically.

The basic component of the staging of *D.E.* was moving panels. Appropriately arranged, they created the setting for one or another episode. The dynamic for the whole production was provided by the high-speed running of M. A. Tereshkovich[38] in the leading role as he encountered the moving panels (a man invisible to the audience was behind each panel, moving it).

D.E. was reminiscent of a movie—so great was its number of different episodes, characters, and so fast paced was the tempo. Despite the fact that the company was a large one, many of us had to play several roles. For instance, Érast Garin[39] played seven different agents, who arrived one after another with each agent's proposition. Meyerhold constructed the episode "Seven Agents" like a circus illusion act using the

38 Maksim Abramovich Tereshkovich (1897–1939), actor at the RSFSR 1 and Theater of the Revolution 1920–33, in satiric and caricatural roles; began directing 1927 and organized the Lunacharsky Studio Theater (after 1931 the Ermolova Studio Theater), which he ran until 1936.

39 Érast Pavlovich Garin (1902–80), actor, an agile comedian much used by Meyerhold, who cast him as Gulyashkin in *Credentials,* Khlestakov in *The Inspector General,* and Chatsky in *Woe to Wit*; he later worked at the Leningrad Comedy Theater and the Moscow Satire Theater.

principle of quick-change. Exiting behind a panel after playing a given role, Garin, assisted by dressers, changed clothes with lightning speed, and when the show was on tour, this whole kitchen of stunts was visible to the spectators, because the panel opened accordingly. It's curious that, bowing to the audience, he raised his arms and made a "compliment" like a bona fide circus performer.

This production had lots of hits for actors. I. Il'insky was unforgettable in the role of the capitalist Tvaift. The scene "Tvaift's Morning" was especially successful. Lying in bed, Tvaift gave orders to his secretary, played by me, while a masseur (V. Maslatsov[40]) "massaged" him, walking up and down his prostrate body. This scene was noteworthy first of all for the fact that it was performed with complete belief in the given circumstances, with a feeling that it couldn't be done any other way.

In the scene "In the Bar" M. Babanova and her partner, D. Lipman, danced magnificently. Lev Sverdlin danced the chechotka [tap dance] excellently.[41] For this production, an original jazz band was created, which included among the players the pianist Evgeny Gabrilovich, the poet Valentin Parnakh (later a famous screenwriter), and the shock worker Aleksandr Kostomolotsky,[42] a master of walk-on roles and caricature, later an actor at the Mossovet Theater.

Despite a certain rectilinearity and even primitive quality in the play, the production enjoyed great success with the spectators. But Il'ya Érenburg,[43] I recall, greatly disliked Podgaetsky's play and even quarreled with Meyerhold over it.

All my life I'll remember a unique charity matinee of D.E. when Meyerhold came onstage. He and Zinaida Raykh[44] were supposed to act in the "Desert Scene." The theater was packed, and all the actors poured into the house to see this sensation. But a bitter disappointment awaited us. Vsevolod Emil'evich rode out of the audience on a motorcycle with a sidecar and was raised to the stage by a trapdoor elevator. He was in a leather overcoat with the invariable scarf around his neck. His entrance was met with thunderous applause. Not having acted for many years, Meyerhold got a bit fuddled, looked at Raykh for a long time in torment, trying to say something to her but evidently forgetting his lines, and, without saying a word, walked offstage.

40 Vladimir Aleksandovich Maslatsov (1897–?), actor.

41 Lev Naumovich Sverdlin (1901–69), actor at the Theater of Revolution from 1926, often in crowd scenes and secondary roles; later at the Vakhtangov Theater 1937–41 and the Mayakovsky Theater 1943.

42 Evgeny Iosifovich Gabrilovich (1899–1993) played piano for Meyerhold for four years, before becoming a successful screenwriter; as a war correspondent, he witnessed the uncovering of Hitler's corpse in his Berlin bunker. Valentin Yakovlevich Parnakh (actually Parnokh, 1891–1951), creative director of music and choreography at Meyerhold's Theater, whose jazz band appeared in D.E.; emigrated to Paris 1925–31 but returned to the Soviet Union as a translator. Aleksandr Kostomolotsky (1897–1975), actor and painter, friend of Shostakovich.

43 Il'ya Grigor'evich Érenburg (Ehrenburg, 1891–1967), author and journalist, a favorite of Stalin; lived in Berlin 1921–24 and Paris 1924–34, retaining Soviet citizenship; evacuated to Moscow 1940. One of his novels coined the term The Thaw to indicate the shift in Soviet cultural policy.

44 Zinaida Nikolaevna Raykh (1894–1939), a student in the Theater Workshops who became Meyerhold's second wife; he made her the female lead in all his productions from 1923, exploiting her sex appeal. She was mysteriously murdered after her husband's arrest.

MEYERHOLD'S INVENTIONS were not always appreciated or even understood by the proletarian audience.

> Rabkor[45] Nikolaev, "The meaning of *D.E.*," *Rabochy i Teatr* [Worker and theater] 37 (September 15, 1925), 15.

There is no integral and definite impression of *D.E.* as a performance. This is explained, for the most part, by the flaws in the subject matter. This *agitka,* magnified to the dimensions of something huge, is not always successfully performed. The very scheme of the play is rather diffuse, without unity of plot, the individual episodes almost totally unconnected to one another. The performance has not yet lost its agitational power and conviction, despite the comparatively long (relative to our conditions) time that has passed since the first performance. Individual moments are fully contemporary and totally grip the spectator. If we address the method of the director's concept, applied by Meyerhold in this staging, one can, as in all his works, point out the sweep, audacity, and success of the devices used. The moving panels (screens), on which, in essence, all the "sets" are built, make possible the dynamics of the action. Despite the bizarre nature of the stage experiments, the spectator quickly gets used to them and in future follows them with impatient enjoyment.

Very good is the jazz band (a noisy orchestra), although, at times, awfully deafening for our northern ears. Its use does not always seem appropriate and necessary, at times it also impedes the unfolding action, and even in the front rows of the stalls you cannot make out the words spoken onstage. Some episodes might be recognized as classical by the power of their agitational–artistic pressure ("Propagate Rationally," "Fox-trotting Europe," "Lackeys of French Capital"). The episode "Hand Over Europe" gives a particular impression of the prominence and depth of the stage. The sports moments are also very good. [...]

> John Dos Passos, "Moscow theaters October and November 1928," *Theater 1929* (January 1929), 8. The American novelist John Roderigo Dos Passos (1896–1970) was a committed socialist when he visited the Soviet Union in 1928; what he saw turned him into a Trotskyite who militated against Stalinist show trials.

D.E. [...] a play about the conflict between American capitalist world dominion and the revolution, a little play like Lawson's *The International,*[46] although set in a very different key. A fantastic play in numberless scenes, playing to the music of the only

---

45 *Rabochy korrespondent* or working-class reporter.
46 John Howard Lawson (actually Levy, 1894–1977), American playwright and Communist, who, with Dos Passos, founded the short-lived Workers Drama League 1926 and the more durable New Playwrights Theater 1929; *The International* (1928), with sets by Dos Passos, ran for twenty-seven performances. Lawson was later blacklisted as one of the "Hollywood Ten."

good jazz band east of the millpond, that was from the director's point of view the most interesting and the least successful of Meyerhold's productions. The scenery was ten big polished red wooden screens about twelve feet high and fifteen broad that scooted about continually, revealing small bits of the stage set with the furniture necessary for each scene. Meanwhile maps and headlines are continually shown on a movie screen in the top of the proscenium arch. In the course of four hours, every effect possible to the Elizabethan Theater, to the Japanese and Chinese theaters, to the burlesque and melodrama of the west was squeezed dry and poured into the shaker. [...]

———————

FOR THE 1924–25 SEASON, the Theater of Revolution staged *Quadrille with Angels,* based on Anatole France, directed by Meyerhold's epigone Aleksey Gripich (1891–1985), and featuring Mariya Babanova. The critics, tiring of this sort of agitstyle, joked.

Mikhail Levidov, "Simple truths," *Novaya zritel'* 39 (1924), 4.

Q: What does a European bourgeois spend his time doing?
A: He dances the fox-trot and prays to God.
Q: What is the bourgeois system?
A: The restaurant and the cabaret...
Q: What is the revolution?
A: It is when, at the end of the third part, during approximately the twentieth episode, the lights go out, the newsboy shouts: general strike; sometimes during this they shoot blank cartridges and foul the air in the theater, where the ventilation was bad enough without that.
Q: And what is the vice punished?
A: It is always the enchanting Babanova, who, although she is vice, still always makes the greatest hit.

———————

THE TEACHER BUBUS (*Uchitel' Bubus,* 1924) by Aleksey Fayko was described by the composer Shostakovich as "wild and crazy." This comedy is set in an unnamed European capital rocked by revolutionary uprisings. Bubus, a tutor in a wealthy household, wavers between the various factions. In this respect he resembled a great many other protagonists of Soviet drama in the late 1920s and early 1930s. The critics were equally divided, their attention drawn more to Meyerhold's employment of biomechanics than to the intrinsic qualities of the play.

Pavel Markov, "*Bubus* at Meyerhold's," *Rabochy i teatr* 6 (February 9, 1925), 15–16. Pavel Aleksandrovich Markov (1897–1980), critic and director, a collaborator with Mayakovsky on the Satire Studio, became head of the literary department of the MAT from 1948.

This was not a production. It was a lesson in directorial pedagogic mastery. The performance might be called "The Teacher Meyerhold." The play served as a pretext for educating actors and constructing individual scenes. The director was disdainfully divorced from the author.

Fayko[47] wrote in good language an uncomplicated, light comedy, almost a farce, shifting in the last act into melodrama. It tells of the teacher Bubus, an inept proponent of "the principles of virtue and honesty," a cowardly fighter against "violence," a wavering defender of everything "eternal" about someone who might now be called by the nominal name "Bubus." It is a comedy of a toy government.

But Fayko's play is not for Meyerhold. His temperament feels constrained in its narrow frames and bored in its small dimensions. He tried to compensate for its absence of monumentality, which crushed the rapid light comedy of Fayko. The farce comedy moved in a slow tempo to the ironic accompaniment of music by Chopin and Liszt. Posters and political slogans vainly tried to underline the elements of political satire, which do not exist in this simple "comedy of manners." The lack of a meeting between author and director destroyed the play and rendered the director's work fruitless.

All that is left is to admire the directorial brilliance of Meyerhold's doings, as one admires an abstract combination of sounds and colors. How he built a system of actors' movements; how he moved them around the stage; in what combinations he staged things; how he used the bamboo scenery; how from the simplest combinations of color and light he created a beautiful picture; how the musical accompaniment forced the actors to build their speech musically; how the principle of "preacting"[48] led to a distinct art of pantomime—all this was a lucid lesson in the laws of directorial mastery.

A cold and magnificent Meyerholdian production evokes a cold response: delight at Meyerhold's mastery and wearisome indifference to the fates of the characters in the play. But most of all: a thirst to see the Meyerhold who hopes, hates, laughs, agitates passionately, loves—the Meyerhold of *The Forest* and *Earth Rampant,* more profound and significant than this magnificent and ironic "stage instructor," as he showed himself to be tonight.

MEYERHOLD had already staged Aleksey Fayko's first full-length play *Lake Lyul* in 1923. This "detective melodrama" has been called by Konstantin Rudnitsky "the first 'genuine,' 'well-made' play to appear on the Soviet stage." It revolved around a conflict of ruthless capitalists, a bogus ex-revolutionary, and a set of actual revolutionaries, intended to display the "collapse of individuality." Meyerhold's production at the Theater of Revolution had been a highly influential success two years before it toured to Leningrad, where its welcome was more measured.

47 Aleksey Mikhailovich Fayko (1893–1978), whose early conspiracy dramas appealed to Meyerhold, but whose *Man with a Briefcase* (1928) had a longer stage life. His playwriting petered out after the war.

48 A device Meyerhold borrowed from Asian theater: a "momentary pause for aim," a static freeze preceding a significant action.

Rabkor V. Dolgintsev, "The Theater of Revolution," *Rabochy i teatr* 17 (April 26, 1925), 7.

I've never seen a Meyerhold production except for *Lake Lyul'*, and all the same I'll make bold to speak my mind about the Theater of Revolution. Whether or not the production of *Lake Lyul'* is successful, it appears to be typical of the theater and gives one the right to judge the whole tendency of the theater.

The subject matter of *Lake Lyul'* will not sustain criticism. A vapid adventure melodrama, devoid of even a pretension to being revolutionary. Questions of class struggle, internal contradiction of capitalist society, questions of personality and the masses are treated so superficially, so falsely, that you feel like advising the author to take a course in political economy and read an anthology of class struggle to write at least with a bit more "politeracy."

And yet, despite the vacuity and poverty of the subject, this production gripped me completely. The tempo of the action, its dynamics, the very process of the unfolding action were gripping. And involuntarily you ask yourself the question: is this the aim that justifies the existence of the Theater of Revolution and its name? Undoubtedly: yes!

The whirlwind of Revolution has so wound us up, life has taken on such a rapid tempo, with the eternal tension of muscles, ideas, in the upsurge to the sublime, that the forms of the old theater are no longer capable of presenting the dynamics of our life nowadays. We need new forms, as broad and high as skyscrapers. Meyerhold creates these forms. Maybe the creation of these new forms will appear to be the means to create a revolutionary production?

P. K—y, "Theater of Revolution," ibid.

Modern art, striving to re-create this turbulent life, destroys old forms and tries to find a new one to transmit the feverish, agitated rhythm of the European capitalist city. This attraction to Americanism also constitutes the entire interest in the production of *Lake Lyul'*, first staged by Meyerhold in 1923.

Two years ago, such a production was a real sensation, but time flies, and what yesterday staggered us with its novelty has today already lost the sharpness and freshness of its impressions. Elevators, sirens, horns, telephones, jittery spotlights, shouts, an American tempo—all this holds the spectators in a tense state of attention, creates an atmosphere of the seething life of a huge city.

The stage atmosphere is literally drenched in all sorts of honking horns, flashing lights, the keen struggle of boundless energy. A dynamic beauty, born in the urban milieu, saturates the whole stage. Lightning swift movements are interwoven with the nonstop, restless strolling of the crowd. They all talk quickly (thereby abusing clear enunciation), speedily, wonderfully darting about, everything bubbles, flashes, and lives.

[...] It is easy, pleasant, engrossing to watch this well-wrought, wittily contrived constructivist production. Brilliant moments, distinctive, individual numbers (as in the circus), everything is put on show, craves approval, but after every act (and there are five of them) the spectator rightly asks: "Where is the social–political task of a theater which it promised to reveal in 1923, what is the meaning of such a production?" There is no answer by the time the production ends.

———————

HAVING PILLORIED Western capitalists as the villains in his recent productions, Meyerhold now mounted a comedy that skewered the "ex-people" and "wannabes" of his own society. The young sketch writer Nikolay Érdman presented him with his first full-length play, *Mandat*. (The title is often translated as *The Mandate* or *The Warrant*, but, in light of the action, means *Credentials* or *The Party Card*.) Using a forged document, a young nitwit tries to impress a bourgeois neighbor to marry his sister, but the intended bridegroom prefers their cook, who is believed to be the Grand Duchess Anastasia. It opened at Meyerhold's theater on April 20, 1925.

"Érdman's *Credentials* at the Meyerhold," *Rabochy i teatr* 22 (May 31, 1925), 14.

A scheduled meeting of the theater section of the Govt Acad. of Arts & Sciences was devoted to a discussion of the production of N. Érdman's *Credentials* at Meyerhold's Theater. [...] P. A. Markov considers that Meyerhold did not appreciate the first two acts, portraying them in the style of light comedy. Then in Act III the director was able to raise Érdman's play to the level of tragicomedy, making an indelible impression on the spectator, as the Art Theater once did with *The Seagull*.[49] This is our first play—this is the start of our theater. [...]

V. G. Sakhnovsky moved to a profound discussion of the director's concepts. In this production Meyerhold discovered a new form of theater, a new realism. In this production Meyerhold destroyed the man without a face, the man who still dreams about the beauty of old Russia, the burned estate, or who, like Pavel Gulyachkin, shouts hackneyed slogans. Without presenting a single positive character, he drenches the spectator in irony, inveigles the spectator to rebel against such a life. Therein lies the social significance of the production.

Yury Kobrin, "The actor in Meyerhold's Theater as a social activist [*obshchest-vennik*]," in *Teatr imeni Meyerkhol'da* [Meyerhold Theater] (Moscow: Moskovskoe teatral'noe izd., 1926), 29–30, 32.

The revolutionary theater is educating a new actor. "Cliché" acting has retreated into the distant past; the old actor, the bygone old school had different worldviews. Its professional actors considered it indispensable to perform "on command" of the director or the author and confined themselves to that. The new actor in every role, depicting one "type" or another, expresses his relationship to it. By this the theory of "acting as pure art" is discarded in the revolutionary theater.

49 *The Seagull* (1895–96) by Anton Chekhov was a qualified failure when it first opened at the Alexandra Theater in St. Petersburg but made the reputation of the MAT when it was revived there in 1898.

The reflection of passing reality, the reflection of the class struggle, the reflection of the everyday life of the workers is possible only if the actor will express his relation to that stratum of society that he depicts. [...]

Indeed, *The Forest, Credentials,* and other productions were able to captivate, win over the working-class spectator only thanks to the fact that the "old" background and the "new" background received there their greatest reflection, were able to captivate exclusively by the "ironical" performance of the actors. [...]

To be with the working class, to reflect its life, its struggle on our theatrical boards is the goal of the revolutionary theater. But when the revolutionary theater can fulfill that great role, which we impose on it to be a theater "of agitation and propaganda"—it can do this *only when* the actor becomes a social activist, merges with the working class, will move against its background, will be linked indissolubly with it. This is no easy task. We know that most of our actors represent the old school, that there are few new actors, actors of the proletarian background among us, and those actors, who emerge from a proletarian environment, often lost contact with their own class, and that is why it is still necessary in great measure to be linked to the working masses, by means of work in working-men's clubs, cultural commissions at factories and plants, participation in drama circles, organizing worker's performances, etc.

An actor outside the proletarian class is not a socially active actor and is incapable and inept at knowing how to present the new life, the struggle for "new culture."

In Meyerhold's theater the acting is taken to be acting that manifests a definite social aspect.

Meyerhold's theater strives to manifest social functions of stage art. In the revolutionary theater the actor must be a tribune, from his theatrical tribunes he must exert agitational influence on the worker spectator. As a propagandist, leading agitation among the worker spectator, there must be a new actor. The years 1918–1919–1920 were years when open-air theater was the agitpoint.

Now the proletarian revolutionary theater must become a center of agitation and propaganda.

Meyerhold's theater, besides the manifestation of the actor's role as tribune-agitator, demands that the actor be a prosecutor.

The actor-prosecutor, indicting old society, indicting our cultural obsolescence, indicting our bureaucracy, etc.

The actor must be a social activist—this motto found its practical application in Meyerhold's theater.

The actor-tribune, actor-"prosecutor," actor, showing his relationship to the rebuilding of society he depicts, is our unhackneyed, proletarian actor.

In Meyerhold's revolutionary theater the actor is a social activist—therein lies the reason that the theater vividly notes our reality, depicts it not "on command" but actually presents, educates the new working-class spectator.

The struggle for a purposeful actor, for the social purpose of acting, is the task of the revolutionary theater.

Konstantin Fel'dman, "From bio-mechanics to the Caspian roach," in *Sem' dney MKT 1–20* [Seven days of the Moscow Chamber Theater] (Moscow: ZIK, 1924). Konstantin Isidorovich Fel'dman (1881–1967), journalist, screenwriter, and critic, had been a member of the Menshevik faction and participant in the battleship *Potëmkin* mutiny.

This passion for the special effects of "theatrical discovery" defines the very nature of the discoveries of V. Meyerhold: in his creative work it is hard to trace the logical progression of the artist's ideas, moving along a clearly mapped path. Meyerhold "is seeking"; therefore he himself can have the vaguest idea of what he is actually seeking; in the pursuit of discovery he has no qualms about using any available means, caring little whether it is theatrical or not; like Gogol's Osip,[50] he picks up every bit of rope "for in housekeeping every little bit of rope can come in handy."

For a long time now, has not Meyerhold fought against naturalism with the frenzy of a berserk Vissarion? For a long time now, haven't we heard loud proclamations of "biomechanics" and the war against aestheticism onstage? In *Tarelkin's Death,*[51] instead of fish, we're inundated with cardboard squares reading "Shark," "Sheatfish," etc., instead of letters and documents—signs with the mottos "biomechanics," "photocinema," etc.

But the possibility of "discovery" is limited first of all by the techniques of the theater, and the desecrated aesthetic takes its revenge.

Already in *Lake Lyul'*, the spectator was surprised by Meyerhold's return to naturalism.

That "urbanistic production" completely failed to cohere what with the disorderly hustle and bustle of the crowd scenes, the naturalism of the costumes, and chiefly the acting, built on reexperiencing. In this show V. Meyerhold had shaken to its foundations the essential law of any artistic work: unity of style.

In *The Forest* Meyerhold crudely broke that law. To put it baldly, there is no performance as such in this new "discovery" of Meyerhold; no play, no interpretation of it.

Let me make myself clear: I have nothing against so-called perversion of the author onstage, and I am not offended on Ostrovsky's behalf. The author is only one element of the theatrical creative work, and of course the theater has the right, more, the obligation to adjust any stage work to its own laws. An author may conceive his play along the lines of drama and comedy, the theater may choose to treat it as farce.

However, a *plan* is necessary, for without a plan, there is no work of art. In *Forest*, there is no such plan; it's not by chance the play is broken into thirty-three episodes; these episodes make up thirty-three acts of a single evening's program at Meyerhold's theater. For in front of us there was no performance but an evening of music hall, miniature theater with its many numbers. And nothing was missing in this program: scenes of everyday life, comic skits, atmospheric scenes, a concertina and giant staircase, a pedicure and acrobatics.

50 Osip, Khlestakov's shrewd man-servant in *The Inspector General*, who, in Act IV, relieves the town's tradesmen of everything they are carrying.
51 *Tarelkin's Death* (1869; first produced 1900), the third play in Aleksandr Sukhovo-Kobylin's grotesque comic trilogy. Meyerhold staged it in a constructivist manner in 1922.

The critics have noted that in the performance, there were two scenic dimensions: one on the bridge, where eccentric acts reigned, the other on Gurmyzhskaya's estate, where the everyday life of an old-fashioned Russian estate unfolded. To be blunt, the whole production is built on aesthetic effects with the aid of naturalistic techniques. To begin with the props, there are real "dinner tables," underwear hung on a clothesline, rubles and a wheelchair and a real pumpkin which Gurmyzhskaya is actually pickling; nor is the situation saved by the "Caspian roach," which Neschastlivtsev hands to Arkashka instead of money, for this effect is treated as entirely "natural," an actor's gag. And in the scene with the pedicure, when Gurmyzhskaya actually bares her feet, noticeable was the orgiastic joy with which Meyerhold seized on that naturalistic effect, literally resting on it from his long journey into the cold, abstract poles of stylized and biomechanical theater.

[...] And in the scenes between Pëtr and Aksyusha, in the scenes with the concertina and the giant staircase, there is clearly a marked return to the aesthetics of the "Art Theater," built on mood and exploited hundreds and thousands of times by the innumerable miniature theaters of the former Nevsky Prospect.

[...] However, the story goes that in one of his discourses Meyerhold explained that the production of *The Forest* was done to show that a return to Ostrovsky is impossible.

Tairov and the Kamerny Theater

After a 1921 staging of *Romeo and Juliet* that was overwhelmed by Aleksandra Ékster's complicated sets and costumes, Tairov chose Racine's *Phèdre* as his next production. It opened in February 1922, again designed by Vesnin in a far more chastened form of constructivism. Relying on the emotional power of Koonen's acting in the lead, Tairov managed to achieve his first solid post-Revolutionary hit. It did not silence his enemies but bestowed a good deal of prestige on the theater.

> Anatoly Lunacharsky, "Theater and revolutionary Russia," *Vestnik Iskusstv* [Herald of the arts] 1 (1922), 4.

Tairov is basically conducting very serious research into the content of his theatrical experiments. Look over his whole repertory, and you will see that three-quarters of it consist of masterpieces of world literature or adaptations of those classics. Nor is this enough. Tairov, moreover, moving toward a synthetic theater, intends to stage Racine's *Phèdre* and endows this production with a particular significance. Here, evidently, the theater earnestly hopes to reach a harmonic combination of extremely profound psychological tragedy with a corresponding form. We shall see what becomes of this, since the failure of *Romeo and Juliet,* I suppose, does not provide us with the degree of certainty we should like to have. But, I repeat, all the same, there is much to be learned from Tairov.

But Tairov comes from the leftist intelligentsia, infected with futurism, that is, with a perversion of form, which has developed owing to a vacuum of content. Hence the abyss of affectation. One may be technically acute and polished, but does one always have to behave so affectedly? Almost all of Comrade Tairov's productions are distorted by affectation. One must free oneself of this at any cost. Perhaps only a repertory of new plays could free him.

In conclusion I say: nowhere will such new plays appear so well prepared, nowhere will they find such a welcome, nowhere could they be awaited with such firm confidence as in Russia.

> Anatoly Lunacharsky, "*Phaedra* at the Kamerny Theater," in *Sobranie sochineny v 8 tomakh* [Collected works in eight volumes] (Moscow: Iskusstvo, 1964), 3:108–10.

I also had a rather negative view of the experience of the Kamerny Theater, although, following my general principle never to be guided by my personal opinions, always acknowledging the collective's stability and belief in itself, its plan, its capacity for work, I supported the Kamerny Theater to the best of my ability. I, like many others, was put off by the affectations characteristic of this theater, the exaggerated role of gestures, implemented by Tairov in word and deed under the name "neorealism," the cult of external forms, the fervent denial of the symbolic and ideological origins of the theater, contempt for literature—in the name of liberating the actor and the playing area with its effects. [. . .]

Tairov said, even before he staged *Phaedra,* that this is his first production in which the emotional side would be given primacy, as it were, in which many auxiliary elements would be discarded, such as music, elaborate scenery, etc., and the actor would appear before the public fully armed with all his mimetic, plastic, and declamatory art, meant to disclose a profound and significant tragic concept.

Now, after this preview of *Phaedra,* I can say with certainty that this is Tairov's first indisputable triumph. The audience contained persons from the most diverse backgrounds, even pillars of theatrical Old Believers whom I greatly respect—and not for a moment did anyone gainsay the beauty of this performance. [. . .]

First and foremost [among the merits] was Bryusov's[52] translation. I haven't read it but only heard it from the stage. I am not entirely convinced that the translator was right to change Racine's *plot* in several respects, but I must say that Bryusov succeeded in making, as it were, a kind of distinct, surprising miracle. The changes were not all that radical: iambic pentameter instead of alexandrine verses, a few trochees and anapests in the last acts, elevation to rhymed verse in especially emotional passages, substitution of the names of Greek deities for Racine's characteristic Latin names, and, in the end, there was a huge transformation. In the end it turned out that the shortest path to the realm of great primordial myths, to this tragedy of the children and nephews of the gods themselves, to this profound pre-Homeric state of emotion,

---

52 Valery Yakovlevich Bryusov (1873–1920), symbolist poet, who attacked the "unnecessary realism" of the MAT; his own plays went unperformed, but his translations from Maeterlinck, D'Annunzio, Wilde, and others were frequently performed.

to this "deed" committed by Phaedra and others with the staggering awareness that hundreds of generations and millions of people are, so to speak, invisibly present at their sinning and their atonement, in a word, the shortest path to this whole great ancient Hellenistic tragedy, which Nietzsche[53] intuited with tremulous soul, turned out to be Racine's neoclassicism and not, for example, Euripides!

For the very first time, this great, ancient gust of the grandiose collective creation of a myth by a completely unspoiled people began to blow on me from Racine's *Phaedra* in Bryusov's translation, while all the other *Phaedras* and even Euripides's *Hippolytus* seemed more or less like sophisticated literature.

This impression of monumental tragedy was, of course, due, no less than to the translator, to the skill of performers, and, first and foremost, Koonen. No offense is meant to Russian actresses, but I completely agree with the opinion of one of Russia's foremost men of the theater present at the performance that *no other Russian actress would be able to provide such sure and skillful plasticity*. Koonen as Phaedra was always majestic, always regal, despite the awful passion that constantly consumed her. This was the granddaughter of the Sun, daughter of King Minos, most just of men, set to judge the dead in Hades. She is full of an ineffable internal nobility, but she is also the daughter of the ultra-vicious Pasiphaë, victim of Aphrodite; in her blood runs the irrepressible fire of passion, and the clash between this awful, all-consuming passion and her great nobility strikes lightning-like sparks. Koonen in her portrayal of Phaedra rose to this height, bringing to mind names like Rachel or Russian masters of art, long gone but still exceptionally dear to us even by name, the Semënovas and Asenkovas,[54] full of the plangent emotion of tragedy.

THIS WAS A RICH PERIOD for theatrical debates over current productions. It was also a heyday of satire and caricature, and, as a hit of the season, *Phaedra* was ripe for ridicule, particularly since most theatrical journalists were adherents of Meyerhold.

Ivan I. Startsev, "A public debate on *Phaedra* at the house of the press (a shorthand transcription of the main points)," *Teatral'naya Moskva* [Theatrical Moscow] 30 (1922), 14–15. Ivan Ivanovich Startsev (1869–1967) was a popular humorist.

From the editors. The colleague we entrusted with providing an account of the debate on *Phaedra* at the House of the Press for the last number of our journal carried out

---

53 Friedrich Nietzsche (1844–1900), German philosopher, whose first book *The Birth of Tragedy Out of the Spirit of Music* (1872) suggested that Greek tragedy arose from a conflict between Apollonian and Dionysian principles.

54 Ekaterina Semënovna Semënova (1786–1849), actress, daughter of a serf, reputed to have popularized French neoclassic declamation on the Russian stage. Varvara Nikolaevna Asenkova (1817–41), actress, who specialized in breeches roles and created the role of the Mayor's Wife in *The Inspector General* and Sof'ya in *Woe from Wit*.

his assignment very diligently, but on the way to the press room he fell victim to a sudden attack by unknown assailants who stole this historical document from him. Since all the accounts of this debate hitherto have been *absolutely inaccurate,* we shall here give the authentic shorthand report of the debate, admitting in advance it has been tightly condensed. Water and everything superfluous (repetition, stamping on the floor, uncalled-for gestures, sidelong glances at Tairov and Lunacharsky, borrowed opinions and overheard judgments, thanks for complimentary tickets, and so on)—all this has been abridged, leaving only what we print here.

KOGAN: I got hold of the gavel, which means I am the chairman. I didn't use to like the Kamerny Theater, I mean it lacked emotion. Now both my wife and I and my friends like it, I mean it's good. It's a big show—I liked it. It's a democratic show, with emotion, that is, an emotional show, just like the Maly Theater. To sum things up in general: it's a good show. Bryusov will discuss it in more detail.

BRYUSOV: Ten thousand years ago there were no myths. Nine thousand years ago there weren't any either. And well, seven thousand years ago there weren't any then either. But now, that is, in the third century B.C. everyone started to write about Phaedra—Evreinov, Racine, even me. In general, people loved with a criminal love. Tairov staged *Phaedra* very well, especially original was the headgear which was copied from images on vases. For a long time I didn't know whether to call the tragedy *Hippolytus* or *Phaedra,* and then, just to be original, I decided simply to call it *Phaedra.* No one else has named it that, well, only Racine. And, well, he doesn't count. It is a wonderful myth, especially in my translation.

AN UNIDENTIFIED MEMBER OF THE PUBLIC: I would like to say a few words about the show. In Racine the character's name is "Aricie," but at the Kamerny it's "Arikia." I don't think this is a good idea.

MARGOLIN: Phaedra stands on buskins. The Kamerny Theater stands on buskins. The set design stands on buskins. Emotion stands on buskins. Buskins, buskins, buskins. I wound up on buskins. Details in the last issue of *Screen* stand on buskins.

VOLKOV: The Kamerny Theater is the theater of Koonen and Tseretelli,[55] because it stages plays only by French authors, for example, Hoffmann's *Princess Brambilla,* Schnitzler's *Pierrette's Veil,* Lothar's *King Harlequin,* and Shakespeare's *Romeo.* In these plays they die onstage seventeen times, and get married six and a half times. Therefore it is a tragic theater. I was there 76.18 times—which means—well, it must mean something. If you think this is nonsense, you're wrong. I'll prove it.

FERDINANDOV:[56] The Kamerny Theater is my father, because it is extremely respectable, the production is extremely wonderful, but the Kamerny Theater is extremely

55 Nikolay Mikhaylovich Tseretelli (1890–1942), tall, lanky actor, who played most of the leading male roles at the Kamerny Theater 1916–28, opposite Alisa Koonen; a virtuoso, capable of singing, dancing, and declaiming. Played Hippolytus in *Phaedra.*

56 Boris Alekseevich Ferdinandov (1889–1959), actor, director; cofounder in 1921 of the Experimental Heroic Theater; worked at the Kamerny Theater 1916–21 and 1923–25, designer of *King Harlequin, The Toy Chest,* and *Adrienne Lecouvreur.* A film director from 1925.

3.6. Alisa Koonen as Phaedra, directed
by Aleksandr Tairov, Kamerny Theater,
Moscow, 1922.

messy, and Phaedra is extremely indecent, although she is extremely respectable. Theseus has an extremely long beard.

ÉGGERT:[57] A few words to the point. I haven't taken off my hat because they're staging *Be Kind to Horses*[58] here and they'll make off with my hat for sure. But at the Experimental Heroic Theater, there's music with hymns.

(*Noise. Some Scythian*[59] *expressions.*)

KOGAN: Since Éggert refuses to take off his hat, I am stepping down from the duties of chairman. Basta. Put out the light.

SHERSHENEVICH:[60] Put on the light or I'll unscrew the lightbulb.

BRYUSOV: Kogan, turn it on or he'll unscrew it.

THE PEOPLE: We want to go on with the debate.

HOUSE OF THE PRESS: We declare that the debate is herewith closed.

SHERSHENEVICH: Then I want my money back.

BRYUSOV: Kogan, they'll take their money back, true, the ruble is in the toilet, but they're willing to take toilet paper.

HOUSE OF THE PRESS: We insist that the debate proceed.

TAIROV: I don't want to speak. I still have not cooled down from *Phaedra* and I'm afraid to speak. I feel sorry for Ferdinandov. In general, I feel sorry for anyone who isn't Tairov.

57 Konstantin Vladimirovich Éggert (1883–1955), joined the Kamerny Theater as an actor 1917 and, after a good deal of work in and around Moscow, returned to it 1921–23; directed the New Dramatic Theater from 1925.

58 *Be Kind to Horses* (also known as *Kind Treatment of Horses*), a parody of music hall, staged by Foregger at his workshop, Mastfor, in 1922, with sets by Sergey Yutkevich and costumes by Sergey Eisenstein.

59 Scythian, a poetic term for "savage." Aleksandr Blok's poem "The Scythians" revived the ancient use of the name of these nomadic peoples of the Black Sea to imply barbarism.

60 Vadim Gavrilovich Shershenevich (1893–1942), poet and playwright, translator of plays by Claudel, Shakespeare, and Brecht staged by Tairov; cofounded the Experimental Heroic Theater in Moscow 1921.

3.7. Lecocq's *Giroflé-Girofla*, directed by Aleksandr Tairov, designed by Georgy Yakulov, Kamerny Theater, Moscow, 1922.

FROM THE PUBLIC: I love the Kamerny Theater, but Tairov doesn't want to speak. That's bad: I will not love the Kamerny Theater.

BRYUSOV: Since all the speakers have had their say about *Phaedra,* I hereby declare the debate closed.

To DEMONSTRATE the validity of his theories of the actor's versatility, Tairov turned from French neoclassic tragedy to French operetta. After eight months' rehearsal, he opened Charles Lecocq's *Giroflé-Girofla* in Yakulov's cubist design with moving parts on October 3, 1922. The comic opera of 1874 involves twin sisters (both played by Alisa Koonen) and their avoidance of marriage to a marauding Moor.

> Aleksandr Tairov, interview about *Giroflé-Girofla, Teatr* 2 (October 10, 1922).
> In *Stat'i, besedy, rechi, pis'ma,* 292–93.

It is pretty well known that we conceive of the new actor as a professional who has mastered the whole intricate complex of his means of expression and is capable of using it in any sphere of stage art.

Hence it is clear that, in staging an operetta, we have no intention of inviting specialist performers and choristers for this particular production. To perfect the actors' mastery, it was important that the same actors who performed the mysteries of

Kalidasa and Claudel, Racine and Shakespeare, the harlequinades of Hoffmann[61] and pantomimes, be able to take on the performance of an operetta. [...]

We are treating operetta as a musical stage eccentricity, not as a comic opera, we do not want to pour out feelings in arias, duets, and choruses, but, as before, we are striving for a new stage composition, based on the organic confluence of sensations, movements, words and sounds. [...][62]

The stage space is simplified to its furthest limits, which is absolutely necessary for mounting the production, and reworked on the principle of central and auxiliary combinations of screens, which play a certain ancillary role in developing the needed movement. The central screen, besides, also has a special acoustical significance. The primary consideration of the costumes is the naked form of the human body and its movement, which means that the main basic costume is jersey and tights, over which, depending on the tasks set for the forms and movements of individual characters or the ensemble, will be put those costume pieces and props that can more precisely help the actor fulfill his tasks. The costume is constructed so that the actor's body is freed from frills that impede his movement, but at the same time it provides the form he requires. [...]

THE RESPECTFUL RECEPTION given to *Phaedra* and the rapturous audiences at *Giroflé-Girofla* emboldened Tairov to take the fight to the enemy camp. Casting a jaundiced eye on Meyerhold's biomechanical experiments, he published an article condemning his rival's *fokusnichestvo* (fakery, charlatanry).

Aleksandr Tairov, "Hocus-pocus in the science of theatrical art," *Vremennik Kamernogo Teatra* [Annals of the Chamber Theater] 1 (1922), 26–28.

I recently attended a lecture by Meyerhold on this topic and witnessed a demonstration of his work that tried to confirm the scientific basis of his hypotheses. It has been a long time since I've come across such poverty of ideas, with such ignorant elementary proofs and such flagrant complacency as on that evening.

Meyerhold began with an analysis of existing theatrical theories. Here are some excerpts of this analysis: the theory of the *inner core* [*nutro*],[63] he says, is based on self-narcosis and the fact that before he comes onstage the actor drinks cognac, black coffee, or asks the extras to shake him up, so he can make his entrance in a disheveled manner. While playing Ivan the Terrible, from early morning the actor frequents

---

61 The Kamerny Theater had opened with Konstantin Balmont's adaptation of the ancient Sanskrit drama *Shakuntala* by Kalidasa. Ernest Theodor Amadeus Hoffmann (1776–1822), German writer, composer, and painter, had been the inspiration for *Princess Brambilla* (1920).

62 This shaft was directed at Nemirovich-Danchenko, who was directing Lecocq's *La Fille de Madame Angot* as a comic opera with true-to-life emotions.

63 *Nutro* (the inside), an important concept in traditional Russian acting, referring to spontaneous emotion generated from the actor's own experience.

churches, kisses icons, crosses himself, and thus gets into the mood of the performance.

His entire "scientific" criticism and analysis of theories of the actors' nature comprises these few provincial anecdotes for young actors. It is absurd to object that I have personally known actors, convinced atheists, who have played Ivan the Terrible brilliantly [...] The same method of "scientific *analysis*" has also been applied by Meyerhold to Stanislavsky's theory.

[...] Having destroyed all the old theories, Meyerhold has begun to propose his own. [...]

Rejecting the creative principle of art in general and the actor's art in particular, Meyerhold is inclined to regard the actor's expertise as a sort of mechanical process, composed of a series of tried and true mechanical movements and special stage tricks. To prove this, he cites the famous leap onto the chest, used in *Othello* by the tragedian Grasso,[64] claiming, merely on the basis of a private conversation with him, that this leap is a mere stage trick, produced by using the appropriate mechanical techniques.

This single example ruthlessly exposes the whole myopia and preconception of Meyerhold's proposition. Of course, it should be clear even to a tyro in the theater that without knowing a series of techniques and the appropriate training, such a leap cannot be performed and repeated invariably from performance to performance. But to pose the question correctly, we must not only understand how it is done but also *why* Grasso did it, despite the fact that a whole team of Othellos previous to him never resorted to it.

During the process of an actor's work, there exist two distinctly different moments: (1) the constructively creative and (2) the creatively performative. With the help of the latter the actor can confidently reproduce it from performance to performance, thanks to a precisely learned construction of the role. Here the technical or, if you like, mechanical factor plays a significant role. The actor must master his mechanism so that even the most complicated of his movements is perfected automatically. Only in this case is he free to use his creative talents without risk. However, this is only a derivative result, derived from the first factor in the actor's work, i.e., the creatively performative.

When constructing his role, the actor (I include the director's assistance here), in varied and complicated ways, requiring serious scientific study, finds the outline of his role. Herein lies the most essential moment of his creative work. Before taking the leap it is imperative that the *thought* of leaping occur beforehand. Without the birth of this thought the leap would not exist, and the birth of this thought can in no manner be explained mechanically. [...]

THE KAMERNY THEATER left Moscow on February 21, 1923, for the first of three European tours. The authorities may have felt that its Western repertoire could

---

64 Giovanni Grasso (1873–1930), Italian actor, who performed in the Sicilian dialect. He toured Germany, England, France, and Russia. Lunacharsky called him "a real wonder! Incredible, unparalleled temperament..."

make it more accessible and acceptable than the constructivists' extreme interpretations of minor works. Critics in France and Germany responded enthusiastically, endorsing Tairov's approach that so irritated his Soviet reviewers.

Gabriel Boissy, "*Phaedra* at the Kamerny Theater," *Comœdia* (March 12, 1923), 1107. Gabriel Boissy (1879–1949), French theater critic and translator of Sophocles and Shakespeare, expert on ancient drama, initiated the idea of a tomb of the Unknown Soldier at the Arche de Triomphe.

In this strange production, where influences from the Far East and the theater of Dionysus are combined in a strange regression, how can we recognize this Racinian work of art, at once both monumental and realistic, this tragedy which at moments becomes humane, when the heroine attains a particular level of greatness in her heroism, this tragedy whose internal life burns with such power that it brings us close, as if we were family, to the most divine of its characters?

So, Tairov, for all his manifest respect, could not and did not do anything but distort Racine; still, there is some point to explaining how. This explanation will establish first and foremost the reasons for the distortion; this will help me to be fair to the efforts of the Kamerny Theater, efforts that were truly marvelous; it will help me, finally, to orient several members of the audience to the true path of the performance which seemed seriously to trouble them. It was very entertaining to watch these spectators vacillating between delight and outrage, wavering before making one choice or another; this, it is true, was not so simple, since it represents a reaction against realism, a return to abstract and heroic art.

First let us analyze the scene design. There was nothing to remind one of anything past or present, except for a few general cubist settings. There were pyramidal forms to the left and cylindrical ones to the right. These created the impression of massive blocks, slabs for very modern naval constructions, and lent the stage gigantic proportions.

Downstage right, the forms arranged in a semicircle serve as seats, and a few large steps come down from there or, more accurately, serve as an abstract means of descent. Further upstage, with a bold stroke, the playing area, which resembles the deck of a ship, rises into the distance and ascends over the pale blue abyss.

The impression is intensified thanks to a brightly painted triangular flat that descends with the bulge reminiscent of a sail.

So it is as if the characters are situated between earth and sky, amid distinctive signs and shapes that served to build legendary architectural works. And this was truly mythical, for however prepared I was for the entrance of Hippolytus and Theramenes, I shall never forget the appearance of Phaedra. What a holy and at the same time barbaric manifestation! [...]

Her feet shod in raised Japanese footgear; her head framed by a red wig, ornamented with enormous golden bands; her bust suppressed, eliminated by a golden breastplate, which half-covered a long skirt of black-and-white stripes, and in particular this symbol of eastern idols—a red cape, a fantastical cape with fiery pleats which at times blew about frantically, at other times calmly dragged behind her. This is Phaedra according to Tairov.

I also have to add that the features of her face were completely altered, stylized, that the outline of her nose was emphasized by cardboard phalanges, and the face itself turned into an antique mask, while cothurnoi were reinstated as footwear.

All the other characters were presented in the same sharp, distinct style. Their bodies, the characteristic parts of their bodies, were effaced or reduced to a minimum by the dominance of costume, makeup or cardboard. Theramenes, reminiscent of a grotesque figure from Myrrhine, has a hooked nose, a wavy beard, and a dwarf's body. Hippolytus, dressed like a warrior off a Mycenaean vase, is adorned with a helmet of cubist planes and a golden crest reminiscent of one of those horse's manes that so terrified little Astyanax.

This japonoiserie is revealed even more obviously in Oenone's costume. With her long white face, with extended eyes and aquiline nose, with a white angular cone framing her face, with a cascade of cloth forming a skirt, this Oenone is reminiscent of certain demonic faces from the ancient kakemons of Nara.

But despite all these seemingly disparate echoes, there is no disharmony. Everything is unified by a heightened monumental style, connected with an impulse of extraordinary unity. Indeed, one cannot say whether these tragedians are good or bad or what spiritual essence they impart to their characters. They do not act their roles. Each of them performs a dance following a score provided by the director. Their movements and gestures are inexorably predetermined. The mark of a fixed expression is on their faces. Their walk is a rhythmical one imposed by the cothurnoi. The impression was strengthened even more thanks to the stern figures of warriors frozen in the background in poses reminiscent of vase painting [...]

Setting aside Racine, setting aside the whole Sorbonne and all the monuments, you unexpectedly come face-to-face with the myth. Out from under the gilding and seductive colors the demigods of heroic Greece rise up. [...]

There is much to be said about discoveries in the realm of stage movement: the moment in Act IV when Phaedra falls to the ground on the edge of the abyss, giving the feeling that the playing area where she speaks with Minos is listing; the moment of Phaedra's death, which is becoming clear from her first words and gradually attains its highest expression. Tairov makes innovations everywhere, and these last two serve as a restraint even for our French Phaedra.

How desirable it would be for all our young actors, all our tragedians to aspire to this production. How poor they would feel in the presence of this exceptional richness! Let those who would be moved wait no longer. The tragedy does lose every virtue of emotion, but it recovers its original strength and once again becomes, despite the unfamiliar plasticity, *heroic exultation.* And this leaves far behind the attractive but narrow realism of Stanislavsky.

"A. Ya. Tairov's report on the results of the foreign tour of the Kamerny Theater," early September to late December 1923. *STDM 21–26*, 250–52.

The theater's trip abroad, which lasted seven months, led to an extremely valuable and
meaningful sociopolitical and artistic outcome, but, unfortunately, was not accompanied by corresponding material success, which meant that the Kamerny Theater was
unable to pay numerous debts [...]

5. The foreign press and Western European public opinion considered the great
success of the Kamerny Theater naturally to be the cultural success and achievement
of Soviet Russia. With high estimations of the theater's work, they made conclusions
as to the great creative strength and work capability of the new Russia. Along with this,
the appearance of the Kamerny Theater from Russia gave cause to certain groups to
suggest that the Kamerny Theater was under orders to make Bolshevik propaganda
as a kind of challenge by the Soviet government to the countries of the West in the
sphere the West considers its monopoly—the cultural sphere.

In this regard, the following excerpts from numerous press articles about the
Kamerny Theater, including French and German, as well as Austrian, Belgian, and
American, are telling:

a. London, *The Outlook*: "It turns out that those who claimed that the Bolsheviks
destroyed art were most ill informed about what is going on in Soviet Russia. And here
now is a specimen of their art—the Moscow Kamerny Theater which directly refutes
this lie." "I have never seen more accomplished achievements."

b. Paris, *Comœdia*: "The Kamerny Theater is Lenin's ballet."

c. Vienna, *Neue Freie Presse*: "This theater was propaganda for the Soviet government."

d. *Gallic News*: "Once again the old saying has come to pass—a light from the east."

e. New York, *New York Times*: "Its (the Kamerny Theater's) basis is purely cosmopolitan, like most of the ideas coming out of Moscow from the moment of Bolshevism."

f. New York, *Observer*: "Like Moscow, whence it came, the Kamerny Theater is just
as completely revolutionary and international."

g. Berlin, *Neue Volkische Zeitung*: "They have brought us from Moscow the far from
impotent Proletkul't. Like Chicherin[65] and his staff, who caused universal surprise when
they entered the Geneva convention hall in beautifully fitted tailcoats, so Tairov's art
astonished us with its masterfully virtuosic command of the stage."

h. Munich, *Volkische Kommentator*: "The dispatch of a Bolshevik theatrical company." "We have learned that the famous MKT must either leave or be expelled. The
Munich police in collusion with the Office for the Registration of Foreigners discovered
that the MKT is composed of very peculiar Russians ... According to our sources, there
can be no doubt that we are dealing with a purely Bolshevik theater troupe, and the
outward appearance of the scenery confirms this. Obviously, beneath the fig leaves

---

65 Georgy Vasil'evich Chicherin (1872–1936), former member of the Socialist Democratic Labor
Party, Soviet commissar of foreign affairs, who resigned in 1930 allegedly owing to illness. After
his death he was made a nonperson.

of art, Bolshevist propaganda was aimed at Munich—to the great joy of Moscow and Berlin leaders, Bolshevist prophets in Germany, who once again had the opportunity to unfurl the red banner with the Soviet star in Munich."

As a result of these attacks, the theater was expelled from Munich. A theater that arose from Bolshevist Russia and was in keeping with its revolutionary achievements turned out to be unacceptable to England, Switzerland, Czechoslovakia, Lithuania, and Latvia; these governments refused to give the theater visas, which led to the cancellation of confirmed contracts and concrete proposals that had promised to provide the theater unconditional financial success, especially since most of the governments had offered a high amount of foreign currency; and tours on their territory could have not only covered the costs of the theater but also made a profit.

6. Germany, where the Kamerny Theater resided from April to September, suffered, for political reasons, an uncontrollable downturn of the exchange rate of the Deutschmark. When the theater arrived in Germany, it was eighteen thousand marks to the dollar, and when it left, it was more than one hundred million. Therefore, despite the enormous interest shown in the theater by the German critics and public, which filled the theaters even during the summer off-season, the box-office takings gradually became virtually worthless, barely able to allow the theater to cover its routine expenses. [...]

In view of all this, which constitutes the enormous cultural and social significance of the Moscow Kamerny Theater's last tour, the recognition by numerous (about two thousand) reviews by the foreign press in all languages, as well as our own press, which corroborate the opinions of the government of the USSR in Paris and Germany, and also of the People's Commissar of Enlightenment, and, taking into account that, because of present circumstances, the Kamerny Theater at this time lacks the financial resources needed to pay its debts, we request your involvement in clearing the very numerous debts incurred by the foreign tour.

Perhaps you will deem it possible to take into consideration the circumstance that in December of this year we will be facing the tenth anniversary of the work of the Moscow Kamerny Theater, from the moment of its foundation (1914) under the extremely difficult conditions of war and revolution.

Pavel Markov, "The return," *Teatr i Muzyka* [Theater and music] 35 (1923), 1105.

The Kamerny Theater has returned from its foreign travels. They were short-lived, not more than half a year; however, during this brief period, Moscow's theatrical life took on a more distinct outline. It has become clear that the year 1923–24 in the Russian theater was a year of vital experiments, sustained toil and apprenticeship. Almost every theater embarked on the path of self-examination and the adoption of new forms born of other theaters. This entails the question of theatrical culture, how the theater is born out of the depths organically and logically. That which in the past was a specific quality of individual theaters has become the stage technique common to most theaters. It is as if a leveling of theater is occurring. The creative idiosyncrasy of each theater is beginning to disappear and become blurred—the very idiosyncrasy that ought to justify its existence and for whose sake it works. The wonderful and profound achievements of the last few years—*The Magnanimous Cuckold, The Dybbuk,* and *Phaedra*—have predetermined the fate of the Russian theater. [. . .]

MARKOV may have been right. Back in Moscow, the Kamerny continued down its eclectic path, with a dramatization of G. K. Chesterton's allegorical novel *The Man Who Was Thursday,* Ostrovsky's classic of Russian domestic despotism *Thunderstorm,* and a caricatural rendering of Bernard Shaw's *St. Joan.* The Chesterton, with scenery suggesting a modern cityscape, was a nod to the fashion for "urbanism" and plays of modern city life; *Thunderstorm* was a direct response to Lunacharsky's appeal "Back to Ostrovsky." Critics continued to be hostile, but, even with ticket prices raised, the theater played to 78 percent capacity in 1924–25.

"From a shorthand transcription of a debate on contemporary theater, 16 November 1924." From "Khronika," *Izvestia* 261 (November 15, 1924). *STDM 21–26, 252–55.*

A. Ya. Tairov's speech. [. . .] Anatoly Vasil'evich [Lunacharsky] is a magnificent speaker, everyone knows this and no one better than himself. Anatoly Vasil'evich has his own manner of public speaking: he begins like this in a slow tempo—I know him well and am very fond of him as a public speaker—and so he begins in this kind of slow tempo, then gradually begins to expand, and swell, and then launches a brilliant cascade of salvos all of which hit their target. He turns into a wonderful marksman who doesn't waste a single bullet. I was lucky—as it happens I was right in his speech's line of fire. (*Laughter, applause.*) And so Anatoly Vasil'evich let off shot after shot very steadily, very zealously, and very happily. Of course, when the marksman is lucky, the targets are probably lucky too, I suppose. (*Laughter, applause.*) But the target is alive, and this living target not only wants to be happy but wants to say a little something in response.

First of all, as to neorealism, Anatoly Vasil'evich says that this is the slogan that I promote. This is correct. He says that I gave it up. I deserted it and now am not repeating it. I never retrace my steps. Why should I repeat this slogan, it is now being repeated right, left, and center without exception? If people talk about the theater, it's true, they talk not about neorealism but about a new realism. I don't think there's much difference, either in terminology or essence. I have never—there were probably several misunderstandings here on Anatoly Vasil'evich's part—understood neorealism to be as A. V. described it. He said that I claimed that an actor is an actor, his business is mastery of technique, and therefore he should demonstrate his technique. Tseretelli is Tseretelli and nothing more. Yes, maybe, this may be right applied to one actor, but not as applied to my theory. I gave primary importance to the dramatic character, that is, the actor is a master because he doesn't replicate his own self but [. . .] turns into an entirely different dramatic character, and sustains and embodies this stage character with all his vast technique. This is what I have always said and written, and this lay at the basis of the work we carried out.

I do not deny theatrical illusion, I merely said that there can be all sorts of theatrical illusions: fantastical, naturalistic—which is a super-theatrical illusion. And there are authentic theatrical illusions based on theatrical art. And when I referred to neorealism, I was referring to a realism confined to no particular sphere of influence. I have never deviated from this position and never will, and the most recent work of the Kamerny Theater shows this. Again, I have never denied emotion, as is obvious from my book. I spoke of theatrical emotion, and I will insist on it now. And, of course, if anyone in the audience says, "How artfully he weeps," that would be an entrechat in its purest form; but if the spectator himself starts to sob because an actor onstage is weeping brilliantly, that would be nasty, mawkish, I would never advocate that. But if the spectator becomes worked up so that his pain is mixed with joy, for this art comes to him from the stage and is not nervous weeping, that will be truth, the only truth. There are no, can be no other truths for me. [...]

Lunacharsky's concluding remarks. [...] With Tairov, the actor and the actor's art are central and not what is called collective will, collective thought, which uses the theater as the instrument of its expression. But I have to say that the Kamerny Theater was born when there were not such enthralling subjects for playwriting. He took the aesthetic possibilities and gave us substantial achievements. This will not be forgotten and is no doubt merging with the theatrical mainstream as a part of a general restructuring. But our current trend toward new realism is dictated by the fact that subject matter is now appearing that did not exist in the days of Nevezhin, Krylov,[66] etc. When there are no enthralling plays, then at least let there be coloratura; neorealism is exactly this kind of coloratura. You are enthralled by a singer's coloratura, but do not think that it will touch your heart. And now that we know we have the subject matter, coloratura can be developed as an auxiliary, that is, we shall return to a didactic theater. [...]

THE KAMERNY still enjoyed enough official favor that it was allowed to tour Germany and Austria between April and August 1925 and was awarded a medal from the University of Cologne.

Robert Benchley, "Vienna letter," July 19, 1925. In *Life* (August 10, 1925). Reprinted by permission of The Estate of Robert Benchley, Nat Benchley, executor. Robert Benchley (1889–1945), American humorist, was theater critic for the comic journal *Life,* for *Vanity Fair,* and for *The New Yorker.*

66 Pëtr Mikhaylovich Nevezhin (1841–1919), playwright, expert at sensational society melodramas. Viktor Aleksandrovich Krylov (1838–1906), the dominant playwright on the Russian stage in the latter part of the nineteenth century, in charge of the St. Petersburg repertoires from 1893; a hack who put his hand to any genre.

3.8. Alisa Koonen as Joan and Vladimir Sokolov as the Dauphin in Shaw's *St. Joan*, directed by Aleksandr Tairov, designed by the Stenberg Brothers, Kamerny Theater, 1924.

We haven't got very much money left, but we would gladly give fifteen or twenty dollars of it (a little over a million kronen in vanilla money) to watch George Bernard Shaw's[67] face at a performance of his "St Joan" such as is being given here by the Russians of Tairoff's *Kammertheater*. If he is the man that he ought to be, he would laugh his head off.

For these Russian boys have taken his sacred script, which the New York Theater Guild[68] nearly bled itself to death over, and have it on with boards and gunnysack and made a circus of it. The characters, with the exception of *Joan*, are clowns. The settings are thrown together out of ill-fitting laths. The *Dauphin*, in actual clown makeup, with a little hat on the side of his head and a long feather trailing to one side, sits on an arrangement of boards like the bleachers at the Polo Grounds, clad in skin tights with a tiny dab of imperial ermine on the shoulders, and giggles pleasantly while huge, bulbous-nosed churchmen discuss the state of the realm. The soldiers wear flannel uniforms, with nominal tin fittings to suggest armor, and tomato-can helmets. The *Maid* alone is immune from the devastating parody.

All this, of course, sharpens the satire to the point of burlesque and makes it a hundred times more malign. If Shaw really means to kid his countrymen, if the centuries and centuries of repetition of the same old historic formulas, the pomp and ceremony

67 George Bernard Shaw (1856–1950), Irish playwright, whose plays were frequently performed in Russia in the years before the Revolution; his socialist views made him popular afterward. He never saw Tairov's production.

68 The Theater Guild in New York had staged the world premiere of *St. Joan* in December 1923, with Winifred Lenihan in the lead.

and the majestic clash of arms, are to him the bunk that they seem to be, then he ought to adopt these Russians as his sons. If he is sore at what they have done, he doesn't understand his Shaw, that's all. [. . .]

Eccentrism and Circusization

The designer Georgy Annenkov, drawing on the Manifesto proclaimed in 1913 by the Italian F. T. Marinetti, declared the music hall the foundation of revolutionary theater. Marinetti's manifesto of Futurism had called for the annihilation of all existing forms of establishment art and pointed to popular entertainment, with its rapidity, sensual appeal, and physical action, as the model to emulate. The cult of the café concert, music hall, and circus, as well as that for technology and machinery—a characteristic trait of futurism—was to have for long years an enormous influence on the Soviet theatrical aesthetic. Annenkov's manifesto of December 5, 1921, for the Free Comedy Theater, Petrograd, called for a celebration of the machine, maximal improvisation, and moving scenery.

"Eccentrism" won over almost all the theaters in Moscow. In addition to Meyerhold's Theater of Revolution, founded to be an "agitational theater" in his special sense, which became the authorized arena for the German expressionist repertoire, there were the Moscow Proletkul't Theater, Granovsky's Jewish Chamber Theater, and the Theater of Popular Comedy in Petrograd, run from 1920 to 1922 by Sergey Radlov and V. N. Solov'ëv. Former collaborators of Meyerhold, they sought to base their people's theater on the principles of improvisation (another nod to the commedia dell'arte) and the "circusization" or "music-hallization" of the classics. Nikolay Foregger's Studio (Mastfor) specialized in parody with the latest Western music. Petrograd's FÉKS (Factory of the Eccentric Actor) wholeheartedly participated in this trend. It is no coincidence that many proponents of eccentrism, among them Eisenstein, Kozintsev, and Trauberg, eventually abandoned the theater for the more manipulable medium of film.

> Viktor Shklovsky, "On the birth and life of the FÉKS," *Gamburgsky shchët* [A strict accounting] (1928). Reprinted in *Za 40 let* [After forty years] (Moscow: Iskusstvo, 1965), 91–92.

This was a time when frostbitten troops on trains drank from locomotives as if they were samovars. People played skittles in front of the Hermitage . . . Factories emitted no smoke . . . The air was rarefied by revolution . . . St. Pete (not yet Leningrad) was suspended between the present and the future, just as in the space between the earth and the moon there was no equilibrium. This gave scope to experimentation . . . Experiment was directed against tradition . . . The demand for changes in tradition spoke against the obsolescence of the old and its usual association with an outworn way of thinking . . . Nowadays it is hard to trace precisely why it should be eccentrism via

Eisenstein, "the FÉKS group," and to some degree Meyerhold that created new devices of post-October art... Eccentrism is based on a selection of impressive moments and on their new, not automatic, connections. Eccentrism is the fight against the staleness of life, a repudiation of its traditional perceptions and assumptions.

NIKOLAY MIKHAYLOVICH FOREGGER (in full Foregger von Greifenturn, 1892–1939) believed that human movement must be modeled on machinery. He had worked at the Crooked Mirror cabaret and the Kamerny Theater before he staged the agitprop Political Carousel as the Second Moscow State Circus in 1919. With Vladimir Mass he created the Foregger Workshop (Mastfor) in 1922, which staged episodic plays featuring "social masks." Foregger was later attacked for "inveterate formalism."

Nikolay Foregger, "Avant-garde art and the variety theater," *Érmitazh* 6 (1922), 5–6.

1. In the general evolution of culture, there are front-line battalions, scouts, who are not even the vanguard: light, quick to appear, quick to disappear, they seem to leave no trace.

Such are the arts that address only our formal perception, sensuous in the wider meaning of the word, arts which, to be appreciated, do not require the work of the mind.

They are light, but, through repetition, they make breaches in the old foundations of habits and norms, they prepare the ground for the consolidation of solid, completed masses which form the totality of an era.

[...] So with the applied arts, which, among the plastic arts, reveal the humdrum, needs, trends, and present all the outward signs of style of a given era, so with the music of dance halls and popular holidays, and finally, in the realm of theater, the revue, the platforms of fairground booths, the music hall and variety.

I omit circus, insofar as its aim is to demonstrate, to put in evidence the qualities and possibilities of the human body, the sports aspect, though I include in the aforesaid group the eccentrics, clowns, and all those who create, in place of a bare demonstration, an accomplished mechanics of spectacle.

2. They are the pioneers in the assault, which is why those avid for new values, those who create them, attentively study those arts, convinced that they alone can reveal the features of the style of the age in which one lives. The French, who, more than anyone else, seek out the precise meaning of words and definitions, merely distinguish the art of the avant-garde from the rest, without, as we do, putting in opposition old art, new art, right-wing art, left-wing art.

When the powerful waves of art reflect a predefined actuality, those "minor" forms, not unlike the foam on the crest of billows, surge forward, bearing in their spindrift the aroma and taste of the new waters that are to wash the world clean. In the theatrical realm, the "music hall" must play this role (let us use this American term in its broad sense, as a collective to amalgamate all the meanings listed earlier).

3.9. Graphic design for the Foregger Studio, 1922. The letters read "Mastfor" and "Senderov."

The circus has shown the actor the importance of the body as instrument, supple, obedient, and expressive; it has taught him its methods for surpassing the material. The music hall will teach him its manner of attacking work and the characteristics of the modern theater's cast of characters, their precise formation and the rhythm of stage action. [...]

FÉKS WAS ORGANIZED in Petrograd in 1922 by the young directors Grigory Kozintsev, Georgy Kryzhitsky, Leonid Trauberg, and Sergey Yutkevich. On September 25, 1922, it offered its first production, loosely connected to Gogol's comedy *Wedlock*, but titled *Wedlock ("Not from Gogol"); a Stunt in Three Acts* "to a stunned Petrograd audience." It was "engineered" by Kozintsev and Trauberg.

> Grigory Kozintsev, *Ékstsentrizm* [Eccentrism] (Eccentropolis, formerly Petrograd, 1922). Georgy Mikhaylovich Kozintsev (1908–73), director, had studied with Aleksandra Ékster in Kiev; in 1924 he and the rest of the FÉKS turned to filmmaking. At the Pushkin Theater in Leningrad he staged Shakespeare in the late 1940s and early 1950s and made movies of *Don Quixote* (1957), *Hamlet* (1964), and *King Lear* (1972).

Eccentric: a clown; also a term for any ridiculous and irrational novelty act with surprise effects.

[...] ART IN LOWERCASE LETTERS, A PEDESTAL OR A FIG LEAF

Life demands art that is

> hyperbolically coarse,
> aggressive, nerve-wracking,
> openly utilitarian, mechanically precise,
> instantaneous, rapid,

otherwise people won't listen, won't see, won't stop. All of this together adds up to art of the twentieth century, art of 1922, art of the up-to-the-moment

> *Eccentrism.*

[...] The forebears of FÉKS are

> In language—the chansonette, Pinkerton,[69] an auctioneer's spiel, street brawls.
> In painting—the circus poster, the cover of a pulp novel.
> In music—the jazz band (a Negro makeshift orchestra), the circus march.
> In ballet—American dance music.
> In theater—the music hall, the movies, circus, dance cafés, and boxing. [...]
> THE AMERICANIZATION OF THE THEATER
> in Russian means
> ECCentriSM

Playbill for Kozintsev's *Wedlock,* Petrograd, September 25, 1922.

Stunt in 3 acts, completely improbable occurrence by the eccentric Serge.[70]

Time is Money!!! Allo! Eccentric Theater! Eccentrism presents: operetta, melodrama, farce, movies, circus, variety, puppetry in a single performance! # Revue of contemporaneity—1. Charlie Chaplin. 2 Albert Einstein # Completely improbable occurrence of N. V. Gogol' # Fex-Music-Hall: American dances # The death-defying rain # Orchestra of alarms # Conference automatique # Action by electro-radio-steam mechanisms # Stagehands for the performance Grigory Kozintsev—Leonid Trauberg.[71]

A. V. Sergeev, "Theater-circus-movies," quoted in Leonid Trauberg, "On the production *Wedlock,*" *Iskusstvo kino* [The art of film] 3 (1991), 121.

The two main characters—Albert and Einstein—were played by the circus eccentrics Serge and Taurek. [...] Eccentrism was the principle of organization of the whole spectacle. The troupe was brought to life with the help of clysters: Miss Agata danced, accompanied by a ballroom pianist "Down the street a bunch of people marched

---

69 Stories about Pinkerton detectives were immensely popular. Because the Pinkertons were often used in the United States as strikebreakers, Nikolay Bukharin recommended to the komsomols that they develop "Red Pinkertons."
70 Aleksandr Sergeevich Aleksandrov-Serge (1892–1966), acrobat and animal tamer, second generation of a circus dynasty and in charge of the workshop at FÉKS 1921–24. Later developed a spectacular equestrian act.
71 Leonid Zakharovich Trauberg (1902–90) became a leading Soviet filmmaker, whose work included *New Babylon* (*Novy Vavilon,* 1927–29) and the Maksim trilogy (1934–39).

crocodile-file," with . . . a crocodile; a Gogol who bore no resemblance to Gogol came onstage and talked in a Ukrainian accent, and was generally "some beanpole with a moustache." The eccentricity travestied the plot, characters, theater as such. No villain, no hero, no dead man, no circus act per se preserved its original meaning, when put through an ironic or parodic interpretation.

Trauberg: "Serge and Taurek were greeted by the audience with a howl of joy. They played scientists, who set themselves the task of bringing a dead body to life. And suddenly this dead body turned out to be—Chaplin! They were very happy. 'He's deesist,' said Taurek. 'What'd ye mean, deesist—not deesist, but dis-eased.' Anyway, all sorts of circus stunts, malapropisms. 'Gotta revive him.' They ran somewhere offstage to the utter delight of the audience."

> Letter of Grigory Kozintsev to L. M. Kozintseva-Érenburg,[72] Petrograd, September 27, 1922. In *Perepiska G. M. Kozintseva 1922–1973* [Kozintsev's correspondence] (Moscow: Artist-Rezhissër-Teatr, 1998), 8–9.

. . . *Wedlock* finally came off on the 25th, and I exerted tons of effort on it (for example, I painted scenery three nights in a row, and rehearsed all day long). Strange as it seems, we triumphed indisputably and definitively.

This is how it started: in the house there was a hyperbolically large audience, absolutely everybody. The whole Alexandra lot (even Evtikhy Karpov,[73] etc.) turned up in a group intending to spoil the show, for instance, I don't know if you know Kolya Peter (N. V. Petrov);[74] and until the curtain went up, there was a crazy uproar. A wild din, balls people had brought with them fly through the air, somebody's caterwauling and so on. I go into Serge's dressing room, he's in a savagely spiteful mood, asks: "Do you mind if I overact just a little bit, I'll show them what 'Eccentric Theater' is all about?"

The first scenes take place to the accompaniment of balls and noise, and when it's time for Serge's entrance, he comes on and starts to howl, outshouting the audience, then the audience starts to quiet down, then Serge grabs a chair and starts to do death-defying feats with it all over the stage, I've never seen such a sight in my life, the silence turns to wild applause, Lyusini[75] comes on. Some actress from the Alexandra gets up and tries to say something, then Serge does a remarkable circus number—he takes the

---

72 Kozintsev's sister had married Il'ya Érenburg in 1919 and was living in Berlin.

73 Evtikhy Pavlovich Karpov (1857–1926), director and playwright, a leader of the Alexandra Dramatic Theater 1896–1918, staged the failed premiere of Chekhov's *Seagull* in 1896; he was a symbol of deadly, outmoded theater.

74 Nikolay Vasil'evich Petrov (1890–1964), Meyerhold's assistant on *Dom Juan* and *Masquerade* at the Alexandra Theater; in the 1920s (to 1933), artistic director of the Leningrad Academic Drama Theater and the Moscow Transport Theater 1938–48; head of the acting and directing faculty of GITIS.

75 Stage name of Aleksey Yakovlevich Kapler (1904–79), playwright and screenwriter, a childhood friend of Kozintsev. In the 1920s he published short stories, worked as a cabaret dancer, and served as assistant director to Les' Kurbas. Later he wrote the scripts for such patriotic films as *Lenin in October* and *Lenin in 1918*.

chair and acts as if he's about to chuck it into the audience, the lady drops in fear. All the rest of the entrances take place to accompaniment of applause. The entrance of our best actress Tikhomirova;[76] she came on in her own frock. When I saw it at the dress rehearsal, I almost fell into the orchestra pit. Imagine a half-naked woman, wearing a frock more revealing than any music hall costume, and covered with green sequins. On her entrance an excited whisper runs through the crowd, she tap dances and sings, exclamations break out, "Where did this glamour-puss come from?"

The first act ends to applause. The same thing happens in the second act, and when the third act ends in a general call for the author, I come on, bow, and say that I thank the audience for its scandalous reaction to our scandalous work. Now about the show itself. It's hard to describe, but I'll try (by the way, I consider the chief trophy of our production to be a note Tikhomirova got inviting her to have supper in a private room of a restaurant).

The scenery. The backdrop with garish advertisements, on it a portrait of Chaplin, at the left a wooden dummy—an automaton with a megaphone covered with a mass of graffiti, it emits sandwiches, a cup of tea, a cigarette lighter, a mailbox, a mirror, a telephone, etc. It explains the action and shouts out preprepared witticisms. On the right a row of taut wires, bearing the letters "Matrimonial Bureau." In addition, they push on a platform on springs with Gogol sitting on it, he's shot up to the ceiling, and a revolving chair.

I can't write any more, because I have to run. Yes, there is more news. Kryzhitsky and Serëzha Yutkevich[77] are leaving our depot [...] because Kryzhitsky plans to open a "Philosophic Showbooth" theater, and we aren't interested in being involved in such a project. [...]

Sergey Radlov, "The future of FÉKS," *Teatr* 3 (1923), in Radlov, *Desyat' let v teatre* [Ten years in the theater] (Leningrad: Priboy, 1929), 19.

[Petrograd] In the course of the season, FÉKS will carry on work as an independent studio within the Petroproletkul't. FÉKS productions will autonomously begin in November with *Foreign Trade on the Eiffel Tower*[78] with a completely new script and a new team of performers. The production will sum up all theatrical innovations in the way of Americanism, music-hallization, and primitive eccentrism. Next will come a play of the new plan, *The Shot at Lenin*.

Experimental theater at the present time is busy solving the problem of new theatrical lighting, owing to the circular shape of the stage. The theater has succeeded in

76 Nina Vasil'evna Tikhomirova (1898–1976), student of Vakhtangov at the Gunst Studio (from 1918) and the Third Studio; played a Zanni in *Princess Turandot*; in 1924 moved to the MAT 2.

77 Sergey Iosifovich Yutkevich (1904–85), a student of Meyerhold who worked closely with Foregger, Eisenstein, FÉKS, and the Blue Blouse troupes; directed the first revivals of *The Bathhouse* and *The Bedbug* (1954–55).

78 *Vneshtorg na Éyfelevoy bashne, ili printsip sego dnya*, with a nod to Jean Cocteau's *Les Mariés de la Tour Eiffel*, shows the Soviet Union saving Europe for a glorious future.

interesting and attracting to work a series of engineers, among them the president of the Electrotechnical Soviet in Petrograd N. A. Shatelen.[79]

> Grigory Kozintsev and Leonid Trauberg, "Our enemies are—who?," *Teatr* (Petrograd) 7 (1923), 14.

Out of the way—bad taste! Petrograders! Don't suppose that larding the programs with "Crinoline girls" and "Violet girls," people in half-masks + transparencies + pocket flashlights + interpolated music hall songs (*Wedlock,* September 23) makes you a modern theater! Rappoport![80] Are you sure of the "stunning novelty" of packing Shaw with bars, jugglers, nightclub dancers and generally inoculating the Petrograd public with a taste for American cabaret? Greenwich Villagers of all lands and nations! Give up hope of being inventors: you use detectives, pop songs, and agit so affectingly that they would pass for inventions, if it weren't for the competition from the Alcazar vaudeville house in Tambov! The ultimate—the liveliest of them all—is Timoshenko.[81] He should—piece of advice—bear in mind: using boxing matches, short scenes, Grand Guignol, etc., is needed only when it leads to a concrete Soviet goal, and not meant as a cheap stunt. When the goal is in proportion, we'll tip our hats. It's not about the use of foreign things. It's about the misuse. After all, we don't protest when in Moscow Eisenstein beautifully uses our devices from *Wedlock* for *Wise Fool.*[82] But our targets are money changers and fashionistas. [. . .]

[. . .] You think eccentrism means turning somersaults? Piffle. Torkhovskaya's dance with Martinson[83] (*Foreign Exchange*) is more authentic than thousands of Serge's saltos. The goal of eccentrism is quite simple: "the organization of a new everyday life." [. . .]

PROLETKUL'T was headed from 1922 by Sergey Eisenstein, who demanded from the actor an acrobat's technique. His staging in 1923 of a Russian classic, Ostrovsky's satirical comedy *No Fool Like a Wise Fool,* transformed by him into a circus spectacle, with the addition of filmed elements and the substitution of contemporary political figures for characters in the play, was the very type of futurist experimentation. In Eisenstein's words [a personal statement, 1926], the three plays he staged for the First Moscow Worker's Theater were directly opposed to Proletkul't aesthetics and meant to support LEF, their staging "a mathematical calculation of the elements of affect, which at that time I called 'actions.'" The

---

79 N. A. Shatelen, academician, member of the Politechnical Institute of Leningrad.
80 Iosif Matveevich Rapoport (1901–70), student of Vakhtangov at the Third Studio from 1920, played a Sage in *Princess Turandot*; later at the Vakhtangov Theater.
81 Semën Alekseevich Timoshenko (1899–1958), master of ceremonies and director at the Petrograd Free Comedy Theater and the "Little Showbooth" cabaret; later a film director.
82 See below.
83 Sergey Aleksandrovich Martinson (1899–1984), grotesque actor at GosTIM and the Theater of Revolution from 1924, often playing caricatural Americans; in the 1930s, at the Moscow Music Hall, created the role of the clown Skid in *Burlesque* and then played only in cabarets and films.

first production, *Wise Fool,* was an attempt at "a cubist dissection of a classical play into distinctly affective 'attractions.'" The second production, *Do You Hear, Moscow?,* "used essentially technical means to try to realize theatrical illusions with mathematical calculations." The third production, *Gas Masks,* was staged in a gasworks, during working hours. "The machines were at work and the 'actors' were at work; for the first time the success of an absolutely real, highly objective art was demonstrated."

Sergey Eisenstein, "The montage of attractions for *No Fool Like a Wise Fool,*" *LEF* 3 (1923), 70–75.

An attraction (in our diagnosis of theater) is any aggressive moment in theater, i.e., any element of it that subjects the audience to emotional or psychological influence, verified by experience and mathematically calculated to produce specific emotional shocks in the spectator in their proper order within the whole. These shocks provide the only opportunity of perceiving the ideological aspect of what is being shown, the ultimate ideological conclusion. [...]

The attraction has nothing in common with the stunt. The stunt, or, more accurately, the trick (it is high time that this much abused term be returned to its rightful place), is a finished achievement of a particular kind of mastery (acrobatics, mostly) and it is only one kind of attraction that is suitable for presentation (or, as they say in the circus, "putting across"). Insofar as a trick is absolute and complete in itself, it means the direct opposite of the attraction, which is based exclusively on something relative, the reactions of the audience.

Our present approach radically alters our opportunities in the principles of creating an "effective structure" (the show as a whole) instead of a static "reflection" of a particular event dictated by the theme, and our opportunities for resolving it through an effect that is logically implicit in that event, and this gives rise to a new concept: a free montage with arbitrarily chosen effects (attractions) independent (of both the PARTICULAR *composition and any thematic connection with the actors) but with the precise aim of a specific ultimate thematic effect—a montage of attractions.* [...]

The school for the montage maker is cinema and, principally, music hall and circus, because (from the point of view of form) putting on a good show means constructing a strong music hall–circus program that derives from the situations found in the play that is taken as a basis.

Sergey Eisenstein's diary, December 9, 1923, in *Mnemozina. Istorichesky al'manakh,* ed. Vladislav Ivanov (Moscow: Éditorial URSS, 2000), 2:255.

Tret'yakov has neatly formulated something that I was planning to write in *Izvestia* concerning this year's repertory—"the subject of the play" is not in the play but in the audience—the play only "includes" moments necessary to the objective of the production and which are put before the spectator "to achieve the condensation of the necessary emotional effect" (conversation with Zalkind[84] at the rehearsal of *Gas Masks,* December 13).[85] Of course, he said it better. Conclusive for drama from the viewpoint of the theater of attractions. (A few days ago I spent the night at his place—once again he emphasized that it was a swinish trick not to show him one's hand in the attraction method of the theater before the premiere of *Wise Fool*—theatrical attraction is *my* invention. It's good to have a theorist close at hand, but I'm afraid that he will get the credit for this achievement. [...]

> Description of Sergey Tretyakov's *Do You Hear, Moscow?* (*Slyshish, Moskva?*), staged in Moscow in 1924 by Sergey Eisenstein, who intended "to collect into one strong-willed fist the diffuse emotions of the audience and to instill in the spectators' psyche a purposeful directive, dictated by the current struggle of the German workers for Communism." *LEF* 4 (August–December 1924), 218.

The second and third acts worked up plenty of tension in the audience that was discharged in the fourth-act scene showing [German] workers storming the Fascist platform. In the audience, spectators leaped from their seats. There were shouts: "Over there, over there! The count is escaping! Grab him!" A colossal student from a worker's university, leaping to his feet, shouted at the cocotte: "What are you fussing about? Grab her," accompanying these words with a salty curse. When the cocotte was killed on the stage and shoved downstairs, he swore with satisfaction, adding, "She had it coming." This was said so forcefully that a lady in furs sitting next to him could stand it no longer. She jumped up and blurted in fright: "Good heavens! What is going on? They'll be at it here, too," and ran for the exit. Every killing of a fascist was drowned in applause and shouts. It was reported that a military man, sitting at the back, pulled out his revolver and aimed it at the cocotte, but his neighbors made him see sense. This fervor affected even the stage. Extras in the stage crowd, students . . . placed there for decoration, unable to hold back, joined in the assault on the installation. They had to be dragged back by their legs.

> The birth of the Moscow Satire Theater. N. Kolin, "On satire and the Satire Theater," *Teatr* 3 (1938), 83–90.

The Moscow Satire Theater is one of the most remarkable entities demonstrating the growth of Soviet satire. It was born in 1924 out of the remnants of "The Bat," "Crooked Jimmy," and other "miniature-miniaturistic" theatrical organisms. Its organizers were the talented playwrights L. Nikitin, Ardov, Aduev, Argo, Gutman, and Tipot[86] and the

---

84 Aron Borisovich Zalkind (1889–1936), early Soviet Freudian psychologist, sexologist, and educational theorist.

85 *Protivogazy* by S. M. Tret'yakov, at the First Proletkul't Theater, based on George Kaiser's expressionist drama *Gas*. Staged by Eisenstein at an actual gasworks, it opened on February 28, 1924.

86 Lev Venyaminovich Nikitin (1891–1967), prolific and versatile playwright. Viktor Efimovich Ardov (actually Zigberman, 1900–1976), caricaturist and sketch writer, coauthor of the revue *You're Not a Hooligan, Are You, Citizen?* (1927). Nikolay Al'fredovich Aduev (1895–1950), satiric

actors Kara-Dmitriev, Pol', Volkov, Milyutin, and Neverova.[87] It was born as a theater of revue. [...]

Moscow from a Point of View ([with contributions by Nikolay Érdman] 1924) was the first of such productions. Its success defined the profile of the theater. In the course of three years, revues exclusively held the stage at the Satire Theater. Their ideological tendency was at times remarkably shaky; often they tried only to provoke laughter by whatever might make a philistine laugh. Workers at the Satire Theater don't care to remember this, but over the course of a few years their theater was enthusiastically attended, especially by an audience of Népmen. Such remarkably popular revues of the time, such as *Oy, Gritsa, Don't Get Involved in the Empress's Conspiracy, Quiet—I'm Stealing, Europe, That's What We Need,* and others, never rose to the level of highly ideological, originally satiric works. [...]

Vitaly Lazarenko, "Circus and clown," *Rabochy i teatr* 69 (January 12, 1926), 15.

I think it necessary to state with satisfaction the great achievements and enormous evolution made by the circus over the last eight to ten years. A series of puzzling stunts, the impeccable purity of the work, the high-quality technique of the circus performers, at the present time, is granted by everyone. Russian circus artists occupy far from the last place in the world arena; one need only recall the names of Durov, who set a world record in his time, the leaper Sosin, the equilibrist Stepanov,[88] and many others, affirming the glory of the Russian circus. But one frank admission has to be made:

"We have few clowns."

[...] The first basic reason seemed to be the total lack of literary material. Literary "specialists" of all sorts of weaponry, from versifiers to chroniclers, write articles, columns, dramas, comedies, verses, ballads, whatever you like, but not one of them has yet managed to write a script for a clown, a scenario for a pantomime, etc. We, circus workers, isolated from literary men and journalists, deprived of support, truly pose the question: under such conditions, how can we be rebuked for triteness, lack of culture, and so on? It's not a matter for us but for the men of letters: let them work with us to create a new, Soviet repertoire.

The Achilles' heel of the clown's work is the absence of a director, of course, not

---

poet, author of monologues and pantomimes. Argo (actually Abram Markovich Gol'denburg, 1897–1968), author of agitprop sketches and puppet satires. Viktor Yakovlevich Tipot (actually Ginzburg, 1893–1960), cabaret actor and director; wrote for the Blue Blouse.

87 Dmitry Lazarevich Kara-Dmitriev (1888–1972), banjoist and drummer, who chatted with the audience. Yury (Georgy) Sergeevich Milyutin (1903–68), actor at the Kamerny Theater, pianist and composer for the Blue Blouse. E. N. Neverova, P. N. Pol', and Ya. M. Volkov, cabaret artistes with the Bibabo, Crooked Jimmy, and Bat cabarets.

88 Vladimir Leonidovich Durov (1863–1934), clown and animal trainer, who applied Pavlovian principles to the work in his menagerie. Aleksandr Iosifovich Sosin (1893–1978), acrobat and clown, who worked internationally 1925–28; famous for his leap over twenty-four soldiers with bayonets. Stepan Vasil'evich Stepanov (actually Krivoshein), known for performing balancing acts at the top of a five-meter-high tower.

a generic theatrical one, but a circus specialist, who could, thanks to his experience and knowledge, effectively and divertingly provide a number. The ideal for us would be the joint study of a number by the performer, the author, and the director: then we would avoid lots of failures and roughness in the work.

In conclusion, about so-called Soviet satire. "So-called," for we are nowhere near authentic Soviet satire; maybe there is a whole series of successful and witty literary skits, which satisfy all the demands of modern satirical works, but there are very few suitable for circus performance. A special difficulty consists in the fact that every routine that we perform has to be saturated with a keen dynamic, or else it would not get to the spectator. [...]

———————

IT WOULD BE A MISTAKE to think that the younger generation wholeheartedly welcomed these experiments. Among those who felt that they ran counter to the socialist project was Nikolay Pavlovich Okhlopkov (1900–1967), who had been inspired on hearing Mayakovsky to join a theater group in his native Irkutsk, where he staged a mass action and ran its youth theater. In the early 1920s he was in Moscow studying at GITIS and Meyerhold's studio, playing minor roles in almost all of Meyerhold's productions between 1922 and 1926.

> Nikolay Okhlopkov, "Ob uslovnosti" [On stylization], 1959, in N. P. Okhlop-kov, *Vsem molodym* [To all that's young] (Moscow: Molodaya Gvardiya, 1981), 80–81.

I haven't always intelligently and boldly fought against formalistic "experimentation," I have not always found a way to oppose it, but I was always organically sickened by "Gogol on a bike" (FÉKS), and the tight-rope walking—as in the circus—in Ostrovsky plays at the Proletkul't, and the green wig in *The Forest* at GosTIM, and a lot of that sort of thing (although even so, that nasty green wig made the whole forest of Meyerhold's general concept for the production clear to me). I was not yet ready for the struggle, I did not have the appropriate strength to combat personally, loudly and boldly, for instance, "metro-rhythm" in the theater, led by Ferdinandov, in which even the text of Ostrovsky's *Thunderstorm* was chopped into tiny bits, forcing the actors to rap out every syllable mechanically, or to fight against Foregger's theater, organized somewhere on the Arbat. At that time, the best thing my callowness could find to do was attend the show at that theater, simply stop their action and loudly proclaim for all to hear that this was not a theater but a mess. Then I would invite all the spectators into the lobby so that we could debate Foregger's "principles of theater." I did this out of extremely deep-seated motives. Youth raging within me, on one hand, and fury at the aesthetes, on the other. When I was forbidden entry to the theater, I disguised myself in all sorts of costumes unknown to the ticket takers, even women's clothes. I simply couldn't stand those aestheticizing theatricians.

FANS OF IMPROVISATION Anatoly Vladimirovich Bykov (1892–1943), a mathematics and physics student at Moscow University, and Anastasiya Aleksandrovna Lëvshina (1870–1947) cofounded an improvisation studio in 1917 and reorganized it as Semperante in 1919 in an apartment by the Nikitsky Gates in Moscow.

> Boris Golubovsky, *Bol'shie malen'kie teatry* [Big little theaters] (Moscow: Izd. im. Sabahnikovykh, 1998), 337–38. Boris Gavrilovich Golubovsky (1919–), an expert on acting technique, was director of GITIS Front Theater and the Miniature Theater "Ogonëk" in World War II; director in chief, Moscow TYUZ, 1957–65; headed the Gogol Theater, Moscow, 1965–87; then taught at GITIS (later RATI).

In my time, "Semperante" played in a big auditorium of the Polytechnic Museum almost without a mise-en-scène—the "naked" actor on a bare stage. Before us rose the miracle of theater—brilliant improvisations by two expert actors, getting drunk on their time onstage. I don't know which to prefer—Bykov more conspicuous because he played the leading roles; the theater was created for him, on account of him, and he reigned over it by right. Here was someone who could be called a tragic clown! He could do the most difficult thing—maintain a mask without a mask, as a living human being. Bykov was somewhat reminiscent both of the American "unsmiling clown" Buster Keaton and the suave and dazzling Max Linder,[89] Chaplin's forerunner, captivating the whole world with the art of drawing room comedy. And suddenly—through the sparkling comedy, a clownish super-seriousness was perforated by malicious little notes, a terrible force surged forward, sweeping everything from its path. In "The Human Squid" (from Fëdor Gladkov's[90] story), Bykov incarnated the fantastical figure of a certain Klyuev, attached by suction to a government bureaucracy, wrapped in clouds of bootlicking, blackmail, and squabbling, and thereby making a vertiginous career: so this title—"The Human Squid"—was really quite accurate: you didn't know which part of him was the body, he so coiled and twisted, transforming himself into something humanoid, without losing a true-to-life credibility. A virtuoso! And what a contemporary—even now—theme!

Partnering him, Lëvshina was the brains of the theater, enjoying fame as a wonderful pedagogue, [...] homely and not hiding that fact, but, on the contrary, knowing how to turn her defects into qualities and precisely in that way becoming charming and attractive.

---

89 The films of the comedians Buster (Joseph Francis) Keaton (1895–1966) and Max Linder (actually Gabriel-Maximilien Leuvielle, 1883–1925) were widely distributed in Russia.

90 Fëdor Vasil'evich Gladkov (1883–1958), author of *Cement,* the first Soviet novel to describe the reconstruction of Russia after the devastation of the Civil War.

3.10. "The Death of the Sun" at Semperante, with Bykov as the Yankee and Lëvshina as the Chinaman.

A. Menshoy, "Jazz band, shimmy, cocottes, currency speculators or symbols of modern Europe," *Teatr* (Petrograd) 13 (December 25, 1923), 12–14. Menshoy was a correspondent to *Novy Mir* and a former member of the Russian Socialist Federation.

The most up-to-date Berlin cabaret (an exact copy of the Parisian one) is made up of the following basic elements:

A jazz band.
The shimmy.
Cocottes.
Foreign currency exchange. [...]

The jazz band is a dream conjured up by some insane idiot and brought to life. It's a wild thing, frenzied by cocaine ... They've said it's Negro. But this is wrong: Negroes are very cultured people (I've lived among Negroes a long time), one of the most cultured peoples in the world. Negro folksongs and dances are true art ... But the jazz band was thought up by an insane idiot—a civilized one, moribund and out of his mind from syphilis ... The jazz band (in its most up-to-date formation) consists of fiddles, cellos, an upright piano, a bass, fourteen drums, cymbals, accordions, penny whistles, and other things that have nothing to do with music: there are some broken pots, knives, forks and spoons, old shoes, spectacle cases, horse brasses, tin cans, shards of glass, name plates, combs, sticks, an old top hat. The fiddler dances and plays—he plays the fiddle and dances through the hall, between the pillars. He plays the devil knows what—you can't make it out. And every time he has to hold out his hand to get a tip, the playing is interrupted—and then—resumes, but it's already something else, from some other opera. It had been weeping and sobbing, and now it's a dance tune and hilarity. [...]

A jazz band seems to me a symbol of modern Europe, postwar, post-Versailles. An insane cacophony. [...]

The shimmy is not a dance, but onanism, a surrogate for the sex act. [...] The shimmy is not danced like a waltz, or even like a cake walk, but follows no rules, no "one, two, three, one, two, three." [...] The shimmy is sick, abnormal, inhuman lust.

The shimmy is danced by half-dressed women with upturned eyes, lips painted blood-red, and pale, pale faces. The men are in evening dress, also with upturned eyes and reddened lips, also pale. The shimmy is wearying, it dislodges one from life. Two hours of the shimmy—and then a mild swoon. [...]

So many dramas in modern Europe are unwatchable—and horrible to the point that if you knew all, all of them, you'd put an end to your life by suicide. This is not phrase making. I write these lines sincerely. [...]

The Two Moscow Art Theaters

For several years, the Moscow Art Theater had suffered a serious crisis in its repertoire; after the Revolution, it was really at pains to find a work that would suit both its traditional standards and the new political situation. It first turned toward classical plays, which condemned the old order or protested against social injustice. The climate around Stanislavsky and Nemirovich-Danchenko was very strained; they were assailed by violent criticism on the part of the innovators for whom they represented an outdated aesthetic. To that was added a serious element of disorganization: the Art Theater had been cut in half by the Civil War in 1919. Luckily, its classification as an academic theater gave it some breathing space.

Annenkov, *Dnevnik*, 280–82.

My understanding of theater definitely differed from Stanislavsky's views, but I never disdained his enormous talent and the influence he had on the rebirth of the theater of his time on a worldwide scale. [...] The work [on Tolstoy's comedy *Fruits of Enlightenment*] was prolonged and painstaking. Every detail of the production, even the most trivial, became the theme for our discussions: how the tablecloth was to be laid on the table, how a frockcoat was to be unbuttoned, and so on. In discussion, Stanislavsky not only gave all sorts of advice but kept expecting new ideas all the time and, occasionally, accepted them, even if they contradicted his theories. He loved to collaborate, in the literal meaning of the word, and not give instructions or orders. When in our études we got to the scene of the spiritualist séance in Act III, I proposed to take advantage of the revolving stage (at that time the Moscow Art was the only theater in the Soviet

Union equipped with a revolving stage). Tolstoy's play is extremely realistic, of course, but the spiritualist scene evoked a feeling of a certain slippage of consciousness, a certain head-spinning. If at the moment when Leonid Fëdorovich Zvezdintsev puts out the candles, and in the ensuing darkness, I mean the conventional theatrical blackout, Tanya crawls out from under the divan and takes the dangling cord in her hands—if at that moment the whole setup of the stage along with the characters suddenly spun round and finally froze in the original position, when Semën coughs, Tanya hides back under the divan, and Leonid Fëdorovich lights the candles again—it seemed to me that such a device would underline that psychological moment of the stage action. Stanislavsky looked at me in wonder and said that the revolving stage had been installed in the theater exclusively for technical reasons, to facilitate scene changes during the intermissions, behind a closed curtain, and hence was not for the demonstration of "effects" and any possible scenic "gimmickry." I was dismayed: all the ingenuity and all the novelty (as it seemed to me) of this act of the play vanished for me. But three or four days later, Stanislavsky, at lunch hour in the theater's cafeteria, sat at my table and almost whispered in my ear:

"I've thought it over, I agree, let's risk it. Go ahead!"

In one of the next rehearsals the stage began to revolve.

"Great! All right! It works!" Stanislavsky cried out, roaring with laughter, and added in French, "Ça va!"

However, when the rehearsals were already in full swing, a representative of the People's Commissariat for Enlightenment showed up at the office unexpectedly and explained that this play by Lev Tolstoy did not correspond to the "general line of the political moment" and that, therefore, the production of *Fruits of Enlightenment* should be stricken from the repertoire. Our work was cut short. This was clear proof of "the creative freedom" and "absence of censorship" in the Soviet Union.

"We are living through 'historic' times, which are always full of surprises," Stanislavsky smiled with bitter irony.

SEVERAL MEMBERS of the Kachalov group, including Kachalov himself and Knipper-Chekhova, returned to Moscow in 1922 after three years abroad. Those who stayed in Europe, among them Pëtr Shatrov and Mariya Germanova, called themselves the Prague Group of the Moscow Art Theater (they had a subsidy from the Czech government) and traveled widely, to the chagrin of the parent company, which felt they had usurped the name and reputation of the original.

Sergey Bertenson, *Vokrug Iskusstva* (Hollywood, Calif.: S. Bertenson, 1957), 338–39.

After an eyeful of smart, tidy Europe, how gray and unattractive the streets appeared, how badly and poorly dressed the people. [...] At the theater we were greeted with a big reception with all the comrades and colleagues at a dinner set up in the lobby. Our theater caterer, everyone's friend A. A. Prokof'ev, connected with the theater from the first days of its origin, had organized a regular feast, and it was hard to believe that this very Moscow, which comparatively recently had been starving, could provide so many varieties of foodstuffs.

Stanislavsky treated us with a certain coolness. There had been plenty of time for people to whisper to us that he did not fully believe in the involuntary nature of our exile, somewhere in the crevices of his soul suspecting that we had acted according to a preconceived plan. Besides, he considered that our group had earned a success that by right should belong not to it but to the theater as a whole, whenever it might go abroad. [...] On the other hand the meeting with Nemirovich-Danchenko was of quite another character, simple and heartfelt. [...] From talking to him it was clear what an important role his new Musical Studio[91] had played in sustaining the very existence of the theater, when the activity of the dramatic troupe left in Moscow had narrowed to a minimum and the repertoire had been thrown into disarray. It had not been easy to bring to life the idea of the Musical Theater. He had had not only to organize a new troupe on completely new principles, pour new elements into it, but also to overcome the skeptical sneers of some and the dissatisfaction of others that the frivolous tunes of operetta should resound within the walls of the Art Theater. However, the production of *The Daughter of Madame Angot* dispelled all doubts and not only lightened the position of the theater in the hard times of crisis but even gave a jolt to its very art, which needed a new rhythm and a release from many stale old habits. [...]

WITH a fully constituted acting company, the MAT proposed to accept invitations from impresarios in Europe and North America for a tour. Its purpose would be not only to spread the renown of "Soviet" art but also to make much-needed foreign currency (*valyuta*) and, in Stanislavsky's case, through lectures and private lessons, to earn the money to keep his tubercular son Igor' in a European sanitarium. The tour, enthusiastically supported by Lunacharsky, was opposed by Feliks Dzerzhinsky, head of the Cheka, on the grounds of "brain drain." Many other artists permitted to go abroad had not returned.

F. F. Dzerzhinsky, "Memorandum to the Central Committee," April 19, 1921. In *Soviet culture and power: A history in documents 1917–1953*, ed. Katerina Clark and Evgeny Dobrenko, with André Artizov and Oleg Naumov (New Haven, Conn.: Yale University Press, 2007), 9. © 2007 by Yale University.

According to very reliable information, a group of artists from this theater is in close contact with American circles intimately connected to intelligence agencies. The the-

91 The MAT Musical Studio was founded in 1919 by Nemirovich-Danchenko to apply Art Theater methods and principles to staging opera and musical comedy, with an emphasis on psychological truth and historical accuracy. His first productions included Lecocq's *The Daughter of Mme Angot* (1920), Offenbach's *La Périchole* (1922), Aristophanes's *Lysistrata* (1923), and *Carmencita and the Soldier* from Merimée and Bizet (1924). They were toured to the United States in 1924–25.

ater has been promised material assistance abroad. The artist Sukhacheva has been in close contact with a number of these individuals. [...]

Allusions to rest and treatment are by no means convincing, since the artists could easily use their vacations for trips to the provinces.

Firmly opposed to such petitions, the VchK [Cheka] asks the Central Committee to treat this matter with all seriousness.

LUNACHARSKY then suggested that the Art Theater's First Studio be allowed to travel abroad and, if it returned, the parent company would be given permission; his proposal was voted down. A flurry of letters, notes, and memoranda ensued, concerning artists' foreign travel. Chaliapin was allowed to tour and never returned; Aleksandr Blok was forbidden travel to Finland for his health and died shortly thereafter.[92] The First Studio was allowed to tour to Germany and then the parent company to Germany and the United States, primarily for economic reasons, with a repertoire that was nearly twenty years old. Lunacharsky had won this round, but the government's attitude toward theatrical touring became increasingly negative. And, as it happened, some younger members of the Art Theater (Akim Tamiroff, Maria Ouspenskaya, and Leo Bulgakov) did stay in New York.

The Art Theater's absence made it all the more vulnerable to attacks on its "irrelevance" and "bourgeois tendencies." Rumors ran that it hobnobbed with White émigrés. Lenin and Trotsky both questioned the need to preserve it. Trotsky's *Literatura i revolutsiya* (1923) laid down guidelines for the Party's policy in administering culture, insisting that it, not historical progress, guide the proletariat in the proper direction. However, in the realm of art, the Party should not command but "indirectly guide" its political course. To this end, it should pick and choose among the cultural elites, preferring some, opposing others. The leaders of the Moscow Art Theater were among the undesirables.

Leon Trotsky, *Literature and Revolution,* trans. Rose Strunsky (heavily rev.) (New York: International, 1925), 32.

The most indisputable "insulars" are the members of the Moscow Art Theater group. They do not know what to do with their highfalutin technique, or with themselves. They consider everything going on around them as hostile, or, at any rate, alien. Just imagine: these people are living, in this day and age, in the atmosphere of Chekhov's plays. *Three Sisters* and *Uncle Vanya* nowadays! While waiting for the bad weather to blow over—bad weather does not last long—they played *The Daughter of Madame Angot,* which, apart from all else, gave them a little chance to show off their opposition to the revolutionary authorities. Now they are disclosing to the blasé European and the

---

92 For the exchange of correspondence, see Katerina Clark and Evgeny Dobrenko, with André Artizov and Oleg Naumov, *Soviet Culture and Power: A History in Documents 1917–1953* (New Haven, Conn.: Yale University Press, 2007), 9–21.

all-paying American how beautiful was the cherry orchard of old feudal Russia and how subtle and languid were its theaters. What a noble moribund cast from a gem of a theater! Doesn't the very gifted Akhmatova[93] belong here too?

Nemirovich-Danchenko to O. L. Bokshanskaya, November 18, 1923. In *Tvorcheskoe nasledie,* 3:43.

We are at war with the Glavrepertkom [...] which wants to impose on the theater a censorship such as never before. [...] It won't license a play whenever it finds it counter-revolutionary, and whenever it finds it insufficiently Soviet, and whenever the play has a king ([Ostrovsky's] *The Snowmaiden*) or tsarist officials ([Ostrovsky's] *The Voivode*), and whenever there is a beautiful past or church ([Turgenev's] *A Nest of Gentry*), and whenever anything in general bothers it, the Glavrepertkom, and whenever it is useful to flex its muscles.

IN VIEW OF THESE ATTACKS, Lunacharsky decided to protect the former Imperial Theaters, the MAT, and the Kamerny once and for all by creating a special category of academic theaters, part museum, part production company.

Anatoly Lunacharsky, "Moim opponentam" [To my opponents], 1920, in *Teatr i revolyutsiya* (Moscow: Gosizdat, 1924), 43.

Now that the tiny theatrical October is here, it would, of course, be ridiculous to hand over to it the treasures that were preserved not without great labor at the time of the gigantic tempest in the real October [of 1917] ... I can entrust Comrade Meyerhold with the destruction of what is old and bad and with the creation of what is new and good. But I cannot entrust him with preserving whatever is old and good.

"The paths of the Academic Theater," *Teatr* [94] (Petrograd) 1 (September 29, 1923), 3–4.

The task of the academic theater is to be the BEST THEATER in modern times. [...]
    The theater must tread three paths to achieve its purpose.
    PATH 1—to preserve as carefully as possible the legacy of past centuries, trying through tradition to present to a new generation of actors past mastery.
    This is the path of the *museum theater and theatrical traditions.* [...] If the theater wants to live, it has to create its own school, or rather, a school of its best actors, and *conserve* the technique, transmitted to the students from the old masters. Isolated in its

---

93 Anna Andreevna Akhmatova (actually Gorenko, 1889–1966), poet, married to Nikolay Gumilëv and fellow member of the Acmeist movement; in the early 1920s her work was rarely published, and in 1930 her son was sentenced to a labor camp; in 1946 she was expelled from the Writer's Union and rehabilitated only after Stalin's death.
94 Journal founded to support the newly named academic theaters.

own everyday concerns, cut off from the objective conditions of the era, the theater of tradition inevitably is doomed to decadence, its expertise will be lost, and the upshot is its inevitable rupture with modern times and its ruin.

PATH 2—is experimental. The search for a new repertory, new formal principles and the construction of the actor's expertise on the bases of a new pedagogic system. This is the path of the *studio theater*. [...]

The more daring the experiments carried on, the more significant can be the achievements and results; but they can be completely without results or insignificant. This in great measure depends on the chance coincidence of objective conditions with subjective premises of the experiment. [...] This, of course, is not a path for the academic theater.

PATH 3 is the compilation and involvement in the work of the theater of everything significant that is created by the era, whatever seems most *indisputable, integral,* and *consummate,* in its mastery.

This is the path of the ACADEMIC THEATER.

[...] The path of the academic theater is not in a synthesis of old and new (museum and experiment), which would seem to be utopian, but in a constant growth and organic renewal of the theater.

FOUR DRAMATIC STUDIOS and a musical studio revolved as satellites around the sun of the Moscow Art Theater. The First Studio, founded by Stanislavsky and Sulerzhitsky in 1912 to be a testing ground for a new system of acting, was composed of a constellation of talented young actors and two actor-directors, Mikhail Chekhov and Evgeny Vakhtangov. In 1922 Chekhov became the director of the First Studio, which, in 1924, was renamed the Second Moscow Art Theater.

The Second Studio, founded in 1916 and which would be folded into the bosom of the Art Theater in 1924—and the Fourth, founded in 1922, which was to become in 1927 the Realistic Theater—were of lesser importance.

> The First Studio visits Berlin. Harry Kessler, *In the Twenties: The Diaries of Harry Kessler,* trans. Charles Kessler (New York: Holt, Rinehart, and Winston, 1971), 190–91. Count Harry Clément Ulrich Kessler (1868–1937) was a keen observer of the arts throughout Europe between the wars.

Wednesday, August 2, 1922, Berlin. First night of the Moscow Experimental Theater at the Apollo Theater [...] Dramatized Dickens. Marvelously spirited and realistic acting for all that it is strictly stylized. They are entirely free of that artificiality which is so distracting about our Expressionists. The impression is of pure naturalism. The masks are an astonishing achievement, their faces real works of art where the painting and modeling is concerned, yet without interfering with the play of the features. The actor Chekhov is unforgettable.

Mikhail Chekhov to Konstantin Stanislavsky, August 1923, from Berlin. In
M. P. Chekhov, *Vospominaniya* [Memoirs] (Moscow: Iskusstvo, 1986), 315.

In the course of the last year some serious changes have taken place in the studio, in
part in its external life, in part in its internal, invisible, spiritual one. And that's the most
important thing. The direction of the studio has changed. Certain dangers came into
being, certain distressing perspectives hove in view. However, something appropriate,
true, is taking shape. If you, Konstantin Sergeevich, remember your words, especially
those you uttered last year, about art, about theater and the actor in general, then you
will see the *direction* I write about. We are still *following* you a bit, at a certain *distance,*
a delay (that you don't want to permit us, which makes things very hard for us). In
short, the time has come to take a step forward, not only in words but in deeds. [. . .]

Giatsintova, *S pamyat'yu naedine,* 226.

It is hard to recall how matters developed day by day, but in the summer of 1924 Bersenev, who had become at that time one of the most active members of the [First] Studio,
informed the administration that he had signed a contract with the Administration of
the Bol'shoy Theater to transfer to the First Studio the building of the New Theater on
Theater Square (now the Central Children's Theater), in confirmation of our autonomy.
The administration granted that the contract "in full measure corresponds to the interests of the Studio" and conveyed to Bersenev deep thanks, signed by Chekhov and
forty performers. [. . .] Lunacharsky had been so impressed by *The Spendthrift*[95] that
he himself helped us to acquire the new building. And even Nemirovich-Danchenko,
who had earlier insisted that the Studio merge with the Art Theater, agreed that it
had matured to an autonomous existence. And it was he, Vladimir Ivanovich, who
proposed to call the Studio detached from the MAT the MAT 2.

Stanislavsky reacted dramatically and angrily to our transformation. He called the
First Studio Goneril, the Third, Vakhtangov's, Regan, and the Second, incorporated
into the Art Theater at that time, Cordelia.

THE FIRST PRODUCTION of the Moscow Art Theater 2 was *Hamlet,* with Mikhail
Chekhov in the lead. After the general rehearsal, the actors were given an ovation,
and Lunacharsky made a speech to Chekhov, praising him for his contribution to
Russian stage. The Moscow press was unanimously laudatory. Stanislavsky's sour
opinion was that he could not play tragedy.

95 *Rastochitel'* by Nikolay Leskov (1874), a moral melodrama, had been produced the previous year.

3.11. Michael Chekhov as Hamlet, Moscow Art Theater 2, 1924.

Andrey Bely,[96] letter to Mikhail Chekhov, November 13, 1924. In *Vstrechi s proshlym* [Encounters with the past] (Moscow: Sovetskaya Rossiya, 1982), 4:226–28.

When you appeared, or more accurately, when the curtain parted, I didn't even notice you, although I knew, of course, as the action proceeded, that you were onstage. But you faded into the background; when Hamlet began to speak, he didn't stand out from the rest; and in general in the first scenes Hamlet was *"one of"*; and all the time the question posed itself to me, where in the world was *Chekhov*? Either *Chekhov* at that time doesn't stand out the way he used to or the *"whole"* in which he is only a note is swallowing him up, and he is dissolved in the sound of an enormous unforgettable *"whole"*; what's going on? In the middle of the act it became clear to me that *Chekhov-Hamlet* is quite surprising: not what others and not what my fancy painted (that is my representation of Chekhov-Hamlet; along with that, it was clear that in Hamlet you weren't producing a single sound of Erik's, while it would seem that it would have been so easy for you to give a hint of Erik). And my wonderment grew: this Hamlet is not *Hamlet,* not the feeble, weak-willed, sort of neurasthenic, sort of fantast, but sober, intelligent, observant, active Hamlet; and there came to mind: "Hasn't he rationalized Hamlet?" By the end of the act it had become conclusively clear that this externally active, sober, and intelligent prince is intelligent with a great intelligence, that is, I

96 Andrey Bely (actually Boris Nikolaevich Bugaev, 1880–1934), symbolist poet and critic, whose dramatization of his Joycean novel *Petersburg* (1925) provided a juicy role for Mikhail Chekhov; his interpretation of Gogol (1925) exercised considerable influence on Meyerhold.

sensed through him from the distant future (perhaps the mid-twentieth century) his penetrating Impulse of Life: the Impulse acted in him (the scene with his mother, at Ophelia's grave, etc.).

[...] It's astonishing what you've done with Hamlet: you acted as if on two separate planes; your own individuality and that of the others. You were in all the "*atmosphere*"; and this expansion of you resulted precisely from a certain conscious diminution of all that is effective and outwardly theatrical in Hamlet; your Hamlet is almost uninterest-ing from the point of view of all the outwardly; and precisely from the diminution of "self" as an actor Hamlet has expanded, taken on colossal dimensions in my conscious-ness; and perhaps you will not be displeased to hear a final, indisputable conviction: today *for the first time* I understood Shakespeare's Hamlet; and this improvement in my understanding came about through you. I didn't see Chekhov, "*the terrific actor*"; I saw Hamlet and forgot about Chekhov. [...]

"M. A. Chekhov—Hamlet," *Rabochy i Teatr* 11 (December 1, 1924), 9.

Nikolay Volkov, *Trud (Labor)*: This choice of play is so audacious and significant that, regardless of the result, the *very fact* of the *Hamlet* premiere forced us to regard it as an artistic and cultural event in advance. [...] Of course, the fact that *Hamlet* seemed contemporary we owe entirely to the theater that staged it. And perhaps it's not so much *what* it has done as how it approached the grandiose task, with what feeling it set to work. Hence the creative profundity in which the *seriousness* of the tragedy seemed melded with the *seriousness* of the production.

Chekhov's Hamlet in his black-and-white garb, scrawny, with a muffled and husky voice, with expressive hands, very simplified, translated the whole tragedy to the level of such human simplicity, such silence, that the luxurious frame of the performance hindered him as an actor.

Khrisanf Khersonsky,[97] *Izvestia*: M. A. Chekhov [...] clearly contends within himself with the danger of hysteria in this role and in many ways overcomes it, especially at the end of the play, when Hamlet the neurotic has to overcome his weakness. Chekhov reveals Hamlet's spiritual passion with nervous tension, but also without shouting, in a quiet, muffled voice. In *Hamlet* he displays the spiritual culture not of the sixteenth but of the twentieth century; the costume of the Prince of Denmark is only the outer theatrical convention, but by nature he is a modern intellectual.

His soliloquies are the quavering of spiritual chords plucked to their limit. Their melody is deeply troubling—it is the moan of grief. His face and eyes importune with inner striving, he sees the world with the "mind's eye." Remarkably expressive is that mute face when it falls silent. In Chekhov, silence is no less eloquent than outbursts of speech. With unusual subtlety and force he delivers the speech rehearsing the players, when one unspoken movement of his eyes, hiding tears, is unforgettably moving. And

97 Khrisanf Nikolaevich Khersonsky (1897–1968), theater scholar and critic, expert on Vakhtangov.

with an outburst of anger after a tense silence, Hamlet rises up afterward, to chastise the king and his mother. [. . .]

NIKOLAY LESKOV'S COMIC TALE of the left-handed smith from Tula and the steel flea was turned into a zany and uproarious evening in the theater by Evgeny Zamyatin, directed by Aleksey Diky, in 1925. It drew on folk art and the current trend for physical comedy.

Evgeny Zamyatin,[98] "On *The Flea,*" *Rabochy i Teatr* 47 (November 23, 1926), 9.

For a long time now, our Russian masters in every field of art have been imbibing the water of life from the springs of the people's creativity.

Russian wood carvings, Russian icons and penny prints, Russian folk tales and epics, Russian songs and dances inspired the creativity of Konenkov, Roerich, Kustodiev, Petrov-Vodkin, Leskov, Remizov, and Stravinsky.[99] And only the Russian folk theater has so far remained as if it were a bypath on the highways of arts. True, the *themes* of Russian folk theater have been used a bit, but almost no one has tried to take the *form* of the folk theater. Almost the only exception to this appears to be Remizov—his *Spring Rites for the Dead [Rusal'nye deystva].*[100] But, meanwhile, it struck me that the forms of folk theater, created by the folk itself, its ancient and rich culture, could provide stage material very close to our new spectator.

The Flea is an experiment in building such a folk theater, an experiment in using the forms of Russian folk comedy. Like every folk theater, this is, of course, not a realistic theater but a stylized one from start to finish, which is why I called *The Flea* a *game* [*igra*]. In concept this ought to be just that, a game, a high-spirited, mountebank's game, in which all sorts of transformation, wonders, surprises, anachronisms are permissible. The subject of the game is taken from tsarist times, but the anachronisms generously open the door in the game to topicality.

As in every Russian folk comedy, *The Flea* mixes comic and dramatic elements:

98 Evgeny Ivanovich Zamyatin (1884–1937), novelist and playwright, best known for his dystopian novel *We,* which influenced Aldous Huxley and George Orwell; his later plays were aborted in rehearsals, and he was severely reprimanded for formalism.

99 Sergey Timofeevich Konenkov (1874–1971), monumental sculptor, who lived in the United States 1923–45 and was brought back to the Soviet Union at Stalin's behest. Nikolay Konstantinovich Roerich (1874–1947), painter, designer, philosopher of mystical bent; from 1921 lived in the United States and India. Boris Mikhaylovich Kustodiev (1878–1927), painter, designer, who specialized in nostalgic re-creations of prerevolutionary merchant life. Kuz'ma Sergeevich Petrov-Vodkin (1878–1939), painter, studied with V. A. Serov and took part in the World of Art; after the Revolution, designed for Leningrad Drama and Meyerhold theaters. Nikolay Semënovich Leskov (1831–95), author, a master of the *skaz* or first-person narrative style. Aleksey Mikhaylovich Remizov (1877–1957), symbolist poet, who composed sophisticated versions of folk dramas. Igor' Fëdorovich Stravinsky (1882–1971), composer and conductor, whose *Sacre du printemps, Les Noces,* and *Renard* were inspired by Russian folklore.

100 *Spring Rites for the Dead* is better known in its dance form as *Le Sacre du printemps,* staged by the Ballets Russes.

the last two acts *half admit* openly the drama of a master craftsman, a working man from Tula, who loves his work as only a real artist can love what he produces. However, the comic element appears basic to *The Flea*. This element is united with satire, also a constituent, indispensable attribute of Russian folk comedy.

The thematic material for *The Flea* came from the Russian folk tale about the residents of Tula and the flea, reworked by N. S. Leskov in his splendid story *Lefty*.[101] However, not much of Leskov's version is left in the play—especially in the script I gave to the Bol'shoy Dramatic Theater (the original script of *The Flea* has been running at the Second MAT since February 1925).

Other Stages

After *Earth Rampant*, the next production of the Theater of Revolution was Ernst Toller's *The Machine Wreckers*. Meyerhold ostensibly turned the actual directing over to his young student P. Repnin but created the mise-en-scène and sat in on rehearsals.

Komardenkov, *Dni minuvshie*, 95–96.

When the actors not involved in the play learned about Meyerhold's presence at rehearsals, they asked permission to stop by the theater and be in the auditorium, and he gave it. Many actors assembled, the director P. Repnin[102] assigned the characters their places, and the rehearsal began. It went rather lamely, although the actors did their best. Vsevolod Émil'evich watched the action very attentively. When a section was over, he would run onto the stage, saying that it was good. But sometimes with his characteristic temperament he would start to concoct a staging, demonstrating postures, gestures, and an interpretive image. Those in the auditorium would watch his every movement tensely. The stage came alive, he united everything in a single whole, it was all invested with meaning, and, after saying, "There, that may be it," he would leave the stage to the thunder of applause and sit back in his seat. These rehearsals were a good schooling for many, and Vsevolod Émil'evich very quickly achieved importance and recognition for the Theater of Revolution.

[...] It was determined that the scenery for *The Machine Wreckers* would be stylized. Much attention was paid to the lighting. A ceiling was hung over the stage from girders on the sides, through which the light was filtered. The greater part of the action took place in a textile factory. In the center we set up two cruciform screens, which revolved on a central axis; each of the four parts could emerge from the center on casters, which provided a number of combinations. When the action took place

---

101 Leskov's "The Tale of Cross-Eyed Lefty from Tula and the Steel Flea" ("Skaz o Tul'skom kosom Levshe i o stal'noy blokhe," 1881) ends unhappily, but Zamyatin provided a happy ending.

102 Pëtr Petrovich Repnin (1894–1970) worked as an actor at the RSFSR 1 1920–24 and as a director at the Theater of Revolution 1922–24; later joined the Realistic Theater under Okhlopkov 1934–38; had a long and distinguished career as a comic film actor.

in the street, then from behind a screen, silhouettes of houses would move out, and there was a cityscape. This was a very interesting concept. [...]

SERGEY RADLOV, another of Meyerhold's students, called for the dictatorship of the director and became head of the Leningrad Theater of Drama (1923–27), which also had an expressionist agenda.

Sergey Radlov, "Who needs constructivism?" *Teatr* 11 (1923), 2–3.

Maybe it is time to ask, "What is constructivism in the theater?"

Meaning no offense, I expect many readers of this respected magazine have this sort of idea:

"If there is a box set with three walls, a ceiling, rugs, armchairs, and a sofa, then 'that is the normal way.'

"But if there are machine tools and ladders and terrorized actors running all around them more or less deftly, then, surely, that must be the most radical 'constructivism.'"

But, believe me, it is not so.

Setting up ladders, making it possible for actors to move, not only right, left, and forward, but also up and down, is the favorite activity of directors of all trends and orientations. Arbatov in his time was famous for this in his Moscow productions, Georg Fuchs[103] intentionally used this practice in his "Künstlertheater," and Meyerhold formulated these principles in his article on producing *Tristan und Isolde* in *1909* (fancy that!), where he writes:

"Let the stage floor be molded just as a sculptor molds his clay, so that the stage floor will be transformed from a wide open space *to a compactly placed series of planes of various elevations.*"

And after this, no matter how many times Tairov assures us he invented the model for his trash.

No. I took constructivism to mean something totally different, when, preparing the production *Wretched Eugene*[104] with the designer Dmitriev, I rejected this principle of staging.

I should comment that in this case I am using the word *constructivism* as it is generally used—to mean a method of stage design. I am sure that constructivism can also mean the movement of actors who are taught this principle.

Primarily, constructivism is connected with new tendencies in the arts, along with easel painting, three-dimensional works of various materials like Tatlin's[105] "counter-

103 Nikolay Nikolaevich Arbatov (actually Arkhipov, 1869–1926), director and teacher at the Vera Komissarzhevskaya Theater 1904–6, later at Suvorin's Theater and the Petrograd People's House. Georg Fuchs (1868–1949), German playwright and director; author of the influential *Stage of the Future* (1904) and *The Revolution in the Theater* (1909); founded the Munich Art Theater.
104 *Hinckemann* (1922) by Ernst Toller, a play about the return of a German soldier, castrated in the war, who becomes a carnival geek.
105 Vladimir Evgrafovich Tatlin (1885–1953), constructivist designer, who became highly popular

reliefs." The meaning of the essence of these materials is one of the main characteristics of this art. We must say that most stage constructions made so far are very far from such strict and severe works as Tatlin's counter-relief made of [?] and ropes, exhibited for the second time last year at the "Exhibit of New Movements."

[...] I say all this not because I am an opponent of constructivism properly understood. On the contrary, I think that constructivism, as the spatial incarnation of the dramatic (temporal) structure of a play, has not developed even half of its hidden capability. I just do not think that it is a panacea—the only and usual method for creating a play.

[...] And perhaps the most important thing in stage constructivism is its essential abstraction. Constructivism does not seek to portray anything: it exists *on its own*. That is why there is such a large number of constructions on which it is possible to perform any play. Ékster's *Romeo and Juliet*, Rabinovich's *Lysistrata*, Levin's *The Fall of Elena Ley*,[106] I don't remember whose *Earth Rampant*—all these constructions, practically unrelated to the dramatic structure, let alone the plot, of these plays. But if we follow this path, isn't it more logical to make a stage construction once for all and perform the whole repertory on it practically without any scenery? This was the setup of the Shakespearean and ancient stages.

[...] The utter rejection of representation is now thought to be in good taste (except in those cases when constructivism accidentally turns into naturalism—*Man and the Masses*,[107] obviously, *Lake Lyul'* at the Theater of Revolution). Dmitriev and I decided to violate this taste in *Wretched Eugene*, especially because the nature of the play threatened to make the production excessively abstract and schematic.

Konstantin Tverskoy, "*Pazukhin's Death*,"[108] *Rabochy i Teatr* 2 (September 30, 1924), 7–8. Konstantin Konstantinovich Tverskoy (actually Kuz'min-Karavaev, 1890–1944) studied with Meyerhold; he became the chief director and designer at the BDT 1927–35; transferred to Saratov and then repressed.

It would be hard to make a more successful choice of play to open the season at the Academic Drama Theater than *Pazukhin's Death*.[109] Despite its venerable age, the satiric comedy of Saltykov-Shchedrin has lost none of its point and is ideologically close to the contemporary spectator.

---

after his model for the Tower of the Third International won a gold medal at a Paris exhibition; in 1926 he headed the Tea-Kino-Foto Department of the Art Institute of Kiev.

106 Ékster's *Romeo and Juliet* (Kamerny Theater, 1921), Isaak Moiseevich Rabinovich's *Lysistrata* (MAT Musical Studio, 1923). Moisey Zeligovich Levin (1895–1946), constructivist designer who later shifted to realism in the late 1920s; designed *The Rout* (1927) at the BDT and a metaphoric *Joy Street* (1932). *Padenie Eleny Ley* by A. N. Piotrovsky had been a success at the Theater of New Drama (March 31, 1923), but Radlov could not get it produced at the Academic Drama Theater.

107 *Man and the Masses* (*Masse Mensch*, 1921) by Ernst Toller presents the revolutionary mob as inimical to humanity.

108 Staged at the Academic Dramatic Theater by Leonid Viv'en with designs by M. Z. Levin.

109 *Pazukhin's Death*, a savage satire on greed by Mikhail Saltykov-Shchedrin (1857), was not produced until 1893; the MAT made a success of it in 1914.

The staging indubitably reveals the influence of the spring tours of Vs. Meyerhold: the desire to "rejuvenate" a classic play, to make it more "contemporary," lies behind the director's concept. To fulfill these tasks the simplest and easiest path was chosen: a left-wing designer was invited to operate a cure. The designer did his own thing: he set up onstage design installations, dressed the actors in grotesque costumes, but ... the rejuvenation did not occur.

It was immediately clear that the whole outward configuration of the production (sets, costumes) in no way fulfilled its basic task—*to aid the actor in his acting*. All the performers—actors of the old, academic school, accustomed to a level stage space, to ordinary, well-fitting costumes, to psychologically justified situations onstage, etc., in short, everything that the new school ("leftist" theater) is rebelling against.

The result was a completely mechanical joining of the "old" actor with expressionist scenery, which led to the loss of the old actor's power of performing, while the expressionism of the designer seemed superfluous and unnecessary ballast.

[...] But the main thing, which evokes the greatest doubt: in our times, when simplicity, clarity, and accessibility are so necessary, the application of sophisticated forms intelligible only to a small circle of the initiate, can it help the theater carry out its task in organizing the mass spectator?

ZAUM or transmental language had been promoted by the futurists before the Revolution as a universally comprehensible protolanguage hidden in the sounds, disjointed vowels, and consonants of words. Its postrevolutionary existence was tenuous and kept alive mainly by its inventors and the OBERIU (Ob'edinenie Real'nogo Iskusstva or Union for Realistic Arts), a Leningrad literary group supported by Malevich. That they were allowed to publish their esoteric ideas speaks volumes for the relative tolerance of this period.

A. Kruchënykh, *Fonetika teatra* [The phonetics of the theater] (Moscow: MAF, 1923), 5, 9, 11–12.

Boris Kushner:[110]

Transmental language is first of all a language of public action, whose tempo and rhythm in its speed and dynamism far outstrip the slowness of ordinary human speech.

Theater, as a public action, has reached an impasse, fallen into a patch of stagnation and patent degeneration, perhaps exclusively because the spoken recitation of roles makes the theatrical action impotent in rhythm and tempo. [...]

Transmental language is the only means of developing the potential of the dramatic stage and blazing new trails of development, prosperity, and rebirth for the theater. [...]

Transmental language is triumphing and will triumph as a socialist dialect.

110 Boris Anisimovich Kushner (1888–1937), futurist poet and theorist, contributor to the journal *The Art of the Commune (Iskusstvo kommuny)* of Narkompros; enthusiast for the collectivization of artists. Died in the Gulag.

Aleksey Kruchënykh:[111]

For the actors, transmental language is the most expressive kind, because it is born of oral speech (sonic-aural) [...] Transmental language is created and forged by the artist and is not passively adopted as a burdensome legacy of the ages; it is the one and only constructivist language (it cannot be compared with official acronyms, because they are accidental and do not stray far from the existing language, although they at times provide valuable word formations). [...]

"Your transmental words are incomprehensible!"

"But what if they were comprehensible to only five persons!" "That's antisocialist (!!)."

So the Bryusovs grumble [pun: *bryuzhat'*], as do the sub-Bryusovs, the Krauts [*nemaki*] and old-timers.

But the theater knows better than anyone that if the actor is unable to persuade by means of phonetics alone (sound, intonation, rhythm), then no concept is possible to him. For the benefit of the actors themselves and the education of the deaf-mute public, *we must stage transmental plays—they will allow the theater to be reborn!* [...]

IGOR' GERASIMOVICH TERENT'EV (1892–1937), a lawyer, had been a mover and shaker in the futurist movement in Tbilisi in 1919. He worked with Aleksey Kruchënykh, published in *LEF,* and studied under the mystic Georges Gurdjieff in Paris. In 1924 he staged *John Reed* at the Leningrad Red Theater, a success, halfway between Foregger and Meyerhold. In 1984 K. L. Rudnitsky[112] wrote to Terent'ev's collaborators and contemporaries to reconstruct his work.

> K. A. Guzynin[113] to K. L. Rudnitsky, after March 20, 1984. In Konstantin Rudnitsky, "Replika Terent'eva" [The Terent'ev response], *Moskovsky nablyudatel'* 7–8 (1995), 78–93.

As for *John Reed,* that show had been staged by Terent'ev at the Red Theater, located at the time in the Lenconservatory hall, where there was a very big, well-equipped stage. And if [his later productions of] *Natal'ya Tarpova* and *Inspector General* were, so to speak, chamber performances, *John Reed* on the big Conservatory stage was a monumental production, with the same sweep with which A. D. Diky staged Vishnevsky's *The First Cavalry*[114] in 1929 on the stage of the People's House in the same Red Theater.

---

111 Aleksey Eliseevich Kruchënykh (1886–1968), leader of the Russian futurist movement and collaborator with Velimir Khlebnikov on *Victory over the Sun* (1913). Promoter of a "transmental" (*zaumny*) language of disjointed vowels and consonants.

112 Konstantin (Lev) Lazarevich Rudnitsky (1919–88), theater historian and critic, worked for nearly thirty years at the GI art studies, with special attention to Stanislavsky, Tairov, and Meyerhold, on whom he wrote a magnum opus; a leading contributor to the six-volume history of the Soviet theater (1963–71).

113 Konstantin Alekseevich Guzynin (1900–1993), playwright, collaborator with the Leningrad Musical Comedy Theater and the Variety Theater.

114 Aleksey Denisovich Diky (1889–1955), student at the MAT First Studio; director of *The Flea*

One of the episodes of the play made an unforgettable impression on me my life long. On the background of a night sky the whole enormous stage was occupied by the *tëplushki* [heated goods vans for human passengers] of the railway gang, with wide open doors, filled with soldiers in their overcoats. At the end of this episode it gradually grew dark, evening turned to night. The train began to move. Clouds scudded across the sky. Corresponding sound effects created a complete illusion of a moving train. The soldiers shook in time to the movement, their figures outlined in silhouette. And distinctly visible were only the tiny lights of the innumerable cigarettes they smoked. These lights in the aggregation of all the increasing sounds of the moving train created a unique picture, whose emotional influence was unusually powerful. [...]

IN THE EARLY YEARS of the BDT the only Soviet play produced had been Lunacharsky's *Faust and the City* (1920). During the NÉP era it moved from classics to German expressionism, and only gradually began to be infiltrated by revolutionary dramas by contemporary Russian playwrights.

> Boris Lavrenëv,[115] "*Revolt*; the author on himself," *Rabochy i Teatr* 40 (October 6, 1925), 5. Boris Andreevich Lavrenëv (1891–1959), whose early historical plays were staged by the BDT 1925–29, welcomed the advent of socialist realism and spearheaded a movement for heroic revolutionary plays.

I wrote *Revolt* on commission for the BDT, and it seems to me to be the first theatrical experiment on a large scale.

I was very attracted by the idea of a romantic tragedy and, so far as possible, I tried to compose *Revolt* on that plan. There is an inexhaustible supply of material for tragedy in the not-so-distant past.

At the basis of *Revolt* lay a factual event—a revolt of the narkom of the Turkestan Republic Osipov[116] in January 1919, extremely interesting and idiosyncratic. Of course, all that is left of the facts in the play is the basic plot and place of action: the rest is completely reinvented.

The basic thread of *Revolt* is in the tragic characters, the opposition of the two heroes of the play: Glavkom Liperovsky and commander of the Partisan Squadron Ruzaev. The former appears to be a typical representative of the white movement, an extreme individualist, revolting against the intellectuals—the second is a power of the

---

at the MAT 2, he often came in conflict with Mikhail Chekhov. In 1937 he was sentenced for espionage to ten years in a labor camp but was released after four years and became one of Stalin's favorite portrayers of himself. *First Cavalry* (1929) was a typical epic drama by Vsevolod Vital'evich Vishnevsky (1900–1951), broken into episodes and devoid of a fully rounded hero.

115 Boris Andreevich Lavrenëv (1891–1959), whose early historical plays were staged by the BDT (1925–29); he welcomed the advent of socialist realism and spearheaded a movement for heroic revolutionary plays.

116 Konstantin Pavlovich Osipov (1896–?) led an anti-Soviet riot of revolutionary socialists in Tashkent in January 1919; it was put down by Ivan Belov.

black earth, molding the collective with an iron will, a quick-thinking macho peasant, colossally stubborn in achieving his goal.

[...] I am the first to present the figure of the White Guard in a tragic light. Up to now white guards have appeared onstage only as farcical buffoon characters and have been made out to be perfect idiots. [...] In *Revolt* I also tried to give only the artistic truth of the struggle and to reveal the reasons that led to the crushing defeat of the Whites, consisting by no means in their stupidity but in their absence of a uniting will, a united goal, enthusiasm, in the extreme individualism and inner spiritual disintegration and sense of doom. [...]

> Andrey Lavrent'ev and I. Kroll', "The directors on their work," *Rabochy i Teatr* 40 (October 6, 1925), 5. Andrey Nikolaevich Lavrent'ev (1882–1935), actor at the MAT 1902–10, then at the Alexandra, was one of the founders of the BDT. Isaak M. Kroll, director at GOSET, staged the popular *Restless Old Age* (1938).

Lavrenëv's play is characteristic of the parallel development of two themes: the tragedy of the individual and the masses, from which all of an individual's experiences flow and are organically bound with his class attributes and that mass, so that he appears to be an expression of them.

The task of the director is to realize in full measure the author's tasks with every means at the disposal of the modern theater; the set models prepared by Acad. Shchuko[117] were done in a realistic mode and offered the possibility to unfold the crowd scenes on which the play is built.

We treat the production in the style of artistic realism, whereby a manifestation of the class essence of the performance is placed as the very cornerstone of the work.

> G. K—y, "Tragedy on stage of the BDT," *Rabochy i Teatr* 47 (November 24, 1925), 5.

The author of *The Wreck of the Five*, Andrey Piotrovsky,[118] is unquestionably an expressionist—perhaps the only representative of this tendency now in Russia, an undoubtedly talented dramatist with his own profile. A brilliant stylist, already in *The Fall of Elena Ley*, with a brilliant control of dramatic devices. Both in manner and in technique *The Wreck of the Five* borders on the new German school of expressionist dramatists and bears traces of Toller's[119] influence. Andrey Piotrovsky is a European. But in his creative work this "Europeanism" is turned into a sort of completely personal style, Russified,

---

117 Vladmir Alekseevich Shchuko (1878–1939), architect and stage designer, who did most of his work in St. Petersburg and then with the Leningrad BDT; his style developed from the painterly and pictorial to the constructed setting.

118 *Gibel' pyati* by Adrian Ivanovich Piotrovsky (1898–1938), a founder of TRAM; attacked for his ballet libretto *Limpid Stream* 1936, arrested 1938. Directed by Pavel K. Vaysbrem of the Leningrad TYUZ.

119 Ernst Toller (1893–1939), German expressionist playwright and poet; emigrated to the United States 1933.

3.12. *Revolt* by Boris Lavrenëv, directed by Lyubimov-Lanskoy, designed by Boris Volkov, Moscow Trade Unions Theater, 1925.

harmonious as a song, and the main charm of *The Wreck of the Five* lies precisely in its language, its manner of speech. Unfortunately the aroma of the text is remarkably dissipated by putting the play on the stage. Is this the fault of the imperfect diction of the immature actors, and in general, can this style be transmitted theatrically? are questions for debate. In any case, the play in its stage adaptation is indisputably heavy-handed.

The play is constructed on a sharp contrast of scenes, unfolding "in a Western power," with scenes that are played out in Alatyr, on the dreadful night of July 18. As often happens, the "Western" grotesquely farcical scenes work more successfully than the "Red," sustained in a more naturalistic spirit. The figure of the attaché of the Western power is sketched by the author with great humor, and his gibberish French is incredibly funny. And perhaps the main quality is that everyday life plays no autonomous role in it, that everyday life is shown not for the sake of everyday life, but that it possesses a certain "necessity from without," tragic emotion, alternating with sharp grotesquerie. [. . .]

———

THE CASE OF the MGSPS Theater (Theater of the Soviet of Unions of the Moscow Region) was somewhat different. Created to bring works of social and political education to factory clubs and to encourage the amateur "self-realizing" theater, it was bound to the working masses and directly influenced by the agitational movement and Proletkul't.

Golubovsky, *Bol'shie malen'kie teatry,* 139–40.

Vladimir Bill'-Belotserkovsky's[120] play *The Squall* [1925] had been put on at many theaters, but none of the directors had understood its qualities. Even at the MGSPS Theater the play had its opponents. That *The Squall* opened was due to Lyubimov-Lanskoy.[121] After the MGSPS *The Squall* made a mighty progress through many theaters in the country.

At the Maly Theater *Lyubov' Yarovaya*[122] opened after *The Squall* [...] The sailor Svandya was played by the remarkable professional S. Kuznetsov,[123] who had, by the way, once worked at the MGSPS Theater: brilliant theatrical work. I emphasize theatrical, but not lifelike. Vanin,[124] who played Bratishka in *The Squall,* said, "I can't hold a candle to Stepan Leonidovich—a real expert! [...] But as Bratishka I can beat the pants off him." [...]

The best scene was the last one, when, after the fight, Bratishka has entered the Ukom [regional party committee] and seen his friend the chairman lying on the table. "Vas'ka, get up! We've beat 'em!" he whispered.

In *The Squall,* as in a film newsreel, the authenticity of everyday life won people over: a small black pot-bellied stove, wooden benches, red calico banners with slogans, plywood structures. No ornaments on the costumes: dark jackets, felt boots, kerchiefs. The style of the production was virile, rugged, like an unsanded plank—not a production for aesthetes. Indeed, that roughly drawn poster "Are you a registered do-gooder?" showing a hare staring directly at the spectator. The only form of punishment is to be shot up against the wall, by firing squad. No time for reflection or pity: "for undermining morale, for treason, for weak resistance to typhus..." No time for personal emotions: the chairman of the Ukom is informed of the murder of the kulaks, his relatives.[125] A moment's pause. A dry answer: "Duly noted." [*K svedeniyu.*] The characters live on the verge of typhoid fever, they can't get a night's sleep or enough to eat.

120 Vladimir Naumovich Bill'-Belotserkovsky (1885–1970), sailor who took part in the Revolution and Civil War and, from 1920, composed Bolshevik agitprop plays. *The Squall* (1925) is credited with being the first realistic play about the Soviet state.
121 Evsey Osipovich Lyubimov-Lanskoy (actually Gelibter, 1883–1943), director, who joined the Trade Unions Theater in 1922 to stage the work of young Soviet writers; an expert at crowd scenes, he injected excitement and plausibility into crude scripts.
122 *Lyubov' Yarovaya,* play in four acts by Konstantin Trenëv from his novel (1925–26); revised into five acts 1936. It had its premiere at the Moscow Maly December 22, 1926; Stalin saw it ten times. See chapter 4.
123 Stepan Leonidovich Kuznetsov (1879–1932), at the MAT 1908–10, but left because he could not get accustomed to psychologized acting; at the Maly Theater from 1925, where he was a master of makeup and external details and of farce comedy.
124 Vasily Vasil'evich Vanin (1898–1951), after acting at the Crooked Mirror and New Drama Theater in Petrograd 1921, entered the MGSPS Theater (later the Mossovet) 1924–49; did his best work under Lyubimov-Lanskoy, one of the first actors to specialize in Soviet types.
125 *Kulaks,* literally, "fists," a term used to denote wealthy or tightfisted peasants; the Soviet authorities applied it to anyone who refused to join a collective farm, fating them, along with their families, to be deported to camps or remote regions or simply liquidated.

Walter Benjamin, "What a Russian theater hit looks like," *Die literarische Welt* [The literary world] 6 (January 17, 1930), 7. Reprinted in *Gesammelte Werke* (Frankfurt-am-Main, Germany: Suhrkamp, 1972), 4:561–62.

Dramatic criticism which in Europe is a means of influencing the audience is in Russia a means of organizing it. [. . .] No one knows better how a theatrical hit in Moscow looks than my partner, Bill'-Belotserkovsky, the creator of *The Squall*. *The Squall* was not only the biggest success in Soviet Russian theater history but was also the first to be achieved with a purely political drama. Incidentally, in common with much Western European drama, the experts were firmly convinced it would be a flop. I myself saw Belotserkovsky's play in Moscow many years ago. *The Squall* is a sequence of scenes that depict the Revolution in a small town. [. . .] *The Squall* employs the new Russian naturalism, which might be called a naturalism less of milieu and psychology than of the political situation of the moment. To anticipate: the part taken by professional dramatic criticism in this event was evanescent. There are no prominent journalistic critics in Russian, at least not for theater. That is no accident. [. . .] Of all types of literature, political tensions can hardly be more conspicuous than in the theater. The mass public brings them to expression. Anyway, in a country like Russia, permeated with politics, it would be hopeless for an individual, by dint of his mere capacity as a reviewer, to try to control these energies. Now and then, at important turning points, the great theorists themselves will often adopt a slogan that Bukharin once uttered in *Pravda* about a Meyerhold production; that has an influence. But journalistic dramatic criticism has almost none. Its place is taken by the articulations of preliminary eruptive, wordless mass judgments. At the end of the premiere the theater stays open for one or two hours, and debates about the evening take place on the spot. This is no opening-night sensation. The attempt to pin down and clarify, to relive the impression, is organized and leads to all sorts of organized interrogations of important plays. The topics of the questionnaires submitted to playgoers distinguish between the production and the play and range from the most primitive questions—"How did you like the play?"—to the most subtle: "How would you have ended the play?" Not to mention ideological–aesthetic questions, appraisals of actors and direction. A personal signature is not necessary, but the respondent is expected to indicate to which class he belongs. Extracts from such questionnaires are published in the bulletins of the various theaters. But here, too, one ought not to expect a definitive consensus of public criticism. Instead, that is provided by the reports of worker correspondents, the so-called *Rabkor*, which on behalf of factory cells take up the word on current questions in daily papers, trade union and factory publications, etc. There are 1,200 of these in Moscow at the moment. Their positions can be decisive, but again only because they are open to public scrutiny. The *Rabkor* organizes discussions of the play—so-called trials—in their own spheres of activity, to which, however, the theater, and especially the playwright, are invited. Here he has the opportunity to develop his ideas unmediated to the worker public, to receive fresh stimuli. The influence of the *Rabkor*, its agitation for or against a play, has finally become so great that many a theater endeavors, before it begins rehearsals, to put itself in harmony with them. Of course its veto has no decisive significance, but mostly people strive to align themselves with its criticism in the form of a preliminary compromise.

IN MAY 1918 a permanent office and a periodically convened council of theaters for children and children's festivals were instituted in the TEO. Natal'ya Sats, appointed director in 1921 of the Moscow Children's Theater, then of the Central Children's Theater founded in 1936, was the leader in the field. Eventually, there were a hundred children's theaters throughout the Soviet Union.

> Children's Theater, *Sovetskaya kul'tura, itogi i perspektivy* [Soviet culture, sources, and perspectives] (Moscow: Izvestiya TsIK SSSr i VtsIK, 1924). Quoted in Annenkov, *Dnevniki*, 275.

The group of Academic Theaters also includes the State Children's Theater (run by Henrietta Pascar).[126] Children's theaters, exclusively intended for school and preschool age children, are a completely new phenomenon [...] In Soviet Moscow two have arisen. This shows the entire modernity of the phenomenon, but because this is something new, it presents its leaders with remarkably difficult and responsible tasks. The State Children's Theater has not accomplished them. The first years of its existence were notable for wavering in the choice of repertoire. A basic problem has still not been decided: what should be the content of a performance for children? Should it avoid modernity and stay within the bounds of fairy tales or history plays, or, on the contrary, should it be enriched with subject matter torn from the heart of current events? Kipling's fable *Mowgli*, a dramatization of Hoffmann (*The Nutcracker*), Andersen (*The Nightingale*), and even the biblical parable of "Comely Joseph,"[127] put on in the first seasons, apparently could not respond to the needs of the juvenile audience. And this year, along with a dramatization of the famous novel for young people, Mark Twain's *Tom Sawyer* (adapted by Vl. Lidin), we saw S. Auslender's play *Kol'ka Stupin*,[128] wholly modern in its attitudes and, for all the flaws in its scenario, satisfying to the school public, which found in it an echo of modernity, in the atmosphere of a child's life.

---

126 Henrietta M. Pascar, active in the KhPSRO, artistic director of the First State Children's Theater in Moscow; emigrated to Paris.

127 *Iosif Prekrasny* by Vasilenko, a parable of innocence in a corrupt world, was first directed by Boris Goleyzovsky for the Bol'shoy Theater on the stage of the Experimental Theater 1925.

128 Vladimir Germanovich Lidin (1894–1979), prose writer, often attacked as "bourgeois" in the 1920s; war correspondent for *Izvestia* in World War II. Sergey Abramovich Auslénder (1888–1943), poet connected with the World of Art movement; a disciple of Mikhail Kuzmin, he introduced lesbian themes into his writing. *Kol'ka Stupin* is about a street kid who refuses to join a gang, goes to America to work in a factory, and returns to the USSR in time to foil a plot to blow up a power station. He has been described as an early version of the "positive hero."

3.13. The audience in the Leningrad Theater for Young Spectators.

IN 1921 the Jewish Chamber Theater moved to a five-hundred-seat theater on Malaya Bronnaya. There it began its ironic, parodic versions of folkloric themes.

Walter Benjamin, "Granovsky tells his tale," in *Gesammelte Werke,* 4:520–22.

The influential organs of the press did not support Granovsky until his great success with *The Witch*,[129] the first play that he brought to an unbroken run of one hundred performances; only then was his victory declared. This was the external turning point in the history of this theater. The internal one, however, lay a year before. It was a production of *Middlemen* [*Luftmenshn*] by Sholem Aleichem. In Granovsky's hands the trivial figures of this comedy were depicted as all the types that over time composed the irresistible horde of ghosts of this stage. For the first time it became decisively clear to Granovsky, as he put it himself, that only by a detour across the negative—across satire and grotesque—could the Yiddish theater advance to valid, living forms, meaning, the only ones capable of impressing themselves on a mass audience and winning it over. [...]

This ensemble was created in almost 10 years of work, but in those years the working day ran 18 to 20 hours. [...] "My actors," says Granovsky, and to their credit, "would be accepted at no other theater. They would have to learn (or relearn) for the first two years. Between us, all that's needed to change a scene is a facial expression, often only a wink, which a third party would perhaps not notice. If another director came in today, my actors wouldn't understand him. They understand me and learn to understand themselves through me. In our ensemble we have put everyone under the microscope, studied him through and through. Each of his roles is a function of his

129 *Di Kishufmakhern* (1878), a comic opera by Abraham Goldfaden, was staged by GOSET 1922.

place in the collective and moves toward a common interpretation of any given play." (That the given text of this play is treated only as a blueprint, a libretto, is something Granovsky's theater shares with all the leading stages in Russia.) "Because that is the case, we don't cast to type. That's why we can, indeed, must forgo stars as well. That's also, by the way, why we do not feel bound slavishly to greater or less 'talent' in an individual actor, we can allow ourselves to take into account, besides the original abilities, the absolute power the ensemble wields over the individual. I believe the average talent of my actors is modest compared with that of a leading ensemble in a Berlin season. But the individual with us is a human being first, and only then an actor. We draw him into our work with all his strengths, according to his whole being. That's why the entry of a 'newcomer' is such a big event."

———

ONE OF Mikhoél's best roles at this time was the tailor Soroker, whose life is turned upside-down when he wins a fortune in a lottery in Sholem Aleichem's *200,000* (*Dos grosser gevin*, 1923).

> Osip Mandel'shtam, "Mikhoéls," *Vechernaya krasnaya gazeta* [Evening red gazette] (Leningrad) (August 10, 1926), reprinted in *Sobranie sochineniy v 3-kh tomakh* [Collected works in 3 volumes] (Moscow: Terra, 1991), 3:107–10. Osip Émil'evich Mandel'shtam (1891–1938) was an Acmeist poet who stressed the importance of culture as a condition of human dignity; a satiric poem about Stalin got him exiled to a camp in Siberia, where he died.

Both the basic plasticity and force of Jewishness lie in the working out and transmission over centuries of a feeling for form and movement that governs all aspects of fashion—intransigent, millennial . . . I am not talking about the cut of one's clothes, which does change and is not worth evaluating, nor have I taken it into my head to offer an aesthetic justification of the ghetto or the style of the shtetl. I am talking about the inner plasticity of the ghetto, its vast artistic force which is surviving the ghetto's destruction and will ultimately flower only when the ghetto is fully destroyed.

[. . .] Violins accompany the wedding dance. Mikhoéls comes down to the footlights and stealthily, with the cautious movements of a faun, lends an ear to the minor chords. The faun, which has happened upon a Jewish wedding, hesitantly, is not yet intoxicated but always aroused by the caterwauling music of the Jewish minuet. This moment of hesitation is, perhaps, more expressive than all the rest of the dancing. Frozen in place, this is where the inebriation comes in—a mild inebriation brought on by two or three sips of a sweet wine, but quite enough to make a Jew's head spin: the Jewish Dionysos is not demanding and bestows gaiety at once.

In the course of the dance, Mikhoéls's face takes on an expression of sagacious weariness and mournful ecstasy, as if indistinguishable from the mask of the Jewish people drawing near to antiquity.

Here the dancing Jew is like the leader of the ancient chorus. All the force of Judaism, all the rhythm of abstract dancing ideas, all the pride of the dance whose sole incentive, in the last analysis, seems to be a fellow feeling for the earth—all this flows into the trembling of the hands, the vibration of the thinking fingers, animated like articulate speech.

Mikhoéls is the pinnacle of national Jewish dandyism—the dancing Mikhoéls, the tailor Soroker, the forty-year-old child, the blissful loser, the wise and affectionate tailor...

And yesterday on this very stage, there were svelte dancing girls wearing caftans anglicized into jockey coats, patriarchs drinking tea in the clouds like old geezers on a balcony in Homel...

[...] And all of GOSET's plays are constructed to reveal Mikhoéls's masks, and in each of them he accomplishes the infinitely difficult and glorious journey from Judaic meditation to dithyrambic ecstasy, liberation, the unshackling of the dance of wisdom.

LES' KURBAS'S NEW THEATER, the Berezil Artistic Association, made its debut in Kiev in March 1922 and began to proliferate in studios throughout the Ukraine.

Les' Kurbas, "'Berezil' manifesto," *Barikadi teatru* [Theatrical barricades] 1 (1923). Reprinted in Russian in *Stat'i i vospominaniya o L. Kurbase* [Articles and remembrances of L. Kurbas] (Moscow: Iskusstvo, 1987), 367–68.

Berezil is not a dogma, although there is dogmatism in it. Berezil is a movement, and when it stops being one, it will stop corresponding to its name, it will end its existence. It is the free association of dynamic slogans. It is a process. And not only in the theater, in art, but in culture, in life. The theater is closer to it than anything else, because it strives to clothe its concept of the world in an emotional form. Knowing that the morrow is beautiful, it aspires to tomorrow and wants to bring alien emotions and alien consciousness close to its concept of the world. Berezil does not judge its presentation of the morrow's culture by making specific recommendations, although every "Berezilian" has the right to create his own concrete recommendation, effective for a certain period of time. Until the time when life will revoke it. The criterion is the effectiveness of the application of the prescription. The only success that is justified is the one that bears within itself "something unknown." The means, deprived of a keen influence on the spectators, is stagnation and cliché, it contradicts development and distances the audience from us. In this way the art of Berezil theater is only a method for propaganda of social and artistic ideas, whose delta is communist culture, and whose techniques are constantly in flux. Berezil does not set itself the goals of creating a culture of the communist today. Or building a communist theater for our today. Although those who are involved in those kinds of games and a metaphysics bound up with them are accepted into its bosom, since they too are in process.

The fact is that Berezil simply does not know whether the theater will survive in the future. And the solution to this question points to the natural progress of events connected with the differences among the groups that enter into Berezil. It is the most interesting for it today—for the general tomorrow. It is not afraid of mistakes. It is movement. And movement is a universal principle.

Berezil firmly stands on the platform of October. It unites only those who see in the proletariat the one and only genuine force, in whose hands are found the solution to its chief problem. [...]

Berezil is for activity, organization, tempo, Americanization, the latest word in science, contemporaneity.

Skeptics can drop dead!

Some biographical data:

Founded in March of last year. Its roots are in the Youth Theater. Develops along the straight line of artistic tendencies of the new Ukrainian theatrical idea from its origin in the Youth Theater as transfigured into an October guise. Unites around itself those and many others.

"*Gas* at the Kiev theater, April 1923," *Chervonyi Shlyakh* [Red path] 4–5 (1924), 282–83.

Gas undoubtedly laid the foundation of the theater of the Revolution, which, until the present, existed only either in theory or in the unsuccessful attempts of other Ukrainian directors. [...]

Gas is the product of a year's work by the Berezil Studio. Kurbas placed the basic emphasis of the presentation on the problem of showing social class dynamics in their dialectic process. Without the least exaggeration, it can be stated that Kurbas solved this problem brilliantly. The form of the presentation impresses one with its scholarly development. Kurbas studied in their minutest details all the rules of utilizing his actors for mass presentation as well as the minimum and maximum technical possibilities of his actors and, on the basis of his findings, set himself the goal of presenting an artistic and rhythmic synthesis based on the elements of the various categories of rhythm in the developing process, the elements of a mass meeting, and the collective sorrow during the explosion.

IN NOVEMBER 1923 Kurbas staged his dramatization of Upton Sinclair's novel about a persecuted American socialist worker, *Jimmie Higgins*, using expressionist techniques and film. "Onstage the actor exists in a limited space. To overcome this limitation we have to search for those forms of stage expression that could transmit the limitless world of a person."[130]

---

130 *Iryna Avdiieva*, quoted in Vasyl' Vasyl'ko, ed., *Les Kurbas: spohady suchasnykiy*, trans. Virlana Tkacz (Kiev: Mystetstvo, 1969), 154.

Les' Kurbas, *Dzhimmi Higgins* [Jimmie Higgins] (Khar'kov: Shliakh Ostvity, 1924), 53–54. Minus light and music cues. An explosion in the last scene of Act II.

GROUP [OF WORKERS]: That's somewhere nearby.
    Could it be the power plant?
    No, it's probably the munitions factory.
    It's over in that direction.
JIMMIE: Oh!
(*On screen we see a street in a working-class neighborhood. Then Jimmie's house.*)
JIMMIE: Listen, fellows, I've got to go.
(*On screen we see Jimmie's wife, Lizzie, playing with the children.*)
JIMMIE (*shouts*): Let me go! (*Runs out.*)
GROUP: Why did he shout?
    He lives over there.
    Where?
    There.
    Next to the munitions factory.
(*On screen Jimmie runs through the same street to his house. Around the corner he sees the ruins of the factory. Terrified, he keeps running. Instead of his house and family, he finds a huge crater. On screen a close-up of Jimmie's face—dreadful despair. The stage is empty. Jimmie runs on.*)
JIMMIE: Damn war! Damn capital!
    I don't want to live.

KURBAS had staged the first Ukrainian production of *Macbeth* in 1920 at the Youth Theater; it had not been an unqualified success. In 1924 he restaged the tragedy for Berezil.

Les' Kurbas's *Macbeth*, 1924. From the diary of Vasyl' Vasyl'ko, *Shchodennyk* 5 (January 1, 1923–May 14, 1924). Ms. V. Vasyl'ko papers SMTMCA (April 3, 1924), 121, as quoted in Irena R. Makaryk, *Shakespeare in the Undiscovered Bourn: Les Kurbas, Ukrainian Modernism, and Early Soviet Cultural Politics*, trans. Irena R. Makaryk (Toronto: University of Toronto Press, 2004), 82. © University of Toronto Press Incorporated 2004. Reprinted with permission of the publisher. Vasyl' Stepanovich Vasyl'ko (actually Mylaiv, 1893–1972) was a young actor in Berezil who had played Banquo in Kurbas's 1920 production of *Macbeth*. After Berezil was dissolved, he performed leading roles in theaters throughout Ukraine.

First scene of witches. Bare stage draped in black; in the middle a green screen four by four meters with red text, "Precipice," and beside it a green raised platform two and a half meters long by one and a half meters wide by one and a half meters. The frame attached with four knots to the flies. And that's the whole set. The witches in blue-gray costumes (with wide trousers) and in red peaked wigs. The idea was to create all the wigs out of fabric, but, because of the cost, regular wigs were retained. The witches perform in an exaggerated theatrical manner without any pretentions to mysticism; [they are] "witchy" in a cliché sense of the word.

About the audience. The auditorium was not full . . . Lots of intelligentsia, few workers. I sat not far from L. M. and O. M. Starytsky.[131] When, after the first scene, the screen with its title raced up to the flies in full view of the audience, and the actresses-witches walked out into the wings using their normal walk (as normal actresses, no longer as witches), Ludmyla Mykhailivna exclaimed in terror, "O God!" and I felt that she must have crossed herself.

> Mykhailo Mohyliansky, "The Berezil *Macbeth*," *Chervonyi shliakh* (Kharkiv)
> 4–5 (April–May 1924), 282–83. Quoted in Makaryk, *Shakespeare: Les Kurbas*,
> 105.

Kurbas's production of *Macbeth* at the beginning of April was really a spring delight, although sages and specialists attempted to drown it in a whole flood of questions about "principle," the first of which is: may the classics, and especially Shakespeare, be modified? All the questions of "principle" stank of boredom because, really, is it so important whether joy is derived in accordance with principles or contrary to them? As long as there is joy, so long as there is artistic achievement? With the production of *Macbeth*, the great directorial talent of Kurbas achieved a great victory, passed a by no means easy test, and by giving the spectator a classic tragedy with kings, witches, and so forth, preserved (in the impressions made on the spectator) the main characteristics of the profound intentions of the dramatic genius and poet of human passions . . . What more can be asked of a director? [. . .]

BETWEEN 1925 AND MID-1927 Moscow housed a number of meetings and conferences dedicated to what should be the government's role in the theater. Stenographic records were made and published. Debates raged over controversial plays and theaters, such as Bulgakov's *Days of the Turbins*, the MAT 2, Érdman's *Suicide*, and the Bol'shoy Theater. The Bol'shoy's very existence was questioned. Lenin characterized Lunacharsky's decision to preserve it "utterly indecent" (January 12, 1922),[132] and the Politburo voted to shut it down. It was a balletomane, the official head of the Soviet state M. I. Kalinin, who demanded that the decision be reconsidered; and, on financial grounds, the Bol'shoy was preserved.

---

131 Lyudmila Mikhailivna Starytska, a scion of the old Kievan aristocracy and herself a playwright. Her reply to the theater questionnaire read in part, "What are you doing with Shakespeare, obscuring the content of his play and in particular making idiots of Duncan and his son, shows that you don't have a director who understands how such a treatment destroys the play." Vasyl' Vasyl'ko, *Shchodennyk*, April 3, 1924, 123.
132 For the relevant documents, see Clark and Dobrenko, *Soviet Culture and Power*, 23–31.

The Komsomol of the Bol'shoy Theater, *Ryadom s Stalinym v Bol'shom Teatre (zapiski voennego komendant)* [Next to Stalin at the Bol'shoy Theater (notes of a military commander)] (n.p.: n.p., 1995), 14–15.

The creation of a komsomol cell at the Bol'shoy Theater was a very complicated matter. Daughters of factory owners, former ladies in waiting of the court of his imperial majesty were still working at the theater. The first five members to join the komsomol in 1923 were, first, its leader, the designer V. Luzhetsky, who was sent from the Krasnopresnensk worker–peasant komsomol, and then the carpenter A. Utkin, the stagehands I. Piskarev and K. Kalinkin, and the wardrobe woman A. Lukina.

The prominent dancer M. Gabovich had his own way of understanding the komsomol and the Party. He reasoned thus: "Performers ought not to be members of the Party, for their work is not for profit. It's quite a different thing from a steel worker in a factory, or an engineer, toiling to smelt steel." E. Malinovskaya had to go to a great deal of trouble to show such performers as M. Gabovich, V. Tikhomirov, A. Messerer, and A. Ermolaev[133] that they are indeed engineers in their field.

In 1928 the prima ballerina I. Chernetskaya[134] entered the komsomol and was quick to be warned by E. Gel'tser:[135] "Who knows, instead of a tutu, you may have to wear a coarse woolen dress, boots, and a sword-belt to go out and dance Odette in *Swan Lake*."

All the same the members of the theater's komsomol carried out urgent agitational work among the youth. [. . .] Soon the organization turned into a powerful political force, its numbers reaching 300.

Anatoly Lunacharsky, "O politike Narkomprosa v teatral'nom dele" [On the Narkompros' politics in theatrical matters], *Sovetskoe Iskusstvo* [Soviet Art] 3 (June 1925), 6, 408.

Repertkom . . . has taken an incorrect line, and instead of protecting the theater from counterrevolution, pornography, incitement of national hatred, or religious prejudice, it has started down the path of prohibiting anything that could in any way be faulted. [. . .]

I do not have the slightest intention of tolerating at the present time any organized and much less any official *opposition* in the apparatus of Narkompros.

---

133 All ballet dancers, choreographers, and teachers. Mikhail Markovich Gabovich (1905–65), *danseur noble*, student of Gorsky; at the Bol'shoy Theater 1924–52; first interpreter of major roles in such Soviet ballets as *The Fountain of Bakhchisaray* and *The Red Poppy*. Vasily Dmitrievich Tikhomirov (actually Mikhaylov, 1876–1956), at the Bol'shoy Theater from 1893, head of the ballet troupe 1925–30; cocreator of *The Red Poppy*. Asaf Mikhaylovich Messerer (1903–92), ballet dancer and choreographer, lead soloist at the Bol'shoy 1921–54, with a very wide repertoire. Aleksey Nikolaevich Ermolaev (1910–75), in Leningrad 1926–30, at the Bol'shoy 1930–58, in romantic, heroic roles.

134 Inna Chernetskaya, a pupil of Isadora Duncan, choreographed *Rienzi* for Meyerhold 1923 and wrote the libretto for the futurist ballet *Iron Foundry* (1926–27).

135 Ekaterina Vasil'evna Gel'tser (1876–1962), ballerina, much influenced at the St. Petersburg ballet by Marius Petipa; at the Bol'shoy Theater 1898–1935, then toured the Soviet Union widely.

Anatoly Lunacharsky, "On Glavrepertkom censorship," *Rabochy i Teatr* 41 (October 12, 1926), 9.

From time to time rumors run wild about some allegedly odd prohibitive measures of our Soviet theater censorship. Categorically they declare that two plays of Shakespeare, Ostrovsky, old popular operas, and so on have been prohibited. All such rumors are based on obvious misunderstandings easy to clear up.

The repertoire is inspected by the Glavrepertkom as well as by the theatrical section of Narkompros and the artistic–political soviet specially created by the administration of Gosaktheaters, not only with an eye to general-censorship licensing or general-censorship prohibition of this play or that—*the repertoire is inspected in regard to its value and artistic organization, and in co-ordination with the repertoire of the individual theaters.*

You can meet people who start telling you excitedly that the Repertkom tried to ban *The Marriage of Figaro*, whereas the fact is that, next year in Moscow, we will have three productions of *The Marriage of Figaro* at different academic theaters. Of course, one has to give a moment's thought to the expediency of such a phenomenon. Or they'll tell you that one or another Ostrovsky play is banned, when in fact it turns out that the given theater wants to put on seven or eight plays of Ostrovsky and that in the repertoire one of these plays, less appropriate, is replaced by another more appropriate; or they find that such a number of Ostrovsky plays is excessive and doesn't allow enough opportunity to stage new productions and so on.

It is also fitting to remember that independent of the great political and artistic competence of the Glavrepertkom, theatrical management has the right to dispute its reasoning, in which case the colleagues of the Narkompros always examine the dispute attentively and decide it expeditiously.

It is time to leave off more or less maliciously disingenuous exaggerations relative to the allegedly unlimited inflexibility and peremptoriness of the Glavrepertkom.

Audience resistance to bad drama. Session on theatrical issues called by the Central Committee of CPSU. S. N. Krylov, ed., *Puti razvitiya teatra: sbornik* [Paths of theatrical development: Anthology] (Moscow: Teakinopechat', 1927), 35–36, 234, 151, 89–90, 72.

LISOVSKY, *Communist critic*: the theaters "are obviously not accepting our revolutionary playwrights. Anything that smacks of the class struggle is not accepted."

R. PEL'SHE,[136] *head of the Political Enlightenment Division of the People's Commissariat of Enlightenment*: I have a whole portfolio of complaints made by our revolutionary playwrights ... about the theater directors. They are complaining that many of the theaters in Moscow are not staging their plays despite the fact that they have not only been found ideologically useful but are even sufficiently artistic. Some plays

136 Robert Andreevich Pel'she (1880–1955), Communist journalist and art critic, head of the Glavrepertkom; originally installed by Lunacharsky, he proved to be a disappointment and was quickly replaced; one of the leaders of the Glavpolitprosvet from 1924.

have been reviewed by the official organs or by individual Communist authorities on the theater arts, but nevertheless many of them have not been produced in the city of Moscow. What is the reason? . . . To a large extent, it is a certain desire by the large theaters not to stage works whose class nature is expressed clearly.

LUNACHARSKY, *Commissar of Enlightenment, complained to Party members*: Some people are saying that the plays our repertory committee licenses are sometimes not accepted by the theaters themselves . . . Of course, no theater will say: "We do not want to take your play because we find it revolutionary." A loyal theater will say: "We are not accepting it because it is not artistic." The theaters can be hypocritical about it. [. . .]

One of these plays cost us twelve or thirteen thousand rubles. It was 100 percent useful ideologically, but it was taken off at the end of the year because only twenty or twenty-five people had come to see it.

[. . .] We are telling the theaters: "Support our ideology," and we not only fail to help them but even try to obtain some kind of income from them. But you know this is impossible under these conditions; there is a great danger that the theaters will be [ideologically] useful—and shut down.

Worker and Peasant Theater

Kerzhentsev, after serving in a number of administrative Party positions, in 1926–27 became chair of the Editorial Union of the USSR, a foundation stone of Soviet censorship; in 1928–30, he was deputy administrator of the agitprop division of the Central Committee, advancing through various offices until, in 1936, he was made both head of the Committee for Artistic Affairs and a team member of SNK SSSR. He led the propaganda campaigns against "enemies of the people" and Stalin's rivals, persecuting art workers and supporting only those who toed the Party line. Removed from office in 1938, he ended as editor of the *Great Soviet Encyclopedia*.

> P. M. Kerzhentsev, "Theatrical politics [1922]," in *Tvorchesky teatr*, 5th ed. (Moscow: Gos. Izdatel'stvo, 1923), 223–28.

The anomaly of our theatrical politics becomes especially evident if we try to answer the question—do we, in the last analysis, have a state theater?

Evidently, we do. And not just one, but five in all. At least in the budget of the Socialist Republic up to this moment, some tens of millions are being spent on the matter of state theaters. The People's Commissariat of Enlightenment even has a special "Division of State Theaters."

And yet were there and are there real state theaters here? Not "formerly imperial," but specifically state theaters, responsive to the spirit, tasks, striving of the worker–peasant power and responsive to the whole system of the Socialist Republic?

Of course not! Certainly not! [. . .]

Where is our heroic revolutionary theater, which would provide not only aesthetic pleasure but would also satisfy our revolutionary temperament? There is none. It is still to be created.

Let the repertoire of this heroic theater be slight, but let it be very strictly, punctiliously select. Let the productions be impeccable and the makeup of the troupes the best that can be created.

I cannot define exactly what is to go into this theater. The repertoire will probably have to be published anew. Let there be in the repertoire only three or four plays, but they must be staged as if they were masterpieces.

However, the new theater must not be confined within the bounds of pure drama. It inevitably will be connected with music. Specifically, building a new state theater on the basis of the dramatic theater, it is possible to achieve a synthesis of art, harmonically to unite opera, ballet, pantomime, etc. Every kind of mass spectacle compels special attention to turn to the harmonic movement of the crowd, to its rhythm—so logically the art of the ballet (in the widest meaning of the word) will enter drama. [...]

Such a dramatic state theater will be created in two ways. The first, the quickest—but this is idealistic and hopeless—is to put together the best possible troupe from all the available teams of actors in Russia. To select from the professionals all who are lively, ardent, young, seeking, to recognize the best (not by authority but by questing and daring) musicians, directors, designers. [...]

The second way is slow but sure. One must create a troupe of proletarian actors, to discover directors and other leaders who not only adhere to a school but possess a revolutionary temperament and communist views, and try to build a theater without traditions, with new scenic materials, a new foundation.

The new theater is to be born not on the boards of the "Marinka" and "Alexandrinka" but in the workers' quarters. [...]

Sergey Radlov, "What kind of art is to be shown to workers?" (April 1922), from Radlov, *Desyat' let v teatr,* 40–45.

There now exist two extreme points of view. The first derives from the quite correct sense that new organic forms of art can be created only by someone who has felt the world to be catastrophic, destructive, reforming, who has not slept through the greatest changes and shocks in the social life of the people. Only by accepting the world war and revolution as the start of a new epoch can a new era make new art.

But it is quite wrong to forge ahead regardless of obstacles and, instead of an organic bond, identify the Left in politics and in art *mechanically,* as Mayakovsky and Meyerhold do.

In the end, with the Left all over the place, "comfutism"[137] is a dangerous play on words, and one should not declare political anathema on all artistic opponents on the Right! Even as an agent of the Left front in the theater, I should, however, energetically protest against *forcible* elimination of all right-wing art, wherever it hasn't quite been eliminated.

137 A portmanteau word made up of *communism* and *futurism.*

3.14. "Right to Life" parade, Moscow, May Day, 1920s.

True, there is a lot of excitement and nothing is happening. On the contrary, let us admit that 99 percent of all factory and club theatrical organizations are in the hands of arch-rightist workers. Unfortunately, this is not academic art but often only pale drafts, weak copies of it. Not Davydov, not Yur'ev, not Kondraty Yakovlev[138]—most of the time not their students but only their imitators.

The defenders of this trend understandably refer to the *taste* of the workers. Very weak evidence! Artistic taste is formed by a man's whole life and his artistic impressions. No one will venture to affirm that the life of the Russian worker before 1917 was normal in its progress. His taste was not so much developed as degenerated by the surrogates of art. Healthy intuition can fight through all conditions, but the modern-day taste of the workers is not a conclusive norm for us. We must heed it, cultivate it, but not blindly follow it.

On the other hand, we see in both extremes a desire, no matter what, to *protect* the worker, to keep him in line, to palm off one's own personal tastes on him and on no account to introduce him in full earnest to the very conflict of movements which is indeed the fundamental life of art. It's either–or: either art is mere entertainment,

138 Three luminaries of the Moscow Maly Theater before the Revolution: Vladimir Nikolaevich Davydov (actually Ivan Nikolaevich Gorelov, 1849–1925), rotund character actor who created Chekhov's Ivanov; Yury Mikhaylovich Yur'ev (1872–1948), romantic leading man, especially in classical drama; and Kondrat Nikolaevich Yakovlev (1864–1928), famous for his feline Porfiry Petrovich in *Crime and Punishment*.

and then it's best to put on all sorts of *Mysteries of New York,* or it must broaden the prospect, and it is wrong to conceal its basic essence. The eternal transformation of genres and their conflict, the unceasing revolution, dissatisfaction with yesterday's art and a quest for tomorrow's—that is what the worker must be dedicated to, once he has been invited to inquire into this by himself and on his own. To strive to show the worker only unquestioned and generally accepted art means to give him only yesterday's wares. Not so much generally accepted as dead! After all, Euripides's contemporaries booed him; everybody hissed Racine's *Phèdre,* except Boileau; Blok was mocked; and when Pushkin wrote *Boris,* people pitied the decline of the talent that had created *Ruslan and Lyudmila*! Now we applaud *Turandot.* Ten years ago, nobody wanted to hear about Italian comedy. On the other hand, many leaders of the Kul'tprosvets, remembering that they in their youth were attracted by *The Deluge* and *Cricket on the Hearth* at the MAT Studio, promote the productions most resembling that style, completely forgetting that the authors of those productions have moved on to the most stylized stagings and have long disavowed their earlier work.

Let us not try to set up a despotism of one or another tendency in art we prefer but invite the worker to judge for himself, showing him, interpreting to him the most varied kinds of product. Let us *cultivate him, and not shelter him as if he were a child and a dimwit.*

Twelfth Congress of Communist Party 1923, *VKP (b) v rezolyutsiakh i resheniakh* [Resolutions and decisions of the VKR(b)], part 1, 522.

The question of utilizing the theater in systematic mass propaganda in favor of the ideas of struggling for Communism must be stated in a practical form. Suitable forces must be attracted, both in the capital and in the provinces, to strengthen the creation and selection of a suitable revolutionary repertoire [...]. The theater must also be utilized as a means of antireligious propaganda.

Serge Orlovsky, "A note on Kolkhoz-Sovkhoz theaters," in Martha Bradshaw, *Soviet Theaters 1917–1941* (New York: Research Program on the USSR, 1954), 113–26.

At the beginning of the twenties, I traveled with a small group of professional actors around the towns and countryside of the Moscow, Yaroslavl' and other districts. The peasants received us very well, although they looked a little condescendingly on people who earned their bread by so doubtful a trade. [...] Far more than in the city, the village playgoers demanded costume plays, and a production in which the tsar and tsaritsa were characters caused a real furore. The peasants at that time did not care for plays of contemporary life, and still less for those in which the characters were simple people or muzhiks. For example, our production of Gorky's *The Lower Depths* was a decided flop, and we had to remove it from the repertoire after two performances. [...]

The actors lived in separate rooms, which they rented from the peasants, dining all together at the common table of one peasant who was well off and who fed us very simply but nourishingly for fifty kopeks a day. [...] An unusual contrivance was used as advertising: since the theater in the city of Sergach was located at the foot of a hill, its iron roof was easily seen, and so the announcement was painted in huge letters on this roof. Hand-drawn posters were stuck on all houses and signposts. One of the actors had the idea of painting *Woe from Wit* on the backs of pigs rooting not far from the theater. [...]

> Sergey Radlov, "Mass spectacles," in *Stat'i o teatre 1918–1922* [Articles on theater 1918–22] (Petrograd: Mysl', 1923), 41–45.

The government has got to realize that truly magnificent and impeccable spectacles are not created in five days, that monumental memorials do not spring up like mushrooms, and I am sorry that the pitiful erection of a giant on Kamenny Island did not appear to be the last experiment in too hurried a sweep.

Directorial work with the masses is complicated by the fact that, of course, there are no professional veteran actors. True, if there were professionals, the work would be even more difficult, because every actor would like to act in his own way, and his individual role and pointless detailing would destroy the synthetically generalized production.

[...] It would be better if the groups that took part in mass spectacles were not fortuitously introduced military units but theatrical clubs (of which there are now a great many), made up of people who are already fond of the theater, so that enforced mobilization does not compromise the valuable idea of a people's celebration, so that these clubs take part in the action en bloc, assuming this or that group of characters, so that, in that way, competition can arise between these clubs, for the agonistic principle is the most important element of any artistic *play*.

> "Liquidation of collective theaters, [because of economic difficulties]," *Teatr* (Petrograd) 13 (December 25, 1923), 15–16.

L. I. PUMPYANSKY,[139] *economic sector Sorabis* [Union of Art Workers]: The theatrical collectives in their present form do not meet economic goals. To Sorabis, they even appear to be an outworn and useless form from a professional standpoint. The task of Sorabis, like every profunion, is obviously to unify the workers on the payroll, whereas collectives represent the unification of petty owners.

In view of this, the Central Committee of Sorabis has proposed through its *gubotdels* [gubernia divisions] to carry out a reregistration of all theater collectives, as a way of licensing general assemblies of the latters' workers to question the further existence of the enterprises.

Three paths lie before the workers in the collectives:

---

139 Lev Ivanovich Pumpyansky (1889–1943), art historian, dean of the art history faculty of the All-Russian Academy of Arts in Leningrad; he stayed at his post during the siege.

First, the preservation of the earlier form of the collective, but this entails the exodus of all the members from the union, who will henceforth be considered handicraftsmen [*kustary*], while the collective will continue to exist in the capacity of a legal entity, with the obligation to enter into a collective contract with all those who work for pay.

The second solution appears to be the liquidation of the collective. In this case, all workers are obliged to reregister with the Labor Exchange as unemployed persons, who can organize through their artel.

Finally, the third solution is to look for an entrepreneur in the guise of an organization or a private individual.

On the basis of this resolution the Cent. Com. Petrograd Gubotdel of Sorabis, in agreement with the Petrogubopolitprosovet, proposes the liquidation of the Petrograd theater collectives. The two largest collectives, "Musical Comedy" and "Passage," are already run as a general assembly, as is "Free Comedy." The assemblies have unanimously declared themselves an enterprise and have elected liquidation-efficiency committees (*lirakko*), which are tasked with finding new "owners."

> B. F—n, "A worker's budget," *Rabochy i Teatr* 3 (October 7, 1924), 16. Based on government statistics, the magazine attempted to work out what portion of a worker's budget might be devoted to theater and film.

Dues to clubs (membership dues) are an extremely insignificant portion of a worker's budget. But theater and movies occupy a very considerable place in a worker's budget, true, not all that high, but all the same, there is a gradual annual rise.

According to 1922 data, on average a laborer spent on his cultural needs no less than 2 percent of his earnings. At the same time an office worker spent twice as much, i.e., 3.9 percent of his earnings.

	Laborer	Office worker
Theater and other entertainments	0.9%	1.8%
Books, newspapers, etc.	0.7%	1.6%
Children's education	0.4%	0.5%
Total	2.0%	3.9%

[...] This table makes clear that theater and other entertainments take first place in the cultural outlay of laborers and office workers. Within this, unmarried laborers' and office workers' expenses are twice as high as those of family men.

In 1923, some growth in expenditures on cultural needs can be observed, viz., up to 2.5 percent of earnings, in which expenditure on theater and other entertainment constitutes an average of 1.3 percent. Among clerical workers as well, expenditures on theater and other entertainment have also increased, to an average of 2.2 percent.

It needs to be noted that the greater part of the expenditure on "theater and other entertainments" is meted out to the movies, which make up 65 percent of these expenditures.

[...] An increase in this outlay may be made only at the cost of the laborer's expenditure on alcohol, [which] in 1922 constituted 2.7 percent of wages, and in 1923, 2.5 percent. We consider that a decrease in outlay for alcohol depends in great measure on our cultural organizations, which must skillfully and thoroughly interest workers so that they genuinely begin to prefer theater, movies, etc. [...]

RABOCHY I TEATR and TKhB Kul't-Otdel LGSPS distributed questionnaires about the living newspaper *Workbench* and the plays *John Reed* (Red Theater) and *The Devil's Disciple* (LGSPS Studio, directed by A. N. Orbelov).[140]

> B. Fel'dman, "Questionnaire of the Profsoyuz spectator," *Rabochy i teatr* 15 (December 29, 1924), 4.

The questionnaires' data are unsatisfactory, first because the working-class spectators filled them out carelessly. For many the individual bullet points were not clear or comprehensible.

To the extremely interesting question when it was most convenient in the week for the worker-spectator to attend a show (theater and club), most replied that the best day seemed to be *Saturday*, followed by Friday and Tuesday. Many declared that theater parties organized by unions should take place precisely on those days.

To the question "where would you want to go and what do you like best: opera, drama or ballet," the answer was:

To the former Maria Theater, opera 35 percent of respondents, ballet 30 percent, drama 25 percent. [...] However, a great many who filled out the questionnaire also indicated that they preferred to see a *show* at the club. Staged plays at clubs were the least liked. [...]

It is very characteristic that to the question "of all the plays you've seen which did you like best," the worker-spectator gives no specific answer. [...] In general, everyone who testified to attending one theater or another also notes *his fondness for the movies* (they especially like *The Red Imps*[141]). A number of worker-spectators complain that at the club it's hard "on account of no quiet" "to watch a play, you see it all, but don't hear much—too much noise." Therefore serious spectators prefer the playhouse to the club. They express satisfaction with the circus: "very good," "really satisfying," "not a waste of time," etc.

140 A. N. Orbelov, founder of the LGSPS or Leningrad State Proletarian Actor's Studio Theater; also headed the Living Book (Zhivaya kniga) Theater, which adapted works of literature.
141 *Krasnye dyavolyata* (1923), directed by Ivan Perestiani, was an immensely popular Georgian adventure film from the novel by Pavel Blyakin, about three children (one of them a boy of color) who help defeat the Ukrainian anarchist renegade Makhno.

Some worker-spectators were dissatisfied that the living newspaper *Workbench* performs without scenery and the actors without makeup and appropriate costumes:

"What kind of theater is this," is the discontented question of one spectator (foundry worker Egorova), "if there's no makeup and scenery? I liked it a lot, only it's a shame there's no scenery." The power of tradition!

The same worker Egorova, to the question "Which performer did you like best?" stated, "Chaliapin, if only he was still a citizen of the USSR." [...]

Lots of complaints about the distribution of Profsoyuz theater tickets: "Look at who gets them!" "Are there really so many profworkers in Leningrad that they fill the theater on Profsoyuz days?" ... However, most of the complainers do admit that "it's got a bit better now." But all the same, there are too few tickets, especially in acad. theaters of ballet and opera. They are very fond of the ballet: "didn't understand much, but it's good!" "very pretty" etc. [...]

> Rabkor I. Ya—vich, "Respect the theater!," *Rabochy i teatr* 19 (January 26, 1925), 9.

Of course there are people who dance in the mud, which fortunately does not go on in our worker's clubs and theaters. *Rabkor* Pivovarov deplores the good order at the Gosznakov Theater; he complains that there, you're not allowed to chew sunflower seeds, go to sleep, but mainly that it lacks the "gray spirit of the worker."

In the eighth year of revolution, when the authorities in every way are fighting ignorance, when vast funds are being spent on beautifying worker's clubs, when workers are creating self-governance, there are comrades who assert that a worker has a "gray spirit."

I don't know on which workers' behalf Pivovarov speaks. I, as a worker, having toiled 18 years at the workbench, think: the true proletarian must not be described that way. The worker loves and values beauty and cleanliness everywhere, but especially in the theater. If by different material circumstances a worker cannot achieve perfect cleanliness and coziness in his own home, in his own domestic circle, then in the theater he wants, besides the pleasures of seeing and hearing, to relax and breathe in pure air, undefiled by shells of sunflower seeds and uninfected by the "gray" spirit of the worker, which he breathes all day at his factory. [...]

> "How to overcome a lack of repertoire," *Rabochy i teatr* 9 (March 2, 1925), 5.
> A debate had raged in this journal about the inadequacy of literary works in serving a proletarian stage.

There are still no proletarian dramatists. This is explained by the fact that, first of all, the doors to theater before the Revolution were closed to the working masses. To write a play, the proletarian writer had to know the stage to some extent, its possibilities and condition. Those plays now presented to us by dramatic specialists are as "contemporary" as they are themselves. But if they are to some degree actually contemporary, then the "workers" they depict, their interests and questions, are whatever you please (rather like the authors themselves) but not real workers.

[. . .] Of course, all this is comprehensible and clear: to depict a worker, you yourself first of all have to come from a working family, or in any case be rather deeply infused with the interests and problems and life of the working class.

It is stupid and ridiculous to suggest to the dramatic specialist of today to "write contemporary plays and put onstage authentic workers." What is the theater to do until these authentic proletarian playwrights turn up? Of course, not close it down and certainly not drive it away. The technique and achievements of the theater, handed down to us as a legacy, are too great: actors, old actors (when authentically proletarian plays appear, we may need new performers, which we need to think about right away) are so interesting that we must in every way protect and preserve them. But how are we even somehow to modernize these theaters and bring them closer to the real interests and problems of the broad masses of those who toil? The way, truly, is meandering, difficult, but it does exist. It is to adapt works by young and old proletarian writers. Such works of literature, especially those that have had wide circulation (stories, tales, epics), exist in sufficient quantity that the selection can be broad and interesting.

[. . .]

Such work in its first phase allows us to improve the health of regional and factory theaters. It is necessary to gather around them groups of local literary talents and systematically set about the realization of this important task. In this way we will succeed simultaneously in making known and preparing for future authentic proletarian dramatists. [. . .]

B. Fel'dman, "What do the numbers say?", *Rabochy i teatr* 29 (July 21, 1925): 1.

The distribution of complimentary prof-union tickets in the past 1924–25 theatrical season, as before, is done exclusively through the Gubotdel of Unions. Therefore it stands to reason that the number of tickets distributed for this or that theater first of all depends on the size of a given union. It is obvious that the big Leningrad Union of Metalworkers turns out to be the most in demand of prof-union theater tickets. But irrespective of the size of the Union of Metalworkers, a remarkable role in the demand for complimentary theater tickets is played by the average cultural level of the mass of members of one or another union.

The smallest role, of course, is played by the choice of plays—individual unions that belong to the arrangement of TKhS Kul'turotdel LGSPS can select performances of shows they want to see, within limits—but this, in a lesser degree, relates to academic theaters, where the demand was so great that the selection became extremely difficult. [. . .]

As to the number of complimentary theater tickets to Acad. theaters received and distributed for the whole past season, first place is held by the Union of Metalworkers

(49,670 tickets), then the unions of Sovtorg[142] Workers (32,033 tickets), Chemical Industry Workers (22,176 t.), Education (18,592 t.), and Food Industry Workers (19,061
t.). Such large unions as Textile Workers, Municipal Employees, etc., lag far behind
the aforementioned group of unions. It is curious to note here that, if we except the
railway workers scattered along the rail lines far from Leningrad, last place in terms
of number of Prof-union theater tickets received and distributed is held by the Union
of Art Workers.

[...] Thus, Acad. theaters, attended by almost five hundred thousand worker-
spectators (up to 50 percent of all guaranteed box office) must [...] decisively "turn
their countenance" upon the new spectator, selecting for him, by the unfailing means
of the prof-unions, an appropriate repertoire, realizing it with their best talents. Not the
worker-spectator for the acad. theaters, but acad. theaters for the worker-spectators!

B. G., "O khalture" [On hackwork], *Rabochy i Teatr* 9 (March 2, 1926), 10.

On February 2, in Philharmonic Hall, the usual outrage occurred, and it is high time
to put a stop to it.

The agencies that hand out permits to organize concerts, the agencies that sanction
these concerts, the managements of the concert halls that rent out the premises, and
finally, the performers themselves who appear at these or other concerts are obliged
to protect society from encroachment on people's nerves, time, and money. Whoever
arranged the evening with the participation of Kachalov, Moskvin, Samoylov, Timé,
and Khodotov[143] on February 21 at Philharmonic Hall I don't know. The names of the
managers responsible are not printed on the poster. All that is known is that by mid-
concert, the audience was already shouting:

"This is a disgrace!"

And some of the more impassioned and audacious, i.e., those in the balcony,
shouted:

"Respect the audience! We demand respect for the audience!"

Judge for yourself: the evening ended at nearly one o'clock. By this time Kachalov
had made two appearances, having taken up less than half an hour in all. Moskvin
made one appearance, having taken up around eight and a half minutes. The rest of
the time was divided into the longest intermissions, fits of yawning, coughing, carrying off dirty screens, tables, divans and armchairs, and finally, brief appearances by
P. V. Samoylov, E. I. Timé, and . . . the long-awaited N. N. Khodotov.

Don't suppose that the number of participants in the evening already enumerated
is the total. I deliberately kept in reserve the evening's leading hero:

---

142 Sovremennaya torgovlya (Modern Trade).
143 Three luminaries of the Alexandra Theater before the Revolution: Pavel Vasil'evich Samoylov
    (1866–1931), a performer of passive dreamers; Elizaveta Ivanovna Timé (1884–1968), who
    distinguished more than two hundred roles with her deep voice and attractive manner; Nikolay
    Nikolaevich Khodotov (1878–1932), who played neurotic youths and then pioneered the new
    genre of melodeclamation.

"The free-lance young man!"

I don't know who he is. There are lots of these snappy young men. They shove their way into institutions and with various rights and wrongs finagle permits to organize concerts. They also lecture. [. . .] There he is before and after Kachalov, before and after Moskvin, in general before—and after everyone, and he stomped onto the platform more than anybody. There with his own inaccurately stressed pronunciation he insulted the ears of the spectators after the most musical monologues of Kachalov and Moskvin as Bolkonsky.[144] [. . .]

We insist on the need to put an end to these disgraceful hacks, this exploitation of the names of those whom every cultured person loves and respects for his qualities. All the agencies that issue licenses to organize concerts must pay the greatest attention to the programs of the evening organized and hold the representatives of the specific agencies responsible for a well-balanced performance of the evening's program.

> A. S. Makarenko, "The theater in the Gorky Corrective Camp, 1923–24," in *Pedagogicheskaya poéma* [The epic of pedagogy] (Moscow: Svetlana Nemolya, 2003), n.p. The ideas of Anton Semënovich Makarenko (1888–1939), pedagogue and reformer, influenced the Soviet educational system; he served as director of the Gorky Corrective Labor Colony 1920–28 and the Dzerzhinsky Corrective Camp, Khar'kov, 1927–35 for homeless children and juvenile delinquents.

In the new colony, we got our hands on a real theater. It would be hard to describe the delight we felt when the mill shed was placed at our full disposal.

Our theater could have seated as many as six hundred people—equal to the number of spectators from several villages. The importance of the dramatic club increased, and the demand for it increased in proportion. [. . .]

We put in all sorts of iron stoves and heated them only during performances. They were never able to heat the stage area, since all the heat flew up and escaped through the iron roof. So, even though the stoves themselves always got red hot, the spectators preferred to sit in their overcoats, taking care only that the side next to the stove did not get scorched. [. . .] The only prohibitions were against chewing sunflower seeds and showing up drunk. Following an old tradition, any townsman found, after the most thorough examination, to smell of the tiniest bit of vodka was deemed to be drunk. [. . .]

We made a real stage—roomy, high, with a complicated wing system and a prompter's box. Back of the stage was a large open space, but we were unable to make use of it. To provide a tolerable temperature for the actors, we screened a small room off this space, put a makeshift stove in it, and there we made up and dressed, somehow maintaining an order of precedence and a division of sexes. In the rest of the backstage space and on the stage itself it was as cold as outdoors.

In the house were a few dozen rows of plank benches, a vast sea of seats, a splendid field for cultural work, just asking to be sown and reaped. [. . .]

144 Prince Andrey in *War and Peace.*

During the winter season we produced about forty plays, but we never went in for the usual light entertainment found in clubs, offering only full-length, serious, four- and five-act plays, mostly taken from the repertoires of theaters in the capital. This may have been the most outrageous gall, but it was certainly not hack work. [...]

Performances took a heavy toll on the colony's funds. Forty or fifty rubles went for costumes, wigs, and other accessories. One way or another, we spent about two hundred rubles a month. This was a considerable expenditure, but we never stooped so low as to charge our spectators a single kopek for admission. We were aiming at the youths, and the village youngsters, particularly the girls, never had any pocket money. [...]

We tried to pick plays with a long cast of characters, for a great many of the colonists wanted to act. [...] It was hard to get actresses. [...] We auditioned all the wives, sisters, aunts, and other relatives of our staff and the mill workers and persuaded friends in town to give us a hand, and even then, we fell short of our needs. [...]

When it came to obtaining props for a performance, the colonists behaved more like ravaging beasts than human beings. If a lamp with a blue shade was needed for the stage, they would raid not only the staff rooms but the rooms of friends in town, and a lamp with a blue shade was sure to be had. If they sat down to a meal onstage, the meal must be a real one, with no exceptions. [...] For wine we used cider.

But as a rule, the actors were not eager to stay onstage too long, for it was as cold as outdoors. In *The Revolt of the Machines*[145] Karbanov had to stand onstage a whole hour, with nothing on but a loincloth. The performance took place in February, and unfortunately for us, the thermometer sometimes fell to thirty degrees below zero. [...] Sometimes the cold did stand in the way of our artistic development. We were presenting a play called *Comrade Semivzvodny*.[146] The scene took place in a landowner's garden, and there was supposed to be a statue. 6-P Mixed could find no statue, although they looked in all the local cemeteries, so we decided to do without. But when the curtain went up, to my astonishment I beheld a statue—there was Shelaputin powdered with chalk and wrapped in a sheet, looking slyly down at me from a draped stool. I lowered the curtain and shooed the statue off the stage, to the great disappointment of 6-P Mixed.

The Living Newspaper and the Blue Blouse

The living newspaper was one of the means of the early agittroupes of informing an illiterate public of the crucial events of the day. It became a major device of the Blue Blouse movement, founded in 1923 by Boris Yuzhanin, an instructor at the Moscow Journalism Institute. It was named after the factory worker's overalls,

---

145 *Bunt mashin* by A. N. Tolstoy opened in Leningrad April 14, 1924; he was sued by Kroll, the translator of Karel Čapek's *R.U.R.*, for plagiarism.
146 *Tovarishch Semivzvodny*, a popular military play by Golichikov.

which, in the early period, were the actors' standard costume. By the late 1920s it counted nearly 5,000 teams of nearly 100,000 members and had spread to other countries.

Vladimir Filippov, "More about 'the living newspaper,'" *Rabochy i teatr* 10 (November 24, 1924), 6–7. Vladimir Aleksandrovich Filippov (1889–1965), historian and theater critic; served as chairman of the theatrical section of Narkompros 1920–29.

The "living newspaper" is a necessary and modern theme of the theater nowadays. Firmly established in working men's clubs, the "living newspaper" is becoming the most acceptable form of work of the "United Artistic Circle."

Actually the United Artistic Circle centers on the so-called group of current politics, and in this way it faces conspicuous new tasks of theatrical staging of current politics, the politics of today.

The "living newspaper" has changed styles of staging. If we track the development of amateur theater, rooted in the club platforms, we shall see that club shows played an enormous role in the organization of [...] class agittheater [...]

The "Red Theater," created by a talented group of club instructors, grew entirely out of those shows. And only the use of realistic devices endows its works with an idiosyncratic character.

This fallback to a realistic position is noticeable at the present time even on the front of amateur theater. If, to reflect political events, the "living newspaper"—the most up-to-date form of amateur theater—sometimes makes use of conventional dramatic characters—"masks" of the bourgeois, fence-sitter, general, worker, etc.—then in relationship to the presentation of everyday life, we can observe the purest waters of realism. [...]

As to the significance of the "living newspaper" in organizing agittheater. Just as club shows demonstrated their influence in the course of developing agittheater, so the amateur "living newspaper," built on the collective creativity of the masses, plays a significant part in the creation of agittheater.

The cultural growth of the worker demands from the theater the creation not of a newspaper but of a "living magazine" or even a "living book," with profoundly thought-out political content.

Zhivaya gazeta [Living newspaper], 1925, 3, 7–8.

The "living newspaper" can be an extremely effective weapon of educational propaganda for hygiene in a worker's club. Only one must remember that, in exploiting a theatrical form of propaganda, we must observe all the laws of the stage: in no case must the "living newspaper" turn into a dramatized lecture or trivial sermon, broadcast from the stage even if in verse. [...] Liveliness and varied action and humor—those are the indispensable conditions for success of the "Newspaper" and its agitational activity. [...]

Dust and Tuberculosis

(*The worker* FEDOTOV *coughs. A second worker enters.*)

2ND WORKER: What, Fedotov old pal, working too hard, took sick or what?

FEDOTOV: Ugh, this damned cough is killing me. I'm kind of weak, can't get any work done, no appetite, at night I'm soaked in sweat . . . but the cough keeps getting worse.

2ND WORKER: Yes, pal, you're in a bad way, you're a goner . . .

FEDOTOV: This damned cloud of dust. You take one breath of it and you can't stop coughing.

2ND WORKER: Maybe you've got TB? Check in to the outpatient clinic, pal, they'll cure you there.

FEDOTOV: I did go, they prescribed some powder . . . I took the powder—it made things a bit better, but as soon as I get to my machine, I breathe in that dust—my chest and throat start to get raspy. (*Enter the* FOREMAN.)

FOREMAN: Listen here, lads, today the whole gang is going to the clinic for a checkup— the doctor wants to have a look!

FEDOTOV: What's the good of a checkup? I'm coughing, can't catch my breath . . . is a checkup going to make that easier? (*Exits.*)

2ND WORKER AND FOREMAN (*sing to the tune of "Parting"*):

> TB, oh, TB, TB
> Is the worker's enemy,
> The proletariat's wicked foe.
> The friend of hazardous jobs.

[After a chorus that points out that "smokers, grinders, textile workers, and stone breakers" are especially susceptible, the lights go down and come up again. The chairman of a committee for the protection of labor enters.]

CHAIRMAN: So, comrades, we move the following resolution: "Pursuant to the decision of the infirmary to heal his diseased and tubercular lungs, to send the worker Fedotov to a health resort for lung disease in the Crimea; on his return from the resort to transfer Fedotov to work unconnected with the production and inhalation of dust." Against? Carried unanimously.

[The sketch ends with a mixed chorus of "cells for the improvement of the health of labor and everyday life."]

Sapogi (Boots), comedy in one act by G. Subbotin. In *Derevensky teatr* [Village theater] (August 1, 1925), 14–17, 19. Gavriil Mikhaylovich Subbotin (1883–?) had worked at the MAT and the First Studio; later he became an actor and director of the All-Russian Touring-Concert Union (VGKO). The play involves three komsomols, eighteen to twenty years old; two of them tease a layabout and incipient delinquent into becoming a useful member of society.

"How to Act This Play"

What is this play supposed to show the spectator, what is its underlying idea, with what ideas and feelings should the spectators leave? This question should concern everyone who starts work on this play.

At the present time the peasantry everywhere, in all its life, is exchanging the old for the new. It is making a transition to new methods of farming—to crop rotation, machines; from illiterate and benighted it is becoming literate and enlightened; old slavish customs are changing to another, rational way of life. But all this is not happening at once, obviously, and not always smoothly. It is understandable that young people are passionate, always moving forward, and that sometimes they gallop ahead pointlessly, with very sudden deviations, and so they harm not only themselves but often the whole village.

Mischief making, hooliganism, debauchery, bullying, vanity, loafing around—all this must end. Our Union, all the peasantry first of all, needs serious, thoughtful, honest, persistent work.

With kids often everything new boils down to their simply moving away, breaking loose, shirking their own basic peasant work, their own farming, on which all peasant life depends.

There are such kids who only talk and do little, and one of them is made fun of by this playlet.

How are you to act this little playlet so that this basic idea is understood, to show Vasya as ridiculous? Let us divide the play into scenes. [. . .]

G. Silaev, "How to act a sketch," *Éstrada* [Variety stage] (1944), 3–4.

A sketch is an original staged anecdote, therefore to play a sketch like an ordinary play, in which the action develops slowly and consecutively, is impossible. In a sketch, as the saying goes, one must take the bull by the horns, i.e., from the very beginning the acting must be dynamic and filled with inner rhythm. Therefore the first condition is a firm memorization of the lines, because in a sketch empty pauses and draggy tempos are inadmissible.

The second condition is an instant reaction to your partner's words and action, without any psychological preparation, therefore you must listen to and observe your partner very closely and to the point, so you can instantly reply in tune to his words and actions.

The third condition is the heightened rhythmical saturation of the acting, i.e., a heightened tone without shrillness, general excitement but without hecticness and garbled words. To live to a full rhythm means to feel more keenly, to react more sharply to everything that goes on. One small example—you are pouring water from a decanter to slake your thirst, that's one rhythm, but if you are pouring water for the man next to you who has lost consciousness, you will live and act in a completely different, more heightened type of rhythm.

3.15. "Fordism and NOT," performed by a Blue Blouse Troupe. The Nauchnaya Organizatsiya Truda (Scientific Organization of Labor) was a movement to introduce efficiency and assembly-line methods to Soviet factories and everyday life.

Comrade Novitsky, head of the Artistic Division of the Glavnauka, "What is the 'Blue Blouse,'" *Sinyaya Bluza* 1 (January 1928), 9–12.

1. The "Blue Blouse" is a classic form of dramatized living newspaper, whose growth springs from the living report (from the oral newspaper).

2. The "Blue Blouse" is an agitform, a topical spectacle, born of the Revolution, a montage of political and everyday phenomena in the light of class proletarian ideology.

3. The "Blue Blouse" is a versatile, living, juicy, bright, portable itinerant form that can work in any public space under any conditions.

4. The "Blue Blouse" is a club, cabaret form, a special aspect of amateur artistic work in worker's clubs. It was born spontaneously and in the clubs has supplanted the bourgeois play, "insularity," and amateurishness.

5. The means of influence in the "Blue Blouse": speech, catchphrases; gesture, the mechanization of gesture; the poster, appliqué work; music; song; agitmovement; physical culture movement; acrobatics; eccentric dance movement, etc.

6. The techniques of the "Blue Blouse": exposure; contrast; acting with objects; uninterrupted work.

All this derives from the "small forms," the "music hall," the leftist experts Meyerhold and Foregger.

7. The forms of act in the "Blue Blouse": the blow-off—entree—exercises, contact with the spectator; editorial oratory (mass action); international reportage; skit of everyday life; dialogue, monologue; revue; jingles [*chastushki*], etc. [...]

10. The actor of the "Blue Blouse" is synthetic, he is a singer, a physical culturist, a quick-change artist. [...]

After 1926, all the "Blue Blouse" groups carried out the tasks of the Soviet propaganda organizations Sotsstrakh, Gostrakhovanie, Sberkass, and MOPR, of cooperation, Fordization, production quality, economic regime, etc. [...]

> Standard Soviet Blue Blouse Program, in L. Hoffmann and D. Hoffmann-Ostwald, *Deutsches Arbeittheater 1918–1933* [German Workers' Theater] (Munich, Germany: Rogner and Bernhard, 1973), 1:247–49.

1. Prelude
2. Parade of the Soviet Press
3. An incident in China (sketch)
4. Gymnastics (attraction)
5. Ford and us (sketch)
6. Ten years of October
7. The Red Army
8. IWA (International Workers' Aid)
9. Jazz band
10. For a new way of life
11. Sovnarkom (a meeting of the People's Commissariat)
12. Dances from Europe (parody)
13. Russian traditional dances
14. Chorus of Russian folksongs
15. Solo concertina number
16. After-hours amusements
17. The working girls
18. Peasant women (from the paintings of Malyavin[147])
19. Chastushki [jingles]
    a. Electrification of the USSR
    b. Introduction of the metric system to the USSR
    c. Puppets
    d. Penny prints (Marionette-folk pictures)
    e. Toys (models of costumes of the cottage industries of the Tula region)
    f. Sailor songs of 1918–19 with acrobatic stunts and dances.

> V. Mrozovsky, "Nina Ayzenberg's work for the Blue Blouses," *Sinyaya Bluza* (1926), trans. in Alla Sosnovskaya, "Nina Aizenberg (1902–1974): Russian designer," *Slavic and East European Performance* 20 (Fall 2000), 48–73. Reprinted with permission of Martin E. Segal Theatre Center.

The special needs of Blue Blouse actors—the quick-change roles and their constant presence onstage—have long required the skills of an innovative designer. Of course,

---

147 Filipp Andreevich Malyavin (1869–1940), whose gaudy peasant canvases were painted after the Revolution; he settled in Paris 1922.

it is also recognized that Blue Blouse actors need to wear their characters' costume pieces over the still-visible background of their "professional clothes." Even well-known Muscovite artists, such as the Stenberg brothers and Boris Érdman,[148] who designed for the Blue Blouse movement, failed to solve this problem. The spectacular costumes that they created turned out to be appropriate for conventional theater but did not take into account the nature of Blue Blouse actors. It was only Nina Ayzenberg,[149] an extremely young artist, a product of the stormy years of the VKhuTEMas, who, by using reversible appliqué patches, managed to find an appropriate solution to the requirements of this acting style and to create bold, original designs that met the specific costume needs of the Blue Blouse.

Dovzhikova, "Blue Blouse," *Rabochy i teatr* 16 (January 5, 1925), 9.

Cheerfulness, confidence, and precision movement make an impression from the outset. Bawdiness and gaudiness [*sochnost' i krasochnost'*]—this is part of the performance. But what is there of "living newspaper" in this? We were led to understand beforehand that the newspaper does not bear a local character, but even the general political moment of topical interest is absent or, more accurately, *not heard*. Beginning with jingles, ending with importunate ditties from every imaginable operetta, all this with uninterrupted humming and noise was dinned into our ears and *prevented* comprehension. And if music and songs can serve only as subsidiary material in the whole chain of artistic techniques that exert influence on the spectator, then in this case, music is an annoying obstacle. [...] Definite ends demand definite means to be achieved. And besides, Leningrad has its own style—quite distinct from Moscow's. "What is wholesome in Moscow is bad for red St. Pete." And it's a pity because individual numbers (*rabkors*) are very well done and have an effect on the spectator. One thing or another ... A politicocabaret or else a "living newspaper"—a mixture of the two styles is impossible—is a dangerous permutation. A correctly staged whole must provide both a definite artistic and theatrical formation.

Walter Benjamin, *Moscow Diary,* 77.

December 28, 1926. We decided ... to stop in at some *pivnaia* [alehouse] that was featuring evening entertainment. As we were entering, there were a few people at the door struggling to cart off a drunk. The room was not that large or crowded, and people were sitting alone or in small groups over beers. We took seats fairly close to the plank stage, whose backdrop consisted of a charming blur of meadow with a hint of a

---

148 Stenberg Brothers: Georgy Avgustovich (1900–1933) and Vladimir Avgustovich (1899–1982), designers who called themselves constructivist engineers; they worked for both Meyerhold and Tairov, their best work done on his O'Neill productions. Boris Robertovich Érdman (alias Druzki, 1899–1960), brother of the playwright Nikolay Érdman; he designed for Meyerhold, Foregger, the Blue Blouse troupes, and many theaters; chief designer at the Moscow State Circus (1941–45).
149 Nina Ayzenberg (1902–74) studied at VKhUTEMas and worked as a stage designer from 1924; she was a member of the October group of constructivist painters 1930–32.

ruin that seemed to be dissolving into air. Still, this vista was not enough to cover the entire length of the stage. After two song numbers, the main attraction of the evening began—it was an *intsenirovka*, i.e., material adapted for the stage from other sources, such as epic or lyric. In this case the dramatic framework seemed to serve as a pretext for a medley of love songs and peasant songs. First a woman appeared onstage alone and listened for a bird. Then a man entered from the wings, and it went on like this until the entire stage was full and everything ended in a chorus of song and dance. The whole thing did not differ all that much from a family festivity, but since such occasions are gradually disappearing from real life, they are probably all the more alluring to the petit bourgeois when they occur onstage. Odd what they serve with beer: little bits of white bread or black bread with a crust of salt baked onto them, and dried peas in brine.

> Boris Tenin, *Furgon komedianta* [A comedian's caravan] (Moscow: Iskusstvo, 1987), 97–100. Boris Mikhaylovich Tenin (1905–90), after work with Meyerhold, joined the Blue Blouse, taught in the circus school, and became a comic actor, ending up at the Leningrad Comedy Theater 1937–46, the Moscow Satire Theater 1955–62, and the Malaya Bronnaya 1962–74.

When I joined the "Blue Blouse," at first I appeared under the auspices of the Mossel'prom [Moscow United Enterprises for the Distribution of Agricultural Industrial Products], having my own group to make appearances in restaurants and beer halls. The fact is that the leadership of the Mossel'prom also wanted to renovate the so-called beer vaudeville [*pivnaya éstrada*] to effect a change in the gypsy and Ukrainian choruses in restaurants and the accordionists in beer halls. But the ordinary Blue Blouse programs were too cumbersome and serious for restaurants. Something more entertaining was required. The leadership of the Mossel'prom turned to Osip Maksimovich Brik[150] with a proposal to reorganize such groups. He took on the work.

[...] Brik wrote a pamphlet "Variety Confronts the Café Tables" [*Éstrada pered stolikami*], published in 1927. There he wrote, "The earliest appearance of the 'Blue Blouse' in beer gardens provoked bewilderment, but interest as well. It was a surprise that amid the beer, shellfish and dried peas people in blue smocks would show up and instead of scabrous verses and double-entendre songs begin to sing and speak on topical and political themes."

[...] [Our] program began with topical political themes, gleaned from the latest newspapers. With one or sometimes two partners I performed jingles. We were dressed peasant-style. I wore a red peasant blouse outside my trousers, with big bright yellow sunflowers sewn on it. On my head was a peaked cap, on my feet bast slippers. My female partners were in sarafans, peasant kerchiefs, and bast slippers as well. But our jingles were not necessarily on village themes, though there were a few. [...] The image of a peasant seemed very successful for a jingle act. It endowed a good characteristic, allowed one to be a bit wily or naively ingenuous, "to speak blunt home truths" to their faces, and dance where necessary.

150 Osip Maksimovich Brik (1888–1945), writer, critic, theorist of the LEF group.

Later, moving into a big Blue Blouse collective, I played skits, danced, took part in oratorios, but the jingle act remained for me the crowning and most favorite. [...]

[...] Originally the "Linkage" company performed jingle acts in an original manner. A quintet of actors of both sexes, standing in a row, would come out onstage hidden up to the neck by a black cloth. Only our heads were visible. When we came to a stop, each one would yank a small rag doll torso with little arms and legs that was in front of the cloth concealing himself. It was attached to the neck of the performer. They were figures of peasant men and women and lads. It might be a drunkard, a janitor, or someone else—the figures changed depending on the nature of the jingles. The actors' heads were covered with appropriate caps, hats, and kerchiefs.

Slits in the cloth allowed us to direct the puppets' arms and legs. We could adjust kerchiefs or caps on our heads, wipe our noses, palm a cheek, or simply swing the puppets' arms.

Prison Theater

In 1922 Pzheval'sk concentration camp was established near Lake Issyk-Kul', along with a second camp on the shores of the White Sea, about thirty-five miles west of Arkhangel', where the city of Severodvinsk now stands. The regime was rigorous with starvation rations and frequent beatings.

Beginning in 1923, the Solovetsk camp, on islands in the White Sea, grew at a rapid pace. Every year its population increased several times over. In 1924, there was a total of four thousand inmates; by 1929, a typhus epidemic could kill off seventeen thousand inmates without significantly reducing the total number. There was a "Cultural–Educational Section": not a regular troupe, although its members were assigned to lighter work. The professional directors Vladimir Evtikhevich Karpov and Bor arrived in 1923.

> Natal'ya Kuz'yakina, *Teatr na Solovkakh 1923–1937* [Theater on Solovki 1923–
> 37] (St. Petersburg: Dmitry Bulanin, 2009), 52–54.

[Despite primitive conditions], on October 23, 1923, the theater on the island offered its first show—I. Myasnitsky's light comedy *The Treasure*.[151]

Shiryaev in *The Unextinguished Lamp* eloquently described the leading role played by the provincial actor Sergey (Ivan Andreevich) Armanov in creating the theater.

The lanky, gaunt fellow loved art like a fanatic and, thanks to a boundless passion for the stage, considered everything possible. "While under investigation in Butyrka prison, he contrived even there, in a common cell crammed to capacity, to create something in the nature of a variety troupe with dancers, singers, reciters, and a Chinese conjurer." [...]

151 Ivan Il'ich Myasnitsky (actually Baryshev, 1852–1911), house dramatist at Korsh's Theater, Moscow, before the Revolution.

The theater was actually begun by another individual—probably G. I. Nikitin, who first worked under the pseudonym "Vecherin" and later acted under his own name. In all likelihood he was either an amateur with a strong background or a professional actor no longer young. On June 1, 1924, on Solovki, a benefit was advertised "for Nikitin—the first director, one of the creators of the theaters." The *bénéficiaire* staged the prerevolutionary popular melodrama by P. Nevezhin, *The Profaned,* and played the leading role of Victor.

Nikitin in the first year produced more than ten traditionally realistic shows but later showed a capacity for development. A reviewer praised him for the choice of a short comedietta *Deviltry,* probably from The Bat repertoire, played before drapes, with a simplified staging and a widespread use of cinematic dynamics in the scene changes. [...]

A cultural–educational, instructional section was created (KPCh, KVCh) and charged with supervision of the theater. The greater part of the tickets was distributed to the administration. In the hall, people waited for hours until "somebody" from the leadership would appear and the director would give the signal to begin.

Those who slept on bare boards in the enormous cathedrals stinking of sweat and muck (13th co.), those who were dying of scurvy and injuries from hard labor—it was impossible for the doomed to go to the show. They didn't have the strength. Circumstances did not allow the theater, created by the convicts for their own kind, the KRs [counterrevolutionaries], to support them.

The actors entertained the happy few who had avoided hard labor—the tally clerks, secretaries, bookkeepers, and other camp staff. M. Z. Nikonov-Smorodin[152] has written about this: "Here the proletariat was barred entry... Chekists of every stripe, a small portion of the specialists who had managed to shirk hard labor, the lucky dogs who had pull, the supervisors and guards—that's who filled the theater, used the library, bathhouse number one, and other camp privileges."

An angered Tiberius spewed malice:

"Some managerial 'punk' considered it especially chic to sit where everyone could see him, before the very eyes of the officials. And the closer this 'punk' squirmed, the bolder he felt in sitting in the best seats in the first rows of the hall."

He also noted a revoltingly nasty tradition—

"the inordinate zeal of the commanding officers in drilling their subordinates... when, having made it into the forbidden hall, you carefully look for a seat, for the best seats were earlier reserved by the 'select public'... you hear the threatening 'Quiet'—'That'll do'—'Silence'—at every cough (and almost all of us coughed, for the autumn season had made itself known)..."

152 Mikhail Zakharovich Nikonov-Smorodin (1889–?), former White Army commander who led a peasant insurrection; arrested 1927; his death sentence was commuted to hard labor in the Gulag; escaped to Finland 1935.

Prison variety songs. Gabriel Ramensky, "The theater in Soviet concentration camps," trans. Gene Sosin, in Bradshaw, *Soviet Theaters,* 201–2.

Prison, prison, what a word,
It is shameful and terrible,
But for me it's quite different,
I've known the prison for a long time.
I know the narrow little cell,
I know the prison ration well,
I know the iron grating and
I know the prison lock.

—

Our land, our Solovetsky
A wondrous land for *ka-ers* and *shpany!*[153]
Sing a song of camp life,
Smiling bravely like a child!

The gnats are very good in spring.
The view from Sekirina Mountain's[154] fine,
Where happy people take their rest
From all the cares of useless work.

To all who rewarded us with Solovetsky
We say, "Come here yourselves
And sit here three or maybe five years;
You will remember it with joy."

153 *Ka-er* [K. R.] is "counterrevolutionary" or political prisoners. *Shpany* is "riffraff" or criminal prisoners.
154 Location of a solitary confinement cell with a strict regimen; imprisonment there was for a six-month term, but not everyone survived that long.

CHAPTER FOUR

Stalin Consolidates Power, 1926–1927

W HEN STALIN EXPELLED TROTSKY, Zinov'ev, and Kamenev from the Party and came to power in January 1927, he urged the rejection of classical Russian art along with modern Western culture. The cultural establishment, however, upheld the classics at the same time that it fought against nonrealistic styles and "abstract" humanism, and it demanded the creation of works loyal to and glorifying the official order. Ideological and political interests determined the country's culture. On the Left, the proletarian writers' organization RAPP contended with LEF, whose leaders numbered former futurists and constructivists, casting the Proletkul't into the shade. Defeat of this far-left opposition accompanied the end of NÉP. Thousands of Népmen were imprisoned or driven from their homes, families were expelled from state housing, and their children were barred from Soviet schools and universities. This included many members of the "cultural front."

All cultural organizations were reengineered to inculcate principles of Communist morality. The intention of the Soviet leadership was to create a new type of personality wholly devoted to Communism. Religion was attacked on every front, to be replaced by a new morality. Conscience could no longer be a private matter, for the individual was subsumed into the public welfare. The seeming tolerance for opposing viewpoints under the NÉP evaporated.

For the first time, a real attempt was made to bring the theater completely under Party control by appointing Communists as producers and administrators, establishing "artistic councils" within the theater, and emphasizing the role of "activist" groups such as Party, Komsomol, and trade unions to wage "civil war in the theater" and end the "spiritual NÉP." Party officials and proletarian representatives from factories and unions served on the councils to prevent deviation from the Party line.

Meyerhold's *Inspector General* is the dominant production of this transitional period, marking the apogee of his power and influence. The stripped-down and minimalist mechanism of his earlier productions was replaced by opulence and maximalism. By forging his own idiosyncratic version of a national classic, he was establishing his prerogative to be the *auteur* of the spectacle, whose vision encompassed every aspect of the interpretation. Stalin could not help but regard such presumption with distrust.

Overview

> Walter Benjamin, *Moscow Diary*, ed. Gary Smith, trans. Richard Sieburth (Cambridge, Mass.: Harvard University Press, 1986), 20–21, 59.

December 13, 1926. [The director of the Theater of Revolution V. S. Starukhin] is a former Red Army general who played a decisive part in the annihilation of Vrangel[1] and was twice named in Trotsky's general orders. Later he committed a stupid political blunder that brought his career to a standstill, and since he had earlier been a man of letters, they gave him this position as a theater director, which, however, demands little effort. He appears to be fairly dumb.

January 2, 1927. Illés's[2] play *Attentat* was to be performed for the press at one o'clock in the Theater of the Revolution. Misguidedly taking the public's thirst for the sensational into account, they had subtitled the play *Buy a Revolver,*[3] thereby giving away at the very outset the final twist in which the White Guard assailant is discovered by the Communists just as he is about to commit his deed, at which point he tries at least to palm his revolver off on them. The play contains an effective scene done in the style of Grand Guignol. It also has serious politicotheoretical ambitions, since it is supposedly meant to depict the hopeless situation of the petit bourgeoisie. But this was not conveyed at all by the production, given its lack of principles, its uncertainty, and its countless little winks at the audience. It even threw away its best trump cards, which were guaranteed by the suggestive settings—a concentration camp, a café, a barracks in the decaying, sordid, bleak Austria of 1919. I had never seen a more inconsistent handling of stage space: the entrances and exits were inevitably ineffectual. One could clearly observe what happens to Meyerhold's stagecraft when an incompetent director tries to appropriate it to his own purposes. The theater was packed. One could even see people wearing something like formal dress for the occasion.

> Basil Dean, *Seven Ages: An Autobiography 1888–1927* (London: Hutchinson, 1970), 293. Basil Dean (1888–1978), prominent English stage director of West End hits, visited Moscow in early 1926, under the auspices of the Foreign Office and the Russian embassy in London.

1 Baron Pëtr Nikolaevich Vrangel' (1878–1928), Russian general who supported Kornilov's attempt to overthrow the Petrograd soviet. After his defeat by the Red Army in the last major battle of the Civil War, he fled abroad.

2 Bela Illés (1895–1974), Hungarian writer, had lived in the Soviet Union since 1923; subsequently, he became general secretary of the International Union of Revolutionary Writers 1925–33 and a general in the Red Army during World War II.

3 *Kupite revol'vera,* directed by B. D. Koroleva, sets designed by S. Efimenko; premiere December 30, 1926.

At Madame Kameneva's own Theater of the Revolution a mock trial, directed for her by Meyerhold, is being presented, using the most advanced production methods; actors dispersed among the audience, mostly working class: an old woman with a basket of groceries plops down in the seat beside me; she follows the action of the play with shouts of approval or disapproval—I'm not sure which—a form of audience participation of which the current "nouvelle vague" would heartily approve. At the Red Army Theater, a play about the 1905 revolution; a caricature of the late Czar is greeted with howls of derision. In the Theater of Satire an actor impersonates Trotsky so to the life that he is greeted with loud cheers. [...]

> Vladimir Pavlov, "On the threshold of 1927," *Novy zritel'* [New spectator] 1
> (January 4, 1927), 1–2. Vladimir Aleksandrovich Pavlov (1899–1967) was both
> a theater critic and a sociologist.

And so today one may distinguish three completely distinct ideological tendencies and one crossroads.

One is the idealistic mood, shading into decadence, bordering on mysticism. Here one must put the system of the MATs in the first rank.

The second is the fellow traveler, who accepts reality, for the most part, superficially, like a philistine, and by dint of this is in danger of joining the decadent tendency block.

The third is the stabilized one, in principle consolidating the up-to-date and healthy results of revolutionary art—the principles of material culture and proletarian ideology—and likewise adapting the best achievements of the past to the construction of the present.

But there is danger even here. A theater that may suddenly balk at progress on the road to projected revolution, and at times give in to theatrical "fashion," will inevitably miscarry and trade what has value for small change.

And, finally, the crossroads. This is today's TIM [Meyerhold Theater], whatever it may have been, but which is in fact set on its own path of development. [...]

> Anatoly Lunacharsky, "On theater censorship," *Teatr segodnya* [Theater today]
> (1927), 53.

The philistine who dabbles in liberalism is very fond of comparing the GPU with the Corps of Gendarmes,[4] the police with the old constabulary, and Glavlit and Glavrepertkom with the old censorship. This comparison is cheap and comes naturally to the lips of the philistine [...] Everyone realizes how hard it is to be a "censor." Everyone realizes the mass of animosity usually aimed at censorship. But we should not

4   Glavnoe Politicheskoe Upravlenie or Chief Political Directorate, which replaced the Cheka as the principal instrument of political control over the Soviet population, a secret police used to suppress intraparty opposition. Corps of Gendarmes (Otdelny korpus zhandarmov), the uniformed security police of the tsarist regime, responsible for state security; after 1902 it was merged with the Okhrana or secret police.

aggravate the situation of our comrades who have been charged with this job. [...]

No one should conclude from this that I consider that the activities of our Glavrep-ertkom merit full approval. Quite the contrary. I have often had to intervene in all types of conflicts with our theater "censorship" and to point out its mistakes. But, after all, nothing gets done without mistakes, in particular something so difficult.

ON MAY 16, 1927, the Sixth All-Union Congress of Art Workers resolved that salaries be raised across the board. This led to a rash of articles in the press and a definite proposal from the Central Committee of Rabis for economic reforms.

V. Melik-Khasparov, "A system for a pay scale," *Rabis* 11 (1927), 4.

Groups of theaters	Theater budget (rubles per month)	Fund for salaries (rubles)
I	over 20,000	over 15,000
II	18,000–20,000	10,000–15,000
III	14,000–18,000	7,000–10,000
IV	9,000–14,000	5,000–7,000
V	4,000–9,000	3,000–5,000

A New Soviet Drama

Lyubov' Yarovaya, a play in four acts by Konstantin Trenëv, based on his own novel, was the first Soviet play to be enthusiastically welcomed by audiences. It also relieved the Maly Theater of a reputation for bourgeois values, although there was nothing new about the plot or the staging. It opened on December 22, 1926. Stalin saw it ten times and, in 1935, insisted that a five-act version be staged by the Moscow Art Theater.

V. Ashmarin, *"Lyubov' Yarovaya," Novy zritel'* 1 (January 4, 1927), 6.

The Maly Theater's latest production, the play *Lyubov' Yarovaya,* immediately evokes comparison with the MAT 1's production of *Days of the Turbins* by M. Bulgakov. [See later.]

If Bulgakov's *Days* seemed to be a play alien to Soviet contemporaneity, ideologically inclined to a right-wing Smenovekhov–Ustryalov[5] persuasion, *Lyubov' Yarovaya* by Trenëv[6] and the Maly Theater's interpretation can be considered a production 100 percent satisfactory for the Soviet community.

5 Nikolay Vasil'evich Ustryalov (1890–1937) founded the Smenovekhovstvo movement (from his published letters *Smena vekhov* [Moving the landmarks] [Prague, n.p., 1921]), which declared the Civil War at an end and urged that Russians unite under the Bolsheviks, without necessarily accepting Communism. Arrested and shot 1937.
6 Konstantin Andreevich Trenëv (1876–1945), whose first play about the Pugachëv rebellion failed

The Maly Theater forged *Lyubov' Yarovaya* into a performance full of harmonious contemporaneity, able to resurrect a few episodes of the Civil War and illuminate them correctly from the viewpoint of a fighting proleteriat, and not the viewpoint of that specific "intelligentsia" that fought against the workers and peasants at the fronts, but then, broken up and deceived by its generals, importunately crawled with Judas-like embraces to "acknowledge" the Soviet power. [...]

During the rapid evacuation of a Rev[olutionary] Com[missariat] the Bolshevik commissar Vikhor' has committed special atrocities. The teacher Lyubov' Yarovaya, having lost her husband in the imperialist war, has devoted herself to her work—a member of no party, she carries out the tasks of the PresRevCom [Chairman of the Revolutionary Commissariat] Koshkin, works with the Bolsheviks, and hates the Whites. She is left in the city to maintain a link with the Reds and the Greens.

And then, once the RevCom has been evacuated, Commissar Vikhor' removes his mask: he's a dyed-in-the-wool S.R. [Social Revolutionary], a counterintelligence officer, and has undermined the Soviet power and contributed to the advent of the Whites. The defeated teacher learns to her horror that he is her husband, Yarovoy. The town in the hands of the Whites, the demoralization of the intelligentsia and the proprietor classes, the Bolshevik underground and the conditions of their savage and ruthless hunting-down by the counterintelligence led by Yarovoy, and, finally, the disintegration of the command team of the Whites—all these tableaux proceed before the spectator in an authentic and artistic stage incarnation, born of a sincere sympathy of the spectator with the Bolsheviks and hatred and scorn for the "men of goodwill."

And when an offstage explosion and the arrival of the cavalry destroy the power of the Whites—when the officers hurriedly rush to the foreign steamship—Lyubov' Yarovaya, as a witness, maligned as a counterintelligence agent, turns her husband, Yarovoy, over to the Cheka, and wholeheartedly joins the group of Bolsheviks who have been through the crucible of hard work and struggle and are called on to build a new life.

The romantic plot by no means dominates the foreground, the complicated intrigue of interrelationships does not overshadow the most important and essential thing in the performance—the passion of the struggle and the *patriotism* characteristic of fighters for "*a socialist fatherland.*"

Both the material aspect and the actors' performances in the play are given in the style characteristic of the theater—this is, artistic realism as it is understood in an academic theater. The sedulous execution of the scenery, the carefully well-kept costumes, all this makes the stage production almost *naturalistic.* After all, these themes are already familiar to the spectator as treated by constructivism, by what the light hand of Vs. Meyerhold has introduced into the Theaters of Revolution, the MGSPS, the Proletkul't, and so on. [...]

---

at the MAT in 1925; his second, *Lyubov' Yarovaya,* was such a success that it earned him one hundred thousand rubles a month for years.

Mikhail Zagorsky, "*Lyubov' Yarovaya* at the Moscow Maly Theater," *Zhizn' iskusstva* 1 (January 4, 1927), 10–11. Mikhail Borisovich Zagorsky (1885–1951), theater critic and historian, was Meyerhold's literary manager 1925–35.

Moving to an artistic evaluation of *Lyubov' Yarovaya,* one has to say that the playwriting of K. Trenëv, the author of *Pugachëv Times,* suffers from all the usual faults of plays written by men of letters, accustomed to the very loose techniques of plot construction of novels and novellas, with their legitimate digressions, masses of episodic characters, retarded development of the intrigue, and so on. In *Lyubov' Yarovaya,* of course, there is no understanding of the original laws of the stage or awareness of how to reveal characters theatrically by means of intensifying dynamic and active conflicts and situations. The play has no auxiliary and central points for actors to perform; a series of seemingly central figures suddenly fade into the background; episodic figures push aside what is important; a series of plot twists are sewn with white thread and do not succeed onstage. But all the same, beneath all the clumsy and incoherently built dramatic fabric courses the healthy blood of stage animation and passion, and there is distinctly heard the quickened beating of the heart of our own times and how we understand our era.

[. . .] As to the acting, this production is also extremely curious and valuable for the fact alone that many actors of the Maly Theater here appear for the first time in a modern repertoire, creating images and characters of people of our time. Even for such a great actor as *Stepan Kuznetsov,* the character of the Bolshevik sailor Shvandya was a kind of experiment, because there are no classical traditions and practices here, and the new theatrical material has to be worked out anew, proceeding only from the actor's personality and observations of life. Stepan Kuznetsov brilliantly coped with that problem, having created the lusty, lively, and smiling figure of a simple man with a pure heart and a daring soul, who does not even suspect that he is a "hero" and who risks his life with the smile of an upright lad for whom the revolution is something of his own breed and blood, and Karl Marx is a clever, lively granddad with a gray beard, whom it's no sin to learn from and who should be affectionately embraced, if you run into him on life's highway. [. . .]

Vera Pashennaya, "The way I have to work on a role," *Teatr i Dramaturgiya* [Theater and playwriting] 7 (1933), 61–64. Vera Nikolaevna Pashennaya (born Roshchina-Insarova, 1887–1962), a leading comic actress at the Moscow Maly Theater 1907–62, toured with the MAT 1922–23.

I pictured the outward appearance of Lyubov' Yarovaya all at once. I didn't even have to grope for an image–it was so clear that this was no coarse, vulgar female. My task was to make Yarovaya in every way an amiable, feminine, and kindhearted woman. She speaks softly but decisively, somehow even a bit bashfully, when she speaks with Commissar Koshkin, but she is unbending in her relations with the enemy. [. . .]

Yarovaya smokes in her scene with Panova; this comes from the author—and so I worked out the whole "process" of smoking as a careful external signifier. Finding a

4.1. Stepan Kuznetsov as the iconic sailor Shvandya in *Lyubov' Yarovaya,* Maly Theater, 1926.

pack of cigarettes in a small bundle and selecting one, I look for matches first in my overcoat, then in the pockets of my dress, and I even rummage through the bundle only to find that there are none. And only after this, as if on compulsion, I cross to Panova's little table to get a light. Lighting up from the match Panova holds out to me, I don't thank her, not even with a nod of the head, and sink into a chair near her table, almost turning my back on her. I play the whole scene barely glancing at her, and only once—on the line "There are even worse parasites than lice"—I stare straight into her eyes and immediately, again withdrawing into myself, I take a long drag on the cigarette and after the words "They ate up my husband" I blow out the smoke, slowly knock off the ashes, and gazing straight ahead, after a pause, I add, "And made a meal of my little boy." And this sequence of movements, this purely outward form derived from inner experiences, but carefully worked out and set in their outward form, always "grabs" the audience in an extraordinary way. In that scene you can always "hear a pin drop." [. . .]

Konstantin Tverskoy, "*Lyubov' Yarovaya* at the Construction Workers' Theater," *Rabochy i Teatr* 11 (March 15, 1927), 11.

The clamorous Moscow success of K. Trenëv's new play, whose staging here in Leningrad caused a fight to break out between two theaters, the exceptional attention paid it by the theater critics—all this has really raised interest in the premiere and expectations of a remarkable production and a high quality of playwriting. It would seem that is precisely where Trenëv's play is very lame. *Lyubov' Yarovaya* is a rather disorganized series of scenes from the Civil War with characters typical of that period. A good literary text needs considerable abridgement and directorial adaptation. This, unfortunately, was not done . . . For all that, the production at the Construction

Workers' (staged by G. Énriton [a film actor]) was by and large met with a substantial and profitable reception. The great successes lie in the details, and the little that seems questionable is, evidently, easy to eliminate. Quite a pitiful impression is made by the play's finale—the device of bringing onstage military squadrons, once applied in *Semivzvodny*, is now old-fashioned and, besides, demands rather a large mass of people. The scene of the workers goes by superficially, and in general all the crowd moments are underdone. [...]

The Construction Workers' Theater—the leading theater in the suburbs—has already won over its audience. The attendance now is remarkably high. Presumptions of its modernity, its necessary and actual capabilities for carrying on serious *permanent* work in the suburbs, have been confirmed with distinction. Of course, to make a start, funding is indispensable. Under our conditions, attempts to organize theatrical enterprises without spending basic capital and to count solely on exploiting the labor of actors who take part are quite hopeless [...]

> John Dos Passos, "*The Mutiny* at the Trade Union Council Theater," in "Moscow theaters October and November 1928," *Theater 1929* (January 1929), 6–7.

The Mutiny, a chronicle play dealing with the revolt of a Red Army division in Turkestan in 1924, written by Furmanov,[7] who was the commissar against whom they revolted. The boundaries between the audience and the stage have disappeared altogether, the boundaries between life and art have disappeared. That's why this is the most important play in Moscow. It's probably no literary masterpiece; the action, in spite of the superb use of masses and the flexibility offered by a visibly revolving stage, a wide apron, and a gang-plank, is often as creaky and schematic as in a Drury Lane melodrama, but the thrilling vividness of its direct hammer blows opens up such possibilities for the workers' theater as have hardly been imagined. [...]

EVSEY OSIPOVICH LYUBIMOV-LANSKOY (actually Gelibter, 1883–1943), director at the Trade Unions Theater in Moscow from 1922, staged the work of young Soviet writers, with tumultuous crowd scenes and raw topicality.

> Lyubimov-Lanskoy at the MGSPS Theater. In B. G. Golubovsky, *Bol'shie malen'kie teatry* (Moscow: Izd. im. Sabashnikovykh, 1998), 143–44.

The production of *The Rails Are Humming* [1927], based on one of Kirshon's[8] first plays, immediately brought the spectator into an atmosphere of tense hard work.

---

7 Dmitry Andreevich Furmanov (1891–1926), Red Army commissar, whose best-known novels were *Chapaev* (1923) and *Mutiny* (*Myatezh*, 1924).

8 Vladimir Mikhaylovich Kirshon (1902–38) provided some of the most durable plays of the Five-Year Plan and, as secretary of RAPP, argued for greater psychological depth in Soviet drama. Arrested for Trotskyism 1937 and executed by firing squad.

Against a background of black velvet shone a glass roof leading far upstage, through which sunbeams penetrated into the factory shop. Downstage part of a locomotive undergoing repairs, at the sides high metal ladders. An unusual industrial beauty, a feeling of space, the rich atmosphere were appealing. The stage, freed of wings and backdrops, open to its limits, had been turned into the boiler shop of a big factory. I recalled the work of the designer Boris Volkov[9]—you could feel the scale of it. A symphony of metal, steam pipes, patches of light, people, living in the tense rhythm of workers—one of the directors was correct in saying of the production, "It's riveted nice and tight." A propos, Vl. I. Nemirovich-Danchenko, after he saw *The Rails Are Humming*, invited Volkov to his musical theater.

Today the play's plot seems primitive—a new "red" manager, a former locksmith in this same factory, Novikov combats technical obsolescence, Népmen attached to the factory, and outright saboteurs. We share Novikov's experiences, sympathize and rejoice in his final success. The actor Georgy Kovrov,[10] in the role of Novikov, was not a rock-ribbed Communist, moving through obstacles without quailing. He suffered, got nervous, put himself through hell—for several years it was forbidden to *perezhivat'*[11] a positive hero. [...]

"Summing up the season," *Novy Zritel'* 22 (1927), 12.

A. Khoral, "The Proletkul't Theater." All the work of the theater is based on contemporary drama and a system of orders. The playwrights *Afinogenov*,[12] *Krepusko, Byvaly,* and *Glebov*[13] are associated with the theater.

An abundance of widespread agencies place an expensive overhead on the theater and reduce the possibility of lowering prices. Besides this, the chief theatrical box offices—TRB and TsTK—are agencies that, for the most part, serve theaters that are part of their organizations. That is why theaters such as Proletkul't, which do not belong to any of the existing theatrical organizations, do not get the requisite attention for distribution. In this regard, the idea of forming its own controlling agency has been put forward.

9   Boris Ivanovich Volkov (1900–1970) began designing for the theater in 1922; at the MGSPS Theater 1924–40, where he designed a number of iconic Soviet plays, including *The Squall* (1925) and *Mutiny* (1927); after stints at various other companies, at the Maly Theater from 1951.
10 Georgy Ivanovich Kovrov (actually Kuvshinov, 1891–1961), acted at the MGSPS Theater 1924–29, 1931–34; Theater of Revolution 1930–31; Maly 1934–39; one of the first to play military types from the Civil War.
11 *Perezhivat'*—the Stanislavskyan concept of "living through" or "reexperiencing" emotions in acting.
12 The first plays of Aleksandr Nikolaevich Afinogenov (1904–41) dealt with historical industrial uprisings outside Russia; he ran the literary department of the First Moscow Worker's Theater of the Proletkul't 1927–29. He fell from grace 1935 and was arrested as a Trotskyite agent 1937, but was returned to favor. He died in the bombardment of Moscow.
13 Sergey Mikhaylovich Krepusko (actually Martynov) had his play *Along the Way (Put'-doroga)* staged by the Proletkul't October 7, 1926; Grigory Semënovich Byvaly (known as Lote) had his play *Rubber (Kauchuk)* staged 1927. Anatoly Glebovich Glebov (actually Kotel'nikov, 1899–1964) made his debut at the Maly with *Zagmuk* (1925), about a slave revolt in ancient Babylon; his play for the Prolet'kult was *Power* (1927), about the October Revolution.

4.2. Lyubimov-Lanskoy's staging of *Konstantin Terëkhin* (alias *Rust*) by V. Kirshon and N. Uspensky, a melodrama of Soviet youth, designed by Nikolay Man'shutin and G. F. Mukhin, Trade Unions Theater, Moscow, 1926. In this meeting of the Communist cell, the sign reads "Look Life Straight in Face. Do Not Be Afraid of Hard Work."

Of the eighty-eight performances staged in the season, eight special performances were sold out, three touring performances to the suburbs took place, and there were seven free performances. Up to 50 percent were complimentary tickets distributed to suburban box offices. The Prolet-study groups were provided with three hundred tickets every day at fifty kopeks a ticket for various areas of the auditorium and thirty kopeks for the matinees.

The issue of reducing prices is directly related to the future normal functioning of the theater at six performances a week, which is impossible without state support.

Dos Passos, "Moscow theaters November and December 1928," 7–8.

PROLETCULT is also a workers' theater. Originally the actors were amateurs from the factories, but now all but the supers are professionals.

Power, a chronicle play about the October revolution, is interesting as a combination of New Realism and Meyerhold. The idyllic lyrical scene where the red sailor goes to make propaganda in the villages seemed to me one of the best things I saw in Russia. All attempts at dramatic false tension have disappeared. The actors are no longer playing to the audience. The audience is a prolongation of the supers. The actors are as sure of themselves as Negro soft shoe dancers or headliner comedians in vaudeville. The sailor sits on a seesaw, playing round with the village girls, peasants who've deserted from Kerensky's army keep drifting in. The local landowner tries to stem the tide; a company of Kerensky's soldiers comes in to keep order and gradually melts away in the reds; everything is played very casually with singing and bits of dance; the gigantic struggle has reached a moment of balance, like a spring day in January, like the moments of infantile happiness soldiers at the front sometimes felt while the barrage rumbled like a steel roof over their heads. It's theater at its simplest, at its nearest to its roots in a dance or a religious festival or a lot of drunks amusing each other with comic pantomime. [...]

Nikolay Evreinov, "Summing-up the club season," *Novy zritel'* 20 (1927), 12.

The past year is characterized by a turning point as to improvement in the quality of club work in general and artistic work in particular.

The clubs staged a number of important things that were earlier worthy only of prof-theaters. For instance, the production of the opera *Rusalka*[14] in Reugov. Favorable notices by experts show that even serious things, of course after long preparation, are within the grasp of the club stage. Important serious plays were staged in other clubs as well: *Squall, Cement,*[15] and others from the classical and revolutionary repertoire. The same thing can be observed in the provinces.

The so-called minor forms were also developed in scenic work in the clubs. At the present time we are observing a crisis in the "Blue Blouse" and the living newspaper in general, but it is possible to say definitively that minor forms will emerge from the crisis only more firmly in place. There is already a rise in the club operetta (*Petrukha the Red Army Man* in the Vorovsky club) and the vaudeville (*The Quick-Witted Stocking-Darners* with the female textile workers), which enjoyed success with the working spectator. The recently held LGSPS competition of living newspapers showed that this genre is far from obsolete. [...]

THE FIRST AVATAR of TRAM (Theater of Working Youth) appeared in 1922 as an amateur studio at the House of Communist Education, headed by Mikhail Sokolovsky. Plays were not to be performed traditionally but rather "dramatized." In the words of the Proletkul't theorist Adrian Piotrovsky, "the dramatization of a remembered event or asserted slogan was the linchpin onto which were threaded actions, movements, dialogues and songs."[16] This theater form sought not "to show" but "to prove," "to persuade," to change lives. In 1925, it took on the name TRAM under the auspices of the Russian Association of Professional Writers (RAPP), and

---

14 *Rusalka* (1856) by A. S. Dargomyzhsky, based on Pushkin's poetic drama about a miller's daughter, seduced and abandoned, who turns into a water nymph. The first professional revival under the Soviets took place November 30, 1929.

15 A dramatization of *Tsement* by Fëdor Vasil'evich Gladkov (1925), a novel about gender equality among the workers in a new cement factory.

16 Adrian Piotrovsky, *Teatr. Kino. Zhizn'* (Leningrad: Iskusstvo, 1969), 93–97.

it took on the same opponents as the Proletkul't did: the classical and professional theater considered as a product of capitalist society. The narrow liaison between TRAM and the Komsomol organization assured it a rapid rise: eleven TRAMs in 1928, seventy in early 1930. The aim of the movement was to stage productions of political education illustrating from day to day the tasks imposed by the Party and the Komsomol. Although they had no mission to train professionals, the TRAMs gave their members a very extensive theatrical education. In 1928 the Leningrad TRAM was transformed into a professional troupe.

> S. Mokul'sky, "Amateur workers' theaters of Leningrad," typescript in Dana collection, Harvard Theater Collection. Stefan Stefanovich Mokul'sky (1896–1960) was a literary critic and theater scholar.

At present there are approximately 100 dramatic clubs and circles in Leningrad, consisting of up to 5,000 workers. This figure is double the total number of professional actors in Leningrad (as of January 1, 1928, there were 2,381 actors and 190 directors in Leningrad, according to data provided by Gubrabis). Club theaters cater to over a million viewers per month, while, according to ticket sales, the established professional theaters are patronized by only seven hundred thousand viewers, a huge percentage of whom are not laborers but white-collar workers, whereas the number of spectators not belonging to the working class is very low in dramatic clubs. The given data clearly show that club theaters serve the laborers of Leningrad far more than do professional theaters. If we add that the role of the club theater is expanding and enlarging, along with the number of spectators, while the professional theaters are constricted and lack full houses, the picture becomes crystal clear. The future undoubtedly belongs to the worker's club theater, which is flesh of its flesh with the proletarian masses. Which is precisely why the issues of improving the worker-actor's qualifications, of distinguishing the most talented individuals from the mass of amateurs and of creating a new group of professional worker-actors from among them, become especially important. Such work is being carried out and has already shown tangible results.

The primary cell of the worker's theater was the so-called "Amateur Theatrical Workshop" (Samodeyatel'naya teatral'naya masterskaya or Satemas), where thorough study-training work was carried on with the aim of improving the qualifications of the most capable members and of giving a professional technique to their work. At the same time, at this phase, members are still associated with their factory and study at the theater workshops only in their spare time. The amateur theatrical workshops later gave rise to worker's theaters, whose participants finally turned professional and were released from the factories. There are two such theaters in Leningrad: (1) the Worker's Theater of Leningrad's Proletkul't (Rabochy Teatr Leningradskogo Proletkul'ta or RTP) and (2) the Leningrad Theater of Youth Workers (Teatr Rabochey Molodezhi or TRAM).

The first of these emerged in 1925 from the Proletkul't's theater workshop and consists of workers taken from the plants with the intention of specializing in the art of acting. [...]

TRAM's move to professionalism is somewhat less distinct, as a specifically Komsomol theater, which originated the widespread theatrical workers' movement *solodezhi* which our critics christened "Tramism." TRAM is somewhere halfway between an amateur theater workshop and a worker's theater. Engaging the Komsomols in an everyday training routine and developing professional skills in them, TRAM, however, only partially takes its komsomols off the production line and, unlike RTP, does not go on to work on purely professional drama, but continues to maintain the traditions of amateur "minor genres," from which all the productions of their theaters grow. TRAM thus means to create a new type of professional theater by following a different path from the Proletkul't Theater, maintaining a strong link with the Komsomol organization and continuing to serve its daily needs. Both paths, however, lead to one and the same goal—to overcome the antithesis between professional and amateur theaters by means of a synthesis, which is envisaged as a new type of professional theater of the proletariat, which will eventually replace the pro theater inherited from the bourgeoisie. In this way, an important dialectical process is unfolding before our eyes. [...] As the tenth anniversary of the October Revolution rolls around, the workers' theaters can consider themselves as finally established. They are no longer a dream or a prediction but rather a totally *actual fact.* They are equal participants in the struggle for revolutionary theater, a struggle that hitherto was undertaken only on the left front of the professional theater. [...]

Meyerhold's *Inspector General*

Gogol's comedy *Inspector General* (*Revizor,* 1836, revised 1842) was considered by many the best Russian play ever written, a work every educated Russian knew by heart. Meyerhold, who dubbed himself "author of the spectacle," was offering a challenge in the profound transformations he wrought on it. He was not interested in yet another interpretation of the text but wanted to make it a compendium of the entire Gogolian world. To this end, he was inspired by the symbolist exegeses of the play that saw Khlestakov as a petty demon, his nullity bespeaking an existential void. Mikhail Chekhov's Khlestakov in the MAT production of 1921 had also impressed him by its freewheeling improvisation. Gone were the sparse scenic constructions and clown routines of earlier Meyerholdian shows; there was a recourse to real objects, not military impedimenta this time but antique furniture, polished mahogany doors, elegant props reminiscent of the prerevolutionary *Masquerade.* Gogol's five acts became fifteen episodes and his dusty provincial town a capital city. After a year's rehearsal *The Inspector General* opened on December 9, 1926, and became the most discussed, debated, decried staging of a classic for years.

V. Meyerhold, "Explication," October 20, 1925. In *Meyerkhol'd repetiruet* [Meyerhold rehearses] (Moscow: Artist-Rezhissër-Teatr, 1993), 2:40–45.

The difficulty of this production is that the actor works as the chief figure in it and the whole weight of the performance lies on the actor. Therefore the task is to find the easiest path for the actor so as to present the acting without any kind of complicated obstacle. The stage has to be so organized to make it easy for the actors to act. In *Bubus* it was easy to act because a musical background was created, hence a chain of technically structured mises-en-scène [...]

Act I, scenes 1 and 2. Onstage only a very big sofa that can accommodate a lot of people. They sit on it, squeezed tightly together, people of different sizes, fat and thin. [...]

These people sit, but the most important thing is that the stage space will be steeply raked and the furniture will be on an incline, sloped. In front of the sofa a table with polished surface, so close to the sofa that it cuts them off at the waist. Under the table, perhaps their feet may be visible. We will light it so that their faces and hands will be the most visible.

I'd like to remind you of Dürer's picture "Gesu che disputa con i dottori,"[17] in which the basic thing is the hands and faces. This provides a clear understanding of what I would like to achieve in *The Inspector General* in the sense of the acting style. No one has noticed this, but it is a very interesting problem of stage acting.

This play of the hands is also shown in *The Coward*.[18] There, the first duelist, who is later killed, builds the acting in this way. Like a conjurer, he wipes his glasses—makes a few passes to deflect attention; he is hoodwinking plain and simple, by making passes. His play with the cigar is beautiful.

The play of the hands and the associated mime will become the basic device of acting in this play. The polished surface of the table will provide a beautiful background for the play of a bunch of hands, which must be especially sharply visible on such a surface. [...]

> Ol'ga Bokshanskaya to Nemirovich-Danchenko, December 8, 1926, In *Pis'ma O. S. Bokshanskaya Vl. I. Nemirovichu-Danchenko* [Letters of O. S. Bokshanskaya to Vl. I. Nemirovich-Danchenko], ed. I. N. Solov'ëva (Moscow: Izd. Moskoskogo Khudozhestvennogo Teatra, 2005), 1:520–21.

During the day I went to Meyerhold's for the public preview of *The Inspector General*— and was so tired out by that performance that yesterday I was quite destroyed. It is impossible to call this show anything but a mockery of the public. Few of our folks sat it out to the end, but I decided conscientiously to see the whole thing—and paid for it with a headache. Tonight is the last preview, and tomorrow the show will open. Before it was shown, there was great interest in the production, because a great deal was said of those gimmicks Meyerhold would put in the play. But I think everyone will soon

---

17 Albrecht Dürer's oil on wood painting *Jesus among the Doctors* (1506) shows a meditative youth surrounded by grotesque old men.

18 *Trus'* (1914), a silent film based on a story by Aleksandr Kuprin and directed by Boris Glagolin and R. Ungern.

4.3. Meyerhold rehearses Zinaida Raykh as the Mayor's Wife in the interpolated scene in *The Inspector General*, in which lovelorn lieutenants pop out of the furniture, Meyerhold Theater, Moscow, 1926.

be disillusioned and the show will not make money, as was earlier expected. There's no way to give a brief report of the show, because it's all been so amplified. Both a new script (partly from Gogol's first manuscript, partly Meyerhold's invention) and new characters: an Officer in Transit, who follows in Khlestakov's footsteps, and a kind of charwoman, to whom Osip speaks his first monologue (Osip is a young fellow). And then the Mayor's dialogue in the last act with the merchants in this production is delivered by the Mayor alone, in the form of an address to imaginary tradesmen and the sacks, fish, and hams piled up on the table and sofa. Inserted into the show are ten officers lovelorn for the Mayor's wife, who burst into her room and out of the chest of drawers, and even—with a crash and a gunshot—out of something that looks like an aquarium. The play is broken into fifteen episodes, roughly five episodes to each section. Meyerhold calls himself "the author of the spectacle." Of course, music is introduced. This is how the finale is done: the Mayor's last monologue is delivered to the nonstop whistling of the policemen surrounding him. A doctor steps out from the side and holds a straitjacket. And suddenly all the characters pass in a row from one end of the stage to the other, in a kind of frenzied dance, then they cross, still dancing, into the aisle in front of the first row of seats, and meanwhile a canvas drop cloth with enormous letters—the gendarme's last line—reels down from above and hides the stage. The actors, moving in front of the first row, vanish through the side doors. When the drop has curtained the whole stage, they all issue from under it and run madly along the side aisles of the parterre. They run all around the parterre and disappear into opposite side doors. The drop cloth is raised and reveals onstage a frozen tableau of terrified officials and guests, but they are all wax figures, not actors. They are very well made. The audience applauds, and the living actors appear next to the wax figures. The music plays a fanfare. Meyerhold himself comes out, leads forth his assistants, applauds the troupe. Yes, it's possible to fool the audience to the top of their bent.

Benjamin, *Moscow Diary*, 11, 56–58.

December 9, 1926. . . . A violent argument breaks out [amid Viktor A. Shestakov, Asja Lācis, and Bernhard Reich[19]] in Russian about Meyerhold's production of *The Inspector General*. The major point of contention is his use of velvet and silk, fourteen costumes for his wife; the performance, moreover, lasts five and a half hours.

December 19, 1926. Even though it had been shortened by an hour following its premiere, *The Inspector General* still ran from a quarter to eight until midnight. The play was divided into three parts, with a total (if I'm not mistaken) of sixteen tableaux. Reich's many accounts had prepared me for the overall visual effect of the production. Nonetheless I was amazed at its extravagance. In fact, the most remarkable thing about the production was not its sumptuous costuming but rather the stage sets. With very few exceptions, the scenes were played on a tiny area of an inclined plane on which, at every shift of scene, the sets would change into different Empire-style mahogany decors with different furnishings. The net effect of this was the creation of a number of charming genre pictures, which is in accordance with the basic intent of this nondramatic, sociologically analytical production. People ascribe a great deal of importance to this production as an adaptation of a classical play for the revolutionary theater, but they also consider the experiment a failure. The Party, moreover, has come out against the production, and even the moderate review by *Pravda*'s theater critic was rejected by the editors. The applause in the theater was restrained, and perhaps this was due to the official line more than to the audience's actual reaction. Certainly the production was a feast for the eyes. But this is no doubt linked to the general atmosphere of cautiousness here when it comes to openly revealing one's opinions. If you ask people whom you barely know what they think of some insignificant play or film, the answer is that "the word here is this or that" or "people have mostly been of such and such an opinion." The guiding principle of this production, the concentration of the action into an extremely restricted area, creates an extraordinarily luxurious density of dramatic values, without, however, neglecting the acting dimension. The high point of all this came in a party scene, which was a masterpiece of staging. There were about fifteen people huddled in the tiny performance area, grouped between barely suggested pillars made of paper. (Reich spoke of the abolition of linear arrangement.) On the whole,

19 Bernhard Reich (1894–1972), Austrian-born playwright, director, and critic, Asja Lācis's life partner; became a Soviet citizen in mid-1920s.

the effect is like the architecture of a cake (a very Muscovite simile—only the cakes here could explain the comparison) or, better yet, like the grouping of dancing puppets on a musical clock whose chimes are played by Gogol's text. There is, moreover, a great deal of actual music in the play, and the little quadrille that occurs toward the end would be an attractive number in any bourgeois theater; in a proletarian one, it comes as something of a surprise. The latter's forms are most clearly evident in a scene in which a long balustrade divides the stage in two: the Inspector General stands in front of it, while the masses remain behind, watching his every movement and playing a very expressive game with his coat—now grabbing it with six or eight hands, now tossing it over the shoulders of the Inspector General as he leans against the parapet.

THE SYMBOLIST WRITER ANDREY BELY was more closely associated with Mikhail Chekhov and the Moscow Art Theater 2, for which he had adapted his Joycean novel *Petersburg* (1925). His admiration of Meyerhold was such that he offered him its counterpart *Moscow*. He would write a magisterial work on Gogol, published in 1934.

> Andrey Bely to Meyerhold, December 25, 1926, Moscow. In V. Meyerhold, *Perepiska* (Moscow: Iskusstvo, 1976), 256–58.

Dear and deeply respected Vsevolod Émil'evich, I didn't see you at the dress rehearsal of *Inspector General*; and kept silent; meanwhile, during these weeks, my mind has been working the whole time on that enormous body of material you offer as *The Inspector General*. And even now, at this remove, I see the contours of the whole, cleansed of the personal "*delights*" of the first moments and the "*weariness*" at the riches of the production (in every sense), and from a purely physical fatigue from a protracted performance, and from the great number of "idiotic" first-nighters. [...]

And only in the days that followed did the impression of *The Inspector General* pour forth, grow steadily, freed from the "*babble of voices*," the purely physical weariness (after all, the dress rehearsal ended at half past one in the morning). Now I can say firmly, simply, and clearly: Thank you for *The Inspector General*.

Actually: this is an event; actually, *The Inspector General* is being seen for the first time; and it might be worth troubling the grave of the late Gogol so that the deceased might rise from the grave and support you by his presence at the performance, because he would support you against that backbiting that for a whole week spewed from mouths in the newspaper columns. As if you had killed Gogol's laughter—that wholesome, merry laughter—and let loose symbolic deviltry in the play. [...]

All your attempts to move *The Inspector General* far in the direction of a screamingly funny [*khokhota-grokhota*] revue are only a manifestation of Gogol himself. And you provide this in the production superbly: the *placard* proclaiming the arrival of the official, the diabolical bounding around the room down to the straitjacket and the other details—everything resurrects *The Inspector General* to the thunder of "*the trumpets of the Apocalypse.*" This is what Gogol wanted; you are only extricating Gogol from the *cotton-wool* in which he had to muffle the *thunderous* action, so that in Nikolaevan Russia the Gogolian utterance could be more or less made possible: Gogol pretended to be a simpleton so that the bitterly toxic trenchant laughter would be muffled and only *laughter* would be heard. This whole line—the line of the transubstantiation of laughter and nothing but laughter in the prophetic utterance of Gogol, inspiriting, massacring—this whole line is impeccable in your *Inspector General.* And now, when many people are abusing you (because they are hit: some Gogolian dart has hit them), I would like to bark at the top of my lungs: "You're wrong: Meyerhold's production is an event (1) in the history of the Russian theater, (2) in the very understanding of Gogol."

I have lived Gogol all my life, I love him, he's always on my mind; but you have opened new horizons to me; I am seeing *The Inspector General* for the first time; and probably will be reading him for the first time. [...]

WALTER BENJAMIN attended the public debate on *The Inspector General* on January 3, 1927, and made a note of it in his journal; he later expanded that description to explain the controversy to the educated German reader.

Walter Benjamin, "Disputation bei Meyerhold [January 3, 1927]," *Die literarische Welt* 3, 6 (February 11, 1927), 3. Reprinted in *Gesammelte Werke*, ed. Tillman Rexroth (Frankfurt-am-Main, Germany: Suhrkamp, 1972), 4:481–83.

There is no doubt that Meyerhold is Russia's most distinguished director. But he has an unfortunate personality. Which is why a new version of *The Inspector General* has landed him in an unfortunate situation. Some tough weeks are in store for him now. One of the last literary directives of the [Communist] party is called Conquering the Classics. The masterpieces of Russian literature are, on one hand, to constitute the prestige of new Russia, and on the other, to be responsible for educating its hundreds of thousands of newly literate. Naturally the leading role in the full working-out of this falls to the theater. However, in Russia (as in Europe), there is only a dwindling number of "classic" plays. Anyone who selects one of them is staking a lot on a single card. When a year ago Meyerhold ventured Ostrovsky's *Forest* [*Les*], he won. This year with *The Inspector General* he lost. His achievement as director was also very considerable. But despite his radical revision, he did not conquer the play for the proletarian stage. On the contrary: no one could see in this theater anything that (with some cutting) could not be put on in some little playhouse on the Kurfürstendamm with a greater prospect of success. He also adapted the shape of the stage. On the steep rake of a mahogany centerpiece (*Aufsatz*) one little living picture after another was slid out. Naturally (naturally for Moscow, that is) all the furnishings were authentic in material and style. Every little item in the collection shouted out its glass case in a museum. Unheard-of was the extravagance with which he treated himself to human matériel. Everything that came on was densely packed together in an instant. This massing on the steep rake suggests in the event the influence of contemporary deflation. All that made this production problematic enough. Through the revision it became even more so. Not that the Russian director has that crippling, bred-in-the-bone respect for every writer's word fixed in black on white that is still current in Western Europe. What ruined the dramatic adaptation is not the act of revision per se, but how it turned out. It hounded the famous Gogolian laughter out of *The Inspector General.* Bobchinsky and Dobchinsky are not comic figures but the two-faced goblin of a nightmare, the leading figures are not Gogolian caricatures but the orchestra of a *Ghost Sonata*[20] before the fact. For this reason or others Party and press reject Meyerhold's work. To legitimize it (but also to gather his friends around him), Meyerhold made his own theater available for a disputation. The surprising progress of the evening was that a few persons spoke against *The Inspector General,* no one enthusiastically, and yet his opponents triumphed all down the line. Not Lunacharsky nor Mayakovsky nor Bely could save him. Meyerhold owed this to his unfortunate temperament. It was painful to watch the maneuvers of his friends in an attempt to come to the rescue of someone hopelessly sinking beneath the foaming tide of the popular mood. This went beyond *The Inspector General.* People wanted a highly celebrated name like Meyerhold not to give in to the lowest common denominator. The control lay in very capable hands. And the average level of the ordinary Russian public speaker is so high that even in a four-hour debate, on the whole, a bad speaker is followed by a good one. Mayakovsky is far and away the best. At the right moment he takes the audience in hand, for fifteen minutes acts the part of an intellectual rowdy who boxes a few rounds with it for the sheer pleasure of the fight and still knows how to stay reasonably objective. This sort of thing: "Anyway, he cast his wife in the best part. Protectionism?!"—"But what if he married her because she's a good actress!" And masterfully, stalwartly, he takes his seat again at the green speaker's table—Andrey Bely, the famous author of *Petersburg* and *Moscow.* He should be on exhibition in our literary–historical seminars: the romantic decadent in a velvet jacket and tie like something out of Gavarni.[21] You couldn't turn up his equal in all modern Paris. Here, on the most revolutionary stage in Moscow, he, the "eternal reader of Gogol," danced an old-fashioned gavotte. Hands, which in 1850 would have been filling an opium pipe, here splayed themselves imploringly before the audience. Then the "man of the people." Short trousers, Manchester jacket, riding boots, bass voice. "Where is the Gogol for the workers, the Gogol for the peasants? There's no point in discovering him for the bourgeoisie a second time." About midnight, people tempestuously called for Meyerhold. The applause on his entrance told him that there was still much to be won. But in under ten minutes he had lost any contact with the masses. The Opposition's slogan: "Moscow has its yellow journalists." Meyerhold exposed "agendas": secret conspiracies, acts of revenge. From the rows where the youths, the Komsomols, were sitting came the first whistles: "Dovolno" [Enough].

20 *The Ghost Sonata (Spuksonaten,* 1907), one of August Strindberg's "chamber plays."
21 Paul Gavarni (actually Sulpice Guillaume Chevalier, 1804–66), French graphic artist who skewered the manners and morals of the Parisian bourgeoisie.

Lots of people got up and left. In vain he clutched at the red file folders and tried to be impassive. A quarter of the auditorium is empty by the time he stops. To eradicate the bad impression, a couple of speakers are sent on after him. But the conflict is decided. Now the "Controversy over *The Inspector General*" will go through official channels. The journalists of Moscow have appealed to the Party. From now on, there is a front against Meyerhold.

ON JANUARY 27, 1927, the "fig-tree association" of writers devoted to Zamyatin put on an evening in honor of Meyerhold, where he was roasted with "Greetings from the Mestkom of Deceased Writers" by Evgeny Zamyatin and Mikhail Zoshchenko.[22]

Yury Annenkov, *Dnevnik moikh vstrech* (Moscow: Zakharov, 2001), 319–20.

Shocked by the second death of our late lamented N. V. Gogol, WE, the great writers of the Russian land, to avoid a repetition of deplorable incidents, propose to dear Vsevolod Émil'evich, with a view to bringing them back to life, to take on destroying the traditions of these our classics, whose obsolescent titles we have adapted to the present instant:

1. D. Fonvizin, The Mentally Defective Retard (formerly, The Minor).
2. A. S. Pushkin, A Course in Economics (formerly, The Miser Knight).
3. Ditto: Grishka, Leader of a Self-Styled Bloc (formerly, Boris Godunov).
4. M. Yu. Lermontov, The Petty-Bourgeois Party (formerly, Masquerade).
5. L. N. Tolstoy, Electrifying the Village (formerly, The Power of Darkness).
6. Ditto: El-Cee or Cee-El (formerly, The Living Corpse).
7. I. S. Turgenev, Four Weekends in the Country (formerly, A Month in the Country).
8. A. P. Chekhov, Can't See the Forest for the Trees (formerly, The Cherry Orchard).
9. A. S. Griboedov, Roar, Griboedov (formerly, Woe from Wit).
10. Comrade Ostrovsky insists on retaining his original titles: No Fool Like a Wise Fool, Talents and Admirers, It's a Family Affair, Paddle Your Own Canoe...

B. Mazing, "Meyerhold's speech at the Ac. Theater of Drama," *Rabochy i teatr* 5 (February 1, 1927), 8.

"The theater doesn't have to appeal to philistines!" was the admonitory slogan of the speech [...] Why do most plays nowadays dwindle into photographs of scenes from the People's Court? That's a place the philistine goes to with the same satisfaction as to the theater. Wouldn't it be better for the new regime in the theater to kick out the philistine spectator by building one last special "Philistines' Theater," a grandiose building where all kinds of matters brought before the People's Court will be investigated.

---

22 Mikhail Mikhaylovich Zoshchenko (1894–1958), humorist, much of whose material was performed in cabarets; in 1946 he was attacked as "alien to Soviet literature" but was rehabilitated 1953.

[...] "When I call for work on the classical repertoire, am I calling for a step backward?" many people ask. Indeed, it seems to be a familiar truism that to construct the scaffolding of a new culture, we must master and rework the best of the old cultural heritage. Reworking is not slavish copying. In classic works, there will always be material for the creation of a powerful modern performance.

[...] What the theater needs right now is not the tiresome grotesque and not a realism false to the stage. It needs to find a new, untheatrical realism. It needs to take, as Chaplin and Keaton have done in the movies, from the sum total of gestures, movements, behaviors, only what rings true for the masses, basing the staging on collective emotion. *The Inspector General* is built in the mode of realism, but only of a musical kind. The whole performance is a symphony, constructed according to the rules of musical composition.

The Inspector General has evoked references to mysticism and eroticism, as if there were any in the production. Unfortunately, here in Russia, the fantastical is often called mysticism, which is not the same thing. Without the fantastic, there is no creative work, no striving forward. And the assertion that the dummies in the production spell "mysticism" is truly absurd.

The same holds true for eroticism. To see such a thing in the production is possible only for someone who likes to read between the lines. [...]

S. Voskresensky, "*The Inspector General* and concerning *The Inspector General*," *Rabochy i teatr* 9 (March 1, 1927), 9.

In a speech about his production of *Inspector General*, Meyerhold explained the aim of his work to be the desire to oppose an earlier "amusing" treatment of *Inspector,* to give it a contemporary denunciatory one. It has to be said that he has not carried out this task. Almost nothing "denunciatory" has, in our opinion, been added, but a great deal has been diminished: first of all, the indifferent reception of the production. The failure in carrying out the tasks he set himself includes the remarkable difficulty in the reception of *Inspector*; it is extremely difficult to watch this production. The characteristics of the dramatis personae not only fail to emphasize the new type of treatment but seem likely, to some degree, to erase the satiric concept of the work. This chiefly concerns Khlestakov and the Mayor. If you accept the treatment of Khlestakov as the "principal mystifier," this does not gibe with the type of half-witted youth, a sort of "punk," who figured in the production. Perhaps this is supposed to be "contemporary," but it bears absolutely no relation to the characteristic times and types of the Nikolaean era. Equally improbable is the Mayor, a Mayor *of a county seat,* depicted as some kind of retired general. This last circumstance is directly connected with an obvious attempt to satirize not the bureaucratic small fry of the Nikolaean provinces but the bureaucratic bosses. Hence the luxuriousness of the staging uncharacteristic of the attributes of a county seat, and so forth. The whole meaning of the play contradicts this concept of the director, hence some of the general dissent clearly felt during the performance. [...] This production is reactionary in its very nature.

THE MASSIVE EFFORT put into *The Inspector* left Meyerhold sufficiently drained to turn over the direction of Tret'yakov's *Roar, China!* (*Rychi, Kitai!*) to one of his students, Vasily Fëdorov. A topical melodrama, with the British as the villains and Chinese coolies as the heroes, it was based on an incident in which a British gunboat demanded that two innocent Chinese workmen be executed for the accidental death of an American businessman. It opened on January 23, 1926. Almost immediately, Fëdorov disowned the production and resigned, complaining that Meyerhold had altered his staging beyond recognition. Even so, the production proved successful, touring widely, and its gunboat setting influenced a number of foreign revivals.

Basil Dean, *Seven Ages: An Autobiography 1888–1927* (London: Hutchinson, 1970), 293–94.

At Meyerhold's theater, originally a music-hall, no curtain, no draperies or scenery of any kind, stage-hands encouraged to lurk at corners of the stage to watch the show; artists, too, waiting to make their entrances. Something theatrical in the flaunting untheatricality. We are told the actors are called every morning for a daily work-out in a nearby gymnasium. Physical fitness is certainly necessary for actors continually running up ladders and leaping from rostrum to stage in the effort to add dimension to their performances. The play is an absurd melodrama called *The Cry of China* [sic]; propaganda against the gunboat diplomacy of Britain. At the back of the stage is a vast girder mast, and what purports to be the quarter-deck of the British gunboat, *Cockchafer*. At certain moments this contrivance is made to advance and to swing the muzzles of two large guns over the audience with menacing effect. In front of the gunboat is a tank of real water, and nearest the audience, platforms and steps for the incidents on shore. The British captain strides about his quarter-deck smoking an enormous briar pipe. When an American guest leaves the ship he has a dispute with a Chinese boatman, falls into the water, and is drowned. The captain demands two Chinese lives in place of his guest. He attends the public execution with a squad of marines to see justice done, still smoking pipe. [...]

Sergey Radlov, "Roar, China!" *Desyati let v teatre* (Leningrad: Priboy, 1929), 145–55.

The theme of Chinese events is so up-to-date, so exciting to every thinking person, that by itself it guarantees the play the spectator's taut attention. The shocking incident of the execution of boatmen innocent of the death of a white man would be capable of rousing the auditorium, even if couched as a newspaper bulletin. If before the start of any performance an actor came out and read the text of the just-received news that yesterday the captain of an English vessel demanded the execution of two members of the boatmen's union in the place of a fugitive ferryman, allegedly guilty of the murder of an American, such information, especially in these days of our remembrance of Sacco and Vanzetti,[23] would produce the most powerfully agitated reaction. In essence S. Tret'yakov evidently counted on such an effect when he wrote a very laconic, epically simple and unvarnished text.

The question is, is it enough in the theater to build a whole production out of such episodes with such simplicity and artlessness? Of course, to present the life of the East in the theater is a risky and difficult task. [...]

It was tempting to present the sounds of Chinese speech—at moments you seemed to be listening to original Chinese language—but this is the dead end of naturalism; the next words, spoken in Russian, sound somehow especially greasily Muscovite, and at times the Chinese call to mind Ostrovsky's merchants. There's something phony—the only slightly pidgin dialogue ("You pay, me pull") with the American, the same boatman articulately and with grammatical correctness discussing matters with his comrades, and the coolie boiler man, I suppose as the most aware, keeps talking and acting like the purest Russian with the least connection to the rest of the Chinese. And all the same, despite these defects—the scenes of everyday Chinese life were staged with a kind of painstaking mastery and often even tenderness. It is the most powerful thing in the performance. The European portion was far inferior. Admittedly, Tret'yakov deliberately wrote it in a schematic and rectilinear fashion. But, staged in the spirit of the most elementary and intentional grotesque, it splits the production into two halves completely disjunctive in style. By all means, offer a contrast, but do not paint some of the figures in oils, some in scene paint. When a group of "lived-through," "lifelike" Chinese is encountered by a couple of terrified male and female tourists (playing neither a character nor an attitude to the character), the result is a completely incomprehensible combination of a clichéd poster with a good painting of the Repin[24] school.

When the Chinese are so human, without inflated and cardboard heroism (the boatman's fear of death and self-sacrifice!), why depict the Europeans as such bogeymen for little children? Really, if they were to speak their nastiness more casually and quietly, without barking, screaming, and hammering on every word (that is, a bit more like Englishmen!), they would be more terrifying and more convincing and would not break with the realistic tendencies of the whole production. How discomfiting to see in Meyerhold's theater an application of devices already outworn in all the amateur drama clubs, and the bourgeoisie, rotting in the inevitable foxtrot, evokes not anger but dismay. [...]

---

23 The 1921 trial of Nicolo Sacco and Bartolomeo Vanzetti, Italian immigrants to the United States, for bank robbery and murder became an international cause célèbre because of their anarchist views; they were executed 1927, and the Soviet Union invited Sacco's wife for a visit.

24 Il'ya Efimovich Repin (1844–1930), realist painter and sculptor, member of the Peredvizhniki or Itinerants school, famous for his genre scenes and portraits of Russian celebrities.

The Two Moscow Art Theaters

In 1925, Stanislavsky brought out a book of memoirs, *Moya zhizn' v iskusstve* [*My Life in Art*, a revision and expansion of an English version he had published in America in 1923], which introduced the reading public to his ideas on acting. His so-called system was less a philosophy than a patchwork of professional jargon and psychological terms that launched several durable concepts ("the super-task," "the magic if," "the through action") to codify a standard language for actors. The main purpose was to uncover the sources of the actor's creativity, what he referred to as "re-experiencing" (*perezhivanie*).

This transitional period saw the Moscow Art Theater finally manage to recover much of its creative vitality. Stanislavsky experienced an upsurge of comic flair in his productions of Ostrovsky's *Ardent Heart* (1926) and Beaumarchais's *Marriage of Figaro* (1927), the latter purportedly interpreted as a revolutionary statement. Aleksandr Kugel's *Nicholas I and the Decembrists* and a French satire on profiteers, *Merchants of Glory*, were less well received. The Art Theater convinced the Ukrainian physician-turned-writer Mikhail Bulgakov to adapt his novel *The White Guard* into a play. The result, *Days of the Turbins*, turned out to be highly controversial.

Benjamin, *Moscow Diary*, 11, 25.

December 9, 1926. . . . Stanislavsky's staging of a White Guard play; how it was initially submitted to the board of censors, only one of them taking notice of it and returning it, recommending certain modifications. Then months later, having made the necessary modifications, the play is finally performed for the censors. Banned. Stanislavsky to Stalin: I'm ruined, all my capital was tied up in that play. Stalin deciding: "the play is not dangerous." It premieres, protested by the Communists, who are kept at a distance by the militia.

December 14, 1926. The naturalistic style of the sets was remarkably good, the acting without any particular flaws or merits, Bulgakov's play itself an absolutely revolting provocation. Especially the last act, in which the White Guards "convert" to Bolshevism, is as dramatically insipid as it is intellectually mendacious. The Communist opposition to the production is justified and significant. Whether this final act was added on at the request of the censors, as Reich claims, or whether it was there all along has no bearing whatsoever on the assessment of the play. (The audience was noticeably different from the ones I had seen in the other two theaters. It was as if there were not a single Communist present, not a black or blue tunic in sight.)

Aleksandr Orlinsky, "Theater: The Civil War on the stage of the MAT. ('Days of the Turbins'—'The White Guard')," *Pravda* (October 8, 1926); reprinted in *Moskovsky Khudozhestvenny Teatr v russkoy teatral'noy kritike 1919–1943*, ed. O. A. Radishcheva and E. A. Shingareva (Moscow: Artist. Rezhissër.

4.4. Act IV, scene 1, of *Days of the Turbins* by Mikhail Bulgakov, directed by Il'ya Sudakov under Stanislavsky's supervision and designed by N. P. Ulyanov, Moscow Art Theater, 1926.

Teatr, 2009–10), 1:193–94. Aleksandr Robertovich Orlinsky (actually Krips, d. 1938?) was an influential collaborator of Glavrepertkom and critic; editor of *Sovremenny Teatr* 1927–28. He was repressed during the purges of the 1930s.

The whole "historical action" ends happily to general satisfaction with a petty-bourgeois wedding of the heroine, separated from her husband, who betrayed his White Guard duties, and falling right into the arms of the former Hetman's adjutant, a jolly opportunist and singer. Just as in goody-goody American films . . . The only problem is that the play comes across as a tendentious display of pseudo-mass-White heroism, idealizes the White Guard, perverts, in essence, the era of the Civil War, creates a conciliatory and romantic aureole around the professional White officer class, so cruelly and deservedly punished by history and the revolutionary proletariat. They will say in mitigation: there is spread over all the action of the heroes a thick, greasy layer of squalid philistinism, which comes to a climax in the last act; but as a matter of fact, this philistinism, oozing from the author's inner being, is so presented onstage by the theater, which unfortunately bears a close likeness to its author, that this only contributes to the emotional conciliation of the spectator with the characters. The efforts of author and theater clad the play's tendentious conception not only in heroics but even in exculpatory humor and virtue. What could have produced such a cruel perversion of *artistic truth,* which was always the MAT's pride and joy? [. . .]

A POLEMICAL DEBATE about *Days of the Turbins* that involved Mayakovsky and Kirshon took place at the House of the Press on February 7, 1927. Stanislavsky responded at the All-Union Congress of Theater (May 9–13, 1927), complaining that the effort to implement new policies was leading to a dearth of plays. Lunacharsky, unconcerned by the success of *Turbins* with audiences, chastised the Repertory Committee at the meeting on theater questions called by the Central Committee of the CPSU. Vilified by the critics, the play was finally taken off in 1929.

> Anatoly Lunacharsky, *Puti razvitiya teatra* (Moscow: Teakinopechat', 1929), 23–24.

You let it happen. And after the theater had spent thousands on it, and the actors had worked into their roles, you decided to take off a play that had got this far thanks to your ... collusion! What could we say? That our Repertory Committee ... allowed *Days of the Turbins* up until the dress rehearsal and did not stop it before there had been enormous expenditures? The morale of the theater would have suffered a blow that would have had worldwide significance. Could we have said that, despite all this, we were forced to correct the error of the Repertory Committee in regard to the state and the theater? ... The People's Commissariat of Enlightenment had a discussion about it and decided that, under these circumstances, *Days of the Turbins* must be allowed. We decided to greet the play with certain criticisms. [...] Certainly the production was a feast for the eyes. But this is no doubt linked to the general atmosphere of caution here when it comes to openly revealing one's opinions. If you ask people whom you barely know what they think of some insignificant play or film, the answer is: "the word around here is this or that," or "people have mostly been of such and such an opinion."

UPSET by the *Turbins* controversy, Stanislavsky tried to avoid contemporary issues and backslid in his choice of the creaky melodrama *The Two Orphans* (*The Sisters Gerard*) for his next production, on the grounds that it took place on the eve of the French Revolution. The proletarian theater groups had no patience with the Art Theater's avoidance of reality. In 1927 the MAT toured to Leningrad with an outdated repertoire.

> N. Konsky, "*Uncle Vanya*," *Rabochy i Teatr* 23 (June 7, 1927), 5.

Unabashed, [the MAT] comes before the new spectator with *Uncle Vanya*, with a mood so far from modern, a play of Chekhov so far from the whole ideology of our day and so removed to a sad page of Russian reality, to the leaden life of spiritual vegetation of the country, to the unendurable atmosphere of stagnation. This Chekhov polarity, with its twilight life, hopelessness and tragic trauma, with its superfluous people, that whole nightmare world of impotence and perplexity of the 1880s and 1890s, has sunk into the distant past and is completely foreign to the modern spectator. [...]

The spectator of today no longer knows those tears that the Chekhovian shadows once evoked; they have lost their rich, gloomy coloration, they are gone with the wind, and what is gripping all over again is the joy, the high excitement at the wonderful theatrical technique, in the presence of that living poetry, which the artists of the stage so carefully revealed in Chekhov's play. [...]

Korneev, Shebalov, Pavlenkov, "*Rabkors* on the MAT," *Rabochy i Teatr* 24 (1927), 7.

After the theater presented Hamsun's play *At the Gates of the Kingdom*,[25] one can and must speak not about *how* the Art Players perform but *what* they perform. It's 1927 and these plays have an "industrial work record" of fifteen to twenty years. Ten years of proletarian revolution and two and a half decades from the day of the first performances of *Tsar Fëdor*.[26] Somehow none of this connects with our times or sinks into the consciousness of a contemporary. Ten years have gone by since the embittered war of the old capitalist world with the new world a-borning, which found expression in our Soviet regime, but this struggle has passed by the Art Theater: in the old auditorium no echo resounds of the fight of dying and borning worlds. In an epoch of titanic building, such petrified inertia of the theater, congealed as it were on the heights of artistic achievement, is not only incomprehensible but can hardly find a justification in the history of the theater. [...]

We welcome the visit of the MAT to the workers' district, the desire to show its rare mastery to dwellers on the outskirts—all the same we have to say that the Moscow Art Theater in its present form represents an enormous artistic collection, like a treasure house of stage experience, like a museum. But nothing more.

The theater's ignorance of contemporaneity makes it a theater of a bygone era, far from modern life.

The Art Theater can be called modern only when it speaks the language of a revolutionary playwright, the language of the present day.

THE YEAR 1927 marks the first genuine step toward transforming the Moscow Art Theater into a Soviet institution with *Armored Train 14-69* by Vsevolod Vishnevsky, performed to celebrate the tenth anniversary of the Soviet regime. Its protagonists are Bolshevik partisans in Siberia during the Civil War. Kachalov, in the role of the partisan leader, and Khmelëv, in the role of the Bolshevik intellectual, created characters whose images were to become iconic. The play is regarded by many historians as marking the beginning of the Sovietization of the Art Theater.

25 Knut Hamsun's *At the Gates of the Kingdom* (*Ved Rigets Port*, 1895) had been produced at the Moscow Art Theater before the Revolution, with Vasily Kachalov as its Nietzschean hero.
26 *Tsar' Fëdor Ioannovich* (1864), a blank-verse chronicle play by Aleksey Konstantinovich Tolstoy; it was banned until 1898, when it was simultaneously staged by Suvorin's Maly Theater in St. Petersburg and by the Moscow Art Theater, as the latter's very first production. Its rich costumes and choral singing remained a showpiece.

4.5. *Armored Train 14–69* by Vsevolod Ivanov, directed by Il'ya Sudakov under Stanislavsky's supervision and designed by Viktor Simov, Moscow Art Theater, 1927. The scene on the church roof: the American soldier in down right, in eyeglasses and puttees, and Nikolay Batalov as Vaska Ukorok is beside him.

Nikolay A. Abalkin, *Sistema Stanislavskogo i sovetsky teatr* [Stanislavsky's system and Soviet theater] (Moscow: Iskusstvo, 1954), 205.

[Nikolay Khmelëv dissociated the Bolshevik character Peklevanov from stereotyped "Party members."] Every tendency to declamation was removed from the character. Peklevanov appeared on the stage unpretentiously, spoke in a low voice, was near-sighted, and seemed odd, but beyond his outer sociability, there were concentration, a good mind, and a gentle spirit. All this seemed much more convincing than theatrical heroism, pathos, and declamation.

André Van Gyseghem, *Theatre in Soviet Russia* (London: Faber and Faber, 1943), 38–43.

Naturalism runs rampant and only falls short in perfection in its own particular *métier* in the design of the room [in Act One]. It is shapeless and without point...it straggled across the stage untidily and is masked-in untidily by two false prosceniums that give it a slipshod air. In direct contrast to this is the minute attention to detail...the furniture, pictures, and all properties in the room are chosen with the nicest sense of period [...] The acting, too, is in tune with the naturalism of the setting. [...]

But as the play continues and the main action shifts over to the activities of the partisans [...] we experience a growing sense of disappointment, of dissatisfaction. It is not the acting which worries us—that is impeccable—it is that the theatrical form of naturalism is the wrong medium for this play. There is no unity of form and content.

[In the railway embankment scene] it is an embankment of canvas and wood painted to resemble so closely as possible the rocks and stones of reality, and consequently attracting our attention more sharply to its falsity. The slope is padded to the shape of rocks in the manner of scenery fifty years ago. We look at it flatly, from a two-dimensional viewpoint. There is none of the urgency and flow of steel rails sweeping across the country. When the poor little Chinaman creeps up the slope and lies down in front of the advancing train we are merely watching him do it, whereas we should feel that those thundering wheels rushing nearer and nearer will tear across us, too, in another minute. [...]

The naturalism of the setting tends to romanticize the scene, and [...] contradictions of this nature leap out at one throughout the entire play, and are to some degree softened in the scene on the church roof. [...]

AUDIENCES THRILLED to the scene in which, on the church roof, partisan Vaska Okorok propagandizes a captured American soldier (neither knows the other's language). This is the first mention of the name "Lenin" on a Soviet stage. Stanislavsky directed the actor to pronounce it "as the most treasured, most precious, most important thing in life... for you must put into speaking the word Lenin your soul, your love for humanity and your country."[27]

> Vsevolod Vishnevsky, *Bronepoezd 14-69*, in Konstantin Trenëv, Vsevolod Ivanov, and Vsevolod Vishnevsky, *P'esy* (Moscow: Moskovsky rabochy, 1979), 121–22.

OKOROK (*suddenly waves his arms happily, beckons the American toward him, and yells right in his face*): Hey, you, fellow!... Listen... Le-nin... Lenin...
AMERICAN: Lenin... Hurrah!
OKOROK (*strikes his own chest*): Us, you bum, we're the Soviet republic!
AMERICAN: Republic... Hurrah! [...]
(*Okorok brings an icon of Abraham going to sacrifice Isaac out of the church.*)
OKOROK: Listen. This one here, with the knife—that's a bourgeois. [...]And this one here, this young fellow lying tied to the logs—that's the proletariat. Savvy? Proletariat...
AMERICAN: Proletariat? Me worker from Detroit auto works! Worker... me... worker... motor car! [...] Down with imperialism!

27 Quoted in A. Ya. Trabsky, ed., *Russky sovetsky teatr 1926–1932. Dokumenty i materialy. Chast' pervaya* (Leningrad: Iskusstvo, 1982), 184–85.

Stalin, a shrewd judge of plays, not least from the political standpoint, had no illusions about *Armored Train's* deviations, but defended it and its author on February 12, 1929, in a speech at a meeting with Ukrainian writers, when he repeated his earlier opinions about Bulgakov as well. Katerina Clark and Evgeny Dobrenko, with André Artizov and Oleg Naumov, *Soviet Culture and Power: A History in Documents 1917–1953* (New Haven, Conn.: Yale University Press, 2007), 61–63. © 2007 by Yale University.

Take Vsevolod Ivanov's *Armored Train*. He's not a Communist, Vsevolov Ivanov. Maybe he considers himself a Communist [*noise, comments*]. Well, he's a sham Communist [*laughter*]. But that hasn't kept him from writing a good piece that has great revolutionary significance, its educational significance is indisputable. What would you say—is he right wing or left wing? He's not right wing or left wing because he's not a Communist. You can't apply purely Party measures mechanically to the writers' sphere.

Stanislavsky interviewed by Theodore Dreiser, November 19 and 22, 1927. *Dreiser's Russian Diary*, ed. T. P. Riggio and J. L. W. West III (Philadelphia: University Pennsylvania Press, 1996), 113–17, 130. © 1996 by the University of Pennsylvania Press. Reprinted by permission of the University of Pennsylvania Press. The eminent American novelist Theodore Dreiser (1871–1945) was a dedicated socialist who had taken part in a number of progressive causes; his visit to the Soviet Union in 1927 resulted in his book *Dreiser Looks at Russia* (1928).

Decorations and settings have been much enriched since the revolution, but to the inner art of the actor, the revolution has brought nothing. To the surface actor's art has been added,—movement, gymnastics, dancing, singing, all very valuable. [. . .] Our theater uses only such decorations as support the art of the actor: for the futurist actor we use futurist decorations.

"Has communism produced any really good plays?" *I asked.*

"No, but as chronicles, *The Days of the Turbines* [sic] and *The Armoured Train* are good, and a new play in preparation in our theater by Leonov,[28] is really of the best. *How soon I would be able to do it I cannot say.*"

And then he added:

"Art itself is organic and therefore slow to change, but the revolution brought many changes in content. Art will play, and is already playing, a big role politically and educationally in *Russia.* In every factory there is a theater, in every workers' club a theatrical circle. All Russia now plays.

[. . .] *Stanislavsky's secretary wanted to know if I would not give them a play. I suggested the* American Tragedy (N.Y. Play form) *and promised to submit a script.*[29]

28 *Untilovsk* (1927) by Leonov was a dark drama about an icebound backwater, a refuge for social outcasts, that has a hard time coming to terms with change; after 181 rehearsals, it ran little more than a week before being banned.

29 He did so, but when the MAT considered staging *An American Tragedy* in 1931, it turned to Erwin Piscator's adaptation. Legal problems prevented it from going forward.

AS THE First Moscow Art Theater struggled to take on an acceptable Soviet profile, the Second Moscow Art Theater was drifting further into the eddies of Party
censure and critical anathema. Both its choice of plays and its production style
were condemned as reflections of Mikhail Chekhov's adhesion to the teachings
of Rudolph Steiner and anthroposophy. This was considered a direct challenge
to the government's policy of atheism. *Hamlet* and Andrey Bely's dramatization
of his novel *Petersburg* were taken as provocations, overindulgence in mysticism.
Oresteia was the last straw.

> Sadko, "Aeschylus flops at the MAT 2," *Zhizn' iskusstva* 3 (January 18, 1927), 8.
> Sadko was the pseudonym of Vladimir Ivanovich Blyum (1877–1941), critic
> and head of the theater and music section of Glavrepertkom; he savagely at-
> tacked Bulgakov, the MAT, and Meyerhold and proclaimed satire an enemy
> of the Soviet Union.

If you seriously believe that God, fate, immutable truth, etc., exist and "toy with mankind," that there are extraterrestrial entities with objective existences, then you have to
set them in motion so that . . . we shake in our boots with fear. But even the MATians live
in the twentieth century, in a godless Soviet nation . . . Besides, they know that however
much they try to terrify the modern spectator with god ("heathen" or "Christian") or
the Fates or Moira (in capital letters!), no one's going to be scared by these bogeymen.
No wonder that when they put on those passages in the tragedy where any decent
Greco-Roman ancient would feel quite "shaken to the core" à la Aristotle, the action
on the Soviet stage slumps to an almost comic level. [. . .]

For us religion is the absence of political thought and any other rather elementary
literacy. Where are we supposed to get a tendency to "be shaken to the core"?

Perhaps for someone the spectacle of an intellectual who learned nothing in the
October Revolution, which he's been chattering about for many years, and is bogged
down in the emigration, might seem a subject worthy of Aeschylus—we need no
"tragic" motivations to explain this: we scan this "tragic hero" from top to toe; for us
it's a "comic" subject.

And you won't scare us with any Moira, insofar as we long ago brought all those
transcendental gimcracks down to earth. Wherever biology and sociology exist, when
we've recast the roles of the ancient Greco-Roman gods with all manner of reflex behaviors and industrial relations, there's no time and place for the "pathos" of tragedy.
Ours is another kind of "pathos!" [. . .]

"In the lower depths of the MAT 2," *Zhizn' Iskusstva* 14 (April 5, 1927), 1–2.

The Sovietization of the theater is a long and complicated process. And the 10-year
experiment has shown that the administration's equipping this or that theater with

party forces, the presence of an embryonic Soviet community in the form of the Mestkom, clubs, MOPR[30] cells, Il'ich corners [reading rooms], etc., are still no guarantee of the authentic Sovietization of the theater. We see a bunch of the greatest theaters, outwardly, seemingly, sufficiently Sovieticized and, at the same time, dispirited by the backwardness and anachronism of their products.

In short, "revolution from above" is still not enough—one needs a regeneration of the fabric of *theatrical everyday life,* a certain "revolution from below." It is necessary that *inside the theater* there is a living force, which, relying on the forms of the new community, would realize the "revolutionary" in an organized way. A whole series of reasons hampers the process of Sovietization of theatrical everyday life, so that on the tenth anniversary of October the extratheatrical relations represent quite a special microcosm—with a structure, worldview, and traditions that frequently originated in the days of Shchastlivtsev and Neshchastlivtsev.[31]

But history penetrates even this decrepit world. In this respect the recent events taking place at the MAT 2, to the astonishment of the entire Moscow theatrical community, are especially noteworthy.

For the last few months everyone has known that a sort of "opposition" has taken shape within the MAT 2. Recently fragments of news of this began to appear in the press. The opposition group is very small in number. It is headed by the actor Diky and consists, in addition, of six persons in all: Klyucharev (*predmestkom* [chair]), Volkov, Pyzhova, Bibikov, Muzalevsky, and Tsibul'sky.[32]

The opposition fomented a "mutiny" against the so-called rightful heads of the theater—the administration, headed by Chekhov. The opposition group put up a struggle for a more wholesome atmosphere in the everyday life of the theater, to turn its face to *Soviet contemporaneity* against the ever more sharply defined tendency of its repertoire to mysticism, idealism, etc., an atmosphere that is clearly leading the theater's work into an inevitable dead end. At the same time the opposition has intended to organize possibilities to realize the Sovietization of the MAT 2 not only de jure but finally de facto. But the administration succeeded quickly in rallying round itself the overwhelming majority, and the opposition failed to achieve not only a voice in the media of self-government but even . . . roles in the latest productions.

"If you don't beat 'em—the ox and the mare won't budge."

And suddenly a scandal broke out in the noble MAT family. The press published an open letter from the administration of the MAT 2 to the whole Soviet community by Chuprov,[33] an actor of that theater.

30 Mezhdunarodnoe Obshchestvo Pomoshchi Revolyutisoneram (International Russian Red Aid), an organization to support revolutionary movements.

31 Shchastlivtsev and Neshchastlitsev (Fortunate and Unfortunate) are the strolling comedian and tragedian who bring about a happy ending in Ostrovsky's *The Forest.*

32 Actors in the First Studio and MAT 2: Viktor Pavlovich Klyucharev (1898–1957), Leonid Andreevich Volkov (1893–1976), Ol'ga Ivanovna Pyzhova (1894–1972), who quarrelled with Mikhail Chekhov and joined the Theater of Revolution, Boris Vladimirovich Bibikov (1900–1986), Georgy Vasilevich Muzalevsky, and Mark Il'ich Tsibul'sky (actually Tsyvul'sky).

33 Mikhail Pavlovich Chuprov (1893–?), actor at the MAT 2 to 1927.

This is not so much a letter as almost the hysterical cry of a suffocating man. And the appearance of this is all the more unexpected and impressive in that, until now, the actor did not belong to the opposition. The effect produced was remarkably powerful. The greatly splintered majority closed ranks even more tightly and united with the administration, having felt the growing danger. Editorial pages were bombarded with resolutions, refutations, expressions of indignation, etc.

Chuprov in his letter accuses Chekhov and the administration with the establishment and jealous maintenance of the unwholesome regime, destroying the theater as a collective, and carefully keeping it from any contemporary influence. Has this regime actually been consciously advanced by Chekhov and the administration subservient to him? Does it have a place in a theatrical "fellowship"? Perhaps there is a connection between the depressing atmosphere of the theatrical regime and the suicide of the actor Vereshchagin? Is everything living actually denatured and stifled there? All these questions are to be answered by a special commission, created to investigate this incident.

The whole Soviet theatrical community is awaiting its definitive answer. At the moment it is important for us to note the thing in this letter of Chuprov that the MAT 2 opposed and that for a long time now has been a subject for notice and discussion in the theatrical press: the sway of the disheartening atmosphere in this theater, expressed both in the attraction to the mystical interpretation even of wholesome plays and characters, to a repertoire more or less saturated with "idealism," and that long-drawn-out and hopeless repertorial crisis that this theater, so rich with talents, is experiencing. Chuprov's letter lifts the curtain on the internal life of this theater and demonstrates its specifically anthroposophical atmosphere, which has enveloped everyone and everything there.

On the other hand the press demonstrated the connection between the anthroposophical leanings of the leaders of the theater (Andrey Bely, close to the theater through *Petersburg*,[34] as everyone knows, is an inveterate Steinerite) and their theatrical practice. In one article, "Flirting with the Divine," it is shown, e.g., that the interpretation of Hamlet proceeds from an idea about Hamlet by R. Steiner himself... Let every man be foolish in his own fashion, but, when the Soviet theater is transformed into a sort of citadel of reactionary, depressive "sects," when its performances are transformed into organized propaganda for "god-bothering" [*bozhenki*] in all its guises, then a great deal becomes understandable. The MAT 2, with its brilliant talents and internal decay, reminds us of that rich man whose luxurious garb concealed a fatal bleeding ulcer. "Neither will he quicken nor will he die." Not to depart from the circle of religious phraseology, let's say that talents will not be hidden in the earth but, on the contrary, will be transplanted to another healthy organism and will be given a lush Soviet growth.

The Soviet community is able to uproot anything harmful to the organization of Soviet theatrical culture.

34 Although far from a success, Bely's dramatic adaptation of his novel of the 1905 Revolution, *Petersburg* (1925), was astonishing for Mikhail Chekhov's performance as Senator Ableukhov. Chekhov was a devotee of the anthroposophy of the Austrian mystical philosopher Rudolf Steiner (1861–1925).

Mikhail Chekhov to Glavrepertkom, September 22, 1927, Moscow. In M. Chekhov, *Vospominaniya*, in *Literaturnoe Nasledstvo* [Literary legacy] (Moscow: Iskusstvo, 1986), 2:343–44.

The Peerless Beauty (*Krasa nenaglyadnaya*), a fairy-tale pantomime.

The production will consist of a pantomime performed to music. It will differ from an ordinary pantomime by the fact that at a few climactic moments the performers will speak necessary explanatory phrases.

The material in the scenario offers a wide possibility to bring out the profundity and native beauty of folk creativity; previously, the theater's attempts to reveal this went no further than the depiction of clichés petrified over time. The picturesqueness, the bright and rich Russian fantasy, the combination of lyric moments with the melodramatic reality of the situations, wholesome Russian humor and an abundance of the quasi-tragic—these are elements that comprise the proposed fairy tale. All this sets the theater new tasks for the display of folk creativity. The tempo of the events depicted is bound to have the lustiest and merriest effect on the audience.

The artistic goal of the production is to develop the actors' technique along three basic lines:

a. Musicality, rhythmicality, and metricality in movement.

b. Artistic speech related to the musical shaping of the production.

c. A search for aesthetic forms of movement, words, and sounds.

In addition, the production will pursue the goal of abandoning the usual stage devices, ordinarily used in opera and pantomime (ballet), taken separately.

The aforementioned concept of the production is to be an artistic secret, not advertised in publicity.

I earnestly request that a reply be forthcoming, because work has got to begin now, in view of its complexity and the extended time it will take. [...]

Glavrepertkom to Mikhail Chekhov, October 17, 1927.

The attempt of the scenario *The Peerless Beauty* to bring out the profundity and native beauty of folk creativity must be held to be a failure ...

Other Stages

In this interim, for all the uncertainty of the political outcome, theaters continued to function with much the same freedom they had under the NÉP. Several important experiments and polished productions took place in these years.

At the Leningrad House of the Press, which he headed, Igor' Terent'ev staged *Foxtrot* by Vasily Andreev, his own play *The Nodule*, and, in 1927, Gogol's *Inspector General* and *Natal'ya Tarpova* from the novel of Sergey Semënov.[35] After Meyerhold's *Inspector*, Terent'ev's version seemed especially freakish and dangerous, with

35 Another adaptation of the novel *Natal'ya Karpova* would later be staged at the Kamerny Theater in 1929, with the author's collaboration.

characters breaking into song (everything from gypsy ballads to Rimsky-Korsakov) and wearing "speaking" costumes, emblematic of their functions.

K. A. Guzyni to K. L. Rudnitsky, after March 20, 1984. In Konstantin Rudnitsky, "Replika Terent'eva," *Moskovsky Nablyudatel'* 7–8 (1995), 78–93.

I. About *Natal'ya Tarpova.*

1. Since this was a staging of a novel by Semënov, sometimes the actors talked about themselves and their experiences in the third person, and then addressed their partners in the name of the characters they were playing. At the time this device was an innovation, but it was seldom employed in the performance and did not get in the way of the spectator's reception.

2. How was the mirror used? First, it was not a gimmick [...] but a very witty directorial concept for one of the scenes in the production. It looked like this: the episode took place on a train. Downstage there was a cross section of a corridor in a railway car, whose wall stretched from wing to wing, along the footlights, and was about two meters high. Center stage was a door to a compartment. Characters, entering through it into the compartment were hidden behind a door, and at that moment, like the lid of a box, the roof of the compartment (a big mirror the whole width of the compartment) rose at a 45-degree angle. In this mirror, which reflected the action of the character inside, the spectator continued to follow the course of the action. So far as I recall, the mirror was used only in this episode. [...]

II. About *Inspector General.*

1. There was no curtain for the production. It was replaced with multipaneled polished screens. At the end of Act I, when the screens moved (they were a bit taller than life size), at the top of them often ran real live white mice, evidently as they had appeared to the Mayor in his dream.

2. In Act II, Osip, as usual, lay on the bed, strumming the strings of a guitar, to the strains of which he spoke his soliloquy. When Khlestakov entered, Osip greeted him with the famous gypsy "Song of Praise," accompanying himself on the guitar. [...]

3. In Act I, when the mayor plans to go to Khlestakov at the inn, before his dialogue with Derzhimorda, he goes into the privy and converses from there with him in this way:

MAYOR (*evidently suffering intensely, straining*): Take in hand...(*making an effort*) a street...What am I saying? Take...(*straining*) in hand a broom...(*straining*) and sweep (*with relief*), och...the street...

As you see, there was a sufficiency of directorial shock tactics. But in those days no one took the classics seriously. [...]

Igor' Terent'ev to A. Kruchënykh. In M. Levitin,[36] *Menya ne bylo* (Moscow: Izd. Teatr Érmitazh, 2005), 277.

"Kruch! *The Inspector General* turned out many times better than I had expected. First, the end—the return of Khlestakov—evoked howls from the audience.[37] The critics are trying to get me imprisoned and close the theater. The present moment is very dangerous for everyone in the whole House of the Press because there are some disapproving directives from above. We are beginning a savage fight. All the scum felt that it smells of the transmental [*zaum*]. You can't even utter this word. Things seem to be more horrible than ever! I have to go to Moscow, but for that I'll at least have partially to return fire in Leningrad. That's why I wrote a letter to Mayakovsky asking him to come. The directors of the House of the Press sent a similar letter to Bukharin.[38] We need authorities from Moscow. I won't call on you, because the situation is tough enough without that. For the time being I myself will make no appearances anywhere for the same reason, because there's no time. The most righteous people of all categories, both Com. and non-Com., old and young, will stand up for *Inspector General*. Such a to-do even in the enemy camp. Power and expediency [*operativnost'*] are on the enemy's side. We shall take (all possible) measures to turn the circumstances in our favor.

We have to gain time, now that we've broken through the door of the editorial office, which is furiously discussing my "criminal" work. A series of positive articles and notices is being written, and these have to be published wherever they can.

Money for the House of the Press ended with the appearance of *Inspector General*, they're putting on pressure in that way. We haven't a penny for publicity. No money for the lights at the entrance to the theater! The situation is the most difficult!

TERENT'EV moved to Moscow and preached an "anti-artistic theater." He was arrested in 1929, 1931, and 1936 and was accused of using *zaum* and other futurist techniques to send anti-Soviet messages to foreign powers. He died in a labor camp in 1937.

Having failed to interest Lenin in his idea of "Christian communism," the prerevolutionary star Boris Glagolin had been directing at the Moscow Theater of Revolution from 1923, introducing such innovations as no props and direct address to the audience. Eventually, he used the excuse of an art exhibition in Germany to emigrate to America.

---

36 Mikhail Zakharovich Levitin (1945–), director and playwright, a student of Yury Zavadsky, teacher at GITIS and director at the Hermitage Theater, Moscow, from 1977. He has devoted much of his career to rehabilitating Aleksandr Tairov and Igor' Terent'ev.

37 At the end of this staging, when the "real" Inspector is announced, instead of a Petersburg official, Khlestakov reappears.

38 Nikolay Ivanovich Bukharin (1888–1938), a colleague of Trotsky, who became a high Communist Party official and member of the Politburo, until he broke with Stalin in 1928 over the collectivization of the peasantry. Tried for espionage 1937 and executed.

Boris Glagolin to Vsevolod Meyerhold, late April 1927. In *Mnemozina. Do-kumenty i fakty iz istorii otechestvennogo teatra XX veka*, ed. V. V. Ivanov (Moscow: Indrik, 2009), 4:26–27.

Closer acquaintance with the Theater of Revolution whither I have drifted has led me to the decision to refuse to be its chief or main director, as an unworthy function. I have already informed the new manager I. S. Zubtsov[39] of this. I find it tiresome to tilt against windmills. Especially since I am living in a closet at the theater literally among Soviet theater rats, with no electricity, which was turned off for nonpayment, and I wear myself out in asinine arguments.

So I decided, since I have the savings, to go to Magdeburg for the exhibition, and then, maybe, go and give two or three lectures in New York. For a long time I've had invitations there from my Khar'kov student L. I. Luganov (Kopelevich), married to Less's sister.[40] At the Theater of Revolution, on my return, I'll stage Morozov's *Ape Island*.[41] That's the only way I can free myself from this crucifixion on mattresses.

But there are difficulties:

1. I have no sponsorship to enable me to get a passport for abroad—Drop me a line: whom should I contact?

2. L. I. Luganov asks—with the intention of popularizing me—for testimonials about me from Russian celebrities, but my archives are in different cities and, by and large, this comes as a very difficult and stupid matter, but (horribly) indispensable for America!—Please, write one of your nicest sentences about me.

3. This seems to be all the more necessary because this same Luganov writes: a certain M. Gering[42] has been advertising himself in New York as a representative of your theater, and to prove that he personally "staged with Meyerhold a great many plays, that plans of Meyerhold productions belong to him," this Gering lodged a protest in the press against my lecture, advertised by Luganov, "On Meyerhold's productions." In his protest this son of a bitch, obviously, discredits me as well—as Luganov's letter makes clear—Request: write to this representative to stop telling lies and take pity on us from the height of his greatness. [...]

I remember how I asked V. É. to go with me to America and how he said, "We'll go in ten years." My fate is to be the forerunner: in all the cities you will visit and which

39 Ivan Sergeevich Zubtsov (1890–?), worked at the Meyerhold Theater as a directorial lab assistant and from 1925 as administrator. Appointed manager of the Theater of Revolution June 1927, where he worked until 1937, when he was transferred to the Kamerny Theater.

40 Lyubov' Lazarevna Less (1900–?), actress; started 1919 at the Soviet Theater created by Glagolin on the basis of Sinel'nikov's theater; taught at GITIS and the State experimental theatrical workshops 1922–26; took part in Meyerhold's productions.

41 Unpublished play of Dmitry Nikolaevich Morozov (1927). Zubtsov objected to the bad science in it: apes turn into human beings, "irrelevant to the ordinary spectator."

42 Marian Maksimilianovich Gering (1901–?), director, started in Rostov-on-Don 1920–21. From 1921, took part in the state higher theater workshops and GEKTEMAS. In summer 1923, took a three-month leave to learn about U.S. theater. His leave became extended. He staged shows at the Jewish People's Institute, Chicago, 1924–25, and lectured on behalf of Meyerhold, who did not sanction it. He was directing in Chicago and New Haven in 1944.

will pay homage to you, I will have proclaimed, "Just you wait until Vsevolod gets here!" But time's a-wasting, we must escort the Revolution through the world (perhaps literally, perhaps figuratively)—only we should not end up in bed or at Romashov's[43] Theater of Revolution. Greetings to Zinaida Nikolaevna.

Your *B. Glagolin*.

SOVIET ARTISTS were fascinated by the dynamic modernism of the American city with its skyscrapers and rapid transit. There was a peculiar taste for American culture in the 1920s, with multiple productions of *Chicago* and *Machinal*. Tairov initiated a cycle of Eugene O'Neill plays with *The Hairy Ape* (January 14, 1926), in appropriately expressionist settings, followed by *Desire under the Elms*. Tairov explained its style as "concrete realism," a reconciliation of constructivist form with naturalistic behavior and psychology.

Benjamin, *Moscow Diary*, 55–56. Trans. rev.

December 30, 1926. The production [of *Desire under the Elms*] was very poor, and Koonen was especially disappointing, completely uninteresting. What was interesting (but as Reich correctly pointed out, wrongheaded) was the fragmentation of the play into single scenes (cinematization) by means of dropped curtains and lighting changes. The tempo was far more rapid than is usually the case here and was further accelerated by the dynamism of the decor. The set consisted of a cross-sectional view of three rooms: on the ground floor, a large room with a view to the exterior and an exit. At certain points, one saw its walls slide up at a 180-degree angle, and the outdoors seemed to stream in from every side. There were two more rooms on the second floor, reached by a stairway that was partitioned off from the audience's view by laths. It was fascinating to follow the characters making their way up and down the stairs behind this lattice. There are six headings on the asbestos curtain advertising the program for the coming week (the theater is closed Mondays).

Dreiser attends *The Robbers* at the Leningrad Theater for Young Spectators, November 28, 1927. In *Dreiser's Russian Diary*, 173–76.

The entry was buzzing with boys and girls ranging in age from eight to fourteen. [...] The stage director [Evgeny Hackel] had revised it somewhat for the children, had written a prologue to each act which connected the play with the life of Schiller, and was very proud of the results. The theater was exceedingly well-built for the young audience, the broad seats in a semi-circle like an amphitheater, so that no spectator was far from the stage. I like the stage sets very much, the scene was very quickly changed

---

43 Boris Sergeevich Romashov (1895–1958), leading comic playwright of the period, who spearheaded the movement away from his own mordant brand of satire to "cheerful comedy like lemonade on a hot day."

4.6. Schiller's *The Robbers* at the Leningrad Children's Theater, directed by Evgeny Hackel and designed by M. A. Grigor'eva, 1927.

by shifting long silver pillars, swung on ropes into different positions, and some slight change of properties. But my first impression of the play was very bad. It seemed to be old-fashioned declamation, but after the first act, I began to get accustomed to the shouting and came to the conclusion that the style of acting suited the play. Judging from the deafening applause, the laughter, sighs and tears, the young audience like it. [...] There are forms which the children fill out giving their opinions, and these, as well as observation of the spectators during performance, are the basis for [the administrators'] conclusions. [...] [After the performance, Dreiser interviewed the director Aleksandr Bryantsev[44] in his office.]

—Does the Soviet government wish to make this kind of theater a part of the educational plan?

This is a provincial theater and so does not get direct support from the center, but our local Soviet supports us. (The theater costs the government 250,000 roubles a year.) We try to educate the spectator so that when he grows up he will be trained to go to the new theater. The local Soviets try to organize more of such theaters and apply to us for advice so that the general ideas will spread.

—From where do the actors come?

First the founders were a small group, including the actors, who had been dreaming of this idea a long time. We at first got money from the Central Department of

44 Aleksandr Aleksandrovich Bryantsev (1883–1961), an actor with the Itinerant Theater before the Revolution, had begun directing for children as early as 1918; founded the Petrograd TYUZ 1921 and staged forty-eight productions there until his death. It is now named after him.

Education in Moscow, and then after two years from Leningrad. During the famine, we got only bread and herring. For two years the actors gave 30% of their salaries to the theater fund. The director had been a teacher in a children's school and had been a well known stage manager. Besides this first group there is a whole line of actors who come to the director and apply for places, but we cannot take casually, we take only specially qualified graduates of Actors' Universities and those who have the ideal of the children's theater. We have no school, but all actors receive special training here. In the craft of the actor it is necessary to follow one school. We follow the system of Stanislavsky, as do most of the Russian theaters, including Meyerhold. [...]

We then fell to discussing the present craze in Russia for Sovietizing all plays—twisting the psychology so as to inculcate communistic ideals. Seeing a stage setting for Uncle Tom's Cabin & inquiring when & how that was done, I finally asked—"How does your production of it differ from the American standard. Have you preserved it intact?"

"No," was the reply—and I immediately sensed international complications.

Here We must adapt play to audiences. In Uncle Tom's Cabin the attention *should* not center on Tom, who is a passive character, but on the active hero, George. [...] The sentimental part is thrown out. Eva doesn't exist [...]

FOLLOWING MEYERHOLD'S LEAD with *The Magnanimous Cuckold,* Les' Kurbas turned to Ferdinand Crommelynk's *Les Tripes d'or,* under the title *Zlatopuz,* as the premiere production of the Khar'kov Berezil. It opened on October 16, 1926. It is a grotesque comedy about a miser who swallows his gold. Kurbas meant it as an exemplary work, illustrating the five stages of production: "preparation of the play, table work, planning the staging and first run-throughs with scenic elements, dress rehearsals with an audience, and the final version of the production."

> Les' Kurbas, *The Ukrainian Theater of Today and Berezil'* (Khar'kov: RUKh, 1927), in Ukrainian; in Russian *Vecherny Kiev* (1927), in Kurbas, *Ukrainian Theater of Today,* 393–417.

There are more philistines in the theater than nonphilistines, which is the case everywhere. For that reason the Ukrainian director en masse has fallen behind the demands of contemporaneity. In most cases, when it comes to expertise, he is a dilettante. His equipment is only more or less a well-defined orientation to the most "current" forms of theater: en masse he is a mainstream conservative, pining for the "good old days," having a hard time accepting those innovations that have been assimilated even by philistines.

There prevails the same self-esteem, self-satisfaction, lack of self-criticism, which have recently been expressed in part by Ukrainian actors. [...]

In the Ukraine it is impossible and injurious to talk about realism. En masse the Ukrainian theater worker simply does not understand this word yet. He slips into the usual involuntary naturalism and coarse "from the inside out," that primitive amorphousness that, as a rule, suits only a play that contradicts that striving for the categorical life-forms that characterize our era. Such "realism" is especially intolerable here in the Ukraine, where the proletariat seeks a contemporary face for our nation, lost in the village thickets over the course of centuries of slavery. [. . .]

Zlatopuz was a caricature that outlined that special theatrical plan, which can be reduced neither to the grotesque nor to buffoonery. It issues from a new, unpassive, life-altering setup. And therefore few, very few people appreciated the qualities of *Zlatopuz*—no more than one and a half reviews. This was documented in articles by Mikola Khvylevy and Oles' Dosvitny,[45] whose article for some reason no one wanted to publish. True, *Zlatopuz* seemed only an unfinished sketch. The original plan for the role of the landscape was rendered dryly and occasionally; the sound montage, on which special tasks were imposed, was only half realized. Compositionally, the play was not restructured and shortened, the ideological moments were not emphasized, as was first intended. But even in such form *Zlatopuz* for a literate and intelligent director of a productive theater can become methodological fodder for a good five years. By its imperfection, *Zlatopuz* became the prototype for the whole season. A whole month and a half of rehearsals, an ordeal with the VUFKU,[46] which released the actors involved in the performance in major roles from filming almost on the day of the premiere; the atmosphere of scandal and disappointment on both sides of the footlights, so power-fully magnifying our narrow-mindedness, the prospect of apolitical relations to all our staging concepts in future—all this knocked us off our feet and deprived the troupe of the openness and cheerful mood with which it arrived in Khar'kov. And only the realization that this is just a phase gave us the strength to emerge from the season with honor, without surrendering our basic positions.

———

IN 1927 Meyerhold invited Kurbas to attend *The Inspector General* and asked the audience to applaud the best director in the Soviet Union. They gave him a standing ovation.

The year 1927 saw Granovsky's last important work for GOSET, *The Travels of Benjamin III,* a vehicle for the great actors Mikhoéls and Zuskin. The following year, Granovsky took the company on a European tour, but when it returned to Moscow in 1929, he stayed in Germany, directed *Uriel Acosta* for Habima, and devoted himself to filmmaking.

45 Mikhola Khvylevy (actually Fitilëv, 1893–1933), proletarian Ukrainian poet and Cheka officer; committed suicide under pressure of Stalin's anti-Ukrainian campaigns. Oles' Dosvitny (Russian name Aleksandr Fëdorovich Skripal', 1891–1934), Ukrainian writer, lived abroad 1914–18; member of "Vallite" and author of the novel *The Americans* (1925).
46 The All-Ukrainian Photofilmdirectorate, which ran all the film studios in Odessa and Yalta.

Natalia Vovsi-Mikhoéls, *The Travels of Benjamin III,* in *Mon père Salomon Mikhoéls,* trans. Erwin Spatz (Montrichet: Les Éditions noir sur blanc, 1990), 49–51. Natalya Solomonovna Vovsi-Mikhoéls is the daughter of Solomon Mikhoéls and wife of the composer Mteczysław Weinberg.

In 1927, [Robert] Falk[47] began the sets for *The Travels of Benjamin III* from Mendele Moikher-Sforim.[48]

[...] I still remember two hovels, on either side of the stage, the roofs decorated with bedbugs and cockroaches, little benches under each little window and an enormous yellow moon rising way off on the horizon.

Sleeping on the benches, the travelers imagine in a dream that they have already reached the Promised Land. Then, instead of birch trees, palm trees swayed above the houses and the crowd of beggars met on the road was transformed into warriors and captains dressed in fantastic costumes.

Papa discussed his makeup with Falk for a long time. On a sketch by the latter, Benjamin looked like a redhead. "Well, I think he has a white beard and you can't see any hair under his skullcap," Mikhoéls insisted and, unbeknownst to Falk, glued on a white goatee. "Yes, I admit you're right, Solomon Mikhailovich," remarked Falk with his timid smile. Mikhoéls requested that the costume be "tight in the shoulders, as if one were trying to take flight while one's wings were clipped."

These "clipped wings" turned up throughout his characters, in the shriveled hands squeezed against the thighs, which turned their palms up in impotence when he spoke, in the hesitant and cautious gait, in the frightened and inquisitive look directed toward the "enchanted distance."

Zuskin[49] as Senderl looked like the logical complement to Mikhoéls's Benjamin character. But they decided to delineate his silhouette differently: Benjamin represented the active element, the bearer of ideas that tend upward. He was vertical. Senderl remained devout, submissive, obedient, passive, entirely downward, outspread, horizontal. They managed to achieve their goal: Zuskin tall in real life became a little, broad Senderl next to a Benjamin stretching upward.

[...] Listening to a worn-out old record, *The Duet of Benjamin and Senderl,* I can see again scenes from this play unreeling like a film. Here they are arriving together, shielding their eyes with their hands as if staring at unfamiliar and attractive distances. One, in his tattered black caftan, tight in the shoulders, with his skullcap, his skimpy goatee pointed upward and tied up with a string, "so that it doesn't sway on the road." The other, in his gray sacklike smock, cinched in as on a woman, blindly following

---

47 Robert (actually Roman) Rafaelovich Falk (1886–1954), painter and scene designer, chiefly at GOSET; Stanislavsky's son-in-law.
48 Mendele Moikher Sforim (actually Sholom Yankov Abramovich, 1835/6–1917), whose fictions helped make Yiddish a literary language; his Benjamin III has been described as a Jewish Don Quixote.
49 Veniamin L'vovich Zuskin (1899–1952) joined GOSET 1921; tall and hefty, he was often teamed with the diminutive Mikhoéls; noted for his bittersweet comic talent. Became head of GOSET 1948 but was arrested and executed on trumped-up charges of espionage.

the former on his bandy legs. We were dealing with two aspects of the same person, Benjamin personifying the mind and Senderl-the-biddy the body of the naive dreamer. The events in their life were stupid and insignificant, and those in their soul sublime and tragic.

[...] According to the testimony of the dramatic critics of that time, "the day after the premiere of *Benjamin,* Mikhoéls woke up famous." He truly became the public's pet. Jews and non-Jews headed for the State Theater to see the same show again and again. From that moment, Mikhoéls played a major part in the theater and its success. In the internal hierarchy, nothing had changed. Granovsky continued to manage the theater, with his customary authority, and Mikhoéls continued to obey him as always. An unspoken but durable redistribution of tasks took place: Granovsky looked after the theater and Mikhoéls the actors.

CHAPTER FIVE

The First Five-Year Plan, 1928–1932

I N A MAJOR ARTICLE announcing the first Five-Year Plan for modernizing industry throughout the Soviet Union, Stalin called this period the "Great Break." Most of the breakage took place in the bodies and minds of the population. The immediate impact was felt in the farming regions, where enforced collectivization caused intense hardship. Anyone labeled a *kulak* (literally, a "fist"; figuratively, a rich peasant; in actuality, any farmer above the poverty line) was liable to be persecuted, exiled, or murdered. In first two months of 1930, sixty million people were herded onto collective farms. It is estimated that by that time, fourteen million peasants had been slain as the result of government agricultural policies. The USSR had been an agricultural nation, and collectivization overturned centuries of traditional knowledge, practice, husbandry, and living conditions. Beginning in 1933, grain quotas impossible to fill led to mass starvation, most dire in the Ukraine and the lower Volga area.

The Five-Year Plan was launched to make the USSR an industrial nation, with equally unrealistic goals set in this sphere and equally intense strain on the populace. One difference was that, whereas collectivization had little effect on the arts, except in subject matter, industrialization required their full participation as impetus and propaganda. The dramatic poet of the first five-year plan was Nikolay Pogodin, who employed schematic characters in sharp opposition and direct address; in *The Epic of the Axe* (1930), the "manager of the theater" invites the spectators to visit a steel foundry.

Two important policy changes effected in 1928 had a considerable impact on the theater. Sovnarkom created an Arts Sector of the Commissariat of Enlightenment (Glavnoe Upravlenie delam khudozhestvennogo literatury i iskusstva), known in short as Glaviskusstvo. Glavrepertkom was incorporated as an office within it and was charged with monitoring and approving all plays prior to production. In September 1929 its name was changed to the Council for Belles-Lettres and Art (Sovet po khudozhestvennom literatury i iskusstv), and it was moved from Narkompros to Sovnarkom. A massive censorship machine was another new project under construction. Lunacharsky was removed from office and, in 1930, appropriately for a man who had written a play called *Don Quixote Liberated*, was appointed ambassador to Spain.

The "Bolshevization of literature" was consolidated by the creation of RAPP (Rossiyskaya assotsiatsiya proletarskikh pisateley; Russian Association of Proletarian Writers). It had begun in 1925 as a splinter group of the All-Russian Union of Writers (VAAP) and took its name in 1928, forging several smaller groups into a federation on an equal footing. Militant to the point of fanaticism, its members claimed proletarian origin and asserted the "hegemony of the proletariat" in literature, with a mission to create a genuinely new, revolutionary culture. They believed that a mystical union with the proletariat could lead to the blissful liberation of the isolated intellectual. The Party fanned the flames of RAPP's fervor, and in 1929, it embarked on a campaign of terror aimed at breaking the will of the fellow travelers in its rival institution, the All-Russian Union of Writers. "Unwholesome forces," "saboteurs," and "wreckers" were to be extirpated, as was the "anti-Soviet intelligentsia." Scapegoats were singled out and picked on (among them the novelist and playwright Evgeny Zamyatin). The theme of the realization of the Five-Year Plan was declared to be the only one worthy of a Soviet writer's attention.

The year 1930 was another pivotal date when literary disputes and discussions revealed the emergence of Stalinism. The Union of Writers was purged, and RAPP held total sway over the literary scene. Mayakovsky was treated with disdain, typical of the suspicion of outsized genius, and psychological realism was denigrated in favor of revolutionary romanticism and the cult of the positive hero. The critical chorus of opposing opinions that characterized the New Economic Policy (NÉP) period was reduced to a single voice; the open debates that had enlivened the premiere of every interesting production were replaced by private deliberations by official agencies and public denunciations of chosen victims.

The Five-Year Plan also promoted physical fitness, a counterpart to the Strength through Joy movement. Modeled on sports competitions, the first pan-Soviet Olympiad of the arts of the peoples of the USSR, at which seventeen national theaters participated, took place in Moscow in 1930. Thereafter, periodically, the federated republics exhibited the best work of their drama and opera theaters in Moscow during "decades of national art."

In April 1932 the Central Committee's resolution "on restructuring literary and artistic organizations" marked the official end to radical experimentation in the arts; an inflexible framework was constructed in which culture was to perform its prescribed functions. On April 13, the Politburo resolved to liquidate independent organizations of writers, who were to be replaced by a now monolithic Union of Writers. After it denounced Meyerhold, the MAT, and several other theaters, RAPP was suddenly disbanded without any warning. The socialist realism prescribed for literature was now the approved method for every branch of culture, centralized under a rigid bureaucracy.

The New Repertoire

Western observers were cynical about the chances for the Plan. Resettled in Berlin, Aleksandr Granovsky freely expressed his opinion on the contradiction between Slavic torpor and Stalinist policies of "dynamism."

> Walter Benjamin, "Granovsky tells his tale," *Die literarische Welt* 4, 17 (April 27, 1928), 1f. Reprinted in *Gesammelte Werke* (Frankfurt-am-Main, Germany: Suhrkamp, 1972), 4:518–22.

In the latest debates on the theater, "dynamism" plays, as everyone knows, a great role. Grounds enough to treat the concept gingerly. This seems to be Granovsky's intention as well. In any case the skeptical smile that always lies in ambush on his face appears more clearly when he notes in answer to a question, "And in what way *is* the Russian theater dynamic? Does it seem so to you? Meyerhold is something quite different; at least, if you ask him, he is not looking for a human dynamic but for a coming collective to move and act to the rhythm of the machine. And anyway, can Slavs turn the dynamic into an intrinsic principle? Their most familiar postures are procrastination, dragging things out, letting things distend and strain, not the explosive, the immense, the abrupt."

THE INFLUENCE OF RAPP and the power of the proletarian culture grew considerably during this period. It made bolder attacks on nonconforming playwrights such as Bulgakov. ("Remember *The Crimson Island, The Conspiracy of Equals,* and similar pulp fiction, which the Repertkom enthusiastically allows in the repertoire of the actually bourgeois Kamerny Theater.") However, Meyerhold seemed to remain above the fray.

> Proletarian Theater Association to I. V. Stalin, December 1928. In Katerina Clark and Evgeny Dobrenko, with André Artizov and Oleg Naumov, *Soviet Culture and Power: A History in Documents 1917–1953* (New Haven, Conn.: Yale University Press, 2007), 53–55. © 2007 by Yale University.

Esteemed Comrade Stalin!

While wholly confident in you as the spokesman for a definite political line, we, the undersigned members of the Proletarian Theater creative association, would like to know your opinion on the following issues [...]

1. Do you think the right-wing danger in politics established by the Party, while feeding off the same roots, is also seeping into various ideological productions, in particular, literature and theater? [...]

2. Do you find it opportune, in the given political conditions, instead of pushing such a major artistic force as the MAT 1 toward revolutionary themes, or at least a revolutionary interpretation of the classics, to do everything possible to make it easier for this theater to slip to the right, to disorganize intellectually that part of the young

MAT that already can and wants to work with us, to knock them off track, to push back that portion of theater specialists who are staging a play like Bulgakov's *Flight*[1]—which according to the unanimous response of Glavrepertkom's arts and politics council [. . .] is a weakly masked apology for White heroics [. . .]?

4. How are we to assess the actual "greatest goodwill" toward the most reactionary authors (like Bulgakov, who has got four blatantly anti-Soviet plays staged in the three leading theaters of Moscow; moreover, plays that are by no means outstanding for their artistic qualities but that are, at best, on an average level? [. . .])

THE ELEVEN SIGNATORIES of this letter included the playwrights Bill'-Belotserkovsky and Glebov, the director Lyubimov-Lanskoy, and the Latvian activist Asja Lācis.

> I. V. Stalin to Bill'-Belotserkovsky, February 1, 1929. In I. V. Stalin, *Sobranie sochineny* (Moscow: Gos. Izdat. Polit. Lit., 1949). In Clark and Dobrenko, *Soviet Culture and Power,* 326–29.

1. I consider the formulation of the question about "right-wing" and "left-wing" in literature (which means the theater too) incorrect. [. . .] "Right-wing" and "left-wing" refer to people who deviate in one direction or the other from the purely Party line. There it would be strange to apply these concepts to such a non-Party and incomparably broader sphere as literature, theater, etc. [. . .] It would be most correct to operate in literature with concepts of a class nature, or even the concepts "Soviet," "anti-Soviet," "reactionary," "antirevolutionary," etc.

2. [. . .] Bulgakov's *Flight* [. . .] cannot be considered a manifestation of a "left-wing" or "right-wing" danger, either. *Flight* is a manifestation of the attempt to evoke pity, if not sympathy, for certain strata of pathetic émigrés, probably an attempt to justify or semijustify the White cause. *Flight* in its present form is an anti-Soviet phenomenon. Actually, I would have nothing against staging *Flight* if Bulgakov were to add to his eight dreams one or two more dreams depicting the internal social springs of the Civil War in the USSR so that the spectator could understand that all these, in their own way "honest," Serafimas[2] and various university lecturers were chucked out of Russia not due to the Bolsheviks' caprice but because they were living off the people (despite their "honesty"), that in driving out these "honest" exploiters, the Bolsheviks were carrying out the will of the workers and peasants and therefore acting perfectly correctly.

3. Why are Bulgakov's plays produced so frequently? Probably because we don't have enough of our own plays good enough for staging. In a land without fish, *The*

---

1 Bulgakov's *Beg* (also translated as *On the Run,* 1927–28), "eight farcical dreams" about the end of General Vrangel's army and the escape of White Russians, was forbidden and not produced until 1957—in Volgograd.

2 A sensitive lady of Petersburg who becomes an émigrée because of her love for an idealistic intellectual.

Days of the Turbins is a fish. [...] *Days of the Turbins* is a demonstration of the crushing force of Bolshevism. Of course, the author is not at all "guilty" of this demonstration, but do we care about that? [...]

MAN WITH A BRIEFCASE (*Chelovek s portfelem,* 1928) brought Aleksey Fayko to full prominence as a controversial dramatist. It portrayed the intelligentsia as supporting the Soviet system in public and abusing it in private. Granatov, an old-school professor, pays lip service to the Revolution but remains uncommitted until circumstances bring about a conversion. The play, when it was produced at the Theater of Revolution, had a mixed reception: critics were torn between seeing it as a condemnation of fellow travelers or a defense of them. Although it marked the start of a four-year hiatus in Fayko's work, it was momentous for the future of Soviet drama.

> Concluding speech. Aleksey Fayko, *Chelovek s portfelem; drama v 5 aktakh* (Moscow: Modpik, 1928), 132.

GRANATOV: I was prepared to speak to you today about the evolution of the intelligentsia, its stratification, its inner contradictions, and its social significance. I was prepared to speak about the ruin of the old intelligentsia and the birth of the new, youthful intelligentsia that is triumphing over the old. I had an awful lot to say. But at the last moment I find I have left my notes in my study—my quotations, my plan of attack. You see, my briefcase is empty... and instead of the lecture I had prepared, let me fix your attention on a single case in point—myself. A living human being is a thousand times more interesting than mere abstractions, warm crimson blood flowing through living veins is far more exciting than a chemical preparation in a test tube... (*cries of protest from his students.*) No... I am not going to be frivolous... I shall be merciless to myself and my subject. Today I am going to fight a duel with myself before your eyes, and the greater my victory, the greater will be my defeat. [The students try to stop the lecture, but Zina demands that the chairman let Granatov speak. After admitting to a murder and driving his wife to suicide, he expresses his failure at breaking with the past.] Why? Because I attacked the problem merely externally... I assimilated the mere formalities, still harboring within me the poison of past generations, the poison of individuals, the poison of so-called privilege. I began to serve the Revolution and the new dominant class like a crafty hireling who is able to ingratiate himself with any master. Instead of trying to make myself part of the process, with all the hardship and agony of mind that it engenders, to asset my individual self. [He warns them of all such men with briefcases in the society.] Oh, no one is so much in evidence when there is talk of Soviet construction, and no one is so clever at participating in it without contributing a single thing toward it. [...] It is your business to take the necessary steps. [He leaves and shoots himself offstage.]

John Dos Passos, *"The Man with a Briefcase,"* in John Dos Passos, "Moscow theaters October and November 1928," *Theater 1929* (January 1929), 7.

The method of production is an adaptation to the stage of the camera eye. In fact movies are used twice in the play to give the effect of a train clattering across the country. From a writer's point of view this is probably one of the best plays now running in Moscow. [...] The method is a development from [Georg] Kaiser's expressionism. "New realism" might be a name for it. Here again, there is no picture frame, rather an adaptation of the movie screen worked in three dimensions, plus the auditorium. All detail and all "beauty" have been scrapped for a series of effects that will make the audience participate directly in the tragedy. The tragedy happens "actually" in the theater the way the miracle of the Mass is supposed to happen "actually" in a Catholic church.

YURY KARLOVICH OLESHA (1899–1960) adapted his novel *Envy* (1927), a satire on consumerism, for the stage as *A Conspiracy of Feelings.* (See later for his *List of Benefits.*) Two weeks before it opened at Vakhtangov Theater, Yury Olesha reviewed it in comparison with his novel and then, after it opened, defended it in a speech at the Leningrad BDT.

Yury Olesha, *"A Conspiracy of Feelings.* Auto-review," *Sovremenny teatr* [Contemporary theater] 9 (1929). Reprinted in Yu. Olesha, *P'esy. Stat'i o teatre i dramaturgii.* Moscow: Iskusstvo, 1968), 257–58.

The theme of the play is the struggle for emotional engagement [*pafos*]. Was emotional engagement a monopoly of the old world, did it disappear with the advent of our era, or will it be equally an attribute of new, rational people? In the play, two refined men fight with an "idol." The spectator has to decide: is it the idol that these refined individuals hate? Or is it only a result of the invincibility and righteousness that makes it seem awesome and terrible? It is historical legitimacy that cannot be vanquished. Therefore, instead of a living face, the doomed heroes see a ghastly mask, "history's ugly mug." This face is radiant, but to them it looks hideous, and, blinded by it, they drag themselves to it to vandalize it before perishing.

The play is not realistic, its tone is ecstatic, overemotional. It relies on a preconditioned spectator. I can already predict the opinion of the bureaucratic spectator that all the heroes in my play are insane. [...]

Yury Olesha, "The author on his play," *Zhizn' iskusstva* 52 (1929). Reprinted in Olesha, *P'esy,* 260.

The first set of accusations flung at me concerned my main hero, Andrey Babichev. He is a sausage maker, wrote the critics, a sausage maker and nothing more. I deliberately gave my Communist hero an eccentric profession to make him theatrical, vivid. Next, in opposition to the coruscating dialogue of people of the past, I wanted to make my hero's diction coarse, ironic, and wanted to contrast a mere sausage with Ophelia, something concrete with aimless romanticism [...]

Sergey Radlov, "What's wrong with our drama?" (April 1929), in Radlov, *Desyat' let v teatre* (Leningrad: Priboy, 1929), 61–65.

Now is the time to total up the early returns.

Soviet drama does exist.

That is to say, there exists a number of plays that dominate our repertoire and possess a unity of devices, styles, a similarity of themes.

The qualities of this drama:

first, contemporaneity and topicality in the themes treated;

second, the presence of remarkable true-to-life observation;

third, clear-cut, well-defined sympathy and antipathy, making it easy and uncomplicated for the most unsophisticated spectator to draw conclusions, although this is attained at the cost of an extremely elementary approach to treating issues.

Its defects:

first, absence of strong dramatic concepts;

second, extreme photographic qualities, headline topicality, purely journalistic officialese in characters and the language spoken onstage;

third, a rift with the superb technique of contemporary Soviet production, the extremely formalistic "oversimplification" of our stage.

There is no point in arguing over whether the plusses or the minuses weigh more heavily. The qualities speak for themselves; we are obliged to speak about the defects— and all the more loudly the more eagerly we want to eliminate them.

Two of them relate to the wonderful absence of our theatrical literature both from the theater and from literature, i.e., from the techniques of the modern stage and the formalistic level of our poetry and prose.

The childish naturalism of our drama is a terrifying phenomenon that compels our affectionate dismantling of the classics, Tairov and Nemirovich-Danchenko ever more frequently hide behind operetta, I have escaped to the opera,[3] Terent'ev in his panic grabs hold of a fat novel, having despaired of dramatic art, and this whole list of deserters threatens majestically to confine Stanislavsky to his opera studio.

What's the trouble?

Gathering all my courage, I dare to speak my opinion.

Plays in Russia are written not by the right people, that is, not by those who ought to be writing plays today. [...]

Who is writing in Russia? Prose writers and journalists. But it would appear that lyric poetry is better training for the stage than the leisurely novel: appreciate the catastrophe of *Untilovsk* and the excellent *Badgers* of Leonov.[4]

3 At the Leningrad Theater of Drama, Radlov staged operas by Alban Berg and Sergey Prokof'ev 1923–27.
4 Leonid Maksimovich Leonov (1899–1994), whose first play *Badgers* (1927) was a formulaic

Werfel, Hasenclever,[5] even Toller are poets. They parsimoniously situate a word in time and space. We scatter dialogues any old how with the same garrulousness as on the trolley. In our plays the word never tries to congeal and become unique.

Moreover: why doesn't anyone write a play in verse? Naturalism devoured it? But we put up with operetta as a genre, and we read verse. After all, verse and operetta are equally unnatural. And besides, you'd have to be deaf not to hear that Mayakovsky's poetic technique is literally born for modern high comedy.

The experiment of the young Leningrad poet D. Tolmachev[6]—but, unfortunately, in a play too occasional in theme—proved to me the accuracy of my conviction. Meanwhile, we have frivolously driven verse into the living-newspaper routine. But, of course, the gist of the matter is not whether a play is in prose or verse. The question actually is, a refined text or a slapdash one? In the plays of Blok or Kuzmin, a spare prose was as good as poetry.

The theater demands the economy and restraint of Pushkin's prose (i.e., a poet's prose) and not the garrulity of a journalist. And it is characteristic that the best specimen in the contemporary agit-press is *Gas Masks,* written by Tret'yakov, i.e., a man of futurist and poetical literary culture. [...]

Hallie Flanagan, "The Soviet Theatrical Olympiad," *Theatre Guild Magazine* (1930), 10–13, 62. Hallie Flanagan (actually Ferguson, 1890–1945) studied European and Russian theaters on a Guggenheim grant in 1926; she wrote about her impressions in *Shifting Scenes of the European Theaters* (1928) and re-created them in classrooms at Vassar; she ran the Federal Theater Project 1935–38.

The first Soviet Theatrical Olympiad is on in Moscow and twelve hundred actors, directors, and designers, representing twenty different Soviet nations, many of which a decade ago had no national existence, are competing in the field of theater, cinema, music and the dance. [...] Plays in eighteen different languages fill the afternoons and evenings, while the mornings are reserved for cinemas, lectures, and theatrical exhibits...

[...] The theater, like every organization in Russia, is committed to a five-year plan, some conception of which may be gained from the banners flung across streets and the facades of buildings:

Art must understand socialism before it can serve it.

---

adaptation of his novel about revolutionary partisans versus the White Guard. The MAT chose to stage his gloomy drama *Untilovsk* in 1928, but it was banned after ten performances.

5 Franz Werfel (1890–1945), Prague-born writer, whose play about the Mexican Revolution *Juarez und Maximilian* (1925) was staged by the Theater Guild in New York; emigrated to France and the United States 1938. Walter Hasenclever (1890–1940), German expressionist writer, whose play *Der Sohn* (1916) was a manifesto of a rebellious younger generation; self-exiled to France 1933 and committed suicide in an internment camp.

6 D. G. Tolmachev, film animator, member of the OBERIU; his realistic verse play *Dead Center* (*Mërtvaya tochka*), an "industrial tragedy," was included in the BDT repertoire for 1925–26, to be performed by the younger actors.

The Theater and Cinema must combine to liquidate the two enemies of scientific progress—vodka and religion.

Where is our new theater architecture? Loges are anachronistic in Soviet Russia.

Wanted: a Theater for every village, school and factory in Soviet Russia.

[...] The Olympiad lays great stress on the importance of each nation retaining its individual culture and mode of expression. In the words of Anatole Glebov of the Art Section of the USSR:

> At this Olympiad the progressive revolutionary art works of all the nations of the Soviet Union will meet one another for the first time and become convinced, first of the unity of their aims, and second of the necessity of respecting national cultures. Not separating from one another in a narrow spirit of chauvinism, but teaching and enriching one another, the various Soviet theaters will jointly lay foundations for socialist culture.

[...] [Nikolai] Petrov, who entitled his address [which opened a roundtable discussion on the second day of the conference] *Various Illnesses of Modern Playwriting*, said:

"Why is it important to speak of art today? The only significant thing in Russia today is the Five-Year Plan involving collectivization of farms, communization of industry, and liquidation of ignorance. Art is important at present only as it serves some aspect of this plan.

"The theater is not serving industry as well as it should, and the object of this meeting is to discover the cause and to suggest a remedy [...]

"First of all, our dramatists have not succeeded in mastering the new tempo. The pace of our life today is more rapid than the pace of our plays. [...] Our playwrights live too little in the theater. They realize too little the possibilities of our new stage. How absurd for a dramatist to imprison his ideas in the small painted scenes of the past when the stage is now of any size, form, and rapidity he desires. Why should he continue to use a polite whisper when he has at his disposal the loudspeaker? Why should he be less bold in plan and execution than his fellow worker who is building farms and factories overnight? Let the dramatist take possession of the theater! Let him use all the forces at his disposal—cinema, radio, machines, lights, acrobatics! Perhaps in so doing he can assist the director in one of the most pressing problems of our stage—that of finding a new method of acting suitable for peasants and workers. So far no such method has been devised, and consequently our mise-en-scène outstrips our acting. [...]"

Petrovsky[7] gave his address the characteristic title *On the Playwriting Front*. He said: [...]

"Remnants of past dramaturgy which still hamper our playwrights are as follows:

1. Family or love intrigue.

2. Idealistic motives, untrue to our materialistic conception of life.

---

7   Andrey Pavlovich Petrovsky (1869–1933), skilled in secondary roles; director at the Zamoskvorech'e Theater in Moscow 1926–29, at the Bol'shoy, and in the provinces.

3. Stress on the importance of personal intellectualism.

4. Emphasis on the individual rather than the group.

"All of these elements are based on principles of psychological realism, a dramatic method which Konstantin Stanislavsky and the Moscow Art Theater brought to perfection before the Revolution. Admirable for plays of the past, this method is unsuited to plays of the present because, in its absorption with personal problems, it is unaware of the existence of the mass mind and mass consciousness and hence incapable of serving the aims of the expanding present.

"[...] Furthermore, symbolic generalization is bad because, by its metaphysical character, it can alter the meaning of a political theme or change the entire direction of a play. Today is no time for generalizations in life or art."

> Érdman's *The Suicide*[8] at the Vakhtangov Theater, transcript of a meeting of the Artistic-Political Council of the Vakhtangov State Theater, September 17, 1930, after a reading of the play. RGALI, fond 2570, opis' 1, delo 139. First published and translated in Nikolay Érdman, *A Meeting about Laughter: Sketches, Interludes, and Theatrical Parodies...*, ed. John Freedman (Luxembourg: Harwood Academic, 1995), 191–204.

KAZACHENKO: Comrades, I'm not going to focus on several errors of a purely ideological order, a whole series of expressions—clearly unnecessary for us and alien to our ideology—which are put forward in this play. I don't want to say this was done on purpose, but they are alien to us. For example, take an expression like "Where else can an unemployed worker shoot himself, except in the bathroom," "Stores are being closed," or "Public opinion is nothing but a factory of slogans." All of this wouldn't carry so much weight if something would counteract these words and ideas. But since nothing counteracts them, these expressions and thoughts are nothing but food for the bourgeoisie, which will watch this play with pleasure and laugh at it. [...]

LEMBERG:[9] We are so lacking, so poor in talented plays that it seems to us that we have found an author who has a brilliant command of the pen. And it would seem that we should be happy to have found such a talented play. But, at least as it concerns me, I don't experience any such joy. The author constantly walks the sharp edge of a knife, drawing his spectator along after him. And the double entendres, of which this play is full, invariably fall off this knife's edge—not in the direction of ridiculing the bourgeoisie but in the direction of ridiculing the Soviet public. [...] This play is unacceptable for the Vakhtangov Theater, or for any other Soviet theater for that matter.

ARTAMONOV:[10] [...] The play is written with great talent, although I must admit, it's

---

8   *The Suicide* (*Samoubiytsa*, 1930) was rehearsed separately by Meyerhold and Stanislavsky but was banned 1932; it was first publicly staged by Valentin Pluchek in Moscow 1982. See later.

9   K. F. Lemberg, member of the factory committee at the Moscow Regional Electric Plant.

10 Georgy Adamovich Artamonov, deputy director of the Vakhtangov Theater in 1930.

not for us. If a play like this were to be presented onstage for the spectator, it would cause a reaction that would be extremely disadvantageous for us. [...]

AYZENSHTADT:[11] [...] The play's basic flaw is that its people are too petty and insignificant to waste a whole full-length play on doing battle with them. They are not drawn with sufficient clarity. Their own harmfulness is too insufficient. They have no place in our life. [...]

ZAKHAVA:[12] [...] The most fallacious method of evaluating any work negatively is merely to list phrases without taking into account who is saying them and what the function of a given image is. It's obviously impossible to go about selecting random phrases from various voices that have a counterrevolutionary, anti-Soviet tone, etc. [...] Georgy Adamovich uttered the phrase that Podsekalnikov appears to be a philistine and tells reactionary stories. What kind of stories does a philistine tell, other than reactionary ones? If we take that approach, then we are shut off from every possibility of portraying a negative character onstage. [...]

SHVARTSMAN:[13] [...] I think there is absolutely no way we can give permission to this play. The author mobilizes all these characters around this anecdotal incident of Podsekalnikov's suicide. But we know that there are attempts to capitalize on Mayakovsky's death.[14] [...] I consider that this play is an absolutely seditious play, thanks primarily to its talent. Because it is written wittily, because the spectator will understand everything and all these lines are capable of unnoticeably feeding the philistines. If a worker went to see it, then, in any case, he doesn't need it. It doesn't mobilize any tasks or problems of our reality at all. [...]

KUZA:[15] [...] We haven't seen a [talented] contemporary play since *A Conspiracy of Feelings*. Therefore, this play primarily attracted us as a brilliant example of dramatic literature that provides the opportunity of creating a splendid production that is near and dear in its form to our theater. That is the main idea that ruled the Vakhtangov Theater. I want to emphasize that.

[...] I must admit that I have yet to hear an exhaustive Marxist analysis [or] a coherent and ideologically exhaustive analysis. [...] Why such panic? [...]

GORKY had advised the MAT to rehearse the play so that, on the fifteenth anniversary of October, the best writers could be represented.

11 Ayzenshtadt, secretary of the Artistic–Political Council of the Bol'shoy Theater in 1930.
12 Boris Evgen'evich Zakhava (1896–1976), actor and director, a student of Vakhtangov and head of the Vakhtangov Theater 1923–25. He was later head of the Shchukin Acting School in Moscow.
13 Shvartsman, delegate of the union of worker-journalists to the Artistic–Political councils of several theaters.
14 The reference to "death" rather than "suicide" (just five months earlier) indicates the touchiness of the subject. The suicide was not acknowledged for decades after Mayakovsky was canonized by Stalin in 1935 and made part of the school curriculum. He was, in Pasternak's words, "introduced forcibly, like potatoes under Catherine the Great."
15 Vasily Vasil'evich Kuza (1902–41), handsome leading man and director at the Vakhtangov Theater from 1921; also directed at kolkhoz and factory theaters. Killed in a German bombing raid on the Vakhtangov Theater.

K. S. Stanislavsky to I. V. Stalin, October 29, 1931. In Nikolay Érdman, *Pésy. Intermedii. Pis'ma. Dokumenty. Vospominaniya sovremennikov* [Plays. Interludes. Letters. Documents. Remembrances by contemporaries], ed. A. Svobodin (Moscow: Iskusstvo, 1990), 283–84.

Deeply respected Iosif Vissarionovich!

Knowing your abiding interest in the Art Theater, I turn to you with the following request.

You already know from Aleksey Maksimovich Gorky that the Art Theater is deeply interested in Érdman's play *The Suicide,* in which the theater sees one of the most remarkable works of our era. In our view, Nikolay Érdman has managed to expose the various manifestations and ingrown roots of the philistinism that opposes the construction of the nation. The device by which the author has shown the philistinism of living people and their monstrosity represents an original innovation that is, however, fully in keeping with Russian realism in all its best representatives, such as Gogol and Shchedrin, and is close to the traditions of our theater.

Therefore, after the author completed the play, the Art Theater thought it important to apply its expertise to reveal the comedy's social significance and artistic authenticity. However, at the present time, this play is banned by the censor.

So we would like to request your permission to set to work on the comedy *The Suicide* in the hope that you will not refuse to inspect it prior to the release of its performance by our actors. The fate of this comedy could be decided after such a showing. Naturally the Art Theater will not involve you in any expense prior to the showing.

Letter of I. V. Stalin to K. S. Stanislavsky, November 9, 1931

Most respected Konstantin Sergeevich!

I do not have a very high opinion of the play *Suicide.*[16] My closest comrades consider that it is vapid and even harmful. The opinion and reasons of the Repertkom you can learn from the appended document. It seems to me that the comments of the Repertkom are not far from the truth. Nevertheless, I do not object to the theater making an experiment and showing off its mastery. I do not rule out that the theater may succeed in achieving its goal. The Kultprop of our Party's Central Committee (com. Stetsky)[17] will assist you in this matter. The supervisors will be comrades who know about artistic matters. I am an amateur at this stuff. Regards.

I. Stalin

[Attached was a devastating evaluation of the play by the Repertkom.]

THE SIXTH WORLD (*Shestaya mira*), staged with Rodchenko's designs, in early 1931, the "completion" year of the first Five-Year Plan, was a combination of circus

16 Stalin gets the title wrong, calling it *Samoubiystvo* (the act of suicide rather than the perpetrator).
17 Aleksey Ivanovich Stetsky (1896–1938), head of the Division of Culture and Propaganda of Leninism of the Central Committee.

and variety acts, song and dance, by Aleksandr Zharov and Nikolay Ravich.[18] A contrast between Moscow and New York, it offered "A Museum of Russian Bygones" with tsarist policemen, lords, and Bolsheviks; dances on kettledrums; and crowd scenes with komsomols. The motto was "Let Us Overtake and Surpass America." The critics didn't care for it.

> N. Ryazhevsky, "Explanation of the agitational part of the production *Sixth World*, addressed to A. Rodchenko,[19] 1931." Typescript, Rodchenko and Stepanova Archive, quoted in A. N. Lavrent'ev, "Pozdny konstruktivizm v teatre" [Later constructivism in the theater], in G. F. Kovalenko, ed., *Russky avangard 1910-kh—1920-kh godov i teatr* (St. Petersburg: Dmitry Bulanin, 2000), 362.

Apotheosis: drill, panorama, the march of socialism.

When, after the American leaves, the komsomols declare to the song of the drill that we must catch up to America only by the path to knowledge, they transform the blast furnace, etc., turning around the side that depicts a section of the blast furnace and the process of shaping "belts" by fusion. A serious lecture is given on cast iron smelting. We move to Magnitogorsk. A film about it is shown, the screen for the overhead projector shows documents. An enormous blueprint is let down—the plan of a factory. And after the explanation of what is to be found where, the whole set pulls apart. In the lower part is a panorama (a model) of Magnitogorsk. It revolves. The size is about three by three meters. Here we have to provide a triumphant conclusion with a mass of people and parades of everything made out of metal, including weaponry. The parade includes the army.

> S. V., "Music-hall in passing," *Vechernaya Moskva* [Evening Moscow] (March 2, 1931).

Sixth World is a caricatural reflection of anti-Soviet campaigns and the world capitalist crisis, served up in an interesting way. Having made the central figure the American Fish, the survey immediately intrigues the spectators and leads to a comic collision of the meeting of the millionaire with the Soviet Fish. This plot rather audaciously, without fear of losing its "moral," interweaves individual choreographic, musical, and circus acts. And to tell the truth, it does not seem a bad idea when the same undraped Chorus Girls spruce themselves up a bit and turn into respectable Soviet nationals or militarized komsomols.

18 Aleksandr Alekseevich Zharov (1904–84), proletarian and komsomol poet, author of the *Anthem of the Young Pioneers* (1932); served in the navy 1941–45. Nikolay Aleksandrovich Ravich (1899–1976), head of the theater–musical section of Glavrepertkom 1929; screenwriter for *Suvorov* (1940).

19 Aleksandr Mikhaylovich Rodchenko (1891–1956), constructivist artist, designer, and photographer, married to Varvara Stepanova; close collaborator with Mayakovsky on *LEF* and *Novy LEF* 1923–28; expelled from the October movement for "formalism."

ON FEBRUARY 7, 1931, the Theater of Revolution enjoyed one of its greatest successes with Pogodin's *The Epic of the Axe.*

> Mariya Knebel', *Rezhissër, uchitel', drug* [Director, teacher, friend] (Moscow: VTO, 1966), 43. Mariya Osipovna Knebel' (1898–1985), trained by Stanislavsky and Mikhail Chekhov, acted at both the MAT and MAT 2; she began directing in 1935. She was dismissed from the MAT 1950 and became head of the Moscow Central Children's Theater. Her teaching at GITIS was immensely influential in handing down the undiluted ideas of her mentors.

How to describe that feeling of love, tenderness, and excitement that gripped the audience when Babanova as Anka burst into the shop, when, guarded by one of the foundry workers, Stepashka was sleeping a sound sleep? Babanova as Anka understood that he was not to be awakened, but it was also impossible for her to cope with the storm of happiness that gripped her. And she flew into a dance. I did not know another dramatic actress whose physical flexibility was so perfect. She made the most complicated movements with phenomenal lightness. Her dance seemed to be an improvisation made up on the spot . . . It seemed that this dear creature, dancing in a frenzy around the sleeping Stepashka, was ready to dissolve into the air with happiness. All this lasted a few seconds, and when she suddenly disappeared, the house rocked with applause.

THE FIRST "SOVIET" PLAY written by Maksim Gorky (and his first play since 1915) was *Egor Bulychëv and the Others (Egor Bulychëv i Drugie),* the account of a wealthy timber merchant dying of cancer in spring 1917. He is surrounded by legacy hunters, religious charlatans, and faith healers and dies to the sounds of the approaching Revolution, welcomed by his illegitimate daughter Shura. The premiere opened simultaneously in Moscow and Leningrad on September 25, 1932, with Boris Shchukin as Bulychëv, at the Vakhtangov Theater, directed by Boris Zakhava, and with Nikolay Monakhov at the BDT, directed by Vl. Lyutse and K. K. Tverskoy. The former bore away the laurels. Shchukin's performance was considered a benchmark in Soviet acting, with all the elements of the actor's talent merged into a profundity of thought and depth of humor, with strictly controlled technique lightened by free improvisation.

> Aleksandr Afinogenov, *Sovetskoe iskusstvo* 44 (September 27, 1932), quoted in Gorky, *Polnoe Sobranie Sochineny* [Complete collected works] (Moscow: Nauka, 1968–82), 9:50.

What perplexity on the faces of those of our "critics" who are accustomed to identifying a concept of the "positive" with the "absolute." They cannot conceive that such an old fox as a profligate and tyrant of a merchant can fulfill a relatively positive social function, even when it amounts to fundamental criticism, itself emerging from an animal-like fear in the face of death, of existing society and the human maelstrom it creates.

André Van Gyseghem, *Theatre in Soviet Russia* (London: Faber and Faber, 1943), 106–7.

One cannot speak too highly of this performance. It is as fine a piece of collective work as can be found on any stage, even on that of the Moscow Art, for in addition to the consummate care for detail and psychological grasp of the characters which distinguishes the Art Theater, there is also a more highly colored, more theatrical approach to the play which makes it, if possible, more alive. The performance of Bulychëv by Boris Shchukin[20] is a triumph of acting. He maintains a perfect blend of humour and tragedy, and builds up the character in so real a way that his mannerisms, his walk, and the way he holds his arms, stay with you long after you leave the theater. When the Theatre Festival visitors saw *Egor Bulychëv*, in 1935, they held up the play with wild cheers and prolonged applause for Shchukin's performance.

Harold Clurman, "Moscow Diary," in *The Collected Works of Harold Clurman: Six Decades of Commentary on Theater, Dance, Music, Film, Arts, and Letters*, ed. Marjorie Loggia and Glenn Young (New York: Applause Books, 1994), 11–12. Harold Clurman (1901–80), a playreader for the New York Theatre Guild, in 1931 cofounded the Group Theater, which embraced and adapted Russian acting techniques; a refined director and skilled writer, whose pointed theater criticism appeared in *The New Republic, The Nation*, and *The Observer*.

May 16, 1935. Went to see *Egor Bulychëv* again at the Vakhtangov Theater. Last year I was impressed by the element of stylishness in this production, because it was much freer in its treatment of a realistic play than we are accustomed to in America. But this time I was impressed with the realness of the production: the observation, the concrete detail, the quiet truth. Everything is done lovingly, cleanly, and clearly: nothing is missed, nothing is overstressed, nothing neglected. Shchukin's Bulychëv is still superb. He dominates the play by his part and his personality (which is vigorous and young without a trace of coarseness or vulgarity), and yet he brings a perfect ensemble feeling to the stage. His spiritual attitude in the performance (and this counts a great deal in the first impression created by an actor on the audience) breathes dignity, simplicity, and a masculine sweetness. He is universally loved by audience and fellow actors. And because I know he is no miracle man but an honest theater worker of talent who by force of a real desire to grow (he was an illiterate boy and is almost completely self-educated) has risen to the point of his present performance. [...]

20 Boris Vasil'evich Shchukin (1894–1939), actor, a pillar of the Vakhtangov Theater 1926–38, versatile and moving; his range stretched from the buffoon Tartaglia in *Princess Turandot* to the first stage portrayal of Lenin (*Man with a Gun*, 1937).

5.1. *Egor Bulychëv and the Others* by Maksim Gorky, Vakhtangov Theater, directed by Boris Zakhava, with Boris Shchukin as Egor (far right), 1932.

Reader Bullard, *Inside Stalin's Russia: The Diaries of Reader Bullard 1930–1934*, ed. Julian and Margaret Bullard (Oxfordshire, U.K.: Day Books, 2000), 36, 105, 137. Sir Reader William Bullard (1885–1976), British career diplomat, consul general in Moscow and Leningrad 1931–34, ended his career as ambassador to Tehran.

June 15, 1931 [Moscow]. I used to wonder whether the people themselves do not get sick of this propaganda, and recently I had one proof that they do. I went to see a play about the socialisation of the fishing industry. When it was due to start a typical communist with a black blouse and high Russian boots began a political speech. Soon the audience began to clap. The speaker at first looked flattered, but then he realised that the applause was a sign of boredom and not enthusiasm, and he yelled at the audience that they ought to listen to "the truth." Finally the speaker had to retreat in a fury.

April 6, 1932. [The consular office had been moved to Leningrad in late 1931.] Cave[21] and I managed to get tickets on March 30 for a play, *Strakh*[22] (*Fear*). It was well we did, for it has now been taken off. It is not a great play, but it gives a good picture of

---

21 A. J. Cave had been British acting consul in Vladivostok 1918–19, Leningrad 1924, and Riga 1927; during this period also vice-consul in Leningrad. His appointment was terminated 1934.

22 *Fear* (1930) by Afinogenov had a successful premiere at the BDT and a less successful one at the MAT 1931. It focused on the individual case of a scientist who believes that Communism works through fear but comes around in the end. The key speech was that by Clara, the old Bolshevik: "Yes, the working class knows what fear is . . . under capitalism and under imperialism. That fear has produced and is producing the fearlessness of the revolutionary sturggle, the fearlessness of the struggle of a new, classless society, and the fearlessness of revolutionary victories!"

5.2. *Fear* by Aleksandr Afinogenov, Moscow Art Theater, directed by Il'ya Sudakov and designed by Nisson Shifrin, with Leonid Leonidov as Professor Borodin (far right), 1931.

present-day Russian life. The central figure, Borodin, was a physiologist, an elderly non-Party man who is director of a research institute. Proof of sabotage comes to light, and a member of the staff accuses the director, who is interrogated by the OGPU—of course in the kindest manner. Are the OGPU deceived? The OGPU are never deceived. No criminal ever escapes them, but no innocent person they interrogate is ever punished. In no time the informant is unmasked as the real criminal, and the old scientist returns to his post at the institute. Even more interesting was a secondary plot revolving around a man who is high up in the Party. He would never have been admitted to the Party at all if it had been known that his father had been a small landowner. So far as he knows the only person who is aware of his secret is a very old friend. He speaks to this friend of his guilty past and his dread lest it should be discovered. The conversation is overheard by his twelve-year-old daughter, who is a Young Pioneer. She gives him away to the OGPU and that is the end of papa. She is patted on the back and walks about with a self-satisfied smirk. I saw the play from a side gallery with a view of the whole audience. The sight of the ideal Soviet child did not seem to make them happy.

September 18, 1932 [Leningrad]. The principal dramatic theater, closed for six months for repair and renovation, was reopened tonight—a sad frost. Bubnov[23] (one of Stalin's Old Guard and Commissar for Education) *read* a speech which lasted for an hour and a half. An actor assured the Government that when the capitalist world attacked the Soviet Union, actors would be in the front line of defense. There were speeches by

---

23 Andrey Sergeevich Bubnov (1884–1940), state, military, and Party official, narkom for enlightenment of the RSFSR 1929–37.

delegates from the principal theaters. Poor old Karpinsky,[24] aged eighty-six, President of the Academy of Sciences, read an inaudible speech. A telegram was read in which Bernard Shaw said how wonderful it was that this Russian theater should have run for a hundred years: in England it was remarkable if a theater ran for a hundred weeks. At 11:30 p.m. I ran away. The man in the cloakroom was much troubled by our leaving.

THE IMPROVISATIONAL, satiric theater Semperante was one of the casualties of the new order.

> Boris Golubovsky, *Bol'shie malen'kie teatry* (Moscow: Izd. im. Sabashnikovykh, 1998), 337–38.

In the early 1930s the Semperante Theater spun its wheels: the method of "improvisation" was finally compromised by bad scenarios. The presence of two talented actors could not hide the incapacity of the whole troupe, without the remotest clue of what improvisation is all about. A schism arose in the theater, which led in 1932 to a new collective—the Moscow Dramatic Theater. Bykov and Lëvshina, with a small group of enthusiasts, or more accurately, with a few very bad actors who had nowhere to go, still dragged their cross a bit to clubs, repeating their now long, rambling "improvisational" performances, in which the leaders' mastery still glistened.

TWO DIFFERENT ADAPTATIONS of A. Fadeev's[25] novel *The Rout* were on, at the Moscow Maly Theater and the Lensovet Theater.

> N. Oruzheynikov, *"Razgrom"* [*The Rout*], *Sovetsky Teatr* 12 (December 1932), 14–16. Nikolay Oruzheynikov (actually Kolesnikov), literary and theatrical editor of *Vechernaya Moskva* and RAPP spokesman, in 1931 accused Boris Pasternak's *Safe Conduct* of being "an attack on Communism," and in 1937 charged Kirshon with "Trotskyist diversionism"; he was repressed in turn and his name erased from publications.

There are two ways to adapt fiction for the stage. The first is to make the heroes say what they think about themselves. This method is devoid of psychological verisimilitude. Thoughts, as they work their way outward, find a different means of expression. True, there is the dramatic tradition of the device of the soliloquy. The hero explains himself to himself in isolation. But the use of the soliloquy demands a corresponding

---

24 Aleksandr Petrovich Karpinsky (1847–1936), geologist, president of the Academy of Sciences 1916–36; responsible for preserving the autonomy of the Academy of Sciences until 1929.

25 Aleksandr Aleksandrovich Fadeev (1901–56), proletarian writer influenced by Lev Tolstoy, influential member of the Cultural Committee and general secretary of the Writers' Union 1946–55; played a leading part in Zhdanov's postwar campaign for socialist realism. Committed suicide after Khrushchëv's denunciation of Stalin at the twentieth Party Congress.

punctuation throughout the work. Therefore neither the prolix soliloquy of Levinson in the dramatization by Narokov and Fadeev at the Maly Theater nor the equally verbose soliloquy of Mechik at the Lensovet Theater convince the spectator: for a while an artistic recitation prevails onstage, not acting. But there is another way: a dramatic composition that supplements the images of the main characters through their confrontation with secondary ones, by alternating situations, through the tension of action. [...] Let's take an episode such as the one of catching fish. At the Lensovet Theater we behold a detachment of exhausted, weakened men. Dissatisfaction is already boiling over. When they force a freezing, defenseless lad to crawl into the water, notes of taunting and a covert challenge can be heard. This home-grown bullying [*samodurstvo*] is not simply a dodging of unpleasant necessity but a sketch of its partisan scope. And Levinson's decision to force the most hard-bitten partisan to crawl into the water too is definitely not pity for the frozen lad, at least not primarily. Levinson realizes that the hoops of discipline are falling apart, that his influence over the men is faltering, and therefore he pulls his Mauser out of its holster. What do we see at the Maly? With jokes and wisecracks the partisans suggest to a young lad that he climb in the water. He is reluctant, but there is nothing you'd call a conflict. Levinson appears upstage. No anxiety, indifferent intonations, measured and premeditated gestures. The *samodurstvo* turns out to be Levinson's and not the partisans.' The whole situation becomes flat, anemic, offering nothing toward a psychological character sketch of Levinson or the emotional coloration of the action.

THE UKRAINE had long been under a cloud because of its unrepentant nationalism. Les' Kurbas moved Berezil to Khar'kov and there staged Mykola Kulish's *The National Malakhyi* in 1928: its characters are all victims of the Bolshevik regime, with no positive characters. Audiences were stirred up, but Marxist critics were predictably negative. After the 1929–30 season it was prohibited and the author compelled to undergo a regimen of self-criticism.

> Mykola Kulish, *Literaturnaya gazeta* 8 (February 28, 1931), quoted in Martha Bradshaw, ed., *Soviet Theaters 1917–1941* (New York: Research Program on the USSR, 1954), 315. Mykola Gurovich Kulish (1892–1937), Ukrainian writer, organized schools under the People's Education movement and gave aid during the 1921–22 famine; his plays were widely produced in Ukraine and southern Russia; editor of *Chervony Shlyakh* [Red path]. During the famine of 1933, he began to oppose the establishment; his plays were denounced, and he was condemned as a bourgeois-nationalist. He was deported to the Solovetski camp, where he died.

Malakhyi Stakanchuk, in demanding the immediate reform of man, voices politically oppositional sentences that are very reminiscent of the Trotskyite theories of the time. [...] Besides this the hero is armed [...] with nationalistic aphorisms [...] I did not oppose "Malakhianism" with our revolutionary creative activity (the reconstruction period), the socialistic successes and great achievements of the Party in the field of cultural–national growth. And in such a form the play assumed a politically harmful meaning by taking a stand against the Party through its expressions of Ukrainian national deviations. I eventually recognized all of my errors, and I now condemn them as I condemn all those who were identified with them during my entire literary activity during 1927 and 1928.

> Mykola Skrypnyk, *Radyans'kyi teatr* 23 (1929), 7–8, quoted in Bradshaw, *Soviet Theaters*, 315. Mykola Oleksiyovych Skrypnyk (1872–1933) was a Bolshevik functionary who ran several Ukrainian commissariats; as commissar of education (1927–33), he promoted Ukrainianism, including a new orthography; purged 1933.

Comrade Kurbas believes that the work *The National Malakhyi* by Kulish is rooted [...] in the entire history of our culture. Comrade Kurbas wants to merge his theater with these historic ideological traditions of Ukrainian culture, to join and bind it. And in this we differ with Comrade Kurbas. [...] In the national question Comrade Kurbas is repeating the old arguments, the same ones that Khyl'ovyi supported when we fought against him.

Peasants' and Workers' Theaters

> P. Barkovsky, "On the collectives of unemployed actors," *Zhizn' iskusstva* 2 (1928), 5.

The Leningrad Posredrabis runs a series of collectives of unemployed actors. The state of most of these collectives is a dismal one. [...] The "New Theater" [...] has a permanent building (155 Raz'ezhdaya). As the theater's artistic director frankly admits, the basic purpose of the collective's existence is to earn a crust of bread, by giving the public a more or less decent production. Therefore the collective "cooks up" no fewer than one premiere a week. It stands to reason that even with the most conscientious intentions, nothing can be expected except "hackwork." Example: on one Sunday they rehearse *Khamka* during the day, and at the end of the rehearsal the actors immediately make up and "whip through" *Tsar Fëdor* twice without a break (two separate sessions)!

With costume plays things usually work like this: the costumes show up only at the performance itself. I was convinced of this, when I arrived at the inspection of the play *The Dagger* and saw the notice backstage: "Today at twelve o'clock a run-through rehearsal without makeup and costumes, and at eight o'clock the performance." The performance was canceled and the run-through moved to the next day.

Now, a few words about the "New Dramatic Theater," which is housed in the Goznak Club. The situation there is no less miserable. The inspection of the work of this collective began with the fact that two productions, *Lyubov' Yarovaya* and *The Execution of Salva,* had been dropped from the work schedule, one after another, for they seemed completely unacceptable in terms of directorial and design concept, and the ideological treatment, so to speak, "limped along on all fours." This definitely raises the question of the need to change the directors and, in some part, the performers, or rather, to create a new collective. But, on the other hand, what can possibly be done, if mounting the play *Lyubov' Yarovaya* did not permit spending more than 100 rubles in all, and if the means of the collectives are not enough to attract a properly qualified director? That's the impasse from which only Posredrabis can and should find an outlet.

Of course, when you consider the importance of the struggle with unemployment, hackwork cannot be fought only with administrative measures, but in fact the attempt to "straighten out" ideological and artistic lines of the collectives is significantly paralyzed by the fact that, with the current state of affairs, the collectives cannot carry out the demands made on them. For this they need to be given the possibility (1) to increase their membership, (2) to stage no more than two premieres a month, and (3) to set as their basic task work on a flexible plan. [...]

AFRICAN AMERICANS who arrived in the Soviet Union as either immigrants or tourists were warmly welcomed by officialdom. Racism and Jim Crow in the United States fed anticapitalist propaganda. One of these visitors was the tenor Roland Hayes (1889–1977), son of ex-slaves; he toured internationally and was given a hero's welcome in the Soviet Union in 1928.

> Ronald Hayes at a village theater. MacKinley Helm, *Angel Mo' and Her Son Roland Hayes* (Boston: Little, Brown, 1942), 252–53.

I was taken to see a government-sponsored play entitled *A Window Facing the Village.*[26] There was practically no sense of theater in that production. There was no curtain, for example. The argument of the piece was projected upon a moving-picture screen, the actors moved silently into their places on the stage, the lights went up and the performance began. There was no play of the imagination, no tug of fancy: it was all as matter-of-fact as a cold-storage warehouse. The author of the play intended to show that the Party had established schools in rural districts everywhere and had carried scientific methods from the factories to the farms. What he wrote was simply an account of a forum in which a forensic address was broken up into parts and assigned to players representative of various proletarian types.

Opera in Moscow was hardly more artistic than the theater, although the opera house itself retained something of its Czarist magnificence, with its frescoes and draperies and richly upholstered seats. It was packed with working people on the night we attended a performance of "Boris Godunoff"—men and women who had come straight from mill and factory, still dressed in their dirty blue and black blouses and aprons.

---

26 *Okno v derevnyu* (1927) by Rodion Mikhaylovich Akulshin (1896–1988) concerns the introduction of electricity, radios, tractors, and airplanes into a rural village. A fervent fan of collectivization, he repented in the 1960s.

5.3. *A Window Facing the Village* by Rodion Akulshin, 1928; a play about the introduction of tractors, radios, airplanes, and electricity to a remote village. Photo: L. Tomorin, Moscow.

St. Nikonov, "Toloka-Moroka" [Fallow fields are fellow fiends], *Krasnaya Niva* [Red cornfield] 14 (1928), 4.

"What they showed us here, comrade peasants, is a book written in great big letters so even an illiterate can read it."

This was the beautiful and neat way a peasant who took part in an improvised debate appraised the meaning of the performance just seen at the Central House of the Peasant.

The hour was already late, the young folks—obviously, Muscovites—were in a hurry to leave the hall, the drop-in public had left. But those who had come for social business even from here, Moscow, try to bring the "newest thing" to their remote villages, settled deep into the comfortable seats of the Peasants' House . . .

In a far corner with wondering, uncomprehending, but still joyously awakened eyes, a Korean peasant, just arrived in Moscow, a political emigrant, gazes around the room. He doesn't get the subject of the debate, but onstage he had seen a cow and a horse; onstage a pernicious thistle was engaged in combat with profitable maize, and after the triumph of the latter—onstage a canny little farmer and his fat livestock rejoiced—and the Korean gave a broad grin, nodded his head in approval, and applauded.

You bet! The talk was after all about what they understood and what was familiar to them. The performance as a mere demonstration spoke of one of the forms of the best land tenure, the struggle with the age-old predilection for *toloka* [grazing fallow fields], for leaving allegedly infertile fields "as resting acreage." The performance explained in the most elementary way that it is more profitable to plow up and sow grass for fodder as a standing crop, more beneficial for the peasantry to cultivate, instead of useless rape and burdock, Sudan grass, maize, and beetroot.

Hence we do not intend here to consider this performance as an exemplary model. It is no more than a schematic *agitka,* true, beautifully and smartly costumed and quite literate agronomically. But this *agitka* makes us think, it stimulates serious ideas, it actively leads to a mass of wholesome agro-ideas. In this sense the experience of the Rostov comrades, who made the acquaintance of Moscow only a few days ago, deserves all manner of attention.

This agronomic theater is organized by a group of members of the Rostov drama clubs, works with the Don administrative district House of Peasants, and has already presented upward of sixty performances in the hamlet. In the repertoire of this theater there are eight plays in all (five of them written by the leader of the theater—the journalist Dmitrievich), but some of them have been shown 153 times (*Increase Income*), others more than 50 times (*Death by Drought*). Before it is sent to the hamlet, the performance is offered for revision to the peasants who come to the Rostov House of Peasants. So every play of this theater fully and accurately responds to the demands and special conditions (geographically and ethnographically) of the land.

"I can confirm it... in '21 lucerne[27] saved our cattle," a Samarian peasant hastened to share his experience after the performance. One from Tver' told how they had switched to crop rotation in his parts. Each of those who stood up spoke of his own husbandry—whether it went well or ill—and they all concluded with one and the same wish:

"The peasantry needs agronomic enlightenment. A theater like this can be understood even by an illiterate... It can help the peasantry... Give our village a theater like this." [...]

Sergey Tret'yakov, "On the Blue Blouse," *Sinyaya Bluza* 1, 73 (January 1928), 6.

The "Blue Blouse" is very sick.

And it did this to itself.

Its ailment is in part growing pains, in part the general current disorganization of the exchange of aesthetic products in the social organism. [...]

Passion (solemnity, lofty heroism) is so limited in "Blue Blouse" that it rings out in any of its everyday-cabaret or comic numbers in its program not as normal portions of the program but as intentional padding between animated acts.

Is this good or bad?

Bad—if passion petrifies into boring generalized constructions.

That is the dead end of bombastic clichés. [...]

27 A cloverlike plant used for animal fodder.

5.4. Meeting of a village Communist cell at the theater in the village of Medvenka, Kursk Gubernia. Painting by E. M. Cheptsov, 1928.

An impassioned variety stage can arise only in a country of fanatical social structuring. It can create heroes, emphasize the red feature of the slightest concrete moment of that structuring. It can be the loudspeaker of social praise or blame, address every industrial collective, every two-legged molecule of that collective. [...]

The pivot of the "Blue Blouse" is that the wit of its numbers be based not in the aesthetic (humorous, melodramatic) wit of the performance style but in the factuality, topicality, and concreteness of the given material.

This means—

Grounding in fact. A local theme. A local incident. A local sin. Called by its first and last names. Dated. Addressed. Engraved in the memory. Packed into our structure, as a whole. [...]

M. Voztochnaya, "Elektro-chastushki" [Electro-jingles], *Sinyaya Bluza* (1929), in Boris Yuzhanin and V. Mrozovsky, eds., *Sovetskaya éstrada. Sbornik repertuara moskovskogo teatra "Sinyaya bluza"* [Soviet variety: Pieces from the repertoire of the Moscow Blue Blouse Theater] (Moscow: Tea-Kino-Pechat', 1929), 64. Boris Semënovich Yuzhanin (actually Gurevich, 1900 to after 1954), instructor at the Moscow Institute of Journalism, created the "living newspaper" and Blue Blouse troupes 1923; sentenced to the gulag for espionage 1936; returned to Moscow.

[Sung by two girls in peasant costume and a lad with an accordion.]

> On the wood's edge cuckoos three
> Reporting to a jackdaw say:

Electro-jingles are what we
Sing in a new and diff'rent way.

A pretty girl sits on the roof—
Could anything be sweeter?
Why, in the house there hangs a proof
Of progress: an electric meter.

Three kilowatts, I have to state,
Make the icon lamp now out of date.
Like an electro-diamond gleaming,
Dun'ka winks with her left eye.
It would drive you madly dreaming,
If she didn't have a stye.

Forsake me not, Varvara sweet,
For you I've risked my all—
I've stole the streetlamp off the street
And 'lectrics did install.

The factory committee's bloated,
To cure its sickness we're devoted.
A proletarian power line
Replaces the red-tape one just fine.

Egor' to Tanya: "I'm aspiring
"To a kiss." "Don't be a fool.
"You have got defective wiring.
"I'd be shocked, I learned at school."

Serëzha, drop it, don't tell lies,
To joke 'bout love ain't right.
This ain't a lamp inside my eyes,
What glows is a searchlight.

Yankees love th' electric chair,
Or so it's often said.
We should tuck each millionaire
In an electric bed.

Natal'ya Il'inichna Sats (1903–93), daughter of the composer Il'ya Sats, was the artistic director of the Moscow Central Children's Theater from 1921 to 1936. Her repertoire reveled in exoticism, intended to make the imagination of the young audience soar and give it an "international education." This taste for fantasy led her to concoct very lush spectacles, combining all forms of art in a synthetic theater. She was the first in the USSR, in 1929, to use animated cartoons onstage. In the

5.5. Parade of the Workers Club of Communal Employees, Park of Culture and Recreation (later Gorky Park), Moscow, May 23, 1931.

mid-1930s, the Party condemned art specifically designed for children. The number of classic and didactic plays had to be increased. In 1936 Sats was arrested and sent to a labor camp (1937–42) and was allowed to return to Moscow only in 1958.

The first children's political production. *The Buzonade,* 1930, at the Moscow Children's Theater. In Golubovsky, *Bol'shie malen'kie teatry,* 255–57.

[Leonid] Bochin brought the Moscow Children's Theater in 1930 a "drama for pioneers," earmarked for amateurs. Natal'ya Il'inichna Sats, who had a keen instinct for talented people, understood that it might work out to be a real play about modern youngsters, school, the Pioneer movement,[28] which few professional playwrights knew anything about ... The word "BUZA" had a very broad meaning, both favorable and unfavorable: delinquency, escape from the influence of the rules of discipline. For us, young spectators, the second meaning was considered far from compromising, rather, on the contrary, attractive! ... BUZA was involvement in life, a struggle with stagnation, formalism; the eternal theme ...

Lin'ka Smekhov, the hero of *The Buzonade,* does not want to endure the deadly boredom of endless meetings and comes in conflict with the Pioneer leader Tipa (what

28 Pioneer Movement, a Communist organization for children aged nine to fourteen, founded 1922 as an adjunct of the komsomol movement and somewhat resembling the Scout organization, which had been suppressed. Its heyday was during the Five-Year Plans, when, though not compulsory, its membership was almost universal.

a name!) Motylina, a young bureaucrat with her brains in mothballs. Tipa Motylina (she spins [*motaet*] tedium and red tape) is a commander and a dictator who gets by "on lung power," the youngsters are becoming accessories of voting machines. For her *buza* is hooliganism, a token of disfavor. [...]

Lin'ka Smekhov (splendidly played by Natasha Parkalab) is absolutely logical in his views of life, his *buza* is the organic rejection of a heartless system. Tipa orders a trial of Lin'ka—we, the spectators, took part in the trial. At one of the performances I saw some young fellow on his own bat vote for Lin'ka's expulsion from the Pioneers. This only heated up the others. Today I wonder if this was concocted as a theater "of provocation," to express divergent points of view? [...]

The author, through the character Evgeniya the Genius, throws a question to the spectators: "Is a *buzoteer* a slacker, a hooligan, a trouble-maker? ... What do you think, kids?" [...]

Sats made the production gaudy, with a satirical tinge rare in children's theater: the stage was hidden behind a sheet of paper with the inscription "Minutes of the Thousand and First Meeting." The council of the Pioneer detachment was a long table, behind it sit kids in identical blouses with strings attached to their hands. Tipa is above them, pulling the strings, and they all vote unanimously "Pro" or "Con." Downstage a spider is spinning, enveloping the children's lives. This was all thought up by the irrepressible Lesha Bochin. [...]

The production was called "controversial"—and that's true. It excited both the child and the adult audience—no one remained indifferent! I personally remember that pedagogues and youth leaders were not so enthusiastic about recommending going to it.

Natal'ya Sats, *Nash put'. Moskovsky teatr dlya detey i ego zritel'* [Our path: The Moscow Children's Theater and its audience] (Moscow: Moskovsky oblastnoy otdel narodnogo obrazovaniya, 1932), 54–55.

In February 1930 a brigade of actors of ours [Moscow Children's Theater] left for a month and a half of service to all the villages of the Kolomensky district of the Moscow province. The brigade traveled with a specialized agit-repertoire and gave seventy performances. Despite the bitter cold and our actors putting up and taking down the scenery themselves, sleeping on the ground in their clothes and moving the shows several kilometers from one village to another, mostly on foot, they carried out the work with great enthusiasm. Here are some excerpts from the diary of the brigade actress N. Parkalab about our trip: "The kolkhoz organization had active assistants in the person of pioneers and schoolchildren, which is why the best received of our whole program was *About Granny Avdotya,* which shows how Pioneers carry out the work of explanation, as a result of which Granny Addotya joins the kolkhoz...

"From a letter of Anna Monakhova, age eleven: 'Thank you for the show and please come back again. As schoolchildren and young Pioneers we will support our parents in the Leninets kolkhoz.'

"Lyuba Zaytsev, age twelve: 'I liked best how the Pioneers convinced Granny Avdotya to join the kolkhoz and liquidate illiteracy, and we will do the same thing with our parents.'

"A prominent inspection of the Nepetsenk, Mukhinsk, and Pobleevsk schools, as well as others, showed that the schools are very clean and in every class there is a sanitary commission of children, all the walls are hung with its slogans, beautifully executed.

"The issue of hygiene is brought out in our production *About Little Epishka*. In another show, *Town and Country*, we discuss the union of town and country."

––––––––––––––

THE COMINTERN organized an affiliate called the International Union of Revolutionary Theaters (Mezhdunarodnoe ob'edinenie revolyutsionykh teatrakh, MORT). It proclaimed an International Worker's Theater Day on February 15, 1931. In May 1933 it organized the first and only International Olympiad of Revolutionary Theaters in Moscow: eleven foreign troupes joined fifteen companies from the Republics of the Soviet Union to perform works exemplifying socialist theatrical techniques.

"Instructions for the preparations for the International Workers' Theatrical Olympiad, organised by the IWDU," Bulletin no. 1 of the Organization Committee of the International Workers Theatrical Olympiad, Cooperative Publishing Society of the Foreign Workers of the USSR, 1932, 29–30.

On the basis of the decision of the enlarged Presidium of the IWDU of July 1931, the International Workers' Theatrical Olympiad will be held on October 15, 1932, in Moscow. This Olympiad is to serve as a review and mobilization of the forces of the proletarian and left-wing theater for the struggle against fascism, social fascism, and imperialist war, and for the defense of the Soviet Union.

The International Workers' Theatrical Olympiad will make it possible to reveal the creative forces of the revolutionary theatrical front in all countries, and will help to generalize this experience of the struggle of the workers' theater, to attract the toilers into the mass revolutionary proletarian organizations. Moreover, the Olympiad will help to reveal the general line of development of the revolutionary and workers' theatrical movement to raise the workers' theater to a higher political level and help to educate cadres of the revolutionary theatrical front on the basis of Marxism–Leninism.

Together with this, the Olympiad is intended to help win over separate groups of art workers who are affiliated with the Left theater (stage managers, artists, actors, musicians, etc.) among whom, because of the aggravated economic crisis in the capitalist countries, quite a revolutionary trend has developed during the last few years. [. . .]

4. Selection of theaters must follow the line of the organization of revolutionary competition between all the affiliated workers and sympathizing theaters, groups, and agitation and propaganda troupes of the sections of the IWDU.

B. Fatelevich, "Theatres of Workers' Youth (TRAM) in the struggle for a new level of quality," International Workers' Theatrical Olympiad Bulletin no. 2, International Union of the Revolutionary Theatre, Moscow, 1932, 28–29.

The low theoretical level of the members permitted certain erroneous theories to penetrate into the movement. [...] The gist of these hostile class theories, which penetrated into the TRAM movement and through it into the whole system of mass amateur theatrical circles, consisted in a tendency to underrate the importance of the TRAM as a theater. [...] The TRAMs were led to keep aloof from the professional theaters; they failed to understand the necessity of mastering the cultural heritage of the past; the members of the various groups were diverted from the struggle for mastering their profession.

[...] We must, however, acknowledge the creative powers of the movement. With the aid of the Party and Young Communist League, the members of the TRAM struggled against and finally overcame these "theories." [...] A clear understanding of the mistakes made and a program of action designed to eliminate them—such were the results of the historic resolution adopted by the Central Committee of the Communist Party of the USSR with regard to the organization of literary and artistic bodies and of the resolutions adopted by the Central Committee of the Young Communist League with regard to the TRAM movement. [...]

The following were the leading slogans of reconstruction adopted by the plenary session:

"Struggle for a critical mastering of the cultural heritage."
"For the creation of a dramaturgy worthy of the epoch of social construction."
"Struggle for new creative cadres and a militant union with the Soviet professional theater."

Lenin's theory of a critical mastering of the cultural heritage had to a certain extent been ignored by the members of the TRAM. [...] The study of theatrical culture was treated by the TRAM as a purely theoretical subject. Being out of touch with the experience of other theatrical systems, the TRAM stage managers were obliged to fall back mainly on the method of improvisation. They struggled against the idealistic tendencies of the Moscow Art Theater and Meyerhold machinism, while in practice, in consequence of their theoretical weakness, they fell into both errors without being able to ascertain the reasons for it. [...]

[...] In view of the "theories" that previously existed in the movement to the effect that the members of the TRAM were not actors but only stage reporters and that the TRAM's function was to train mass propagandists, the various TRAM troupers came to include many earnest and reliable people, good or steadfast Communists and Young Communists who might have been useful in many branches of socialist construction but had no talent whatever for the stage.

Every TRAM group must carefully consider whether we are not spoiling these comrades' lives by leading them away from their trade or occupation when it is impossible to train them to be actors of the Soviet theater. [...]

The Red Army Theater

In 1929 the Political Administration of the Red Army decided that it should have its own theater to indoctrinate military personnel with propaganda about the glorious victories and discipline of the Soviet forces. The actors were to be drawn from the companies that had been entertaining in clubs. At first it was located in the Central House of the Red Army. From June 1930 it was known as the Theater of the Worker-Peasant Red Army (TRKKA), according to the press of the time. The first seasons, bulky with historical and heroic dramas performed amateurishly, were failures.

> K. Podsotsky, "The Red Army Theater is created," *Krasnaya Zvezda* [Red star] (September 6, 1929), 16.

The Red Army Theater over the course of the last two or three months has started work. [...]

The season obviously ought to open with an historical play. Plays reflecting the contemporary condition of the Red Army do not exist yet. In this regard one needs to hope for the remarkably great assistance and cooperation on the part of organizations that can provide this material. True-to-life material can be provided by military tribunals, the public prosecutor's office, Party committees, especially in connection with purged Party organizations, individual commanders, and soldiers. It is indispensable that every military unit take an interest in the repertoire of our theater and give thought to what it could provide for reflection onstage of the contemporary condition of the Red Army. Sociopolitical organizations ought to help us create a modern repertoire. [...]

In the current year the Red Army Theater will work in the Red Army Hall of the TsDKA. Preparatory work is already under way for the appropriate equipping of that hall. The equipping can be finished by the end of October, i.e., when the theater begins work. [...]

> I. Gamazov and S. Dashkevich, "On the threshold of a great mistake (a matter of discussion)," *Krasnaya Zvezda* 215 (September 18, 1929), 15.

The most important thing right now is to plan correctly "the whole setup" of the new theater, to define its tasks. All is not right with the organizers of the theater, and they are on the threshold of a serious mistake.

How do its organizers define the role and tasks of the Red Army Theater in their documents and public statements? "The theater must be a weapon of the military, international, class education of the RKKA [Worker-Peasant Army]." "The theater must be one of the weapons of the fighting ranks of the army." All this which is, in general, correct in relation to the RKKA is wrong in that it completely ignores the civilian spectator—the worker, the civil servant, the komsomol member, the reserve officer. Those statements are infused with the inaccurate idea that there is no part for the civilian spectator to play in the theater, that the theater will in essence be only an intra-army matter. "The Red Army Theater sets itself educational tasks only in regard to the Red Army itself"—that's what this setup will lead to in essence. [...]

All these mistakes must be corrected as soon as possible. Once the Red Army Theater is created, there will be no sense to creating in Moscow an independent theater for the goals of military propaganda among the civilian population (there have been such attempts). [...] The Red Army appeared to be the initiator of the creation of this new theater, and the realization of the basic leading principle in its work ought to belong to it. But not only does this not exclude; it presumes the widest benefit for the theater as one of the weapons of military propaganda and the widest (and not only material) participation of the organizations of workers' communities in its creation. [...]

> Workers of the Red Army Theater, "Theaters, what have you done to protect the country? An appeal from the Red Army Theater," *Rabis* (1931), 3.

Workers of all the shops of the Red Army Theater ask the army of Moscow art workers: what will you show on the day of the thirteenth anniversary of the Worker-Peasant Red Army? Hastily written and badly prepared sketches? Or perhaps special exhibits on the texts of *Ruslan and Lyudmila, The Swamp, Woe from Wit, Louis the... teenth, Love and Intrigue,* and *Napoleon II?*—Except for Vs. Meyerhold's theater (*The Ultimate Decisive*),[29] there is not a single contemporary play in the repertoires of all the rest of the Moscow theaters that has given a thought to the matter of the military danger approaching us from the west, plays that mobilize the spectator to protect the one and only government of socialist labor in the world. [...]

Our Concrete Suggestions

1. Headed by the Red Army, a parade of all the Moscow theaters to the TsDKA—for "military technique."

2. A hundred percent introduction to the Osoavnakhim of the workers of the Moscow theaters.

3. Excursions of theaters to the Work.-Peas. Red Army Museum.

4. Outings of each theater to the Red Army barracks no fewer than once every six months.

5. To expand the work of circles of military knowledge into theatrical enterprises. To achieve the maximum involvement of the workers.

6. To organize a military corner in the clubs of theatrical workers.

The Red Army Theater will take up the challenge of any of the Moscow theaters for the best performance of this work. Our referee will be the Cent. Comm. of our Union of Art Workers.

---

29 *Posledny reshitel'ny* (1931) by Vsevolod Vishnevsky, in which the deaths of a few heroic sailors are shown to be expendable in view of the Soviet Union's vast population and resources.

THE THEATER became central in relation to the eleven neighboring TKAs existing in the USSR (from talks with the official of the theater V. I. Papirov, August 1932). From that time the theater was abbreviated TsTKA in the press and on posters.

> I. Kruti, "The Theatre of the Red Army," International Workers' Theatre Olympiad Bulletin no. 2, International Union of the Revolutionary Theater, Moscow, 1932, 34–35. Isaak Aronovich Kruti (1890–1955), Ukrainian theater critic, correspondent to *Teatr i dramaturgiya*, translated Korneychuk's plays into Ukrainian.

The Central Theater of the Red Army in Moscow is a combination of three theaters of different kinds: drama, revue, and a group performing Red Army songs. During the winter, all three theaters are open in Moscow, playing to audiences of workers and Red Army men. In summer, when the army is in camp, all these theaters are transferred to the camps, where, besides giving performances, they also perform a great work in instructing mass amateur study circles, comprising in all as many as five hundred thousand persons. In many military districts of the USSR, similar theaters have been organized on the model of the Central Theater of the Red Army.

The group performing Red Army songs constitutes a peculiar kind of agitation and propaganda brigade. This group, which comprises twelve singers, three dancers, three reciters, and two accordion players, presents its half-hour programs as a sort of dramatized tale, punctuated by songs and dances, organically connected with the subject of the given performance. [. . .]

The Revue Theater is a [. . .] small portable theater giving witty performances interspersed with singing and dancing [. . .] It reflects all the burning questions of the day, questions of current politics within the USSR and urgent questions of military development. In the same manner, the songs performed by the singing group are designed to find their way from the stage into the everyday barrack life of the Red Army men, so *the repertoire and the methods of staging employed in the Revue Theater should enrich the amateur art of the Red Army drama.*

With this object in view, many of the performances and the majority of the concerts are staged by this theater with a maximum of simplicity, the materials used being the objects that come to hand in the daily life of the Red Army. [. . .]

The Theater of Drama [has as its] principal task [. . .] to create *a realist performance of the great ideological exaltation in the grand style.* The theater is well aware that no "special" method exists for the production of a military play. [. . .] In its performances the theater deals with the history of the Civil War, tries to reveal its international content and to create a common type of the hero in the recent struggle. The theater also tries to explain the army's present processes of development. [. . .]

Meyerhold

Official displeasure with *The Inspector General* made it imperative for Meyerhold to stage a Soviet play, but the scripts he submitted to Glavrepertkom—a dramatization of Bely's novel *Moscow* and Tret'yakov's *I Want a Baby*—were turned down. He was forced to revive *The Magnanimous Cuckold,* with Zinaida Raykh in Babanova's role.

> Iosif Stalin to RAPP. In *Sobranie sochineny,* 9:329. From the archive of V. Stavsky.[30]

As to Meyerhold, [Bill'-Belotserkovsky] is more or less wrong—not because M. is a Communist (there are plenty of "good-for-nothing" people among the Communists) but because he, M., as a theater worker, despite some disgusting traits (affectations, mannerisms, surprising and harmful gallops away from real life in the direction of the "classic" past), is undoubtedly bound to our Soviet community, of course, and cannot be numbered among the category of "aliens."

AS A STOPGAP MEASURE, Meyerhold turned again to the classics with Griboedov's verse satire *Woe from Wit* (*Gore ot uma*). He tried to distinguish it by using an earlier title *Woe to Wit* (*Gore umu*) and giving it some political point by hinting that Chatsky, the protagonist, was allied to the Decembrists. Much of the business seemed extraneous, an effort to give some interest to lines the audience could recite from their own memories.

> V. Smyshlaev, *Pechalno i nekhorosho v nashem teatre . . . Dnevnik 1927–1931 gg.* [*Things are painful and unpleasant in our theater . . . diary 1927–31*] (Moscow: IGS, 1996), 136–37.

March 22, 1928, Moscow. Last night I was at Meyerhold's production of *Woe to Wit.* There have been a lot of debates and strange rumors around this performance. They say there was a terrible scandal at GAKhN on Monday: Piksanov[31] showed up with a lecture in which he insulted Meyerhold in every possible way. In reply Meyerhold called Piksanov a "nitwit," which, in Gabrichevsky's[32] opinion, is the honest truth. Unfortunately, I was not at the lecture, but some say that Meyerhold was carried out of the Academy in a faint, others that the audience threw galoshes at Meyerhold . . .

My interest in the production was heightened. I liked it a lot. I accepted it as a *lyrical* work of Meyerhold. Chatsky is Meyerhold. And all of Chatsky's lines resound through

---

30 Vladimir Petrovich Stavsky (actually Kirpichnikov, 1900–1943), general secretary of the Soviet Writer's Union 1936–38 and editor of *Novy Mir* 1937–41; died at the front as a war correspondent.

31 Nikolay Kir'yakovich Piksanov (1878–1969), literary historian and professor at Moscow University from 1921; his important monograph on Griboedev was published 1934. He had also objected to Stanislavsky's performance of Famusov 1912.

32 Aleksandr Georg'evich Gabrichesky (1891–1968), art historian and friend of Boris Pasternak.

Meyerhold's individuality—even down to "Away from Moscow, I go to seek throughout the world..." And when at the end Garin (made up as Meyerhold—that can't have been accidental) left the stage with his trunks, I whispered to Olin'ke [Smyshaev's wife, Ol'ga] seated beside me, "That's Meyerhold leaving for America!" [...]

The whole performance is fresh, subtle, original, and wonderfully musical! It's beautiful! After this production I have fallen in love with the theater again! I wanted to work in it again and again! Meyerhold is brilliant. And that canine howl that the Moscow critics set up around this production reminds me of the barking of Krylov's pug dog.[33] [...]

> "Stenographic record of the debate over the staging of Griboedov's comedy *Woe to Wit* at the Meyerhold Theater, 2 April 1928," in *Mnemozina. Dokumenty i fakty iz istorii otechestvennogo teatra XX veka*, ed. V. V. Ivanov (Moscow: Indrik, 2009), 4:360–65.

B. G. SUSHKEVICH:[34] Art is not created for the mob, not to be a sedative, but art is made for those who move toward change, for those who appear as the creative intellect of future life. [...] What strikes me as really awful about the modern theater is that situation when the spectator can go to *Lyubov' Yarovaya* and *Armored Train, The Adjoining Room,* and *The Rout, Mutiny, The Rails Are Humming,*[35] and *Woe to Wit* in exactly the same way. He goes everywhere and enjoys in the same way with more or less the same satisfaction whatever the case. This is a dreadful moment in art, a dreadful moment in the development of theater, for it is philistinism. Here is this man who goes to be entertained, this man who goes to everything indifferently, who will go whether they present something new or not. When we propose that art should somehow foresee the man of the future, the intellectual of the future, who wants his own means of understanding life, his own relation to the life around him, this probably does not correspond to what currently satisfies the inveterate playgoer. So that this new man can feel himself excited by the performance, the first thing that has to happen is that the theater respond to the rhythm of life. Formally, with the viewpoint of the special understanding of the very work onstage, not the text, not only the words uttered but the rhythm of the action, the rhythm of the organization of this entire space you see, the rhythm of the mise-en-scène's choices, the rhythm of the individual sections, the rhythm of the whole production—which is the genuine action. And then, when we

---

33 Refers to Ivan Krylov's fable "The Elephant and the Pug Dog," in which, by barking at an elephant, a pug dog gets a reputation for courage.

34 Boris Mikhaylovich Sushkevich (1887–1946), actor at the MAT from 1908 and the First Studio from 1912; director at the MAT 2 until 1932. Artistic director of the New Theater from 1937, instilling Stanislavskian principles.

35 The biggest hits of 1927–28—*Armored Train 14-69* [*Bronepoezd 14-69*] by V. V. Ivanov, *The Adjoining Room* (*Prokhodnaya komnata*) by V. Pushmin, *The Rout* (*Razgrom*) by B. Lavrenëv, *Mutiny* (*Myatezh*) by A. A. Furmanov and S. Plivanova, *The Rails Are Humming* (*Rélsy gudyat*) by V. Kirshon—all deal with events in the Revolution and Civil War or else with current industrialization.

look at the production we are discussing today, the first thing anyone present should notice about the arrangement of the director's plan, the first thing that appears to the theatrical observer, are those new conditions that are created for the rhythmic sounds of those themes that live in Griboedov's *Woe to Wit*. That's what's interesting. [...]

This means that the sensitive directorial barometer that is Meyerhold felt that vibration in the artistic atmosphere which told him that it is appropriate with all passion to change the very ground plan of the stage and the very meaning of those scenic relations that offer a new solution to a new mise-en-scène and new configurations. This shows that we are perhaps reaching a critical moment in the theater. He who does not hear this, does not feel the theater right now at a kind of dangerous moment, he will answer for this before history, because it no longer behooves us to sit as we are sitting now, as you see and hear me, because now it is no longer possible to receive a performance as we do receive it. We have to reorganize inside and out, form things differently to fall in line with the rhythm beating throughout the land. And for that reason I consider that the work of destruction carried out by Vsevolod Émil'evich is a positive moment in the work of creation, is also a positive moment, but I say both destruction and creation, and therefore I will not be among those who sit with a handkerchief and wipe away tears and say, "Goodness me, how awful, they don't act *Woe from Wit* here the way they do at the Maly Theater." [...]

IN SPRING 1928, when Glaviskusstvo was being organized, the Komsomol and part of the Moscow press were engaged in an impassioned attack on the Bol'shoy Theater. The next theatrical cause célèbre (the first in which Glaviskusstvo was closely involved) concerned the Meyerhold Theater.[36] While Meyerhold enjoyed a five-week vacation in France in 1928, the box-office receipts at his theater dropped to 40 percent. Glaviskusstvo ordered him to cease negotiations for a foreign tour and, fearing a repeat of Mikhail Chekhov's defection, continued his theater's subsidy only on the condition that he return and put it on an even keel.

In reply, Meyerhold mounted three plays that were violent attacks on the bureaucracy and petty bourgeois conformity in Soviet society: *The Shot* by Aleksandr Bezymensky (1929) and *The Bedbug,* "a fairy-tale comedy" (1929), and *The Bathhouse,* a "drama in 6 tableaux with circus and fireworks" (1930), both by Mayakovsky.

> Meyerhold, telegram to Mayakovsky, May 4, 1928, Sverdlovsk. In *Stat'i, pis'ma, rechi, besedy,* 2:176.

Last time I call on your good sense. Theater perishing. No plays. Need to lay off classics. Don't want to reduce repertoire. I ask serious question: can we count on getting your play this year. Wire direct Sverdlovsk, Central Hotel.

Meyerhold

36 See "O Meyerkhol'de i Chekhove: Nasha anketa," *Novy zritel'* 38 (September 16, 1928): 8–13.

THROUGHOUT THE 1920S Mayakovsky had been active as a public poet, a world traveler, a poster propagandist, and an avant-garde filmmaker and prolific screenwriter. Beyond the revision of *Mystery Bouffe,* his activities in the theater had been limited to a few agit-prop sketches and circus scenarios. In 1926 he signed an agreement with the Meyerhold Theater to compose "A Comedy with a Murder" in two weeks. Instead, by late December 1928, he had completed a new play, *The Bedbug,* which was read at the Meyerhold Theater on December 28.

Aleksandr Rodchenko, "Work with Mayakovsky," in *Aleksandr Rodchenko. Opyty dlya budushchego: dnevniki, stat'i, pis'ma, zapiski* [Experiments for the future] (Moscow: Grant, 1996), 254–55.

I particularly remember how Mayakovsky began reading *The Bedbug.* It was so surprising and so brilliantly original . . .

He picked up the manuscript and began:

V.

Mayakovsky

The Bedbug

a fairy tale etc.

That very harsh, surprising, and very loud *V,* and the rest done the same way, flabbergasted me.

Apparently Meyerhold objected to me as designer, and therefore the rehearsals had already begun and the first four parts, which were contemporary and everyday, were done by Kukryniksy,[37] while the future—the 70s and parts 5, 6, 7, 8, and 9, were not quite done.

But Volodya [Mayakovsky] evidently convinced Meyerhold and they invited me to be designer. I quickly came up with a model, and while the assistants built it, I rapidly made sketches for costumes, and there were quite a lot of them.

Meyerhold is a brilliant director; it's very interesting to watch his rehearsals, when he himself shows the actors graphically how he creates the roles, the stage movement.

Meyerhold does everything himself and therefore he loves young, unknown designers, whom he can control.

But he knew that that wouldn't work with me and gave me complete freedom of action and contradicted me in nothing. Only in the last few days, when they brought the construction from the workshop and it sat for a while in the auditorium, did he announce that it was very depressing and that none of it would do.

Similarly, when some new costumes showed up onstage, he announced that they would not do at all.

37 Kukryniksy (Porfiry Nikitch Krylov, Mikhail Vasil'evich Kupryanov, Nikolay Alekseevich Soko-lov), a trio of cartoonists who had met at VkhUTeMAS and worked from 1924 for the humor magazine *Krokodil*; they became world renowned during World War II for their cartoons and posters pillorying the Axis leaders.

But I quietly remarked, that's all right, let's look at it all onstage at night, and then we can argue and decide.

The workers began to set it up, and after it was all installed, I went home for dinner. That night, a rehearsal was called with the construction and the costumes.

I was deliberately late, and when I entered the hall, the rehearsal was going on. The first person to come up to me was Volodya; he shook my hand, said "thank you" and that he liked everything.

I remarked gloomily that Meyerhold was dissatisfied.

Volodya said that, on the contrary, he was in seventh heaven.

Meyerhold similarly greeted me as if nothing had happened during the day.

Interview with Meyerhold, *Vechernaya Moskva* (February 11, 1929), on the eve of the premiere.

The staging will realize a basic concept of the author: to show the play as a satiric comedy and a fairy-tale comedy. The author and director establish a sharp division between Parts I and II; consequently, the physical production is assigned to designers of different schools: the Kukryniksy (realists) and Rodchenko (constructivists). To divide the parts of the performance more sharply, the composer D. Shostakovich[38] has written a special intermezzo, which will be performed before the second part of the performance begins as an autonomous musical number by the GOSTIM orchestra under the leadership of Yu. S. Nikol'sky.[39]

THE PREMIERE took place at the Meyerhold Theater on February 13, 1929, with Mayakovsky billed as assistant director. The reactions of the general public were mixed, but the press was almost exclusively negative, if not belligerent, particularly about the scenes set in the future.

N. Osinsky, "'The Bedbug' at the Meyerhold Theater," *Izvestia* (February 26, 1929), 47, 3583. N. Osinsky (actually Valerian Valerianovich Obolensky, 1887–1938), Party official, economist, was also a staff journalist for *Izvestia* 1917–35 and *Pravda* 1917–32.

The second part is worse not only in the writing but in the directing. And the defects are the very same in both: the socialism comes out scraggly, feeble, leftist-intellectual. The characters are either muted abstracts or, on the contrary, they dance their movements as at the Kamerny Theater in days gone by.

---

38 Dmitry Dmitrievich Shostakovich (1906–75), composer; worked as head of the musical division and as pianist of GosTIM 1928. Mayakovsky had wanted him to imitate the march rhythms of fire brigade bands and was less than pleased with his music for *Bedbug*. In 1936–37 and again in 1948 he was accused by Party critics of formalism (see chapter 6).

39 Yury Sergeevich Nikol'sky (1895–192?), composer and conductor.

P., "*The Bedbug* at Vsev. Meyerhold's Theater," *Prozhektor* [Spotlight] 10, 180
(1929), 28.

The Bedbug as seen at Meyerhold's Theater is light and merry. Wisecracks, comical
situations, the splendid acting of Igor' Il'insky, and, compared with earlier productions, good acting from the rest of the actors—all this elates the spectator, weary of V.
Meyerhold's "academic" productions.

Many have rebuked the author and the theater for showing the new life of people
in 1979 as bloodless, schematic, so that one can't help but think that it will be boring
to live in this future society, and this explains why the "bacillus of love" (according
to Mayakovsky—philistinism as well) spreads throughout the new people with such
unusual ease. This is hardly a substantial rebuke: the theater did this accurately, without
having taken on the impossible task of showing the new society "with all its details."

Review of *The Bedbug*, *Rabochaya Moskva* (*Moscow at Work*) (February 24,
1929).

Incomprehensible . . . No good for anything. Except taking children to.

Vsevolod Meyerhold, "The reconstruction of the theater," from lectures given
in Leningrad, Kiev, and Moscow, 1929. In *Stat'i, pis'ma, rechi, besedy*, 2:194–207.

Doesn't it seem to you that from the moment when film began to talk, the international significance of the screen disappeared. A Chaplin, who now is understood in
America and Holland and the USSR, becomes incomprehensible as soon as he starts
to speak in English. The Russian peasant will refuse to accept an English Chaplin.
Chaplin was close to him and comprehensible, so long as all he did was mime. So we
regard this achievement as a surrender of cinema's position in its struggle with the
dramatic theater. [. . .]

We, in building a theater that must compete with cinema, we say: let us pursue to
the end our task of cinefying the theater, let us realize onstage a whole series of technical
devices of the cinema screen (not meaning that we will hang a screen in the theater),
give us the possibility of transferring to a stage equipped with the latest technology,
suiting those demands that we will make of the theatrical spectacle, and we will create
such productions as will attract as many playgoers as the movies do.

A revolution in the realm of reconstructing the forms and content of the contemporary theater has been halted in its progress only because of the lack of funds for the
reequipping of the stage and auditorium.

What's more: we must study the demands of the contemporary spectator and
consider a performance not for three hundred to five hundred persons (the proletariat
does not want to go to so-called intimate or chamber theaters) but for tens of thousands (look at how sports stadiums are filled to bursting, where nowadays footballers,
volleyball players, hockey teams show off their skills and where tomorrow theatric'
sports events will be shown). The contemporary spectator wants to get a thri'

production so grandiose that its intensity is to the power of thousands, not hundreds. Every performance that is created now is created with the intention of summoning the audience to take part in the consummation of the performance, and both playwriting and the technique of modern directing activate their machines with the assumption that the performance will be created not only by the abilities of the actors and the stage machinery but also by the abilities of the audience. We now build every production with the consideration that it will appear unfinished. We do this, knowing that the spectator will produce the most remarkable improvement. [...]

We regard the participation of the masses in creating productions not at all from the viewpoint, quote, that we are swelling our ranks and the whole country will turn into one enormous army of thespians. The theater is becoming a bridgehead for the formation of a new human being, the theater is helping to launch a new training program for the people. For the conclusive conquest of the forces of nature by human beings, the new human needs that agility that is easily provided by training in theatrical recreation, in clubs and their laboratories, in games in stadiums, in parades of our revolutionary holidays. Here, fighting on the front lines of the cultural revolution, the creative initiative of the masses will flourish luxuriantly. [...]

The actor today occupies the central role in the theater because all the most complicated questions of theatrical culture of our time are tightly linked to one supreme question, namely, the question who and what format will intensively provide the audience with that thrill of the will without which any composition of an audience is today unthinkable, an audience organized not so that the production is composed as some commercial fiction but so that the morning after the performance, the machine of construction will be put in motion with even greater energy.

Our great progress along the road of socialist construction is impeded by a great portion of humanity that easily yields to such vices as Oblomovitis,[40] Tolstoyan nonresistance to evil, banditry, alcoholism, religious narcosis, counterrevolutionary grumbling...

It's a funny thing: there are 36,805 religious associations in the RSFSR. The number of religious communities in comparison with 1922–23 has nearly doubled. Sectarian organizations of every stripe are increasing: Evangelists, Christians, Baptists, Tolstoyans, Seventh-Day Adventists, Dukhobors, and so on. No fewer than 1.7 million young people are under their influence.

Read the newspapers from day to day, and you will be convinced: almost daily, urgently, maliciously, the village kulak plunges a "knife in the back" of the Communist, the rural correspondent, the representative of Soviet authority.

If we juxtapose this reality with what our contemporary repertoire "puts forward as life," we have to admit that our theater is still woefully remote from life!

We had already renounced apoliticism in the theater; we know how to react quickly and in good time to the most important political, economic, and cultural events in the country (the dangerous work of miners, the fight with the demobilized mob, the

---

40 Oblomov is the lazy, phlegmatic landowner in Goncharov's novel of that name.

class struggle in the countryside, the women's struggle for emancipation), but who is ready to give the spectator of theatrical productions that thrill, which, to our mind, appears to be the best way of saving the sick part of citizens of our union from the poison gases of the clerics and the village kulaks or from the decadent narcotics of the urban petty bourgeoisie?

[...] The answer is the actor hand in hand with the playwright.

Now, when the tempo of the Five-Year Plan is tightly bound to the tempo of the cultural revolution, we cannot remain indifferent to the diseases of the portion of humanity that prevents us in our progress on the path to socialism. [...]

The theater is faced with a new task.

The theater must put the spectator through a work-over that, over the course of the performance, will stir up and ripen in him the strongest will to struggle, which will help him to overcome the Oblomovitis, Manilovitis,[41] hypocrisy, erotomania, and pessimism within himself. [...]

To RECONFIRM his Soviet credentials, Meyerhold then staged a verse tragedy about the Civil War, *The Second Army Commander* by Il'ya Sel'vinsky.[42] Director and author clashed from the start: Meyerhold wanted to create "a monumental musical tragedy," while Sel'vinsky accused his staging of "agit-prop primitiveness." It opened in Khar'kov on July 24, 1929, and, thanks largely to the striking stage pictures, it was a success.

> Vsevolod Meyerhold, *The Meyerhold Theater and the Red Army*, 1929. In *Stat'i, pis'ma, rechi, besedy*, 2:179.

The Meyerhold State Theater (GosTIM) from its very inception has been closely connected with the Red Army.

In the days of the first performances of the first production of our theater (when it was called "RSFSR 1 Theater"—*Dawns*—the Red Army by its capture of Perekop brought to a victorious close the Civil War in the south. In the course of the action, during the performance, we included news about the heroic storming of Perekop. This first experiment at introducing into a performance a current-events portion was greeted by the spectators with great enthusiasm.

MEYERHOLD'S NEXT COLLABORATION with Mayakovsky, *The Bathhouse*, was a satire on bureaucracy. When it was read to the Artistic Political Council of the Meyerhold Theater on September 23, 1929, it was met with roars of laughter and applause. The writer Mikhail Zoshchenko reported, "Rarely have I seen such an

---

41 Manilov is a dreamy, sentimental landowner in Gogol's comic epic *Dead Souls*.
42 Il'ya L'vovich Sel'vinsky (1899–1968), poet and playwright; author of memoirs about Meyerhold.

utterly positive reaction." Nevertheless, the play was held up for two months by Glavrepertkom.

Vladimir Mayakovsky, *Ogonëk* (November 30, 1929).

The Bathhouse is a "drama in six acts with circus and fireworks."

    The Bathhouse has journalistic aims, and that is why its characters are not so-called living people but tendencies come to life.

    [...] The theater has forgotten that it is a show, a spectacle.

    [...] The point of my work in the theater is an attempt to restore spectacle to the theater, an attempt to transform the stage boards into a rostrum. [...]

———

ONCE THE BARBS were blunted, the play was given its first production at the Theater of the House of the People in Leningrad on January 30, 1930, directed by V. Lyutse.[43] It was, again in Zoshchenko's words, "greeted with a killing coolness." Rumor ran that the Moscow production would be banned. However, it was licensed on February 9, 1930, just three days after Mayakovsky had joined RAPP. There had been considerable pressure on him to do so.

Igor' Il'insky, *Sam o sebe* [Myself about myself] (Moscow: Iskusstvo, 1973), 277.

I saw Vladimir Mayakovsky for the last time at the first night of *The Bathhouse* at the Meyerhold Theater. After the performance, received with no great warmth by the audience, or at any rate, Mayakovsky painfully felt this was the case, he stood alone on the porch of the lobby, letting the departing audience pass him by, looking straight into their eyes. That is how he has remained in my memory.

———

DURING the postpremiere debate, the critic V. Ermilov[44] complained that Act III contained parodies of RAPP's literary slogans: "For the living man" and "Learn from the classics." They were subsequently removed. Again, the critical consensus in the press was extremely hostile.

"Account of an editorial conference, with the participation of workers of the Burevestnik works, theater critics, and the author of the play," *Vechernaya Moskva* (March 31, 1930).

Advice to the Meyerhold Theater and Comrade Mayakovsky
Scrub Out The Bathhouse

43 Vladimir Vladimirovich Lyutse (1904–73), a pupil of Meyerhold and actor at the RSFSR 1; he was a member of the team that helped create the scenery for *A Doll's House* in 1922.

44 Vladimir Ermilov (1904–65), a member of the editorial board of RAPP's literary journal *At the Literary Post* (*Na literaturnom postu*); notorious for his declaration, "What's beautiful is our life."

5.6. Maksim Shtraukh as the bureaucrat Podsekalnikov and Zinaida Raykh as The Phosphorescent Woman from the future in *The Bathhouse* by Vladimir Mayakovsky, directed by Vsevolod Meyerhold at his theater, Moscow, 1930.

Mass Audiences Fail to Understand the Play
Questionable characters: where are the Communists, where are the workers?
[. . .] *The Bathhouse is unintelligible for mass audiences*—this was the almost unanimous statement of the workers who took part in the conference. Not only specific moments in the play but also some of the basic ideas and characters (the "time machine," the "phosphorescent woman") remain obscure for a considerable part of the audience. [. . .] As comrade Voytsekhovich said, the spectator gets no idea of the main theme of the play. According to comrades Sazonova and Moselkova, the Burevestnik workers walked out of the performance of *The Bathhouse* completely disappointed. [. . .] Why is the bureaucrat not countered by the working masses or Party members? Comrade Zuev asked, Why don't they give the bureaucrat a bath, as happens in real life?
[. . .] In reply to what was said, the play's author, Comrade Mayakovsky, declared, first of all, that he did not regard *The Bathhouse* as a failure; on the contrary, he considered the production a great success of the Meyerhold Theater. [. . .] Mayakovsky rejected the imputations concerning the absence onstage of the working masses, the Party, trade unions, pointing out that the play had been written and staged from the standpoint of workers and Party members [. . .] sitting in the auditorium. In conclusion Mayakovsky admitted the need for further work on the play.

ON APRIL 14, 1930, Mayakovsky killed himself with a revolver, a prop from one of his silent films. His suicide note mentioned Ermilov and the RAPP critics.

In spring 1930, Meyerhold and his troupe were allowed to go on a three-city tour of Germany and then on a tour of Paris; the German response was cool, the French enthusiastic. On his return, Meyerhold was desperate for a striking new play. Vishnevsky's *The Ultimate Decisive,* an idealized picture of life in the Red Navy, was a hodgepodge of theater tricks and manipulated emotion. It was most memorable for the final stage picture of a surviving sailor chalking on a screen the population numbers "162,000,00 − 27 = 161,999,973," while a music hall song by Maurice Chevalier played over the radio.

> Vsevolod Meyerhold, "From talks with participants in *The Ultimate Decisive,*
> 15 January 1931." In *Stat'i, pis'ma, rechi, besedy,* 2:242–47.

I happened to see a Kabuki troupe in Paris, and I was struck by the fact that they were exhibiting an art I had never yet seen. I knew Kabuki in theory—from books, from visual material—I knew the techniques of Kabuki, but when I saw Kabuki, it seemed to me that I had never read or known anything about it.

The most basic element of their techniques is that they approach every enactment with a necessary naivety—it doesn't matter whether they are playing a highly dramatic, tragic, or comic position. The actor first of all assumes a situation, an expression that would be understood by the most naive person, unschooled in any subtleties, who happened to be in the audience. Chaplin mastered that kind of technique. He too selects stage effects that are the simplest, most naive, and most familiar to everyone. He discards anything that will not be accessible to everyone. This is also done by the Kabuki actors. In addition, they have moments—moments of ritual, stage ritual—when the actors need to display masks, figures; they enter, show themselves off as participants in a given performance. It is something like the parade when the circus comes to a small town, and instead of putting up posters, the performers ride horses, donkeys, camels, and elephants, don their costumes and defile through the town. [...]

Such naive devices exist in this play, they are in Vsevolod Vishnevsky. If we are to compare him with other playwrights, we will first of all be struck by the ingenuousness, and then the choice of what is peculiarly familiar to everyone—there is nothing sophisticated, everything is simple, simple, simple, and simple. The emotions are simple and the expression of the emotions is very simple. [...]

The plot is the same kind as in the simple Japanese drama played by Kabuki. But look at how the Kabuki actors treat such a simple plot. The more ingenuous the situation, the simpler the plot, the more necessary to present it powerfully, to come up with lots of little effects. What does Chaplin do? When Chaplin is building to a climax, he acts economically, tensely and expressively, he gives all of himself, all his technique. [...]

Vsevolod Meyerhold to Yury Olesha, August 6, 1930, Hendaye-Plage, Basses-Pyrénées, France. Meyerhold, *Perepiska* (Moscow: Iskusstvo, 1976), 308.

Dear Yury Karlovich, yesterday I got a letter from Moscow with the news that you intend to give *A List of Benefits* to the Vakhtangovians. The letter puts forward a reason: "Raykh didn't like the play." [...]

How so, my dear fellow?

I have put your play at the center of the repertorial plan for the 1930–31 season. Traveling with the company to Western Europe, amid all the difficulties that stood in the way of our tour, weary, enervated, ill, all the same I found time to work on your play. I came up with a lot of splendid details for the directorial plan of your play. A couple of times, in relating the subject of your play to friends of our theater here in the west, I caught myself saying that no play had ever so gripped me as *List of Benefits*. What has happened? Lack of faith as a professional? The failure of *The Bathhouse*? Is that my fault? Zoshchenko's treachery? Is his example contagious? Perhaps our office offended you in some way? It didn't send you the promised money? I entreat you let me know at once (definitely by telephone): is the rumor true? or is it malicious gossip? And then: what nonsense, as if Zinaida Nikolaevna would not like the play. Who is conspiring to make us quarrel? Zinaida Nikolaevna is even more excited by the play than I am. I saw with my own eyes how she conveyed the tragic plan of your new great tragedy and how excited she was by your lyrical effusions in it.

When I learned of Zoshchenko's treachery, I was upset, but not hurt. Because Zoshchenko is an occasional guest in the theater. But you were created for the theater. And there are not many of those. They are unique. Mayakovsky is gone. Érdman is depressed. Sel'vinsky is coming back to us, but when—who knows?

Dear friend, think it over! [...]

OLESHA WROTE BACK that he was convinced he had written a bad play and was as depressed as Érdman.

Yury Olesha, "The theme of the intellectual," *Stroyka* [The line] 3 (1930), 6.

"In printing this interesting article by Yu. Olesha, the editors stipulate their disagreement with a whole series of positions in this article and, in the next issue of *Stroyka*, propose to insert an article laying out the editors' viewpoints on the theme put forth by Com. Olesha."

I have written a play commissioned by the Vs. Meyerhold Theater. The play will be called, in all likelihood, *A List of Benefits*.

In every intellectual, especially in the intellectual who works in the realm of art, there resides a certain "idea of Europe." Perhaps this attraction to so-called pure art is an attraction that labor has made obsolete. Perhaps this idea that everything ought to be permitted to a talented person is an idea about the importance of personality, the aspirations of the individual. Perhaps because we are now cut off from Europe, this idea rages in the soul of the intellectual especially powerfully, leading the mind along the border between nostalgia for the lost importance of personality and self-hatred, hatred of one's own ego, which can in no way be assuaged.

The action of the play takes place in the USSR (Part I) and Europe. But all of it—in the USSR and Europe—exists as it were in the mind of the leading character, the hero, or rather the heroine, because the leading character in the play is a woman, an actress, who dreams about Europe. She is sent on a mission abroad, but the day before she leaves, a delegation of workers comes to her with the request to set off with a shock-worker brigade to a kolkhoz. The actress agrees but does not keep her promise, and, instead of going to the kolkhoz with the theater's agit-troupe, leaves for abroad. This is the first part of the play, in which the heroine is ambivalent, tormented by contradictions, secretly protesting against "the enslavement of the individual." And now she is in Europe. Just yesterday she considered herself torn in two. Her mind held a belief in the triumph of Communism and the rise of a new world. But her feelings were against it. The struggle between mind and feelings made her life in her homeland ambivalent. Having escaped to Europe, she seems to go within herself. The repressed half of her soul—feelings—become the more important, turned from half into whole, into a unity. [...]

She is ready to commit treason. But, well on the road to treachery, she begins to understand that outside those conditions that yesterday seemed unnatural and unbearable, she cannot exist. Here, as it were, the other half—the mind—becomes important, here the heroine steps outside for the second time and dreams, panic-stricken: to return! return! But there is no way to return, because the shadow of treason already lies on her. And the heroine seeks a means of rehabilitation and finds it.

The play is divided into three parts.

I have never been to Europe. I do not claim to depict Europe. The theme of the play is "the Europe of the mind," if I may so express it.

I call the play a melodrama of emotional engagement.

FOLLOWING A SPEECH at the First All-Union of Writers in 1934, Olesha fell into disfavor, and his literary activity dwindled to a trickle.

> Vsevolod Meyerhold, "Creative methodology of the Meyerhold Theater," December 25, 1930. In *Stat'i, pis'ma, rechi, besedy*, 2:229–40. This is an excerpt from a stenographic record of four days of discussion at the State Academy of Art Studies (November 13, December 3, 17, 25) in which Meyerhold took part.

Yes, first you have to adjust your muscles, build up your skeleton correctly, learn to move rhythmically, hold your head properly foreshortened, and then the moment comes when we say, "Comrade, why are you walking around mindlessly, why aren't you thinking?" When speech comes, it will be at the third stage: first movement, then thought, then speech. First comes the training in an acrobatic or biomechanical system, so that a person in a well-ventilated building will adjust his muscles, learn to breathe properly, cry as naturally when moved as a baby cries. Then we send him into another room where the time comes to control certain means of expression an actor needs. Suppose I give you the phrase "to hell with you"—do you know how to utter this phrase? Do you know how to differentiate the phrase spoken by a fascist from a phrase spoken by a communist, do you know how to fortify your consciousness, adapt to the whole staging that provides you with the given dramatic context, do you perceive all the nuances? This, too, is the realm of training. Don't imagine that the actor can saunter down the street and collect observations, and then show up onstage. We need training in the realm of movement, training in the realm of thought, training in the realm of speech. This is magnificent work, it is beyond the power of any but a special- ized theater that must be regarded as a scientific research institute, in which there is a movement laboratory, a movement operation that enables one to execute it. Until then, what we have (and this can be confirmed by the comrades from my theater who are present here) is mere shrubbery. What the hell does movement training matter, what the hell do speech or thought training matter—it doesn't mean a damn thing, it's not a theater, it's simply a toilet (*laughter*). That's all I wanted to say (*applause*).

A *LIST OF ASSETS* opened on June 4, 1931, with Zinaida Raykh playing the émigrée actress, based on events in the life of Mikhail Chekhov. It was fated to be the last production of the Meyerhold Theater in the old Sohn playhouse.

Tairov

The Kamerny Theater became more and more isolated, as Tairov tried to maintain its artistic program without alienating the state organs of control. More operetta (*Day and Night, Sirocco*), more O'Neill (*All God's Chillun Got Wings*), more clas- sical tragedy (Hasenclever's version of *Antigone*) failed to meet the demand for topical plays. A turn to new Russian drama was unsuccessful: Bulgakov's satire of the censorship *The Crimson Island* was quickly banned, while M. Levidov's *The Conspiracy of Equals,* based on a French original, was taken off after a single performance.

> Vladimir Pimenov, "Dve sud'by" [Two fates], *Teatr* 6 (1990), 124–25. Vladimir Fëdorovich Pimenov (1905–?), head of the USSR Central Theater Administra- tion and vice-chairman of the Playwrights' Council, was the editor of *Teatr* during the Thaw; he left when Krushchëv was deposed in 1964 and became rector of the Gorky Literature Institute.

But in those days every innovator was suspect, every experimenter was a potential adversary, every talent was disturbing in its potential for intractability. They were look- ing for enemies everywhere, they looked for them in the world of art, they looked for them even in the theater. One of the "enemies" turned out to be Aleksandr Yakovlevich Tairov. His artistic palette was too broad, his talent too irrepressible, his way of thinking creatively too independent, too opposed to the MAT, whose artistic penmanship, so to speak, was declared the general, genuine one, prescribed for the pages of every theater.

Aleksandr Tairov lived, as it were, under a Damoclean sword. Not only did they ignore him and his theater but of course the most awful thing at the time were the words of Stalin, who in 1929 called the Kamerny "bourgeois" in a famous letter to Bill'-Belotserkovsky. A figurative iron slab was laid on the theater, a heavy slab of Stalin's displeasure. In essence, the theater was condemned. And at the same time it lived, lived off of Tairov's inexhaustible energy.

The Kamerny existed in a milieu of hostile criticism, crude, abusive, anti-intellectual, uncreative. In essence they insulted whatever Tairov did. [...]

You would think that Tairov, harried and hounded by the critics, should have been more passive than water, more lowly than grass. But all the same he remained a leader of the creative theatrical process; as before, he dreamed about his future productions. And he never hid behind foreign backs, never fell silent or was afraid to utter his opinions openly [...]

FOR ALL THE HOSTILITY the Kamerny was allowed to make its third and last tour, to Europe and South America, from March to July 1930. When it returned, RAPP called Tairov on the carpet, but what began as an attack turned out to be the theater's salvation, a new play called *The Optimistic Tragedy*. Before it could be produced, Tairov staged three other Soviet dramas: *Line of Fire* by N. N. Nikitin, *Sonata Pathétique* by N. G. Kulish, and L. S. Pervomaysky's *The Unknown Soldier*, each attacked in turn by RAPP and the press for political immaturity and error, primitive production values, and negative characters granted as much depth as positive ones. Tairov broke out of this circle of mediocrity with an American expressionist piece, Sophie Treadwell's[45] *Machinal*.

Golubovsky, *Bol'shie malen'kie teatry*, 227.

A. Tairov's production was magnificent and monumental, but it was boring to watch (for me!). Everything was obvious from the very start. The production was constructed impeccably, although not without vulgar sociology. Ellen—the great actress A. Koonen—immediately showed herself to be a distinguished individual, languishing in bondage. Koonen could never be anything but distinguished. Tarasova's[46] Ellen was an ordinary woman and therefore familiar to everyone, and there was infinite pity for her.

Tairov took for the basis of his production an image—everything is "machinal,"

45 Sophie Treadwell (1884–1970), American journalist, playwright, and actress, known almost exclusively for *Machinal* (1928), an expressionist drama in which an oppressed young woman murders her husband and dies in the electric chair.

46 Alla Konstantinovna Tarasova (1898–1973), leading actress at the MAT and a favorite of Stalin; played the heroine in Nemirovich-Danchenko's production of *Machinal*. Other roles include Anna Karenina 1937 and Masha in *Three Sisters* 1940. She was made a deputy to the Supreme Soviet 1943.

everything is the same: costumes and remarkable sky-scrapers by Ryndin. There is the office, the clerks sit in identical waistcoats, in a row, and behind them on coat-hangers hang identical jackets. Each one behind identical typewriters—it's obvious that it's "machinal." In all the windows, identical couples, fates. "A mechanized psyche" is how Tairov defined the kernel of the production.

Alisa Koonen, *Stranitsy zhizni* [Pages of life] (Moscow: Iskusstvo, 1975), 352–60.

At a meeting of RAPP in 1930, devoted to the theater, after Tairov's speech to us, Vsevolod Vishnevsky[47] stepped up. He introduced himself. Short, stocky, with a pointed nose, squinting eyes beneath beetling brows, he greatly appealed to me.

"What you've said is hale and hearty," he addressed Tairov. "Dynamic realism—that's the position, directly corresponding to the times. [...] Your fight against naturalism, which keeps all of us from advancing the big problems is correct. One has to fight."

[...] The atmosphere at rehearsals of *Optimistic Tragedy* was unusual: Tairov was attracted to the work of the navy. It had to be followed so that in the production there would be no mistakes in naval rules and regulations. Our actors in turn were given the possibility to observe characteristic sailors on leave. They had their own way of walking, their own bearing. Getting acquainted with sailors provided us with a lot: we felt as if we were actually on a warship. The presence of the sailors personally brought me great good luck. I urgently looked for a leather jacket for the commissar, I couldn't imagine the commissar without a leather jacket. But the ones they brought from the shops didn't work at all. They were of quite another cut, unlike the jackets worn at the time of the Civil War. Besides, they were made of stiff material that stuck out, "leatherette." It was very distressing. The sailors were aware of our concerns as actors. And so once, when we were rehearsing onstage, a little middy ran into the house with a bundle under his arm, and, panting, joyously shouted at me with all his might:

"Alisa Georgievna! I got you a jacket! A real one! A Civil War one! A commissar's one!"

[...] The preview at the theater was attended by members of the Revvoensovet [Revolutionary Military Council], headed by K. E. Voroshilov.[48] In the pit, at the suggestion of Klimenty Efremovich, sat Red Army soldiers and sailors from our sponsorship groups.

This was an unforgettable performance. The spectators greeted it with exceptional enthusiasm. During the action they would jump up, shout "Hoorah!" and applaud. The atmosphere in the auditorium, of course, leaped across the footlights to the stage, the performance went with great élan. When it was over, there was not even a discussion. The production was accepted unconditionally. The theater received permission to print on the poster "Dedicated to the Red Army and Navy." [...]

47 Vsevolod Vital'evich Vishnevsky (1900–1951), playwright, gave *Optimistic Tragedy* to the Kamerny after quarreling with Meyerhold; his later play *Unforgettable 1919* (1949) was a paean to Stalin.
48 Klimenty Efimovich Voroshilov (1881–1969), commissar of the Soviet Army and Navy from 1925 and a member of the Politburo 1926–62. Pensioned off by Khrushchëv 1962.

The design for *The Optimistic Tragedy* by Vadim Ryndin[49] was one of the high points of his beautiful art. A rigorous simplicity of line and the magnificent splendor of a wide-open stage space created a generalized and at the same time specifically realistic shape for the production. The lighting was remarkable. Here we were shown the great expertise of our chief lighting designer Georges Samoylov,[50] who always as a true artist deeply penetrated the concept of a production. The lighting extended the footlights of the stage space. It emphasized the very tonality of the production, conveying its most subtle nuances.

This production was one of the first attempts to create a new genre—contemporary Soviet tragedy. [...]

Aleksandr Tairov, "*The Optimistic Tragedy.* Speech to the Kamerny Theater Troupe," October 2, 1932. Tairov, *Zapiski rezhissëra. Stat'i, besedy, rechi, pis'ma,* ed. P. Markov (Moscow: VTO, 1970), 331–50.

Vs. Vishnevsky's play *The Optimistic Tragedy* [...] is dedicated to the birth of the Red Army as one of the first organizing and organized principles of Great October. The play's theme is the struggle between life and death, chaos and harmony, negation and affirmation.

Therefore all the emotional, plastic, and rhythmic lines of the production must be built along a distinct curve, leading from negation to affirmation, from death to life, from chaos to harmony, from anarchy to conscious discipline. [...]

This is a tragedy because the whole tone of the action is located on the verge of a rolling boil.

There is no serenity in the play, no people in ordinary situations; here human passions rage and melt, the passions of the individual and the masses flung into the maelstrom, the result of the social displacements of Great October. [...]

But it is an optimistic tragedy because death is not the consummation of the whole cycle of events [depicted in the play]. Events and incidents, reaching their utmost limits, vanquish death and affirm life, its power, its renewing and organizing principle; therein lies the optimism of the given tragedy, an optimistic tragedy.

Here we have a double catharsis. The first catharsis is the oath ("We, sons of the working people...")

Why this catharsis? Because what we are dealing with here is a group of people, some of whom up to now have been ruled by doubt, ruled by fear of death; the result is a characteristic confusion of concepts and experiences. This confusion is resolved in harmony, emancipation, and purification, expressed by the revolutionary oath.

And the second catharsis is the death of the commissar itself. The commissar perishes, but perishes as a seed, cast into the earth to become the origin of a new life

49 Vadim Fëdorovich Ryndin (1902–74), chief designer of the Kamerny Theater 1931–34, who avoided constructivism; later chief designer at the Vakhtangov Theater 1935–44, 1947–53 and the Bol'shoy Theater 1953–74.
50 Georgy Konstantinovich Samoylov (1897–?), lighting designer.

of a plant, so that the death of the commissar gives birth to new life, [the start of new paths] leading to generational change.

In this unusual catharsis death is transformed into new life. [...]

Only our Revolution has properly posed the question of a collective made up of individual human lives; only our Revolution is leading to a new social consciousness, and therefore only now can such a double catharsis arise, in which the collective eclipses the personal and an individual death is consummated in the name of the collective life, the life of new generations, the life of a class, the life of the Revolution. [...]

The commissar arrives—a woman. Approach of the sailors. The provocation of Vozhak and the practical joke. The woman appears. In this case it's immaterial that this is a provocation by Vozhak, it doesn't matter that the sailors are playing a joke on the commissar, what matters is that they have seen—a woman, for them something unusual, interesting, impressive, involuntarily and powerfully arousing in them a thirst for the fullness of life in the presence of a person possibly about to die. Hence the desire for this woman, hence what the author's stage direction describes—"guffawing, an explosive horse laugh"—the blatant outward signs of the erotic principle, bloodshot eyes, gaping mouths, outstretched arms, taut muscles—an outpouring of lust in every man's body and in the general body of them all.

If it is like that, it will be not funny but horrifying, and if it is horrifying, that is what the production needs. [...]

THE OPENING of *The Optimistic Tragedy* at the Kamerny on December 18, 1931, is considered one of the red-letter days of the Soviet theater. Although the events were shown as historic (in parallel with the Kronstadt rebellion), the treatment was epic. Ryndin's monumental set, depicting the foredeck of a battleship, became iconic. Koonen's commissar was not a waxworks saint but an attractive human being. The production was widely honored and played for eight hundred performances. Overnight, the despised aesthetic Tairov was at the forefront of socialist progress. He was named a People's Artist of the USSR.

The Two Moscow Art Theaters

The Second Moscow Art Theater had a turbulent life, rent from inside and out. It was regularly attacked by the Communist press for "aestheticism" and "eclecticism" at the same time as it suffered internecine conflict. The malcontents who had created a separate cadre in 1927 left the following year, but in 1928, another controversy broke out between Boris Sushkevich and Mikhail Chekhov, whom the collective accused of mismanaging the theater. Chekhov emigrated to Latvia, and Ivan Bersenev then reorganized the MAT 2, which became a showcase for Soviet hackwork.

Smyshlaev, *Pechalno i nekhorosho v nashem teatre*, 122–25.

March 16, 1928, Moscow. Right now the theater is undergoing hard times. On the night of the 12th (Tuesday) to the 13th (Wednesday), after *Sundown*,[51] a meeting of the core company, at which Sushkevich castigated Chekhov for ruining our theater. After Sushkevich's speech, almost everyone there spoke, and almost everyone (with the possible exception of Giatsintova) one way or another supported the basic positions laid out by Sushkevich. Chekhov was disgusting. This was all fully unexpected by him, and he tried in vain to justify himself and suggested to us that we ought to have protected and loved him. But that night no one believed him. Chekhov could not wriggle out of the fact that he knew nothing of what was going on in the theater. [...]

Everyone spoke more or less sharp words. Chekhov replied to all of it sullenly and in dismay. He didn't expect that the truth could be presented to him in all its nakedness. Chekhov said that he is an emissary of God and that we ought to listen to him and learn, but we busy ourselves with protests. All these speeches [...] persuaded him that he had neglected things. [...]

At the end of the session Sushkevich spoke candidly, directly, gratefully; he talked of how the theater had to be saved and requested Chekhov to forget what was personal on behalf of them all, for they definitely have faith in him and want to see no one but him as administrator.

Mikhail Chekhov to the Collective of MAT 2, from Berlin, August 29, 1928.
Chekhov, *Literaturnoe nasledie* (Moscow: Iskusstvo, 1986), 1:350.

Please post this letter in the greenroom.

Although the reasons for my departure from the MAT 2 should be understood by every member of the theater, I nevertheless think it my duty to state them in a clear and concrete form.

The last years of our work together were full of complicated and difficult experiences. Destructive and harmful tendencies contended within the walls of the theater with fruitful and wholesome tendencies. In this struggle the collective strove to define and manifest its will. Most recently the will of the majority of the collective of MAT 2 finally found its concrete formulation, and I saw that this will did not correspond to the ideal and the artistic goals that I as leader had in mind for the theater. I faced a difficult problem; I had either to do violence to the will of the collective, inoculating it with principles of a new art (as I understand it), or else resign and allow the majority of the collective easily and freely to realize its own conceptions. I chose the latter course, as that most corresponding to my worldview. After long and serious consideration, I came to the conclusion that any *forcible* reeducation of the MAT 2 collective is pointless.

To remain in theater as an actor, *merely* playing a series of roles, is impossible for me because long ago I got over that phase of enthusiasm for specific roles. I can be

51 *Zakat* (1916) by Isaak Babel' (revised 1928 for performance by the MAT 2) is a racy panorama of life in the Jewish underworld of Odessa before the Revolution.

attracted and roused to creativity only by *the idea of a new theater in totality, the idea of a new theatrical art.* I am sure that if it is in my power to return to Moscow (within a year) and it is fated that I show myself in the theater, then the results of my work will again unite those of us who already even now feel close to my art.

For the day and years of our creative joy together, I thank you.

Mikh. Chekhov

WHEN THE MAT 1 celebrated its thirtieth birthday on October 27, 1928, the premier of the Soviet government, Mikhail Kalinin, exhorted it "to walk hand in hand with the working class . . . in the struggle to create a new human being."[52] Stanislavsky, befuddled by the socialist pomp of the occasion, made reference to Savva Morozov, the self-made millionaire who had floated the Art Theater in 1898, a blunder that led to denunciation and sent him to bed with a heart attack.

> Joshua Logan, "Stanislavski," introduction to Stanislavsky, *Building a Character* (New York: Theater Arts Books, 1949). Joshua Logan (1908–88) was a prominent American director and playwright, whose many successes include *South Pacific* (1949) and *Picnic* (1953).

Stanislavsky was an invalid, lying on a couch in his living room, when I first saw him in Moscow in [January] 1931. He was forced to conduct his rehearsals at home with his back propped against the raised end of his couch and his feet stretched along its length, covered with a lap robe. [. . .] He greeted us in French. He apologized for not being able to entertain us as well as he could in former years. The Five Year Plan was strict and did not encourage entertainment, that is, not at home. He pointed to an old woman-servant of his who was arranging chairs at the other end of the room. "It is very loyal of her to be working for me because her occupation is not considered essential and she therefore gets almost no rations, half a loaf of bread a week!" [. . .]

This particular morning Stanislavsky was going to rehearse some scenes from the opera *Coq d'Or* by Rimsky-Korsakov. He was preparing it for presentation at the Stanislavsky Opera Studio,[53] a small theater which was one of the off-shoots of the Moscow Art Theater. [. . .] The actor-singers were young and inexperienced. [. . .] Most of them were in gray turtle-neck sweaters and drab woollen clothes. Their faces were gray too. They had the kind of pallor which I remember thinking came from the lack of proper food. [. . .]

---

52 M. Kalinin, "Kollektyu MKhATa, 27 oktyabrya 1928 g.," in A. V. Solodvnikova et al., eds., *Moskovsky khudozhestvenny teatr v sovetskuyu épokhu. Materialy i dokumenty* (Moscow: Iskusstvo, 1962), 9.

53 Not quite: Stanislavsky founded an opera studio as an affiliate of the Bol'shoy Theater in 1918, and it was given his name in 1924, becoming the Stanislavsky Opera Studio-Theater in 1926 and the Opera Theater in 1928; in 1941 it was merged with the MAT Musical Studio to become the Moscow State Musical Theater named for Stanislavsky and Nemirovich-Danchenko.

The first part of the rehearsal was an aria sung by the king sitting on his throne, accompanied by a pianist at the end of the room. He sang the aria with the traditional gestures, grimaces, and diaphragm posture that I had noticed in the singers at [Western opera houses]. He even had that theatrically pained expression in his eyes when he hit a difficult note. Stanislavsky stopped him before he had reached the end of the aria, cutting him off in the middle of a note and of a Mephistophelian gesture which consisted of bringing one hand, fingers trailing, from his diaphragm through an upward arc until the forefinger was pointing magnificently at the ceiling. Stanislavsky spoke sharply to him, even sarcastically. The actor argued vehemently, pointing to his diaphragm, waving his arms and generally indicating that what the director had asked him to do was impossible. Stanislavsky spoke again and this time seemed to be giving him an order. Sulking, the actor put both of his arms to his side and sat on his hands. He began the aria over again. [...] Every once in a while Stanislavsky would shout at him and the actor would sing louder and finally, with his hands beneath him, he was singing full and clear but with a pained and martyred expression. After this he was forced to sing the same aria with his hands lying in his lap. Every time his hands would involuntarily move in a stereotyped gesture Stanislavsky would stop him. By the end of half an hour he sang the aria simply and sincerely. His hands were under control, his face in repose, and, although I could not understand the words, I could see by his eyes that he had begun to think what he was singing. He had taken one step nearer the truth. But it had been an exhausting struggle on Stanislavsky's part to get him there.

IN SEPTEMBER 1929 a thirty-six-year-old bureaucrat, Mikhail Sergeevich Geytts, took up the political and administrative duties of the Art Theater, posting a banner, "We shall transform the entire Komsomol into shock brigades in order to fulfill the Five-Year Plan." Every collective had to sponsor some industrial organization, so the Art Theater wound up as big brother to the Moscow Ball Bearings Factory. Nemirovich wearied of the constant meetings and eventually attended only those on artistic matters, skipping the finance and the trade union sessions. The "red manager" Geytts was dismissed on Stalin's order in September 1931, and the following December the MAT was attached directly to the Central Executive Committee. On January 19 it was renamed the Gorky Academic Art Theater, although it had not staged a play by Gorky for nearly thirty years. Over the next five years, it would stage four of his works.

Bulgakov was driven to distraction by his untenable position in Soviet culture. Besides *The Day of the Turbins,* his comedies *Zoya's Apartment* and *The Crimson Island* were banned after a few performances. When the Art Theater agreed to stage *Flight,* about White Russians in exile, Platon Kerzhentsev, the deputy head of agit-prop, denounced him in a letter of January 1929.[54] After investigation, the

---

54 An English translation of the complete letter can be found in Clark and Dobrenko, *Soviet Culture and Power,* 98–103.

Politburo decided that it was politically inexpedient to have the play produced. The correspondence between Bill'-Belotserkovsky and Stalin was a result of this incident. Bulgakov continued to be persecuted in the press, his writings could not be published, and the OGPU never returned the notebooks they had confiscated in 1926. In desperation, Bulgakov composed an appeal to the government in late March 1930. The contents were well known and circulated widely in samizdat before being published in the late 1980s. It had been typed by his third wife-to-be, Elena Shilovskaya, on an Underwood, the only typewriter with a Cyrillic keyboard.

> Vitaly Shentalinsky and John Crowfoot, *The KGB's Literary Archive* (London: Harvill Press, 1995), 84–85. The underlining is by the pencil of Genrikh Ya- goda,[55] head of OGPU.

March 28, 1930

TO THE USSR GOVERNMENT

After my works were banned, many citizens who know me as a writer could be heard all offering the same advice.

Write a "communist play" [...] and also send a repentant letter to the USSR govern- ment, recanting the views I had formerly expressed in my literary works, and giving assurances that henceforth I would work as a fellow-traveling writer who was devoted to the idea of communism.

The purpose: to save myself from persecution, poverty, and, ultimately, inevitable death.

I did not heed this advice. [...]

For me the starting point of this letter is provided by my lampoon, *The Crimson Island*. [...] I shall not take it on myself to judge how witty my work is. I will admit, however, that a menacing shadow looms through the play. And this is the shadow of the Central Repertory Committee. It has reared up those helots, eulogists, and cowed "lackeys." It has killed artistic thought. It has damaged Soviet playwriting and will end by destroying it altogether. [...]

When the German papers write that *The Crimson Island* is the "first call in the USSR for freedom of the press" they are telling the truth. I admit this. It is my duty as a writer to battle against censorship, no matter what form it takes and under what regime, as it is my obligation to issue appeals for freedom of the press. [...]

ANY SATIRIST IN THE USSR MUST QUESTION THE SOVIET SYSTEM. [...]

I AM REQUESTING THE USSR GOVERNMENT TO ORDER ME TO LEAVE THE COUNTRY IN THE SHORTEST POSSIBLE TIME ACCOMPANIED BY MY WIFE LYUBOV' EVGENIEVNA BULGAKOVA. [...]

55 Genrikh Grigor'evich Yagoda (1891–1938), deputy chairman of the OGPU from 1924 and commis- sar for internal affairs (NKVD) from 1934; as Stalin's chief agent in the security organs, conducted the early purges but was accused of slackness and removed. Arrested 1937 and, after a show trial, shot.

If [...] I am doomed to a lifetime's silence in the USSR, then I request the Soviet government to give me a job. [...]

I am offering the USSR the services of a thoroughly honest specialist, an actor and director who, without a shadow of sabotage,[56] undertakes to stage any play conscientiously, from Shakespeare down to contemporary works. [...]

THERE FOLLOWED the famous phone call from Stalin on April 18, 1930, that implicitly offered Bulgakov a post as dramaturg at the Art Theater. The playwright acceded and was added to its literary staff. Two years later, Stalin announced his desire to see *Days of the Turbins*: the scenery was hastily taken out of mothballs and the cast rehearsed. The play reentered the MAT's regular rotation and was ultimately performed. Stalin saw it fifteen times.

> M. Bulgakov to P. S. Popov,[57] January 25, 1932, quoted in A. Smelyansky, *Mikhail Bulgakov v Khudozhestvennom teatre,* 2nd ed. (Moscow: Iskusstvo, 1989), 212.

In mid-January 1932, as a result of reasons unknown to me and into an examination of which I cannot enter, the government of the USSR sent the MAT a remarkable directive to revive the play *The Days of the Turbins*. For the author of this play this means that he, the author, has been given back part of his life.

Akimov's *Hamlet*

Nikolay Pavlovich Akimov (1901–68) began as a designer in Khar'kov in 1922, moving the next year to Leningrad; throughout the 1920s and 1930s he created sets for important productions at the Leningrad Theater of Drama and the Moscow Theater of the Revolution. He was well known as a designer of cartoonlike concision and a taste for the grotesque when he initiated a career as a director at the Vakhtangov Theater, where his first independent work as a director was *Hamlet* in 1929. It ran counter both to romantic tradition and the intellectual princes of Kachalov and Michael Chekhov. Much of the rest of Akimov's career was spent at the Leningrad Theater of Comedy (1935–49, 1955–68).

> Golubovsky, *Bol'shie mal'enkie teatry,* 31–35.

First of all, the Hamlet of Anatoly Goryunov[58] ... So stout and life-loving a Hamlet could not represent universal melancholy. This Hamlet, if allowed to live, would have

---

56 An allusion to the campaign against "bourgeois" specialists. In May 1928, fifty-three engineers and technicians at the Shakty mines in the Donbass regions were publicly tried and sent to prison for "sabotage" and "economic counterrevolution."

57 Pavel Sergeevich Popov (1892–1964), philosopher, historian of logic and Bulgakov's admirer and would-be biographer.

58 Anatoly Iosifovich Goryunov (actually Bendel', 1902–51), nephew of Ivan Moskvin, at the Vakhtangov Studio and Theater 1920–51, infusing his roles with joie de vivre.

become Falstaff, with his fleshly life-loving cynicism and mischief making. [...] I would define the genre of Akimov's Hamlet as a political detective story in which everything is built on a bitter power struggle: Hamlet has organized a conspiracy against Claudius, who seized the crown that belonged to the prince after the death of his father, whom Claudius, according to the laws of the gangster film, had villainously poisoned. To start with, Hamlet decided to make up the legend of his father's ghost; he creates the nonexistent ghost's voice by speaking into a jug, forcing his friend Horatio to take part in the action and kicking him with his foot when the latter doesn't come up with the lines fast enough, sedulously spying on the actions of his opponents. A brilliant invention of the director: Hamlet meets Ophelia in a park, notices Polonius hiding behind a tree spying on him, and immediately switches to the role of a madman.

Long before the postwar Leningrad Hamlet of the director G. Kozintsev and Okhlopkov's Hamlet, Akimov decided to liken Hamlet and Horatio to humanists, learned natural scientists. Horatio is reading *The Praise of Folly* by Erasmus of Rotterdam, scenes in *Hamlet* are transferred to the library, a large globe stands in his study. On the walls of the court hang paintings of the late Renaissance. [...]

The most grandiose (that's the best thing to call it) scene was the "Mousetrap": an enormous staircase, leading up to a hall where the troupe of strolling players put on their play. A procession of courtiers, headed by Claudius and Gertrude, proceeds in that direction. The king is wearing a mantle of scarlet velvet, which is held by a few courtiers. The king mounts the stairs, and the courtiers do not move from the proscenium, holding the mantle in their hands. Finally, Claudius reaches the top of the stairs, and the enormous mantle seems to cover the stage to its very height, scarlet velvet like a sea of blood floods the space of the court. The king and queen move into the distance, individual lines of dialogue reach us from the hall, our attention as audience, corresponding to the reactions of the royal pair, which we receive via the prince and Horatio. We are not distracted by the plot of the play-within-a-play which we know [...]

The play is interrupted—the king rushes headlong from the hall, the courtiers have no time to follow him, and he, like a beetle on a pin, stuck in that damned huge mantle, streaming around him like a river of blood, cannot free himself from it, from the crime pursuing him with irresistible force—a tiny little figure shedding blood—an image of overpowering strength!

Another scene: Claudius greets Rosencrantz and Guildenstern in the studio of an artist painting his portrait. On a tall pedestal is set a canvas of enormous dimensions: a nearly finished full-dress portrait of a great monarch in a magnificent cloak, calculated to look like a giant king out of Swift's[59] satire. Claudius stands behind a special [stand], sticking his head through a opening, just the way itinerant photographers work on street corners or at fairs [...]. Servants hold the orb, scepter, and crown over his head. Then he leaps out from behind the [stand]—a satirical effect contrasting the monumental portrait with the everyday appearance of the business-like monarch. [...]

Akimov was trying to strip the play of its "classical" dryness and sought to color the action with devices of everyday life and physical action, not very exactly understanding

59 The King of Brobdignag in Jonathan Swift's *Gulliver's Travels.*

the point of Stanislavsky's system. Therefore Hamlet during his soliloquy smoked a pipe like a ship's captain, and shaved himself; Gertrude knit stockings, like a staid matron, while Claudius busied himself with matters of state; Laertes sharpened his sword.

Pavel Markov, "'Hamlet' staged by Akimov," *Sovetsky Teatr* 7–8 (1932), 15–18.

The archaeologist of theater Akimov has examined the theatrical intrigue exclusively, pruning away characters and images and excising the problem of Hamlet. After dismissing prior discussions, Akimov has advanced nothing new. After eliminating Hamlet's philosophical soliloquies, Akimov has preferred a Hamlet who is unthinking and unreflecting. Horatio's concluding words about Hamlet the thinker and his sublime soul sound unexpected to the spectator, who over the course of five hours has observed onstage an ironic pretender to the throne, trying by ingenious means to unseat the king. [. . .]

Akimov's directorial idea derived from "topsy-turvydom." It was from the start an idiosyncratic academic "reductio ad absurdum." Shakespeare is reduced to absurdity. Akimov *has entered into a polemic* with Shakespeare in support of, so to speak, "polemic for polemic's sake."

CHAPTER SIX

The Second Five-Year Plan and the Great Terror, 1933–1938

A SECRET CIRCULAR from Stalin in 1933 proclaimed the victory of agrarian collectivization; the mass deportations and harsh repression in the countryside abated. However, as the second Five-Year Plan was put into gear, the chasm between public and private life grew wider. Many of the social reforms of the early revolutionary period—female emancipation, easy divorce, tolerance of free love and homosexuality—were rescinded. There was a return to traditional family values among a new middle class. The assignment of housing and communal apartments allowed for greater scrutiny of family life and the repression of individuality. The population became more passive in its obedience to dictates from above. A cult of Stalin began to take shape.

In 1933 Hitler became chancellor of Germany. The establishment of another powerful fascist state alarmed the *apparat*. As Geoffrey A. Hoskins has put it,

> Communist officials, devoted to unity, strict discipline, ruthless crushing of enemies, were in their element. In 1933, they knew they would now have to prepare themselves and the population for what might prove to be the most destructive war of all. They reacted by closing ranks and projecting an image of complete unity and absolute resolution. Any collective, even outside crisis conditions, tends to generate its own mode of discourse, which becomes obligatory for anyone who wishes to remain an active member. Private doubts are pushed aside, inappropriate or dissenting notions are suppressed, and everyone reproduces the jargon—and therefore the sentiments—of those in charge. Rhetoric becomes virtual reality and then reality itself.[1]

The sense of impending war and the need for preparation contributed to Stalin's own paranoia, which played no small part in the government's policies. The reason given for the dissolution of RAPP was that the proletarian cadres were now sufficiently strengthened, as a result of progress in socialist construction, so that it was no longer necessary. The salient factor was Stalin's distrust of leftist fanatics

---

1 Geoffrey A. Hoskins, "Cards on the Table, Comrades," *Times Literary Supplement* (January 28, 2000), 3.

and Marxist fundamentalists. The All-Russian Union of Soviet Writers, founded in 1934, was purported to offer writers more latitude than RAPP ever had. Ultimately, however, it was Stalin's power that spread through every aspect of Soviet life.

The diminution of individuality in private life was replicated in the arts. Leveling and standardization were the bywords. An abrupt end was put to the revolutionary experimental period that had flourished in the 1920s. In August 1934, at the First Congress of the Writer's Union, Maksim Gorky and A. A. Zhdanov pronounced socialist realism to be *the* style for Soviet art. It differed from realism *tout pur* in its rosy and optimistic view of the eventual socialist victory worldwide. A continual social competition was in play, a battle for the attainment of Communist ideals. Since the triumph of Communism was historically inevitable, the outcome at any given crisis was only superficially in doubt. Socialist realism could be most easily discerned in literary works, so, at first, those aspects of the performing arts that came under scrutiny were playtexts, opera and ballet libretti, and screenplays rather than performance practices.

Specific works were singled out as exemplary models; Gorky's style of writing had been extolled at the First Congress, since socialist realism was supposed to be logically evolved from it. Vsevolod Vishnevsky's portentously titled play of 1933, *The Optimistic Tragedy,* was cited as a paradigm (although Stalin had his doubts). In this work, which perpetuated the "popular heroic" genre, a commissar and her supporters all die, but do so defending the historical need for social revolution. It managed to synthesize epic narration and the romantic style that Gorky had prescribed during the Civil War period.

At the same time that tradition was gaining the upper hand over the avant-garde, text won over spectacle, the author over the director. The dominant theme of Soviet playwrights of this period was the construction of socialism, in its various forms. Besides dramas devoted to agriculture and industrialization, the victory of socialism, and the reinforcement of political cohesion, plays were devoted to the "ideological front." Typical examples are *Fear* (1931) by Afinogenov, which addresses the problem of winning the intelligentsia to the cause, and a play by Pogodin about the reeducation of political prisoners and common law in the work camps of the Cheka, *Aristocrats* (1933).

As Gorky demanded, the Soviet theater provided images of the new "hero of our times," culminating in the appearance onstage of Lenin and Stalin. Over time, a characteristically Stalinist imagery and the distention of Stalin's role in relation to Lenin's were to take on considerable dimensions. Stalin's own taste was for the opulent and magniloquent; the acting style for these titans was appropriately large scale, as were the settings that showcased them.

Censorship was reconfirmed on November 1, 1935, by a joint decree of the RSFSR Commissariat of Enlightenment, the RSFSR Commissariat of Justice, and the NKVD. Plays, films, ballets, and other performances were to be reviewed by the censors at least ten days before their official opening. The management of each theater had to reserve for the censors two seats at every performance, no farther from the stage than the fourth row.[2]

Between 1932 and 1936, "the pursuit of happiness" became the aim of "a new political and industrial elite" that had developed during the first Five-Year Plan. Because the second Five-Year Plan invested more in consumer industries and rationing was relaxed, a consumer culture began to develop. In a Communist society, however, money accomplished less than did favors dispensed by the government. Loyalty to the regime, not least among the deftest practitioners of socialist realism, was rewarded with lavish royalties, political preferment, medals and honors, and, the greatest inducement, material benefits—apartments, dachas, automobiles, extended spa vacations, perquisites for relatives. The Party became the universal patron of the arts. Not surprisingly, some artists and intellectuals exhibited more dissatisfaction with lack of recognition and recompense than with censorship and repression.

Conversely, bad examples to be avoided were pilloried. In the second half of the 1930s, the ideological organs of the Communist Party and the state, which carried out both the social orders of the Central Committee and the personal orders of Stalin, took steps to weed out nonrealistic elements in Soviet art. In 1934 Glavrepertkom was reorganized as an independent directorate and was renamed Glavnoe Upravlenie po kontrolyu za zrelishchami i repertuarom (Chief Directorate for the Inspection of Spectacles and Repertoire, or GURK) but was still referred to as Glavrepertkom. On December 16, 1935, the All-Union Committee for Artistic Affairs (Vsesoyuzny Komitet po delam iskusstv) was established under the Sovnarkom to bring every aspect of cultural life together under one roof. It consolidated power even over the Writer's Union and eclipsed the Ideological Section of the Central Committee and, in 1936, over Glavrepertkom. This latest phase of centralization turned the spotlight more directly on the performing arts, as all the theaters were put under the committee's supervision in December 1936.

The committee's director was Platon Kerzhentsev, a fanatical journalist and political operative who has been described as "the Communist Robespierre." Between January 1936 and January 1938, when he was dismissed, he used the committee to spearhead attacks on "formalism" and naturalism, leading to the condemnation of Shostaskovich's opera *Lady Macbeth of Mtsensk* and ballet *Limpid Stream*. First used as a pejorative in 1930, formalism was a catchall term, its very lack of definition enabling it to be used to scapegoat surviving left-wing artists of the 1920s, among them Diky, Eisenstein, and Meyerhold. More than half the new plays and productions produced by the leading theaters of the Soviet Union in the 1936–37 season were forbidden by Glavrepertkom as insufficiently socialist–realistic or too formalist.

2   L. G. Fogelevich, *Osnovye direktivy i zakonodatel'stvo o pechati. Sistematicheskii sbornik,* 5th ed. (Moscow: Sovetskoe zaknodatel'stvo, 1935), 125.

Individuals and institutions branded with formalism or "Meyerholdism" were severely reprimanded, transferred, stripped of authority, arrested, exiled, or, in the most extreme cases, executed. Denunciations, the gloating of the favored, and the demoralization of the rest were the order of the day. Scrabbling for favor and internal quarreling among intellectuals served as a prologue to the Great Purge, which began with the murder of Sergey Kirov in 1934 and did not end until 1939. An estimated ten million citizens were arrested, interrogated, and banished to labor camps. In February 1936 the Second Moscow Art Theater was closed, followed in September by TRAM. Gorky died in 1936, possibly poisoned. Shut down were the Meyerhold Theater, the experimental theater of Les' Kurbas in the Ukraine, and the theater of Sandro Akhmeteli in Georgia. Theaters of the most opposite tendencies, such as the Kamerny and the Realistic, were yoked together willy-nilly. The attack on Meyerhold was replicated in the fates of Tret'yakov, Babel, and, less lethally, Érdman. Vsevolod Vishnevsky carved another notch in his sycophantic career by denouncing fellow playwright Vladimir Kirshon in the April 26, 1937, issue of *Literaturnaya Gazeta* for "having worked with Trotskyists." The condemned became "nonpersons," their names and images erased from history. Even Lunacharsky, who died in his bed in France in 1940, underwent this oblivion.

Meanwhile, Stanislavsky's system of acting was converted from a living, evolving art form into a dogma. The rapidly rigidifying principles of the Moscow Art Theater were reconfirmed as the correct aesthetic system for the development of Soviet theater: the directive to actors and directors was "study at the MAT," a tenet of conformity that severely stunted the stage's artistic development. The balance of power shifted from the innovative theaters of Meyerhold and his epigones to the academic theaters, which took on greater importance.

Even as the purges and "wrecker" trials were taking place between 1935 and 1938 and thousands were being shot or sent to labor camps, the official Party slogan was "Life has become more fun, comrades!" As life was more hermetically sealed for Soviet citizens, certain chosen sites were opened to travelers from abroad. Theatrical tourism was sponsored by the Intourist Agency in precisely those years; annual festivals were visited by interested parties from Europe, Asia, and America, who reported back on the achievements of Stanislavsky, Meyerhold, Tairov, Nemirovich-Danchenko, Mikhoéls, and Okhlopkov, blithely unaware of the conditions under which they worked.

Projection and Reality

In 1933 alone, 248 "Soviet" plays were staged in the Soviet Union. There were 551 theaters, which, by 1938, had increased to 800. That year, admissions totaled seventy-six million rubles, with a profit for the state of twenty-four million rubles.

O. Litovsky, "Sixteen years," *Teatr i dramaturgiya* 8 (November 1933), 1–11. Osaf Semënovich Litovsky (1892–1971), editor and theater critic of *Teatr i Dramaturgiya, Sovetsky Teatr,* and *Rabochy i Iskusstvo,* columnist for *Pravda, Izvestia,* and *Sovetskoe Iskusstvo;* chairman of Glavrepertkom 1930–37; managing director of the Moscow Lensovet Theater 1937–41. He was an inveterate opponent of Bulgakov and his work.

The number of professional theaters in the USSR at the present time is 560. In the Moscow region alone (not counting Moscow), there are sixty-four theaters. In the Leningrad region, there are thirty-two theaters, in the Ukraine eighty, in the Northern Caucasus nineteen, in the Urals twenty-seven, in Kazakstan twelve, and in Yakutin two.

In Moscow, there are now five opera theaters, forty-nine dramatic theaters, three operetta houses, two of mixed type, one satire theater, and Tatar, Jewish, Ukrainian, Lett, and Gipsy theaters. In tsarist Russia, in 1914, there were 154 theaters.

The theaters of the USSR employ an army of theatrical workers of forty-seven thousand persons. But even that is not enough to satisfy fully the gigantically increasing demands for theater workers.

[. . .] The national theaters of the USSR do their work in 40 languages. Every year, the number of national theaters is growing. In Georgia, there are now fourteen national theaters, in Uzbekistan fifteen, in Armenia seven, in Belorussia thirteen, in Azerbaizhan ten, in Kazakstan twelve, in Bashkir three, and in Yakutia two. The Tatar theater in Simferopol is celebrating in the current year its tenth anniversary.

[. . .] In Moscow alone, there twenty-eight theater schools. They include Tsetetis, the technicum for amateur art, the regional theatrical technicum, the technicums of the Maly, Kamerny, Vakhtangov, MOSPS, Revolution, Red Army, and GOSET theaters, etc. [. . .]

The Five-Year Plan for art projects the building of 115 new theaters in the RSFSR, with 182,000 seats. [. . .]

"The creative growth of the arts during the second Five-Year Plan," International Workers' Theatre Olympiad Bulletin no. 2, International Union of the Revolutionary Theatre, Moscow, 1932, 40.

According to the control figures [of the People's Commissariat of Education], an Institute of Arts will be opened in Moscow in 1933, together with a Theatrical Institute and Gorky University in Leningrad [. . .]

During the second five-year period, 115 theaters will be built in the RSFSR and the various autonomous republics: 22 in the Urals, 17 in Western Siberia, 13 in the Moscow region, 6 in the Leningrad region, 5 in the Far East, 6 in Kazakstan, 2 in Bashkiria, 2 in Tataria, 2 in Karelia, 1 in Kara-Kalpakia, 1 in Kirghizia, and 1 in Mongolia. According to the plan, 277 million rubles are to be spent for the construction of new theaters. Besides this, many of the existing theaters will be repaired and reconstructed. More than three hundred million rubles will be spent for the construction, repair, and reconstruction of theater buildings.

The attendance at theaters will also grow to a considerable extent. In 1937 the performances will be attended by no fewer than 380 million persons, the figure during 1932 being 37 million persons.

Twenty-five circuses will also be constructed during the coming five years. [...]

André Van Gyseghem, *Theatre in Soviet Russia* (London: Faber and Faber, 1943), 63–64.

The Central Ticket Office will frequently buy up a whole production for six months. They then proceed to sell blocks of seats to Trade Unions at the same prices at which they bought them, and the Trade Unions sell them to their members at reduced rates. Thus it is often impossible for the casual spectator to buy a seat at the Theater Box Office, all booking being sold for months ahead. When the Box Office manager sells this whole production to the Central Office, he reserves a certain number of free seats for each performance, naturally, since there are always fellow artists or foreign producers to be accommodated! The Theater Office will guarantee to sell 93 per cent of his seats for the six months: frequently it actually sells 98 per cent, and this profit they keep themselves. They became very rich recently on their deal with the Vakhtangov Theater: both sides were satisfied since the theater was assured of its 93 per cent and the office made a profit for itself. Actually 3,000,000 rubles profit which they made on the Vakhtangov Theater was devoted to helping the Gipsy Theater[3] and various provincial theaters which visited Moscow in the summer [1934].

"From the theater notebook," *Rabochy i Teatr* 13 (May 1933), 24.

Recently it became apparent that the box-office receipts at theaters were beginning to lessen. At the Gosdram, there was even a case of a show being replaced (a matinee, it's true) on account of no audience.

And the decrepit state of the repertoire is far from being the only reason for this. "Fresh" productions—*Carmen, The Trial, Rheingold*[4]—don't always attract a full house.

[...] At a time when distribution of theater tickets demanded a certain know-how and hard work, when the spectators still weren't coming to the theaters in any numbers that made for full houses, the theatrical budget was to a remarkable degree predicated on the assumption of organized groups of spectators.

Despite discounted prices, theater parties [*kul'tpokhody*] were *economically* essential to the theaters, allowing houses to be filled 100 percent.

3 Romén (Romany) Theater, Moscow, organized in 1931 as the "Indo-Romany Theater Studio" under Ivan Rom-Lebedev; most of its productions were folkloric celebrations of an idealized gypsy life. It was professionalized 1937–41 under the direction of MAT actor Mikhail Yanshin.
4 *The Trial* (*Sud*, 1932) by Vladimir Kirshon was a play about the class struggle in Germany. *Das Rheingold*, the prologue opera to Richard Wagner's Ring Cycle, was directed in 1932 by Sergey Radlov at the Leningrad Academic Opera and Ballet Theater (the former Maria) with scenery by Isaak Rabinovich.

Then the situation altered. Aiming to raise profits, theaters lost sight of the *political* meaning behind attracting new cadres of organized spectators, the political meaning of the theater parties and special performances—and the quality of theater parties was artistically reduced. The results of such shortsighted management can be felt especially keenly at the present time.

Of course, the regulation of staffs is indispensable: in many theaters the staff has swollen out of all proportion. But that remedy by itself cannot prevent the debacle.

Parallel work on two fronts, tours and, mainly, a broad involvement of the working spectator—all these measures taken to achieve the profit side of the estimate (and not only by cutting expenses) can help to fulfill the financial plan.

But for this, special measures have to be taken. The naive inscription on posters "A decade of May First theater parties" will not save the situation. Economic factors must force management to think about reinforcing the weakened bonds between the theaters, on one hand, and the factories and plants, on the other. The initiative must be the theater's, as the party with the greater stake in every respect.

What is being done in this respect? So far, nothing! . . .

A. A. Andreev, "Light, color, and movement," *Sovetskoe iskusstvo* 210 (May 8, 1933). Andrey Andreevich Andreev (1895–1971) was secretary of the Central Committee of the All-Russian Communist Party 1935.

There was a time when attempts were made to strictly regulate the lighting, the size of materials used, the emblems and decorations used on the facades of buildings. The streets were marked out like constructivist textbooks, and they had to be read like books.

And every time the decorations for May First caused disappointment. It seemed as if all the slogans and themes had been used, as if all points had been decorated with numbers, paint, and photodocumentation, and as if all the public squares had been submerged in real motor cars and models of products, and yet somehow all this work failed to provide a unified artistic and political effect.

Only this year, despite much more modest work on the part of the May First head-quarters, has Moscow achieved a truly festive decor. A picturesque splendor, an artistic expressiveness, and a clear political statement all blended together harmoniously.

What is the secret of the success of the 1933 May Day decorations that have been so admired by the masses themselves, who have stood for hours in front of different subjects attentively scanning the details of the city's festive decor?

[. . .] Up until last year, the artist has always been trying to compete with the city. [. . .] This year the May First headquarters chose a different method—a more economi-cal outlay of decorative emphases. More attention was paid to the central squares and streets at which the districts meet on May First. Light, color, and movement became the basic means of expression. Crudely painted decorative panels and vast abstract wooden structures with diagrams and photographs occupied a much less important position than before. [. . .]

This year shop windows were widely used for purposes of artistic campaigning.

Kuznetsky Bridge was turned into a "street of satire." [...] Also interesting was the "parade" of Moscow theaters. Unfortunately the exhibition of pictures in the windows on Gorky Street must be admitted to have been unsuccessful. [...]

IN 1935, control was transferred from the Narkompros to the newly founded Committee for Artistic Affairs.

Spravochnik rukovodyashchikh materialov Komitet po delam iskusstv pri SNK Soyuza SSSR [Instruction manual for the Committee for Artistic Affairs of the USSR] (Moscow: Iskusstvo, 1941), 5.

Approved by the Council of People's Commissars of the USSR no. 1542, September 25, 1939.

I

1. The Committee for Artistic Affairs under the SNK of the USSR is to function as the leadership of all forms of art in the USSR, excluding the cinema, to manage directly the most prominent artistic endeavors and establishments of All-Union significance based on a specific list confirmed by the Council of People's Commissars of the USSR, and, through the administration of artistic affairs under the SNK of the republics of the union, will run the artistic enterprises of the republic and local subordinates.

II

2. The Committee for Artistic Affairs under the SNK of the USSR:
a. is to oversee and confirm the repertoire of theater and concert establishments of the subordinate unions, as well as through the administration for artistic affairs under the SNK of the united republics direct and inspect the repertoire of artistic and entertainment enterprises of the republic and local subordinates. [...]
g. will exercise government oversight of the spectacles and the repertoire (theater, music, variety stage, circus), theatrical publicity, artistic sound recording, the production of paintings and sculptures, confirm plans for phonograph recording of all organizations that issue phonograph records, the catalog and editions of phonograph records.
h. in coordination with the appointed governance will regulate the price of tickets in theaters, circuses, concert halls, and museums. [...]

IN 1933 a massive summer theater was opened in Moscow's Gorky Park. It was moved into a building in 1954.

Yakov Vorob'ëv, "A theater without performances," March 14, 1938. Unidentified clipping, Dana Collection, Harvard Theater Collection.

In 1933, when, on the initiative of Lazar' Moiseevich Kaganovich,[5] the construction of the gigantic Green Theater was undertaken, it was presumed that this would become

5 Lazar' Moiseevich Kaganovich (1893–1986), secretary of the Central Committee 1928–39; in

a performance center in its own right, where the greatest of the USSR's artistic troupes would be able to exhibit their artistry.

Various attempts in this direction were made during the first five years of the Green Theater. Special productions from Moscow's Bol'shoy Theater, Leningrad's MALEGOT,[6] and a number of other dramatic theaters show that the Green Theater's stage was not simply an enlarged platform, that this theater was not simply an "enterprise" with an enormous auditorium. *Carmen,* performed by the combined efforts of the Moscow Bol'shoy Theater and MALEGOT in 1935 on the Green Theater stage, sounded different than when performed at the Bol'shoy. The crowd scenes of this brilliant, passionate opera were arranged on the Green Theater stage with an artistic panache that "ordinary" theaters could not even dream about.

The Green Theater set the most inspired and talented directors of the country the challenge of creating a new performance style based on the technical possibilities offered by the enormous and unique stage and an auditorium seating thousands. Not only *Carmen* but other shows, such as operas, ballets, and dramas, staged in the Green Theater (*The Flame of Paris, Glory, The Quiet Don, The Fair at Sorochints,*[7] individual acts of *Prince Igor', The Maid of Pskov*) became, in every sense, great artistic events in the life of Moscow. And each of these productions brought in tens of thousands of spectators. Bearing in mind the work experience of the Green Theater, one can project preliminary plans for the artistic performances to be staged in the future Palace of Congresses. [...]

The Vakhtangov Theater was invited to put on an anniversary performance of *Man with a Gun*[8] on the Green Theater stage. However, the theater turned down the invitation, stating that the performance "would not sound good" on the stage of this enormous open-air theater. But this was not the real problem. The Vakhtangov simply did not want to take the extra trouble.

The Moscow Operetta Theater was more candid when it refused to perform *The Wedding at Malinovka*[9] on the Green Theater stage, unceremoniously citing "box-office" considerations.

"The performance would be seen by hundreds of thousands of spectators in the

---

charge of the collectivization of agriculture 1929–34 and the Party Purge 1933–34; one of Stalin's chief lieutenants, his influence waned after the general secretary's death, and in 1957, he was expelled from the Central Committee.

6   Leningrad Academic Maly Opera Theater, formerly the Mikhailovsky or Grand Duke Michael Theater.

7   *Plamya Parizha* (1932), a ballet by Boris Asaf'ev about the French Revolution, and *Tikhy Don* (1935), an opera by Ivan Dzherzhinsky from Mikhail Solokhov's novel, were both favorites of Stalin (he saw the former fifteen times). *Sorochinskaya yarmarka* (1936), from Gogol's story, is not the unfinished opera by Modest Musorgsky but a kitschy musical comedy by A. Ryabov.

8   The prize-winning *Chelovek s ruzh'em* (1935) by Nikolay Pogodin was the first play in which Lenin appeared onstage as a dramatic character.

9   *Svadba v Malinovke* (1937), a folk operetta by Boris Aleksandrov, set in a Ukrainian village and making fun of Makhno's uprising; it was played to the troops at the front and to beleaguered city dwellers 1941–42.

summer at the open-air Green Theater and later no one would come to see it inside a theater building."

It seems to us that a performance such as *Earth*,[10] staged by the Art Theater on the twentieth anniversary of the Great Proletarian Revolution, would have an excellent effect on the large stage of the Green Theater. But the theatrical board of the All-Union Committee on the Arts considers it to be more expedient for the MAT to limit its "touring season" to an autumn tour to Leningrad this year.

No one in the All-Union Committee for Artistic Affairs plans to show the best national and other theatrical performances on the Green Theater stage. And yet one could show *Arsen* from the Rustaveli Theater or *From a Spark*[11] from the Mardzhan-ishvili Theater or the best productions of the Azizbekov Dramatic Theater of Baku or the Sverdlovsk opera, etc., etc. The expediency of such tours to Moscow can hardly be doubted. The capacity of the Green Theater's auditorium exceeds even the boldest designs of our theater architects. The technical equipment of its stage has been considerably improved this year, especially the newly installed sound system. (Incidentally, the architectural renovations to the Green Theater are not yet complete. The matter of covering the theater in case of inclement weather is yet to be resolved. Where are the masses of sculptures, fountains, and porticos discussed by our architects when the idea of building the Green Theater first arose? So far none of this is forthcoming.)

A long time ago a question arose of creating a new distinctive mass heroic spectacle, in which elements of theater, circus, symphonic and choral music, and movies would be synthetically combined. At one time, there was talk of performing one of the classical Greek tragedies at the Green Theater. At present, there is a more realistic issue of staging in 1938 one of two heroic epics—either the *Epic of Tsaritsyn*, based on a scenario by A. N. Tolstoy,[12] or the epic *Rus'* based on Pavlenko's[13] scenario. To accomplish this, one of the best theatrical troupes of the country has to be put to work in a timely fashion. However, theaters are loath to go to any trouble, they don't want to "overwork" themselves. [. . .]

Julian Bullard and Margaret Bullard, eds., *Inside Stalin's Russia: The Diaries of Reader Bullard 1930–1934* (Oxfordshire, U.K.: Day Books, 2000), 179, 183–84, 198–99, 231, 251.

10 *Zemlya*. It's unclear if the writer is referring to *Earth (Zemlya)* by Perets Markish (1931), *Earth* by Nikolay Virta (1937), or *Heaven and Earth (Zemlya i nebo*, 1935), a detective play about astronomy, by the teenaged Tur' Brothers (Leonid Tubel'sky and Pëtr Ryzhy), staged by the MAT 2.
11 Prize-winning Georgian plays: *Arsen* (1936) by Sandro Shanshiashivili and *From a Spark...* (1937) by Shalva Dadiani, about Stalin's recruitment of workers in Baku to the cause.
12 Aleksey Nikolaevich Tolstoy (1882–1945), known as the Red Count; popular for his science fiction, he pillaged history for his melodramatic plays, including a view of Ivan the Terrible that praised Stalin.
13 Pëtr Andreevich Pavlenko (1899–1951), whose short stories and novels deal with the eastern reaches of the Soviet Union and the defense of the homeland; he wrote the screenplay for *Aleksandr Nevsky* (1938) and then became a war correspondent.

April 30, 1933 [Leningrad]. I go to the theatre with Pott[14] quite frequently. It only costs a few pence, and we can now get good seats by telephoning the theatre. Perhaps because people have less money. Not only were wages cut heavily in January, but salaries are always in arrears. Many people have not yet received their March pay. [. . .]

The man who runs the hand-puppets, Eugene Demmeni,[15] is one of the few people here I should like to see more of if conditions were different. He is a pleasant, quiet man, very enthusiastic about his work, and he showed us all his figures and costumes. One of the plays they do is *Little Black Sambo*. Demmeni worked the tiger for our benefit. It had dreadful claws made out of quill toothpicks. It was one of the worst days of the trial [of MacDonald[16]], but nothing could have been less offensive than Demmeni's manner, and afterwards he returned to us by a roundabout channel the money we had paid for our tickets—as the only way in which he could show his sympathy.

May 20, 1933. We thought we ought to go and see a play about life in England: *Joy Street*.[17] We came out at half-time finding it more than our digestions could stand. The first two scenes were in a London slum. There was a strike with the trade union leader "betraying the workers," the police arrested the strike committee, a boy delivering washing is knocked down by a motor-car and discharged for soiling the washing, which included Lady Salisbury's lace knickers. A girl is raped. There is much hypocritical church-going. Bailiffs evict the washerwoman for being behind with the rent . . . We had had enough. The cloakroom attendant asked why we were leaving. "England isn't like that." "Ah," he said, "I know a little too."

June 26, 1933. On the 22nd I took Miss Goyer and Mrs. Diedrichs[18] to see *Dniy Turbiny* [sic] (*The Days of the Turbin Family*), a play that was banned for some years, but has been put on again recently because, it is said, Stalin likes it. It is not a great play, but it is of poignant interest. It is set in the Ukraine in 1918. Mrs. Diedrichs was much moved. I offered to lend her the book on which the play is based, but when she saw it was published in Paris, she did not dare to borrow it.

January 14, 1934. Sunday. While Miss McEvoy[19] was staying with me I took her to the theater with a young American actor, Page. We saw *The Marriage of Krechinski*[20]

---

14 Leslie Pott was appointed British vice-consul to Leningrad in 1933; a fluent Russian speaker, he delivered candid reports on the famine in the Ukraine.

15 Evgeny Sergeevich Demmeni (1898–1969) organized the Leningrad Puppet Theater in 1930 and initiated puppet theaters in collective farms in the vicinity.

16 On March 11, 1933, OGPU arrested six British engineers of the Metropolitan-Vickers electrical engineering firm and charged them with espionage and sabotage on behalf of the British Intelligence Service. One of them, William Macdonald, whose trial began on April 12, confessed to the charges and was sentenced to a term of three years' imprisonment. This led to a British embargo of the USSR.

17 *Dzhoy Strit* (also known as *Ulitsa radosti*), a "social melodrama" by Natan A. Zarkhi, was directed by I. Yu. Shlepyanov at the Theater of Revolution in 1932.

18 Miss Goyer was doing research in a physics laboratory; Mrs. Diedrichs was Bullard's Russian teacher and an Intourist guide.

19 The eighteen-year-old daughter of the artist A. A. McEvoy.

20 *Svad'ba Krechinskogo*, the first part of Sukhovo-Kobylin's satiric trilogy, first performed in St. Petersburg in 1856.

performed for the first time since the Revolution. Page says that Russian acting is a great contrast to English and American. Here nothing is left to the imagination of the audience, every point is underlined, and the actors often play to the audience instead of to each other. He may modify his opinion a little after seeing the First Art Theater in Moscow perform *The Cherry Orchard* but in the main I agree with him. The audiences need to have the drama driven in in the same way as politics—with a club.

April 6, 1934. I saw a very amusing play last week—*Somebody Else's Child.*[21] Except at one point it has no Marxist ideology in it, and is correspondingly popular.

Yu. Shiroky, "The theater serves the navy," *Iskusstvo i zhizn'* 11 (1933), 15–17.

The theater of the Red Army Baltic fleet is one of the interesting creative collectives that has taken shape and evolved during the last few years. [...] The theater has existed for 10 years now. [...] In 1928, at the Kronstadt House of the Red Army, a studio of small forms was organized which at first pursued extremely modest goals. [...] In late 1929, nearly ten Red Navy men were transferred from the ship to make up one of the Baltic semiprofessional brigades. With the help of the symphonic orchestra created for DKA, a plain revue was organized here, in the course of which the performers sang topical verses and arias, set to the tunes of popular operettas. Nearby this troupe there lived and worked a drama club whose repertoire consisted of uncomplicated works of then still young Soviet playwrights. From the works of these two homegrown groups a collective soon formed, devoted to the creation of dramatic shows. [...]

[A movement for a more literary drama led to a performance of *The Adventures of the Good Soldier Švejk.*[22]] However, the demand for a defensive show, a show that reflects the heroic past of our country, was felt ever more keenly. And so in 1933 the theater brought out *Red Verdun,*[23] a production devoted to the defense of Tsaritsyn. In this production the actors succeeded in using those variegated stage skills they had used in the studio of small forms. Ensemble and solo dances here were relieved by music, dueling matches, and powerful choruses. The dialogue took only second place in *Red Verdun,* basically the vocal part of the basic spectacle. Consequently, *Red Verdun* underwent a certain adaptation and entered the repertoire of the theater as the fruition of creative achievements from the first period of the collective's activity.

A. Olgin, "Physical culture theatre combines music and acting with athletic grace," *Moscow Daily News* (September 17, 1935), 3–4.

21 *Chuzhoy rebënok* (1933), also known in English as *Father Unknown*; a comedy by Vasily Vasil'evich Shkvarkin (1894–1967) about an actress who passes herself off as an unwed mother; it became a standby of the Moscow Satire Theater, with fifteen hundred performances.

22 An odd choice, since Jaroslav Hašek's unfinished Czech comic novel (1923) features a crafty simpleton who continually thwarts the militarist establishment; perhaps it was inspired by Erwin Piscator's antiwar German dramatization of 1928.

23 *Krasny Verdun,* a term for the battle for Tsaritsyn during the Civil War; Stalin had fortified the town against the Whites for a while, but the dramatizations never pointed out that General Vrangel' eventually recaptured it.

6.1. General Secretary Stalin, Party officials Kirov and Ordzhonikidze, and Maksim Gorky watch a physical culture parade in Red Square, May 28, 1932.

Combining the athletic perfection of the ancient Greeks, the art of the contemporary theater, and the educational purposes of the Soviet physical culture movement, the new Leningrad Physical Culture Theater is as unique as it is entertaining.

Its object is to popularize all forms of sport, from football and boxing to parachute jumping and tennis. Its performers are athletes, acrobats, and actors. At the same time they are as skilled as a ballet artist in interpreting the music that accompanies the extraordinary rhythm of their dance–sports pantomime. [. . .]

The first number on the program is like a sculpture from the classic section of a museum—the athletes of antiquity appearing before the audience as a living bas-relief [. . .], the warriors and runners of Sparta. [The following acts include tennis and comical boxing.]

The scene changes. Fifteen young men and girls, each wearing a GTO badge, again flood the stage with youth and health. For twenty minutes, their muscles rippling under their sports jerseys, they go through the GTO complex—acrobatics, swimming, shooting, running [. . .] to the accompaniment of music. [. . .] As a Red Army paper said of it, "The arrival of this theater on tour is an event. Our men will have to learn physical culture from actors."

Socialist Realism

At the First Congress of Writers, Gorky had defined the subject matter of socialist realism as "deeds, creativity . . . the uninterrupted development of the priceless individual faculties of man," leading to the conquest of nature and the unification of humanity as a single faculty. In the face of this vision, Zhdanov had to declare that the socialist form of "realism" was not opposed to romanticism. Rather, it was hostile to any kind of "modern" arbitrarily vilified under the name "formalism." According to Zhdanov, literature and art had to be tendentious, to show "reality...in its revolutionary development," to promote "the ideological transformation and education [of the public] in the spirit of socialism." (And subservience to the Party line by the "engineers of the human soul.")

Valery Kirpotin, "Success of Soviet drama," *Teatr i dramaturgiya* 8 (1934), 1. Valery Yakovlevich Kirpotin (1898–1997) was chief of the Literary Division of the Party Central Committee and, from 1932, organizing secretary of the Union of Soviet Writers; tasked with promoting socialist realism, he attacked Mikhail Bakhtin and organized the Pushkin Jubilee in 1937 as a festival celebrating Communist ideals. These remarks were made at the First Congress of Soviet Writers.

Soviet drama differs from that of the prerevolutionary and the contemporary bourgeoisie in content. The prerevolutionary and contemporary bourgeois dramas concentrate on the life of egotistic individuals. The self-infatuated savoring of narrowly individual experiences, the abnormally exaggerated individualistic principle...adultery, eroticism, and crime are most typical of the content of the bourgeois drama. The idea that private property and money are the highest blessings on earth...forms one of the basic themes of bourgeois drama. That is true both of its classics and of its period of decline.

The ideas of Soviet drama are new. Its theme is collective toil and the collective struggle for socialism...Soviet drama depicts man in a new way, as a participant in the class collective, as a creator of new social forms, as the discoverer of new techniques that immeasurably expand his power over nature...It concerns the class struggle of the working class against its exploiters, the civil war, socialist industrialization, the collectivization of agriculture, the role of the intellectuals in the Revolution.

"The growth of the repertoire of the revolutionary theatre," *International Theatre* 3–4 (1934), 17–18.

The contest opened by the Soviet government in February 1933 for the best play is over. One thousand two hundred plays were submitted; the judges, prominent people in public life, writers and producers (including Meyerhold and Aleksey Tolstoy) have reached the following decision:

To award no first prize, as none of the plays submitted conforms fully to the conditions of the competition [...] The first prize was not awarded, because despite all the success of recent years, Soviet dramaturgy is still behind the enormous demands made on it by our great epoch. Soviet playwrights are fighting for quality, ridding themselves of schematism and oversimplification, gradually mastering the molding of live artistic characters.

To award second and third prizes as follows:

6.2. *The Wreck of the Squadron* by Aleksandr Korneychuk, designed by Nisson Shifrin, Red Army Theater, 1934; an attack on Ukrainian nationalism that depicts the Red Navy's sinking of the fleet to thwart the White Russians.

Second prize to *The Wonderful Alloy* by V. Kirshon and *The Wreck of the Squadron* by A. Korneychuk.[24]

Third prize to *Fighters* by B. Romashov; *Shahnahme* by M. Dzhanan; and *The Watchmaker and the Hen* by I. A. Kocherga.[25] [...]

The Wonderful Alloy by Kirshon is a gay, buoyant comedy of Soviet youth, of the life and struggle of the Young Communist League in socialist construction. *The Wreck of the Squadron* by Korneychuk is a drama of one of the most tragic episodes of the Civil War. It is written with real fervor and is directed with all its force against Petlyura Ukrainian nationalism.

24 Vladimir Mikhaylovich Kirshon (1902–38), author of melodramas of Soviet youth and industrialization, including *The Rails Are Humming* (1927), *Bread* (1930), and *The Trial* (1932); in 1937 he was accused of Trotskyism and executed by firing squad. Aleksandr Evdokimovich Korneychuk (1905–72), Ukrainian playwright, whose play was an outright attack on Ukrainian nationalism; he continued to churn out one-dimensional patriotic dramas into the 1960s.

25 *The Book of Kings* by M. Dzhanan, an Armenian actor, revealed how Great Britain pulled the strings on politics in Persia. *The Watchmaker and the Hen,* by the Ukrainian playwright Ivan Antonovich Kocherga (1881–1952), was a farce offering revolutionaries as the real "masters of time."

Sergey Tsimbal, "Three productions of *The Wonderful Alloy*," *Rabochy i teatr* 30 (1934), 8–9. Sergey L'vovich Tsimbal (1907–78), theater critic for *Rabochy i teatr, Iskusstvo i zhizn'* 1932–38, chief dramaturg at the Leningrad Comedy Theater 1946–47; he led debates on problems of Soviet drama.

The success of Kirshon's *Wonderful Alloy* eloquently illustrates the demand for a comic play bubbling up in our general public. The drought in our comic drama is being remedied slowly and with great difficulty. There are many reasons for this. Before a Soviet comedy of really new quality can be created, before mature comic techniques of Soviet drama can take shape, no small amount of time has to pass. The very genre of comedy takes hold only in those periods when reality itself has become relatively stable and in the artist's field of vision the traditions, customs, and conventions formed in this reality are turned upside down. But our reality is growing and changing with such speed that yesterday's characteristic signs of normality have by tomorrow already become obsolete, outmoded, overwhelmed, whereas comedy, all comedy and especially comedy of character, is built on the artist's vivid observation, on the ability to select what is essential and *typical* in what he sees and notices around him. And when these typical details are undergoing daily changes, the dramatist willy-nilly is like a pedestrian trying to sketch an automobile driven at top speed. To overcome this difficulty, our dramatists too often are constrained to have recourse to the traditional, readily available devices of bourgeois comedy and with their aid make their spectator laugh.

Kirshon's comedy—which deals with the new young creators of our reality, relating how a jolly brigade of life-loving engineers who know how to rejoice, love, work, and relax is fighting for the technological independence of their country, a comedy whose basic theme is the greatest joy of creative work, a joy discovered in its fullness only by people in socialist lands—with irritating candor uses ruthlessly outworn farce situations, played out in drama, the most essentially primitive devices to entertain the spectator, devices that strikingly contradict the whole breath of youth, the whole excitement and power of its material. But the spectators laugh. They laugh until they drop every time a merry confusion of characters takes place onstage. They roar until they cry at every proverb garbled by the good-hearted Latvian Jan Dvali, they laugh at such simple-minded devices of the dramatist as the game with Brigadier Gosha's trousers. They laugh, in short, wherever the slightest pretext for laughter is provided.

[...] Theatrical practice of the last few years has been so poor in productions of Soviet comedy that we are directly threatened with the impoverishment of the comic actor's technique on our stage—an impoverishment that cannot fail to be expressed in playwriting. [...] Comic roles must be written that take direct account of comic actors. A new quality of comic acting will prompt our comedy writers with new comic devices. It would be perilous to underestimate the mutuality of this process, for a new reality creates its own new typical characters, and consequently, in new Soviet comedy, the chief situations must involve not old-fashioned dotards, simpletons and lovers, fostered by bourgeois comedy, but new characters, fostered by our reality, through whom the dramatist is able to reveal and decipher in typical circumstances its whole remarkable idiosyncrasy.

Stella Adler on *The Wonderful Alloy.* Janet Thorne, "It makes you weep: An interview with Stella Adler on Soviet actors," *New Theater* (October 1934), 8. Stella Adler (1903–92), American actress in the Group Theater and wife of its founder, Harold Clurman, had questioned Stanislavsky in Paris about his system and from 1949 became a formidable teacher at her own studio in New York.

I went to the opening of *The Wonderful Alloy* by Kirshon [at the Moscow Art Theater]. Everybody in Moscow—all the theatrical people—were [*sic*] there. And they clapped. And they cheered. And the play *wasn't* very good. I had to say something. I began, bewildered, to one of the directors from another theater. "This isn't as good as most of the plays I've seen here."

"No," he said.

"The acting isn't so good."

He said, "We know it."

Diffidently, I mentioned, "At home this would be a flop."

"It's a flop."

On the stage Danchenko was pressing the actors' hands. Kirshon was kissing Danchenko. The house bravoed.

"It's a flop," said the director, "but it's the work of a talented writer in whom we are interested. The designer shows a growing gift. Here are some of our best actors in new roles—not their best, but interesting. There is an audience which will want to see this step in the development of this theater and these people. The play will stay in the repertory for a while, perhaps two nights a week, later once a month, long enough to reach this audience."

So the work isn't wasted. It's seen. It's criticized seriously. Because serious work has gone into it, it isn't kicked and annihilated the morning after. I tell you, I could weep. It's an actors' paradise.

THE LENINGRAD LECTORIUM opened in September 1934, and Meyerhold spoke there the next day, defining the fight between "socialist culture and fascist non-culture," arguing for a culture "of taste." He came down particularly hard on the play *Someone Else's Baby.*

"Meyerhold on the tribune at opening of the Lectorium," *Rabochy i teatr* 29 (1934), 12–13.

I know nothing more vulgar and worse than this play.

I slip into the back of the auditorium and I see how so-called witty, vulgar wisecracks wander through the hall. As the innate vulgarity that permeates this work infects the spectator.

Laughter. We need laughter. Oh, we need laughter, it lightens the brain, it aids relaxation, it exposes the enemy. But isn't it time to raise the question of the dosage and type of laughter?

I always remember the story of a certain doctor who prescribed laughter without a specific dosage. One boy so tickled another that he laughed and laughed and finally died. Laughter is all very well, but if we don't regulate the dose, then an apoplectic fit will strike. I only hope that Shkvarkin doesn't have the same susceptibility as that boy.

> Nikolay Oruzheynikov, "Soviet drama," *VOKS Socialist Construction in the USSR* 6 (1934), 11, 18–20. Rev. trans.

One of the plays enjoying genuine success before Soviet audiences bears the title of *My Friend.*[26] The playwright deliberately states his ideological view of the hero and reminds us that he is dealing with a contemporary character who might be found right here in the audience. Gay, the hero of the play, and chief of construction of a large new factory, has not been invented to demonstrate some thesis nor for purposes of propaganda. He has been drawn from the living stream of real people, unadorned with all his peculiarities and foibles. Gay is not like those characters of Communists that were schematically patterned in the plays of the first years of revolution. He is in no way deprived of individuality, only the heroic background of the great industrial construction sets off his big and unique personality. N. Pogodin[27] has succeeded in getting close to the artistic truth about the real heroes of our time.[28] [...]

The birth of the new hero cannot lead to the rise of a new Faust or Hamlet, for in the Soviet Union the class that stands behind the personages developed by literature is not given to metaphysical speculation, nor is it afflicted with skepticism, but is full of the juice of life. Knowledge for this class is not a "sweet poison" but a weapon for the transformation of the world. It is a hero who endeavors to master the treasures of the whole of human culture, who endeavors to master the treasures of the whole of human cultures, who endeavors to possess the whole heritage from Plato to Hegel, and from Pythagoras to Einstein. It is a hero who breaks free from all the shackles of the past, who is full of the buoyant joy of the free man imbued with the intense emotion of creation. [...]

In all cases, however, the Soviet spectator wants a joyful play alive with laughter, buoyancy, and bright colors. Such is the keynote of our life, and this determines the quests of our playwrights who are turning more and more often to comedy as a form which admits of an optimistic figure of the new man [...] the new hero, the Gulliver of the socialist society who rises above the Lilliputians of the old play. [...]

---

26 *Moy drug* (1932) by Nikolay Pogodin deals with the difficulties in getting a factory up and running.
27 Nikolay Fëdorovich Pogodin (actually Stukalov, 1900–1962), playwright, whose work was considered the pattern for socialist realism and whose heroes were devoted to fulfilling the Five-Year Plan; his plays about Lenin were particularly popular.
28 In the same issue, Pogodin predicted that "the theater will by the very nature of things become transformed into a place wherein the spectators will be infected with the jovial spirit of the great construction of socialism. That is why the playwrights and the theaters should bring onto the stage the heroes, the best people of our epoch" (57).

Samuil Margolin, "The artist and the theater," *VOKS Socialist Construction in the USSR* 6 (1934), 42–46.

The spirit of realism is felt in nearly all the models and designs of productions in preparation for the current season. And although it is scenic architecture that is more and more freeing our theater from abstract constructions, nevertheless these realistic tendencies found a perfect expression also in the work of the designers who formerly stood up for the principles of conventional stylization. The best testimony to this is furnished by Fëdorovsky's[29] settings for the opera *The Maid of Pskov* [*Pskovityanka*] by Rimsky-Korsakov, which was produced at the Bol'shoy Theater. Here we have the Pskov of the epoch of Ivan the Terrible [...] conveyed with the convincing force of a great art that penetrates the heart of the historical events and expresses them in effective and clear-cut images. [...]

Constructivism has already become a thing of the past [and] has now almost ceased to exist as an independent style. The constructivists have given up the theater, either turning to the cinema or engaging in such varied activities as printing, aviation, furniture making, etc. Of those of the constructivists who have remained in the theater, some have become directors and producers, others have become architects. [...]

The new spectator in the Soviet theater demands a setting that discloses the substance of the play and of its epoch. [...] What the spectator wants of the designer is that he get as close as possible to real life; that he tell in the brightest scenic images about living facts and peoples; but these requirements by no means should limit the artist's imagination. Dmitriev has shown himself a master in his scenery for the performance of *North Wind*[30] at the Nemirovich-Danchenko Musical Theater[31] and in his convincing realistic stage design for the production of *Queen of Spades* (Bol'shoy Theater). In his next works he will no doubt overcome his tendencies toward naturalism. [...]

The Soviet spectator can be impressed only by a generalized image that sheds light on the entire epoch; this alone he considers great art. Naturalism, the heritage of the bourgeoisie, is fundamentally alien to the tendency of the Soviet theater toward the style of socialist realism. [...]

"The creative path of the Maly Theater," *Teatr i Dramaturgiya* 11–12 (1934), 15–20.

Our heroic epoch demands a theater worthy of it. Soviet theater seems to be the best theater in the world, but it is still not at the level of the Soviet epoch. The Revolution

---

29 Fëdor Fëdorovich Fëderovsky (1883–1955), prize-winning designer, who provided lush and colorful sets and costumes for productions at the Bol'shoy Theater 1921–41, 1947–53, particularly for Russian opera and the cossack epic *The Quiet Don* (1936).

30 *Severny Veter* (1930), an opera by Lev Knipper based on Kirshon's *City of Winds*, used a melodeclamatory form that was attacked by main-line critics.

31 Nemirovich-Danchenko founded a Musical Studio at the MAT in 1919, which toured widely; in 1926 it became the Nemirovich-Danchenko Musical Theater with its own building on Bol'shaya Dmitrovka Street and absorbed the corps of the Art Ballet in 1939.

demands that the stages of the Soviet theater display the psychology of the new man and the new socialist community. Such a theater does not exist. Such a theater must be created.

Where is such a theater to come from? What elements of the old theater can be used to create a theater of the Soviet epoch?

A. Lunacharsky, speaking about theater of the past, wrote, "Not biomechanics nor neorealism nor idealistic symbolism nor impressionism with its nuances and details will be fit for such a theater. Similarly the poster is as unsuitable for it as is a miniature. It needs a fresco, i.e., great artistic subtlety to capture its monumentality. This theater will probably trample over those models provided by the Maly Theater, but it will travel the same path [...]"

The Maly Theater is carrying on a decisive fight against the decline of the ideological and artistic quality of its repertoire, against a false interpretation of tradition. Making higher demands on its repertoire, the Maly Theater has eliminated a whole series of productions that do not satisfy the new, higher artistic demands, productions that did not answer to the best traditions of the Maly Theater. The Maly Theater notes with satisfaction that a number of its shows—*Lyubov' Yarovaya, A Disorderly Street, Don Carlos, Enemies, Fighters, Skutarevsky*[32]—were greeted by the Soviet community and press as a series of triumphs in putting on the classics and in revealing a Soviet repertoire. [...]

The production of *Fighters* at the Maly Theater showed the Red Army and the whole Soviet community that the theater is capable of taking on topical themes from real life, even the military specifics unfamiliar to it.

Skutarevsky is the next phase of the theater's intensified work on the social image of Soviet reality, on the culture of highly artistic speech. The theater shows how the objective reality of the Soviet land is refashioned by the best representatives of the old intelligentsia, gives it a new, socialist life, and how this reality rejects hostile elements that have become the rubbish heap of history. [...]

Working on *Fighters* and *Skutarevsky,* the theater is leaving behind the patina of kitchen-sink literalism [*bytovizm*], characterized by specific productions of the last few years, and is striving to create a collective realistic language of stage art. [...]

Boris Golubovsky, *Bol'shie malen'kie teatry* (Moscow: Izd. im. Sabashnikovykh, 1998), 148, 343–44.

Lyubimov-Lanskoy understood that a new methodology was needed, but he resisted, like Tairov and other masters, the destructive, violent "evacuation" propagated by the leadership of the Committee for Artistic Affairs, and he could not find his own,

---

32 *Rasteryaevaya ulitsa,* a dramatization of Gleb Uspensky's 1866 novel of proletarian bad behavior *The Mores of a Disorderly Street. Don Carlos* (1782), Schiller's verse drama of intolerance and tyranny. *Vragi,* Gorky's 1906 play about a factory strike put down by the military. *Bortsy* (1933), by Boris Romashov, about a Red Army commander brought up among partisans. *Skutarevsky* (1934), Leonid Leonov's dramatization of his novel about a contentious scientist.

different means of expression. Even before the war, Lyubimov-Lanskoy decided to set in motion "an old, but faithful weapon": to revive the hits of the 1920s–1930s. It was clear that in *Mutiny*, many devices had aged badly—the prologue, the address to the audience; the crowd scenes had lost their monolithic quality, their temperament. [...] *The City of Winds*[33] in a new directorial recension had lost its luster, its romantic tonality. The attempt to "work in MAT style," in halftones, didn't suit the genre—the play turned out to be more powerful than the production. Even Afinogenov, a friend and colleague of Kirshon, confessed that the play, once it was stood "on the ground," had dimmed, the production turned out to be primitive, folkloric [*ashug*], the author's and theater's pride and joy had become unnecessary and bombastic. [...]

The chief reproach leveled at dramatists, directors, and actors, although the last were the least to blame for this, consisted in the absence onstage of a modern hero. They expected from the theater new Pavel Korchagins, the Commissar from *Optimistic Tragedy*, Lyubov' Yarovaya, Bratishka, Chapaev, etc. But this had no effect on dramatists. In the mid-1930s at the Art Theater, a hero of our modern times came from the Ukraine—the romantic *Platon Krechet* by Aleksandr Korneychuk. The insatiable semi-official organ had temporarily spoiled our appetite. *Platon Krechet* attracted spectators with its melodrama. No serious social program spent a serious minute in the play. We greeted Krechet's monologue almost as a parody:

"Krechet (*mechanically puts a hand on the skull, stares at it*). Not always are we strong enough to stop your cold, your eternal laughter ... You inexorably close the circle. You annihilate geniuses of the people in this, our heaviest hour ... Who gave you the right for the time being to deal death to man's happiness with your breath? I challenge you to a duel. Today you have triumphed cruelly ... But tomorrow who will triumph? Who? You or I." Beautiful. Much too beautiful!

I cannot compare Krechet with Grigory Gay from *My Friend*, optimistic but full of irony and not speaking bombastic words. Astangov[34] as Gay was for me the ideal modern hero.

IN 1935 Akimov was named chief director of the Comedy Theater. He decided to stage Evgeny Shvarts's satiric fairy tale *The Princess and the Swineherd*.

Nikolay Akimov, "The path of the Comedy Theater," November 17, 1962, quoted in Evgeny M. Binevich, "Na puti k 'Drakunu,'" [On the way to *The Dragon*], *Neva* 10 (1996), 171–72.

In earlier times, there was a certain reassuring formula: why are you complaining to the Repertkom that it has banned a play? They do not ban good plays. Show us a good play that the Repertkom has banned. I intend to show one—in 1934 Shvarts

---

33 *Gorod vetrov* (1929), Kirshon's play about the defense of Baku during the Civil War.
34 Mikhail Fëdorovich Astangov (actually Ruzhnikov, 1900–1965), intellectual actor at the Theater of Revolution 1925–27, 1930–41, then at the Mossovet 1943–45, and from 1945 at the Vakhtangov.

wrote a very good play, *The Princess and the Swineherd*,[35] which was once forbidden, then permitted, and when I had got halfway through work on it in this theater, it was forbidden again. No one explained the reason. Certain nuances had upset somebody.

[Between March 27 and April 3, 1936, all the theaters held meetings of "self-exposure" in the campaign against formalism. At a meeting at the Pushkin Theater, Akimov said:]

I do think that Shvarts belongs to the number of playwrights who are probably not devoid of certain formalistic tendencies, but, nevertheless, he has, I think, a lot of very valuable qualities, and it is there that the creative individuality of the theater, the theater's creative energy, has to be expressed in knowing how to extract what we need from this man and to discard what we do not need. I think that in the play *The Princess and the Swineherd* it would be possible to do that.

[March 28] Shvarts's play is very witty, very comical, interesting, ideological in its content. The fact that it is composed in the form of a fairy tale is not formalism. What will most convince the spectators of the slippery problem of fascism in Germany—a display of real princes, a performance of *Professor Mamlock*,[36] or a performance of *The Princess and the Swineherd*? The last will be the most persuasive. It is wrong to accuse *The Princess and the Swineherd* of formalism.

> Boris Tenin, *Terenty Ivanovich*, directed by Akimov at Theater of Satire and Comedy, from *Furgon komedianta. Iz vospominanii* (Moscow: Iskusstvo, 1987), 185–86.

Terenty Ivanovich[37] is a play about the Civil War in the Far East, the struggle of the partisans against the White Guard and interventionists. With splendid theatrical know-how, a good character actor himself, Yu. Svirin invented an entertaining, adventure-filled plot with involved narrative gambits, disguises, effective climaxes, and comic reversals. The character of Terenty Ivanovich, leader of the regional partisan movement, was intriguing in himself. Neither the other characters nor the spectators knew him by sight until almost the end of the show. They didn't know where he was or where he was leading them. They all became acquainted with him at the same time. Then it turned out that Terenty Ivanovich had been onstage all along, successfully hidden in the White high command behind the mask of Officer Esaulov. [...]

The production had to be prepared very quickly—for the celebration of the twentieth anniversary of October. So far as I know, this was the first time Akimov staged

---

35 Evgeny L'vovich Shvarts (1896–1958), associated with the Oberiu group, began to write children's literature with a blend of realism and fantasy. His satirical fairy-tale plays had a rocky time getting produced, owing to their satiric edge. *The Princess and the Swineherd* was eventually produced in 1960 by the Sovremennik as *The Naked King*.

36 In *Professor Mamlock* (1933) by Friedrich Wolf a distinguished Jewish surgeon in Germany is so devoted to reason and humanity that he is blinded to Nazi anti-Semitism until it is too late. The play, written by Wolf in exile, was first produced in Yiddish in Warsaw (1934) and was filmed in the Soviet Union in 1938.

37 *Terenty Ivanovich* (1937) features a Bolshevik insurgent who disguises himself as a White officer.

a Soviet play. Therefore the most powerful aspects of his directorial talent—irony, sarcasm, elegant form—seemed irrelevant to the given play. If it hadn't been a jubilee piece, he probably would have relegated it to someone else.

Akimov read the company a detailed exposition of the future show. Understanding that in this play there was no reason to look for special psychological grounds for the characters' actions, he suggested looking at the actual events of the play through the haze of joyful memories of those heroic and victorious days. [. . .] "We're dealing with a kind of fairy tale," said Akimov, "a people's legend of how it was. After all, that Terenty Ivanovich is leading the partisans directly from the White high command is already something of a legend. What matters in the production is the popular element of the characters, like popular heroes of fairy tales. Courage, gumption, humor, derring-do, and sometimes recklessness [. . .]—that's how we can justify all the actions of the play's heroes. This is the key to the comic bent of the production."

> Yu. Yuzovsky, *Richard III* at the Leningrad Bol'shoy Dramatic Theater, 1935, in "Leningrad letter," *Sovetskoe iskusstvo,* 1936, reprinted in *O teatre i drame* (Moscow: Iskusstvo, 1982), 1:112–14. Yu. (actually Iosif Il'ich) Yuzovsky (1903–64), theater and literary critic whose career began in the 1930s, paid close attention to Gorky and Soviet drama; latterly, he was accused of "cosmopolitanism," and his works went unpublished and unreprinted.

At *Richard* something happened that I had not foreseen: that the spectator should be "buttonholed" before he barely had time to sit down, even before he had heard Richard's soliloquy, even before Richard himself appeared—but as soon as the curtain went up! I don't know whether on opening night there was applause at that point; I don't think there could have been, the attention was too powerfully fixed even for applause, the reaction would have been expressed more profoundly: by an awe-stricken silence. I don't recall whether I have ever experienced such a sudden and nakedly spontaneous collision with the awesome name of Shakespeare. The excitement was caused by a designer. His name is Tyshler.[38][. . .]

Onstage were three enormous turrets whose brickwork is given by Tyshler the character of ponderous, looming uniformity, while the crimson color of the walls casts its reflection on the very air, the sun, the sky. The walls pull apart, revealing galleries, passages, dungeons, throne rooms. The drawbridge falls, the walls come together— and again the even more inaccessible, fortified, lowering turrets, as if ready to take part by leaping into the bloody feud of Red and White roses . . . The scenery became a continuation of the Shakespearian soliloquies or even their origin. Anyway, that's what it looks like in Tyshler. [. . .]

---

38 Aleksandr Grigor'evich Tyshler (1898–1980), designer influenced by cubo-futurism and constructivism, he did his best work for Shakespeare, especially *King Lear* (GOSET, 1935), *Richard III* (BDT, 1935), and *Twelfth Night* (1951). His vision encompassed the whole production: scenery, costumes, makeup, props, coloration, and structure.

The Moscow music hall. Golubovsky, *Bol'shie malen'kie teatry*, 284–86, 288–96.

It is impossible to imagine Moscow in the 1930s without it. Even its failures stirred up interest... For the theater they rebuilt a venue on Triumphal Square of the former circus of the brothers Nikitin, which had become the second State Circus. One group of critics spoke of the attractions of the music hall as bad images of the decadent art of the West, another stigmatized it for the vulgar sociologization of the variety stage and, mainly, rebuked it for being boring. Such a rebuke was irresistible. At the music hall first-class directors staged a satirical vaudeville genre: D. Gutman, creator of the Satire Theater, N. Gorchakov of the MAT—his production of *Squaring the Circle*[39] on the little stage of the MAT was the pinnacle of comic performance in the early 1930s; the ubiquitous A. Arnol'd,[40] a genius of the circus, variety stage, racing, and billiards. [...] The ballet master–innovator Kas'yan Goleyzovsky[41]—kicked out of the Bol'shoy Theater and creator of the classic variety act "Thirty Chorus-Girls"—adorned the performances with his inventions. For designers they invited the best practitioners— N. Akimov, the brothers Stenberg. As the saying goes, "the management has spared no expense"... Nevertheless the music hall was boring. [...]

One of the last programs of the music hall before this period was far from boring. Vladimir Khenkin[42] graced it with Homeric laughter. He would strenuously run out of the proscenium and greet the spectators in the hall, often making them up on the spot, inventing surprising names, and admonishing, "Just don't laugh ahead of time, or else I'll find it funny myself!" Then, coquettishly and proudly, he would shake his long-absent locks: "I am an ex-brunet." "In kindergarten I was the tallest boy!" He would look at the spotlight, squint: "The spotlight is an anti-Semite, it knocks your eye out..." "I'm fifty-four years old, but no one would think I'm more than fifty-three!" [...]

[Leonid Utësov[43]] considered "The Music Shop" the best work in this genre for all his creative life. I believe him unconditionally.

The play's plot is barebones. Various customers come to a music shop: a foreign conductor, a peasant with his horse ("played" by two jazz tap dancers, mistiming their steps). The horse fell down, and when it got up, it looked as if it had got twisted around. Then came the comic process of untwisting it back again. The action was led by the

---

39 *Kvadratura kruga* (1927–28) by Valentin Kataev, a comedy about the housing shortage in Moscow, enjoyed an international success.

40 Arnol'd Grigor'evich Arnol'd (actually Barsky, 1897–1969), circus and variety artiste; he started as a dance act, then, after work with the magician Kio, became a popular conjurer.

41 Kas'yan Yaroslavovich Goleyzovsky (1892–1970), dancer, choreographer, with his own studio, the Chamber Ballet 1919–25; he reformed dance costume to make it more erotic. He staged the ballet *Pierrot and Columbine* and the spectacular hippodrama *Makhno's Mutiny* (*Makhnovshchina*, 1929) at the Moscow Circus.

42 Vladimir Yakovlevich Khenkin (1883–1953), music hall performer who also worked at the Moscow Operetta 1928–34 and from 1934 at the Moscow Satire Theater; popular for his recitations of Zoshchenko's writing.

43 Leonid Osipovich Utësov (actually Vaysbeyn, 1895–1982), song writer and band leader, the most popular musician in the Soviet Union; with his comic jazz band he was a combination of Paul Whiteman and Spike Jones.

salesman Kostya—Leonid Osipovich himself, in addition to playing other roles. This is when he drew on his theatrical past! Each of the characters made a satiric point and was connected with a musical number. In this way, jazz was almost transformed into real theater. The jazzmen-actors played lightly, not trying especially to transform themselves, but made merry to the top of their bent. Such a jazzman as the first-class percussionist Nikolay Samoshnikov—and in jazz a percussionist is the leading man!—turned out to be a splendid eccentric actor. [...]

An American conductor (played by Utësov) made a jazz arrangement of the Russian classic "Do Not Count Diamonds in Caves of Stone," turning it into a lovely foxtrot. A peasant (Utësov again) came in to exchange dung at Torgsin[44] because an agronomist had told him that manure is gold. Kostya mocked the composers in the Russian Association of Proletarian Musicians, their narrow-mindedness and inhibitions, by performing "A Meeting at the Engine-shed"—so-called assembly-line music: it turned out to be factory hooters, noises, shouting, the screech of metal—total bedlam! Kostya wept: "I feel sorry for the elephant, imagine a tropical forest, through it walks a young, civilized elephant. Suddenly bing-bang! shots ring out. The elephant falls. People run in, cut off the elephant's tusks, make keyboards out of them, and then play this kind of rubbish on them." Samoshnikov played a suicidal composer. They saved him, pulled him out of the water, and he played the rescuers his piece on a clarinet—unimaginable sounds, reminiscent of yowling cats. The musicians, headed by Kostya, silently take him by the arms, carry him to the bridge and just as silently throw him back in the water. Samoshnikov would stare inimitably, absurdly, incomprehensively, first at one, then another of the musicians carrying him.

[Nikolay Osipovich Volkonsky,[45] enfant terrible of the Maly Theater, took over the music hall and published a manifesto "Fairground Booth, Pamphlet, Melodrama" (*Soviet Iskusstvo* 30 [January 1933]): the féerie, tragicomedy, revue, and fairground booth must be blended.]

He took the American melodrama by George Watters and Arthur Hopkins, *Burlesque,* which had been staged in Germany and Vienna by Max Reinhardt[46]—the biggest "box-office" director in the West. It had everything needed for a commercial success: love, jealousy, explosive passions—an alternation between the too attractive world behind the scenes and the no less seductive scenes from the "everyday life of millionaires." Variety, circus, dance, hit songs... Volkonsky seriously reworked the play, imbuing it with a big dose of socialism that even at that time seemed excessively schematic. The capitalist world, debauching poor performers, was unmasked to a

44 *Torgovlya s inostranami* (foreign trade), state hard-currency stores for the exchange of gold and jewelry 1931–36.

45 Nikolay Osipovich Volkonsky (actually Murav'ëv, 1890–1948). In 1927–30 one of the organizers and leaders of the Profklub Workshop. In the Maly productions of *A Profitable Job* and *The Minor* he attracted attention by his revision of the classics.

46 *Burlesque* (1927), an American backstage melodrama by Arthur Hopkins and George Marker Watters; the original has a happy ending. Max Reinhardt (actually Goldmann, 1873–1943), from 1902 to 1933 the leading director in the German-speaking world, with a vast repertory and theaters in Germany and Austria; emigrated to the United States 1934.

fare-thee-well. However, this was not what excited the spectators. Pure melodrama—the pork packer–millionaire Harvey steals the singer Bonny from her husband, the famous eccentric clown Skid, while hired killers kill Skid himself—gripped hearts sick and tired of problems of industrialization, epics of the ax, tempi, armored trains, etc. [...]

The role of Skid suited Martinson to a T; he moved superbly, danced variety dance exquisitely, and, most important, was an actor of rare gifts, who could walk the tightrope between eccentricity and psychology. [...] Skid comes onstage and his body moves as if on hinges; he dazzles with a slapstick of physical tricks, abruptness, conveyed with refinement. The ditty about jealousy, a broken heart, and bitter loneliness rang with such human distress that it moved even unsentimental students. [...] Then Skid comes with the clown Bozo to his ex-wife. An improvisation develops: Skid sings a ditty full of pain that turns into the unforgettable tango "Jealousy." For this tango alone we, rightly or wrongly, entered the auditorium of the music hall a great many times.

[As the clown Bozo, Boris Tenin] came up with an interpolated number—in the character of a war veteran he sang a Brecht[47] song:

> I want you, ladies and sirs,
> To burst out laughing,
> The way you laughed when you
> Unleashed the laughing gas at us!

Brecht's lines resounded with enormous power, like a gunshot aimed straight at the audience. The role of Bozo became a watershed in Tenin's life; he immediately moved up a rung as an actor.

The Arts Under Attack

Shostakovich's four-act opera of adultery and murder among the nineteenth-century merchant class, *Lady Macbeth of the Mtsensk District* (*Ledi Makbet Mtsenskogo Uezda*), opened on January 24, 1934, at the Leningrad Maly Opera Theater and ran for eighty-three performances. This success was duplicated at the Nemirovich-Danchenko Opera Theater in Moscow (a production Shostakovich preferred), where it ran for ninety-four performances.

> E. Braudo, "Opera and ballet in the Soviet Union," *VOKS Socialist Construction in the USSR* 6 (1934), 34–35.

A great advance as compared with *The Nose*[48] is Shostakovich's[49] latest opera *Lady Macbeth of the Mtsensk District,* after the story of the same name by Leskov, in which

47 Bertolt Brecht (1898–1956), German poet and playwright of Communist sympathies, who, at this period, was best known for his sardonic musical *Der Dreigroschenoper* (1928) and his didactic plays; with the Nazi advent to power he moved to Finland and the United States.
48 *Nos,* Dmitry Shostakovich's ingenious setting of Gogol's fantastic short story, opened at the Maly Opera Theater in Leningrad January 18, 1930, and was condemned as "formalist."
49 Dmitry Dmitrievich Shostakovich (1906–75), composer, had begun his career under the auspices

6.3. "Seeing Off the Husband" in *Lady Macbeth of the Mtsensk District* by Dmitry Shostakovich, directed by Vladimir Nemirovich-Danchenko, Nemirovich-Danchenko Musical Theater, Moscow, 1935. A. Tulub'eva as Katya is on the floor; S. Ostroumov as Sergey is far left.

the composer for the first time carries out the principles of socialistic realism, i.e., presents the living characters in the atmosphere of the life of a whole epoch profoundly analyzed. It is at the moment the most talked of opera in our musical world and is produced by three theaters in Moscow and Leningrad simultaneously. [...]

The music of *Lady Macbeth* was known even before the production from a number of preliminary concert performances. There have been found in it the new features of broad melodiousness and emotionality on the basis of realistic portrayal. [...] The melodic prinicple, which Shostakovich used to relegate to the background, now flows in a broad stream. The central female role is one of the strongest in all opera. A considerable place is taken by choruses, vital and expressive, in no way reminiscent of the sumptuously decorative choruses of the traditional opera. The orchestra of *Lady Macbeth* is full and multifarious; and in emotional passages it rises to huge climaxes.

Bullard and Bullard, eds., *Inside Stalin's Russia*, 243.

March 11, 1934. Pott and I got much pleasure out of the new opera *Lady Macbeth of the Mtsensk District.* The music is completely unconventional. I was in the front row and could see the orchestra scores. They had no key signatures and obviously there was no fixed key in any part of the music. I suppose that theoretically the piece was full of what we call disharmonies, but we did not find that either ugly or out of place. It must be a difficult piece to play and still more to sing—the intervals being so unusual. The performance was broadcast the night we were there, and the composer was present. After the first act Shostakovich came forward from the audience and bowed. He looked like a studious English undergraduate of about twenty-one.

---

of Trotsky and worked for TRAM but was regularly attacked for his political apathy; his response to the attacks on *Lady Macbeth* was his musically conservative Fifth Symphony (1937) and the heroic Seventh Symphony (1941); but he was again attacked for formalism in 1948.

> [?[50]], "Muddle, not music: About the opera *Lady Macbeth of Mtsensk District*,"
> *Pravda* (January 28, 1936), 1–2.

The listener can, from the very first moment in the opera, sense a deliberately *dissonant muddled stream of sounds.* Snatches of melody, fragments of musical phrases submerge, reemerge, and then vanish once more amid the grinding and screeching racket. It is hard to follow such "music" and to remember it, impossible.

So it goes throughout the whole opera. Onstage the singing is *completely replaced by shrieking.* If the composer chances to tread the path of a simple, comprehensible melody, then, as if scared by this misfortune, he hastily throws himself back into the *musical muddle,* which, in places, turns into *cacophony.* The expressiveness the listener demands has been replaced by a *demonic rhythm.* The musical *noise* is supposed to be expressing passion.

All this is not because the composer is untalented or incapable of expressing simple and powerful feelings in music. This music has deliberately been composed *"back to front"* so that nothing may remind us of classical opera music, nothing may be in common with symphonic resonance, with simple commonly accessible musical speech. This is music that has been composed on the very same principle *of rejecting opera, on which basis leftist art in general rejects simplicity in theater along with realism, the concept of character, and the natural sound of words.* This is transferring the extremely negative features of "Meyerholdianism" in a magnified form into opera and music. This is a *leftist muddle* instead of natural human music. Good music, which has the ability to enchant the masses, is being *sacrificed by the petty bourgeois formalist attempts and pretensions to create originality by using devices of cheap originality.* This is toying with *intellectual matters,* which can come to a very bad end.

For Soviet music the danger in taking such a direction is clear. *Leftist deformation of opera has derived from the very same source as that in art, poetry, pedagogy, and science. Petty bourgeois "innovation" has led to a break with original art, original science, and original literature.*

The author of *Lady Macbeth of Mtsensk District* had to borrow *from jazz its nervous, convulsive, hysterical music so as to endow his protagonists with "passion."*

At a time when our critics, including even the music critics, are hailing socialist realism, the stage is presenting us with the *crudest naturalism* in Shostakovich's composition. Monotonously, both the merchants and the people are shown as beastly caricatures. The predatory merchant's wife, grabbing wealth and power through murder, is portrayed as some sort of "victim" of bourgeois society. Leskov's realistic story has a meaning imposed on it that is not in it.

And all this is *crude, primitive, and vulgar.* The music shrieks, hoots, pants, and sighs to depict love scenes as naturalistically as possible. And "love" is smeared throughout the opera in the most vulgar way. The merchant's double bed occupies center stage.

50 For a long time the authorship of this earth-shaking article was attributed to Stalin himself. In the Thaw period, David Zaslavsky, a staff journalist on *Pravda* 1928–65, confessed at one time to polishing a finished piece presented to him, at another time to writing the review. Another possible candidate is Platon Kerzhentsev.

All the "issues" are resolved on it. In the same crudely naturalistic style, deaths by poisoning and stabbing are shown, almost on the stage itself.

The composer has apparently not set himself the tasks or paid heed to what the Soviet audience expects and looks for in music. He has, as if on purpose, *encoded this music, confused all the notes in it in such a way that his music may reach only the aesthetic formalists who have lost their wholesome taste.* He has ignored the demand of Soviet culture to drive out coarseness and savagery from all corners of Soviet life. Some critics call this glorification of a merchant's lust a satire. There can be no talk of satire here. By every means of musical and dramatic expression, the author is trying to engage the public's sympathy for crude and vulgar aspirations and actions of the merchant woman Katerina Izmaylova.

Lady Macbeth is winning kudos from the bourgeois public abroad. Isn't the bourgeois public praising it because the opera is *a muddle and absolutely apolitical?* Isn't it because it *tickles the perverted tastes of the bourgeois audience by its fidgety, shrill, and neurotic music?*

Our theaters have expended no small effort on a careful staging of Shostakovich's opera. The actors displayed remarkable talent in overcoming the noise, shrieking, and grinding of the orchestra. By means of dramatic acting they have tried to compensate for the melodic mediocrity of the opera. Unfortunately, this has made its crudely naturalistic features all the more evident. The talented acting deserves acknowledgment, but the wasted efforts—pity.

ARTISTS AND WRITERS were outraged and confused by the article and wondered on which of them the axe would next fall. The secret police reported Meyerhold as saying, "What would Mayakovsky have done if they'd told him: write this way, well, like Turgenev. [. . .] I'm working on a production of *The Bedbug* and several times during work I've caught myself thinking—no this would be Meyerholdism, it needs to be different."[51] The arts community barely had time to absorb this shock, when a second accusatory article appeared.

"Against formalism and 'leftist deformity' in art," *Komsomolskaya Pravda* [Young Communist League truth] (February 14, 1936).

Art plays an immense role in educating the new socialist. That is precisely why issues of art and its creative development are so close and so important to the Lenin Komsomol. A Komsomol member cannot ignore Soviet art, he must be aware of its tasks and must promote its flourishing.

[. . .] The authors of this ballet [*The Limpid Stream*][52] aimed at depicting life and

---

51 Report from the Secret Political Department on responses from artists and writer, no later than February 11, 1936. Quoted in Clark and Dobrenko, *Soviet Culture and Power*, 235.
52 Shostakovich wrote the music to *Svetly Ruchey*, with a libretto by F. V. Lopukhov and A. I. Piotrovsky; it opened at the Leningrad Maly Ballet Theater on April 4, 1935.

festivals on the collective farms. But they did not bother to study either ballet or collective farming. They applied an old balletic cliché to a new subject, and what showed up onstage was a kitschy, saccharine puppet show. Balletic phoniness and mindlessness prevail onstage and in the orchestra. But perhaps *Limpid Stream* shows most clearly why Shostakovich writes such formalistic music, why he turns out twiddly bits, stunts, and capers, confusing these with real art. He neither knows and esteems the people's creativity nor does he love and respect the musical speech of the people. [...] Only that kind of art which in its supreme artistic form accurately reflects reality, only that kind of art is favored by the masses. *"It must move from its deepest roots into the very heart of the broad laboring masses"* (Lenin).

[...] There are people in this country who are dreadfully confused that Shostakovich's opera simultaneously displays both naturalism and formalism. They say that formalism and naturalism are mutually exclusive. But actually both naturalism and formalism are blood-brothers and often accompany one another.

[...] Never before have prospects for Soviet art been as clear and bright as in these days. Discussions of the people's leader Comrade Stalin and the prime minister Comrade Molotov[53] with the composer Dzerzhinsky[54] and the conductor Samosud,[55] the criticism by the central organ of the Party of Shostakovich's opera and ballet pose great and difficult tasks for Soviet art. Socialist realism in art can be born only out of fertile, rich juices and powers of the soil of the people's creativity. A combination of the great classic masterpieces of the past with the simple, infinitely rich, powerful, and clear language of national artistic creativity, only such a combination can breed lofty socialist realist art. To learn from Shakespeare and Beethoven, Pushkin and Glinka, Ostrovsky and Musorgsky, to scoop up from the inexhaustible source of creativity of all the peoples of our motherland—that is now the task of the art worker, from the young apprentice to the grizzled master.

"Against formalism and 'leftist deformity' in art," *Komsomolskaya Pravda* (February 14, 1936). Reprinted in *Protiv formalizma i naturalizma v iskusstva. Sbornik statey* ([n.p.]: OGIZ-IZOGIZ, 1937), 15–19.

For us, the petty bourgeois "Westernized" roots of formalism are clear in all their forms and mutations. The poisonous rot of formalist mold is creeping perniciously into our country with stealthy steps. [...] And in art the dead take hold of the living, all the more so when

53 Vyacheslav Mikhaylovich Molotov (actually Skryabin, 1890–1986), a close ally of Stalin, operative in organizing the mass purges of the 1930s; premier of the USSR 1930–41, foreign minister 1939–49, 1953–57. Dismissed in 1956 by Khrushchëv and expelled from the Party in 1962.

54 Ivan Ivanovich Dzerzhinsky (1909–78), a composer of more traditional music, had composed *The Quiet Don* (*Tikhy Don*), an opera based on Sholokhov's epic novel of heroic Cossacks; Stalin had seen it six days before he attended *Lady Mtsensk* and found the comparison deleterious to Shostakovich.

55 Samuil Abramovich Samosud (1884–1964), conductor at the Leningrad Maly Opera Theater 1918–36 and the Bol'shoy from 1936, conducted the premieres of *The Nose, Lady Macbeth of Mtsensk,* and Prokof'ev's *War and Peace,* among others.

we are struggling against the class-enemy tendencies that arise in art and ooze toward
us from the bourgeois formalists of the capitalist West and at other times camouflaged
by all sorts of laudatory verbiage. [...] (emphasis original)

> Aleksey Gzovdev, "On the cult of the director," *Rabochy i Teatr* 9 (May 1936),
> 10–11. Aleksey Aleksandrovich Gvozdev (1887–1939) was one of the founders
> of Soviet theater studies, especially of Western Europe, where he had studied
> 1925 and 1928; he was much influenced by the methodology of German *The-*
> *aterwissenschaft*. He was the first chronicler of the Meyerhold Theater 1927.
> In 1932 his school was accused of being "bourgeois formalist," and studying
> dramatic form was forbidden.

A sharp deficit in directorial culture can be observed in the production of *Taming of*
the Shrew at the Comedy Theater. Evidently the theater considered that presenting
Shakespeare's comedy in its original forms might be "boring" to that theater's spectators. Therefore they introduced into the production supplementary comic "figures,"
who were furnished with a whole assortment of ordinary obtuse "little jokes," scattered
throughout the play and the spectators over the course of the whole performance. These
"little jokes" were offered to Sly, seated in the auditorium, whereby this episodic role
in Shakespeare's play (Sly) grew into the pivotal character in the performance. At the
base of this "concept" lay a profound distrust of the classics, incomprehension, and a
dislike for "thinking along with the poet."

Another typical characteristic of a number of our directors is to strive to demonstrate their creative initiative by exposing (sometimes very acutely and freshly) a
number of *peripheral* and *collatoral themes* that exist in the play. In such cases the talk
is of the "displacement of themes" as the principle of the director's approach to the
play. One theme or another, found in the play, begins to be developed at the expense
of the main and central ideas of the play. [...] This kind of collision has, for rather
a long time, "afflicted" the LOSPS Theater. [...] For instance, the secondary role of
Fëklusha (in Ostrovsky's *Thunderstorm*) appeared onstage in the newly discovered
and original profile of a frenzied hysteric. But the expansion of this role to the limits
of independent action inevitably led to the ruin of the perspective and proportion
established by the playwright. [...]

> Investigation no. 12690 of the Ermolova Theater actors Georgy Yul'evich
> Baumshteyn (Bakhtarov) and Evgeny Anatol'evich Bonfel'd (Kravinsky) for
> anti-Soviet activity, 1936. Boris Sopel'nyak, "Teatr kontsa tridtsatykh," *Mos-*
> *kovskie novosti* 12, 24 (March 31, 1996), 35.

G. Yu. Baumshteyn is sufficiently convicted of exhibiting anti-Soviet attitudes, for he
systematically carries on among his circle of acquaintances malicious, counterrevolutionary, and Trotskyite agitation, directed against the measures of the parties and
the government, and spreads provocative rumors. As a measure of suppression, the
subject is to be taken into custody.

[Of Bonfel'd, besides counterrevolutionary activity] Among his coworkers he has expressed clearly terrorist sympathies in relation to the leaders and heads of the Party and government.

[At his first interrogation Baumshteyn admitted that he had said that Hitler and Mussolini were powerful leaders and forceful personalities.]

"With whom did you talk about this?"

"I remember talking about it, but I've forgotten with whom exactly."

"The investigation states the facts that you talked about it with actors of your theater Nikolay Losev and Vera Leonenko. Do you confirm this?"

"Yes."

"What kind of counterrevolutionary discussions did you have with Bonfel'd and Grudnev?"

"None. Although I remember that I once in their presence called Trotsky our most popular personality. Next to Lenin, of course."

"Maybe you remember that you praised Kamenev and Zinov'ev, asserting that they had no part in the murder of Kirov?"

"No, I never said anything about Kamenev or Zinov'ev."

"You did, you did . . . We know all about it. And what did you remark in relation to the liberation and arrival in the USSR of the Bulgarian Communists Dimitrov, Popov, and Tanev?"[56]

"I remarked . . . I said that Germany had slipped up in this. Here with us for such a deed as burning the Reichstag they wouldn't have been let go, but would have been shot long ago."

[The two actors were sentenced to what at the time was a light sentence: three years' exile to a region of Kazakhstan (in 1939 Baumshteyn began teaching at the Brest Children's Music School). The colleagues they had named in their testimony and others were interrogated in turn throughout 1937 and 1938 and sentenced to eight or ten years in the camps. The Ermolova Theater had to be closed: the leading actors were in camps, the best productions were removed from the repertory, and the public avoided this "anti-Soviet" hangout.]

> Yury Lyubimov, *Rasskazy starogo trepach* [Tales of an old chatterbox] (Moscow: Novosit, 2001), 138–39. Yury Petrovich Lyubimov (1917–) studied at the MAT Second Studio and the Vakhtangov Theater School before being enlisted in the song-and-dance unit of the NKVD. He was one of the leading romantic actors at the Vakhtangov Theater 1946–64 before metamorphosing into an innovative and controversial director.

Then I acted with great success in an episode of *Man with a Gun*.

This was a sort of tinsel, Christmas-tree, New-Year's-greeting-card story with a

56 The Bulgarian Communist leaders George Dimitrov Mihaylov, Blagoi Popov, and Vasili Tanev were on trial in Germany in 1933 for setting the Reichstag fire; they were traded to the Soviet Union for several German aviators who had been secretly training in the USSR.

happy ending: a soldier from the front meets Lenin. It all followed the standard formula: there was the soldier from the front, a peasant, there was a proper worker who was for some reason escorting this soldier. There was Smolny, as the headquarters of the Revolution, and Lenin. Later an order was given to put Stalin in it. Still later at the MAT they staged a similar play, and it had begun as a movie... There is a genealogy of Leninoids and Stalinoids. A saga for the Soviet people.

There was a whole series of plays, tableaux from life—Lenin–Stalin. And whole discussions went on: how to stage Lenin and Stalin. And should they put Lenin just a bit higher... If there were two steps: who should stand higher. Later a whole commission had to approve a production, and already they were trying to decide:

"No, let's put them on an even keel. You mustn't put Lenin higher. After all Stalin is the Lenin of today, let them be side by side."

Later Stalin came to some show and made the remark:

"Why is Vladimir Il'ich always running around me like that? It should be done more calmly somehow. We often sat together, conversed in a friendly fashion, settled problems, and here he is always bustling about. He ran things, at that time I only helped."

Nikolay Pogodin, "From a playwright's workshop," *International Literature* 7 (July 1938), 67–69.

How did I approach the development of Lenin as a character? I fully realized that in this task lay my chief test. I decided that the figure of Lenin, without a convincing representation of the masses among which and for whom he lived and struggled, would be incomplete. [...]

The scene of Lenin's first appearance [in *Man with a Gun*] opens with the words: "Missing your tea, eh?" Shchukin, in the role of Lenin, enters. The entire audience rises and applauds his superb interpretation of this difficult role. Shchukin's attainments in the part of Lenin mark him indisputably as one of the most ingenious artists in the modern theater. When he first approaches us from the depths of the corridor, his head slightly inclined to one side, we at once feel the conviction this characterization of Lenin carries. After the first storm of applause, Shchukin says, "Missing your tea, eh?" with such simplicity that there is nothing left for us to wish in the way of improved interpretation. [...]

As to the style of speech employed for Lenin in my play, I was governed by the opinion that to lend myself to lifting literal quotations from his works onto the stage would be a gross error. I decided that a scrupulous imitation of Lenin in text might bring results diametrically opposed to those desired; might lead to a caricature effect. Therefore I took his general vocabulary and the idiosyncrasies of his speech and allowed my imagination to picture just how Lenin might express himself under given circumstances. In conversation with Shadrin about the German soldier, Lenin has the phrase: "Will he make peace with us? Eh?" Among Lenin's letters I frequently encountered this very typical expression: "Eh? What do you think?" [...]

Playing Lenin and Stalin in Pogodin's *Man with a Gun,* Vakhtangov Theater, 1937. Yury Elagin,[57] *Ukroshchenie Iskusstv* [Taming the arts] (New York: Izd. imeni Chekhova, 1952), 137–38.

Shchukin's position was a difficult one; he had to play Lenin in Stalin's presence. The position of Ruben Simonov, however, was even more difficult; Simonov had to play Stalin in Stalin's presence! Where has there ever been anything like it in the history of the theater? ... Simonov's nerves could not take it, and they gave way. Some three days before the performance, he became unable to take food. His extraordinary state of nerves did not permit him to swallow, and his stomach refused to work. His face became drawn, he grew thin, and his complexion turned sallow.

The worst moment came when Simonov, as Stalin, came onstage that fateful evening, looked at the government box directly before him, and caught sight of the real, flesh-and-blood Stalin. Even Simonov's vocal cords stopped working. He was so terrified that he lost his voice. Simonov uttered his send-off speech to the Red Guardsmen who were going off to battle in an inaudible whisper. He moved his lips ridiculously and gesticulated with his right hand like a broken toy.

The Two Moscow Art Theaters

A suggestion was made that the Second Moscow Art Theater be moved to Kiev. In the face of refusal, Kerzhentsev confirmed the theater's liquidation on February 28, 1936, in a document that stated that it in no way lived up to its name and was a mediocre theater undeserving of preservation.

> E. G. Dulova to V. D. Buturlin, March 2, 1936. In MS. RGALI, *MKhAT 2. Opyt vostanovleniya biografii* [MAT 2: Experiment in establishing a biography] (Moscow: Moskovsky Khudozestvenny Teatr, 2010), 833. Vladimir Dmitrievich Buturlin was a member of the MAT 2 1927–36; he was appointed head of a special bureau to deal with that theater in 1934.

You know about the situation of the so-called MAT 2. It's all the fault of Bersenev; when they offered him Kiev, he declared that they are the Moscow Art Theater, that it is an *academic* theater and they cannot be anywhere but Moscow, and if a transfer is insisted on, they will protest in the press. And the question of Kiev was not put to the general meeting nor to the board of directors. Bersenev took it all on himself, obviously adopting the principle of Louis XIV "I am the State." [...]

I think that now you are sorry that you didn't leave the theater in time.

Total consternation in the theater.

The building already belongs to the "children's theater," they are rehearsing and Bersenev is evicted from his own Olympus, everything is huddled together in the

---

57 Yury Borisovich Elagin (Jurij Jelagin, 1910–87), violinist at the Vakhtangov Theater; his memoir *Taming the Arts* (*Ukroshchenie iskusstv,* 1951), written and published in emigration, spread a number of legends about theater and music under Stalin.

Mestkom building. On [February 29] I was at the funeral of the MAT 2. Despite the sold-out house and the aisles and circles crammed to overflowing, a crowd stood before the theater, hoping by any means possible to get inside the house. Every appearance of Bersenev and Giatsintova was accompanied by an outburst of applause, and by the end of the performance[58] ovations had been organized such as the theater hadn't remembered since the time of Mikhail Aleksandrovich [Chekhov].

MATTERS at the Moscow Art Theatre 1 had also come to a crisis.

> Nemirovich-Danchenko to S. L. Bertenson, July 22, 1935, Karlsbad. In V. I. Nemirovich-Danchenko, *Tvorcheskoe nasledie*, ed. I. N. Solov'ëva (Moscow: Moskovsky Khudozhestvenny Teatr, 2003), 3:451.

But the internal life of the Art Theater is just as bad as ever it was. There is no real administrator, although there are two of them. The relationship between us, i.e., me and Stanislavsky, has never been so prickly. All because he has surrounded himself with people who, to my way of thinking, are unfriendly. Suffice it to say that all year long we have met only once. True, he will never go out anywhere, but I as a healthy man will go wherever I have to. Such relations may have existed for a long time now, but before I tried all the same to "overcome" the barrier, to mitigate his artistic absurdities. But now it has worn me out. Besides, I don't have the strength to fight with the nonsense and in this struggle lose my own good things. But the main thing is that art itself has only suffered from this. That is, from my concessions and my silences. [...] People think that the kernel of the hostile relations is only the result of Konst. Sergeevich's ambition or something personal on my part, in short, that two bears don't get on in one den. In fact that isn't it. The main thing is different understandings of art itself. I have long made no secret of the fact that when I'm at work, I fight against the teachings of Zinaida Sergeevna[59] and the apologists for Konstantin Sergeevich's "system." The greatest eyewash is going on. I cannot act against it, but when I'm at work, I show concretely what it leads to . . . That's the meaning of *Enemies, La Traviata, Katerina Izmaylova.*[60] It's only just beginning to be understood. [...]

MIKHAIL BULGAKOV'S TENURE at the MAT was less productive than he had hoped; he found himself relegated to the task of dramatizing great works of literature, even, he joked, the Brockhaus–Ephron encyclopedia. Although he was allowed to play the Judge in an adaptation of *The Pickwick Papers,* most of his efforts at

---

58 *A Plea for Life* (*Mol'ba o zhizni*) by Jacques Deval, a legendary production that gave Bersenev and Giatsintova the opportunity to play lovers over the course of a lifetime.

59 Stanislavsky's sister Zinaida Sergeevna Sokolova (1865–1950) worked with students of his Opera Studio on "the system" and, in the opinion of many, vulgarized it.

60 Nemirovich's most recent production had been Gorky's play of capital–labor relations *Enemies,* and at his opera studio *La Traviata* and Shostakovich's *Lady Macbeth of the Mtsensk District,* also known as *Katerina Izmaylova,* from its heroine.

creativity were thwarted by Stanislavsky and the prevailing taste for socialist realism. Tasked with dramatizing Gogol's *Dead Souls,* he came up with an interesting treatment, employing the author as narrator. After a year, Stanislavsky attended a rehearsal, tossed out all the preliminary work, and, eager to confute Meyerhold, turned Gogol's epic into a series of tableaux, vehicles for veteran character actors to show their stuff.

Harold Clurman, "Moscow diary," in *The Collected Works of Harold Clurman: Six Decades of Commentary on Theater, Dance, Music, Film, Arts, and Letters,* ed. Marjorie Loggia and Glenn Young (New York: Applause Books, 1994), 9.

May 6, 1935. At night we saw the Moscow Art production of Gogol's *Dead Souls,*[61] one of its more recent productions. There were excellent scenes in this and two or three superb characterizations in small parts. Nearly all of it had the usual Moscow Art maturity of acting, which is very satisfying—almost like a lesson. Yet I did not feel that it was important: I shall not think of it as much as I have about some of Meyerhold's poor productions. One sees these Moscow Art productions as one picks up a well-bound classic sometimes: one reads a little, one says "this is first-class stuff" and stifles a yawn. There was no *drive* in this production, no creative fire. One did not feel as if all the actors were saying or the director had thought, "With this production I want to achieve something and say something that it is impossible to say in just this production alone, that it may take all our lives to say and to achieve." One does not sense some other world outside the frame of the production to which the actors belong and which they are making every effort to express.

One organizational element that interested me in the production of *Dead Souls,* however, was the fact that a good many important actors were playing bits in the large cast.

BULGAKOV'S PLAY about Molière, *The Cabal of Bigots* (*Kabala svyatosh*) had been passed by Glavrepertkom in 1931, and rehearsals began in 1932. They were still going on in 1935, and the playwright was continually locking horns with the director, the elderly and unsympathetic Stanislavsky. Bulgakov's play is about the compromised position of an artist in an autocratic society; Stanislavsky wanted to turn it into a romantic melodrama about a misunderstood genius.

From the diary of Elena Bulgakova, in M. A. Bulgakov, *Zapiski pokoynika* [Notes of the dear departed] (St. Petersburg: Akademichesky Proékt, 2002), 386–91. Elena Sergeevna Bulgakova (1893–1970), third wife of Mikhail Bul-

---

61 *Mërtvye dushi,* a dramatization of Gogol's comic epic, was begun by Mikhail Bulgakov and directed by Boris Sushkevich; Stanislavsky objected to its "Meyerholdian" aspects, insisted on a more straightforward adaptation, and took over the direction. It opened at the MAT 1932.

gakov (1932), the alleged model for Margarita in *The Master and Margarita*, was the preserver and promoter of his literary heritage.

March 5, 1935. Misha's had a tough rehearsal . . . He came home broken and frantic. Stanislavsky, instead of sorting out the actors' acting, began in the actors' presence to sort out the play. He speaks naively, imagines Molière the way a high school student might and therefore demands insertions in the play.

March 10. At Stanislavsky's again. The little opera hall in Leont'ev [Lane].[62] St. began by stroking Misha's sleeve and saying, "You need stroking." Evidently, he'd already been informed about Misha's bitter reaction to his critique in the actors' presence. They haggled for about three hours. Stanislavsky's idea is to show throughout that Molière is the creator of a brilliant theater. Therefore one has to insert the things Misha considers trivial or unnecessary.

Ferocious argument with Stanislavsky and Livanov.[63] [. . .]

April 7. A rehearsal of *Molière* is going on at Stanislavsky's in Leont'ev [Lane], finally driving Misha out. Instead of rehearsing scenes from the play, he gets involved in pedagogic exercises with the actors and says a bunch of irrelevancies, which advance the play not at all. Misha demonstrates to me that no system, no authorities can make a bad actor act well. [. . .]

April 22. Today Misha and I read the minutes of the *Molière* rehearsals, which I received last night . . . They make it clear that Stanislavsky is determined to break up the whole play and create it from scratch. In the "Conspiracy" scene, for instance, "have D'Orsini put on a mask and from his seat move into the Conspiracy." The cup of patience overflowed and Misha immediately dictated to me a letter to Stanislavsky and Gorchakov with a categorical refusal of revisions and with the explanation that if the play doesn't suit the theater in the form he wrote it, he asks them to remove it and return it to him.

Rehearsal transcript, Stanislavsky working on *Molière*, May 4–11, 1935. Bulgakov, *Zapiski pokoynika*, 425–26.

May 4, 1935.

STANISLAVSKY (*to the Shoemaker* [Batashov,[64] whose role was later cut]): Here's another remark—it's a foreign play, so why are there such Russian terms of abuse—*svoloch'* [scum] and so on. We need to put in some other terms of abuse.

LIVANOV (Moiron): But I hate this play, so I'd like to quit it. I'm so knackered by this play that I hate it.

---

62 The ballroom in Stanislavsky's home in Leont'ev Lane had a pillared stage, where he conducted lessons.

63 Boris Nikolaevich Livanov (1904–72), actor at the MAT from 1924, alternating comic roles such as Shvandya in *Lyubov' Yarovaya* with heroic parts. His piratical interpretation of Solëny in Nemirovich-Danchenko's revision of *Three Sisters* (1940) became standard.

64 Mikhail Nikolaevich Batashov (1900–1991), actor at the MAT 1933–56.

STANISLAVSKY: [...] This play is very difficult, but overcome this obstacle. You were born into an age when you have to cope with difficulties. That's why the government turns to the Art Theater—because it considers that this theater will not present tasteless things, all sorts of hocus-pocus. We are set a dreadfully difficult task, let's carry it out so that it will give us enormous technique, victory. If the actor doesn't love his technique, of course... he's not an artist. Nothing will come of it then. Don't put yourself in that position.

May 5, 1935.

STANISLAVSKY: Mikhail Afanas'evich has set the actor a horribly difficult task: "You're playing the play's hero and you show only his flaws." He actually gives us nothing positive. Molière is a coward, an egoist, he's whimsical—in short, everything's negative. The author gives us very few of his positive qualities. That he loves his new bride, that's only natural, she's a beautiful woman. Actually there's nothing positive. In other words—what can we build a hero on? That's the difficulty with the role. Actually something like cowardice, onstage... you know how that suits a comical character, but it's hard to play a cowardly hero. Show me a hero in all literature who's a comic type? Bulgakov's hero is presented in ultranaturalistic tones. Actually there are only two or three patches of brightness, the rest is all black. [...] If I were you [to Stanitsyn[65] as Molière], that aspect—the cowardice—I wouldn't emphasize it.

May 9, 1935.

STANISLAVSKY (*to Stanitsyn*): [...] I don't understand why Bulgakov insists that you be a coward?

GORCHAKOV: He doesn't say anything about the absolute need to fight. He says: "they draw their swords." They themselves requested a fight.

STANITSYN: He actually insulted me. "You, my good sir, are a scoundrel!" So his status as a gentleman is insulted... "I call you out." We've done it in such a way that Molière has thrown away his sword because the authorities forced him and he had to throw away his sword. There I don't even throw away the sword, but I drop it, because my heart is broken. [...] So we have to determine this task: it's important that he's a hired killer, a murderer provocateur. If this is useful, then we have to find it.

STANISLAVSKY: We have to do it so that it gets to that point. Then it's necessary to have a real duel, in which at first the battle is joined in full force, and then someone gets the upper hand. Then in my eyes you turn from a coward simply into a less technically proficient man. But how to join the battle? Actually, there's always something unbelievable about it. Take *Faust*, do you really believe it there? They invariably cross swords and move back and forth...

PODGORNY: Could we do lunges?

STANISLAVSKY: It would be good if you did something surprising, unexpected, then it wouldn't be stagy. In short, try it out.

---

65 Viktor Yakovlevich Stanitsyn (actually Gëze, 1897–1976), actor, director; at the Second Studio and the MAT from 1918 to his death, especially in character parts.

BULGAKOV ANNOUNCED his intention to withdraw the play, so in May Stanislavsky stepped down and allowed Gorchakov and Nemirovich-Danchenko to finish the job. First submitted to the theater in early 1930, it finally opened on February 16, 1936.

Bulgakova's diary, in *Zapiski pokoynika*.

December 21. Rehearsals of *Molière* are going on. It makes your head spin! Misha told me ... about the tantrum Koreneva[66] threw when they compressed some of her scenes, rushing to Mariya Petrovna Lilina,[67] screaming hysterically, behaving with exceptional impertinence.

When they began to rehearse with the cuts and said, "Put the lights on her," she screamed:

"Ah! I don't need any light!"

Her acting is ghastly. [...]

February 6 [1936]. Yesterday, after countless torments, the first dress rehearsal of *Molière* was held, the dry tech. Present were the secretary of TsIK Akulov,[68] Litovsky, as well as the theater's manager designate, Arkad'ev.

It is not the performance I've been anticipating since the 1930s, but it was a success with the rehearsal's audience. [...] Magnificent: Yanshin (Bouton) and Bolduman (the King).[69]

Hideously bad—Koreneva, Gerasimov[70] and Podgorny. It's a crime to show such actors.

Vil'yams[71] is good. In some places they applauded the sets. They applauded after every scene. A noisy success by the end of the play. Misha left to avoid a curtain call, but they extricated him from the vestibule and brought him onstage.

He came out to pay his respects to Nemirovich (he's awfully pleased).

THE FIRST PERFORMANCES were well received, but an unfavorable review in *Sovetskoe Iskusstvo* led to its removal from the repertoire after seven performances.

---

66 Lidiya Mikhaylovna Koreneva (1885–1985), actress at the MAT 1904–58, her best role Verochka in *A Month in a Country* (1909); as she aged, her behavior grew more temperamental and hysterical.

67 Mariya Petrovna Lilina (actually Perevoshchikova, 1866–1943), actress, wife of Stanislavsky, at the MAT from 1898, specializing in lyric and comic roles.

68 Ivan Alekseevich Akulov (1888–1938), secretary of the TsIK SSSR.

69 Mikhail Panteleymonovich Bolduman (1898–1983), after work in Kiev, actor at the MAT from 1933; best in the heroic, virile mode preferred by Stalin.

70 Georgy Avdeevich Gerasimov (1900–1961), at the MAT from 1924 to his death, mainly in secondary roles; codirected *Death of a Salesman* 1960.

71 Pëtr Vladimirovich Vil'yams (1902–47), designer, working at the MAT 1929–43 and then as chief designer at the Bol'shoy 1941–47; the first Russian designer to use scrim to achieve effects of distance.

This was followed by a damning notice in *Pravda* on March 9, 1936, titled "Outward Glitter and False Content."

Pavel Kerzhentsev to I. V. Stalin and V. M. Molotov on *Cabal of Bigots,* February 29, 1936. Katerina Clark and Evgeny Dobrenko, with André Artizov and Oleg Naumov, *Soviet Culture and Power: A History in Documents 1917–1953* (New Haven, Conn.: Yale University Press, 2007), 268–70. © 2007 by Yale University.

Despite the whole veil of hints, the political meaning Bulgakov invests in his work is sufficiently clear, although most reviewers may never even notice these hints.

He wants to evoke in the viewer an analogy between the writer's status under the dictatorship of the proletariat and under the "arbitrary tyranny" of Louis XIV. [...]

If we set aside the author's political hints and the apotheosis of Louis XIV, the play is a total ideological vacuum—the play poses no problems, does nothing to enrich the viewers, but then it skillfully offers up poison drops in an opulent but barren flower. [...]

All the theater's energy went into *externals.* The sets (Vil'yams), costumes, and mises-en-scène—all this has as its aim amazing the viewer with the costly genuine brocade, silk, and velvet. (It's no accident the production cost 360,000 rubles, whereas *Thunderstorm* cost 100,000 rubles.) [...]

My recommendations: Have the MAT filial remove this production not by formal prohibition but through the theater's conscious rejection of this production as mistaken and a distraction from the line of socialist realism. For this, place in *Pravda* a sharp editorial on *Molière* in the spirit of these comments of mine and analyze the production in other organs of the press.

Let the theaters see from the example of *Molière* that we are trying to achieve not outwardly brilliant productions where the acting is technically clever but productions that are ideologically saturated, realistically full-blooded, and historically accurate— from the leading theaters *especially.*

[*Stalin's notation*: "To Molotov: I think Com. Kerzhentsev is right. I approve of his proposal. I. Stalin."]

A. S. Shcherbakov to the secretaries of the Department of Cultural–Educational Work, September 17, 1936. (Stalin ordered that the contents be discussed.) Clark and Dobrenko, *Soviet Culture and Power,* 219–20. Aleksandr Sergeevich Shcherbakov (1901–45) was head of the Department of Cultural–Educational Work.

The theater's situation is no better and no worse. The MAT leadership, K. S. Stanislavsky and V. I. Nemirovich-Danchenko, take no interest in the theater whatsoever. They are more involved with their opera theaters. The mutual squabbling between them, which gets increasingly intense, has completely destroyed any unified leadership at the MAT. The theater now has two lines, two camps recruiting their own supporters, drawing actors and directors into petty intrigues and quarreling. [...]

There is no firm repertoire plan, the theater lives on a day-to-day basis. [...] The actor corps, with rare exceptions, is in a depressed state. The theater has eight staff directors and the same number of assistants, but they are staging only a few performances, and the others, while receiving a salary at the Art Theater, are working only on the side. [...] No creative work is being done with the actors, who are left to their own devices. The situation is particularly bad with the so-called young actors (with ten years' seniority at MAT): they are completely at a loose end, don't get new roles for years, no one is teaching them, no one is interested in their needs and requests. [...]

PANICKED BY THIS REPORT, Stanislavsky asked Stalin to appoint a Communist director to keep the theater on an even political keel. The chosen one was Mikhail Pavlovich Arkad'ev (1896–1937), an official in the Theater Department of the NKP RSFSR, opposed by Nemirovich-Danchenko. His advent in 1936 was trumpeted in *Pravda* as a red-letter day in the history of the Art Theater. The influence of the "Red manager" was felt in the introduction of mass-produced propaganda into the repertoire. Korneychuk's *The Banker,* after 173 rehearsals, was canceled following its preview. Stalin had demanded that the MAT revive *Lyubov' Yarovaya,* which opened in December 1936 to unanimously bad reviews. Regularly urged by *Pravda* to promote socialist realism, the MAT personnel publicly endorsed the new policy, despite private misgivings.

Even though the NKVD's files on the MAT's members swelled daily, it became clear that it had become Stalin's favorite theater and would not be purged by Beria. On the occasion of its fortieth anniversary, the MAT sent a celebratory telegram to the general secretary, thanking him as "the man who inspires us in our work [...] who confidently leads the way toward Communism, the friend of art."

Another Soviet imposition was Nikolay Virta's play *Earth* (1937), his first play for the MAT, based on a novel of his. *Zemlya* deals with the rebellion of Tambov peasants against the Soviet power during the Civil War. Cast with the MAT's strongest actors, it opened on November 5, 1937, to celebrate the twentieth anniversary of the Revolution.

> The director Leonid Leonidov to the assistant director Medynsky. A. Antonov-Ovseenko, *Teatr Iosifa Stalina* (Moscow: Gregori-Peydzh, 1995), 144–45. Anton V. Antonov-Ovseenko, son of an Old Bolshevik liquidated in 1938, was twice arrested and interned in a labor camp 1941–53; he became director of the State Museum of GULAG history.

When I received from the management the order to work on this play, I thought: is it worthwhile to fling open this stinking pit again now? But reading Stalin's words, "Remember and never forget that so long as there is a capitalist weapon, there will be wreckers, saboteurs, spies, terrorists, remember and carry on the struggle with those comrades who underestimate the strength and significance of sabotage." I understand that this is an eternal, constant theme.

Klavdiya Nikolaevna Elanskaya:[72] They do not school us to think creatively, on the contrary, they break us of the habit of creative thinking. Our theater is a house of the dead . . . The artist-actor—he has somehow to catch fire, to dream, to burn. But with us the actor can only dream, act into his pillow, for if he told his comrades, they would make him a laughingstock. If he told the management, it would be considered a crime—he warmed to dream of something, at a time when the theater does not require any reveries—they will mark everything for you and call you when you're needed.

THE ONLY TWO REAL SUCCESSES of the MAT prior to the war were both staged by Nemirovich-Danchenko: an adaptation of *Anna Karenina* in 1937 and an "optimistic" renovation of *Three Sisters* in 1940. In the former case, audiences flocked to view the set pieces and costumes, crowd scenes and special effects of a bygone tsarist era. (The actors had been taught deportment by ex-count Volkonsky, a former court factotum.) Alla Tarasova, the Anna, was awarded a Stalin Prize and made a deputy of the Supreme Soviet.

M. Tverskoy, "*Anna Karenina*," *Sovetskoe iskusstvo* (April 23, 1937), reprinted in *Moskovsky Khudozhestvenny Teatr v russkoy teatral'noy kritike 1919–1943*, ed. O. A. Radishcheva and E. A. Shingareva (Moscow: Artist. Rezhissër. Teatr, 2009), 2:258–64.

The performance is genuinely realistic; it is exciting, calls forth tears, it moves you, stirs up ideas, poses and helps to solve major problems, which have not lost their acuteness even now. The production of *Anna Karenina* is a major event in the cultural life of the land of socialism not only because our best theater has brought onstage a brilliant work by a great artist and enriched our knowledge of the past.

The performance raises problems of new human relationships. We become fully aware of new relationships of men and women, husbands and wives. Love, as Engels brilliantly foresaw, will become genuine love only in a socialist society. We are constructing new bases for morality through our experience, we often pay with our suffering. A structure of relationships is already being created immeasurably superior to anything that existed before, because the falsehood that lay at the base of marriage, the family, love in the old society, the falsehood that inevitably flows from the exploitative character of that society, has been extirpated. But the vestiges of capitalism in people's consciousness have remained, they are alive and hard to eliminate. [. . .]

---

72 Klavdiya Nikolaevna Elanskaya (1898–1972), actress, in the Second Studio 1920–24 and the MAT, where her roles included Katerina Maslova in *Resurrection* and Ol'ga in Nemirovich-Danchenko's 1940 recension of *Three Sisters*.

Vsevolod Ivanov, "The MAT is the national Russian theater," *Teatr* 4 (1937), reprinted in *Moskovsky Khudozhestvenny Teatr v russkoy teatral'noy kritike 1919–1943*, 2:268–70.

This psychologism in the MAT style comes not from Dostoevsky nor from Sukhovo-Kobylin, it is the style of Chekhov organically assimilated by the theater, absorbed into its blood and brains. The whole MAT theatrical tradition (even when the MAT stages modern works) is permeated with those noble elevated feelings. [...]

I want to emphasize the utmost sincerity of the MAT. One of the reasons for the stunning, nationwide success of *Anna Karenina* lies, in my opinion, in the all-conquering sincerity of Tarasova as Karenina. Our country, our whole nation, were not long ago witnesses of the unexampled in the history of humanity, treachery, and double dealing of enemies of the people Tukhachevsky[73] and other sons of bitches, bartering away our country.

Righteousness, sincerity, honor, inner spiritual beauty—that's what we demand from people, that's what the spectator demands in the theater. And the outstanding Soviet actress Alla Konstantinovna Tarasova has known how, through her flair as an artist, to capture this inner thirst, this longing of the Soviet spectator, and she has satisfied his expectations by her performance of the role of Anna Karenina. People in the audience, with bated breath, get upset, "share the experience," many unabashedly weep... The stage provides the audience an answer to its question, releases its internal tension. This is the original "catharsis" of which the ancient Greeks spoke. Therefore, *Anna Karenina* is a national performance on the stage of the Russian national theater. [...]

In conclusion, I want to say that the national in art cannot be cultivated. And it is impossible to write anything national intentionally and with purpose aforethought. Pushkin, Repin, Tchaikovsky, Gorky, Mayakovsky hardly ever set themselves the conscious task of creating a national work of art. But everything they created is deeply human in its subject matter and connected precisely to our country. Unfortunately, only after the death of Vladimir Vladimirovich Mayakovsky did we understand that in his person the Soviet land lost its national poet. And the theater of V. Meyerhold, having staged his plays (the only one, I believe, in our country to do so), could not create national productions out of them...

The success of *Anna Karenina* and the general truckling to government policy enabled the MAT to be sent as a national treasure to the Paris Exposition of 1937, partly to compete with Nazi Germany's cultural products. Despite the fact that each member of the troupe was accompanied by minders to prevent association with White Russians, the "Red manager" Arkad'ev got in trouble by providing

---

73 Mikhail Nikolaevich Tukhachevsky (1893–1937), marshal of the Soviet Union, from 1936 first deputy of the narkom of defense of the USSR. Arrested in May 1937, accused of taking part in a "military–fascist conspiracy," and shot in June, along with other colleagues in the Red Army. Later rehabilitated.

information in interviews that had not been approved in advance by the government. He was dismissed in June 1937 and liquidated.

The prominence of the MAT forced it to serve as an auxiliary to the government. The veteran character actor Ivan Moskvin was made a deputy of the first convocation of the Supreme Soviet in 1937. He was thus compelled to make speeches, meet delegations, visit factories, and serve as a go-between. His inability to intercede for Meyerhold made the director's stepdaughter a bitter enemy.

"Moskvin addresses art workers' meet," *Moscow Daily News* (February 3, 1938).

People's Artist of the USSR I. M. Moskvin, deputy to the Supreme Soviet, addressed yesterday's meeting of the All-Union Congress of the Art Workers Union [...]

"I receive letters from children twelve, thirteen, fourteen years of age. 'We have decided to devote ourselves to the theater,' they write. Among them are some who write that they are now in the ninth class but have decided not to go on in the tenth, because their heads are occupied with the theater and there is no room in their thoughts for their lessons. You can see that we must especially seriously think about this. I do not know how to organize admission to the dramatic schools, but from my own experience I know that it is impossible to decide in one examination whether the candidate has talent or not. [...] It will be necessary that young people should be tested over a period of two, and perhaps three, or even six months. [...]

"We were one single family united in our faith in Stalin. That is precisely why, every moment of our life, all our thoughts, feelings, and eyes are turned toward him who created the great Constitution and called the entire people to the administration of the country. Let us then continue to live united, to live as one big family, and let our watchword be: One for all, all for one!"

STANISLAVSKY, whose health was rapidly deteriorating, spent most of his time working at home with the students of the opera studio or else in sanitarium. While developing an acting system of "physical action," he grew even more remote from day-to-day events and the changing political landscape.

Lyubimov, *Rasskazy starogo trepacha*, 147–48, 170–71.

Although Stanislavsky was very ill ... as soon as actors began to carry on very frank conversations in rehearsal, he quickly stopped them:

"Stop at once, otherwise they'll send us all to GUM."

He was confusing the GPU with GUM, the department store. He was so isolated that he confused these concepts; he lived in a private residence: his residence was his theater. They didn't touch him, for he had no dealings with them.

Once Stalin invited Stanislavsky to his box. Stanislavsky said in terror:

"My real name is Alekseev." Stalin looked at him and said:

"Dzhugashvili."

Black humor.

Then Stalin said:

"It's boring around here."

The whole retinue began to say:

"How can you stage such things? It's boring . . . You should give this some thought."

Stalin paused, then said:

"During the intermissions."

And everyone went: ha, ha, ha! and offered congratulations [. . .]

Aleksandr Galich, *General'naya Repertitisya* (Frankfurt, Germany: Posev Press, 1974), 74–75. Aleksandr Arkadievich Galich (actually Ginzburg, 1918–77) was in the last class Stanislavsky taught at his home. Stymied in his attempts at playwriting, in the 1960s Galich became a controversial chansonnier and emigrated to Paris.

How did it happen that not a single even moderately distinguished actor emerged from Stanislavsky's studio? There were thirty of us students hand-picked from three thousand candidates. There were two more auditions later on, bringing the number of students in the drama section [. . .] to about fifty altogether. We were the cream of the crop, the chosen few, the lucky dogs, envied by students of all the other theater schools. But with the possible exception of Mikhail Kuznetsov,[74] who left the theater to work in film as soon as he graduated from the studio, not even a single slightly distinguished actor emerged from our ranks.

I now realize the answer is simple. No one really cared whether the students would become actors. We were, of course, taught the actor's art, but we were essentially only wooden pawns on the chessboard grandly called "Theater as Temple." We were the guinea pigs on whom Stanislavsky tested his latest theory, the so-called theory of physical actions.

Much has been written about this theory, but in a few words it came down to this: the correct physical actions would bring the performer to the correct behavior, the correct behavior would bring about the correct state of mind, and the correct state of mind would help find the correct words [. . .]

Stanislavsky was holed up in his mansion, walled off from the rest of the world. He lived in a completely illusory, fictional universe, where the only sacred thing, the cornerstone of everything, the creed of all creeds was a certain Theatrical Art, in capital letters, which he still continued to serve zealously despite his advanced age, whereas "out there" . . .

A contemptuous smile and a magnificent wave of a large and elegantly manicured hand indicated that "out there" referred to the current Moscow Art Theater, where

---

74 Mikhail Artem'evich Kuznetsov (1918–86), much honored film and TV actor. Played in Eisenstein's film *Ivan the Terrible* (1944–45).

Vladimir Ivanovich Nemirovich-Danchenko presided, and where they staged all sorts of absurd modern plays with ridiculous names. [...]

And mesmerized by the talent of our great teacher, enthralled by his incredible charm, his prominence, his fame, and his sheer physical presence, we too lived in an imaginary, unreal and illusory world. It goes without saying that we still had our unavoidable Komsomol meetings, we still read newspapers (Stanislavsky himself did not read any newspapers), we still listened to the radio, we still went to the movies. But all of this was done somehow as a matter of course: it was not important. It was as if the crushing events of those terrible years had absolutely nothing to do with us, the students—or so it seemed.

Many of us, many, if not most, were to pay a steep and bitter price for all those early years we lived as if we were deaf and blind. Many of us were to pay for those years with general disillusionment, with loss of both talent and faith in ourselves. [...]

STANISLAVSKY DIED on August 7, 1938. His book *An Actor Works on Himself* was published posthumously, edited by his student Grigory Kristi, who eliminated such words as "soul" and "spirit" from the text.

> The Moscow Art Theater's fortieth anniversary tribute to Stalin, 1938. Antonov-Ovseenko, *Teatr Iosifa Stalina*, 140.

Dear Iosif Vissarionovich!

The workers of the Moscow Art Theater, gathered today after the summer vacation and beginning its forty-first season, in all its profundity recognize the responsibility and wide-ranging tasks that stand before Soviet art. Our ideas involuntarily turn to You, to the man who inspires us in our work, in the surmounting of any difficulties, in audacity in creative experiments. We promise you to apply all our powers, to expand our creativity even further and with each of our productions offer an answer to the inquiries of our spectator.

... And on the first day of our work, cheerfully, fully rested, gladly gathered again between the walls of our beloved theater, we send our heartfelt, grateful greetings to the man who confidently leads us toward Communism, the friend of art—You, Iosif Vissarionovich.

> The actor Boris Babochkin at the All-Russian Stage Director's Conference, 1938. Quoted in Dmitry Kalm, "Problems of the Soviet theatre," *International Literature* 10 (October 1939), 78.

There is but one method in the Soviet Union. It is Stanislavsky's method, the method of the realistic theater, in which is summed up a century's experience in the Russian theater. We have no other method. This is perhaps unfortunate—and perhaps it is fortunate.

Isaak Babel's experience had been fortunate in working with the MAT 2, which staged his black comedy about Jews in prerevolutionary Odessa, *Sundown*. His experience with the MAT 1 was unfortunate. His *Mariya* was scheduled to open there in 1935 but was banned. On May 15, 1939, Babel was arrested, and, after a twenty-minute trial, shot on January 25, 1940. This excerpt from his NKVD interrogation indicates how the MAT had become the official theater of the USSR and how to criticize it adversely was now seen as an act of lèse majesté.

> Babel interrogated by NKVD. Vitaly Shentalinsky and John Crowfoot, *The KGB's Literary Archive* (London: Harvill Press, 1995), 52.

My talks with Mikhoéls, who was trying by fair means and foul to get my banned play *Sundown* back into the repertoire, were of the same kind. So were those with Goryunov, one of the managers of the Vakhtangov Theater, who wanted my play *Mariya*, banned by the State Repertory Committee, to be permitted again. Their efforts to get my plays back on the stage went hand in hand with our propaganda against the current Soviet repertoire and its supporters and against the new policies of the Moscow Art Theater. Its productions of plays such as *Enemies, Earth,* and *Dostigaev and Others*[75] were, we declared, inevitable and predictable failures. The attention devoted to the best theater in the country had created a hothouse atmosphere, we said, and this was dulling the brilliance and innovation that formerly distinguished its work . . . Our love for the People was artificial and theoretical and our concern for their future simply an aesthetic category. We had no roots among the People, hence the despair and nihilism that we disseminated.

The Decline and Fall of Meyerhold

No one mourned the passing of the Sohn Theater, but when Meyerhold moved his troupe into a building on lower Gorky Street (now the Ermolova Theater) in summer 1932, it was considered a temporary measure. Plans were put in motion for a grandiose new theater building to seat three thousand spectators. However, there were endless delays and cost overruns, and, ultimately, the Meyerhold Theater would be liquidated in January 1938, even before it opened. Meanwhile, Meyerhold spent the last years of his creative life in a poorly equipped playhouse with a standard proscenium opening and no stage depth to speak of. The physical inadequacies severely limited what Meyerhold could put on. The inaugural play, Érdman's comedy *The Suicide*, was proscribed, even after two months of unauthorized rehearsal. So Meyerhold turned to *Prelude* (*Vstuplenie,* 1932), a dramatization by the young Soviet writer Yury Pavlovich German (1910–67) of his novel. It had

---

75 The MAT had staged Gorky's *Enemies* 1935–36, *Earth* by Nikolay Virta 1937–38, and Gorky's *Dostigaev and Others* 1938–39.

been praised by Gorky because its hero is a German chemical engineer, compelled to transfer his work from Shanghai to an enthusiastic Soviet Union. It was adapted into what Meyerhold called *"a realistic musical theater"* (his emphasis) and opened on January 28, 1933.

> Vsevolod Meyerhold, *"Prelude* at the Meyerhold Gostheater," April 6, 1933, in *Stat'i, pis'ma, rechi, besedy* (Moscow: Iskusstvo, 1968), 2:261–62.

The pandemonium of insinuations directed at the Soviet Union by the "civilized" West, the catastrophic position of the proletariat and the repressed portion of the intelligentsia in capitalist countries, the ideological impoverishment of life with its convulsive wailing for a crust of bread, torn from the mouths of the proletariat in conditions of crisis—those are the premises to the fact that the best part of Western European and American intelligentsia, especially its avant-garde (Henri Barbusse,[76] Bernard Shaw et al.), look with affection and hope to the Soviet Union, seeing in it the way out of the impasse into which capitalism has driven humanity. The best people of Western Europe and America become more and more aware of the correctness of the socialist system, which opens to humanity a great road to a bright future—a future in which an unprecedented flowering of science and art, culture in general, will come about.

IN DECEMBER 1933 the Kul'totdel VTsSPS organized a seminar of the heads of independent Moscow theater collectives. Meyerhold delivered the first lecture.

> Vsevolod Meyerhold, "On ideology and technology in the theater," December 1933, in *Stat'i, pis'ma, rechi, besedy,* 2:268–69, 274–75, 279–81. Translated in *The International Theatre* 2 (1934), 6–8.

Both director and actor must *understand clearly the purpose of the performance.* There is no such thing as a play without a purpose. An outstanding play is exceptional mainly in its profound ideas; i.e., it is clearly polemical—it tries to "persuade" the audience.

The purpose of each role must be clearly understood. There must be a *political* (*ideological*) idea in the rendering of each role. To this there must be added *agitational performance*: the actor not only performs his role in conformity with the general purpose of the play but also desires to propagate his part of that purpose with particular feeling.

This clearly reveals the defects of the system of "living one's role." It is dangerous to submerge oneself entirely in a part, losing control of oneself. In entering into a part, the actor has no right to forget that he is the bearer of definite ideas. The actor must be either the defender or the prosecutor of the character he enacts; otherwise, he will not take his true place in the conception of the performance. [. . .]

Our approach to the construction of images, mise-en-scène, and performance as

---

76 Henri Barbusse (1873–1935), French writer and reformer.

a whole is *profoundly realistic*. Every movement has its motivation, which is bound up with the idea of the performance and with the psychology of the figure. We use conventional methods, but within the framework of the conventional theater, we build up profoundly realistic figures.

We speak of the conventional theater because, being a realistic theater, we do not cease to be enemies of naturalism. The theater cannot reproduce life photographically; it is necessary to select what is most typical and to show connections and interactions. [...] We do not want to be naturalists or to make naturalists in our audience. *The theater is conventional by its very nature.* [...]

A number of incorrect ideas have also grown up around *biomechanics*. Biomechanics is a system of training worked out on the basis of the long experience of my work with actors[,] a course for preparing the actor for the stage, like our work in the field of speech [...] It gives the actor the habits he must have. It takes into account that the actor is at one and the same time organizer and organized and it shows him the way to direct his acting, to cooperate with his partners and with the audience, to foreshorten his acting, and so on. [...]

FOR SEVERAL MONTHS Meyerhold was thrown back on revivals. Since most of the Soviet plays he had proposed had been rejected, he decided to dust off a melodrama that had been one of the biggest hits of the nineteenth century, *La Dame aux ca-méllias* by Alexandre Dumas *fils,* featuring Zinaida Raykh as Marguerite Gautier.

> Vsevolod Meyerhold, "A production about the fate of a woman", 1934, in *Stat'i, pis'ma, rechi, besedy,* 2:285.

Having made it our task to put on a cycle of productions devoted to Woman, we have included in our repertoire A. Dumas *fils*'s play *The Lady of the Camellias* as one of the best plays of the French nineteenth-century theater, which marks the start of the realistic tendency in the French theater.

The leading character in the play, Marguerite Gautier, is a country girl who has barely learned to write her name when she winds up in Paris. In the exposition of the play it is said of her that she once worked in a milliner's workshop. "The worst of all situations for women," writes Bebel,[77] "in those trade associations of industry in which they primarily are occupied, as for instance, in the production of dresses and millinery... Women working in this branch of industry, are compelled (because of the paltry wages for the work) to supplement their income by selling their bodies."

Our concern was to show in the play the milieu, all the elements of that idiosyncratic legalized inquisition to which bourgeois society condemns woman.

The bourgeois debauches a girl, sacrifices her to satisfy his vanity, promotes her to first place when he needs her, but when she seems superfluous, ruthlessly turns her away.

---

77 August Bebel (1840–1913), German social-democratic political reformer.

In his memoirs of Lenin, Lyadov[78] relates that Vladimir Il'ich and Nadezhda Konstantinovna attended a production of *The Lady of the Camellias* in Geneva. And when during the performance Lyadov turned around to Vladimir Il'ich, sitting at the back of the box, he saw that Il'ich was shamefacedly wiping away tears. It is not hard to guess what in this drama provoked those tears of Lenin's. In it he saw an artistic representation of the slavish plight of women under capitalism. We know the displeasure with which Vladimir I'lich regarded the mechanism of oppression of woman in bourgeois society. [...]

By putting on Dumas *fils*'s play *The Lady of the Camellias,* we raise the question of the attitude to women in our country in relation to the attitude to women in capitalist countries. Anyone who sees this show will fight with renewed vigor for the confirmation of a new life, for the reinforcement of a new morality, that same Communist morality about which Lenin spoke so often.

> Aleksandr Matskin, "Time to go: A chronicle of the tragic years," *Teatr* 1 (1990), 25–51. Aleksandr Petrovich Matskin (1906–96), chief theater critic at *Sovetskoe iskusstvo* 1933–37, actively engaged in theatrical journalism and debates and cofounded *Teatr* 1937.

I recall that the experiment began by changing the period of the play—not the 1850s, as in Dumas, but the 1870s. This was a tremendous advantage for the director. Before him lay a different era, different music ("the age of cancan," Offenbach's heyday), different painting (Renoir and especially Manet). On this level Dumas's grandiloquent text demanded a certain deepening, a "Flaubertization," as Vsevolod Émil'evich would say, but carefully, without overloading it, without modernizing it, so that it is Dumas onstage and not someone else. [...]

He changed the social status of Armand Duval, raising him a few strata higher in the hierarchy of Parisian society ("Armand Duval in our production is not the son of a tax assessor but the son of a major industrialist"). This is no longer the demimonde of cheap cocottes in garrets and shady apaches. The theater turned into a scintillating society where vice has greater luxury and greater scope. [...] With such a treatment the outer design of the production was essential—everything was collector's pieces, antiques, top quality—furniture and porcelain and expensive knickknacks and all the rest of the furnishings of the highest maker's marks. And this was not the commission store in Stoleshniky Lane, where at the time the richest assortment of rarities was piled up cheek by jowl haphazardly. In the theater strict taste was observed, as if the things had been selected by fussy consultants, connoisseurs of the style and the material world of the Third Republic. [...] The juxtaposition of the frozen and exquisite beauty of the things and the squalor of the moving, drinking, gobbling, reveling crowd, governed by sinister instincts, set up the two polarities of the production—the individual and the herd—where the drama of Marguerite Gautier is played out. [...]

---

78 Martyn Nikolaevich Lyadov (1872–1947), leader of the Moscow Workers League 1895; veteran Bolshevik and delegate from Saratov; party historian and head of the Comintern.

Just as rehearsals for *The Lady of the Camellias* were beginning, the newspaper where I worked proposed to send me and two other comrades to southern Ukraine, where there was a famine, mowing down whole districts and gubernias. [...] I have never seen anything more horrible before or since. [...] I got back to Moscow. Of course it was impossible to write about anything I had seen. Who would print such things? I told Meyerhold of my impressions. He became distracted, which rarely happened with him. Then I plucked up my courage and said that I had read more than once that beauty will save the world. Where is that beauty? Meyerhold, having regained self-control, replied, "It hasn't been discovered yet." After a brief pause, he added, "It won't save us from famine, but it can save us from savagery, brutality, and vulgarity."

THE PRODUCTION opened on March 18, 1934. Predictably, the irony of its emphasis on surface glamour eluded the critics, who accused Meyerhold of offering vice as a model. Meyerhold refused to write an article supporting Shostakovich's attackers shortly after one of Stalin's close personal assistants had made it known that Stalin failed to attend *The Lady of the Camellias* because the theater did not have an official box. On March 5, Meyerhold and his wife, Zinaida Raykh, conferred with Boris Pasternak and Aleksandr Gladkov to decide whether to meet with Stalin or attempt to defend Shostakovich.

> Aleksandr Gladkov, "Encounters with Pasternak," *Meyerkho'ld* (Moscow: Soyuz teatral'nykh deyateley, 1990), 2:349–50.

I of course said that he certainly must try to bring about that meeting, and that V. É. must talk with Stalin not only about GosTIM and himself but about all of the vital problems of art. [...]

Zinaida Nikolaevna supported me, but cautiously added that it would be better for Meyerhold to limit himself to the question of Meyerhold's own work and not touch on Shostakovich, whom only time and his own efforts could help. But Pasternak[79] didn't agree with either of us. In a long and prolix speech [...] he gave the advice not to seek a meeting with Stalin because nothing good could come from it in any case. He told about the sad experience of his telephone conversation with Stalin after the poet Mandel'shtam was arrested, when Stalin, not hearing him out, hung up the receiver. Heatedly, he pointed out to V. É. that it was unworthy of him, Meyerhold, to go to Stalin looking like a petitioner, and he couldn't be in any other position at that time. That people such as Stalin and Meyerhold must either speak as equals or not meet at all. [...]

... To my great amazement, Meyerhold agreed with Pasternak; he said that he understood that right now, indeed, was not the time to seek such a meeting, and he asked all of us to forget this conversation. He in fact refused to take steps to be received [...]

---

79 Boris Leonidovich Pasternak (1890–1960), one of Russia's greatest poets, whose translations of Shakespeare became standard.

MEYERHOLD'S PRODUCTIONS IN 1935 were a radical revision of Tchaikovsky's opera *Queen of Spades* for the Leningrad Maly Theater and an evening of three Chekhov farces called *33 Swoons*. The former was reasonably successful, but the latter failed to be funny. With the war on formalism in full swing, the director felt it necessary to confess his errors in a speech in Leningrad on March 14, 1936, called "Meyerhold versus Meyerholdism," but it turned out to be more a fulmination at his imitators and opponents than a mea culpa. His rejection of socialist realism was even more blatant in his next public utterance.

> Vsevolod Meyerhold, "Speech at the Meeting of Theatrical Workers of Moscow, 26 March 1936," in *Stat'i, pis'ma, rechi, besedy,* 2:348–57. An abridged version was published under the title "Against formalism and naturalism" in *Teatr i Dramaturgiya* 4 (1936), 207–10.

The theatrical community is waiting for me in my speech to move from criticism of other theaters to detailed self-criticism.

My entire creative path, all my practice on this path is nothing other than detailed self-criticism. I never embark on a new project until I have freed myself from the captivity of my latest work. The biography of an original artist is the biography of a man ceaselessly torn by dissatisfaction with himself. An original artist becomes such not only by the power of his nature-given abilities but also by the power of enormous work on polishing his natural abilities. An artist begins an original master, constantly learning, constantly observing and reflecting and strengthening constantly what lies in the sphere of his worldview. He does not uproot himself from reality, knowing that he is part of the class with which he lives and works, that with them he is blazing the trail to socialism. The life of such an artist experiences joy on the day when the last stroke is flung on the canvas and the greatest suffering the next day when the artist sees his mistakes. [...]

The passion of the lofty demands on our art as on any clear, simple art we see in the articles of the central organ of our party. And we know that these articles are evoked by the same relation to art as there was in Lenin.

The most important thing in art is simplicity. But each artist has his own representation of simplicity. In the search for simplicity the artist must not lose the specificity of his personality. [...]

MEYERHOLD PLUNGED into work on *One Life (Odna zhizn')*, Evgeny Gavrilovich's dramatization of the novel *How the Steel Was Tempered* by Nikolay Alekseevich Ostrovsky (1904–36). With Evgeny Samoylov as the purblind hero Pavka Korchagin, it reached dress rehearsals and received preliminary approval. Before it could be opened to celebrate the twentieth anniversary of the October Revolution, a second showing was damned by the Party organs, headed by Kerzhentsev.

Platon Kerzhentsev, "An alien theater," *Pravda* (December 17, 1937). Quoted in Yury Elagin, *Tëmny genii: Vsevolod Meyerkhol'd* (New York: Izd-vo imeni Chekhova, 1955), 399–407.

On the twentieth anniversary of the Great Socialist Revolution, only one theater out of the 700 Soviet professional theaters seems not to have scheduled a special production for the October celebration and does not have a Soviet repertoire. This is the Meyerhold Theater.

[...] Year after year V. Meyerhold, in reply to the accusation that his theater lacked a Soviet repertoire, replied, "There are no suitable plays," and again, "There are no suitable opportunities."

[...] In a series of plays staged by the theater, Soviet reality has been presented in a crudely distorted, mockingly hostile manner. [...] Over a number of years, Meyerhold stubbornly tried to stage the play *I Want a Baby*[80] by the enemy of the people S. Tret'yakov, which was a hostile slander on the Soviet family, and the play *The Suicide* by Érdman, which defended the right of the middle class to exist and lodged a protest against the dictatorship of the proletariat. It is characteristic that during the discussion of this latter play at his theater V. Meyerhold insisted that the play is "particularly timely," and one of the leading female workers of the theater, defending the play, referred to the Five-Year Plan in a clearly anti-Soviet spirit. [...]

Our press has more than once turned the attention of the leaders of the theater to the abnormal situation in which the theater's work was heading. A long time ago, *Pravda* wrote about the antisocial atmosphere of the Meyerhold Theater. In 1933, at the time of the party purges, the theater's departure from Soviet reality and an unwholesome trend in the theater were noted. Connected to that abnormal situation, the intensification of the political and artistic errors of theater, connected to the system of nepotism and the regime of self-criticism, no small number of Soviet actors left the theater (D. Orlov, Babanova, Shtraukh, Glizer, Garin, Okhlopkov, Tsarëv,[81] etc.). [...]

In its earliest articles about formalism *Pravda* especially mentioned the formalist errors of V. Meyerhold, but he usually referred to this criticism frivolously and irresponsibly. V. Meyerhold was more susceptible to formalist errors than anyone else, but he drew no conclusions about himself from the articles in *Pravda*. Instead of criticism

---

80 Tret'yakov's play of eugenics *Khochu rebënku* (1926) was rehearsed by Meyerhold 1926–27, but the Repertkom refused to release it. Brecht translated it into German, but it went unproduced.

81 Dmitry Nikolaevich Orlov (1892–1955) had met Meyerhold in Novorossiysk and was invited to join him; acted at the Theater of Revolution 1922–41. Babanova left because Meyerhold had bestowed the leading female roles on Zinaida Raykh. Maksim Maksimovich Shtraukh (1900–1974), one of Meyerhold's favorite comedians, had left for the Mayakovsky Theater in 1932 after the failure of *The Bathhouse*. His wife, Iudif Samoylovna Glizer (1904–68), grotesque character actress at the Moscow Proletkul't 1921–28, before moving to the Theater of Revolution, had never worked for Meyerhold. Garin did not leave voluntarily but was transferred to the Leningrad Comedy Theater 1936. Okhlopkov had left Meyerhold in 1930 to become a director. Mikhail Ivanovich Tsarëv (1903–87), who had worked for Meyerhold from 1933 and played Armand in *The Lady of the Camellias*, was transferred to the Maly Theater 1937, eventually rising to become its artistic director 1985.

of his political errors and an examination of his erroneous artistic path, V. Meyerhold devoted himself to empty scoffing at the "Meyerholdian errors" of other theaters. He did not correct the ideological perversions and formalist affectations in plays of the standard repertoire [...]

V. Meyerhold and his theater have isolated themselves from general work reflecting Soviet reality in artistic images. As a result, he has made himself an alien body in the organism of Soviet art, he has become alien to the theater.

Do Soviet art and the Soviet spectator need a theater like this?

> "Resolution on the liquidation of the Vs. Meyerhold Theater," *Teatr* 1 (1938); *TASS* and *Pravda* (January 8, 1938); reprinted in *Teatr* 1 (1990), 142.

1. The Meyerhold Theater over the course of its entire existence could not free itself from positions alien to Soviet art, thoroughly bourgeois and formalistic. As a result, to suit ultraleft craftiness and formalistic mannerisms, even classical works of Russian drama were presented by the theater in distorted, anti-artistic guise, with a misinterpretation of their ideological substance (*The Inspector General, Woe to Wit, Tarelkin's Death*, etc.).

2. The Meyerhold Theater has appeared to be entirely bankrupt in the staging of plays of Soviet dramatists. The staging of these plays offered a perverted, slanderous presentation of Soviet reality, subsisting on double entendres and even out-and-out anti-Soviet ranting (*The Suicide, A Window on the Village, Second Army Commander*,[82] etc.).

3. During the last few years Soviet plays have entirely disappeared from the theater's repertoire. A number of the best actors have left the theater, while Soviet dramatists have turned away from a theater isolated from the entire social and artistic life of the Union.

4. On the twentieth anniversary of the October Revolution the Meyerhold Theater not only failed to prepare a single production but made a politically hostile attempt to stage a play by Gabrilovich (*One Life*), which anti-Sovietically misinterprets the famous work of art by N. Ostrovsky, *How the Steel Was Tempered*.

Apart from anything else, this production was a misuse of government funds on the part of the Meyerhold Theater, accustomed to living on government financial subsidies.

In view of this, the Committee for Artistic Affairs under the Sovnarkom USSR has decreed:

a. the liquidation of the Meyerhold Theater as alien to Soviet art;

b. to employ the theater's company in other theaters;

c. the question of the possibility of Vs. Meyerhold's further work in the realm of theater is to be considered separately.

> Vsevolod Meyerhold, "Lecture in the director's courses of the dramatic theaters, 17 January 1939," in *Stat'i, pis'ma, rechi, besedy*, 2:470.

---

82 *Kommandarm 2* (1929), Il'ya Sel'vinsky's verse tragedy, had been Meyerhold's attempt to display a modern Soviet hero.

It's a shame that we conducted all our experiments in public. It would have been good if there had been a sort of hidden laboratory, where we, the directors, could work with accompanying lectures, as at the Planetarium. [...]

———————

AFTER MEYERHOLD'S THEATER was liquidated in January 1938, he would have been unemployed had not his former teacher, director, and erstwhile artistic opponent Stanislavsky taken him on as artistic director of his Opera Theater.

Lyubimov, *Rasskazy starogo trepacha*, 147–48.

For years Stanislavsky had not gone to his own theater. [...] And when Meyerhold's theater was closed, the only man who wasn't afraid and took him to work in his own studio was Stanislavsky. And he spoke the bitter sentence:

"I can't set you up at the MAT; I'm rarely there myself, but I can place you with me in the studio."

Vsevolod Meyerhold to Stanislavsky, January 18, 1938. V. Meyerhold, *Perepiska* (Moscow: Iskusstvo, 1976), 348–49.

Dear Konstantin Sergeevich,

N. V. Gogol, describing an occurrence in one of his novellas, after having difficulty in putting down on paper what had just happened in his novella, suddenly stops short and exclaims, "No!... I can't do it!... Give me another pen! My pen is feeble, dead, too finely cut for this picture!"

Intending to write you a letter on your birthday, I seem to be in Nikolay Vasil'evich's plight.

For you—my dear teacher—my feelings are such that to express them on paper, any pen would seem feeble and dead.

How can I tell you how much I love you?

How can I tell you how great is the gratitude I owe you for everything you have taught me in that ever so difficult matter that is the art of the director?

If I possess the strength to overcome all the difficulties put in my way by the events of the last few months, I shall come to you and you will read in my eyes my joy that you have recovered from your illness, that you are hale and hearty once more, that you are once again setting to work for the benefit of our great homeland. [...]

———————

AT THE STANISLAVSKY OPERA THEATER, after Stanislavsky's death, Meyerhold took charge of the final rehearsals for *Rigoletto,* which opened on March 10, 1939. He was planning a move to the Pushkin Theater in Leningrad, heartened by certain changes in Party policy, including the replacement of Ezhov by Beria as people's commissar for internal affairs. The prominent proletarian writer Aleksandr Aleksandrovich Fadeev (actually Bulyga, 1901–56), as a member of the Central

Committee of the Communist Party, exercised great influence over Soviet literature. He was calling for greater freedom for artists and cited Meyerhold in particular. (After the war, as general secretary of the Writer's Union from 1946 to 1955, he championed Zhdanov's policy of socialist realism and committed suicide during Khrushchëv's de-Stalinization campaign.)

> Aleksandr Fadeev, final speech at the meeting of the Presidium of the Writer's Union, April 1939. In M. P. Kotovskaya and S. A. Isaev, eds., *Mir iskusstv: almanakh* [The world of art: An almanac] (Moscow: Gos. Institut teatral'nogo iskusstva, 1991), 414.

Meyerhold is an outstanding artist who carries on with his work in the Soviet theater. His work must not be covered up. We need to form a clear attitude as to what he is doing and what he has done in the past, frankly criticizing what is incorrect and wrong but acknowledging what is progressive and capable of enriching the Soviet theater.

FOR THIS, Fadeev was privately rebuked by Stalin, who announced his intention of arresting Meyerhold as a foreign agent. At the first All-Union Conference of Theater Directors, convened in Moscow on June 13, 1939, Meyerhold was not on the program. When he was called on to speak, he responded with a sorry display of self-incrimination, disowning his past masterpieces and lauding Dovzhenko's film *Shchors* at the model for a new heroic, patriotic drama.

> Meyerhold's speech at the first All-Union Conference of Theater Directors, Moscow, June 15, 1939.[83] From the stenographic transcripts, Kotovskaya and Isaev, *Mir iskusstv,* 441–50.

We are here, comrades, so that, having discovered the root of the errors made by formalists and naturalists, we can tell the people, the government, and the Party time and again how we can keep from committing these errors in future. [...] Knowing you very well—there are among you many of my friends and students—I must tell you [...] we errant artists, artists who have made more than a little trouble for that remarkable unity in which form and content are indivisible, we errant artists were concerned with the honing of form, much admired form, at the expense of content which we drove into

83 Although brief quotations from Meyerhold's speech were printed in *Vechernaya Moskva* (June 16, 1939), his disappearance and obliteration made the speech the stuff of legend. A brief, relatively accurate summary appeared in Alexander Kaun's *Soviet Poets and Poetry* (Los Angeles, n.p., 1943), but Yury Elagin, in his *Tëmny geny: Vsevolod Meyerkhol'd* (New York: Izd-vo imeni Chekhova, 1955), published a spurious version that was defiant, not to say heroic. It was reprinted in English in Nikolay A. Gorchakov's *The Theater in Soviet Russia,* trans. Edgar Lehrman (New York: Columbia University Press, 1957). Extracts of Meyerhold's actual speech appeared in the journal *Teatr* in 1974, but only with the publication of the full stenographic transcript in 1991 was the extent of Meyerhold's capitulation made clear to the world at large.

the shadows . . . But see what happened? We, comrades—myself, and Shostakovich, and Sergey Eisenstein—are allowed every opportunity to go on working and correct our errors by labor alone (*applause*). Comrades, tell me—where, in what other country on the globe are such things possible?

[. . .] Constructivism? What is it? On one hand, we can, of course, defend certain innovations that developed in the period of constructivism—well, say, the actor was liberated, he wanted to appear without makeup, he wanted to come onstage unencumbered by a stylized costume, well, in our classes this goes on all the time. But we wanted to foist this onto the new spectator, to impose it as a kind of problem that, you see, was intended to eliminate the whole array of theatrical collectives that were moving in other directions.

[. . .] The experiments I carried out on *The Forest* and *The Inspector General* should not have been shown to a general public, but only to a narrow circle of actors, directors, etc. But what happened? *The Forest* and *The Inspector General* were succeeded by the Vakhtangov Theater *Hamlet,* and if we hadn't been stopped in time, the devil knows how badly we might have mutilated the classics (*applause*).

Hard as it is for me subjectively to lose my theater, I must consider the decision to close it made by the Party and our government to be correct (*applause*). I think, comrades, that it is a lesson—a good lesson for all those today who would like to smuggle in an insidious formalism, and I can say with certainty that not everyone is yet cured of this disease. I can reel off a whole list of names of directors, a whole list of productions in which insidious formalism is still being smuggled.

[. . .] Comrade Stalin's remark that we must learn to live like Lenin is especially necessary to us the workers in the realm of theater. [. . .] So, comrades, when we talk about socialist realism in our creative work, let us bear in mind that this is possible only on the certain condition that our worldview has a firm foundation, for if our worldview does not, then there can be no such work. Hence a grasp of the bases of Marxism–Leninsim seems to be utterly indispensable. [. . .]

Golubovsky, *Bol'shie malen'kie teatry,* 48–49.

Everyone was waiting for the Master's appearance. Meyerhold, contrary to his tradition of being always elegant and smart, wore no jacket, was in a striped shirt with a loosened necktie. He began his speech—dead silence in the hall, strained attention. In the opinion of many, he didn't know what to say—he was so packed with grief, confusion, and fear. [. . .]

Many of Meyerhold's opinions were received variously by the audience. Some, like, for instance, the Vakhtangov's director B. E. Zakhava, considered that when the Master cited *Princess Turandot* among the formalist productions, it was [. . .] black humor. We the youth, admirers of Vakhtangov's masterpiece, didn't understand how one could say such things. "Is he that scared?" the young director Pavel Syrov, sitting beside me, asked. [. . .] We were staggered by his admission that it was right to close his theater. We wanted to shout, "No! It's wrong!" [. . .] Here and there a faint noise of marginal conversation sounded. It was painful and difficult to hear the Master offer the example that Lenin at a hunt compared the ducks at which they were shooting with the bourgeoisie, the enemies. May the memory of the great Master forgive me—but at that point laughter broke out in the hall, ironic smiles appeared on faces. [...]

At the end of the speech Meyerhold left the auditorium. They had stopped listening to him.

> Chairman Khrapchenko responds to Meyerhold's speech. In Kotovskaya and Isaev, *Mir Iskusstv*, 461. Mikhail Borisovich Khrapchenko (1904–86), chairman of the Committee on Artistic Affairs 1938–48, had been unable to suppress the ovation that had greeted Meyerhold's election to the platform committee or to push a motion to prohibit "all applause, laughter and comments during speeches."

Comrade Meyerhold [...] referred to his errors, but his admission of them was to some extent formal. The Party teaches us that it is not enough merely to confess our errors; we need to demonstrate their nature and their essence so that others may learn from them, above all young people. We need to show them where such errors lead, how they arise, and where their true nature lies, why such errors are harmful and how they can be overcome. He said nothing about the nature of his errors, whereas he should have disclosed the errors that led his theater to become a theater inimical to the Soviet people, a theater that was closed by order of the Party.

> From the collective letter of the Dramatists' Section of the Union of Soviet Writers to I. V. Stalin (unfinished text, no earlier than June 20, no later than June 26, 1939). In *Teatr* 1 (1990), 145.

At the directors' conference the entire house gave Meyerhold an ovation. One must understand the reason for this ovation and remove that reason. What is Com. Khrapchenko doing? He allows Meyerhold to speak, having previously written him a crib—what to say and how to say it, what to cover. Of course, after Meyerhold's poor and helpless speech, this achieves the reverse result. Instead of really unmasking the defects of formalism, the petty-bourgeois rebelliousness and hyperindividualism in Meyerhold receives its justification by these ovations. Moreover, stung by this "wave of applause," M. B. Khrapchenko tries on the third day's session of the conference to forbid applause, laughter, and backtalk at the conference in general. This attempt is made so seriously and urgently that it evoked from the whole house general indignation and demonstrative applause following the speaker. Such "experiments" in the milieu of workers in art can be made only by a man absolutely devoid of a sense of humor! We write about this only because this small fact very clearly hides the bureaucratic, resolution-bearing style of the leadership of the VKI "to conceal," "to forbid," "to delete," "to prescribe."

A WEEK LATER, Meyerhold was arrested, confined in the Lubyanka Prison in Moscow, and tortured into a confession that he later tried to recant. On July 14, Zinaida Raykh was stabbed to death in their Moscow apartment and her eyes gouged out, allegedly by "hooligans."

> Meyerhold from prison to Soviet Premier Molotov,[84] January 2 and 13, 1940.
> In *Sovetskaya kultura* [Soviet culture] (February 16, 1989), 5; reprinted in
> *Teatral'naya zhizn'* 5 (1989), 1–3.

Immediately after my arrest [...] I was plunged into the deepest depression, obsessed by the thought "it serves me right." I began to persuade myself that the government felt that the sins I had committed had not been punished sufficiently (the closure of my theater, the dissolution of my troupe, the sequestration of the new theater I was planning and that was under construction on Mayakovsky Square), and that I should undergo further punishment, which was now being administered through the agency of the NVKD. "It serves me right," I persuaded myself, and that "I" split in two. One began to search for the "crimes" of the other, and when it failed to find them, it began to make them up. In this process my interrogator proved to be an aide of considerable experience, so that together we set about to invent things in close collaboration. [...]

They beat me, an ailing sixty-year-old man. They lay me face down on the floor and beat the soles of my feet and my back with a rubber truncheon. When I was sitting on a chair, they used the same truncheon to beat my legs from above with great force, from my knees to the upper parts of my legs. And the days following, when my legs were bleeding from internal hemorrhages, they used the rubber truncheon to beat me on the red, blue, and yellow bruises. The pain was so great that it was like boiling water being poured on the most tender part of my legs (I screamed and wept with the pain). They beat me on the back with the truncheon; they beat me about the face with blows from above [...]

Lying face down on the floor, I learned how to cringe, writhe, and howl like a dog being whipped by its master. [...] Whenever my imagination dried up, my interrogators would work in tandem [...] and draft statements, sometimes rewriting them three or four times. [...] My interrogator questioned me constantly, "If you refuse to write (meaning 'fabricate'?!) we shall beat you again, leaving your head and right hand untouched, but turning the rest of you into a shapeless bloody pulp of mangled flesh."

[...] I recant the confessions that were beaten out of me in this way, and I implore you as Chief of State to rescue me and return me to my freedom. I love my country and I will serve it with all my strength in the years left to me.

---

84 At this point Molotov's position was second only to Stalin's. He was chairman of the Council of People's Commissars, a post equivalent to prime minister, 1930–40.

> Verdict of the Military Collegium of the USSR, presided over by Judge Virikh and held *in camera,* January 14, 1940. In *Teatral'naya zhizn'* 2 (1990), 33. Virikh sent tens of thousands of innocent people to their deaths throughout the 1930s.

Meyerhold-Raykh, Vsevolod Émil'evich is to suffer the ultimate degree of criminal punishment by firing squad, with confiscation of property. The sentence is final and not open to appeal.

FOLLOWING HIS CONVICTION, Meyerhold was shot in the basement of the Military Collegium on February 2, 1940. Immediately thereafter he became a nonperson, his name expunged from all publications, including a jubilee volume devoted to his production of *Masquerade.* The sentence was quashed on November 26, 1955, thanks to the efforts of Meyerhold's granddaughter Mariya Valentey. He was not publicly rehabilitated until 1958.

Tairov Stumbles

Tairov's newly acquired prestige gave him breathing space to pursue his own interests. Instead of following up the success of *The Optimistic Tragedy* with another patriotic epic, he compiled *Egyptian Nights,* a collage of Pushkin's unfinished romance with scenes from Shaw's *Caesar and Cleopatra* and Shakespeare's *Antony and Cleopatra,* and music by Profok'ev. Even though Tairov professed a Marxist interpretation of history, the production was assailed by negative reviews that complained of its diffuseness and superficiality. He reached the artistic level of *Optimistic Tragedy* again only with an adaptation of *Madame Bovary* in 1939. It has to be said that he was hardly helped by the prevailing school of criticism that considered him the last Mohican of bourgeois estheticism, not hesitating to launch against him unjustified political accusations.

> Aleksandr Tairov, "The Kamerny Theater," International Workers' Theatre Olympiad Bulletin no. 3, International Union of the Revolutionary Theatre, Moscow, 1933, 55–56.

In molding our stage models we were guided by the following principles:

a. The three dimensions of the scenic box were made to correspond organically to the cubic measurements of the actor.

b. For each new play we constructed a new stage that corresponded to the dynamic, rhythmical, and plastic structure of the play and that served as a sort of *claviature* for the development of the actor's action.

c. Expediency in the utilization and apportionment of the floor space of the stage, not only horizontally but also vertically.

d. To light and music in the theater we assigned a new functional role. We strove to give each of our new performances its particular rhythmical base.

e. The costumes were conditioned by the structure of the movement of the actor in question, emphasizing the basic aspects of this movement. Also, where necessary, the costume gave the actor an auxiliary outlet for his histrionic ability. [...]

Our presentations, each within its own special realm, whether in tragedy or in eccentrics, strive to solve the problem of dynamic realism, in which content and form ought to be synthetically united by the social feeling and artistic style of our epoch.

ONE OF THE OFFICIAL TENETS of Soviet culture was *narodnost'*. To be accessible to the masses and to inspire them with loyalty to the nation, art had to be imbued with folk traditions, popular customs, and patriotic sentiments. The converse was a distrust of "Western-bourgeois" culture.

Condemnation was showered on *Paladins* (*Bogatyry*) by Dem'yan Bedny,[85] because it was a satirical treatment of the tenth-century conversion of Russia to Christianity. This had already been the subject of a successful revue at the Satire Theater, but now such treatment was seen as an offense to the resurgent national-ism glorifying the nation. Tairov reacted to the committee's decision to remove *Paladins* with a heart attack. Artists came to his home to express their condolences as if to a wake. Bedny, utterly dumbfounded, stayed at home for three days, and then summoned Party secretary Viktor Stavsky for a confidential discussion. It was clear that Bedny, preferring not to deal with Stalin in person, wanted to use Stavsky to transmit his explanations and justifications. Stavsky took along a stenographer to record his remarks, which thoroughly confused Bedny.

Inquiry of the Secret–Political Section of GUGB NKVD SSSR, "On the re-sponses of men of letters and art works on the removal from the repertoire of D. Bedny's play *Paladins*," no later than November 16, 1936. In Svetlana Sboeva, *Tairov. Evropa i Amerika 1923–1930* [Tairov: Europe and America, 1923–1930] (Moscow: Artist-Rezhissër-Teatr, 2010), 517–28.

A. TAIROV: I confess I made a great mistake. I take all the responsibility on myself, even despite the fact that the Committee for Artistic Affairs, which accepted the production, approved it. My mistake consists in that I, as an artist, should have foreseen all the consequences. It is offensive that my mistake is taken to be a provocation [*vylazka*] as some have written. The mistake came about because I put great faith in Dem'yan Bedny as an old Communist. I could no more think that D. Bedny's script might harbor a pernicious tendency than I could be a commissar under D. Bedny. Such mistakes did not occur in *The Optimistic Tragedy* and in *Homeland*,[86] whose authors were less authoritative, and I exposed their plays to

---

85 Dem'yan Bedny (actually Efim Alekseevich Pridvorov, 1883–1945), the most popular proletarian poet after Mayakovsky, journalist, author of scenarios and librettos.

86 *Rodina* (1935) by B. M. Levin.

the criticism of responsible workers. I will go to the TsK VKP(b), where, I hope, they will understand me. There I will put the question about showing new plays not only to the committee but to the TsK. This is necessary as a guarantee. What really frightens me is whether they will allow me to go on working. What upsets me is this desire to exhibit me as a renegade of the people. It is so horrible that I cannot even think about it calmly.

A. KOONEN: This is a lesson for Tairov. You cannot count on his strength. Otherwise it wouldn't matter so much to us.

TSENIN, meritorious artist of the Kamerny Theater:[87] So long as the monarchy in our theater continues, so long as all questions are decided exclusively by Tairov, without considering the leading workers in the theater, so long will the theater pursue political fiascos. [...]

DEM'YAN BEDNY: The farcical tone of the subject and the treatment of *Paladins* are to be explained by the nature of the music; so, for instance, the "paladins" sing arias from popular operettas. The farcical showing of the Christianizing of Russia and its erroneous interpretation are explained by the customary antireligious propaganda to which Dem'yan Bedny's practice tends. On the other hand, he'd been stuck with work on historical questions that have a far from Marxist character.

Dem'yan Bedny, admitting that he has made a huge mistake, explains it by his misunderstanding the material and his stupidity. However, in conversation, he repeatedly returned to the role of the inspecting agencies, that at the very start of the work on *Paladins* a year and a half ago the original text had not satisfied him, struck him as frivolous and stupid, but Tairov and Litovsky encouraged him, asserting that the text would turn out brilliant as a stage piece. [...]

STANISLAVSKY, People's Artist of the USSR: Bolsheviks are geniuses. Whatever the Kamerny Theater does is not art. It is formalism. It is a narrowly pragmatic theater, it is Koonen's theater.

LEONIDOV, People's Artist of the USSR: When I read the committee's decision, I got in bed and put my feet up. I couldn't get over my excitement: the lusty way they lit into Litovsky, Tairov, Dem'yan Bedny. A more ghastly bunch than the MAT 2. [...]

MEYERHOLD, People's Artist of the USSR: Finally they smote Tairov because he deserved it. If I were to draw up a list of plays at Tairov's to be prohibited, *Paladins* would be the pearl. And Dem'yan needs it too. But the main thing is that the committee and Boyarsky[88] are personally to blame. He is exterminating me. So long as the committee is in charge, art cannot develop.

NATALIYA SATS, meritorious artist of the Republic, artistic director of the Central Children's Theater: Tairov made mistakes. He used unfinished music by Borodin. Dem'yan Bedny shouldn't have been commissioned because he is a bad playwright.

---

87 Sergey Sergeevich Tsenin (1884–1964), after time in the provinces, acted with the Kamerny Theater 1914–16 and 1919–49, toured abroad with the theater three times.

88 Yakov Osipovich Boyarsky (actually Shimshelevich, 1890–1940), chairman of the Central Committee of RABIS 1929–35; deputy chairman of the Committee for Artistic Affairs 1936; administrator of the MAT 1937–39. Repressed 1939, rehabilitated posthumously.

The invitations to Palëkh painters to be the designers is playing with form without the possibility of correcting its content. The theater can have nothing to say to the spectator. [...]

TRENëV, playwright, author of *Lyubov' Yarovaya*: I am delighted by the decision. I am proud of it as a Russian. You cannot spit in our faces. I myself could not go to the performance but sent my wife and daughter. They did not sit through it but left and were thoroughly disgusted. A pile of muck this big makes an impression. [...]

VSEVOLOD VISHNEVSKY, playwright: It serves Dem'yan right, he shouldn't be doing hackwork [*khalturit'*]. It's the lesson of history: "don't stir us up." History will still come in handy, and soon enough. They're already preparing the opera *Minin and Pozharsky—Rescue from Intervention*.[89] [...]

L. TRAUBERG, film director: The Soviet government is becoming ever more national and even nationalistic. By dint of this, completely unexpected things find themselves defended by the Party leadership. It becomes all the more difficult to work when leading individuals—members of both the Glavrepertkom and the Committee for Artistic Affairs—cannot accurately decide the meaning of plays, which they go and remove after they have accepted them. [...]

YU. OLESHA, writer: The play does not play the leading role here. Dem'yan was the one, Dem'yan got punched in the snoot. Him today, tomorrow someone else. There's no special reason to rejoice. Dem'yan's being paid off for his former sins.

OL'GA FORSH:[90] Can't a writer be of two minds? It's wonderful, remarkable, that they taught Dem'yan a lesson. Only now, if you please, it's become hard for those of us who write plays. Litovsky, they say, has quite lost his head, is unsure of anything. Even without that, the members of the Glavrepertkom are forcing me to cross out and correct my play about Kamo.[91] [...]

EISENSTEIN, meritorious art worker and film director: I didn't see the production, but all the same I'm extremely pleased that they have given Dem'yan a sound drubbing. He needed it, he's been putting on airs. It's also good that they gave it to that lickspittle Litovsky, who took a tumble with his rave notice. In all this business one question interests me: where were they earlier, when a counterrevolutionary play was allowed onstage? [...]

SIMONOV, Vakhtangov Theater, meritorious artist: The committee's decision is correct. Tairov's theater is hanging by a thread. It would have been closed long ago, were it not for Litvinov,[92] who protected it. [...]

89 This didn't prevent Vishnevsky from paying a condolence call on Tairov.

90 Ol'ga Dmitrievna Forsh (1873–1961), novelist, playwright, screenwriter, often wrote about the events of the Revolution.

91 Kamo (actually Semeno Aržahovitš Ter-Petrossian, 1882–1922), Georgian-Armenian revolutionary Bolshevik, an early comrade of Stalin; took part in the Tiflis bank robbery of 1907.

92 Maksim Maksimovich Litvinov (actually Meir-Khenokh Movshevich Vallakh, 1876–1951), Bolshevik, Soviet statesman, and diplomat; deputy narkom for foreign affairs 1921–30; narkom for foreign affairs 1930–39; deputy narkom for foreign affairs 1941–46; ambassador to United States 1941–43; died in an automobile accident.

GORCHAKOV, director, meritorious artist of the USSR: This play is mere verbiage. Nothing interesting about it. The decision is a correct one. [...]

OKHLOPKOV, artistic director of the Realistic Theater: Now we have to be on our guard. This is a sign. Plays have to be given to the collective to read. We must be careful in our relation to the repertoire. For our fellows this is a great lesson. [...]

LITOVSKY, chairman of Glavrepertkom: I will not appear at a non-Party conference. At the conference of the members of the Party I will say that Litovsky is not alone to blame, but also the committee: Kerzhentsev, Boyarsky, as well as Gorodinsky,[93] who all accepted the production.

M. BULGAKOV, author of *Days of the Turbins*: This is the rare instance, when Dem'yan, despite his personality, will not gloat: this time he himself has fallen victim—and can't chortle over others. Now let him feel what it's like himself.

AFTER THE PRESS ATTACK on *The Paladins* in November 1936, an indignant Mikhoéls organized a debate in which he defended Tairov's work and demanded that the critics of Tairov include him in their criticism. His chivalrous remarks were completely distorted in the reportage the next day.

> Pravda 323 (November 24, 1936). Quoted in Natalia Vovsi-Mikhoéls, *Mon père Salomon Mikhoëls. Souvenirs sur sa vie et sur sa mort*, trans. Erwin Spatz (Montricher, Switzerland: Les Éditions noir sur blanc, 1990), 61–63.

On November 23 a meeting of theatrical workers and actors took place dedicated to the play *The Paladins*, staged at the Kamerny Theater under the artistic direction of Tairov.

People's artist Mikhoéls asked the following question: why has this theater fallen so far? Comrade Mikhoéls answered that criticism has not played its vigilant and educational role and that the actors had no team spirit.

If we add to that an intellectual impasse and a relapse from the discipline familiar to Tairov, unacceptable relations between the actors and the director, the absence of the least self-criticism, all added to vanity and vulgar ambition, the reasons for the failure of Tairov and the Kamerny Theater become patent.

Speaking in his turn, Tairov expressed his regrets.

Okhlopkov Survives

Nikolay Okhlopkov was the first outstanding Soviet director to have formed his entire career after the Revolution. A Siberian provincial inspired by a Mayakovsky

---

93 Kerzhentsev published an article "Falsification of the People's Past: About *Paladins* by Dem'yan Bedny" in *Pravda* (November 15, 1936). Viktor Makovich Gorodinsky (1902–59), conductor of the Moscow Philharmonic 1934–35, assistant leader arts sector of Kul'tprosvetotdel TsK VKP(b) 1935–37; member of the editorial board of *Komsomolskaya Pravda* 1936–37; editor of *Muzyka, Sovetskoe Iskusstvo* 1937–40.

reading to take up theater, he gained most of his training under Meyerhold and by acting in many of his productions. In 1931 he was appointed chief director at the Theater on Krasnaya Presnaya (formerly the MAT Fourth Studio); it reverted to an earlier name, the Realistic Theater, in 1934. He hoped to make it a "theater of great passion and experimentation" by applying original uses of space and Eisensteinian montage to achieve intimacy between actor and audience. At a time when the school of Meyerhold was in disgrace, Okhlopkov was the most inventive innovator of this period. Drawing on some of the same theatrical traditions as Meyerhold, he sought to render the spectator "active." To do that, he suppressed the "box set" and dispersed the action throughout the spectators so as to mingle stage and auditorium. A large part of his repertoire was confected from adapted novels.

Golubovsky, *Bol'shie malen'kie teatry,* 177.

Okhlopkov's name as an innovative director first echoed throughout all Moscow at the Realistic Theater in 1932. It was his first theatrical love. So what if the building was absurdly small. (It didn't even satisfy Sergey Obraztsov,[94] who accepted the building for his puppets after the Realistic Theater closed.) But in it theatrical passions seethed, authority was overthrown, new forms were sought, critical lances were crossed, productions sprang up and were trampled down. Okhlopkov was called a naturalist, an eclectic, a formalist, an esthete, a primitive . . . But the spectators increasingly loved this theater. It seemed as if the director had set himself insoluble problems: how to figure out how the *Iron Flood* can flow through here, the whole Cossack village in *Running Start* can be squeezed in? But all this was accomplished, despite the negativity of the critics, the distrust of the authorities. A theater cannot exist without failures, flops, mediocrity. Okhlopkov had them too. Nevertheless I more than once heard from Nikolay Pavlovich nostalgic reminiscences about the difficult but happy days of his theatrical youth, the boisterous, brimming hopes.

RUNNING START (*Razbeg*), V. P. Stavsky's play about class war in a village during the process of collectivization, opened on March 30, 1932. Inspired by a mass action he had staged in Irkutsk as his first theatrical effort, Okhlopkov bent every effort to bring the spectators into the action. Yakov Shtoffer's[95] "environmental design" fragmented the stage and flooded it with light and color. While it granted the "revolutionary" nature of the concept, Okhlopkov was severely attacked by the critical establishment for abandoning ideological realism in favor of entertainment and theatricality.

94 Sergey Vladimirovich Obraztsov (1901–92), puppeteer, who headed the Central Puppet Theater from 1931, specializing in musical numbers.
95 Yakov Zinov'evich Shtoffer (1906–51) designed at the Realistic Theater 1932–34, and then produced work for many major Moscow theaters.

Nikolay Okhlopkov, "Ob uslovnosti" [On stylization] (1959), in Nikolay Okhlopkov, *Vsem molodym* (Moscow: Molodaya Gvardiya, 1981), 71.

When I staged a "mass action" on an open town square in 1921, there was nothing in
the stage space other than individual stage pieces. There was no scenery. It would have
been impossible to hang it in any case—overhead there was only the sky. No wings.
There would have been no way to lean them against and nail them to a wall—in fact,
there were no walls. On the square, on every side, there were thousands of spectators.
But I will never forget how these thousands of spectators, as if at the beck of a sorcerer's
magic wand, began to believe in everything that took place onstage, began to see those
places of action, which were barely hinted at by the details and stage pieces. This miracle,
performed by the spectacle, was consummated with the help of ancient, primordial
power of the theater—a power tested by the centuries and called imagination! [...]

> Okhlopkov remembers *Running Start*. From *Hamlet* rehearsal notes, October
> 3, 1945.

Once I was summoned by RAPP. *Running Start* was debated for three days. Averbakh[96]
was a speaker who loudly announced to a large meeting for writers, directors, and
actors that he, and with him all proletarian art, ends with Okhlopkov. Back then we
didn't know that he was an enemy of the people. On the contrary, we knew that he had
a lot of authority in the world of writers, that he spoke as an official representative of a
huge organization. Only Vsevolod Vishnevsky defended me during this discussion, and
Stavsky, who was confused, said something that was not very clear or comprehensible.
Only Vishnevsky actively fought for me. The debate lasted three nights. When I came
to the theater I burst into tears. It was bitter and painful for me, because this was the
first play about a kolkhoz. Later on the Vakhtangov and Lyubimov-Lanskoy theaters
started to stage plays about kolkhozes. My play was the first one, and the audience
greeted it enthusiastically. No matter what kind of mistakes I made in the play, I was
deeply hurt by the feeling that I was done for, that people thought I had committed a
base or evil deed. I was sobbing. My tears were not yet dry, when I banged my fist on
the table and said, "Wait, I will prove to you once again, I will struggle all the same,
and I will work no matter what. But I am not a Titan. I am an ordinary man, and I do
not possess the spiritual depth and richness of a Hamlet."

AFTER A DRAMATIZATION of Gorky's *Mother* that also broke the stage frame, in
1933 Okhlopkov staged another adapted novel, *The Iron Flood* by A. Serafimovich,[97]

96 Leopol'd Leonidovich Averbakh (1903–37), literary critic, general secretary of RAPP 1928–32.
   Liquidated.
97 Aleksandr Serafimovich (actually Aleksandr Serafimovich Popov, 1863–1949), writer of Cossack
   ancestry, whose fiction deals with peasant life; his best novel *The Iron Flood* (*Zhelëzny Potop*, 1924)
   concerns the inhabitants of a Red village battling Whites to get to their allies during the Civil War.

about the 1918 anabasis of the Taman army and its followers to meet up with the Red Army.

Van Gyseghem, Theatre in Soviet Russia, 190–91.

Babel. A theater more full of sound than was the crowded foyer. Women shrilling across to one another—babies crying—men shouting orders—lovers quarreling—a group of men singing to a harmonica. The savory smell of cooking assails our nostrils as we stagger dazedly into the hubbub, looking for our seats. Seats, did I say? We can't see any seats—anyway, they're looking the wrong way, surely?—pardon, madame, was that your child I stepped on? There are some seats—but a rocky promontory has first to be navigated; we dodge under the muzzle of a gun that is being cleaned by a young man singing lustily as he polishes, only to find our heads entangled, as we come up, with a mass of washing hanging out to dry. [. . .] Perspiring and muttering our apologies to an inattentive ear, we pass on, see a seat number—no, ours is the next group. Here we are—careful—mind that loving couple at our feet—if you would just move your dress a little—thank you—gosh, that's a pretty girl, did you see?—yes, yes, all right, I'm coming! We throw ourselves into what we hope are our seats, first taking care to remove the frying pan left there for a moment by the young man attending the campfire at our side. [. . .] The clamor dies down and lines of dialogue begin to emerge that are obviously part of a text and not extemporary. The bald, general lighting fades and spotlights pick out the costumed actors. The play begins—or, should I say, continues at the point interrupted by our entrance?

There is no proscenium stage—in fact, no stage at all as we know it. The whole of one side of this rectangular-shaped auditorium has been built up into a bank, rising to above five feet at its highest point. It is rocky, uneven, a sort of semimountainous terrain, and long tongues of it jut right out into the center of the hall and curl round at the ends. In between these jutting tongues the audience sits. The wall behind the rocky bank—which is in fact the stage, acting area, call it what you will—is plain sky. There are entrances at either end of the hall. [. . .]

> Boris Shumyatsky to Comrade Énukidze, Secretary of TsIK, August 22, 1934. Boris Zakharovich Shumyatsky (1886–1943), official of the Chief Directorate of the Film Industry 1930–37, was in 1936 deputy chairman of the Committee for Artistic Affairs. Avel' Sofronovich Énukidze (1877–1937), an "Old Bolshevik," was to be expelled from the Party in 1935 for suggesting that Stalin step down; he was arrested and shot in 1937.

Dear Avel' Sofronovich:

Commissioned by the Politkatorzhans' [political prisoners'] Society, I am addressing you as the director of the Historical-Revolutionary Theater named after the society, with a request to legalize the unification of the two theaters with a resolution of TsIK, namely, of the State Historical-Revolutionary Theater [GIRT] named after the Politkatorzhans' [political prisoners'] Society and the Realistic Theater, or the so-called Fourth MAT Studio.

I venture to provide a few reasons to support such an amalgamation:

1. The subject matter of these two theaters is historical–revolutionary in its essence. For instance, the special task of GIRT is to show the revolutionary struggle in artistic plays, and several plays which have already been staged by GIRT as well as the whole plan for future productions are based exclusively on historical–revolutionary themes.

As for the Realistic Theater, such plays as *The Iron Flood,* Gorky's *Mother,* and *Running Start* are undoubtedly plays that deal with the historical–revolutionary theme.

2. Until now, GIRT has been going through the early stages of organization in the sense of staffing the theater with both an artistic team and artistic and administrative management. Lately it has undergone a crisis in directing because of the absence of an artistic vision in the acting troupe. At the same time, owing to the talented artistic leadership of the Realistic Theater by Comrade Okhlopkov, all these defects can easily be corrected.

In this regard, I inform you that Comrade Okhlopkov was the first one to express his opinion about the need to unite these two theaters. According to our common opinion in this case, without disrupting our artistic plans and achievements, we will be able to manage a single, very good, serious theater.

3. The Realistic Theater does not have the space needed to produce serious plays, especially if they require crowd scenes. It is true there are proposals to give even the Realistic Theater the Manege Building, but this is a vast prospect. At the same time the Politkatorzhans' Society has almost finished constructing a building for the GIRT, which undoubtedly will be a valuable improvement in the realm of stage equipment. Like other theater directors, Okhlopkov refers to our building in the most positive terms. And finally

4. The government provides significant subsidies to both the GIRT and the Realistic Theater. At the same time, if these two theaters are united, there is reason to suppose that the subsidy will not be needed. In any case, a huge savings will be achieved.

That is why, as a director, I would like to ask you to legalize this case with the appropriate resolution. This is necessary because, as the Soviets see it, the Historical-Revolutionary Theater is under the Narkompros, while the Realistic Theater is under the UMZP. It is clear that, despite all our wishes, some disputes may arise. Nevertheless they can be easily resolved, if only you will write "Agreed" on this declaration.

With Communist regards:
Shumyatsky

[The request was turned down.]

––––––––––––––

NIKOLAY POGODIN'S *ARISTOCRATS* (1935) concerns the construction of the White Sea–Baltic Canal by political prisoners and ordinary criminals under the watchful eye of the GPU; this experiment in forced labor was propagandized as an effective method for turning outlaws into useful Soviet citizens, a proper topic for socialist realism. On the page, Pogodin's play is, in Ernest Simmons's words, "amiably dull," no *Beggar's Opera* of the Gulag. It was Okhlopkov's ingenious production that made it a major hit of this period.

> The Union of Soviet Writers of the USSR to the Editorial Board of *Izvestia,*
> October 28, 1934.

The Playwrights' Section of the Union of Soviet Writers invites your representative to attend the reading and discussion of Comrade N. F. Pogodin's new play *Aristocrats.*

The reading of the play will take place on October 31, 1934, at 7:00 p.m. in the Large Hall of the House of Soviet Writers.

At the same time we request that an announcement of the upcoming reading be made in the next issue of your newspaper in the CHRONICLE section.

Secretary: *Kashinsteva.*[98]

> Nikolay Okhlopkov, "*Aristocrats* at the Realistic Theater," *Rabochaya Moskva*
> (November 3, 1934).

We believe that the Soviet theater should master the traditions and methods of festive popular folk theater.

In this light N. Pogodin's new comedy *Aristocrats* represents a priceless play for us. Its goal is to move contemporary spectators with its intelligent and deep joy. This is a play about the transformation of people who are "lost to society" and "incorrigible"— bandits, thieves, and prostitutes. The contemporary spectator, a participant in socialist construction, a living witness to huge historical victories achieved by the working class under the leadership of the Party of Lenin and Stalin, has the right to demand of the theater a play in which it is possible to laugh the victors' laugh of energetic joy. And if we are able to educe such laughter from the audience with the play *Aristocrats,* then we will consider that we have achieved the artistic task that has been placed before us.

> Nikolay Okhlopkov, "The carnival play: N. Pogodin's *Aristocrats* at the Realistic
> Theater," *Izvestia* (January 16, 1935).

In our play we are making an attempt to create special conditions of an actor's "life onstage" to achieve the fullest ideological and artistic revelation of the dramatic work, and to arm the theater with the strongest and, in our opinion, the deepest and most theatrical methods.

The production has to resolve another problem—the problem of creating, in a draft version so far, a carnival play. Themes such as the rescue of the crew of the *Chelyuskin* by our brave pilots,[99] the construction of the Moscow subway, the Taantsy's glorious iron

---

98 Mariya Aleksandrovna Kashintseva (1903–83), wife of the writer Andrey Platonov.
99 In 1933 the SS *Chelyuskin,* a steamship attempting to break a maritime route through polar ice,

6.4. The women's barracks scene in *Aristocrats* by Nikolay Pogodin, directed by Nikolay Okhlop-kov and designed by Ya. Shtoffer, Realistic Dramatic Theater, Moscow, 1935.

march during the Civil War, the theme of workers' growing revolutionary consciousness that Gorky brilliantly reflects in his *Mother,* the construction of the Belomor–Baltic Canal named for Stalin or the construction of the Volga–Moscow canal, etc., can and must be developed by theaters not only on a small scale but also because of their grandiosity, on the scale of carnival performances for tens of thousands of spectators with thousands of participants.

[...] We conduct experiments in this field as theatrical "drafts for production." But even on this scale we hope to excite in our spectators the joyous and proud passion of a participant and a witness of the huge historical victories of the Party and working class in the transformation of the people's consciousness.

Yu. Yuzovsky, "A festive play: *Aristocrats* at the Realistic Theater," *Literaturnaya Gazeta* (February 2, 1935).

A gong is struck. A light goes off and instantly goes back on. A dozen figures in light blue tights scatter across the stage. Without giving the audience a chance to recover its senses, they start throwing clouds of white confetti at the audience and at each other. The music is a snowstorm. There are thousands of small white dots in the air. The

became crushed by ice floes; its crew built a primitive runway with a few crude tools. The pilots who rescued them were honored as the first Heroes of the USSR.

figures appear more and more possessed. The same is happening with the music. It is impossible to see a thing through the dense flashing of the little dots. A blizzard. It abates. We look around. The whole auditorium is covered in snow.

One spectator has two little dots stuck to his eyelashes. He can imagine that they are snowflakes and so they even start melting. And when several figures pressed against each other appear onstage caught in the blizzard, the spectator can honestly believe that they are cold. That this is the North. That it is the wild region between the White and Baltic seas. That these are exiles who have come here to build a canal. Such is the concept of the play.

A gong. A female skier. She stands on a piece of carpet that is thick and white as snow: ski boots, skis, a sports outfit, and a curl falling from under her hat. The young woman shuffles her skis in place while the same light blue figures run past her. Bending over, one carries a branch of a fir tree past her, a second one a pine branch, a third one, touching her hat, and a fourth, a fifth and more, more, faster and faster . . . You end up seeing a huge northern forest before your eyes and an athletic young woman running through the forest into the wind.

Applause. The spectator is grateful not only for a poetic picture. He is grateful that he, so to say, has taken part in this skiing. That he is not only an observer but also in some sense a participant.

A gong. Two Chekists. An old one and a young one. The old one is rebuking the young one for some sort of misconduct. His voice is strict, official and steely. "Yes, sir," the young one answers abruptly while turning around on his heel. In a fatherly way the old man grabs the young man's belt from behind and says in a quiet, friendly tone of voice, "Come and see me tomorrow, we'll talk." That is all. The spectator is filled with associations. An entire life is presented in a single moment. A picture of the Chekists' life at the canal, with iron discipline and warm friendship.

Here, as well as in many other scenes, the spectator takes aesthetic satisfaction in the working of his imagination, the fledging of wings for the flight of his own fantasy, not only his emotional but also intellectual enjoyment. The spectator catches the hint thrown to him by the theater to develop it into a picture, aglow with brilliant colors. This is theater. This is real theater. [. . .]

Okhlopkov does not stand in place. And he gets restless when the protagonist is afraid to stick his head out of the room lest, Heaven forbid, he should catch cold. He is attracted to broad epic canvases. Epic, that is popular folk, that is those where a picture of humanity which is conquering or creating life is presented. There, losing his mind but loyal to the idea that inspires him, he throws himself into such seemingly unencompassable epics as Serafimovich's *Iron Flood* or Stavsky's *Running Start*. He is constantly drowning in this flood, constantly, so to speak, taking only running starts but not reaching his cherished goal. He realizes this and every time persistently declares the following about his productions: "This is not a performance, but just sketches for a performance, just simple practice versions of a theatrical show I dream about." But in each such practice you see the enormous thirst to give expression to the modern epoch.

[...] In *Iron Flood*, the actor was often buried in the mise-en-scène. But, because the actor suffered, the director also suffered. [...] How strongly, simply, courageously, lovingly the Chekists are portrayed—the young one played by Abrikosov and the old one by Novikov.[100] Here the strange theory that the vitality of the positive hero is created by his inadequacies meets with disaster. [...] Varvara Belen'kaya[101] plays the bandit Son'ka. She gives the character a wonderful feminine soul, but broken and crippled, suffering from this contradiction, but hiding it from other people's eyes, and therefore always exaggeratedly proud, independent, conceited... [...] A strange feeling grasps you when you see the performance, surrounded on all sides by spectators. As if for the first time you are really gripped by the essence of the theater. [...] Perhaps this architecture of the stage is questionable. But what is unquestionable in this play is that this is a real theatricality bursting with health.

[...] The theatricality in this play is not just a tendency to provide a smart and effective show, and not a tendency to the grotesque at all costs. This is an attempt to express theatrically the real essence of facts, events, people, to express it positively. This type of theatricality is fruitful. That is why an Okhlopkov play is a celebration.

ALTHOUGH it was the hit of the season, *Aristocrats* came under the usual critical fire, this time for romanticizing criminals, but in the public debate Okhlopkov defended his work so fervidly that the press began to publish ecstatic raves. Even so, "whither Okhlopkov?" became a concern for the ideologues.

> Iogann Al'tman, "A victory of drama and theater," *Izvestia* 26 (January 1, 1935). Iogann L'vovich Al'tman (1900–1955), theater critic, editor of *Sovetskoe Iskusstvo* 1936–38 and *Teatr* 1937–41, was a prolific writer on dramatic theory. After 1947 he was repressed during the attack on "cosmopolitans."

Okhlopkov does not need wings-and-borders onstage, a curtain or footlights. His actors need barely any makeup. But more than anyone, they do need a knowledge of life. And so a "pseudo-correct" directing style. "Closer to life" is accepted by the theater as a call to naturalism. On the stage everything happens "as in life." A child's bodily functions. Young people kiss each other as nightingales sing. People fall bloodied and carry off the corpses of their nearest and dearest. People are desperate, unite, take mountains by storm, are victorious. A tin mug, a metal can, sheepskin coat, boots, pillows, blankets, yoke and carriage—everything is dumped onto the stage. The only thing missing is live horses.

The naturalism of *The Iron Flood* consists also in the interpretation of the artistic

---

100 Andrey L'vovich Abrikosov (1906–73), acted in many companies, including the Realistic, before joining the Vakhtangov Theater 1938; distinguished by his laconic simplicity. Vasily Konstantinovich Novikov (1891–1956), acted at the MAT 1924–55.

101 Varvara Vasil'evna Belen'kaya (actually Belyakova, 1902–?); after provincial work acted at the Realistic Theater 1934–37, the Kamerny to 1950, and the Pushkin to 1962.

images. Anguished hysterical crises often are substituted for people's internal tension, and rollicking reckless shouts substituted for the joy of collective victory. This reduced the enormous internal epic passion onstage.

But, despite these mistakes and failures, *The Iron Flood* was a victory for the theater. First, mass theatrical action was reborn, the possibility of such a production was proven using specific material that was not, actually, drama. Second, the possibility of creating a new style of acting was proven, where "theatricalization" moves into the background. Third, the unsatisfactory condition of contemporary drama, which does not give the theater the opportunity to develop, was announced.

It is as if the theater said: Here are three productions, and they are all made out of literary prose reworked for the theater. Here are three productions, and all of them say that we need witty and complicated material about life. Here are three productions, and all of them say that the curtain, footlights, and other such things are not necessarily required, and sometimes even interfere. [. . .]

Okhlopkov tries to create a new theater. The destruction of the stage is not the only thing. The stage has been destroyed before, but that did not create a new theater. Okhlopkov is trying to create a theater of mass action, where the drama would depict social conflicts, where comedy would be presented in a carnival procession, in masks, in popular jokes, in the merriment of the masses, where laughter is not quiet and hushed but is provocative and bellicose as during the time of Rabelais. Okhlopkov sees in his contemporary theater a precursor of the future theater of mass action where the stage is a large arena, the audience is huge, the performance occurs amid the spectators, maybe with the participation of the spectators themselves. *Aristocrats* in the Realistic Theater was an expression of these aspirations. And it must be recognized that on the path to this future theater the production of Pogodin's *Aristocrats* was the clearest landmark, a play of great power and significance was created. [. . .] *Aristocrats* is the outstanding play of the current season, an indisputable victory of Soviet drama and theater.

Okhlopkov was unable to follow up this success with equivalent achievements: of the two productions of 1936, *Othello* was regarded as an empty pageant, and *Colas Breugnon*, from Romain Rolland's novel *Jean-Christophe*, a forced effort at merrymaking. Many of Okhlopkov's best actors deserted him. In August 1937 the Realistic Theater was merged with the Kamerny and its building turned over to the puppeteer Sergey Obraztsov. It would have been impossible to find two directors of more incompatible temperament or two theaters of more incongruous aesthetics.

Okhlopkov, "On stylization," 75.

The Realistic Theater had barely been in existence five years, in which my first tryouts of "realistic stylization" took place, when our theater for some reason was "merged" with the Kamerny Theater.

I remember my first conversation with A. Ya. Tairov after the "merger."

"Shall we be friends?" Tairov said with an affectionate smile.

"No, let's be enemies," I replied.

THIS "SHOTGUN WEDDING" was of short duration. In 1938 Okhlopkov and half the Realistic Theater troupe went to the Moscow Theater of Drama for a short period. Okhlopkov was then recruited to join the directing staff at the Vakhtangov.

The Red Army Theater

Overextended in its many performance activities, the Red Army Theater eliminated its cabaret, puppet, and song divisions in 1932. Its first effective director was Yury Zavadsky, who exempted the staff from wearing uniforms and tried to reconcile Vakhtangov's theatricality with socialist realism. In 1935, when he declined to merge his acting studio with the Red Army Theater, he was dismissed and exiled to Rostov. It was his successor Aleksey Popov, the director from 1937 to 1958, and his designer Nisson Shifrin who brought the theater to artistic maturity. Aleksey Dmitrievich Popov (1892–1961) had studied at the MAT and with Vakhtangov and directed at the Vakhtangov Theater from 1923 to 1930 and at the Theater of Revolution from 1931 to 1935. He was a past master at crowd scenes and the dynamics of the Soviet hero.

> Aleksey Popov, Artistic Director of the Central Theater of the Red Army [TsTKA], to Com. F. E. Rodionov, Commander of the Central House of the Red Army [TsDKA], Moscow, May 13, 1937.

By the end of my second year at the theater, I came to realize that I was turning into a clerk who was simply and honestly carrying out his chores. That is not enough for any Soviet job, especially in the theater. My feeling has two major causes.

Despite its excellent acting company, the TsTKA is incapable of achieving its artistic goals on our ghastly concert hall–like stage. We are unable to meet adequately the high standards set for the company by the new building and by its own future in general.

As a director I always have to rein in both my creative imagination and the capabilities of the company when working on this stage. Over the last couple of years our theater had every reason to turn into a profound theatrical institution, and yet it never did so owing to a number of objective reasons.

When the TsTKA, despite unbelievable conditions, managed to put on *The Petty Bourgeoisie* and *The Year '19*[102]—neither production the best we could do, but still quite competitive with the best productions of other Moscow theaters—we were not even

---

102 *Meshchane* (1901), Gorky's first play, about the political inertia of urban Russians, was staged originally by the Moscow Art Theater. *God '19* (1936), by Iosif Leonidovich Prut, was yet another chronicle of the Civil War.

6.5. The star-shaped building of the Central Red Army Theater, Moscow, designed by K. S. Alabyan and V. N. Simbirtsev, 1939.

given an opportunity to show these productions to our narkom and our government, which will soon be making decisions about the future destiny and prospects of our theater.

The theater will need a lot of their help. The theater will need to be advanced by and obliged to these people. What real decision can be taken if the theater's work has not been seen?

Those two reasons cause a lack of perspective and loyalty within the company.

The fact that the date for completing construction has not yet been set and therefore there is no specific work plan for the theater prevents us from working with playwrights, set designers, and the acting company. The work on stage machinery has not yet been started, and by now it is clear to all of us that the building of the stage lags a long way behind general construction.

The ways of employing the new facilities are rather complicated. As practitioners, we are aware of the serious forthcoming fiscal and logistical difficulties. How they are to be resolved will be decisive for the sort of work we do and the acting company we select.

There is a lot of very reliable gossip about an opera troupe to be housed in the new building. The company has ignored this gossip for a long time. However, in the last year, considering the delay in supplying stage machinery not needed by an opera company, combined with the neglect of our work and a complete lack of any specific plans concerning transfer to a new building, the company has of course become demoralized. You can see it yourself, I don't have to go into detail. [...]

THE MASSIVE new theater building, in the shape of a Red Star, was constructed by gulag prisoners. Plans were begun in 1932, but owing to the usual bureaucratic interference, it was not completed until 1938. It sat two thousand spectators and had a giant stage, thirty meters wide by fifteen meters high by sixty meters deep, best suited for epic battle scenes. The company moved in in 1940.

Comrade L. Z. Mekhlis, *In re:* the construction of the Central Theater of the
Red Army, February 16, 1938. Lev Zakharovich Mekhlis (1889–1953), state and
Party official, was narkom of Goskontrol' 1940–50.

In June 1933, TsTKA was presented a plan for the theater designed by the architects
Fridman and Glushchenko. It appears that this design plan had already been examined
by PUR, and it was assumed that the construction would be conducted according to
this plan. Some time later, the head of the TsTKA received an order from PUR to show
this design plan to Lazar' Moiseevich KAGANOVICH,[103] who inspected it in the TsDK
building. After one of his reports of the heads of the political sections of the MTS,
Com. KAGANOVICH did not approve the design; he found it banal and unsuitable to
the spirit of the Red Army.

After this a closed planning competition was organized, in which architects Fridman and Glushchenko, academician of architecture [Ivan Aleksandrovich] Fomin,
and Prof. [Lev Vladimirovich] Rudnev were invited to participate. Architects [Ivan
V.] Zheltovsky, [Aleksey Viktorovich] Shchusev, [Vladimir Alekseevich] Shchuko, and
others refused to participate because of their full workloads.

On examining the projects with the participation of People's Commissar Com.
VOROSHILOV and Com. KAGANOVICH, Prof. Rudnev's design was declared to be
the best. Rudnev was charged with revising his design, adding the changes indicated
during the judging. At the same time, Com. KAGANOVICH and Com. VOROSHILOV
inspected the site planned for the construction.

The cubic capacity of all project designs was limited to 140–80 thousand cubic
meters.

By the year's end, this work was completed and exhibited in the conference hall
of the Narkomat. The inspection of the project by the narkom was participated in by
Com. KAGANOVICH, on whose orders a scale model was displayed there of the new
design of the theater, which is shaped like a star. In view of the fact that a doubt was
expressed as to whether a building of such shape could accommodate a theatrical
facility, it was decided to give the architects, Comrades [Karo Semënovich] Alabyan
[1897–1969] and [Vasily Simbirtsev] Simbirtsev [1901–82], a two-month period to
prepare a working draft of the project. Simultaneously, the same task was given to a
group of architects from the Mossovet studios, such as Comrades Vaynshteyn, Kessler, El'kin, and others. At the final inspection of the projects, which took place at the
TsDKA on February 23, 1934, in the presence of Com. VOROSHILOV, KAGANOVICH,
KHRUSHCHËV, BULGANIN,[104] and others, the draft design made by Comrades Alabyan
and Simbirtsev was accepted for construction. This fact was registered by a document,
a copy of which is attached. After the revision of this design, it was finally presented to

103 Lazar' Moiseevich Kaganovich (1893–1991), secretary of the Central Committee of the Com-
     munist Party from 1924 and active in both the collectivization campaigns in the Ukraine in the
     early 1930s and the purges in the late 1930s. Expelled from the Communist Party in 1957.
104 Nikita Sergeevich Khrushchëv (1894–1971), at this time first secretary of the Moscow Party Com-
     mittee. Nikolay Aleksandrovich Bulganin (1895–1975), former Chekist, at this time a member
     of the Central Committee of the Communist Party.

the People's Commissar at the conference hall on June 20, 1934, when oral permission to begin construction was given. [...]

During the revision of the technical design, the capacity of the auditorium (eighteen hundred persons) and the size of the building (three hundred thousand cubic meters) were specified.

During the period before Alabyan's plan was shown, the cost of construction mentioned in oral discussions was no more than twenty million rubles. After Alabyan's project was officially accepted for construction, higher cost estimates (relating to the cubic size) of thirty-five million rubles were reported, but Gamarnik, referring to Com. VOROSHILOV and KAGANOVICH, ordered that the budget be limited to twenty million rubles.

Therefore, in one of the reports concerning the theater construction, there was a firm resolution of the narkom to keep within the budget of twenty million rubles. However, Gamarnik, who knew it was impossible to keep within the budget, gave no orders for further construction work.

Then, on October 4, 1936, cost estimates of the theater in the range of thirty-five million to forty-eight million rubles were considered. The figure of forty-eight million rubles was reduced to thirty-six million rubles, owing to a decision not to use marble facing on the frontage. The sum of thirty-six million rubles was reported to the government. But the figure was not approved by the government, and the sum of 20.1 million, which was set at the end of 1934 and introduced into the budget estimates [*titul'nye spiski*] of 1935, continued to be shown in the budget estimates.

Finally, at the end of August 1937, yet another report was submitted to the government about increasing the budget estimate for the theater to thirty million rubles. The result was an order to the NarKomFin to examine the construction budget estimate and present its conclusions. The NarKomFin studied the theater budget estimate of 30,168,000 rubles, using the Tsekombank staff, and acknowledged it as the sum of 31,850,000 rubles, taking into account the cost reduction that was to be given in 1937 and 1938.

When considering the budget estimates for 1938, the government decided to reconsider the theater issue, and meanwhile to withdraw the credits that were included in the budget estimate. [...]

The total spent through 1/1/38 was 20,415,000 or 67 percent [of the total project budget].

Another 11,385,000 rubles is necessary to complete the work.

IN 1938, while still at the Central House of the Red Army, Popov staged one of his most popular productions, a lively reinterpretation of *The Taming of the Shrew*.

Aleksey Popov, *The Taming of the Shrew: Vospominaniya i razmyshleniya o teatre* [Memoirs and reflections on theater] (Moscow: VTO, 1963), 236.

The play confirms the power of love, from which is born a great feeling of respect for and not the subjugation of women. Just at the end of the 1930s in the Far East, the "Khetagurov" movement arose,[105] focusing attention on questions of family life. The wives of our commanders were breaking out of the closed circle of family interests into the arena of social activity. And strange as it seems, *The Taming of the Shrew* as an authentically profound classical work could come across as very contemporary. Many of the play's ideas responded to the question of what makes for family happiness. [. . .]

Moscow saw *The Taming of the Shrew* almost a year after we had performed the play in the Far East. [. . .]

> Yury Kalashnikov, "*The Taming of the Shrew* at the Central Red Army Theater," *Pravda* (October 26, 1938), 19. Yury Sergeevich Kalashnikov (1909/10–?), a theater historian, headed the Chief Directorate of Theaters 1944–48; from 1956 was deputy administrator of the Research Division of the Institute for Art History.

Shakespeare's vivacity, optimism, richness, and motley colors have been incarnated on-stage with talent and authentic temperament by the collective of the Central Red Army Theater. The stage director A. D. Popov, the assistant directors P. V. Urbanovich and V. S. Blagoobrazov, and the designer N. A. Shifrin have created a bright, cheerful show.

The essence of the characters of Katharina and Petruchio has been correctly understood.

The actors Dobrazhanskaya (Katharina) and Pestovsky[106] (Petruchio) strive to present all the complexity and contradiction, the idiosyncratic nature of the heroes of Shakespeare's comedy. Dobrazhanskaya succeeds better at transmitting the growth of feelings, the triumph of love over malice and obstinacy than Petruchio. For too long, coarseness and strength appear to be for Petruchio-Pestovsky not an outward shell, not the means, but the essence, the inner nature of the character. His Petruchio is of a small-minded nature, too rigid and coarse. Pestovsky does not know how to use Petruchio's later behavior to refute his tirade at the start of the play about a rich dowry as his one and only interest. [. . .]

The Soviet stage has not yet seen a Shakespearean production in which the servants have been so organic, so high-spirited, so infectiously merry, such a bright folkloric "plebeian background." The best of the servants is Aleksandrov as Tranio. He is young, merry, witty, picturesque. [. . .] The servants in Petruchio's house make a beautiful ensemble, in which each is in his place. The actors and directors have found lush, almost Flemish colors for the servants. [. . .]

---

105 The Khetagurov movement of patriotic girls promoted women's participation in Soviet progress, 1937–39.

106 Lyubov' Ivanovna Dobrazhanskaya (1908–80), from 1924 toured with the old barnstormer Pavel Orlenev; from 1934 at TsTKA, noted for the audacity of her sharply etched heroines. Viktor Nikolaevich Pestovsky (1901–45), a student of the MAT Fourth Studio, acted at the MGSPS Theater 1923–24, the Red Torch 1925–32, and the Red Army Theater from 1936.

6.6. Backdrop for *The Taming of the Shrew*, designed by Nisson Shifrin, Red Army Theater, Moscow, 1937.

P. Korzinkin, "A joyous spectacle: *The Taming of the Shrew* at the Central Red Army Theater," *Krasnaya Zvezda* [Red star] (October 26, 1938).

The Central Theater of the Red Army has taken an active part in the creation of the best works of military playwrights. But to be a theater of the Red Army does not mean talking only about the army. The scope of interests of the people in our army is enormous. Therefore it was not by chance that the theater turned to the works of Shakespeare—"the classic of classics" of drama. [. . .]

The show scintillates with sparkling merriment. The spectator keenly follows that agile warlike wit, frequently interrupting the action with loud applause. The theater beautifully highlighted one of Shakespeare's special points of genius—his ability to put characters into conflict, into action, in all their lifelike integrity. Carefully addressing the author's text, conveying every word to the spectator, the theater knew how to reveal the treasured thoughts of the playwright about the triumph of a freedom-loving human individual.

The actress Dobrazhanskaya offered a new, accurate image of Shakespeare's heroine. In her performance Katharina is not simply a quarrelsome, headstrong woman, tamed by a male despot. She is not subjugated involuntarily, not simply broken by a stronger will. A real woman from the Renaissance era—intelligent, energetic, of powerful character—she understands her husband, figures out his game, and, fighting for her feminine dignity, assists him. [. . .]

Every scene in this show breathes with high-spirited mastery, freshness and novel, creative thinking. The delightful harmony, the remarkable resonance of the whole ensemble, the finish and inventiveness of every situation speak of the great labor put into the production by the whole collective of the theater. [. . .]

I. Bachelis, "*The Taming of the Shrew*: Premiere at the Central Red Army Theater," *Izvestia* (October 26, 1938). Il'ya Izrailevich Bachelis (1902–51), journalist and theater critic, edited the literature and art section of *Komsomol'skaya Pravda* 1935–38. After the war, he made the film of the Belsen concentration camp for the Nuremberg trials.

Aleksey Popov, who staged *The Taming of the Shrew* [...] totally cut the prologue. The play is not performed by "strolling players" but by real actors, and not before Sly but directly for the audience. The acting of those who, in Hamlet's words, "tear a passion to tatters" became serious acting, as if they had already mastered the instructions later offered by Shakespeare via Hamlet. They portray characters and not masks. True, this forfeits the idiosyncratic brilliance and impetuous tempo of the performance, its sparkling merriment, but even so, there is plenty of joking and laughter in the performance.

So, we can be reconciled to the loss of the prologue. But farther on we encounter another particularity of A. D. Popov's production. Italy, depicted according to the tradition of Shakespeare's times, is also taken seriously, as a "real" Italy. Nothing *English* showed up in Shakespeare's play. Meanwhile, as Shakespearologists have shown, Katharina and Petruchio are genuine English actors; [...] Shakespeare's Italy was a conventional country, a pseudonym for England—in Popov's production, this convention has disappeared; in everything (costumes, sets, manners) a realistic Padua is seduously produced.

Carefully and insistently Popov emphasizes that this is not a farce, not the performance of comic masks, but a profound, serious, intelligent, realistic play, revealing the natures of people of the Renaissance. He wants to show us a "rehabilitated" Shakespeare, who, in the opinion of Prof. A. Smirnov,[107] "bursts the action from within" and, while seeming to act out the Domostroy,[108] in essence reveals the psychology of proud and bold people, fighting for their dignity. [...]

GOSET

Although GOSET retained the best of Granovsky's productions in its repertoire after his defection, under the artistic leadership of Mikhoéls it turned to contemporary Yiddish plays and a more realistic acting style. The high point came in 1935 with a strikingly original *King Lear,* with Mikhoéls in the lead and Zuskin as the Fool.

---

107 Aleksandr Aleksandrovich Smirnov (1883–1962), professor of literature, whose book on Shakespeare's works (1934) offers a Marxist interpretation of the playwright as a progressive "bourgeois humanist."

108 *Domostroy* (*Domestic Order*), a sixteenth-century Russian manual of household instructions, advice, and homilies; husbands are advised to beat disobedient wives, but with affection.

Clurman, "Moscow diary," 12–13.

[On *The Witch*][109] ... There is almost no story left of the original material, and what story there is is absurd and dramatically without function. What we see is a grotesque harlequinade—angular, distorted, abstract, garish, noisy. It is full of gestures, leaps, somersaults, nonsensical rhymes, bewildering propos, heterogeneous songs, dances, and a kind of crazy choral comment conveyed through strange sounds, stranger bits of mimicry, and all sorts of corkscrew contortions.

This production was worked on for two years and is relatively short: two and one-half hours. The first minute I looked at the stage I said to myself "All this is stuff and nonsense," the next minute I thought "Why shouldn't it be" and as the scenes progressed I felt myself thinking "how much charm and life there is in it?" The fact is that it is all very clear, simply, even concrete, when one relates it to the period with which it was concerned. It is a folk picture or ballet of the old Jewish Ghetto [...] an unbelievable memory of the past, an impossible dream, half nightmare, half joke. [...]

Even the set which at first sight looks like a perfectly arbitrary arrangement of surfaces is based on the definite reality of a Russian Jewish village before the revolution with its poverty-stricken wooden materials, its ramshackle architecture, its cockeyed helter-skelter, tattered effect. Though it is essentially a stage construction which permits the varied acrobatics of all the strange characters, the set gives the feeling of the kind of place the old Ghetto was. [...] Not that this production is without its blemishes of flatness, of "modernistic" sophistication and of mere bizarrerie. Today the actors play it coldly, without much inner urge, youthful plasticity or sense of fun. They have no emotion, and it is all a little like a bad reproduction of a bright painting. Granovsky never did work emotionally with his actors but they had emotion at first that came from their personal relation to the period and to the situation. Now only the form remains, but as an actor of the company explained, it remains technically accurate because Granovsky worked it out so that if the actor turned the wrong way he was likely to get a crack on the nose, or if he made a badly timed cross he might have one of his colleagues crash down on his head. "Granovsky did this on purpose," the actor said, "he wanted every movement to be as strictly coordinated as a machine." Indeed the production has something of the precise nature of a cuckoo clock.

[...] When we came out of the dressing room onto the stage-landing I saw a big call-board all plastered with typewritten material. "What is that?" I inquired. "That is the theater newspaper. It is used as a means of mutual criticism. Actors may write their criticisms of one another, of the director, the organization, anything they feel strongly or clearly about. The directors can do the same, as well as any member of the collective—including stage-hands." [...]

---

109 *The Witch of Botoşani* or *Di Kishefmakhern* (1878), a Yiddish-Rumanian musical comedy by Avram Goldfaden; the title role is traditionally played by a man.

Solomon Mikhoéls, "Finding the way to a character," 1935, in *Stat'i, besedy, rechi. Stati i vospominaniya o Mikhoélse* [Articles, talks, speeches: Articles and recollections of Mikhoéls] (Moscow: Iskusstvo, 1965), 49–59.

Into the cauldron in which I boil up my work, when it comes to spices and seasonings, I add whatever I have experienced and know about. If I were to be asked, what stuff do you use to create your role, I would say: I create them out of Mikhoéls. I sculpt them from myself, that is, my view of the world, which is continuously taking shape, changing, growing, deepening, from my own disposition, from my sorrows, passions, and joys—out of myself—and, of course, I am not something apart from everything else. I seem to be the sum total of everything around me, the entire reality permeated with the struggle, passions, tasks, victories, defeats, that surround us today [...]

I strictly segregate and separate the character's image from myself. As the Bible teaches us, God created Eve from Adam's rib. I've just said that "I create" a character's image "from myself." But I create it from one of my ribs, not from my whole self. In other words, when I approach any character, any creative task, I try to be taller, bigger, and wider than the task. [...]

A character's image is greater than a person and lesser than a person. A character is something integral, but a character is also an element. Sometimes it is only one facet of a person, the facet that characterizes him to the greatest degree. And there is always one facet that predominates in a person, and all his other attributes are molded around it. The search for this "kernel," the most essential trait of a given person, is one of the main tasks of an actor [...]

A character's image is, consequently, a disclosure (in the realm of one's view and attitude toward the world) of whatever most interests me today, and most engages me at any given moment.

Therefore the timeline of a role is the timeline of my life. [...]

The people I see and know I analyze, as if assessing them, and afterward, like God in the Bible, I take a rib and out of that rib I create Eve. [...]

Solomon Mikhoéls, "My work on *King Lear*" (1939), in *Stat'i, besedy, rechi,* 76–83, 92, 106.

To play King Lear was my long-standing dream from adolescence itself. At the time I was studying at a technical high school in Riga, where great attention was paid to the study of world literature. The literature instructor often made us read classical works aloud in class. He usually gave me poetry. Dramatic works we always read out loud in the roles. When it came time for Shakespeare's *King Lear,* I was instructed to read the role of Lear. I well remember what an impression the last scene made on me. Out of the whole tragedy it disturbed me the most. This was obviously reflected in my recitation, because when I read it, our teacher shed tears. On that day I swore to myself that if ever I became an actor, I would definitely play King Lear [...]

In 1932, there was a great deal of grief in my life. [His wife had died.] Over a very short period of time I lost several people who were close to me. These difficult losses

6.7. Solomon Mikhoéls as King Lear, GOSET, 1935.

unsettled me to such an extent that I began to consider quitting the stage forever.

To go out and stage play my old roles became unbearable to me. There were comic episodes in these roles that were funny to the whole audience. To me, this laughter seemed alien. I was envious that people could laugh. At the time I was inwardly devoid of that capacity. I firmly resolved to leave the theater. [...]

[...] ... the point of departure of my concept of the tragedy lay in the king's summoning his daughter and appearing before them with a *premeditated intention*. The ease with which he relinquishes his great power led me to the conclusion that, for Lear, many universally recognized values had become devalued, that he had found some new, philosophical understanding of life.

Power is nothing compared to what Lear knows. For him human beings represent something of ever-decreasing value. This reveals Lear's purely feudal conception of human beings. Having sat on his throne for so many years, he trusted in his own sagacity, decided that his sagacity surpassed absolutely everything known to humans, and decided that he alone could oppose the whole world after previously joking, "Well now, children, tell me how much you love me, and I'll pay you for it."

The very fact that he has decided to pay for flattery proves that he puts absolutely no stock in the word love. In just the same way, he puts no stock in those territories and riches which he has decided to parcel out. So he divides his kingdom into portions. [...]

I remember with absolute clarity that the first gesture was this: the king passes his hand over his bare head, as if he wants to touch his lost crown. I had already come up with this gesture in 1932, although the production was not realized until 1935.

Vovsi-Mikhoëls, *Mon père Salomon Mikhoëls*, 95–97.

I attended more than a hundred performances. I knew the play by heart. But the impression left by the first appearance of the king has stayed with me all my life, as one of my strongest experiences.

To the sound of a triumphal march, the courtiers arrive with great pomp. Suddenly, the music stops. In the most profound silence, the old king appears discreetly. Hunched over, muffled up unceremoniously in a plain cloak, King Lear moves, his head bowed, toward the throne, looking at no one.

The fool is already on the throne. Lear takes him delicately, nonchalantly, by the ear to make him get off with a mild irony, before finally looking up and running his eyes over the bowed heads of the courtiers. For the first time, one can finally observe his face. It is not made up. He does not wear the traditional beard. The face of a skeptical monarch.

With an easy gesture, the king counts those present. He does not notice Cordelia, hidden behind the throne. But then she appears and he bursts out in a hearty old-man's laugh. This laugh becomes one of Lear's leitmotifs. He repeats it several times over the course of the play.

[...] At the most dramatic moment of Lear's inner life, at the time of his cruelest defeats, this little laugh is heard again. Why? Because, now, when the earlier beliefs have been shattered, all the former values destroyed, Lear remembers the only inarguable value, the balance sheet of his whole life, Cordelia.

In the last scene, Lear's last gasp ends on the laugh. But this is not the careless laughter of the first act. Now it's hard to know whether this is a laugh or a sob. [...] Lear appears carrying the dead Cordelia in his arms, and moving past the silent warriors, he quietly utters his triple "woe, woe, woe," then delicately places his daughter's corpse on the ground, saying, "A dog, a horse, a mouse, they live, while you, my child, you no longer live, you breathe no more!" Turning away from her for a moment, he lets a feeble sigh escape, which is prolonged. Then, as if he was remembering his past life, he briefly hums a tune he used to sing returning from the hunt, two or three measures, and the song becomes a laugh which sounds like a plaintive cry. He lies on the ground next to Cordelia, puts a finger on her lips, and repeats very quietly, "Her lips . . . her lips . . . you see?" before dying. In Mikhoels's concept, these last words of Lear signify that from those lips he heard the truth for the first time.

This scene was stupefying. While the curtain came down slowly, a deathly silence reigned in the audience, and only when the audience came out for their curtain call did the audience unleash deafening applause. That is how every performance of *King Lear* ended, from the dress rehearsal to the last one on January 18, 1944.

B. Zingerman, "Mikhoéls-Lear," in Matvey Geyzer, *Solomon Mikhoéls* (Moscow: Prometey, 1990), 369. Boris Isaakovich Zingerman (1928–2000), theater critic, editor of *Teatr* 1955–62, combined a sociological approach with research into form; among his many works are a monograph on Shakespeare on the Soviet stage and a penetrating analysis of Chekhov.

His Lear entered the tragedy with a skeptical smirk on his lips, sure of himself and his opinions—and later, on the heath, howled like a dog. There appeared before the audience a derisive little old man challenging history to a duel and playing a daring, dangerous game with it. Disproving the individualistic claims of his character, his views formed at a great distance from life, Mikhoéls believed in man's capacity to know. He called to overcome the gap between what we think of the world and what it is really like. He asserted the beneficence of knowing, as if knowledge would never come with difficulty or lead to any tragic revelations. In Mikhoéls's performance, he astounded his contemporaries with the sustained emotion of knowing, going all the way in the ruthless logic of his deductions. In the process of this proactive, pragmatic—firsthand—palpable knowing, the shroud of abstract appearances was supposed to fall away. All this naturally was complicated in Mikhoéls by one more theme, which was related to the social standing of his character.

An individualist and a scholiast, Lear is an autocrat as well; his exclusive social position reinforces in him the awareness of his personal exceptionality. In the old king, as Mikhoéls played him, there dwelt the concept that he is the chosen one, called on in his special qualities to carry out a certain important mission. Besides being accustomed to opposing all other persons with his will, he has decided to oppose it to the reality around him. In Mikhoéls's interpretation, the crux of Shakespeare's tragedy lies in Lear's wanting to impose a willful experiment on life . . .

Van Gyseghem, *Theatre in Soviet Russia,* 176–77.

For me the high spot of this production was the performance of V. Zuskin as the fool. This was a piece of sheer genius—such a performance as one sees only once or twice in a lifetime. This fool was no age, of no time—he was on this earth but not of it, a pathetic tormented spirit caged for a while in this quicksilver body but always with half of him away on other, more brilliant worlds—tied to this earth by a bright love for his master. [. . .]

The settings by Tyshler contributed greatly to the mood of the play. They had a monumental, a doomlike quality that was in some strange way a synthesis of the Hebraic and the Druidic. The stage was divided as in the Elizabethan manner: the upper stage was supported by solid, carven figures of wood. The immobility of these figures, the simplicity of the carved folds of their drapery, the fixity of their eyeless gaze as they stared past and above the cavorting mortals round them—here Tyshler's imagination has captured and reproduced something of the immensity of the tragedy, some brooding quality that was extremely impressive. The upper stage was revealable by the front wall opening like a window—steps let down to the lower stage, steps that were concealed inside the carven figures. The exteriors were painted in a formal brick pattern—the insides were decorated in extreme simplicity with wooden figures in carved relief. This use of natural material, in its natural color—for neither the wooden reliefs nor the monumental figures were painted—is one of the distinguishing marks of Tyshler's work. [...]

Worker and Peasant Theater

Difficulties for the TRAM organization had begun as early as 1929, when *The Shot,* a satire on the Soviet bureaucracy, was attacked for "deviationist leftism" and banned. Once socialist realism was installed as the approved style, TRAM was condemned for formalism and overvaluing the director at the expense of the actor. It was liquidated. Part of the Leningrad Collective joined the Red Army Theater, and in 1938 the Moscow TRAM became the Lenin Komosomol Theater.

Golubovsky, *Bol'shie malen'kie teatry,* 233–34.

The ruin of the TRAMs occurred naturally and inevitably. It was not at all a matter of their not possessing culture, professionalism, talented youngsters in need of a school, a serious mastery of their craft. The spectators saw clearly that many actors repeated themselves, banking on their charm and familiarity. All this might have been tolerated and dealt with. The fact was that the naughty company, unrestrained by the rules of good taste, the implied decorum in art, fell out with the semiofficial organs of the press, which controlled Soviet theater. Among the TRAMists, along with the primitive playwriting, the rectolinear resolve there often burst out an acute thought, a social protest, hatred of formalism, innate in the life of the youth. The TRAMs demanded standardization, and as a result, not a single theater evolved from the TRAMs—either in Moscow or in Leningrad.

E. M. Delafield, *I Visit the Soviets: The Provincial Lady in Russia* (New York: Harper and Brothers, 1937), 65, 71–74. E. M. Delafield (actually Edmée Elizabeth Monica Dashwood, born de la Pasture, 1890–1943), English writer, made a hit with the semiautobiographical *Diary of a Provincial Lady* (1930); in 1936 she spent six months in Leningrad and on the Seattle Communal Farm near Rostov, which had a total population of 728, of whom 530 were farmers. One night, a concert party was held.

The comrades sat at the little tables in groups of four or five—it was like a kind of skeleton café chantant, without glamour, music, drinks, or excitement...the whole effect was curiously drab, even though most of the women had put on their best dresses for the occasion. [...]

The stage, to my surprise, had a very good drop scene and back cloth, both well painted. I asked who had done them, and Eva said that "an artist" had once visited the commune, but had only stayed a very short time.

The entertainment was nearly all provided by the Ukrainians. About twelve men and women, all wearing national costume, came in and sang. It was very pathetic to see the gay red silk skirts and beautiful embroidered aprons and wreaths of artificial flowers, so carefully kept and so seldom worn, and so unlikely ever to return to the lands whence they had been brought.

The songs were part-songs, sung in a minor key and very, very slowly. There was no accompaniment, and the singers kept wonderfully in tune and, so far as I could trust my ear, did not end up by singing flat. But the songs were of incredible length. [...] They sang several times, and one couple danced—a very attractive peasant dance. Then they all danced a "wedding dance" with a pair in the middle, and all the others joining hands in a ring round them. [...] Then there was some balalaika playing by two Russian boys—but they were not very good—and one or two more songs.

Finally the Ukrainians, obviously feeling that they had not taken all the trouble of dressing themselves up for nothing, took possession of the stage again and sung more, and even longer, part-songs. Although they were too long, they really were effective in a strange, plaintive way.

Just before midnight, the electric light—which was made on the estate—gave its three customary warning flickers, and the meeting broke up. [...] The comrades were so exhilarated by their night's entertainment that they remained out of doors, singing what they remembered of the Ukrainian choruses while somebody twanged a balalaika, for what seemed to me like hours afterward.

Nataliya Sats, "18 years of Soviet children's theater," *Moscow News* (May 27, 1936), 10.

Spring 1936 was marked by a new event in the life of the Soviet theaters for children. March 5 saw the opening of a new central children's theater created according to a decision of the Party and government.

"In the very center of Moscow, next to the Bol'shoy and Maly theaters—that is where our new theater is," children proudly told each other. They came to the theater in holiday attire, in special streetcars, trolleys, and autobuses. They entered the new theater, the huge staircase of which was lined on both sides with great bushes of white lilac, palms, and creepers. At the entrance to the foyer they were met by the actors in costume, the favorite characters of children's productions. Every child present received a badge with red berries, which was pinned to his clothing by the actors. On the sides of the staircase sat child entertainers in brilliant, colorful costumes, musicians of a toy orchestra who sang verses specially written for the occasion. [...]

In the children's foyer grew huge plants with yellowish bananas—made of silk. Spectators of various heights found tables to suit their various sizes. Huge dolls on the buffet counter gave the children a good laugh. The tea tasted especially delicious; it was served in cups painted by artists of the children's theater, beautiful cups reminding the children of their favorite plays.

The climax came when the curtain rose on a large, well-equipped stage, when grown-up actors who played the parts of schoolboys in *Serëzha Strel'tsov* [by Valentina

Leykina] fused in one spirit with the schoolchildren who sat in the theater, when the footlights ceased to exist, as it were, and the stage and audience merged in a single, common life, a life of high emotions.

The Central Children's Theater has 397 workers, including 80 skilled actors, 40 musicians, a number of pedagogues and others. [...]

IN 1937 Sats was sent to a labor camp and not released until 1942. She settled in Alma Ata, where she founded the first Kazakh children's theater.

> Molière on ice, unidentified clipping, 22, 428, February 20, 1938, from V. S. Karelin, *Dva reisa* [Two voyages] (n.p.: Glavsevmorput', 1938). Dana Collection, Harvard Theater Collection.

On the sea of Finland [...] a fleet of ships was making its way to open waters through thick ice. The ships sailed in a column led by the icebreaker *Krasin*. Sharply changing course in a zigzag, the icebreaker slid onto the ice, crushing it with all the strength of its hull and plowing into the water with a loud crack. The other ships quickly made their way into this narrow strip of open water. [...]

The *Krasin* and the *Smolensk* remained, smoothly rocked from side to side half a mile apart. The *Krasin* had to return to the mouth of the Kolyma in Ambarchik Bay for the rest of the ships [...] to take on fifteen hundred tons of coal. The command set the time for the loading at two days. One hundred personnel from the komsomol crew of the *Krasin* and 270 passengers of the *Smolensk* formed brigades of 10 each. "All hands on deck" was sounded. The Moscow polar theater brigade no. Twenty-eight worked like Stakhanovites.[110] Instead of 100 hoists per brigade, they averaged 120–130. Theater artists M. I. Orlov and V. S. Karelin turned into real winchmen and kept at the windlasses sometimes for two or three shifts in a row. Engineers, geologists, scientists, and artists all turned into coal heavers. The windlasses creaked, the shovels scraped, and the scuttle-buckets quickly transported coal onto the icebreaker.

Meanwhile, in the fourth hold of the *Smolensk*, work was going on, with no more slacking than on deck. The brigades relieved of hauling were preparing a platform scaffold for the Moscow Polar Theater's show. On the upper deck the hold was screened off as a performance space, hung with a curtain. Brightly colored flags lent the improvised stage a festive look. The ship's electricity provided the requisite lighting. The hold deck was cleared of garbage and covered with clean mats. The stalls were made up of chairs and armchairs from the staterooms, while the pit was of boards placed on boxes and barrels.

Playbills with the following message were posted in the staterooms of the *Krasin* and the *Smolensk*, in the sailors' quarters, and on deck:

---

110 Stakhanovite, a movement allegedly created by a coal miner, Aleksey Stakhanov (1906–77), in 1935 to increase industrial production. It was in fact invented and promoted by the Soviet media, offering a model by which to justify an increase in production targets for all workers.

"Today in Hold no. 4 of the 'Smolensk' *Tartuffe*, a comedy in five acts, will be staged, by the Moscow Polar Theater. Show time 8:00 p.m. Tickets available from the ship's deputy commander for political affairs."

Eight o'clock. The siren sounded three times and the curtain went up. The audience gazed avidly at the stage.

On the upper deck the windlasses continued to creak, steel hawsers clanged, the coal heavers' cries filtered through, but no one even heard them.

During the fourth act, the ship pitched forward. Heavy swells were felt as the ice broke up. The coaling stopped, but the show went on. The pitching became stronger. The ship began to list to one side, but the actors did not even think of halting the performance. The audience, seeing their determination, encouraged them in all sorts of ways. When in Act V Orgon lost his balance and fell off his chair, the audience shouted in chorus a phrase he had used earlier: "Stick to your guns, Orgon . . ." And Orgon and the rest of the cast did stick to their guns and performed the play to the end.

And then the show was over. The audience warmly thanked the actors; not knowing how else to express their appreciation, sailors and passengers presented the performers with cookies, lemons, and fruit preserves. These touching gifts included the most valuable one of all—a sincere love of art.

Other Republics

Mardzhanov had defended his former student Sandro Akhmeteli from a death sentence in 1924 and had him appointed codirector at the Rustaveli Theater in Tbilisi. The two men failed to get on as partners, so Mardzhanov left to found a new theater in 1926. A hot-tempered modernist, Akhmeteli had come under fire from the OGPU for "anti-Soviet activities," but his immense success at the Moscow Festival in 1930 preserved him for a few more years.

GOSET toured to Tiflis, Minsk, Khar'kov, Dnepropetrovsk, Nikolaev, and Odessa, with the old Labiche comedy *Trente Millions de Gladiator*. They were accompanied on the first leg of the tour by a French theatrical journalist.

> Léon Moussinac, *Avec les comédiens soviétiques en tournées. Notes de voyage* (Paris: Editions sociales internationales, 1935), 50–52. Léon Moussinac (1890–1964), French Communist playwright and film critic, on the staff of *L'Humanité*, founded Les Amis de Spartacus and boosted Eisenstein; he had attended the RAPP conference in Moscow in 1927.

May 18 [1935]. At the Rustaveli Theater, the doors will always be open to us. Akhmeteli's[111] hospitality is entirely cordial . . . I attended a performance of *The Summit* at the Rustaveli Theater. This play comprises a kind of oratorio and is very representative,

111 Aleksandr (Sandro) Vasil'evich Akhmeteli (actually Aleksandre Akhmetelashvili, 1866–1937) ran the Rustaveli Theater 1924–35.

with its imposing and original staging, of the effort undertaken to implement shows of national format and revolutionary content. But there seems to be a certain mysticism inherent in the lyricism of such a work, and the ending, which suddenly contrasts the legends of Kazbek with central electricity, does not strike me as organic. [...]

Another night I got lost in the crowd at the Mardzhanov Theater. They were playing a new comedy that provoked the audience to prolonged laughter at every moment. Participation was total; although my neighbor whispered, for my guidance, that these laughs could not be high quality, the play being mediocre. In a stage box there was pointed out to me an old woman with white hair and a dignified, simple face, in national costume, who was observing both the stage and the audience at the same time: Stalin's mother.

BY THE TIME the English writer John Lehmann saw Akhmeteli's best productions, the director was already under arrest, and foreign visitors were told that he had retired, a lie perpetuated even after his death.

> John Lehmann, *Prometheus and the Bolsheviks* (London: Cresset Press, 1937), 77–87. John Lehmann (1907–87), highly regarded English novelist, memoirist, and traveler and a member of the Bloomsbury Group, edited *New Writing* and *Penguin New Writing* and founded his own publishing house.

Vakhtang[112] got me tickets a few nights later for one of the Rustaveli Theatre's most famous productions, *Anzor*. The achievement of Akhmeteli, Vakhtang explained to me during the intervals, was to have created a special style of representation. *Anzor*, a translation into a Caucasian setting of Ivanov's civil war play, *The Armored Train*, was a particularly successful example of this style. Anzor himself is a sort of Chapaev of the mountains, a natural leader of the clans, who comes over to help the Bolsheviks in their struggle against the Whites. Akhmeteli's aim was to bring out the freedom and vigour of the life of these Caucasian mountaineers, the fierce pulse of the revolutionary awakening. The emphasis on movement and gesture, in a strongly rhythmic way, struck me at once in the opening scenes. The actors seemed more to chant their words than to speak them; they sprang about the various levels of the main set, which represented a mountain, in a carefully controlled pattern, and the whole effect was in some ways more like a ballet than a play. This effect was heightened by the magnificent mass scenes of songs and dances, which broke and varied the rhythm. Akhmeteli's technique certainly fitted such a heroic, revolutionary play down to the ground, and made out of it something entirely unlike anything else that I had ever seen. It was, I realised even then, a style that came naturally to the quick, temperamental, song and dance loving Georgians, but neither that, nor the slight absurdity of certain minor incidents that fitted the "translation" badly, lessened my admiration and pleasure.

112 Vakhtang Kldiashvili, an assistant producer at the Mardzhanishvili Theater, who had spent time in Paris and New York.

6.8. *Anzor* by Shanshiashvili, directed by Sandro Akhmeteli, Rustaveli Theater, Tbilisi, 1928.

This rhythmic emphasis, the ballet-like effect, was I learnt after further visits to the Rustaveli Theater, a characteristic of all the plays Akhmeteli had produced, and I began to see that, superb as were the results the method achieved with the proper material it was, on the whole, rather limited. Plays about the struggles, old and new, of the Georgian mountain-folk, and plays of rather similar character from abroad, such as Schiller's *Die Räuber,* which was given under the title of *In Tyrannos,* came off brilliantly; but it was not every day that a Georgian audience wanted heroics and highly-coloured epics. Like any other theater-enthusiasts, the Georgians also liked plainer fare sometimes, something a little less tense, a little more every day—comedies, and psychological studies of a quieter sort [...]

It was instructive to come from *Anzor* to *The Eclipse in Georgia* at the Mardzhanishvili Theatre. This was an adaptation of an old comedy, by Antonov,[113] which had been extremely popular in the nineteenth century. [...] The lively movements and subtle intonations were so expressive, that I felt I hardly needed to understand what was being said, and laughed as much as anyone. Moreover, the beauty of the grouping and the décor would have been obvious to me even if I had been totally deaf; and the delicate blending of humorous passages with music and poetry was profoundly satisfying... The charm and point of the play is in its picture of Tiflis life, the light sketches of numerous citizen types, and the satire on Georgian gullibility. It was clear to me, the first time I saw it, that [...] it remained pure comedy, without any trace of propaganda grafted on to it. But afterwards, when I could follow what was being said more closely, I saw that it was nevertheless not entirely without its wider social implication: the relations of the rising Georgian bourgeoisie to the old landed-proprietor

113 Zurab Antonov (1820–54), Georgian playwright with a strong comic bent.

class were gently but effectively suggested in one of the most amusing scenes, taking place [...] on the flat roof of one of the houses.

"Did you notice the drunken Russian soldier with the big red nose and the vodka bottle in the main scene?" Vakhtang asked me afterwards [...] "That's an amusing relic of the earliest dramatic festivals that took place in Tiflis with nearly the whole town participating. There was always a 'foreign tyrant' who was represented in the worst light possible; at the beginning it was a Turk, but after the Russians arrived the Turk turned into a Russian, and there always had to be a Russian clown in every popular show. But you mustn't think it's a sign of chauvinism: Mardzhanishvili had a great belief in preserving as much as possible from the popular medium."

"And there's no interference from outside, from the politicians, with the actual methods of production?"

"No. We're allowed almost complete liberty to experiment. When I say 'almost complete' I mean that we naturally listen to what the critics say, thrash out their objections among ourselves, and in replies to the papers; but there are no 'orders from above' which we blindly and silently obey."

"And what about interference with the actual plays, with a classic, for instance?"

"Well, there was a time when attempts were made to doctor the classics: that was in the days of RAPP [the Union of Proletarian Writers], when the extremists were in the saddle, people who had theories as to how an author in the past *should* have written. [...] I myself, soon after I returned, was told to alter a character in an English seventeenth-century play, because it was felt that no one except a proletarian or a peasant could be shown as a hero, and my hero was unfortunately well-born. I made a fight about it, and eventually won my point. To-day I shouldn't have to fight about it at all..."

A few nights later I saw *Guria,* one of the most popular pieces in the repertoire of the Mardzhanishvili Theatre.[114] It had been constructed by the playwright Dadiani, from four novels by a famous Georgian writer, Ninoshvili.[115] Vakhtang told me that Ninoshvili, whose chief work was done in the quarter of a century after 1880, went himself to live with the peasants of the province of Gria, in Western Georgia, for many years [...] The play was extremely simply staged, in contrast to the rather florid scenic effects of *Arsen,* and the whole production was quieter, almost flat at times, with unemphatic curtains to the quick-changing scenes. The sets were reduced to a minimum, a house being represented, for instance, by a small painted wall brought forward to one side of the stage, on to which the lighting was concentrated while the rest of the stage remained in darkness: a wooded mountain by a slightly sloping ground on which one or two dark-painted pillars stood for trees. The action worked up peasant risings, the tense atmosphere of the 1905 Revolution, but, by easy stages, impressionistically, details of life being depicted with real economy and expressiveness of movement and gesture—a peasant girl, seduced by a young nobleman, being

114 Koté Mardzhanishvili State Dramatic Theater, founded by its namesake in Kutaisi 1928; moved to Tbilisi 1930.
115 Egnate Fomich Ninoshvili (actually Ingorovka, 1859–1941), Georgian writer of working-class background, cofounder of Mesana Dasi (Third Group) of authors; a devoted Communist, he portrayed oppressed peasants and depraved aristocrats.

persuaded by the obscene go-between to set out for the city brothels—an old peasant, a railway worker, falling asleep while guarding the line, and being run over—a love scene between two young peasants—the mountain highwaymen in their lair reading a daily paper in which Ninoshvili describes their life exactly—a wine-festival and the special Gurian dances accompanying it. The more intimate scenes, between two or three people, were particularly carefully worked out. This treatment was a natural result of the play's origin in novels, but at the same time, it was thoroughly characteristic of the theatre's style, and I couldn't help feeling that, though Akhmeteli's Theatre—Akhmeteli had then retired but nearly all the productions were still his—achieved grander and more forceful effects, the other gained very much in depth and richness by seeking out the heart of each play's meaning and developing its production from that core, rather than imposing a "grand style" on everything that was attempted.

AKHMETELI was arrested on the night of November 19, 1936, and, despite torture, denied the charges of espionage and plotting the murders of Stalin and Beria. The investigation was especially brutal, led by Beria himself and under the control of the narkom for internal affairs of Georgia Golidze.

The charges against Akhmeteli. Antonov-Ovseenko, *Teatr Iosifa Stalina*, 152.

[Akhmeteli] carried on espionage on behalf of the English secret service and turned out to be a member of a Trotskyite–Zinovievian counterrevolutionary terrorist organization, and in the field of art, he developed widespread harmful activity. Under the pretext of sponsoring national theaters of other republics and regions he created militant groups in Baku, Sukhumi, Grozny, Staliniri, and other areas of Georgia. Into these groups he personally recruited thirty-five persons. In the Rustaveli Theater he created a terrorist organization, to complete acts of terrorism against Beria. Moving his residence to Moscow, he there tried in actors' circles to organize a terrorist group to complete acts of terrorism against Stalin and other members of the Politburo.

TWENTY-FIVE more persons were implicated: the men were executed the next day; the women were given ten years in a labor camp.

V. Tikhonovich, "Theatrical culture of the Peoples of the USSR," *VOKS Socialist Construction in the USSR* 6 (1934), 70–71, 75. V. Tikhonovich, a specialist in amateur theater, had been prominent in Proletkul't and directed *Macbeth* in Moscow in 1921 with designs by Eisenstein.

Characteristic of the attitude of the bourgeoisie toward its own national theater is the fact related by the eminent Azerbaijan actor Hadji-Aga-Abbasov.[116] He tells how

116 Hadji-Aga Abassov Mutalib ogli (1868–?) organized the Baku agitsatire theater 1921–24; worked for Rabis and ran the Azibekov Theater in Baku 1925–27, the Technikum Theater 1930–37.

the proprietor of a Turkic theater in Baku obstructed in every way the holding of performances in Turkic. The Turkic theater was also opposed by the Moslem clergy. First of all, they forbade women to act on the stage, and the Turkic dramatists had to write plays containing no feminine roles. If, however, feminine roles were introduced, they were usually played either by men or by women of other nationalities—Russian, Armenian, or Jewish. Even after the October Revolution two of the actresses of the Uzbek national theater were slain by their fanatic relatives for disobeying the dictates of the clergy. [...]

... After the October Revolution the first to be created were the theaters of Tadjikistan and Turkmenistan. [...]

Many of the nationalities that had no theater before the Revolution are finding a rich store for the development of their theatrical art in the so-called ethnographical culture consisting of the folk songs and dances that have come down from the hoary past.

Thus, the first all-Crimean Kolkhoz Olympiad held in October 1933 has introduced us to the treasures contained in the national cultural heritage. The Olympiad disclosed the dramatic historic past of the Tatars [...] The Tatars have evolved something in the nature of a "folk opera," consisting of a marriage ceremony lasting for three days, and a wealth of folk songs—philosophical, lyrical, romantic, and satirical; also a choreography in which, besides the feudal love song of "Haitarma," the industrious life of the people is reflected in a number of folk dances [...]

Attempts were made to adopt the folk songs and dances of the prerevolutionary period to modern themes. At times this was done mechanically, the old tunes being sung to a new text, or the old dance being given as an illustration of a new theme. But more frequently, the adaptation was of a deeper character. Remarkable and successful attempts in this respect were made by the Uzbek State Musical Theater, in which such eminent artists as Tamara Petrosiantz[117] and Kari Yakubov[118] are working. The theater has made use of the folk and classical music and choreography of its country for the creation of new melodies, new dances, and various scenic productions on the themes of the Civil War and socialist drama (*Halima*) and musical comedy (*Comrades*); there was also created and produced the first Uzbek ballet *Cotton*.[119]

[...] The Uzbek troupe got its theatrical education from pupils of Vakhtangov; Glaznek (known under the stage name Glazunov),[120] an actor of the Vakhtangov Theater, is the art director of the Latvian theatrical organization Skatuve; the regisseur of the Armenian Theater Simonov is also a member of the Vakhtangov company, etc.

---

117 Tamara Artëmovna Khanum (actually Petrosyan, 1906–91), Uzbek dancer, studied in Moscow and began a professional career 1926; the first Uzbekistani woman to perform publicly and without a veil, she formed companies in Tashkent 1926–28 and in Samarkand and Kokand 1928–34.

118 Mukhitdin Kari-Yakubov (1896–1957), Uzbek baritone, who sang at the Universal Exposition in Paris and Berlin 1921; organized an ethnic ensemble to perform folk music 1926.

119 *Pakhta* (1933), music by Roslavts, choreographed by Bek and U. A. Kamilov.

120 Osval'd Glazunov (actually Glaznek, 1891–1947), Latvian actor, senior disciple of Vakhtangov; interned for three years in Riga by the Germans during the war; he and his wife were then sentenced to the Gulag for ten years for treason.

THE RUSSIAN-LANGUAGE THEATER in the capital of Turkmenistan, Ashkabad (Ashgabat), was the Pushkin Dramatic Theater, founded in 1926. It admitted women to its troupe in 1929 and often performed in Moscow. Unemployed directors from Moscow and Leningrad eager to run a theater of their own might apply for posts in the remote republics. One such application got a basting from a journalist.

> Yakov Vorob'ëv, "Director Fëdorov's memorandum," *Sovremennoe Iskusstvo* (April 28, 1938), 4. Vasily Fëdorovich Fëdorov (1891–1949), a former collaborator of Meyerhold, had headed the directorial section of the Theater of Revolution 1927–28 and directed at the Fourth MAT Studio (Realistic Theater) 1928–29.

"The present memorandum has been drawn up in accord with the suggestion made to me V. F. Fëdorov by the administration of the Board of the Pushkin State Russian Dramatic Theater in the person of its administrator Mr. Nechaev, to take on the leadership of the theater's artistic division in future seasons."

[...] The section "Statement of Facts" paints an epic picture of the unattractive situation in the theater... The author of the memorandum uses such terms as "extremely unsatisfactory, revolting and superficial plays such as *Someone Else's Child* by Shkvarkin slip (?!) into the repertoire." He is dissatisfied with the technical equipment onstage, the lighting and the economic foundation of the theater. Next we read, "It has been made clear that for a number of years the theater has been unable to win over the favor and the love of an audience of workers."

[...] Let us say a few words about how the author of the memorandum thinks of himself as "the artistic profile of the theater." Frankly speaking, the resultant profile is rather blurry. It seems that V. F. Fëdorov does not really know what he wants. The matter does not go any further than the bromide that "a theater's artistic profile is formed, above all, by the repertoire the theater has" and that the "theater's repertoire defines all the formal specialties of the given artistic organism, viz. the theater."

In the section "Repertory Plans for the Next Three Years," fifteen classical plays and three Soviet plays are listed. In 1939 the artistic boss plans to acquaint the Ashkabad public with *The Squall*, in 1940 with *The Optimistic Tragedy*, and in 1941 with *The Wreck of the Squadron*.[121]

V. F. Fëdorov believes that including classical plays in the repertoire will "guarantee the theater's development along the lines of socialist realism."

Is that so? If the matter were that simple, there would be nothing easier than guaranteeing the development of all our theaters along the lines of socialist realism.

Does V. F. Fëdorov explain his fundamental approach to the stage interpretation of the classics? By no means. Does he discuss anything regarding a system for training actors or processes for working on form? Not a word. On the other hand, he does not forget to stipulate in this document that the velvet drapes onstage should be "impec-

---

121 The theater had staged *Platon Krechet* in 1936 and *Lyubov' Yarovaya* in 1937 and was to put on *Othello* in 1940.

cable." This may indeed be of great importance. But it seems to us that the director's work with the actors is also important. [...]

The most piquant section of the memorandum has been modestly located at the end. It is titled "Regarding My Material Daily Claims for the Future." Fëdorov has composed this section with great precision. It seems that here he knows clearly what he wants. He wants to receive three thousand rubles a month. He wants to work at the theater for half a year, to spend three and a half months on leave and two and a half months posted to Moscow on behalf of the theater. Finally, he would like the administration to provide him a good suite at a hotel and for some reason definitely one with "a good view of the street." [...]

> Langston Hughes, "The Soviet theater in Central Asia," *Asia* (October 1934), 590–93. James Mercer Langston Hughes (1902–67), African American poet, playwright, and activist, had strong Communist sympathies; he visited the Soviet Union in 1932 to make a film, never realized, and met Arthur Koestler in Turkmenistan.

In Samarkand, Bokhara, Tashkent, Ashkhabad, and many other cities in Central Asia north of the Persian and Afghan border, the people's theater has become a vital and exciting force since the Soviet regime established its flow of life through that once backward part of the Orient. [...]

It was only after the Revolution that women appeared on the native stage. The ice was broken by Tamara Khanum, now a famous dancer, who first dared to perform in public—under guard. After her, other women, newly liberated from their harems, went into the theater. Some continued to wear their veils at home, although they took them off onstage. Several actresses were murdered by reactionary relatives. At Bokhara, Tucson-oi, a talented native woman who had studied in Moscow, was killed by her husband for refusing to desert the theater; and in Samarkand, as recently as 1930, another young actress, Nurhan, was put to death by her parents for appearing unveiled onstage. Her funeral was made the occasion for a stirring appeal to all women to take off their veils, to refuse to remain in harems or to submit to the slavelike customs of the past. Today there are a great many women in the theaters of Soviet Asia, and they are an important factor in freeing others from the chains of the old life.

At Ismailov's[122] invitation I attended a national congress of playwrights who came together in Tashkent to discuss the problems of the Uzbek stage and its relation to the second Five-Year Plan. Ways and means of devising plays and pageants that would further the plans for industrializing the land and pushing on to complete socialism were taken up by the assembled young men and women interested in creating a theater to meet the specific needs of the day.

Ismailov's own famous play, *The Spoilers of Corson*, reflects the new social order. It is important not only because it is an excellent drama but because it shows clearly the value of cotton, Central Asia's main crop, to the economics of socialism. It pictures

122 Ismailov, Uzbeki dramatist and chairman of the Writer's Union.

vividly the fight that had to be waged against the counterrevolutionary elements that sought to destroy and sabotage cotton production, in an effort to break down the first Central Asian worker's republic.

Halima, another drama popular with Uzbek audiences, has for its theme the closing of the harems and the unveiling of the women—one of the most amazing transformations since the Revolution. [...] *Halima* has been presented for a number of years, and at each performance fewer veiled faces are seen. At the production of *Halima* that I attended in Tashkent I counted only twelve veiled women among the two or three hundred in the audience—many of them schoolgirls who have never been and never will be veiled now. [...]

The Mongolian players at the International Olympiad of Workers Theaters (nonprofessional) held in Moscow a year ago last June created the greatest interest of any group present. For eight or nine days they had traveled from Ulan Bator, in Outer Mongolia, to the Red Capital, bringing their silken costumes and exotic musical instruments via the Trans-Siberian. When the curtains of Moscow's vast music hall parted to the low monotone of Chinese pipes and fiddles, the Mongolian actors were welcomed with a prolonged burst of applause by the Russian public. Their play, *Dark Power,* pictured the sufferings of the Mongols under their former princes of the golden tents and the lamas of the corrupt temples. It was a revolutionary play acted to native music in the formal Chinese tradition, except that women took the feminine roles in the cast, not men, as in the old Chinese theater.

[...] As Ismailov, the Uzbek playwright, said, "We must use the theater to teach our people how terrible and dangerous the beys and the priests and the Cossacks were in the past, and how beautiful life can be in the future when all workers get together." [...]

CHAPTER SEVEN

The Great Patriotic War, 1939–1945

I N SEPTEMBER 1938 the Central Committee Directorate for Propaganda and Agitation (Upravlenie propagandy i agitatsii Tsk VKP[b]) was reorganized under Andrey Zhdanov's leadership to bring the arts even more closely under Party control. This measure, as well as the concerted attacks on specific artists and works, resulted, to some degree, from a keen awareness of an impending war. The need to direct the arts to propagate a sense of nationalism was taken to be urgent. Plays and films had to present themes from Russian history, demonstrating the defense and expansion of the Russian land.

At the same time, diplomacy between Germany and the Soviet Union made it bad form for writers to comment on such fascist policies as anti-Semitism and anti-Communism. German works were often prescribed for performance. Eisenstein, for example, was commanded to stage a monumental *Walküre* at the Bol'shoy in 1937, shortly before he caricatured Nazi savagery in the nightmare figures of the Teutonic knights in his film *Aleksander Nevsky*.

The Molotov–Ribbentrop pact, confirming strict neutrality between the USSR and the Third Reich, was signed in 1939; it privately promised Russia all the territory it had lost after World War I. The compact enabled the Nazis to march into Czechoslovakia and Poland and the Soviets into Finland and the Baltic nations with impunity. Then, on June 21, 1941, Hitler launched Operation Barbarossa, taking Minsk, Smolensk, and Kiev and pushing within fifty miles of Moscow.

From the first days of the onslaught, in a tradition shaped in the Civil War, the theater actively participated in the defense of the country, first by continuing to play at any cost; then by sending tours into the front zone; and finally, by delegating its artists as instructors in "self-realizing" brigades. The care taken in preserving cultural institutions, instigated by Lunacharsky in the first years of Soviet power, was revived during the war; the theaters were evacuated as the Germans advanced, which had the unforeseen effect of implanting high-quality creative activity in such backwaters as Tashkent, Sverdlovsk, Kuybyshev, Chelyabinsk, Fergana, Irkutsk, Omsk, and Barnaul.

Russian culture was also reaffirmed by performing the classics, especially the Russian classics, thereby reminding the Soviet combatants what they were fighting for. Some 24,240 productions of Russian classics alone were performed in 1940.

Though it had no deep-seated influence on performance style, the war altered the repertoire, loosening the hold of censorship and allowing better plays to be staged. Soviet leaders were anxious to enlist the support of all loyal citizens, which meant concessions to peasants and churchgoers but also to the intelligentsia. The wartime alliances led to the inclusion of French, British, and American playwrights. The need for relief also encouraged the staging of light entertainment, along with the spate of patriotic dramas.

First place was allotted to nationalistic, resolutely psychological works consecrated to the struggle against the German invader. They explored the moral ideals and inner convictions of the fighter, the partisan, and the Soviet civilian. Simonov's fiercely patriotic *The Russian People* (1943) chronicled the courage and patriotism of ordinary civilians and soldiers in the face of death. (The emphasis on the "Russian people" was in step with wartime propaganda but, after the war, was denounced as bad taste when "Soviet patriotism" again became the Party slogan.) Halfway through the war, a new heroic drama appeared, in the line of the stirring, if crude, Civil War melodramas of the 1920s. Typical were plays dedicated to the defense of Sebastopol, Leningrad, and Stalingrad, such as Lavren'ëv's *Song of Those of the Black Sea* (1942), Vishnevsky's *Beneath the Walls of Leningrad* (1943–44), and Yury Chepurin's *Those of Stalingrad* (1942–44). Drama was distended to epic dimensions.

The war was propitious to historical drama. Preexisting plays were revived and revised to accentuate their anti-German character. All the eminent military commanders and victories of the past were celebrated, with strong parallels drawn between bygone triumphs and the ongoing war. Generals Kutuzov, Brusilov, and Bagration and Admiral Nakhimov were always characterized by their great love of the people. The new plays were of very uneven quality; the prerevolutionary Russian past was not only rehabilitated but embellished, and the class divisions in bygone Russia were elided in favor of chauvinistic imagery. In this spirit, several works were devoted to Ivan the Terrible, attempting to show the progressive aspect of his reign. This idealization of the tsar's personality suggested a tacit identification with Stalin, as in the bipartite play of Aleksey Tolstoy (1942–44).

Theater at the front became a civic duty, a form of military service. Performing under the most difficult of circumstances, on truck platforms, in the open air, with rudimentary equipment, gave rise to diverse forms. The most elementary was the highly mobile concert brigade (*kontsertnaya brigada*), capable of performing, in shelters and clearings, a repertoire composed principally of poems, songs, scenes from well-known plays, monologues, one-acts, sketches, and the like. The mobilized spectators were also offered, whenever possible, the standard theatrical "fit-up" of the prewar period, with curtain, wings, makeup, costumes, and sets. Much of this was improvised, since no attempt had been made since the civil war to systematize production methods born of war conditions.

From August 1939 to September 1940, some twenty-nine thousand performances of plays and concerts were given by various theatrical units before Soviet soldiers and sailors. Of this number, 3,377 concerts and plays were performed within a single ten-day period dedicated to the twenty-first anniversary of the Red Army and Navy. Once evacuated to Sverdlovsk, the Red Army Central Theater sent out a number of teams to fifteen points along the front, to stage scenes from classical drama for three weeks in winter 1942. The Front branch of the Red Army Theater gave more than twenty-five hundred concerts during the war years.

On the Eve

Order no. 625, December 1, 1939. In *Spravochnik vukovodyashchikh materialove Komiteta po delam iskusstva pri SNK soyuz SSSR* (Moscow: Iskusstvo, 1941), 19–20. Reprinted in A. Antonov-Ovseenko, *Teatr Iosifa Stalina* (Moscow: Gregori-Peydzh, 1995), 144–45.

1. The Committee for Artistic Affairs for the Sovnarkom of the USSR forbids rehearsal of "plays with characters of a leader" without special permission of the Chief Department of Theaters. To the authorized petitions presented by the Department for Artistic Affairs to the SK of the United Republics, there must be affixed a detailed description of the creative profile of the theater as a whole and the essential performers in the show; photographs of the interpreters of the leading roles—without makeup and in makeup; and a short directorial character sketch of the production. It is categorically forbidden to begin work on plays with characters of a party leader until these plays are authorized by the Glavrepertkom.

2. A production prepared by a theater will be accepted by the Department for Artistic Affairs of the United Republics only with the obligatory involvement of the representative of the republic or regional party organizer. [. . .]

3. A list of plays (productions) subject to authorization in the aforementioned order is especially established.

A DECREE of January 28, 1940, gave the Committee for Artistic Affairs power to organize new theaters and liquidate existing ones. A projected third Five-Year Plan intended to increase the number of theaters to 1,150 by 1943. A total of 270 million rubles had been assigned for the construction of fifty-six new playhouses, whereas 30 million rubles were designated for apartment houses for actors. The war would redirect those funds to other uses. A later decree turned its attention to the repertoire.

"On the improvement of the leadership of theater repertoires," Order no. 779, December 24, 1940. In *Spravochnik*, 14–17.

These last few years, the theater repertoires have been enlarged by a number of plays by Soviet authors, and a series of remarkable works of Soviet drama have appeared. Plays with characters of leaders of the Revolution are especially significant—*Man with*

7.1. *Kremlin Chimes* by Nikolay Pogodin, Moscow Art Theater, 1942, designed by V. V. Dmitriev, with A. N. Gribov as Lenin in his office at the Smolny Institute.

a Gun and *Kremlin Chimes* by N. Pogodin, *Lenin in '18* by Kapler and Zlatorovova, *The Bolshevik* by Dél',[1] etc., reflecting the passion and heroics of our party's struggle for the victory of the socialist revolution. [...]

Other than these Soviet dramas, there are few plays of high quality on modern Soviet themes. A series of plays in which the authors try to come to grips with problems of everyday life, family, morality, are faulty both in their ideological content and in their artistic values. The repertoire of some theaters seems clogged with works that are vulgar, anti-artistic, and even hostile to our nation. Only as a result of relaxed political oversight could such hostile works as Leonov's *Snowstorm* [*Metel'*], Kataev's *Cottage* [*Domik*], Glebov's *Cleanliness* [*Nachistota*], and a few others been permitted to penetrate theatrical stages.

Many managers and artistic directors of theaters have started on the path of commercial adjustments to the repertoire on behalf of the "box office," staging such vulgar, mindless plays as *Charley's Aunt, Sonny Boy* [*Synishka*], *The Spy's Throne* [*Trona shpiona*], *His Wife* [*Ego zhena*], etc. Catering to the taste of the backward portion of the audience discredits a theater and leads to ideologically artistic and financial collapse. [...]

The Administration for Artistic Affairs under the SNK of the United Republics must devote special attention to the everyday operative leadership of the theater, decisively combating irresponsible relationships to questions of repertoire on the part

1   They were performed in Leningrad: *Lenin v 1918 gody* (1940) is a stage version of a screenplay by Aleksey Yakovlevich Kapler (1904–79), adapted by Taisya (Tat'yana Semënovna). Zlatogorova (1912–50). *Bol'shevik* (1940) by D. Dél (actually Leonid Solomonovich Lyubashevsky, 1892–1975), an actor and playwright at various youth theaters.

of individual heads of theaters, who give pride of place to narrowly commercial goals, ignoring the cultural–political needs of the spectator.

With the aim of decisively improving the leadership of the theatrical repertoire, I order:

1. That the Glavrepertkom carry out a two-week inspection of the theaters' current repertoires and cleanse them of plays that distort Soviet reality and that are artistically bankrupt.

2. That the Glavrepertkom and the Chief Administration of Theaters select the best plays from Soviet and classic drama and draw up a hand-list of them for theaters. [...]

6. That the State order plays by the foremost playwrights on the themes: (a) the defense of the USSR, patriotism, love of one's country; (b) the successes of Soviet construction; (c) the victory of building collective farms and people of the new Soviet villages; (d) the moral temper of Soviet man; (e) the Soviet school and education of the younger generation; (f) the Soviet family. [...]

Konstantin Rudnitsky, "Ivan Bersenev," in Boris Poyurovsky, ed., *Zvezdy moskovskoy stseny. Lenkom* [Stars of the Moscow stage: Lenkom] (Moscow: Tsentroligraf, 2000), 17, 20–21, 29–32.

In 1938 Ivan Nikolaevich Bersenev headed the Moscow Theater of Working Youth, which was soon renamed the Lenin Komsomol Theater. [...] He wrote, "To put on a modern production is not only a duty of the theater but its organic necessity. Without modern drama a theater cannot live a normal creative life and develop. To display our Soviet life onstage, to reveal its depths, is as essential a need for the theater as it is for the poet—to sing of our land, its heroes, its aspirations. The citizen-actor cannot be satisfied with roles of a classic repertoire alone. In the great dramatic legacy of the past, there are colossal plays, titans of poetic creativity, which affirm noble human aspirations to freedom and truth and teach selfless devotion to one's homeland, sublime honor, and civic valor. We stage and perform these plays. But can they exhaust the theater's desire to incarnate the spectator's need to see onstage what he lives today and will live tomorrow? The Soviet theater is capable of putting on such a production."

[The play in question turned out to be *Front* by A. Korneychuk, which Bersenev directed.] This play was printed in *Pravda* and the actors learned their roles straight from the pages of the newspaper. The tempi, which Ivan Nikolaevich showed in work on this play, was again wonderful: the production was created in three weeks. [...] The play was written with passion, explosive anger, and belief in victory—this passion was conveyed to the director, the actors, and everyone wanted to convey it to the spectator.

Bersenev wanted to transmit to everyone who showed up in the audience, an audience packed with soldiers of the Soviet Army, heading for the front, the wounded just come out of hospitals, mothers and wives of defenders of the fatherland—to transmit to them, as he himself said, the "play's truth"—to show how talented military commanders are setting out to do battle, how selflessly and heroically they are fighting our war, how decisively they are extirpating from the army anything that is unnecessary, alien, or an obstacle to a successful struggle.

"I remember," related S. I. Giatsintova, "how this production was received: quite normally, with no attention paid to the actors' performances or the scenery, generally forgetting the theater, devoting oneself wholeheartedly to the subject of the play, accepting its events as utterly real facts of life. What was going on before their eyes was so gripping that our spectators forgot the stage. They themselves were, in a manner of speaking, 'transformed' and felt themselves to be not playgoers but participants and judges in this conflict unfolded in the play."

[Bersenev played the role of the manager of an airplane factory Miron Gorlov.] "When there came onstage a man in civilian clothes, not yet old but already extremely grizzled, with serious, observant eyes," wrote L. Vendrovskaya,[2] "he immediately made the spectator attend to his words with interest. The sluggishness and self-conceit of his brother, General Ivan Gorlov, he criticized directly, succinctly, with conviction" . . .

[Bersenev said:] "At first I was always afraid of slipping into the moralizing tone of a *raisonneur*. But then I suddenly realized what was important. I wanted this gravitas, this conviction in every word to be born as a result of Miron's great experience of life, the result of a heartfelt pain—because he really loves his brother!—and the feeling of the enormous responsibility which Miron has for him" . . .

In Act I, when Miron is a silent presence during Ivan's dialogue with Gaydar, Ognev, and others, Bersenev clearly showed how accurately Miron appraises his brother's egoism and self-love. Behind Miron's restraint one could feel his great passion and spiritual depths. And the more upset he was, the more restrained he became. At the party at Gorlov's, after all the guests had gone, Bersenev as Miron stood in deep thought, smoking a hand-rolled cigarette, and to his brother's question, "A penny for your thoughts?"—with restrained agitation, striving to be outwardly calm—he answered, "I'm thinking: Lord, when will our land be cleansed of fools, ignoramuses, toadies, nitwits, lickspittles." Then when Ivan left, tossing him a laugh and a crude remark in reply, and Miron was alone, there came an outburst, a discharge of his pent-up consternation. "We have to beat them, these self-centered ignoramuses, beat them until they bleed, beat them to smithereens and quickly change them into different beings—new, young, talented people," said Miron ardently and angrily.

And at the end of the play, when, irritated by Miron's forthrightness, Ivan rudely showed him the door, Bersenev significantly remarked, turning to Gorlov's adjutant, "Don't worry about me. I know my way perfectly well. You stay with the commander, I think he will soon have to be seen out himself." And in the glance he threw Ivan,

---

2   Lyubov' D. Vendrovskaya, curator of the Vakhtangov Theater Archive.

there was no offense at a personal insult but grief and sympathy for people such as Ivan Gorlov. Miron sauntered out of the room, with a sense of enormous dignity.

> Boris Poyurovsky, "A man in his place" [Valentin Pluchek[3]], *Moskovskaya Pravda* (September 2, 1984), reprinted in *Chto ostalos' na trube... Khroniki teatral'noy zhizni Vserossiyskoe Teatral'noe Obshchestvoroy poloviny XX veka* (Moscow: Tsentroligraf, 2000), 84–86.

His first and constant attachment is for Meyerhold, with whom he first studied acting technique, and then directing. Pluchek's debut onstage in the wordless role of the officer who jumps out of a bedside table in Meyerhold's *Inspector General* was noticed by Mayakovsky. Later Pluchek took part in *Bedbug* and *Bathhouse*. Even now he relates with rapture how the author read both plays to the company. And it begins to seem to you that it was only yesterday and you yourself were present.

Simultaneously the young director Pluchek headed TRAM (theater of young workers) as an electrician. And then with Aleksey Arbuzov he organized a studio, the very one that, on the eve of war, captivated theatrical Moscow with the legendary *The Town at Daybreak*.[4] This play about the builders of Komsomol'sk-on-the-Amur was created by art students themselves—young actors, university students, TRAM workers. Each one invented his role, and then A. Arbuzov reduced them all to a common denominator. In age he was almost a coeval of the rest of the art students. But not in status: his *Tanya*[5] had already resounded throughout the land.

The studio received the right of citizenship and began proudly to be called State; it was granted a club stage in Likhovoy alley and some funding. Pluchek was already dreaming about *Ruy Blas,* but the war broke out. The men immediately went to the front, in the army in the field, and many failed to return. And at the front Pluchek headed the Theater of the Northern Fleet.

The director's lyrical gift, his optimism, his intense emotion, first so clearly revealed in *The Town at Daybreak,* could not be seen to better advantage than there and then, on the very rim of his homeland, where the front line stood, in such productions as A. Kron's *Naval Officer,* Yu. German's *The White Sea,* and especially *Long, Long Ago* by A. Gladkov.[6] Moreover, for the first time, Pluchek turned to comedy and staged Lope de Vega's *The Dog in the Manger* and Carlo Goldoni's *Servant of Two Masters.*

3   Valentin Nikolaevich Pluchek (1909–2002), later director of the Moscow Satire Theater 1950–2000, where he staged Mayakovsky's trilogy, Bulgakov's *Flight, The Threepenny Opera,* along with more conventional Soviet fare, putting together a brilliant company of actors in the meantime.
4   *Gorod na zare* (1939) was an improvised play, written in collaboration with the actors of the Moscow Theater Studio, cofounded with Aleksey Nikolaevich Arbuzov (1908–86), who became the leading dramatist of the postwar generation. After its premiere at the studio a few months before war broke out, it played before front-line troupes 1941.
5   *Tanya* (1938), about a new woman overcoming obstacles, was produced at the Theater of Revolution with Mariya Babanova in the lead.
6   *Ofitser Flota* (1945) by Aleksandr Aleksandrovich Kron (actually Kreyn, 1909–83); *Beloe More* (1944) by Yury Pavlovich German; *Davnym-daleko* (1941), a heroic comedy in verse about the Napoleonic invasion of 1812, by Aleksandr Gladkov.

Where, one wondered, at such a tragic moment could one have the will to laugh? But in fact the demand for comedy in those days was even greater than before the war . . .

IVAN SUSANIN was the original title of Mikhail Glinka's opera *A Life for the Tsar* (1836), concerning the expulsion of the Poles and the inauguration of the Romanov dynasty in 1613. Its title hero is a peasant who misleads the invaders and undergoes torture to save the fatherland. The final chorus is a paean to the emperor. Glinka changed the title as an ingratiating gesture to Nicholas I. The tsarolatry proved to be a problem when the opera was revived in 1939, as war clouds gathered.

> *Ryadom s Stalinym v Bol'shom Teatre (Zapiski voennogo komandantova)* (n.p.:
> n.p., 1995), 15–16.

As war came closer, a patriotic repertory was needed. Its apogee was the operas *Ivan Susanin, Prince Igor'*, etc.

The opera about the heroic feat of the hero of Kostroma was born in torments, arguments, doubts. The first complication lay in the fact that the Committee for Artistic Affairs fixed bayonets against the finale "Praise be." The second was a sequel to the first—nobody knew how the finale would be interpreted by the government. And if the finished production was not approved, what would become of the enormous expenses? In their calculations one need only mention that it was necessary to build 2,709 costumes, as many headdresses, 5,418 pairs of shoes, complicated scenery and props . . .

S. Samosud took all this on himself. In Leningrad, such a concept was unrealizable. [. . .] There was an enormous risk: to stage the opera with the "Praise be," you could say good-bye to the theater.

But then fate took a hand. A ten-day festival of Leningrad art was going on in Moscow. Sholokhov's *The Quiet Don* and *Virgin Soil Upturned*[7] were brought to the capital. Samosud came to court. He explained his idea for a production of the opera *Ivan Susanin,* and the idea was supported. [. . .]

A public commission was created, which included nearly thirty persons [. . .] It had the right to carry on an inspection of any theatrical section, its preparedness for the forthcoming production. A total of 325 specialists worked on the production, and 390 experts in ninety-two specialties worked in the workshops. The enormous collective was headed by B. Mordvinov; the designated designer was Pëtr Vil'yams.[8] [. . .]

Everything went according to plan, but sparks of the argument about the finale flew up to the Kremlin. The chairman of the Committee for Artistic Affairs P. Kerzhentsev ordered, "Stage the opera without the finale 'Praise be.'" Samosud refused point-blank

---

7   Mikhail Sholokhov's popular epic novels about Cossacks *Tikhy Don* (1928–40) and *Podryataya Tselina* (1932) were turned into operas by Ivan Dzerzhinsky in 1935 and 1937, respectively, and were lauded as models of socialist realism in music.

8   Boris Arkad'evich Mordvinov (actually Sheftel', 1899–1953), began as an actor at the Second Studio from 1921, the MAT 1924–38; director at the Bol'shoy Theater 1936–40.

to stage the opera in such a truncated form. Stalin showed up at the theater and invited Kerzhentsev, Samosud, and Leont'ev[9] to a conclave. The factions stated their positions, arguments pro and con. Stalin listened to them with great attention, pacing in the stage box. Then Kerzhentsev asked, "Just who is Pozharsky?" And he answered himself, "A prince. In 1612 he was the inspirer and leader of the Russian people in a struggle against the Polish occupiers. And who was Minin? A merchant, just another tradesman. Who stood behind him? All the clergy, nobles, merchants, the entire Orthodox Russian world. Only by uniting their strengths could they defeat the Polish invasion. And just who is Ivan Susanin? The elected elder of the village of Domnino. He was chosen by the poor, and the rich, a priest, and they were all baptized. So stage *Susanin* in the theater with real historical accuracy, without any juggling with facts. Minin and Pozharsky should enter from the Kremlin on horseback with a religious procession, and the defeated Poles should be forced to throw their banners at the feet of the victorious Russian Orthodox people."

Only one scene was deleted, in which at the Spass gates Antonida and Susanin's foster son Vanya mourn the death of their father. It prolonged the opera and expressed private grief when the whole populace was exulting and celebrating the victory over the Poles.

The premiere of the opera took place on February 21, 1939. It had an unprecedented triumph. The entire government was present at the show.

Susanin ran throughout the war. He was cut down with sabers and burned on a bonfire—that was an invention of Samosud. And it happened that a not quite sober aviator with a pistol in hand came out of the audience to save Susanin. He reached the stage but was surrounded by members of the chorus, who forced him into the wings and then out of the theater.

After the war in meeting with veterans, I. Kozlovsky[10] related, "M. Mikhaylov[11] sang Susanin's aria in Act IV a thousand times, five hundred of them in felt boots at the front and in hospitals. It was the wonder of the twentieth century. He was inimitable, a second Chaliapin as Susanin."

IN LEONID LEONOV'S DEFENSE, in a play about a family conflict, *The Orchards of Polovchansk*, character determines events, as in most socialist realism.

B. Rostotsky, "Sovetskaya dramaturgiya na stsene MKhATa," in *Ezhegodnik MkhATa* [MAT yearbook] (Moscow: Izd. Muzeya Moskovskogo Khudozhest-

---

9 Yakov Leont'evich Leont'ev (1890–1948), administrator of the Maly Theater studio, deputy administrator of the MAT 1933–34; then at the Bol'shoy Theater.
10 Ivan Semënovich Kozlovsky (1900–1993), lyric tenor; at the Bol'shoy Theater 1926–54; Stalin's favorite singer, he was famous for his high notes.
11 Maksim Dormidontovich Mikhaylov (1893–1971), bass, at the Bol'shoy Theater 1932–56, became Stalin's favorite performer of the role of Ivan Susanin.

vennogo Akademicheskogo Teatra SSSR, 1947), 160–61. Boleslav Norbert Iosifovich Rostotsky (1912–81), theater critic, teacher at GITIS from 1944, authored several books about the MAT.

The Orchards of Polovchansk[12] breathes with the spirit of bright optimism growing from a deeply patriotic faith . . . in the victorious power of Soviet people. In this play, we meet representatives of the old way of life, and living corpses who try to hamper the construction of the new life. But they do not determine the atmosphere of the action. It concentrates on Soviet people who are honest and devoted to our country: the director of the Soviet state orchard—Adrian Makkhaveev[13]—and his sons . . . The play definitely rings with the conviction that Soviet people will resist the military threat with all the weapons in their power, with a fiery hatred of the enemy, and with a love for their socialist homeland.

ORDER 134 of March 19, 1940, stipulated work conditions, salaries, and costs for concert organizations, which were rapidly becoming the most widespread form of performance.

In 1940 Yury Lyubimov was drafted into the army, becoming an actor in the song and dance unit of the NKVD.

Yury Lyubimov, *Rasskazy starogo trepacha* (Moscow: Novosti, 2001), 170–71.

Once Beria[14] even visited us [the military ensemble] and selected the program for the Kremlin. Dunaevsky, brother of the "great" Dunaevsky,[15] was trembling all over. Upstairs in the administrator's office sat Shostakovich, Yutkevich, Tarkhanov,[16] Sveshnikov, Goleyzovsky—just in case Beria wanted to give instructions to them all—they all sat and waited. Of course, no one was allowed in the auditorium, only the actors onstage. Everyone waited in trepidation. Suddenly all the doors opened, guys in civilian clothes appeared, hands in their pockets. Then the door was flung wide open, Himself entered in a cap, an overcoat that he didn't remove. No "hello" or "good-bye" to anyone. He shouted in a Georgian accent:

"Get going."

And everyone began to twist and turn and dance and sing. This went on for about half an hour. Then a pause. And he said:

"Here's how it'll go at the Kremlin: first the song about the Leader, next the song

12 *Polovchanskie sady* (1939), in which each member of a Soviet family learns to be of use.
13 The Russian version of Maccabees.
14 Lavrenty Pavlovich Beria (1899–1953), first secretary of the Georgian Communist Party 1931–34, replaced Ezhov as head of the NKVD 1938–53, directing the administration of the forced labor camps and the development of atomic weaponry. Arrested and executed 1953.
15 Isaak Osipovich Dunaevsky (1900–1955), director of the Song and Dance Ensemble of the Central House of Culture of Railway Workers 1938–48; prolific songwriter, especially for films.
16 Mikhail Mikhaylovich Tarkhanov (actually Moskvin, 1877–1948), actor, director at the MAT from 1919 (in the Kachalov troupe) to 1948; brother of Ivan Moskvin.

about me: 'Shary bary, veriya, Beria'—in Georgian, there will be Georgians there, they'll dance and sing—Sukhishvili-Ramishvili—then there'll be the Moldavian dance and then there'll be the Russian dance, where the peasant girls spin around, and you can see their sexy thighs. That's all!"

And he left. All the doors slammed shut, the guys disappeared. And in the stillness an official of the ensemble said:

"Now that's what I call style! Let it be a lesson to you!"

THE Red Army Central Theater company, apart from sending two units to the new territories of Western Ukraine and Western Belorussia (part of Poland), remained in Moscow preparing the opening of the new theater building, which took place at a gala on October 14, 1940. Daily expenditures amounted to twenty-five thousand rubles, whereas the daily take with a capacity audience amounted to only twelve thousand rubles. The small rehearsal hall was turned into a separate theater to increase the audience.

> To the Official of the Ninth Section of the PURKKA Colonel Commissar Com.
> V. I. Maksimov, January 1, 1939. Copy to Partburo TsDKA Com. Sukharëv.

The reports of the partburo, as I reported, note that the collective of the troupe of the Central Theater of the Red Army is swollen, and even testify to the bad mood owing to the unemployment of many actors. It was proposed that the theater free itself of ballast. As of today the question has been dealt with in the following way: when a list was drawn up the troupe contained 107 persons, including students; at the present time 6 persons have already been let go and another 11 individuals will be let go [. . .]

Moreover, coms. Kruchinin and Trushin are immediately transferred from the troupe into the auxiliary team, and in this way today the troupe consists not of 107 persons but of

actors—90
students—6
auxiliary team—12 persons.

By releasing six persons, the savings come to 4,550 rubles per month, 54,600 rubles per year, and the theater will in no way suffer by this.

> *Urgryumov,* Official of the Central Theater of
> the Red Army Battalion Commissar.

A PRIME EXAMPLE of turning historic events into patriotic themes was Lukovsky's[17] *Battle at Grünwald,* which dramatized a conflict of 1410. Known to the Germans

---

17 Igor' Vladimirovich Lukovsky (1909–79), whose cliché-ridden play and screenplay *Admiral Nakhimov* (1941) were considered object lessons of this sort of dramaturgy.

as the Battle of Tannenburg, it was an occasion when a Polish–Lithuanian army inflicted a crushing defeat on the Teutonic Knights.

> Yu. Osnos, *Sovetskaya istoricheskaya dramaturgiya* [Soviet historical drama] (Moscow: Sovetsky pisatel', 1947), 270–71. Yury Aleksandrovich Osnos was a theater historian and playwright.

The entire historical situation on the eve of the famous battle is fictitious; it is presented like the international situation at the start of the Second World War. The play contains a "fifth column"—in the spy Fabrias, who bounces around from capital to capital. It has a cowardly political figure named Jagiello, who seeks peace at any price and keeps repeating, "If only Cracow were mine!" Wallendrodt, the Grand Master of the Teutonic Order, is depicted as an ordinary Hitlerite bandit.

> A. N. Tolstoy's play *Ivan the Terrible*. A. S. Shcherbakov, secretary of TsK VKP(b), to I. V. Stalin, April 28, 1941. *Glasnost'* 48 (November 28–December 4, 1991).

After deliberation on the play, it was denied the award of the Stalin Prize both for formal considerations (the play has not been published or performed in any theater, the Soviet public doesn't know it, the critics have not responded to it, etc.) and because of its essence, for the play distorts the historical profile of one of the most prominent Russian statesmen, Ivan IV [...]

The problem is that *Ivan the Terrible* was written at the special request of the Committee on Artistic Affairs, following the TsK VKP(b) instructions on the need to restore to Russian history the authentic historical profile of Ivan IV, which has been distorted by aristocratic and bourgeois historiography. [...] Therefore the staging of this play or its publication would increase the confusion in the minds of historians and writers on the issue of Russia's history in the sixteenth century and of Ivan IV.

Relative to what has been set forth here, we must ban the staging of A. N. Tolstoy's *Ivan the Terrible* in Soviet theaters, as well as the play's publication in print.

[Tolstoy "kissed the rod" and sedulously revised his play until it conformed to the appropriate line on Ivan IV as a destroyer of feudalism and builder of a centralized Russian state. He won the Stalin Prize in 1946.]

> Nikolay Akimov, "Our author Evgeny Shvarts" (March 1965), in M. L. Slonimsky, Z. Nikitina, L. N. Rakhmanova et al., *My znali Evgeniya Shvartsa (Ne tol'ko o teatre)* [We knew Evgeny Shvarts (not only about theater)] (Leningrad: Iskusstvo, 1966), 269–70.

This remarkable teller of tales was constantly tormented by a problem—to write a comedy about our times without any fantasizing. Our Comedy Theater [...] was also eager for such a play from him.

And then, a few months before the Patriotic War began, Shvarts wrote such a play. He called it *Our Hospitality*. The political situation was at that time rather complicated: a heroic, patriotic play was needed, directed against our enemies, enemies whom everyone knew but who could not be named. The historical reasons for this are notorious. And with that task Shvarts coped brilliantly. A foreign reconnaissance aircraft with a crew that spoke Russian with a thick accent makes a forced landing on our territory in a deserted steppe in the southwest of our land. A small group of Soviet youths led by an old teacher who has undertaken a natural history excursion comes across it.

The main task of the enemy team is to repair the plane and to hide what must not be discovered. Therefore our unarmed group is captured by the crew of the aircraft, behaves heroically, and, at the end, achieves a moral and actual victory. So, the very narrow frame of a small circle of characters on the eve of war showed a page from the struggle which in the ensuing year took on the dimensions of a world war.

The nationality of the aircraft could be surmised, but nowhere named, and on that score the play received no reprimand. But it did not manage to get staged, because it was banned by the Glavrepertkom for another reason.

The fact of a flight by a foreign aircraft across our borders was considered unrealistic and humiliating for the dignity of our government.

No arguments that, at a high altitude, at night, a single plane, which, in any case, was discovered and rendered harmless by the end of the play, could cross the border had any effect. "Haven't you read," they said to us sternly, "that our border is closed? Consequently, the basic situation of the play is improbable and impossible!"

On June 22, 1941, we ruefully became convinced that no precautions on the borders could stop enemy aircraft and that Shvarts's hitherto banned play could and should be staged.

JUNE 22, 1941, was the first day of the war, and mobilization of the arts began immediately. On day 2 of the invasion, the Central Committee of RABIS (the Union of Art Workers) sent out a circular to embarkation points, recruiting offices, and railroad stations informing troops that "where units of the army or navy can be found, art workers will be sharing their lives. Now as never before, art will be a mighty and warlike means of victory of communism over fascism."[18] The Red Army formed a song and dance ensemble within weeks of the German invasion. Over the course of the war, variety artistes offered 1.35 million concerts, more than 473,000 in close proximity to the front lines.

Evacuation of the Moscow Theaters

The German army, trying to get within artillery range of Moscow, were constantly harassed by Russian aircraft and raids, with great losses to the Soviets, and also

18 O. A. Kuznetsova, "Éstrada v periode velikoy otechestvennoy voiny," in *Russkaia sovetskaia éstrada*, ed. E. Uvarova (Moscow: Iskusstvo, 1976), 2:372.

suffered greatly from bivouacking in a freezing forest; on December 1, 1941, the Germans were definitively halted.

At the Moscow Circus, the clown Karandash invented an act called "How the Fascists Came to Moscow and Back."

> Mikhail Rumyantsev, *Na arene sovetskogo tsirka* [In the ring of the Soviet circus], ed. Evgeny Kuznetsov (Moscow: Iskusstvo, 1954), 126–28. Mikhail Nikolaevich Rumyantsev (1901–83), the clown known as Karandash (Pencil), progressed from Charlie Chaplin imitation to his own comedy, often using small animals.

I got an idea for an act about the failure of Hitler's attack on Moscow.

Taking an ordinary barrel of large dimensions, I put it on a goods truck, whose wheels I covered with painted canvas, depicting a long line of tanks. The tank's tower was represented by another ordinary box stuck on top with a chunk of log sticking out. In front on the little bottom of a can I painted a skull and crossbones. Then I got into this tank. On entering the ring, as if approaching Moscow, the tank exploded and burst into pieces, and, laboriously extricating myself from the debris, my clothes in ragged tatters, I ran back to where I'd come from.

Technically it was a simple setup: all I had to do was disconnect the hoops that held together the barrel composed of tiny wooden slats, for the "tank" to fall to pieces instantly. At that moment I only had to throw up my arms and legs sharply, as pieces of "the tank" flew in all directions, and at the same moment I made a forward somersault to one side as if propelled by the force of the explosion. This effect was strengthened by the boom of the explosion, accompanied by thick smoke. While the "tank" moved to the center of the ring, where the explosion occurred, I had time to pull off the loosely fastened costume covering, which concealed the tattered rags, and in that guise I flew out of the tank at the moment of the "catastrophe."

...But how was I to transfer this theme to my own comic persona [...] so that the Hitlerite would be portrayed not by me, the actor Rumyantsev, but by Karandash.

Finally I decided on a very simple means [...] I would show it to the ringmaster [...] just as children show their improvisations to grown-ups. [...]

I began to devise a costume: covered with a sack, on my face I fastened a half-human, half-canine mask, on my head a cast-iron cooking pot for a helmet, and, arming myself with an enormous prop axe, cudgel, and knife carved from wood, I marched straight ahead with legs wide apart, staring in the distance. Meanwhile behind my back men in uniform brought in my tank. I got into it and with the shout "Nach Moskau" rolled forward in the tank. In the center the tank, as I've already recalled, broke apart, after which, having pulled myself out from under the heap of rubble, I stood stock still for a second as if not understanding what had happened. Then, recovering, I quickly bound up my head in a kerchief, grabbed a crutch and stick, and hobbled off on one leg into the wings.

IN JULY 1941 a German air raid completely destroyed the building of the Vakhtan-gov Theater, the playhouse closest to Nazi artillery, during a performance of *Fieldmarshal Kutuzov*. The company was allowed to use the secondary stage of the Moscow Art Theater, which was trying to maintain normal practice under trying circumstances. The theater created a brigade that debated whether a classical repertoire of Pushkin, Dostoevsky, Chekhov, and Gorky would appeal to the troops; it was heartened by the enthusiastic reception it received.

> Ol'ga Bokshanskaya's reports to Nemirovich-Danchenko,[19] in *Pis'ma O. S. Bokshanskaya Vl. I. Nemirovichu-Danchenko*, ed. I. N. Solov'ëva (Moscow: Moskovsky Khudozhestvenny Teatr, 2005), 2:531–32, 536.

August 29, 1941. Moscow. [. . .] On the night of the 19th there was a raid, with bombs. Once that night Nezhny[20] called to tell me that so far no luggage is available. To tell the truth, somehow this didn't bother me particularly—I was tired, the previous night the all-clear had been sounded at 5:00 a.m., and tonight, actually, at 2:00. But I got home exhausted. And no sooner had I talked to Nezhny, when intense shooting started again. True, no alarm was sounded, but nobody slept at home, and even without an alarm, many hurried along to the shelters, and the tramping of feet was distinctly heard in the street—many running feet. After that night there was no alarm until the night of the 28th. This did not save us from nights "with one eye open." The nights are dark, very dark. To be close to the shelter, I and many others arrive at the theater between 9:00 and 10:00 p.m., when we can still see the way on the street. We sit in the theater—we chat, then we start to doze off on the sofas, benches in the lobby, on bunks specially set up in the new rehearsal spaces and in a separate part of the lower lobby. I never go in these last two places, because these bunks are rather dirty, and there is a good number of bedbugs in them, as everyone admits. I wake up a couple of times, and when I'm wide awake around 4:00, I head for home, undress there, and lie in bed about four hours. Some of those who come to the theater sleep there until morning and head for home at 8:00 to 9:00—to wash, change clothes. Then, on the night of the 27th to the 28th, the alarm was sounded for nearly two nights and the all-clear at 1:30. No bombs were dropped. There was shooting, but not before they sounded the alarm, and none during the alarm. Last night, in a pouring rain (as there had been during the day, rain and more rain), went by without an alarm. In the interval between the 9th and the 18th I didn't write, because there were alarms nearly every day and there was news about them in the papers and on the radio. All of us are coping splendidly. [. . .]

August 30. [. . .] (By the way, at the present time, of the total number of 160 actors, we have only 50: some have been called up, some are in the home guard, some are sick, some on duty or short-time leave. But the troupe is fully adequate for the single stage

---

19 Nemirovich-Danchenko had already evacuated to Nal'chik, capital of the Kabardino-Balkhar Republic in the Caucasus. He had left it by the time the Nazis overran it in 1942.
20 Igor' Vladimirovich Nezhny (1892–1968), assistant, then administrator, at the MAT 1940–52.

available, even more than necessary, and Kalish[21] enthusiastically hands out leaves, if an actor is not overoccupied. This is so that at the end of the year they won't have to pay out wages for leaves untaken.) Anyway, *Pushkin*[22] is in rehearsal—getting ready to be shown to the Committee. The theater is very concerned that it open: it will assure box-office takings, a new premiere, satisfied actors who get to play new roles, and once Stanitsyn is free as a director, it might to possible to use him for a comedy, which they're looking for and definitely want to find, he's a very good comic director. But all the same, *Pushkin* won't open all that quickly, because all the productions are jostling each other onstage. In effect we have the stage for on-stage rehearsals three times a week: Tuesday, Wednesday, and Thursday. On Friday, Saturday, and Sunday we perform the daily shows: at 10:00–11:00 for the subscription groups and 3:00–4:30 for the general public. Monday is a day off. Let's say Iv. Yak.[23] now starts to stage *Pushkin* to show the Committee, and there's no way to do anything more because the branch stage is full of Vakhtangovians. And now our stage is assigned roughly in this way: meanwhile Acts I, II, and III of *Reconnaissance in Depth*[24] "were being formulated" (Kedrov's[25] expression). Now they've partially conceded the stage to *Pushkin*. After this time they will prepare insertions to *Chimes,*[26] and *Chimes* will have the stage until it is open to the public. Later, even if *Pushkin* is allowed, *Reconnaissance* will get the stage, and, once they're free of [*Kremlin*] *Chimes,* the actors will begin to rehearse *Suvorov*[27] in the lobby. And *Pushkin,* again supposing it's licensed, will go onstage and open right after *Reconnaissance.* [...]

Now obligatory military studies have been introduced for actors. That is, not only for the actors, but generally for all persons of a certain age. So that the actors have to deal with this, and they often make the point that they are being worked to death: what with war readiness and day duty at the theater and at home on the roof, and rehearsals, and performances, and concerts. But it isn't hard to make them see reason, if you remind them that many millions now have it much worse.

The Battalion Marches Westward (*Batal'on idët na Zapad,* 1941) by the Georgian playwright Georgy Davidovich Mdivani (1905–81) concerns a Georgian collective farm before and after militarization. It was staged by the Kamerny Theater.

---

21 Grigory Mikhaylovich Kalishyan, assistant manager of the MAT 1938–42.
22 *Pushkin* is better known as *Last Days* (*Poslednie Dni*) by Mikhail Bulgakov; it had been licensed for performance as early as 1935 but was not performed by the MAT until 1949.
23 Ivan Yakovlevich Gremislavsky (1886–1954), son of the MAT's original makeup artists, director at the First Studio, later designer at the MAT 1918 until his death.
24 *Glubokaya razvedka* (1941) by A. A. Kron was performed by the MAT 1943; it was his last play.
25 Mikhail Nikolaevich Kedrov (1893–1972), actor, director, at the MAT from 1924, whose best role was Tartuffe 1939; head of the Stanislavsky Dramatic Theater 1939–48 and served in various administrative posts at the MAT 1940–63.
26 *Kremlevskie Kuranty* by Nikolay Pogodin was first performed by the MAT in 1942; a hagiographic play about Lenin, it became one of the standards in their repertoire well into the 1960s.
27 *Polkovodets Suvorov* by I. Bakhterev and A. Razumovsky, about the eighteenth-century general, was performed at the MAT 1948.

"G. Mdivani's *The Battalion Marches Westward,*" *Pravda* (September 23, 1941).

Hundreds of eyes in the auditorium were glued to the stage. Everyone became a participant in the action. Everyone saw his own home, his own hopes, his own good-byes, and
his own military experience in his mind's eye [...]. The audience took the presentation
to be a continuation of the military day. It breathed courage and conviction.

AFTER THE WAR the critic Yukovsky, in *Znamya* (Banner), rebuked the author
and actors for being evacuated east, while their characters stayed and fought on
the western front.

> Memorandum from the TsK VKP(b) Propaganda and Agitation Administra-
> tion to Secretary G. M. Malenkov, August 7, 1944. Quoted in Katerina Clark
> and Evgeny Dobrenko, with André Artizov and Oleg Naumov, *Soviet Culture
> and Power: A History in Documents 1917–1953* (New Haven, Conn.: Yale Uni-
> versity Press, 2007), 377. © 2007 by Yale University.

Spectacle was badly needed—the war had begun. The play had the instructive, result-
oriented title *The Battalion Heads Westward.* We have to say, because it is instructive,
albeit offensive, that while *The Battalion Heads Westward* was heading for the stage,
its author and actors were evacuated eastward.

[Remarks such as these were held against Mdivani after the war during the purge
of theater critics.]

SHORTLY AFTER the destruction of the Vakhtangov Theater, the Bol'shoy was twice
damaged by German bombs. Evacuation "bases" in the eastern part of the USSR
had been planned before the war, primarily for heavy industry, with shelter for the
machinery but not the workers. Government departments moved to Kuybyshev,
and the Bol'shoy opera and ballet companies, along with the costumes and scenery,
accompanied them. As the German advance went deeper, the provincial theater
companies closed down and hastened eastward in an unorganized fashion. A
great many actors stayed and waited for Germans. In the big cities the evacuation
of the theaters was the responsibility of their individual administrators, since officialdom had made no special provision for artists (or the Jews who dominated
the performance professions). The Red Army Theater abandoned its new building
and evacuated to Sverdlovsk, the Maly to Chelyabinsk, the Kamerny to Irkutsk,
the Mossovet to Alma Ata. On October 13 two groups from the MAT were told
they would be evacuated to Tashkent but wound up in Saratov.

Sergey Lemeshev, *Put' k iskusstvu* [The road to art] (Moscow: Iskusstvo, 1968), 206–7. Sergey Yakovlevich Lemeshev (1902–77), lyric tenor, sang at the Bol'shoy Theater 1931–65, a rival of Kozlovsky.

In autumn our collective [of the Bol'shoy Theater] prepared for evacuation, which began in the second week of October.

Anyone who was not in Moscow at that time has no idea what it went through on the night of October 15–16. The alarm began in the early morning. Buses had disappeared from the city transport—that was immediately apparent. People stood in queues for bread—silently, sullenly. The police had vanished somewhere. In their stead one found civilians with weary faces, clumsily holding rifles by their straps. A wet snow mixed with rain fell on and off. Hundreds of cars, tearing along toward Gorky Embankment, churned up filthy geysers of heavy spatters... An unprecedented, suspicious silence lay over the city. Moscow's nighttime silhouette was dark and mournful. The balloons overhead increased this impression, a motionless mass frozen over the lowering roofs. All night long, there was no lessening in the movement in the streets. And there was something inexplicably uncanny about this: after all, a curfew was in effect in Moscow. It meant that something had happened at the front that had caused people to break the rules.

Under the streetlamps groups of people collected. Suitcases, sacks of belongings at their feet... They were waiting for some conveyance. At 6:00 a.m. a loudspeaker crackled, and the unwontedly sullen voice of Levitan[28] pronounced, "The situation outside Moscow has worsened..." I stopped listening. It had all become clear.

On the 17th I was to leave with the third and last group from the theater. In the morning we came to Komsomol Square. People were sitting on suitcases waiting for the order of embarkation. Our send-off was led by Mikhail Borisovich Khrapchenko, president of the Committee for Artistic Affairs. I remember the performers kept seeking him out in the square and making inquiries, when we were finally put on the train. The weather was very cold, and I was for some reason dressed very lightly and very quickly froze. Mikhail Borisovich advised me to go home and get warm, saying:

"Go ahead, we won't be leaving in a hurry, the roads have been trampled down and are in a terrible state."

So I went home twice, and a third time, having left the station about ten o'clock at night. I drank some hot tea, and ... fell asleep. In the morning, there was no one to go with. In three days I began to get inflammation of the lungs, followed by pleurisy. On November 7, I remember, I was already feeling well enough to listen on the radio in our den to the broadcast of the parade in Red Square and Stalin Square. There was a 25-degree frost, and the radio brought to our ears the crunch of tank tracks on the first snow that had fallen the night before. The troops went straight from the parade to the front, into battle... I lived on Gorky Street and saw the tanks, those monsters of war, on the move. A makeup of camouflage and snowballs gave them a somber "worker's" look.

28 Yury Levitan (1914–83), "the voice of Moscow," was a much-loved announcer for the All-Union Radio; Hitler so hated him that he swore he would personally wring Levitan's neck when Moscow fell.

I began to work, sang at concerts for units forming at the front, went into hospitals, call-up stations.

In Kuybyshev the Bol'shoy Theater opened its new season.

But some people stayed in Moscow. Mikhail Markovich Gabovich received permission to organize the work of an affiliate. We came to the first meeting with a certain excitement. How many of us? Not so few, as it turned out. [...] In short, a company. If not large, at least not so small that it was impossible to work. Even an orchestra and a chorus were made up.

In these difficult days we literally discovered in Gabovich an irreplaceable "front" director. A remarkable dancer, a brilliant performer, he, it turned out, possessed an innate talent as an organizer and leader [...]

So on November 19, when the front was no more than thirty or forty kilometers away from the capital, we opened our first season in the affiliate with a great concert. All the big names were represented in it. I won't conceal that I intended to join the "Kuybishites" as soon as possible. Restlessness, darkness, cold, especially harsh that winter, were oppressive. And then, too, I felt I was of no importance. [...]

Evgeny Simonov, *Nasledniki Turandot* [The heirs of *Turandot*] (Moscow: Algoritm, 2010), 64. Evgeny Rubenovich Simonov (1925–94), son of Ruben Simonov, managed the Vakhtangov Theater after his father's death (1968–87); he founded the Ruben Simonov Studio Theater in Moscow 1988, which became the Simonov Dramatic Theater 1995.

On October 14, 1941, the train pulled out of Yaroslavl' station, carrying into evacuation the collectives of the Maly and Vakhtangov theaters. The Maly Theater was headed for Chelyabinsk, the Vakhtangov for Omsk.

Nikolay Pavlovich Okhlopkov and his wife, Elena Ivanovna Zotova, traveled in the carriage next to ours. Okhlopkov often paced the corridor and looked out the window for a long time. His face was taciturn and stern. [...]

"I could strangle Hitler with my own hands... I could," Okhlopkov suddenly burst out and then sank back into his ruminations.

Natalia Vovsi-Mikhoëls, *Mon père Salomon Mikhoëls. Souvenirs sur sa vie et sur sa mort,* trans. Erwin Spatz (Montricher, Switzerland: Les Éditions noir sur blanc, 1990), 170.

On October 16, at six o'clock in the morning, the greater part of the company of the State Jewish Theater was evacuated to Tashkent.

It was suggested that Mikhoéls leave for Nachik, where they were sending the best actors of the Moscow theater, what they were calling their "gold reserve." But my father refused. It may seem corny, but he really could not imagine life outside his theater. That very night, he sped to Kuybyshev, and from there to Tashkent. He probably chose that itinerary to get official confirmation of the theater's arrival in Tashkent: all the government offices were in Kuybishev at the time.

IN DECEMBER 1941 Mikhoéls was appointed chairman of the Jewish Anti-Fascist Committee, and from April 1942, he traveled through North America, Mexico, and Great Britain, raising millions of dollars and great amounts of matériel and medical supplies for the war effort.

The Russian counteroffensive began on December 5, 1941.

On times for beginning and ending performances, Order of the Committee for Artistic Affairs no. 802, December 31, 1941. In *Spravochnik Komiteta* [Committee Handbook], 105.

With the aim of improving service to the spectator *I order*:

1. At all theaters subordinate to unions, from January 10, 1941, evening performances are formally to begin at 8:30 and finish no later than 12:15.
2. In connection with this the managers of theaters are to examine the schedule set by the production and shorten the intermissions as much as possible.
3. The ending of specific performances later than the appointed time is to be allowed only with prior permission by an official of the Chief Administration of Theaters. [...]

THE EVACUATED THEATERS tried to carry on as normally as possible, often finding the places of evacuation more comfortable and well supplied than they were used to.

Ol'ga Bokshanskaya to Nemirovich-Danchenko. In *Pis'ma O. S. Bokshanskoy,* 2:589.

January 24, 1942. Saratov. [About *Kremlin Chimes*] The question of the role of Stalin was rather difficult to resolve. Did I write you that they decided to rehearse Gerasimov?[29] [...] When it was shown to the Khudsovet, Gerasimov did not satisfy many members of the council, and it was decided to show him a second time a day later. But almost nobody came to the second showing, and it was easy for Gerasimov's supporters to convince those committee members who were present. The question was, in this way, decided almost by itself in favor of Gerasimov. Khmelëv has taken a lot of time with Gerasimov and will achieve good results, he (Gerasimov) has made enormous successes for himself. And besides, outwardly (especially from the front), with the help of Faleev,[30] he greatly resembles portraits of Stalin from that period, and besides he is fastidious about the text (remember how Bolduman's text went awry because of the characteristic speeches he left out?)—the result will be quite proper and thoroughly

---

29 Georgy Avdeevich Gerasimov (1900–1961), actor and pedagogue; at the MAT from 1923, usually in secondary roles.
30 Mikhail Grigor'evich Faleev (1884–1956), makeup artist and wigmaker; at the MAT from its founding in 1898 to 1955.

dignified, accurate. He doesn't catch fire, there's none of the infectiousness of a leader in him, but when it comes to the external likeness—that's there.

THE Art Theater director Vasily Sakhnovsky had been arrested during the night of November 4–5, 1941. He explained later to Nemirovich-Danchenko that, not having left for Saratov with the rapidly evacuated Art Theater, the authorities figured that "he will be around to work when the Germans take Moscow." A rumor had spread that the German command intended to put him on the team of a provisional government, after the fall of Moscow. All this had come about because he had had unsupervised meetings with émigrés in Paris in summer 1937, during the MAT tour. Two days after Sakhnovsky's arrest, the dramatist Afinogenov, about to leave on a propaganda trip to America, was killed by a Nazi bomb. By mid-March 1942, the front was stabilized forty miles west of Moscow.

> V. I. Nemirovich-Danchenko to Stalin, December 18, 1942. In Inna Solov'ëva, ed., "Pis'ma naverkh," *Moskovsky nablyudatel'* 3–4 (1996), 71.

Most respected, dear Iosif Vissarionovich!

For several months I have been wrestling with my reluctance to direct your attention away from the most important matters that concern you. I decided only because I understand the interest you always show to the fates of our theaters. For a long time it seemed to me that I dare not do otherwise.

The Art Theater keenly needs a major director. I myself am capable only of heading it. And although I have not left the stage, I am trying to sort out the future. I especially prize this present time, which literally demands right now that I take my bearings, remove the accumulated sores, and organize myself from scratch.

And in the meantime the best of the two or three I have with me, V. G. Sakhnovsky (*Dead Souls, Anna Karenina,* et al.), has been exiled from Moscow. I know only too well the reason why, during the theater's evacuation in October of last year, he did not leave—he lay ill in his dacha after an attack of angina pectoris.

(There is no way I can suspect him of malice aforethought!)

Meanwhile he has not been stripped of his title (People's Artist) nor his medal (the Red Banner of Labor) nor his property. And he lives in Alma Ata—a climate especially harmful to him.

He was my primary stage director and my deputy artistic director. In the latter case Khmelëv has been a fine replacement for him, and remains so, but as a stage director Sakhnovsky is irreplaceable. Suffice it to say that the work on *Hamlet*[31] has been completely frozen. But I have hastened to prepare a detailed plan for Shakespeare's *Antony and Cleopatra.* And the responsibilities of the chief stage director with us hang in the air.

---

31 *Hamlet* was a pet project of Nemirovich-Danchenko; rehearsals ended with his death.

If possible, our dear patron, if it is not a present danger, help to bring him back. And I pray excuse me for the time I have taken.

Sincerely yours *Vl. Nemirovich-Danchenko.*

SAKHNOVSKY was freed on December 22, 1942, and returned to work at the Art Theater.

The seaport of Odessa was besieged for seventy-three days in August and September 1941. By government command, a concert brigade was recruited, which performed five or six times a day, every day. When the population was finally evacuated by ship, the performers were among the last to be removed, as Hitler's Romanian troops swarmed into the city. The brigade continued its activities in the Northern Caucasus.

The Siege of Leningrad

Hitler's plan was to besiege Leningrad and starve it into submission. Three million inhabitants were trapped, and supplies of food, drugs, and other necessities could only be brought across an ice road on Lake Ladoga. By the time the siege was lifted on January 27, 1944, nine hundred thousand Leningraders had died. Still, throughout the three-year blockade, Leningrad witnessed twenty-five thousand musical and dramatic performances.

> G. I. Sukhanov, *Teatr, lyudi, zhizn'*... [Theater, people, life...] (St. Petersburg: n.p., 1992), 140–41.

[About the Leningrad Pushkin (formerly Alexandra) Theater] I remember one bright frosty January Friday. There were performances in the theater—a matinee and an evening one. Trams were moving along the Nevsky Prospect. German artillery shells hit the Eliseev store and went through the very bottom of an overcrowded tramcar. [...] I cannot describe how many victims there were, how the car was practically cut in half, front and back, how the snow absorbed the blood, taking on a strange reddish-pink tint, nor can I describe the suffering of the wounded, writhing in the snow, with blood flowing like manganese and iodine. [...] In the theater the show was stopped and we, actors and staff, all who could, ran to the scene of the catastrophe to save whomever we could. It was very sunny and frosty. Because there were very few stretchers, we transported the wounded in our arms to the theater's first-aid station. We put them right on the floor. When the first-aid station area became filled to overflowing, we put them on the floor in the adjacent corridor. I was wearing a beat-up old overcoat of sheet wadding—a winter one. When I transported the last person, I remember the frantic beating of my heart, the tears freezing on my face, and my stiffening arms, because the sleeve of my overcoat was thoroughly drenched with blood, which froze there. To bend my arms at the elbow, I had to tear off the frozen sleeves.

The brilliant artiste of the Alexandra Theater Nina Mikhaylovna Zheleznova[32] reigned over our first-aid station. She and her husband, an actor at the same theater, did not evacuate with the company but lived in the theater in a "pseudo-barracks situation," as such a way of life was then called. Nina Mikhaylovna, a highly cultured individual, supervised the medical stations too, stood in at the theater for doctor and nurse, helping everyone she could. I remember that on that day she was up to her elbows in blood. After first aid was rendered in our station the wounded were removed to a hospital. We called that day "Bloody Friday."

[...] A performance of Kálmán's *Circus Princess*[33] was under way. During the third and last act an artillery bombardment unexpectedly began. Heavy shells burst one after another in the immediate proximity of the theater. By the instructions of the PVO the spectators had to be evacuated quickly from the auditorium into the corridors and lobby of the theater, because the ceiling over the auditorium was unreliable, whereas the walls of the Alexandra Theater were, on the contrary, very thick, good old-fashioned masonry that served as a decent shelter even from direct hits. A shell, exploding in a full audience, would have caused tremendous human casualties. Our audience was inured to any combat situation that might arise and, at the first powerful explosions, would rise from their seats and file out during the bombardment into the corridors adjacent to the parterre and the circle.

Akimov, "Our author Evgeny Shvarts," 270–72.

Shortly after the war began, the academic theaters were evacuated from Leningrad, but four theaters—the TYUZ, Musical Comedy, Radlov's theater, and the Comedy Theater—were left to sustain the populace of the city. Beyond the basic repertoire, it was desirable, naturally, to perform what would respond to the conditions experienced. Such a play had to be created, because nothing like it had been prepared. I turned to my two favorite playwrights, Evgeny Shvarts and Mikhail Zoshchenko, with the appeal to create energetically in a comic framework a combative work that would lift the spirits of the spectators. After brief discussions they decided to collaborate, splitting up the scenes of a scenario created as a team.

The work of the theater and the playwrights progressed at a feverish pace, the scenes were rehearsed as soon as written, without waiting for the completed play, and in a month and a bit a desperate production was born (at times I couldn't even recall its title), a grotesque show called *Under the Lindens of Berlin*. Hitler appeared in it with his henchmen, who predicted a quick defeat—remarkably quicker than it seemed in fact! After performing this show a few times, we removed it from the repertoire. Events

---

32 Nina Mikhaylovna Zheleznova had played Nina in the 1926 revival of Meyerhold's *Masquerade* and appeared in silent film.

33 Emmerich Kálmán's operetta *Die Zirkusprincessin* (1926) contains several interpolated scenes set in a circus.

had intensified, the ring of the blockade had closed up around Leningrad, and witty mockery of overconfident fascism seemed to be poorly received in the midst of air raids. The decision to remove the show was completely unanimous with the authors and our leading organizations.

Autumn 1941 saw such rapid changes in the situation, living conditions, and the aspect of the city that it was difficult to plan ahead.

Our theater moved into the building of the Bol'shoy Dramatic Theater, which had left Leningrad at the very outbreak of the war. The move was dictated by the presence in the building on the Fontanka of bomb shelters for spectators caught in air raids and the lack of them in our building on the Nevsky. It soon turned out that for performances to take place, the actors and the whole staff had to live in the theater itself—otherwise no one could be sure of showing up on time for a performance or rehearsal. With the advent of cold weather, snowfalls, and the gradual reduction of electric power, connections with friends became very difficult, the distances in a city without public transport became palpable in all their primitive force.

[With difficulty Akimov persuaded Shvarts to leave the city.]

A month after the Shvartses left, in late December, when it had become utterly impossible to perform shows because of the want of light and water, the Comedy Theater was evacuated in five Douglas aircraft to Bol'shaya Zeml'ya and, after trekking through the Urals and the Caucasus, settled down to regular work in the capital of Tadjikistan. Shortly thereafter we managed to make contact with Evgeny L'vovich. He turned out to be in the town of Kirov in sorry straits.

After a few months' work in Dushanbé, meeting with a very hearty welcome from the authorities of Tadjikistan and great interest on the part of the spectators, among them more than a few of our old Leningraders who had also been evacuated there, our theater was so strengthened after the blockade both physically and creatively that I had no hesitation in sending out a call to Shvarts, inviting him to run the literary section of the theater. Soon he and his wife joined us, almost as emaciated as we had left him in Leningrad, but enthusiastic, joyful, and warmly welcomed by the whole theater.

Testimony of Evgeniya Mezheritskaya. In *Teatr Muzykal'noi Komedii v Gody Blokady* [The Musical Comedy theater during the blockade] (Leningrad: Iskusstvo, 1973), 20–23.

The organization of the performing service of the front was headed by the municipal Military Patronage Commission.[34] From spring 1942 it was run by an official of the Department of Artistic Affairs, B. I. Zagursky.[35]

The commission, working on a voluntary basis, was located on the premises of the School of Choreography on Architect of Russia Street. Here all the performers from

34 The Military-Patronage Commissions were the local equivalents of the USO, organizing entertainment for the troops.

35 Boris Ivanovich Zagursky, chief of the Department of Artistic Affairs in Leningrad and director of the Maly Opera Theater; illness confined him to the Bol'shoy Theater in winter 1942.

the theaters, philharmonics, conservatories, and music halls who remained in the city assembled. Here the claims of *politotdels* were turned in. It was the headquarters of Military Patronage work.

On the books of the commission were nearly 300 performers, including those left in Leningrad, students of the conservatories, the Theater Institute, oldsters who frequented the Choreographic Institute.

Each participant of a front brigade would show his repertoire to a special inspection committee. It was made up of representatives of the City Committee party, the repertoire committee, the Department for Artistic Affairs, and the municipal military-patronage commission.

[. . .] In some cases it was necessary to intensify hatred for the enemy, to stir up the fighters before the fight. So we would include works of a patriotic nature—Susanin's aria, Simonov's poem "The Artillery Man's Son,"[36] or Bezymensky's[37] "Letter Enclosed in a Parcel."

In other cases, fighters, after heavy combat, required relaxation, recreation, and so the concert included sketches, arias, duets, and scenes from operettas. Lidiya Aleksandrovna Kolesnikova,[38] for instance, often sang Délibes's "Bolero" and Blanter's lyrical song "On the White White Mountain." They loved the singing. In myriad letters they asked us to send them the words scored for the bayan.

On national holidays, up to forty brigades had to be put together, each of which gave two to three concerts a day. [. . .]

A Captain Levchenko wrote from the front: "*. . . a group of artists of the Theater of Musical Comedy [. . .] gave twenty-one concerts under extremely difficult conditions in forward positions. The concerts frequently took place in the rain, in conditions prevailing at the front, at night, by the light of automobile headlights and bonfires. The participants in the concerts, enthused by the fact that they were being heard by thousands of men and officers, worked with high spirits, a feeling of patriotism, proper to Soviet artists.*"

WHEN the only remaining theater in the city, the Musical Comedy, reopened, it was filled every night despite cold, hunger, shelling, and the exchange of bread rations for tickets.

Teatr Muzykal'noi Komedii v Gody Blokady, 24–27.

[*Aleksandr Ivanovich Orlov* (1873–1948), from 1929 conductor of the Grand Symphony Orchestra of All-Union Radio:] On the night of September 8–9, our house on Liteiny

36 The writer Konstantin (Kirill) Mikhaylovich Simonov (1915–79) served as an artillery commander and war correspondent; his most famous war poem "Wait for Me" ("Zhdi menya") was carried by soldiers in their tunics and mailed home to their loved ones.

37 Aleksandr Il'ich Bezymensky (1898–1972), a RAPP writer, published a Front Line Notebook during the war; his play *The Shot* (*Vystrel,* 1930) had been singled out by Stalin as a model for Soviet drama.

38 Lidiya Aleksandrovna Kolesnikova, lyrical soprano at the Musical Comedy Theater in such operettas as *The Black Domino* and *Silva*.

7.2. Queuing at the Theater of Musical Comedy in blockaded Leningrad.

Prospect was bombed out, and I wound up in Kuybishev Hospital. This district was often bombed. The surgeon advised me to move to a safer place. I resettled in the bomb shelter of the Maly Opera House and even became its commandant.

On December 6, my name day, A. N. Feona[39] paid a call. Congratulating me, he offered me as a gift a little piece of bread the size of a matchbox. I was very moved.

[*Tamara Sal'nikova:*] On December 7, 1941, the theater, then still on Rakov Street, was presenting *The Three Musketeers* [by Varney]. It had been snowing since morning. I left my home on Petrogradskaya before nightfall. It was hard to walk: my hands and feet froze, my head spun with hunger. On Kirov Bridge I ran into an artillery bombardment. Some women, shoveling snow, quickly fell flat on the snowdrifts. I followed their example. And suddenly one of the women cried out and crawled over to a lamppost. Behind her a red patch spread on the fresh snow.

The shelling went on nonstop. Only by creeping, helping the wounded woman, we got down off the bridge. On the Field of Mars volunteer air wardens ran over to us. My wounded companion fell into their caring arms. Barely able to drag my feet from what I'd experienced, I reached the theater. I can imagine how I looked: overcoat drenched, ski pants torn at the knees . . . But in those days no one paid any attention to such things.

In the dressing rooms and throughout the theater it is palpably below zero. But the electricity is working. That means one can warm one's theater slippers on the light-bulbs. I try with my hands to smear on the congealed makeup. One more effort lies ahead: to force oneself to slip into the elegant costume of my heroine Marie. The one for the first act, as bad luck would have it, has short sleeves and a plunging neckline. After this "operation," having thrown on my overcoat, I climb onto the sofa with my feet up to get warm, if only a bit. Our dresser Zhenya sets on my head a bonnet with

39 Aleksey Nikolaevich Feona (1887–1963), actor who worked in operetta from 1911, chiefly in Leningrad: Musical Comedy Theater 1919–29, Maly Opera Theater 1919–27. As a director at the Musical Comedy Theater, he tried to introduce realism into the staging.

an elegant ribbon. Then—a few vocal exercises, singing warm-ups, and I'm onstage. I try to convey the serene feelings of meek, submissive Marie.

In the intermission I rush to my dressing room to change for Act II, this time (thank the author!) into a warmer dress with a mantle, for the action takes place in a nunnery. On the stairs the worried voices of Grisha Butman and Grisha Krut'ko. They come closer. And suddenly next to the hot water tank I saw the chorister Sasha Abramov lying with the chained mug in his hands. A kind, very dear man. He had died during the intermission . . .

[*Nikolay Nikolaevich Radoshansky* (1887–1963), operetta baritone who worked in Moscow and Leningrad 1912–36 and then directed opera throughout the provinces 1936–48:] Day by day the food shortage got worse . . . It was hard to go to the theater and back, and Ogareva and I moved to a cellar of the Philharmonic, fitted out under the bomb shelter. [. . .]

One night we learned about a dreadful fire. In the People's House park the "American mountains" [roller coasters] were burning. We rushed out into the square. It was as bright as day. I took a few steps forward and felt my legs fail me.

That evening in the theater Louis Varney's operetta *The Three Musketeers* was on, with an excellent libretto by M. Zoshchenko. I played Porthos. In Act III, at the moment when a slightly tipsy Porthos, lying behind a bush, says, "Who the devil is treading on my foot?" a siren sounded . . . And the same thing six times in a row. Each time the audience and actors left their places and went down into the bomb shelter.

It was hard for me to walk with swollen feet, and therefore I stayed behind, lying in back of the onstage bush and waiting for the end of the air raid. The seventh time, when we began the show with the same episode, a rather shrill voice called out from the audience:

"Radoshansky, cut that damned line!"

I followed the advice. The show went on without a hitch and ended without incident.

Duration and Aftermath

The Soviet victory at Stalingrad on January 31, 1943, is considered the turning point of the war on Russian soil. The Party leadership flexed its muscles in a new surge of confidence and began to reimpose Communist ideology. "The people" again became eclipsed by Marx, Engels, and Stalin.

"'Immortality' is new Soviet stage production about activities of young guerrillas," *Moscow News* (March 3, 1943).

SVERDLOVSK, RSFSR (by telephone). Jack Warner believed in immortality. He maintained that all Americans are romanticists, and he proved his point when he died from a fascist bullet on the snowy expanses of the Soviet Union during the German offensive on Moscow in 1941.

Jack Warner is one of the characters in *Immortality*, a new play by A. Arbuzov and

A. Gladkov produced by the Central Theater of the Red Army, which is now playing in his Urals city. An American newspaperman, Warner [. . .] jumps at the opportunity to join a group of Moscow students going out of town to help bring in the potato crop. [. . .]

One fine day they learn that the Germans have advanced and that they are cut off. For three weeks they roam the forest looking for a way out of encirclement, [before they] take the place of a group of guerrillas wiped out by the Germans. [. . .]

They have no weapons, no fighting experience and no plan of action. [. . .] But they know that the guerrillas must not die, and with the unquestioning romantic heroism of youth they take up the fighting standard of the former detachment. [. . .] Tonya, a girl tractor driver from the local state farm, and Ivanych, a wounded Red Army sergeant, who have also been stranded behind the enemy lines, share the patriotic enthusiasm of the students and join their detachment. [. . .]

A fierce battle follows. Warner is killed, and so is the group's leader, Sasha Slavin, a talented young pianist. Others also die, and they die happy in the knowledge that that for which they lived—art and creative labor, the country, a fact which lends peculiar charm and freshness to this play about a little detachment that is a particle of the formidable guerrilla movement so valiantly helping the Red Army drive out the German fascist invaders.

BY LATE AUGUST the Germans had been begun to retreat and were in full rout by June 1944. Gradually, the evacuated theaters began to move back to their homes. The government resumed control of the theater buildings, and the Committee on Artistic Affairs took over organizing theater units for the front: eleven front theaters, not to mention circus and vaudeville units. The Red Army Theater returned to Moscow in June 1943 after nearly two years in Sverdlovsk.

The lifting of the siege of Leningrad was celebrated by a burst of red, white, and blue rockets on January 27, 1944. Slowly, as the decimated city tried to retrieve a sense of normality, evacuees returned to a scene of devastation.

> Georgy Kozintsev to his sister L. M. Kozintseva-Érenburg, Leningrad, June 12, 1944. In *Perepiska G. I. Kozintseva 1922–1973* (Moscow: Artist-Rezhissër-Teatr, 1998), 52. Just before the war, Kozintsev had staged *King Lear* at the Gorky BDT in Leningrad; when the theater returned from evacuation, the production was renovated.

When I got here I went to see *King Lear*. The scenery had been burned, the designs were gone, and everything had been done from memory by the chief of the directorial unit. They played Shostakovich's music in accordance with all the revisions occasioned by rationing, by experienced musicians. My modest creation was renovated not without the inclusion of a few personal ideas by the theater's manager,[40] in my opinion in

---

40 Lev Sergeevich Rudnik (1906–?), the Gogol Theater's artistic director 1940–44; later worked in Moscow as a film director.

7.3. Military spectators at the front.

collaboration with the chief of the fire brigade. This show will have to be taken off and done over again. I'm waiting for Al'tman.[41] The problem is that all this was done by people who care about the show and who respect all of us. It's not their fault, but their headache, so that it's hard to get things off one's chest even using kind words. [...]

WHILE IN DUSHANBÉ, Shvarts had completed his finest play, *The Dragon,* begun at a time when the Hitler–Stalin pact prevented explicit presentation onstage of the Nazi peril. When the situation changed in 1942, he could be more audacious in his writing. In 1944 the Comedy Theater moved back from Tadjikistan to Moscow and suggested that *The Dragon* be performed. The government readers were aghast at an allegory that could as easily be applied to Stalin's Russia as Hitler's Germany. Akimov was summoned by a very worried committee chairman, who informed him that it was not to be performed. He later learned that a highly placed official had seen something in it that wasn't there. Not until 1962 would it be offered to the public.

41 Natan Isaevich Al'tman (1889–1970), chief designer for GOSET 1922–28; worked in Paris 1928–35 but returned to Leningrad to create scenery for Shakespeare and Pushkin at the Pushkin Theater and the BDT.

The Committee for Artistic Affairs judges Evgeny Shvarts's *The Dragon,* August 4, 1944. Transcribed from the diary of N. N. Chushkin[42] by E. Binevich, "Na puti k 'Drakonu,'" *Neva* 10 (1996), 174–77.

B. V. MOLCHALIN:[43] The play can be understood in different ways. It mixes the most diverse subjects. There's something appealing about it . . . The conception, set against a fairy-tale canvas, the main fault with the play is it requires constant explanation and interpretation . . . There's too much exposition. Shvarts has got to come up with more precise answers for himself. There's a lot that's unclear, obscure, the theater cannot help the author. If the production were to be put on right now, it would be an affront to the spectator . . .

A. V. SOLODOVNIKOV:[44] It is impossible to concur with the author's prognosis as to what will come after Hitler. The situation has changed. The play was meant for the prewar period or the very start of the war, and the current play has to answer the following questions [. . .]

SHVARTS (*responding privately to these criticisms later*): Hatred for Hitler . . . They are asking me to be as precise as a pharmacy, but I'm as precise as a song. There is a precise conclusion in the play, the one and only one that the spectator can draw from *The Dragon*—Hitler is a bastard, and his circle are also bastards, and they will answer for what is going on now.

Meeting November 30, 1944, discusses the second variant of the play.

NIKOLAY POGODIN: That this is a talented play goes without saying. It is wholesome, in places simply brilliant . . . and as a playwright and an author Shvarts is to be congratulated. This work is not for today, but perhaps for five years from now. This work ought to stay in the author's desk drawer, to be lovingly worked on even more. This, to my mind, is a genuine and great work of literature . . . but there are some things that evoke associations of ideas that are, perhaps, uncalled-for. Government is government, and especially in such critical times, and if an author has set himself such an awfully heavy task, beyond his strength, he may sometimes blow bubbles. And these bubbles can be interpreted as politically uncalled-for associations of ideas . . . If we ourselves were somehow contaminated and couldn't tell right from wrong, I would regard this as a brilliant, exciting, free, remarkable work for the stage. But is this the right time for it? I don't understand this point, as I nowadays don't understand a good deal about our theatrical life.

SERGEY OBRAZTSOV: The first version was clearer in concept. Maybe this concept was wrongheaded. Maybe it was debatable, maybe even harmful, but it was rather clear, you have to save people even when they don't want to be saved . . . And for the sake of people who don't want to be saved, Lancelot, risking his life, kills the

---

42 Nikolay Nikolaevich Chushkin (1906–77), theater historian and archivist; worked at the MAT Museum 1937–41.

43 B. V. Molchalin, head of the Repertkom.

44 Aleksandr Vasil'evich Solodovnikov (1904–90), journalist; from 1936 official of the Chief Administration of Theaters under the Committee for Artistic Affairs of the SNK USSR.

Dragon... Once he's killed him, it becomes clear to him that he made a mistake and that, evidently, this isn't enough. It is evident that the people are so infected by the Dragon that the next step is to destroy the next Dragon in the form of the criminal... It's impossible to avoid associations of ideas. They are there, the author doesn't hide them. And in this I see a certain, maybe, very daring but associative truth. [...]

IL'YA ÉRENBURG: Artistically I rank the play very highly. But I think, by and large, the present discussion is not about how well it is written—it would seem everyone is in agreement about that, and there's no need to discuss it... I liked the first version better artistically, it is better. But the first version was—on a political level—an absolute mishmash, so much so that I had to keep figuring out what it was talking about: a government usurped by fascists or a fascist government. This fairy tale has confused two worlds. France and Germany... Now for me it's clear from the second version that it's talking about a government usurped by fascists and the outrages perpetrated by this disguised semifascist camouflaged group—that's what's important for us. This has to be totally uprooted in every nation, and not by weapons but by exposure. And in this respect the play has a career ahead of it. I see it in all the theaters of Europe... The political meaning of this play is enormous. So what needs to be done? First—throw out everything that leaves an impression that this is Germany. That is a result of the names... Let Lancelot be one of those knights errant who is not obsessed exclusively with liberation... We can only *pretend* to this. And then the associations of ideas can begin—where he is and why he has no weapons. Which means, it has to be made fantastic, stylized. Lancelot in my conception is the people... We artists can have nothing to do with the political destruction of fascism. We can be concerned only with the moral destruction of fascism. Neither the army nor the government is concerned with that. The moral destruction of fascism is our concern. And this is the first work of art devoted to that question, that is, the fundamental task of tomorrow.

NIKOLAY AKIMOV: I am very pleased that this great new work of E. A. Shvarts has been morally acknowledged and artistically appreciated by most of those present. And second, I have always been and am still convinced of the political necessity of this play. When I was asked if it's worth messing with the theme of philistinism [*meshchanstvo*] against which it's directed, I was convinced that it's worth messing with European philistinism, it will mean a great deal tomorrow... The need for this play is undeniable. And if this play is needed, if we basically agree, then we have to complete and correct it. A number of correct observations have already been made here... If those general tendencies expressed here, that is, the interpretation, the elaboration of this second version, as it now exists, if it will be done by the theater with the help of the Repertkom and all the other officials who will assist us, then in no time at all we can bring the submitted script of the play to the point where not one extra word of it will evoke uncalled-for associations of ideas and doubts. After this the theater will finish the work of the production on the submitted version, because I have not stopped believing in the eventual success and triumph of the given undertaking.

EVGENY SHVARTS: Strictly speaking, Nikolay Pavlovich said in a nutshell what I wanted to say. Really, the very argument whether this is a fairy tale or a satire seems to me academic and pointless. There are all sorts of fairy tales, there are fairy tales that resemble a play, a satire, and there are fairy-tale satires, and none of this runs counter to the fairy-tale genre. And actually, to remove everything political from a fairy tale has no interest for me. I recently said, and I'll repeat it again, that we are a unique generation, maybe the only one that has been able to observe not only the fate of individuals but the fate of a government. Before our very eyes the government survived exceptional tragedies, and these things touched us personally. We were as linked to them as if they happened next door. The fate of many friends in Leningrad depended on the behavior of France, Norway, Romania. So not to profit by the experience provided by this war does not interest me.

Vovsi-Mikhoels, *Mon père Salomon Mikhoëls*, 202–3.

The war was over. On April 29, in the premises of the Russian Theater Society on Gorky Street, the first conference in four years to be dedicated to Shakespeare was held. [...]

The hall of the Russian Theater Society was packed. What an odd, forgotten feeling to sit and listen to peaceful words about the immortality of Shakespeare! For over four years, from morning to night, from all the media, on the radio, out of all the loudspeakers, all we heard was: "Everything for the front, everything for victory!" The cruelest, most interminable war was coming to an end. Numerous participants were seeing one another for the first time after acquaintance with the front, the exodus, the prolonged separations. Most of them met in the corridors, excited by the events of the last few days: Berlin about to fall! But all the chairman had to announce was "Mikhoéls has the floor" for the hall to fill immediately.

[...] The sound of his voice always provoked a thunder of applause. It was the same this time. My father lit a cigarette, waiting for the hall to calm down, then declared with emotion: "The radio has just announced that there is fighting in the streets of Berlin. It is the beginning of the end of Germanic madness, of the German convinced of his superior origins. Man has beaten superman."

Poyurovsky, "A man in his place," 85–86.

And then the war ended. Pluchek returned to Moscow. They assigned him to head the Touring Theater, which was quickly liquidated. And the director remained unemployed. The very man who had astonished everyone on the eve of the war. Who in the war years had shown himself to be a mature independent artist. And suddenly M. Nikonov[45] and N. Petrov, who at that time ran the Satire Theater, invited Pluchek to stage something there. From that time on it was his place of work.

45 Mikhail Semënovich Nikonov (1916–64), chief director at the Meyerhold Theater 1937–38, then at the Ermolova 1945–50, Satire 1950–56, and Mossovet 1957–65; president of the VTO 1942–44; played a major role in reviving Mayakovsky.

[...] A Pluchek production is provocatively poetic. It contains a lot of grief and pain. But faith and hope as well—Pluchek could never stage anything without them. Even Mayakovsky.

OKHLOPKOV'S CONTRIBUTION to the war effort had been a production of Vladimir Solov'ëv's verse chronicle *Field Marshal Kutuzov* at the Vakhtangov in 1940. He and the theater were evacuated to Omsk, where he staged *Cyrano de Bergerac* with designs by Vadim Ryndin. On the return to Moscow, actors of the former Realistic Theater approached him to head a new collective under the Theater of Drama banner; he did so in late 1944, with mixed results. Pogodin's *The Ferry Girl*, a siege-of-Leningrad drama, became a prime target for new attacks on the theaters.

Throughout the evacuation and later, Okhlopkov had devoted much time to a project for staging *Hamlet*. The play had not been produced in the Soviet Union since Akimov's zany version of 1932. It was reputed that Stalin disliked the play, first, because it dealt with regicide, and next, because its hero was indecisive. Okhlopkov's concept was heavily influenced by his experience of the war.

Nikolay Okhlopkov, "Explication of play HAMLET," May 29, 1945. Transcript of talk by the Artistic Leadership of the [Moscow Drama] Theater with the creative collective.

Rehearsal room 11:00 a.m.

Living through the last three years forced me to ponder many things, my own life, the life of our country. I saw in our war features that are repeated from century to century. These are features of the struggle of two worlds, two systems, two views of the world, two concepts of the world.

Let's take the sixteenth century, or a time after the sixteenth century, or any time, we notice how every so often literal volcanic eruptions, the greatest catastrophes, occur— wars. This is by no means a chance phenomenon. It is explained by the fact that the struggle between two worlds is aggravated. The world of humanistic ideals collides with the greedy pretensions of a world where vileness, deceit, prevail, where the human rights of a decent existence are annihilated, where man is a wolf to his fellow man. All this has taken on a barefaced, cynical guise in the form of fascism.

... I began to look for a shelter where I might understand *Hamlet*. I sought, if not a hearth, then in the conditions of evacuation, a warm stove to take cover from the Siberian blizzard, which howled and moaned outside the window, to hide from the bloody impressions of war, to immerse myself in nothing but Shakespeare's *Hamlet*. It seemed to me that this was the very way in which I could manage to lay Shakespeare bare.

[...] I began to understand this because *Hamlet* burrowed into my soul as soon as my thoughts turned to the front, to the line of two enemies, enormous camps. There I began to understand and began to fantasize. I transported myself to where the cruelest fighting was going on, where the greatest battle was raging. There I found the key. Without contemporizing Shakespeare in any way, without leveling him to a false base, I understood what constituted the power of *Hamlet*.

[...] I'm excited today. I've been working for many years and living for many years, and I'm excited today like a little kid, and I'm nervous. I ride on the trolley and feel my hands tremble and my heart flutter. I'm glad of it, because you can't approach Shakespeare calmly. For this is work one must undertake in fear and trembling; and, if this explication is of any help to you, it means my years of preparatory work were not in vain. [...]

If you write "a prison," no one will go there. It's a gloomy paradise. This paradise seems ready to breed happiness, but it breeds monsters. That's the kind of world it is.

It seems to me that everything, including the frame, must be stripped down to be one big window. No, not a window—a door, portals to this world, there must be two halves to these portals, and so people can go through them, they have taken keys, begun to open the locks with all sorts of screeching, howling. It's a rusty lock, it skreeks, they've unlocked it, but it is impossible to open the doors because they are more like the covers of a Bible and need some score of muscular men to apply themselves, half naked, apply themselves to these doors, and then the doors open with a great screech. And so the world of Hamlet's tragedy opens. And below, the floor will be covered with iron or metallic slabs, and when anyone passes, his steps echo over the whole stage. All is empty. We open a wall of this prison, and there is an enormous fireplace, and Claudius is sitting, warming his feet. Claudius enters, and nobody else. He walks across the enormous stage, drops his handkerchief, and courtiers scurry like rats to pick it up and disappear at once.

This world is vast. Enormous arches, daylight filters in. But as soon as light penetrates, Rosencrantz and Guildenstern fear the light, they try to keep it from touching them.

That sort of world.

[...] Here everyone, both myself as director, and you as actors, must have a heightened rhythm, everything must be highly charged. You know outside Moscow stand enormous towers and on them small notice boards with a skull and crossbones and a bolt of lightning, and you feel that if you but touch it, you will cease to be.

What I'm talking about is high tension. [...] I'd like this production to infect the spectator with breathtaking excitement, mental stimulation, ideas or passions that can be invested even in a very cool format.

That's what *Hamlet* means to me. [*Applause.*]

THE SUDDEN DEATH of forty-four-year-old Nikolay Khmelëv, one of the most interesting of the second generation of MAT actors, might be reckoned a symbolic end to this era. His multidimensional portrayal of a Communist Party member in *Armored Train 14–69* had changed the theatrical interpretation of such characters. He had been a steely Karenin in *Anna Karenina,* and in 1943, on the death of

Nemirovich-Danchenko, he assumed the leadership of the MAT. The stresses of the previous two decades proved to be too much.

> Marina A. Raykina, death of Khmelëv. In *Moskva zakulisnaya. Zapiska teatral'nogo reportëra* [Moscow backstage: Notes of a theatrical reporter] (Moscow: Vagrius, 2000), 173–74. Marina Raykina, theater critic for *Moskovsky Komsomolets*, ran the Gavroche Children's Art Theater.

November 1, 1945. Moscow. Nikolay scheduled the dress rehearsal for the new production *Hard Times* [*Trudnye Gody*]. He had already put on his costume, was made up, and even posed for a photographer, who never suspected that he was taking the last photo of the celebrated actor. They started to rehearse, and suddenly Khmelëv fell down. Everyone who was onstage at that moment rushed over to him, sat him in the first row of the stalls. The doctor called in examined the patient and said that it was impossible to move Khmelëv. And then they lay Nikolay Pavlovich on a couch in the front box, the one where invited guests of high rank usually waited for the show to start. Khmelëv wasn't involved in the show that was on that night: *Dead Souls.* He died while it was being performed.

CHAPTER EIGHT

The Cold War Begins, 1946–1953

T HE POSTWAR PERIOD represents the absolute nadir in creativity in Soviet literature and art, owing to a straitjacket of restrictions and government policies. Wartime had brought about a "spontaneous de-Stalinization," and its horrors became linked with a sense of internal initiative; many Russians had also come into contact with a reality different from Soviet propaganda, especially in the standard of living; ideological optimism cautiously raised it head. The public that was emerging from an unheard-of ordeal was offered a theater of distraction.

This did not last long. Victory had legitimized the power structure beyond debate. Although "the people's" patriotic efforts and a holy defense of the motherland (*Rodina* replaced *Otechestvo*) independent of the Party had been stressed, it had never been to the detriment of the Party leadership. Now reaction set in in all fields to protect the purity of Communist ideology from alien influences. In 1946 Stalin appointed Andrey Zhdanov to lay down the law on cultural policy. Andrey Aleksandrovich Zhdanov (1896–1948) had been active in the purges, had served as a defender of Leningrad, and was second secretary of the Communist Party of the Soviet Union (1941–48). The Zhdanov era opened in summer 1946 with three decrees of the Party Central Committee. Significantly, these were public proclamations, not resolutions made and implemented behind the scenes. The first, of August 14, attacked the journals *Zvezda* and *Leningrad* as "devoid of ideas and ideologically harmful"; it proclaimed that "the task of Soviet literature is to help the state to educate youth correctly, to meet its requirements, to bring up the new generation to be strong, believing in its cause, not fearing obstacles, ready to overcome all obstacles."

The second, issued on August 16 and titled "About the Repertoire of the Dramatic Theaters and the Means of Improving It," stiffened the powers of Glavrepertkom. It reprimanded the theaters for moving away from contemporary themes and for presenting weak plays without ideological content, in which honest Soviets were presented as primitive caricatures, with the tastes and manners of the petty bourgeoisie, while the negative characters were depicted in vivid colors. It criticized the infatuation with historic plays, so popular during the war, and condemned the blind idealizing of great figures from the past. It also condemned the introduction of a foreign bourgeois repertoire on Soviet stages. Plays about "gangsters and dance hall girls" that praised "adultery and the exploits of all kinds of adventurers" were thought to distract the audience from the political struggle. The Soviet repertoire had to be purged of all plays by authors who attempted to remain aloof from politics. Too much light entertainment, too much attention to the so-called psychological, was harmful to the body politic.

Authors and theaters were called on to "represent in their plays and their shows the life of Soviet society in its uninterrupted movement forward, to contribute in every way to the ulterior evolution of the best features in the character of Soviet man, those features which appeared with particular strength during the Great Patriotic War." This involved the vilification of all things bourgeois and the glorification of all things Soviet, particularly Stalin. The young were to be politically educated through optimistic works designed to inculcate a spirit of courage, devotion to the fatherland, and faith in the victory of Communism. More positive heroes were needed. It also stipulated that theaters were obliged to stage annually "at least two new spectacles of highly ideological and artistic quality on Soviet contemporary themes."

The Zhdanov purge was the culmination of Party attitudes toward literature and art that had begun with socialist realism and was reiterated in 1943 after the victory at Stalingrad. In response, many theaters resorted to the classical Russian repertoire: up to 1953, the classic Aleksandr Ostrovsky was reportedly the most popular playwright, despite the fact that Zhdanov rejected nineteenth-century plays as serving the interests of "bourgeois culture." The struggle against imperialism, particularly "American imperialism," spawned a whole series of plays offering distorted pictures of life in capitalist countries, where espionage on the USSR and other social democracies is stigmatized. In almost all these plays, the positive characters are didactic straw men, while the enemy characters are absurdly caricatured. The result is a melodramatic and implausible drama.

This denatured drama was further vitiated by the concept of the conflictless play. Nikolay Virta, a Stalin Prize winner and "accepted" playwright, advanced the idea that since negative characters were no longer typical, the only conflicts that could be represented on the stage were those between the "good" and the "better." This "theory of lack of conflict" was urged on antipatriotic critics and playwrights and resulted in a host of very poorly written plays that tried to follow this ideological recipe. Despite their weaknesses, many of these plays were performed at theaters throughout the country, including the MAT, which in the years following the war became a kind of official laboratory for new Soviet plays. "Conflictness" combined with the cult of Stalin paralyzed the theater.

A two-day conference in late 1948 held jointly by the Union of Soviet Writers, the Committee on Artistic Affairs, and the All-Russian Theatrical Society deplored the weaknesses of Soviet drama, the lack of a personal voice, and genuine conflict. The unforeseen result was an attack not on playwrights but on critics, spearheaded by Fadeev, secretary-general of the Writers' Union. Negative reviews were judged "antipatriotic" and demeaning to Soviet prestige. Similar vague accusations of "formalism" and "bourgeois estheticism" rained down on the chosen victims. Since many of these critics were Jewish, they became sucked into the wider attack on "rootless" or "nationless cosmopolitans," an ironic term, since one of the irritants to the government was the foundation of the state of Israel. GOSET, the State Jewish Theater in Moscow, was closed after its leaders had been murdered. Leading Russian writers, such as Anna Akhmatova and Mikhail Zoshchenko, were attacked for being anti-Soviet. Akimov was dismissed from the Leningrad Comedy Theater. In 1950, the last bastion of "formalism," the Kamerny Theater, disappeared and was rebaptized the Pushkin Dramatic Theater. Literally thousands of people wound up in work camps as a result of such accusations, and thousands more simply lost their careers.

As the repertoire worsened, the Party intervened in 1952 to condemn the theory of the absence of conflict, and Malenkov, in his report on the activity of the Central Committee at the nineteenth Communist Party Congress, called for "Soviet Gogols and Shchedrins," a contradiction in terms. However, the actual conditions for the development of drama had to be postponed until after the death of Stalin in 1953 (the year *The Bathhouse* was revived, beginning a return to Mayakovsky). They were affirmed after the twentieth Communist Party Congress in 1956.

Theater administration was also reorganized. After World War II, the Ministry of Culture, carrying out the directives of the Central Committee, took on itself the control of theaters in the country. The structure of all theaters was to be based on the organizational model of the MAT, which, in the late 1930s, had become a benchmark for the development of other Soviet theaters. Subsidized by the government, all theaters were to have permanent companies that would stage ten different shows each month. This single model remained in effect through the mid-1980s. Before 1946, the administrative head of the theater was responsible for its political conformity; the artistic director was his subordinate. Now a third individual was added, the "deputy artistic director in charge of literature," the Zavlit, charged with organizing the repertoire. In 1949 the functions of the artistic director came to an end, being replaced by the chief producer, explicitly subordinate to the administrator, usually a political boss with little or no knowledge of the theater (as had been the case at the Imperial Theaters in tsarist times). Often chief producers were drawn from "among party or government officials who had been a failure at their jobs" or from actors active in local Party committees.[1]

Geographically, each district was to have a dramatic theater as well as a puppet theater. In major cities, those with populations close to one million, musical theaters and theaters for young people were also to be operative. Touring theaters would exist as well to perform in rural areas. Across the country, theaters were to

---

1   G. Georgievsky, "How I Became a Theatrical Administrator," *Teatr* 1 (January 1957): 118–19.

play in the various national languages, though at least one theater performing in Russian was to be in operation in each republic.

Stalin also decided to economize. The 960 theaters that had existed in 1941 fell to about half; most of those that disappeared were ethnically non-Russian theaters. A decree of the Council of Ministries on March 4, 1949, cut subsidies to make theaters self-supporting. Unable to select their own repertoires, stage new plays, and maintain the artistic integrity of their theaters, managers also had to fulfill their financial plans, like factory managers. Audiences responded by staying away in droves.

The Repertoire

"The dramatic repertoire and measures to improve it: Decision of the Central Committee, CPSU (B), 26 August 1946," in *Decisions of the Central Committee CPSU (B) on Literature and Art (1946–1948)* (Moscow: Foreign Languages, 1951), 11–20.

The principal defect of the present dramatic repertoire is that plays by Soviet authors on contemporary themes have actually been crowded out of the country's leading theaters. Out of twenty plays currently being staged in the Moscow Art Theater, only three deal with present-day Soviet life; the figures for the Maly Theater are twenty and three, respectively, nine and two for the Mossovet Theater, ten and two for the Vakhtangov Theater [...] The obviously abnormal position in regard to the dramatic repertoire is exacerbated by the fact that among even the small number of plays on contemporary themes produced by our theater, some are of an inferior artistic and ideological standard [...] As a rule, these plays draw an ugly caricature of Soviet people, depicting them as crude and uncultured, with philistine tastes and manners. On the other hand, negative personages are portrayed as possessing strong character, will power, ability, and ingenuity. The plots of these plays are artificial and false, with the result that they present Soviet life in a false and distorted light. [...]

The Central Committee, CPSU (B), is of the opinion that the Committee on Arts has been pursuing a wrong policy in introducing plays by foreign bourgeois authors into the drama repertoire. [It is] an attempt to use the Soviet stage for propaganda of reactionary bourgeois ideology and morality, an attempt to poison the minds of Soviet people with a world outlook that is hostile to Soviet society and to galvanize survivals of capitalism in the people's minds and everyday life. [...]

The Central Committee, CPSU (B), resolves: [...]

3. The principal practical task of the Committee on Arts shall be to ensure the production by every drama theater of no fewer than two or three new plays annually of high ideological and artistic standards on present-day Soviet themes. [...]

4. The Committee on Arts is instructed to delete from the repertoire all idealess and unartistic plays and to exercise constant control in order that puerile, idealess plays, propagating erroneous views and of low artistic value, shall not appear on the Soviet stage. [...]

8. The Committee on Arts is authorized to arrange in 1946–47, in conjunction with

the Board of the Union of Soviet Writers, an all-USSR competition for the best plays dealing with contemporary Soviet life. [...]

> Mikhail Kozakov, *Risunki na peske. Aktërskaya kniga* [Sketches on sand: An actor's book] (Moscow: AST, Zebra E, 2007), 100–101. Mikhail Mikhailovich Kozakov (1934–2011), while still in the Studio School of the MAT 1952–56, became an inveterate theatergoer, seeing all that was on in Leningrad and Moscow. He was picked by Okhlopkov in 1956 to play the youngest Hamlet in Russian history; acted at the Sovremennik 1959–71; and, most importantly, was leading man at the Malaya Bronnaya 1971–80. He emigrated to Israel in 1991 but returned to Russia five years later.

[...] About contemporary plays, there's almost nothing to be said: at this time, the theory of lack of conflict ruled our stages like Mamay the Tatar.[2] With very few exceptions you could count on one hand, Soviet drama was represented either by assembly-line plays about the struggle between the good and the best (produced by such masters of the genre as A. Surov, A. Sofronov,[3] N. Virta, and others) or, even more, about the struggle for peace and untarnished ideals: this was the era of the "cold" war, and like an all-consuming epidemic, K. Simonov's anti-American mendacity *The Russian Question* appeared on almost every stage. They tried to compensate for the triviality of the contemporary theatrical repertoire with classics and occasionally permitted performances of modern plays in translation.

But even national classics had to know their place. The basic role was to be played by the unmasking of tsarism. Of the foreign plays, "cloak-and-dagger" comedies were especially prolific: after the hardships of war the Soviet spectator deserved a complete vacation. Never before or after had we so loved the Spaniards Lope de Vega, Calderón, and Tirso de Molina. The main Moscow hits were the romantic *The Dancing Master* [*El maestro de danzar*, 1594] with Vladimir Zel'din[4] and *The Dog in the Manger* with Mariya Babanova. In Leningrad, though not by de Vega, but also about Spanish life, *Don Cesar de Bazan* with Vladimir Chestnokov[5] at the Dramatic (formerly the Blockade, later the Komissarzhevskaya) Theater, and at others *The Girl with the Pitcher* and *The Crack-Brained Caballero.*[6]

2 Mamay (d. 1380), chieftain of the Blue Horde of Mongols, defeated by Dmitry of the Don 1378. His name is proverbial in Russia for tyranny and devastation.

3 Aleksandr Surov (1926–), hack playwright of anti-American dramas, lead attacker on "cosmopolitans"; expelled from the Writer's Union after Stalin's death (reinstated 1982). Anatoly Vladimirovich Sofronov (1911–90), a factory worker turned playwright, who served the regime with crude propaganda pieces between 1946 and 1957 and, in the 1970s, turned to writing farces.

4 Vladimir Mikhaylovich Zel'din (1915–?), after acting in Moscow transport and trade unions theaters, entered the Red Army Theater in 1945, where he played Aldemaro in *The Dancing Master*; much appreciated for his virtuosity.

5 Vladimir Ivanovich Chesnokov (1904–68), noted for his restrained temperament; at the Lenin Komsomol Theater 1937–42; Theater of the Baltic Fleet 1942–45; and Leningrad Dramatic Theater 1945–54.

6 *Don César de Bazan* (1843), a comic melodrama by A. Dennery and Dumanoir, based on a char-

Actually a different spirit prevailed at the Comedy Theater, the spirit of a real theatrical holiday with the directing and designs of Nikolay Pavlovich Akimov. Leningraders loved Akimov's theater, singled it out, for which Akimov was made to pay soon enough. But even his repertoire contained neither *The Dragon* nor *The Naked King*, although E. L. Shvarts had written them specifically for this, "his very own" theater. The comedy hits of those years were *M. Perrichon Takes a Trip* by E. Labiche, an adaptation by L. Malyugin[7] of an American scenario *The Road to New York*, an episodic comedy by S. Mikhalkov, and that same triumphant *Russian Question* by Konstantin Simonov, which was still running at two or three theaters.

> I. Kruti, "*The Dancing Master*: Premiere of a play by Lope de Vega at the Central Red Army Theater," *Krasnaya Zvezda* (October 1, 1946). Isaak Aronovich Kruti (1890–1955) was a theater critic and historian.

A powerful, simple, sincere love removes all obstacles from its path and celebrates a victory over the dogmas of medieval morality—such is the basic theme of Lope de Vega's play *The Dancing Master*, staged by the Central Red Army Theater. [. . .]

The Central Red Army Theater is to be thanked for its initiative in enriching the repertoire of the Soviet theater by *The Dancing Master*, a play we had never seen, translated by T. L. Shchepkina-Kupernik.[8] The talent of the translator and the culture of the theater, directed to the same artistic ends, ensured the production its best qualities—the nobility of the general tone and refined merriment. [. . .]

The production of *The Dancing Master* enjoys a great and deserved success with the spectator. He is attracted and excited by the profound humanist theme of this performance, caroling the integrity and clarity of human nature, plain dealing and honor, in affirmation of his right to happiness, elevated understanding of honor, pledged to a steadfast righteousness and inviolable loyalty.

> B. Emel'yanov, "*The Dancing Master*: A production of the Central Theater of the Red Army," *Sovetskoe Iskusstvo* (January 1946).

When you see this production, filled with life and light, where dialogue, music, and dance come out in unique rhythms, the question involuntarily arises, why is the spectator so entranced and why does he follow with such fixed attention the adventures of Lope de Vega's amorous heroes? It would seem that this play, its theme, its heroes, are infinitely remote from us, from today's interests, excitements, and passions of the spectators. After all, we are watching only one of the innumerable "cape-and-sword" comedies typical of the golden age of Spanish drama. [. . .]

---

acter in Hugo's *Ruy Blas*. Lope de Vega's comedies *La moza da cantero* (1625–26) and *El caballero de milagro* (1593).

7 Leonid Antonovich Malyugin (1909–1968), critic attacked for "cosmopolitanism"; playwright of popular comedies.

8 Tat'yana L'vovna Shchepkina-Kupernik (1874–1952), actress, poet, and translator, granddaughter of the great actor Mikhail Shchepkin.

ПРОГРАММЫ МОСКОВСКИХ ТЕАТРОВ

№ 6-а
5—11 февраля 1946 г.

«Учитель танцев» Лопе де Вега
в Театре Красной Армии
Артист В. Зельдин в роли
«учителя танцев» Альдемаро
Рис. А. Главштейна

ИЗДАНИЕ ГАЗЕТЫ
«СОВЕТСКОЕ ИСКУССТВО»

8.1. Programs of Moscow Theaters for February 5–11, 1946, featuring B. Zel'din in the title role in *The Dancing Master*, Red Army Theater, Moscow.

But the comedy *The Dancing Master* is written on a rather important theme. True love and loyalty must always triumph. All obstacles are nothing in the face of human emotion, if it is sincere and powerful. This is what almost every line of Lope de Vega's comedy says to us. This theme is rather old but remains eternally new, like the character of a man who always in everything acts only in accord with the voice of his honor and his feeling. [...]

The translation of T. Shchepkina-Kupernik can serve as a model, for it fully satisfies all the specific demands made by a poet of the theater. Every line and pause in it is stage worthy. The production by the Red Army Theater is one of the best productions of Lope de Vega in our theater.

FROM FEBRUARY 23, 1951, the theater was renamed the Central Theater of the Soviet Army, or TsTSA.

The Russian Question by Konstantin Simonov (1947), staged in six hundred theaters, became a focal point for early Cold War tension. Simonov, a popular wartime poet and reporter, was also an apparatchik who wrote a vile diatribe in *Pravda* against the "antipatriots" in the Soviet theater, listing names, mostly of

8.2. Poster for *The Russian Question* by Konstantin Simonov, Russian Theater, Riga, 1947, showing a wide array of American types.

Jews. He campaigned for "an active and relentless ideological offensive" against the United States. The play's leading characters are a down-on-his-luck American journalist named Harry Smith, a political progressive who once wrote a friendly book about Russia, and his antagonist, MacPherson, a despotic American newspaper publisher in the mold of William Randolph Hearst. Taking advantage of Smith's need for money, MacPherson commissions him to write a negative report about life in Moscow, but once in Russia, Smith cannot betray his principles. "Have you noticed that more and more often the word 'red' is coming to mean the same thing as 'honest'?" is a typical line. This drama, after receiving bad notices in the West—except from *Le Monde* ("*une pièce vivante*")—helped to win Simonov the Stalin Prize and caused a scandal in Berlin, where its staging was regarded by the U.S. and Western European officials as an unprecedented act of outright cultural aggression by a previous ally. "Politics have returned to the Berlin stage in as crude and crass a form as in the heyday of Hitler and Goebbels," opined the *Times* of London.

> Smith's final dialogue, dictating to his colleague Hardy. Konstantin Simonov, *The Russian Question*, authorized trans. Eva Manning and Sergey Kozelsky, *Soviet Literature* 2 (February 1947), 25–26.

SMITH: Write, then. (*Dictates, walking up and down the room.*) Today I visited the notorious Harry Smith, a former Macpherson employee. He tried to fight Macpherson and was thrown off the paper. He wanted Kessler to publish his book, but Kessler refused. He wanted to print it in a series of articles in Williams's paper, but Williams didn't want to take it. He has lost peace of mind, comfort, home, car, and money. His friend has died and his wife has left him. When I came to him, I was forced to write standing up—he could not even offer me a chair, because all his furniture has been taken away. There are rumors that in a few days he will go back to work on Macpherson's paper as a police reporter. But these rumors . . . these rumors are without foundation. The aforementioned Smith does not intend to retreat. He is mad as the devil, clean through, as his dead friend used to say. The aforementioned Smith will not go to work for Mr. Macpherson as a police reporter, he will not hang himself, or cut his throat, or jump from the twentieth floor. The aforementioned Smith, on the contrary, intends to begin his life anew.

Why have you stopped, Hardy? Go on writing. I've not finished yet. The aforementioned Smith intends to make the attempt to establish finally whether a man who was born an honest American can live honestly in the land of his birth. Yes, yes, write it down, Hardy, write it down. Though to hell with you, for that matter! If you don't write it, then I shall write it myself, and in the end I'll find a place in America that'll print it. For a long time the aforementioned Smith naively thought that there is one America. But now he knows—there are two. And, if, fortunately for him, yes, fortunately for him, there is no place for the aforementioned Smith in the America of Hearst, then he'll find himself a place in that other America—the America of Abraham Lincoln, the America of Roosevelt!

Curtain.

Yury Lyubimov, *Rasskazy starogo trepacha* (Moscow: Novosti, 2001), 189–90.

In the production of *All My Sons*[9] [at the Vakhtangov Theater, 1948] I played the role of the American flyer Chris. It was one of my best roles. Mekhlis,[10] minister of Gos-kontrol of the USSR, had a viewing of this production when the theater was on tour in Sochi. And he said, "And just why are they playing this? Here's this young actor—he acts beautifully, but why? These are our enemies. I would have thought we had flyers like this here. He's so upset over his air power that he beats up his father." [The actor playing the father was always terrified that Lyubimov would kill him, and his fear read to the audience.]

"That's what our enemy is like, he wouldn't spare his own father."

[. . .] And later at the district committee in Moscow they provoked me: "How can you, a candidate for party membership, stoop so low as to make a hero of our enemy?"

---

9 *All My Sons* (1947) by Arthur Miller is an Ibsenite drama about the sins of the fathers being uncovered by their sons.

10 Lev Zakharovich Mekhlis (1889–1953), much despised commissar who tried to cover up his Jewish origins by being "holier than the Pope"; editor of *Pravda* 1930–37; military adviser responsible for the defeat of the Crimean Front 1942; rabid persecutor of Party enemies.

SERGEY MIKHALKOV, author of the words to the Soviet national anthem, composed a typical "anticosmopolitan" play, *I Want to Go Home* (*Ya khochu domoy*) in 1949. In it, "British imperialists" and "Latvian traitors" conspire to prevent a Soviet child, Sasha Butuzov, from escaping a displaced persons camp in Germany. Soviet authorities aid his escape, and as he is about to fly to Moscow, he is questioned by Captain Peskaev.

> S. Mikhalkov, *Ya khochu domoy* (Moscow: Iskusstvo, 1949), 24.

PESKAEV: Do you want to go to Moscow?
SASHA: I want to go home.
PESKAEV: You will soon be home.
SASHA (*looking at Comrade Stalin's picture*): Stalin!
PESKAEV: Yes, that is Comrade Stalin.
> *A pause.*
SASHA: Is Stalin in Moscow?
PESKAEV: Yes, in Moscow. You will be in Moscow too.
SASHA: I want to go home.

A reaction set in, demonstrated by an article in *Pravda* titled "Do Away with Bureaucratic Obstacles to the Development of Theater" (1952), by three journalists, V. Zaleski, V. Kuznetsov, and V. Mlekhin. They questioned the value of centralization, pointing out that state funds had been wasted on state-commissioned plays, while the managers shirked responsibility by staging classics. Even Malenkov, at the nineteenth CPSU Congress in October 1952, said, "The Soviet people . . . will not tolerate dullness, art that has no message, and falsity . . . Our remarkable authors must scourge the faults, defects, and sores still to be found in our society . . . We need Soviet Gogols and Shchedrins, who with the fire of their satire will burn away everything that is undesirable, rotten, and moribund, everything that retards our progress." (He was echoing an editorial "Nikolay Vasil'evich Gogol," which had appeared in *Pravda* on March 4, 1952, the centenary of the writer's death.) In response, Mikhalkov wrote a comedy in the style of *The Inspector General,* titled *The Crayfish.*

> E. Surkov, "On the way to satirical comedy," *Literaturnaya gazeta* (April 11, 1953), 3.

The Presidium of the Soviet Writers' Union met on April 8 to discuss the development of Soviet satirical comedy, a renewal of the tradition of Gogol and Shchedrin. Plays under discussion were *The Fall of Pompeev* by N. Virta, *The Crayfish* by Mikhalkov, *Anonymous Author* by S. Narinyani, *Naming No Names* by V. Minko, and *A Frank Conversation* by L. Zorin.

LITTLE came of this. Virta's *Smert' Pompeeva* was dismissed as irrelevant to Soviet life; Mikhalkov's *Raki* was relegated to children's theater and as *The Crayfish and the Crocodile* was produced in 1960.

The Ubiquity of Stalin

> Natal'ya Korneeva, *Ekaterina Furtseva. Politicheskaya melodrama* [Ekaterina Furtseva: A political melodrama] (Moscow: Algoritm, 2007), 42.

In May 1945 Stalin at a banquet made a toast "to the health of the Russian people." And from that moment everything Russian came into fashion and everything non-Russian began to be extremely out of favor in society. A year later, at a gathering at the Kremlin, Stalin gave out a directive about the ousting of Jews in leadership roles. It was carried out by Georgy Malenkov,[11] who prepared a circular that listed the posts to which Jews were not to be appointed.

> A. Antonov-Ovseenko, *Teatr Iosifa Stalina* (Moscow: Gregori-Peydzh, 1995), 181–82.

[The new campaign against the intelligentsia] opened on August 26, 1946, with the establishment of the Central Committee of the All-Union Communist Party (Bolsheviks) concerned with theatrical repertoires. After this the formation of a repertoire fell under the strict control of Party overseers. Theaters were rebuked for staging plays by Shkvarkin (*The Last Day*) and Gladkov (*New Year's Night*), Maugham (*The Circle*) and Hervé's operetta *Mam'zelle Nitouche* . . . Blow-ups in committee, slatings at meetings ensued without interruption. Along with excoriation of the offending directors. Two years went by, and then, in December 1948, at the twelfth Plenum of the governing board of Soviet writers, with a report on how to implement "the historical Resolution of Cent.Com.," there stepped forth Anatoly Sofronov, author of the play *The Moscow Character,* which he offered as nothing less than the requisite political model. This forward-looking hypocrite was cautious, for he still knew nothing about the aforementioned directive. Therefore he limited himself to attacks on specific theater critics who had written unflattering reviews of his plays and the potboilers of Romashov (*Great Power*) and Anatoly Surov (*Green Street*)[12] . . .

Stalin bestowed the role of chief figurehead on Aleksandr Fadeev. According to Konstantin Rudnitsky, himself a witness to and victim of this campaign,

> . . . Gray hair flopped over the high forehead of the chief of the writer's guild, steely eyes angrily flashed. Fadeev began modestly: it would appear that "our drama is a new word in the artistic development of humanity," but he added that

---

11 Grigory Maksimilianovich Malenkov (1902–88), prominent in the purges of the 1930s, a member of the Politburo 1941 and of the State Defense Committee, by 1946 was deputy premier of the USSR, a position second only to Stalin. Expelled from the Communist Party in 1957.

12 *Zelënaya ulitsa* was produced at the MAT 1948. It was so bad that at the first rehearsal it drove the actors to drink.

we "acknowledge only party drama and only party criticism." ... Whereupon to this end he quoted Lenin and his theory of class morality: the teacher taught us to distinguish proletarian morality from bourgeois morality.

... Fadeev appeared to the writers in the guise of a frenzied fanatic for the first time. One of the most responsible persons there, in the Central Committee, wound him up to the limit. Otherwise, would Fadeev have uttered the strident threat: "But there are non-Party critics here among us!"? Otherwise, would he have named first among many destined for the sacrifice his own friends Abram Gurvich[13] and Iosif Yuzovsky? So what, betrayal was always highly prized at the court of the Kremlin. Afterward, when the spat-upon critics and fingered journalists were stripped of work, bereft of a crust of breast and awaiting arrest, Fadeev would offer them his aid and sympathy ...

Nikolay Akimov, "Put' Teatra Komedii" [The path of the Comedy Theater], in *Akimov—éto Akimov!* [Akimov—is that Akimov!], ed. Z. I. Zaytsev et al. (St. Petersburg: Rossiyskaya Natsional'naya Biblioteka, 2006), 34.

I myself became a member of the Artistic Council of the Committee for Artistic Affairs and a member of the Committee for the Stalin Prize. [...] Two productions, *Peace Island* and *About Comrades and Friends*,[14] were nominated for a Stalin Prize [in 1947]. I was privy to all the details. The production *About Comrades and Friends* was voted first prize. Our photos were appearing everywhere already—TASS,[15] etc. The cultural officials congratulated us, but when the prize was announced, this production was not mentioned on account of an interesting episode of considerable historical meaning. When the official of the committee reported these candidates to the Politburo, Stalin, on hearing *About Comrades and Friends,* confused it with *Old Friends,* which had received the prize the previous year, and said, "We've already honored it last year." But in the crazy atmosphere of that time, nobody dared correct him and say that we were dealing with a different play and playwright, and this mistake had serious consequences.

Konstantin Simonov, *Glazami cheloveka moego pokoleniya* [As seen by a man of my generation] (Moscow: Izd. Agentsva pechati Novosti, 1989), 56.

[Meeting of the Politburo, March 1948, to choose candidates for Stalin Prizes; in attendance were Fëdor Panferov, Vsevolod Vishnevsky, Valery Druzin,[16] and Konstantin Simonov. The last recalled the following:]

13 Abram Solomonovich Gurvich (1897–1962), chess master, proficient at the end game; theater critic from Baku who, in the 1930s, had called for a new genre of Soviet drama.
14 *Ostrov mira,* a propaganda play by E. P. Petrov; *O druziakh-tovarishchakh,* a lyrical comedy by V. Z. Mass and M. A. Chervinsky; both were staged by Akimov 1947.
15 Short for Telegraphic Agency of the Soviet Union, the official (and only) Soviet news agency, founded in 1925 as a subordinate of the Propaganda Department of the Central Committee of the Communist Party.
16 Fëdor Ivanovich Panferov (1896–1960), author of novels about collectivization; editor of *Oktyabr'*

After a short pause faded away Stalin asked,

"Who wrote the play *The Crows' Stone*? It was printed in issue forty-four of the journal *Star* [*Zvezda*]. I think it's a good play. At the time no one paid it any attention. But maybe we should give the prize to Comrades Gruzdev and Chetverikov?[17] What do you think?"

Druzin, the only one who had read the play, anxiously jogged Simonov's elbow and whispered:

"What should we do? We printed it, but Chetverikov is under arrest in prison. Should I say so or keep silent?"

"Of course, say so," whispered Simonov. He thought: Stalin can free the author of the play. If Druzin keeps silent, he won't be pardoned.

"We still have to decide which prize to give the play, which level? I think..."

Then Druzin blurted out desperately:

"He's in prison, Comrade Stalin."

"Who's in prison?" The general secretary didn't understand.

"One of the authors of the play. Chetverikov's in prison, Comrade Stalin."

The leader fell silent, riffled through the magazine in his hand, closed it, and put it down, prolonging the silence. Then he glanced at the list of prizes and said,

"Let's move on to literary criticism."

STALIN first appeared as a character onstage when Nikolay Pogodin wrote him into his Lenin play *Man with a Gun* at the Vakhtangov Theater (1937). Thereafter he became a fixture in plays and films about the Revolution and its aftermath, and a number of unfortunate actors were condemned to play him to his face.

> Boris Golubovsky, *Bol'shie malen'kie teatry* (Moscow: Izd. im. Sabashnikovykh, 1998), 90.

Diky played Stalin monumentally, he magnified him physically, not playing down his powerful build but presenting him as a leader. [When asked by Mikhail Romm[18] why his performance was so static, Diky replied, "I am playing a monument."] This magnification could be felt even more in the theater than on film. In *Unforgettable 1919*[19] by Vs. Vishnevsky, at the Maly Theater (1949), everyone grimaced in fear, recalling the

---

1931–60; deputy to the Supreme Soviet. Valery Pavlovich Druzin, militant socialist-realist critic; editor of *Zvezda* 1947–57; removed as deputy editor of *Literaturnaya gazeta* 1959.

17 Il'ya Aleksandrovich Gruzdev (1892–1960), former member of the Serapion Brothers literary group, survivor of the Siege of Leningrad; an expert on Gorky. Boris Dmitrievich Chetverikov (1886–1981) was interred at a labor camp 1945–56.

18 Mikhail Il'ich Romm (1901–71), after a military career, became a film director and ran the Studio Theater for Film Actors 1942–43; his movie *Everyday Fascism* (*Obyknovenny fashizm*, 1965) was widely seen.

19 *Nezabyvayemy 1919*, one of the most Stalinist plays in the Soviet repertoire, rewrites the history of the fight against Yudenich outside of Petrograd. It had been accepted by Maly on the personal recommendation of Stalin, who didn't care for the eventual production.

blocking that the director had clearly calculated as praise of the leader: Diky as Stalin was enthroned in an armchair by a desk, while Lenin, badly played by Babochkin, walked around him. (Babochkin was quickly replaced. Film stars had no luck in the character of Lenin: B. Chirkov, V. Vanin, and B. Babochkin[20] seemed to have conspired brilliantly to fail in the role! And if you add the much later scandalous episode with I. Il'insky as Lenin in the show *John Reed,* a play written and staged by E. Simonov, when at the first appearance of the leader the audience cordially burst into laughter and started to applaud, clearly without respect for the great prototype, the picture turns out to be impressive! Il'insky was also replaced.)

[...] Stalin loved the actor Diky. [The Maly Theater had staged] *Southern Liaison* [*Yuzhny uzël*], a play by the writer Arkady Perventsev[21] forgotten by God and man, a very tiresome "chronicle" about the liberation of Sebastopol. Everything in the performance went along as usual in such productions, boring and correct, but the chief snag was that Diky played Stalin without any accent at all. How could this be? To go against historical truth? [The official from Repertkom] Surkov[22] did what was at the time an heroic deed and decided to cancel the production. He was upset, not knowing the reaction of Stalin, who had seen it performed, and finally [Aleksandr Nikolaevich] Poskrebyshev[23] informed him that Comrade Stalin asked that his gratitude be conveyed to the whole theater collective and especially to the artist Diky for the fact that he was first to understand and to show that "Comrade Stalin belongs to the whole Russian people and the great Russian culture." Diky triumphed. Another prize.

Boris Babochkin, "From the autobiography," in *Vospominaniya. Dnevniki. Pis'ma* [Recollections, diaries, letters] (Moscow: Materik, 1996), 39–40.

[In 1949 he joined the Moscow Maly Theater.] The first time I played Lenin was in Vs. Vishnevsky's *Unforgettable 1919.* A phony, boot-licking "patriotic" play with a covert meaning that nobody surpassed Stalin, of course, in venerating Lenin, but the whole thing wasn't about Lenin, it was about Stalin. He was the genius of all geniuses! Diky played Stalin monumentally. He had already got the Stalin Prize for his interpretation.[24]

20 Boris Petrovich Chirkov (1901–82), expert buffoon, acted at the Leningrad TYUZ 1925–30, 1935–39 and at the Gogol Theater from 1966, but most successful in music hall and movies. Vasily Vasil'evich Vanin (1898–1951), actor, especially good in productions of Lyubimov-Lanskoy at the Moscow Trade Unions Theater, he perfected the type of the energetic proletarian "buddy" exemplified by Chapaev. Boris Andreevich Babochkin (1904–75), actor, at the Leningrad Pushkin Theater 1931–36, shot to fame as the hero of the blockbuster film *Chapaev* (1933); at the BDT 1936–40 and the Vakhtangov 1940–46.

21 Arkady Alekseevich Perventsev (1905–81), second cousin of Mayakovsky; war correspondent, screenwriter, and novelist, best known for *The Ordeal,* about the transplantation of an aircraft factory.

22 Evgeny Danilovich Surkov (1915–88), theater critic and journalist; took a special interest in the work of Anatoly Éfros.

23 Aleksandr Nikolaevich Poskrebyshev (1898–1965), major general, Stalin's right-hand man, head of the Special Section of the Central Committee; he played a leading role in the Great Purge of 1936–38.

24 For playing Stalin in the film *The Third Stroke (Trety udar),* directed by I. V. Savchenko, Diky

In this production he contrived to be a different person. And no one had any doubts about it. The role of Lenin was small and was in just one act. I think I played it rather badly, but surely no worse than any other actor. At least I didn't try to strut and fret as much as they did, I tried to be more modest and human. Diky wanted to crush me with his massiveness. After the premiere, there was not only an ovation but an emergency meeting of the company. Shapovalov[25] described the production as a watershed in the history of the Maly Theater and especially noted the success and "magnificent achievement" of the actors who played Lenin and Stalin. We were congratulated beyond all bounds. The show "caught on." Diky and I would enter to approving applause, which was repeated throughout the show, of course. The theater was packed. The papers—we knew about this—were preparing appropriate reviews. Everything went as it should over the course of, I think, the first month. We performed it probably about ten times.

And then one fine Sunday, before going onstage, I adjusted my appearance in a mirror, hurried to my place as usual, and quickly came onstage where Lenin's study in the Kremlin had been reproduced. I came on . . . and was greeted by no applause. "Accident!" I thought and told them to show in Comrade Stalin, as my role required. Enter a monumental Stalin—Diky. And he too seemed a bit nonplussed. Nor was he greeted by applause. I glanced at the audience. It was half empty. I cast my gaze to the left to the government box. There sat Stalin and Malenkov. Obviously, that was why the spectators who half-filled the auditorium had failed to react to the people coming onstage—it was discharging an official duty. However, at the end of the play, there was government-issued applause.

I went home, for the most part rather calmly. I returned to the theater only two days later, on Tuesday morning. And on the producer's doorstep I immediately ran into Shapovalov and Zubov.[26] They had just returned from the Kremlin. Malenkov had summoned them. I don't remember the details of the conversation with Shapovalov and Zubov. We were curtly informed that Diky and I were relieved of the roles: "Comrade Stalin didn't like it."

I asked rather calmly:

"What didn't he like? Maybe we can rework it or redo something?"

They answered:

"No, that would be awkward. It all has to go."

All means all. I went home. On the notice board hung an announcement for an emergency meeting of the company. My private dressing room was quickly taken from me. It didn't bother me. But I understood the kind of storm cloud that was gathering over me.

This story would be of little interest were it not for its unexpected ending, quite in

---

received the Stalin Prize second class 1949, and for the same role in the film *The Battle of Stalingrad* (*Stalingradskaya bitva*), directed by V. M. Petrov, the Stalin Prize first class 1950.

25 Leonid Emel'yanovich Shapovalov (1902–55), deputy chairman for cadres of the Committee on Artistic Affairs from 1940, later administrator of the Maly Theater.

26 Konstantin Aleskandrovich Zubov (1888–1956), after acting in the Far East, became an actor and chief director of the Theater of Revolution 1925–31, excelling in the comedies of Romashov; at the Moscow Lensovet 1932–38, at the Maly Theater from 1936, becoming chief director in 1947.

the spirit of Saltykov-Shchedrin. The theater feverishly began to look for new actors to play the roles of Lenin and Stalin. Performers from all over the Soviet Union were summoned to the Maly Theater. For two months in the dressing rooms I kept running into two dozen bald actors—Lenins—and Georgian-looking actors—Stalins. Finally, for the role of Stalin, they chose B. Gorbatov[27] of the Satire Theater, but the Lenin search had evidently come to a standstill. And then one morning I got a phone call at home:

"Boris Andreevich, it's Zubov."

"Hello, Konstantin Aleksandrovich."

"Dear Boris Andreevich, please come to rehearsal."

"Which rehearsal, Konstantin Aleksandrovich?"

"The one for *Unforgettable 1919*."

"And which part should I rehearse?"

"What do you mean, which? Lenin."

Pause.

"I don't understand, Konstantin Aleksandrovich. I was relieved of that role."

"Boris Andreevich, my dear man! Who told you such nonsense? No one was talking about you. There wasn't a word about you. They removed Aleksey Denisovich. So you'll be here?"

"Konstantin Aleksandrovich, I don't understand..."

"Boris Andreevich, I'll explain it all to you when you get here. And I'll tell you the new idea I've come up with for that scene."

I went to the rehearsal and saw that Zubov had come up with no new idea. Everything was exactly the way it had been. I thought it over and refused to rehearse. Once and for all. And I consider this one of the few righteous moves in my life. Shtraukh played Lenin in the play. In the reviews that the papers had prepared, only the names were changed. Nothing else.

Directors under Fire

> Evgeny Simonov, "The new generation," in *Nasledniki Turandot* (Moskva: Algoritm, 2010), 307–8.

Observing the clash of the great masters, I often prayed within myself: let this cup pass from me! But it is probably decreed that everyone who has trod the theatrical boards drain this cup to the dregs. My generation—a group of people of a single school, who came to art in the postwar years—had not endured the ordeal of what was possibly the hardest of all the ordeals that time had predestined to humanity. And so we all fell foul of one another, seeking a guilty party. In actuality, there was no reason to seek, for everyone was guilty! WE were guilty! Somehow this word has disappeared

---

27 Boris Fëdorovich Gorbatov (1917–87), acted at the Moscow Theater of Satire from 1945; his performance as Stalin at the Maly Theater in *Unforgettable 1919* in 1949 enabled him to join that troupe.

imperceptibly from our vocabulary and has been replaced by the shorter but more dangerous word "I"! [...]

And everything turned to dust. We obliterated our own history, we did not cherish our glorious past, we scattered each to his own corner, we stopped being artists and turned into absurd bureaucrats with cars and villas, into those very bureaucrats whom we had mocked when young and with whom we had fought so desperately.

> Adol'f Shapiro, "The Petersburger from Khar'kov," in *Kak zakryvalas' zanaves* [As the curtain goes down] (Moscow: Novoe Literaturnoe Obozrenie, 1999), 128–29. Adol'f Yakovlevich Shapiro (1939–), a student of Mariya Knebel', became chief director of the Riga State Youth Theater in 1964, where he introduced ideas of Vakhtangov, Brecht, and Mikhail Chekhov; when the theater closed in 1992, he went freelance.

Nikolay Pavlovich Akimov, with whom I studied at the Leningrad Comedy Theater, was never numbered among the nationalists. He was among the Westerners and formalists. In his experiments one always glimpsed an avoidance of toeing the general line. At the time of the compulsory indoctrination of the distorted Stanislavsky system, Akimov splayed his hands at the lectern, "Somehow Botticelli never declared that he was working according to the Giotto system." All his life he was drawn beyond the bounds of the commonplace. This was what drew me to him in particular. A stage designer of high quality, an original director, a brilliant graphic artist, a portraitist, a poster designer, a journalist, a photographer, a theorist of art—Akimov carried the torch of that daring time in the theater that almost was extinguished with the destruction of Meyerhold and Terent'ev, the excommunication of Tairov and Zoshchenko. How did he survive?

> Akimov, *Akimov—éto Akimov!*, 35–38.

In 1949 the [Comedy] Theater was 20 years old. The theater's situation was stable and happy. The reviews were splendid. The theater was subordinate to a union, and, taking into account summer tours and an autumn jubilee, I had been officially asked to present lists for jubilee awards, to air my views on who should get which title or reward, etc. Then we toured to Moscow and things went wonderfully. After that we had a good stint in Sochi, and in August there was an article in the *Leningrad Pravda*,[28] disowning the theater and its leaders, which appeared totally unexpected for the whole Leningrad leadership and the whole Committee for Artistic Affairs. The reason for this upset comes across like an anecdote from a thriller and has little relation to history, but it happened.

The reasons for what I consider a ridiculous episode came about because in 1949 a campaign was unleashed against cosmopolitans—one of the most unsuccessful concepts

---

28 G. Grakov, "Recurrences of Formalism: On the Tours of the Comedy Theater to Moscow," *Pravda* (August 5, 1949), 10.

one could imagine. We had survived this campaign happily, for it was limited to the theater critics and their slaughter and didn't affect the theaters. But during the repercussions of this wave a fatal mistake by one of the Kremlin chauffeurs brought about this result. We were touring at the time in Moscow simultaneously with the Pushkin Theater. The Pushkin Theater was showing *Boris Godunov* on the main stage of the MAT, I believe, and the same day we were at the MAT affiliate with [Labiche's farce] *M. Perrichon Takes a Trip*. And the chauffeur drove the members of the Politburo to the affiliate. They got to the government box, decided that this was no sort of *Boris Godunov*—neither in costume nor in text—quietly got up, and left. The building custodian noted that they stayed eight minutes, removed their coats, took a look, and realized their mistake. But the fact remained that members of the Politburo had walked out of a performance, and at that time this was enough that, when, for other reasons, they had to find a victim on whom to visit all the severity of critics and self-critics, we seemed a rather appropriate object.

Generally speaking, our theater was in a special situation, which deserves mention. The fact is that over the past thirty years of the theater's existence, there had been many campaigns. Now, a campaign could never be abstract. It had to have concrete examples and malefactors who could be exposed. When concrete examples were chosen, some entities seemed to be sacrosanct, and no matter what went on in them, they could not be attacked. No one took it into his head to sniff out formalism at the MAT. Anything that went on *there* was wonderful. Other entities, though not to be spared, were too petty, and to persuade the whole Soviet Union that some director somewhere in Voronezh was dabbling in formalism just wouldn't do. Our theater, for one thing, was not academic or under special protection, and besides that, it was remarkably popular. It had all the requirements for being made an object lesson, and if, in 1949, its perfection for this purpose reached its height, long before this, there was a well-beaten track that the critics enthusiastically took as an effective example.

The Committee for Artistic Affairs was in dreadful fear and trembling—what were they supposed to do, and what decisions were to be made? But the thunder rumbled from too high a chimney for the committee to do nothing, so it published a twenty-five-page order—a whole dissertation, in which I was fired from my post for formalism, lack of interest in the Soviet repertoire, and Western influences. And the upshot was that, in ten days, I was replaced in my post by a chief director of the realistic school. So for the course of some years my path diverged from the theater's. I carried on as a freelancer. For two years I could work only in one city where they were not afraid to give me work—Moscow. In Leningrad they feared me like the plague. I worked as a designer at the Vakhtangov Theater for Okhlopkov. Then I worked there as a director. In 1952 they summoned me to Leningrad and offered me the New Theater, now the Lensovet Theater, at that time in parlous straits.

Matters there had got so bad that the management, depressed by the poor box office, removed a row of seats from the balcony, writing them off so there would seem to be fewer empty seats. Twice a week they showed movies instead of plays. There was nearly one million in debt. In short, it was a very unenviable situation. Who would rush to take over such an enterprise? But insofar as my appointment to the theater at the time appeared as a kind of official amnesty, to refuse it would have been politically awkward.

[. . .] In 1955 a formal offer was made to me to return to the Comedy Theater, which had come unscrewed in its own way. It had been impossible to obey the order of the Committee of Artistic Affairs to find a great realistic director in ten days. In the ten years of my absence, 19 directors had been brought in. [. . .]

My return to this theater was and remains of interest, because it is the only case in the life of the Soviet theater of the return of a leader who had been removed with such fanfare.

Vladlen Davydov,[29] "The death of Dobronravov, 27 October 1949." Quoted in Marina A. Raykina, *Moskva zakulisnaya. Zapiski teatral'nogo reportera* (Moscow: Vagrius, 2000), 173–74.

[The MAT was performing *Tsar Fëdor*, with Boris Dobronravov as the fourth member of the Art Theater to play this role.] I was employed in my second season in the theater and was standing among the guards in a crowd scene. Boris Georgievich had just finished acting in the sixth scene, in which the tsar loses his temper: "Let them rot in prison!" he shouts and bangs his fist on the table. He finished the scene, left the stage. He was supposed to change his costume in the makeup room to go on in the eighth and final scene "Archangel Cathedral." He always came off with a candle in his hands. That day the candle "blazed" badly, that is, the contact had come loose on the electric light. The actor growled and, as he passed, snarled at the ASM: "This is the last time I act with candles like these."

In a few hours, these meaningless words would be repeated throughout the theater as fatal or clairvoyant. Meanwhile, Dobronravov got to the door to the dressing rooms, pushed it open, and . . . collapsed. While they were waiting for the first aid doctor, Boris Georgievich was laid in the front box on that same couch. Then he passed away, not from cerebral thrombosis like Khmelëv, but from a heart attack.

STANISLAVSKY'S WRITINGS had undergone considerable editorial intervention before publication. *An Actor's Work on Himself*, essentially ghost written by Lyubov' Gurevich, had had such words as "soul" and "spirit" excised. His unfinished manuscript on creating a role was put together by his student Grigory Kristi to make it a manifesto of socialist realism. A new edition of his autobiography *My Life in Art* also required reinterpretation.

---

29 Vladlen Semënovich Davydov (1924–2012), actor with the MAT from 1947 in a variety of roles; curator of the MAT Museum 1985–2000.

Vitaly Vilenkin, "Editorial report on Nikolay Dmitrievich Volkov's[30] introduction to the 1952 edition of Stanislavsky's *My Life in Art*," April 22, 1952, 45–47. Bakhrushin Theater Museum. Vitaly Yakovlevich Vilenkin (1910–97), at the MAT from 1934, was one of the founders of the MAT Studio School in 1943.

The school of self-criticism, which Stanislavsky initiated with his experiments and which he practiced on himself throughout his lifetime, is so stupendous, instructive, and so necessary at this time in mobilizing everyone who works in the arts that it would be a crime to overlook it, it cannot be understood neutrally. One must bring out the theme of Stanislavsky's brilliant self-criticism. [...] How else can one understand this life, which consists of continuous failures, slumps, fiascos, and shortcomings... A naive reader, approaching this book, may actually believe that everything Stanislavsky did at the Art Theater and prior to the Art Theater was a continuous pointless groping or a series of failures. In this regard one must reveal honestly the real state of affairs of the book self-critically and didactically, because Stanislavsky here stands forth as a teacher in another stupendous function. [...]

One would like to read about what gives a special meaning to Stanislavsky's book nowadays, today, in our times?... What does it teach us about its profession, how does it go beyond the narrow frame of professionalism, how does it inspire lofty civic feeling in a person, how does it teach one to relate to technique? It is absolutely necessary to draw such conclusions.

[...] When Nikolay Dmitrievich says *My Life in Art* is an artistic confession, it stirs protest. Not because this is inaccurate in terms of style but because it does not correspond with what Stanislavsky meant to say in this book. There is too much teaching in this book, too much contention to call it an "artistic confession"... Here the reader might easily be misled by a chance formulation. [...]

DURING THE WAR, the Kamerny Theater had been evacuated to Barnual in western Siberia, and then to Balkash in the Karaganda steppe. Despite the impoverished conditions, it premiered G. D. Mdivani's *The Battalion Heads Westward* and four other war plays. In October 1943 the theater returned to Moscow and put on a concert version of *The Seagull*. Various projects were aborted, and plans for J. B. Priestley's *An Inspector Calls* were dashed by the Zhdanov ban on foreign plays.

Vladimir Pimenov, *Vospominaniya, vstrechi*... (Moscow: Pravda, 1967), 15–17. At this time Pimenov was a member of the Committee for Artistic Affairs.

Tairov stubbornly and bravely sought a Soviet play and didn't find one, despite the fact that for some time his deputy for repertoire and the basic author of the theater was the inspired playwright Vsevolod Vishnevsky. But Tairov wanted to find a specifically modern play with a sharp conflict about the present time. [...] During one of our

---

30 Nikolay Dmitrievich Volkov (1894–1965), theater scholar and critic on *Kul'tura teatra*, *Ogonëk*, *Teatr*, etc.; adapted *Anna Karenina* (MAT, 1937) and *War and Peace* (1946).

lengthy discussions about modern drama Aleksandr Yakovlevich told me about the tragic fate of a group of Simferopol actors, who were tortured by the Gestapo during the occupation of Crimea.

A group of actors, among them the theater's designer, Nikolay Baryshev, his wife, the honored actress of the Republic Aleksandra Fëdorovna Peregonets,[31] and a host of other theatrical colleagues, both actors and workers on the technical staffs, created an underground partisan organization. They helped the partisans of the Crimea, handed over plans for where fascist groups were stationed in Simferopol, and transported first aid supplies to the partisans. Aleksandra Peregonets received permission to organize a theater studio and, accepting young people into it, saved them from transportation to Germany. The Gestapo tracked down the underground partisans and, the day before they evacuated the Crimea, had them shot.

"What a dramatic story! This is a genuinely clear-cut conflict, unusually dramatic and tragic and, incidentally, it's already a play!" said Tairov. A play had actually been submitted to the theater, and Tairov accepted it. He said he wanted to find an heroic role for Alisa Koonen, and he saw her in the play in the role of the heroine, whose prototype was Aleksandra Peregonets.

However, the play, written by A. Vasil'ev and L. Él'ston,[32] did not live up to Tairov's hopes. It was shallow, superficial, show-and-tell, complicated human feelings were reduced to declamatory outbursts, stale gimmicks depicted the conscription and execution of dangerous missions. And yet, though Alisa Koonen tried to create a heroic image of an actress–partisan, she could not do it. And again the theater suffered a failure.

Interest in the play was stimulated not only by its title—*Actors* with its leading heroine an actress, but by a new understanding of the role of the actor in society. The actor now, in this play, became a citizen, a hero. They were no longer Shmaga or Shchastlivtsev, poor vagabonds in the plays of Ostrovsky [. . .], Nina Zarechnaya, even Edmund Kean,[33] depicted in plays as people broken, destroyed by the imperfection of the world. The characters in *Actors* were now heroes, emerging from the people, mingling with art and society. However, such a directorial conception of the play, laid out to me by Tairov, unfortunately received no artistic realization in the production, because the play itself was too schematic and psychologically shallow.

But the most dramatic chord in the dying fall of the creative path of Tairov and his theater was considered to be the production of *Lady Windermere's Fan* by Oscar Wilde. Tairov had often mentioned this play in talking about his new conceptions. He spoke of possibilities of a new social reading of it, his desire perhaps for the last

---

31 Nikolay Andreevich Baryshev (1907–44), designer at the Crimean Russian Theater in Simferopol from 1930; Aleksandra Fëdorovna Peregonets (1896 or 1897–1944), after acting work in Khar'kov, Petrograd, Moscow, Kazan, etc., joined the Simferopol troupe in 1931 in dramatic and comic roles. During the Nazi occupation they headed an underground group, were arrested by the Gestapo, and were shot.

32 Lev Mikhaylovich Él'ston (1900–1986), director, worked mainly in the provinces from 1922.

33 Shmaga and Shchastlivtsev, itinerant comedians in Ostrovsky's *Innocent though Guilty* and *The Forest,* respectively; Nina Zarechnaya, the young actress in Chekhov's *The Seagull*; and Edmund Kean, hero of Alexandre Dumas *père*'s play *Disorder and Genius,* a favorite role for romantic actors.

time to appear together with his friend and wife, Alisa Koonen, when the actress and her director would again combine their ideas and thoughts onstage. Despite the fact that Tairov's proposal received no backing, he began to prepare the production. [...]

The inspection took place. There was a sparse audience. There were representatives of the Committee for Artistic Affairs, critics, writers, and other theater people. Everyone was alarmed to realize that they were witnessing a great tragedy for the director. The production had no effect. Onstage were actors in tailcoats, the heroine wept, everything was gloomy and trivial. But it seemed that Tairov saw not what was going on onstage, but something other than what we saw—he was seeing the drama of a mysterious woman as the drama of an actress. Who knows, maybe, if we were to see Tairov's production nowadays, we might find more in it than we did then, both the human feeling and the social themes, more than in a modern production of the Maly Theater, which copies the surface beauty of poses, faces, and costumes and melodramatic tears. [...]

Everyone was convened at the Committee for Artistic Affairs. The leaders of the theater, the leading actors came. No one mentioned *Lady Windermere's Fan,* as if it did not exist. Our task was to offer a proposal for improving the theater's work. It was not very comfortable, all the more for me, an intimate of Comrade Tairov, to give advice to a famous director and a senior theatrical worker. Everything I said was meant to provoke discussion and activate Tairov himself to support his proposals. I wanted these proposals to come from him. The main thing (Tairov himself understood this) had to be to invite new actors and directors to the theater, without diminishing the leadership of Aleksandr Yakovlevich himself. But it all turned out unexpectedly difficult for Tairov. The actors launched into caustic criticisms of the artistic direction, namely, Tairov himself. His closest comrades did not support him. [...] In total silence Tairov's voice rang out: "So that's it. I have no theater. I can no longer go into it. I accept any criticism and I probably might still go on working. But with comrades who have turned their backs on me I cannot work."

Two days later, Tairov sent a letter with the request to release him from his duties as artistic director of the theater. He declined any discussion of his letter.

Aleksandr Tairov to Mikhail Andreevich Suslov,[34] March 1950. Autograph and typescript in RGALI.

As the result of a meeting about this matter in the Committee for Artistic Affairs of the Soviet Ministries of the USSR, May 19, 1949, I was turned out of this theater, after leading it without interruption for thirty-five years.

If, the day before, they had told me that such an outcome was possible, I would not have believed it, as I do not at times even now, although it is an indisputable fact! Why? First of all, because there were no proper grounds for it, second, because, despite

34 Mikhail Andreevich Suslov (1902–92), "Chief Ideologue of the Communist Party," deeply conservative member of the Presidium, head of the Central Committee Department for Agitation and Propaganda from 1946; led the attack on the Jewish Anti-Fascist Committee.

the protracted scrutiny of the theater by the district committees of the Party both of Moscow and the committee, not only did no one speak with me personally on this theme, but even my repeated attempts to set up such discussions invariably met with failure, and, third, because the Party gave us in this plan directives of quite a different order. I know this also from my own experience, when, after a great mistake committed by my production of Dem'yan Bedny's play *Paladins*, the Party, after accurate and acute criticism, left me as the leader of the theater, with the possibility of taking the theater farther down the correct path; I also know the examples of the first versions of the motion pictures *Admiral Nakhimov* and *Michurin*,[35] when the Party, after subjecting them to appropriate Bolshevik criticism, still gave the directors the possibility to correct the demonstrated flaws and in this way create works worthy of Stalin Prizes. So Com. Stalin not only theoretically but practically teaches us to expose modern errors, root and branch, and draw all the necessary conclusions so as not to repeat them in future.

I even suggested that, after the serious criticism of my mistakes, I should have been able to correct them and lead the theater to the necessary heights. All of my complex, almost 45 years of creative life, I thought, spoke for this.

When in early 1929 I learned that Com. Stalin, in his reply to Bill'-Belotserkovsky, characterized the Kamerny Theater as bourgeois, this had a staggering effect on me. I could not at once understand the whole truth of this description, but simultaneously I could not think about anything else. And only gradually, by way of a difficult and complicated process of self-criticism, did I become convinced that this description was as accurate as it was acute. I understood that, despite the conspicuous success of specific productions, I, as a whole, as an artist, was under the sway of a bourgeois aesthetic. I created the Kamerny Theater in the prerevolutionary period, on the eve of the First World War, when the artistic intelligentsia was undergoing great internal upheaval and, wobbling from side to side, turbulently exchanged one "ism" for another. I ardently took on the reform of the theater, subjectively proposing that I would advance its progress, but objectively I isolated it from life and turned it into a thing unto itself. This and much else I began to realize only after Com. Stalin's reply, which became for me, in this way, a foundational moment in my theatrical work.

Having set myself the task of freeing my mind from the practices of bourgeois aesthetics and reconstructing a creative method for the theater along the plan of socialist realism, I announced to the collective the struggle against formalism, aestheticism, Western tendencies in the repertoire, of which both the theater and I were undoubtedly guilty in the preceding period. Now, looking back at the past, I cannot say that this was an easy and immediate success, but the turn-around was achieved and this rapidly produced beneficial results. We concentrated our work on Soviet drama and deliberately, from production to production, were confirmed in the new position, and achieved serious successes, especially with the staging of *The Optimistic Tragedy* of Vs. Vishnevsky, which was praised by *Pravda* as "the triumph of the theater."

---

35 *Admiral Nakhimov*, a film about the naval hero of the Crimean War (directed by Vsevolod Pudovkin, 1947); *Michurin*, a film about the botanist (directed by Aleksandr Dovzhenko, 1948).

Associated with this new turn in the work of the Kamerny Theater, its twentieth anniversary was celebrated in 1935, at which time the government awarded a number of its workers the honorable titles of People's and Meritorious Artist. From that time the theater kept firmly to the course of Soviet plays and themes. When we turned occasionally to a Western theme, it was only with the aim of exposing its bourgeois ideology and politics. So, in 1939, the Kamerny Theater was the first to stage the anti-fascist play by Aleksey Tolstoy *The Devil's Bridge*, in 1947 Kozhevchikov and Prut's play *The Fate of Reginald Davis* against Anglo-American intervention, and in 1948 I. Érenburg's play *The Lion in the Square* against the Marshall Plan.[36] In the years of the Great Patriotic War, while evacuated, we staged exclusively plays devoted to our people's struggle for liberation. I write about this not to boast about the positive aspects of the theater but to make it clear how unexpected we found the sudden and excited accusations of Westernizing against me and the theater in the speech of Com. G. M. Popov[37] to the Moscow Committee Bureau in 1947, which he repeated later at the Moscow Committee Plenum.

[...] I do not mean by this that our work was devoid of flaws. We did deviate, for instance, with Wilde's play *Lady Windermere's Fan* in 1948, when a number of Moscow theaters were working on Western plays, which, as with us, never reached an audience. All the same, this error, like the other shortcomings in the theater's work, hardly dictated that outcome of the committee meeting of May 19, 1949, as a result of which I was turned out of the Kamerny Theater.

[...] It was immediately assumed that from July 1 I be transferred by the committee to the Vakhtangov Theater as a stage director. However, in actual fact, things happened quite differently.

We, i.e., the people's artist of the RSFSR A. G. Koonen, who, approved by Com. Lebedev, also left the Kamerny Theater, was later transferred by the committee to the same Vakhtangov Theater, and I assumed that we would go there for active creative work, which was assured us by the management of the theater. For my part, I suggested appropriate plays: *Unforgettable 1919* by Vs. Vishnevsky (with the author's agreement) and *Manuela Sánchez* by the Spanish Communist writer C. Arconada[38] about the partisan movement in Franco's Spain. The theater did not consider it feasible to produce Vishnevsky's play. As to Arconada's play, despite the fact that the management of the theater and its Party organization both liked it, and I proposed to carry on this work simultaneously with the other productions in the theater, so as in no way to prevent their opening, the theater actually gave me no opportunities to set about it, but, on the

---

36 A dramatization of Mark Aldanov's novel *Chortov Most* (1925). *Sud'ba Rezhinal'da Dévisa* (1947) by Kozhevchikov and Iosif Leonidovich Prut (1900–1996), playwright and screenwriter. *Lev na ploshchade* (1948) by Il'ya Érenburg was a nasty attack on American behavior in postwar Europe.

37 Georgy Mikhaylovich Popov (1906–68), after World War II first secretary of the Moscow Communist Party Committee and secretary of Central Party Committee; under investigation in 1949; later, as party boss of Leningrad, he opposed some of Khrushchëv's reforms.

38 César Muñoz Arconada (1898–1964), Spanish Communist writer of the Generation of 27, lived in Moscow, where he worked with the Gypsy Theater; *Manuela Sánchez* went unpublished but was broadcast in fragments on Radio Moscow.

contrary, persistently used every pretext to delay it until January 1950, when something new got in the way.

I refer to the government granting A. Koonen and me personal pensions of unique importance. It hardly needs to be said that we both accept that pension as a special honor, as a singular act of the concern of the Party and government for the performing arts in general, and in the given case for us, for which we will always be infinitely grateful and recognizant. Which makes all the more incomprehensible to us the order of the Committee for Artistic Affairs, published by them in this respect, a copy of which I here append. In it the grant of our pensions is adjudged to be the result of all our work "concerning the development of theatrical art," and simultaneously it is stated that we as the most senior (which does not correspond to reality) masters of stage art are "retired from the stage." This is not only difficult for us but is impossible to reconcile, all the more since this, as was explained to me by the legal department of both the committee and the Ministry of Social Security, does not correspond to Soviet legislation, that no one asked us about this and that we actually never intended this, and after the granting of the pensions it could not be. We are used to thinking otherwise, and to answering the government's care with earnest work. But now we are explicitly and automatically deprived of this. Deprived at a time when in other theaters comrades older than we are by more than a decade are still working.

We are both healthy, vigorous, and eager to contribute to the advancement of our culture.

More than ever before, we have tested our creative aims and know firmly and unwaveringly that our work can be really useful.

We know that the Soviet theater and, in particular, the Moscow theaters are rich in artistic forces, but this can hardly serve as a basis for depriving two artists who have given their whole lives unstintingly to Soviet art of the possibility of working.

For us idleness is unbearable, especially now, in the period of a bitter struggle between two worlds, when our Soviet motherland, under the brilliant leadership of Com. Stalin, is taking gigantic strides toward Communism. We cannot at this time stand aside from its seething life and be mere onlookers of the great upsurge. We must be participants in the process and in a Soviet way, i.e., *by our labors* thank the Party and the government and implement the progress of our culture. But our *labor is theater.* Alienation from the theater is not life for us. And yet we are now placed precisely in such a situation.

From the moment we received our pensions, we were actually dismissed from the staff of the Vakhtangov Theater despite the promises of its management that we were contracted to produce a production of Arconada's play in 1951, not to mention the fact that right now, when not only a year but even a week of work is important, we have in essence lost the whole season.

Of course, you understand that for us the question has nothing to do with the financial aspect of the matter, especially now when we are guaranteed pensions, nor even in working specifically for the Vakhtangov Theater.

We are Soviet artists and can work in any Moscow theater, insofar as all our lives we have been tied specifically to Moscow. The question is not only about the Vakhtangov Theater but about the position of the committee, which is actually removing us from any further life in art, depriving us of the inalienable right of every Soviet citizen—the right to work. It is guaranteed to us by the Great Stalinist Constitution. As artists we cannot give it up, and as citizens of our socialist motherland we have no right to do so. Therein lies the tragic nature of our situation, from which we ask the Central Party Committee to extricate us.

If I am required to provide any additional data, I am always ready to produce them.

I would be infinitely grateful if we could talk person to person, for which I feel a serious need. [...]

IN AUGUST 1950 the Kamerny Theater was renamed the Pushkin Dramatic Theater, under the leadership of Vasily Vanin; it opened the next year with a revival of *Krechinsky's Wedding*. Tairov died in a Moscow hospital on September 25, 1950. Koonen continued to act and perform in recitals until her death in 1974.

The End of GOSET

Before the war, anti-Semitism had not been a state policy. In fact, it was among the evils of capitalism attacked by socialist indoctrination. After the war, as the Jewish Anti-Fascist Committee began to collect testimony of the Holocaust, Stalin's personal anti-Semitism came to the fore. Jewish leaders and organizations were ruthlessly eliminated, culminating in discovery of the so-called Doctor's Plot of 1952. Only Stalin's death prevented a nationwide pogrom.

Mikhoéls, who had been named a People's Artist of the USSR (1939), People's Artist of the RSFSR (1935), and Meritorious Artist of the State Academic Theaters (1926), had also won the order of Lenin (1939). After serving as president of the Jewish Anti-Fascist Committee, winning a medal "for valorous labor in the Great Patriotic War," he became a member of the Presidium of VTO and of the Cent. Comm. of the profsoyuz of art workers. He won the Stalin Prize (1946) for the production of *Freylekhs*. He was killed in Minsk on January 13, 1948, at the dacha of Lieutenant General Lavrenty Fomick Tsanava (1900–55), the minister of state security of the Belorussian Republic; then his body was driven into town and tossed onto a roadway to give the impression that his car had collided with a truck. His murder had been planned by Beria and agents of the KGB of the USSR, led by deputy minister Sergey Ogol'tsov.

> Svetlana Allilueva, *Only One Year* (New York: Harper and Row, 1969), 154. Svetlana Iosifovna Allilueva (1926–2012), Stalin's daughter, defected to the United States 1967; after a brief return to the Soviet Union in 1984, she continued to live in the West.

One day, in father's dacha, during one of my rare meetings with him, I entered his room when he was speaking to someone on the telephone. Something was being reported to him and he was listening. Then, as a summary of the conversation, he said, "Well, it's an automobile accident." I remember so well the way he said it: not a question, but an answer, an assertion. He wasn't asking; he was suggesting: "an automobile accident." When he got through, he greeted me; and a little later he said: "Mikhoéls was killed in an automobile accident." But when next day I came to my classes in the university, a girl student, whose father had worked for a long time in the Jewish theater, told me, weeping, how brutally Mikhoéls had been murdered while traveling through Belorussia in a car. The newspaper, of course, reported the event as an "automobile accident."

He had been murdered and there had been no accident. "Automobile accident" was the official version, the cover-up suggested by my father when the dark deed had been reported to him. My head began to throb. I knew all too well my father's obsession with "Zionist" plots around every corner. It was not difficult to guess why this particular crime had been reported directly to him.

Natalia Vovsi-Mikhoéls, *Mon père Salomon Mikhoéls. Souvenirs sur sa vie et sur sa mort*, trans. Erwin Spatz (Montricher, Switzerland: Les Éditions noir sur blanc, 1990), 235–36.

In December 1948 the troupe left for a guest stint in Leningrad. Zuskin, who acted in almost every production, as well as running the theater, naturally could not stay in Moscow. But to the general surprise, he obstinately refused to leave. A few days after the company left, on one of those lowering winter evenings when somber forebodings burst upon you, almost physically weighing you down, the manager of the theater passed through us like a gust of wind to announce that Zuskin was going to receive a visit from an important delegation charged with persuading him to go to Leningrad. The manager hesitated a moment to suggest that artistic personalities are whimsical, before going upstairs to take part in the decisive meeting. A few moments later, Zuskin rang at our door in an agreed-on manner. Pale as death, but animated with an unusual energy, he demanded that we all leave the room where the telephone was. Barely two minutes went by. Once this mysterious conversation was over, he left the room without a word and went back upstairs to his flat. From that moment one could read in his eyes the terror that in those accursed times we were used to recognizing in those condemned. As we later learned, Zuskin was committed in writing not to leave the city, and the telephone call had served to confirm this sentence.

A few days later Zuskin was hospitalized for a sleep cure necessitated by his nervous exhaustion. He left at home his little girl of twelve in the company of two old maids, the child's aunts, sisters of his wife who had gone on the tour to Leningrad.

On the morning of December 28, a knock on the wall awoke us. We listened in. Upstairs they were hammering unmercifully on the door. Everything gave way inside me, but I kept hoping against hope. In anguish I stared at the ceiling when, about nine o'clock, the theater called to say that they had continually phoned Zuskin's place but no one had picked up the receiver. They had sent the administrator, who was delayed for some unknown reason. Could we go upstairs and see what was going on?

At that moment we heard a noise on the stairs, a shout, a dog barking. Opening the door, we saw the second-floor neighbor hurry downstairs, literally dragged by his dog. He sank into a chair, gripped by emotion, and murmured in a barely audible voice, "It's them." We had understood that much ourselves. What about Zuskin? Surely they weren't going to arrest a sick man out of his bed!

Yes, they were. They picked him up that night, sick and sleepy. They dragged him from the hospital directly to the Lubyanka. We learned all this years later, from the very mouth of the doctor on duty that night at the hospital. Zuskin remained imprisoned for questioning for three years and eight months, before being shot on August 12, 1952.

A man with the touching naivety of a child, the best actor the Yiddish stage had known, killed at the age of fifty-three. Why? Back then one did not ask such questions.

> From Venyamin Zuskin's interrogation. V. F. Kolyazin and V. A. Goncharov, eds., *"Vernite Mne Svobodu!" Deyateli literatury i iskusstva Rossii i Germanii—zhertvy stalinskogo terrora. Memoral'ny sbornik dokumentov iz arkhivov byvshego KGB* ["Give me back freedom!" Literary men and artists of Russia and Germany as victims of Stalin's terror: Memorial anthology of documents from the archives of the former KGB] (Moscow: MEDIUM, 1997), 335–36.

[*December 24, 1948*. Zuskin speaks:] On the day of Mikhoéls's funeral *Zhemchuzhina*[39] came to the Jewish Theater where the coffin with Mikhoéls's body was, and until the moment it was taken out of the building she stood by the coffin.

When I saw *Zhemchuzhina*, I went up to her at once to share the grief that had befallen us, and which I took very hard. *Zhemchuzhina*, as I saw, had herself felt Mikhoéls's death strongly. In talking to me next to the coffin, she asked me at length about the state of Mikhoéls's family, whether we should take measures for their welfare, and when she was done, she asked, "What do you think happened here—an accident or a murder?" Having no facts concerning the matter, I answered *Zhemchuzhina* that we should believe the official version. *Zhemchuzhina*, however, objected to that and said the matter was not so cut-and-dried as they were trying to make it seem.

[Another session:]

PRESIDING JUDGE: Later you testified, "Having fallen under Mikhoéls's influence, I absorbed his nationalistic anti-Soviet attitudes and finally crept down the narrow road of enemies."

ZUSKIN: I didn't discuss these things with him...

P.J.: But isn't that the testimony you gave?

ZUSKIN: Yes, I did, because some of the investigators stated they didn't believe me.

P.J.: But you just told us that your evidence was trustworthy.

39 Polina Semënovna Zhemchuzhina (actually Perl Karpovskaya, 1897–1970), Communist official married to Molotov; first female narkom 1939 and an associate of the Jewish Anti-Fascist Committee; arrested for treason 1948 and in a labor camp to 1953.

ZUSKIN: I'm not asking the court for any leniency, I'll tell my life story, and you can judge me not by reports but by my own actions.

P.J.: It's impossible to ignore such testimony. The court's job is to verify your testimony.

ZUSKIN: But all my testimony is a lie.

P.J.: Yet when you denounced other defendants here and stipulated your nationalistic [i.e., Zionist] activities, the repertoire of the theater, your roles in that theater, did you put any questions to anyone or testify to their inaccuracy?

ZUSKIN: I want to make only one correction. Granovsky was artistic director of the Jewish Theater for ten years, Mikhoéls for nineteen years. Together that makes twenty-nine years, and I was artistic director of the theater for a few months in all. Whoever organized the repertoire, whoever's responsible for it, did I have any dealings with him? I did not because I was an actor. Granovsky took exclusive part in the work of the Jewish Theater, besides for seventeen years Litvakov[40] was the ideological head of the theater. For three years running it could have been cleared up that so-and-so Zuskin was in the theater, but this was not done, although I asked about it.

P.J.: You asserted that having fallen under Mikhoéls's influence, you entered an anti-Soviet enemy path.

ZUSKIN: I categorically deny it.

P.J.: You said yourself that in a conversation with him the two of you said that Jewish culture was stifled in the Soviet Union.

ZUSKIN: I deny it because I never talked about that with him. [...] No, I don't know how to make speeches, I can recite a role, I can read what is written down. [...] I was prompted to say all that. [...] Because I was taken to the interrogation in a totally stupefied condition in my hospital pajamas. After all, I was arrested in the hospital where I was undergoing a cure, and besides, my illness was such that I spent a long time in a deep sleep. I was arrested while I was asleep and only when I woke up in the morning did I see that I was in a cell and realized I'd been arrested...

[January 11, 1949]

I confess myself guilty of expressing hostile attitudes against the Soviet government; I maintained a criminal connection with the Jewish nationalist underground and its leader Solomon Mikhaylovich Mikhoéls.

The Jewish Anti-Fascist Committee, of whose presidium I was a member, was set up as an organization hostile to the Soviet government and was used by us to carry on active anti-Soviet activities among Jews who live in the Soviet Union. [...] The Jewish Anti-Fascist Committee maintained a close connection with America, which sent us various materials about the Soviet Union.

Question. Concerning espionage?

Answer. Yes.

---

40 Moyshe Litvakov (1879–1939), Yiddish journalist and politician, editor of *Der Emes*; helped adapt *The Witch* at GOSET. Arrested in 1938, he died in prison.

Committee of Artistic Affairs, order no. 959, liquidating the Jewish State Theater, November 14, 1949. Quoted in Jeffrey Veidlinger, *The Moscow State Yiddish Theater: Jewish Culture on the Soviet Stage* (Bloomington: Indiana University Press, 2000), 270–71. © 2000 by Jeffrey Veidlinger. Reprinted with permission of Indiana University Press.

[Ostensibly the reason was that the theater had not met its plan, absurdly inflated for profits, though in fact it lost only 446,000 rubles in the face of the arrests of its artistic director, chief writers, and the fading away of much of its audience base.]

The Moscow State Yiddish Theater finished the 1948 year with losses of 1,247 thousand rubles and for the ten months of 1949 has allowed losses of the sum of 815 thousand rubles.

Attendance at the theater, both in the years 1948 and 1949, has been at a completely unsatisfactory level and is currently at 13.7 percent capacity. For many performances only thirty to forty spectators are at the theater. The opening of a new production did not raise the audience's interest. The allocation of subscription tickets for the theater's performances in the same period has brought a general debt in excess of one million rubles.

I order:

1. The liquidation of the Moscow Art Theater as of December 1, 1949, on account of its unprofitability.

2. The formation of a liquidation committee [...]

3. The liquidation commission to direct the liquidation of the theater as of December 15 of this year; to present a liquidation balance to the Head Management of Dramatic Theater; to organize with the Moscow Yiddish Theater a systematic tour and farewell show; to secure the maintenance of the theater's building, administration, and service personnel; and to pay its way in full without any subsidy.[41]

The War against Cosmopolitan Critics

Zhdanov had invited the critics to be bolder in supporting "the Party spirit" in the theater; it was not until after his death in August 1948 that a full-throated hue and cry hounded individual members of the critical establishment itself.

Konstantin Rudnitsky's diary, November 30, 1948. Quoted in N. P. Balatova, "From the archive of a theater critic," in *Teatral'naya periodika v Rossii* [Theatrical periodicals in Russia], ed. A. A. Kolganov (Moscow: Tri kvadrata, 2009), 89.

On our way back from Bolshev, at the Yaroslavl station, we bought a copy of *Pravda* and in the article by S. N. Durylin read about Boyadzhiev[42] and myself: "Like-minded

---

41 In fact, all theatrical activity was stopped the next day; after the theater's assets were sold off, its building, the Malaya Bronnaya Theater, was turned over to the Theater of Satire.

42 Sergey Nikolaevich Durylin (1886–1954), literary historian and critic, who wrote journalism under a number of pseudonyms; author of numerous monographs on playwrights and actors. Grigory Nersesovich Boyazhdiev (1909–74), theater critic and historian, prolific author.

critics from *Soviet Art* urge the Maly Theater in the wrong direction." This was how it began, and it is worth writing a wee bit more about it in detail—how an article on Ostrovsky mentioned how Tanya [Bachelis][43] and I attended the Maly Theater's *A Lucrative Post* in the manager's box and across in the government box we saw Beria, Mikoyan, Andreev,[44] Malenkov... they applauded. My derogatory articles about this production and about *The Dowerless Bride* were already set up in type. Right after the performance, I went to the printer's. I could have changed a lot, but didn't correct a line, didn't touch a thing. [...] The next day it appeared. To understand what came after, I have to tell you about the plenum of the Writers' Union of December 15, 1948.

ON THAT DAY Executive Secretary A. A. Fadeev, in his keynote address, accused the theatrical critics I. I. Yuzovsky, A. S. Gurvich, G. N. Boyadzhiev, E. G. Kholodov, A. M. Borshchagovsky, L. A. Malyugin, and Ya. L. Varshavsky of not supporting the Soviet playwriting of A. V. Sofronov, N. Ya. Virta, A. A. Surov, and B. S. Romashov. This initiated the fight against cosmpolitanism, although that word was not spoken.

Some critics, however, made their careers at this time in the journal *Sovetskoe iskssutvo* (Soviet art). N. I. Gromov wrote "The Aestheticizing Antipatriot Varshavsky," the panegyric article about *Unforgettable 1919* that lauded Vishnevsky's play as the source of research for new forms of theatrical expression. Gromov became a deputy president of the Soviet for Playwriting for Theater, Movie, and TV for the Writers' Union Board. Yu. V. Malashev worked at the VTO, then at the Ministry of Culture, and, in 1965, was deputy editor in chief of the journal *Moscow*. T. A. Chebotarevskaya worked at the *Literary Gazette* and wrote monographs about actors.

Antonov-Ovseenko, *Teatr Iosifa Stalina*, 184–85.

The year 1949 came. It began with articles in *Soviet Art*, an article under the monitory title "Bolshevist Party Spirit Is the Basis of Creative Work of Dramatists and Critics." Within a fortnight, on January 28, came an article in *Pravda* like a shot from a high-caliber weapon: "About a Certain Antipatriotic Group of Theater Critics." Within a day, a second voice chimed in, the newspaper *Culture and Life*. All three articles, unsigned, were meant as directives. A series of directives.

That Stalin had a hand in the *Pravda* article can be surmised from the free-and-easy tone, the choice of insults, and the absence of any sense of style: "vile slander," "hostile

---

43 Tat'yana Izraelevna Bachelis (1918–1999), theater critic and historian, author of innumerable articles about modern theater; married to Konstantin Rudnitsky.

44 Anastas Ivanovich Mikoyan (1895–1978), Armenian Bolshevik, member of the Central Committee of the Communist Party from 1921, chairman of the committee for supply for the Red Army during World War II, and minister of trade 1953–55; titular head of state 1964. Andrey Andreevich Andreev (1895–1971), commissar of agriculture and deputy chairman of the Council of Ministers 1946–53; later headed the commission to review the fates of those sentenced during the purges of the 1930s and 1940s.

taunts," "fishy eyes," "attempts to defame . . . to swindle . . . to carp," "cosmopolitan, putrid relation to Soviet art" . . . And at the end—an appeal to expose and to smash this anti-Party group. Do you recognize the language, the temperament of an inveterate thug? . . .

In *Pravda* there sounded for the first time the explicit term "nationless cosmopolitans." Thus was born a cut-and-dried label that could immediately be applied to every critic "to be crushed." The greater number of them "happened to be" Jews. The fact that the list of new victims included a single Armenian and a single Russian could fool nobody: genocide against the creative intelligentsia went hand in glove with the ignition of anti-Semitism. Stalin remained faithful to this "principle" to the end.

THIS CLUTCH OF CRITICS smeared by Fadeev, most of them on the staffs of *Teatr* and *Sovetskoe Iskusstvo,* had made frivolous references to Surov's *Far from Stalingrad,* Chirskov's *The Victors,* and Sofronov's *Moscow Character.* Their "perfidious and slanderous attacks" were aimed mainly at Stalin Prize winners, often by maintaining silence. And silence, Stalin had stated, was a stupid and absurd form of criticism. These writers were first tarred with the brush of "cosmopolitanism" in the article "About a Certain Antipatriotic Group of Theater Critics," published in *Pravda* on January 28, 1949. In February 1949 Rudnitsky was also named a cosmopolitan and fired.

> "To destroy and expose the group of anti-patriotic theater critics," *Teatr* 1 (February 1949), 3–4.

A group of antipatriotic theater critics, whose activities were subjected to a severe and just condemnation in the pages of the Party central organ *Pravda* (January 28, 1949) and the newspaper *Culture and Life* (January 30, 1949), has persistently ignored these Party orders and has followed its own line, antipathetic to the Party line concerning issues of art. [. . .]

By rejecting the method of socialist realism, which is the basis of Marxist–Leninist aesthetics, and by ignoring the decisions of the Party as to issues of art, this group has propagandized a cosmopolitan method of aesthetics and formalist criticism that is uninterested in depicting the vital content of art and in shaping socially progressive tendencies. The group has been "inspired" by the system of A. Veselovsky's[45] bourgeois, cosmopolitan school, which, toward the end of the nineteenth century, put forth pernicious "concepts" about the origin and evolution of Russian theater and art. Its forerunners were the "leaders" of Western European modernism and decadence. Its instructors were the liberal bourgeois professors actively fighting against Marxist–Leninist aesthetics. Its enforcers were prerevolutionary nihilist critics such as A. Kugel.

Weaned on the putrid crumbs of cosmopolitanism, decadence, and formalism, this

---

45 Aleksandr Nikolaevich Veselovsky (1831–1906), literary theorist whose ideas of the mythic origins of poetry influenced the Russian formalists; condemned by the Soviets for "ethnographism" and overemphasis on "source study."

antipatriotic criticism took to decrying and discrediting all that was new and progressive, all that originated, grew, and gained a foothold in Soviet theater and drama [...]

[...] The editorial board of the journal *Teatr* and its staff displayed a political myopia incapable of realizing that the scribblings of these antipatriotic critics included "not just accidental isolated errors but a system of antipatriotic views detrimental to the development of our literature and art, a system which must be destroyed" (*Pravda*, January 28, 1949) [...]

In particular, *Teatr* committed a serious error in publishing the critic V. Zhdanov's[46] baneful article "The Topical and the Artistic" (*Teatr*, 10, 1947). In this article, Zhdanov, allegedly arguing for "a synthesis of the artistic and the topical," denied to V. Romashov's play *The Great Power* (*Velikaya sila*) both topicality and artistry. Moreover, the author of the article reproached V. Romashov for, for all intents and purposes, not putting onstage any of Soviet science's priority issues or the struggle with sycophancy; for depicting topical issues of modern life in the play without profound philosophical and artistic sensitivity; and, finally, for contaminating the characters' real conversational speech with allegedly official jargon and clichés. After treating the play this way, razing it to the ground, the critic suddenly recovers his memory and notes that, "bad" as it was, this play still enjoyed a success with the audience. However, this success the critic attributes to "society's interest in the production" and the novelty of its theme.

Having taken this conciliatory and corrupt position toward antipatriotic theater criticism, the editorial boards and staff of *Teatr* failed to fulfill their basic task: to rally around the magazine cadres of Party critics and nurture a young cadre of critics in the tradition of the Bolshevik press. [...]

We must, decidedly and inarguably, break with liberal tolerance for all the aesthetic nonentities who vilely slander Soviet drama and theater. The duty of Soviet critics is to destroy these stateless cosmopolitan aesthetes, to clear the field for the fruitful activities of the Soviet theater. We must shine into all the nooks and crannies of theater criticism and theory the ruthless light of militant Bolshevik criticism, to smoke out from all the cracks the antipatriots [...]

Labor Camp Theaters

A fresh wave of convicts inundated the camps—soldiers and officers who had spent time in the West, prisoners of war, victims of the anti-Semitic and anti-Western campaigns.

> N. Éydel'man, "About my father," in *Teatr Gulaga. Vospominaniya* [Gulag Theater: Memoirs], ed. M. M. Korallov (Moscow: Memorial, 1995), 156–61. Yakov Naumovich Éydel'man (1896–1978) was an atheist critic of Jewish parentage.

46 Vladimir Viktorovich Zhdanov (1898–?), literary critic and biographer; not to be confused with Andrey Zhdanov.

A Party member and decorated tank commander in the war, he was arrested November 4, 1950, under statute 58-10, sentenced to ten years in the Vorkut camp, and released July 12, 1954.

A short time went by—and blows rained down on the theater critic–cosmopolitans, a new "ice age" set in. My father was ejected from the Party for "inadmissible talk" about the weakness of many officially authorized productions.

Nowadays it would probably get a laugh, but at that time no one was laughing when loud accusations were aimed at a wide range of utterances, among them the words "yes, Sofronov is no Chekhov!" In the group, led by the then-pillars of radio broadcasting Chernyshev and Shelashnikov, it was said, "Yes, we know that Chekhov is superior to many Soviet writers, but this kind of backbiting has a hostile character."

Expelled from work (for the wife as schoolteacher, for the son as student), my father tried for a year and a half to find a job without any success. [...] On the night of November 3–4, 1950, [...] the order was presented, father quickly collected his few things and said good-bye: "We'll probably never meet again." Mother in tears: "He isn't guilty!" (probably at that time a more widespread Russian cry than Tsvetaeva's "My love, what I have done to you!"[47]).

[...] The fifty-four-year-old man was sent to Lubyanka, after eight months to Butyrka, got ten years under statute 58-10, and was sent to a camp, "as a student at Stalin's Vorkuta Academy." [...] Explaining why he stopped writing about theater, Ya. N. many years later exclaimed, "What the hell is the theater compared to what I saw in Vorkuta!"[48]

Probably, all the theatricality of the 1920s and 1930s was transferred to Arkhangel'. [...]

To entertain the higher ranks, concerts and shows were organized with the participation of the pretty good strengths of the All-Union and International class. In one small work camp the superior officer ordered the MC (also a convict) to announce the acts like this: "Rachmaninov. Polka. Played by Ivanov, international spy, statute so-and-so... Mayakovsky. Poem about the Soviet passport. Recited by Rabinovich, statute 58-10... Mozart. Turkish march. Played by von Ecke, Sturmbahnführer of an SS unit; statute so-and-so..."

In this worst of places they roared with laughter more than when free, because of the absence of fear of being imprisoned or sent to a camp.

Kamil Ikramov, "Unwritten history" [recorded by O. Sidel'nikova-Ikramova], in Korallov, *Teatr Gulaga*, 88–89. Kamil Akmalevich Ikramov (1927–89), writer and journalist, was arrested November 12, 1943, for anti-Soviet agitation, sentenced to five years, and freed 1948. He was rearrested 1951 and sentenced to five years in the Kargapol camp; freed April 1955.

47 A line from the poem "Still Yesterday He Met My Gaze" by the émigrée poet Marina Ivanovna Tsvetaeva (1891–1941).
48 Vorkuta was the largest of the internment areas, with 192 subcamps.

The day of the election of the Supreme Soviet was drawing nigh. But the head of the camp, our Yury Gavrilovich Konchev (naturally, the most respected man in the region not hidden behind barbed wire), was president of the electoral committee. And as chairman of the electoral committee, he had to put on an amateur artistic concert at the polls on election day. And where was he to get amateur artists, when there was nothing in the region but dogs? And the camp garrison. The local population, besides, lived appallingly. They were starving to death, they lived worse than us in the camp. (Our camp was a good one. We had one problem—when one of us was sent from the camp to the transit point, it was a tragedy: people sobbed, chopped off their hands, feet, not to leave the camp—that's the kind of camp it was.)

[...] So there had to be an amateur show. And where was it to come from? The camp garrison couldn't sing, because they were all kept isolated in the turrets. There was no way they could rehearse, and besides, they had all had colds from the frost. We, on the other hand, were all together.

[...] But the soloists in our collective did not want to sing in unison. Then I understood why the Party didn't care for the intelligentsia—it does not want to sing in unison. And who does sing in unison? It turns out that those who sing well in unison are Banderites, Vlasovians,[49] the German polizei. All Ukrainians are particularly fond of singing. If they could be got to "jine in de chorus," they would agree to sing whatever you please. About Stalin, Molotov, Beria—it wouldn't matter, so long as they "sang in unison." [...]

So these were the "men's voices." Whereas the "women's voices" were basically those of prostitutes—either our Soviet ones or Germans. But the intelligentsia refused to sing in unison.

Election day dawned. I remember a clear, frosty sunny day—they lead us out, the dogs bark, strain at their chains with all their might, the convoy hold automatic weapons. They escort us to the polling sector. The program was the same for us as for them. They bring us in. It's the regimental mess made over into a club. [...]

A small stage, the kind you see in schools, a curtain that had to be pulled by hand. And, while the chorus was setting up, I came out and announced, "We shall begin our concert"—I understood at the time that the more unnatural the voice, the more the audience liked it. "The poem about the Soviet passport" [by Mayakovsky]. You probably remember what this poem is about, but just let me remind you of its text. Basic passages. It begins with the profound self-criticism, "I would gnaw like a wolf on bureaucracy, I've no respect for credentials . . . ," and it ends with the following lines: "I take out of wide trousers the duplicate of a worthless weight. Read, envy me, I am a citizen of the Soviet Union." And such was the power of art that the regiment envied me.

After this I open the curtain, where the chorus is already standing. Volodya Tyshko is ready to wave his conductor's baton. Verka Bushueva [a common criminal], [the

---

49 Banderites (from Stepan Bandera), Ukrainian nationalists. Vlasovians (from General Vlasov, who commanded the Ukrainians in the Wehrmacht), Ukrainians who surrendered to the Germans near Leningrad.

Pole] Postek, and someone else are already sitting with their bayans and fiddles. I announce: "the composer, winner of the Stalin Prize, Serafim Tulikov. A song about Stalin." I don't remember all the words, but I do remember the chorus, which went: "And our song flies across the wide expanses (*prostitutes*: "paa-a-nses"), to the top of the Kremlin (*prostitutes*: Kre-e-mlin . . .), thank you Comrade Stalin (*Tyshokov*: Sta-a-a-li-i-n), sing out the towns and fields (*all together*)." [...]

> Valery Frid, "*Gogol's Wedlock*: A play by Ostrovsky," in Korallov, *Teatr Gulaga*,
> 106–7. Valery Semënovich Frid (1922–), arrested April 8, 1944 (article 58-10,
> chapter 2; 58-11, 17; 58-8; ten-year sentence), Kargaganda camp (OLP-15),
> Mineral'ny camp; released January 1954.

In Kargapol,[50] in the fifteenth OLP, the head of the KBCh was a kind-hearted, not very literate sergeant-major. It was said that he once announced the show as:

"*Gogol's Wedlock,* a play by Ostrovsky."

[...] He ordered me to run the amateur show—as double-duty; at the time I was working in the office. The sergeant-major honestly admitted that he wasn't up to that sort of thing . . . Ah, if only in our time all the cultural bigwigs, including the ministers, had been so self-critical!

I agreed; on performance days, and sometimes during rehearsals, we were released from work duty. This was a very inspiring incentive, especially for those who worked in the genpop [general population].

In the collections of one-act plays that the KBCh provided us, the main characters were saboteurs and Chekists. We played one and the other with equal enthusiasm: the subject matter of these plays had no more relation to our lives than to any Soviet reality. Their protagonists were purely conventional figures, the same as cowboys or pirates.

As to the programs of the camp concerts, anything went, no one was bothered by clashing genres. I recall the amateur clown Eremeev—as is traditional, in life an introverted, gloomy peasant, no longer young. He delighted his audience with antediluvian fairground gags and tricks. We also had a couple of acrobats: the strongman Jan Ehrlich and his young partner, a professional circus artiste, so weakened by malnutrition that he had a hard time holding the support bar with his scrawny arms.

Remarkable was the tap-dancing pickpocket Val'ka. Normally a self-respecting thief, a lifer [*polnota*], would not take part in an official camp amateur night: it would be a rude breach of "the law." But Val'ka was "damaged goods" [*porchak*], that is, a thief with a shady reputation, and besides, he was very proud of his talent as a tap dancer.

Serious thieves organized their own "concerts"—in the prison cells, in the thieves' barracks—*shalmany*. Sometimes even we genpop [*frayer*] had a chance to witness these performances for an elite circle. And I have to admit: there was something to them. [...]

---

50 In northwest Russia, one of the largest camps, with around eight hundred thousand inmates in the 1938–40 period.

Tamara Petkevich, "An accidental profession," in Korallov, *Teatr Gulaga,*
133–40. Tamara Vladislavovna Petkevich (1920–) was arrested January 30, 1943,
under statute 58-10 and sentenced to a seven-year term, with a further three
years' loss of civil liberties, and confiscation of property. She was confined to
camps in Central Asia (Dzhangidzhir), Belovodsk, and Komi SSR. Released
January 3, 1950, she made it back to her hometown of Leningrad 1959, and
published a memoir *Life Is a Pair of Unmatched Boots* (*Zhizn'—sapozhok
neparny*) (1993).

[Despite having no talent or experience, in 1946 she was assigned to the theatrical
barracks in the Komi[51] camps TÉKO (theatrical-variety collective or agitbrigade). She
was cast as Shipuchina in Chekhov's one-act farce *The Celebration*.]

We toured. We traveled south as far as Sol'chevygodsk and then much farther
southward. Then I saw the [Shezham] camp SzhDL, stretching out as far as Pechora
itself. The colonies were hidden in the taiga and were spread out across the tundra.
We stuck in the mud of the road and the marsh; we got bogged down, kept moving
and dragged along exhausted under the weight of the suitcases. Our escort squeezed
us pedestrians into passenger trains, emptying a few compartments for us so that we
wouldn't mix with the others. The passengers themselves kept their distance. At first
this hurt. Then we got used to it.

The barracks at the colonies were overcrowded. They stowed us wherever they
could: in tiny closets in the office, in the infirmary or the club. We slept on the floor
or on tables. In the morning we rehearsed. In the evening we gave a concert.

The men back from working the timberland, once they learned of our arrival,
hastened to wash, have a quick supper, and fill the assembly or mess hall transformed
into a clubhouse. Not everyone, of course, would go to the concert. Immersed in their
despair, many wholly rejected any idea of entertainment. In the first rows sat the camp
guards. Behind them the prisoners.

The concert would begin and everyone would fall silent. They would listen, holding
their breath, just as, not far away, a spectator too, I listened as well. The good-looking
soloists Serëzha Alliluev and Makary Golovin, a tenor and a baritone, came onstage:
"Farewell, beloved city, we go to sea tomorrow..." They were followed by splendid
Tamara Slanskaya. Her repertoire was full of arias from operas and operettas. I peeped
through a little hole in a side scene and could not tear myself away as I stared at the
people reciting and dancing, wiping away my tears. Only belief in our need for one
another somehow damped down the unflagging feeling of guilt that things were immeasurably easier and better for us than for our audience.

[...] At times we were on the road for three to five months.

North of us other camps were scattered: Ust'vym, Ukhtinsk, Abez, Inta, Vorkuta.
Each had its own theatrical collective or agitbrigade. Of Vorkuta, they said, "They've
got a real theater. The famous Tokarevskaya's there"; about Ukhtinsk, "They've got

---

51 Komi Republic, twelve hundred miles from Moscow and one hundred miles above the Arctic
Circle.

the famous cellist from the Moscow Philharmonic Kreyn. Éggert[52] runs the theater there (many knew his name from the movie *The Bear's Wedding*), there are lots of Kerzhentsev's victims there."

[...] The war had ended. In 1947, most of those convicted from 1937 on had been released. The look of the camp changed substantially. The camps teemed with troop trains with a wartime "replenishment": soldiers from the front who had been POWs; those who had lived in occupied territory; an enormous number of Balts appeared. [...] In the camp now the young were in the majority. [...]

Very often our tours brought us face-to-face with unusual circumstances, out of the ordinary. Over the intercom we were ordered by the head of the Political Section to make a detour from our itinerary and "serve the colony of German POWs." We did not realize that there were any such in SzhDL.

We walked on foot a long way from the station. In small groups we crossed the rickety suspension bridge connecting the banks of a rivulet unfamiliar to us. The road stretched into the far taiga.

The Okhrana commander requested us with scant courtesy to hand over in the zone knives and "anything sharp," if we had that sort of thing. He promised to return them when we left the colony. With no hope of getting any of it back, we handed over our possessions.

The roads into this colony were swept clean and strewn with sand. The barracks were raised on foundations. Instead of glass, there was mica in the window frames. The club struck us as different as well: spacious, well lit, capacious.

A German showed up to translate: he began to study the program. Occasionally he would ask a question, such as, "What is a 'cabbie'? What is a 'hack-stand'?"

The guards and their families had long been sitting in their places. The concert was ready to begin, but no one else had come into the hall. The Germans had refused to enter the club. Confusion ensued. The guards began to run around. After a short while, rows of Germans were led into the club in serried ranks. They settled onto the benches in an orderly fashion. In a hostile and tense silence we finally began the concert.

The first, second, and fifth numbers were performed. Not a sound, not a hand clap. The guards tried to applaud, but these scattered attempts sounded ridiculous.

The concert was played out in deathly silence.

This was just after the war. We had been behind barbed wire and, for a short time now, so were the Germans. The feeling of hatred and animosity blinded both sides.

The concert was over. As if to apologize for the embarrassment, the highest-ranking officer turned to us with great punctilio and invited us to supper.

---

52 Aleksandr Abramovich Kreyn (1883–1951), cellist and composer, scion of a famous dynasty of klezmer musicians. Konstantin Vladimirovich Éggert (1883–1955), prominent silent film actor and director; *Medvezhaya svad'ba* (1926), based on a play by Lunacharsky, is a lurid melodrama about a nobleman who murders obsessively while clad in a bearskin.

The table was already laid. There were heaps of sliced white bread, which we had not seen for many years ... There were bowls of buckwheat porridge, meat, and, what was most improbable, jelly doughnuts.

We stood there unable to believe our eyes. Did the Germans eat like that?

"Take a seat!" they said.

And suddenly our tenor Serëzha Alliluev, in an unusually shrill voice, said to the company:

"We won't eat this German swill! Feed it to them! Let them have it, see how they like it!"

"What's so 'German' about it? These are Soviet products. You should understand what politics requires."

Possibly, possibly.

Humiliated, disheartened, we walked away from the place. Most of us were crying. Some were cursing savagely, obscenely, shouting as loudly as they could; some wept.

But, as a rule, when we traveled, we felt better than when we were on home base.

Antonov-Ovseenko, "The theater at the Krasnovod camp c. 1950," in *Teatr Iosifa Stalina,* 236.

The Krasnovod camp ... consisted of twelve colonies, each in its own zone. We dug by hand enormous pits—receptacles for petroleum, which was to be brought by sea from Baku. Exhausted even before this, debilitated by illness, I couldn't fulfill the set quota, or even half of it. A cell loomed before me, after it the sick bay, and there complete deliverance from the cares of life. The last few days I dragged myself from work to the zone at the far ridge. The escorts, shouting and threatening with their rifle butts, urged on the tail of the column. And I trudged on, barely lifting my feet, and sang. What I sang, some ballads, I don't remember. But I sang. Somebody informed the head of the KVCh—the cultural–educational section [for camp subdivisions]—about the singing goner, and in the morning the brigadier sent me to the barracks: "Someone from the KVCh will be coming for you soon."

The KVCh ensemble was located at the very end of a one-story wooden building, the House of Culture. Here they rehearsed, here they rested on two-tiered bunk beds. The pianist Boris Ozerov, a baritone from a local philharmonic, who landed in the camp on charges of "agitation"; two dancers, who badly "tapped out" a chechotka; a couple of circus artistes—the clown Jean and the gymnast Giro, musicians (bayan, accordion, balalaika, dombra, guitar), and a few choristers—I believe that was the whole crew. With these forces we had to give concerts for the free hired hands and guards and also entertain the prisoners. At first they put me in the general chorus, then they assigned me to draw up the program. There was no repertoire, and once the chief asked me to write a literary–musical montage on a military theme. Either my thick glasses had made a reassuring impression on him or something else, but the chief expected a scenario from me.

... As if it were yesterday, this premiere goes by. We, the two MCs, stand in front of the curtain. Dzeen-n-n ... Behind the curtains someone strikes brass plates.

first MC: The year is 1242. On the ice of Lake Chudskoy Alexander of the Neva routed the Teutonic knights, driving them from the Novgorod territory. Cla-a-ang ...

second MC: The year is 1380. Dmitry of the Don in a battle with the Tatars on Kulikovo Field established the independence of Old Rus'.

And so year after year, through the ages up to our own times. Up to the tragedy of 1941, which we had to present as the greatest achievement of Stalin's leadership. Every statement by an MC was accompanied by music, song, or a dramatic action. This was greatly reminiscent of the once extremely popular living newspaper shows or the "Blue Blouse."

CHAPTER NINE

The So-Called Thaw and the Refrigeration, 1954–1963

T HE FIRST MAJOR SHOCK was the death of Stalin in 1953. The one sure thing in the lives of Soviet citizens vanished. Then came the arrest and execution of Beria. The Gulag system slowly began to be dismantled with amnesty for criminals with less than five-year sentences; returning convicts offered fresh disclosures about how the system worked. After the first period of national grief and covert relief, a cautious liberalization, later dubbed the "Thaw" from Il'ya Érenburg's novel of that name, began in 1955, as government policies detached themselves from their Stalinist carapaces. Even the Kremlin was opened for the first time to anyone who could buy an admission ticket.

The next year, Khrushchëv's secret speech to the Party Congress, denouncing Stalin as a despot, opened up a world of possibilities, along with a good deal of confusion. For educated Russians, "a world of certainties came to an end, now that core beliefs and commonly accepted wisdom had turned to dust."[1] Each new revelation about the past had to be digested, each new crisis confronted, the promised freedoms assayed and evaluated. De-Stalinization also opened wary overtures to the West, encouraging intellectuals to look abroad for wider horizons. Except for Khrushchëv himself, the regime never quite approved of these efforts and often showed undisguised hostility to them. The brutal crushing of the Hungarian revolt in November 1956 and the repudiation of Boris Pasternak's novel *Doctor Zhivago* in 1957 showed that. The defection to the West of the ballet dancer Rudolf Nureyev in 1962 was a widely publicized embarrassment. The complex interplay between Soviet foreign and domestic policy created not only opportunities but also unforeseen setbacks.

Although artists were champing at the bit to explore new territory, lip service continued to be paid to the traditional formulas of socialist realism. Even in the mid-1950s, the party line insisted that works of art had to be easily accessible to the people, and this doctrine survived well into the 1980s. Any experimentation had to be carried out within the bounds of Marxist–Leninist ideology, a true oxymoron.

1   Vladislav Zubok, *Zhivago's Children: The Last Russian Intelligentsia* (Cambridge, Mass.: Harvard University Press, 2009).

Figures and movements whose names had not been heard for years were gradually rehabilitated. As the ideas of Meyerhold, Vakhtangov, and other inadmissible experimenters began to filter into the debates over the future of theater, more dissatisfaction was expressed with the MAT model, not least because its current leaders were incapable of casting off official rhetoric and ways of thinking. Vakhtangov's student Ruben Simonov attempted to resurrect his mentor's nonnaturalisic teachings, developing an Aesthetics of Celebration and a vision of tragicomedy. Meyerholdian directors emerged: in the annus mirabilis 1956 Boris Ravensky, at the Maly, directed an impressive production of Tolstoy's *Power of Darkness,* whose religious message had caused it to be ignored since the Revolution, and cast one of Meyerhold's favorite actors, Igor' Il'insky. Valentin Pluchek, director of the Moscow Satire Theater, revived all three of Mayakovsky's comedies. At the same time, the famous Leningrad director and artist Nikolay Akimov, a master at survival, promoted satirical traditions in his interpretations of Russian classics and the fairy tales of Evgeny Shvarts. Bulgakov and Dostoevsky were rediscovered, and the barnacles were scraped off the good ship Anton Chekhov, most notably by Tovstonogov and Éfros.

In 1953 Glavrepertkom had been disbanded and its functions apportioned to Glavlit and the newly founded Chief Administration for Theaters and Musical Institutions of the USSR Ministry of Culture (Glavnoe Upravlenie teatrami i muzykal'ny uchrezhdeniyami Ministerstva kul'tury SSSR). This move to decentralization in favor of "collective leadership" was speeded up by a reform of the 1956 Party Congress. The Committee for Artistic Affairs disappeared, its duties transferred to the Ministry of Culture. Controls began to be relaxed, but a fresh reaction was caused by the Hungarian Revolution of 1956, which the KGB alleged had been sparked by subversive literary debates. The idea that intellectual interchanges might lead to counterrevolution always consternated the government and was to be countered by greater doses of Soviet nationalism. Yet this reaction was followed by the hugely successful World Youth Festival in 1957 and the launching of Sputnik. Throughout this period, there was a constant push-me-pull-you tug-of-war between greater freedom and the reimposition of government authority.

More responsibility was invested in the administrators and directors of individual theaters. Member of the Writers Union were allowed to submit their plays directly to the theaters and publishing houses and editorial boards of literary periodicals. Rewriting was now done in the theater and not in committee. The Ministry of Culture examined plays only after they had been accepted by a theater's *zavlit* (literary manager) or published. Once approved, they were "recommended as good to be played everywhere."

It was not easy to alter the hierarchy of existing theaters, but changes of leadership often effected the necessary improvement, and even established masters sought to enlarge the scope of their artistic quests. Many new plays openly challenged the cult of personality created by Stalin and examined events related to his regime, reconsidered the early revolutionary period and the Civil War, and tried to reexamine accepted orthodoxies. The official version of the Great Patriotic War was challenged, with attention turned to the tragic price the people had had to pay for the victory. Still, there was no real treatment of Party conflicts or the Stalinist period, even if antitotalitarian values informed the dramas.

While the Stanislavsky system became more mummified as a required course in the theatrical curriculum, one of his last students, the actress Mariya Knebel', imparted much of his living heritage in her classes and productions. Her staging of Nikolay Pogodin's *The Third Pathétique,* significantly in 1956, put on the MAT stage a Lenin play that was less than hagiographic. She also was the first to revive Chekhov's early play *Ivanov* (Pushkin Theater); its hero's passivity and feckless divagation became a metaphor of the predicament of the post-Thaw intellectual, and a dozen different theaters offered their own interpretations.

The year 1956 also saw the opening of the first new official theater since the 1930s. The well-named Sovremennik, or Contemporary Theater, under the aegis of the MAT, was a troupe of young actors who threw themselves enthusiastically into a repertoire of plays by Viktor Rozov, Aleksandr Volodin, Mikhail Roshchin, and Leonid Zorin as well as a number of English and American playwrights. The recurring theme, which was current at other theaters as well, pitted the hopeful and unsullied idealism of youth against the cynical compromises of the older generation. It loudly reaffirmed human individuality.

Backing and Forthing

The first breach in the theatrical Iron Curtain was made in 1954, when the Comédie Française appeared on the stage of the Maly Theater in Moscow. Its tour opened with *Tartuffe.*

> Pierre Descaves, *Molière en U.R.S.S.* (Paris: Amiot-Dumont, 1954), 29–31. The radio pioneer Pierre Descaves (1896–1966) was general administrator of the Comédie Française 1953–59.

Intermissions in the modern Russian theater are of long duration. One of my Soviet guides could even confide to me, in a moment of abandonment, with great humor:

"Most of our programs could be advertised as 'Tonight, a play in two intermissions and five acts.'"

The intermission is tremendously important and, you will see why, socially important. [...] In the orchestra, the exodus to the corridors was a slow one; people were willing to stand in front of their seats, bowing all round; they might change the trajectory to greet a celebrity or locate a friend. The evening was a diplomatic one: the whole staff of the French embassy, the head of foreign missions; that night was also one for the national *apparat.* In a box, quite recognizable, Marshal Zhukov, attentive and benevolent; further on, in another box, MM. Gromyko and Zorin, the two vice-ministers of foreign affairs; near the forestage, the powerful profile and encyclopedic brow of Mr. Aleksandrov, Minister of Culture.[2] [...]

"Tonight," commented one of the members of the French embassy in Moscow, "a highly select audience: lots of officials, professors, critics, military men."

Few uniforms, however; no dress suits; not the shadow of a tuxedo; no evening gowns. This "preview" is like a "dress rehearsal," informal, no standing on ceremony or ceremonial. A few swift introductions, at the foot of the reserved enclosure which is located as a last-minute addition at the top of the orchestra seats, in a graceful fan shape. There was so little protocol this evening that I saw, seated sedately in the third or fourth row of the orchestra, Mr. Vinogradov,[3] the Soviet ambassador to France, who made the trip specially to be present at the start of the tour he had negotiated so patiently.

> Mikhail Kozakov, *Risunki na peske. Aktërskaya kniga* (Moscow: AST/Zebra E, 2007), 129–34.

It was a sensation. From the third-tier gallery I saw *Le Cid* and was glad to have penetrated there with other students, forcing the ranks of the Maly ticket-takers. The brilliant André Falcon[4] who played Rodrigue, declaiming Corneille's verse according to all the rules of the French academy, seemed beautiful to me, if only because he recited the monologues in French. [...]

Next came the New York Everyman Opera.[5] They put on *Porgy and Bess*. When the curtain parted and the first chords of George Gershwin's "Lullaby" were heard, when on the operatic (!) stage we saw living passions, living people, when it became obvious that the opera, for all the conventions of the genre, could be modern, emotional, stunningly interesting—a gust of serious wind, what I am saying, a hurricane burst into the auditorium and literally blew a few spectators out of it.

"This isn't our music!" Alla Konstantinovna Tarasova said, scandalized, and demonstratively walked out of the theater.

Yes, of course, the music wasn't ours. [...] But the choruses, and the plasticity of

---

2   A pleiad of Soviet officialdom: Georgy Konstantinovich Zhukov (1896–1974), conqueror of Berlin, Soviet defense minister, the most decorated officer in the USSR; Andrey Andreevich Gromyko (1909–89), minister of foreign affairs 1957–85, known in the West as "Mr. No"; Valerian Aleksandrovich Zorin (1902–86), permanent Soviet representative to the United Nations Security Council 1952–53, and again during the Cuban missile crisis, and Soviet ambassador to the Federal Republic of Germany 1956–65; Georgy Fëdorovich Aleksandrov (1908–61), appointed by his ally Georgy Malenkov to be first minister of culture in 1954 and removed from office the next year by Khrushchëv, who exiled him to Minsk to teach dialectical materialism.

3   Sergey Aleksandrovich Vinogradov (1917–70), a KGB general, after serving as Soviet ambassador to Turkey and Egypt, was appointed to the French mission 1953; a close friend of Charles de Gaulle, he was hugely popular in Paris.

4   André Falcon (1924–2009), French actor, member of the Comédie Française 1946–66, playing in the roles of young heroes (Britannicus, Hippolyte, Ruy Blas, etc.).

5   The Everyman Opera of New York, sponsored by the American National Theater and Academy (ANTA), brought *Porgy and Bess* to the USSR in 1956 by invitation.

the performance, and the music, singing, dancing, Negro performers, the plot, at last! Open-mouthed, we greedily gulped down the fresh air [...].

Then in autumn 1955 the MAT advertised the tour of an English dramatic troupe, led by Peter Brook.[6] They were bringing *Hamlet*. [...]

In Okhlopkov's production Hamlet[7] takes long strides to music, dreaming behind the grille. Then he rushes to the bars, grabs them in his hands, and "... To be (pause) or (pause) not to be? (pause). That is the question." (Pause). And after he has declaimed for a second time, "To die, to sleep!" he pulls out a dagger. Hamlet himself at this time is behind the barred door, and only his hand with the dagger is visible to the spectator. Pause. The dagger falls from his hand to the ground, and the auditorium rings with a cry of alarm: "Perchance to dream?" And the face distorted by the cry is seen through the bars. Further along the denunciation, "Who would bear the whips and scorns of time, the oppressor's ills, the proud man's contumely..." etc., with the summing up "So conscience does make cowards of us all," and then in Samoylov's[8] most tender tremolo: "But soft... the fair Ophelia? Nymph, in thy orisons, be all my sins remembered!" And, of course, applause!

Paul Scofield[9] entered and we barely had time to notice before he had uttered:

> To be or not to be,
> That is the question.

But the intonations were quite different from those in Act One, they were more bitter, deeper, they sounded magically seductive.

The "Mousetrap" scene was played like a detective story. [...] Finally, the duel between Laertes and Hamlet. Of course, no pizzicato. Not even a duel, but a hand-to-hand combat. No! A sports contest, only Laertes' rapier was pointed and deadly. [...]

Moscow began to buzz. Opinions, ecstasies, arguments, rejections, praises, misunderstandings, ecstasies, arguments. Tickets, of course, were not to be had. [...] In Moscow a serious clash of opinion flared up. It all seemed too unusual: from the staging and style of performance to details of props. Especially after Okhlopkov's *Hamlet*, which just a year before had been staggering in its novelty. [...]

6   Peter Brook (1925–), leading English director of the twentieth century, had gone directly from Oxford University to the Shakespeare Memorial Theater in Stratford, where he met Paul Scofield, who became his favorite actor.

7   After a ten-year incubation period, Okhlopkov's *Hamlet* opened at the Mayakovsky Theater on December 16, 1954. Its basic metaphor was "Denmark is a prison."

8   Evgeny Valerianovich Samoylov (1912–2006), a student of Leonid Viv'en, he acted for Meyerhold (1934–38), then for Okhlopkov at the Theater of Revolution 1940 (from 1954, the Mayakovsky Theater); known for his heroic roles, he played the Danish prince for Okhlopkov in 1954 in the tradition of "tempestuous Hamlets." At the Maly Theater from 1968.

9   Paul Scofield (1922–2008) had played his first, contemplative Hamlet 1948; his 1955 revival was the first English-language production of the play to appear in Moscow since 1917.

Descaves, *Molière en U.R.S.S.*, 92–95.

The Moscow scene:

Destroyed by bombardment during the war (it is situated in an "elegant neighborhood" of modern shops and office buildings, in the Chicago–Buffalo Bill style), [the Vakhtangov Theater] has been rebuilt with the most modern appurtenances, no frills in the audience, no boxes or balconies; a vast, extremely luxurious orchestra and a formidable "mezzanine." It is akin to some movie palace of our Parisian boulevards. This theater presents a classic repertoire with Gorky, Shakespeare, and the modern repertoire with several plays about kolkhoz life.

The Soviet army has its own stage; or rather, stages, grouped in an immense building, in the style of a gigantic Pantheon. [. . .] This is a creation of the Soviet era, a vision of the big, the high and the wide. Its large auditorium is one of the curiosities of this establishment, where modern technology triumphs in all its forms. Eclectic programs: "among the military" they present Gogol's *Inspector General,* Lope de Vega's *Dancing Master,* or recent creations such as Baratashvili's *The Mayfly . . .*[10]

In this rapid census of the resources of Moscow's theatrical life, one must list the Lenin Komsomol Theater, where Roger Vailland's play *Colonel Foster Will Plead Guilty*[11] is on, although for the most part they "mount" only classic Soviet plays such as Chekhov's *Cherry Orchard*; the Ermolova Theater, a "dramatic" stage [. . .] created by the merger of the Ermolova Studio and the Khmelëv Studio [in 1937]. This theater has an original mission: beside the traditional Russian classics, it has staged Balzac's *The Stepmother* and Kuo-Mon-Jo's *Tsu Yan*; the Pushkin Theater (a Moscow dramatic theater) is the former Kamerny, specializing in a modern repertoire, with Saltykov-Shchedrin's *Shadows*; the Mayakovsky, formerly the Theater of Revolution, famous for presenting *The Legend of Love* by the poet Nâzim Hikmet; the Romén Theater, the State gypsy theater, which performs plays and especially operettas devoted to gipsy life; the Stanislavsky Drama Theater alternating Dickens's *Little Dorrit* and Ostrovsky's *The Dowerless Bride*; the Soviet Theater of Moscow, refuge of the last great black and red dramas, and where *The Merry Wives of Windsor* has long held the boards; the Satire Theater, whose specialty is obvious; this is where they perform *Monsieur Duroy* (a modernized version of Maupassant's *Bel Ami*) and where one of the biggest hits of the last few years was put on: Mayakovsky's *Bathhouse*. All these theaters are "major firms" in full operation.

Beside these big firms, one might highlight the activity of stages that are less important but extremely popular: the Transport Theater of Moscow, subsidized by the Ministry of Transport and Communications, as innumerable troupes are by numerous state agencies; the director Sudakov has accomplished excellent work there, staging

10 A dramatization of *The Gadfly* (1897), a novel about an Italian revolutionary, by the Irish novelist and translator Ethel Lillian Voynich (née Boole, 1864–1960), which was immensely popular in the Soviet Union and Communist China.
11 *Le Colonel Foster plaidera coupable* (1952) by Roger Vailland (1907–65) is an antimilitarist play about the Korean War; it was banned in France after one performance.

notably Aleksey Tolstoy's *The Roads of Torment,* Voynich's *Ovod,*[12] *Storm* by the Lett writer V. Latsis;[13] the Dramatic Theater of Moscow, essentially made up of young actors; the Moscow Theater of Drama and Comedy; the Stanislavsky and Nemirovich-Danchenko Theater, where opera and ballet alternate; the Opera Studio of the Moscow Conservatory; the Studio Theater of the Cinema Actor. To close out this list, one must note Obraztsov's Puppet Theater; [...] the Moscow Puppet Theater with its marionettes; the Central Children's Theater, which performs plays suitable for children from seven to fifteen; and finally, the Theater of Young Spectators.

The list may seem, if not impressive and exhausting, at least long. It would appear quite tiny if one were to consider that Moscow is a capital of nearly nine million inhabitants and contains some forty cinemas, Houses of Culture (rather abandoned and numbering about fifty). If you consider on one hand the "appetite" of the Soviet public for theater and, on the other, the limited number of institutions that can satisfy it, you will understand both the drama of the modern Soviet theater and its social importance!

IN 1955 the Deputy Minister of Culture, Vladimir Semënovich Kemenov (b. 1912), a Zhdanov lieutenant, complained that the theaters were abusing their newly gained autonomy in the choice of repertoire. At the Ninth Congress of the All-Union Theatrical Society, he asserted that most plays were of a low ideological and artistic level; the *glavrezh* (*glavny rezhissër,* chief director) ought to be the "ideologue" of the theater and exercise a veto when necessary; he bore full responsibility for the plays produced. The following year, the Ministry of Culture officially condemned the state practice of commissioning dramas. Rates were fixed for payments to playwrights, up to fifteen thousand rubles.

The playwright Aleksandr Kron revealed that all theater contracts contained a clause requiring a playwright to accept any modification or correction required by a theater manager; he was not allowed to withdraw his work if he disagreed. Texts could be changed even during the run, edited by *redaktors* whose names accompanied the author's. "It seems that for every book there is an officer and a political commissar. Innumerable 'instructors' and inspectors were accustomed to give orders in a decisive manner as if they were preceptors or supervisors."[14]

The artistic councils created in 1955 became partly elective, but their role remained conservative, and the administrator remained the real head. The problem of the *glavrezh* versus the administrator was widely discussed in 1956–57, and the incompetence of many of the latter was pointed out. The ministry made an effort to appoint more competent administrators, but the conflict between satisfying the political authorities and fulfilling a financial plan by attracting audiences was still very real.

---

12 See *The Gadfly,* note 10.
13 A dramatization of his three-volume epic novel. Latsis had been championed by Stalin a year before the general secretary's death.
14 Aleksandr Kron, "Notes of a Writer," *Literaturnaya Moskva* (1956), 789.

In late 1955 a theater-goer's strike took place. The result was an effort to create a more "progressive" repertoire and to attract theater parties with reduced prices.

Order of the Central Committee of the Soviet Army Theater, December 13, 1955.

Starting on January 1, 1956, the Moscow Municipal Department of Theatrical-Performance Booking Offices will issue group subscriptions for attendance at Moscow theaters, at privileged prices. Among the Moscow Theaters the Central Army Theater of Soviet Drama is also included.

In this respect, privileged prices for seats in the auditorium of the TsTSA for performances included in the group subscriptions from January 1, 1956, are set as follows:

> For the Large Auditorium   1,827 seats at 19,127 rubles.—
> For the Small Auditorium   471 seats at 5,316 rubles.—

> Official of the Central Theater of the Soviet Army,
> *Colonel Tsaritsyn*

A. G. Orlov, *O trude rabotnikov teatral'no-zrelishchnykh uchrezhdeny* [On workers' labor at theatrical and performance institutions] (Moscow: Profizdat, 1976), 35–36.

The extension of daily work for all theatrical coworkers cannot exceed 7 hours. Breaks for rest and meals during working hours are not included. Rules for regulating workers' time regarding participation in performances, rehearsals, and traveling and touring productions, as well as rules for regulating the work of individual categories of workers, are to be established.

If the nature of the work does not allow for strict regulation of the worker's time, an abnormal working day may be established. The Ministry of Culture of the USSR in accordance with the Cent. Comm. of the profsoyuz of workers of culture has drawn up a list of the duties of theatrical workers with an abnormal workday. [...]

A list of the duties of workers with an abnormal workday in the extracategorical theaters (the Bol'shoy Theater and the Kremlin Palace of Congresses, the MAT of the USSR and other theaters, on a par with the aforenamed) is established by the Ministry of Culture of the USSR in accordance with the Cent. Comm. of the profsoyuz of cultural workers.

THE INTRANSIGENCE of state policy on the arts was made clear when Valentin Pluchek decided to stage Nâzim Hikmet's *And Was It Ivan Ivanovich?* (*Ivan Ivanovic var midi yok muydu,* 1956) at the Moscow Satire Theater. The Turkish poet, an admirer of Mayakovsky and Meyerhold, had become a world hero of communism during his imprisonment by the Turkish government from 1938; on his release in

1950, he received the International Peace Prize and moved to Moscow. The play is an attack on the cult of personality and the replacement of the old *apparat* by a new one, just as despotic.

Government reports, September 1956, in *Literaturnaya gazeta* (1994), reprinted in Nina Velekhova, *Valentin Pluchek i Prival komediantov na Triumfal'noy*, 2 [Valentin Pluchek and Comedians' Rest at 2 Triumphal Square] (Moscow: Rutena, 1999), 121–22.

The basic defect of N. Hikmet's play consists in his trying to show the presence in our country of a "hierarchy," opposed to the people. The main character Sergey Konstantinovich Petrov has "over him" a certain bureaucrat Konstantin Sergeevich, and "under him" a careerist secretary, hoping in future to take Petrov's job. They all insist on "tightening the screws," "nipping in the bud," "poking holes," while the people "insist on a respectful distance from them." Therefore the sentence uttered by the Man in a Cap (representative of the working people), for example, sounds ambiguous, in the closing line: "The end will be the way we want it . . ."

It is considered indispensable:

1. To direct the attention of the Ministry of Culture of the USSR to the serious ideological defects in N. Hikmet's play *And Was It Ivan Ivanovich?* and to suggest that the Ministry investigate the public presentation of the production of this play in a national theater.

2. To insert a critique of this play into one of the central newspapers.

We ask your instructions.

> Head of the Department of Culture Central Committee Communist Party
> Soviet Union   *D. Polikarpov*
> Deputy Dept Head   *B. Ryurikov*
> Head Dept Secretary   *B. Yarustovsky*
> September 26, 1956

[The Moscow Satire Theater held the premiere on May 11, 1957.]

[. . .] A viewing of the production prepared by the Moscow Satire Theater shows that insignificant changes have been made in the play's subject matter. The play as before preserves a deliberate, strident critique of our shortcomings, connected with the consequences of the cult of personality. Specific lines sound ambiguous and anti-Party.

It is necessary to note that the ideological defects of the play are in large part aggravated by the directorial choices in the production. An impression is created that the director of the production (Comrade Pluchek) ostensibly strove specially to emphasize the negative side of the activity of the leaders of Soviet institutions, to compact the defects in the lives of Soviet people. The offenses of the production are intensified by the nature of its staging, which appears to be openly formalistic.

The Department of Science, School and Culture of the Central Committee of the Communist Party of the Soviet Union for the Russian Soviet Federal Socialist Republic notes that the Ministry of Culture of the USSR and the RSFSR, as well as the Moscow Institute of Culture, were irresponsible in allowing the said production to open. Without having organized a preliminary inspection in good time, the Moscow Institute of Culture and the management of the Satire Theater advertised the production widely and allowed a preliminary sale of tickets. Moreover, having received no sort of approbation, the production was included among those taking part in the "Moscow Theatrical Spring."

[...] The Department finds the performance of the production *And Was It Ivan Ivanovich?* undesirable in the form in which it is staged by Moscow Satire Theater.

> Head Department of Science, School and Culture
> Central Committee of the Soviet Union for the
> USSR *N. Kaz'min*
>
> May 14, 1957

THE PRODUCTION was banned, and the play failed to appear in the two-volume Russian-language edition of Hikmet's works that appeared in 1957. It was eventually published in 1962 but remained off the stage as a relic of Stalinism worthy of oblivion.

> Nâzim Hikmet to the Presidium of the Central Committee of the Communist Party of the Soviet Union, Moscow, October 1, 1958. Velekhova, *Valentin Pluchek,* 124.

Respected comrades!

I entered the ranks of the All-Union Communist Party (Bolsheviks) in 1923 in Moscow. From that time on I committed no action unworthy of a Communist.

Never and nowhere have I acted against the Soviet Union and the Communist Party of the Soviet Union.

From 1951 I have lived in Moscow. I consider the Soviet Union my second homeland.

Recently there have been many unsubstantiated facts which discredit me as a Communist and a member of society.

In addition, I have the impression that you have been incorrectly informed about my political and artistic activities.

I could be more useful in the fight for communism, if this false information about me were dispelled.

With communist greetings.

Nâzim Hikmet

THE STANISLAVSKY SYSTEM had become a theatrical paradigm of the postulates of Marx and Lenin. Official promoters of the system spent their time trying to eliminate any contradictions and weaknesses they could find in it and reconciling its ideas with those of socialist doctrine. Attempts to improve the system could be made only outside the MAT, and even then, one had to proclaim allegiance to it. This was the approach taken by those who had worked with Stanislavsky, such as Aleksey Popov, head of the Soviet Army Theater from 1935 to 1960; Mariya Knebel', who left the MAT for the Central Children's Theater; and Yury Zavadsky, director of the Mossovet Theater from 1940 to 1977.

Mariya Knebel', "Is Stanislavsky's system universal?" *Teatr* 6 (June 1957), 11–19.

Stanislavsky's system has often been introduced forcibly; his authority had been used to suppress artists of other tendencies who tried to go their own way. [...] meanwhile the name of Stanislavsky was the sole password for gaining admittance to the flock of "orthodox realism."

[His system should be used sparingly, like antibiotics. As for Meyerhold, he should not be reviled as a formalist, even if he could not be called a socialist realist.]

FROM THE TIME of his play *Tanya* (1938), Aleksey Arbuzov was considered one of the country's leading and most versatile playwrights. He initiated the most vital phase of his career, undermining the clichés of Stalinist drama, with an unscripted speech at the Russian Conference of Theater Practitioners in 1958.

Poyurovsky, "Aleksey Arbuzov," *Chto ostalos'*, 16–18.

From October 7 to 9, 1958, the All-Union Conference of Theater Practitioners was held in Moscow. The first and last days' sessions took place in the Columned Hall of the House of Unions. The plenary sessions by sections went on in the Actor's House and the Central House of RI USSR on October 8.

On the first day the keynote addresses were made by the Minister of Culture of the USSR. N. A. Mikhaylov, the secretary of the Writer's Union of the USSR and playwright B. A. Lavrenëv and the chief director of the Mossovet Theater Yu. A. Zavadsky. On the dais was a member of the Presidium and secretary of the Central Committee of the Communist Party of the Soviet Union Ekaterina Alekseevna Furtseva,[15] which gave the conference special weight. The hall was full to capacity. Such a representative forum of theater people in the postwar years had never before been convened. Besides, it was a special time: the country lived under the influence of the resolution of the XX Communist Party Congress.[16] And we hoped for changes for the better in the theater.

The conference ran rather smoothly, without special arguments. And after the sec-

---

15 Ekaterina Alekseevna Furtseva (1910–74), first woman elected to the Central Committee of the Communist Party, and Minister of Culture 1962–74, famous for her philistinism, irresolute opinions, and susceptibility to leading men.

16 The first congress held after the death of Stalin in February 1956 contained a denunciation of

ond interval the center of gravity, as often happened, imperceptibly shifted to the lobby. That was where passions raged! But suddenly the presiding officer B. S. Rzhanov[17]—at that time head of the Profsoyuz of cultural workers—gives the floor to Arbuzov and asks him to introduce the director L. M. Litvinov[18] from Kazan. Arbuzov put down his text in front of him and began to read. The audience listened to the first few sentences with polite attention: he was the author of *Tanya*, *The Town at Daybreak*, and *Years of Wandering*. But within a few minutes, there could be no more talk of politeness. The columned hall turned into a stadium and those assembled into sports fans. Applause, tempestuous applause, thunderous applause turned into an ovation. Laughter, hilarity, more laughter! The crowds rushed through all the lobby doors, blocking the aisles, violently occupying the seats. In the middle of Arbuzov's speech not one empty seat remained in the hall, but people kept arriving and arriving.

The chairman gives the signal: time is up!

The hall actually demands: extend the time!

Arbuzov went on. Now his historic speech is widely famous. But at that time it was heard only by delegates and guests of the conference.

What did Aleksey Nikolaevich talk about? What got everyone so excited? Now it's called *glasnost'*. But then, in 1958, to take a stand against A. V. Sofronov himself in defense of a certain A. Volodin,[19] author of a "questionable" play *The Factory Girl*, was no joking matter and rather dangerous. Especially since Arbuzov went beyond the limits of a private conflict and opened the question more broadly:

> Serving the muse does not tolerate vanity:
> Beauty must be magnanimous . . .

Arbuzov finished, left the podium, but the hall was in an uproar. It was a genuine demonstration of insurbordination and solidarity, which at the time united in its ranks those who were far from being like-minded. It seemed as if people forgot about their careers, ranks, ages, at last. At that moment, everyone seemed united in his rush for the truth, his refusal to accommodate lies. Arbuzov expressed that secret thing he had suffered himself, about which many had thought, but no one meanwhile had resolved to speak aloud.

A pause. The chairman patiently waited until passions died down.

"The floor passes to the playwright G. D. Mdivani, Moscow. He will introduce comrade L. M. Litvinov, Kazan."

---

the former general secretary, specifically in Khrushchëv's speech at a secret session; though not published, it was read at meetings throughout the country and opened up the possibility of public criticism and vocal opposition.

17 B. S. Rzhanov, chairman of the Central Committee of Trade Unions.

18 Lev Markovich Litvinov (actually Gurevich, 1899–1963), director of romantic tendencies at the Belorussian State Jewish Theater 1927–48, then at the Jan Kupala Theater in Minsk 1948–50, and from 1950 at the Kazan BDT.

19 Aleksandr Moiseevich Volodin (actually Lifshits, 1919–2001), screenwriter, whose controversial first play *The Factory Girl* (1956) was successfully staged by many theaters, including the Red Army Theater, through the 1957–58 season; he became the house dramatist of the Leningrad BDT, then the Sovremennik, where he launched a new genre, the "parable play."

Laughter in the hall: after all, everyone knew that, now after Arbuzov, Litvinov had to put in an appearance.

On the podium Mdivani. He turns to Arbuzov as a friend, on a first-name basis. And he starts to argue, but not to the point, but immediately starts sticking on political labels:

"What, Alësha, are you against the party, against the Central Committee, against our beloved government? Then say so straight out! . . ."

He is speaking without written notes, passionately, trying to outshout the hall, which at first met his words with a faint murmur, then began to utter individual exclamations, then there was heard an uproar, whistling, general whooping and hollering. The chairman tries to calm the hall, appeals to party conscience, even asks the communists to rise, finally calls for help . . . to the militia. After this Rzhanov conclusively loses control over the assembly, and Mdivani, whistled down, has to abandon the podium, cutting himself off in mid-word . . .

Late at night in the Actor's House a cabbage party was thrown for the members of the conference. Arbuzov seemed to be a new man. Everyone rushed to congratulate him. He was cheerful and joking. Then he drew me aside and gave me the text of his speech, adding:

"I doubt if I'll survive until it's published, but you may possibly still 'see heaven all over diamonds . . .'[20] God grant it!"

[. . .] The next day the newspaper *Soviet Culture* ran a detailed account of the conference, reporting that Arbuzov's disgraceful behavior produced dissatisfaction from all those present [. . .] and that Mdivani had received the unanimous support of the hall. [. . .] To his credit B. A. Lavrenëv, who came to the podium with brief concluding remarks, felt bound, without wishing to engage in polemics, to turn to the editor of *Soviet Culture,* who was sitting there on the dais, and say—and I quote:

"In this hall today the theatrical community of the nation is gathered. Can it be assumed that after such a publication anyone present will go on harboring the least illusion about the objectivity of information broadcast by the newspaper you edit?"

ARBUZOV'S SPEECH was the first salvo in a barrage of unofficial pamphlets and journals and exhibits of experimental work. An exhibition of paintings and sculpture by nonconformist artists in December 1962 set off the next blowback from the government. The KGB invited Khrushchëv to visit one such exhibition, where he vilified the artists as "pederasts" and their work as "dog shit." He called a gathering of the cultural elite at Kremlin to proclaim: "The Thaw is over! This is not even a light morning frost. For you and the likes of you it will be the *Arctic* frost."

Theater groups that lacked official recognition tried to supply the need for freer expression.

---

20 A line from the end of Chekhov's *Uncle Vanya,* when Sonya consoles her uncle that after a lifetime of drudgery "we will see heaven all over diamonds." It became a catchphrase.

Boris Poyurovsky, "Segodnya ya snova zovu vas v dorogu!" [Today again I call you to the road!], *Russkaya mysl'*, 4150 (1996); reprinted in *Chto ostalos'*, 101.

Some assert that the Variety Studio Theater MGU "Our House" under the leadership of the same Mark Rozovsky[21] should be considered the great-grandfather of the Theater "At Nikitsky Gates." It opened in 1958. At that time the small club on Mokhovaya occasioned no small headache for the administrators of Moscow University. There for the first time after the catastrophe they set up an evening devoted to Vsevolod Meyerhold, and the next day this was called "a crude anti-Soviet provocation." There they staged "dubious" plays by "dubious authors," from Brecht to Shvarts and Kohout,[22] as if there were no value to the works of Sofronov or Mdivani. [...]

Sukhanov, *Teatr, lyudi, zhizn'*..., 108–9.

Until Gorbachëv[23] came to power this party agency [the Obkom Bureau] was very important. In Leningrad, after the protracted single combat between V. S. Tolstikov and G. I. Popov,[24] who were the first secretaries of the Obkom and Gorkom, respectively, the Obkom bureau definitively became the last resort in settling all questions. Here they doled out punishments and rewards, but never caresses. Let me make the proviso that I am referring to the tenure of "the bosses" Tolstikov and Romanov.[25] In the 1960s, in my capacity as president of the Lensovet Commission for Culture, they invited me to all the meetings of the Obkom and Gorkom bureau, whenever cultural issues were on the agenda. [...]

That was when I began to realize how everything was decided by one man, and not by the bureau, which had only to support its "boss." If members of the bureau did intervene or comment on the issue under discussion, then, as experienced tacticians of the *apparat*, wholly familiar with their boss's likes and dislikes, they always intervened to help him resolve the issue to his liking. They didn't argue with Tolstikov and Romanov. They didn't flatter them to their faces, for both men were far from stupid [...], and of course, wouldn't have put up with crudely obvious soft soap. All either of them needed was that the answers to questions were the ones they considered correct. And

21 Mark Grigor'evich Rozovsky (1937–), playwright and director, cofounder of the studio "Our House" 1958–69, which sought a "Soviet absurd"; at the Leningrad BDT he originated *Story of a Horse*, but it was co-opted by Tovstonogov. Staged the first Soviet rock opera *Orpheus and Eurydice* (1975). In 1983 created the Nikitsky Gates Studio Theater.

22 Pavel Kohout (1928–), Czech playwright and cofounder of the dissident Living-Room Theater; exiled to Austria in 1970.

23 Mikhail Sergeevich Gorbachëv (1931–), a member of the Central Committee from 1971 and full member of the Politburo from 1980; became general secretary of the Communist Party on Chernenko's death in 1985 and, in 1990, president of the USSR. Lost his position when the Soviet Union disintegrated in November 1991.

24 Vasily Sergeevich Tolstikov (1917–2003), first secretary of the Leningrad Provincial Party 1962–70 and an adherent of Khrushchëv; appointed ambassador to China 1970. Georgy Ivanovich Popov (1912–), first secretary of the Leningrad Party Committee from 1971.

25 Grigory Vasil'evich Romanov (1922–2008), first secretary of the Leningrad Party Committee 1970 and member of the Central Committee 1971; Gorbachëv's chief rival to be general secretary.

so the members of the bureau, ostensibly maintaining independence and autonomy, masterfully grasped the task before them, and arrived at decisions in complete accord with the "chief's" wishes. [...]

I remember Leonid Sergeevich Viv'en,[26] who ran the Pushkin Theater at that time. A shrewd man, a fine actor, director, and teacher, Leonid Sergeevich was occasionally invited to the bureau's meetings. He would listen attentively with an interested expression to everything that was said, but when his own work in the theater came under discussion, Viv'en would usually "doze off." He played all his roles brilliantly, including the role of someone who nodded off at office meetings.

An excellent psychologist, Viv'en understood that no one would choose to disturb his nap, not even the "boss." He would "wake up" when the matter had been resolved, having learned the range of opinions expressed, but without having expressed his own opinion.

Poyurovsky, "Catherine the Great: Ekaterina Furtseva," in *Chto ostalos'*, 119–21.

In the early 1960s the most active members of theatrical Moscow would gather in the Great Hall of the Central House of RI. The first deputy minister of culture of the USSR, A. N. Kuznetsov,[27] would come to give a lecture. People said that earlier he had worked for many years in the *apparat* of A. A. Zhdanov—the chief ideologue and subtle "connoisseur" of literature and art, the persecutor of Shostakovich, Prokofiev, Akhmatova, Zoshchenko, and other distinguished exponents of national culture. This was the period that the wise Il'ya Érenburg prophetically christened "the Thaw," for which he immediately got in trouble: "What does 'thaw' mean? Don't you believe in the irreversibility of our times, are you afraid of new frosts?" Érenburg's adversaries tormented him with such questions. Those were interesting times!

The main emotional content of modern plays could be formulated this way: in the old days people were imprisoned justly but nowadays they are released, also justly. [...]

Kuznetsov actually handed out rankings. Those who particularly caught hell from him were Volodin, Rozov, Shteyn, and Shatrov,[28] and the patterns set up for them, as usual, were Korneychuk, Sofronov, Mdivani, and Solodar'.[29] In debates, speakers, chosen well in advance, would include "ideological warriors" drawn from case-hardened

---

26 Leonid Sergeevich Viv'en (1887–1966) had made his name as an actor at the Imperial Theater before the Revolution; moving to the Soviet repertoire, he became director of the Pushkin Theater 1937–57.

27 A. N. Kuznetsov was director of the State Committee for Cultural Relations with Foreign Centers, then deputy minister of culture under Furtseva and her successor in that post.

28 Viktor Sergeevich Rozov (1913–2004), playwright, whose career was promoted by productions at the Sovremennik; most of his plays have the same theme, the privileged hypocrisy of adults redeemed by the hopes of modern youth. Aleksandr Petrovich Shteyn (1906–93), editor of the magazine *Iskusstvo i Zhizn'* (*Art and Life*), devoted most of his plays to glorifying the Russian navy, until he wrote an uncharacteristic comedy *Springtime Violins* (1959). Mikhail Filippovich Shatrov (1932–2010) made his name with revisionist plays about Lenin that often broke taboos.

29 Tsezar' Samoylovich Solodar', composer of popular songs and musical comedies, such as *In a Lilac Grove* (1954).

actors, directors, playwrights, and critics. By the way, they all sat on the Presidium, to which, of course, no one was elected. And center stage, herself, the only woman, Catherine the Great, as Furtseva was facetiously nicknamed by Maretskaya and Plyatt,[30] sometimes even in her presence.

The author of the immortal poetic work about Uncle Steppe stepped up to the podium and tried carefully to defend his comrades, especially Shatrov and Shteyn. Of Shatrov's play *Gleb Kosmachev,* [S. V.] Mikhalkov[31] noted that although it was not officially banned, still, so far as everyone was concerned, it was clearly "disapproved for publication." But why, exactly? What was dangerous about it? Still less, in Sergey Vladimirovich's opinion, could one understand the criticism aimed at the hero of Shteyn's play *Ocean.*

"What's the crime in one of them calling the other 'fool' and blaming his comrade for having 'sawdust for brains,'" asked Mikhalkov. "You've got Kachalov in *Lower Depths* calling Knipper 'Slut'! And yet nowadays the play is studied in middle school as a classic."

An uneasy, unhealthy excitement in the hall, that clearly sympathized with the ideas of one of the authors of the words to the Soviet National Anthem. From her seat Ekaterina Alekseevna made a curt rejoinder:

"Dear Sergey Vladimirovich, remember what Gorky's play is called[32] and when it was written?! What can it have in common with young officers, who are entering naval college by way of the Komsomol? Can't you perceive the difference at all?"

1:0 to the Minister. A brief pause.

"Agreed," replied Mikhalkov. "It was a long time ago. But remember what granddad Shchukar' says in Sholokhov."[33]

Again a roar of laughter, applause.

Charming, clever Furtseva again parried:

"Granddad Shchukar' is a remnant of the past, and we are talking about our contemporaries."

Mikhalkov did not want to give in, and rather out of desperation, he launched his last argument:

"Well, fine, you're right, Granddad Shchukar' is a remnant of the past. But look at Nikita Sergeevich—isn't he our exact contemporary! Yet didn't he make that remark about Kuz'ma's mother [*Kuz'kinu mat'*]?"[34]

30 Both eccentric comic actors who had studied with Yury Zavadsky at the Vakhtangov school. Vera Petrovna Maretskaya (1906–78) acted at the Mossovet from 1940. Rostislav Ivanovich Plyatt (1908–89) performed at the Lenin Komsomol, then at the Lensovet Theater 1941–43, then at the Mossovet for the rest of his career. .

31 Sergey Vladimirovich Mikhalkov (1913–2009), co-lyricist of the Soviet national anthem (1943) and author of children's books.

32 In Russian, *Na dne* or *At the Bottom* (1902).

33 Granddad Shchukar' is a Falstaffian peasant in Sholokhov's epic novel *The Quiet Don,* a braggart and tale-teller who keeps referring to himself as "a martyr to Soviet power" and makes fun of Communist organizers.

34 An idiom short for "*pokazhu gde zimeet Kuz'kinu mat'*" (literally, "I'll show you where Cosmo's

It is hard to depict the reaction of the audience. Bear in mind: the theatrical activists had not progressed to the present era of everything being permissible, while Khrushchëv, having rid himself of opposition, at that moment was occupying the posts both of head of the government and leader of the party. To raise one's hand—and to whom? That was no laughing matter!

The terrified Furtseva was no longer smiling. She abruptly rose and, having lost all her feminine charms in a flash, angrily said:

"Talking's all right, but don't start raving!"—Whereupon she stressed her words with expressive gestures: first she wagged a finger at the disturber of the peace, and then put it to her temple and made a slight circular movement...

Silence and order quickly prevailed in the hall, and Mikhalkov, without saying another word, quietly withdrew.

Everything went on as usual...

THE PROPORTION of Russian prerevolutionary plays performed fell from 26 percent in 1953 in Moscow to 17 percent in 1956 and 15 percent in 1961. Ostrovsky, who had been the most prominent in 1953, fell from 274 performances of twenty plays in 1953 to 25 performances in 1960; similarly, Gorky's plays declined from 127 performances in 1953 to 10 in 1961. Suddenly adaptations of Dostoevsky appeared for the first time in years, with thirty-five in the first half of 1961. Foreign playwrights fluctuated in popularity, with full-fledged communists such as Howard Fast and Roger Vailland, sympathizers such as Shaw and Arthur Miller, and even Shakespeare and Noël Coward conspicuous. Soviet drama was tentatively questioning the system.

Unlike Stalin, Khrushchëv preferred to delegate cultural matters to others, until gross abuses were brought to his attention. Growing concern over theatrical activism finally got a rise out of him. At a meeting of the Presidium, which also discussed the bard Bulat Okudzhava and the dissident Solzhenitsyn, the repertoire came up for discussion.

Meeting of the Presidium of the Central Committee of the Communist Party of the Soviet Union, April 25, 1963. Koreneva, *Ekaterina Furtseva*, 241–43.

QUESTION: on improving the organization of the leadership of ideological work and cultural matters. On increasing radio broadcasts abroad...

COM. KHRUSHCHËV: Shuysky told me that Ekaterina Alekseevna phoned him and said that someone advanced the idea of liquidating the Minkul't [Ministry of Culture]. We need to preserve the Minkul't, because it is to be a department of the Central

---

mother spends the winter"), meaning "I'll show you a thing or two." A favorite phrase of Khrushchëv, who used it to refer in 1954 to the super hydrogen bomb the Russians were developing, in 1959 in the kitchen debate with Richard Nixon, and again in 1962 with John F. Kennedy during the Cuban missile crisis.

Committee, and right now we are dealing with questions of greater international relations in culture.

... We somehow need to organize work on ideological questions along broader lines. Right now this aspect is out of control.

... Take the theater. It has an organizational significance. Look here, they put on *The Inspector General*. Did they ask anyone? Who needs it? It's all right, it was revolutionary in its time. I'm convinced that the idea was Igor' Ilin'sky's. But Igor' Il'insky is a grumbler. What kind of repertoire will he run, when he shows up on different stages? Crap, nothing but crap. No one will pay attention and this aspect of the front is out of control.

... Even the Art Theater, they just put on *Mary Stuart*. I've seen it twice. Exceptional, but this show is not for our benefit, but for Tarasova's. She really is ... the queen of Scotland, magnificent for her age. You think this kind of show would be put on anywhere else in the world except here? But why is it here? Once upon a time they used to stage for us *Armored Train*, once they would stage *Bread, Kremlin Chimes, Lyubov' Yarovaya*—that's a wonderful play, right now it would draw better than *Mary Stuart*.

Tovstonogov

With the death of Nemirovich-Danchenko in 1943, there was no stage director with a sufficiently Olympian stature to challenge state controls or to impose his vision on a major theater. The situation altered with the appointment of Georgy Tovstonogov to lead the Leningrad BDT in 1956. A student of Aleksey Popov at GITIS, he had served an apprenticeship at the Griboedov Dramatic Theater in Tbilisi. There followed a difficult "Moscow period" (1946–49) with few productions and artistic isolation. In 1949 he was made chief director at the Lenin Komsomol Theater, where he won a Lenin prize for his monumental but anti-Stalinist revival of *The Optimistic Tragedy* (1955).

> Dina Shvarts, *Dnevniki i zametki* [Diaries and notebooks] (St. Petersburg: Impress, 2001), 251–55, 110–11. Dina Morisovna Shvarts (1921–98), dramaturg at the Leningrad Lenkom (1949–56), head of the literary department of the BDT from 1956, collaborated with Tovstonogov on many productions, including *The Idiot, The Quiet Don,* and *Three Sacks of Unsorted Grain*.

When he was appointed chief director of the BDT in 1956, G. A. Tovstonogov[35] was already famous, a winner of two prizes, young, talented, vigorous. He was sure that the principles of Stanislavsky and Nemirovich-Danchenko were uniquely true, that

---

35 Georgy Aleksandrovich Tovstonogov (1913–89) published two books on the theory and practice of directing, *The Director's Profession* (1965) and *Circling Thoughts* (1972), which express his belief that the director is the auteur of a production, free to reinterpret a text in polyphonic, cinematic ways.

humanity had come up with nothing better. From this position he went about creating a troupe. After seven long years of crisis (following the removal of N. S. Rashevskaya[36] in 1949), a once celebrated theater had not only frittered away its past traditions but seemed unable to uphold any standard. The spectators jumped ship. There was good reason why one of the city "cabbage parties" showed how soldiers who had been punished and put in the guardhouse were promised to be freed if they attended a show at the Bol'shoy Dramatic Theater. This prospect terrified them, and they asked to go "back to the brig."

The performances made a horrific impression. Overacting reigned supreme, which was all the more shocking given the sparsity of spectators. [In one case] there were fewer spectators than actors onstage. [...] There were talented actors in the BDT troupe who were not very fastidious or had become hackneyed in "their special" line of business or let themselves do whatever they thought right. This number included V. P. Politseymako,[37] a distinguished actor who nevertheless had no right to the position of all-powerful "master" in which he found himself at the moment of G. A.'s arrival. [...]

"I shall try to begin by making an example of Politseymako when I talk to the company," said G. A. "Of course I could find plenty of 'scapegoats,' but I consider and have always considered it bad form to put a 'minor' actor in a negative light, even if my intention is the important aim of re-educating the company" [...]

And he began as he meant to go on! ... At every gathering, at every rehearsal G. A. sharply and pitilessly analyzed Politseymako's role, pointed him out as a bad example, in comparison with the methodology of realistic, psychological, authentic theater. Vitaly Pavlovich kept silent the whole time, grinding his teeth. Many "comrades" reveled in this, others awaited "practical conclusions." And to cap the climax, G. A. gave the "lead actor," who had never played a small role, the episodic part of an innkeeper in the production of *The Punishment of Anthony Graham*. This was a shock. V. P. submitted without a murmur. Still grinding his teeth, he waited for his entrance and humbly sat on the revolving stool of the innkeeper, as if it were the electric chair. [...]

Then in early 1957 Guilheme Figueiredo's play *The Fox and the Grapes*[38] [...] landed in the theater over the transom, without prior negotiations, simply mailed in by the Moscow translators. [...] Late at night G. A. phoned me:

"A brilliant play. I'll stage it at once. Tomorrow I'll read it to the company." [...]

G. A. read it brilliantly. The play stunned the actors. After Aesop's last words, "Where's the cliff that they throw freedmen from?"—a long pause. And applause rang out.

Then the discussion began. Everyone praised the play a good deal. But almost every-

---

36 Natalya Sergeevna Rashevskaya (1893–1962), from 1921 to the end of her life, acted at the Pushkin Dramatic Theater; from 1946 to 1949 she was artistic director of the BDT and staged a few productions there.

37 Vitaly Pavlovich Politseymako (1906–67) entered the BDT in 1930 and became noted for his fiery temperament, magnificent voice, and broad emotional palette; he played important leads under Tovstonogov.

38 *A raposa e as uvas* (1953), by the Brazilian playwright Guilheme Figureido (1915–97), is an allegory about human freedom, featuring the slave-fabulist Aesop.

9.1. Vitaly Politseymako as Aesop in *The Fox and the Grapes,* directed by Georgy Tovstonogov, BDT, Leningrad, 1956.

one ended with the pessimistic remark, "We can't put on this play. We have no Aesop."

Politseymako was sitting there too. Silence. The eyes behind his glasses expressed the habitual modesty of his new fate. His teeth were clenched.

G. A. let everyone have his say, never once interrupted. And in conclusion he said:

"I'm glad you welcomed this play so warmly. I like it a lot too. [...] But, comrades, I was surprised that you think you don't have someone to play Aesop. I'm sure that in our company there is a remarkable actor, an actor of great temperament, with a magnificent voice, who 'by acclamation' must play Aesop. This actor is Vitaly Pavlovich Politseymako. Moreover, his fiftieth anniversary comes in May and I'm glad things have fallen out so that he can play the premiere for his jubilee. But even if there weren't an anniversary, I wouldn't confide this role to anybody else in the country."

Dumbshow. G. A. was inwardly savoring the effect he'd produced.

He thanked everyone there and went to his office. In a few minutes V. P. Politseymako entered and tumbled to his knees. He was weeping. From that moment, G. A. had no more devoted actor than Politseymako. And then the company, all the "well-wishers" got the point.

[...] [Tovstonogov] possessed a special vision that penetrated to the heart of a problem, to the depths of a man's spiritual life, which defined his behavior and actions. As the saying goes, "he had a piercing eye."

I think it was precisely this quality of his personality that basically defined his success as a director. He knew what today's theatergoers needed and what he himself wanted to talk about. He understood how far to connect these principles. On this understanding he founded his repertorial politics. Better than anyone else, Tovstonogov understood the need to preserve the methods of an actor's work formulated by

Stanislavsky, in harmony with new esthetic categories, evolved over time. He considered the method of physical actions of the actor a constant category, but directly dependent on the esthetic norms born of the times.

[…] He was not only a brilliant director, but a leader of exceptional wisdom. He was the builder of the theater. In this sphere in the history of the national theater I can compare him only with Vl. Nemirovich-Danchenko. Like him he understood how to "collectivize a group of people."

This means not only actors but workers in other sectors. All the heads of the various aspects of the theater were under Tovstonogov actually "collective," and these people worked with Georgy Aleksandrovich for decades.

His authority among all the workers of the theater was indisputable. In the staging of his productions, the choice of the repertory's direction, each of his organizational decisions, Georgy Aleksandrovich proved to those around him that he was always right. He proved this over the thirty years of his life devoted to the Bol'shoy Dramatic Theater. […]

At meetings of the Artistic Council when Georgy Aleksandrovich heard a point of view that did not agree or fully fall in with his own, he reacted very spontaneously and sometimes lost his temper. But if he felt that another person's opinion had at least some point, meaning utility, he quickly appraised the situation and turned sometimes to quite different matters. Then, to the surprise of many, he would return to the original question, offer various positions and accept the one genuine solution, but only after presenting it in such a variant that it never came into anyone's head that his decision had been taken by adopting an opponent's opinion. He was very wily. […]

DOSTOEVSKY had been condemned by Soviet ideology as obscurantist, monarchist, and Christ-ridden. He began to enjoy a revival and some of his novels were dramatized. Tovstonogov led the trend with his version of *The Idiot* (1957), introducing the film actor Innokenty Smoktunovsky in the role of Prince Myshkin.

> Naum Berkovsky, "*The Idiot* staged by G. Tovstonogov," *Teatr* 6 (1958), in *Prem'ery Tovstonogova* [Tovstonogov premieres], ed. E. Gorfunkel' (Moscow: Artist-Rezhissër-Teatr, 1994), 82–967. Naum Yakovlevich Berkovsky (1901–72) was the author of innumerable works on European literature.

[…] The secret of Smoktunovsky's[39] success lies in coming onstage out of the novel, the depths of the novel, which he understands and feels without omissions, in all its episodes in sequence. Smoktunovsky plays not a scenario, he plays the novel—through the scenario. […]

Smoktunovsky is an actor of careful inner inspiration, everything about him moves lightly, freely. At the same time every gesture is clear-cut; one has a firm memory of

39 Innokenty Mikhailovich Smoktunovsky (actually, Smoktunovich, 1925–94), a former prisoner of war, acted first at the Red Army Theater 1945–46, then in films; at the BDT 1957–60, he left to go back to filmmaking and then joined the MAT in 1972.

9.2. *The Idiot* from the novel by Dostoevsky, with Innokenty Smoktunovsky (center) as Prince Myshkin, directed by Georgy Tovstonogov, BDT, Leningrad, 1957.

how the prince holds his beggar's bindle in his outstretched hand, how he hands it over to the servant in General Epanchin's hallway—that bindle, those belongings wrapped up in a plain, homely checked bandanna contain his entire social position, everything that enables him to hold on to the outer world, and the gesture with the bindle has to be incised deep in the spectator's consciousness. When Smoktunovsky takes his dark hat off his head the first time, the spectator makes a new discovery. At last Prince Myshkin's whole face is before him: the brow is loftier, his long, lank hair, hanging in shocks, is fully visible, the characteristic hair of a poet, perhaps a missionary, an itinerant preacher of some still unknown truths. There is a moment when Smoktunovsky almost holds his head on display, allowing the spectator to inspect him more closely. [...]

In the dramatic composition the parodic episodes with the "nihilists" have been omitted. In those episodes Dostoevsky sealed up the only possible way out of the tragedy—the way out via a realistically intelligent, mass revolutionary struggle—and insisted thereby that the significance of the tragedy is absolute. By purging the plot of the episodes with Burdovsky, Ippolit and the rest, the author of the dramatic adaptation again makes possible a way out, and then the very tragedy of Prince Myshkin presents us with its genuine, historically relevant nature.

G. Tovstonogov deserves first-class honors for this production, directed with great energy, an understanding of Dostoevsky's ideas, a real devotion to the great writer. [...]

VOLODIN'S *FIVE EVENINGS* (1959) was produced at the Leningrad BDT; it was an optimistic declaration of faith in the potential of ordinary human beings. The critical establishment decried it, but their attacks on this and his subsequent plays could not dissuade Georgy Tovstonogov from staging them and audiences from adoring them.

Volodin, quoted in Solomon Volkov, *St. Petersburg: A Cultural History,* trans. Antonina W. Bouis (New York: Simon and Schuster, 1995), 499.

Even before I completed the play *Five Evenings,* they came up with the formula that this was malicious barking from around the corner. However, there was no barking at all, no criticism of reality—it is beyond that, either beneath or above it, as you like. Then they changed the formula: "These are just little maladjusted people, pessimism, petty themes." And they all repeated it every time: whatever I did, it was a petty theme and pessimism.

Vadim Gaevsky, "A Petersburg Candide," in *Teatr* 7 (1984), reprinted in *Fleyta Gamleta: Obrazy sovremennogo teatra* [Hamlet's recorder: Images of the contemporary theater] (Moscow: Soyuzteatr, 1990), 93–94. Vadim Moiseevich Gaevsky (1928–), ballet and theater critic, held the chair of theater studies at RGGU; editor of *Moskovsky nablyudatel'* (1990–98).

We look back on [Tovstonogov's] whole life, the life of a director who as far back as the 1950s was seeking a path to a living theater, to the free music of human speech and human relations. There's a good reason why the guitar ballad "My darling, take me with you" became the refrain of *Five Evenings,* and the voice of Zinaida Sharko,[40] who sang it thirty years ago, resounds in the memory even now, like a voice reverberating with clear-eyed hope. And along with it the unforgettable Kopelyanov[41] baritone, a masculine Hemingwayesque intonation (Hemingway at that time dominated our minds), in which there were so many surprising overtones, so much music and so much yearning, a bit tipsy, even somewhat boorish, but wonderfully tender, confused, with a tinge of vague guilt feeling, a strange thing to hear in the voice of someone not quite an ex-convict, not quite a worldly-wise front-line fighter. The production based on the play by A. Volodin was staged at a time when people who had vanished and names that had been forgotten were returning from nonbeing, when what had seemed a forever-vanished feeling of humanity was also returning. It revealed to us then that human souls, half-frozen in the long, cold night, were all still alive, and the old song was still alive, and the production was replete with this revelation, was infinitely convulsed by it, and therefore it convulsed us infinitely as well.

---

40 Zinaida Maksimovna Sharko (1929–), after touring and cabaret work, entered the Lenkom Theater 1952–56 and was at the BDT from 1956; a versatile actress who played Ol'ga in *Three Sisters* inter alia.

41 Éfim Zakharovich Kopelyan (1912–75), at the BDT from 1935, playing Bob Murphy in *The Russian Question;* with the advent of Tovstonogov, he became famous for his powerfully ironic performances.

TOVSTONOGOV'S FEATS of resuscitation included blowing the dust off the plays of Gorky and classic Russian drama, which he infused with contemporary meaning.

> Tatyana Doronina, in *Barbarians* and *Woe from Wit*. Édvard Radzinsky, *Moya teatralnaya zhizn'* [My theatrical life] (Moscow: ACT, 2007), 104–5, 141. Édvard Stanislavovich Radzinsky (1936–) was a favorite playwright of Anatoly Éfros, who staged his acrid comedies of modern life from the 1960s to the 1980s; with *glasnost'*, he became an acclaimed historian.

In a flaming red wig Tat'yana Doronina[42] [in *Barbarians,* opened 1959] stood against the back wall, stretching out her arms as if crucified. A pagan Venus, crucified by the wretched barbarians. [. . .]

The next day I saw *Woe from Wit* [opened 1962].

Since that time I have seen a great many productions. But up to now I am convinced that anyone who was not in the theater at Tovstonogov's *Woe from Wit* has never been in a theater. Onstage there was a mirage of Pushkin's Petersburg. At that time I considered Griboedov's play a collection of brilliant lines, magnificent aphorisms, brilliantly written roles. A troupe could be formed from this play, since it contains all the lines of business. But for me its subject was absolutely conventional and the central conflict utterly contrived. Sof'ya is a clever, malicious, arrogant beauty, beloved by a brilliant, victorious Chatsky. But for some reason she prefers the bootlicking Molchalin, who is obtuse and, for the most part, pathetic.

That night at Tovstonogov's theater I understood for the first time the dangerous subject of the play. More precisely, the director understood, and even more precisely— our era instructed him.

On the curtain was an epigraph, spelling out the meaning of Tovstonogov's production: "It was foretold to me that a devil with soul and talent will be born in Russia!" The audience at the time recognized that these words were written not by some malicious Russophobe but by "our very own"

—the illustrious *A. S.* [*Griboedov*].

The production featured a quite surprising Molchalin and Chatsky. Chatsky (played by Yursky[43]) with a quiff, impetuous, greatly resembled the academician Landau.[44] Just like a modern intellectual from a scientific research institute, with rapid offhand speech. And opposing him the clever Molchalin! Or rather, the rational. Rational . . . with our sort of reasoning. If Chatsky fights against circumstances, Molchalin, played by Kirill

---

42 Tat'yana Vasil'evna Doronina (1933–), first a leading actress for Tovstonogov at the Lenin Komsomol and BDT, moved to the MAT 1963, then to the Mayakovsky 1972, and returned to the MAT 1983, invariably seeking out prominent roles. She led the Gorky MAT from 1987.

43 Sergey Yur'evich Yursky (1935–) joined the BDT 1957 and became a leading player of physically expressive odd men out, while appearing on the cabaret stage; joined the Mossovet as actor and director 1978. In 1992 he organized the Actor's Guild (ARTel' ARTistov).

44 The theoretical physicist Lev Davidovich Landau (1908–68) had a gaunt face surmounted by bushy eyebrows and a cowlick of gray hair.

Lavrov,[45] confidently follows them, he is a man of his times. And if today one has to lick boots, he is ready to stoop before the porter's dog. But if tomorrow is the time for audacity, in a moment he will become a super-Chatsky...

[...] Doronina was the first actress to make sense of Sof'ya. She played a dangerous, arrogant beauty. Her haughtiness and willfulness are at the limit, or rather unlimited. A willfulness that increases in proportion to the rebellion! Doronina played her love for Molchalin as the triumph of an unlimited "I want." [...]

Chatsky rails against society and authority, and Sof'ya by her love rebels against society and authority. They turn out to be closely linked—Chatsky and Sof'ya: both relentlessly clever, both sarcastic and malicious. Both too alike, too great to come together. [...] In this rebellious Sof'ya there was already a glimmer of the future Nastasya Filippovna in *The Idiot,* which was soon to be brilliantly performed at the BDT.[46]

Akimov and the Comedy Theater

Throughout all the changes in artistic policy and political leadership during the Five-Year-Plans and even the hardships of the siege of Leningrad, from 1935 Akimov had managed to survive as chief director and designer of the Leningrad Comedy Theater without truckling overmuch to the regime. In 1949 he was abruptly dismissed when a number of officials walked out of a performance halfway through. He then served a brief stint at the Lensovet, where he infused the nineteenth-century satires, Saltykov-Shchedrin's *Shadows* (1953) and Sukhovo-Kobylin's *The Case* (1955), with up-to-the-minute innuendo. He was brought back to the Comedy Theater in 1956 and remained there until 1968.

Adol'f Shapiro on working with Akimov. *Kak zakryvalas',* 130–31.

At this time he was working on D. Ugrëmov's comedy *The Trunk with Travel Stickers* [*Chemodan s nakleykami*]. Few remember it (and for good reason), but I'm afraid, if I again dropped in on the first rehearsal and listened to Akimov, I would reassert that I was present at a historic event. The theme of his speech might have been defined as "World Comedy Writing and *The Trunk with Travel Stickers.*" Then strange rehearsals began. At any given moment the elegant, always fashionably dressed Nikolay Pavlovich would show up, holding a small file folder. Sometimes he would squint slyly, greet us, drop a few caustic remarks concerning the academic Pushkin Theater visible through the window and the unseen academic Gorky Theater [the MAT], sit on a throne (a stage piece from some production), and propose to begin. The blocking was done, the actors knew their lines. They crossed the stage and the director proclaimed, "Scene

---

45 Kirill Yur'evich Lavrov (1925–2007) acted chiefly as an extra until entering the BDT 1955, where he began playing adolescents and then spent the rest of his career in leading roles.

46 Radzinsky's chronology is not incorrect. Although *The Idiot* had opened in 1958, it enjoyed a major revival in 1966.

Two." Nikolay Pavlovich watched his beautiful actors with unconcealed satisfaction, laughed at their improvisations, and every so often with a malicious smile jotted something down on a cigarette packet. As far as I could tell, something that had nothing to do with the play. Then they went through the third scene and then it was time to prepare for the evening's show. The actors finally expressed their excitement with the rehearsal, talked about what new thing they had discovered for themselves that day, and we would leave.

But there was one rehearsal that was unforgettable. Akimov showed us costume sketches. It was depressing to think that they were going to the tailor's and wigmaker's workshops. These were not simply characters, not even images, but detailed portrait sketches of actors in roles. The actors were overwhelmed, they seemed to be unable to figure out how such perfection of form could be achieved onstage. But Akimov himself would not accept that—otherwise he wouldn't have gone from painting to theater. The only conclusion: sarcastic Akimov was an innocent. An innocent, but a true artist. He dreamed of putting a chair onstage that would make the audience burst into tears.

[...] Akimov was no creator of a movement or a school. He was unabashedly opposed to the academicism connected with the educational process.

THE DRAGON finally went into rehearsal at the Comedy Theater on December 7, 1961.

Nikolai Akimov addresses the participants. Quoted in Evgeny M. Binevich, "Na puti k 'Drakonu,'" *Neva* 10 (1996), 178.

I think that Shvarts is becoming a classic of literature. Staging a classic, we should consider its status at the present time. But to adapt a classic to the petty phenomenon of "today" is trivial. I propose . . . to stage *The Dragon* about human dignity. Those ideas, scattered throughout the play, should be addressed by all . . . The kingdom of the Dragon left behind corrupt souls, wherein dragonets reside. To kill the dragon residing inside us all is Shvarts's concept. One must extirpate the evil he leaves behind him . . . The play is very complicated, and so is its production . . . To confront all the difficulties of the work means staging the fairy tale as a fairy tale, and anyone who wants to draw conclusions will draw them for himself. We will not allude to the past, because that's cheap and dissipates the theme, which is important and meant for "tomorrow." *The Dragon* will not have a Georgian accent . . .

Human feeling must be deep and realistic. The most fantastic characters must be, as in a psychological drama, characterized by psychological depth—something between Dostoevsky and Anatole France. A dead earnest attitude to all the fantasy is absolutely necessary. Just as it is in the author. Here the passions are original and powerful. Not a single role can be played as a joke.

THE LENINGRAD PUBLIC stormed the theater to see *The Dragon* for fear it would be closed out of hand. They chose to see Khrushchëv in the time-serving Mayor who knuckles under to the Dragon in its lifetime and then assumes its power after its death.

The Sovremennik

In 1956 a group of young critics and theater people, inspired by Jean Vilar's Théâtre National Populaire, met in Moscow with the idea of creating a new theater devoted to truth and innovative production values. It included two members of the Central Children's Theater, Oleg Efremov, a young actor, and Anatoly Éfros, a young director. Efremov wanted an artistic democracy, Éfros a directorate. The critic Vladimir Sappak kept notes of their late-night meetings.

> Vl. Sappak, *Bloknoty 1956 goda* [Notebooks 1956] (Moscow: Moskovsky Khudozhestvenny Teatr, 2011), 36–37, 111–12. Vladimir Fëdorovich Sappak (1921–61), theater critic on several journals, including *Teatr*, was one of the first Soviet television reviewers.

June 27, 1956. [...] This is Efremov's[47] position:

The theater is a cooperative fellowship of actors. We have to test out this setup. The most important thing in the theater is the collective, built and led democratically. An elected artistic council, an elected administration. All questions to be decided by vote. One for all and all for one. Hence a feeling of responsibility to the collective.

"For me the question of the collective is a very interesting one," Oleg says, "from my earliest childhood I've thought about it. For its sake I have even organized a new theater, a theater where the least actor and the chief director are equals. I am for the dialectical origin of the collective. Psychologically this is very important. Without it we can stage nothing. Everything will be smashed to smithereens" ...

Éfros[48] takes a different position. He speaks reasonably, without losing his composure, even smiling. He sits in a soft armchair, his legs crossed. He asserts: "I simply want to understand. As soon as you convince me—I will quickly renounce my own point of view."

This is Éfros:

"We are organizing a new theater. This is our idea, our initiative. We will invite actors: you want to, come, you don't want to, you don't have to. The main thing is the community of artistic aspiration. If someone comes to us—that means we are the

47 Oleg Nikolaevich Efremov (1927–2000) organized the Young Actors Studio at the MAT 1956; when it became the Sovremennik, he was its director and leading actor; he took over the MAT in 1970 and, in 1987, split the company in two.

48 Anatoly Vasil'evich Éfros (1925–87), a student of Mariya Knebel', did his apprenticeship at the Central Children's Theater, before becoming the controversial director at the Moscow Lenin Komsomol Theater 1963–67, the Malaya Bronnaya 1967–84, and the Taganka 1984–87.

authorities for him. Will we become more authoritative if they 'elect' us? And how is this going to look: we come to the collective and say—we created you, so now elect us! There's something phony about this. We have to act simply and business-like. We are all very tired of all sorts of pseudo-social processes. What Efremov proposes, in essence, is in no way different from what already exists . . . I am for the enterprise. We will pick the actors, stage the production; we will approach the question honorably and in a business-like way. We will proclaim a fight with bureaucracy in art, we will smash ossified forms. In short, I am for Peter Brook's method; only our enterprise will not be privately but governmentally supported, and not commercial but artistic."

"That's a nightmare, what you're saying," Oleg leaps up, turns red, tears his hair, he almost shouts [. . .].

October 15, 1956. [. . .] This was the evening that excited everyone. All of us, as if on command, arrived freshly shaven, in neckties, carefully knotted, and wearing white shirts—a rarity these days. Everyone felt the solemnity of the moment—the first selection of the company. Before we began—we negotiated—no presidium, no speeches. We moved the tables aside. We sat in a circle. Efremov spoke first. He got so excited, turned red, couldn't begin for a long time and out of excitement spoke almost in a whisper. [. . .] The basic intervention, of course, was Éfros's. He also stammered, chose his words carefully, but, to my mind, spoke wonderfully well—everything from himself, significantly, simply and accurately. Then, after it all, he asks me: "Did I speak very badly? Damn being tongue-tied! It shouldn't be like that!" I assured him that it had all been outstanding.

We broke up early—still had time to get to the subway. [. . .]

THE GOVERNMENT suggested they be a studio or a television theater, but they held out to be accepted as a full-fledged dramatic theater. When it became clear that Éfros would not be allowed to direct Bulgakov's *Molière*, he dropped out of the project. Efremov and the others organized a Studio of Young Actors, made up of players from various troupes, under the aegis of the Moscow Art Theater. They rehearsed in the MAT Studio-School building and performed on the stage of its affiliate. Their principles were those of the 1920s: team spirit, devotion to art, strict discipline, and a natural style of acting. They intended to open in 1957 with two plays about the Great Patriotic War: Aleksandr Galich's *Sailor's Rest*, about the Jewish contribution to the war effort (as *The Serebrisky Family*, it had been banned in 1942), and Viktor Rozov's play about the pain and loss of ordinary Russians in wartime, *Alive Forever*. The preview of Galich's play was held at the Palace of Culture.

Aleksandr Galich, *Dress Rehearsal* [*General'naya repetitsya*] (Frankfurt-am-Main: Posev, 1974), 14, 19–20.

It turned out that Aleksandr Vasil'evich Solodovnikov,[49] the managing director of the Moscow Art Theater, had not only given strict orders that absolutely no one be allowed to attend the dress rehearsal, except persons named on a special list, but had also convened the ticket takers of the Moscow Art Theater and drilled them to be as uncompromising as Kremlin security, to assist the easygoing guards of the Palace of Culture. [...]

I will never forget that feeling of bleak desolation that came over me as soon as I crossed the threshold of the auditorium. The large chandelier had not been lit, and only about fifteen people were sitting in the huge auditorium meant for fifteen hundred. [...] The largest group sitting in the Palace of Culture auditorium, about ten people, consisted of several Moscow Art Theater administrators and some insignificant bureaucrats from the Board of Culture. [...] Off to the side, completely apart from everyone else, sat Georgy Aleksandrovich Tovstonogov, the artistic director of Leningrad's Gorky Bol'shoy Theater. He was sitting with his head thrown back, apparently closely examining something at the top of the ceiling. It was not clear how and why he came to be at that particular dress rehearsal [...].

A genuinely talented man, Tovstonogov achieved a leading position in the theatrical world due to his talent, energy, and even a bravery of sorts.

But it is one thing to fight your way to the top and an altogether different matter to remain up there.

Because neither talent nor energy, nor even bravery, can help you once you have reached the top. And so begins the shameful path of compromises, of making deals with your own conscience, of rationalizations like, "Fine, all right, I'll produce this crappy play for such-and-such an anniversary or red-letter day, but after that..."

But after that there will be another anniversary, and yet another red-letter day (in our country they follow one another in a never-ending daisy chain), and the command goes out, "All the masters of culture, all the artists of theater and cinema must respond, elucidate, reflect, immortalize, and glorify!..."

And so they respond, elucidate, reflect, immortalize, and glorify!

Never will the cherished "afterward" arrive; talent fades, energy runs out, and even the word *courage* becomes obsolete.

THE PLAY was prohibited. When Galich went abroad, he published his account of the banning of the play as *Dress Rehearsal*. It was finally performed by Oleg Tabakov's students as *My Big Land* in 1988 and filmed in 2004.

---

49 Aleksandr Vasil'evich Solodovnikov (1904–90), a factory worker, was, in 1937, assigned to cover cultural matters for *Pravda* and serve on the Committee for Artistic Affairs; in 1948 he was made administrator of the Bol'shoy Theater but was dismissed four years later. He served as administrative director of the MAT from 1955 to 1963.

Kozakov, *Risunki na peske*, 225–26, 235–36.

Up to the day of the premiere, the performance of *Alive Forever* was still not at the MAT affiliate but in the big hall of the Studio-School, the actors were on the verge of physical and nervous exhaustion. They were jokingly referred to as "Alive for Now."

I remember the first performance. Rumors ran through Moscow. The curtain went up at midnight, but the hall was full. Everyone was there: directors, actors, writers, critics. And it was understood: "For the last fifty years not one young studio organization has arisen. This is criminally uneconomical," wrote the playwright Aleksey Arbuzov. Many people agreed with him. And then at last . . .

The premiere of *Alive Forever* has been described repeatedly. People expected "something new," and saw "something old." The production was influenced by adherence to the MAT school, but in the way that Efremov and his actors understood it. Then what made the production exciting? In *Alive Forever* the studio actors had felt the pulse and intuited the philosophy of the times, transmitted in subtle, everyday intonations. The "something new" in the Young Actors Studio (as the Sovremennik was first called) consisted in an intuitive acceptance of the contemporary rhythm of life, the problems it poses, that they were all, luckily, living people, and this defined the manner of acting and something else—in contrast with the MAT—a quality of stage truth, which I literally call "neorealism," without making art-critical analogies, say, to the neorealism of Italian cinema. Although the neorealism of the Italian cinema was particularly attractive to us. The second most important quality was a sense of civic integrity—something at that time almost banished from the stage.

[In September 1958 the newly named Sovremennik Theater-Studio moved into the concert hall of the Soviet Hotel for its first independent season.] Efremov proposed a new economic model, which he forwarded to the cultural establishment. It stipulated that "the Sovremennik" was ready to work much more intensively than at present and double the number of productions, the actors would contract not to make movies or moonlight on the radio or in concerts but would give their all to the theater—but then their work had to be rewarded commensurately. The theater proposes that its financial plan be enlarged, but after this plan is fulfilled, it requests that the "surplus" money remain in the theater, to be distributed among the actors on the "share system." The actors will become, so to speak, "sociétaires," shareholders, as was the case, among others, at the old, pre-Soviet MAT under Stanislavsky and Nemirovich-Danchenko. [. . .] In this way, "the shareholder" will be genuinely concerned about the quality of the actors playing beside him, the principle of a financial common interest will enable the company to develop and support the Rules, which would otherwise rest on an unstable foundation.

Oleg Nikolaevich's proposal, unanimously supported by the troupe, was taken by the government to undermine the foundations of the socialist system. It prompted the remark "Hungary all over again!" (nothing horrified bureaucrats more than Hungary after the events of 1956), and the economic project was, of course, buried. But they remembered Efremov for it for a long time, whenever they wanted to put a scare into

9.3. Igor' Kvasha, Oleg Efremov, and Oleg Tabakov (left to right) in *The Legend Goes On* (*Prodolzhenie legendy*), from a story by Anatoly Kuznetsov, Sovremennik Theater, Moscow. Photo: Vladimir Perel'man.

him. [. . .] Some high official in the Ministry of Culture answered curtly and concisely when Efremov turned to him with a question of life-or-death importance:

"Why do you keep harping on 'the collective, the collective'? . . . Who've you got in this collective of yours? It isn't serious! For me it's one man! Remember: Oleg Popov![50] Oh, sorry! Oleg Efremov!"

You might say he was the buffer between the uncompromising young collective and the leaders of the ministry, which never took seriously the "boys and girls" of the Sovremennik. An official of the department reproached Oleg:

"You've put together just a bunch of Jews: Kvasha, Evstigneev. There's just one Russian and she's a female—Volchek."[51]

Oleg Tabakov, in *Teatr Anatoly Éfros: Vospominaniya, stat'i* [The theater of Anatoly Éfros: Reminiscences, articles] (Moscow: Artist-Rezhissër-Teatr, 2000), 152. Oleg Pavlovich Tabakov (1935–), known for quick-change roles and social grotesques, headed the Sovremennik (1970–76) after Efremov's departure. He created an independent studio theater and, in 1983, joined the MAT, whose artistic director he became in 2000.

The clutch of roles I managed to play at the "Sovremennik" in the first years naturally resulted from my physical, kinetic, psychological, and other attributes. In general, my

50 Oleg Konstantinovich Popov (1930–), clown who personified the folkloric Ivan the Simpleton.
51 Evgeny Aleksandrovich Evstigneev (1926–92), actor, who developed an improvisational style based

line of business was called "the lyrical hero" or "the young hero," but the Soviet era had insisted on its own version: the young hero was obliged to be directly engaged in production, earning authority in shock production, at the open-hearth furnace or the machine bench. My heroes were entering life as school boys or students—different sorts, but united by a desire to find their own calling in life. One might think that the clutch of roles I played had to lead inevitably to the subsequent stereotyping of myself in various hypostases. But this, luckily, didn't happen.

My other actor's attributes were also discovered and exploited.

And this happened at the Sovremennik.

A skeleton of the future "Sovremennik" was organized and structured, of course, around Efremov. The skeleton crew included Galya Volchek, Igor' Kvasha, with the addition of Zhenya Evstigneev, who had been in a class below them and above me, Vitya Sergachëv, and Lilya Tolmachëva,[52] at that time an actress at the Mossovet Theater, joined up ... I was the youngest.

ON APRIL 1, 1961, the Sovremennik moved into a permanent building in the center of Moscow on Mayakovsky Square, where the Variety Theater had previously performed.

The Origin of the Taganka

Yury Lyubimov had been a leading actor at the Vakhtangov Theater from 1946 as well as a popular matinee idol in films. In 1959 he began teaching at the Shchukin Theater School and revealed a talent for directing with a production of Galich's *How Much Does a Man Need?* (*Mnogo li cheloveku nado?*). He then made waves by choosing Brecht's *Good Person of Sichuan* as the graduating class project for 1963. (The authorities could not ignore Brecht's prestige in the German Democratic Republic but regarded him as doctrinally unsound.)

> Boris Zakhava, as rector of the Shchukin Theater School, to Lyubimov about permitting his production of *Good Person of Sichuan,* October 25, 1963. Yury Lyubimov, *Rasskazy starogo trepacha* (Moscow: Novosti, 2001), 228, 233, 238.

In your staging of the production *Good Person of Sichuan* in its original form (the form it had as a classroom exercise at the end of the last school year), along with its positive

---

on jazz improvisation; prominent at the Sovremennik 1957–70; eventually joined Efremov at the MAT. Igor' Vladimirovich Kvasha (1933–2012), played young heroes at the Sovremennik; later became a television personality. Galina Borisovna Volchek (1933–), actress, director, became the Sovremennik's leader in 1989; known as the "Iron Lady."

52 Viktor Nikolaevich Sergachëv (1934–2013), after work at the Red Army Theater, joined the Sovremennik in 1957. Lidiya Mikhaylovna Tolmachëva (1932–) worked at the Saratov TYUZ, then at the Mossovet 1955–56, and was a charter member of the Sovremennik in 1957 in a wide range of roles.

9.4. Act I of *The Good Person of Sichuan* by Bertolt Brecht, directed by Yury Lyubimov, Taganka Theater, Moscow, 1963.

aspects, serious flaws were noted. The most substantial of these was the presence in the performance of moments that served as occasion for demonstrations in the audience on the part of those who enjoy taking postures of political skepticism and contumacy.

This is all the more intolerable in the given production since the ideological spirit of Brecht's play is wholly directed against a society where man exploits man, and consequently, a production which expresses that idea must not only include no elements of any criticism whatsoever aimed at a socialist society but, on the contrary, must awake in the spectators a feeling of pride in our country, where the exploitation of man by man had become a matter of history. No sort of ambiguity, used to make reference to our Soviet reality, has any place whatsoever in this production.

At my insistence you made emendations to the production, intended to remove the indicated failings.

However, my order that the song "About Power and the People" be absolutely excised from the production was, for some reason I do not understand, met with on your part with dogged resistance.

I consider that the additional lines inserted into this song[53] do not change the gist of the matter. Therefore I am compelled, in my rights as rector, categorically to demand the excision of that song from the production. Take this as my official command. [...]

[*Lyubimov picks up the story*:] For Moscow this was unusual playwriting. Brecht was very rarely staged, and Moscow barely knew him. I had never seen the Berliner Ensemble[54] and was completely free from influence. In other words, I did it intuitively,

53 The lines in question were "The powers march along the road... / Some corpse is on the road. / "Hey! That must be the people!" The school audience would stamp its feet and shout "Encore! Encore!"
54 The Berliner Ensemble, East Berlin troupe located in the Theater am Schiffbauerdamm, founded

freely, without the pressure of Brechtian tradition. [...] And because I had seen no Brecht, I was a virgin and came up with a Russian variant of Brecht. The production was what my instincts and my flair prompted in me. [...] Because it seemed to me that the Brechtian structure itself, the principles of his theater were absolutely those of a political theater, somehow they forced the students to see the world around them more clearly and situate themselves and their relation to what they see in it. Because there was no other way to play Brecht.

The Good Person had an enormous resonance. And drew in everyone. Poets, writers came. We even contrived to perform *Good Person,* despite the faculty prohibition, at the Film House, the Writers' House, for physicists in Dubno. We acted five times at the Vakhtangov Theater. They allowed it because the production had such success, and besides, my old schoolmate and friend, even as far back as the Second MAT, Isay Spektor,[55] was the business manager of the theater, a practical man, and the Vakhtangov troupe was on tour at the time. And people broke the doors down there. And I was sent away to act somewhere else, although they had another performer for the part. So I didn't see how these shows went at the Vakhtangov. And only afterward they let me know that Mikoyan was there and made the remark: "Oh!! This isn't a school play, this isn't a student production. This is theater and extremely idiosyncratic." So you see, a member of the Politburo got it.

Boris Poyurovsky, "Vakhtangov-style!" [Po-vakhtangovski!], *Moskovsky kom-somolets* (December 15, 1963); reprinted in *Chto ostalos',* 144.

Take the episode in the tobacco factory at least. A large number of stools onstage. They are arranged in a single row, as if on parade. And it seems as if there's no beginning or end to them. Each stool is a worker's seat. But we do not see the faces of those who work here. And only through the hunched backs and monotonous movements in time to the same monotonous sounds do we feel how tired everyone is. Robot people, machine people.

Everything in this episode is subordinated to the concept and the feeling: the actors and the mise-en-scène and the rhythm. Without this well-defined form we would not sense so distinctly the social meaning of Brecht's play.

Lyubimov's production rejoices us by its democratic quality, where the peculiar poetry of workers' quarters can be felt at every step. Here humor combines with tragedy, tragedy with optimism.

---

and run by Bertolt Brecht (1948–66), where he experimented with theories of Epic acting and distanciation.

55 Isay Isaakovich Spektor (1916–) began as an actor at the Moscow Realistic Theater 1931–34 and, after further study at the MAT 2 school, joined the Vakhtangov Theater in 1939 as an actor. As the theater's deputy administrator and administrator from 1965, he fell afoul of Minister Furtseva. Married to the actress Iuliya Borisovna.

CHAPTER TEN

Innovation within Stagnation, 1964–1984

ONE OF THE interesting paradoxes of Soviet culture is that the period known as Stagnation, owing to the smug, stolid, and increasingly arteriosclerotic leadership of Leonid Brezhnev, also saw the most exciting upsurge in theatrical creativity since the 1920s. This was all the more unlikely because Brezhnev's accession in 1964 was followed by more arrests. After the trial of the allegedly anti-Soviet writers Andrey Sinyavsky and Yuly Daniel, sentenced to a labor camp, a creeping re-Stalinization was evident. Resistance to the regime was diagnosed as a mental disorder and its "sufferers" interned in psychiatric wards. The Prague spring was brutally ended by the Soviet troops' invasion of Czechoslovakia in 1968. "Celebrity dissidents," such as the nuclear scientist Andrey Sakharov, the writer Aleksandr Solzhenitsyn, the musicians Galina Vishnevskaya and Mstislav Rostropovich, and the dancer Mikhail Baryshnikov, wound up in exile, internal or external. For the most part, the intelligentsia sank into compliant passivity.

The Ministry of Culture, under the unpredictable leadership of Ekaterina Furtseva, maintained the mechanisms of censorship efficiently in the realm of the arts. The ministry purchased the rights to plays from the national playwrights' association; theaters had to negotiate with it. A play, even a classic, could be added to a theater's repertoire only after permission was received from the appropriate cultural body, whose decisions in turn had to be approved ultimately by the Council of Ministers of the USSR. Khrushchëv had begun to open the frontiers to a two-way traffic for cultural exchange; Furtseva continued this policy for orchestral music, opera, and ballet but was less open handed with theater.

The exceptional status of the theater during this period was that audiences flocked to it to hear messages they could not hear anywhere else. Often veiled in "Aesopic language" (a term from the nineteenth-century satirist Saltykov-Shchedrin) or scenic metaphors, antiestablishment attitudes could be conveyed from the stage. It was easier to censor texts than directorial interpretations or inventions. In Leningrad Tovstonogov still dominated the scene. In Moscow in the late 1960s, new directors were appointed: Goncharov at the Mayakovsky Theater in 1969; Efremov at the MAT in 1970; Zakharov at the Lenkom in 1973. Turning away from the mediocre repertoire, many directors adapted prose and played the classics: Éfros staged Gogol's *Wedlock* and *The Cherry Orchard* in 1975; Chekhov's *Ivanov* was seen as a forecast of the current mood and enjoyed multiple revivals.

The only new theater to be officially recognized, after the Sovremennik, was the Taganka in Moscow. Yury Lyubimov, popular actor at the Vakhtangov Theater and teacher at the Boris Shchukin School, was given the ramshackle Theater of Drama and Comedy on Taganskaya Square. There he and his students established a company that swore allegiance to Meyerhold, Vakhtangov, and Brecht; it became a theater of poetic metaphor, relatively open in its liberal politics. There he fostered the genius of the raw-voiced bard Vladimir Vysotsky. Vysotsky's protest songs were widely distributed by the new phenomenon *magnitizdat,* bootleg tape recordings, seized by the KGB wherever it found them.

If Lyubimov, for all the international renown of his theater, was barely tolerated by the authorities, Anatoly Éfros was regularly persecuted. Both at the Lenin Komsomol Theater (1963–67) and the Malaya Bronnaya (1967–84), his innovative stagings of the classics and his introduction of new plays, performed by a highly talented company, were undermined by the authorities and attacked by the critical establishment. Lyubimov preferred to shape plays out of literary material; Éfros encouraged daring new playwrights, among them Mikhail Roschchin, Ignaty Dvoretsky, and Édvard Radzinsky.

Other prominent directors had their favorite playwrights as well. Efremov, first at the Sovremennik, then at the Moscow Art Theater, favored plays about problems of modern economic life by Aleksandr Gel'man and revisionist interpretations of Soviet history by Mikhail Shatrov. Both Efremov and Tovstonogov were enthusiastic fans of Aleksandr Vampilov, the short-lived Siberian whose wry comedies were often called "Chekhovian." Dvoretsky and Aleksey Arbuzov set up a playwriting workshop; its best exponents were dubbed "post-Vampilovian" by Anatoly Smelyansky in *Literaturaya Gazeta* in 1978. Their plays spoke bitter truths about the absurdities of private life and survival in Soviet society, so that the censorship prevented the work of Lyudmila Petrushevskaya from appearing on state-subsidized stages. It is significant that their first productions often took place in studios and unofficial spaces, directed by recent drama school graduates, such as Anatoly Vasil'ev, who had not been given berths in major theaters.

After the fiftieth anniversary of the USSR, the twenty-fourth Party Congress of 1971 promulgated the term the *Soviet people* (*Sovetsky narod*) as a "new, historic, social and international society" with one state and one economy, united in socialism. Although it recognized the "many facets of national identities," it in fact was dissolving the individual claims to cultural autonomy among the republics. The struggle for democracy and de-Stalinization in Soviet art was promoted as a return to pure, revolutionary values and a realization of the ideals of Communism. Soviet cultural workers defended humanitarian ideals in both decision making and self-examination and the right to challenge Soviet orthodoxy. The utopian ideals of socialism were reintroduced, along with a recognition of the importance of making art as it had existed in the first decade after the Revolution.

Nevertheless, the constitution of 1977 reinforced the primacy of the Communist Party over the legislative and executive powers. In the words of the songwriter Andrey Yurchak, "until the mid-1980s, it never even occurred to anyone that in our country anything could change. Neither to children nor to adults. There was a complete impression that everything was forever."[1]

Cracks in the Foundation

The exploitation of oil and mineral resources brought in hard currency. The *nomenklatura* had cars and drivers, spacious apartments, abundant rations, the ability to send their children to special schools. The average Soviet worker, on the other hand, had a standard of living one-third that of an American and one-half that of a German. That was a huge improvement over previous years, but there was an ongoing shortage of consumer goods, owing partly to the immense expenditures on defense and the support of Cuba. New regulations attempted to ameliorate working conditions in the arts.

> A. G. Orlov, *O trude rabotnikov teatral'no-zrelishchnykh uchrezhdeny* [On the labor of workers in theatrical-performing arts institutions] (Moscow: Profizdat, 1976), 35–36.

The extension of daily work for all theatrical coworkers cannot exceed 7 hours. Interruptions for rest and meals during work hours are not included. Rules are established for regulating workers' time, in relation to participation in performances, rehearsals, traveling, and touring productions, as well as rules for regulating the work of individual categories of workers.

If the nature of the work does not allow strict regulation of workers' time, an abnormal working day may be established. The Ministry of Culture of the USSR, in agreement with the TsK of profsoyuz of workers of culture, has drawn up a list of the duties of theatrical workers with an abnormal workday. [...]

A list of the duties of workers with an abnormal workday in the extracategorical theaters (the Bol'shoy Theater and the Kremlin Palace of Congresses,[2] the MAT USSR, and other theaters on a par with the aforenamed) is established by the Ministry of Culture of the USSR in agreement with the TsK profsoyuz of cultural workers.

---

1 Television interview, June 24, 1994, quoted in Alexei Yurchak, "Soviet Hegemony of Form: Everything Was Forever, Until It Was No More," *Comparative Studies in Society and History* 45, 3 (2003): 480.

2 The Palace of Congresses in the Kremlin was built 1959–61 on the orders of Khrushchëv, who wanted a massive venue for Communist Party meetings; it is the largest building in the world with a stage for performances; its auditorium seats six thousand.

LITTLE BY LITTLE, the voices that had been silenced under Stalin began to be heard, occasionally through official publications but most often through the reminiscences of survivors. One of Mariya Knebel's students and a fervent admirer of Vakhtangov, Adol'f Shapiro, became the youngest chief director in the USSR, when, in 1964, he was appointed head of the State Youth Theater of Riga, which he forged into a strong company.

> Adol'f Shapiro, "He laughs at everything," in *Kak zakryvalsya zanaves* (Moscow: Novoe Literaturnoe Obozrenie, 1999), 148–49.

In the years when I was getting my start a famous film director predicted the ruin of the theater. He goes, movies, TV, blah blah blah. He is wrong. The theater is tenacious of life—because it is constantly dying. There are no pretensions to eternal life in its nature. And throughout history, performance is but a flash of artistic thought.

One of my classmates would rave about Meyerhold, another about Kurbas. Yet another about Terent'ev. This youthful ardor did not pass without consequences. They became persons of note. So far so good, but then it turned out that the result of the return of the glorious directors from being nonpersons was the explosion of a renascence. We hoped that the experiments of the legendary Masters would help us to walk as professionals in their footsteps . . . We wanted to gain strength by drinking at this source.

But the landscape of life changes, the old rivulets dry up. We scattered in embarrassment after the revival of Meyerhold's *Credentials* and after the resuscitated *Turandot*. The theater sneered at our youthful illusions. It is idiotic to grieve—one can seal a painting with varnish and preserve the paint, one can restore a film, but a production cannot be revived.

The theatrical language decays over time—metaphors wear out and take on elements of parody. The fishermen's net in which Othello became entangled,[3] the canary beating its wings against a cage when life has closed in on the hero, a storm bursting into a room at the moment a symphony is created, once excited the spectator but now raise a smile.

Vlasyuk alluded to such an episode when demonstrating the genius of Kurbas. A young director was rehearsing a scene in which interventionists are plotting an invasion scheme. On the table a map, staff officers all around. The little table was now moved downstage, then put to the side upstage, the arrangement of the officers was altered, but nothing worked. And then Les' Stepanovich hurried through the orchestra pit to the stage—remove the little table. Leave the map. Give me your saber! He put on a sword belt, fastidiously picked up the map of the Ukraine, threw it on the floor, and triumphantly planted a foot on it. Then he pulled the saber from its sheath and used it to shred the map. The enemy, so to speak, was trampling, divvying up, and hacking about the Ukraine.

---

3   The reference is to the movie *Othello* (1955), directed by Sergey Yutkevich, with Sergey Bondarchuk in the leading role.

This scene from Irchan's[4] *The Bridgehead* [*Platsdarm*] is recalled by Kurbasites as often as Meyerholdians do the finale to *The Ultimate Decisive*.

EKATERINA FURTSEVA'S APPOINTMENT as minister of culture was a demotion from her position on the Central Committee, and after Khrushchëv's removal she lacked a powerful protector. A former textile worker who had worked her way up through the ranks by total devotion to the Party, she had only a rudimentary knowledge of the arts. Her policies were erratic; she tried to insist on a rigid Party line but could be swayed by concerted resistance, handsome leading men, and her taste for luxury. Her mercurial moods ranged from matronly commiseration to an off-with-their-heads fury. In 1974 she was to commit suicide after accusations of financial peculation were leveled at her family.

> Boris M. Poyurovsky, "Catherine the Great," *Moskvichka* [The little Muscovite] 17 (1998), reprinted in *Chto ostalos' na trube . . . Khroniki teatral'noy zhizni Vserossiyskoe Teatral'noe Obshchestvoroy poloviny XX veka* (Moscow: Tsentroligraf, 2000), 114–18.

In October 1967 the All-Union festival was held, devoted to fifty years of the Great October Socialist Revolution. All the theaters in the country took part in it, including, naturally, the Maly. On its stage the director in chief at that time, Evgeny Simonov, staged his own verse play titled *John Reed*. Enthusiastic opinions about it were quick to appear. The reviewers included Aleksandr Korneychuk[5] and other people no less famous and influential at that time. [. . .] However, word of mouth differed remarkably from the written opinions, which at that time was a fairly frequent occurrence. So I was in no hurry to see the production.

[Poyurovsky chose not to review it, because he would have had to tell the truth, but his editor at *Vechernyaya Moskva* insisted.] What I saw in the first act plunged me into complete despair. However, the habit of sitting through to the end stood me in good stead, though I confess, it had been a long time since I had seen such a mass exodus of spectators. The capstone of all was a verse monologue of Lenin to the delegates of the second All-Russian Congress of Soviets, recited by Igor' Ilinsky with the familiar intonations of Comrades Ogurtsov and Byvalov[6] combined.

The performance was a long one, in 3 acts. I came home late. [. . .] Out of friendship, Seva Shevtsov offered to read the [galley sheets of the] article over the telephone. It

---

4 Myroslav Irchan (actually Andrii Babiuk, 1897–1937), Ukrainian Communist writer, active in émigré politics; arrested 1933 for counterrevolutionary activities and sentenced to ten years in a labor camp.

5 Aleksandr Evdokimovich Korneychuk (1905–72), playwright, whose pro-Communist hackwork held the stage from the era of the Five-Year Plans into the 1960s.

6 Fictional bureaucrats played by Il'insky in musical comedies on-screen: Ivan Byvalov in *Volga-Volga* (1938) and Ogurtsov (Pickleton) in *Carnival Night* (*Karnaval'naya noch'*, 1956). Ogurtsov's catchphrase is "I don't like jokes and won't let anyone tell them."

was all exactly as written. Only they changed the headline. My original had read "An Attempt on the Life of John Reed," the galleys "Play No Success . . . for Director" (seeing that Evgeny Simonov had not only staged the play but written it as well).

[On return from a vacation, Poyurovsky was given the cold shoulder by Furtseva at a performance of the touring Bol'shoy Theater and was ordered to come to her office. After a sleepless night:]

I showed up to the reception desk ten minutes before the appointed hour. The receptionist knew about it but asked me to wait. At nine on the dot she said:

"You may go in." And immediately rang up: "Grigory Ivanovich, good morning, please look in on Ekaterina Alekseevna."

I understood: a confrontation was in store.

Entering the minister's office, I said good morning, but evidently did so too timidly. In any case, no one answered me. Ekaterina Alekseevna was sitting at the back of the room behind an enormous desk covered with file folders. She was studying something attentively. This pause was prolonged, probably, not very long in fact, but it seemed an eternity to me: such summonses were not issued every day, luckily. Finally Vladykin[7] came in, and Furtseva's aide as well.

"Ah, you're here already," Ekaterina Alekseevna said cheerily, springing up from behind the desk and coming to meet us. Her mood was clearly a good one, quite unlike the one in which she had conversed with me at the Bol'shoy Theater. "Do you know one another?" she asked Vladykin and me simultaneously.

And we both nodded in the affirmative.

"Then, please, Grigory Ivanovich, repeat what Comrade Poyurovsky replied when you presented him with my request."

And Grigory Ivanovich repeated word for word the very same thing I had already heard.

"Well, what do you say now?" asked Ekaterina Alekseevna.

"Nothing, except what I've already said."

"So it seems Grigory Ivanovich is lying?"

"I don't say that, but no one ever asked me to meet with you."

And suddenly Furtseva, with a nasty glint in her eye, said to the aide:

"Invite Grigory Ivanovich's assistant here, and be sure he brings the appointment book with him."

In a few minutes the assistant was in the minister's office.

"When was your article on *John Reed* published?" Furtseva asked me.

I gave her the date.

"Look at roughly two or three days later, whether you phoned Comrade Poyurovsky, on which telephone, and what he answered."

All this time the participants in this discussion, including the mistress of the office, were on their feet.

---

7 Grigory Ivanovich Vladykin, deputy minister of culture, had served on Stalin's anticosmopolitan committee; a bibliophile and expert on Aleksandr Ostrovsky.

"Please take a seat," Ekaterina Alekseevna offered. And she added, "There's no truth on one's feet, and it is absolutely necessary for us to get at the truth."

We sat around the table, the assistants peaceably submerged in reading, and Furtseva withdrew somewhere.

"Well, what about it?" she cheerfully inquired, having suddenly returned to the office. Silence. "Did you find anything?" Stillness. "All right, everyone can go," Furtseva pronounced with a kind of new, malicious intonation. And added, "Except Vladykin and Poyurovsky." We had already stood up but had to sit down again. "Well, aren't you ashamed? Get out and don't let me see you again!" she blurted at Vladykin. And he, like a whipped dog, beat a retreat. I would have liked to follow him, but Furtseva ominously asked, "Where are you off to? Our conversation is still to come."

From a lower drawer of the desk she drew out an envelope, with a letter fastened to it, and handed it to me:

"Read it!"

"What fresh disaster?" I thought and plunged into reading.

Of course, I will not attempt to quote from memory a letter written almost thirty years ago. But I well remember its gist. [...] Evgeny Rubenovich [Simonov] repeatedly addresses Ekaterina Alekseevna in the hope that now she will surely decide to post him to his beloved Vakhtangov Theater. But if the minister considers as before that father and son must not work together, he is ready even today to move to any other collective, even outside of Moscow, and not necessarily as director in chief—only he will have to leave the Maly, since, now that my article has come out, he cannot remain: someone daily sends to his home address (postage due!) cuttings with the review. And at the end quite a moving P.S.: he agrees to run even a folk theater.

"Well, what can you say in your defense?" Ekaterina Alekseevna inquired. And added, "Or shall I appoint you director in chief of the Maly Theater?"

I didn't begin to justify myself. I simply replied that I was very sorry that a dear friend was hurt. However, my evaluation of the play and the production had nothing to do with my commiseration. And then, for some reason, I suspected that Furtseva herself had not seen *John Reed*.

"I haven't got the time to go everywhere. You know how busy I am—in over my head! But how dare you take such a tone in discussing the oldest Russian theater?! Do you understand what they've accomplished?"

And then I had recourse to an inadmissible ploy:

"In the first place, there are three theaters in all in Moscow in direct subordination to the Ministry of Culture of the USSR. In the second, you are offended on behalf of the oldest Russian theater, but that is indeed a coincidence—because I am concerned on that very account! I'm the one who saw the production, and you haven't... Besides, I was humiliated on behalf of the Revolution, Lenin, and John Reed, and for some reason you haven't mentioned that."

My last words made Furtseva think things over for a moment. And, taking advantage of a certain perplexity, I unexpectedly proposed:

"In such cases your predecessor Anatoly Vasil'evich Lunacharsky first of all personally went to see a controversial work. And only afterward would he render his judgment. If, after you see the performance, you consider that I acted improperly, I give you my word never more to work as a theater critic. After all, a theater specialist can be an editor and a teacher and a *zavlit* [literary manager of a theater] and an organizer. Believe me, this is all that I can promise. But you must agree: this is no small matter for a man who from youth chose his profession, received a special education, and has done nothing else for fifteen years."

To my surprise, Furtseva accepted the rules of the game, but added:

"Just see to it that you don't repent of it later!"

With that we parted. But, as ill luck would have it, the next performance of *John Reed* was scheduled for February 20, on a Soviet Army day. True, and for a few times running thereafter: on such days theater parties were organized, and free tickets distributed to the audiences.

Furtseva dropped in on the Maly Theater not the first night and, to tell the truth, I thought she had forgotten all about it; after all, forty days had gone by. But suddenly a phone call at night: Ekaterina Alekseevna from the management's box. I tore along to the end of Act I and saw, in the lobby at the buffet, everywhere, an unusually large number of drunks. Apparently, before the show started, Viktor Vasil'evich Grishin[8] had awarded medals here, in the Maly Theater, and the Red Banner to the leaders of the Chief Board of Trade of the Mossovet—Tregubov and his cronies. It would have been a sin not to celebrate such consideration by the beloved Party and government for the humble toilers of the countinghouse. And so attention please! to make matters exceptionally festive, the spectators were treated to an open bar, specially those who dealt with the deficit.[9]

In the second act I went into the auditorium: there were empty seats galore! The administration's box looked empty, in any case, Furtseva was not to be seen in it. By the third act people were still leaving, while those who remained might just as well have left—they made so much noise that nothing could be heard. Finally the curtain came down, there was barely time to open it to the sparse applause of the most steadfast theater buffs from the Board of Trade, and quietly they dispersed. [...]

That night *John Reed* was played for the last time. Leaving the theater after a short explanation with Simonov, Furtseva asked [her aide] to convey to the administration that the production was never again to be put on under any circumstances.

VALENTIN PLUCHEK, who had created an experimental studio with Aleksey Arbuzov in 1939, where they staged the improvised *The Town at Daybreak*, was made director of the Moscow Satire Theater in 1950. He revived Mayakovsky's comedies

8   Viktor Vasil'evich Grishin (1914–92), member of the Politburo, hardline leader of the Moscow Communist Party 1967–85; often blamed for Chernenko's death by forcing the ailing chairman to go to the polls.
9   *Defitsitny*, "in deficit," was a catchphrase of the period, referring to the constant shortage of consumer goods and the inability to fulfill quotas.

with great success in the 1950s, though he got into trouble with Hikmet's *Was It Ivan Ivanovich?* In 1969 he staged another watershed, Beaumarchais's *Marriage of Figaro*, which had last received serious attention in 1927 with Stanislavsky's production.

Valentin Pluchek on staging Beaumarchais and Mayakovsky. Nina Velekhova, *Valentin Pluchek i Prival komediantov na Triumfal'noy*, 2 (Moscow: Rutena, 1999), 178, 287–88.

When I staged *Figaro*, it was just the period that had begun in the 1950s with the English "angry young men" (Osborne's *Look Back in Anger*).[10] A type of young cynic, a skeptic with a cigarette in the corner of his mouth, had come into fashion: his fathers had cheated him, so had the Revolution, and so on. That's where the boys in Rozov's[11] plays came from. I remember a certain case. A friend and I, vacationing in Ruza, were walking in the woods and arguing about something so passionately that we almost came to blows. Flushed with anger, continuing the argument, we walked into a café called *The Cozy Corner*, having decided to have a drink and finish our verbal duel. We walk in shouting, making a racket, berating one another, and there sit students, boys and girls, on their holidays. And all quiet as quiet could be, flabby slackers, barely uttering a word... We had dropped into another world.

And it suddenly seemed to me that quite another kind of hero was needed—an active hero, who replies to intrigue with action, taunts with wit, cleverness, like Figaro!

[Flush with the success of Figaro, Pluchek then decided to give Gogol a modern twist by making *The Inspector General* a depiction of contemporary Russia, by staging "the whole author."]

In those days, preparations were being made for a tour of the Satire Theater to France. Don't assume, however, that the Ministry of Culture was sending us, far from it: it opposed the tour in every way. Our tour was the work of Georges Soria and Louis Aragon[12]... They were in Russia, saw our *Bathhouse*. They took an interest in Mayakovsky, and after they'd seen the show, in the theater Georges Soria said, "We want to show the Satire Theater to the French, otherwise, we really don't need anything." Our ministry, as everyone knows, was rigid in character, but you'd not be surprised if the French didn't want to have something palmed off on them they didn't want. In short, they "waited it out," and we began to discuss contracts and prepare for the tour.

[...] A whole commission was created under Ekaterina Alekseevna Furtseva, and this commission inspected our shows. They look, look, but finally—I don't know what

10　John Osborne (1929–94), English playwright, whose *Look Back in Anger* (1956) is taken to be the opening salvo in the "Angry Young Man" attack on the British establishment.

11　Viktor Sergeevich Rozov (1913–2004), playwright, whose career was promoted by productions at the Sovremennik; most of his plays have a similar theme, the privileged hypocrisy of adults redeemed by the hopes of modern youth.

12　Correspondents to the French Communist magazine *L'Humanité*: Georges Soria (1914–91), author of the play *La Peur* (1954) and director of the Agence Littéraire et Artistique Parisienne; Louis Aragon (actually Andrieux, 1897–1982), a former surrealist and husband of the Russian translator Elsa Triolet.

happened—at the last moment it seems—the commission failed to see *The Bathhouse.*

What came next is hard to describe.

Infuriated, Furtseva summoned Kuznetsov, who was both her deputy and the official in charge of theaters, and blew up such a scandal that he probably remembered it to the last day of his work at her ministry. Everyone knew well: her tantrums were something unforgettable. Officials trembled as they entered her office. She knew how to lose her temper, this woman of character. And when she screamed at the lackadaisical official, the veins stood out dangerously on her sleek neck.

No one and nothing could come near her on his own initiative, and she made no exception for anyone. It was simply impossible to burst in upon Ekaterina Alekseevna like a gunshot. She even replied to one of the most famous actresses of modern times, who asked her for an audience, "in the regular rotation."

And as the artistic director of the theater, they immediately summoned me to Kuznetsov, they sent a car for me.

Now listen: this is the big scene.

I entered Kuznetsov's office.

And, I swear to you that such a thing has happened to me only once in my life. What I saw before me was an unretouched scene from *Inspector General,* when the Mayor meets Khlestakov and cannot pronounce a single word out of fear.... I see before myself a tall fat man trembling with fear, who obviously wants to say "Valentin Nikolaevich," but cannot pronounce anything except the first syllable and stammers "Va-va-va-va..."

... Finally, recovering, this important, powerful official turns to me beseechingly and pleads, "If Ekaterina Alekseevna asks you about *Bathhouse,* tell her that the commission did see that production."

Now that Russian companies were allowed to tour abroad, the publicity had to be controlled.

> Extract from "Memorandum to leaders of collectives of the Russian Federation, about to go on tour abroad," no. 136, July 18, 1977, 1A–2.

Plan for Informational-Propaganda Measures Abroad

Informational-propaganda measures taken abroad must be directed at a broad exploitation of the media of mass information (television, radio, the press) of foreign countries to introduce workers in Soviet culture and art to the foreign audience, holding meetings with the workers' and democratic communities, with the creative intelligentsia, with the aim of propagandizing the achievements of the Soviet Union after sixty years.

The plan must include the preparation of:

—creative information about the collective,

—publicity film reels, slides, posters, booklets, prospectuses,

—photo albums about the collective,

—photo exhibitions of the people's economies and cultures of the republics, regions, provinces, towns,

—materials for the foreign press and television (creative portraits of the leading actors, directors, designers, heads of the ensembles, ballet masters, choir masters, conductors, articles about the history and development of the collective, etc.),

—talking points for interviews with press reporters, and on radio and television,

—the shaping of productions, the choice of variety acts, the programs of concerts for appearances on radio and television, at artistic gatherings,

—the selection of material for talks:

about the development of culture and art in our country, republic, region, province,

about the great achievements of communism,

about the heroic cities,

about Moscow, the Olympic city for 1980,

about the peace-loving foreign policies of the Soviet Union (carrying out the resolves of the Helsinki accords),

—meetings with representatives of culture and art, progressive communities, the active members of Friendship Societies,

—meetings at Houses of Soviet Science and Culture,

—meetings with workers' organizations, agricultural communities, the youth, students,

—visiting organizations, academic institutions,

—laying bouquets and wreaths on historic monuments.

Tovstonogov in Charge

Throughout this period Tovstonogov consolidated his position, learning when to bend to the administration and when to capitalize on opportunities for more openness. "I am a realist by conviction," he declared, "and my productions should prove that the most daring forms of expression do not come into conflict with realism." So saying, he relied on psychological acting and highly theatrical mises-en-scène without doing violence to the texts. This was his heyday, beginning with a reinterpretation of *Three Sisters* that highlighted their selfishness and used cinematic blocking to create "closeups" and "long shots." He then revived *The Idiot*.

Dina Shvarts, *Dnevniki i zametki* (St. Petersburg: Inapress, 2001), 186–87.

April 2, 1966. A viewing of *The Idiot* in its new redaction. The performance has become more subtle, more laconic. Rogozhin has become very good, especially in Lebedev's[13] interpretation. But Innokenty [Smoktunovsky] is something unfathomable. He is

13 Evgeny Alekseevich Lebedev (1917–97), actor who worked under Tovstonogov at the Lenin Komsomol Theater and went with him in 1956 to the BDT; later became internationally famous as the gelding Kholstomer in *Story of a Horse* (1975).

beautiful. You never want to take your eyes off him. Maybe because it is impossible to record. You can take photos, describe the role, ultimately make a movie. And yet not one of these mnemonic devices will present the brilliance of the actor at every second of his existence. How to convey the intonations? How to express in words his scene with Aglaya when she appoints a rendezvous? The desire to remember the location of the future meeting and the stupefaction at her words. And the "Is she asleep?" in the last scene. Only he could get away with it—to put it bluntly. Hope in the face of complete conviction that everything has gone wrong. Physically tangible the last, very last hope.

The shock of the audience. More than that—a psychopathic state, bruised by contact with this brilliant power all-penetrating into the character. Complete merger with Dostoevsky—the child, the man, the poet, the victim, the one responsible for everyone's ruin (yet guiltless). Elegance and ungainliness. Everything, everything— Jesus Christ, in the most modern guise, in an elegant suit, closely cropped hair, dyed blond. And the face?

GORKY'S FIRST PLAY, *The Petty Bourgeoisie* (*Meshchanʹe*), had been neglected since its production by the MAT in 1901. The critical consensus was that it was an awkward and tendentious bit of apprentice work. Tovstonogov turned it into the longest-running play at the BDT to date.

> Georgy Tovstonogov, "On *The Petty Bourgeoisie*" (1966), in *O professii rezhissëra* [On the profession of director], reprinted in *Zerkalo stseny* [A mirror of the stage] (Leningrad: Iskusstvo, 1984), 1:136–48.

Paradoxical though it may seem, the impulse for new reflections on *The Petty Bourgeoisie* came to me from the theater of the absurd. It forced me to get concerned with the very problem of modern philistinism as the problem of a definite philosophy of life, and I began to look for a play in which this problem was expressed most fully and most intricately and in an artistic format familiar to me, in which it was presented full-length, so to speak. And as I thought about it, I suddenly rediscovered *The Petty Bourgeoisie* for myself. But the principles of the interpretation, the possibility of angling it to our own times arose unexpectedly. [...]

The principal interpretation of the work was for me imbedded in Nil's line that the Bessemenov family again, for the umpteenth time, "were playing out the dramatic scene from the eternal comedy titled 'Neither One Thing nor the Other.'"

To uncover the cycle of delusion into which these people had fallen and that rendered their very existence absurd was for me the most important thing in the work process. That is why the tragedy of their senseless floundering lies in the fact that most people are apt to yield to delusion, create these vicious circles for themselves, in which they flounder futilely, submit to fetishes they have dreamed up themselves. It is like hypnosis, or rather, self-hypnosis.

[...] The culminating development of this theme in the production became the scene in which Bessemenov begins to move the potted plants around, as a serious cry for help, a shout of "Police!" At the moment when he realizes that his own strength is not enough to keep the world of his own home from collapsing, when his family's internal conflict comes to a climax, he sedulously and pedantically moves the potted plants around, because everything has to stay in its place, the established order must prevail now and forever in everything. [...]

This world and its people were obsolete, psychologically and objectively—that comprises the revolutionary resonance of the play, and there is no need to bring onstage the singing of *The Marseillaise* to illustrate the idea of the coming revolution. Such emphatic and primitive symbolism is counterindicated in this play. For me, beyond the walls of the Bessemenov home there exists only a drunken working-class suburb and nothing more. From my point of view, *The Marseillaise* in the Bessemenov home can have only an ironic resonance. [...]

TOVSTONOGOV also cultivated modern playwrights, among them the prolific Leonid Genrikhovich Zorin (1924–), a favorite at the Sovremennik as well. His early works had been banned until *The Guests* (1953) benefited from Stalin's death to present a generational conflict; under Brezhnev, Zorin was subsidized by the KGB, a fact that was revealed only many years later.

Édvard Radzinsky, *Moya teatral'naya zhizn'* (Moscow: AST, 2007), 123–24.

At this time Goga the great was preparing one of his most brilliant productions. It was Leonid Zorin's *Roman Comedy,* where every word was directed at the national Caesars and the national empire.

After the dress rehearsal the discussion took place right there in the auditorium. The representatives of society discussed it. As was common then, these were people who had a superior understanding of art—the distinguished lathe operator from a factory and other experts plus the subservient critics and officials who ran art. And they annihilated the magnificent production and taught the first director in Europe how he ought to stage it. In short, it was suggested that Tovstonogov discard the production. So now he had two paths. The first was insane: to play Georgy Tovstonogov, godfather of the theatrical world of that time, and refuse. And the second was our own, the usual one, that is the reasonable one: to think of the future of his theater, that there was much that lay ahead, and to play another Tovstonogov—the laureate of the Lenin and State prizes. That is, to get on his knees to the authorities and discard the production.

And he discarded it.

SIBERIAN-BORN Aleksandr Valentinovich Vampilov (1937–72) had tremendous success with his comedies in the late 1960s, until his untimely death in a boating accident on Lake Baikal. *The Elder Son* (1967) enjoyed more than sixteen hundred performances throughout the USSR in 1974. The Chekhovian *Last Summer in Chulimsk* (1971) explored the frustrations of the inhabitants of a small Siberian town. Tovstonogov rehearsed it from September 24, 1973, to February 15, 1974.

Tovstonogov, "Address to the cast on Vampilov's last play," in *Zerkalo stseny*, 2:238–39.

September 24, 1973. We are starting to rehearse Aleksandr Vampilov's play *Last Summer at Chulimsk,* at a time when the author is no longer alive . . . This play turned out to be the last creative work of this gifted playwright and remarkable man, our comrade Sasha Vampilov. He was full of projects, wrote two plays and screenplays at the same time, but the play we are beginning today is his last . . .

We managed to make him happy in his lifetime—we were the first to stage his *Provincial Anecdotes.* Aleksandr Vampilov came to Leningrad, took part in the rehearsals, along with the theater created a new variant of the play, was at the opening, and experienced the joy of success. He acknowledged our production to be "his own," and our friendship was to continue for many years.

This time the author won't be around, he won't see the opening, our toughest, most well-meaning, most interested and subtle critic . . . He wanted to do something more in this play. In his letter of June 12, 1972, he wrote, "I send you the last page of *Chulimsk.* As a matter of fact, nothing has been changed, of course, it simply crossed my mind that the very, very end (the finale) might be more precise and more natural in form."

We didn't get that page . . . And no one can guess exactly what he wanted to do, because for all the simplicity and clarity of Aleksandr Vampilov's thought, like nobody else he was surprising in every dramatic twist and turn. This surprise factor in the face of irreproachable logic is another sign of a great talent, the trailblazer of new paths in art.

He was no older than thirty-five, but he knew life like a sage. And if we want our *Chulimsk* to be worthy of the memory of Aleksandr Vampilov, we have to accomplish an enormous task, plunging into life of a taiga settlement remote from us. And before we seek the universally human in the characters and clashes of people, we must sense their reality, their flesh and blood, their difference from all the other people on earth, their precise social and moral nature. Let's treat this modern play as if it were a classic, it deserves it.

Tovstonogov was a shrewd exploiter of young talent. He preferred actors who had not studied at GITIS or who had served their apprenticeships in the provinces. He spotted Mark Rozovsky as a talented product of the new studio movement, co-opted his project of dramatizing Tolstoy's *Kholstomer: Story of a Horse,* and, with the BDT's house designer Eduard Kochergin, turned it into a masterpiece.

Mark Rozovsky, "Work on the production," in *Delo o "konoradstve"* [A case of "horse theft"] (Moscow: Vagrius, 2006), 196–97.

The theatricality of *Kholstomer* had to be sought first of all in the elements of folk art. The genre of the parable is apposite, therefore the whole iconographic system of the production-to-be had to have roots in the most real folk theater.

A tragic enactment.

Defining *The Story of a Horse* as tragedy, we had to approach this play with all the measures present in tragedy. For instance, the role of the Chorus in some degree can be like the role of the Chorus with the Greeks—the theme of fate, the torments of the hero, catharsis must be present in the show! . . . However in no case must the tragic progress prevail over the natural truth taking place onstage—in that case it wouldn't be Tolstoy! . . . Our obligation is to do everything so that the spectator will feel, so to speak, the reverberation of tragedy, but to fall into the pseudo-emotional expression half-and-half with fake profundity means to exchange theatricality for theatricks, that is, to make the very thing that Tolstoy so hated. This danger is increased by the fact that the tragic quality cannot be *forgotten,* we have to try to find a symbol, but a symbol that breathes *life,* and not something abstract. [. . .]

The countenance of *Story of a Horse* is like a medieval mystery play. The task is to merge the elements of the fairground show booth, in which the "mystery play of a horse" is played out, with the psychological theater, which will result in the "mystery play" turning into "a story." Striving for clarity and transparency, we should not forfeit the complexity and refinement of the form we select. This form offers instantaneous transitions from the grotesque to the lived experience, from representation to the deepest reproduction of an inner life. [. . .]

Nikolay Zaytsev, "By theatrical means," *Neva* 11 (1976), reprinted in *Prem'ery Tovstonogova* [Tovstonogov's premieres], ed. E. Gorfunkel' (Moscow: Artist. Rezhissër. Teatr, 1994), 264–69.

In a surprising theatrical synthesis, visible, tangible metaphors and actor's psychologies, tragic feeling and almost vaudevillian pantomime, trenchant lyrics and soul-searing gypsy fiddles, spring up from a stylistically integrated production, whose main characters and choric herd constitute an organic ensemble.

The stage is draped in gray burlap, hung on blocks and pulleys. There are saddles, horse collars, harnesses. The grooms pour real oats into hollowed-out wooden troughs. A naturalistic environment for horses. A stable. But also an arena for joy and grief, a hippodrome of life and death. The universe itself. The gray burlap of the walls resembles the hide of an old gelding with swollen scabs and scars. It is streaked with the crimson color of wounds, when at the end Kholstomer is slaughtered.

[. . .] During the blackout, you hear the clattering of hooves and the neighing of galloping horses. And there they are, in the stable.

Center stage is E. Lebedev. Like the other actors, he is dressed in burlap. Only his "hide" is dappled. The actor is dragged away from the spectator, bows down, raises his tail (which so far he has been holding in his hand) behind his back, swishes it back and forth a bit, shudders the skin on his shoulder blades, as if shaking off bugs, and

10.1. Evgeny Lebedev as Kholstomer (Strider)
in *The Story of a Horse* by Mark Rozovsky,
from a story by Lev Tolstoy, directed by
Georgy Tovstonogov and designed by David
Borovsky, Leningrad BDT, 1975.

before us stands the old skewbald gelding. Kholstomer begins the tale of his destiny.

M. Rozovsky's adaptation is constructed so that the action is intermingled with the author's narrative, which is conducted by the characters themselves, speaking in the third person: "The skewbald gelding stood on his own..." [...]

G. Tovstonogov by his own admission has recourse here to a Brechtian mannerism: "This is Tolstoy hyphen Brecht, for I think that in Tolstoy's parable there is present what Brecht called 'the distancing effect.'"[14] [...]

The end brings us back to the beginning of the performance: the master leads the scab-covered gelding to slaughter. The knife blow—the blood of a crimson ribbon pours from his breast to the ground. Soaring above the beams, Kholstomer's soul literally lights up. As if all life flashed before him at that moment, finally bringing relief. Blackout... The spectators think that the show is over. But the lights come up, and E. Lebedev, already abandoning the image of Kholstomer, speaks Tolstoy's concluding words about what happened to the old gelding's hide. O. Basilashvili,[15] also "dropping" his stage image, speaks of the funeral of Prince Serpukhovsky. Unwinding the silk ribbon like a bright butterfly fluttering away again, the "double" ending may perhaps insist on its "artifice" or, on the contrary, its "lack of artifice." [...]

We have before us a tragedy of kindness—naive, deceived kindness. But also a

14 *Verfremdungseffekt*, Bertolt Brecht's version of the formalist literary theory of *ostranenie*, promoted by Viktor Shklovsky, in which a work is "made strange"; usually mistranslated as "alienation effect."

15 Oleg Valeriyanovich Basilashvili (1934–), actor, at the BDT from 1959, playing Andrey in *Three Sisters* and an infantile Khlestakov in *The Inspector General*. In *The Story of a Horse* he played the horse's owner, Prince Serpukhovsky.

passionate loathing of cruelty, evil, absence of spirituality. As well as the polyphonic liveliness, the contemporary keen emotional effect of high morality. In aggregate, the indivisibility of the themes is the strength of the production, a token of the rarity of its stylistic integrity. This is a clear and disarming testimony to the rich expressive possibilities of the modern theater, an art that both lives and brings to life.

Shvarts, *Dnevniki*, 189.

A conversation of G. A. [Tovstonogov] and R. Nikolaev.[16]

In veiled terms it was proposed that G. A. announce that he was about to leave. Nikolaev referred to Lenin's remark: "One mistake is a mistake, two mistakes is two mistakes, three mistakes is a policy."

"And you've made four: *Last Summer at Chulimsk, Energetic People, Three Sacks of Unsorted Wheat,*[17] *Story of a Horse.*"

(Incidentally—one of our happiest, most successful seasons!)

"Your plus—*Minutes of a Certain Meeting*[18]—is the exception. You yourself don't appreciate that production."

In a few days R. Nikolaev was removed from the Obkom and transferred to television.

G. A. remained at his post. What was going on?

WITH *Story of a Horse,* Tovstonogov had reached the pinnacle of his creative career and his influence within the profession. From this point on, he would be increasingly eclipsed by younger talents.

Lyubimov at the Taganka

The Moscow Theater of Drama and Comedy on Taganskaya Square was founded in 1946 and made no particular stir under the leadership of Aleksandr Plotnikov (1946–63). It became known affectionately as the Taganka after Yury Lyubimov took it over in 1964 (this became the theater's official name in 1989). He dismissed the existing staff, troupe, and repertoire and transferred his school production of *The Good Person of Sichuan* there, along with most of the graduating class, who became the core company. By posting in the lobby large portraits of Stanislavsky, Meyerhold, Vakhtangov, and Brecht, he emblazoned his artistic manifesto. His

16 Rostislav Vasil'evich Nikolaev in the early 1970s was chief of the Department of Culture in the Leningrad Regional Committee of the Communist Party and then demoted to chairman of the Leningrad Committee for Television and Radio.

17 *Énergichnye lyudi* (1974) by Vasily Makarovich Shukshin (1929–74) is a Gogolian indictment of Soviet society. *Tri meshka sornoj pshenitsy* (1974) by Vladimir Fëdorovich Tendryakov (1923–84) pits a collective farm leader against a corrupt bureaucrat.

18 *Protokol odnogo zasedaniya* (1976) by Aleksandr (Shunya) Isaakovich Gelman (1933–) is made up of arguments over returning a prize given in error to a work brigade.

commune was devoted to a more improvisational, rough-hewn, and confrontational style than the Soviet stage has been used to since the 1920s.

> Yury Lyubimov on *Ten Days That Shook the World* (1965). From *Rasskazy starogo trepacha* (Moscow: Novosti, 2001), 246–47.

I conceived the idea of staging a show based on John Reed's *Ten Days That Shook the World*.[19] There was a sort of obstinacy in this: the book, with which one could do nothing, is a kind of charade; there's no clear way to work with it. And the show has nothing in common with the book. The show is a series of attractions.

This show was a pure polemic against theatrical monotony. At that time the slogans went: here's your greatest theater in the world, the MAT, here's this model—and now, please, everybody dance to it. And I decided as a counterweight to show the whole range of the theatrical palette. Why precisely? The theater can be extremely variegated, because all the genres are in it: specialty acts [*khodoki*], there's the naturalistic theater, the clown show, the circus, the shadow theater, the hand puppet theater—so whatever inspired my imagination, I did. And, oddly enough, though at the time I hadn't staged a single opera, I intuitively worked along the same lines as operas do—that is, I rehearsed the episodes separately, and then put it together.

[...] In the lobby hung two ballot boxes: a red and a black: "Vote. If you liked it, 'yes,' if not, 'no.'" And most people, 90 percent, were positive, but at first we even copied out what was written on the negative tickets, because the abuse was appalling: "How can you! It's high time you were stopped, what is this—is this how you show the Revolution? When will the government finally deal with you? What kind of mockery is this? It's exasperating! A definite 'no' to such art! I'd close the theater. How disgraceful: where is the bright image of Vladimir Il'ich at the entrance to the theater? And what we saw next!" and so on. Or in lipstick on one ticket: "Abomination!"—some lady was indignant that it was a carnival atmosphere.

> Arthur Miller, "On the theater in Russia," © 1969 by Arthur Miller, from *The Theater Essays of Arthur Miller*, ed. Robert A. Martin (New York: Viking Press, 1978), 331–33. Used by permission of Viking Penguin, a division of Penguin Group (USA) Inc. Arthur Miller (1915–2005), American playwright, is best known for *Death of a Salesman* (1949) and *The Crucible* (1953), works which expatiate on crises of conscience and the stifling of human potential.

No one who goes to the theater in Russia can fail to be struck by the audience. It is not bored and it is not uncritical, but it is passionately open to what it has come to see. Outside on the street there are always dozens of people pleading with each arrival for an extra seat. Young people make up the majority of the audiences, and particularly if the production offers something new and contemporary there is almost an atmosphere of adoration in the house, and open gratitude to the author, the actors, the director. It is

---

19 *Ten Days That Shook the World* (1919) is the vivid reportage of the Russian Revolution written by the American radical John Reed (1887–1920).

as though there were still a sort of community in this country for the feeling transcends mere admiration for professionals doing their work well. It is as though art were a communal utterance, a kind of speech which everyone present is delivering together.

The earthiness, the bodiliness, so to speak, of Russian acting even extends into its stylizations. Yury Lyubimov's production of *Ten Days That Shook the World* in his Taganka Theater is a sort of visualization of the atmosphere of the Revolution, rather than a play. From time to time a white screen is lowered over the whole stage, and, lit from behind, it shows the silhouettes of the actors, the people of the city caught up in the chaos. The detail of each silhouette instantly conveys not only that one is a prostitute, another a bourgeois, another a worker, another an old querulous gentleman, but somehow their attitudes toward the Revolution, and the impression comes from body postures, particularly of gestures, the way a head is held or a finger points. And as the light is moved back and more distant from the actor, his silhouette grows on the screen, so that at the end the figures of the new Red Army men, the defenders of the Revolution, move like giants as tall as the proscenium, dominating the whole theater.

Much of the production is sheer choreography and neither better nor worse than its counterparts elsewhere, but is always some explosive conception which instantly speaks of this particular Russian genius for physicalizing. A young man is being held before a firing squad. He is let go to face his death. The rifles rise to sight him. There is no explosion of bullets, but the young man rises onto his toes, then comes down on his heels. Then he rises again, a little higher this time, and comes down harder. Now he jumps up a few inches off the floor and comes down; then he jumps up about a foot off the floor and comes down; now he is springing, higher and higher, his hands behind his back, until he is flying upward in a movement of both escape and pride, of death's agony and life's unbelievable end, until one imagines he will succeed in simply flying upward and away—and then he comes down and crumples to the earth, and no sound is heard.

David Borovsky on his work with Lyubimov. Quoted in Alma Law, "The trouble with Lyubimov," *American Theater* 2 (April 1985), 4–11. David L'vovich Borovsky (in full, Borovsky-Brodsky, 1934–2006) was the house designer at the Taganka, where he worked from 1968 to 1999; noted for his use of raw and untreated materials.

I try to find an object lying around under our feet and to translate it into a new meaning. The object is what it is, and yet it pulls along behind it a whole series of new meanings. [The harrow in *Wooden Horses*, 1974.][20] That's what seems to me most valuable in the theater, that this body of a machine abandoned somewhere suddenly turns into something symbolic through the strength of the audience's and the theater's imagination, and yet it doesn't lose its primary nature for man.

20 *Derevyanie koni* (1969), based on three stories by Fëdor Abramov, features two peasant women in a village seen at different periods in the Soviet era.

Yury Lyubimov, "The algebra of harmony: A meditation on theater aesthetics followed by a note on actors and the acting profession," trans. Aline B. Werth, *Cultures* 5, 2 (1978), 65–81.

Looking back over the first ten years of my work in the new theater, I see that it falls into three main stages.

The first stage was marked by the continuation of the Brecht–Vakhtangov line, with the production of *The Good Woman of Sichuan, Ten Days That Shook the World* (based on the book by John Reed), *Mother,* and *What Is to Be Done?*[21]—all of which reflect the Brechtian conception of the theater as I understand it, inspired by folk tradition, carnivals, life in the marketplace. This conception accounts for our frequent use of prose works in the theater, in addition to the fact that I consider that our prose and poetry are more interesting than our dramatic works. And also, prose, of course, gives me more opportunities for creating stage settings on a number of levels.

The second stage began when Andrey Voznesensky[22] and I set out to adapt his poems to the theater. We planned a special performance which we called "The Poet and the Theater": Voznesensky read his poems, and they were enacted on the stage. I wanted to bring the poet into our theater; although he was in no sense theatrical, and did not even like the theater. He simply used to say, "Here are some poems for you. Make what you like of them." And we made a poetry spectacle, which was later called *Antiworlds.* It is still being put on. It was the first of our series of poetry spectacles, to be followed by others: *The Fallen and the Living* (verses written by wartime poets), *Listen* (about the poet Mayakovsky), *Pugachёv* (based on Esenin's poem), and another presentation of works by Voznesensky titled *Protect Your Faces!*[23]

The last spectacle, *Protect Your Faces!,* is worth describing in greater detail. It was an experiment, based on the principle of open production, and it consisted of fragments, without any subject. Before the performance I warned the audience that what they were about to see was not really a performance but a public rehearsal, and that they must regard it as such. Naturally, our performance was in fact prepared beforehand, and it was only on exceptional occasions that I interrupted it to explain to the actors and the audience if a mistake had been made. We adopted this form of presentation to familiarize the audience with the creative preparatory work of the actors and show

---

21 Although Gorky's *Mat'* had often been dramatized, the adaptation by Lyubimov and Boris Glagolin 1969 was regarded by the authorities as insufficiently revolutionary. *Chto delat'?,* a turgid novel by Nikolay G. Chernyshevsky (1828–89), intellectual leader of radical Russian youth in the midnineteenth century who spent twenty years in Siberian exile, had been a major influence on Lenin. The Taganka adaptation 1969–70 put the characters in contact with the author's commentary.

22 Andrey Andreevich Voznesensky (1933–2010) was the most publicly confrontational poet of this period, who won worldwide fame from his platform performances. Khrushchёv deemed him a "pervert." *Antiworlds* (1965) was a collage of his poems.

23 *Pavshie i zhivye* (1966), a stage composition by D. S. Samoylov, B. T. Gribanov, and Yury Lyubimov. *Poslushayte!* (1967), a collage of Mayakovsky's poetry by Lyubimov and Valentin Smekhov, was the first Taganka production to antagonize the critical establishment. *Pugachёv,* Sergey A. Esenin's (1895–1925) play about the eighteenth-century peasant revolt, was banned until new interludes by Nikolay Érdman were removed. *Beregite vashi litsa . . .* (1970), another revue drawn from Voznesensky and Vysotsky, was removed after three performances.

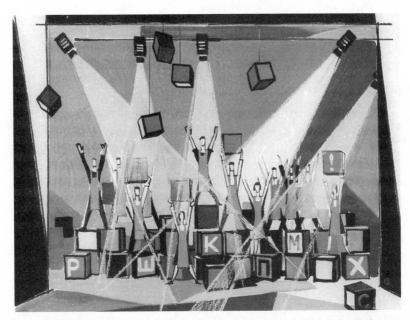

10.2. The design for the "Music and Light" episode in Mayakovsky's *Listen* by Éduard Stenberg, directed by Yury Lyubimov, Taganka Theater, Moscow, 1967.

them more clearly the purpose of our experiments. [...] During the performance, the lights were left on in the theater, and I gave directions as in a public rehearsal, sometimes even making the actors repeat the verses several times, explaining their mistakes. [...]

The third kind of show we put on comprised performances of the classics. These included, first and foremost, works of Molière, Shakespeare, and Ostrovsky, also of Gorky, Chernyshevsky, and Brecht. [...] We took three Ostrovsky plays—*Thunderstorm, The Marriage of Balzaminov,* and *No Fool Like a Wise Fool*—and mixed them up, like a layer cake. [...] The production was staged in the style of a benefit performance, juggling with historical fact and making the actors play their parts in the presence of the dramatist. [...] The actors play their parts, and Ostrovsky sits there on a chair in the center and makes his comments. Some he praises, to others he says "you've got the tone wrong" or "you're overacting." [...]

B. Mozhaev's[24] *Alive* at the Taganka (1968). Lyubimov, *Rasskazy starogo trepacha,* 266.

Mozhaev wrote his story "From the life of Fedor Kuz'kin" in 1964–65, and in 1967, it was printed in *Novy Mir,*[25] we turned it into a production, and they closed it on us.

24 Boris Andreevich Mozhaev (1926–93), naval officer, then prose and screenplay writer, whose works were rarely released for publication after 1974.
25 *Novy Mir* (*New World*), a mass-circulation Soviet periodical founded in 1925; in the 1950s and

They took me off the work. Then they reinstated me. It was spring 1968, during the events in Czechoslovakia.

Not long before the showing of *Alive,* we were received by Ekaterina Alekseevna Furtseva, minister of culture. She was not alone—together with some of her deputies. The discussion proved to be heated and thoroughgoing. Ultimately we succeeded in convincing her that the production should go on. She waved her hand: "Well, all right, rehearse. Work on it—we'll come and take a look." [...] It was like inviting all the mayors in Russia to judge Gogol's *Inspector General.*

> From L. V. Zotova, *Dnevnik teatral'nogo chinovnika 1966–1970* [Diary of a theatrical official] (Moscow: n.p., 2003), 154, 161. Lyudmila Vasil'evna Zotova, a graduate of GITIS, was assigned to be an inspector in the Theater Department of the Ministry of Culture 1964; from 1973 to 1988 she worked at Soyuzgoskontsert, planning theatrical tours abroad. She called herself "a cog in the bureaucratic machine."

June 28, 1968. I learned that in answer to Lyubimov's letter "to the higher-ups," a phone call ensued, which reversed the decision of the [Kirov] District Committee Office, and instead of the formulation "to reinforce the leadership of the theater," it was simply determined "to show" Lyubimov, and so they phoned him and said that he should go on working as before.

July 18, 1968. Kogan, the manager of the TYUZ, provided details about the Lyubimov affair. Allegedly Brezhnev's assistant phoned Lyubimov at home, Tselikovskaya[26] picked up, he asked her to put Lyubimov on, that all the questions about him have been removed, that the proper instructions have been given, and he called because Brezhnev would very much like to meet him, etc....

The other day the secretary of the Kirov District Committee was transferred to the general editorial board of television...

> Valery Zolotukhin, *Tagansky Dnevnik* [Taganka diary] (Moscow: OLMA-PRESS, Avantitul, 2002), 1:214–15. Valery Sergeevich Zolotukhin (1941–2013), actor at the Taganka from 1966 in sharply etched character roles and an indefatigable diarist, played Fëdor Kuz'kin in *Alive.*

March 3, 1969. At 1:00 p.m. the run-through of *Alive* began. Present were Boyadzhiev, Roshchin,[27] Ryzhnev, Dimka, and a few more theater people, also very intelligent. [...]

The run-through went sloppily, after a two-week interruption you start right in acting, forget bits, the performance is still not ironed out, etc.

1960s the editor, Aleksandr Tvardovsky, published a number of forbidden and controversial works by Solzhenitsyn and others.

26 Lyudmila Vasil'evna Tselikovskaya (1919–1992), an actress of great charm and humor, at the Vakhtangov Theater from 1942.

27 Mikhail Mikhailovich Roshchin (1933–2010), playwright, a favorite at the Sovremennik.

THE BOSS: Sloppy, it doesn't flow, it's fallen to pieces... You had good moments, but also... in general, I'm not very pleased with you today, there've been better rehearsals.

Voynovich[28] is completely excited, he doesn't remember anything like it in the last 25 years—the best production of all times and nations.

VOL'PIN:[29] Congratulations on the brilliant work, wonderful, delightful...

BOYADZHIEV: Let me kiss you... Congratulations, exceptional, magnificent. For a long time we've been discussing what to do so that the production will open, and this is what we've come up with. Two basic moments.

They must be made to watch, they might get upset and walk out, therefore one must tone down the beginning. So, let's assume, you haven't entered as an actor but as the Kuz'kin you've become by the end, i.e., leading a decent life, when he got kitted up in a new jacket, cap, etc .This removes the tension and underlines the point—this is how I live now, but I didn't achieve such a life all at once, but here it is now and I'll show you, etc. That's the first thing, the second—if Act I is a man falling under the wheel and pressured and poisoned, and for a wonder he survives, then the second-act Kuz'kin, not that far from being an oppressor himself, must make an active move to enter the fray, knowing that he is right and therefore will triumph.

As a critic, of course, I should not advise you, because I wholly and fully accept and understand that tragic intonation with which you fill the whole affair, but in appearance with a smile, a joke. But whatever you do, they may bury the production, and we have to come up with ways to save it. It is a huge victory for the Soviet theater and so on. Let me kiss you... [...]

RYZHNEV: Well, I've never seen anything like it in my life. I'm moved to my core. Good for you, but as a Party member I tell you—what are you doing, with this moaning and groaning? Do you realize what you're about, they'll give you what-for for this production, right away, on the spot.

As later developments revealed, he was closest of all to the truth.

Lyubimov, *Rasskazy starogo trepacha*, 266–67.

At the presentation of the production in April 1969, nobody showed up; instead Mozhaev and I were summoned to the Ministry of Culture. Furtseva did not receive us, but her deputies without beating around the bush explained to us that no one had authorized the production, so on what grounds were we proposing it? We reminded them about the previous meeting with the minister, at which our

28 Vladimir Nikolaevich Voynovich (1932–), dissident writer of satires and dystopian fiction, whose work remained unpublished; emigrated 1980 but returned ten years later.
29 Mikhail Davidovich Vol'pin (1902–88), author of screenplays and satiric verse, collaborator with Nikolay Érdman, V. Mass, and others; in a labor camp 1933–36; in the Song-and-Dance Ensemble of the NKVD 1941–46, with Lyubimov and Érdman.

interlocutors had been present. Right to our faces they said they didn't remember. [...] Suddenly the next morning a phone call to the theater: the minister is coming! Ekaterina Alekseevna showed up, her Persian lamb cape draped from her shoulders, with a retinue of thirty-four persons. Everyone was turned out of the auditorium, so a mouse couldn't creep in.

At the run-through they did not allow either the designer, David Borovsky, or the composer, Édison Denisov,[30] to attend. As it happened, Voznesensky sneaked in. There sat the minister's deputy, Vladykin, and somebody else. There was also the young official Chausov.[31] And esteemed Ekaterina Alekseevna sat there.

For our side, there were seated the manager of the theater, Dupak, the partorg, Glagolin,[32] the author, and myself.

Zolotukhin, Tagansky dnevnik, 1:215–19.

March 6, 1969. [Lyubimov:] "Don't expect any reaction, I'm warning you—you'll perform as if to an empty house. This doesn't matter, let's keep ourselves in check, act for yourself, an ordinary rehearsal, act to your own satisfaction, catch fire from your partners, as if there's a fourth wall—for once there will be one today."

"Well, they're not living people, if somehow, somewhere we can't get through to them."

"Don't count on it and don't flatter yourself, trust my experience. Look at me sometimes. I'll use my hand to show where you should heighten the rhythm, speed it up, the way I look should let you figure out how it's going. Well, God help you!" [...]

[Furtseva after Act I:] "Author! Do you like it?"

"Yes, quite a lot."

"Call the party secretary of the organization."

... And then it began. This is an outrage, this is unheard-of effrontery. No, it's not audacity, it's anti-Soviet, it's not even covert. [She's having hysterics...]

Vladykin with hysteria in his voice: "We have for a long time coddled Comrade Lyubimov, we tried in every way to help him, we supervise in a good way, we advise, we request, nothing works—Com. Lyubimov stubbornly goes his own way, a disreputable way of oppositional theater. What are you fighting against, Com. Lyubimov? You have fostered an apolitical collective and no one will forgive you for that. Today's performance is the apotheosis of all these harmful tendencies, which Com. Lyubimov sticks to in his creative work. This is a harmful performance in every sense—anti-Soviet, anti-Party."

MOZHAEV: That's your opinion.

VLADYKIN: Yes, it is mine.

30 Édison Vasil'evich Denisov (1929–96), composer, strongly influenced by European music; black-listed 1971, moved to Paris.
31 Mikhail Chausov, graduate of GITIS and subaltern at the Ministry of Culture.
32 Nikolay Luk'yanovich Dupak, administrator of the Taganka 1963–77, 1978–90. Boris A. Glagolin, director at the Taganka, secretary of the Party office.

MOZHAEV: And my opinion is opposed to yours, so let's arbitrate.

FURTSEVA: I came, word of honor, with good intentions. I wanted somehow to help, to reconcile everyone somehow... But no, I see nothing will come of it! You are absolutely out of agreement with everything and completely reject our words.

She kept addressing Mozhaev as "my dear" and Lyubimov as "dear comrade."

FURTSEVA (*to Mozhaev*): My dear! You have still done nothing in literature or in art or in theater, you have still done nothing to behave properly.

LYUBIMOV: Why do you say that, this is a respected writer, one of our favorites, one person may like this, another one that, why do you speak so groundlessly against one of our best writers?

MOZHAEV: E. A.! I write a comedy, it's a condition of the genre that repulsive characters be caricatured, mocked. They are written that way, they are played that way. If this were a drama or something else, this would be a different discussion. But I'm a writer, I write a comedy about a bad kolkhoz... we have to ridicule our defects, uproot them and eradicate them... The performance supports those people who put together and led the March plenum.[33] It changed a great deal in the life of our peasants and kolkhozniks.

FURTSEVA: How is this a comedy, it's the most genuine tragedy! After this people will go out and say—What's going on here, have we really spilled blood for such a life, a revolution, built kolkhozes which you here subject to such ridicule? A great deal is hidden and understood behind this. And these kolkhozes have stood the test of time, have withstood the war, collapse... The brigadier is a drunk, the chairman is a drunk, a drunken chairman, the head of the district committee regiment is a skunk.

MOZHAEV: How is he a skunk?

FURTSEVA: What else, they called him that on the phone—you figure it out. What right does he have, being on Party work, to treat people so inattentively... Lots of times I've been on Party work and I know that Party work demands efficiency of all one's heart for the people.

    —You were a good worker, but this is another kind of worker...

MOZHAEV: Well, fine, the chairman bothers you, and Kuz'kin doesn't bother you?

FURTSEVA: No.

MOZHAEV: Then what's the problem? He's my main hero, all the ideas are in him, all the meaning—Kuz'kin triumphs, a simple peasant, his truth triumphs. If the negative characters had triumphed, it would have been a tragedy. The Party is on Kuz'kin's side, it turned to another basis the life of the peasant in our collective.

SOMEBODY: The performance is set up so that it is not the Party that helps Kuz'kin; not its measures, but his own resourcefulness and chance...

FURTSEVA: One good man in the whole production—and everyone beats him, poisons him, so you feel sorry for him and sympathize with him in every way.

---

33 In March 1965 a special Central Committee Plenum on agriculture, convened by Brezhnev, dismantled many of Khrushchëv's reforms and declared that plan fulfillment was more important than and incompatible with the shift to the production principle.

MOZHAEV: That's correct. This is the author's concept, with whom else would you sympathize—Motyakov or who?

FURTSEVA: And what do you say about the 1930s? The 1930s—industrialization, collectivization, and you talk about them with such taunts. No! This show will not go on, it is very harmful, an inaccurate show. And you (Lyubimov), dear comrade, give some thought to where you're leading your collective.

LYUBIMOV: You don't have to scare me. It's not the first time you've removed me from work, don't worry about me—I'll find work. [...]

FURTSEVA: I give you my word, wherever you turn, right up to the highest levels, you will find support nowhere, it will only be worse—I assure you.

LYUBIMOV: Respected persons, academicians have seen this. Kapitsa[34]...they have a different opinion, they fully accepted the show as a Soviet, Party, deeply artistic show.

FURTSEVA: Academicians are not responsible for art, I am. Let academicians answer for their own work, they have authority in their own spheres. Comrades! There may be another opinion about the show, maybe somebody liked the show?

Pause. A timid voice from the house. "I liked it."

"Who is that? Ah, Voznesensky, well, that stands to reason."

They did not give the floor to Andrey. Mozhaev became indignant.

"Among other things, he's the best Soviet poet. Why can Com. Zashkiver speak, have an opinion of his own, while Voznesensky can't? What is this—stand at attention all around?

VOZNESENSKY: I watched the rehearsals of this show four times. I considered that is a deeply Russian—national production. Wonderfully poetic in all its elements and deeply Party. It shows wonderfully triumphantly and optimistically that the Russian people are alive and will never fail, no matter what the bureaucrats do to them.

FURTSEVA: Thank you, as if we thought the Russian people would fail. Thank you for your belief in the Russian people. (To Mozhaev.) Don't think that you're such a fighter for truth—"a man of the 'sixties."[35]

VLADYKIN: What I saw today is vulgarity, political vulgarity. [...]

Mishka Chausov was there, blathered something about Belorussia[36]... as if he were rattling off a machine-gun belt of cartridges. [...]

Lyubimov, *Rasskazy starogo trepacha*, 269–72.

"Ekaterina Alekseevna, may I speak from the heart?"

She said, "Speak, as the voice of youth."

He says to her:

34 Sergey Petrovich Kapitsa (1928–2012), physicist and mathematician, son of the academician Pëtr Leonidovich Kapitsa.
35 A historical reference to the Narodniki or "People's Party" of the 1860s and 1870s, which traveled the countryside, introducing the peasants to literacy.
36 Furtseva was a Belorussian.

"Ekaterina Alekseevna, what is this stuff they dare to show us! This is like serfdom! You can't keep your temper!"

She says to him:

"Yes, speak, speak out boldly."

And then he got more and more excited, but then Mozhaev stepped in. He walked over to the aisle and said to Chausov:

"Sit down!"

He sat. And Mozhaev wagged his finger at him:

"Ay-yay-yay-yay-yay, young man, ay-yay-yay, so young and already behaving like a wretched careerist. What will become of you?" And to the minister: "Aren't you ashamed to instruct a person, to train a person like this?"

They were stunned, while he walked around and read them a lecture about the state of affairs and how they allow themselves to talk to us that way. He became enraged and turned bright red. He went off on a whole harangue.

They accidentally forgot to turn off the Tannoy, and the whole theater heard this fulmination.

Then Ekaterina Alekseevna recovered and said to Mozhaev, "Fine, we know all about you too, sit down."

And then she turned to me:

"What can you say to all of this? What do you think: they're stringing up *Novy Mir* from a sour-apple tree and you want to make tracks away from it?"

And I didn't think, and my tongue ran away with me:

"And do you think you're getting all that far from your *October*?"

And then she shut up. She didn't understand that I was thinking of the magazine *October*, run by Kochetov.[37] Because there was a rivalry between Tvardovsky's *Novy Mir* and Kochetov's *October*. But she figured I was referring to the October Revolution. And she went berserk:

"Ah, that's what you're like . . . I am going straight to the general secretary and informing him of your behavior. So this is how things are . . . this is how far you let things go . . ."

And she ran off . . . The lovely big Persian lamb cape had fallen from her shoulders. Someone picked it up, and it vanished . . .

And with him disappeared the production of *Alive*.

For this "slanderous" production they removed me from work and expelled me from the Party. And then I wrote a letter to Brezhnev. And he was merciful and said, "Let him work." In a couple of weeks they let me back into the Party: "Well, Yury Petrovich, well, we got a bit worked up, you'll forgive us . . ."

---

37 Vsevolod Anisimovich Kochetov (1912–73), dogmatic Party officer and socialist realist novelist; editor *Literaturnaya gazeta* 1955–59, *Oktyabr* from 1961.

NEVERTHELESS, *Alive* was not licensed for performance, and Lyubimov was still trying to bring it before the public when he was dismissed and his citizenship was revoked in 1984.

Hamlet at the Taganka (1971). Lyubimov, *Rasskazy starogo trepacha*, 294–96.

Reasoning and thinking about *Hamlet* and talking a great deal with Vladimir [Vysotsky],[38] I realized I had to get him to go more deeply into the role, because at first he really didn't understand the whole Christian line, that Hamlet is the first real intellectual. [...] There is no other play of Shakespeare's in which religion has such an influence on the development. There isn't a scene without talk about faith. [...]

The curtain was conceived of before the rehearsals. It looked enormous, although it was nine by five and a half meters. The Taganka is a small theater. It is very multipurpose: simply a stage curtain—that's how it started—it stood to one side, because Hamlet was sitting by the wall, and they were all exiting with mourning bands: as if just after the death of his father. Then it moved forward, separating Vysotsky and the downstage coffin from everyone else. There stood a big broadsword, on which they swore later on. And Vysotsky sang a verse of Pasternak's: "The din's died down, I've come out on the boards..." But most important to me were the lines, "I fish in a distant echo for what happens in my time."

Then there was powerful tragic music, the curtain moved to the back wall. And the King's speech from the throne began, as if on Red Square—the curtain moved forward. "Although of our dear brother's death the memory" is a speech from the throne to the whole square. Then, slowly, slowly, afterward the curtain was raised by all the participants in the performance, the royal couple came out, and Hamlet was on one side. Then the King dismissed everyone with a bow, swords slid out of the curtain, and they sat in the curtain on swords, while Hamlet sat on the old coffin, on the old planks of the coffin. The planks were so old, old, as when they demolish a building. And the grave was fortified with planks, to keep it from caving in, the way gravediggers arrange things. Then a very old tree was made ornamental, as in Tudor houses. And across the whole wall, on the back wall went an enormous—cross. Across the whole wall and through the center. And Hamlet began his dialogue with the King—the first scene.

Vadim Gaevsky, "Hamlet's recorder," in *Pravda teatra* [The truth of the theater] (Tbilisi, 1980), reprinted in *Fleyta Gamleta* (Moscow: Soyuzteatr, 1990), 120–21.

Vysotsky's voice as instrument: he sets the tone of the performance. He has the aggressive and defenseless tone of reality. And he has an overtone—of unheard, unusual fate. This is Shakespeare, made comprehensible and intimate—and at the same time mysterious, inscrutable Shakespeare. Vysotsky's role comprehends the inner motifs

---

38 Vladimir Semënovich Vysotsky (1938–80), actor and singer-songwriter, prominent at the Taganka; his protest songs, sung to his own guitar accompaniment, circulated widely on cassette tapes.

10.3. Vladimir Vysotsky as Hamlet, Taganka Theater, Moscow, 1972. Photo: Vladimir Plotnikov.

and secret, inner light. "I am alone, all sink into Pharisees," he sings in the despair of Pasternak's verses. And he ends calmly and sorrowfully, "To live a life is not to cross a meadow." "To live a life" in Elsinore means living along a dangerous line: here it is easy to let yourself be killed, even easier to become a murderer yourself. The role is exceptionally dramatic, because Vysotsky's Hamlet is a very young Hamlet. Paul Scofield's Hamlet is a youth with an old man's wrinkles on his face. Vysotsky's Hamlet is a youth without a single wrinkle. The production catches him unawares with a guitar in hand, on the threshold of careless years, away from great tragic fates. Vysotsky plays a youth at war, the drama of youth made a sacrificial victim. This charming young man is created for song and love but has to repel and bear blows. Mortal blows he receives from his nearest and dearest, and he smites his nearest and dearest indiscriminately. What sinister demon possesses his musical soul? The destiny of ancient tragedy? The evil of Shakespearean or romantic drama? The aggressive will of modern sociopsychological plays? None of the above. Vysotsky's Hamlet is not a fatalistic hero, nor a villain nor a superman. This youth is in the mousetrap. After blind outbursts of enraged passion he does not want to live, in his hoarse fury and in his silent grief he is disarmingly human. The better, the more tragically the actor acts, the less he is like a tragedian of ancient or modernist style. Theatrical and literary types fail to understand this. However, in the mousetrap into which Hamlet has fallen, productions are not staged and books are not written.

The choice of Vysotsky for the role of Hamlet is a happy and pointed choice. His past roles—rebellious and scandalous—shed an extra light around him. Hamlet in the

Taganka production is Hamlet defamed. He is surrounded not only by treachery but by vicious gossip. He cannot count on being understood or on solidarity. [...] At the Taganka Elsinore is not a prison so much as a reform school. [...] Vysotsky's voice is the indomitable voice of a street singer. And his soul is the almost convulsively tense soul of a poet. Vysotsky recites verse as if he were standing on the brink of an abyss. He throws his head back, he seems to fall. Vysotsky plays the expiring energy of the soul that has leaped up with wonderful strength and is just on the point of falling head over heels. [...]

> Alla Demidova, *Dnevnik*. In *Zapolnyaya pausu* [Filling the gap] (Moscow: AST, 2007), 25–34. Alla Sergeevna Demidova (1936–), a student of Lyubimov with an electrifying stage presence, was leading actress at the Taganka from 1964. She played Gertrude in *Hamlet*. Later worked with Anatoly Vasil'ev and Roman Viktyuk, and created Theater A 1993.

1974.

March 19. Hamlet. It went horribly. I don't like it when Vysotsky is in such a happy-go-lucky mood—it doesn't come out a tragedy.

April 18 ... Hamlet went vilely. Lots of clinkers. The curtain just barely crawled along and is warped into the bargain. We're afraid that it will collapse again. The rhythms were jagged, especially in "To be or not to be." Volodya was nervous, acted "from a position of strength"—which I like least of all in him—aggression. Everyone acted as if in cotton wool. The audience shouted "bravo" ...

June 13 ... At night *Hamlet*—our scene—went well. Vysotsky after his time abroad for the last few days has been living a different rhythm. Obviously, a different track to our life.

October 8 ... In the morning rehearse *Hamlet*. Renovation for the new stage.[39] We rehearse in basic light with the curtain, as the most important thing. ...

October 9 ... In the morning another rehearsal of *Hamlet*. The curtain jams—at night we were in torment. A tiff with Vysotsky. It was spoken of at the evening show. I am playing pretty-pretty, especially in the first act. I have to be more concerned about my son. How we all are tied together in our relations!

October 26. Hamlet. Vysotsky and I try to change the pacing. It doesn't work. I had had a haircut, played with short hair—it gets in the way, then I had to change the whole design of the role ...

November 30. Hamlet. We played well. Before the second act—we didn't start for a long time, Vysotsky and I sat on his grave, talked about death, about what is to come—afterward. He said he'd write a song about it.

1975.

[Anatoly Éfros had been invited from the Malaya Bronnaya to stage *The Cherry Orchard*.]

---

39 In 1972 a new building for the Taganka was planned at the corner of Garden Ring and Upper Radishchev Street; it was not open for performances until 1983.

May 26 ... Vysotsky arrived. With a beard, he said he'd grown it especially for Lopakhin.

May 28 ... Vysotsky shaved off his beard—Éfros had suggested it. Rehearsal of *Cherry Orchard.* Vysotsky immediately joined in.

June 6 ... Rehearsal of *Cherry Orchard.* I was staggered by Vysotsky: he learns his lines quickly and grasps the staging ...

June 12. Rehearse *Orchard.* Vysotsky quickly picks things up, plays the beginning well—worried and quick. After this I run in—a feverish rhythm with no empty movement. At night the 600th *Antiworlds.* Voznesensky recited after we finished.

June 19. Ran through *Cherry Orchard* for Lyubimov. Lyubimov watched with his face half turned away and ill-disposed, for everything annoyed him. So, of course, this made us play repulsively. At night *Wooden Horses.* Lyubimov came backstage, asked me why I play Ranevskaya so young, after all she's an old bag. I reply that Ranevskaya is obviously only thirty-seven or thirty-eight (her oldest daughter is seventeen). He was surprised, had probably never thought about it. He asked why things were so listless in all the rhythms—I started to explain something, he interrupted and started to talk about Chekhov, but actually about something else ...

June 26 ... Rehearse *Orchard* stop-and-start ... Then we ran through two acts. Élem Klimov[40] was there—he was bored by it. Obviously, he, like Lyubimov, doesn't accept this kind of Chekhov. Éfros's notes are wonderfully subtle and to the point. Many people don't accept his design, maybe they can't manage it. Our talk about this afterward—he said that he used to try to get out of the actors what he saw and wanted, but with time he understood—an actor cannot jump higher than his own capacities, and here for him what matter most in the production are Vysotsky, Zolotukhin, etc.

June 27. Run through *Cherry Orchard.* Instead of Vysotsky, Shapovalov.[41] Very difficult ... Sluggish rhythms. I fuss around on this background. Without Vysotsky I'm losing it. An observation. The dispute of Éfros–Lyubimov (Chekhov–Tolstoy). A beautiful speech by Éfros about Chekhov the intellectual. Lyubimov was annoyed but restrained himself. Of course they're incompatible ...

June 28. Run through of *Cherry Orchard* for the artistic council. They didn't understand any of it. They came out against it. Lots of protestations of loyalty to Lyubimov ...

July 6. Opening night of *Cherry Orchard.* It went well, to my mind. Lots of flowers. Éfros was excited behind the scenes. After Lopakhin-Vysotsky's monologue ("I bought it")—applause, after my scream—also. Banquet. Lyubimov wasn't there. Conflict.

October 31 ... A night rehearsal of *Cherry Orchard*—before the season begins. Half the actors aren't there. Vysotsky still hasn't returned, and Shapovalov didn't show up. Éfros was downcast. He's thinking of transferring the production to his own stage with his own actors.

---

40 Élem Germanovich Klimov (1933–2003), film director, whose work was usually sidelined or banned by the authorities.

41 Vitaly Vladimirovich Shapovalov (1939–), actor at the Taganka from 1968, playing Mayakovsky, Pugachëv, Rybin in *Mother,* and Pilate in *Master and Margarita*; moved to the Sovremennik 1985–87, before returning to the Taganka to appear in *Alive* and *Vladimir Vysotsky.*

10.4. Setting for Chekhov's *The Cherry Orchard* designed by Valery Levental', directed by Anatoly Éfros at the Taganka Theater, Moscow, 1975.

November 3. In the morning a rehearsal of *Hamlet.* Lyubimov clearly doesn't like our *Cherry Orchard*—he constantly talks about it in place and out of place. At night *Hamlet.* Vysotsky acts "full steam ahead," not looking at anybody. Very aggressive. I think he's stopped heavy drinking again.

November 4 . . . Tonight a run through of *Cherry Orchard.* I was late. Everyone was waiting for me. Éfros said nothing. The first act was good, the second act very bad: I don't know how to speak the monologue about "sins." Vysotsky listens badly, plays "superman." Dreadful! Third act average, we were indicating, fourth not so bad. I have to be calm.

December 23 . . . At night *Cherry Orchard*—instead of *Fasten Your Seatbelts.*[42] The audience was the usual. Various reactions . . . Now the performance goes worse. I play the first act badly, it is unclear to me. The relationships are fuzzy, Ranevskaya's "illness" is forced. Vysotsky has started to play the beginning quietly, obviously he has decided to go contrary to my heightened rhythm; and you can't have that in this production; we all act alone, bound by "a single rope." I'll try and talk it over with him . . .

Alla Demidova, "Rehearsing *Cherry Orchard*," in *Teatr Anatoliya Éfrosa. Vospominaniya, stat'i* (Moscow: Artist, Rezhissër, Teatr, 2000), 108.

42 *Pristegnite remni (Chetyre minuty v éfir,* 1975), a political satire by Georgy Baklanov and Lyubimov.

Lopakhin's monologue in Act III, "I bought it . . . ," was played by Vysotsky at the highest tragic level of his best songs. From him this monologue was a song. And sometimes he even almost sang some of the words: he'd draw out and draw out his consonants in a wheeze, and then all of a sudden snap sharply. And how frenzied was his dancing in that monologue! How he leaped up at a branch of flowering cherry, trying to break it off, on the forestage! He didn't go down on his knees in front of Ranevskaya—he actually seemed to dance on them in front of her and immediately changed the tone when he addressed her. For a moment he sobered up. Immeasurable tenderness: "Why, oh why didn't you listen to me? . . ." About five times in the course of his monologue Varya threw her keys at his feet, before he noticed them, and once he'd noticed—carelessly, as if it were unimportant, as if it were perfectly natural: "She threw away the keys, wants to show she's not in charge here any more . . ." And again with an eruption: "Well never mind . . . Music, play . . . Music, play so I can hear you!" Lopakhin's love for Ranevskaya is tormented, self-flagellating. An absolutely Russian phenomenon. After all, we have no tradition of troubadours, chivalric love, Russian literature knew no loves of Tristan and Isolde, Romeo and Juliet. Our love is always an eruption, a torment, a suffering. In the love of Lopakhin, as Vysotsky played him, it was also all tortured, benighted. He wasn't understood, he wasn't accepted, and in reaction—riot, suffering, ruin. There can be no middle ground. [. . .]

Master and Margarita at the Taganka (1977). Lyubimov, *Rasskazy starogo trepacha*, 304–7.

I wanted to do something interesting for the tenth anniversary of the theater. And I believed that the most interesting thing for me and the theater would be to put on *Master*. [. . .] The conviction arose in me that I had to combine the best the theater had done in the way of progress, the theater's aesthetics and manners. And I took the things dearest to me from those years—the *Hamlet* curtain, the Molière picture frame[43]—but the reason I took them was because I thought: in the frame I'll place Pilate—Rome, gold, the Caesars, the procurator will sit there through the whole show. From the Soviet era, a small tribune on the left, on which Berlioz will exercise, speechify out of *Alive*, cubes out of *Mayakovsky* for Woland to sit on—well, as it happened, over the course of time they were cut. The only thing left was that cross, crucifix, which had been in *Hamlet*. [. . .]

I wanted it for the tenth anniversary of the theater, but they wouldn't permit it. I only managed to get it on for the thirteenth anniversary of the theater—April 23. [. . .]

It was Simonov and the commission that passed this show, I think Kaverin[44] was in on it too—I've forgotten, a very authoritative commission on the creative heritage of Mikhail Afanas'evich [Bulgakov] helped me a lot, because they acknowledged that the

43 Molière's comedy of religious hypocrisy *Tartuffe* (1971) was one of Lyubimov's few productions of a classic play; the characters entered through life-sized portrait frames.
44 Veniamin Aleksandrovich Kaverin (actually Zil'ber, 1902–89), satirical playwright, whose *Two Captains* (1948) became the basis for the rock musical *The "Juno" and the "Avos."*

10.5. Yury Lyubimov (seated) in rehearsal at the Taganka with Dmitry Pokrovsky; Nikolay Gubenko stands between them. Photo: B. Kremer.

staging was well done and it appeared as a kind of document of the struggle with the authorities. This was their official report on the staging. Positive. But cautious, with a knowledge of how things are done, etc., etc. And this forestalled the authorities, who, of course, didn't want to license it. But it seemed to the commission that the epilogue was unnecessary. My third act wasn't really a third act. It was, rather, a short, twenty-five-minute epilogue. A denouement. And it ended: "Manuscripts don't burn"—the scene in which Woland reads his novel and there's a Prokof'ev march. And both the committee that passed it, I remember, and the heritage committee, they both agreed that "manuscripts don't burn" was beautiful. But because somewhere inside me I was protesting that they do burn, unfortunately, they still do burn, I did not agree and stubbornly played the whole finale. But I think I was right, because a finale like that flowed from the whole concept.

Éfros

Anatoly Éfros had been working with Mariya Knebel' at the Central Children's Theater, developing a version of Stanislavsky's system based on improvisation and motivational truth. In 1964 he was appointed director at the Moscow Lenin Komsomol Theater, which, after Bersenev's death in 1951, had passed from hand to hand with no clear direction.

Viktor Rozov, "A producer after my own heart," trans. Melinda Maclean, *Soviet Literature* 9 (1977), 57, 59.

Every talented artist becomes a creator only when he breaks away from established, traditional standards in art and makes a step forward, creates something new. And

Éfros did exactly that when he put on Aleksander Khmelik's wonderful play *My Friend Kol'ka*.[45] What a fascinating play it was! It aroused the noblest feelings in everyone who saw it, young people and grown-ups alike, filling them with an implacable hatred for everything bad. And isn't that the main and only meaning of our work, if one looks at it from the educational point of view: to stimulate noble feelings and suppress base ones? [...]

Éfros did away with the room walls used in his previous productions of my plays and others too. The stage set was a spacious school yard with a place for games in it. And everything that was necessary during the course of the play—a classroom, a Young Pioneers' room—appeared with the help of almost symbolic partitions. In his previous works Éfros had won recognition, but in *Kol'ka* he found freedom, he discovered himself. [...] The years of apprenticeship were over and the years of exploring began. Later Éfros was to free himself of many things. And in the play *The Outsider* by Ignaty Dvoretsky,[46] there would be not only no walls on the stage but nothing except chairs and table—bare side curtains and the harsh, unmasked top lighting that is lowered down. There's nothing, only actors. And the performance is powerful and intelligent, also magnetic, united from within.

Antonina Dmitrieva,[47] "On Éfros," unpublished interview with Dina Goder, typescript, 1–4, 7.

On the whole I think the period at the TsDT [Central Children's Theater] was remarkable, bright, and for him as well. For we were all young and he was young. At night we'd get together and rehearse *Romeo and Juliet,* playing all the roles in succession. For instance, I overacted just about everyone, including both Juliet and Romeo. Some scene would be selected and he would ask, "Who wants to play Tybalt?" Of course, I would shout, "I do, I do!" There was an unbelievable sense of improvisational work at the TsDT—they even came to us from other theaters: Vitaly Solomin and Borya Shchedrin,[48] lots of folks ran to us. They were all young, students. We worked a lot, three performances a day—not like now. And all the same we rehearsed at night. It didn't matter. Because there was the happiness of creativity. [...]

And then came the Lenkom.

[...] At the Lenkom he had already departed from the improvisational method

---

45 Aleksandr Grigor'evich Khmelik (1925–2001). *Drug Moy Kol'ka* was about a group of bored children who reform their Pioneer group; made into a popular film in 1961.

46 Ignaty (Izrail) Moiseevich Dvoretsky (1919–87), a former lumberjack, whose plays raise moral issues; chairman of the playwriting section of the Leningrad Writer's Union in the 1970s, he was instrumental in exposing the inhuman conditions of the Stalinist labor camps.

47 Antonina Ivanovna Dmitrieva (1929–99), studied at the Shchukin School and acted at the Central Children's Theater; with the Lenin Komsomol 1966–67 and the Malaya Bronnaya from 1967.

48 Vitaly Mefod'evich Solomin (1941–2002), actor, director, who served at the Maly from 1963, playing "positive" heroes and character parts; at the Mossovet 1986–89, returning to the Maly. Boris Efimovich Shchedrin (1939–), director at the Mossovet from 1968; introduced the Russian audience to García Lorca.

and began "to stage a production." He had already staged both *The Seagull* and *Molière* quite differently. And when we chided him, I even said, "Anatoly Vasil'evich, remember how well we used to work..." And he was annoyed. He considered this to have been apprenticeship and wanted to work as a stage director. He came to the start of the work with an already prepared concept and did not develop it in work with us. And when I would chide him, he would say: "Tonya, I was fooling you all. I only pretended that you were also creating something and working—it was a cheat." And I would say to him, "Cheat me some more, Anatoly Vasil'evich!" But he never returned to the improvisational method. All this happened so abruptly.

I felt very bad about such an abrupt demolition of his method of work. Perhaps this is what spoiled our relationship. In *Seagull* I played Masha, and I remember how he came onstage and showed me—before, he never let himself do that. I was supposed to repeat his intonations, and if I didn't, he was dissatisfied. At one moment he even wanted to take the role away from me. [...] Whether he was in a hurry or had become bored with educational methods I don't know. It seems to me that he had already thought everything out, and now we only had to carry it out. On the whole, once he had opened a production, he threw it away. Like a doll. He never looked at his productions. Even if there were insertions or we played in a different, unsuitable space. [...]

I go to the MAT to see *Uncle Vanya*—and the moon rises, cocks crow, clouds sail by, and a Russian folksong resounds somewhere, but there is no atmosphere at all. Éfros knew how to create an atmosphere not for the eyes—a designer would make sketches for him—but through the actor. He enters and the rhythm of the scene and all that, the way it's built, and lots more. [...] He tuned the actors up to the right intonation. That's why he didn't like insertions—even to the point of canceling a production. A foreign body had entered, destroying the atmosphere. [...]

Radzinsky, *Moya teatral'naya zhizn'*, 78, 99–100.

[Aleksandr Shirvindt[49] in *22 to You, Old Men!*] In his role there was an uncomplicated preamble to an anecdote: "There are these tomatoes..." He scattered this preamble throughout the script. But before every repetition he would fall into thought, stare into the audience with a hypnotic gaze and after this philosophical musing changed "tomatoes" to something like, "There are these cucumbers..." And for some reason the audience began to laugh. Before every new preamble his cogitation in search of a new fruit or vegetable increased... There were cornichons, dates, pomegranates... He was recherché. He had barely to open his mouth and the audience was already roaring with laughter... And when, on his way offstage, he suddenly turned around and said, "There are these..." and stopped in his long, agonizing musing, a sort of insane laugh rocked the house. But he maintained the agonizing pause of meditation. And

---

49 Aleksandr Anatol'evich Shirvindt (1934–), comic actor and cabaret artist, at the Lenin Komsomol 1957–66 and briefly at the Malaya Bronnaya 1967–70, before entering the Moscow Satire Theater, becoming its artistic director in 2000.

finally he quite elegaically ended by saying, "... bush pumpkins." The house burst into hysterical laughter. [...]

For this production the Lenin Komsomol Theater was (a rare occurrence at the time) full.

[...]

I brought the play [*104 Pages about Love*] to the Lenin Komsomol Theater. The manager read it with a kindly smile...The smile meant: you want us to be hauled before the ideological commission again, but I don't!

And it probably would have ended there, if only...If only at that time Anatoly Vasil'evich Éfros hadn't been assigned to the theater as director in chief. He had a quirk, which at that time was odd, even wild. If he read a play and liked it, he immediately started to rehearse it. He didn't care in the least about what was considered to be the most important thing—whether it would be permitted. [...]

In the role of *She*, after many doubts of mine and his, Éfros cast Ol'ga Yakovleva.[50] He was far from convinced, but there were no other young leading ladies at the theater.

When she uttered the first line, all doubts disappeared. His and mine.

The rehearsals were wonderful. Éfros barely had to make a remark to her. He watched the stage with a kind of wonderment. She was, actually, the very girl from the Moscow streets. Later I rarely saw anyone take over a role so immediately—make it her own life. [...] She revealed certain female secrets from the stage. The tears mixed with laughter *in the aftermath,* frenzied hysterics...To my mind, this perplexed Éfros horribly—he knew none of this.

So Yakovleva came onstage as a beginner and ended rehearsals as the leading actress of his theater!

Ol'ga Yakovleva, *Esli by znat'*... [*If you only knew*...] (Moscow: ATR-Astrel, 2003), 96–101.

With the arrival of Éfros at the Lenkom a real jolly "club" formed of his former actors Shirvindt, Zburev,[51] and others who came from the Central Children's and who had already worked at the Lenkom [...] There were also at the Lenkom two remarkable persons, Nikolay Nikolaevich Sosunov, the theater's chief designer, and Valentina Izmaylovna Lalevich,[52] his wife, also a designer. He was a legless veteran; he moved around in a vehicle with hand controls. A desperate maximalist—any compromise that, as it seemed to him, Éfros allowed during the course of these three or four years invariably called forth an intransigent reaction from Nikolay Nikolaevich. In the face

50 Ol'ga Mikhaylovna Yakovleva (1941–), Éfros's leading lady at the Lenin Komsomol 1962–67 and the Malaya Bronnaya 1968–84 and briefly at the Taganka, giving fresh, modern interpretations of classic roles. Joined the MAT 2004.

51 Aleksandr Viktorovich Zburev (1938–), at the Moscow Lenkom from 1961; a specialist in uncompromising heroes of ironic wit, he played the title role in Arbuzov's *My Poor Marat*.

52 Nikolay Nikolaevich Sosunov (1908–?) and Valentina Izmaylovna Lalevich (1918–?) collaborated as designers at the Central Children's Theater 1943–63, the Lenin Komsomol 1964–66, and the Ermolova Theater from 1966.

of our own friendly artistic relations they very often slammed doors and scattered into various offices. [...]

The deputy manager of the theater was Grigory Salay, a proper creep. Whenever Anatoly Vasil'evich was freed from administrative duties (said to be "for ideological reasons"), Salay would say, "I'll leave the theater too—for idealistic considerations, because they removed Éfros!"—and dragged through the corridor two heavy bushels of documents from the bookkeeper! [...] It's hard to believe in the telling.

For instance—the tours to Kislovodsk. We played *Making a Movie, 104 Pages, Goodbye, Boys, My Poor Marat*[53]—popular productions, and we enjoyed full houses, of course. Maybe not 100 percent, but close to it. However, for some reason, in the report it was marked down as 75 percent! (Incidentally, for the authorities, this additional drop was to get rid of Éfros. [...])

On the tours to Kiev the public simply flocked in droves, the auditorium was almost filled twice over: the administration took it into its head, allegedly by mistake, to sell two sets of tickets for the same performance! And those who came first took their seats and at every seat stood the "latecomers" who made a scene: "This is my seat!" The performance was held up for half an hour, somehow everyone got seated, they were shoved in somewhere—and again in the reports, "Attendance—75 percent." [...]

We knew not to expect anything good from the already opened *Making a Movie*—by itself, on the part of the authorities. And Anatoly Vasil'evich approached this, one might say, consciously—he understood perfectly that the result would be a not very "admissible production": the hero is a film director whose film "is shut down"; this touched the authorities and the critics and ideology.

But this production gave rise, so to speak, to an "exceptional" case. Even among officials, it seems, there are wonderful people.

The production was accepted by Evseev himself—I think he was a bureaucrat of the municipal department of culture. (I recall he had only one leg and walked with a cane.) [...] He simply fell in love with *Making a Movie*—and banned it! He could not release it "out of duty to the service." In front of the whole company he said the production will not open, but on the other hand, he could not ban it—he liked the production, and we had to find a way out, maybe we could redo something, and besides, there's been an anonymous letter—and so on.

And bureaucrat Evseev fell ill! He was so torn between his responsibility as a Soviet functionary and the bidding of his heart that he even took to drink and went into a hospital. [...] Even from the hospital, through Édik Radzinsky, he kept up a connection to the theater, how necessary it was to change something, smooth it over just a bit, and Édik communicated with us. [...]

When the production finally opened, Evseev was so delighted that he sent to the

53 *Snimaetsya kino* by Edvard Radzinsky, a Felliniesque study of censorship; and his acrid romance *104 Stranitsy pro lyubov'* (both 1973). *Do svidaniya, mal'chiki* (1962) by Boris Balter from his novel, a tale of three teenagers trying to join the army in World War II. *Moy bedny Marat* (1964) by Aleksey Arbuzov, a love triangle set during the Siege of Leningrad, known in English as *The Promise*.

premiere a case of champagne, flowers to Giatsintova, and for me a big, big box of some special candy. Obviously from the official stores. Éfros snatched the box away from the messengers and said, "She doesn't eat chocolate!" (He knew I had Botkin's disease, hepatitis.) Of course, we did drink the champagne.

Chairman of the KGB Vladimir Semichastny[54] to Brezhnev about the state of ideology in the USSR. From Aleksandr Yakovlev, *Sumerki*. Quoted in Radzinsky, *Moya teatral'naya zhizn'*, 129.

The Lenin Komsomol Theater is running a production of *Making a Movie* by the playwright Radzinsky. This ambiguous play is full of allusions and allegories about what kind of difficulties a creative worker runs up against under conditions here, and in essence comprises the ideas, enthusiastically propagandized for in the West, about the lack of creative freedoms in the Soviet Union and the need to fight for them. This lack of the alleged "freedoms" is associated with our demand for "partyness in art."

[Radzinsky: "It decided the fate of the theater."]

Édvard Radzinsky, "Rehearsal," in *Teatr Anatoliya Éfrosa*, 70–1, 73.

... Mid-1960s. Giatsintova phoned. She said, "They removed Éfros."

How confused is the past. The stage of the Lenin Komsomol Theater that night had on Brecht—*Fear and Misery of the Third Reich*.[55] Fascist marches rumbled, backstage worked-up actors were fleetingly glimpsed. An actress with a bundle of papers: petitions to certain parties with the request not to remove Éfros. Someone drove to Dubno, to Peredelkino and other places, where famous representatives of the scientific and artistic intelligentsia dwell in the bosom of nature. To those who valued the Lenin Komsomol Theater and its chief director. To sign. In Dubno, apparently, everybody signed. But in Peredelkino not everybody. And they explained, "This way now it will be better for Éfros." Since that time I've often heard that enigmatic phrase: "It'll be better for him, if we behave worse."

... In the empty rehearsal hall—Éfros, Lyubimov, Efremov. They propose something... They presuppose something. But they can do nothing. So nothing can be done: Éfros is removed.

Three leaders, three pillars of the theater of that time. Powerless before the will of overweening bureaucrats. A symbol of what went on in those days.

[...] "Why did they remove him?" friends unfamiliar with the theater would inquire.

A curious formula evolved:

"Because he turned the Lenin Komsomol Theater from the most unattended to the

---

54 Vladimir Efimovich Semichastny (1924–2001), chairman of the KGB 1961–67, a hard-bitten enemy of intellectuals, who persecuted Sinyavsky and Daniel and *Dr. Zhivago*; he was instrumental in the removal of Khrushchëv and destroyed documentation of the Great Purges.

55 *Furcht und Elend des Drittes Reich* (1938), Brecht's first outspokenly anti-Nazi plays, a series of one-act scenes from everyday life.

most attended. Because he staged clever plays. Because he didn't stage quickly dated ephemera, didn't compromise."

In short, because of everything that the people who removed him asked for in their speeches and actions. Absurd? I promise you: it gets even more absurd.

... But how can you explain this to people unfamiliar with the theater? The initiates knew: they had removed him correctly. He did not know how to sidestep, he found it boring to perform our favorite dance: a little step to the left, then two to the right. He was ashamed to answer demagoguery with unforgivable demagoguery and boorishness with boorishness.

Everything that's known as bad politics. [...]

But I promised to tell you something absurd.

His production of *Romeo and Juliet* went unlicensed for a long time. Because of its pessimism. Well, the authorities weren't cheered up by the story of star-crossed lovers. In the discussion someone boldly remarked that there was a line: "No tale of more woe than this..." They answered, "Demagoguery," and ordered him to work on the optimism.

> After Éfros left the Lenkom. L. V. Zotova, *Dnevnik teatral'nogo chinovnika 1966–1970* (Moscow: n.p., 2003), 162, 45.

July 18, 1968. The City Council analyzed the work of the Lenin Komsomol Theater and "squeezed out" that it is alive due only to Éfros's productions. And Dneprov,[56] who had written that *Molière* had to be removed for ideological reasons, is now playing Molière himself.[57] It was resolved to remove Miringof[58] and pension him off. The murderer has done his work.

October 27, 1968. At ten o'clock we went to the Lenin Komsomol Theater to inspect *Smoke of the Fatherland.*[59] We head to the theater with Shumov[60]—not a single person around, while before (under Éfros) you could hardly get past the stage door. We walk, talk about this, pass Anurov of the City Council, who joins the conversation: "Yes, if we'd deal with the Sovremennik and Taganka the same way, that would be the life," he says quite seriously. In the theater, no one, 40-some persons, all "regulars."

ÉFROS was transferred to the Theater on Malaya Bronnaya in 1967 with ten of his actors. His first production there, Chekhov's *Three Sisters,* confirmed his reputation as an enfant terrible.

---

56 L. Dneprov, Party theater organizer.
57 In 1967, Éfros staged the first production of Bulgakov's *Molière* since the MAT in 1936, making the protagonist a Christ-like figure.
58 Mikhail Miringof, theater critic for *Teatral'naya zhizn'*, on the theater's literary staff.
59 *Dym otechestva* (1944), a dramatization of Konstantin Paustovsky's novel of the intelligentsia on the eve of war.
60 N. Shumov, official in the Comptroller's Department of the Ongoing Repertoire.

Vadim Gaevsky, "Invitation to the dance [*Three Sisters*]," *Teatral'naya zhizn'* 12 (1987), reprinted in *Fleyta Gamleta. Obrazy sovremennogo teatra* (Moscow: Soyuzteatr, 1990), 55.

This painful production about people who need to erect a cross for themselves begins with such joy, such a glittering prologue as we have never chanced to see in the staging not only of a Chekhov play but even of a cloak-and-dagger comedy. They seem to have come straight from somewhere else, from Tirso de Molina, from *Don Gil of the Green Breeches*,[61] these three ladies in green, as if they were dressed by Somov or Bakst or Golovin,[62] in exotic gowns with high, puffed sleeves. Only then, after a close look, do we grasp how much simplicity, how much bitter knowledge of life these three butterflies, three princesses, three brides awaiting grooms, contain, and how humiliated, how beaten down by life are their companions, the merry musketeers in green, roisterers from a fairy-tale Sea Strand, from an ever-greening land—how they themselves, defenders and heroes, need comfort and support. As to the green color that decorates the proscenium, the uniforms of the officers and the gowns of the sisters, it must be declared it was chosen not without reference to Masha's famous lines ("a green oak-tree," "a green tomcat"); it creates a joyous background for the nonjoyous observations (typical set designer's irony), but in addition, it opens up to us anew our Chekhov the impressionist (the designers are V. Durgin and A. Chernova[63]).

However, the striking color choice for a Chekhov play is not the only surprise in the new production. Color is given an unusual role in it, but even more unusual is dance. Chekhov's characters, defective chatterboxes, talk in this production without seriousness and without enthusiasm, literally compelled from without, but they dance, whenever they chance to dance, joyfully and enthusiastically. One might think that they are given to know what the director does not forget: that here words cause separation, breed quarrels, misunderstanding, and hostility, that a careless joke is half a step to death here; perhaps they know in advance the Baron's fate—conversations don't attract them, dancing does. The element of dance enters the Prozorov house like springtime, Tusenbach becomes its harbinger, his gesture, an invitation to a waltz, essentially opens the performance. How much refinement, how much theatrical brilliance there is in this surprising, banal waltz, which gradually draws in the characters and in which they all—the disinherited sisters, old Chebutykin, gloomy Solëny, homely Tusenbach—feel beautiful and young. [...]

---

61 *Don Gil de la calzas verdes* (1635), a comedy of cross-dressing, by Tirso da Molina.
62 Three designers connected with the World of Art movement: Konstantin Andreevich Somov (1869–1939), much inspired by eighteenth-century European art; Léon Bakst (actually Lev Samoilovich Rozenberg, 1866–1924), chief designer for Diaghilev's Ballets Russes, famous for the highly colored exoticism of his sets and costumes; Aleksandr Yakovlevich Golovin (1863–1930) designed for the Bol'shoy Theater, worked closely with Meyerhold at the Alexandra, and, after the Revoluton, worked with Stanislavsky at the MAT.
63 Viktor Yakovlevich Durgin (1937–) and Alla Iosifovna Chernova (1943–) had designed *Molière* for Éfros at the Lenkom.

Yakovleva, *Esli by znat'...*, 128–30.

One would think it such an outwardly serene, stylized production. Stylized sets and, in my view, beautiful ones. Of course, something in the design might completely upset the authorities—for instance, an upside-down tree with golden leaves.

The designer had dressed the women "provocatively." At the time I had not yet seen a coordinated ensemble in scenery and costumes in theaters. Well, Lyubimov did have his idiosyncratic ensemble, they all ran around in quilted jackets and striped jerseys. Or everybody in military greatcoats with bayonets in *Ten Days That Shook the World*.

I understand how it might confuse our critics: why are all the women in green tones and those stylized, exaggerated skirts—and they all have big, puffy sleeves. I heard remarks: "What are those sleeves they've got on, they look like brassieres?" I really don't understand the kind of imagination that sees the erotic in everything. "And why are they all water nymphs? Why is there an ottoman downstage?"

What, is an ottoman a taboo object? Is a sofa preferable? It's comfortable to act on a roomy ottoman—and that's all. It's all functional. Why the confusion, I don't understand.

But—from the great height of a commission headed by E. Furtseva, I can understand. With Furtseva came actresses from the MAT: A. Tarasova and A. Stepanova[64]— those are the ones I remember. They came, went—after this performance we played a few more times. And with great success. It may be that the success was stoked by scandal—"see, the director got fired and this is his first staging at another theater." It may be that many people came to support us or simply out of curiosity—what kind of a director do you fire, transfer, and so on. I was in the production, and it's not for me to judge.

In short, the production was canceled. And this is how it happened.

An already opened, running production was inspected without an audience, in an absolutely empty auditorium. We played to deathly silence and a hostile attitude—they kept whispering all the time, which was rather off-putting. They observed, the actors left, and Furtseva discussed something with Éfros in the manager's office. There were ministerial officials with her—Ekaterina Alekseevna could not discuss it on her own: she was probably afraid that if she were alone, the theater would win. She arrived with a retinue. The palace guard versus the theater.

We stood outside the door to the office of Manager M. P. Zaytsev and eavesdropped on what she was saying in shrill tones. We heard the cries: "It's your fault, Anatoly Vasil'evich, that Tusenbach pronounces the speech about work ironically."

Yet I remember how in rehearsals Anatoly Vasil'evich quarreled with Leva [Krugly]:[65] "More serious! Maybe light in style, but less irony, less irony! Leva, this is very serious! Excuse me, Leva, but why do you allow yourself such irony in relation to work?" [...]

---

64 Angelina Iosifovna Stepanova (1905–2000), actress at the MAT from 1924, had played Irina in Nemirovich-Danchenko's 1940 production of *Three Sisters*. Tarasova had appeared as Masha.

65 Lev Borisovich Krugly (1931–2010), who played at both the Sovremennik and the Malaya Bronnaya, one of Éfros's favorite actors. Worked abroad as a director and pedagogue after 1979.

And Éfros answered Furtseva, "Yes, Ekaterina Alekseevna. It is my fault. I'm to blame! We'll try to correct it." [...]

The chief charges were, of course, ideological: "a very pessimistic production." Although how one could play it optimistically, I don't know... [...]

Passing by me, Furtseva said, "And to think they praised you!" And went down the stairs. Those standing by called after her, "Weaver"![66]

Zotova, *Dnevnik*, 26, 78–79, 98–99, 100, 152–53, 162, 351.

September 30, 1967. Somehow it's all shameful, I feel as if I'm taking part in an indecent game—all around scandalmongering, malice, hatred.

December 2, 1967 [about the second inspection of *Three Sisters* by the Ministry of Culture]. The production again thrilled me, a lot of yelling, but the fourth act is probably really the best. But Lyubimov told L'vov-Anokhin[67] that Chekhov is a bad playwright and no one needs him and he's pointless and he doesn't like him.

January 29, 1968. Shumov got from Tarasov an anonymous lampoon on *Three Sisters* and shoved it at everybody, and I was cheered a great deal by Spektor (the assistant director of the Vakhtangov Theater), who, when he learned that it was anonymous, refused to read it. It was like a slap in Shumov's face. It's nasty but, because I have to note everything down, I cite it as testimony to the badgering "of the creative intelligentsia," and cowardly as well, unsigned by a name known to officialdom.

February 1, 1968. Conference at the VTO.[68] After A. V. Éfros's appearance... appearing at the end of the meeting, Tovstonogov nervously had an adverse reaction and explained that he had always defended Éfros, but now he wouldn't, that his latest productions are a loss of ideological position, and that Éfros could consider his appearance as a breakup. L'vov-Anokhin feels that Tovstonogov behaved badly. It's very convenient now, isn't it—to hide behind his back all sorts of scum... our people were delighted by the scandal... in the morning Tarasov came to our room and said to me: "There, you see, your lefties themselves are beating up Éfros, both Tovstonogov and Pluchek." I: "Who is this lefty Tovstonogov? He's been upright and correct all his life."

May 14, 1968. At eleven Furtseva and the commission watched *Three Sisters.* [...] On their way back, Shumov told about the discussion—the Art Theater folk had "suffered" the most. I shall only note Zharov's[69] funny remark: "Éfros is a recidivist, for a long time they've been saying that he is ideologically incorrect, and that keeps me from looking, then I see something good, and it occurs to me that this has got to be Éfros and nobody else!"

---

66 Furtseva had begun her political career in the textile industry.
67 Boris Aleksandrovich L'vov-Anokhin (1926–2000), dance critic and director at the Red Army Central Theater under Popov, then at the Stanislavsky 1963–69, the Maly 1979–89, and the New Drama Theater in Moscow from 1991.
68 Vserossiyskoe Teatral'noe Obshchestvo (the All-Russian Theatrical Society).
69 Mikhail Ivanovich Zharov (1899–1981), after playing comic roles for Meyerhold, entered the Kamerny Theater 1931–37 and then the Maly from 1939 in character parts.

May 31, 1968. A sad entry. Yesterday, May 30, *Three Sisters* was played for the last time. It will not be revived next season, a firm decision at every level by the leadership.

Boris Poyurovsky, "Catherine the Great," in *Chto ostalos',* 112.

They are mistaken who think that the initiative for prohibition and repression always came from governmental and Party officials. Of course, they were paid a salary to "be vigilant." But was it not the famous old-timers of the MAT who demanded in the 1960s that officials remove *Three Sisters* of Anatoly Éfros from the Malaya Bronnaya Theater? Was it not a "group of comrades"—actors of the Ermolova Theater—who by turns "chewed up and spat out" Andrey Lobanov, Leonid Varpakhovsky, and Aleksandr Shatrin?[70] I say this not to rebuke anyone, for in the given cases, none of them is still alive, neither those who could not live in peace without committing some vile act nor those who suffered at their hands.

Dmitrieva, interview, 8.

At the Malaya Bronnaya, there was a production *The Happy Days of an Unhappy Man*[71] based on Arbuzov. For some reason it all sounded like music. How Éfros achieved this I don't know. The set had a flight of stairs on which sat a chorus, consisting of Durov,[72] Martynyuk, and somebody else. They commented on the action. The way the chorus entered, the way it mounted the steps, the way it spoke its lines—it was a musical show. No one else could have done anything like it. In general he had a remarkable sense of rhythm, he loved music a lot and staged it very subtly. For instance, in *Othello,* at the most piquant moment, Ella Fitzgerald sings "Airport." In *Othello!* But she was interpolated so precisely, she sounded so grandiose and so added to the action! Later he chided himself for this. At the end, staging some show, he said, "No, no, no music. I'm fed up: as soon as you have to lay it on in some scene, they add music." [...]

THE SELF-GOVERNANCE of theater led to endlessly protracted meetings to deal "democratically" with the problems that arose.

---

70 Andrey Mikhaylovich Lobanov (1900–1959), a reliable director of socialist realism and teacher of Georgy Tovstonogov and Mark Zakharov, was artistic director at the Ermolova 1945–58; the hostile reaction to his production of *The Guests* (1954) put him in the hospital. Leonid Viktorovich Varpakhovsky (1908–76) began as a director with TRAM; at the Ermolova 1957–61, from 1962 at the Maly. Aleksandr Borisovich Shatrin (actually Abram B. Shapiro, 1919–78), at the Ermolova 1960–64, whose production of De Filippo's *Saturday, Sunday, Monday* was a success there for ten years.

71 *Shchastlivye dni neshchastlive cheloveka* (1967) by Aleksey Arbuzov.

72 Lev Konstantinovich Durov (1931–), scion of a famous circus family, actor at both the Lenin Komsomol and the Malaya Bronnaya, where he played important character roles.

Minutes of the meeting of the Artistic Council of the Moscow Dramatic Theater on Malaya Bronnaya, November 21, 1968.

Agenda: 1. Discussion of the rude behavior of the actress A. V. ANTONENKO[73] at a performance of *Go So As to Stay,* November 20, 1968.

M. P. ZAYTSEV: Yesterday in the show *From One to Midnight* [at the Taganka Theater] A[nna] V. Antonenko was assigned the role of Alëna, the result of the illness of N. M. Nikonova. And on the main stage, in the show *Go So As to Stay,* the repertoire office officially assigned N. F. Zinov'eva to the role of Irina (instead of Antonenko). At four o'clock A. V. Antonenko phoned me at home to say that she refused to act, she had a medical certificate. I left for the theater specifically to prevent the disruption of the performance. I spoke to Nikonova by phone, promising to send her a car; I asked her to perform somehow, so as not to disrupt the performance. Thirty minutes before the show *Go So As to Stay,* I had to meet with the actress N. F. Zinov'eva and settle the question of her participation in that performance, so that putting her into that performance was done deliberately. As to what happened next, I ask the head of the troupe, G. M. Lyampe,[74] to inform the Artistic Council.

G. M. LYAMPE, *actor, head of troupe:* I'm very upset. I've worked 20 years in the professional theater and never come up against anything like this.

On November 19 N. M. Nikonova was supposed to show up for a rehearsal, but declined, because after fainting she felt very bad. Shortly before two o'clock she phoned and explained that her condition was so bad that she could not play in that night's performance. Perepel'kina[75] came to the rescue and played a role other than her own in *The Wedding of a Marriage Broker.* The next day N. Nikonova's health had not improved. And because there were two performances, the only recourse in *Go So As to Stay* was Zinov'eva, who was officially cast by the director of the theater in that role in the P-m team, and had rehearsed it earlier. Antonenko got upset by this. As a result, A. L. Dunaev[76] phoned me to ask, What's going on? I replied that Nikonova was ill and had let me know beforehand. On November 20, at two o'clock, Antonenko addressed me with her request to phone N. M. Nikonova to ask her to perform. I phoned, but Nikonova's blood pressure had gone up. Forty minutes later, Antonenko screamed at me that she had a doctor's note too, but she did not declare that she refused to act. Soon Mikhail Petrovich phones me and informs me that Antonenko refuses to act today, but she herself cannot phone G. M. Lyampe. I phoned Antonenko and listened to her complaint—why, she says, do they believe N. M. Nikonova and don't believe that *she* is ill? I phoned Nikonova yet again on behalf of Mikhail Petrovich's office, in the presence of N. N. Volkov.[77] Then Mikhail

73 Anna V. Antononeko played Masha in *Three Sisters.*
74 G. M. Lyampe played M. Dimanche in *Dom Juan.*
75 L. A. Perepel'kina, actress, president of the theater's Mestkom.
76 Aleksandr Leonidovich Dunaev (1920–85), director, who served a long apprenticeship in the provinces before coming to the Soviet Army Theater 1959–61; at the Malaya Bronnaya 1968–84.
77 Nikolay Nikolaevich Volkov (1934–2003), student at the Shchukin School, acted at the Malaya

Petrovich asked N. N. Volkov to take a taxi and pick up N. M. Nikonova. When A. V. Antonenko learned that Nikonova was going to go on, she came to the theater and began to make up for *Go So As to Stay,* but the director, M. E. Beskin, told her that Zinov'eva was to go on and was already made up. Antonenko screamed that only she was to act or else she'd go to the police. Ten minutes before the start of the show, the chief director agreed to let Antonenko act after talking to her. [...]

A. L. DUNAEV, *chief director of the theater:* This is an unusual situation, I am very upset and rescheduled today's rehearsal. On talking to Antonenko I said that she wouldn't act today and ordered her home. She was in a nervous state, on the brink of making a scene, she hung around a while before the show started, I didn't want a scene and decided to let her act and preferred that this performance be fraught with all the ensuing consequences. When it became clear that Nikonova was ill, Antonenko demanded that the production *From One to Midnight* be changed. I replied that this would not happen, because it had an alternative actress. I can find no justification for such an occurrence. Antonenko is not a beginner, she's a Party member, a leader of the Komsomol Organization of the theater, her behavior goes beyond all the bounds of decent conduct. Today is to take the strictest measures to decide whether she is to continue at the theater.

[A. V. Antonenko explains that it was a one-time occurrence, Lyampe was rude to her, and she values the theater above all...]

A. M. PESELEV,[78] *actor, secretary of the party organization:* [...] No one in the theater is allowed to pull such stunts, lots of us have bad personal lives and unpleasantnesses in the theater. Today our theater is attracting everyone's attention. If we value the collective, we do not have the right to let everything pass—that's the ruin of morale, ethical norms of behavior, my personal position in the theater [...] This was a tough year for the theater. The Artistic Council has to render its strictest verdict. We are suffering an external and spiritual lack of discipline. [...]

[For several hours the discussion continues as more than a dozen members of the troupe, actors, administrators, even stagehands, express their negative opinions, demanding punishment and dismissal for outrageous behavior. Near the end, Éfros speaks up:]

A. V. ÉFROS: This is uncharacteristic of her. I don't think she's like that, an accident happened, an idiotic female complex. She never before overstepped the mark in regard to a role. Maybe her behavior was out of keeping with us—some have this mistaken opinion that the environment in which Anya mixes and works is business-like, unspoiled, industrious, honorable. Apparently in the collective no one ever gets demoralized, everything is healthy. Everyone is working hard. Ninety-nine percent of the actors behave correctly. Anya had a fit of quasi-theatrical vulgarity; this could happen to lots of people. [...]

Bronnaya 1962–87, playing Vershinin in *Three Sisters, Dom Juan,* and *Othello.* Then transferred to the Mayakovsky Theater.

78 A. M. Peselev, actor and secretary of the theater's Party committee; played Kulygin in *Three Sisters,* M. Dimanche in *Dom Juan,* and the Doctor in *Brother Alësha.*

M. P. ZAYTSEV [the last word]: I don't agree with some people that the theater is being torn apart. I have worked in many theaters, I believe ours to be the most creative theater. This is my official statement. Of course there are shortcomings. We work hand in hand with Dunaev, which makes me very happy, but I am against Aleksandr Leonidovich's allowing Antonenko to go on yesterday . . . She merits the most serious punishment. I declare that there will be no more instances of such behavior. [. . .]

Yakovleva, *Esli by znat'* . . . , 234–35.

There was a period at the Malaya Bronnaya when Anatoly Vasil'evich produced a series of theatrical masterpieces: *Dom Juan, Wedlock, A Month in the Country, Brother Alësha.*

When Anatoly Vasil'evich began to carry on open rehearsals—not restricted—the theater simply let everyone in. Anyone who applied, almost off the street—Anatoly Vasil'evich's idea was not to restrict anyone from attending rehearsals. Therefore the auditorium and the balcony were constantly filled with university students, degree candidates, and well-known actors, and friends of friends, and the merely curious. As a rule, at each rehearsal, there were thirty to forty persons. People sat, even if the process was far from the moment when the actors were beginning to rehearse something onstage. And long before the actors remained onstage without the director. Because the period when the director is onstage all the time is the most substantial at rehearsals; all the responsibility lies on him alone, he tries by his narration and demonstration to inculcate his concept into the actors.

But the actors, I among them, were annoyed by the presence of extraneous people in the house. We even teased Anatoly Vasil'evich, saying, another couple of troop trains pulled in today. Or "A troop of builders . . . or cleaners has shown up. They've also asked to be present!" He reacted very proudly, but we did not lay off. And once, when I saw somewhere in the back rows a man sitting with a suitcase on his lap, I said, "There, the station waiting room is open, people are hanging out here!" Anatoly Vasil'evich got very angry with me.

Mikhail Kozakov, "In a space of one's own," in *Teatr Anatoliya Éfrosa,* 118.

Dom Juan [by Molière, 1973] was wonderfully harmonious. Everything in it was harmonious—Borovsky's set designs, the costumes, the music (ancient Spanish melodies and tunes). The production was a bit ascetic, but very beautiful, with a mobile, musically plastic, somewhat refined mise-en-scène, with a precisely controlled rhythmic tempo . . .

Another thing that astounded me in working with Éfros: he allowed extraneous people to attend rehearsals. For me this was very unusual and at first unpleasant: it was not easy to take criticism in the presence of spectators. But I quickly understood that it was very useful, for opening night the actors would come on fully prepared—there was no fear of the audience, no difference between the empty rehearsal room and the packed auditorium of the first performances.

Éfros demonstrated things beautifully in rehearsals. He demonstrated both the

10.6. Mikhail Kozakov as Molière's Dom Juan, directed by Anatoly Éfros and designed by David Borovsky, Malaya Bronnaya Theater, Moscow, 1973.

concept and the rhythmic tempo. The nuances had to be worked out by the actors themselves. And anyone who could do this in the director's key would win as a result. It was necessary to insert one's own personality, but, as jazz players say, in one's own space. And these limited improvisations of the actor "in his space" struck me as wonderfully accurate. After all, if all these "spaces" were united, as always happened in Éfros's best productions, by the will of the director, the performers had no possibility to pull apart the action. Unfortunately, actors, by dint of their nature, always try to "pull the covers to their side," if they are not harshly restricted. And over time this would start to happen in Éfros's productions, which really annoyed him. Maybe that's why he didn't like to watch his old productions.

> Mikhail Kozakov, *Risunki na peske. Aktërskaya kniga* (Moscow: AST/Zebra E, 2007), 473–75, 487.

What struck me about Anatoly Vasil'evich's rehearsals? First, the complete absence of idle chatter. In the last years of my work at the Sovremennik and even at the MAT, there was brought into rehearsals something like "a plebiscite"—little was done, but on the other hand, lots was said. And this, in my view, is the first sign of a theater's downfall. [. . .] In this sense the way Éfros ran rehearsals constituted the most important of professional lessons.

At the first rehearsal Anatoly Vasil'evich arrived absolutely prepared and never began by speaking about the author—what he knew and thought about him—as most directors do. He immediately began to make a performance out of a single actor—Éfros. At the start of the rehearsal he already had his opinion on the play as a whole—on its tone, rhythm, style. All this might be refined later on, but in essence the whole production was thought out by him in advance. It was obligatory for Éfros to read the play himself. We did not read our roles, as often happens, helplessly floundering in the text, but he "walked us through" the play, tried out its sounds, traveled its line of action. And we were not to ask questions but to listen and make notes. When I, still not dedicated to this, tried a couple of times to "meddle," my colleagues, students, and companions-in-arms of Anatoly Vasil'evich—Yakovleva, Volkov, Durov—stared at me in wonderment. Later I, too, always took notes on Éfros, tried to explore his vision of the production. And he read the play like a remarkable actor, created before our eyes, in our presence sought the correct tone, made adjustments, often said:

"Wait, I'll sort myself out right now..."

He without fail had to "sort himself out" and never made a decision by cold rationality. He moved down a different path—of feeling and intuition. This by no means excluded a sort of abstraction—quotations from poetry, references to films of Fellini or Bergman, or to yesterday's television program—but the main thing was his immersion in the play, its influence on him. In this way the read-through took two or three days, sometimes four. During this time he made progress getting through the whole play. And at the end he could say:

"Maybe something isn't understood—ask questions. But it's better to wait a bit, until tomorrow."

And tomorrow the second phase began. I was used to taking a play to pieces. There was nothing like that here. He immediately got the actors on their feet, some still didn't have their lines by heart. It was easy for me, I liked to work from the page, but some found it hard. Éfros rehearsed, eschewing the table period. Sometimes he would work through an improvisation, but even in this he was very concrete, always oriented to the situation given by the author in the play. And there we were, moving around, scripts in hand, cooperating on our feet, so to speak. We sweated, in the true meaning of the word, immediately, without preliminaries, we began the actor's hard labor, real hard labor.

Éfros considered (and I was not always in agreement with him, and we argued a lot) that in working on a character, the actor must move only from himself, that the character is born "within oneself." He proposed that creating a character was part of the theater's past, that the kernel of the role must grow exclusively out of oneself. In this sense he was more royalist than the king, I mean Stanislavsky, who loved creating characters, and he completely rejected the way of Mikhail Chekhov, who, as everyone knows, worked from the outer to the inner.

Spencer Golub, "Interview with Anatoly Éfros," *Theatre Quarterly* 26 (Summer 1977), 29, 31, 33. Spencer Golub, professor of theater at Brown University, is a noted authority on twentieth-century Russian theater.

1977.

You know I've worked with these people for a long time. We respect one another very much. They are in many ways "infected" by me and I by them. I understand their

10.7. Ol'ga Yakovleva as Agaf'ya Tikhonovna in Gogol's *Wedlock,* directed by Anatoly Éfros and designed by Valery Levental', Malaya Bronnaya Theater, Moscow, 1975.

original personalities. The communication between us is still not complete, but there exists a solid basis of interdependence between us. I know that I have a certain actor who projects masculine weakness very well on the stage—Nikolay Volkov. I know that I have an actor who is able to express an almost hysterical level of energy—Lev Durov. And I know that in my troupe there is an actress who clearly understands the psychology and emotional make-up of the contemporary woman—Ol'ga Yakovleva. When I conceive a new idea, a new approach, it arises out of them. They are more than performers: they are the material from which I create. There is almost always the sense of these actors being parts of a consistent whole, the continuation of one and the same set of reactions, one and the same large theme which concerns us. It is the theme of the inter-relationship between weakness and strength, energy and weakness—or rather the lack of energy. [...]

It's important to me that the actors not only understand in an intellectual sense my approach to a particular scene or action, but that they physically enter into the action, the scene, and establish a physical system of associations. Then the approach becomes practical rather than theoretical... It must all come out of the flesh... The most important thing for the actors is mobility—both inner and outer...

Actually, I would prefer to work with an empty stage. Again to use the image of the boxing ring, the ring is always the same, but the boxers who come to fight in it are different each time. The stage, like the boxing ring, should be empty and unchanged from contest to contest. What transpires within this space can be of the most diverse nature. Thus, we must deal with the stage as it is, as an empty box. But the nature of the stage is such that it does not simply reproduce everyday reality, but instead offers us a condensed, heightened and almost symbolic picture . . .

———————————

THE NEW DISPENSATION of artistic councils proved to be very cumbersome. In practice, it meant that the theater had to filter a new production through several revisions to make sure that it was immaculate before it would be presented for approval to the authorities. This entailed endless discussion and alteration. It began to frustrate Éfros, whose creative concepts could be distorted by this chopping and changing.

Minutes of the meeting of the Artistic Council, May 14, 1977, 1–7.

DUPAK: We have determined the 1976–1977 season. We can settle the budget. The following productions are approved:

1. G. Zavol'skaya, *The Four of Them*
2. O'Neill, *A Touch of the Poet*
3. N. Dumbadze, *The Guilty Verdict*
4. I. Turgenev, *A Month in the Country*[79]

On June 22 we have to present to the Governing Board of Culture the production of *Enemies,* which we are preparing for the sixtieth anniversary of Great October. That way our entire directing team has produced shows that display all the basic strengths of our troupe and even the "newcomers." By the way, our experiment in inviting actors for specific roles is supported by the Ministry of Culture of the USSR and the Chief Governing Board of Culture.

P. The question of publicizing the current repertoire from the standpoint of finances and the question of the run of productions from the standpoint of creativity.

Sh. Plan for the 1977–78 season.

1. *Enemies* will be transferred, as a running show, to the autumn.
2. *Peter Pan.* We are planning to do this show for young people. A young director, young designers, and the initiative for its preparation and release must come from young people. What's responsible for the need to stage this show by December 25?
3. Alëshin, *If . . .*
4. Dvoretsky, *A Veranda in Summer*
5. L. Tolstoy, *And the Light Shineth in Darkness.* We should end the next season with this show, opening it before the break.

Besides A. L. Dunaev's production of the Tolstoy play, we are not planning any projects for the classics. But we do have some. We would like to persuade A. V. to

———————————

79 The Eugene O'Neill play was first produced in the United States in 1958. Nodar Dumbadze (1928–84) was a distinguished Georgian novelist. Of these plays, Éfros directed only the Turgenev.

do a Gogol not at the Sovremennik but "at home." Likewise, we have seriously to consider L. K. Durov's proposal for a production of *The Forest.*[80] [...]

The variety of the repertoire thematically and in terms of genre is not only an ideological task, about which we must constantly think, but our paramount creative task. Only in a thematically and generically diverse repertoire can actors develop their individualities to the fullest extent. [...]

We need expeditiously to open the Small Stage on the stage of the House of People's Creativity.

As of today, the repertoire plan is as follows:

1. É. Radzinsky, *The End of Don Juan,* dir. A. Éfros.
2. F. Dostoevsky, *Itsy-Bitsy,* work of L. Krugly.
3. The poetry of D. Samoylov[81]—proposed by M. Kazakov.
4. A proposal by L. Durov, who can get down to preparing a show for the Small Stage this very day. [...]

DUROV: There's something I don't understand. [...] Why do you put us in a situation, turn us into marionettes? I'm not allowed to stage a classic. I'm kept away from work the whole year. I will spend a whole year looking for some mythical Soviet play, I'm not allowed to stage a classic. Free me from work. Someone else can stage it, and I can sit idly by.

DUNAEV: A legitimate question. Somehow we're acting ridiculously. All this resulted from the extreme need for a children's production. This will be investigated.

I don't want to be a pain in the neck. If Durov comes up with a play tomorrow, he can start to stage it right away.

We can't turn this into a memorial theater. The Soviet repertoire is absolutely necessary. [...] We need a Soviet play. We need it ahead of anything else.

PESELEV: The Art Council had to hold a discussion. The problem is that in 1976 we didn't do a single Soviet title. This fact we learned in our work on the future. The theater cannot exist if we don't open two Soviet shows a year. [...]

DUROV: I understand perfectly. I didn't come to the management with a proposal for *Forest,* because I know the theater needs a Soviet play. The search for one will go on for another three months. So I won't do *The Forest.* I have an itch to work. I need to show myself as a director in something solid. I turn to the council. [...]

A. N. Kotkin's stenographic record of the meeting of the Artistic Council concerning the ongoing repertoire, December 2, 1977, 2.

A. V. ÉFROS: I devised a certain path which I followed, whatever it cost me. I want to make a small preamble before we start a specific discussion ... I take this on myself.

80 The actor L. K. Durov was eager to become a director, which he did in 1979, after taking the course at GITIS.
81 David Samoylov (actually David Samuilovich Kaufman, 1920–90), lyric poet, who composed a lyrical cycle about the Great Patriotic War 1960–75.

[Written into the report: I make no reservations in what I am about to say. This is not known to any of you.]

Many people believed that in every case as director I treated most people with creative trust, with as much respect, love, and attention as I am capable of, although I have favorite actors, and joyfully greeted the appearance of every actor I didn't know before. I've worked with many actors earlier, there was a long list of them, and I want to talk about this. When people say that this isn't so . . . remember nothing I say is out of malice.

I've decided to put the question of the theater's ongoing repertoire more broadly. I'm not interested in which actor speaks more loudly or softly or acted better or worse. I will talk about something else that is upsetting us. I came to the theater yesterday and was flabbergasted and upset to learn that Dupak hadn't been elected to the Party Committee.

CHAIRMAN (DUPAK): I ask that this subject be deleted from the agenda and not be dealt with.

A. V. ÉFROS: I ask that you allow me to say what I want to say. I can take part in communal work the way I understand it. [. . .] We do not have people, some of whom make jet aircraft and others of whom make chairs. If they do things well, they are equal; if they do things badly, they are also equal.

But it so happens that they make jet airplanes well, and chairs badly. [. . .]

You are some of the very best, most honorable members of the collective. I love you very much, but sometime you do horrible things. [. . .]

A good theater is a theater that arouses interest, that people go to, that has resonance, and it's often hard to get in. Such a theater without daring productions, without good stage direction, without first-class actors is unthinkable. Volkov left, and we had to restage *Othello*. Performers were found for that production. Instead of feeling that we were enriched by this, instead of supporting this, they said, "Ah, they're putting the squeeze on us!!"

One time [Gogol's] *Wedlock* works as a comedy, another time as a tragicomedy. I would like it to work as a tragicomedy.

What I'm talking about is that everyone should advance and develop and that a science should be constructed on dialectic, that no one stands in place but everyone develops. For art must go forward every year. What athletes do the theater also does. We are distinguished by the fact that we have living people, not mummies. We have managed this, whereas other theaters have mummies. But all the time someone wants to halt this movement. And some people think only about their own benefits. But you wouldn't receive those benefits from any other management. [. . .]

Minutes no. 5. Meeting of the Artistic Council of the MDT on Malaya Bronnaya, May 13, 1979 (from the stenographic copy).

Agenda

Inspection and discussion of the production of É. Radzinsky's play *The Sequel to Dom Juan,* on prospects for work on productions for the small stage. [...]

KOGAN:[82] The long-awaited opening of the Small Stage has taken place. I would like to discuss the quality of work in all its aspects, i.e., the possibility of showing a production. The possibility of leasing it out. The space, how to work in it further.

SAYFULIN:[83] It's possible to establish a good level of quality in this space. You receive aesthetic pleasure. The audience will try to get to see this production, because it is serious art and not a scandalous event.

An interesting play, with great philosophic subject matter, constitutes a novelty, remarkably contrived. It is in the best sense of the word an "absurd" play. At the end a serious theme emerges—harmony is destroyed and a castrated man arrives, the advent of the "Age of Sganarelle"...

Our Small Stage is highly original. I haven't seen anything like it. Not to mention A. Mironov,[84] but I liked him. He acted with such power! Pretensions of tasteful order are there. But it's great work! Durov was in danger of repeating himself, but sincerity, organic quality, commitment make me forget repetitious intonations.

This production sets up a balance between Dom Juan and Sganarelle. It would be interesting to see it with Yakovleva and Kanevsky. There are longueurs, repetitions in Act II. With the death of the Commendatore I began to lose the thread of the meaning.

PEREPEL'KINA: I didn't like this play when I read it. I love Bulgakov, but he constructs his idea very precisely, whereas in Radzinsky, there's a carelessness, and dramatically speaking, some of the ideas are sloppy. A single theme is varied multiple times. Abstraction after abstraction—I don't understand, I lose the thread.

Mironov did not convince me, a woman. He isn't Don Juan. There's something concrete in Durov, and I experienced things along with him. I don't understand Mironov and the rest. Koreneva[85] didn't come off, either in costume or in the role. It's neither concrete nor abstract. There has to be precision, and it has to come from the playwright, otherwise it isn't exciting. [...]

DUNAEV: I would like to note the persistence of Anatoly Vasil'evich and Dima in creating this space. The perspectives are great and interesting. This arena provides great possibilities. [...]

ÉFROS: At the moment I do not feel self-confident. Something happened... and a great deal has to be considered... and I'd like to do something else, something new. I'll go on thinking about it.

---

82 I. A. Kogan, the administrator of the theater and chairman of the Artistic Council.

83 Gennady Rashidovich Sayfulin (1941–), acted at the TsDT 1961–64, at the Lenin Komosol 1964–67, and from 1967 at the Malaya Bronnaya, playing Cassio in *Othello* and Alësha Karamazov.

84 Andrey Aleksandrovich Mironov (1941–87), a remarkable comic actor, from 1962 at the Moscow Satire Theater; he died in the wings of a Riga theater after delivering Figaro's last-act monologue.

85 Elena Alekseevna Koreneva (1953–), acted at the Sovremennik 1975 and the Malaya Bronnaya 1977–78; lived in the United States 1982–94, then returned to Russia and starring roles.

[...] I will not give in, but at this moment I feel alienated. There is that phenomenon when nothing seems new and interesting. This exists both in spectators and in artists. But if nothing amazes people, it means they're not artists. [...]

Something very interesting might be done in this space. A production of Blok's *Little Show Booth*. To preserve this little stage. To think up something for it.

RADZINSKY: What happened? Five actors knocked themselves out working for the spectators. Mironov worked beautifully, but Durov worked superbly. Durov worked ruthlessly. Mironov is not ruthless. This show is unbelievable, but it's special to me. We don't live in isolation. And this is definitely literature and it became understood at once. The world has changed for this time. And it became understood—it is done in the highest degree artistically. I only wonder if they, the spectators, will sit here without air-conditioning?

ÉFROS: Everyday there's something that has to be sorted out. I am on the outs with three actors and nobody wants to look into it. [...]

The Artistic Council resolved:

To recommend to the leadership of the theater to present the production for submission to the Central Directorate on May 17. The director's team will take into account the wishes and remarks made by the council for the perfection of the production.

Before the end of the season, to define the plan of work of the Small Stage for the next season.

> Minutes of the meeting of the Artistic Council of the MDT on Malaya Bronnaya, July 29, 1980, 1–8.

Agenda

Appraisal of the run-through of *Summer and Smoke* by T. Williams.[86] Directed by A. Éfros. Designed by D. Krymov.[87]

A. V. ÉFROS: The actors and I were of one mind: to show this to the Artistic Council long before the opening, so I would like you to say whatever you think. You have understood that there are no costumes, but the sets are all finished. [...]

M. M. KOZAKOV: This production has to be opened. There are no counterindications to its being submitted [for opening]. The audience will greet and welcome it. I think it will be welcomed with great interest for a number of reasons, including T. Williams and a good translation, literary and unpretentious, unlike other translations. You come into the auditorium, you see it's beautiful, tasteful. Éfros interprets

86 Tennessee (actually Thomas) Williams (1911–83), American playwright, famous for dramatic confrontations among emotional characters, as in *The Glass Menagerie* (1945), *A Streetcar Named Desire* (1947), and *Cat on a Hot Tin Roof* (1955). *Summer and Smoke* (1948) was later revised as *Eccentricities of a Nightingale* (1952).

87 Dmitry Anatol'evich Krymov (1954–), painter and designer, the son of Anatoly Éfros and the theater critic Natal'ya Krymova (he chose his mother's name to avoid anti-Semitic prejudice); at the Malaya Bronnaya from 1976, where he designed most of his father's productions. Moved to the Taganka in 1985, then became freelance.

the play according to his lights, and the work that was put into it is outstanding. O. M. Yakovleva gives an interesting performance. To find this way of speaking, not simply to play an hysteric. It's hard to draw the line, but she does it. As to the rest, not one piece of work calls forth a sharp protest. I understand how hard it is for Kachan[88] to enter a new collective, but I regard his work respectfully. These are the positive effusions of my brain. But there were other considerations. Everything I'm going to say now is highly personal, perhaps meaningless.

I was not personally moved by this show, didn't weep and laugh. This has to do perhaps with the author—T. Williams is not my favorite author. For me any Western play is interesting in itself but gets under my skin only when it evokes associations. This did not evoke a strong reaction in me, so I sat and reasoned: who on earth is Alma? Whom does she stand for nowadays? What about the boy? Who is he? A rambunctious American male? Then I have to imagine a Nicholson[89] or a young Brando. I couldn't pin things down concretely. I began to be annoyed by Ostroumova's[90] walk, the stylized stage crossings. I thought about the play, I thought a lot about whether Kachan was the character I could identify with. Act II grabbed me more, the first was a bit of a bore and too long.

M. I. ANDRIANOVA: I was excited by the polyphony. The way everything flowed into a single stream, the way everything was thought out! The work is complex, there's a lot that's new in the director's work. This work is great and beautiful. O. Yakovleva has done remarkable work. The feminine theme is so exciting, I simply sobbed. And it's very contemporary. And it isn't Russian. That's a minor concern. And this is a great victory for the actors. O. Yakovleva first of all and V. Kachan. I saw the thought process in his eyes, he is also fine in his passions, his feelings. [...]

T. P. SAYFULIN: Yesterday at Vysotsky's funeral I heard lines from the end of Hamlet... Today we see on our stage something similar. The theme of eternity cannot help but provoke thoughts of what is beyond, what more is there... People will come to this show because it's an Ol'ga Yakovleva show. She and this author were created for one another. As to the composition of the show itself, I think it needs a prologue. It took me a long time to figure out who's who, why they're here. If there were a prologue, the expositional stuff wouldn't bother me. There is no Americanism in the production. That is fine. [...]

I. YA KASTREL' [actor]: I didn't understand why A. V. Éfros picked this play. By the end of the show I was convinced. I understood it all, it all excited me. There's a lot of prolixity in Act I. The distance between the hero and heroine doesn't lessen

---

88 Vladimir Andreevich Kachan (1947–), actor, author, and songwriter, who sang in Utësov's orchestra for seven years while acting at the Moscow TYUZ; at the Malaya Bronnaya 1980–84, where he played Chichikov in *The Road*.

89 Jack (John Joseph) Nicholson (1937–), American film actor, who at this point was known in the Soviet Union for *Easy Rider* (1969), *Five Easy Pieces* (1970), *Chinatown* (1974), and especially *One Flew over the Cuckoo's Nest* (1975); he appeared with Marlon Brando in *The Missouri Breaks* (1976).

90 Ol'ga Mikhaylovna Ostroumova (1947–) acted at the Malaya Bronnaya 1973–83; moved to the Mossovet 1984; played Rosa Gonzalez in *Summer and Smoke*.

over the course of two hours and gets boring. Act I needs cutting, in the interests of the show itself. [...]

A. V. ÉFROS: Thank you. I have taken in all your feelings. There are a few things to consider. I too am under a great impression from yesterday's funeral. We have lots of stupidities that keep us from realizing our own essences. People cherish the truth about themselves. Soul and body—they will talk about this at home. And about this play. I love everyone with whom I've worked. [...] Now about the style. Over in America there is none of this excess. We want to overdo things. But it's not necessary. Yes, they came and took a look and understood that we with our own art know something too.

I wanted to put on a production that wasn't tragic by Western–American means of expression, but surreptitiously.

We need to make powerful changes in our art. [...]

Stenographic transcript of the discussion of Tennessee Williams's *Summer and Smoke* at the Chief Administration for Culture (of the Ispolkom of the Mossovet), August 8, 1980, 1–16.

L. S. YONOV: We have internally discussed among ourselves the inspected production, and the general consensus is that this is the best work of Tennessee Williams to appear in Moscow, and I think it is also the best work of the director Éfros of the last few years. It may be a return to his best years, it may the apotheosis of a still greater experiment. This is very high-class work of great culture. There is a very subtle psychological working out of the characters. The whole production is of high culture. The chief success of the production is first of all the work of Yakovleva, a defining step in the actress's work. [...]

So when you talk about the other work, and in particular Kachan's work, for all their pluses they don't seem so perfect. They have their good points, but today this actor is still holding back. [...] Then, too, it seems to me that his eyeglasses hid certain human feelings and in some way changed the essence of his character, changed his behavior. [...] When he acts crudely, I think the actor ought to feel nauseated. But inasmuch as I've seen this production twice, I've felt that all this will appear and develop as things evolve. [...]

The main thing is the end of the performance. The whole structure of Alma's character, what Yakovleva does in the theater, is the moral victory in the performance. Even John says that she has triumphed, and this moral high point illumines us. In the performance you don't lay special stress on the social atmosphere, and there isn't much in the play; you are excited by moral, universally human problems, and from that standpoint, suddenly at the end, something happens. Whether it's the partners, or it's your decision, but as I read the play, there are lines that resolve a great deal in the end, when he says that their eyes met and they felt an extraordinary closeness, which is rarely born, that is, a kind of human spontaneity. But in this case, when we get there—what have we got? A casino? A kind of spontaneity and honesty. She decides that she has to go into that casino. She doesn't have to behave today the way she did two years before. And when she says farewell to the past, she moves as if to a sacrifice, it seemed to me, that this decision of yours would more exactly probably be different, different—it's a flop. There will be no new love. There are critics who say that Alma is a future Blanche. But I wouldn't like to see that. And in this second showing it seemed to me that this is the most important thing for you to work on.

M. L. RUZHININA: [...] It seems to me that, by removing the prologue to the production, the theater has lost something, because it's in the prologue that the theme of eternity begins to resound, concretely expressed in the statue of the angel, and a certain statement of eternity which is expressed over the course of the play. Or by a concrete object, as when the gift of the handkerchiefs is made.

M. S. SHKOLIN: [...] The comrades are correct in saying that you have to alter the development of [the character John]. But in the second part you have to get rid of his pathology in the monologue by the [anatomical] chart, when things simply get disgusting and you look at that poster and think that this is a butcher chopping meat. You don't have to do the chart so naturalistically, because it gives rise to unpleasant associations. [...]

I think you've got to have more discussions with the actors and clarify a few details onstage. Many of our comrades were given pause by the scene of the young people's get-together. It didn't produce a particularly negative impression on me. Perhaps the actors could create their roles here without words? [...]

So we have decided today that we shall support the production, taking into account all the comments and requests that have been made. Anatoly Vasil'evich will make certain scenes more comprehensible and clearly projected, especially the final scene. And on the whole we think that this will be a clear and interesting piece of theater.

M. I. Savvina, Ministry of Culture. Act of Acceptance of a Production, August 7, 1980.

[*Summer and Smoke* is accepted, subject to the following conditions:]

1. To carry on work with the actor V. A. Kachan on a clear expression of John's character and the dialectic of his behavior.

2. To eliminate the supernumerary actors' fussily overdoing things in the so-called conversation scene.

3. To present in the finale a clearer picture of Alma's state and behavior (actress O. Yakovleva) so as to show a victory at the end of the play and not a collapse of the heroine's moral principles.

4. To change the anatomical chart of the human body to another, less graphic one.

By THIS POINT Éfros had left the Malaya Bronnaya (see later), and the chief director was Evgeny Nikolaevich Lazarev (1937–), actor at the Mayakovsky Theater from 1961 in comic roles; he joined the Malaya Bronnaya in 1984 but returned to acting at the Mossovet in 1987. Under his guidance, the repertoire deteriorated.

V. I. Shchadrin and O. D. Shiryaeva, "Plan for financing new productions at the Moscow Dramatic Theater in 1984."

Title	Author	Opening date	Budgetary cost
1. *The Theater Manager*	I. Dvoretsky.	1st quarter	3.0
2. *Request Concert*	L. Korsunsky	3rd quarter	4.0
3. *What're You Up To, Old-Timers?*	B. Vasil'ev	4th quarter	12.0
4. *Soldiers Are Not Born*	K. Simonov	Carried over from 1st quarter, 1985	7.0
		Sum total	26.0

The Sovremennik and the Moscow Art Theater

The Sovremennik rapidly became the best-attended theater in Moscow, famous for its intimate acting style and uncluttered productions, its championing of principle in the face of compromise. *Always on Sale* (*Vsegda v prodazhe*, 1965), the first play of the novelist Vasily Aksënov, was a great hit, not least for Oleg Tabakov's multiple roles, including a blowsy refreshment-counter salesgirl. It was reminiscent of the mordant satires of the NÉP period, contrasting a cynical journalist with a naive dreamer in a Moscow tenement. The official critics were careful to praise the comic value of the production, while distancing the theme from everyday Soviet reality.

Yu. Rybakov,[91] "Kistochkin and the rest," *Literaturnaya gazeta* (June 15, 1965), reprinted in A. P. Svobodin, *Teatr "Sovremennik"* (Moscow: Iskusstvo, 1973), 66. Yury Sergeevich Rybakov (1931–), editor in chief of *Teatr* 1965–69, member of the VNII (All-Russian Scientific-Research Institute) 1969–2000, was a Zhdanovito theorist and prolific writer on theater.

Cynicism and cynics, egoists and egoism, philistines and philistinism (in its most up-to-date variety)—all this has attracted the attention of our writers more than once.

---

91 Rybakov, a supporter of the dramatization of literary works and of Lyubimov's work in particular, was hounded from his post at *Teatr* by his more doctrinaire colleagues.

The author of *Always on Sale* offers his take on this theme. He is not writing a story from real life but a satiric fantasy.

The actors' work in the production *Always on Sale*, the subtlety of the directorial devices (the director is O. Efremov), are uniformly excellent. The role of Kistochkin is one of the best or, perhaps, the very best acting work of M. Kozakov. [...] Kistochkin, Treugol'nikov, and Professor Abroskin each take a position on the leading questions of life. The last tries to contradict the worldview of the cynic Kistochkin. There is a discussion of the problems of war and its moral consequences: Kistochkin puts forth his concept that "anything goes" because of its so-called inevitability. But the play has a third level, so to speak, a prophetic one. There the action takes place in an imaginary world, created by Kistochkin's malicious, antihumanist imagination. [...]

In those scenes the author and the theater show what Kistochkin's theory could lead to in real life. The intention is a noble one, but one has to say that there may be too strong a dose of the fantastic onstage.

So, V. Aksënov[92] has written a play, and O. Efremov and the actors have played a performance, packed with civic-minded hatred for cynicism, philistinism, and indifference.

ONE OF THE STRONGEST statements of the Sovremennik's favorite theme came in 1966 in an adaptation by Viktor Rozov of Ivan Goncharov's *The Same Old Story* (*Obyknovennaya istoriya*), his 1847 Bildungsroman about how an ingenuous young man is corrupted by his cynical uncle and his society. Oleg Tabakov was so familiar in roles of fresh-faced youngsters than his transformation into a sleek, impassive opportunist was terrifying.

> N. Lordkipanidze, "Sentimental education," *Pravda* (September 13, 1967), reprinted in Svobodin, *Teatr "Sovemennik,"* 72.

The theater and the actor Oleg Tabakov, who plays the role of Aleksandr, have, of course, studied the works of V. Belinsky[93] and, furthermore, have seen in them one of the foundations of their personal artistic stance. Specifically personal in taking into consideration the views of the new spectator. Specifically, therefore, the same old story—a story of how a young man "rolling along" the road of life lost his illusions one by one—this story is presented by the theater as not so much normal as tragic.

Remember how, in fact, Aleksandr Aduev appears before us at the start? O. Tabakov sketches his hero for us as absolutely positive, absolutely attractive, absolutely sincere

---

92 Vasily Pavlovich Aksënov (1932–2009), whose parents had been interned in labor camps, began writing about rebellious youth. His later plays were not produced, and he emigrated to the United States in the early 1980s.

93 Vissaron Grigor'evich Belinsky (1811–48), liberal critic who believed the theater is "the wellspring of the people's education" and should express the social and spiritual demands of the nation. He preferred progressive messages in the arts and was adopted by the Soviets as a forerunner of socialist realism.

10.8. Minister of Culture Furtseva (center) after the opening night of *The Bolsheviks,* Mikhail Shatrov's controversial play about an attempt on Lenin's life; Sovremennik Theater, Moscow, 1967. Oleg Tabakov stands behind her, hands clasped. She had released the production on her own responsibility and declared it "the best Party meeting I ever attended." Photo: Vladimir Perel'man.

in his aspirations and pledges. And the love that he inspires in the spectator seems to be one of the most important aspects of the directorial concept. We have to believe in him so that we will experience all the bitterness of disappointment later on.

[...] The ending, in which Aleksandr Aduev presents us with a completely "formed" personality, is imprinted all the more powerfully in contrast with another ending on offer—the ending of the life of his uncle Pëtr Aduev, whose character is interpreted with passion and acuity by Mikhail Kozakov. Here we seem to be witness to a bitter paradox: a man who at first poured cold water on Aleksandr's enthusiastic head comes to a standstill in dismay before the consequences of his own teachings. [...]

Galina Volchek has staged an intelligent production.

THE SOVREMENNIK'S ORIGINAL SPONSOR was thrown into full eclipse by its protegé's popularity.

Ever since Nemirovich-Danchenko's death in 1943, the Moscow Art Theater had gone into a decline, its repertory made up of unexciting chestnuts and prize-winning Soviet boilerplate. Its showpiece at this time was *Steelworkers,* a paean to heroic Bolshevik foundrymen. In 1970 the administration brought in Oleg Efremov to improve the situation. The appointment and his acceptance of it appalled both his colleagues at the Sovremennik and the old guard at the MAT. Boris Livanov protested against Efremov—he later referred to him as "the Pretender Grigory Otrepev"—and attacked him for founding a theater artistically opposed to the MAT.

Boris Livanov to the general secretary of the CP USSR, August 19, 1970. In Anatoly Smelyansky,[94] *Ukhodyashchaya natura* [Departing nature] (Moscow: Iskusstvo, 2001), 300–301. Anatoly Mironovich Smelyansky (1942–), literary manager of the Red Army Central Theater 1975–80 and the MAT 1980–87, where he became dean of academic studies; he is a popular television interviewer.

The creative practice of the Sovremennik Theater and its leader O. N. Efremov consistently and persistently confirms a definite line, to wit: in the ideological realm pretentious fault-finding, in the artistic realm a polemic with the art of the MAT ... Not to improve socialism, "to make it useful for mankind," but to improve mankind, "to make it more useful for socialism."

Oleg Tabakov, *Moya nastoyashchaya zhizn'* [My real life] (Moscow: Éksto-Press, 2000), 268–72.

In 1970 Oleg Nikolaevich, leaving the Sovremennik to run the MAT, invited the troupe to go with him. In my view the proposal was purely formal, insofar as there was no way to absorb the whole troupe into the MAT—in the best case, they could have taken five, seven, or four and a half persons, while the remaining forty would have remained unemployed. They would have been left to disintegrate and decay over the course of time. And this would be to deal with them dishonorably.

The creative triumphs of the Sovremennik of that time were not regarded in the best light. Efremov's productions *From Night to Noon*[95] and the first variant of Chekhov's *Seagull* were "sun bleached," I might say. And there was no hope that this situation would change or alter if we moved. On the contrary, the MAT had its own enormous troupe of 120 persons, even without us ...

The playgoers made different sorts of demands on these two theaters: even then, in a period of a certain lull, people queued up all night for tickets to the Sovremennik, while at the MAT, tickets were handed out for free, and the house was rarely full, I am careful to point out.

And to put it plainly, I was offended that the fourteen best years of my life, given to the Sovremennik, somehow would become the tail wagging the dog.

I refused. Zhenya Evstigneev also refused. I think the decision of the rest of the Sovremennik actors not to follow Efremov to the MAT was influenced by my and Evstigneev's position. And something deliberate had to be done, some action or plan so that the Sovremennik would live on.

Then I decided to become the theater's manager. I didn't suggest this myself but agreed to the suggestion—otherwise I would hardly have decided on my own to sacrifice myself. What for? To prove to ourselves and to Oleg Nikolaevich that we could survive

94 Smelyansky's *The Russian Theatre after Stalin* (Cambridge University Press, 1999) was one of the earliest detailed accounts in English of that period written by someone who had observed or participated in many of its major events.
95 *S vechera do poludnya* (1968) by Viktor Rozov.

without him. The question was not whether we could live better without Efremov but how we could preserve the theater. [...]

After six or eight months Evstigneev, who had agitated with me for autonomy, triumphantly moved to the MAT. In explanation he wrote that he had always dreamed of playing the role of the leader of the worldwide proletariat Vladimir Il'ich Lenin. But I knew Zhenya: he was too talented to dream of playing Lenin. It was just a clever formulation, prescribed by Oleg Nikolaevich, to end any discussion. Of course, the leaders understood that this was an attempt on Efremov's part to destroy our theater. Evstigneev was too potent a figure, whose absence would immediately weaken the Sovremennik. For all my respect for the camaraderie of the Sovremennik, Evstigneev and I played in different productions, but equally attracted audiences.

Kozakov, Kalyagin,[96] and Sergachev left with Efremov. Losses, indeed, but what was one to do . . . [...]

My conflict with Efremov went on for two years. We were not even reconciled at the grave of our teacher Vasily Osipovich Toporkov,[97] didn't speak. [...] Sometime later, Oleg Nikolaevich came to the hundredth performance of *Always on Sale* and asked my forgiveness. I forgave him; we shed tears and buried the hatchet.

IN 1973 the Sovremennik moved from central Moscow to a building on Chistye Prudy (Clear Ponds).

The Sovremennik had not been allowed to stage *Molière* when it opened, but Efremov was eager to put it into the Moscow Art repertoire with himself in the lead. He added Smoktunovsky to the company to play Louis XIV and reverted to the alternative title.

> *The Cabal of Bigots* at the MAT. Shapiro, *Kak zakryvalsya zanaves'*, 86–87, 281–82.

[Smoktunovsky] sensed his control over the spectator. At times he made contact with it contrary to the logic of the action. Coming onstage, Smoktunovsky took an enormous pause. He stared intently at the audience, as if focusing its attention on what constituted the real meaning of the beginning performance—"You see, today I play the king. I am Louis!" The actor was so filled with a sense of the significance of this event that the hall subsided in reverential silence and waited. It waited precisely as long as Smoktunovsky thought necessary. Only after he was sure that the spectators were fully aware of how lucky they were did Innokenty Mikhaylovich begin to act. After the performance, in the makeup room, I often reminded him of the awkwardness of such a pause. He would drawl in surprise, "Re-eally? Well, I thought . . ." At the

96 Aleksandr Aleksandrovich Kalyagin (1943–), after stints at the Taganka, the Ermolova, and the Sovremennik, became a fixture of the MAT in a wide range of character roles. In 1993 he created his own theater, the Et Cetera.

97 Vasily Osipovich Toporkov (1889–1970), joined the MAT 1927 and became an adept of Stanislavsky's system; author of *Stanislavsky in Rehearsal* (1948).

next performance the pause would be abbreviated, but it soon started to distend once more. And again, "Re-eally? Well, I thought..." He tried to take account of my note but could not refuse the spectator the right to realize that there was only one king in the place—Smoktunovsky.

Oleg Efremov in *Cabal of Bigots* played better than anyone else the penultimate scene ("Tyrant, tyrant..."), which was the one that got to him most. With a tinge of guilt at rehearsals he insisted that we stick to Bulgakov in every way, but this scene had to be supplemented, another resonance had to be sought. In terms of current affairs the danger of acting a conflict between artist and authorities forced us again and again to return to Molière's fate. Efremov, Tabakov, and I reinterpreted the scene with Bouton first one way, then another. We called to our aid examples both remote and close at hand. The two infernally talented Olegs endlessly recalled their Sovremennik, the productions banned, the viewings for the authorities and so forth; from the distance of years they analyzed once more what they had experienced, the situations and behavior of individuals that stuck in their memory. They tried to merge all this with Bulgakov's text, and as a result it began to sound from Efremov as if uttered for the very first time. The inescapable pain of Molière's position in his advanced years forced him to reevaluate the path he had taken. [...]

IN 1973 the government offered the MAT a technically well-equipped new building on Tverskoy Boulevard, capable of an audience of 1,370; it vast size overwhelmed the actors.

The end of an era is summed up by Leonid Brezhnev's visit to *That's How We'll Win!* by Mikhail Shatrov at the MAT in 1981. The story comes from Burkov,[98] who played the worker who meets with Lenin.

Radzinsky, *Moya teatral'naya zhizn'*, 322–24.

Brezhnev and the members of the Politburo appeared in the box. Applause broke out.
[...]
The performance began.

"Lenin," recounted Burkov, "the director's concept was to have Lenin enter his office modestly, sort of sidling in."

As soon as Lenin appeared in the office, in the silence of the auditorium was heard a voice, known by millions to the point of agony.

"Is that Lenin?"

"Yes," someone in the box whispered in reply.

"Should we greet him?" asked the general secretary.

"No need," one of the members of the Politburo whispered rather loudly.

Meanwhile Il'ich's secretary came onstage.

98 Georgy Ivanovich Burkov (1933–90), shrewd comic actor, at the Stanislavsky Theater 1967–70, 1972–80, the Sovremennik 1970–71, and the MAT 1980–88.

"Who's that?" the general secretary immediately inquired of the whole theater.

"The secretary" came a whisper in the box.

"She's a pretty little thing," remarked Leonid Il'ich.

The audience listened in alarm.

But again the familiar voice:

"Who's that?"

"Krupskaya," replied the whisper.

"Krupskaya? A young one," Brezhnev wondered.

Then came Burkov's turn. He made his entrance and spoke his lines.

"Have him repeat it. I didn't hear," Brezhnev's voice broke out.

In reply someone's soothing whisper was heard.

But the general secretary clearly enjoyed managing the performance. And when a woman in opposition onstage dared to retort to Lenin, Brezhnev was categorical:

"Get rid of her!!" the audience heard.

After this the general secretary was quietly escorted from the box for a while. But he was stubborn and soon returned. And an obsequious member of the Politburo explained what was going on onstage:

"That's Armand Hammer[99] talking to Lenin."

"Hammer's in Moscow?" the general secretary genuinely wondered to the whole theater.

At that someone couldn't hold back any more, or, more precisely, dared not to hold back . . . or didn't need to hold back. Someone's laughter erupted. And immediately the tense silence of the auditorium turned into a general, very nervous roar of laughter.

After that they took Brezhnev to see his favorite hockey game. [. . .]

And the next day, "all Moscow" was talking about Brezhnev's senility.

Hard Times at the Taganka

Demidova, *Dnevnik*, 38–39.

1980

July 13. Play *Hamlet* for the 217th time. Very muggy. And our strength is spent—it's the end of the season, not long ago we had our stressful and onerous tours to Poland. We played *Hamlet* there too. Volodya does not feel well; he runs offstage, gulps down medicine . . . Backstage a Red Cross doctor is on duty. During the show Volodya often forgets his words. In our scene, after the line "Confess yourself to heaven," he quietly asked me, "What's next, I've forgotten?" I prompted him, he went on. He acted well. In the same scene the heavy curtain caught on the tomb on which I was sitting, the tomb moved, and I found myself face-to-face with the ghost of Hamlet's father, whom I am not supposed to see in the performance. Volodya and I successfully made use of our "hitch." In the intermission we talked about how the "hitch" should be well fastened,

99 Armand Hammer (1898–1990), American oil tycoon, art collector, friend of Lenin, and philanthropist; imported pharmaceuticals to the early Soviet Union; although a Republican, he maintained regular business contacts with the Communists.

our general state of feelings, and how—thank God—we could soon go on a break and take it easy. Volodya was in a mild, good-humored mood, rare lately . . .

July 18. Hamlet again. Volodya is inwardly calm, not so excited as on the 13th. Focused. Doesn't forget his lines. Although in the "Mousetrap" scene he ran offstage again—felt bad again . . . Ran onstage very pale, but exact in his cues. Played evenly in our scene. Again very hot. Muggy. Poor audience! From time to time we run into the air in the theater's courtyard, but they sit quiet and tense. However, they're wearing summer clothes, while we're in all-wool, handcrafted, very heavy sweaters and gowns. Everyone is soaking wet from the start. By the curtain call we can barely crawl out from exhaustion. No one even smiles, and only Volodya suddenly stared at me: "Weak, you say. So what, not weak!" Understanding that this was at most only "words, words, words . . .", but, knowing Volodya's excitement, in any case I extricate myself: "Well, no, Volodechka, we'll manage to play it the last time on the 27th . . ."

July 25–27. I arrive at the theater at 10:00 for the rehearsal. I run, late as always. At the door with tears in his eyes Alësha Poray-Koshits,[100] who heads the production unit. "Don't rush." "Why not?" "Volodya's dead." "Which Volodya?" "Vysotsky. At four in the morning."

The Vysotsky tribute in 1981. Lyubimov, *Rasskazy starogo trepacha*, 417, 428–29.

Top secret

Central Committee of the Communist Party of the Soviet Union

On the possible antisocial manifestations connected with the anniversary of the death of the actor Vysotsky July 13, 1981.

According to reports from the operative sources, the director in chief of the Moscow Theater of Drama and Comedy on the Taganka Yu. Lyubimov, in preparing a new production about that theater's actor Vysotsky, who died in 1980, is attempting from tendentious positions to show Vysotsky's creative path, his interactions with the organs of culture, and to represent the actor as a great "combative" artist, ostensibly "unrewarded and deliberately forgotten by the authorities."

The premiere of the production is planned for July 25, the day of the anniversary of Vysotsky's death. On that day the unofficially created "Committee on the Creative Legacy of Vysotsky" at the Theater on the Taganka [. . .] intends to take action devoted to the actor's memory on the site of his burial in Vagan'ka Cemetery in Moscow and at the site of the theater at the conclusion of the performance, which may provoke unwholesome agitation on the part of Vysotsky's admirers in the areas near the theater and create conditions for possible demonstrations of an antisocial character.

Communicated as a point of information.

Chairman of the Committee on Govt Security *Yu. Andropov.*[101] [. . .]

---

100 Aleksey Evgenevich Poray-Koshits (1941–), stage designer at the MAT and the Taganka, but primarily for Lev Dodin at the Leningrad TYUZ and then at the Maly Theater of St. Petersburg from 1984.

101 Yury Vladimirovich Andropov (1914–84), ambassador to Hungary 1953–57, responsible for

November 10, 1981.

Central Committee of the Communist Party of the Soviet Union

On the behavior of the director Yu. P. Lyubimov in relation to the preparation for the production *Vladimir Vysotsky* at the Taganka Theater.

[...] Vysotsky's popularity, particularly after his death, distinctly contains an element of unhealthy sensationalism, vehemently whipped up by hostile circles abroad, interested in enlisting Vysotsky in the category of dissidents, "outsiders."

Vysotsky's poetic and sung legacy is uneven and extremely contradictory, caused by his narrow-minded worldview. The artistic fate, behavior, and frame of mind of Vysotsky had pernicious utterance in his ideological immaturity, seen as well in such personal specifics as his marriage to a French actress, M. Vlady,[102] and his proneness to alcoholism, which aggravated his mental drama and split focus and led to a religious and creative crisis.

[...] In fact the whole content of the script aims to prove that the poet "was hunted down," to depict his conflict with our society, the predestination and inevitability of his ruin. A remarkable number of his songs, included in the script, are taken from records released abroad, from Vysotsky's archive, which have not received authorization from Glavlit.

Included in the script are excerpts from Shakespeare's *Hamlet* used tendentiously, with definite subtext.

This same aim is underlined by excerpts from the works of the American [*sic*] dramatist Stoppard,[103] famous for his anti-Soviet views and works.

The series of poems and songs has been inserted into the script with the admitted preconception of creating the "oppressive" atmosphere in which Vysotsky ostensibly lived. [...] The culmination of this theme is reached in Vysotsky's song "The Wolf Hunt," which metaphorically depicts the situation of the artist in Soviet society. [...] The creators of the script oppose Vysotsky's work to the art of socialist realism. [...]

THE VYSOTSKY TRIBUTE was forbidden, and a series of preemptive bans were laid on planned productions of *The Suicide,* Dostoevsky's *The Devils,* and Pushkin's *Boris Godunov.* Lyubimov, who had already taken his company on a tour of Paris in 1977, went to London in 1983 to stage *Crime and Punishment* at the Lyric Theater. Using the pretext that he made anti-Soviet remarks in a newspaper interview, the

---

crushing the Hungarian uprising of 1956; head of the KGB 1967–82; succeeded Brezhnev as general secretary of the Communist Party. His attempt at reforms was aborted by a sudden death from kidney failure.

102 Marina Vlady (actually de Poliakoff-Baidaroff, 1938–), French film actress of Russian parentage who married Vladmir Vysotsky in 1969; she joined the Communist Party to ease their long-distance relationship.

103 Tom Stoppard (actually Tomáš Straussler, 1937–), Czech-born British playwright; at this point he was best known for *Rosencrantz and Guildenstern Are Dead* (1966), *Jumpers* (1972), and *Travesties* (1974). He visited the Soviet Union in 1977 with Amnesty International and became a protestor against state censorship.

government withdrew his Soviet citizenship. For four years he wandered the globe, staging plays and operas in various languages.

Demidova, *Dnevnik*, 274–77.

1983

September 1–15. After the premiere of *Crime and Punishment* in London there was a press conference, at which one of the workers at the Soviet Embassy snidely whispered, "Yu. P., you may be staging the crime here, but when you get back to Moscow, punishment will be waiting for you." Lyubimov told the assembled reporters that he is staying in London and hasn't decided to return to Moscow.

December 10. Lyubimov phoned [from London] to know if his name is still on the poster. So far—yes.

December 17. Artistic council at theater … What to do next? We decided to write a letter to Andropov, to meet with Zamyatin, to phone Lyubimov constantly, for ourselves to perform January 25 the show about Vysotsky. At Lyubimov's request we should start the revival of *Boris Godunov* [...]

December 27. I phoned Andropov's assistant, who told me rather harshly that I had to address Chernenko,[104] he deals with all these matters now.

1984

January 11. Got Chernenko's phone number, phoned—very harsh conversation: "he doesn't deal with these matters by himself, and he can't force Lyubimov to return if he doesn't want to."

January 15. On Dupak's behalf I phoned Lapin[105] on TV with the request to help film our productions. He screamed that he doesn't intend to film anti-Soviet productions, etc. He slammed down the receiver.

January 19. The Vysotsky show was banned on 25 January. We'll do an evening. Lyubimov's in Milan. [...]

January 20. [...] There are rumors that Éfros is coming to the Taganka.

February 9. Andropov is dead.

March 6. Lyubimov's citizenship is withdrawn.

March 11. Decree to appoint Éfros artistic head of the Taganka.

March 13. Galya Volchek invited me to join her theater [the Sovremennik].

March 20. Introduction of Éfros to the troupe. I didn't leave.

March 21. Efremov said he can take me in his company only next season, since he had phoned Anurov (manager of the MAT), Zaytsev (deputy minister), and said he wouldn't take anyone from the Taganka.

April 8. First Éfros rehearsal. *Lower Depths.*

April 18. Our theatrical archive was confiscated and moved somewhere else.

104 Konstantin Ustinovich Chernenko (1911–85), a close associate of Brezhnev, member of the Central Committee and the Politburo from 1978; after Andropov's death, chosen general secretary of the Communist Party but died of emphysema within a year.
105 Sergey Georgievich Lapin (1912–90), Party apparatchik and diplomat; director general of TASS 1970 and chairman of the State Committee for Television and Radio Broadcasting 1970–85.

Yakovleva, *Esli by znat'* . . . , 327–29, 333–35.

When the idea was broached of moving to the Taganka—at the end of February or the beginning of March 1984—Anatoly Vasil'evich invited me to his home. There were Natasha and Dima. Anatoly Vasil'evich said, "I've brought you here because you are dear to me and I want to explain my opinion. I've been offered a transfer to the Taganka. What do you think about this?" Natasha rather definitely said, "I raise both hands for."—"What do you think, Dima?" Dima was sullenly silent. I said, "I raise both hands against." And I explained why: I thought this was not the collective for Anatoly Vasil'evich.

He then said, "I have worked with them, I know this collective. Moreover, they've been without a director a long time, and no one knows if Lyubimov is coming back or not. I staged *Cherry Orchard* with them—it's a remarkable gang of . . . craftsmen."

For some reason, even earlier, while still at the Malaya Bronnaya, he had called them "a craft guild." A kind of "combat team." To the general dissatisfaction of disciples and other actors, he told us, "You understand, it's a kind of worker's craft guild." Into this term *craft guild* he put something meaningful.

Vysotsky was alive at the time, and the association with him had evidently retained pleasant memories.

But from rumors I knew how they lived both backstage and in everyday life. I had heard what goes on in all sorts of theaters, talked with directors, they would say: "No, that place is full of bandits!"—"What about that place?"—"That place is a kind of swamp . . ."—"What about there?"—"There—they drink." Well, and there is something more—for instance, they say in a kind of sleazy actor's slang, "I'm a genius, and you're a genius."

Later I became convinced of much of it myself. In the Theater on the Taganka, because they were in opposition to the authorities, a kind of sinister power took shape. Only here—in this mutinous collective!—did I hear that "under Stalin things were better," "under Stalin there was order."

And of course they did drink there. They also did me an honor. Right next to their theater was a kind of glassed-in booth, with drinks. And some men of the theater—Zolotukhin and the secondary romantic lead Antipov,[106] and someone else—invited me into the glass booth. Right after the first rehearsal: "Come on, you're part of the theater—so let's go!" Éfros waited, not without anxiety, to see what I would do. I said, "Where?"—"Right next door, to the glass booth!"—"What for?"—"We-ell, *you know what!*" I said, "No, I don't engage in *you know what.*" [. . .]

Anatoly Vasil'evich soon agreed to the transfer. He said, "What else am I going to do?" [. . .] He simply couldn't imagine not going every day to a rehearsal somewhere. [. . .]

They didn't strike me as a "craft guild"—they were a half-drunken fellowship in the theater world, constantly creating a situation of scandal and obstruction in relation to the authorities: were it not for this obstruction, half of their social notoriety would have evaporated.

---

106 An odd description of Feliks N. Antipov, a comic talent, who played such character roles as Orgon in *Tartuffe* and Varlaam in the aborted *Boris Godunov.*

A question lingered about this: obstruction is obstruction, but what was the relationship to the authorities? What kind of authority is this, you are ostensibly in opposition to it, you are always giving it the finger—and this same authority builds this oppositional theater an enormous new building? What's the logic in that? Artists who are in opposition, even privately, covertly, rarely receive buildings and a chief directorial staff. And now for this "opposition" they have built an enormous, fully modern hangar of a theater and say, "Take possession of this, our opponents—those who oppose us!" There's a discrepancy here. Or were the authorities nicer than we thought?

Rehearsals [for *The Lower Depths*] began. Of course, the rebellious part of the troupe—consisting, strictly, of four leading actors—continued to rebel even at rehearsals. They demonstrated that they were free to come to rehearsals or not, rehearse or not, or rehearse and mutiny at the same time.

At rehearsals they suggested all sorts of clichés from old Lyubimov productions: to wear a sort of rubber cap with holes, stick hair through the holes—they thought it would be funny and meaningful.

As I have already said, their aesthetic was alien to me. Evidently so was the artistic world of Éfros to them. It would seem there is also a stylized, poetical theater with Lyubimov—but the poetics of these directors were diametrically different. How was one to combine the "craftsmanship," Blue Blouse, sharp-etched manner with the subtle psychology of Anatoly Vasil'evich? Besides, they came to rehearsal either drunk or half-drunk. And didn't come at all. There were three performers for every role. And if today, let's say, the through-line of Kleshch was worked out with one actor, Zolotukhin, the next day Zolotukhin didn't show up and Filatov[107] did. And it was exactly like that with every detail—Éfros again patiently for three hours explained the same ten-minute scene, which had been rehearsed the day before. Then for two days running Filatov didn't show up—a third actor came onstage, to whom again, with the same details, patiently, Anatoly Vasil'evich showed the same design.

[...] He couldn't understand, because it was all alien and incomprehensible to him, the fear, tale-bearing, toadyism. And more—envy. Even though Vysotsky was not there and *Cherry Orchard* had been removed from the repertoire, he could not be forgiven having played Lopakhin for Éfros.

The troupe was variegated: some were talented and well known, others were the run-of-the-mill whom no theater can do without. They behaved modestly, worthily, and more or less creatively. And there were those who usually took almost no part in the creative process, the so-called support group—they took no initiatives, put their hopes in no director, and never expected anything for themselves.

Anatoly Vasil'evich had often compared the theater to jazz. And I was surprised that in this difficult atmosphere of rebellion, with those involved in the work from actor's vanity and those uninvolved from dissatisfaction (no matter how many teams were assigned, you couldn't count on the whole population of the theater), a production

---

107 Leonid Alekseevich Filatov (1946–2003), acted at the Taganka from 1969, with a term at the Sovremennik 1985–87; played the Master in *Master and Margarita,* Horatio in *Hamlet.* He also composed poems, parodies, and plays.

evolved, literally based on a jazz polyphony. The actors submitted to his direction—willy-nilly, there was no way of wriggling out of it. They were already in thrall to his directorial musicality, if I may put it that way.

The production opened. But it came with great difficulty—both psychologically and even simply physically. Before the premiere itself Anatoly Vasil'evich had had a mini heart attack. We visited him in the hospital, and Anatoly Vasil'evich wrote letters to the actors, his instructions to the troupe: how to act, how to hold their ground, how to behave before the performance—a director's pedagogical wishes. [...] But the actors were not very concerned with them. They were already performing and were now interested only in their own success and "the matter of food and drink." They were not much bothered at the opening by the absence and illness of the man who had staged it.

The Soviet Army Theater

The artistic council system was particularly cumbersome at the Central Theater of the Soviet Army, because the latter phases of the inspection process were visited by members of GLAVPUR (Glavnoe Politicheskoe Upravlenie Sovietskoy Armii iVoenno-Morskogo Flota—Chief Political Directorate of the Soviet Army and Military–Naval Fleet). In 1980 a new production by Aleksandr Vil'kin,[108] *Farmers in Armor* [*Usvyatskie Shelmonostsy,* literally *The Helmet-Wearing Villagers of Usvyaty*], dealt with a rural community during the first days of the Great Patriotic War. The subject was a ticklish one, since Soviet troops had just invaded Afghanistan the year before. The year also saw the nuclear physicist Andrey Sakharov exiled to Gorky, Vysotsky's death, and the boycott of the Moscow Olympics. At the first meeting the play was discussed by actors and directors and provisionally accepted. At the second meeting, army staff and Party apparatchiks posed objections. By the third meeting, advice from brass hats played an even greater role. The play did, eventually, enter the repertoire.

> Minutes no. 9 of the meeting of the Artistic Council of the TsATSA, May 7, 1980. Discussion of *Farmers in Armor,* a dramatization by A. Sherel' of a short story by E. Nosov.[109]

BURDONSKY:[110] The production has been accepted today. The tempo-rhythm works. There's a lot of interesting actor's work. But it all has to be polished. Components

108 Aleksandr Mikhaylovich Vil'kin (1943–), actor and director at the Taganka 1968–77, 1983–91, where he played John Reed, Mayakovsky, and both Orgon and Tartuffe in *Tartuffe*; director at the Mayakovsky Theater 1977–82.

109 Evgeny Ivanovich Nosov (1925–2002), novelist; his short story "Uskvatye Shelmonostsy" (Helmet wearers of Uskvyaty, 1980) was so popular that he expanded it into a volume of tales under that name in 1986. Many of the problems with the play came from the pretensions of the adaptor Sherel'.

110 Aleksandr Vasil'evich Burdonsky (1941–), from 1972 director at the Central Army Theater, preferred strong female roles as the focus of his productions.

of the production are very interesting, it seemed to me that A. M. Vil'kin has managed to read Nosov in an interesting and content-rich way. It seems to me that the
exposition of P. I. Vishnyakov[111] in the "Book of Hours" scene is raisonneur-like,
he can probably do the exposition other than by reading a script over the radio. In
terms of lighting, it's an interesting production. But at the very beginning, there's
a dim vacuum light. By and large the theater has acquired a good production for
the big stage on our themes.

ZEL'DIN[112] [leading actor, not cast in the show]: "Do the Russians want war?" That's
what this production answers. Russians are the most peace-loving people. Vil'kin
has made an interesting, profound production, which will create excitement. The life
of the village is well constructed. The performance is very moving. This production
precisely belongs to our theater. I like the actors' work a lot. It seemed to me that
there are some longueurs that need to be abridged, but on the whole it's a beautiful
production. Even the music is very organic, the staging is good. I personally vote
for this production and congratulate the whole staging collective. Very clear-cut
are these peaceful people who don't understand immediately that this is war.

PASTUKHOVA:[113] I too understand that the time period and conditions were complicated
and difficult. What did I like unconditionally? It's the ensemble quality of all the
decisions. To my mind, there is a very serious "but" in the production—its awful
prolixity. I think it has to be shortened.

MAYOROV:[114] I think that this production is greatly needed, the acting team is magnificent. The performance is exciting. But it seems to me too that the production
will only work if it's shortened. To my mind, you have to shorten the last scene in
Kos'yan's home, you could cut Mironov-Prokhorov's monologue. And a serious
problem is that the dialogue is inaudible. But it's a good script and very moving. I
agree with Burdonsky—it's impossible to keep Selivan-Vishnyakov's radio broadcast.

I. S. UNGUVYANU [a director]: Nowadays people rarely stage an author, basically all
directors stage themselves. Today I met with precisely the opposite case—a beautiful narrative, a wonderful clear-cut adaptation, and a careful relation of the director to the author. Not since *Wooden Horses* can I recall such a wonderful Russia.
An epic production is the result—what is rare, it is authentic and national. As to
abridgement, it is necessary, but it has to be carefully deliberated. The actors are
so realistic, antihistrionic, that's why the dialogue is inaudible. To my mind, the
most histrionic and stagy scene is the dialogue of Makhotikha and Kos'yan—and
it seemed superfluous. As to cuts: the beginning of the Book of Hours scene is
superfluous—no loss. In Act II it's more complicated. The main thing is not to lose

111 Pëtr Il'ich Vishnyakov (1911–88), after acting in Voronezh, joined the Central Army Theater
     1956, where he played Chapaev and Lopakhin in *The Cherry Orchard*.
112 Vladimir Mikhaylovich Zel'din (1915–) joined the Central Army Theater 1945, where his acting
     was noted for physical plasticity and musicality. He became the oldest living actor in Russia.
113 Mariya Fominichna Pastukhova (1918–2003) joined the Central Army Theater 1945, where she
     played delicate but emotionally steadfast women.
114 Mikhail Mikhaylovich Mayorov (1906–93), at the MAT 2 from 1930; joined the Central Army
     Theater 1936, playing two roles in the popular production of Lope de Vega's *Dancing Master*.

now that inner sanctity, supplied by all the creators of the performance. I recall the finale being more powerful in the author—those living streams of people, flowing out of the different villages. I was shaken reading Vishnyakov's text—so wise, so subtle, so beautiful. Beautiful work from Pokrovskaya, Petrov, and Zakharov. [...]

SMELYANSKY [dramaturg]: I was excited by this work and because I myself invited Vil'kin and Sherel'. This is not a dramatization but a play, less than 40 percent of the author's text is left, and Nosov himself was surprised. Vil'kin was not afraid to be circumstantial, quiet in the production. The actors' faces were luminous. The beautiful work of the actors—Pokrovskaya,[115] Vishnyakov, I have never seen such quality. To my mind, the work is wonderful, bright, palpitating. Obviously there are things that can be shortened to keep the performance from being boring. This production is honest, that's very important. The power, the enormous spring thaw of the people—that ought to be in the finale. Mironov today overdid the last monologue, but what he had worked on must be preserved. Now the question is whether it is possible for Vil'kin to make cuts and the finale before the 9th, he would have to play the replacement on the 9th. If this is not possible, there's no need to jump-start the actors, and we can wait until May 16.

SABEL'NIKOV: It is a production of our own, on a theme of our own. Russians don't want war, but when necessary, they can defend their Russia. Indubitably there are very powerful things in the production: impressive scenes—the beginning of the performance is a powerful scene, the last in Kos'yan's house.

Objections raised:

1. The episode with the lecturer—by his appearance alone one understands that he is an empty vessel. The scene presents knockabout farce, but this is a tragedy. When does it happen? If 1923, then you have to remove the line about the fact that our guys were beaten, no one in the village knew about that.
2. When Vutoy gets the news about the war, there has to be a "connection" between him and the peasants.
3. There is a lot of drinking, especially in the last scene, but this should have a Christian aspect.
4. The final monologue of the chairman sounded difficult today.
5. The real water distracts attention and grated on me personally.

Finally, the show has to be shortened. I think that there's no need to talk about May 9. After the stipulated revisions it will have be inspected again as to the results.

VIL'KIN: 1. As to the monologue—today Mironov went off the rails—he will do it well.

2. The finale—we'll deal with it.

3. The bathing scene—in any tragic genre, if there are no farcical scenes, the tempo-rhythm can't be maintained. We are piling up the serious scenes as high as possible. Besides, this bathing is taken seriously and purely by men who are

---

115 Alina Stanislavovna Pokrovskaya (1940–) joined the Central Army Theater in 1963, in a wide range of roles; played Natal'ya in *Farmers in Armor*.

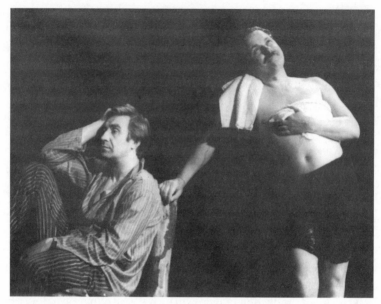

10.9. The bathhouse scene in *Farmers in Armor* by Aleksandr Sherel', directed by Aleksandr Vil'kin and designed by Pëtr Belov, Red Army Theater, Moscow, 1980.

going off to war, and many to their deaths. The main thing in this scene is "a certain stillness."

4. We can cut down Morecheva, but in terms of tonality she is doing it correctly.

Now about the situation—we can't open the production after eight full-stage rehearsals. Before the 16th all I have left are three rehearsals; to open the production on the 16th with a second team, then on the 18th the actors—a large group is going to Germany.

Decision: On the whole the Arts Council has accepted the production. Tomorrow morning, May 10, it will be performed with revisions, and on the 16th the second team will be presented.

President of the Artistic Soviet TsATSA   *V. Strel'tsov*
Secretary of the Artistic Soviet TsATSA   *S. Yarmolinskaya*

Minutes no. 10 of the meeting of the Artistic Soviet of TsATSa, May 16, 1980.

STROEVA[116] [invited critic and historian]: The production moved me deeply. The sensation of national truth, when the simplest folk encounter war. A feeling for Sholokhov's line, Shukshin's.[117] A well-executed beginning—the calendar, the grand-

---

116 Marianna Nikolaevna Stroeva (1917–2006), theater historian, on the editorial board of *Teatr* in the 1950s; her article on Volodin's *Factory Girl* was the first sign of a thaw in theater criticism.
117 Vasily Makarovich Shukshin (1929–74), actor and writer, who during the Thaw wrote popular tales of village life, often filmed.

father clock—the war is beginning. The sensation of great truth of both the work itself and the actors. Moracheva played the old woman splendidly—the element of a holy relationship to troubles. Vishnyakov is the link to the epic perspective of national life. This is a new word in our search for a military theme—no explosions or murders. The theme of readiness, of the approach of what is to happen tomorrow. All this can be read in the clear and spacious directorial inventions. Everything is presented simply and familiarly . . . Tears welled up in everyone and pride at the strength of the people that comes out in this production. The first act is a bit static. If the production is tightened up, it will be more dynamic.

ANIKOVICH:[118] Soldiers have always gone to war all through the ages, and will the spectators understand here why people are going to war?

STROEVA: In the production, there is our time, our people, with whom we faced the war, that and the chairman of the kolkhoz—his fiery speech about the flag. This and the splendid girl—the female komsomol, and the lieutenant and Vasil'ev as Kas'yan. These are Soviet people, our own, and they go to defend the Soviet land—this is indisputable.

ZEL'DIN: The production is very profound, it is antiwar–pro-peace. I am seeing it for the third time—the performance has grown. It moves me. This is not a cerebral [*lobovoy*] production—it's alive, realistic.

PASTUKHOVA: It seems to me that the production stands comparison with those we've seen in the recent past. But to my mind, there are still long-drawn-out moments in the inner rhythm. War demands a greater sense of things happening. There is in this production a certain flatness, a languor. The scene of Davydka and Nyurka doesn't develop. I expected more people in the finale. The production keeps on getting better and better.

UNGURYANU: I believe that this is a real, exceptional triumph for the theater. Not once did I get the feeling that this is not timely, not something Soviet: this is a very human work. There is no belligerence in the Russian nature—we are a peaceful people. The advent of the Soviet power—its first decree about peace—means our power, our Revolution confirmed this—a peaceful existence. This is the second patriotic war after 1812. There are productions that have to be listened to like symphonic music. I understood in this work that our concern is true—we will triumph, and this is not done with slogans, which would be very simple, but flows from the life onstage.

ANIKOVICH: But what in the production paves the way for this triumph? Where do you see this?

UNGURYANU: The most important question the production answers is what do the Russian people want? Being Soviet is what unites us, whatever our roots—whether we are Russians or Moldovians . . .

BURDONSKY: For me, there's no question what these people are going to war for. For their land, for their children, mothers, wives, horses, for all of that. Here there is a

118 Vsevolod Ivanovich Anikovich, an army general and deputy of the Political Directorate of the Soviet Army and Navy (GlavPUR), in charge of all military theaters.

hint of Tolstoy—the intensity of the upsurge of the soul. Here the eternal problem of the world and war, you don't have to look in it for a particular era.

SMELYANSKY: The question is the limits of our Soviet patriotism. Our writers, the so-called village school—Rasputin, Shukshin, Astaf'ev,[119] Nosov, and so on. Soviet patriotism is not divorced from Russian, national patriotism. In times of crisis this theme of *Brothers and Sisters*[120] has always arisen—this was the address to the people at the start of the war. In Nosov the start of the war is like lifting up a club. The transition of Russian patriotism into Soviet. Nosov demonstrated this clearly. First I go to defend child, mother, wife, river, neighbor, then the flag—the nation. That is precisely the reason for the appearance of Prokhor the chairman. This is a completely concrete place and time. In Nosov it is an idyllic, pastoral narrative. This is something concrete; you can't expect it to answer every question—it answers one—if a threat arrives from without, everyone will rise as one man to defend this Motherland of ours. Now as to the actors: the present team—Vasil'ev—this is beautiful work, although it is only his third time onstage. Interesting work from Gulbkina, Seliverstova. Right now the performance has been shortened by forty-five minutes, but there are still passages that may be cut.

UNGURYANU: Here everything happens in the first three days of the war and people haven't had time to understand fascism.

FILIPPOV [commander of TsATSA]: I've seen the third performance. On the evening of the 10th, one-third of the spectators left the hall, but it was a replacement for *The Comic Fantasy*.[121] Today's performance has grown a lot, although there are still opportunities for cuts. The question as to whether this period is Soviet seems strange: clearly this is a Soviet village, there's a chairman of the kolkhoz, a brigadier, a komsomol girl—collective-farm and historical problems predetermine this. It's all familiar. We see with the eyes of the victors. There may still be a bit to trim from the performance, but today it grew.

BELYAEVSKY [responsible for military and Communist propaganda]: Nevertheless there are still doubts about nationalism, party feeling, and socialisticity. From the point of view of nationalism, it's the victory of the collective. And from the socialistic point of view, for me, there isn't enough of a certain element—the Red Star, the Kremlin, the Flag. The comrades haven't learned that this is a performance, it must have an educational significance. You have undertaken to show 3 days out of the whole war. How does the ordinary man prepare to go to war? The supreme level of the ideological acceptance of the war is there, this is in the scene with the banner, but there are still reservations. A sense of moderation in the religious question is somewhat missing. There are lots of shouts of "Lord!" You have to strengthen

---

119 Valentin Grigor'evich Rasputin (1937–) and Viktor Petrovich Astaf'ev (1924–2001) were both rural writers, upholding conservative values against modern moral relativism; Rasputin joined the reactionary *Pamyat'* movement, and Astaf'ev was criticized for his chauvinism and racism.

120 *Bratya i sёstry* (1958), a novel by Fёdor Abramov, concerning the life of a village during and immediately after World War II; later successfully adapted to the stage by Lev Dodin.

121 A play by Grigory Izrail'evich Gorin (actually Ofshtein, 1940–2000), many of whose Aesopic comedies were banned prior to 1985.

the highly ideological side of the production. Chibisov, the representative of the government, should be weightier and not so funny. [...]

SAVEL'NIKOV: If you compare the two performances I've seen, definite steps have been taken. That's understood. Of course, everyone understands what the stage dialogue means. We have to start with Nosov. And when we start adding things, we are at odds with Nosov, we can go on adding things. In the first days of the war, there was no religious upsurge. There is a definite leveling of our heroes—all one height, one psychology, one domestic situation. We can get rid of the word "Lord!" Get rid of the cross and the book. Chibisov has been improved—he's no longer the scoundrel he was before. In the Book of Hours, when Selivan tells about how he killed his first German—he's not used to killing—hatred for the enemy deadened the feeling of revulsion at murder.

ANIKOVICH: The very fact that the production has evoked such a spirited discussion says that it has to be fought for. Work still has to be done on the production—to deal with our misgivings. Chances are it will become our triumph. Gloom, passivity, religiosity are to be reduced. But from what we have seen today, it should not be opened as is. I get the impression that it will bear the chief patriotic commitment for definite corrections.

SMELYANSKY: I think that if we postpone showing this production to audiences, it will be much weakened. Of course we won't advertise performances, but it might be possible to play it as a replacement.

ANIKOVICH: Let the director say what he can do.

VIL'KIN: Make all the revisions needed to perform the production, otherwise the actors will not understand what's expected of them. We are of one mind with you and think the same—so the spectators in the auditorium will become of one mind with us.

SMELYANSKY: We promise you that everything will be corrected, but the production must live.

RESOLUTION: Tomorrow night the production will be performed instead of *30 Days Away*.

BELOV: Today we'll play it as a replacement, then we'll rehearse, we'll play it as a replacement again on May 25, and we'll invite you again.

VIL'KIN: Before May 25, I will open the production with two casts, with revisions.

SHEREL': We'll need two or three days to make the improvements in the script. We have already thought about this ourselves and, practically speaking, we didn't expect today's remarks. Before these changes become the flesh of the production we will have to test them before an audience.

RESOLUTION: To carry on work on the production and on May 25–26 to show it to the leadership of the PUR. [...]

Minutes no. 11 of the Meeting of the Artistic Soviet of TsATSA, May 26, 1980.

ZEL'DIN: This is a very profound patriotic production, a beautiful, pure relation to the motherland.

MAYOROV: The production has grown in strength. It is filled with optimism, sorrow, no depression or dismay. The hearts of these people are full of faith in victory. In the production, there's no deviation from a straight course—there is an inner fullness.

KASATKINA:[122] The dearest thing in the production are those people, the simply Soviet folk, who cannot be defeated. In the production, there is infinite respect for our forebears, for history. It is an important point of contact with history, our motherland. It's very dark, it needs to be lightened up. In general this production is growing, maturing. In Selivan's story about the German I didn't get the words "had to."

SAZONOVA:[123] I liked the production a lot. Anyone who has survived the war cannot fail to be excited. The production is growing by leaps and bounds. The actors had little time to rehearse, and they emerged heroically from a difficult situation. To my mind, Vishnyakov shouldn't read the narrator's text, it should be someone who doesn't play a character. I liked Mironov in this production—very authentic, simple. If you make cuts, it has to be done very carefully and attentively; if you remove the scene of Chibisov and Dus'ka, the fate of that woman will vanish.

BURDONSKY: Beautiful material—literary, living—is brought onstage. Chukhovsky[124] has an expression: "Shy heroism." There's something of that in the production. This is a return to the source—to the peasantry, the man of the soil. Pushkin said, "The Russian peasant shows by his gait that he is not a slave." Faith not in god-bothering, but faith in harmony, the harmony of everyday life. It is precisely this that allowed the Russian, not at all belligerent, to triumph in wars that settled the fate of Russia.

SMELYANSKY: What is important in this remarkable literary material? Of course, we didn't set ourselves the goal of taking in the whole war with all it comprehended. It is a reflection of victory, its sources. The hidden warmth of patriotism—that's what L. Tolstoy said about something similar. This is precisely what interested us in the production—the origin, the sources of patriotism. It is important to us that the accents of the time, the Soviet time, be heard by the spectators.

COLONEL 1: The production has become more dynamic. The excitement of the final scene is palpable. In the Book of Hours scene, there is still a note of pacifism. A healthy peasant asks, "Will there be killing?" This is naive. In the scene of farewells all four huts are identical. Drunken Makhotin grates on the spectator, me in particular. The actors played lustily.

ANIKOVICH: On Saturday I visited the Deyneka[125] exhibition—brilliant works. They move people, stagger them with their inner power: the portrait of a milkmaid, of a steel founder, "The Defense of Petrograd." There is not one little red star on them, but there is no doubt that these are Soviet people.

122 Lyudmila Ivanovna Kasatkina (1925–2012) began her work at the Central Army Theater 1947 under Aleksey Popov; her heroines were noted for simplicity and cleverness.

123 Nina Afanas'evna Sazonova (1917–2004) entered the Central Army Theater troupe 1938 as a student of Aleksey Popov; inclined to comedy even in serious roles.

124 Korney Ivanovich Chukovsky (actually Nikolay Vasil'evich Korneychukov, 1882–1969), popular children's author, once attacked by Natal'ya Krupskaya.

125 Aleksandr Aleksandrovich Deyneka (1899–1969), painter and sculptor, famous for his genre scenes and monumental heroic tableaux from Soviet life.

I've seen the production twice—of course there is growth. And the production moves me. But if we want to preserve this production, we have to move in the following directions:

1. The village is altogether archaic. Twenty-three years of Soviet power, and the villagers haven't matured at all.

2. The leveling of the people—young and old, all turn to this old man, who is excellently played by Vishnyakov.

3. Remnants of pacifism. The second scene with the women. I cannot believe that in their soul they all live to see the victory.

4. The chairman has not matured to be a real chairman. I am not moved by his final monologue. The personality of the deputy from on high—that lecturer—is very unconvincing, and it would be better to cut the last scene with the woman. I don't like the scene of Selivan's tale about killing a German. And I still don't want to hear from the stage abusive words and often one particular word about the German. There's a lot of belief in God. You have already done a great deal. And you have to go on improving. The lighting is very subdued.

SAZONOVA: There is a man who will go to war and even on his own, not by a summons, and there is a man who will never go to war, that's the lecturer who comes to this village of those who will go to war. Why do we need to beautify him? Don't we have such "lecturers" among us?

ZEL'DIN: In this specific case the production is very subtle, but everyone is urging us to provide slogans. In every aspect of our life the means of influencing our people are changing. After all, life is light and shadow, and you want black to be black, red to be red. The production has to open.

SAZONOVA: There is a young commander who opposes this lecturer, he will go to war.

GENERAL 2: There is in the production an ideological meaning—a man has shouldered a duffel bag and gone into action, what feelings were evoked by war in the simple people, the sources of victory. Now we are thinking about what needs to be done so that the production makes these ideas understood. I was excited by the last scene, although the chairman did not speak his speech the best. I think that some reworking is still needed. We don't become overjoyed when it is the lecturer who is criticized. The scene of the story of killing the German—you cannot compare an imperialist war with a patriotic one. You have somehow drawn a veil over specifically Soviet patriotism. I am against the fact that they keep referring to Russia all the time, and not to the Soviet Union. [...]

LIZICHEV:[126] Every single one of us is looking at you—all the departments. When I read the novella, I delighted in E. Nosov's language—what verbal power, what power in portraying an individual. Outstanding literature has dropped onto our stage—of course, this is material after our own heart. The production is moving. The acting is beautiful. The narrative covers a very brief period of time—two to three weeks

126 Aleksey Dmitrievich Lizichev (1927–), army general, the youngest officer to be named chief of the Main Political Administration of the Soviet Army and Navy, by Gorbachëv to put through his reforms.

is one thing, but with you only the 22nd, 23rd, have gone by. The 22nd was both a tragic day and a day of confusion, but also certainly of victory—indeed, there had just been victories in Khalkhin-Gol, in Finland, and so on. And Nosov provides the lecturer too, he reflects what was thought at the time, but where Nosov bids farewell to this lecturer, you make him the representative of the Soviet power and a dirty dog and a slippery human being. After all, he's the only representative of the Soviet power. It would be better for such a one to come from the peasants—there are all sorts in the community, and he's the only one, so that it would be more like the novella.

We are military men—we have taken an oath to this power, for this power twenty million have perished, and we ought to respect that. You have to become reconciled that the period matters —better to be closer to Nosov.

It seems to me that your production might sooner be called not "helmet-wearers" but cross-wearers. The church is barely visible in the original, but with you the church is lit with afterglow, the prayers are performed beautifully, and not just by the old women, understandably, but by the young ones as well; it has to be reduced.

There is a lot of darkness outside and inside—all the whimpering, even the komsomol girl wears a kerchief like the Old Believer woman. And there needs to be more light onstage.

The very idea of the production, the acting, the excitement it provokes is all in the production's favor. But it has to be purified.

VIL'KIN: We are all members of a craft union and work for the general good. I am concerned with the artistic side of this business. Aleksey Dmitrievich, your remarks will be carried out and the preceding remarks about the directing. And the remarks about the text, i.e., that in Nosov it takes two weeks, with us it's over in 1 day. [. . .].

The word "pacifism" in relation to Soviet literature and to the author—a state prize laureate—*is inappropriate.*

I staged the production exactly according to the author. If you can convince us that we have all been working in a rut, you will have to base your decision on the production.

SMELYANSKY: We will act on all your notes and open the production.

BELOV:[127] For the production to grow, it has to be opened, so that it can breathe. The actors are already fading, the production is perishing.

FILIPPOV: There is a proposal to accept the production with the requisite revisions and a commission to inspect the rehearsals or to observe the revised production another time.

RESOLUTION: To accept the production with the requisite revisions, to perform it as a replacement two to three times in June. [. . .]

---

127 Pëtr Alekseevich Belov (1929–88), chief designer at the Moscow TYUZ 1957–67 and the Gogol' Theater 1964–74, at the Central Army Theater from 1974; typical of designers of the 1960s and 1970s in his preference for visual metaphors.

THE PLAY did enter the repertory but was not a success, despite the strengths of the performance, owing to a weak and constantly reworked script. Smelyansky later described the whole episode as "a Molotov cocktail."

P. Titorenko and K. Taraskina, repertoire of the Red Army Theater, 1981.

A. Plays of the current repertoire for 1981, transferred from last year.

Title	Author	No. of perfs.	No. of spectators [by thousands]
1. *The Dancing Master*	Lope de Vega	30	37.2
2. *Long, Long Ago*	A. Gladkov	28	33.6
3. *The Tests Never End*	Eduardo de Filippo	15	16.2
4. *The Comical Fantasy*	Gr. Gorin	17	20.7
5. *The Forest*	A. Ostrovsky	17	18.1
6. *30 Days Away*	A. Mindadze	34	39.2
7. *He Who Gets Slapped*	L. Andreev	10	10.3
8. *The Last Encounter*	A. Galin	19	22.1
9. *The Soldier and Eve*	E. Borisova	36	51.3
10. *The Death of Ioann the Terrible*	A. Tolstoy	12	15.6
11. *Farmers in Armor*	E. Nosov	14	16.1
12. *Snow Fell*	R. Fedenev	14	4.2
13. *Vassa Zheleznova*	M. Gorky	10	3.2
14. *Faryat'ev Fantasy*	A. Sokolova	15	5.5
15. *The Holy of Holies*	I. Drutse	22	7.9
16. *To Forget Herostratus*	Gr. Gorin	30	16.3
17. *At Close of Day*	D. Asenov	20	6.9
18. *Orpheus Descending*	T. Williams	18	7.3
19. *Transit*	L. Zorin	12	5.4
20. *Robin Hood's Arrow*	S. Prakof'eva & I. Tokmakova	28	12.4
21. *Les Parents Terribles*	J. Cocteau	25	10.3
22. *Moments over the Abyss*	N. Miroshnichenko	32	14.2
Tours to Dnepropetrovsk		67	56.2
Subtotal		525	430.2

B. New productions, included in the repertoire in 1981.

1. *The Optimistic Tragedy*	Vs. Vishnevsky	14	13.9
2. *A Man for All Seasons*	R. Bolt	14	4.3
3. *Last of the Red-hot Lovers*	N. Simon	2	0.2
Subtotal		30	18.2
Total		555	448.6

Report of the Finance Office of the Chief Political Governance of SA and KIF on the financial situation of the Red Army, June 15, 1981.

I. On inviting outside directors. [...] The director L. E. Kheyfets[128] mounted the production *The Death of Ioann the Terrible,* which remained onstage no more than two years. The restaging of the original artistic work is correct and competent only when done by its creator, the famous director L. E. Kheyfets, who had been hired to work in the Academic Maly Theater. The civilian directors of TsATSA I. S. Unguryanu and A. V. Burdonsky have neither a legal nor a moral right to restage the given production, i.e., they had taken part in no measure in the creative process of its creation. This is the traditional practice of theatrical ethics. [...]

2. On inviting outside musicians into the body of the civilian orchestra to the number of thirty-two persons. [...] The theater cannot deny the creative right of the composer, invited to provide accompaniment for the production, to fill the orchestral score with instruments that are not in the theater's orchestra (harp, waldhorn, organ, trombone, folk instruments, etc.).

In such cases the management is compelled to invite additional musicians to be paid on that occasion only. [...]

3. On inviting to productions other persons apart from civilian actors. Basically one may invite children who are not in the theater's troupe (the productions *Tests Never End* and *Farmers in Armor*) as well as women to take part in crowd scenes in *The Optimistic Tragedy*. [...]

4. On the use of a leather jacket costing 350 rubles for the actress in the role of the Commissar in the production of *The Optimistic Tragedy,* played by People's Actress of the USSR L. I. Kasatkina. [...] The external appearance and the quality of the garment of the leading character in the production have no small significance. [...]

Official of the Central Academic Theater of
the Soviet Army Colonel *V. Strel'tsov*

128 Leonid Efimovich Kheyfets (1934–), director at the Red Army Theater from 1963; his *Death of Ioann the Terrible,* a major event on the Russian stage, led to his dismissal and reassignment to the Maly Theater 1971–86; he returned to the Red Army Theater 1988–94.

Red Army Theater to Com. Boris Nikolaevich Stepanov, Deputy Chairman, Executive Committee, Moscow City Soviet of People's Deputies, no. 31/42, February 11, 1982.

Dear Boris Nikolaevich,

In 1969 the directorate and union representatives of the Central Academic Soviet Army Theater appealed to the Politburo member, minister of defense of the USSR, and marshal of the Soviet Union com. A. A. Grechkov[129] for permission to initiate construction of a housing facility for the leading actors and theatrical specialists in close proximity to the theater, in consideration of the two-shift work schedule and late evening hours of operation. The theater was ready to take on matters of land allocation and obtaining Mossovet approval of the construction.

At the time the theater was in a very difficult situation as to the housing allotment. According to Ministry of Defense regulations, officers have priority in this matter, and because of that, the theater was not, and still is not, getting any of the annually planned housing for its artistic and service staffs. The designated housing construction seems to be the only solution here.

We received permission from the minister of defense of the USSR and obtained in 1975 a share in housing construction at 10–16 Trifonov St., close to the TsATSA (as per Mossovet ordinance no. 332 of 2/17/75).

According to that ordinance, three thousand square meters out of a total fifteen thousand square meters of housing were allocated to the Ministry of Defense of the USSR to be used for the Central Academic Soviet Theater in the large block, multistory building.

The construction is presently completed (7 Soviet Army St.) and the Ministry of Defense was given about seventeen hundred square meters, of which eight hundred square meters were allocated to the theater to bring the leading cadre closer and improve the living conditions of the veterans and the experienced staff.

AKHU[130] of the USSR Ministry of Defense and TsATSA are allocating the apartments in this building to the following leading artistic and technical staff of the theater provisionally on receiving permission to transfer their present housing to the Ministry of Defense candidates. [...]

Decree of the Ministry of Culture of the USSR, no. 21, January 14, 1975.

For its great services in the development of Soviet art the Central Theater of the Soviet Army has been given the honorary appellation of "Academic."

Minister of Culture of the USSR *P. N. Demichev*[131]

---

129 Andrey Antonovich Grechkov (1903–76), general with an impressive war and postwar record, minister of defense 1967–76; general editor of the official Soviet history of World War II.

130 Department of Administrative Management (Administrativno-khozyaystvennoe upravlenie).

131 Pëtr Nilovich Demichev (1918–86), a loyal cog in the Party machine from 1945 and an aide

ON FEBRUARY 13, 1980, the theater was awarded the Order of Labor of the Red Banner, by decree 1553-X of the Presidium of the Supreme Soviet of the USSR.

Studio Theaters

The studio theater movement was one of the most troubling for the government. No provision had been made for the control or subsidy of the numerous groups that sprang up spontaneously and had great audience appeal.

Mark Rozovsky won a reputation in the 1960s as the leader, dramatist, and director of the cabaret studio of the Moscow State University (MGU) "Our House," famous at the end of the political Thaw for its sharp social criticism.

> Mark Rozovsky, *Samootdacha* [Self-sacrifice] (Moscow: Sovetskaya Rossiya, 1976), 38–41, 60.

[1964] Another scene "Fables in Color" ["Basni-tsvetasni"] also had the character of a parable, and its satire was aimed at reticence and grayness, stubborn obtuseness. This scene was, certainly, the best "artistic achievement" of the show *Listen Up—It's Time!*, because its form was a completely new word in stage art. [...]

"Fables in Color" had no words. But it wasn't exactly pantomime. For the chief means of expression on this stage was . . . color.

The drama of the three short episodes was built on the conflicting interrelations of different patches of color.

Here's the fable "Progress," as narrated by the reviewer of our second production the meritorious artist of the RSFSR Zinovy Gerdt[132] in the article "Tradition in Innovation" with the subtitle "Thoughts on the MGU Amateur Theater." [...]

"A row of seven individuals hand each other little gray plates of quaint geometric forms. One, two, a third little plate . . . This is done monotonously, apathetically. But suddenly the flow of identical gray plates is interrupted by a bright red one. The first three persons cheer up, as they pass it from hand to hand. But the fourth man holds on to the red plate and turns it over to its gray side. The flow of identical gray plates proceeds. Suddenly another bright red little plate appears. Again the first three rejoice. And again the same fourth one reverses it to its gray side. He does it calmly, normally. But the third time, when a bright little plate appears, the fourth man lets it go by. They all let it go by, but after this only bright colored little plates begin to move.

"Everything is clear in this sketch, nothing needs to be explained, analyzed. The form found is clear-cut to the maximum, its expression absolutely precise. *There have never anywhere been* similar fables in color."

---

to Khrushchëv in charge of business and ideology; Furtseva's successor as minister of culture, removed 1986 and given the meaningless title of vice president.

132 Zinovy Efimovich Gerdt (1916–96), puppeteer for Sergey Obraztsov 1945–82 and comic actor at the Ermolova Theater 1983–91, famous for his witticisms.

[...] Aleksandr Svobodin,[133] critic: "A new star has risen on Moscow's theatrical horizon. Your theater, if I may be precise, is a talking point, infectious ... Sources might be found in student cabarets. Here are the traditions of the Blue Blouse and folk pantomime. One might glimpse something from the Moscow studio of Isadora Duncan[134] and other artistic manifestations ..."

Valentin Pluchek, director in chief of the Moscow Theater of Satire: "An hour and a half flew by like a single minute. You have brought out great values and laid low what degrades humanity."

Konstantin Simonov, writer: "The show *Listen Up, It's Time!* is good because it forces one to think about life—one's own and other people's ... The show takes a look at life that, to my mind, is accurate, and there is a cruelty to the rubbish that not only accumulates beneath our feet but exists within ourselves. I sympathize with this cruelty."

Viktor Bukhanov, correspondent of the Russian News Agency: "This is a new theater. New in its exceptional qualities. There are lots of them: emphatic grotesquerie, they wallow in the grotesque ... Complexity, intellectuality ... and dominating it all the idea of a director. This is a synthesis of contemporaneity and tradition ... Laterna Magika[135] and Meyerhold. Marcel Marceau[136] and the Blue Blouse theater. Lots of forebears ... But the baby was born with a character *all of its own making.*"

[...] The last scene is a little masterpiece, worth the whole show. Just like *Fables in Color,* this briefest of miniatures, lasting onstage thirty to forty seconds, became our pride and joy, for it contained enormous content and was completely unusual in form. Its text was a mere proposition, a question: "What can I do on my own?" At first a single actor came onstage with that question, then another, then a third. Each one asked the exact same thing, but with different intonations: addressing the audience or oneself or a comrade ... One would seem to be defending himself, another seemed to be thinking it over ... Gradually a crowd formed onstage, declaring in various voices:

"What can do I on my own? ... But what can I do? ... What can I ..."

Suddenly in the cacophony of shouts one stood out, more resonant, a second immediately linked on to it, then a third ... And then there was no confusion. No mob. There was an organic force. And like a chorus it repeats over and over:

What—Can—I—Do—On—My—Own?!! What—Can—I—Do—On—My—Own?!!

And to the beating of a drum, they all march off, excitedly voicing this single and distinct phrase.

There's a grotesque! ... The spectator understood perfectly what we meant to say. But we spoke succinctly, simply, and intelligibly. And in our own language—the language of the cabaret sketch. And the talk was of something serious: a human

133 Aleksandr Petrovich Svobodin (actually Liberté, 1922–99), prolific critic, on the editorial board of the *Moscow Observer* 1990–98 and chief archivist of the Stanislavsky Center.

134 Isadora Duncan (1878–1927), American dancer, who popularized barefoot, untrammeled physical expression; visited Russia and married the poet Sergey Esenin.

135 Laterna Magika (Magic Lantern), a Prague experimental theater, founded in 1958; through the scenography of Josef Svoboda, it originated full multimedia performances.

136 Marcel Marceau (actually Mangel, 1923–2007), French mime, who created the Pierrot-like Bip and popularized the whiteface form.

being's responsibility for his own actions, his personal responsibility and the fact that, if he loses it, he immediately turns into a machine, reduced to one of its "cogs" and now... Now capable of anything!"

"Our House" was designated as "anti-Soviet" in 1969 and closed.

The studio for young actors run by Oleg Tabakov had begun in 1973 in the Moscow Palace of Pioneers with fourteen hand-picked students. In 1977 they moved to the cellar of an old clubhouse at 1 Chaplygin Street. On October 29, 1978, the premiere of Aleksey Kazantsev's play "... And in Springtime I'll Come Back to You" marked the official opening to the public. As a pun on Tabakov, it came to be known as the Tabakerka, or "Snuffbox."

> Aleksey Popov, "Tabakerka, N. Kaminskaya and A. Popov." in *"Tabakerka."*
> *Istoriya teatral'nogo podvala ili 30 let spustya* ["The snuffbox": History of a
> theatrical cellar or thirty years later] (Moscow: Astrel/AST, 2008), 42–47.

Then Oleg Pavlovich invited to the cellar his old friend David L'vovich Borovsky, a magician of theatrical space and chief designer for the Taganka Theater. David L'vovich thoughtfully inspected the gray walls, the vaulted ceilings, the cement floors swept of debris, and said, "You should paint the walls black and put down a wooden floor. Partition off the pipes with a wooden wall of the same boards. And paint that black too. Everything." So the studio space was arranged and has not changed even today. [...]

The studio's daily life began to take shape, its "scent of life." Besides the diminutive hall, there were also "hot" and "cold" rooms, a small dressing room, and a single toilet—the pride and joy of the artistic administration. For Tabakov a theater begins not with cloak rooms but with a toilet, for, by his own admission, the seriousness and respectful relation of a theater to its spectators may be judged by the cleanliness and absence of foul odors in the lavatories. The cellar had a serious and respectful attitude to its audience. In every aspect. Including the toilet. The smallest room in the studio underwent a complete Euro-redo a couple of decades before that term entered the Russian language. Every night it sparkled with cleanliness and smelled sweetly of imported aerosols, placed there by the thoughtful artistic administration. [...]

At the start of the third course the first production was staged. Aleksey Kazantsev's[137] play "... And in Springtime I'll Come Back to You!..." was brought to the studio by Valery Vladimirovich Fokin.[138] There was no talk of writing "a play on themes from the novel" of Nikolay Ostrovsky *How the Steel Was Tempered*. With a modern theatrical language, the young playwright spoke about the worn-out idea of revolution, the blindness

---

137 Aleksey Kazantsev (1945–2007), director and playwright, whose work enjoyed a certain vogue in the 1990s; editor of *Dramaturg* from 1993.
138 Valery Vladimirovich Fokin (1946–), director at the Sovremennik 1970–85, influenced by Grotowski; the Ermolova Theater 1985–91. He became head of the newly founded Meyerhold Center in 1991.

and sense of doom in those who build a bright tomorrow out of blood and pain. The physical blindness of Pavka Korchagin became at the end his insight, the bitter realization of the mindlessness of the path traveled. The narrow-gauge track, running through a wooded bog, led to a dead end. The central hero of the show turned out to be not Pavka, nor his like-minded friends, but three dear old homebodies, sitting in a corner of the hall on a sofa, as if behind the backs of the audience. The central heroes acted onstage: they fought, went to their deaths, escaped or suffered defeat, but the three on the sofa only commented on what went on. Korchagin should have come off as some sort of victor, but the last word was left to those behind him, the homebodies, and not Pavka. He departed. They remained. Just as in life.

The playwright and the director did not change a word of the original source. They did not have to. They only had to change the tonality so that a hymn turned into a funeral march. If a horrible truth broke in at the end to the sightless Pavka Korchagin, it was simply impossible for us spectators not to see and hear it.

. . . Only those who wished to hear heard it. Both in the days of Nikolay Ostrovsky and in our times it was always more convenient and simple to hear the text rather than the subtext. Most probably that was why the production was not banned or, in Oleg Pavlovich's words, a "granary padlock" hung on the doors to the cellar. The emperor-has-no-clothes effect was in operation—to see meant to agree. Without getting up from their sofa, the authorities had the goodness not to observe the new subtext in an adaptation of an old book. Or they simply overlooked it. But the fact remains. On October 29, 1978, the day when the Lenin Komsomol observed its sixtieth anniversary, the cellar on Chaplygin Street celebrated the premiere of its first production.

Strictly speaking, it is that date, and not March 1, 1987, that should be considered the birthday of the Tabakov Theater. [. . .]

MANY talented young directors, on graduating from GITIS and other official academies, failed to be given permanent appointments to theaters in the bigger cities or else were assigned to remote provinces. Anatoly Vasil'ev was one of the most brilliant of these "nomadic" directors, who kept moving his projects to wherever he was invited.

> Anatoly Vasil'ev, "The open space of reality," *Iskusstvo Kino* 4 (1981), 136–37, 142–43. Anatoly Aleksandrovich Vasil'ev (1942–), a student of Aleksey Popov and Mariya Knebel', directed a number of exciting productions without having a theater of his own; he was given a space at 20 Vorovsky Street in Moscow, where he founded his School of Dramatic Art 1987.

By the early 1960s the teachings of Stanislavsky had become a wholly academic science. To stimulate the actor's living feelings within the framework of that system, in the 1950s and 1960s, the most talented practitioners of Soviet stage directing started to revive the forgotten method of the "étude"; for my part, it was in the 1970s while I was rehearsing *The First Version of Vassa Zheleznova*[139] that I decided to stop using the notion of the main event during the analysis of the role. I stopped talking about the characters' objectives. I preferred to talk about the beginning of the role, about the initial event understood as the source of the action. Trying to elaborate the method I used, I suddenly realized that if the interests, actions, and words of the actor are provoked in a particular way, he finds himself capable of switching on to some subconscious feeling. In other words, the actor is not gradually sliding away from something conscious toward his subconscious mind, but vice versa: he moves from something subconscious toward conscious choices. And it is owing to the initial event of the scene or the whole play, owing to the carefully organized sequence of events (or situations), owing to the physical actions discovered through a series of "études," that the actor begins to have a premonition of the end, even if this final point is still unknown to him. He starts to wander around, looking for the way out and the main event, and if the traps are well laid and sprung the right way, the intuitive "persona" of the actor will surely find the way to exist and arrive at its goal.

[...] Later on, I observed that it is difficult to direct the process of acting if the actor is totally immersed in the sensations of the initial event. But to keep from being totally immersed in one's "feelings and sensations," one must maintain a certain distance. This becomes obvious when dealing with realistic plays, say, those of Gorky, or, in general, all of realistic literature. Those works cannot be performed at all if the actors are unable to keep the necessary distance from the material. [...]

Finally I got what I needed: I was in the presence of an actor who was free, an actor who was able to feel—to feel deeply and inwardly—and at the same time an actor who was able to lay the structure and see the goal of the whole play. That kind of actor would eventually become the poet of his role, an eager traveler in the metaphorical space of reality.

ROMAN VIKTYUK[140] became noted as director of the MGU student theater (which, for a long time, was the most exciting and free of the state theaters, having nurtured many famous playwrights, directors, and actors). Here he staged the soon-to-be-banned production based on L. Petrushevskaya's *Music Lessons,* then, in 1980, set up his own ephemeral studio in the "Moskvoreche" House of Culture in a remote residential neighborhood of Moscow. His productions of this period were notable for harsh and ruthless truthfulness.

139 Maksim Gorky's play of a destructive matriarch, *Vassa Zheleznova,* was first produced 1910; he rewrote it to make it reflect the wrong turn the Revolution had taken 1935. Vasil'ev, after long periods of rehearsal and improvisation, staged it at the Stanislavsky Theater 1977–78.
140 Roman Grigor'evich Viktyuk (1936–), in the 1970s staged unofficially sanctioned authors in Moscow and Leningrad; in 1991 he created the Roman Viktyuk Theater, staging shows noteworthy for their blatant eroticism and over-the-top glamour.

Anastasiya Kas'yannikova, "In the air of dreams. Director Roman Viktyuk: 'To live in truth, kindness and beauty,'" *Moskovsky Komsomolets* (March 27, 1991), 3.

[Viktyuk:] Of course, when I deliberately touched the sore spots, there were even more conflicts. I once directed Petrushevskaya's *Music Lessons* at the MGU Theater. They closed that theater. When they were discussing this issue at the university party committee, Roshchin, Efremov, and Arbuzov came over to defend the theater. Nobody listened to them! The decision was predetermined. Then we moved to the Moskvoreche Palace of Culture. People were coming there to see us, the house was always packed, in fact they were sitting on the floor or standing in the aisles. *MK*[141] was the first to publish a positive review about the nearly banned show. (That's why, no matter what you print in your newspaper nowadays, I am forever on your side.) Then the whole gang of national newspapers rushed to stand up for us. Éfros wrote that it was the best production of the last twenty-five years.

Nevertheless, the city and district Party committees were trying to close the show. It was possible to form an opinion without reading, without seeing, without knowing. They were acting aggressively, with impunity, unconcerned with any evidence. The production was closed down and the company dispersed. That was my first and last attempt to establish my own company. It's fate, I suppose.

THE THEATER OF THE SOUTHWEST was created in 1977 by Valery Belyakovich with nonprofessional young artists in Vostryakovo, a remote suburb of southwest Moscow. For a long time Belyakovich was the only director of what was the most popular Moscow theater studio. Its repertoire was primarily oriented to the popularization of Russian and world classics (Krylov and Sollogub, Gogol', Shvarts, Sukhovo-Kobylin; Anouilh, Ionesco, Goldoni, Camus, Neil Simon), staged in a clear, expressive, often grotesque manner. The shows were accompanied by loud music and dynamic movement and were unusually energetic and emotionally contagious. The group had the most fanatic fans of all ages and social ranks, who would attend each new production ten times or more and would aid it disinterestedly.

From souvenir program, circa 1991.

V. BELYAKOVICH:[142] What did we start with? With what we knew. While still a student in the Theater of Young Moscovites I acted in vaudevilles. And in my collective we decided to start with them [in particular *School for Daughters* by Ivan Krylov and Vladimir Sollogub, 1978]. The two mothers were played by Viktor Avilov and

141 *Moskovsky komsomolets*, popular Moscow newspaper with the largest circulation in town. Sergey Romanovich Belyakovich (1953–2009), co-founder of the Southwest Studio with his brother Valery; became a much-employed film and television actor.
142 Valery Romanovich Belyakovich (1950–), a graduate of GITIS, began acting at young people's and experimental theaters; while serving as a librarian in the Moscow suburb of Vostrakovo, he staged amateur productions; founded the Southwest Studio Theater 1977. In the 1990s he worked in the United States and Japan.

10.10. Part of the all-male cast of the 1805 farce *School for Daughters* by Vladimir Sollogub and Ivan Krylov, directed by Valery Belyakovich, Southwest Studio Theater, Moscow, circa 1980. Photo: Kons. Goryachev.

Sergey Belyakovich.[143] It was staged with animation and performed with excitement, without sidelong glances at authority. And when everything goes so merrily and freely, a normal, living, people's theater is born.

[...] What is Gogol's *Wedlock* [1979] about? About Humanity, about human vulnerability and steadfastness at the same time, about Humanity in its passions and weaknesses, about how important it is to remain true to one's essence, one's nature, knowing how to withstand the inevitable squeezing out of everything alien to your individuality. Why precisely does Podkolësin jump out the window? It's a rebellion, a reaction to "Kochkarëvization."[144] Podkolësin, albeit unconsciously, is rebelling against violence to himself.

[...] [Bulgakov's *Molière*, 1980] We stage it as a bright requiem to the artist—to a man who upholds the truth of life and is true to his destiny. For our theater *Molière* became programmatic and forced us to inspect and reconsider everything we had done up to that time.

[...] [Gogol's *Gamblers*, 1981] With *Gamblers* we continued the theme of *Wedlock*: through laughter and tears Gogol has the same love and suffering for a human being, even when he's lost his moral and spiritual bearings in life. The ridiculous man with a false impression of himself as "a sovereign prince" and who crushes his fellow beings with his cruel and calculated gambling. But in the dramatic denouement of *Gamblers,* with bitter insight, the human being manages to purify his soul.

143 Viktor Vasil'evich Avilov (1953–) joined Belyakovich's amateur troupe 1975 and played Hamlet and Khlestakov; noted for his "magnetic" personality and strong features.
144 Kochkarëv is Podkolësin's married friend who keeps urging him to take a wife.

I. Sikorsky, "The theater of good feelings," *Trevost' i kul'tura* [Temperance and culture] (circa 1987), 10–12. Undated clipping in Bakhrushin Theater Museum.

It takes a long time to find the Southwest Studio Theater. "Got any spare tickets?" like a radio beacon guides you from the subway to the humble doors in the basement of an ordinary Moscow high rise. Tickets—no more than a hundred for each performance—are distributed at the opening of the enterprise. On one day for the whole season.

What's so attractive about this people's collective? There are myriad amateur drama clubs, studios, and theaters in this country. But how often do you attend their productions? And this not infrequently in the great modern palaces of art. And here's a humble basement on the edge of the city with at most a few veteran collaborators...

But before telling you about this youthful studio, I must recall that tiny hall in a suburban library in Vostryakova across the Moskva River, where ten years ago young people of the most varied specialties gathered and organized something like a theater. They had no thought of popularity: just so, to while away the time, to try themselves out in dramatic art. The present-day "star" Viktor Avilov often arrived in a heavy truck with two trailers. Today's famous Tamara Kudryashova ran to rehearsals after attending Class Nine at school. Aleksey Mamonov was studying at the university, Ira Bonchareshvili at the Architectural Institute. Volodya Koppalov[145] was working as a photographer, Oleg Zadorin as a lab assistant... Today they are the heart and soul of the theater. A few left, most remained.

Today the kids will often recall their first performances. The spectators were few. But drunken teenagers congregated around the entrance. Not clear whether they wanted to huddle beneath a roof or simply mingle in the warmth. And they constantly fought among themselves. "We'll have no drunks," shouted Valery Belyakovich, then still a student at GITIS. "We'd rather play for ourselves than entertain this audience." But the teenagers continued to break in. Then all the actors made a "wall" and, in their theatrical costumes, made a full-frontal attempt to send the unwelcome guests packing. By the way, this occurrence is very characteristic of students. And today they reverently preserve their creativity from such visitors, not to mention that from the very start in the theater itself, the word *drinks* was stricken from everyday life.

[Local officials began to attend.] "To protect us at that time, to wish the performance well, was a bit risky," says Valery. "We did not belong to any House of Culture. So, a handful of kids gather together at night by themselves, and stay up too late. Music, noise, arguments... Anything could happen... There were a lot of letters, when with the help of Larisa Mikhaylovna [Ryumina, a local cultural commissioner] we got a new location. [...]"

But the new location, where they settled by order of the muse, was not suitable for a theater. The builders in particular were in no hurry to lend a hand. They looked in a couple of times, brought some materials, and obviously turned their attention to a more important object. Then the actors themselves took on the work. [...]

"Our actors are busy with basic day jobs," smiled Belyakovich. "The theater, if one

145 Vladimir Petrovich Koppalov (d. 2007) began appearing in films in 1996.

can call it that, is for us an amusement, an idiosyncratic form of recreation. It is really very idiosyncratic. If you consider that the core company spends only a few hours in the theater every day. For us it's a very heavy workload. Sometimes the spectators wouldn't be all that responsive. But once any one of us realizes that his place in life is on the stage, the theater, then some of our actors cast off their smoothly worn professions. For instance, my brother Sergey was a first-rate diamond cutter, made a splendid salary. And he up and left. It sometimes happens that your profession gets in the way of your hobby. Then your hobby has become your specialization. Now he's registered in a studio. The wages are paltry, but his soul is free from doubt. [...]"

Self-financing allows the Southwest Studio Theater to manage independently the money made from the sale of tickets. It can begin to pay the work of actors and workers in the auxiliary fields. Greater funds can be spent on the design of the productions and on acquiring equipment and costumes. Otherwise, if we recall the first steps of the studios, the kids have to go to the buildings next door and collect the props from old discards. Incidentally, once the neighborhood took an interest in them, the spectators themselves soon began to offer the costume shop this or that piece of clothing. And one fan gave the actors an upright piano...

AFTER "Our House" was closed in 1970 for its political audacity, Rozovsky collaborated with many theaters as director and playwright. At the time of the studio movement, he was one of the first to open his own studio theater, "At the Nikitsky Gates," in 1983, which has carried on to the present day.

Boris Poyurovsky, "Today again I call you to the road!," *Russkaya mysl'* 4150 (1996); reprinted in *Chto ostalos'*, 101–3.

Some people are inclined to think the birthday of the theater "At the Nikitsky Gates" coincides with International Theater Day and falls on March 27, 1983.

Right in the Palace of Culture of medics, right next to the Moscow State University Palace of Culture, where "Our House" once resided, there took place the premiere of the production *Doctor Chekhov*, theatrical fantasies drawn from the stories of Antosha Chekhonte as staged by Mark Rozovsky.

[...] The professions and occupations of the first studio members seemed the most varied: a locksmith, a French teacher, stagehands from the MAT, a college student, a nanny, a charwoman, a salesman, a typesetter, a medical student, a concrete slingsman, an engineer, and even a schoolboy. Almost all of them were onstage for the first time.

Exercises were carried on daily. Besides rehearsals for the first production *Doctor Chekhov*, regular obligatory lessons on physical movement and stage speech and lectures on the history of theater, painting, and literature were immediately organized.

The specialty of the educational process at the studio was its deliberate combination of the method of aesthetic-improvisational acting with Stanislavsky's "system". [...]

After *Dr. Chekhov*, he presented the literary–musical show *Poor Liza* based on

N. M. Karamzin[146]—a clean, moving story, a sophisticated plaything for grownups, that unconditionally marked the professional growth of the performers.

The third work of the theater "By the Nikitsky Gates" was called *Always Shall You Be* ("The Diary of Nina Kosterina"), which included letters of fallen heroes, documents, songs of the 1930s and 1940s, poetry from the classics and modern poets. It was a requiem performance, devoid, however, of intentional theatricality, which would have seemed insulting under the circumstances, and filled with a profound gratitude to those who challenged death with death.

---

146 Nikolay Mikhaylovich Karamzin (1766–1826), author of an influential history of the Russian state, much drawn on by writers of fiction and drama, and court historian under Nicholas I. *Poor Liza* (*Bednaya Liza*) is the sentimental tale of a peasant girl's unhappy love.

CHAPTER ELEVEN

Glasnost' and Perestroika, 1985–1992

O N THE DEATH of the debile Chernenko in 1985, after barely a year in office, Mikhail Gorbachëv took over as general secretary and presented a younger, more hopeful face of Communism. He was determined to be a new broom, sweeping out corruption and inefficiency and rebuilding the infrastructure, without fundamentally changing the system. To this end, he proclaimed the principles of glasnost', "transparency," and perestroika, "reconstruction." The establishment was reluctant to follow his lead; inertia and corruption neutered many efforts at reform. They were most successful in the realm of the arts.

Faced with de facto turbulence in the theater, the authorities followed Gorbachëv's lead, initiating a series of experimental reforms meant to restructure the economic model without surrendering government control. By this time there were more than six hundred professional theaters in the USSR performing in fifty-five languages, not counting the various unauthorized studios, amateur groups, and "apartment" theatricals. Seven new theaters were founded in Moscow alone, and by 1988, there existed a Soviet "fringe" of more than two hundred companies, under the sponsorship of municipal authorities, art unions, and commercial concerns. Their existence was usually ephemeral.

As a sign that a new policy on the arts was in the offing, in 1986 Minister of Culture Pëtr Demidev was dismissed and given the meaningless title of vice president. On New Year's Day 1987, the Ministry of Culture granted theaters fuller economic and creative independence. The most prominent theaters were still guaranteed their subventions and were still touted as official models. However, several layers of censorship were removed. Previously, it had been the policy of the state and its ideological advisory groups that no less than 50 percent of each theater's repertoire should be made up of modern Soviet plays, and no less than 25 percent should be plays from the national republics, ideally including several Russian classics. No longer was this a requirement. Individual theaters were free to formulate their own repertoires.

Just as Gorbachëv discovered that papering over the cracks caused the cracks to become more prominent, so the theatrical reforms opened up spheres of activity that spread beyond state control. The tripartite division of theaters, classified on the basis of subsidy, ticket prices, and income, had begun to break down even earlier when such unfavored companies as the Taganka and the Malaya Bronnaya were attracting bigger audiences than the historic houses. The academic theaters financed directly by the Ministry of Culture or various republics found their subventions in danger. All theaters had been under the control of the official cultural bodies of each city or district, but the proliferating experimental theaters proved to be too many and too short-lived to be effectively governed from above. Meanwhile, the first independent producing enterprises sprang up, to finance theatrical productions. This was far more radical than the studios. In the past, actors had been indentured to a specific theater and could take outside engagements only by special permission. Now they were becoming free agents. Eager to kick over the traces, clusters of prominent players came together for "all-star" productions, usually with commercial backing.

As the economy and infrastructure began to collapse, a main concern was to save the culture. Over the past decades, theater, less stringently censored than the mass media and journalism, had been looked to as a forum for ideas unavailable elsewhere. Imbued with the prerevolutionary idea that theater was a source of enlightenment, many generations of Soviet people had used it as a surrogate for representative government, religion, higher education, and even an independent press. The privileged position of theater enabled dramatists, directors, and actors to become public leaders. It was in art and literature in the USSR that many felt they could dispute official ideological doctrine and influence politicians.

With the removal of censorship and the lifting of government controls, the press and the mass media suddenly took on new importance. Citizens could debate issues and get information from a wide variety of sources. Theater lost its central role as a haven for dissent and unorthodox thought; being a theater critic or director lost its appeal when other spheres of activity seemed to offer more opportunity for advancement and influence.

Meanwhile, national theaters, which had had to play Cinderella to the Russian-language companies in the constituent republics, began to flex their muscles. They organized in imitation of the All-Russian Theatrical Society, which had been in existence for a hundred years. A National Union of Theatrical Leaders formed to serve as an umbrella organization for all the other unions. These independent organizations undermined the government monopoly on theater and allowed a more active and effective defense of the creative and social rights of theater workers. They offered a form of stability when the superstructure of power was falling apart and uprisings in the republics were fragmenting the Soviet Union.

In January 1992, a Commonwealth of Independent States was declared, ending the single, dominant, all-controlling Soviet theatrical culture both at home and abroad.

Brave New World?

Édvard Radzinsky, "Fleeting," *New York Times* (June 8, 1997), 82.

I remember a conversation I had with one of [the old Stalinists], a true watchdog of the regime. I came to talk about my latest play, which had been banned.

"Who cares about your play? It is not a threat!" he said. "Ideology is suffering a severe setback. American literature is creeping through all the cracks. We don't even realize the horror of it. Yes, I made them change *A Streetcar Named Desire,* [to have a happy ending], and many people laugh at me. But that play has a hidden and dangerous message. The world seems so sad after it, and the viewer starts thinking about his life, too. Our best literature does not deal with pathetic reality but is about a dream, about the life that could be. But we do our work poorly, and Americans do theirs with talent. And that makes them even more of a threat.

"For instance, have you ever heard of Albee's[1] play *Who's Afraid of Virginia Woolf?* Sorry about banning your play, but I'll give you the Albee to read—my gift to you. And believe me, reading it will be much better for you than having your play produced."

[...] At the time I was probably the most successful young playwright in Russia. My last play had been produced in 120 theaters and made into a film [*Jogging,* 1986]. But reading Albee was a catastrophe—I became ashamed of everything I had written. I realized what it was to write as a free man. [...]

MIKHAIL SHATROV had made his name with mildly revisionist plays about the Revolution and its leaders. *Bolsheviks* (1967) had been about an attempt on Lenin's life; in *Blue Horses on Red Grass* (1977) Lenin was played without the actor being made up to resemble his portraits; *That's How We'll Win* (1981) concerned Lenin's political testament. *The Brest Peace* had been written in 1962, but, because Trotsky was one of the characters, it was not produced until 1985, at the Vakhtangov Theater. Shatrov spoke at a constitutional congress of theater works before the Politburo (in Gorbachëv's absence). His speech caused a sensation when published, in part, in *Moscow News* (*Moskovskie Novosti*), for it attacked the governments of Stalin and Brezhnev for silencing innovation and singled out former First Secretary Viktor Grisin as the "iron hand" that could have tipped the scales in favor of fascism on the eve of glasnost'.

From the unpublished portion of Shatrov's speech, 1985. Giulietto Chiesa and Roy Medvedev, *Time of Change: An Insider's View of Russia's Transformation* (New York: I. B. Tauris, 1991), 33.

1   Edward Albee (1928–), American playwright, whose one-acts of 1959–60 *The Sandbox* and *The American Dream* were labeled "theater of the absurd," a taxonomy that did not work for *Who's Afraid of Virginia Woolf* (1962) and *A Delicate Balance* (1966) but did for *Tiny Alice* (1964) and *Seascape* (1974). His adaptation *The Ballad of Sad Café* was surprisingly popular in the Soviet Union.

We cannot forget the danger that weighed on us in March 1985 and that, perhaps not immediately, could have led to a relapse of uncontrolled power. When the problems that suffocated the country could have either been confronted with democratization or pushed back by an iron hand.

Mikhail Shatrov, interview with Natalya Dardynka and Pëtr Spivak, in Mikhail Shatrov, *Dramas of the Revolution* (Moscow: Progress, 1990), 9.

When we speak of the approach to history, the basic principle for me personally is the principle that there exists a historical truth made up of factual truths. And we mustn't hide from a single fact. The most important thing is that we don't have to hide at all. If we've mastered the Marxist–Leninist method, every fact has its place in history, for it existed. You have to understand, analyze, and see the links. It's an enormous job that can only be done collectively: historians do their part, artists go into the areas that historians can't—psychology, etc. All of us, together, serve a common cause: the development of a Communist worldview [...]

In *The Brest Peace* Lenin has a speech in which he talks about the price of mistakes a politician makes—it is human lives. Not wounded pride, not losing a game of chess, but human lives. That play is about the responsibility a leader has to the people. The people are present in the play—they are the audience. The critics didn't understand that an appeal is being made to the audience. They will either be indignant or give Lenin their hearts. I'm sure they'll give him their hearts. [...]

People talk about history as the actions of the masses, but any mass is made up of people with first and last names. Are the laws of history really so decisive that the will and desires of people have no influence? [...] The laws of history always work through people; man is the mainspring. But why has that thesis suddenly reemerged? To keep Stalin from being judged by history.

My understanding of [Lenin] as a politician, as a Communist, as a Russian intellectual is such that when I thought about what happened, about the events that are our sorrow and our tragedy, I thought about what would have happened if he had seen that. And I came to the conclusion that an individual as courageous and honest as that would have first tried to find out where he was to blame: that's axiomatic.

ON JULY 8, 1986, the Ministry of Culture issued a decree describing a complex experiment to reorganize the duties and responsibilities of the theaters, placing more responsibility on the artistic councils of the theaters themselves. A follow-up decree spelled out several of the new reforms.

Supplement no. 2 to the decree of the Ministry of Culture of the USSR, no. 358, September 1, 1986, 9.

[...] I. The order for forming a repertoire.

1. Every theater will work out a prospective plan for new productions for two

years, making provision for creating in artistic collaboration with writers of works on contemporary themes, ordering and acquiring plays to be staged as new productions, work on productions according to government decrees from the Ministry of Culture, the staging of plays of national and foreign classics. [...]

3. Plans for the repertoire will be examined in a statement from the leadership of the theater by the artistic council and will be confirmed by an order for the theater.

4. The text (piano scores) of the work, created by the author in collaboration with the theater, will be presented for a decision about its public performance to the corresponding organizations of the theater's leadership.

II. The order for preparing and opening new productions.

[...] 6. A new production, on the demand of those who staged it, will be inspected by the theater's artistic council, which will make a decision about the possibility of its opening for public performance.

In case the artistic council concludes that further work is needed, productions will be obliged to carry out the recommendations made to them and provide a repeat inspection of the production. [...]

9. The direct responsibility for the creation of a repertoire, its ideological-thematic tendency, the opening of new productions of a superior artistic quality, the maintenance of the current repertoire, and the requisite activity in it of the troupe will be borne by the administrator and the artistic leadership of the theater. [...]

11. The Ministry of Culture of the USSR can implement government orders for the performance of a production by theaters that express a desire to carry out work on the theatrical production of a play or the creative claims of the playwright dealing with the important problems of modern times. [...]

III. Quality control of productions in the current repertoire.

12. Inspection of the ideological-artistic quality of productions in the current repertoire, appertaining to the plan of public performance of the productions, is the responsibility of the administrator (the artistic leadership), the chief stage director, and the artistic council.

13. The chairman of the artistic council will arrange for a systematic inspection by members of the council of the productions open to the public. Notes about the quality of the inspected production will be brought to the attention of those who staged it and the collective of performers. The artistic council will regularly entertain at its sessions information about the quality of productions in the current repertoire and the measures taken to respond to the notes.

Order no. 233 of the Central Academic Order of Labor of the Red Banner Theater of the Soviet Army, Moscow, September 12, 1986.

In accord with the decision of the Artistic Council of 1986 to confirm raising prices by 50 percent for evening performances in the 1986–87 season, viz., *Macbeth, My Profession Is Signor from Society, The Lady of the Camellias, The Idiot, The Article, Last of the Red-Hot Lovers, Trees Die Standing Up,* as well as newly opened premieres. The distribution of seats by zones and prices is adjoined:

Large Auditorium
Parterre:
Zone 1 rows 1–15 478 seats at 3.00
Amphitheater:
Zone 2 rows 1–6 273 seats at 2.70
Zone 3 rows 7–11 248 seats at 2.40
Zone 4 rows 12–15 74 seats at 2.10
uncomfortable seats rows 7–11 10 seats at .90

Small Auditorium
Parterre:
Zone 1 rows 1–10 298 seats at 3.00
Zone 2 rows 11–15 145 seats at 2.70
Box 2 zone 1 row 7 seats at 2.70
vision-obstructed seats row 2, 3 seats at 1.50

Official of the Central Academic Theater of the
Soviet Army Colonel *V. Yakimov*[2]

ON FEBRUARY 23, 1993, the Soviet Army Theater was renamed the Russian, and its acronym became TsATRA, for the Central Academic Theater of the Russian Army.

The new dispensation. *Teatry Strany v usloviyakh éksperimenta. Sbornik materialov* [Theaters of the country under experimental conditions: Collection of documents] (Moscow: Soyuz Teatral'nykh Deyateley, 1988), 3–5, 8–12.

The decision to conduct an experiment to improve the administration and increase effectiveness of theatrical activity and the reformation of theatrical programs was prompted by the problematic situation that existed in theatrical operations throughout the country in the mid-1980s. These problems were widely discussed in the press, so one need only list the most important of them here:

1. The difficulty in generating creative theatrical collectives of the like-minded "from below," the impossibility of radical changes in the structure of existing theatrical collectives, as well as the absence of mechanisms for the dissolution of theaters that have proven their ideological-artistic insolvency.

2. The ineffectiveness of the system of administering theaters, based on the one-man administrator under the undefined sphere of competence of the chief stage director.

---

2   Viktor Ivanovich Yakimov (1941–), secretary of the Creative Union of Cultural Workers of Russia, connected with the Central Army Theater from 1983; author of fifty works devoted to military and naval themes in theater.

3. Administrative limitations relating to the formation of the repertoire, preparation, and opening of productions.

4. The low level of payment for the labor of theater workers (compared with the average pay scale in the national economy) is intolerable. Considerable inequities in the pay for creative work and, consequently, a breach of the principle of payment by quantity and quality of work.

5. Unwarranted limitations in the industrial-financial sphere, leading to the ineffectual use of all manner of resources.

6. The unsatisfactory situation of the system of guaranteeing matériel and technical support for theatrical activity.

As noted in the decree of the Ministry of Culture (August 6, 1986, no. 330), "on the complex experiment to improve the administration and increase the efficacy of theatrical activity," its goal is to increase the ideological and social efficacy of theatrical art, to enlarge its influence in educating the Soviet people in a Communist worldview, aesthetic views, and advanced social activity, the development of initiatives of theatrical collectives, an increase in their responsibility for superior results in creative work and the broadening of audiences by the rational use of labor, material, and financial resources.

To realize these stated goals, the experimental program included the following aspects:

—a new order for shaping a theater's repertoire, including a system of government decrees on preparing new productions

—a new order for organizing the staff of the artistic council of a theater, a substantial expansion of the rights of this body in matters of shaping a repertoire, organizing creative work, control over the quality of the production, as well as in the sphere of political instruction;

—a new order for planning and financing the work of theaters

—the expansion of the potential for the material encouragement of work in the theater (a raise in salary from the wages fund, a new order for the formation and use of a fund for material incentives)

—the formation in the theaters of a creative-industrial fund and social development of the collective

—the formal confirmation of leading workers in the theater

That is how the experimental program begun on January 1, 1987, in the eighty-two theaters of the nine unions of the republic (fifty-eight dramatic theaters, seventeen musical theaters, six theaters of young spectators, and one puppet theater) viewed the situation, offering to settle only the last four of the six problems of contemporary theatrical operations aforementioned. [...]

In accord with the methodology worked out by the VNII of art studies, the work of the theater under the new conditions has not been evaluated simply by comparing those improvements that have taken place in their activity with the preceding experimental year (1986). One calendar year is too brief a time for decisive changes to take place in the life of such a complicated and inertial social system as the contemporary theater seems to be. Therefore, in most cases, in evaluating the sum total of the first year's work of the theaters under the new conditions, there can be no talk of obvious improvements but only of tendencies that have appeared in one or another sphere of the activity of the creative collectives. In addition, it is important to correlate these tendencies with that wider background that constitutes for the experimental collective the whole theatrical operation of our country, to evaluate them in the context of those (often extremely unfavorable) changes characteristic of the theatrical situation of most of the unions in the republic. [...]

I. Dramatic Theaters of Moscow and Leningrad.

1. Repertoire. The conclusions of the professional theater experts regarding the productions of this group of theaters testify that, over the course of the first year of work under the new conditions, no essential improvements have taken place in the repertoire. Both in 1986 and 1987, both on the poster and in licensing [*prokat*], the contemporary Soviet play dominates. The performances of Russian and foreign classics have somewhat diminished. This is especially notable in licensing, where the share of Russian classics in 1986 constituted 12.7 percent and in 1987 9.9 percent of the overall number of performances offered. A somewhat greater interest was shown by theaters in 1987 in modern foreign plays. The percentage of licensing of these works grew from 15.9 percent to 20 percent. [...]

2. Personnel. Theaters that were granted a greater independence in matters of forming staff increased the staff rosters and enlarged the de facto number of workers. The average number in 1987 in comparison with the preceding year grew by almost 2.5 percent. Part of this increase was due to bringing troupes up to strength, but basically it was due to an increase in the number of technical workers. [...]

The ratio of women to men in the troupes is insignificant, but still has changed; if in 1986 women constituted 46.6 percent in the experimental theaters of Moscow and Leningrad taken together, in 1987 it was 45 percent. Such a ratio is very far from optimal. [...]

3. Economic activity. [...] The theaters of Moscow and Leningrad were less active in 1987 in touring activities. On the other hand, there was more intensive work in the away spaces in their own cities (the number of away performances grew by 22.4 percent, and the number of spectators attending them by 24 percent).

The profits of the Moscow and Leningrad theaters in 1987 increased perceptibly— by 1,972.3 thousand rubles or 19.5 percent above the grand total profit of 1986. [...] The total profit of Moscow and Leningrad theaters increased substantially—by 47.1 percent. The greater part of this increase (38.5 percent) represents an increase in their own income and 8.6 percent an increase in actual grants. [...]

IN DECEMBER 1986 Gorbachëv released the prominent dissident Andrey Sakharov from internal exile in the closed city of Gorky. It was not by accident that after his return to Moscow, this Nobel laureate, nuclear physicist, and exceptional defender of human rights made his first public appearance at the Theater of the Young

11.1. *Heart of a Dog* from Mikhail Bulgakov, directed by Genrietta Yanovskaya and designed by Sergey Barkhin, Moscow Theater for the Young Spectator, 1987. At the center is A. Vdovin as Sharik, the canine human, amid dream figures from *Aida*.

Spectators, where he saw the play *Heart of a Dog,* based on a once-banned Bulgakov novel, directed by Genrietta Yanovskaya. Sakharov's first public statement in the Soviet press after a decade of silence was, in fact, his review of this production in *Teatr.* In the late 1980s, works by both Soviet and foreign authors as well as many who had emigrated from the USSR and were previously banned by the censors again began to appear. The theater was slowly freeing itself.

> Andrey Sakharov, "I believe in reason," *Teatr* 8 (August 1987), 113–15. Andrey Dmitrievich Sakharov (1921–89) was awarded the Nobel Peace Prize for his work on nuclear disarmament 1975. He was exiled to Gorky 1980 but was allowed to return to Moscow 1986.

I watched the performance with great pleasure. I cannot consider myself a connoisseur of the theater, but I think that the directing was extremely inventive and impassioned, the actors' work is sharp and clear, the design is successful.

Serving as the basis for the theatrical production is the remarkable novella of Mikhail Afansevich Bulgakov, written more than sixty years ago, and now actualized. Professor Preobrazhensky is trying roughly by those means which we now call genetic engineering to create a new and artificial human being. However, this is a fantasy on the part of the author. But behind the fantastic subject one can glimpse the writer's humanistic concept of the nobility of the intellect, of what cannot be implanted in culture by a rough-and-ready surgical method.

I would like to say what made a special impression on me. Bulgakov, composing his novella in 1925, could not know what was to take place in the country much later, but as an artist, he foresaw the danger and harmfulness of ignorance and boorishness, when combined with the possibility of wielding power. The theater scenically incarnated the creation of Bulgakov so that the performance suggested a sense that it knew about both the ensuing years in our history and its tragic pages.

After the performance I remember a conversation about Bulgakov's novella. My interlocutor refuted the author, so he thought, with the serious argument, "Excuse me, all the same the Soviet power was around then, it protected individuals!" Yes, but the democratic postulates of power had become perverted. The Sharikovs[3] and their ilk nowadays not only spit on the floor but everything is permitted to them—both the principles and norms of existence. You think about the production—and involuntarily come back to the classical idea: scientific and technical progress outstrips everything related to the spiritual growth of a human being. It would be dreadful if the people seated in the spaceships of the future were technically literate but had impure hearts. They may defile the whole universe!

The theater made me think about the fates of the intelligentsia in our country. Even in the 1920s, as well as now, not everyone understands the meaning of the intelligentsia, its role in the creation of culture, science, art.

Nowadays our country is gathering strength for the process of reform. I rejoice over this greatly. I understand that to realize the plans put forward by the government is remarkably difficult. Old stereotyped thinking, pseudo-democratic demagogues, lies and laziness stand in the way.

I work, sometimes I find the time to go to the theater, I read the newspapers with great interest. How good that we have seen the light of works extracted from the archives and desk drawers, and new ones appear that could not have been published, say, some fifteen years ago! The critics of the negative manifestations of the past, the striving to unite all powers of our society around programs of renovation, inspire hope.

There are times that are pompous and cruel, that are difficult and happy. I would like to believe that the rational principles in our reality will get the upper hand over all those evils that linger from the past. I believe in reason.

The Studio Theaters

Rapidly, the margins began to move to the center. In 1985 the Theater of the Southwest was named a people's theater, and in 1986 Belyakovich was named best young director in Moscow. The next year, their *Hamlet* played the Edinburgh Festival, commencing a long series of tours of Europe and the United Kingdom.

---

3 Sharikov (from a common Russian dog's name, Sharik, "Little Ball") is the anthropoid created from a street mongrel in Bulgakov's story.

Valeriya Novodvorskaya, "Why we deserted the Sovremennik and the Taganka: Theater as battlefields" (circa 1986). Undated clipping at Bakhrushin Theater Museum.

In the unforgettable 1960s, at the time of the first Great Stagnation that had overtaken the souls bewitched by the twentieth Congress, souls of those Soviet intellectuals unpolished off in the camps, the theater was upheld by two whales:[4] the Sovremennik and the Taganka. Both theaters were great in form and stagnant in content. At the Sovremennik *The Naked King, The Reunion, Bolsheviks, The Decembrists,* and *The People's Will Party*[5] settled questions about Power—not to its advantage. The Taganka flung out challenges in every word and every pause, it laughed and wept at inadmissible places and inadmissible persons, kept alight the Eternal flame. In the 1970s the pillar of the Sovremennik tumbled down. It turned out not to be a pillar of Hercules after all. Art for us is armor and armaments—we don't fight with swords but with plays, not with pistols but with poetry, not with sabers but with paintings. With one another and with the world. Dostoevsky forgot to say that not just the heart but art is the battlefield of our times. After the desertion of the Sovremennik, the Taganka fought on as the lone warrior on that field . . .

It is terribly typical that the theater of the 1960s had to fall silent in the 1970s at the precise moment when the gag was removed from its mouth. A believing generation is as easy to fool as a religious individual, when you show him a revelation of a weeping icon or an ostensible apparition of the Virgin.

For a thousand years we believed in God, the Tsar, and the Nation, in Communism, Lenin, Stalin, Gorbachëv, and Eltsin;[6] more recently we've caught up to a foreign rubbish dump with two more holy cows, the Market and the West. What for others is a tiresome and trivial reality is for us the subject of a cult. Like cannibal tribes that believe in mumbo jumbo, we are dumbstruck by any shiny tea strainer or glass bead. For those of the 1960s, political and theatrical, uncommonly little was needed: a new faith and a kind master. Look at all that we have today. The master has almost stopped throwing us in prison, never beats us with rods, and doesn't even stamp his feet. Moreover, in the course of the daily saturnalia, we are allowed to be cheeky. In Rome the slaves committed excesses but once a year, and we do it every day! So how can we fail to exclaim with Lao Tze:[7] "A wise emperor does not

---

4   The medieval Russian belief that the world was upheld by whales.
5   *Goly korol'* was a revised version of Shvarts's *Princess and the Swineherd,* performed by the Sovremennik 1959–60. The year 1967 saw *Traditsionny sbor,* Viktor Rozov's contrast of past ideals and current compromise, as well as *Dekabristy* by Leonid Zorin, *Narodovoltsy* by Aleksandr Svobodin, and Shatrov's *Bol'sheviki,* which constituted a historical trilogy about revolutionary ideas.
6   Boris Nikolaevich Eltsin (1931–2007), promoted to high office by Gorbachëv 1985, was expelled from the Politburo and from his post as head of the Moscow branch of the Communist Party but won election as parliamentary deputy from Moscow 1989, chairman of the Presidium of the Supreme Soviet 1990, and leader of the defeat of the August 1991 coup. President of the USSR 1991–99.
7   Lao Tze or Laotzu (fl. sixth century BCE), Chinese philosopher, whose system the Tao or Daodijing prescribes nonaction and a harmonious relation to nature.

forget his intellectuals! Wise intellectuals fail to be loyal to the emperor to the end!"

We of the 1960s all remember the fat officer from *Elusive Avengers*[8] who insisted on kissing every lady's hand. The only difference is that we seek out the hands not of ladies but of governments. The Taganka was never underground, because it was stirred not by despair but by hope. The real underground never hopes for anything. It has no budget, it has nothing to hand out. It is unable to give alms to those of the 1960s in 1986.[9] [. . .]

The underground is easily nauseated—it's kept afloat only by the great force of scorn and spleen. We drained its bottle to the dregs, and at the wedding banquet in honor of the nuptials of Power and Intelligentsia, the hemlock was revealed at the bottom, and two theaters arose as an aftertaste . . . Two new whales, on which, perhaps, the world is to be supported, lest it plunge into the nauseating depths, are happily with us. The Southwest Theater and the Sphere Theater[10] have not failed to darken the celebration and turn the wedding into civic obsequies. For the prematurely deceased Opposition. For the deliberately deceased intelligentsia. Here the burial service is read even over Russia (at the Sphere in *Doctor Zhivago* and *Swan Camp*, at the Southwest in *Walpurgis Night*),[11] and the Age, and the Lorelei. At the Southwest demonic possession has not disappeared, at the Sphere bile has not dried up. The requiem of the Sphere is performed to a score by Bulgakov and Pasternak, it can barely be heard through the sturdy realism, like the bells of sunken Kitëzh.[12] We destroy it, and no one else. The Southwest plays Judgment Day not over Russia but over all humanity; its Ionesco, Camus, Shakespeare are like the trumpets of the archangels, which are to sound on the last day of the universe.

Rhinoceroses need asphalt . . . But this situation contains its own risk and fervor; suddenly everyone is delighted and transformed, but why are they grunting like pigs in their excitement?

The Taganka has been transformed . . . So the Southwest's cellar is not left empty, so every night the Sphere is still filled with effervescent spleen. Hither come the easily bored Chekhovian intellectuals who don't fancy bright lights. They come to ascertain whether their Maginot line has collapsed, whether the theaters are being maintained as a solid defense even though it has become clear that reinforcements are not arriving, and rhinoceroses can be swapped only for the carrion-eating eagles of the defeat of 1918 or 1937.

---

8   *Neulomivye mstiteli,* a romantic film of 1966 directed by Edmond Keosayan that pitted gypsies against Cossacks.

9   The year 1986 saw art and literature liberated from a great deal of censorship, and free "Unions of Theater Workers" were formed. Sakharov was released from internal exile.

10 Sphere Theater, a theater-in-the-round located in Hermitage Gardens, Moscow.

11 *Walpurgis Night, or The Steps of the Commander* (*Valpurgieva noch'*, 1985) by Venedikt Erofeev, is set in a horrific mental ward (a kind of Soviet *One Flew over the Cuckoo's Nest*).

12 Kitëzh is a legendary city, which, threatened by marauding Mongols, prayed for salvation and was submerged under the waters of Lake Svetloyar; its church bells were supposed to be audible on still days. Rimsky-Korsakov turned the story into an opera, *The Legend of the Invisible Town of Kitëzh and the Maiden Fevroniya* (*Skazanie o nevidimom grade Kitëzhe i deve Fevroniem*, 1905).

The programmatic production at the Sphere is Pasternak's *Doctor Zhivago*.

How little the Russian intelligentsia has changed since it crawled out of its sixteenth-century holes, how distinct and wholly alien from the wholesome Soviet optimism of the intellectuals of the 1960s! Well, what's left for us? [...] They no longer deliberately imprison people via paragraph 70![13] The red flags have been taken down, the USSR has been renamed, the Communist Party has been driven out ... Was this the sort of thing we wanted? Where is our gratitude? Why, having said "a" in 1964, don't we say "b" now? [...]

> Boris M. Poyurovsky, "Today again I summon you to the road!," *Russkaya mysl'* 4150 (1996), reprinted in *Chto ostalos' na trube ... Khroniki teatral'noy zhizni Vserossiyskoe Teatral'noe Obshchestvoroy poloviny XX veka* (Moscow: Tsentroligraf, 2000), 101–3.

On January 1, 1987, agreeable to the decision of the Mossovet, the Studio "By the Nikitsky Gates" was received into the number of the other four with the status of self-supporting professional theater! From October 1, 1991, a new joy: henceforth Mark Rozovsky's theater is recognized as not only professional but state supported. Up to now he already had two theater spaces—one in fact at the Nikitsky Gates, very small, sixty seats in all. And another bigger one in a new district, with three hundred seats. In autumn 1995 the municipality of Moscow made the young theater quite a regal gift and endowed it with the building of the former Revival Cinema. They are now preparing a general reconstruction, and, one must believe, the fairy tale is to become reality!

THE CHELOVEK [HUMAN BEING] STUDIO was created in 1974 at the Moscow Electrotechnical Institute. It became famous in 1983 after the premiere of Slavomir Mrożek's play *Emigrants* directed by M. Mokeev. The production was immediately banned, and the studio, relocated to a basement on the fringes of Moscow, now found itself illegal, clandestinely showing select spectators two of its forbidden productions: *Emigrants* and *Vladimir Mayakovsky*. During perestroika, the theater received official recognition, a building, and a subsidy. This period was its heyday. Two very high-level teams arose, the team of Roman Kozak, which staged Petrushevskaya's *Cinzano* and *Elizaveta Bam at the Ivanovs' Christmas Party* from the works of the Oberiu, and the team of Sergey Zhenovach,[14] which staged Nina Sadur's[15] *Pannochka* and Corneille's *The Comical Illusion*. But in 1990 Kozak and

---

13 Article 70 regarding "Anti-Soviet agitation and propaganda" was inserted into the Soviet penal code in 1958. It covered activities meant to undermine or weaken Soviet power, including the dissemination of false information, slander, and anti-Soviet literature. It was under this clause that most dissidents were arrested, tried, and sentenced. The penalty was from six months' to seven years' imprisonment.

14 Sergey Vasil'evich Zhenovach (1957–), after work at the Red Army Theater and GITIS, directed at the Chelovek 1988–91 and then took over the Malaya Bronnaya 1991–98, where he specialized in revivals of forgotten plays.

15 Nina Mikhaylovna Sadur (1950–), playwright, a student of Viktor Rozov, who wrote while a

his team entered the MAT, to constitute its Fifth Studio. A year later, Zhenovach and all his actors joined the Theater at Malaya Bronnaya, and the vitality of his studio faded, although other directors continued to stage works there.

A. Inyakhin, "Cloud flowers," *Teatr* 7 (1990), 71–79.

Over the course of time two artistic currents arose in the productions of the Chelovek theater-studio: a romantic theater and a theater of social skepticism. In one, artistic ideas, vacillating, elusive, and shifting as a cloud, flourished, and in the other were caustic parables, masterpieces of social satire, forbidden in their own time, unknown to a whole generation, and therefore withdrawn into themselves.

One of the dearest qualities of Chelovek is that it is a fellowship of professionals, not too preoccupied with manifestos (never was heard an oath of allegiance to any particular school). Their professionalism begins with a respect for art as such. Arising in whatever creation is a creative idea, let it be as egoistic as you please (for instance, an actor wants to stage a show as director), it is concentrated and peacefully realized, but the results, often extremely worthy, do not become a cause for proclaiming anyone whatsoever as the one and only leader, the production itself is the accomplishment of the whole theater. Although for a while people were convinced that the Chelovek studio was first of all *Emigrants* by S. Mrożek, staged by Mikhail Mokeev,[16] in which the director and the actors Mikhail Kozakov and Aleksandr Feklistov[17] subjugated the audience. In fact, both performers remained for a time actors of the still not divided-in-two Art Theater, where one even played Mozart and Treplëv, and the other, gritting his teeth, appeared in Gel'man's[18] *Zinula* and a host of other plays.

In its early days the Chelovek was for them and some other actors a place where they could unburden their souls, perform what appealed to their souls, inasmuch as such work could be possible in the metropolis and not wait until the end of their lifetime, even if they were being cast in big roles and making substantial salaries. The leader of the studio Lyudmila Romanovna Roshkovan "harbored" them and, no stranger to directing herself (here she once staged *On the Open Sea* and not long ago Mrożek's *Striptease*), treated with great sympathy the directorial experiments of young actors or the early work of recent graduates of the directorial faculty of GITIS, from which a repertoire of this fellowship of professionals gradually took shape. [...]

For all its predilection for the plays of Slawomir Mrożek the Chelovek studio,

---

cleaner at the Pushkin Theater; her plays are often tagged as "magical realism." *Pannochka* is an adaptation of Gogol's ghost story "Viy."

16 Mikhail Dmitrievich Mokeev (1951–), director, founded the Green Goose Theater 1973–79, then acted and directed with the MAT 1983–88, especially at the Chelovek Studio; organized his own theater 1992.

17 Roman Efimovich Kozak (1957–2010), actor at the MAT from 1983, made his reputation as both actor and director at the Chelovek Studio; in 1990 he initiated the MAT "Fifth Studio." Aleksandr Vasil'evich Feklistov (1955–), actor, at the MAT 1982–2001 and the Chelovek Studio 1988–90; moved to the Stanislavsky Theater 1991; an exponent of the grotesque.

18 Aleksandr (Shunya) Isaakovich Gel'man (1933–), former engineer, whose plays about human relations in industrial production were good box office at the MAT between 1976 and 1985.

happily, has not turned into the theater of a single genre, although it still remains true to one theme: here they are ever attentive to the real human consciousness in concrete conditions of *sotsum* [the Socialist mentality]. [...] In this sense the work of the Chelovek studio, surprisingly, shows little "novelty," which is remarkable in and of itself, for it does not divert attention from the content-rich essence of man, or from that to which his soul strives, on which his hopes are based, and ... wherever all this may lead, wherever it goes astray. But chiefly, the productions necessarily raise a question whose answer is the most complex of all: "Who Is to Blame?" [...]

P.S. While this article was in press, it was made known that the A. P. Chekhov Art Theater, or as it was once known, the one in Kammerherr Lane, "laid claim to" such actors of the Chelovek as had been nourished in their ranks. Henceforth the group, under the leadership of R. Kozak, will be called the Fifth Studio of the Art Theater and perform its own shows on its new stage. But the Chelovek will remain itself...

Arkady Tsimbler, "Chelovek Studio-Theater," *Teatr* 9 (1987), 123–24, 126.

Italian Vermouth without an Intermission by L. Petrushevskaya, staged by R. Kozak with the young actors of the MAT G. Monukhov, I. Zolotovitsky, and the actor of the New Dramatic Theater S. Zemtsov.[19] [...] It is a show of garish, clear-cut theatrical form. It is defined by the inner dynamic of the staging, its chief contradiction: the contradiction between a sharp theatrical form and the difficulty of the actors in making themselves "at home" in it. That is what creates the tension between the directorial concept and the very material of the play, often proving to be a steadfast resistance.

Roman Kozak first carried out an experiment with Petrushevskaya's play. He removed the play from the framework of real life, hypernaturalistic copying, and the imitation of reality and plunged it into the element of theatricality, art. It turned out that this play is not only about life but about life and art, their opposition, their confrontation.

The foreground of the production emerged as fantasy, creativity, game playing, "a joy ride"! This trio is not getting drunk, they are creating! This is a unique, accessible, maybe freakish way to manifest their creative ardor. It's lucky there are three of them, because "something" is beginning, because this is an improvisation, and in a strange carnivalesque clown act one can change roles, one can forget the poverty and loneliness of life, the monotonous boredom of everyday activities! This is our present-day "moral sense of hearing," on the verge of deafness. It is no longer as simple as Zilov,[20] late for his father's funeral, boozing it up and making mischief on the day of his mother's death.

19 Igor' Yakovlevich Zolotovitsky (1961–), at the MAT from 1983, then at the Chelovek Studio 1988–90 and the Stanislavsky Theater 1991–92, before going freelance. Sergey Zemtsov (1957–) worked in Gorky before graduating from the MAT school 1983; he acted in a number of Moscow theaters.

20 The antihero of *Duck Hunting* (*Utinaya okhota*, 1970) by Aleksandr Vampilov, who manages to wound and disable everyone with whom he comes in contact. He was a favorite antihero of the Soviet theater in the early 1970s.

Because it is unbearably painful, impossible to live constantly with grief, loneliness, guilt, and sorrow. And the audience is right for whom these three "are inveterate liars and lose faith, and indulge in drink until they turn into beasts, forgetting how to talk, and then of nothing holy," but at the same time something living is in these men: the possibility of play, inspiration, a feeling of honor, and a sense that words have lost their meaning. But suddenly, they sober up. And we hear the quiet whisper of the mother, which can be heard, paradoxically, only by someone who has gone to the edge, for whom, it seems, nothing remains of the human: only the beast. [...]

BORIS YUKHANANOV, the "black fox" with the curly locks, was a striking figure in the Moscow and Leningrad youth circles. Director of myriad action-spectacles and videofilms, leader of the director's lab in the avant-garde "Free University," choreographer of ballets, an arcane theorist as well as a practitioner, he was the all-purpose avant-gardist of the late 1980s.

> Boris Yukhananov, "Backstage at Theater Theater," *Iskusstvo* 10 (1989), 57–60.
> Boris Yur'evich Yukhananov (1957–), assistant director to Anatoly Vasil'ev on *Cerceau* (1984–86), created Theater Theater 1985–86; over the next decade he served freelance at many studios and workshops in Moscow and St. Petersburg.

In winter 1986 we showed up in absolute isolation inside Leningrad. Ours was a unique theater, which in addition to everything else called itself "Theater Theater." Already the theater was despaired of. The theater had spent vast amounts of time and space on my infinitely beloved rehearsals of *The Misanthrope*. We decided to find some way out of this situation in those days when our hope still flickered for its realization (or substantiation), I don't know quite how to put it. *The Misanthrope*. We began to churn out a whole series of different ideas and elaborations for new productions. These were, rather, preparations from which little could result, as it struck me then. But once I saw a notice in the paper (a Canadian one, if memory serves), it was called "The Trick of Mimicry." In that notice they reported how butterflies, to survive, change the color of their wings, have recourse to quite incredible tricks to mimic their environment. I saw in this my own fate. We were all such "butterflies," which had to have recourse to the trick of mimicry in its widest sense. [...] We were a theater caught between two cultures, belonging to neither.

And so we began to rehearse that article. Within the rehearsals a performance came to evolve—I understood that it had to be made within the precise canons of collage. Moreover, this very theme—mimicry—was clear to me, because it spoke of how to survive and how to avoid dying. It was a very essential idea. Quite different kinds of "reality" entered into the collage: the reality of the 1970s, Chekhov's words and spaces, the reality of our poor *Misanthrope* and the history of the land in which we lived. In one of Chekhov's stories I ran across the word *khokorona* [funnyral]. It was the second key word for the performance, because it included both life and death. At the time the idea of death was unusually acute, close to life. The collage, which was presented as a staged scene, consisted of all sorts of texts, actions, interludes. [...]

After that we moved to symbolic, untrodden territory of the Universal Theater Theater Video [...] and, beyond that, to Moscow. And our first performance became *Vertical Flight*. It was done very quickly, it was pure, practically total improvisation. Its only planned idea was expressed in the words "attention—flight!" "World champions" came to our rehearsals and rather freely inscribed their actions in the performance. They hung the whole stage with their literally enormous canvases and dropped them into the auditorium. In the production we used all our costumes and characters from *Misanthrope*. We made up our minds to improvise practically without words, the theme was defined as in music—quickly, intuitively. It was clear to me that the "Champions" were incredibly close to us, and together we created a special energetic tone more important than anything else, even more important that all the visual choices. I think, this is precisely where the possibility for synthetic action lies. We must move on not from what is but from what will be. And this "will be" is arranged into zones and realms that—perhaps not quite exactly—one may call Atmosphere, Energy. And if you think about it, Fate, too, or a Sense of one's own fate. One may say that we were united by a clear need for a life-creating movement. The creation of life seemed at that time the central idea for a whole generation that had come into being.

YUZHANANOV'S ABSTRUSE EXPLANATIONS of his experiments could not be further from the socialist realist demand that the lowliest peasant understand what was taking place onstage.

Boris Yukhananov, "Sketch for *The Cherry Orchard*," *Teatral'naya zhizn'* 24 (1990), 11–12. Transcribed by Oleg Shuranov.

[The Workshop of Individuated Directing (Masterskaya individual'noj rezhissury, or MIR), Moscow. Premiere July 27, 1990. Director B. Yukhananov. The interpretation of the text presented here is the result of work by the actors and director in rehearsal. It is a conspectus of the directorial analysis of the play, the rehearsal cardiogram, which fixes and preserves the living memory of the composition, theme, and roles. The actor selects for himself those exact and nervous words that allow him time and again to evoke feeling and acting.]

The stage is freed of the text and turns into action through its relation to it. [...]

A contradictory principle: a performance organized by the law of flight—a flying wedge of cranes. Cranes never fly in an exact triangle. Every second, it is created anew and broken up. The progress of a performance is not fixed as a requisite for repetition. The performance is realized and rehearsed as a preparation and comes together every time only in the eyes of the spectator. There is action, but in every aspect it is caught up and established already in the form of the model. That is, it is no longer action and especially spontaneous action. This is a mobile model of the performance that is realized like life and, after the performance, returns to the status of a model. Action is something monotonous. The theater I'm talking about is living all the time.

Such an attitude to the theater requires special abilities from the actor. The ability not to repeat, but to give birth, to accept the model and develop it into a new reality. This preserves the performance to an incredible extent and uncovers its variant possibilities.

The creation of such a rehearsal model requires a special theater. We created Theater Theater—a zone in which theater is to take shape on top of the performance. As soon as the performance is actually allowed to develop untended, its evolution takes place—the theater withers away. The theater is able, it has the zone and means to breed such a performance.

Theater Theater realizes the demand of the dramatic theater to be regarded in all genres (opera, ballet, concert, performance art, show, action, cabbage party, happening, etc.), to meditate on them as on itself, to enter them as to enter genres of the dramatic theater, through the methodology I've mentioned, and possibly to disclose in this way the theater of the 1990s. [...]

The theater is devoid of real time. Any of its attempts to live here and now can be experienced only as an idea of the here and now. The theater exists in reality, but this reality is uncontrolled and cannot be preserved forever. And this unfixed, preparatory, provocative, but unprescribed reality is the period of the performance. I mean the period in which theater unites with life, actor with spectator, the period in which the theater lives and does not prepare for life. It can live only in the presence of the spectator, only at the moment the result is consummated. There are no preparations for life. The performance is the result of and reason for the theater. It is also the paradox of Theater Theater.

UNDER the Soviet system, published criticism was intended to be part of a public debate about performances. The establishment critics were often befuddled by the work of studios, and their reviews veered from euphoric to dismissive. The government hoped to bring this confusion under control.

"Inquiry of the Secretariat of the STD into the matter of studio theaters," January 1988, 4.

The commission is concerned that the very difficult phase of the creation of studio theaters and their transition into a new professional regime is insufficiently appreciated by the press.

Many young critics regard the process of creating studio theaters only as a transition of amateur theaters into the next class for successes and expect rapid creative perfection from these theaters. And in not a single article is this new phenomenon regarded as a means of changing the theatrical system. Right now it is especially important to establish principles for a constructive dialogue of the leaders of the studio movement and the critics. Works of the studio theaters require an approach that understands simultaneously both what a transitional period means and the aesthetic individuality of studio theaters working in areas not subject to traditional analysis. The commission considers it necessary together with the commission on criticism to begin planning seminars and meetings of leading representatives of Soviet theater studies and stagecraft with young directors and critics to create preconditions for serious analysis of all the processes of the studio movement. And only then all the losses and complexities may be submerged by very serious positive factors.

———————

THE ALL-RUSSIAN UNION of "Creative Workshops" was organized by the Union of Theater Workers of Russia on September 24, 1987, to support new, experimental theatrical undertakings. "The Workshops" assumed the material and organizational aspects of training and hiring directors and realizing the most interesting concepts proposed to the artistic council. The most promising, after years of work, proved to be the Domino Workshop of V. Mirzoev, the Klim Workshop, the Odd–Even Workshop of A. Ponomarev, the Workshop of M. Mokeev, the Workshop of V. Kosmachevsky Jr., and the Schoolofrussianimposture of Sasha Tikhy.

> "Roundtable: 'Organizing and financing the issue of creating Studio Theaters,'"
> April 19, 1988, Union of Theatrical Workers of the USSR, stenographic copy,
> 12–13, 25–26, 29–29a.

A. RUBINSHTEYN:[21] Studio theaters are being created by the executive committees of the Soviets. Studio theaters can be created wherever you like and by whomever you like. [...]

From the point of view of organizations of theatrical activity—amateur or professional or other theatrical collectives—actors work in collectives, even if the collective retains its amateur status.

The question of professional or nonprofessional is a matter for each individual who takes part in this theatrical process. If he signs the union ledger, he's a professional.

Just a moment. What if studio theaters earn a certain amount? We do not consider this necessary.

But if they do earn something, then that should be left entirely to their own discretion, without any regulations.

And this last principle, which we call the honor system, seems to us absolutely essential; in many ways our economy, our national economic order, in general every branch suffers when this principle is violated; we want a person to be treated according to his work, the work he does. If he works as an actor, he must not become grander than a cleaner or a stagehand. Any work must be recompensed accordingly.

---

21 Aleksandr Yakovlevich Rubenshteyn, director of the All-Union Art Research Institute division of socioeconomic problems and chief expert for the Secretariat of the Board of the USSR Theater Workers' Union.

We apply these principles to the model condition of the studio theater, taking it only as a model. [...] The real principle of the studio theaters is variety.

G. DAMAYAN: Unfortunately, I'm beginning to get the impression today that we are still not ready to understand one another. I am absolutely convinced that the variety of forms of vibrant life, a living movement such as the amateur theatrical movement seems to be, must not be driven into a single standardized form.

I see Isaak Dubov sitting here, he has his own theater, works on specific principles. There sits Sergey Ervandovich Kurginyan [b. 1949], he has quite another theater, quite different principles. For twenty-two or thirty years Grinberg ran his own theater in Ivanovo, and he has a third set of principles. And Belyakovich, who puts on shows in Penza, is the same.

Why do we voluntarily emphasize the logic of old productions in the letter at the KNSS Palace of Culture about the uniformity of possible forms? I don't understand. (*Applause.*)

I do not understand! I honestly say to you. I do not work in a government office, I'm not a representative of the STD like Aleksandr Yakovlevich. I wanted to hear his personal opinion, but he always speaks on behalf of the STD. I want to understand as a human being, as a researcher, as a future spectator of yours.

FROM THE HALL: Did you really pay attention to his position?

G. DAMAYAN: How do you mean?

FROM THE HALL: It provides for a variety of forms. And the fact that the situation must be legally affirmed by a document is also clear to everyone.

VOICES FROM THE HALL: Don't stop him speaking, let the man finish!

G. DAMAYAN: Thank you very much. Good-bye. (*Leaves.*)

A. YA. RUBINSHTEYN: Genady Grigor'evich, I think you are being rude.

FROM THE HALL: This is no way to run a meeting. You bring in six managers, a professor stands up, and you can't ask a young man to behave himself properly and let the speaker finish talking! [...]

[RUBINSHTEYN in conclusion:] The STD, like the Ministry of Culture, like the theatrical community in general, is not satisfied by today's training provided by the theatrical institutions of higher learning. A special program of reforms of theatrical education is being worked out right now. It seems to me that, at the moment, it is too far from real actualization. But whatever steps are taken, this program will soon be published and the main questions will be connected with the reform of theatrical education in principle. The question remains how the theater itself is to implement the training in those courses and curricula connected with finished craftsmanship and convey them from the institutions of higher learning.

L. Lebedina, "We take the costs on ourselves," *Teatral'naya zhizn'* 2 (1988), 22–23.

A roundtable organized by the journal in advance of the implementation of the Secretariat's plans.

VYACHESLAV MAL'TSEV:[22] In our All-Russian Union of the Creative Workshops of the Union of Theatrical Workers of the RSFSR, there is no permanent creative team. We will accept applications and try to help those embryonic troupes that have their own artistic concept.

We have some models for the establishment of collectives.

The first is to achieve a finished production.

We will inspect the production, and if it is professionally constituted and does not contradict the Soviet Constitution (i.e., does not propagandize for violence and pornography), we will acquire it for exploitation. We can even pay for five productions—there is no ceiling.

VLADISLAV IVANOV:[23] All the same, the preference will be given to original literary-theatrical concepts. Our task consists not in circulating hackneyed theatrical productions but in the exhibition of something genuinely new and original.

MAL'TSEV: The second is the apportionment of funds for staging a production by an embryonic troupe. The governing board can negotiate three types of contract with this troupe:

1. A contract per production, which guarantees the payment for the rehearsal process and the production expenses, as well as the exploitation of the finished production.

2. A contract for a paid rehearsal period, with a further inspection of the results of the work.

3. A contract for an unpaid rehearsal period. We provide the space and cover all the expenses connected with the organization of the rehearsals. This is the simplest form: the risk is minimal.

The creative workshop is the highest form of our contracts. In the process of work in association, this or that embryonic troupe (which has already formed its aesthetic, artistic program, its own repertoire) is turned into an independent creative organism within the framework of our union. The collective benefits from our spaces, our shops. And it can exist in that guise for no more than two years. After that we have to make a decision: to petition the Secretariat of the Union of the RSFSR, the Great Union of the USSR, the theatrical fund, organs of culture, whether or not it opens as an independent theater.

DMITRY KRYMOV [designer]: The existing theatrical practice does not allow opportunities for a young director to make a showing. Everything is frozen solid. He's under scrutiny from his very first steps.

Even if he manages to get as far as subsidized rehearsals, the artistic council will still regard his production within the context of the fully developed artistic stereotype of the given theater.

IVANOV: We get the point. But even in the case of artistic failure, the production will

22 Vyacheslav Mal'tsev, director of the Union of VOTM.
23 Vladislav Vasil'evich Ivanov (1948–), critic and theater historian, expert on Habima, GOSET, and Mikhail Chekhov and editor of the miscellanies *Mnemozina*.

still become a fact of theatrical life. Let the theatrical community decide whether the production is to live on. [...]

Resolution of the Secretariat of the Governing Board of Union of Theater Workers of RSFSR concerning "Studio theaters and their role in the development of theatrical activity," December 1989, 1, 3–6.

The Secretariat [...] recognizes the special importance of the studio movement, the part it plays in solving the following problems:

—the creation of conditions for the free birth and natural death of theatrical organisms: the conception of various structures, possible manifestations

—the rebirth of the spirit of the creative collective, the cohesion of theatrical collectives

—overcoming the crisis of directing, the creation principally of new mechanisms for appointing leaders

—the search for new forms of contact of the theater and the spectator

The problem of attracting spectators spreads beyond today's organizational problems. It requires a new rebirth of culture, the formation of a new generation whose interest in the theater will be organic.

The activity of the studio theaters can be remarkably helpful in solving these problems, because they are capable of seeking unhackneyed, unstandardized solutions (with connections to the new high schools and gymnasia, in relation to the creation of theatrical works).

Studio theaters in Russia have become remarkably powerful. Their number today reaches 500, despite serious organizational difficulties.

[...] Serious help is needed by those studio theaters that are becoming centers of theatrical culture in regions of the greatest social disruption [*neblagopoluchie*].

To resolve all these questions, we need to involve the means and forces not only of the STD RSFSR but of all organizations interested in cultural uplift. Many questions can help decide the founding in October 1989 of an Association of Studio Theaters.

With the aim of more actively supporting the studio movement and offering it practical, material assistance, the Secretariat considers the adoption of the following measures to be indispensable:

1. To accept as expedient the foundation of an Association of Studio Theaters of Russia and to offer it assistance; the financing of specific programs and a general amount

2. To call a conference of sponsors

3. To ask the Gosplan of the RSFSR to include in its domestic-building plan the projection of cultural centers with specially equipped small stages (without an increase in expenses of construction)

4. To create in collaboration with the Union of Architects of the RSFSR a commission for the exhibition and working out of projects of reconstruction of venues suitable for the work of theatrical studios [...]

7. To assign the association means to subsidize loans to be paid back by the studio

theaters and the exhibition in Moscow of the best work of the studio theaters of the Russian Federation [...]

Among the new important experiments is the experiment in new forms of training (self-supporting, experimental curricular planning, direct contractual relationships of the studio theaters and VUZ), carried out by the Ministry of Higher and Middle Special Education on the model of the B. Shchukin theater school on the initiative of the schools and the "On the Boards" and "The Chamber Stage" studios. [...]

The problem of the search for new forms of work with the spectator, called on to implement the reinforcement of his social activism under perestroika, appears to be extremely timely. The studio theaters, as a rule, take "spectators" to mean not some abstract entity, put through the "mincing machine" of theatrical-performing arts enterprises, but an individual who has come into the theater for spiritual contact, a human being in need of a specific theater, supporting its ideological and artistic platform—precisely that spectator most powerfully open to the influences of the theater, both ideological and artistic. It goes without saying that the presence of such a spectator became crucial owing to the triumphs of the studio movement, and the demand arose for an increase in the number of encounters of the theater with the spectator. [...]

From informational booklets.

THE ODD–EVEN WORKSHOP LED BY A. PONOMAREV[24]

1. The Odd–Even workshop, founded in May 1989, in practice carries out experiments in Russian avant-garde from Nikolay Gogol (1809–1852) to Vladimir Kozakov (d. 1988). [...]

2. NIKOLAY GOGOL. THE NOSE, from N. Gogol, V. Nabokov, I. Annensky, V. Khlebnikov, D. Kharms, F. Schiller, and E.-A. Hoffmann, is an experiment in comprehending the space of the word, as such, beyond its associative meaning, the realization of words as living means of inhabiting actors.

"In the course of the performance the actors exchange roles... The performance exists as a living, moving organism, the actors literally swim in the text, eliciting ever newer and newer nuances of meaning...

"In the person of A. Ponomarev's group theater we behold a new phenomenon, a new phase in the interpretation of stage art." ("A time has come to create," D. Amlinsky, *Komsomol'skaya Pravda* [December 22, 1988]).

THE KLIM WORKSHOP

The first workshop to be formed within the framework of the VOTM, "Domino," under the leadership of V. Mirzoev,[25] opened on November 1, 1988. But even before,

24 Aleksandr Mikhaylovich Ponomarev (1960–), actor and director at the Stanislavsky Theater 1981–86 and the Moscow Hermitage 1986–88; from 1988 founder and director of the Chët-Nechet-Teatr (Odd–Even Theater), specializing in the Russian absurd.

25 Vladimir Vladimirovich Mirzoev (1957–), after work as a journalist and director in various studios, emigrated to Canada 1989, but returned to Russia 1993 to join the Stanislavsky Theater and was then appointed artistic director of the Vakhtangov Theater.

these two productions by this director were performed in the repertoire of the Union: *Madame Margarita* by Athayde and *Break of Noon* by Claudel.[26]

The ongoing explorations by V. Mirzoev in the realm of avant-garde theater led to the refined production of *Miss Julie* by A. Strindberg. The age-old, mystical battle of the sexes, explored by the Swedish playwright, is reconceived by the director from the viewpoint of contemporary world-perception. The director extrapolated Strindberg's subtle eroticism even into the interpolated fragment of Chekhov's *Uncle Vanya*. The production got deserved recognition from the spectator, the theater public at various festivals, and the festival of Soviet art in Zurich.

In the latest performance created in the Domino workshop, *Possibility A* by [Howard] Barker tends toward the drama of the absurd, alternative possibilities of human perception.

From May 1989 the workshop was headed by the director V. Klimenko. Klim's first production was *Possibility B* by Howard Barker, in which the director principally established new tasks.

The new head of the workshop builds a theater of the actor, who is himself both an instrument and a creator, who, achieving possibilities of levels of word and idea, comes to know the world and himself. The director presents the theater as a way of life, as knowledge that the spectator must acquire, if he wants to sympathize with the action presented to him. [. . .]

Klim: "The theater is a zone of infinite expectation. Inspiration comes to the poet as a means of self-sacrifice, the installation of a special world, that joyous condition, by dint of which the presence of the divine takes shape in us, in the theater becomes the act of a collective. The probability of such a thing happening is catastrophic, it makes such an expectation unbelievably difficult, but there is a scant possibility of it.

"This is the special condition of theater, which makes its special art a bud on the Universal tree of truth. [. . .]"

Secretariat of the Governing Board of the Union of Theater Workers, 1990, and the President of the Governing Board of the STD RSFSR, M. A. Ul'yanov, 1990. *Regulations for the All-Russian Association of Creative Workshops* [VOTM], 1–8.

I.2 To carry out its tasks, VOTM, controlled by the present regulations, sequentially:
—forms temporary creative initiatives of a group for the staging and exploitation of a particular production
—organizes on the basis of the resolution of the Secretariat of STD RSFSR temporary creative workshops founded on creative-initiative groups, which have their individual aesthetic program
—runs festivals, test competitions, and other similar measures with the participation of creative collectives of VOTM [. . .]

---

26 *Apareceu a Margarida* (1973) by the Brazilian playwright Roberto Athayde (1949–) is a one-woman show about a dictatorial school mistress; *Partage de Midi* (1906) by Paul Claudel is a four-character, three-act play about the struggle between flesh and spirit.

I.4 The aforementioned organization of the VOTM is the Union of Theatrical Workers of the RSFSR. The interaction of the VOTM with its aforementioned organization will be regulated by the current Regulations. [...]

2.1.2 The Governing Board:

—defines the direction of the creative and productive activity of the VOTM and analyzes its results, in accordance with the board's goals and tasks:

—submits proposals to the Secretariat of the STD of the RSFSR about the opening or liquidation of the affiliates of the creative workshops and exercises control over their productive-creative and financial activities

—inspects questions of the distribution of centralized funds [...]

—submits proposals for changes in the Governing Board of the VOTM. [...]

2.6 A VOTM affiliate, created by the initiative of the local organization of the STD RSFSR, corresponding to the established Governing Board of VOTM and the resolution of the Secretariat of the STD RSFSR, constitutes a legal entity, acting according to the present Governing Board of the VOTM. [...]

2.7 Temporary creative workshops with the rights of a legal entity, if necessary, will be created by the representation of the Governing Board of VOTM by the decision of the Secretariat. [...]

3.1 [...] On the affirmative decision of the Governing Board, the Secretariat of the STD will accept a resolution for the creation of a creative workshop. A contract for the creation of a creative workshop will be concluded between the administration and the artistic leadership of the workshop. The term of the contract will not exceed two years.

THE LEGALESE in which the various statutes were couched failed to discourage the proliferation of workshops.

S. A. Lerner and I. S. Yusina, Director of the All-Russian Association of Creative Workshops of the STD of the RSFSR, revenue of the VOTM for 1990, January 16, 1991.

I. Moscow department
1. From sale of tickets — 26.6 [...]
4. Receipts (normal payments from funds for the development of theatrical, musical art and concerts) — 831.8
5. Other receipts—residue on Jan. 1, 1990 — 61.3
6. Profits of the Moscow dept of VOTM, distributed: — 934.7
[...]
11. Basic financial funds — 130. [...]
V. Grand totals from Moscow, Leningrad and Karelia

1. From sale of tickets 137.4 [...]
6. Profits of VOTM, spent on: 2174.0 [...]

Foreign tours of Russian studio theaters in 1990. A mimeographed list provided by the All-Russian Theater Society.

"Theater of the Absurd" Studio Theater, Leningrad	Netherlands
"Engagement" Studio Theater, Moscow	Spain
B. Panov's Studio Theater, Arkhangel'sk	France
"Benefit" Studio Theater, Leningrad	Sweden, Finland
"Time" Studio Theater, Leningrad	Germany
"Gungo" Studio Theater, Leningrad	Italy
"Wood" Studio Theater, Leningrad	Prague, Italy, Finland, Holland, Italy, Czech Republic, France, Belgium
"Jazzmen" Performance Collective, Moscow	USA
"Geste" Studio Theater, Leningrad	Denmark
"Chamber Stage" Studio Theater, Moscow	Italy
"Chamber Theater" Studio Theater, Leningrad	Finland, Sweden, Denmark, Germany
PTI Studio Theater, Krasnoyarsk	Germany
"Puppintershow" Private Theater, Leningrad	Finland
"Puppet" Studio Theater, Leningrad	Germany
"Labyrinth" Studio Theater, Chelyabinsk	Germany
"The Bat" Cabaret Theater, Moscow	Poland, Germany
"The Player" Studio Theater, Leningrad	Germany
"The Raspberry Patch" Group, Nizhny Novgorod	Germany
"Mannequin" Studio Theater, Chelyabinsk	USA, Italy
"Mimigrants" Studio Theater, Leningrad	Germany (twice)
"Fashion and Song" Studio Theater, Leningrad	Germany
Youth Theater on Krasnaya Presnaya, Moscow	Poland, Germany
"Spartacus Square" Studio Theater, Moscow	USA
"South-West" Studio Theater, Moscow	USA
"Our Theater" Studio Theater, Moscow	Germany
"Nevsky Prospect" Studio Theater, Leningrad	Spain, France, Belgium, Luxemburg
Youth Studio Theater, Perm	Germany

"Planet" Studio Theater, Leningrad	Sweden
"Prospect" Mime Theater, Chelyabinsk	Germany
Fifth Studio of the MAT, Moscow	Netherlands, Poland, Sweden, Norway, Denmark, Portugal
"Five Corners" Studio Theater, Leningrad	Poland (twice)
"The Fifth Floor" Studio Theater, Moscow	Czech Republic
"Ra" Pantomime Studio Theater, Nizhny Novgorod	Spain
"Rock Opera" Studio Theater, Leningrad	Finland, Cyprus
"Salon Theater of Saint Petersburg" Studio Theater	Italy, USA, Germany
"LEM" Theater, Leningrad	Germany
Rock Theater "Secret," Leningrad	Switzerland
Moscow University Student Theater, Moscow	UK, Germany
O. Tabakov Studio Theater, Moscow	Germany
Dance Theater, Petropavlovsk-Kamchatka	Czech Republic
"Terra Mobile" Studio Theater, Leningrad	Sweden, France
"Tverboul" Actors' and Musicians' Company, Moscow	Finland, Germany, UK
"Timbre Laboratory Theater," Moscow	Denmark, Brazil
Studio Theater, Kyzyl	Poland
"At the Nikitsky Gates" Studio Theater, Moscow	Denmark, Germany
"Unicum" Workshop, Leningrad	France
"Odd–Even" Workshop, Moscow	Germany, Switzerland
"Chelovek" Studio Theater, Moscow	Poland
"Show-BENTs" Studio Theater, Leningrad	Germany
"Experiment" Theater, Leningrad	Germany
"Version" Mime Group, Chelyabinsk	Germany

Anna Tsipenyuk, "Inconclusive declaration," *Teatr* 12 (1990), 48–49.

Despite the idiosyncratic style of each director and even the relative lack of coordination in the current group of "Workshops," certain general elements stand out. The values that in the last analysis seem common to this theatrical consciousness gradually come to light. First of all, there is the principle of manhandling the author's texts. Directors in the "Workshops" try to render their material as synthetically as possible. It is hard to name a production strictly bound within the frame of a single play. So in V. Mirzoev's *Miss Julie*, an episode from *Uncle Vanya* appeared. To *Elizaveta Bam*,

11.2. The opening night at the Tabakov Studio Theater, November 24, 1989, of a dramatization of the surrealist novel *Surplus Barrelware* (*Zatvorennaya Bochkotara*, 1968) by the dissident émigré author Vasily Aksënov (in the Argyle sweater; U.S. ambassador Jack Matlock is in eyeglasses and tie). Photo: Vladimir Perel'man.

A. Ponomarev adds *Kupryanov and Natasha*;[27] *Schoolofrussianimposture* comes across, like all stagings of poetry, as a blatant montage of texts: the montage reorganizes *The Nose* and *On Crime* and a whole Pinter trilogy. This persistent demand for combining various texts, including musical ones, independent of the success or failure of each attempt, clearly defines the most important sphere of the directorial interests, one way or another connected with the experiments of Anatoly Vasil'ev. Behind this stands not only the universal transformation of the theatrical language, orientated to the language of film, but also matters of general significance to a contemporary consciousness: the demand for quotation, the sense of the interconnectedness of all cultural strata, the breakdown of the world into its constituent parts and their consequent recombination into a new order, giving birth to new meaning.

Another element common to the Workshop directors seems to be an inordinate focus on language. In the circle of VOTM productions, "Almanacs" by conceptualist poets make a regular appearance. The work of A. Ponomarev seems the most obvious, but not the sole, example of the director's literary interests (of course, the chain Gogol–Khlebnikov–Kharms–Kazakov speaks for itself). V. Klimenko chooses H. Pinter, staging the show *Three Expectations in a Landscape by Harold Pinter*, a writer for whom the characters' linguistic state seems to be the defining factor. In his productions V. Klimenko approximates words to things and things to words; they both exist in the scenic space, and the characters apply them to themselves; one and the same

27 Two works by the Russian "surrealist" Oberiuts: *Elizaveta Bam* (1927) is Daniil Kharms's disjointed crime story; *Kudryash and Natasha* (1931) by Vvedensky is a two-hander for a couple performing intercourse.

words, lines can be combined with different people, like objects or clothing. [...] In his productions V. Klimenko seeks new means of communication: the characters do not address one another directly but through intermediaries—the alienation of words, space, objects. Language in the productions of the Workshops is situated between two poles: at one we find the slogan, the formula of the Oberiuts and the conceptualists, at the other inconclusive, incomplete utterances. The paradox lies in the fact that both can be assigned to anyone, attributed to any character.

Most of the productions contain shock elements, although shocking in different ways. [...] Any shock signifies an impediment to reception and understanding. The VOTM productions create difficulties in understanding even for the exceptional spectator. This incomprehension constitutes the essence of the work of experimentalists in any art. It is characteristic of any generation to interpret the new through old, familiar language. This is especially important for Soviet art, with its traditional primacy of subject matter. So far, there is a remarkably prevalent willingness to justify extremism and extravagance of form by the adequacy of the subject matter. This implies that the subject matter is something that exists prior to and outside the work. The process of the reception of the theatrical text is perverted, whereby we must make sense of the form, while the content appears to be abstract, extracted from the sum total of the forms. [...]

Directors Old and New

The Gorbachëv era began ominously for the old regime in the theater. Éfros, whose new tenure at the Taganka was an unending torment to him, died in harness.

> Alla Demidova, *Dnevnik*. In *Zapolnyaya pausu* [Filling the gap] (Moscow: AST, 2007), 278–83.

1985

January 5. Éfros was taken to the hospital. Olya says it's a heart attack, but, evidently, it is simply an acute spasm.

January 6. [Dupak] said that Filatov and Shapovalov are leaving the theater.

February 3. [...] Éfros says that he's ready to reorganize the theater. Twenty-five percent are competitive vacancies. Old productions will gradually be dropped from the repertoire. He says it isn't hard for him, but it was hard in the summer when they attacked him...

March 16. [*Cherry*] *Orchard* rehearsal. Éfros sat bored. Then he said that we had aged 10 years, that earlier the production had been made in a merry time and proved to be joyous mischief... He suggested we play it as if Ranevskaya were Lyubimov and Lopakhin were Éfros. [...]

April 7. Édison Denisov said that he had talked with Lyubimov, who said that he wants to come back if they'll give him a theater.

1986

December 17. We learned that Gorbachëv cannot or will not unilaterally decide the question about the reinstatement of Lyubimov's citizenship. A letter with that request has to be sent to the Supreme Soviet.

December 23. [...] Éfros signed the letter. What will happen if Lyubimov comes back? I was calm: a natural division. Éfros with his repertoire on the New stage, Lyubimov on the Old. [...]

1987

January 8. [...] We asked Yu. P. [Lyubimov] to write a letter to the Presidium of the Supreme Soviet about his citizenship. He would not agree, said that everyone is a traitor. [...]

January 13. Éfros is dead. At two in the morning—at home—heart attack. "Quickly." In three hours he was no more. [...] I had the same feeling as after Vysotsky's death. Completely upset.

March 3. Meeting of the collective. Gubenko[28] taken on unanimously.

March 9. Official introduction to the troupe of Gubenko as artistic leader. His speech from the throne: emotional bureaucratese and not to the point.

[After time away in France, Italy, Austria, the United States, and Israel, re-creating old productions and staging opera, Lyubimov returned to Moscow in 1988 to prepare *Boris Godunov* and *A Feast in Plague-time*.]

1988

May 8. Lyubimov arrives in Moscow at Gubenko's personal invitation before May 13. Meeting at the airport. Unforgettable. He is pale, and there are tears in his eyes behind dark glasses.

May 9. Lyubimov comes to the theater. His office—everything as it was. He started to rehearse *Boris*.

LYUBIMOV'S GESTURE on his return was to open the long-banned *Alive* at the Taganka on February 24, 1989. His citizenship was not formally restored until 1991, but that premiere, attended by Moscow's political and artistic elite, amounted to full cultural rehabilitation. One Western diplomat remarked, "If you blew this place up, that would be the end of perestroika."[29]

Oleg Tabakov finally quit the Sovremennik when the authorities refused to give official standing to his studio theater (see earlier) and, in 1983, joined the MAT to partner Efremov in *The Bench* and to play Bouton in *The Cabal of Bigots* and Famusov in *Woe from Wit*. Four years later, the MAT began to split apart.

---

28 Nikolay Nikolaevich Gubenko (1941–), actor at the Taganka 1964–68; made chief director at the Taganka 1987–89; on Lyubimov's return appointed minister of culture 1989–91, forcing a division of the Taganka, creating the Community of Taganka Actors; equally disliked by Communists and intellectuals, he caters to the "New Russians."

29 Michael Dobbs, "Lyubimov Returns to Moscow Theater," *Washington Post* (February 24, 1989), C1, C4.

Oleg Tabakov, *Moya nastoyashchaya zhizn'* (Moscow: Éksto-Press, 2000), 332–34.

The split was organized and, in general, planned as a result of the folly, the absurdity of the existence of a burgeoning, gigantic theater troupe. There were nearly 190 persons, which allowed many actors the opportunity to be seen twice a month—on the days when wages were paid. Of course, there could be no talk of an ensemble or of any awareness of one another.

The troupe was so large, so stolid and so static, that almost everyone in it did business outside the theater—either on radio or in the movies, or on television, dancing, singing, and so on.

The reason for the inordinate growth of the company was the constant need to find performers for one role or another. Suppose they were putting on a performance of *Lower Depths,* and the company had no actor for the role of Alëshka the shoemaker, who in the play is 18 or 19. They find a young man in some drama school, take him into the troupe, he plays Alëshka, and that's where his responsibility ends. They don't give him Chérubin in *The Marriage of Figaro* or Officer Fedotik in *Three Sisters.* Somebody else is cast in those roles. So these actors remain in the theater and go to seed. No one tends to their career, no one is responsible for them. And an actor has to act constantly; otherwise he loses a sense of rhythm and professionalism.

This couldn't go on.

Considering that the whole troupe had to be able to work in a more effective, more interesting, more diverse way, Oleg Nikolaevich made a decision to divide the troupe into two parts, giving each half its own permanent location. At this time the major repairs and reconstruction of the building in Art Theater Passage were completed. Previously the MAT performed for rather a long period on two stages—one on Moskvin Street and on a stage on Tver' Boulevard. According to Efremov's plan, part of the actors were assigned to stay on Tver' Boulevard and part to return to the building on Art Theater Passage, as Kammerherr was known in those days.

Discussions about the division of the troupe flared into a conflagration, and mutual reproaches became utterly scandalous. No one knows how far this might have gone if, at one of these meetings, completely inflamed by skirmishes, I had not gotten up and said, "Look here, colleagues. I ask those who support Oleg Nikolaevich Efremov to step into the next room." I should note that, at the time, meetings were meetings of the collective, that is, the stagehands, firemen, wardrobe people, workmen from all the different workshops of the MAT took part, involuntarily bearing witness to the disintegration of the "creative elite." Well, after I spoke, a group of people got up and followed me. These people informally shared Efremov's point of view and wanted to support him at this moment in the life of the troupe. Now they work at the MAT on Kammerherr.

The other half of the troupe was headed by Tat'yana Vasil'evna Doronina. She found the courage to sacrifice her position as a famous and talented actress, unquestionably one of the leading figures in the theater, simply to heal the breach that had arisen. In this sense her humane behavior seems to me extremely rare and worthy of respect.

After all, what was to become of those people whom Oleg Nikolaevich had not invited? Many of them were powerfully and painfully shocked by this, after they had given the theater their all, and this is what they got in the end . . . Doronina headed a group of people who ostensibly were of no use to anyone.

THE COMPANY was now officially two: the "Chekhov" Art Theater, under Efremov, moved back to its old home on Kammerherr Lane, and the "Gorky" Art Theater, led by Doronina, which stayed in the oversized new building. Taxi drivers referred to them as "His" and "Hers."

After he was welcomed by the Taganka, where he revived *Vassa Zheleznova*, Anatoly Vasil'ev rehearsed Viktor Slavkin's nostalgic play *Cerceau* (The game of hoops) from 1982 to 1985 with unpaid actors and eventually opened it in a tent. It proved to be a landmark production that toured to Europe. In 1987 he was given a space at 20 Vorovsky Street in Moscow, which he called the "School of Dramatic Art," a house for his experiments in rhythm, energy, and the poetic word.

> Anatoly Vasil'ev and Giampaolo Gotti,[30] "Créer le Beau en passant par Eros . . ."
> [Creating beauty while bypassing Eros], *Théâtre/Public* (March–April 2006),
> 40.

What I call the *stage text* is located on the border between concrete structures—arising from the written play—and abstract structures—the conceptual order. But this definition has value only in the frame of a theoretic language: to employ current usage, I would say that the *stage text* evolves not in the realm of the dramatic function but in that of the acting.

As to *Cerceau*, it is certainly the realm of the acting that constituted the locale of its actual existence. This was the first time such an approach to theater appeared, even if it was manifested only gradually over the course of the performance. That's why this work took me three years: I refused to compromise, and that is how I could realize an experimental work. [. . .]

Cerceau was therefore made little by little, step by step. The goal was to experiment with ludic structures. That type of structure was not really known to theater people or familiar to them, either onstage or in life.

Concerning *ludic structures,* I would specify that this concerned more than human relations. It did not exclusively concern exchanges on the horizontal plane, for I tried to introduce as well, on the vertical plane, some exchanges of a cultural order. And that defined the title—which was later considered as postmodern.

That work, engaged in long before I approached *Cerceau*, remains unfinished. Particular circumstances prevented me from doing what I wanted, carrying out the experi-

30 Giampolo Gotti (1961–), Italian director, studied at GITIS and founded Koiné–Transartistic Languages.

11.3. *Cerceau* by Viktor Slavkin, directed by Anatoly Vasil'ev, Taganka Theater, Moscow, 1985. The play was staged in a tent in the theater's courtyard.

ment of presenting dramatic texts—those of Chekhov in particular—with a freedom
appropriate to the forms of the novel. For, for me, at that time, what was at stake was
to destroy any structural constraint by destroying conventional dramatic structures
themselves, of staging theatrical texts (a closed structure) as if one were dealing with
novels (open structure). But, then, internal difficulties in those attempts—which would
have taken a considerable amount of time since I insisted on a perspective of purity, a
refusal to compromise—prompted me not to stage the Chekhovs and to turn the page.

So, it was ultimately the work on *Cerceau* that made possible what followed:
Pirandello, Plato,[31] the advent of *verbal action*. [...]

Ludic structures presuppose a ludic exchange: the *ludic conflict*—and the *object* of
this conflict—can be the situation, relationships, atmosphere... First of all, there are
elements of *psychological structures*, but the *object of acting* can be metamorphosed into
one's inner self, the concrete internalized, and only then does it begin to turn abstract
and become an idea, an idea presented in the shape of an image.

The image is like a negative on film that is revealed as positive on photo-sensitive
paper. The idea crystallizes and starts to shift into an image. But one can go further.
Ideas can be inscribed not only in emotional, still quasi-material images but also,
paradoxically, into abstract formulas, signs. I mean, through our imagination, ideas
come to be translated as signs, ritual images, symbols, hieroglyphs, etc. In this way,

31 At his School of Dramatic Art, Vasil'ev restaged Pirandello's *Six Characters in Search of an Author*
(1986–87) and "a theater of the mind" version of the *Platonic Dialogues* (1991).

while always remaining in the *territory of ludic structures,* the object of our research rises to attain a higher level. It's like taking Jacob's ladder to reach heaven.

––––––––––

ANOTHER up-and-coming director was Lev Abramovich Dodin (1944–), whose productions replaced Tovstonogov's as Leningrad's most interesting work. Employing his students from the Cherkasov Institute for Theater and Film, he made a stir with the seven-hour, two-evening chronicle of village life *Brothers and Sisters* (1979) and gained popularity with *The House* (1980). In 1981 he became the chief director of the Leningrad (later St. Petersburg) Maly Dramatic Theater, where he stressed the actor's "aliveness" and collaboration in the creative process. With a class of male dramatic students, he forged forty hours of improvisation into an interpretation of Sergey Kaledin's novella *Construction Batallion,* which had been banned by Gorbachëv in 1987, even after the abolition of censorship. It was a harrowing account of the forced labor imposed on military conscripts; Dodin turned it into a nineteen-episode gripping metaphor for Russian life past and present.

> Anatoly Smelyansky, "Music lessons. *Gaudeamus* at Lev Dodin's," *Moskovskie novosti* [Moscow news] (November 11, 1990), reprinted in *Mezhdometiya vremeni* [Interjections of time] (Moscow: Iskusstvo, 2002), 180–83.

I doubt that almost any reader of Sergey Kaledin's novella *Construction Batallion*[32] could have imagined the performance played out on its motifs and themes at the Maly Dramatic Theater in Leningrad. "The horizon of expectation," inculcated and limited by the theater we have had over the course of a decade, has accustomed us to simple conformity: real life in the forms of realistic theater. Once upon a time, this aesthetic formula was an explosion, a challenge to the routine stage with all its conventions and rituals. But a realistic theater can exist and evolve only when life is open for review and impassive research. The surrogate we used and "reflected" for so many years under the name "our life" has led to the rebirth of the most important tendency of the Russian stage in the twentieth century. [. . .]

Lev Dodin and his students lay hands on a novella, which, even by the new literary norms, exudes a harsh condensation of what might be called antilife. The method is to describe the construction battalion as normal ordinary life, without a single outlet or irrelevant emotion. All the more graphically, the author's concept requires the image of a kind of monstrous social crucible, in which the human individual, *Homo sapiens,* is remade into the two-legged creature that has gone by the nickname *Homo sovieticus.*

In this story Dodin and his actors have, first of all, subjected the theater to scrutiny. The decision is paradoxical and acute, capable of calling down opprobrium on the

––––––––––

32 Sergey Evgen'evich Kaledin (1949–), considered a *chërnukha* or "dark" writer, who focuses on the seamy side of Russian life. *Stroybat,* based on his own two-year experience as a drafted private, building roads and felling trees in Siberia, was finally published in *Novy Mir* in 1989.

creators of the production. And I have already chanced to hear this opprobrium even in the small hall on Rubinshteyn Street. The objections are made on behalf not of art but, as it were, of living life. How can one run counter to the story this way and make a blood-stained daily life the subject of high school improvisations?! But the director, who has worked for many years precisely in the zone of daily life, is not shedding his skin for no good reason. There is probably a kind of supreme necessity in using the theater to estrange and subdue antihuman daily life, to rise above the chaos and even elicit from it a certain sublime harmony.

[...] Under conditions of total collapse a young theater is trying to preserve the joy of acting, a sense of form, to train expert artists capable of passing on the theatrical gene as such. The performance, played by first-form pupils and special students, is an attempt at the self-preservation of the theater. In this way it is trying to resist the cataclysm. [...]

This production perfects not simply acting but a kind of religious enactment, which elevates Soviet life to a kind of archetype, or something like it. The official military ceremonials—from devotion to war down to laughable political activity on the theme of "who is our enemy in the Near East"—as well as the extralegal criminal rituals are illuminated by rituals of another sort, right on up to the biblical. Deposition, confession, initiation, the corrida, benediction, ecstasy—all this coming from the little routines that illustrate the basic themes of the show. [...]

In the military crucible, not only are all sorts of people fermenting but so are all sorts of languages, cultures, creeds, and ways of everyday life. The motley multitude has its head shaved, coarsens, is drained of color, becomes as uniform as those shorn skulls and faded tunics. This Brechtian method keeps us constantly ambivalent: we understand the life force that feeds the actor's imagination, and we see young intellectuals, artisans, high school students, able to reflect the music of this nightmare. [...] If someone was able to instruct these kids this way, to stage their voices this way, to direct their muscles and brains, then it means our situation is not hopeless. And when at the end the Leningrad students perform "Gaudeamus" and translate from Latin to Russian the graven lines of the medieval university anthem, the understanding of time is suddenly washed clean. You understand the eternity of school, technique, the sublime theatrical drill.

Marie-Christine Autant-Mathieu, interview with Lev Dodin, June 27, 1993, *Théâtre/Public* (March–April 1994), 40–42. Marie-Christine Autant-Mathieu is director of research in Theater Studies at the Centre National de Recherche Scientifique in Paris and author of numerous books on Russian theater.

DODIN: When you make theater, you cannot neglect training, education. It is the tradition of the Russian theater, although, lately, it has tended to disappear. Unfortunately living conditions are difficult, different, but if you like, in the theater, to follow the ideas of Stanislavsky (the theater as spiritual creation, the theater as hearth and home, creativity from the soul), you must welcome and train the young. If the theater has principles, a clear conception of what it wants to do, then it is hard to accept people who have viewpoints different from your own. You must make an effort to create a company whose members are not identical but close in their concept of theater.

Theater prolongs school. Each production is an experiment, a sort of apprenticeship, and we will incessantly discover our incompetence. To make something new, you must leave what is old. Often one does not know how to do it, so you work in the old style. With each production, I begin a training course; it's everyone's will, mine and the actors.'

We worked seven years on [Fëdor] Abramov,[33] three years on Dostoevsky (but, during the rehearsals of *The Devils,* the young students performed *The Old Man*[34] and *Gaudeamus*). For long periods when we are "excavating" an author, we live together, we form a community constituted of different groups but united around a controlling line. [...]

ROMAN VIKTYUK worked at many theaters, including the Sovremennik, where his production of Arbuzov's *Evening Light* was especially successful. From 1988, after his staging of Jean Genet's *The Maids* at the Satyricon Theater, he became one of the most fashionable Moscow directors, staging garish spectaculars with unapologetic homosexual overtones.

> Roman Viktyuk on how he works. *Roman Viktyuk s samim soboy* [Viktyuk on Viktyuk] (Moscow: Podkova, 2000), 47–48, 70, 81–82.

The whole Soviet theater is built on lies, on the primitive, and cannot avoid this. Therefore Vampilov is not understood, we only know how to give an imitation of Vampilov, our versions of his plays, because Vampilov is a poet, and poetry is alien to the Soviet theater. Here the laws of socialist realism, realism, naturalism prevail—very convenient for people with gray instincts. For our theater, art is unimportant, technique is unimportant—the only important thing is a pseudo-truthful idea. But *I* consider the subject of a play to be its very form. Any sort of naturalism excludes imagination, there cannot be an upsurge of the soul into the heaven of poetry—only something pitiful and mendacious results from imitating earthly life. As if God were not above us and everything, absolutely everything goes on on earth. Hence our productions are like mushrooms, grown in some kind of monstrous boxes and in a single variety.

When *I* rehearse, *I* do not invent anything. Every second *I* tune myself like an antenna to the cosmos and listen, receive what they are prompting me with from there. *I* say that as a joke, maybe, *I've* been sent here from another planet. True, sometimes *I'd* really like to be a Martian.

---

33 The production of *Brat'ya i sestry* (1979) an adaptation by Dodin, Bekhter'ev, and Katsman, from Abramov's novel of village life (revived 1985).

34 Dodin used fifteen third-form students from the Leningrad Institute of Theater to rehearse an adaptation of Yury Trifonov's novel *Starik.* It opened March 20, 1988.

Luckily, *I* live without vanity, having long ago recognized the need to create my own personal trench, inaccessible to others. *I,* for instance, will never be part of the staff of a state theater, because I know: just let it grab hold of a finger, and this machine will drag you in, head and all. *I* leap out of the ambush, run to somebody else's trench, hang out there a bit and—back again. [...]

In the stagnation period the real function of the theater was to reopen old wounds, which is why the playwrights of the time were Vampilov, Petrushevskaya, Roshchin—who had the audacity to talk about what was out of favor. Nowadays all this is in the open, and our tasks have changed. It's wrong to talk endlessly to a man about what's bad in his life—he might lose faith. And *I* think that it's the very questions of faith, the spirit, which have come downstage center. Only today they demand new approaches and new forms.

When perestroika started, *I* understood that *I* had to turn people toward what had been taken from them—so *I* staged Jean Genet's *The Maids,* Albee's *Lolita* from Nabokov's novel, and Tsvetaeva's *Phaedra.*[35]

[...] A decision to stage *The Maids* in 1987 can come only from naivety, love of people, a belief that it is needed. It was all crazy. One couldn't even mention Jean Genet, along with Ionesco and Beckett. This threesome of world culture understood the essence of the Communist system and spoke about it openly. What else is the meaning of Genet's play *The Balcony,* where he not only condemned the revolution but equated it with a brothel! The heroine of the brothel became a kind of symbol of revolution.

When *I* read *The Maids* aloud at the Satyricon,[36] nobody understood a word of it. They decided it was a whim of mine, but for the sake of good relations they said: please, go ahead and stage it. Although, as was later explained, everyone was convinced that we would perform the show only once. The most perspicacious of all was Kostya Raykin,[37] who said five times. Because he would be in it. We toured *The Maids* to twenty-eight countries, maybe more. [...] What is *The Maids* about? About the fact that the plebs can never achieve the aroma of aristocracy. With its hatred for the aroma, it would rather destroy itself than be able to understand what proceeds from the sublime, heaven, on wings. [...] The debates in the Supreme Soviet, the pinnacle of

35 Genet's *Les Bonnes* (1946–47) is a one-act for three characters, the maids Solange and Claire and their mistress Madame; Genet wanted them to be played by men, which Raykin accommodated. When Albee's adaptation of *Lolita* opened on Broadway 1981, the New York *Times* said, "This show is the kind of embarrassment that audiences do not quickly forget or forgive." In Tsvetaeva's version of *Phaedra* (*Fedra,* 1928), written in Paris, the heroine is guiltless.

36 Satyricon Theater, originally founded as the State Theater of Miniatures under the comedian Arkady Raykin 1983, was renamed after his death 1987. Led by his son Konstantin, it effected a merger of cabaret and drama and eventually became a showcase for Konstantin's flashy extravaganzas.

37 Konstantin Arkad'evich Raykin (1950–), after acting at the Sovremennik for a decade, joined his father's Theater of Miniatures, becoming artistic director of its new avatar, the Satyricon, 1987; technically proficient and movement oriented, he is one of the most dynamic actor-directors in Moscow.

11.4. *The Maids* by Jean Genet at the Satyricon Theater, Moscow, 1987: Konstantin Raykin as Solange, Nikolay Dobrynin as Claire, and Aleksandr Zuev as Madame.

Communists, all these persons are my maids. They are Claire and Solange. They are all the plebs.

I have seen productions in which the characters are played by actresses. Then it is transformed into kitchen-sink squabbling, a private event, settling scores over some milkman. When male actors play it, it is completely alienated, and at the apex stands Oscar Wilde's aesthetics: art is the envelope of life, art defines life, aesthetics is not verisimilitude but an explosion of the subconscious, then Genet's philosophy is revealed. Then the flowers of evil, as Baudelaire puts it, appear to us. For evil at the end of the twentieth century purloins all the means of beauty. [...]

Alla Demidova on *Phaedra* (1988). In *Zapolnyaya pausa* (Moscow: AST, 2007), 153–56.

Our work went on for a very long time and a great deal changed—Hippolytus, Theseus, the choreographers. Roman would take charge, and then disappear. But I completely understood this—his "disappearances." He didn't follow so-called wrong directions to the end. He disappeared not because he was flighty but because he had gone down a blind alley and couldn't find his way out. He disappeared so as not to mark time or emit something indigestible. [...]

We began with the scene with the nurse. When we started to recite aloud with a certain actress, it became clear that it was turning into a kitchen-sink-realism production—and Roman had quite another vision. We rehearsed to create a single voice—it didn't work. And then it came into his head to cast a man. I don't remember whether Dima Pevtsov[38] showed up right away or there was somebody else before him, but we immediately understood that this was the right device. And the scene with the nurse, when we found its resolution, became a little point of perfection in the production. [...]

In her *Phaedra* Tsvetaeva[39] described her own death in Elabug, when, having endured the evacuation there for no more than ten days, she hanged herself, with her knees doubled under, on August 31, 1941. Why? We can give no definite answer, but this parallel allowed us to unite two fates in the production—that of the Poet herself and that of her Creation. We went and introduced into the production some diary entries from Tsvetaeva herself—about her presentiments of her death, the difficulty of expressing the cry of a soul in words and the impossibility of the ears receiving this expressive verbal moan. To overcome this difficulty, and for the spectacle to be accepted by the spectator, that is, with the eyes, we translated many of the poetic images and metaphors of Tsvetaeva's poetry into a series of pure movements.

Long and doggedly, we dealt with the plastique—we sought the necessary form. We experimented with inviting professional ballet actors, but we had to unite movements and words, and only Maris Liepa,[40] whom Roman invited, succeeded in this; Liepa was very good as Theseus—the power of sketching in movement and the rhythm of poetic lines promised very interesting actor's work, but he, unfortunately, was already very ill and did not play the role at the premiere.

The performance begins with groping for an inner rhythm. I—the Poet—seek it along with three young actors and dispense lines to them, while turning them into characters in the meantime. "Actor in white" is given the line "We have no need of wives..." and gradually turns into Hippolytus. "Actor in black" in the hunting scene kills beasts and takes on himself the function of the dark subconscious of Phaedra and the Poet. The third actor is Theseus. A separate character who is not in Tsvetaeva's play—a man in a modern gray overcoat with a newspaper. At the beginning of the show he recites Mandelshtam's famous poem "I shall not see the famous Phaedra..."—he, too, is a poet, perhaps, a friend of the author or S. Éfron,[41] Tsvetaeva's husband.

The work on the production was very interesting for all of us, we created collectively. The basic task of the production was through rhythm and music (written specially for our show by Édison Denisov) to unite ballet plasticity and the word. Many people

---

38 Dmitry Anatol'evich Pevtsov (1963–), at the Taganka 1985–91, then at the Moscow Lenkom, before freelancing.

39 Marina Ivanovna Tsvetaeva (1892–1941), poet who lived in exile 1922–39; her adaptations of classical drama were written in Prague.

40 Maris-Rudol'f Eduardovich Liepa (1936–89), Latvian dancer at the Bol'shoy Theater from 1962; known for his sculptural, masculine movements; exceptional as Crassus in *Spartacus*, but also outstanding in Fokine's *Spectre de la rose*. Taught choreography in Moscow 1963–80.

41 Sergey Yakovlevich Éfron (1894–1941) married Tsvetaeva 1912; he was inveigled into the assassination plot against Trotsky.

helped us in our unusual work. For instance, Alberto Alonso,[42] the famous ballet master, dropped in to watch one of our rehearsals and remained to work with us every day he was in Moscow.

Viktyuk and the actors went to see Béjart during his tour to Leningrad, because the basic principles of plasticity we took from Béjart[43] and Marta Grech. [...]

The first period of our work—a year?—was very pleasant. I liked Roman's friendly disposition. I understood that his life was in a whirl, but nevertheless every day from morn to night he spent with us. He and I were such "girl-friends." Those times were quite different from now—Roman was very poor then, had only one sweater, sometimes I simply had to feed him. And I had the only car, so we went everywhere together, watched videos, which had only just appeared in Moscow. [...]

I remember a few years ago nobody was talking about God, the Cosmos, energy. The words "energy" and "the psychic pole of tension"—all this penetrated our rehearsals, and later I often heard these words in his vocabulary. [...] Roman Viktyuk is one of the few directors who understands and consciously works with "psychic energy."

PËTR NAUMOVICH FOMENKO (1932–2012) was another "nomadic" director. From 1961 he worked at various theaters in Moscow, Leningrad, and Tbilisi, often running into censorship at the Mayakovsky and Lensovet. For a while he led the Leningrad Comedy Theater (1971–81), promoting the Russian classics. Back in Moscow, he formed a studio at GITIS in 1988, which developed into the Fomenko Workshop Company in 1993. His star-studded production of an old Ostrovsky melodrama at the Vakhtangov Theater in 1993 proved to be a watershed moment for the new era. It was heralded as "the end of ideology."

> Boris Poyurovsky, "The benefit of benefits: *Innocent though Guilty* at the Vakhtangov Theater," *Vek* [The age] (June 4–10, 1993), reprinted in *Chto ostalos'*, 279–81.

While the public is debating whether it is proper in our time to revive actor's benefit performances, the director Pëtr Fomenko and the designer Tat'yana Sel'vinskaya,[44] with the help of Ostrovsky's play *Innocent though Guilty*, have set up in the theater buffet a stupendous spectacle, naturally, with the ingenious participation of the actors and

---

42 Alberto Alonso (1917–2008), Cuban dancer, outstanding in Fokine's ballets; from 1959 at the National Ballet of Havana, the leading choreographer in Castro's Cuba, running his own experimental ballet from 1961; national administrator of performing arts 1974–76.

43 Maurice Béjart (actually Berger, 1927–2007), French dancer and choreographer; ran his own troupe from 1960, featuring ballets based on history or literature, often with a strong homoerotic charge (e.g., *Nijinski, clown de Dieu*, to Tchaikovsky's music, 1971).

44 Tat'yana Il'inichna Sel'vinskaya (1927–2012), painter and designer, designed more than 150 productions at various theaters throughout Russia.

actresses of the Vakhtangov company. The production unexpectedly became a general benefit, except that nobody "insults" the beneficiaries by wearing absolutely unnecessary pearls, diamonds, and rubies, as was once done by benighted, ignorant merchants.

True, the grateful spectators all the same present their idols with flowers, which now equal rubies in price. [...]

The action begins in the foyer of the dress circle, or more exactly, in its balconette, where nearly seventy spectators are seated not without difficulty. Another ten or fifteen by some unknown means manage simply to stand. All these duties are jauntily carried out by the actor Anatoly Men'shchikov[45] as the servant Ivan. He later announces an intermission, and after a break invites all the ladies and gentlemen "to the next room" and again helps everyone to find his seat. In this way a small role suddenly takes on a supplemental meaning, for the actor feels himself to be not only a character in the play but a member of the theater staff.

[...] Never mind that Ostrovsky's first act always seemed to me to be a mere prologue, exposition for the drama to come, which, by the way, many directors have done without. Fomenko, on the contrary, treats it as an absolutely integral one-act play. Therefore the actors involved in the first act perform as if they do not know that we will be seeing another three acts after them, true, with other performers.

[...] Moving after the intermission into the refreshment room, I catch myself thinking that in Act I, the actors involved were basically young, and it was easier for them to return to a classroom situation. But how would celebrated masters, used to quite a different stage space, acquit themselves? How are they to escape the clichés of themselves and others, which lie to hand?

Imagine, even here, everyone managed in the best possible way. Instead of the usual theme of the abandoned child with the obligatory melodramatic flourishes, Fomenko chose a rather different perspective. He decided to side with Kruchinina and, with her, to glorify the people of the theater, even if their behavior toward it is not quite the thing. [...]

Marie-Christine Autant-Mathieu, interview with Anatoly Smelyansky, June 8, 1993, *Théâtre/Public* (March–April 1994), 40.

[Smelyansky:] The 1992–93 season gives every evidence of being a turning point. It's been eight years in the waiting, eight years when one had the impression that all was lost, everything had collapsed, and suddenly, this season—it's the general impression— a hope is born of successful, sometimes even remarkable productions. It appears to be connected to the political turning point that occurred this year.[46] It became clear that Russia would not go backward, that it is going forward for better or for worse:

---

45 Anatoly Sergeevich Men'shchikov (1950–) studied at the Shchukin School and joined the Vakhtangov Theater 1987.

46 The referendum in spring 1993. Smelyansky's optimism was belied by the October events, then by those of December 1993, but his observations on the 1992–93 season remain pertinent.

everything has taken a radically different turn, and this impression has been expressed by the theater in a very interesting way.

Fomenko's production of *Innocent though Guilty* at the Vakhtangov Theater is for me a sort of *Turandot* of today, for it records the changes in taste, mood, taking off from an old melodrama that brings provincial actors onstage. It is not that the production expressed the change, the need to see light, merry things. In the 1922 *Princess Turandot,* people laughed because the Civil War was over and they were still alive. Today, a feeling of relief is dominant, people breathe. Even if everybody goes on complaining and repeating as before that life is hard. Yes, it is hard, but now there's a difference. There's been a *winning of freedom,* and people have started to live in the present. Russian has no exact equivalent to the English "present progressive" tense. In Russia, people always live in the past or in the future. They don't know how to appreciate the present time, it is often considered as an intermediate period.

Some productions of this season have shown the value of the present: we have attained freedom. That is the "present progressive": we are engaged in a process of liberation, a difficult, anarchic, etc., process, but we have already changed. The actors, the directors, have changed. And so have the theaters. People have learned that the theater is not a pulpit or a schoolroom, a place for prophecy, journalistic or political debates. The values of the past have been completely discredited. The audience is no longer interested in them, and the theater has become dependent on the audience, for better or worse. For worse, because one must constantly stimulate the spectator so that he goes to the theater (houses have to be filled for economic reasons). For better, because it's always a pleasure when the audience appreciates what you show them.

For me, this season has historic importance.

The theater has shown that it doesn't have only to deal with political and social themes. It has shown joie de vivre. Mark Zakharov[47] in *The Marriage of Figaro* showed the French Revolution with paper streamers. What was important was not the revolution but the love affairs of Beaumarchais's heroes, whereas Stanislavsky had gone in the opposite direction. In Fomenko's production, Ostrovsky's melodrama, the actors take one another's hands and dance in the theater's refreshment room. It's a sort of Russian carnival.

The audience is not interested in comedy as a genre or in philosophic plays. No. It wants light entertainment. It doesn't want to see in the theater what it sees every day in the street or at home. It wants to have fun and relax. It wants things to be beautiful, funny, witty. And especially no blood, nothing military, no memories of what it's fed up with. The very name Solzhenitsyn[48] makes it jump.

---

47 Mark Anatol'evich Zakharov (1933–), director from 1973 of the Moscow Lenin Komsomol Theater (Lenkom), where he staged hit musicals and spectaculars.

48 Aleksandr Isaevich Solzhenitsyn (1918–2008), writer and dissident, political prisoner, had lived abroad from 1974; in 1990 his Soviet citizenship was restored, and he returned to Russia 1994, when his works became readily available there.

In the productions about the Revolution that one can see today (Kulish's[49] *Isle of the Blest,* staged for the first time in Russia at the MAT), the situation is reversed: it is the lower middle class who are seen as normal creatures, while the revolutionaries are madmen, demons. This period is in the process of becoming mythical. The country has been contaminated for nearly a century by this disease, but now we're rid of it; it wasn't lethal, and it can be remembered with a kind of respect. It was painful, but it was an experiment. It is important to serve an apprenticeship in suffering. A man who has never suffered is a bizarre and even terrifying creature. This does not mean that people feel affection for the Bolsheviks, but we have stopped shouting, "Down with the Reds!" Another life has begun. There is no longer this exaltation in repudiating, in destroying. For seventy years, there was a certain culture; one cannot ignore Gorky or Mayakovsky. When you live in the land of Chekhov, you have to understand that angels do not exist, that things are complex, and that people must stop posing as accusers.

49 Since one of his plays had been staged at the Kamerny Theater in 1930, no work of the Ukrainian dramatist Mikola Kulish had appeared on a Russian stage. The MAT produced *Blazhënny ostrov* February 18–20, 1994.

Bibliography

Archives

All-Russian Theater Society, Moscow
Alma Law Collection, New York
Bakhrushin State Central Theater Museum, Moscow
Center for East European and Soviet Studies in the Performing Arts, Illinois University, Carbondale
Central Research Theater Library, Union of Theater Workers of Russia, Moscow
Central [Russian] State Archive of Literature and Arts (TsGALI, RGALI), Moscow
Central State Archive of the Soviet Army, Moscow
Central State Army Theater, Moscow
Central State Theatrical Library, Moscow
Cherkasov Institute of Theater, Music, and Cinema Research Library, St. Petersburg
Ermolova Museum, Moscow
Gesher Theater Press Department, Tel Aviv
Dina Goder Private Archive, Moscow
Harvard Theater Collection, Houghton Library, Cambridge, Mass.
Nataliya Krymova Archive, Moscow
Lenin State Library, Moscow
Library of the Stanislavsky Palace of Art Workers of the St. Petersburg Branch of the All-Russian Theater Society
Lunacharsky State Theatrical Library, St. Petersburg
Mayakovsky Theater Museum, Moscow
Ministry of Culture of the USSR/Russian Federation, Moscow
Moscow Art Theater Museum
Moscow Drama Theater on Malaya Bronnaya
New York Public Library Rare Books and Manuscripts Division
Russian Academy of Theater Arts Library, Moscow
Russian Union of Theater Workers, Moscow
St. Petersburg Central Institute of Theater, Music, and Cinema
St. Petersburg Museum of Theater and Music
Satyricon Theater Press Department, Moscow
Laurence Senelick Collection, Medford, Mass.
Oleg Tabakov Archive, Moscow
Taganka Theater Museum, Moscow

Theater Museum, Hebrew University, Jerusalem
Vakhtangov Museum Press Department, Moscow
Anatoly Vasil'ev Archive, Moscow

Periodicals

Arlekin
Balagan
Bulletin of the International Theater Workers' Olympiad
Byulletin' Tsentral'nogo komiteta Profsoyuza rabotnikov iskusstva SSSR
Derevensky Teatr
Ékran
Ezhegodniki MKhATa
Ezhenedel'nik Narkomprosa
Gostinnitsa dlya puteshestvuyushchikh v prekrasnom
Gryadushchee
Gudki
Hermitage
The International Theater
Iskusstvo
Iskusstvo kino
Izvestiya
Klubnaya stsena
Kommunisticheskaya revolutsiya
Komsomol'skaya Pravda
Krasnaya Zvezda
Kul'tura Teatra
LEF
Die literarische Welt
Literaturnaya Gazeta
Literaturnoe Nasledstvo
London Daily Telegraph
Mnemozina
Moscow News
Moskovsky Komsomolets
Moskovsky Nablyudatel'
Moskvichka
Na literaturnom postu
Narodnoe prosveshchenie
New York Times
Novosti
Novy LEF
Novy Mir
Novy Zritel'
Odnodnevnaya Gazeta TsTKA
Pravda
Programmy Gosudarstvennykh Akademicheskikh Teatrov

Proletariy
Prozhektor
Rabis
Rabochaya Moskva
Rabochy i Teatr
Repertuarny byulletin'
Sinyaya Bluza
Slavic and East European Performance
Sovetskaya Kul'tura
Sovetskoe Iskusstvo
Sovetsky Teatr
Soviet Literature
Sovremennaya Dramaturgiya
Sovremennoe Iskusstvo
Sovremenny Teatr
Teatr (Moscow)
Teatr (Petrograd)
Teatr"
Teatr i Dramaturgiya
Teatr i Iskusstvo
Teatr i Muzyka
Teatral'naya Gazeta
Teatral'naya Moskva
Teatral'naya Zhizn'
Teatral'noe Obozrenie
Teatral'ny Al'manakh
Teatral'ny Nablyudatel'
Teatry i Zrelishcha
Theater (Yale University)
Theater Arts Monthly
Theater Workshop
Times of London
Tvorchestvo
Vechernaya Moskva
Vek
Vestnik Iskusstv
Vestnik Teatra
VOKS Socialist Construction in the USSR
Voprosy literatury i dramaturgii
Voprosy teatra
Vremya
Di yidishe velt
Za kommunisticheskoe proveshchenie
Zhizn' Iskusstva
Zrelishcha

Books and Articles

Abalkin, N. *Sistema Stanislavskogo i sovetsky teatr.* Moscow: Iskusstvo, 1954.

Abelyuk, Evgeniya, and Elena Leenson, with Yury Lyubimov. *Taganka: lichnoe delo odnogo teatra.* Moscow: Novoe literaturnoe obozrenie, 2007.

Afinogenov, Aleksandr. *Dnevniki i zapisnye khizhki.* Moscow: Sovetsky pisatel', 1960.

Akimov, Nikolay. *Akimov—éto Akimov!* Ed. Z. I. Zaytsev et al. St. Petersburg: Rossiyskaya Natsional'naya Biblioteka, 2006.

———. *Ne tol'ko o teatre.* Leningrad: Iskusstvo, 1966.

———. *O teatre.* Leningrad/Moscow: Iskusstvo, 1962.

———. *Teatral'noe nasledie.* Ed. S. L. Tsimbal'. 2 vols. Leningrad: Iskusstvo, 1978.

Aksënova, Galina G. *Teatr na Taganke 68-i i drugie gody.* Moscow: Pravda, 1991.

Aktual'nye voprosy ékonomiki i organizatsii teatral'noy dela. Sbornik nauchnykh trudov. Moscow: Ministerstvo kul'tury RSFSR, 1996.

Alekseeva, M. P., ed. *Shékspir i russkaya kultura.* Moscow: Nauka, 1965.

Alliluyeva, Svetlana. *Only One Year.* New York: Harper and Row, 1969.

Alpers, Boris V. *Put' sovetskogo teatra.* Moscow: Pravda, 1947.

———. *Teatr sotsial'noy maski.* Moscow: OGIZ-GIKhL, 1931.

Alyansky, Yury. *Uvesel'itel'nye zavedeniya starogo Peterburga.* St. Petersburg: Aurora/Stroy-izda Spb, 2003.

Andreeva, Mariya. *Perepiska, vospominaniya, stat'i.* Moscow: Iskusstvo, 1961.

Annenkov, Yury. *Dnevnik moikh vstrech.* Moscow: Zakharov, 2001.

Antonov-Ovseenko, A. *Teatr Iosifa Stalina.* Moscow: Gregori-Peydzh, 1995.

Arbenina, Stella, Baroness Meyendorff. *From Terror to Freedom: The Dramatic Story of an Englishwoman's Life and Adventures in Russia before, during, and after the Revolution.* London: Hutchinson, 1929.

Arkad'ev, M. P. *Osnoye zadachi teatral'nogo stroitel'stva.* N.p.: Izd. Upravleniya teatrami Narkomprosa RSFSR, 1934.

Aronov, S. *Teatr Yunogo Zritelya v SSSR. Po materialam pervogo tura vsesoyuznogo smotra.* Moscow: Iskusstvo, 1940.

Autant-Mathieu, Marie-Christine. "Interviews. Anatoli Smelianski 8 juin 1993. Lev Dodine et Mikhaïl Stronine, 27 juin 1993." *Théâtre/Public* (March–April 1994): 40–42.

Avangard i teatr 1910–1920-kh godov. Ed. G. F. Kovalenko. Moscow: Nauka, 2008.

Azizyan, I. A. "Aleksandr Bykhovsky v 'Gabima,'" in *Russkiy avangard 1910-x-1920-x godov i teatr.* Ed. G. Kovalenko. St. Petersburg: DB, 2000.

Babochkin, Boris. *Vospominaniya. Dnevniki. Pis'ma.* Moscow: Materik, 1996.

Balatova, N. P. "Iz arkhiva teatral'nogo kritika (K. L. Rudnitsky. Dnevnik 1948–1951 gg.)," in *Teatral'naya periodika v Rossii. Doklady, publikatsii, materialy kruglogo stola.* Ed. A. A. Kolganov. Moscow: Tri kvadrata, 2009.

Balet. Éntsiklopediya. Ed. Yu. N. Grigorovich et al. Moscow: Sovetskaya Éntsiklopediya, 1981.

Bazanov, S. N., and M. P. Kim, eds. *Kul'turnaya zhizn' v SSSR, 1928–1941: khronika.* Moscow: Nauka, 1976.

Bazanov, S. N., T. S. Chanysheva, and M. P. Kim, eds. *Kul'turnaya zhizn' v SSSR, 1941–1950: khronika.* Moscow: Nauka, 1977.

Bazanov, S. N., V. K. Bodisko, and N. P. Khilina, eds. *Kul'turnaya zhizn' v SSSR, 1951–1965: khronika.* Moscow: Nauka, 1979.

Beilin, A. *Nikolay Pavlovich Okhlopkov.* Moscow: Goskinizdat, 1953.

Benjamin, Walter. *Gesammelte Schriften.* Ed. Tillman Rexroth et al. 4 vols. in 12. Frankfurt-am-Main, Germany: Suhrkamp, 1972.

———. *Moscow Diary.* Ed. Gary Smith. Trans. Richard Sieburth. Cambridge, Mass.: Harvard University Press, 1986.

Benua (Benois), A. N. *Moy dnevnik 1916–1917–1918.* Moscow: Russky Put', 2003.

Berezkin, V. *Mastera sovetskogo teatra Vadim Ryndin.* Moscow: Iskusstvo, 1974.

Berkovsky, Naum. *Literatura i teatr: stat'i raznykh let.* Moscow: Iskusstvo, 1969.

Bernik, M., et al. *Vam rasskazyvaet artist: monologi i dialogi.* Moscow: Iskusstvo, 1993.

Bertenson, Sergey. *Vokrug iskusstva.* Hollywood, Calif.: printed by author, 1957.

Binevich, Evgeny M. "Na puti k 'Drakonu,'" *Neva* 10 (1996): 171–81.

Birman, Serafima. *Trud aktёra.* Moscow: Iskusstvo, 1939.

Blok, Aleksandr. *Dnevniki 1901–1921.* Moscow: Gos. izd-vo khudozhestvennoy literatury, 1963.

———. *Sobranie sochinenii v 8 tomakh.* Moscow: Gos. izd-vo khudozhestvennoy literatury, 1960–63.

Blyum, V. *Teatr imeni MGSPS.* Moscow: Tea-Kino-Pechat', 1928.

Bodisko, V. Kh., and M. P. Kim, eds. *Kul'turnaya zhizn' v SSSR, 1966–1977: khronika.* Moscow: Nauka, 1981.

Böhmig, Michaela. *Das russische Theater in Berlin 1919–1931.* Munich, Germany: Otto Sagner in Kommission, 1990.

Bokshanskaya, Ol'ga S. *Pis'ma O. S. Bokshanskaya Vl. I. Nemirovichu-Danchenko.* Ed. I. N. Solov'ёva. 2 vols. Moscow: Moskovsky Khudozhestvenny Teatr, 2005.

Boleslavsky, Richard, in collaboration with Helen Woodward. *Lances Down: Between the Fires in Moscow.* Indianapolis, Ind.: Bobbs-Merrill, 1932.

Boyadzhiev, G. *Teatral'nost' i pravda.* Moscow: Iskusstvo, 1945.

Bradshaw, Martha, ed. *Soviet Theaters 1917–1941.* A collection of articles by Yosyp Hirniak, Serge Orlovsky, Gabriel Ramensky, Boris Volkov, and Peter Yershov. New York: Research Program on the USSR, 1954.

Braudo, E. "Opera and Ballet in the Soviet Union." *V.O.K.S. Socialist Construction in the USSR* 6 (1934): 34–35.

Brown, Ben. *Theater at the Left.* Providence, R.I.: The Booke Shop, 1938.

Buchanan, Meriel. *Dissolution of an Empire.* London: John Murray, 1932.

Bulgakov, M. A. *Zapiski pokoynika. Teatral'ny roman.* Kommentarii A. Kobrinskogo. St. Petersburg: Akademichesky proékt, 2002.

Bullard, Julian, and Margaret Bullard, eds. *Inside Stalin's Russia: The Diaries of Reader Bullard 1930–1934.* Oxfordshire, U.K.: Day Books, 2000.

Carter, Huntley. *The New Theatre and Cinema of Soviet Russia.* London: Chapman and Dodd, 1927.

Catalogue 3: Russia and the Soviet Union. New York: Richard Stoddard Performing Arts Books, 1978.

Chagall, Marc. "Mayn arbeyt in der yidishn teater." *Di Yidishe Velt* 2 (May 1928).

Chechetin, A. "Sinyaya bluza," in *Ot "zhivoy gazety" do teatra-studii.* Moscow: Molodaya gvardiya, 1989.

Chekhov, Mikhail. *Literaturnoe nasledie.* 2 vols. Moscow: Iskusstvo, 1986.

Chulkov, Georgy. *Gody stranstvovaniya.* Moscow: Federatsiya, 1930.

Clark, Katerina, and Evgeny Dobrenko, with André Artizov and Oleg Naumov. *Soviet Culture and Power: A History in Documents 1917–1953.* New Haven, Conn.: Yale University Press, 2007.

Clurman, Harold. *The Collected Works of Harold Clurman: Six Decades of Commentary on Theater, Dance, Music, Film, Arts, and Letters.* Ed. Marjorie Loggia and Glenn Young. New York: Applause Books, 1994.

———. "Soviet Diary." *New Theater* (August 1935): 12–13.

Dean, Basil. *Seven Ages: An Autobiography 1888–1927.* London: Hutchinson, 1970.

Decisions of the Central Committee C.P.S.U.(B.) on Literature and Art (1946–1948). Moscow: Foreign Languages Publishing House, 1951.

Delafield, E. M. [Elizabeth Monica Dashwood]. *I Visit the Soviets: The Provincial Lady in Russia.* New York: Harper, 1937.

Demidova, Alla. "Iz dnevnika." *Moskovsky Nablyudatel'* 3–4 (1996): 65–67.

———. *Zapolnyaya pausa.* Moscow: AST, 2007.

Derzhavin, Konstantin. *Kniga o Kamernom teatre.* Leningrad: Gos. Izd-vo Khudozhestvennoy literatury, 1934.

Descaves, Pierre. *Molière en U.R.S.S.* Paris: Amiot-Dumont, 1954.

Dmitriev, Yu. D. *Teatral'naya Moskva 1920-e gody.* Moscow: Gos. Institut Iskusstvovaniya, 2000.

Dobbs, Michael. "Lyubimov Returns to Moscow Theater." *Washington Post* (February 24, 1989): C1, C4.

Dos Passos, John. "Moscow Theaters October and November 1928." *Theater 1929* (January 1929): 5–8.

Dreiser, Theodore. *Dreiser's Russian Diary.* Ed. Thomas P. Riggio and James L. W. West III. Philadelphia: University of Pennsylvania Press, 1996.

Éfros, Abram, and M. A. Zelikson, eds. *Kamerny Teatr i ego khudozhniki, 1914–1934. Al'bom.* Moscow: Vserossiyskoe Teatral'noe Obshchestvo, 1934.

Éfros, Anatoly. *Sochineniya.* 4 vols. Moscow: Russky Teatr, Panas, 1993.

Egoshina, Ol'ga. *Aktërskie tetradi Innokentiya Smoktunovskogo.* Moscow: OGI, 2004.

Eisenstein, Sergey. "Teatral'nye tetrady S. M. Eyzenshteyna," ed. M. K. Ivanova and V. V. Ivanov, in *Mnemozina. Istorichesky Almanakh Vypusk 2,* ed. Vladislav Ivanov. Moscow: Éditorial URSS, 2000.

Ékonomicheskie pokazateli deyatel'nosti teatrov i kontsertnykh organizatsy RSFSR. Moscow: Ministerstvo Kul'tury RSFSR, 1990.

Ékonomika i organizatsiya teatra. Ed. A. Yufit. 6 vols. Leningrad: Iskusstvo, 1971–79.

Elagin, Yury. *Tëmny geny: Vsevolod Meyerkhol'd.* New York: Izd-vo imeni Chekhova, 1955.

———. *Ukroshchenie iskusstv.* New York: Izd-vo imeni Chekhova, 1952; 1988.

Érdman, Nikolay. *A Meeting about Laughter: Sketches, Interludes, and Theatrical Parodies . . .* Trans. and ed. John Freedman. Luxembourg: Harwood, 1995.

———. *Pesy. Intermedii. Pis'ma. Dokumenty. Vospominaniya sovremennikov.* Ed. A. Svobodin. Moscow: Iskusstvo, 1990.

Éstrada. N.p.: Malaya Politicheskaya Biblioteka, 1944.

Éstrada Rossii XX vek. Éntsiklopediya. Ed. E. D. Uvarova et al. Moscow: Olma-Press, 2004.

Étkind, Mark G. *Nikolay Akimov: stsenografiya, grafika.* Moscow: Sovetsky khudozhnik, 1980.

Ezhegodnik Moskovskogo Khudozhestvennogo Teatra. 6 vols. Moscow: Izd. Muzeya Moskovskogo Khudozhestvennogo Akademicheskogo Teatra SSSR, 1945–56.

Fel'dman, K. *Sem' dney MKT 1–20.* Moscow: ZIK, 1923–24.

Fevral'sky, A. *Pervaya sovetskaya p'esa: "Misteriya-buff" V. V. Mayakovskogo.* Moscow: Sovetsky pisatel', 1971.

———. *Vstrechi s Mayakovskim.* Moscow: Sovetskaya Rossiya, 1971.

Filippov, Vladimir. *Maly Teatr.* Moscow: Tea-Kino-Pechat', 1928.

Finf yor melukhisher idisher kamer teater 1919–1921. Moscow: Shul un bukh, 1924.

Flanagan, Hallie. "The Soviet Theatrical Olympiad." *Theatre Guild Magazine* (1930): 10–13, 62.

Frame, Murray. *The St. Petersburg Imperial Theaters: Stage and State in Revolutionary Russia, 1900–1920.* Jefferson, N.C.: McFarland, 2000.

Fülop-Müller, René. *Geist und Geschichte des Bolschewismus.* Zurich: n.p., 1926.

Gaevsky, V. *Fleyta Gamleta. Obrazy sovremennogo teatra.* Moscow: Soyuzteatr, 1990.

Galich, Aleksandr. *General'naya repetitisya.* Frankfurt, Germany: Posev Press, 1974.

Gavrilovich, Donatella. *Profumo di Rus'. L'arte del teatro in Russia scritti di artisti, pittori e critici 1860–1920.* Rome: Bulzoni, 1993.

Getty, J. Arch, and Oleg V. Naumov. *The Road to Terror: Stalin and the Self-Destruction of the Bolsheviks, 1932–1939.* Trans. Bernard Sher. New Haven, Conn.: Yale University Press, 1999.

Geyzer, Matvey. *Solomon Mikhoéls.* Moscow: Prometey, 1990.

Giatsintova, Sof'ya. *S pamyat'yu naedine.* Moscow: Iskusstvo, 1989.

Gladkov, Aleksandr. *Meyerkhol'd.* 2 vols. Moscow: Soyuz teatral'nykh deyateley, 1990.

Gollenbakh, E. F., and A. I. Golovin. *Teatral'no-dekoratsionnoe iskusstvo v SSSR, 1917–1927. Sbornik statey.* Leningrad: Izd. Komiteta vystavki teatral'no-dekoratsionnogo iskusstvo, 1927.

Golub, Spencer. "The Theater of Anatoly Efros." *Theatre Quarterly* 21 (Summer 1977): 18–33.

Golubovsky, B. G. *Bol'shie malen'kie teatry.* Moscow: Izd. im. Sabashnikovykh, 1998.

Gorbunova, Ekaterina. *Meyerkhol'd repetiruet "Tridtsat' tri obmoroka."* Moscow: AGRAF, 2002.

Gorchakov, N. M. *Rezhissërskie kommentary k knigu Nikolaya Virty "Zemlya."* Moscow: Iskusstvo, 1938.

———. *Rezhissërskie uroki K. S. Stanislavskogo.* Moscow: Iskusstvo, 1951.

Gorchakov, Nikolai A. *The Theater in Soviet Russia.* Trans. Edgar Lehrman. New York: Columbia University Press, 1957.

Gorky, Maksim. *Pol'noe sobranie sochineny.* 26 vols. Moscow: Nauka, 1968–82.

Green, Paul. *Drama and the Weather.* New York: Samuel French, 1958.

Gudkova, Violetta. *Yury Olesha i Vsevolod Meyerkho'ld v rabote nad spektaklem "Spisok blagodeyany." Opyt teatral'noy arkheologii.* Moscow: Novoe literaturnoe obozrenie, 2002.

Gurvich, A. "Zametki o komedii." *Teatr* 12 (1940): 80–83.

Gvozdev, A. A. *Teatr imeni Vsevolod Meyerkhol'da, 1920–1926.* Leningrad: Academia, 1927.

———. *Teatral'naya kritika.* Leningrad: Iskusstvo, 1987.

Helm, MacKinley. *Angel Mo' and Her Son Roland Hayes.* Boston: Little, Brown, 1942.

Hoffmann, L., and D. Hoffmann-Ostwald. *Deutsches Arbeitertheater 1918–1933.* 2 vols. Munich, Germany: Rogner and Bernhard, 1973.

Houghton, Norris. *Moscow Rehearsals.* New York: Harcourt, Brace, 1936.

Hughes, Langston. "The Soviet Theater in Central Asia." *Asia* (October 1934): 590–93.

I vnov' o Khudozhestvennom. MKhAT v vospominaniyakh i zapisyakh 1901–1920. Ed. Mariya Polkanova. Moscow: Avantitul, 2004.

Dos idishe kamer teater: tsu zany erefnung in yuli 1919. Tel Aviv: n.p., 1919.

Il'insky, Igor'. *Sam o sebe.* 2nd ed. Moscow: Iskusstvo, 1973.

Instructions for the Preparations for the International Workers' Theatrical Olympiad, Organised by the I.W.D.U. Bulletin No. 1 of the Organization Committee of the International Workers Theatrical Olympiad. Moscow: Cooperative Publishing Society of the Foreign Workers of the USSR, 1932.

The International Workers' Theatre Olympiad. Bulletin No. 2. Moscow: International Union of the Revolutionary Theatre, 1932.

Ivanov, V. V., ed. *Mnemozina. Dokumenty i fakty iz istorii otechestvennogo teatra XX veka.* Vol. 4. Moscow: Indrik, 2009.

Ivanova, L. V., S. S. Tarasova, and M. P. Kim, eds. *Kul'turnaya zhizn' v SSSR, 1917–1927: khronika.* Moscow: Nauka, 1975.

Kalashnikova, Yu. S., ed. *Rezhissër, uchitel', drug. Sovremenniki o tvorchestve A. D. Popova. Sbornik vospominany.* Moscow: Vserossiyskoe Teatral'noe Obshchestvo, 1966.

Kalm, Dmitri. "Problems of the Soviet Theater." *International Literature* 10 (1939): 71–78.

Kaminskaya, Nataliya, and Aleksandr Popov. *"Tabakerka." Istoriya teatral'nogo podvala ili 30 let spustya.* Moscow: AST-Astrel', 2008.

Katanyan, V., ed. *Mayakovsky. Literaturnaya khronika.* 4th rev. ed. Moscow: Goslitizdat, 1961.

Karelin, V. *Dva reisa.* N.p.: Glavsevmorput', 1938.

Kerzhentsev, P. M. *Tvorchesky teatr.* 5th rev. and enlarged ed. Moscow: Gos. Izdatel'stvo, 1923.

Kerzhentsev, V. *Tvorchesky teatr. Puti sotsialisticheskogo teatra.* 3rd ed. Moscow: Izd. Vserossiyskogo Tsentral'nogo Ispolnitel'nogo Komiteta Sovetov R., S. K. i K. Deputatov, 1919.

Kessler, Harry. *In the Twenties: The Diaries of Harry Kessler.* Trans. Charles Kessler. New York: Holt, Rinehart, and Winston, 1971.

Kharms, Daniil. *Polet v nebesa: stikhi, proza, dramy, pis'ma.* Ed. A. A. Aleksandrov. Leningrad: Sovetsky pisatel', 1988.

Khudozhestvenny Teatr. Tvorcheskie ponedel'niki i drugie dokumenty 1916–1919. Ed. Z. P. Udal'tsova. Moscow: Moskovsky Khudozhestvenny Teatr, 2006.

Knebel', Mariya. *Rezhissër, uchitel', drug.* Moscow: VTO, 1966.

Kobrin, Yury. *Teatr imeni Vs. Meyerkhol'd i rabochy zritel'.* With a foreword by A. V. Lunacharskogo. Moskva: Moskovskoe teatral'noe izdatel'stvo, 1926.

Kogan, P. S. *V preddvery gryadushchego teatra.* Moscow: Pervina, 1922.

Kolyazin, V. F., and V. A. Goncharov, eds. *"Vernite mne svobodu!" Deyateli literatury i iskusstva Rossii i Germanii—zhertvy stalinskogo terror. Memoral'ny sbornik dokumentov iz arkhivov byvshego KGB.* Moscow: MEDIUM, 1997.

Komardenkov, V. P. *Dni minuvshie (iz vospominaniy khudozhnika).* Moscow: Sovetsky khudozhnik, 1972.

Konechny, A. M. *Byt i zrelishnaya kul'tura Sankt-Peterburga-Petrograd XVIII-nachalo XX veka. Materialy i bibliografii.* St. Petersburg: Rossiysky Institut Istorii Iskusstv, 1997.

Koonen, Alisa. *Stranitsy zhizni.* Moscow: Iskusstvo, 1975.

Korneeva, Natal'ya. *Ekaterina Furtseva. Politicheskaya melodrama.* Moscow: Algoritm, 2007.

Kotovskaya, M. P., and S. A. Isaev, eds. *Mir iskusstv: almanakh.* Moscow: Gos. Institut teatral'nogo iskusstva, 1991.

Kovalenko, G. F., ed. *Russky avangard 1910-kh–1920-kh godov i teatr.* St. Petersburg: Dmitry Bulanin, 2000.

Kozakov, Mikhail. *Risunki na peske. Aktërskaya kniga.* Moscow: AST/Zebra E, 2007.

Kozintsev, G. M. *Perepiska G. M. Kozintseva 1922–1973.* Moscow: Artist-Rezhissër-Teatr, 1998.

———. *Sobranie sochineniya.* 2 vols. Leningrad: Iskusstvo, 1963.

Kruchënykh, A. *Fonetika teatra.* Moscow: TsIT, 1925.

Krylov, S. N., ed. *Puti razvitiya teatra: sbornik.* Moscow: Teakinopechat', 1927.

Kryzhitsky, G. *Rezhissërskie portréty.* Moscow: Teakinopechat', 1928.

Kuleshova, V. N., ed. *Khudozhnik s zrelishche.* Moscow: Sovetsky Khudozhnik, 1990.

Kuzmin, Mikhail. *Ésseistika—kritika.* Ed. E. G. Domogatskaya and E. A. Pevak. 3 vols. Moscow: Agraf, 2000.

Kuzyakina, Natal'ya. *Teatr na Solovkakh 1923–1937.* St. Petersburg: Dmitry Bulanin, 2009.

Lācis, Asja. *Revolutionär im Beruf. Berichte über proletärisches Theater, über Meyerhold, Brecht, Benjamin und Piscator.* Ed. Hildegard Brenner. Munich, Germany: Rogner und Bernhard, 1971.

Lartseva, Natal'ya. *Teatr rasstrelyanny.* Petrozavodsk: Petropress, 1998.

Lavrent'ev, A. N. "Pozdny konstruktivizm v teatre. 'Klop' i 'Shestaya mira,'" in *Russky avangard 1910-x-1920-x godov i teatr.* Ed. G. F. Kovalenko. St. Petersburg: Dmitry Bulanin, 2000.

Law, Alma. "The Trouble with Lyubimov." *American Theater* (April 1985): 4–11.

Lehmann, John. *Prometheus and the Bolsheviks.* London: Cresset Press, 1937.

Lemeshev, S. *Put' k iskusstvu.* Moscow: Iskusstvo, 1968; 1974.

Les' Kurbas. Stat'i i vospominaniya o L. Kurbase. Literaturnoe nasledie. Ed. M. G. Labinsky and L. S. Tanyuk. Moscow: Iskusstvo, 1987.

Levitin, Mikhail. *Menya ne bylo.* Moscow: Izd. Teatra Érmitazh, 2005.

Lisitsky-Küppers, Sophie. *El Lissitzky.* London: Thames and Hudson, 1968.

Lunacharsky, Anatoly. *A. V. Lunacharsky o teatre i dramaturgii. Izbannye stat'i v 2-kh tomakh.* Moscow: Iskusstvo, 1958.

———. *O massovykh prazdnestvakh, éstrade, tsirke.* Ed. S. Dreyden. Moscow: Iskusstvo, 1981.

———. *O Vakhtangove i vakhtangovtsakh.* Moscow: Iskusstvo, 1959.

———. *Sobranie sochineny v 8 tomakh.* Moscow: Iskusstvo, 1964.

———. *Teatr i Revolyutsiya.* Moscow: Gosizdat, 1924.

Lunacharsky, S. *Teatr dlya detey kak orudie kommunisticheskogo vospitaniya.* Moscow: Gos. Izd. Khudozhestennoy literatury, 1931.

Lyubimov, Yury. "The Algebra of Harmony: A Meditation on Theater Aesthetics Followed by a Note on Actors and the Acting Profession." *Cultures* 5, no. 2 (1978): 65–81.

———. *Rasskazy starogo trepacha.* Moscow: Novosti, 2001.

M. F. Andreeva. Perepiska. Vospominaniya. Stat'i. Dokumenty. Vospominaniya o M. F. Andreevoy. Moscow: Iskusstvo, 1961.

Macleod, Joseph. *The New Soviet Theatre.* London: Allen and Unwin, 1943.

———. *A Soviet Theatre Sketch Book.* London: Allen and Unwin, 1951.

Makarenko, A. S. *Pedagogicheskaya poéma.* Moscow: Svetlana Nemolya, 2003.

Makaryk, Irena R. *Shakespeare in the Undiscovered Bourn: Les Kurbas, Ukrainian Modernism, and Early Soviet Cultural Politics.* Toronto: University of Toronto Press, 2004.

Makaryk, Irena R., and Virlana Tkacz, eds. *Modernism in Kyiv: Jubilant Experimentation.* Toronto: University of Toronto Press, 2010.

Mally, Lynn. *Culture of the Future: The Proletkult Movement in Revolutionary Russia.* Berkeley: University of California, 1990.

Mandelshtam, Osip. *Sobranie sochineny v trekh tomakh.* Moscow: Terra, 1991.

Mardzhanov, Konstantin. *Vospominaniya.* 2 vols. Tbilisi: Zarya Vostka, 1958.

Margolin, S. "The Artist and the Theatre." *V.O.K.S. Socialist Construction in the USSR* 6 (1934): 42–46.

Marinchin, Pavel. *Rozhdenie komsomol'skaya teatra.* Leningrad: Iskusstvo, 1963.

Markov, Pavel A. *Dnevnik teatral'nogo kritika.* Moscow: Iskusstvo, 1976.

———. *Kniga vospominanii.* Moscow: Iskusstvo, 1983.

———. *O teatre.* 4 vols. Moscow: Iskusstvo, 1974–77.

Martynova, S. S. *Opera-fars "Bogatyri" A. P. Borodina v Kamernom teatre (po nezivestnym arkhivnym materialam i dokumentam). Issledovanie.* Moscow: RAM im. Gnesinykh, 2002.

Mass Culture in Soviet Russia: Tales, Poems, Songs, Movies, Plays, and Folklore 1917–1933. Ed. James von Geldern and Richard Stites. Bloomington: Indiana University Press, 1995.

Massovye Prazdnichestva. Leningrad: Academia, 1926.

Mastera MkhAT. Moscow: Iskusstvo, 1939.

Masterstvo aktëra. Moscow: Goslitizdat, 1935.

Masterstvo teatra vremennik Kamernogo Teatra. 2 vols. Moscow: n.p., 1923–24.

Matskin, Aleksandr P. *Teatr moikh sovremennikov: iz starykh i novyzh tetrady.* Moscow: Iskusstvo, 1987.

Mayakovsky, V. V. *Sobranie sochineny v vos'em tomakh.* Moscow: Pravda, 1968.

Mestechkin, M. *V teatre i v tsirke.* Moscow: Iskusstvo, 1976.

Meyerhold, Vsevolod. "On Ideology and Technology in the Theatre." *International Theatre* 2 (1934): 6–8.

———. *Perepiska.* Moscow: Iskusstvo, 1976.

———. *Rekonstruktsiya teatra.* Leningrad: Teakinopechat', 1930.

———. *Stat'i, pis'ma, rechi, besedy.* 2 vols. Moscow: Iskusstvo, 1968.

Meyerhold, Vsevolod, and V. Bebutov. "Odinochestvo Stanislavskogo." *Vestnik teatra* (May 1, 1921): 1–5.

Meyerhold, Vsevolod, V. Bebutov, and Ivan Aksënov. *Amplua aktëra.* Moscow: GVYTM, 1922.

Meyerkhol'd repetiruet. 2 vols. Moscow: Artist-Rezhissër-Teatr, 1993.

Mgebrov, A. A. *Zhizn' v teatre.* 2 vols. Moscow: Academia, 1932.

Mikhoéls, Solomon. *Dos yidishe kamer teater.* Petrograd: n.p., 1919.

———. *Stat'i, besedy, rechi.* Moscow: Iskusstvo, 1965.

Miller, Arthur. "On the Theater in Russia," in *The Theater Essays of Arthur Miller.* Ed. Robert A. Martin. New York: Viking Press, 1978.

Ministerstvo kul'tury SSSR. *Osnovye problemy sovremennoy sovetskoy dramaturgii.* Leningrad: Leningradsky gos. Institut Teatra, Muzyki i Kinematografy, 1975.

MKhAT Vtoroy. Opyt vosstanovleniya biografii. Ed. I. N. Solov'ëva, A. M. Smelyansky, and O. V. Egoshina. Moscow: Moskovsky Khudozhestvenny Teatr, 2010.

Mogilevsky, A. I., V. Filippov, and A. M. Rodionov. *Teatry Moskvy, 1917–1927.* Moscow: Gos. Akad. Khudozhestvennoy nauky, 1928.

Morozov, Mikhail M. *Shakespeare on the Soviet Stage.* Trans. David Magarshack. London: Soviet News, 1947.

———, ed. *Mastera teatra v obrazakh Shékspira. Sbornik.* Moscow: Vserossiyskoe Teatral'noe Obshchestvo, 1939.

Moskva teatral'naya. Spravochnik-putevoditel'. Moscow: Moskovsky rabochy, 1971.

Moskovsky Khudozhestvenny Teatr v russkoy teatral'noy kritike 1919–1943. Ed. O. A. Radish-cheva and E. A. Shingareva. 4 vols. Moscow: Artist. Rezhissër. Teatr, 2009–10.

Moussinac, Léon. *Avec les comédiens soviétiques en tournée. Notes de voyage.* Paris: Editions sociales internationales, 1935.

Mudrak, Myroslava M. *Russian Theater Holdings at the Humanities Research Center.* Austin: University of Texas Press, 1978.

Muratova, K. D., ed. *Periodika po literature i iskusstvu za gody revolutsii 1917–1932.* Leipzig, Germany: Zentralantiquariat der DDR, 1933; 1972.

Muzalevsky, M. V. *Umolknuvshie muzy.* Vol. 1, part 1. Moscow: RITs "Kavaler," 2009.

Nelidov, V. A. *Teatral'naya Moskva. Sorok let moskovskikh teatrov.* Moscow: Materik, 1931; 2002.

Nel's, Sofiya. *Shékspir na sovetskoy stsene.* Moscow: Iskusstvo, 1960.

———. "'Ukroshchenie stroptivoy' v Tsentral'nom teatre Krasnoy armii." *Teatr* 12 (1938): 73–79.

Nemirovich-Danchenko, V. I. "Pis'ma naverkh." *Moskovsky nablyudatel'* 3–4 (1996): 71–72.

———. *Tvorcheskoe nasledie.* Ed. I. N. Solovëva. 4 vols. Moscow: Moskovsky Khudozhest-venny Teatr, 2003.

Nikitin, Andrey. *Moskovsky debyut Sergeya Éyzenshteyna. Issledovanie i publikatsii.* Moscow: Indergraf Servis, 1996.

Nilsson, Nils Åke, ed. *Art, Society, Revolution: Russia 1917–1921.* Stockholm: Almqvist and Wiksell International, 1979.

O teatre. Sbornik statey. Ed. K. Derzhavin. Leningrad: Academia, 1927.

O teatre: Sbornik statey. Ed. S. S. Danilov and S. S. Mokul'sky. Moscow: Iskusstvo, 1940.

Ofrosimov, Yu. *Teatr.* Berlin: Volga, 1926.

Okhlopkov, Nikolay. *Vsem molodym.* Moscow: Molodaya Gvardiya, 1981.

Olesha, Yury. *P'esy. Stat'i o teatre i dramaturgii.* Moscow: Iskusstvo, 1968.

Orlov, A. *O trude rabotnikov teatral'no-zrelishchnykh Uchrezdeny (Prava po sovetskomu zakonodatel'stvu).* Moscow: Profizdat, 1976.

Oruzheynikov, N. "Soviet Drama." *V.O.K.S. Socialist Construction in the USSR* 6 (1934): 11, 18–20.

Osnos, Yury. *Sovetskaya istoricheskaya dramaturgiya.* Moscow: Sovetsky pisatel', 1947.

Ot balagana do Shékspira. Khronika teatral'noy deyatel'nosti G. M. Kozintseva. Ed. V. G. Kozintseva and Ya. L. Butovsky. St. Petersburg: Dmitry Bulanin, 2002.

Paech, Joachim. *Das Theater der russischen Revolution. Theorie und Praxis des proletarisch kulturrevolutionären Theaters in Russland 1917 bis 1924. Ein Beitrag zur politischen Geschichte des Theaters.* Kronberg im Taunus, Germany: Scriptor, 1974.

Pimenov, Vladimir. "Dve sud'by." *Teatr* 6 (1990): 124–25.

———. *Vospominaniya, vstrechi . . .* Moscow: Pravda, 1967.

Piotrovsky, Adrian. *Teatr. Kino. Zhizn'.* Leningrad: Iskusstvo, 1969.

Pogodin, Nikolay. "From a Playwright's Workshop." *International Literature* 7 (1938): 65–72.

Popov, Aleksey. *Vospominaniya i razmyshleniya o teatre.* Moscow: Vserossiyskoe Teatral'noe Obshchestvo, 1963.

Poyasnenie k spektaklyu dlya shkol'nikov "Printsessa Turandot" v teatre imeni E. V. Vakhtangova. Moscow: Mosgorono, 1935.

Poyurovsky, Boris M. *Chto ostalos' na trube . . . Khroniki teatral'noy zhizni Vserossiyskoe Teatral'noe Obshchestvoroy poloviny XX veka.* Moscow: Tsentroligraf, 2000.

Poyurovsky, Boris M., ed. *Zvezdy moskovskoy stseny. Lenkom.* Moscow: Tsentroligraf, 2000.

Prem'ery Tovstonogova. Ed. E. Gorfunkel'. Moscow: Artist. Rezhissër. Teatr, 1994.

Problemy teatral'noe naslediya M. A. Bulgakova: sbornik nauchnykh trudov. Ed. A. A. Al'tshuller, A. A. Ninov et al. Leningrad: LGITMIK, 1987.

Protiv formalizma i naturalizma v iskusstva. Sbornik statey. N.p.: OGIZ-IZOGIZ, 1937.

Protokoly soveshchanii narkomov prosveshcheniya soyuzhnykh i avtonomykh respublik, 1919–1924 gg. Ed. M. P. Kim, L. I. Davydova, T. Y. Kasovitskaya, and A. P. Nenarokov. Moscow: Nauka, 1985.

Puti razvitiya teatra: Sbornik. Ed. S. N. Krylov. Moscow: Tea-Kino-Pechat', 1927.

5 let raboty Moskovskogo Teatra Yunogo Zritelya. Moscow: Mosoblispolkom, 1933.

Rabota rezhissëra nad sovetskoy p'esoy: sbornik statey. Moscow: Iskusstvo, 1950.

Radlov, Sergey. *Desyat' let v teatre.* Leningrad: Priboy, 1929.

———. *Stat'i o teatre 1918–1922.* Petrograd: Mysl', 1923.

Radzinsky, Édvard. "Fleeting," trans. Antonina W. Bouis. *New York Times Magazine* (June 8, 1997): 82.

———. *Moya teatral'naya zhizn'.* Moscow: AST, 2007.

Ransome, Arthur. *Six Weeks in Russia in 1919.* London: Allen and Unwin, 1919.

Raykina, Marina A. *Moskva zakulisnaya. Zapiski teatral'nogo reportera.* Moscow: Vagrius, 2000.

Red'ko, A. E. *Teatr i évolyutsiya teatral'nykh form.* Leningrad: Sabashnikov, 1926.

"Revizor" v teatre imeni Vs. Meyerkhol'da. Collection of articles by A. A. Gvozdeva, E. I. Kaplana, Y. A. Nazarenko, A. L. Slonimskogo, and V. N. Solov'ëva. Leningrad: Academia, 1927; Sankt-Peterburg: Academia, 2002.

Revolyutsionnaya Moskva. Tret'emu Kongressu Kommunistichestogo Internatsionala. Moscow: Krasnaya Moskva, 1921.

Rezhissër v sovetskom teatre. Moscow: Iskusstvo, 1940.

Rodchenko, Aleksandr. *Aleksandr Rodchenko. Opyty dlya budushchego: dnevniki, stat'i, pis'ma, zapiski.* Moscow: Grant, 1996.

Rostotsky, B. I. *K istorii bor'by za ideynost' i realizm sovetskogo teatra.* Moscow: Academia Nauk SSSR, 1950.

Rozov, Viktor. "A Producer after My Own Heart." *Soviet Literature* 9 (1977): 57–66.

———. *Puteshestvie v raznye storony: avtobiografichesaya proza.* Moscow: Sovetsky pisatel', 1987.

Rozovsky, Mark. *Delo o "konokradstve."* Moscow: Vagrius, 2006.

———. *Samootdachna.* Moscow: Sovetskaya Rossiya, 1976.

Rudnitsky, Konstantin. "Replika Terent'eva." *Moskovsky Nablyudatel'* 7–8 (1995): 78–94.

———. *Russian and Soviet Theatre: Tradition and Avant-garde.* London: Thames and Hudson, 1988.

Rumyantsev, M. *Na arene sovetskogo tsirka.* Ed. E. Kuznetsov. Moscow: Iskusstvo, 1954.

Russkaya sovetskaya éstrada 1917–1929. Moscow: Iskusstvo, 1976.

Russky dramatichesky teatr. Éntsiklopediya. Ed. M. I. Andreev, N. É. Zvenigorodskaya, A. V. Martinova, and E. Yu. Beglyarova. Moscow: Bol'shaya Rossiyskaya Éntsiklopediya, 2001.

Russky sovetsky dramatichesky teatr: annotirovanny ukazatel' bibliograficheskikh i spravochnykh materialov 1917–1978. 3 vols. Moscow: Ministerstvo Kul'tury SSSR, 1977.

Ryadom so Stalinym v Bol'shom teatre (zapiski voennogo komandanta). N.p.: n.p., 1995.

Ryazanov, El'dar. *Chetyre vechera s Vladimirom Vysotskim: po motivam televizionnoy peredachi.* Moscow: Iskusstvo, 1989.

Ryndin, V. F. *Vadim Ryndin. Khudozhnik i teatr.* Moscow: Vserossiyskoe Teatral'noe Obshchestvo, 1966.

Sakhnovsky, V. *Rezhissura i metodika eë prepodovaniya.* Moscow: Iskusstvo, 1939.

Samarin, Roman, and Aleksandr Nikolyukin, eds. *Shakespeare in the Soviet Union: A Collection of Articles.* Trans. Avril Pyman. Moscow: Progress, 1966.

Sappak, V. *Bloknoty 1956 goda.* Ed. E. A. Kesler. Moscow: Moskovsky Khudozhestvenny Teatr, 2011.

Sats, Natal'ya. *Deti prikhodyat v teatr: stranitsy vospominanii.* Moscow: Iskusstvo, 1961.

———. "18 Years of Soviet Children's Theatre." *Moscow News* (May 27, 1936): 10.

———. *Nash put'. Moskovsky teatr dlya detey i ego zritel'.* Moscow: Moskovsky oblastnoy otdel narodnogo obrazovaniya, 1932.

Sboeva, Svetlana. *Tairov. Evropa i Amerika 1923–1930. Zarubezhnye gastroli Moskovskogo Kamernogo teatra.* Moscow: Artist. Rezhissër. Teatr, 2010.

Sbornik rukovodyashchikh materialov po voprosam finansovo-khozaystvennoy deyatel'nosti teatrov i kontsertnykh organizatsy. Moscow: Ministerstvo Kul'tury SSSR, 1976.

Senelick, Laurence. "Embodying Emptiness: The Irreality of Mikhail Chekhov's Khlestakov." *New Theatre Quarterly* 25, no. 3 (2009): 224–32.

———. "A Five-Year-Plan for Taming of the Shrew," in *Shakespeare and the Worlds of Communism and Socialism.* Ed. Irena Makaryk and Joseph Price. Toronto: University of Toronto Press, 2006.

———. *A Historical Dictionary of Russian Theatre.* Lanham, Md.: Scarecrow Press, 2007.

———. "The Making of a Martyr: The Legend of Meyerhold's Last Public Appearance." *Theatre Research International* 28, no. 2 (2003): 157–68.

———. "National on Compulsion: The Moscow Art Theatre," in *National Theatres in a Changing Europe.* Ed. Stephen Wilmer. London: Palgrave Macmillan, 2008.

———. "Recovering Russia's Memory," in *Writing and Rewriting National Theatre Histories.* Ed. S. E. Wilmer. Iowa City: University of Iowa Press, 2004.

———. "Stanislavsky's Second Thoughts on *The Seagull.*" *New Theatre Quarterly* 20, no. 2 (2004): 127–37.

———. "'Thus Conscience Does Make Cowards of Us All': New Documentation on the Ochlopkov *Hamlet.*" *Balagan* 1, no. 6 (2000): 3–22.

———. "A Woman's Kingdom: Minister of Culture Furtseva and Soviet Theatre Censorship in the Khrushchev Era." *New Theatre Quarterly* 26, no. 1 (2010): 16–24.

Sergeev, A. V. "Teatr—tsirk—kino. Odin iz putey teatral'nogo avangarda 1920-x godov," in *Russkaya avangard 1910-x-1920-x godov i teatr.* Ed. G. F. Kovalenko. St. Petersburg: Dmitry Bulanin, 2000.

Shapiro, Adol'f. *Kak zakryvalsya zanaves.* Moscow: Novoe Literaturnoe Obozrenie, 1999.

Shapovalov, L. E. *Tvorcheskii put' Malogo teatra.* Moscow: Pravda, 1949.

Shatrov, Mikhail. *Dramas of the Revolution.* Moscow: Progress, 1990.

Shein, Joseph. *Arum moskver yidishn teater.* Paris: n.p., 1964.

Shentalinsky, Vitaly, and John Crowfoot. *The KGB's Literary Archive.* London: Harvill Press, 1995.

Shklovsky, Viktor. *Gamburgsky schët: ésse 1914–1933.* Moscow: Sovetsky pisatel', 1990.

———. *Khod konya: sbornik statey.* Moscow: Gelikon, 1923.

———. *Za 40 let.* Moscow: Iskusstvo, 1965.

Shvarts, Dina. *Dnevniki i zametki.* St. Petersburg: Inapress, 2001.

Shvarts, Evgeny. *Memuary.* Ed. Lev Losev. Paris: La Presse libre, 1982.

———. *Zhivu bespokoyno—: iz dnevnikov.* Ed. K. N. Kirilenko. Leningrad: Sovetsky pisatel', 1990.

Shverubovich, Vadim. *O starom Khudozhestennom teatre.* Moscow: Iskusstvo, 1990.

Simonov, Evgeny. *Nasledniki Turandot.* Moskva: Algoritm, 2010.

Simonov, Konstantin M. *Glazami cheloveka moego pokoleniya: razmyshleniya ob I. V. Staline.* Moscow: Izd-vo Agentsva pechati Novosti, 1989.

Smelyansky, Anatoly. *Mezhdometiya vremeni.* Moscow: Iskusstvo, 2002.

———. *Mikhail Bulgakov v Khudozhestvennom teatre.* 2nd ed. Moscow: Iskusstvo, 1989.

———. *Ukhodyashchaya natura.* Moscow: Iskusstvo, 2001.

Smirnov, A. A. *Shakespeare: A Marxist Interpretation.* Trans. S. Volochova. New York: Critics Group, 1937.

Smirnova, N. A. *Vospominaniya.* Moscow: Vserossiyskoe Teatral'noe Obshchestvo, 1947.

Smyshlaev, V. *Pechalno i nekhorosho v nashem teatre . . . Dnevnik 1927–1931 gg.* Moscow: IGS, 1996.

Solodvnikova, A. V., et al., eds. *Moskovsky khudozhestvenny teatr v sovetskuyu épokhu. Materialy i dokumenty.* Moscow: Iskusstvo, 1962.

Sopel'nyak, Boris. "Teatr kontsa tridtsatykh." *Moskovskie novosti* 12, no. 24 (1996): 35.

Sosnovskaya, A. "Nina Aizenberg (1902–1974): Russian Designer." *Slavic and East European Performance* 20, no. 3 (2000): 48–73.

Sovetskaya dramaturgiya: sborniki. 3 vols. Moscow: Iskusstvo, 1948.

Sovetskaya kul'tura, itogi i perspektivy. Moscow: Izvestiya TsIK SSSR i VTsIK, 1924.

Sovetsky teatr. Ed. K. L. Rudnitsky. Moskva: Iskusstvo, 1967.

Sovetsky teatr. Dokumenty i materialy. Russky sovetsky teatr 1917–1921. Dokumenty i materialy. Ed. A. Z. Yufit. Leningrad: Iskusstvo, 1968.

Sovetsky teatr. Dokumenty i materialy. Russky sovetsky teatr 1921–1926. Dokumenty i materialy. Ed. A. Ya. Trabsky. Leningrad: Iskusstvo, 1975.

Sovetsky teatr. Dokumenty i materialy. Russky sovetsky teatr 1926–1932. Chast' pervaya. Ed. A. Ya. Trabsky. Moscow: Iskusstvo, 1982.

Sovetsky teatr i sovremennost'. Sbornik materialov i statey. Moscow: Vserossiyskoe Teatral'noe Obshchestvo, 1947.

Sovetskoe dekorativnoe iskusstvo. Materialy i dokumenty 1917–1932. Moscow: Iskusstvo, 1984.

Spravochnik po voprosam oplaty i okhrany truda rabotnikov kul'tury i iskusstva. Moscow: Profizdat, 1964.

Spravochnik rukovodyashchikh materialov Komiteta po delam iskusstv pri SNK Soyuza SSR. Moscow: Iskusstvo, 1941.

Stalin, I. V. *Sochineniya*. 16 vols. Moscow: Politizdat, 1946–67.

Stanislavsky, K. S. *Building a Character*. Adapted by Elizabeth Reynolds Hapgood. New York: Theater Arts Books, 1949.

———. *Sobranie sochineny v devyati tomakh*. Ed. A. M. Smelyansky et al. 9 vols. in 10. Moscow: Iskusstvo, 1988–99.

———. *Stat'i, rechi, besedy, pis'ma*. Ed. G. Kristi and N. Chutkina. Moscow: Iskusstvo, 1953.

Stenogramma zasedaniya nauchno-issledovatel'skoy gruppy NII teatra i muzyki pri MKhAT SSSR 22 aprelya 1952g. Moscow: Bakhrushin Theater Museum Archive, n.d.

Stepun, Fëdor. *Byvshee i nesbyvsheesya*. 2 vols. New York: Izd. imeni Chekhova, 1956–57.

———. *Osnovnye problemy teatra*. Berlin: Slovo, 1923.

Stites, Richard, ed. *Culture and Entertainment in Wartime Russia*. Bloomington: Indiana University Press, 1995.

Sto let. Aleksandrinsky teatr—Teatr Gosdramy. Leningrad: Diretsii leningraskikh gosudarstvennykh teatrov, 1932.

Street Art of the Revolution: Festivals and Celebrations in Russia 1918–33. Ed. Vladimir Tolstoy, Irina Bibikova, and Catherine Cooke. Trans. Frances Longman, Felicity O'Dell, and Vladimir Vnukov. New York: Vendome Press, 1980.

Strutinskaya, E. I. "'Teatr chistogo metoda' Yu. P. Annenkova," in *Russkaya avangard 1910-x-1920-x godov i teatr*. Ed. G. F. Kovalenko. St. Petersburg: Dmitry Bulanin, 2000.

Sukhanov, G. I. *Teatr, lyudi, zhizn'* . . . St. Petersburg: n.p., 1992.

Svobodin, A. P., ed. *Teatr "Sovremennik."* Moscow: Iskusstvo, 1973.

Tabakov, Oleg. *Moya nastoyashchaya zhizn'*. Moscow: Éksto-Press, 2000.

———. "A Soviet Actor and Director Looks at Gogol and *The Government Inspector*." *Journal of Russian Studies* 35 (1998): 24–28.

Tairov, Aleksandr. *The Kamerny Theatre*. International Workers' Theater Olympiad. Bulletin No. 3. Moscow: International Union of the Revolutionary Theatre, 1933, 55–56.

———. *Proklamatsy khudozhnika*. Moscow: Shlugleyt, 1917.

———. *Zapiski rezhissëra. Stat'i, besedy, rechi, pis'ma*. Ed. P. Markov. Moscow: VTO, 1970.

Teatr Anatoliya Éfrosa. Vospominaniya, stat'i. Moscow: Artist, Rezhissër, Teatr, 2000.

Teatr Gulaga. Vospominaniya, ocherki. Ed. M. M. Korallov. Moscow: Memorial, 1995.

Teatr i vremya: vozrastyushchaya rol' teatra i formirovanny sotsializma: sbornik statey. Ed. V. N. Dmitrevsky. Moscow: Vserossiyskoe teatral'noe obshchestvo, 1985.

Teatr Muzykal'noi Komedii v gody Blokady. Leningrad: Iskusstvo, 1973.

Teatr-prostranstvo zhizni. Moscow: VRIB "Soyuzreklama-kul'tura," 1988.

Teatr Yunykh Zritelya 1922–1927. Opyt raboty teatra dlya detey i yunoshestva. Leningrad: Academia, 1927.

Teatral'naya kritika 1917–1927 godov. Problemy razvitya. Sbornik nauchnykh trudov. Ed. S. Bolkhontseva. Leningrad: Ministerstvo kul'tury RSFSR, 1987.

Teatral'naya Moskva: Teatr, muzyka, kino: putevoditel'. N.p.: n.p., 1926–29.

Teatral'naya periodika 1917–1940. Bibliografichesky ukazatel'. Ed. V. Vishnevsky. Moscow: Iskusstvo, 1941.

Teatry Strany v usloviyakh éksperimenta. Sbornik materialov. Moscow: Soyuz Teatral'nykh Deyateley RSFSR, 1988.

Tenin, Boris. *Furgon komedianta. Iz vospominanii*. Moscow: Iskusstvo, 1987.

Thorne, Janet. "It Makes You Weep: An Interview with Stella Adler on Soviet Actors." *New Theater* (October 1934): 8.

Tikhonovich, V. "Theatrical Culture of the Peoples of the USSR." *V.O.K.S. Socialist Construction in the USSR* 6 (1934): 70–71, 75.

Toporkov, V. *Stanislavsky na repetitsii.* Moscow: Iskusstvo, 1950.

Tovstonogov, Georgy. *Zerkalo stseny.* 2 vols. Leningrad: Iskusstvo, 1984.

Trotsky, Leon. *Literature and Revolution.* Trans. Rose Strunsky. New York: International, 1925.

Tsirkovoe iskusstvo Rossii. Éntsiklopediya. Ed. M. E. Shvydkoy, V. V. Koshkin, M. S. Rudina, R. E. Slavsky et al. Moscow: Bol'shaya Rossiyskaya Éntsiklopediya, 2000.

Turovskaya, M. *Babanova. Legenda i biografiya.* Moscow: Iskusstvo, 1981.

Tvorcheskie besedy masterov teatra: S. G. Birman, S. V. Giatsintova. Leningrad: Vserossiyskoe Teatral'noe Obshchestvo, 1939.

U istokov rezhissury. Ed. Yu. K. Gerasimov. Leningrad: LGITMik, 1976.

"Ukroshchenie stroptivoy" v Tsentral'nom Teatre Krasnoy Armii. Sbornik. Moscow: Vserossiyskoe Teatral'noe Obshchestvo, 1940.

Utësov, Leonid. *Spasibo, serdtse!* Moscow: Vagrius, 1976.

Uvarova, E. *Éstradny teatr: Miniatyury, obozreniya, myuzik-kholly (1917–1945).* Moscow: Iskusstvo, 1983.

Vaganova, N. M. *Russkaya teatral'naya émigratsiya v tsentral'noy Evrope i na Balkanakh. Ocherki.* St. Petersburg: Aleteyya, 2007.

Vakhtangov, Evgeny. *Evgeny Vakhtangov. Dokumenty i svidetel'stva.* Ed. V. V. Ivanov. 2 vols. Moscow: Indrik, 2011.

———. *Evgeny Vakhtangov. Sbornik.* Ed. L. O. Vendrovskaya and G. P. Kaptereva. Moscow: Vserossiyskoe Teatral'noe Obshchestvo, 1984.

Van Gyseghem, André. *Theatre in Soviet Russia.* London: Faber and Faber, 1943.

Varshavsky, Ya. *Rezhissura v sovetskom teatre.* Moscow: Vserossiyskoe Teatral'noe Obshchestvo, 1948.

Vasil'ev, Anatoly. *Dem einzigen Leser: Schriften, Vorlesungen und Notate zum Theater.* Berlin: Alexander, 2003.

———. "Razumknutoe prostranstvo deystvitel'nosti." *Iskusstvo Kino* 4 (1981): 131–48.

Vasil'ev, Anatoly, and Giampaolo Gotti. "Créer le Beau en passant par Éros." *Théâtre/Public* 182 (2006): 40–44.

Vasylko, Vasyl, ed. *Les Kurbas: spohady suchasnykiy.* Kiev: Mystetstvo, 1969.

Veidlinger, Jeffrey. *The Moscow State Yiddish Theater: Jewish Culture on the Soviet Stage.* Bloomington: Indiana University Press, 2000.

Velekhova, Nina. *Okhlopkov i teatr ulits.* Moscow: Iskusstvo, 1970.

———. *Valentin Pluchek i Prival komediantov na Triumfal'noy, 2.* Moscow: Rutena, 1999.

Veresaev, V. *Vospominaniya.* Moscow: OGIZ, Goslitizdat, 1946.

Vesnik, M., et al., eds. *Vam rasskazyvaet artist: monologi i dialogi.* Moscow: Iskusstvo, 1993.

Viktyuk, Roman. *Roman Viktyuk s samim soboy.* Moscow: Podkova, 2000.

Vilenkin, V. I. *I. M. Moskvin na stsene Moskovskogo Khudozhestvennogo teatra.* Moscow: Muzei MKhATa, 1946.

Vil'yam Shékspir v tvorchestve sovetskikh khudozhnikov teatra. Moscow: Sovetsky Khudozhnik, 1975.

Vlady, Marina. *Vladimir Visotski.* Tel Aviv: Or Am, 1990.

Volkov, N. *Meyerkhol'd.* 2 vols. Moscow: Academia, 1929.

Volkov, Solomon. *St. Petersburg: A Cultural History.* Trans. Antonina W. Bouis. New York: Simon and Schuster, 1995.

Vol'pert, D., and I. Vol'pert. *Zhivaya gazeta (materialy dlya vecherov Sanitarnogo Prosveshcheniya).* Vol. 1. Leningrad: Izd. Sanprosveta Leningradskogo Gubsdravotdela, 1926.

Voprosy teatra no. 13. Moscow: Rossiysky institut iskusstvoznaniya, 1993.

Vovsi-Mikhoëls, Natalia. *Mon père Salomon Mikhoëls. Souvenirs sur sa vie et sur sa mort.* Trans. Erwin Spatz. Montricher, Switzerland: Les Éditions noir sur blanc, 1990.

Vsevolodsky-Gerngross, V. *Istoriya russkogo teatra.* 2 vols. Leningrad: Teakinopechat', 1929.

Vstrechi s proshlym. 4 vols. Moscow: Sovetskaya Rossiya, 1982.

V. S. Vysotsky: issledovaniya i materialy. Ed. Yu. A. Andreev. Voronezh: Izd-vo Voronezhskogo universiteta, 1990.

Wells, H. G. *Russia in the Shadows.* London: Hodder and Stoughton, 1920.

Wilson, Edmund. "The Classics on the Soviet Stage," in *The Shores of Light: A Literary Chronicle of the Twenties and Thirties.* New York: Farrar, Straus, and Young, 1952.

Woroszylski, Wiktor. *The Life of Mayakovsky.* Trans. Bolesław Taborski. New York: Orion Press, 1970.

Worrall, Nick. *Modernism to Realism on the Soviet Stage: Tairov—Vakhtangov—Okhlopkov.* Cambridge: Cambridge University Press, 1989.

Yakovleva, Ol'ga Mikhailovna. *Esli by znat'...* Moscow: ATR-Astrel, 2003.

Yastrebova, N. A. *Teatr 30-kh zerkaloy i zazerkal'e. Iskusstvo, publika, p'esa, vlast'.* Moscow: Gos. Institut Iskusstvovaniya, 2000.

Yur'ev, Y. M. *Zapiski.* Ed. E. M. Kuznetsov. 2 vols. Leningrad: Iskusstvo, 1963.

Yuzhanin, Boris, and V. Mrozovsky, eds. *Sovetskaya éstrada. Sbornik repertuara moskovskogo teatra "Sinyaya bluza."* Moscow: Tea-Kino-Pechat', 1929.

Yuzovsky, Yu. *O teatre i drame.* Moscow: Iskusstvo, 1982.

Zakharov, M. *Kontakty na raznykh urovniyakh.* Moscow: Iskusstvo, 1988.

Zakhava, Boris. *Vakhtangov i ego studiya.* Moscow: Teakinopechat', 1930.

Zavadsky, Yury. "Conversation with a Young Regisseur." *Theatre Arts Monthly* (September 1936): 726–30.

Zograf, N. *Vakhtangov.* Moscow: Iskusstvo, 1939.

Zolotukhin, Valery. *Tagansky dnevnik. Roman.* 2 vols. Moscow: OLMA-PRESS, Avantitul, 2002.

Zorkaya, N. M. "Sud'by ékstsentrizma. Ot 'Zhenit'by' do 'Gogoliady' Grigoriya Kozintseva," in *Russkaya avangard 1910-kh-1920-kh godov i teatr.* Ed. G. F. Kovalenko. St. Petersburg: Dmitry Bulanin, 2000.

Zotova, E. I., and T. A. Lukina, eds. *N. P. Okhlopkov. Stat'i, vospominaniya.* Moskva: Vserossiyskoe Teatral'noe Obshchestvo, 1986.

Zotova, L. V. *Dnevnik teatral'nogo chinovnika 1966–1970.* Moscow: n.p., 2003.

Index